Federal Administrative Procedure Sourcebook

Fourth Edition 2008

William F. Funk
Jeffrey S. Lubbers
Charles Pou, Jr.
Editors

Cover design by ABA Publishing.

The materials contained herein represent the opinions and views of the authors and/or the editors, and should not be construed to be the views or opinions of the law firms or companies with whom such persons are in partnership with, associated with, or employed by, nor of the American Bar Association or the Section of Administrative Law and Regulatory Practice unless adopted pursuant to the bylaws of the Association.

Nothing contained in this book is to be considered as the rendering of legal advice, either generally or in connection with any specific issue or case. Nor do these materials purport to explain or interpret any specific bond or policy, or any provisions thereof, issued by any particular insurance company, or to render insurance or other professional advice. Readers are responsible for obtaining advice from their own lawyer or other professional. This book and any forms and agreements herein are intended for educational and informational purposes only.

11 10 09 08 07   5 4 3 2 1

© 2008 American Bar Association. All rights reserved.
Printed in the United States of America.

Cataloging-in-Publication data is on file with the Library of Congress.
Federal administrative procedure sourcebook / Frank, William; Lubbers, Jeffrey S.; Pou, Charles, editors

Discounts are available for books ordered in bulk. Special consideration is given to state bars, CLE programs, and other bar-related organizations. Inquire at Book Publishing, ABA Publishing, American Bar Association, 321 North Clark Street, Chicago, Illinois 60610.

www.ababooks.org

Chair's Foreword

I am pleased to introduce the fourth edition of the *Federal Administrative Procedure Sourcebook*. The *Sourcebook* is an invaluable resource for practitioners, judges, and academics. It contains the most significant statutes relating to the fundamental processes by which the agencies of government operate on a day-to-day basis in enforcing the law, making policy, and resolving disputes. The *Sourcebook* describes and analyzes these statutes and provides a ready reference source on their operation, history, and interpretation. The 2008 revision adds two new statutes—the E-Government Act of 2002 and the Information Quality Act—and covers scores of statutory amendments, regulatory changes, and executive orders since the prior edition was published in 2000.

This *Sourcebook* is just one of many services this section offers its members. The section brings together lawyers accomplished in administrative law from government, private practice, and academia of all ideological stripes. I invite you to participate in the many interesting and important activities of the ABA Section on Administrative Law and Regulatory Practice.

Michael Asimow
Section Chair (2007-2008)

Preface

We are pleased to introduce the fourth edition of the *Federal Administrative Procedure Sourcebook*. Initially begun by the Administrative Conference of the United States in 1985, with a second edition in 1992, this revision of the *Sourcebook* is the second under the auspices of the American Bar Association Section of Administrative Law & Regulatory Practice. It reflects dozens of statutory and regulatory changes in the eight years since the last edition was published in early 2000.

With the 1995 demise of the Administrative Conference of the United States (ACUS), the American Bar Association's Section of Administrative Law and Regulatory Practice decided to continue updating and publishing this *Sourcebook*—one of ACUS's most popular and valuable texts—so that the closing of ACUS would not end the utility of this resource guide.

This fourth edition of the *Sourcebook*, like previous ones, provides access to, and explanations of, many of the laws broadly applicable to federal agency officials. It contains new chapters dealing with several statutes and other authorities that were not covered previously. These include the E-Government Act of 2002 and the Information Quality Act. It covers major recent developments under the Administrative Dispute Resolution Act, Contract Disputes Act, Government Performance and Results Act, Paperwork Reduction Act, and Regulatory Flexibility Act. It provides a compilation and description of more than a dozen White House Orders and Memoranda on Rulemaking (including several recent ones), extensive administrative law teaching and research materials, and information on recent cases and articles relating to federal administrative procedure. Also, this edition references information on online materials and web addresses likely to be of use to lawyers and researchers in this area.

The *Sourcebook* is intended for several audiences. A primary audience is comprised of agency administrators, attorneys, and other federal employees. Thus, federal administrators wishing a concise description of a particular statute's operation and effect may refer to the overview section. Agency officials and their attorneys may benefit at other times from a desk book that compiles the major laws and related guidance that affect their operations (apart from authorizing and budgetary statutes, of course). We also hope that private attorneys, reviewing judges, scholars, congressional staff, and others performing research in administrative law or public administration will find convenient starting points in the *Sourcebook*'s overview, legislative history, and bibliography sections.

Although this edition required considerable updating and the preparation of new chapters, we were building on the efforts of our colleagues who contributed chapters to previous ACUS editions. They include Michael Bowers, Gary Edles, Mary Candace Fowler, Kevin Jessar, Nancy Miller, William Olmstead, and David Pritzker. In addition, we benefited from the helpful review of the chapters in this edition by Angela Kung, Brian Stanford, and Mary Underwood, class of 2008, Washington College of Law, American University.

We hope that you will find this offering a helpful one.

William F. Funk
Jeffrey S. Lubbers
Charles Pou, Jr.

Contents

Chair's Foreword iii

Preface v

About the Editors xvii

Introduction xxi

1. **Administrative Procedure Act** 1
   Citations 1
   Overview 1
   Legislative History 8
   Source Note 8
   Bibliography 9
   Agency Procedural Rules 16
   Appendix 21
      1. Act 21
      2. United States Department of Justice *Attorney General's Manual on the Administrative Procedure Act* 39

2. **Judicial Review of Agency Action** 177
   Citations 177
   Overview 177
   Bibliography 184
   Appendix 187

3. **Congressional Review of Agency Rulemaking** 199
   Citations 199
   Lead Agencies 199
   Overview 199
   Legislative History 202
   Bibliography 203

Appendix 205
   1. Act 207
   2. Office of Information and Regulatory Affairs, OMB, Form for Submission of Federal Rules under the Congressional Review Act 215

4. White House Orders, Bulletins, and Memoranda on Regulation 217
Citations 217
Lead Agency 219
Overview 219
Bibliography 226
Appendix 233
  I. Bush II and Clinton Administration Executive Orders 233
    A. Executive Order 12,866, Regulatory Planning and Review 233
    B. Executive Order 12,889, Implementation of the North American Free Trade Agreement 252
    C. Executive Order 12,898, Federal Actions to Address Environmental Justice in Minority Populations and Low-Income Populations 254
    D. Executive Order 12,988, Civil Justice Reform 260
    E. Executive Order 13,045, Protection of Children From Environmental Health Risks and Safety Risks 268
    F. Executive Order 13,132, Federalism 273
    G. Executive Order 13,175, Consultation and Coordination with Indian Tribal Governments 280
    H. Executive Order 13,211, Actions Concerning Regulations That Significantly Affect Energy Supply, Distribution, or Use 285
    I. Executive Order 13272, Proper Consideration of Small Entities in Agency Rulemaking 287
  II. Pre-1992 Executive Orders—still in effect 290
    A. Executive Order 12,372, Intergovernmental Review of Federal Programs 290

    B. Executive Order 12,630, Governmental Actions and Interference with Constitutionally Protected Property Rights 293
  III. Other White House Memoranda 299
    A. Presidential Memorandum "Regulatory Reform—Waiver of Penalties and Reduction of Reports" 299
    B. OMB Director's Memorandum "Federal Participation in the Development and Use of Voluntary Consensus Standards and in Conformity Assessment Activities" 302
    C. Presidential Memorandum "Plain Language in Government Writing" 320
    D. OIRA Guidance on Presidential Review of Agency Rulemaking 322
    E. OIRA Memorandum "OMB's Circular No. A-4, New Guidelines for the Conduct of Regulatory Analysis" 331
    F. OMB's Peer Review Bulletin 332
    G. Final Bulletin for Agency Good Guidance Practices .. 333
    H. Updated Principles for Risk Analysis 378

5. Administrative Dispute Resolution Act **397**
    Citations 397
    Lead Agency 397
    Overview 397
    Legislative History 406
    Source Note 409
    Bibliography 410
    Appendix 414
    1. Act 415
    2. Memorandum for Heads of Executive Departments and Agencies: Designation of Interagency Committees to Facilitate and Encourage Agency Use of Alternate Means of Dispute Resolution and Negotiated Rulemaking 431

6. Agency Practice Act **433**
    Citations 433
    Overview 433
    Legislative History 434

    Source Note 434
    Bibliography 435
    Agency Regulations 436
    Appendix 437
        1. Act 439

7. Contract Disputes Act 441
    Citations 441
    Lead Agency 441
    Overview 441
    Legislative History 446
    Source Note 447
    Bibliography 448
    Agency Board of Contract Appeals Regulations 452
    Appendix 452
        1. Act 453

8. E-Government Act of 2002 469
    Citations 469
    Lead Agency 469
    Overview 469
    Legislative History 471
    Bibliography 472
    Agency Regulations 475
    Appendix 475
        1. Act 477

9. Equal Access to Justice Act 509
    Citations 509
    Lead Agencies 509
    Overview 509
    Legislative History 516
    Source Note 519
    Bibliography 520
    Agency Regulations 525
    Appendix 526
        1. Act 527
        2. ACUS Model Rules for Implementation of the
           Equal Access to Justice Act 527

10. Federal Advisory Committee Act 549
Citations 549
Lead Agency 549
Overview 549
Legislative History 552
Source Note 553
Bibliography 539
Appendix 553
   1. Act 557
   2. General Services Administration, Federal Advisory Committee Management Regulations 573
   3. OMB, Circular A-135, Management of Federal Advisory Committees 614

11. Federal Register Act 619
Citations 619
Lead Agency 619
Overview 619
Legislative History 622
Source Note 623
Bibliography 623
Appendix 624
   1. Act 625

12. Federal Tort Claims Act 633
Citations 633
Lead Agency 633
Overview 633
Legislative History 636
Source Note 637
Bibliography 638
Agency Regulations 643
Appendix 643
   1. Act 645
   2. Department of Justice, Claims Under Federal Tort Claims Act 662

13. Freedom of Information Act **675**
    Citations 675
    Lead Agency 676
    Overview 676
    Legislative History 688
    Source Note 690
    Bibliography 691
    Agency Regulations 693
    Appendix 693
        1. Act 695
        2. Executive Order No. 12,600, Predisclosure
           Notification Procedures for Confidential
           Commercial Information 713
        3. Executive Order No. 13,392, Improving Agency
           Disclosure of Information 717

14. Government in the Sunshine Act **725**
    Legislative History 728
    Significant Case Law 730
    Bibliography 731
    Appendix 736
        1. Act 737

15. Government Performance and Results Act **745**
    Citations 745
    Lead Agencies 745
    Overview 745
    Legislative History 749
    Source Note 751
    Bibliography 751
    Appendix 754
        1. Act 755

16. Information QualityAct **771**
    Citations 771
    Lead Agency 771
    Overview 771
    Legislative History 779

Source Note 780
Bibliography 781
Appendix 783
   1. Act 785
   2. Guidelines for Ensuring and Maximizing the Quality, Objectivity, Utility, and Integrity of Information Disseminated by Federal Agencies 787
   3. Final Information Quality Bulletin for Peer Review ... 812

17. National Environmental Policy Act 851
Citations 851
Lead Agency 851
Overview 851
Legislative History 854
Source Note 855
Bibliography 855
Agency Regulations 862
Appendix 862
   1. Act 863
   2. Council on Environmental Quality Regulations, 40 CFR Parts 1500-1508 873
   3. Council on Environmental Quality Regulations, Memorandum to Agencies Containing Answers to 40 Frequently Asked Questions 907

18. Negotiated Rulemaking Act 941
Citations 941
Lead Agency 941
Overview 941
Legislative History 944
Significant Case Law 946
Source Note 947
Bibliography 947
Appendix 950
   1. Act 951
   2. Administrative Conference of the U.S., Negotiated *Rulemaking Sourcebook*, Table of Contents 961
   3. Administrative Conference Recommendations 82-4 .. 971
   4. Administrative Conference Recommendations 82-5 .. 977

19. Paperwork Reduction Act **981**
    Citations 981
    Lead Agency 981
    Overview 981
    Legislative History 987
    Bibliography 988
    Agency Regulations 988
    Appendix 993
        1. Act 995
        2. OMB, Controlling Paperwork Burdens on the
           Public 1026
        3. OMB, Paperwork Reduction Act Submission,
           OMB Form 83-1 1050
        4. Memorandum for Chief Information Officers, from
           Steven D. Aitken, Acting Administrator, OIRA,
           Data Call for the FY 2007 Information Collection
           Budget (Sept. 29, 2006). Paperwork Reduction Act
           Submission 1057

20. Privacy Act **1073**
    Citations 1073
    Lead Agency 1073
    Overview 1073
    Oversight 1081
    Legislative History 1083
    Source Note 1084
    Bibliography 1084
    Appendix 1088
        1. Act 1089

21. Regulatory Flexibility Act **1111**
    Citations 1111
    Lead Agency 1111
    Overview 1111
    Legislative History 1114
    Source Note 1116
    Bibliography 1116
    Appendix 1118
        1. Act 1119

22. Unfunded Mandates Reform Act 1135
    Citations 1135
    Lead Agencies 1135
    Overview 1135
    Legislative History 1137
    Bibliography 1138
    Appendix 1143
        1. Act 1145
        2. OMB, Memorandum for the Heads of Executive Departments and Agencies, Guidance for Implementing Title II of S.1 1155
        3. OMB, Memorandum for the Heads of Departments and Agencies, Guidelines and Instructions for Implementing Section 204, "State, Local, and Tribal Government Input," of Title II of P. L. 104-4 1165

About the Editors

William Funk is a professor of law at Lewis & Clark Law School, where he teaches administrative law, environmental law, and constitutional law. A graduate of Harvard College, 1967, and Columbia Law School, 1973, Professor Funk clerked for Judge James Oakes of the U.S. Court of Appeals for the Second Circuit. Thereafter, he was an attorney-adviser in the Office of Legal Counsel in the U.S. Department of Justice, a principal staff member of the Legislation Subcommittee of the Permanent Select Committee on Intelligence of the U.S. House of Representatives, and an Assistant General Counsel in the U.S. Department of Energy.

Professor Funk has served as chair of the American Bar Association's Section of Administrative Law and Regulatory Practice and edited the section's newsletter for a number of years. He has also served as chair of the Administrative Law Section of the Association of American Law Schools. He is currently the editor of the *Administrative Law Abstracts* for the Social Science Research Network.

Professor Funk is a co-author of *Administrative Procedure and Practice*, published by West Group, now in its third edition, and is also co-author of a popular student aid, *Administrative Law: Examples and Explanations*, in its second edition. He has also published numerous articles on administrative law and is a frequent speaker on administrative law topics.

Jeffrey S. Lubbers has been teaching administrative law and related courses as a Fellow in Law and Government at American University's Washington College of Law since 1996. He has also taught at the Georgetown University Law Center, the University of Miami School of Law, and Washington and Lee University School of Law. He has degrees from Cornell University and the University of Chicago Law School and is a member of the bars of the state of Maryland and the District of Columbia.

Prior to joining the Washington College of Law, he served in various positions with the Administrative Conference of the United States (ACUS), the U.S. government's advisory agency on procedural improvements in federal programs, prior to the agency's shutdown by the 104th Congress in 1995. From 1982 to 1995, he was ACUS's research director, a position in the Senior Executive Service. In that position, he developed ideas for new studies, hired outside consultants (mostly law professors) to conduct the studies, reviewed reports, supervised staff attorneys, and assisted ACUS committees in developing recommendations from the studies on a wide variety of administrative law subjects. He worked with Congressional committees and agencies to seek implementation of ACUS recommendations and served as Team Leader for Vice President Gore's National Performance Review team on Improving Regulatory Systems in 1993. He is also the author of *A Guide to Federal Agency Rulemaking* (ABA, 4th edition, 2006).

Professor Lubbers has published numerous articles on the administrative process and participated frequently in training programs for government officials in the United States and overseas. He has won several prestigious honors for his work in administrative law, including the Presidential Rank of Meritorious Executive and special awards from both the American Bar Association and Federal Bar Association. He is a fellow of the ABA's Section of Administrative Law and Regulatory Practice and, beginning in 1998, has served as the editor of the first nine volumes of the Section's annual volume, *Developments in Administrative Law and Regulatory Practice*.

Charles Pou is an experienced attorney-mediator and dispute resolution professional in Washington, D.C. He has served as a facilitator and mediator of public policy and other government and private disputes, including negotiated rulemakings, tort claims, contract disputes, and environmental and workplace cases. He has acted as a systems design consultant to the Environmental Protection Agency, the U.S. Postal Service, the Nuclear Regulatory Commission, and many other agencies, setting up new conflict resolution programs and rosters. Mr. Pou has served in leadership positions with numerous national dispute resolution and bar groups, and written extensively on dispute resolution issues.

For more than 10 years, Mr. Pou served as director of the Dispute Resolution Program at ACUS, which Congress designated in the Administrative Dispute Resolution Act of 1990 as the lead agency for promoting federal ADR use. He was the co-author of that act and was until 1995 the individual with lead responsibility for spearheading the federal government's implementation of mediation and consensus processes under it. He headed a team of ACUS attorneys assisting federal agencies' implementation of consensus-based decision-making methods. He chaired the Federal Interagency ADR Coordinating Committee, managed a roster of dispute resolution professionals for government cases, and trained hundreds of government employees. He also served as project director and lead editor for the first two editions of the Administrative Conference's *Federal Administrative Procedure Sourcebook*.

Since 1995, Mr. Pou has mediated and consulted extensively with federal and state agencies. He was recognized by the Washington, D.C., chapter of the Society of Professionals in Dispute Resolution with its annual award for Outstanding Contribution to Improved Dispute Resolution for his impact on the use of ADR by public entities. He is a *cum laude* graduate of Rice University and of Harvard Law School.

Introduction

What a charming life that was, that dear old life in the Navy when I kept grocery on a gunboat. I knew all the regulations and the rest of them didn't. I had all my rights and most of theirs.

Thomas B. Reed (R. Me.)
Speaker of the House, 1890-92, 1895-99

The fourth edition of the *Federal Administrative Procedure Sourcebook* has been compiled as a basic introduction and reference book on major federal procedural statutes. The text of each statute is given, along with explanatory material, legislative history, related guidance documents, sources of additional relevant information, and a bibliography.

The *Sourcebook* is designed to be useful for both lawyers and nonlawyers at federal agencies and for any person who needs to know what any of the key federal procedural statutes is about. While this volume is designed to be a convenient source of statutory, regulatory, and other materials, we emphasize that the commentary is not intended to be a substitute for legal research or for legal counsel. Readers with specific questions may have to consult the statute directly, as well as judicial opinions, legislative history, or, where appropriate, the lead agency or their own attorney.

Though the *Sourcebook*'s organization is largely self-evident, a few preliminary comments may be valuable. These notes follow the format of most chapters:

- **Statutory Citations.** This section includes U.S. Code, Public Law, and Statutes-at-Large citations, including significant amendments.
- **Lead Agency.** This designation is a loose one, because a "lead" agency's role may vary from informal consulting and data collection to issuance of binding regulations, from occasional technical guidance to regular oversight of specific activities. The Overview section usually elaborates on the lead agency's role.
- **Overview.** This section summarizes the content of the statute and its applicability. Any observations or conclusions represent only the judgment of the editors.

- **Bibliography.** The lists presented are not intended to be exhaustive, though we have tried to include most major works and some other useful references in the Bibliography or accompanying Source Note.
- **Note on the Administrative Conference and ACUS Materials.** ACUS was an independent federal agency in the executive branch, established in 1968 to advise and assist regulatory agencies and the Congress on administrative law and procedure. ACUS's activities ceased in October 1995 as a result of the decision of the Appropriations Committees of the 104th Congress to terminate funding for its operations. Its archives are currently preserved in the Library of the Washington College of Law, American University, in Washington, D.C. For further information on the termination of ACUS, see the Symposium devoted to ACUS in 30 ARIZONA STATE LAW JOURNAL 1-204 (Spring 1998).

    All ACUS recommendations and the reports relating to them were published by the Government Printing Office in the *Recommendations and Reports of the Administrative Conference* series (cited as ACUS in the Bibliography (e.g., 2 ACUS 119 or 1980 ACUS 313). This series appeared as four multi-year compilations from 1968 to 1977, and annually thereafter through 1995. Conference recommendations were, upon adoption, published in the *Federal Register* and, until 1993, compiled annually in volume one of the *Code of Federal Regulations*. The complete compilation is now conveniently available online at the American Bar Association/Florida State University Administrative Procedure Database [http:/www.law.fsu.edu/library/admin/acus/acustoc.html]. The database has recently added the newly updated and indexed bibliography of ACUS studies from 1968 to 1995. See http://www.law.fsu.edu/library/admin/acus/PDF/ACUSBIB.pdf. ACUS recommendations and reports can also be found at American University and many federal depository libraries.
- **Statutory Texts.** The texts are taken from the U.S. Code and reflect amendments through September 2007. Notes, cross-references, and the like have generally not been included except where particularly useful.

Administrative Procedure Act

Citations:

5 U.S.C. §§551-559, 701-706, 1305, 3105, 3344, 5372, 7521 (2000); originally enacted June 11, 1946 by Pub. L. No. 404, 60 Stat. 237, Ch. 324, §§1-12.

The Administrative Procedure Act (APA), as originally enacted, was repealed by Pub. L. No. 89-554, 80 Stat. 381 (September 6, 1966), as part of the general revision of title 5 of the United States Code. Its provisions were incorporated into the sections of title 5 listed above. Although the original section numbers are used sometimes, in this volume all references to the Act are to sections of title 5.

Section 552 has been revised significantly and is commonly known as the "Freedom of Information Act." Sections 552, 552a (the "Privacy Act"), 552b (the "Government in the Sunshine Act"), and sections 701-706 pertaining to judicial review are discussed and set forth separately. Two significant amendments to the rulemaking and adjudication procedures of the APA were first enacted in 1990—the Administrative Dispute Resolution Act and the Negotiated Rulemaking Act; the Congressional Review of Agency Rulemaking Act was enacted more recently. All of these laws are discussed separately.

Overview:

Attempts to regularize federal administrative procedures go back at least to the 1930s. Early in 1939, at the suggestion of the attorney general, President Roosevelt asked the attorney general to appoint a distinguished committee to study existing administrative procedures and to formulate recommendations. The Attorney General's Committee on Administrative Procedure, chaired by Dean Acheson, produced a series of monographs on agency functions, and submitted its Final Report to the President and the Congress in 1941. These materials, plus extensive hearings held before a subcommittee of the Senate Committee on the Judiciary in 1941, are primary historical sources for the Administrative Procedure Act.

The Administrative Procedure Act was signed into law by President Truman on June 11, 1946. In the months that followed, the Department of Justice compiled a manual of advice and interpretation of its various provisions. The *Attorney General's Manual on the Administrative Procedure Act*, published in 1947 (and reprinted in the Appendix), remains the principal guide to the structure and intent of the APA. The *Manual* (page 9) states the purposes of the Act as follows:

(1) To require agencies to keep the public currently informed of their organization, procedures and rules.

(2) To provide for public participation in the rulemaking process.

(3) To prescribe uniform standards for the conduct of formal rulemaking and adjudicatory proceedings (i.e., proceedings required by statute to be made on the record after opportunity for an agency hearing).

(4) To restate the law of judicial review.

The Act imposes upon agencies certain procedural requirements for two modes of agency decision making: rulemaking and adjudication. In general, the term "agency" refers to any authority of the government of the United States, whether or not it is within, or subject to review by, another agency— but excluding the Congress, the courts, and the governments of territories, possessions, or the District of Columbia.[1] Definitions of other terms may be found in section 551.

Structure of the Administrative Procedure Act. The Administrative Procedure Act has two major subdivisions: sections 551 through 559, dealing in general with agency procedures; and sections 701 through 706, dealing in general with judicial review. In addition, several sections dealing with administrative law judges (§§1305, 3105, 3344, 5372, and 7521) are scattered through title 5 of the United States Code. The sections pertaining to judicial review are discussed in Chapter 2 of this volume. As noted, sections 552, 552a, and 552b are also discussed in separate chapters, as are the new sections added by the Administrative Dispute Resolution and Negotiated Rulemaking Acts.

The structure of the APA is shaped around the distinction between rulemaking and adjudication, with different sets of procedural requirements prescribed for each. *Rulemaking* is agency action that regulates the future

---

[1] *See* 5 U.S.C. §§551(1), 701(b)(1) for other specific exemptions.

conduct of persons, through formulation and issuance of an agency statement designed to implement, interpret, or prescribe law or policy. It is essentially legislative in nature because of its future general applicability and its concern for policy considerations. By contrast, *adjudication* is concerned with determination of past and present rights and liabilities. The result of an adjudicative proceeding is the issuance of an "order." (Licensing decisions are considered to be adjudication.)

The line separating these two modes of agency action is not always a clear one, because agencies engage in a great variety of actions. Most agencies use rulemaking to formulate future policy, though there is no bar to announcing policy statements in adjudicatory orders. Agencies normally use a combination of rulemaking and adjudication to effectuate their programs. The APA definition of a "rule," somewhat confusingly, speaks of an "agency statement of general or particular applicability and future effect. . . ." The words "or particular" were apparently included in the definition to encompass such actions as the setting of rates or the approval of corporate reorganizations, to be carried out under the relatively flexible procedures governing rulemaking.[2]

Beyond the distinction between rulemaking and adjudication, the APA subdivides each of these categories of agency action into *formal and informal proceedings*. Whether a particular rulemaking or adjudication proceeding is considered to be "formal" depends on whether the proceeding is required by statute to be "on the record after opportunity for an agency hearing" (5 U.S.C. §§553(c), 554(a)). The Act prescribes elaborate procedures for both formal rulemaking and formal adjudication, and relatively minimal procedures for informal rulemaking. Virtually no procedures are prescribed by the APA for the remaining category of informal adjudication, which is by far the most prevalent form of governmental action.[3]

Rulemaking. Section 553 sets forth the basic requirements for *rulemaking:* notice of proposed rulemaking in the *Federal Register*, followed by an opportunity for some level of participation by interested persons, and finally publication of the rule, in most instances at least 30 days before it becomes effective. For a detailed discussion of rulemaking procedures, see Jeffrey Lubbers' *A Guide to Federal Agency Rulemaking*, published by the American Bar Association (4th ed. 2006).

---

[2] For discussion of the inclusion of "or particular" in the definition, see K. Davis, 2 Administrative Law Treatise §7:3 (2d ed. 1978); Morgan, *Toward a Revised Strategy for Ratemaking,* 78 U. Ill. L. F. 21, 50 n.143 (1978).

[3] *See* P. Verkuil, *A Study of Informal Adjudication Procedures,* 43 U. Chi. L. Rev. 739 (1976), for a discussion of informal adjudication.

Excluded from the coverage of the Act are rulemaking involving military or foreign affairs functions and matters relating to agency management or personnel, public property, loans, grants, benefits, or contracts. These exceptions to the Act's general policy of providing an opportunity for public participation in rulemaking, to foster the fair and informed exercise of agency authority, are "narrowly construed and only reluctantly countenanced."[4] They are neither mandatory nor intended to discourage agencies from using public participation procedures. On the contrary, when Congress enacted the APA, it encouraged agencies to use the notice-and-comment procedure in some excepted cases, and many agencies routinely do so in making certain kinds of exempted rules. The Administrative Conference encouraged this trend, and called on Congress to eliminate or narrow several of these exemptions.[5] "Regulatory reform" legislative proposals considered over the years have contained provisions to alter or eliminate several of these exemptions.

Most rulemaking proceedings involve *informal rulemaking,* where all that the APA requires for public participation is an opportunity to submit written data, views, or arguments; oral presentations may also be permitted. The published rule must incorporate a concise general statement of its basis and purpose. Despite the brevity of these requirements, it is important to note that Congress has routinely, through other statutes, added procedural requirements that affect various agency programs. These additional statutory requirements may apply to specific agencies or programs, or may be government-wide (such as the Regulatory Flexibility Act; see Chapter 18). Recent presidents have also imposed additional requirements for rulemaking. (See Chapter 4, White House Orders and Memoranda on Rulemaking.) Though courts have sometimes sought to add procedural requirements, the Supreme Court's decision in *Vermont Yankee Nuclear Power Corp. v. Natural Resources Defense Council, Inc.*, 435 U.S. 519 (1978), has, to a great extent, limited this kind of judicial activity.[6] In *Vermont Yankee*, the Supreme Court held that where rulemaking is governed by the (informal) requirements of section 553, as in the case of the Nuclear Regulatory Commission's regulation of nuclear power plants, the courts may not require additional procedures.

---

[4] Am. Fed'n of Gov't Employees, AFL-CIO v. Block, 655 F.2d 1153, 1156 (D.C. Cir. 1981).

[5] *See* Conference Recommendations 69-8, 73-5, 79-2, and 82-2, at 1 C.F.R. Part 305 (1992). *See generally* the discussion in J. LUBBERS, A GUIDE TO FEDERAL AGENCY RULEMAKING 4th ed (ABA 2006).

[6] For a contrary view, see K. DAVIS, ADMINISTRATIVE LAW TREATISE, §§6:37-6:37-3 (1982 Supp.).

The APA also provides for *formal rulemaking*—a procedure employed when rules are required by statute to be made on the record after an opportunity for an agency hearing. Essentially, this procedure requires that the agency issue its rule after the kind of trial-type hearing procedures (§§556, 557) normally reserved for adjudicatory orders (discussed below). The Supreme Court, in *United States v. Florida East-Coast Railway Co.*, 410 U.S. 224 (1973), held that such a procedure was required only where the statute involved specifically requires an "on the record" hearing. Because few statutes do so, formal rulemaking is used infrequently.[7] However, numerous agency statutes (often called "hybrid rulemaking" statutes) do require some specific procedures beyond the basic notice-and-comment elements of informal rulemaking.

Negotiated Rulemaking. The Negotiated Rulemaking Act of 1990, discussed in greater detail in Chapter 16, establishes a statutory framework for the conduct of negotiated rulemaking—a procedure developed in large part through Administrative Conference-sponsored research. As with other "alternative means of dispute resolution" (ADR),[8] negotiated rulemaking provides a means of using consensual techniques to produce better, more acceptable results, reducing the likelihood of protracted litigation. Numerous agencies have successfully completed negotiated rules in the past several years and the Act's provisions reflect that experience and encourage greater use.

The Negotiated Rulemaking Act clearly establishes regulatory agencies' authority to use such consensual techniques as negotiated rulemaking without limiting agency innovation. The Act identifies criteria for the discretionary determination by agency heads of whether and when to use negotiated rulemaking. It also sets forth basic requirements for public notice and the conduct of meetings under the Federal Advisory Committee Act.

Adjudication. Sections 554, 556, and 557 apply to *formal adjudication* (i.e., to cases for which an adjudicatory proceeding is required by statute to be determined on the record after opportunity for an agency hearing).[9] These

---

[7] *See, e.g.*, 21 U.S.C. §371(e)(3) (issuance of standards under the Federal Food, Drug, and Cosmetic Act). In *United States v. Florida East Coast Railway Co.*, 410 U.S. 224 (1973), a statutory requirement of a decision "after hearing" was held insufficient to make sections 556 and 557 applicable (setting of rates under the Interstate Commerce Act).

[8] *See* discussion of the Administrative Dispute Resolution Act elsewhere.

[9] *See* discussion of the Equal Access to Justice Act, which allows certain parties who prevail over the government in formal adjudicatory proceedings (other than licensing and ratemaking) to recover attorney's fees and expenses.

sections apply, for example, to proceedings by certain agencies seeking to impose civil money penalties as part of a regulatory enforcement program.[10]

Section 554(a) specifically exempts six types of proceedings from the requirements of these sections: matters subject to a subsequent *de novo* trial in court; certain personnel matters other than for administrative law judges; decisions based solely on inspections, tests, or elections; military or foreign affairs functions; cases where an agency acts as agent for a court; and certification of worker representatives. Section 554(b) specifies notice requirements. Section 554(c) provides for an opportunity for informal settlements where practicable. Section 554(d) forbids presiding officers from engaging in *ex parte* (off-the-record) consultations on facts at issue in the case. The subsection also addresses "separation of functions," by restricting agency employees engaged in investigation or prosecution of a case from supervising the presiding officer or participating or advising in the decision in that or a factually related case (with certain exceptions). Section 554(e) authorizes agencies, in their discretion, to issue declaratory orders that would terminate a controversy or remove uncertainty with respect to matters required by statute to be determined on the record after opportunity for a hearing.

Sections 556 and 557 prescribe the specific procedures to be used in formal adjudication.[11] In brief, a there is an opportunity for a trial-type hearing, conducted either by some or all of the members of the agency or by an administrative law judge (appointed under 5 U.S.C. §3105). An administrative law judge (ALJ) is normally the presiding officer in formal adjudication. The APA (§556(c)) spells out the powers and duties of ALJs (formerly called hearing examiners). It also provides for the independence of ALJs by protecting their tenure (5 U.S.C. §7521) and pay (5 U.S.C. §5372), and prohibiting inconsistent duties (5 U.S.C. §3105). In addition, under 5 U.S.C. §1305, the Office of Personnel Management has prescribed a special selection procedure for appointment of ALJs. Currently, there are more than 1000 ALJs in the federal government.

Section 556 also covers disqualification of presiding officers, burden of proof, and parties' rights to cross examination. It provides that the transcript of testimony and exhibits, together with all documents filed in the proceeding, constitutes the exclusive record for decision.

---

[10] *See, e.g.*, 12 U.S.C. §§504, 505 (banking); 42 U.S.C. §1320a-7a (Medicare fraud); 16 U.S.C. §1858 (fishery conversation).

[11] Note that sections 554, 556, and 557 contain some special, more flexible, procedures for cases involving initial licensing and rulemaking.

Section 557 provides that when, as is usually the case, a hearing is not conducted by the agency itself, the presiding officer (normally an ALJ) must issue an initial decision—unless the agency requires the entire record be certified to the agency for decision. An initial decision automatically becomes the agency's decision unless appealed or reviewed on motion of the agency. Section 557 provides, in general, an opportunity for parties to submit for consideration their own proposed findings and conclusions, or exceptions to decisions. The record must show the ruling on each finding, conclusion, or exception presented.

Section 557(d) was added to the APA by the Government in the Sunshine Act in 1976 (see Chapter 13) to prohibit *ex parte* communications relevant to the merits of a pending formal agency proceeding. However, where *ex parte* communications do take place, their content must be placed on the public record, and the presiding officer may require the party to show cause why a decision should not be made adversely affecting the party's interest.[12] Most agencies have adopted procedures applicable to hearings relative to agency programs. (A list of citations appears at the end of the chapter.) The *Manual for Administrative Law Judges* contains a detailed discussion of procedures for the conduct of hearings and a collection of model forms.

Alternative Means of Dispute Resolution. The Administrative Dispute Resolution Act specifically provides agencies the authority to employ mediation, arbitration, and other consensual methods of dispute resolution in resolving cases under the APA and in other kinds of agency disputes. The legislation specifically establishes a federal policy encouraging ADR in place of more costly, time consuming adjudication. While no agency is forced to use ADR techniques, the legislation requires each agency head to undertake a review of typical agency litigation and administrative disputes to assess where ADR techniques will be useful. The Act is discussed in greater detail in Chapter 5.

Miscellaneous Provisions. Section 555 states various procedural rights of private parties, which may be incidental to rulemaking, adjudication, or the exercise of any other agency authority. Section 555(b) addresses appearances in agency proceedings by parties, counsel, and other interested persons. Section 555(c) provides that a person compelled to submit data or evidence is entitled to a copy or transcript, except that in nonpublic investigations this may be

---

[12] While the APA does not forbid *ex parte* contacts in informal rulemaking, the Administrative Conference recommended agency practices for making the public aware of most of those that do occur. See Conference Recommendations 77-3 and 80-6, at 1 C.F.R. Part 305 (1992); A GUIDE TO FEDERAL AGENCY RULEMAKING (4th ed. 2006).

limited to a right to inspect the official transcript. Additional provisions of section 555 relate to subpoenas and to the requirement of prompt notice of denials of applications, petitions, or other requests made to agencies.

Section 558 is a rarely invoked section of the APA. Section 558(b) makes clear the requirement that agency rules, orders, and sanctions be within the jurisdiction delegated to the agency and otherwise authorized by law. Section 558(c) contains some special notice provisions and other procedural requirements for handling applications, suspensions, revocations, or license renewals.

Legislative History:[13]

The legislative history of the Administrative Procedure Act begins with the Final Report of the Attorney General's Committee on Administrative Procedure in 1941. This report led to the introduction in Congress of the so-called majority and minority bills, respectively designated as S.675 and S.674, 77th Cong., 1st Sess. These bills, together with S.918, formed the basis for extensive hearings held in 1941 before a subcommittee of the Senate Committee on the Judiciary. In 1945, the House Committee on the Judiciary held brief hearings on various administrative procedure bills, of which H.R.1203, 79th Cong., 1st Sess., was the precursor of the Act as passed. Also in June 1945, the Senate Committee on the Judiciary issued a comparative print, with comments, which is an essential part of the legislative history. The committee reports on the Act are S. Rep. No. 752, 79th Cong., 1st Sess. and H.R. Rep. No. 1980, 79th Cong., 2d Sess. In October 1945, the Attorney General, at the request of the Senate Committee on the Judiciary, submitted a letter, with a memorandum attached, setting forth the understanding of the Department of Justice as to the purpose and meaning of the various provisions of the bill (S. 7). This letter and memorandum constitute Appendix B of the Senate Committee Report and also appear as an appendix in the Attorney General's Manual.

Source Note:

The Senate and House debates plus the documents mentioned in the preceding paragraph, other than the Final Report of the Attorney General's Committee, are compiled in S. Doc. No. 248, 79th Cong., 2d Sess. (1946), entitled *Administrative Procedure Act—Legislative History 1944-46*. The Final Report was published as S. Doc. No. 8, 77th Cong., 1st Sess. (1941). The

---

[13] The summary of legislative history is taken from the ATTORNEY GENERAL'S MANUAL ON THE ADMINISTRATIVE PROCEDURE ACT 8 (1947).

Attorney General's Manual on the Administrative Procedure Act (1947) is a contemporaneous interpretive guide to the original language of the Act (see Appendix).

Individual agencies have adopted, within the framework of the APA, procedural rules for the conduct of rulemaking and adjudication. A list of citations to these rules appears below.

For articles on judicial review of agency action, see the Bibliography for Chapter 2, below. The comprehensive *A Guide to Federal Agency Rulemaking* (4th ed. 2006) discusses the entire rulemaking process. It was published initially by the Administrative Conference and now by the ABA. The Conference also published a *Manual for Administrative Law Judges* (3rd ed. 1993). The *Manual* is a handbook of practice in the conduct of hearings. Persons interested in negotiated rulemaking or ADR in APA adjudication should consult the separate ACUS *Sourcebooks* on these subjects and the other materials listed in the Bibliography sections of those Sourcebook chapters.

The Administrative Conference also sponsored numerous studies of rulemaking and adjudication procedures, and recommended a variety of improvements in agency practice. Its recommendations appeared in the *Federal Register* and volume one of the Code of Federal Regulations.

Bibliography:[14]

I. Legislative History

1. *Administrative Procedure Act—Legislative History 1944-46*, S. Doc. No. 248, 79th Cong., 2d Sess. (1946).

2. *Administrative Procedure in Government Agencies*, S. Doc. No. 8, 77th Cong., 1st Sess. (1941) (Final Report of the Attorney General's Committee on Administrative Procedure).

3. House of Representatives Committee on the Judiciary, *Report on S. 7*, H.R. Rep. No. 1980, 79th Cong., 2d Sess. (1946), *reprinted in* S. Doc. No. 248 (item 1, above) and in Pike and Fischer Administrative Law (2d), Desk Book Stat.-51.

4. Senate Committee on the Judiciary, *Report on S. 7*, Rep. No. 752, 79th Cong., 1st Sess. (1945), *reprinted in* S. Doc. No. 248 (item 1, above) and in Pike and Fischer Administrative Law (2d), Desk Book, Stat.-11.

---

[14] *See also* the Sources listed in the chapters on "Judicial Review" and the "E-Government Act."

II. Other Government Documents

1. Administrative Conference of the U.S., various recommendations and statements, 1 C.F.R. Parts 305, 310 [*available at* http://www.law.fsu.edu/library/admin/acus/acustoc.html]:

68-1	Adequate Hearing Facilities
68-5	Representation of the Poor in Agency Rulemaking of Direct Consequence to Them
68-6	Delegation of Final Decisional Authority Subject to Discretionary Review by the Agency
69-8	Elimination of Certain Exemptions from the APA Rulemaking Requirements
70-3	Summary Decision in Agency Adjudication
70-4	Discovery in Agency Adjudication
71-1	Interlocutory Appeal Procedures
71-3	Articulation of Agency Policies
71-6	Public Participation in Administrative Hearings
72-1	Broadcast of Agency Proceedings
72-5	Procedures for the Adoption of Rules of General Applicability
73-5	Elimination of the "Military or Foreign Affairs Function" Exemption from APA Rulemaking Requirements
73-6	Procedures for Resolution of Environmental Issues in Licensing Proceedings
74-1	Subpoena Power in Formal Rulemaking and Formal Adjudication
76-2	Strengthening the Informational and Notice-Giving Functions of the "*Federal Register*"
76-3	Procedures in Addition to Notice and the Opportunity for Comment in Informal Rulemaking
76-5	Interpretive Rules of General Applicability and Statements of General Policy
77-3	Ex parte Communications in Informal Rulemaking Proceedings
78-3	Time Limits on Agency Actions
79-1	Hybrid Rulemaking Procedures of the Federal Trade Commission
79-4	Public Disclosure Concerning the Use of Cost-Benefit and Similar Analyses in Regulation
80-4	Decisional Officials' Participation in Rulemaking Proceedings

80-6	Intragovernmental Communications in Informal Rulemaking Proceedings
82-4	Procedures for Negotiating Proposed Regulations
83-2	The "Good Cause" Exemption from APA Rulemaking Requirements
83-3	Agency Structures for Review of Decisions of Presiding Officers under the Administrative Procedure Act
85-2	Agency Procedures for Performing Regulatory Analysis of Rules
85-5	Procedures for Negotiating Proposed Regulations
86-2	Use of Federal Rules of Evidence in Federal Agency Adjudications
86-6	Petitions for Rulemaking
87-1	Priority Setting and Management of Rulemaking by the Occupational Safety and Health Administration
88-7	Valuation of Human Life in Regulatory Decision Making
88-9	Presidential Review of Agency Rulemaking
90-8	Rulemaking and Policymaking in the Medicaid Program
92-2	Agency Policy Statements
93-4	Improving the Environment for Agency Rulemaking
95-3	Review of Existing Agency Regulations
95-4	Procedures for Noncontroversial and Expedited Rulemaking
§310.7	Views of the Administrative Conference on Proposals Pending in Congress to Amend the Informal Rulemaking Provisions of the Administrative Procedure Act
§310.9	Statement on Guidelines for Choosing the Appropriate Level of Agency Policy Articulation

    2. *Administrative Conference of the U.S.: A Bibliography* (revised and updated June 2007), *available at* http://www.law.fsu.edu/library/admin/acus/PDF/ACUSBIB.pdf.

    3. U.S. Department of Justice, *Attorney General's Manual on the Administrative Procedure Act* (1947), reprinted in Edles and Nelson, *Federal Regulatory Process: Agency Practices and Procedures,* at 335. (Also reprinted as a separate volume by Wm. W. Gaunt & Sons, Inc., 1979.)

    4. U.S. Office of the *Federal Register, Document Drafting Handbook, available at* http://www.archives.gov/federal-register/write/handbook/ddh.pdf.

III. Other Resources

a. Major Treatises and Hornbooks

1. Alfred C. Aman & William T. Mayton, *Administrative Law* (2d ed.) (2001 The West Group).
2. William F. Fox, *Understanding Administrative Law* (4th ed.) (2000 LEXIS Publishing).
3. William F. Funk, and Richard H. Seamon, *Administrative Law: Examples and Explanations* (2d ed.) (2005 Aspen).
4. Ernest Gellhorn & Ronald Levin, *Administrative Law and Process in a Nutshell* (4th ed.), (2007 West Nutshell Series).
5. Richard J. Pierce, *Administrative Law Treatise* (4th ed.) (2001 Aspen) (Formerly by Davis and Pierce).
6. Richard J. Pierce, Sidney A. Shapiro & Paul R. Verkuil, *Administrative Law and Process* (4th ed.) (2004 Foundation Press).
7. Peter L. Strauss, *An Introduction to Administrative Justice in the United States* (2d ed.) (2002 Carolina Academic Press).

b. Key Casebooks

1. Alfred C. Aman, *Administrative Law and Process* (2d ed.) (2006 Lexis-Nexis).
2. Michael Asimow, Arthur Bonfield & Ronald M. Levin, *State and Federal Administrative Law* (2d ed.) (1998, w/2007 supp. The West Group).
3. Stephen Breyer & Richard Stewart, Cass Sunstein & Adam Vermeule, *Administrative Law and Regulatory Policy* (6th ed.) (2006 Aspen).
4. Ronald Cass, Colin Diver & Jack Beermann, *Administrative Law: Cases and Materials* (5th ed.) (2006 Aspen).
5. William F. Funk, Sidney A. Shapiro, Russell L. Weaver, *Administrative Procedure and Practice: Problems and Cases* (3d ed.) (2006 The West Group).
6. Charles H. Koch, Jr., William S. Jordan III & Richard W. Murphy, *Administrative Law: Cases and Materials* (5th ed.) (2006 LexisNexis).
7. Gary Lawson, *Federal Administrative Law* (3d ed.) (2004 Thompson/West).
8. Jerry Mashaw, Richard Merrill & Peter Shane, *Administrative Law: The American Public Law System—Cases and Materials* (5th ed.) (2003 Thompson/West).

9. Bernard Schwartz, Roberto L. Corrada and J. Robert Brown, *Administrative Law: A Casebook* (6th ed.) (2006 Aspen).

10. Peter Shane & Harold Bruff, *Separation of Powers Law: Cases and Materials* (Carolina Academic Press, 2nd ed. 2005).

11. Peter Strauss, Todd Rakoff & Cynthia Farina, *Gellhorn and Byse's Administrative Law: Cases and Comments* (10th ed. revised) (2003 Foundation Press).

c. Periodicals (aside from law reviews generally)

1. *Administrative Law Review* (published by Washington College of Law at American University and the ABA Section on Administrative Law and Regulatory Practice) (Website: http://www.wcl.american.edu/pub/journals/alr/).

2. *Administrative & Regulatory Law News* (quarterly newsletter of ABA Section on Administrative Law and Regulatory Practice) (also available, from 1996 online at http://www.abanet.org/adminlaw/news).

3. *Developments in Administrative Law and Regulatory Practice* (Series beginning 1998-99, and continuing to 2005-06) (Jeffrey Lubbers, ed., ABA, Section of Administrative Law and Regulatory Practice).

4. Pike & Fisher, *Administrative Law* (now in its 3rd series):
   a. *Ad Law Bulletin*: (one volume): a biweekly newsletter of administrative law.
   b. *Current Digest*: keyed to analytical index in Desk Book.
   c. *Decisions*: look to Digest Table, which is also keyed to the analytical index.
   d. *Deskbook*—(2 volumes) contains important Administrative Law documents.

d. Articles and Other Sources

1. *A Blackletter Statement of Federal Administrative Law* (2004 ABA Section of Administrative Law & Regulatory Practice) (originally published at 54 Admin. L. Rev. 1 (2002)).

2. Alfred C. Aman, *Administrative Law in a Global Era* (1992 Cornell Univ. Press).

3. Michael Asimow, ed., *A Guide to Federal Agency Adjudication* (2002 ABA Book Publishing).

4. Michael Asimow, *Interim-Final Rules: Making Haste Slowly*, 51 Admin. L. Rev. 703 (1999).

5. Barbara Brandon & Robert Carlitz, *Online Rulemaking and Other Tools for Strengthening Our Civil Infrastructure*, 54 Admin. L. Rev. 1421 (2002).

6. John F. Duffy & Michael Herz, eds., *A Guide to Judicial and Political Review of Federal Agencies* (2005 ABA Book Publishing).

7. Christopher F. Edley, Jr., *Administrative Law: Rethinking Judicial Control of Bureaucracy* (1990 Yale Univ. Press).

8. William Funk, *A Primer on Nonlegislative Rules*, 53 Admin. L. Rev. 1321 (2001).

9. William Funk, *When Is a "Rule" a Regulation? Marking a Clear Line Between Nonlegislative Rules and Legislative Rules*, 54 Admin. L. Rev. 659 (2002).

10. Walter Gellhorn, *The Administrative Procedure Act: The Beginnings*, 72 Va. L. Rev. 219 (1986). Part of Symposium issue on the Fortieth Anniversary of the APA, 72 Va. L. Rev. No. 2 (March, 1986).

11. Elena Kagan, *Presidential Administration*, 114 Harv. L. Rev. 2245 (2001).

12. Ronald M. Levin, *Administrative Procedure Legislation in 1946 and 1996: Should We Be Jubilant at This Jubilee?*, 10 Admin. L.J. Am. U. 55 (1996).

13. Ronald M. Levin, *The Case for (Finally) Fixing the APA's Definition of "Rule,"* 56 Admin. L. Rev. 1077 (2004).

14. Jeffrey S. Lubbers, *A Guide to Federal Agency Rulemaking* (4th ed.) (2006 ABA Book Publishing).

15. Jeffrey S. Lubbers, *APA Adjudication: Is the Quest for Uniformity Faltering?* 10 Admin. L. J. Am. U. 65 (1996).

16. Jeffrey S. Lubbers & Blake Morant, *A Reexamination of Federal Agency Use of Declaratory Orders*, 56 Admin. L. Rev. 1097 (2004).

17. Elizabeth Magill, *Agency Choice of Policymaking Form*, 71 U. Chi. L. Rev. 1383 (2004).

18. John Manning, *Nonlegislative Rules*, 72 Geo. Wash. L. Rev. 893 (2004).

19. Jerry L. Mashaw, *Bureaucratic Justice* (1985 Yale Univ. Press).

20. Thomas Merrill & Kathryn Watts, *Agency Rules with the Force of Law: The Original Convention*, 116 Harv. L. Rev. 467 (2002).

21. Beth Simone Noveck, *The Electronic Revolution in Rulemaking*, 53 Emory L.J. 433 (2004).

22. Edward Rubin, *It's Time to Make the Administrative Procedure Act Administrative*, 89 Cornell L. Rev. 95 (2003).

23. Thomas O. Sargentich, ed., *Administrative Law Anthology* (1994, Anderson Publishing Co.).

24. Reuel Schiller, *Rulemaking's Promise: Administrative Law and Legal Culture in the 1960s and 1970s*, 53 Admin. L. Rev. 1139 (2001).

25. Peter H. Schuck, *Foundations of Administrative Law* (2d ed) (2004 Foundation Press).

26. George B. Shepherd, *The Administrative Procedure Act Emerges from New Deal Politics*, 90 Nw. L. Rev. 1557 (1996).

27. Peter Strauss, ed., *Administrative Law Stories* (2006 Foundation Press).

28. Cass R. Sunstein, *After the Rights Revolution: Reconceiving the Regulatory State* (1990 Harvard Univ. Press).

29. Cass R. Sunstein, *The Cost-Benefit State: The Future of Regulatory Protection* (2002 ABA Book Publishing).

30. Paul Verkuil, Daniel Gifford, Charles Koch, Jeffrey Lubbers and Richard Pierce, *The Federal Administrative Judiciary* (1992 Recommendations and Reports 771-1139 (Vol. II), Administrative Conference of the U.S. (with Professors Verkuil, Gifford, Koch and Pierce) (Served as basis for ACUS Recommendation 92-7.).

e. Web Addresses of Note

1. *ABA Administrative Procedure Database.* Developed and maintained with the cooperation and support of the American Bar Association's Section of Administrative Law and Regulatory Practice and the Florida State University College of Law. Contains links to federal agency home pages, state resources, historical materials, and other useful links. http://www.law.fsu.edu/library/admin.

2. *ACUS bibliography*: http://www.law.fsu.edu/library/admin/acus/PDF/ACUSBIB.pdf.

3. *Federal Web Locator*, administered by the Information Center at Chicago-Kent College of Law, Illinois Institute of Technology. http://www.infoctr.edu/fwl.

4. *Government Accountability Office (GAO) Reports*: http://www.gao.gov

5. *Interagency Working Group on Alternative Dispute Resolution*: http://www.usdoj.gov/adr.

6. *LSU's government website.* An amazingly complete link to federal agencies and subunits from all three branches. http://www.lib.lsu.edu/govdocs/federal/list.html.

16   ADMINISTRATIVE PROCEDURE ACT

7. *National Partnership for Reinventing Government* (archived at): http://govinfo.library.unt.edu/npr/default.html.

8. *Office of the Federal Register.* Contains (searchable) *Federal Register* (1994-forward), Code of Federal Regulations, Semiannual Regulatory Agenda, Public Laws (1994-Forward), U.S. Government Manual (1995-forward), Weekly Compilation of Presidential Docs. (1993-forward). http://www.gpoaccess.gov/nara/index.html.

9. *Office of Management and Budget.* http://www.whitehouse.gov/omb/index.html; OIRA, http://www.whitehouse.gov/omb/inforeg/index.html.

10. *Regulations.gov.* The federal government's "one-stop shop" for filing comments in rulemaking. http://www.regulations.gov.

11. *Regulatory Information Service Center.* (Unified Agenda of Regulations—1995-present). http://www.reginfo.gov.

12. *SBA Office of Advocacy.* http://www.sba.gov/advo.

13. *The Freedom of Information Clearinghouse* (Public Citizen). FOIA links. http://www.citizen.org/litigation/free_info.

14. *The Regulatory Group, Inc.* Useful links. http://www.reg-group.com.

15. *"Thomas."* Legislative Information on the Internet. http://thomas.loc.gov/home/thomas.html.

16. *U.S. House of Representatives Internet Law Library—U.S. Code (searchable form).* http://uscode.house.gov/search/criteria.shtml.

17. *U.S. Office of Government Ethics.* http://www.usoge.gov.

18. *U.S. Supreme Court.* http://www.supremecourtus.gov/index.html.

19. *University of Virginia School of Law Federal Administrative Decisions and Actions Page.* Contains links to the various administrative actions that fall outside the scope of the Code of Federal Regulations or *Federal Register*, including administrative agency decisions, advisory opinions, reports, online documentation and more. http://www.law.virginia.edu/lawweb/lawweb2.nsf/0/10cf17e5c5cc0b13852568f00071119f?OpenDocument.

20. *USAGov.* The federal government's comprehensive portal for government documents. http://www.usagov.gov.

Agency Procedural Rules:

Agriculture . . . . . 7 C.F.R. §§1.27-.28, 1.130-.160, Parts 47, 50, 202, 900
Architectural and Transportation Barriers
    Compliance Board . . . . 36 C.F.R. Part 1150
    Coast Guard (Homeland Security) . . . . . 33 C.F.R. Part 20, 46 C.F.R. §5.501-.807

Commerce
    National Oceanic and Atmospheric
        Administration .... 15 C.F.R. Part 904
    Commodity Futures Trading
        Commission .... 17 C.F.R. Parts 10, 12, 13
    Consumer Product Safety
        Commission .... 16 C.F.R. Parts 1025, 1051, 1052
    Environmental Protection
        Agency .... 40 C.F.R. Parts 22, 24, 25,
                Parts 104, 108, §124.71, Parts 164, 209
    Federal Communications
        Commission .... 47 C.F.R. Part 1
    Federal Deposit Insurance
        Corporation .... 12 C.F.R. Part 308
    Federal Emergency Management
        Agency .... 44 C.F.R. Parts 1, 68
    Federal Energy Regulatory
        Commission .... 18 C.F.R. Part 385
    Federal Labor Relations Authority .... 5 C.F.R. Parts 2422, 2423
    Federal Maritime Commission .... 46 C.F.R. Part 502
    Federal Mine Safety and
        Health Review Commission .... 29 C.F.R. Part 2700
    Federal Reserve Board .... 12 C.F.R. Parts 262, 263
    Federal Trade Commission ...... 16 C.F.R. §§1.7-.26, Part 3, §4.7
Health and Human Services
    Centers for Medicare and Medicaid Services   42 C.F.R. Part 402; Part
                                      405, Subparts G, H & I
    Food and Drug Administration (HHS) .... 21 C.F.R. Parts 10-17
    Housing and Urban Development .... 24 C.F.R. Parts 26, 1720,
                                                  §3282.152
    Interior .... 43 C.F.R. Part 4; 50 C.F.R. Part 11
    International Trade Commission .... 19 C.F.R. Part 210
Justice
    Drug Enforcement Administration .... 21 C.F.R. §§1301.41-.46,
        §§1303.31-.37, §§1308.41-.45, §§1309.51-.55, §§1312.41-.47,
                                §§1313.51-.57, §§1316.41-.68
    Newspaper Preservation Act .... 28 C.F.R. §48.10

Labor
    Black Lung Benefits Cases .... 20 C.F.R. §§725.350-.483
    Longshoremen's and Harbor Workers'
        Compensation Cases .... 20 C.F.R. §§702.301-.394
    Office of Federal Contract
        Compliance .... 41 C.F.R.§ 60-1.21-.26, Part 60-30
    Other Cases .... 29 C.F.R. Parts 6, 8
Merit Systems Protection Board .... 5 C.F.R. Parts 1201, 1203, 1209
National Credit Union Administration .... 12 C.F.R. Part 747
National Labor Relations Board .... 29 C.F.R. Parts 101, 102
National Transportation Safety Board .... 49 C.F.R. Part 821
Nuclear Regulatory Commission .... 10 C.F.R. Part 2
Occupational Safety and Health Administration (Labor) ..29 C.F.R. Parts 1905, 1911
Occupational Safety and Health Review
    Commission .... 29 C.F.R. Part 2200
Postal Regulatory Commission .... 39 C.F.R. Part 3001
Postal Service .... 39 C.F.R. Parts 912-966
Securities and Exchange Commission .... 17 C.F.R. Part, Subpart D
Small Business Administration ..... 13 C.F.R. Parts 101.9, Parts 134, 142
Social Security Administration ... 20 C.F.R.§§404.900-.996,§§410.601-
    .707,§§416.1400-.1494; 42 C.F.R. §§405.701-.750, §§405.801-.872,
                                    §§405.1801-.1889
State .... 22 C.F.R. Part 128

Transportation
    Federal Aviation
        Administration .... 14 C.F.R. Part 11, Part 13, subpart D
    Federal Highway Administration .... 49 C.F.R. Parts 386, 389
    Maritime Administration .... 46 C.F.R. Part 201
    National Highway Traffic Safety Admin ... 49 C.F.R. Parts 511,553
    Office of the Secretary .... 14 C.F.R. Part 302, 49 C.F.R. Part 5
    Pipeline and Hazardous Materials Safety
        Administration .... 9 C.F.R. Part 106, Part 107, subpart D
Surface Transportation Board .... 49 C.R. Parts 1110-1119

Treasury

    Alcohol and Tobacco Tax and Trade Bureau .... 27 C.F.R. Part 71

Comptroller of the Currency .... 12 C.F.R. Part 19
Internal Revenue Service ..... 26 C.F.R. Part 601; 31 C.F.R. §§10.60-.82

Appendix:

1. Administrative Procedure Act, 5 U.S.C. §§551, 553-559, 701-706, 1305, 3105, 3344, 5372, 7521 (2000).

2. U.S. Department of Justice, *Attorney General's Manual on the Administrative Procedure Act* (1947).

Administrative Procedure Act

Title V, U. S. Code

Chapter 5—Administrative Procedure

§551. Definitions
§552. Public information; agency rules, opinions, orders, records, and proceedings
§552a. Records about individuals
§552b. Open meetings
§553. Rule making
§554. Adjudications
§555. Ancillary matters
§556. Hearings; presiding employees; powers and duties; burden of proof; evidence; record as basis of decision
§557. Initial decisions; conclusiveness; review by agency; submissions by parties; contents of decisions; record
§558. Imposition of sanctions; determination of applications for licenses; suspension, revocation, and expiration of licenses
§559. Effect on other laws; effect of subsequent statute

* * * *

§551. Definitions

For the purpose of this subchapter—
(1) "agency" means each authority of the Government of the United States, whether or not it is within or subject to review by another agency, but does not include—
    (A) the Congress;
    (B) the courts of the United States;
    (C) the governments of the territories or possessions of the United States;
    (D) the government of the District of Columbia; or except as to the requirements of section 552 of this title;
    (E) agencies composed of representatives of the parties or of representatives of organizations of the parties to the disputes determined by them;
    (F) courts martial and military commissions;

(G) military authority exercised in the field in time of war or in occupied territory; or

(H) functions conferred by sections 1738, 1739, 1743, and 1744 of title 12; chapter 2 of title 41; subchapter II of chapter 471 of title 49; or sections 1884, 1891-1902, and former section 1641(b)(2), of title 50, appendix;

(2) "person" includes an individual, partnership, corporation, association, or public or private organization other than an agency;

(3) "party" includes a person or agency named or admitted as a party, or properly seeking and entitled as of right to be admitted as a party, in an agency proceeding, and a person or agency admitted by an agency as a party for limited purposes;

(4) "rule" means the whole or a part of an agency statement of general or particular applicability and future effect designed to implement, interpret, or prescribe law or policy or describing the organization, procedure, or practice requirements of an agency and includes the approval or prescription for the future of rates, wages, corporate or financial structures or reorganizations thereof, prices, facilities, appliances, services or allowances therefor or of valuations, costs, or accounting, or practices bearing on any of the foregoing;

(5) "rule making" means agency process for formulating, amending, or repealing a rule;

(6) "order" means the whole or a part of a final disposition, whether affirmative, negative, injunctive, or declaratory in form, of an agency in a matter other than rule making but including licensing;

(7) "adjudication" means agency process for the formulation of an order;

(8) "license" includes the whole or a part of an agency permit, certificate, approval, registration, charter, membership, statutory exemption or other form of permission;

(9) "licensing" includes agency process respecting the grant, renewal, denial, revocation, suspension, annulment, withdrawal, limitation, amendment, modification, or conditioning of a license;

(10) "sanction" includes the whole or a part of an agency—

(A) prohibition, requirement, limitation, or other condition affecting the freedom of a person;

(B) withholding of relief;

(C) imposition of penalty or fine;

(D) destruction, taking, seizure, or withholding of property;

(E) assessment of damages, reimbursement, restitution, compensation, costs, charges, or fees;

(F) requirement, revocation, or suspension of a license; or

(G) taking other compulsory or restrictive action;

(11) "relief" includes the whole or a part of an agency—

(A) grant of money, assistance, license, authority, exemption, exception, privilege, or remedy;

(B) recognition of a claim, right, immunity, privilege, exemption, or exception; or

(C) taking of other action on the application or petition of, and beneficial to, a person;

(12) "agency proceeding" means an agency process as defined by paragraphs (5), (7), and (9) of this section;

(13) "agency action" includes the whole or a part of an agency rule, order, license, sanction, relief, or the equivalent or denial thereof, or failure to act; and

(14) "ex parte communication" means an oral or written communication not on the public record with respect to which reasonable prior notice to all parties is not given, but it shall not include requests for status reports on any matter or proceeding covered by this subchapter.

(Pub. L. No. 89-554, Sept. 6, 1966, 80 Stat. 381; Pub. L. No. 94-409, Sec. 4(b), Sept. 13, 1976, 90 Stat. 1247; Pub. L. No. 103-272, Sec. 5(a), July 5, 1994, 108 Stat. 1373.)

§552. Public information; agency rules, opinions, orders, records, and proceedings [See Chapter 13, FOIA]

§552a. Records about individuals [See Chapter 20, Privacy Act]

§552b. Open Meetings [See Chapter 14, Government in the Sunshine Act]

§553. Rule making

(a) This section applies, according to the provisions thereof, except to the extent that there is involved –

(1) a military or foreign affairs function of the United States; or

(2) a matter relating to agency management or personnel or to public property, loans, grants, benefits, or contracts.

(b) General notice of proposed rule making shall be published in the *Federal Register*, unless persons subject thereto are named and either personally served or otherwise have actual notice thereof in accordance with law. The notice shall include—

(1) a statement of the time, place, and nature of public rule making proceedings;

(2) reference to the legal authority under which the rule is proposed; and

(3) either the terms or substance of the proposed rule or a description of the subjects and issues involved.

Except when notice or hearing is required by statute, this subsection does not apply –

(A) to interpretative rules, general statements of policy, or rules of agency organization, procedure, or practice; or

(B) when the agency for good cause finds (and incorporates the finding and a brief statement of reasons therefor in the rules issued) that notice and public procedure thereon are impracticable, unnecessary, or contrary to the public interest.

(c) After notice required by this section, the agency shall give interested persons an opportunity to participate in the rule making through submission of written data, views, or arguments with or without opportunity for oral presentation. After consideration of the relevant matter presented, the agency shall incorporate in the rules adopted a concise general statement of their basis and purpose. When rules are required by statute to be made on the record after opportunity for an agency hearing, sections 556 and 557 of this title apply instead of this subsection.

(d) The required publication or service of a substantive rule shall be made not less than 30 days before its effective date, except—

(1) a substantive rule which grants or recognizes an exemption or relieves a restriction;

(2) interpretative rules and statements of policy; or

(3) as otherwise provided by the agency for good cause found and published with the rule.

(e) Each agency shall give an interested person the right to petition for the issuance, amendment, or repeal of a rule.

(Pub. L. No. 89-554, Sept. 6, 1966, 80 Stat. 383.)

§554. Adjudications

(a) This section applies, according to the provisions thereof, in every case of adjudication required by statute to be determined on the record after opportunity for an agency hearing, except to the extent that there is involved—

(1) a matter subject to a subsequent trial of the law and the facts de novo in a court;

(2) the selection or tenure of an employee, except a[n] administrative law judge appointed under section 3105 of this title;

(3) proceedings in which decisions rest solely on inspections, tests, or elections;

(4) the conduct of military or foreign affairs functions;

(5) cases in which an agency is acting as an agent for a court; or

(6) the certification of worker representatives.

(b) Persons entitled to notice of an agency hearing shall be timely informed of—

(1) the time, place, and nature of the hearing;

(2) the legal authority and jurisdiction under which the hearing is to be held; and

(3) the matters of fact and law asserted.

When private persons are the moving parties, other parties to the proceeding shall give prompt notice of issues controverted in fact or law; and in other instances agencies may by rule require responsive pleading. In fixing the time and place for hearings, due regard shall be had for the convenience and necessity of the parties or their representatives.

(c) The agency shall give all interested parties opportunity for—

(1) the submission and consideration of facts, arguments, offers of settlement, or proposals of adjustment when time, the nature of the proceeding, and the public interest permit; and

(2) to the extent that the parties are unable so to determine a controversy by consent, hearing and decision on notice and in accordance with sections 556 and 557 of this title.

(d) The employee who presides at the reception of evidence pursuant to section 556 of this title shall make the recommended decision or initial decision required by section 557 of this title, unless he becomes unavailable to the agency. Except to the extent required for the disposition of ex parte matters as authorized by law, such an employee may not—

(1) consult a person or party on a fact in issue, unless on notice and opportunity for all parties to participate; or

(2) be responsible to or subject to the supervision or direction of an employee or agent engaged in the performance of investigative or prosecuting functions for an agency.

An employee or agent engaged in the performance of investigative or prosecuting functions for an agency in a case may not, in that or a factually related case, participate or advise in the decision, recommended decision, or agency review pursuant to section 557 of this title, except as witness or counsel in public proceedings. This subsection does not apply—

(A) in determining applications for initial licenses;

(B) to proceedings involving the validity or application of rates, facilities, or practices of public utilities or carriers; or

(C) to the agency or a member or members of the body comprising the agency.

(e) The agency, with like effect as in the case of other orders, and in its sound discretion, may issue a declaratory order to terminate a controversy or remove uncertainty.

(Pub. L. No. 89-554, Sept. 6, 1966, 80 Stat. 384; Pub. L. No. 95-251, Sec. 2(a)(1), Mar. 27, 1978, 92 Stat. 183.)

§555. Ancillary matters

(a) This section applies, according to the provisions thereof, except as otherwise provided by this subchapter.

(b) A person compelled to appear in person before an agency or representative thereof is entitled to be accompanied, represented, and advised by counsel or, if permitted by the agency, by other qualified representative. A party is entitled to appear in person or by or with counsel or other duly qualified representative in an agency proceeding. So far as the orderly conduct of public business permits, an interested person may appear before an agency or its responsible employees for the presentation, adjustment, or determination of an issue, request, or controversy in a proceeding, whether interlocutory, summary, or otherwise, or in connection with an agency function. With due regard for the convenience and necessity of the parties or their representatives and within a reasonable time, each agency shall proceed to conclude a matter presented to it. This subsection does not grant or deny a person who is not a lawyer the right to appear for or represent others before an agency or in an agency proceeding.

(c) Process, requirement of a report, inspection, or other investigative act or demand may not be issued, made, or enforced except as authorized by law. A person compelled to submit data or evidence is entitled to retain or, on payment of lawfully prescribed costs, procure a copy or transcript thereof, except that in a nonpublic investigatory proceeding the witness may for good cause be limited to inspection of the official transcript of his testimony.

(d) Agency subpoenas authorized by law shall be issued to a party on request and, when required by rules of procedure, on a statement or showing of general relevance and reasonable scope of the evidence sought. On contest, the court shall sustain the subpena or similar process or demand to the extent that it is found to be in accordance with law. In a proceeding for enforcement, the court shall issue an order requiring the appearance of the witness or the production of the evidence or data within a reasonable time under penalty of punishment for contempt in case of contumacious failure to comply.

(e) Prompt notice shall be given of the denial in whole or in part of a written application, petition, or other request of an interested person made in connection with any agency proceeding. Except in affirming a prior denial or when the denial is self-explanatory, the notice shall be accompanied by a brief statement of the grounds for denial.

(Pub. L. No. 89-554, Sept. 6, 1966, 80 Stat. 385.)

§556. Hearings; presiding employees; powers and duties; burden of proof; evidence; record as basis of decision

(a) This section applies, according to the provisions thereof, to hearings required by section 553 or 554 of this title to be conducted in accordance with this section.

(b) There shall preside at the taking of evidence—
   (1) the agency;
   (2) one or more members of the body which comprises the agency; or
   (3) one or more administrative law judges appointed under section 3105 of this title.

This subchapter does not supersede the conduct of specified classes of proceedings, in whole or in part, by or before boards or other employees specially provided for by or designated under statute. The functions of presiding employees and of employees participating in decisions in accordance with section 557 of this title shall be conducted in an impartial manner. A presiding or participating employee may at any time disqualify himself. On the filing in good faith of a timely and sufficient affidavit of personal bias or other disqualification of a presiding or participating employee, the agency shall determine the matter as a part of the record and decision in the case.

(c) Subject to published rules of the agency and within its powers, employees presiding at hearings may –
   (1) administer oaths and affirmations;
   (2) issue subpoenas authorized by law;
   (3) rule on offers of proof and receive relevant evidence;
   (4) take depositions or have depositions taken when the ends of justice would be served;
   (5) regulate the course of the hearing;
   (6) hold conferences for the settlement or simplification of the issues by consent of the parties or by the use of alternative means of dispute resolution as provided in subchapter IV of this chapter;

(7) inform the parties as to the availability of one or more alternative means of dispute resolution, and encourage use of such methods;

(8) require the attendance at any conference held pursuant to paragraph (6) of at least one representative of each party who has authority to negotiate concerning resolution of issues in controversy;

(9) dispose of procedural requests or similar matters;

(10) make or recommend decisions in accordance with section 557 of this title; and

(11) take other action authorized by agency rule consistent with this subchapter.

(d) Except as otherwise provided by statute, the proponent of a rule or order has the burden of proof. Any oral or documentary evidence may be received, but the agency as a matter of policy shall provide for the exclusion of irrelevant, immaterial, or unduly repetitious evidence. A sanction may not be imposed or rule or order issued except on consideration of the whole record or those parts thereof cited by a party and supported by and in accordance with the reliable, probative, and substantial evidence. The agency may, to the extent consistent with the interests of justice and the policy of the underlying statutes administered by the agency, consider a violation of section 557(d) of this title sufficient grounds for a decision adverse to a party who has knowingly committed such violation or knowingly caused such violation to occur. A party is entitled to present his case or defense by oral or documentary evidence, to submit rebuttal evidence, and to conduct such cross-examination as may be required for a full and true disclosure of the facts. In rule making or determining claims for money or benefits or applications for initial licenses an agency may, when a party will not be prejudiced thereby, adopt procedures for the submission of all or part of the evidence in written form.

(e) The transcript of testimony and exhibits, together with all papers and requests filed in the proceeding, constitutes the exclusive record for decision in accordance with section 557 of this title and, on payment of lawfully prescribed costs, shall be made available to the parties. When an agency decision rests on official notice of a material fact not appearing in the evidence in the record, a party is entitled, on timely request, to an opportunity to show the contrary.

(Pub. L. No. 89-554, Sept. 6, 1966, 80 Stat. 386; Pub. L. No. 94-409, Sec. 4(c), Sept. 13, 1976, 90 Stat. 1247; Pub. L. No. 95-251, Sec. 2(a)(1), Mar. 27, 1978, 92 Stat. 183; Pub. L. No. 101-552, Sec. 4(a), Nov. 15, 1990, 104 Stat. 2737.)

§557. Initial decisions; conclusiveness; review by agency; submissions by parties; contents of decisions; record

(a) This section applies, according to the provisions thereof, when a hearing is required to be conducted in accordance with section 556 of this title.

(b) When the agency did not preside at the reception of the evidence, the presiding employee or, in cases not subject to section 554(d) of this title, an employee qualified to preside at hearings pursuant to section 556 of this title, shall initially decide the case unless the agency requires, either in specific cases or by general rule, the entire record to be certified to it for decision. When the presiding employee makes an initial decision, that decision then becomes the decision of the agency without further proceedings unless there is an appeal to, or review on motion of, the agency within time provided by rule. On appeal from or review of the initial decision, the agency has all the powers which it would have in making the initial decision except as it may limit the issues on notice or by rule. When the agency makes the decision without having presided at the reception of the evidence, the presiding employee or an employee qualified to preside at hearings pursuant to section 556 of this title shall first recommend a decision, except that in rule making or determining applications for initial licenses—

(1) instead thereof the agency may issue a tentative decision or one of its responsible employees may recommend a decision; or

(2) this procedure may be omitted in a case in which the agency finds on the record that due and timely execution of its functions imperatively and unavoidably so requires.

(c) Before a recommended, initial, or tentative decision, or a decision on agency review of the decision of subordinate employees, the parties are entitled to a reasonable opportunity to submit for the consideration of the employees participating in the decisions—

(1) proposed findings and conclusions; or

(2) exceptions to the decisions or recommended decisions of subordinate employees or to tentative agency decisions; and

(3) supporting reasons for the exceptions or proposed findings or conclusions.

The record shall show the ruling on each finding, conclusion, or exception presented. All decisions, including initial, recommended, and tentative decisions, are a part of the record and shall include a statement of—

(A) findings and conclusions, and the reasons or basis therefor, on all the material issues of fact, law, or discretion presented on the record; and

(B) the appropriate rule, order, sanction, relief, or denial thereof.

(d)(1) In any agency proceeding which is subject to subsection (a) of this section, except to the extent required for the disposition of ex parte matters as authorized by law—

(A) no interested person outside the agency shall make or knowingly cause to be made to any member of the body comprising the agency, administrative law judge, or other employee who is or may reasonably be expected to be involved in the decisional process of the proceeding, an ex parte communication relevant to the merits of the proceeding;

(B) no member of the body comprising the agency, administrative law judge, or other employee who is or may reasonably be expected to be involved in the decisional process of the proceeding, shall make or knowingly cause to be made to any interested person outside the agency an ex parte communication relevant to the merits of the proceeding;

(C) a member of the body comprising the agency, administrative law judge, or other employee who is or may reasonably be expected to be involved in the decisional process of such proceeding who receives, or who makes or knowingly causes to be made, a communication prohibited by this subsection shall place on the public record of the proceeding:

(i) all such written communications;

(ii) memoranda stating the substance of all such oral communications; and

(iii) all written responses, and memoranda stating the substance of all oral responses, to the materials described in clauses (i) and (ii) of this subparagraph;

(D) upon receipt of a communication knowingly made or knowingly caused to be made by a party in violation of this subsection, the agency, administrative law judge, or other employee presiding at the hearing may, to the extent consistent with the interests of justice and the policy of the underlying statutes, require the party to show cause why his claim or interest in the proceeding should not be dismissed, denied, disregarded, or otherwise adversely affected on account of such violation; and

(E) the prohibitions of this subsection shall apply beginning at such time as the agency may designate, but in no case shall they begin to apply later than the time at which a proceeding is noticed for hearing unless the person responsible for the communication has knowledge that it will be noticed, in which case the prohibitions shall apply beginning at the time of his acquisition of such knowledge.

(2) This subsection does not constitute authority to withhold information from Congress

(Pub. L. No. 89-554, Sept. 6, 1966, 80 Stat. 387; Pub. L. No. 94-409, Sec. (a), Sept. 13, 1976, 90 Stat. 1246.)

§558. Imposition of sanctions; determination of applications for licenses; suspension, revocation, and expiration of licenses

(a) This section applies, according to the provisions thereof, to the exercise of a power or authority.

(b) A sanction may not be imposed or a substantive rule or order issued except within jurisdiction delegated to the agency and as authorized by law.

(c) When application is made for a license required by law, the agency, with due regard for the rights and privileges of all the interested parties or adversely affected persons and within a reasonable time, shall set and complete proceedings required to be conducted in accordance with sections 556 and 557 of this title or other proceedings required by law and shall make its decision.

Except in cases of willfulness or those in which public health, interest, or safety requires otherwise, the withdrawal, suspension, revocation, or annulment of a license is lawful only if, before the institution of agency proceedings therefor, the licensee has been given—

(1) notice by the agency in writing of the facts or conduct which may warrant the action; and

(2) opportunity to demonstrate or achieve compliance with all lawful requirements.

When the licensee has made timely and sufficient application for a renewal or a new license in accordance with agency rules, a license with reference to an activity of a continuing nature does not expire until the application has been finally determined by the agency.

(Pub. L. No. 89-554, Sept. 6, 1966, 80 Stat. 388.)

§559. Effect on other laws; effect of subsequent statute

This subchapter, chapter 7, and sections 1305, 3105, 3344, 4301(2)(E), 5372, and 7521 of this title, and the provisions of section 5335(a)(B) of this title that relate to administrative law judges, do not limit or repeal additional requirements imposed by statute or otherwise recognized by law. Except as otherwise required by law, requirements or privileges relating to evidence or procedure apply equally to agencies and persons. Each agency is granted the authority necessary to comply with the requirements of this subchapter through the issuance of rules or otherwise. Subsequent statute may not be held to supersede or modify this subchapter, chapter 7, sections 1305, 3105, 3344, 4301(2)(E), 5372, or 7521 of this title, or the provisions of section 5335(a)(B) of this title that relate to administrative law judges, except to the extent that it does so expressly.

(Pub. L. No. 89-554, Sept. 6, 1966, 80 Stat. 388; Pub. L. No. 90-623, Sec. 1(1), Oct. 22, 1968, 82 Stat. 1312; Pub. L. No. 95-251, Sec. 2(a)(1), Mar. 27, 1978, 92 Stat. 183; Pub. L. No. 95-454, title VIII, Sec. 801(a)(3)(B)(iii), Oct. 13, 1978, 92 Stat. 1221.)

* * * *

CHAPTER 7—JUDICIAL REVIEW

§701. Application; definitions
§702. Right of review
§703. Form and venue of proceeding
§704. Actions reviewable
§705. Relief pending review
§706. Scope of review

§701. Application; definitions

(a) This chapter applies, according to the provisions thereof, except to the extent that—
    (1) statutes preclude judicial review; or
    (2) agency action is committed to agency discretion by law.
(b) For the purpose of this chapter—
    (1) "agency" means each authority of the Government of the United States, whether or not it is within or subject to review by another agency, but does not include—
        (A) the Congress;
        (B) the courts of the United States;
        (C) the governments of the territories or possessions of the United States;
        (D) the government of the District of Columbia;
        (E) agencies composed of representatives of the parties or

of representatives of organizations of the parties to the disputes determined by them;

   (F) courts martial and military commissions;
   (G) military authority exercised in the field in time of war or in occupied territory; or
   (H) functions conferred by sections 1738, 1739, 1743, and 1744 of title 12; chapter 2 of title 41; subchapter II of chapter 471 of title 49; or sections 1884, 1891-1902, and former section 1641(b)(2), of title 50, appendix; and

  (2) "person", "rule", "order", "license", "sanction", "relief", and "agency action" have the meanings given them by section 551 of this title.

(Pub. L. No. 89-554, Sept. 6, 1966, 80 Stat. 392; Pub. L. No. 103-272, Sec.5(a), July 5, 1994, 108 Stat. 1373.)

§702. Right of review

A person suffering legal wrong because of agency action, or adversely affected or aggrieved by agency action within the meaning of a relevant statute, is entitled to judicial review thereof. An action in a court of the United States seeking relief other than money damages and stating a claim that an agency or an officer or employee thereof acted or failed to act in an official capacity or under color of legal authority shall not be dismissed nor relief therein be denied on the ground that it is against the United States or that the United States is an indispensable party. The United States may be named as a defendant in any such action, and a judgment or decree may be entered against the United States: Provided, That any mandatory or injunctive decree shall specify the Federal officer or officers (by name or by title), and their successors in office, personally responsible for compliance.

Nothing herein (1) affects other limitations on judicial review or the power or duty of the court to dismiss any action or deny relief on any other appropriate legal or equitable ground; or (2) confers authority to grant relief if any other statute that grants consent to suit expressly or impliedly forbids the relief which is sought.

(Pub. L. No. 89-554, Sept. 6, 1966, 80 Stat. 392; Pub. L. No. 94-574, Sec. 1, Oct. 21, 1976, 90 Stat. 2721.)

§703. Form and venue of proceeding

The form of proceeding for judicial review is the special statutory review proceeding relevant to the subject matter in a court specified by statute or, in the absence or inadequacy thereof, any applicable form of legal action, including actions for declaratory judgments or writs of prohibitory or mandatory injunction or habeas corpus, in a court of competent jurisdiction. If no special statutory review proceeding is applicable, the action for judicial review may be brought against the United States, the agency by its official title, or the appropriate officer. Except to the extent that prior, adequate, and exclusive opportunity for judicial review is provided by law, agency action is subject to judicial review in civil or criminal proceedings for judicial enforcement.

(Pub. L. No. 89-554, Sept. 6, 1966, 80 Stat. 392; Pub. L. No. 94-574, Sec.1, Oct. 21, 1976, 90 Stat. 2721.)

§704. Actions reviewable

Agency action made reviewable by statute and final agency action for which there is no other adequate remedy in a court are subject to judicial review. A preliminary, procedural, or intermediate agency action or ruling not directly reviewable is subject to review on the review of the final agency action. Except as otherwise expressly required by statute, agency action otherwise final is final for the purposes of this section whether or not there has been presented or determined an application for a declaratory order, for any form of reconsideration, or, unless the agency otherwise requires by rule and provides that the action meanwhile is inoperative, for an appeal to superior agency authority.

(Pub. L. No. 89-554, Sept. 6, 1966, 80 Stat. 392.)

§705. Relief pending review

When an agency finds that justice so requires, it may postpone the effective date of action taken by it, pending judicial review. On such conditions as may be required and to the extent necessary to prevent irreparable injury, the reviewing court, including the court to which a case may be taken on appeal from or on application for certiorari or other writ to a reviewing court, may issue all necessary and appropriate process to postpone the effective date of an agency action or to preserve status or rights pending conclusion of the review proceedings.

(Pub. L. No. 89-554, Sept. 6, 1966, 80 Stat. 393.)

§706. Scope of review

To the extent necessary to decision and when presented, the reviewing court shall decide all relevant questions of law, interpret constitutional and statutory provisions, and determine the meaning or applicability of the terms of an agency action. The reviewing court shall—
  (1) compel agency action unlawfully withheld or unreasonably delayed; and
  (2) hold unlawful and set aside agency action, findings, and conclusions found to be—
    (A) arbitrary, capricious, an abuse of discretion, or otherwise not in accordance with law;
    (B) contrary to constitutional right, power, privilege, or immunity;
    (C) in excess of statutory jurisdiction, authority, or limitations, or short of statutory right;
    (D) without observance of procedure required by law;
    (E) unsupported by substantial evidence in a case subject to sections 556 and 557 of this title or otherwise reviewed on the record of an agency hearing provided by statute; or
    (F) unwarranted by the facts to the extent that the facts are subject to trial de novo by the reviewing court.

In making the foregoing determinations, the court shall review the whole record or those parts of it cited by a party, and due account shall be taken of the rule of prejudicial error.

(Pub. L. No. 89-554, Sept. 6, 1966, 80 Stat. 393.)

* * * *

§1305. Administrative law judges

For the purpose of sections 3105, 3344, 4301(2)(D), and 5372 of this title and the provisions of section 5335(a)(B) of this title that relate to administrative law judges, the Office of Personnel Management may, and for the purpose of section 7521 of this title, the Merit Systems Protection Board may investigate, prescribe regulations, appoint advisory committees as necessary, recommend legislation, subpena witnesses and records, and pay witness fees as established for the courts of the United States.

(Pub. L. No. 89-554, Sept. 6, 1966, 80 Stat. 402; Pub. L. No. 90-83, Sec. 1(3), Sept.

11, 1967, 81 Stat. 196; Pub. L. No. 95-251, Sec. 2(a)(1), (b)(1), Mar. 27, 1978, 92 Stat. 183; Pub. L. No. 95-454, title VIII, Sec. 801(a)(3)(B)(iii), title IX, Sec. 906(a)(12), Oct. 13, 1978, 92 Stat. 1221, 1225; Pub. L. No. 102-378, Sec. 2(4), Oct. 2, 1992, 106 Stat. 1346; Pub. L. No. 105-362, title XIII, Sec. 1302(a), Nov. 10, 1998, 112 Stat. 3293.)

* * * *

§3105. Appointment of administrative law judges

Each agency shall appoint as many administrative law judges as are necessary for proceedings required to be conducted in accordance with sections 556 and 557 of this title. Administrative law judges shall be assigned to cases in rotation so far as practicable, and may not perform duties inconsistent with their duties and responsibilities as administrative law judges.

(Pub. L. No. 89-554, Sept. 6, 1966, 80 Stat. 415; Pub. L. No. 95-251, Sec. 2(a)(1), (b)(2), (d)(1), Mar. 27, 1978, 92 Stat. 183, 184.)

* * * *

§3344. Details; administrative law judges

An agency as defined by section 551 of this title which occasionally or temporarily is insufficiently staffed with administrative law judges appointed under section 3105 of this title may use administrative law judges selected by the Office of Personnel Management from and with the consent of other agencies.

(Pub. L. No. 89-554, Sept. 6, 1966, 80 Stat. 425; Pub. L. No. 95-251, Sec. 2(a)(1), (b)(2), Mar. 27, 1978, 92 Stat. 183; Pub. L. No. 95-454, title IX, Sec. 906(a)(2), Oct. 13, 1978, 92 Stat. 1224.)

* * * *

§5372. Administrative law judges

(a) For the purposes of this section, the term "administrative law judge" means an administrative law judge appointed under section 3105.

(b)(1)(A) There shall be 3 levels of basic pay for administrative law judges (designated as AL-1, 2, and 3, respectively), and each such judge shall be paid at 1 of those levels, in accordance with the provisions of this section.

(B) Within level AL3, there shall be 6 rates of basic pay,

designated as AL3, rates A through F, respectively. Level AL2 and level AL1 shall each have 1 rate of basic pay.

(C) The rate of basic pay for AL3, rate A, may not be less than 65 percent of the rate of basic pay for level IV of the Executive Schedule, and the rate of basic pay for AL1 may not exceed the rate for level IV of the Executive Schedule.

(2) The Office of Personnel Management shall determine, in accordance with procedures which the Office shall by regulation prescribe, the level in which each administrative-law-judge position shall be placed and the qualifications to be required for appointment to each level.

(3)(A) At the beginning of the next pay period following appointment to a position in AL-3, an administrative law judge shall be paid at rate A of AL-3, and shall be advanced successively to rates B, C, and D of that level at the beginning of the next pay period following completion of 52 weeks of service in the next lower rate, and to rates E and F of that level at the beginning of the next pay period following completion of 104 weeks of service in the next lower rate.

(B) The Office of Personnel Management may provide for appointment of an administrative law judge in AL-3 at an advanced rate under such circumstances as the Office may determine appropriate.

(4) Subject to paragraph (1), effective at the beginning of the first applicable pay period commencing on or after the first day of the month in which an adjustment takes effect under section 5303 in the rates of basic pay under the General Schedule, each rate of basic pay for administrative law judges shall be adjusted by an amount determined by the President to be appropriate.

(c) The Office of Personnel Management shall prescribe regulations necessary to administer this section.

(Pub. L. No. 89-554, Sept. 6, 1966, 80 Stat. 473, Sec. 5362; Pub. L. No. 95-251, Sec. 2(a)(1), (b)(1), Mar. 27, 1978, 92 Stat. 183; renumbered Sec. 5372 and amended Pub. L. No. 95-454, title VIII, Sec. 801(a)(3)(A)(ii), title IX, Sec. 906(a)(2), Oct. 13, 1978, 92 Stat. 1221, 1224; Pub. L. No. 101-509, title V, Sec. 529 (title I, Sec. 104(a)(1)), Nov. 5, 1990, 104 Stat. 1427, 1445; Pub. L. No. 102-378, Sec. 2(32), Oct. 2, 1992, 106 Stat. 1350, Pub. L. No. 106-97, Sec. 1, 113 Stat. 1322.)

Amendments

1990—Pub. L. No. 101-509 amended section generally. Prior to amendment, section read as follows: "Administrative law judges appointed under section 3105 of this title are entitled to pay prescribed by the Office of Personnel Management independently of agency recommendations or ratings and in accordance with subchapter III of this chapter and chapter 51 of this title." 1978—Pub. L. No. 95-454, Sec. 906(a)(2), substituted "Office of Personnel Management" for "Civil Service Commission". Pub. L. No. 95-251 substituted "Administrative law judges" for "Hearing examiners" in section catchline and text.

* * * *

§7521. Actions against administrative law judges

(a) An action may be taken against an administrative law judge appointed under section 3105 of this title by the agency in which the administrative law judge is employed only for good cause established and determined by the Merit Systems Protection Board on the record after opportunity for hearing before the Board.

(b) The actions covered by this section are—
    (1) a removal;
    (2) a suspension;
    (3) a reduction in grade;
    (4) a reduction in pay; and
    (5) a furlough of 30 days or less; but do not include—
        (A) a suspension or removal under section 7532 of this title;
        (B) a reduction-in-force action under section 3502 of this title; or
        (C) any action initiated under section 1215 of this title.

(Added Pub. L. No. 95-454, title II, Sec. 204(a), Oct. 13, 1978, 92 Stat. 1137; amended Pub. L. No. 101-12, Sec. 9(a)(2), Apr. 10, 1989, 103 Stat. 35.)

Attorney General's Manual
on the
Administrative Procedure Act

Prepared by the
United States Department of Justice
Tom C. Clark
Attorney General
1947

TABLE OF CONTENTS

INTRODUCTION 5
    Note Concerning Manner of Citation of Legislative Material 8
I. FUNDAMENTAL CONCEPTS 9
    a. Basic Purposes of the Administrative Procedure Act 9
    b. Coverage of the Administrative Procedure Act 9
    c. Distinction Between Rule Making and Adjudication 12
II. SECTION 3—PUBLIC INFORMATION 17
    Agencies Subject To Section 3 17
    Exceptions To Requirements Of Section 3 17
        Any function of the United States requiring secrecy in the public interest 17
        Any matter relating solely to the internal management of an agency 18
    Effective Date-Prospective Operation 18
    Section 3 (a)—Rules 19
        Separate Statement 19
        Description of Organization 19
        Statement Of Procedures 20
        Substantive Rules 22
    Section 3 (b)—Opinions And Orders 23
    Section 3 (c)—Public Records 24
III. SECTION 4—RULE MAKING 26
    Exceptions
        (1) any military, naval, or foreign affairs function of the United States 26
        (2) any matter relating to agency management or personnel or to public property, loans, grants, benefits, or contracts 27
        Public Property 27
        Loans 27
        Grants 27
        Benefits 28
        Contracts 28
    Section 4 (A)—Notice 28
        Contents of notice 28
        Section 4 (a) and (b) applicable only to substantive rules. 30
        Omission of notice and public procedure for good cause 30
    Section 4 (b)—Procedures 31
        Informal rule making 31
        Formal rule making 32
        Publication of procedures 35
    Section 4 (c)—Effective Dates 35
    Section 4 (d)—Petitions 38
IV. SECTION 5—ADJUDICATION 40
    General Scope of Formal Procedural Requirements 40
        Exempted adjudications 43
    Section 5 (a)—Notice 46
        Responsive pleading 47
    Section 5 (b)—Procedure 47
    Section 5 (c)—Separation of Functions 50
        Exceptions 50
        Hearing officers 53
        The agency 56
V. SECTION 6—ANCILLARY MATTERS 61
    Governing definitions 61

Section 6 (a)—Appearance 61
   Formal Appearance 61
   Informal Appearance 63
   Practice Before Agencies 65
Section 6 (b)—Investigations 66
Section 6 (c)—Subpenas 67
Section 6 (d)—Denials 69
VI. SECTION 7—HEARINGS 71
Section 7 (a)—Presiding Officers 71
Section 7 (b)—Hearing Powers 74
Section 7 (c)—Evidence 75
   Burden of proof 75
   Evidence 75
   Presentation of evidence 77
   Section 7 (d)—Record 79
   Record 79
   Official notice 79
VII. SECTION 8—DECISIONS 81
Section 8 (a)—Who Decides 81
   Appeals and review 83
Section 8 (b)—Submittals and Decisions 85
   Submittals 85
   Decisions 86
   Appeals to superior agency 87
VIII. SECTION 9—SANCTIONS AND POWERS 88
Section 9 (a)—Sanctions 88
Section 9 (b)—Licenses 88
   Applications for licenses 89
   Suspension or revocation of licenses 90
   Renewal of licenses 91
IX. SECTION 10—JUDICIAL REVIEW 93
Scope of Section 10 94
Section 10 (a)—Right of Review 95
Section 10 (b)—Form and Venue of Action 96
   Form of Action 97
   Venue 98
   Review in enforcement procedure 99
Section 10 (c)—Reviewable Acts 101
Section 10 (d)—Interim Relief 105
Section 10(e)—Scope of Review 107
Appendix A—Text of Administrative Procedure Act 111
Appendix B—Attorney General's letter of Oct. 19, 1945 123

INTRODUCTION

June 11, 1946, the date on which the Administrative Procedure Act was approved by President Truman, is notable in the history of the governmental process. The Act sets a pattern designed to achieve relative uniformity in the administrative machinery of the Federal Government. It effectuates needed reforms in the administrative process and at the same time preserves the effectiveness of the laws which are enforced by the administrative agencies of the Government. The members of the Seventy-Ninth Congress who worked so assiduously on the McCarran-Sumners-Walter bill showed statesmanship and wisdom in dealing with the difficult problems thus presented.

The Department of Justice played an active role in the development of the Administrative Procedure Act. In 1938, at a time when there was criticism of Federal administrative agencies, Homer Cummings, as Attorney General, suggested to the late President Roosevelt that the Department of Justice be authorized to conduct a full inquiry into the administrative process. In response to this suggestion, President Roosevelt requested Attorney General Cummings to appoint a committee to make a thorough study of existing administrative procedures and to submit whatever recommendations were deemed advisable. For this purpose the Attorney General appointed a committee of eminent lawyers, jurists, scholars and administrators.

For a period of two years this committee, known as the Attorney General's Committee on Administrative Procedure, devoted itself to the study of the administrative process. Its work culminated in the issuance of 27 monographs on the operations of the more important Government agencies it had investigated, as well as in a Final Report to the President and to the Congress. This Final Report is a landmark in the field of administrative law. In fact, the main origins of the present Administrative Procedure Act may be found in that Report, and in the so-called majority and minority recommendations submitted by the Committee. These recommendations were the subject of extensive hearings held before a subcommittee of the Senate Committee on the Judiciary in 1941.

There was a lull in legislative activities in the field of administrative law during the next few years by reason of the impact of war. But when Congress in 1945 resumed consideration of legislation in this field, the Chairmen of both the Senate and House Committees on the Judiciary called upon this Department for its assistance. The invitation was accepted, and the task was assigned to the Office of the Assistant Solicitor General. For many months the members of that Office assisted in the drafting and revision of the bill (S. 7) which developed into the Administrative Procedure Act.

Finally, in a letter dated October 19, 1945, to the Chairmen of both Committees on the Judiciary, I endorsed S. 7 as revised. I concluded that "The bill appears to offer a hopeful prospect of achieving reasonable uniformity and fairness in administrative procedures without at the same time interfering unduly with the efficient and economical operation of the Government." Sen. Rep. 752, 79th Cong., 1st sess., pp. 37-38. The bill then moved in regular course through both Committees with a few minor modifications (H.R. Rep. 1980, 79th Cong., 2nd sess., p. 57). It was subsequently adopted by both Houses of Congress without a dissenting vote.

After the Administrative Procedure Act was signed by President Truman on June 11, 1946, it became evident that a major phase of our work had just begun. Government agencies were calling upon us for advice on the meaning of various provisions of the Act. We endeavored to furnish that advice promptly and in detail to every agency which consulted us. At length I decided that we could offer a definite service by preparing a general analysis of the provisions of the Act in the light of our experience. This manual is the result of that effort. It does not purport to be exhaustive. It was intended primarily as a guide to the agencies in adjusting their procedures to the requirements of the Act.

George T. Washington, the Assistant Solicitor General, was assigned the tasks I have just described—both the rendition of advice to the agencies and the preparation of the manual. He had assisted in drafting the Act and was familiar with the administrative problems of the agencies. Two members of his staff, Robert Ginnane and David Reich, took the major burden of the work, under the supervision and direction of Mr. Washington and myself. The manner in which the task has been carried out has my full approval.

7

While the manual was intended originally for distribution only to Government agencies, public demand for it has been so great that I have decided to make it generally available. I trust that it will prove helpful to those who find a need for it.

A word of explanation as to the manner in which the manual is arranged should be helpful. It has been prepared mainly on a section by section analysis of the Act. Each of the major sections is treated in a separate chapter. There has been no separate treatment of section 11, covering the appointment of examiners, since the Civil Service Commission is entrusted with the responsibilities under that section and is presently engaged in working out the necessary requirements, assisted by an Advisory Committee of experts designated by the Commission. No chapter as such is being devoted to either section 2 (definitions) or to section 12 (construction and effect) for the reason that by themselves they have little meaning except in connection with the functional aspects of the Act. However, there is a separate chapter on two important phases of section 2, namely, the coverage of the Act and the fundamental distinction between rule making and adjudication.

Tom C. Clark
Attorney General

August 27, 1947

8

Note Concerning Manner of Citation of Legislative Material

The legislative history of the Administrative Procedure Act really begins with the Final Report of the Attorney General's Committee on Administrative Procedure (cited hereinafter as Final Report). This Report led to the introduction in Congress of the so-called majority and minority bills, respectively designated as S. 675 and S. 674, 77th Cong., 1st sess. These bills, together with S. 918, formed the basis for the extensive and valuable hearings held in 1941 before a subcommittee of the Senate Committee on the Judiciary (cited hereinafter as Senate Hearings (1941)). In 1945, the House Committee on the Judiciary held brief hearings (cited hereinafter as House Hearings (1945)) on various administrative procedure bills, of which H.R. 1203, 79th Cong., lst sess., was the precursor of the present Act. Also in June 1945, the Senate Committee on the Judiciary issued a comparative print, with comments,, which is an essential part of the legislative history. The Committee reports on the Act are Sen. Rep. 752, 79th Cong., 1st sess. (cited hereinafter as Sen. Rep.). and H.R. Rep. 1980, 79th Cong., 2nd sess. (cited hereinafter as H.R. Rep.). In October 1945, the Attorney General, at the request of the Senate Committee on the Judiciary, submitted a letter, with memorandum attached, setting forth the understanding of the Department of Justice as to the purpose and meaning of the various provisions of the bill (S. 7). This letter and memorandum constitute Appendix B of the Senate Committee Report and have been printed as Appendix B to this manual.

There may be obtained from the Government Printing Office Sen. Doc. No. 248, 79th Cong., 2nd sess., entitled "Administrative Procedure Act— Legislative History" (cited hereinafter as Sen. Doc.), which contains the Senate and House debates on the Administrative Procedure Act, together with all the documents mentioned above, except the Final Report of the Attorney General's Committee on Administrative Procedure and the Senate Hearings (1941). Wherever appropriate, there will be two citations, one to the particular report or hearing in which the legislative material appears, the other a parenthetical reference to the corresponding page in the Senate Document.

9

I.
FUNDAMENTAL CONCEPTS

a. *Basic Purposes of the Administrative Procedure Act*

The Administrative Procedure Act may be said to have four basic purposes:

1. To require agencies to keep the public currently informed of their organization, procedures and rules (sec. 3).

2. To provide for public participation in the rule making process (sec. 4).

3. To prescribe uniform standards for the conduct of formal rule making (sec. 4 (b)) and adjudicatory proceedings (sec. 5), i.e., proceedings which are required by statute to be made on the record after opportunity for an agency hearing (secs. 7 and 8).

4. To restate the law of judicial review (sec. 10).

b. *Coverage of the Administrative Procedure Act*

The Administrative Procedure Act applies, with certain exceptions to be discussed, to every agency and authority of the Government. Section 2 (a) of the Act reads, in part, as follows:

> "Agency" means each authority (whether or not within or subject to review by another agency) of the Government of the United States other than Congress, the courts, or the governments of the possessions, Territories, or the District of Columbia. Nothing in this Act shall be construed to repeal delegations of authority as provided by law.

It will be seen from the above that agency is defined as each authority of the Government of the United States, whether or not within or subject to review by another agency. This definition was adopted in recognition of the fact that the Government is divided not only into departments, commissions, and offices, but that these agencies, in turn, are further subdivided into constituent units which may have all the attributes of an agency insofar as rule making and adjudication are concerned."[1] For example, the Federal Security Agency is composed of many

---

[1] The legislative history of section 2 (a) illustrates clearly the broad Scope of the term "agency." In the Senate Comparative Print of June 1945, the term agency was explained as follows (p. 2): "It is necessary to define agency as "authority" rather than by name or form, because of the present system of including one agency within another or of authorizing internal boards or "divisions" to have final authority. 'Authority' means any officer or board, whether within another agency or not, which by law has authority to take final and binding action with or without appeal to some superior administrative authority. Thus, 'divisions' of the Interstate Commerce Commission and the judicial officers of the Department of Agriculture would be 'agencies' within this definition." (Sen. Doc. p. 13). And in the Senate Report the following appears at page 10: "The word 'authority' is advisedly used as meaning whatever persons are vested with powers to act (rather than the mere form of agency organization such as department commission, board, or bureau) because the real authorities may be some subordinate or semidependent person or persons within such form of organization." (Sen. Doc. p. 196). See also H.R. Rep. p. 19 (Sen. Doc. p. 253).

authorities which, while subject to the overall supervision of that agency, are generally independent in the exercise of their functions. Thus, the Social Security Administration within the Federal Security Agency is in complete charge of the Unemployment Compensation provisions of the Social Security Act. By virtue of the definition contained in section 2 (a) of the Administrative Procedure Act, the Social Security Administration is an agency, as is its parent organization, the Federal Security Agency.

The Administrative Procedure Act applies to every authority of the Government of the United States other than Congress, the courts, the governments of the possessions, Territories, and the District of Columbia (see. 2 (a)). The term "courts" is not limited to constitutional courts, but includes the Tax Court, the Court of Customs and Patent Appeals, the Court of Claims, and similar courts. Sen. Rep. p. 38 (Sen. Doc. p. 408).

While the Administrative Procedure Act covers generally all agencies of the United States, certain agencies and certain functions are specifically exempted from all the requirements of the Act with the exception of the public information requirements of section 3. Section 2 (a) states, in part: "Except as to the requirements of section 3, there shall be excluded from the operation of this Act (1) agencies composed of representatives of the parties or of representatives of organizations of the parties to the disputes determined by them, (2) courts martial and military commissions, (3) military or naval authority exercised in the field in time of war or in occupied territory, or (4) functions which by law expire on the termination of present hostilities, within any fixed period thereafter, or before July 1, 1947, and the functions conferred by the following statutes: Selective Training and Service Act of 1940; Contract Settlement Act of 1944; Surplus Property Act of 1944; Sugar Control Extension Act of 1947;[2] Veterans' Emergency Housing Act[3] of 1946; and the Housing and Rent Act of 1947."[4]

It will be helpful to consider each of these exceptions separately:

(1) "agencies composed of representatives of the parties or of representatives of organizations of the parties to the disputes determined by them." This definition is intended to embrace such agencies as the National Railroad Adjustment Board, composed

---

2. This exception was added by Public Law 30, 80th Cong., 1st sess.
3. This exception was added by Public Laws 663 and 719, 79th Cong., 2d sess.
4. This exception was added by Public Law 129, 80th Cong., 1st sess.

11

of representatives of employers and employees. In addition, it includes agencies which have a tripartite composition in that they are composed of representatives of industry, labor and the public, such as the Railroad Retirement Board and special fact finding boards. H.R. Rep. p. 19 (Sen. Doc. p. 253); 92 Cong. Rec. 2152, 5649 (Sen. Doc. pp. 307, 355). The exemption, it will be seen, is not limited to boards which convene only occasionally, with per diem compensation, to determine, arbitrate or mediate particular disputes, but also includes similar boards or agencies composed wholly or partly of full-time paid officers of the Federal Government.

(2) "courts martial and military commissions."

(3) "military or naval authority exercised in the field in time of war or in occupied territory."

(4) "functions which by law expire on the termination of present hostilities, within any fixed period thereafter, or before July 1, 1947, and the functions conferred by the following statutes: Selective Training and Service Act of 1940; Contract Settlement Act of 1944; Surplus Property Act of 1944; Sugar Control Extension Act of 1947; Veterans' Emergency Housing Act of 1946; and the Housing and Rent Act of 1947." The functions thus exempted on the ground of their temporary nature may be classified, as to their termination, as follows:

(a) "On the termination of present hostilities"—A considerable number of statutes authorizing wartime programs and controls limit the duration of these functions by such phrases as "in time of war", "for the duration of the war", "upon cessation of hostilities as proclaimed by the President", "upon the termination of the unlimited national emergency proclaimed by the President on May 27, 1941", etc. It is clear from the legislative history of section 2 (a) that the exemption is not to be limited to functions derived from statutes which provide for expiration "on the termination of present hostilities" *sic*, but rather extends to all functions which are limited as to duration by phrases such as those quoted above. House Hearings (1945) pp. 36-37 (Sen. Doc. pp. 82-83); 92 Cong. Rec., 5649 (Sen. Doc. p. 355). It is also clear that this exemption for temporary war functions is in no way affected by the circumstance that they may be continued in existence for a considerable period of time after combat operations have ceased. It is well established that statutes authorizing such temporary agencies and functions remain in effect until a formal state of peace is restored or some earlier termination date is made effective by appropriate governmental action. See *Hamilton* v. *Kentucky Distilleries Co.*, 251 U. S. 146 (1919); and the Attorney General's letter to the President, dated September 1, 1945, in H.R. Doc. 282, 79th Cong., lst sess., p. 49. The conclusion that the exemption is not measured by the duration of actual combat operations is confirmed by the fact that this Act, containing the exemption, did not become law until June 11, 1946.

(b) "Within any fixed period thereafter (after the termination of present hostilities)"—This phrase provides exemption for functions which terminate, for example, "six months after the termination of the unlimited national emergency proclaimed by the President on May 27, 1941." It is unnecessary to repeat the discussion under (a), *supra*, as the meaning of the phrase "termination of present hostilities."

(c) "On or before July 1, 1947"—This encompasses such functions as expire on or before that date.

(d) The functions conferred by the Selective Training and Service Act of 1940, the Contract Settlement Act of 1944, the Surplus Property Act of 1944, the Veterans' Emergency Housing Act of 1946, the Sugar Control Extension Act of 1947 and the Housing and Rent Act of 1947 are specifically exempted, regardless of their expiration date. Thus the War Assets Administration, insofar as its functions are derived from the Surplus Property Act, is not subject to the provision of the Act, with the exception of section 3.

The foregoing agencies and functions have been specifically exempted from all the provisions of the Act with the exception of section 3. This means, in effect, that the rule making provisions of section 4, the adjudication provisions of section 5, and the judicial review provisions of section 10 are not applicable to them. These broad exceptions, accordingly, must be borne in mind in connection with the discussion of the other sections of the Act. Specific exceptions to various sections will be noted in the discussion of such sections.

c. —*Distinction Between Rule Making and Adjudication*

The Administrative Procedure Act prescribes radically different procedures for rule making and adjudication. Accordingly, the proper classification of agency proceedings as rule making or adjudication is of fundamental importance.

13

"Rule" and "rule making", and "order" and "adjudication" are defined in section 2 as follows:

> (c) *Rule and rule making.* "Rule" means the whole or any part of any agency statement of general or particular applicability and future effect designed to implement, interpret, or prescribe law or policy or to describe the organization, procedure, or practice requirements of any agency and includes the approval or prescription for the future of rates, wages, corporate or financial structures or reorganizations thereof, prices, facilities, appliances, services or allowances therefor or of valuations, cost, or accounting, or practices bearing upon any of the foregoing. "Rule making" means agency process for the formulation, amendment, or repeal of a rule.
> (d) *Order and adjudication.* "Order" means the whole or any part of the final disposition (whether affirmative, negative, injunctive, or declaratory in form) of any agency in any matter other than rule making but including licensing. "Adjudication" means agency process for the formulation of an order.
> (e) *License and licensing.* "License" includes the whole or part of any agency permit, certificate, approval, registration, charter, membership, statutory exemption or other form of permission. "Licensing" includes agency process respecting the grant, renewal, denial, revocation, suspension, annulment, withdrawal, limitation, amendment, modification, or conditioning of a license.

Since the definition of adjudication is largely a residual one, i.e., "other than rule making but including licensing", it is logical to determine first the scope of rule making. The definition of rule is not limited to substantive rules, but embraces interpretative, organizational and procedural rules as well.[5] Of particular importance is the fact that "rule" includes agency statements not only of general applicability but also those of particular applicability applying either to a class or to a single person. In either case, they must be of *future effect*, implementing or prescribing future law. Accordingly, the approval of a corporate reorganization by the Securities and Exchange Commission, the prescription of future rates for a single named utility by the Federal Power Commission, and similar agency actions, although applicable only to named persons, constitute rule making. H.R. Rep. p. 49, fn. 1 (Sen. Doc. p. 283).

As applied to the various proceedings of Federal agencies, the definitions of "rule" and "rule making", and "order" and "adjudication" leave many questions as to whether particular proceedings are rule making or adjudication. For example, the question arises whether agency action on certain types of applications is to be deemed rule making or licensing (adjudication), in view of the fact that there is apparent overlapping between the defini-

---

5. Note that section 4 (apart from 4 (d)) is applicable only to substantive rules, i.e., rules issued pursuant to statutory authority to implement statutory policy, as by fixing rates or defining standards.

tion of "rule" in section 2 (c) and of "license" in section 2 (e). Thus, "rule" includes the "approval * * * for the future * * *", and "license" is defined to include "any agency permit, certificate, approval * * * or other form of permission."

An obvious principle of construction is that agency proceedings which fall within one of the specific categories of section 2 (c), e.g., determining rates for the future, must be regarded as rule making, rather than as coming under the general and residual definition of adjudication. Furthermore, the listing of specific subjects in section 2 (c) as rule making is not intended to be exclusive. It is illustrative only. H.R. Rep. 20 (Sen. Doc. p. 254). Thus, in determining whether agency action on a particular type of application is "rule making", the purposes of the statute involved and the considerations which the agency is required to weigh in granting or withholding its approval will be relevant; if the factors governing such approval are the same, for example, as the agency would be required to apply in approving a recapitalization or reorganization (clearly rule making), this circumstance would tend to support the conclusion that agency action on such an application is rule making.

More broadly, the entire Act is based upon a dichotomy between rule making and adjudication. Examination of the legislative history of the definitions and of the differences in the required procedures for rule making and for adjudication discloses highly practical concepts of rule making and adjudication. Rule making is agency action which regulates the future conduct of either groups of persons or a single person; it is essentially legislative in nature, not only because it operates in the future but also because it is primarily concerned with policy considerations. The object of the rule making proceeding is the implementation or prescription of law or policy for the future, rather than the evaluation of a respondent's past conduct. Typically, the issues relate not to the evidentiary facts, as to which the veracity and demeanor of witnesses would often be important, but rather to the policy-making conclusions to be drawn from the facts. Senate Hearings (1941) pp. 657, 1298, 1451. Conversely, adjudication is concerned with the determination of past and present rights and liabilities. Normally, there is involved a decision as to whether past conduct was unlawful, so that the proceeding is characterized by an accusatory flavor and may result in disciplinary action. Or, it may involve the determination of a person's right to benefits under existing law so that the issues relate to whether he is within the established category of persons entitled to such benefits. In such proceedings, the issues of fact are often sharply controverted. Sen. Rep. p. 39 (Sen. Doc. p. 225); 92 Cong. Rec. 5648 (Sen. Doc. p. 353).

Not only were the draftsmen and proponents of the bill aware of this realistic distinction between rule making and adjudication, but they shaped the entire Act around it. Even in formal rule making proceedings subject to sections 7 and 8, the Act leaves the hearing officer entirely free to consult with any other member of the agency's staff. In fact, the intermediate decision may be made by the agency itself or by a responsible officer other than the hearing officer. This reflects the fact that the purpose of the rule making proceeding is to determine policy. Policy is not made in Federal agencies by individual hearing examiners; rather it is formulated by the agency heads relying heavily upon the expert staffs which have been hired for that purpose. And so the Act recognizes that in rule making the intermediate decisions will be more useful to the parties in advising them of the real issues in the case if such decisions reflect the views of the agency heads or of their responsible officers who assist them in determining policy. In sharp contrast is the procedure required in cases of adjudication subject to section 5 (c). There the hearing officer who presides at the hearing and observes the witnesses must personally prepare the initial or recommended decision required by section 8. Also, in such adjudicatory cases, the agency officers who performed investigative or prosecuting functions in that or a factually related case may not participate in the making of decisions. These requirements reflect the characteristics of adjudication discussed above.

The foregoing discussion indicates that the residual definition of "adjudication" in section 2 (d) was intended to include such proceedings as the following:

1. Proceedings instituted by the Federal Trade Commission and the National Labor Relations Board leading to the issuance of orders to cease and desist from unfair methods of competition or unfair labor practices, respectively.
2. The determination of claims for money, such as compensation claims under the Longshoremen's and Harbor Workers' Compensation Act, and claims under Title II (Old Age and Survivors' Insurance) of the Social Security Act.

3. Reparation proceedings in which the agency determines whether a ship per or other consumer is entitled to damages arising out of the alleged past unreasonableness of rates.
4. The determination of individual claims for benefits, such as grants-in-aid and subsidies.
5. Licensing proceedings, including the grant, denial, renewal, revocation, suspension, etc. of, for example, radio broadcasting licenses, certificates of public convenience and necessity, airman certificates, and the like.

17

II

SECTION 3—PUBLIC INFORMATION

The purpose of section 3 is to assist the public in dealing with administrative agencies by requiring agencies to make their administrative materials available in precise and current form. Section 3 should be construed broadly in the light of this purpose so as to make such material most useful to the public. The public information requirements of section 3 do not supersede the Federal Register Act (44 U.S.C. 301 *et seq.*). They are to be integrated with the existing program for publication of material in the Federal Register and the Code of Federal Regulations. The Federal Register regulations (11 F.R. 9833) govern the manner in which documents are to be prepared prior to submission to the Division of the Federal Register. All materials issued under section 3 (a) of the Act will be included in the Code of Federal Regulations and should be prepared accordingly. The Division of the Federal Register is prepared to offer assistance to the agencies in this respect.

AGENCIES SUBJECT TO SECTION 3

This section, unlike the other provisions of the Act, is applicable to all agencies of the United States, excluding Congress, the courts, and the governments of the Territories, possessions, and the District of Columbia. Every agency, whether or not it has rule making or adjudicating functions, must comply with this section. Section 2 (a), defining agencies, states specifically that even the exemption for the functions enumerated in the last sentence of that section does not extend to section 3. Accordingly, agencies performing temporary war functions must comply with this section.

EXCEPTIONS TO REQUIREMENTS OF SECTION 3

Two exceptions have been made to section 3, namely:

"(1) *Any function of the United States requiring secrecy in the public interest.*" This would include the confidential operations of any agency, such as the confidential operations of the Federal Bureau of Investigation and the Secret Service and, in general, those aspects of any agency's law enforcement procedures the disclosure of which would reduce the utility of such procedures. It is not restricted, however, to investigatory functions. The Comptroller of the Currency, for example, may have occasion to issue rules to national banks under such circumstances that the public interest precludes publicity.

It should be noted that the exception is made only "to the extent" that the function requires secrecy in the public interest. Such a determination must be made by the agency concerned. To the extent that the function does not require such secrecy, the publication requirements apply. Thus, the War Department obviously is not required to publish confidential matters of military organization and operation, but it would be required to publish the organization and procedure applicable to the ordinary civil functions of the Corps of Engineers.

"(2) *Any matter relating solely to the internal management of an agency.*" This exception is in line with the spirit of the public information requirements of section 3. If a matter is solely the concern of the agency proper, and therefore does not affect the members of the public to any extent, there is no requirement for publication under section 3. Thus, an agency's internal personnel and budget procedures need not be published (e.g., rules as to leaves of absence, vacation, travel, etc.). However, in case of doubt as to whether a matter is or is not one of internal management, it is suggested that the matter be published in the Federal Register, assuming it does not require secrecy in the public interest.

"Internal management of an agency" should not be construed as intra-agency only; it includes functions of internal Federal management, such as most of the functions of the Bureau of the Budget, and interdepartmental committees which are established by the President for the handling of internal management problems.

It should be understood that the following discussion of the requirements of section 3 is not applicable to the above italicized functions since they are expressly exempted from the section.

EFFECTIVE DATE-PROSPECTIVE OPERATION

Section 3, which took effect on September 11, 1946, is prospective in operation. 92nd Cong. Rec. 5650 (Sen. Doc. p. 357). It has no application to materials issued prior to that date. To the extent that an agency's procedures and organization had been published theretofore in the Federal Register (for example, formal rules of practice), it was not necessary to republish them. Appropriate citations were frequently made to such previously published materials. Under section 3 (a) (3), publication in the Federal Register is required of substantive rules (and statements of general policy and interpretations formulated and adopted by the agency for the guidance of the public) issued on and after September 11, 1946.

The Federal Register of September 11, 1946, Part II, appearing in four sections and containing 966 pages, contains the material prepared by Government agencies in initial compliance with section 3.

SECTION 3 (a)—RULES

Section 3 (a) directs each agency to "separately state and currently publish in the Federal Register" its organization, procedures and substantive rules.

SEPARATE STATEMENT

The three classes of material—organizational, procedural, and substantive rules—must be published in the Federal Register under separate and appropriate headings. Such separate statement, however, should not be carried to so logical an extreme as to inconvenience the public. For example, if an agency grants public benefits, it would be proper to include in the substantive rules relative to those benefits a statement as to the form to be used in applying for such benefits and the place of filing; however, the same procedural information must also be set forth or referred to in the separate statement of the agency's procedure. This may be accomplished by inserting in the procedural statement a notation to the effect that the procedure for obtaining public benefits may be found at a designated part of the substantive rules relative to such benefits.

DESCRIPTION OF ORGANIZATION

Section 3 (a) (1) requires that every agency shall separately state and currently publish in the Federal Register "(1) descriptions of its central and field organization including delegations by the agency of final authority and the established places at which, and methods whereby, the public may secure information or make submittals or requests." It is only delegations of *final* authority which need be listed. In this connection, it should be noted that there is no requirement to list in the rules the names of specific individuals to whom power is delegated, unless such specific designation is otherwise required by law, nor is there any requirement that isolated instances of delegation made on an *ad hoc* basis be published. Senate Hearings (1941) p. 1329. However, the agency should list by title the offices or officers to whom definite delegations of final authority have been made (e.g., Claims Division of the Department of Justice, or Regional Director of the War Assets Administration). Under this subsection, it may be advisable also for agencies to state specifically the powers which may be exercised by persons serving in an "acting" capacity.

An agency's central organization should be described by listing its divisions and principal subdivisions and the functions of each. Field organizations should be described by listing the location of such offices, together with a statement of their functions. For example, if certain field offices have authority to issue interpretative or advisory opinions, this should be specified together with a statement as to whether such opinions are subject to review or confirmation by the agency's central or other office. In general, there should be a statement of the information which may be obtained from, and the applications or requests which may be filed with, the different field offices. In view of the last sentence of section 3 (a), it is important that each agency state clearly the types of applications, etc., if any, which it requires to be filed with designated agency offices.

STATEMENT OF PROCEDURES

Section 3 (a) (2) provides that every agency shall separately state and currently publish in the Federal Register "(2) statements of the general course and method by which its functions are channeled and determined, including the nature and requirements of all formal or informal procedures available as well as forms and instructions as to the scope and contents of all papers, reports, or examinations." This subsection is primarily concerned with the procedures by which an agency discharges its public functions—such as rule making, adjudication, and the administration of loan, grant and benefit programs. No categorical statement can be made as to the manner in which each agency should describe

21

"the general course and method by which its functions are channeled and determined."

Section 3 does not require an agency to "freeze" its procedures, nor does it force the adoption of procedures more formal than those previously prevailing. An agency need not invent procedures where it has no reason to establish any procedures. Senate Hearings (1941) p. 1337. However, the agency must, in accordance with section 3, keep the public currently informed of changes in the actual procedures available. Of course, the published procedures of the agency may provide (subject to applicable law) for emergency or exceptional cases.

Where there is an established procedure for the handling of certain functions, the routing of and responsibility for such functions may be stated with reasonable particularity. Some functions, however, may be exercised so seldom that it will not be practicable to prescribe a definite routine. In such cases, the published information should at least include a statement of the office to which inquiries may be directed.

In brief, section 3 (a) (2) requires an agency to disclose in general terms, designed to be realistically informative to the public, the manner in which its functions are channeled and determined. In this connection, it should be remembered that matters of internal management are exempted from the publication requirements of section 3.

Informal conference procedures used by an agency should be publicized with a view to both serving the convenience of the public and facilitating the agency's operations. Such procedures exist widely and are known to the specialized practitioners. The general public should be informed of their availability and as to how and where to take advantage of them.

Forms for application, registration, etc., and the instructions accompanying such forms need not be published in full; publication of a simple statement of the function and contents of the form, and of where copies of the form, if available, may be obtained, is sufficient. H.R. Rep. p. 22 (Sen. Doc. p. 256).

Attention is called to the last sentence of the section, stating "No person shall in any manner be required to resort to organization or procedure not so published." Should an agency fail to publish, for example, a listing of its field offices with their functions, persons who have not received actual notice of such agency organization may contend that they are not bound to resort to a field office prior to institution of their case in the central office.

SUBSTANTIVE RULES

Section 3 (a) (3) provides that every agency shall separately state and currently publish in the Federal Register "(3) substantive rules adopted as authorized by law and statements of general policy or interpretations formulated and adopted by the agency for the guidance of the public, but not rules addressed to and served upon named persons in accordance with law." This exemption for "rules addressed to and served upon named persons in accordance with law" is designed to avoid filling the Federal Register with a great mass of particularized rule making, such as schedules of rates, which have always been satisfactorily handled without general publication in the Federal Register.

The phrase "substantive rules adopted as authorized by law" refers, of course, to rules issued by an agency to implement statutory policy. Examples are the Federal Power Commission's rules prescribing uniform systems of accounts and proxy rules issued by the Securities and Exchange Commission.

Statements of general policy and interpretations need be published only if they are formulated and adopted by the agency for the guidance of the public. The Act leaves each agency free to determine for itself the desirability of formulating policy statements for the guidance of the public. To the extent that an agency, however, enunciates such statements of general policy in the form of speeches, releases or otherwise, the Act requires them to be published in the Federal Register.

The term "public" would not seem to embrace states. For example, the Federal Security Agency sends interpretative guides to states to assist them in complying with the requirements of the Unemployment Compensation provisions of the Social Security laws. Such guides need not be published since they are not for the use of the "public" but only for the state governments.

Section 3 (a) does not require publication in the Federal Register of statements of agency policy and interpretations which are developed and enunciated only in the course of adjudicatory orders and opinions; such orders and opinions are treated as a separate and distinct body of administrative materials under section 3 (b).

An advisory interpretation relating to a specific set of facts

23

is not subject to section 3. 92 Cong. Rec. 5649 (Sen. Doc. p. 355). For example, a reply from the agency's general counsel to an inquiry from a member of the public as to the applicability of a statute to a specific set of facts need not be published.

SECTION 3 (b)—OPINIONS AND ORDERS

Section 3 (b) provides that "Every agency shall publish or, in accordance with published rule, make available to public inspection all final opinions or orders in the adjudication of cases (except those required for good cause to be held confidential and not cited as precedents) and all rules." Section 3 (b) does not require publication of these materials in the Federal Register or in any other prescribed form. Regular publication of decisions in bound volumes or bulletins, as many agencies are now doing, will suffice; in such cases, however, the agency should publish a rule stating where copies of such orders and opinions may be obtained or inspected during the interval prior to publication. It should be noted that the materials specified by section 3 (b) need not be published at all if, in accordance with the agency's rule published in the Federal Register pursuant to section 3 (a) (1), they are available for public inspection. It is suggested that to the extent section 3 (b) is complied with by making materials available for inspection, such inspection be made possible, where practicable, in regional offices as well as in the agency's central office.

The scope of the phrase "opinions or orders in the adjudication of cases" is governed by section 2 (d) and, accordingly, includes orders or opinions issued with respect to licenses. Adjudicatory orders and opinions which are not "final" need not be published or made available for inspection. However, where intermediate orders and opinions would be useful to the public as, say, procedural precedents, agencies may wish to publish them or make them available for inspection in the same manner as final orders and opinions.

An agency may withhold from publication or inspection final orders and opinions "required for good cause to be held confidential and not cited as precedents." If it is desired, however, to rely upon the citation of confidential materials, the agency should first make available some abstract of the confidential material in such form as will show the principles relied upon without revealing the confidential facts.

The last three words of section 3 (b) "and all rules" include "rules addressed to and served upon named persons in accordance with law" which are excluded from the publication requirement of section 3 (a) (3). See H.R. Rep. p. 50, fn. 7 (Sen. Doc. p. 284). Thus rules involving corporate mergers and reorganizations where all the parties are served need not be published in the Federal Register pursuant to section 3 (a); instead the provisions of section 3(b) apply. It is sufficient, therefore, if such rules are made available for public inspection.

SECTION 3 (c)—PUBLIC RECORDS

Section 3 (c) provides that "Save as otherwise required by statute, matters of official record shall in accordance with published rule be made available to persons properly and directly concerned except information held confidential for good cause found." The introductory saving clause is intended to preserve existing statutory requirements for confidential treatment of certain materials, such as income tax returns.

Each agency should publish in the Federal Register, under 3 (a) (1), a rule listing the types of official records in its files, classifying them in terms of whether or not they are confidential in character, stating the manner in which information is available (as by inspection or sale of photostatic copies), the method of applying for information, and by what officials the application will be determined.

The term "official record" is difficult of definition. In general, it may be stated that matters of official record will include (a) applications, registrations, petitions, reports and returns filed by members of the public with the agency pursuant to statute or the agency's rules, and (b) all documents embodying agency actions, such as orders, rules and licenses. In formal proceedings, the pleadings, transcripts of testimony, exhibits, and all documents received in evidence or made a part of the record are "matters of official record."

Section 3 (c) does not purport to define "official record." Each agency must examine its functions and the substantive statutes under which it operates to determine which of its materials are to be treated as matters of official record for the purposes of the section. Indicative of the types of records which are considered official records by Congress are maps, plats, or diagrams in the custody of the Secretary of the Interior (5 U.S.C. 488),

25

records, books or papers in the General Land Office (28 U.S.C. 672), and registration statements filed with the Securities and Exchange Commission under the Securities Act (15 U.S.C. 77f).

The great mass of material relating to the internal operation of an agency is not a matter of official record. For example, intra-agency memoranda and reports prepared by agency employees for use within the agency are not official records since they merely reflect the research and analysis preliminary to official agency action. Intra-agency reports of investigations are, in general, not matters of official record; in addition, they usually involve matters of internal management and, in view of their nature, must commonly be kept confidential.

But even matters of official record need be divulged only to "persons properly and directly concerned." It is clear that section 3 (c) is not intended to open up Government files for general inspection. The phrase "persons properly and directly concerned" is descriptive of individuals who have a legitimate and valid reason for seeking access to an agency's records. See *United States ex rel. Stowell v. Deming*, 19 F. 2d, 697 (App. D.C., 1927), certiorari denied, 275 U.S. 531. Each agency is the primary judge of whether the person's interest is such as to require it to make its official records available for his inspection.

An agency may treat matters of official record as "confidential for good cause found" and upon that ground refuse to make them available for inspection. Information held "confidential for good cause found" may be either information held confidential by reason of an agency rule issued in advance (for good cause) making specific classes of material confidential, or such information as is held confidential for good cause found under a particular set of facts. The section does not change existing law as to those materials in Government files which have been heretofore treated as confidential. See *Boske v. Comingore*, 177 U.S. 459 (1900); *Boehm v. United States*, 123 F. 2d, 791, 805 (C.C.A. 8, 1941).

III
SECTION 4—RULE MAKING

In general, the purpose of section 4 is to guarantee to the public an opportunity to participate in the rule making process. With stated exceptions, each agency will be required under this section to give public notice of substantive rules which it proposes to adopt, and to grant interested persons an opportunity to present their views to it. Where rules are required by statute to be made on the record after opportunity for an agency hearing, the provisions of sections 7 and 8 as to hearing and decision will apply in place of the less formal procedures contemplated by section 4 (b). With certain exceptions, no substantive rule may be made effective until at least thirty days after its publication in the Federal Register. Section 4 also grants to interested persons the right to petition an agency for the issuance, amendment or repeal of a rule.

EXCEPTIONS

In addition to the agencies and functions exempted by section 2 (a), section 4 itself contains two broad exceptions to its requirements.

"(1) *any military, naval, or foreign affairs function of the United States*". The exemption for military and naval functions is not limited to activities of the War and Navy Departments but covers all military and naval functions exercised by any agency. Thus, the exemption applies to the defense functions of the Coast Guard and to the function of the Federal Power Commission under section 202 (c) of the Federal Power Act (16 U.S.C. 824a (c)). Sen. Rep. p. 39 (Sen. Doc. p. 225); Senate Hearings (1941) p. 502.

As to the meaning of "foreign affairs function", both the Senate and House reports state: "The phrase 'foreign affairs functions,' used here and in some other provisions of the bill, is not to be loosely interpreted to mean any function extending beyond the borders of the United States but only those 'affairs' which so affect relations with other governments that, for example, public rule making provisions would clearly provoke definitely undesirable international consequences." Sen. Rep. p. 13; H.R. Rep. p. 23 (Sen. Doc. pp. 199, 257). See also Representative Walter's statement to the House, 92 Cong. Rec. 5650 (Sen.

27

Doc. p. 358). It is equally clear that the exemption is not limited to strictly diplomatic functions, because the phrase "diplomatic function" was employed in the January 6, 1945 draft of S. 7 (Senate Comparative Print of June 1945, p. 6; Sen. Doc. p.157) and was discarded in favor of the broader and more generic phrase "foreign affairs function". In the light of this legislative history, it would seem clear that the exception must be construed as applicable to most functions of the State Department and to the foreign affairs functions of any other agency.

"(2) *any matter relating to agency management or personnel or to public property, loans, grants, benefits, or contracts*".

The exemption for matters relating to "agency management or personnel" is self-explanatory and has been considered in the discussion of "internal management" under section 3. The exemption of "any matter relating * * * to public property, loans, grants, benefits, or contracts" is intended generally to cover the "proprietary" functions of the Federal Government. 92 Cong. Rec. 5650 (Sen. Doc. p. 358). It will be helpful to consider the implication of each of these phrases separately.

Public Property. This embraces rules issued by any agency with respect to real or personal property owned by the United States or by any agency of the United States. Thus, the making of rules relating to the public domain, i.e., the sale or lease of public lands or of mineral, timber or grazing rights in such lands, is exempt from the requirements of section 4. The exemption extends, for example, to rules issued by the Tennessee Valley Authority in relation to the management of its properties, and by the Maritime Commission with respect to ships owned by the United States. The term "public property" includes property held by the United States in trust or as guardian; e.g., Indian property. H.R. Rep. p. 23 (Sen. Doc. p. 257).

Loans. This exempts rules issued with respect to loans by such agencies as the Reconstruction Finance Corporation, the Commodity Credit Corporation, and the Farm Credit Administration. It also exempts rules relating to guarantees of loans, such as are made by the Federal Housing Authority and the Veterans Administration, since they are matters relating to public loans.

Grants. Rule making with respect to subsidy programs is exempted from section 4. "Grants" also include grant-in-aid programs under which the Federal Government makes payments to state and local governments with respect to highways, airports, unemployment compensation, etc.

Benefits. This refers to such programs as veterans' pensions and old-age insurance payments.

Contracts. All rules relating to public contracts are exempt from section 4. The exemption extends to wage determinations made by the Labor Department under the Davis Bacon Act (40 U.S.C. 276a et seq.) and the Walsh Healey Act (41 U.S.C. 35-45), as conditions to construction and procurement contracts entered into by the Federal Government. See *Perkins v. Lukens Steel Co.*, 310 U. S. 113 (1940).

SECTION 4 (A)—NOTICE

Subsections (a) and (b) of section 4 must be read together because the procedural requirements of subsection (b) apply only where notice is required by subsection (a). It is clear that the requirements of "general notice of proposed rule making" apply only to rule making proposed or initiated by an agency; the filing of a petition under section 4 (d) does not require an agency to undertake rule making proceedings in accordance with subsections (a) and (b). H.R. Rep. p. 26 (Sen. Doc. p. 260).

An agency contemplating the issuance of a rule subject to section 4 (a) must publish in the Federal Register a notice of the proposed rule making, "unless all persons subject thereto are named and either personally served or otherwise have actual notice thereof in accordance with law". The reason for the quoted exception is to avoid burdening the Federal Register with notices addressed to particular parties who have been personally served or otherwise have notice. H.R. Rep. p. 51, fn. 8 (Sen. Doc. p. 285). For example, where a proceeding is commenced to establish rates for named carriers or utilities, if a notice complying with section 4 (a) is personally served upon such persons, publication in the Federal Register is not required by the subsection.

Contents of notice. In both formal[1] and informal rule making, the required notice, whether published in the Federal Register or personally served, must include the following information:

1. "A statement of the time, place, and nature of public rule making proceedings". While section 4 (a) does not specify how much notice must be given by an agency before it may conduct public rule making proceedings, it is presumed that each agency

---

1. As used here, "formal" rule making means those public rule making proceedings which must be conducted in accordance with sections 7 and 8.

29

will give reasonable notice.[2] In this connection, each agency should take into account the fact that section 4 (c) provides that thirty days must ordinarily elapse prior to a rule becoming effective. Accordingly, each agency should schedule its rule making in such fashion that there will be sufficient time for affording interested persons an opportunity to participate in the rule making as well as for insuring final publication of the rule at least thirty days prior to the desired effective date.

The nature of public rule making may vary considerably from case to case. Under section 4 (b) each agency, as this memorandum will indicate *infra*, may conduct its rule making by affording interested persons opportunity to submit written data only, or by receiving a combination of written and oral evidence, or by adopting any other method it finds most appropriate for public participation in the rule making process. However, where an agency is required by statute to conduct a hearing and to reach a decision upon the basis of the record made at such hearing, the formal procedures prescribed by sections 7 and 8 must be pursued. Therefore, the notice, required by section 4 (a) should specify the procedure to be employed, that is, formal or informal hearings, submission of written statements with or without opportunity for oral argument, etc.

2. "Reference to the authority under which the rule is proposed". The reference must be sufficiently precise to apprise interested persons of the agency's legal authority to issue the proposed rule.

3. "Either the terms or substance of the proposed rule or a description of the subjects and issues involved". Where able to do so, an agency may state the proposed rule itself or the substance of the rule in the notice required by section 4 (a). On the other hand, the agency, if it desires, may issue a more general "description of the subjects and issues involved". It is suggested that each agency consider the desirability of using the latter method if publication of a proposed rule in full would unduly burden the Federal Register or would in fact be less informative to the public. In such a case, the agency may inform interested persons that copies of the proposed rule may be obtained from the agency upon request—this, of course, in addition to the "description of the subjects and issues involved" in the Federal Register. Where there is a "description of the subjects and issues

---

2. See section 8 of the Federal Register Act (44 U.S.C. 308) for a general statutory standard of reasonable notice.

involved", the notice should be sufficiently informative to assure interested persons an opportunity to participate intelligently in the rule making process. Final Report, p. 108.

Section 4 (a) and (b) applicable only to substantive rules. The last sentence of section 4 (a) exempts from the requirements of section 4 (a) and (b), unless otherwise required by statute, "interpretative rules, general statements of policy, rules of agency organization, procedure, or practice". Thus, the rules of organization and procedure which an agency must publish pursuant, to section 3 (a) (1) and (2) are not ordinarily subject to the requirements of section 4 (a) and (b). The further exemption of "interpretative rules" and "general statements of policy" restricts the application of section 4 (a) and (b) to substantive rules issued pursuant to statutory authority.[3] See Senate Comparative Print of June 1945, p. 6 (Sen. Doc. p. 19).

Omission of notice and public procedure for good cause. The last sentence of section 4 (a) authorizes any agency to omit the notice required by that subsection (and the procedure specified by section 4 (b)) "in any situation in which the agency for good cause finds ... that notice and public procedure thereon are impracticable, unnecessary, or contrary to the public interest". It should be noted that the reasons for which an agency may dispense with notice under section 4 (a) are written in the alternative so that if it is "impracticable" or "unnecessary" or "contrary to the public interest" the agency may dispense with notice. Should this be done, the agency must incorporate in the rule issued its finding of "good cause" and "a brief statement of the reasons therefor". In general, it may be said that a situation is "impracticable" when an agency finds that due and timely execution of its functions would be impeded by the notice otherwise required in section 4 (a). For example, the Civil Aeronautics Board may learn, from an accident investigation, that certain rules as to air safety should be issued or amended without delay; with the safety of the traveling public at stake, the Board could find that notice

---

    3   In this connection, the following working definitions are offered: *Substantive rules*—rules, other than organizational or procedural under section 3 (a) (1) and (2), issued by an agency pursuant to statutory authority and which implement the statute, as, for example, the proxy rules issued by the Securities and Exchange Commission pursuant to section 14 of the Securities Exchange Act of 1934 (15 U.S.C. 78 n). Such rules have the force and effect of law.
Interpretative rule—rules or statements issued by an agency to advise the public of the agency's construction of the statutes and rules which it administers. See Final Report. p. 27; Senate Comparative Print of June 1945, p. 6 (Sen. Doc. p. 18); Senate Hearings (1941) p. 330.
General statements of policy—statements issued by an agency to advise the public prospectively of the manner in which the agency proposes to exercise a discretionary power.

31

and public rule making procedures would be "impracticable", and issue its rules immediately. "Unnecessary" refers to the issuance of a minor rule or amendment in which the public is not particularly interested. Senate Hearings (1941) p. 828. "Public interest" connotes a situation in which the interest of the public would be defeated by any requirement of advance notice. For example, an agency may contemplate the issuance of financial controls under such circumstances that advance notice of such rules would tend to defeat their purpose; in such circumstances, the "public interest" might well justify the omission of notice and public rule making proceedings. Senate Hearings (1941) p. 812.

SECTION 4 (b)—PROCEDURES

Informal rule making. In every case of proposed informal rule making subject to the notice requirements of section 4 (a), section 4 (b) provides that "the agency shall afford interested persons an opportunity to participate in the rule making through submission of written data, views, or arguments with or without opportunity to present the same orally in any manner." The quoted language confers discretion upon the agency, except where statutes require "formal" rule making subject to sections 7 and 8, to designate in each case the procedure for public participation in rule making. Such informal rule making procedure may take a variety of forms: informal hearings (with or without a stenographic transcript), conferences, consultation with industry committees, submission of written views, or any combination of these. These informal procedures have already been extensively employed by Federal agencies. Final Report, pp. 103-105. In each case, the selection of the procedure to be followed will depend largely upon the nature of the rules involved. The objective should be to assure informed administrative action and adequate protection to private interests.

Each agency is affirmatively required to consider "all relevant matter presented" in the proceeding; it is recommended that all rules issued after such informal proceedings be accompanied by an express recital that such material has been considered. It is entirely clear, however, that section 4 (b) does not require the formulation of rules upon the exclusive basis of any "record" made in informal rule making proceedings. Senate Hearings (1941) p. 444. Accordingly, except in formal rule making governed by sections 7 and 8, an agency is free to formulate rules upon the basis of materials in its files and the knowledge and experience of the agency, in addition to the materials adduced in public rule making proceedings.

Section 4 (b) provides that upon the completion of public rule making proceedings "after consideration of all relevant matter presented, the agency shall incorporate in any rules adopted a concise general statement of their basis and purpose". The required statement will be important in that the courts and the public may be expected to use such statements in the interpretation of the agency's rules. The statement is to be "concise" and "general". Except as required by statutes providing for "formal" rule making procedure, findings of fact and conclusions of law are not necessary. Nor is there required an elaborate analysis of the rules or of the considerations upon which the rules were issued. Rather, the statement is intended to advise the public of the general basis and purpose of the rules.

Formal rule making. Section 4 (b) provides that "Where rules are required by statute to be made on the record after opportunity for an agency hearing, the requirements of sections 7 and 8 shall apply in place of the provisions of this subsection." Thus, where a rule is required by some other statute to be issued on the basis of a record after opportunity for an agency hearing, the public rule making proceedings must consist of hearing and decision in accordance with sections 7 and 8. The provisions of section 5 are in no way applicable to rule making. It should be noted that sections 7 and 8 did not become effective until December 11, 1946, and, pursuant to section 12, do not apply to any public rule making proceedings initiated prior to that date.

Statutes rarely require hearings prior to the issuance of rules of general applicability. Such requirements, where they exist, appear in radically different contexts. The Federal Food, Drug and Cosmetic Act (21 U.S.C. 301) is almost unique in that it specifically provides that agency action issuing, amending or repealing specified classes of substantive rules may be taken only after notice and hearing, and that "The Administrator shall base his order only on substantial evidence of record at the hearing and shall set forth as part of the order detailed findings of fact on which the order is based." Upon review in a circuit court of appeals, a transcript of the record is filed, and "the findings of the Administrator as to the facts, if supported by substantial evidence, shall be conclusive" (21 U.S.C. 371). It is clear that such rules are "required by statute to be made on the record after opportunity

33

for an agency hearing". Accordingly, the rule making hearings required by the Federal Food, Drug and Cosmetic Act, initiated on and after December 11, 1946, must be conducted in accordance with sections 7 and 8 of the Administrative Procedure Act.

Statutes authorizing agencies to prescribe future rates (i.e., rules of either general or particular applicability) for public utilities and common carriers typically require that such rates be established only after all opportunity for a hearing before the agency. Such statutes rarely specify in terms that the agency action musts be taken on the basis of the "record" developed in the hearing. However, where rates or prices are established by an agency after a hearing required by statute, the agencies themselves and the courts have long assumed that the agency's action must be based upon the evidence adduced at the hearing. Sometimes the requirement of decision on the record is readily inferred from other statutory provisions defining judicial review. For example, rate orders issued by the Federal Power Commission pursuant to the Natural Gas Act (15 U.S.C. 717) may be made only after hearing; upon review in a circuit court of appeals or the Court of Appeals for the District of Columbia, the Commission certifies and files with the court "a transcript of the record upon which the order complained of was entered", and the Commission's findings of fact "if supported by substantial evidence, shall be conclusive". It seems clear that these provisions of the Natural Gas Act must be construed as requiring the Commission to determine rates "on the record after opportunity for an agency hearing". See H.R. Rep. p. 51, fn. 9 (Sen. Doc. p. 285). The same conclusion would be reached with respect to the determination of minimum wages under the Fair Labor Standards Act (29 U.S.C. 201), which contains substantially the same provisions for hearing and judicial review.

The Interstate Commerce Commission and the Secretary of Agriculture may, after hearing, prescribe rates for carriers and stockyard agencies, respectively. Both types of rate orders are reviewable under the Urgent Deficiencies Act of 1913 (28 U.S.C. 47). Nothing in the Interstate Commerce Act, the Packers and Stockyards Act, or the Urgent Deficiencies Act requires in terms that such rate orders be "made on the record", or provides for the filing of a transcript of the administrative record with the reviewing court, or defines the scope of judicial review. However, both of these agencies and the courts have long assumed that such rate orders must be based upon the record made in the hearing; furthermore, it has long been the practice under the Urgent Deficiencies Act to review such orders on the basis of the administrative record which is submitted to the reviewing court. *United States* v. *Abilene & Southern Ry. Co.*, 265 U.S. 274 (1924); *Mississippi Valley Barge Line Co.* v. *United States*, 292 U.S. 282 (1934); *Acker* v. *United States*, 298 U.S. 426 (1936). It appears, therefore, that rules (as defined in section 2 (c)) which are issued after a hearing required by statute, and which are reviewable under the Urgent Deficiencies Act on the basis of the evidence adduced at the agency hearing, must be regarded as "required by statute to be made on the record after opportunity for an agency hearing".

With respect to the types of rule making discussed above, the statutes not only specifically require the agencies to hold hearings but also, specifically, or by clear implication, or by established administrative and judicial construction, require such rules to be formulated upon the basis of the evidentiary record made in the hearing. In these situations, the public rule making procedures required by section 4 (b) will consist of a hearing conducted in accordance with sections 7 and 8.

There are other statutes which require agencies to hold hearings before issuing rules, but contain no language from which the further requirement of decision "on the record" can be inferred, nor any provision for judicial review on the record (as does the Natural Gas Act, *supra*). For example, the Federal Seed Act (7 U.S.C. 1561) simply provides that "prior to the promulgation of any rule or regulation under this chapter, due notice shall be given by publication in the Federal Register of intention to promulgate and the time and place of a public hearing to be held with reference thereto, and no rule or regulation may be promulgated until after such hearing". See also the so-called Dangerous Cargoes Act (46 U.S.C. 170(9)) and the Tanker Act (46 U.S.C. 391a (3)) discussed in Senate Hearings (1941) p. 589. In this type of statute, there is no requirement, express or implied, that rules be formulated "on the record".

There is persuasive legislative history to the effect that the Congress did not intend sections 7 and 8 to apply to rule making where the substantive statute merely required a hearing. In 1941, a subcommittee of the Senate Committee on the Judiciary held hearings on S. 674 (77th Cong., 1st sess.) and other administrative procedure bills. Section 209 (d) of S. 674 provided with

35

respect to rule making that "where legislation specifically requires the holding of hearings prior to the making of rules, formal rule making hearings shall be held". Mr. Ashley Sellers, testifying on behalf of the Department of Agriculture, called the subcommittee's attention to the fact that in various statutes, such as the Federal Seed Act, in which the Congress had required hearings to be held prior to the issuance of rules, the obvious purpose "was simply to require that the persons interested in the proposed rule should be permitted to express their views". Mr. Sellers drew a sharp distinction between such hearing requirements and the formal rule making requirements of the Federal Food, Drug and Cosmetic Act. Senate Hearings (1941) pp. 78-81, 1515, 1520.[4] Since this situation was thus specifically called to the subcommittee's attention, it is a legitimate inference that with respect to rule making the present dual requirement, i.e., "after opportunity for an agency hearing" *and* "on the record", was intended to avoid the application of formal procedural requirements in cases where the Congress intended only to provide an opportunity for the expression of views. See Mr. Carl McFarland's statement in Senate Hearings (1941) pp. 1343, 1386. See also *Pacific States Box & Basket Co. v. White*, 296 U.S. 176, 186 (1935).

Publication of procedures. Each agency which will be affected by section 4 should publish under section 3 (a) (2) the procedures, formal and informal, pursuant to which the public may participate in the formulation of its rules. The statement of informal rule making procedures may be couched in either specific or general terms, depending on whether the agency has adopted a fixed procedure for all its rule making or varies it according to the type of rule to be promulgated. In the latter instance, it would be sufficient to state that proposed substantive rules will be adopted after allowing the public to participate in the rule making process either through submission of written data, oral testimony, etc., the method of participation in each case to be specified in the published notice in the Federal Register. H.R. Rep. p. 25 (Sen. Doc. p. 259).

SECTION 4 (c)—EFFECTIVE DATES

Section 4 (c) provides that "The required publication or service of any substantive rule (other than one granting or recog-

---

4. See, also, the statement of Acting Attorney General Biddle citing examples of "statutes which require hearings as a part of the rule making procedure without imposing a requirement of formal adversary judicial methods". Senate Hearings (1941) p. 1468.

nizing exemption or relieving restriction or interpretative rules and statements of policy) shall be made not less than thirty days prior to the effective date thereof except as otherwise provided by the agency upon good cause found and published with the rule." This requirement applies regardless of whether the rules are issued after formal or informal procedure.

The discussion on section 4 (c) in the reports of both the Senate and House Committees on the Judiciary makes clear that the phrase "The required publication or service of any substantive rule" does not relate back or refer to the publication of "general notice of proposed rule making" required by section 4 (a); rather it is a requirement that substantive rules which must be published in the Federal Register (see section 3 (a) (3)) shall be so published at least thirty days prior to their effective date. Similarly, "rules addressed to and served upon named persons", when they are substantive in nature, are subject to section 4 (c). The purpose of the time lag required by section 4 (c) is to "afford persons affected a reasonable time to prepare for the effective date of a rule or rules or to take any other action which the issuance of rules may prompt". Sen. Rep. p. 15; H.R. Rep. p. 25 (Sen. Doc. pp. 201, 259).

It is possible that section 4 (c) will be interpreted as amending the Federal Register Act so as to require, with respect to rules subject to section 4 (c), actual publication in the Federal Register (or service) at least thirty days prior to their effective date, rather than the mere filing of such rules with the Division of the Federal Register as heretofore. In any. event, section 4 (c) applies only to such substantive rules as are not excepted from all the provisions of section 4 by its introductory clause or by section 2 (a) of the Act. It is clear, for example, that the effective date of rules issued within the scope of the functions exempted from all of the requirements of section 4 by the introductory clause of that section, will continue to be governed by section 7 of the Federal Register Act (44 U.S.C. 307), rather than by section 4 (c) of the Administrative Procedure Act. Thus, where an agency issues rules relating to public property, such rules may be made effective upon filing with the Division of the Federal Register.

Also, section 7 of the Federal Register Act is not superseded in so far as there are involved rules granting or recognizing exemption or relieving restriction or interpretative rules and statements of policy. Thus, there still may be made effective upon filing with the Division of the Federal Register statements of policy

37

and interpretative rules. Likewise excepted from the thirty-day requirement of section 4 (c) are rules "granting or recognizing exemption or relieving restriction". For example, if a statute prohibits the doing of an act without prior agency approval and such approval falls within the definition of "rule" in section 2 (c), the action of the agency in approving such act, i.e., removing the restriction or providing an exemption, may be made effective without regard to the thirty-day requirement. Senate Hearings (1941) p. 1296. Also, the relaxation of a restrictive rule by an amendment, or the repeal of such a rule, would seem to be within the scope of the exception. The reason for this exception would appear to be that the persons affected by such rules are benefited by them and therefore need no time to conform their conduct so as to avoid the legal consequences of violation. The fact that an interested person may object to such issuance, amendment, or repeal of a rule does not change the character of the rule as being one "granting, or recognizing exemption or relieving restriction", thereby exempting it from the thirty-day requirement.

The requirement of publication not less than thirty days prior to the effective date may be shortened by an agency "upon good cause found and published with the rule". This discretionary exception was provided primarily to take care of the cases in which the public interest requires the agency to act immediately or within a period less than thirty days. Senate Hearings (1941) pp. 70, 441, 588, 650, 812, 1506. Where the persons concerned request that a rule be made effective within a shorter period, this circumstance would ordinarily constitute good cause. Also, it is clear from the legislative history that for good cause an agency may put a substantive rule into effect immediately; in such event, the requirement of prior publication is altogether absent, and the rule will become effective upon issuance as to persons with actual notice, and as to others upon filing with the Division of the Federal Register in accordance with section 7 of the Federal Register Act. Senate Hearings (1941) pp. 594, 599, 1340, 1455. Nothing in the Act precludes the issuance of retroactive rules when otherwise legal and accompanied by the finding required by section 4 (c). H.R. Rep. p. 49, fn. 1 (Sen. Doc. p. 283).

Where an agency, pursuant to the last clause of section 4 (a), omits the procedures of section 4 (a) and (b) because "notice and public procedure thereon are impracticable, unnecessary or contrary to the public interest", subsection (c) does not thereby become automatically inoperative. If the situation is such as to compel the agency, in addition, to dispense with the thirty-day provision, the rule should also contain the finding required by the last clause of section 4 (c).

Section 4 (c) is not intended to repeal provisions of other statutes which require a period of longer than thirty days between the issuance and effective date of certain rules. For example, the Cotton Standards Act authorizes the Secretary of Agriculture to set cotton classification standards which may not become effective in less than one year (7 U.S.C. 56). The thirty-day period prescribed by section 4 (c) of the Administrative Procedure Act does not supersede the one-year period thus required by the Cotton Standards Act.

SECTION 4 (d)—PETITIONS

Section 4 (d) provides that "Every agency shall accord any interested person the right to petition for the issuance, amendment, or repeal of a rule." Section 4 (d) applies not only to substantive rules but also to interpretations and statements of general policy, and to organizational and procedural rules. It is applicable both to existing rules and to proposed or tentative rules.

The right to petition under section 4 (d) must be accorded to any "interested person". It will be proper for an agency to limit this right to persons whose interests are or will be affected by the issuance, amendment or repeal of a rule.

Every agency with rule making powers subject to section 4 should establish, and publish under section 3 (a) (2), procedural rules governing the receipt, consideration and disposition of petitions filed pursuant to section 4 (d). These procedural rules may call, for example, for a statement of the rule making action which the petitioner seeks, together with any data available in support of his petition, a declaration of the petitioner's interest in the proposed action, and compliance with reasonable formal requirements.

If the agency is inclined to grant the petition, the nature of the proposed rule would determine whether public rule making proceedings under section 4 (a) and (b) are required. However, the mere filing of a petition does not require the agency to grant it or to hold a hearing or to engage in any other public rule making proceedings. For example, under section 701(e) of the

39

Federal Food, Drug and Cosmetic Act (21 U.S.C. 371 (e)), the Federal Security Administrator must provide a hearing on a proposed rule only where an application, stating reasonable grounds, is made by an interested industry or a substantial portion of the industry. Section 4 (d) was not intended to modify that statute so as to require the Federal Security Administrator to hold a hearing on the petition of a single individual.

The agency need act on the petition only in accordance with its procedures as published in compliance with section 3 (a) (2). The denial of a petition is governed by section 6 (d). Sen. Rep. p. 15; H.R. Rep. p. 26 (Sen. Doc. pp. 201, 260). Accordingly, prompt notice of such denial should be given to the petitioner, together with a simple statement of the procedural or other grounds therefor.

Neither the denial of a petition under section 4 (d), nor an agency's refusal to hold public rule making proceedings thereon, is subject to judicial review. Sen. Rep. p. 44 (Sen. Doc. p. 230).

This subsection (as in the case of the preceding portions of section 4) does not apply to rules relating to the functions and matters enumerated in the first sentence of section 4. The reports of the Senate and House Committees on the Judiciary state that "The introductory clause exempts from all *of the requirements* of section 4 any rule making so far as there are involved (1) military, naval, or foreign affairs functions or (2) matters relating to agency management or personnel or to public property, loans, grants, benefits, or contracts." (Underscoring supplied). Sen. Rep. p. 13; H.R. Rep. p. 23 (Sen. Doc. pp. 199, 257). The petition procedure of section 4 (d) is not applicable, for example, to the rules which an agency has issued or is empowered to issue with respect to loans or pensions.

IV
SECTION 5—ADJUDICATIONS

Section 5, together with sections 7 and 8, governs the procedure in formal administrative adjudication. In addition, section a lists the types of adjudication which are exempted from the detailed procedural requirements of sections 5, 7 and 8. It is to be noted that the excepted types of adjudication are exempt from all of the provisions of section 5, as well as of sections 7 and 8. Thus, if a particular matter is "subject to a subsequent trial of the law and the facts de novo in any court", subsection (d), authorizing agencies to issue declaratory judgments, is not applicable.

GENERAL SCOPE OF FORMAL PROCEDURAL REQUIREMENTS

"Adjudication" is defined as "agency process for the formulation of an order"; "order" is in turn defined as "the whole or any part of the final disposition (whether affirmative, negative, injunctive, or declaratory in form) of any agency in any matter other than rule making but including licensing" (section 2 (d)). Thus, investigatory proceedings, no matter how formal, which do not lead to the issuance of an order containing the element of final disposition as required by the definition, do not constitute adjudication. For example, accident investigations conducted by the Civil Aeronautics Authority pursuant to Title VII of the Civil Aeronautics Act do not result in orders, and therefore do not involve adjudication within the meaning of section 5.[1]

After examining the definition of "rule making" in section 2 (c), it is apparent that the residual definition of "adjudication" in section 2 (d) might include many governmental functions, such as the administration of loan programs, which traditionally have never been regarded as adjudicative in nature and as a rule have never been exercised through other than business procedures. The exclusion of such functions from the formal procedural requirements of sections 5, 7 and 8 is accomplished by the introductory phrase of section 5 which limits its application (and, therefore, the application of sections 7 and 8) to cases of "adjudication required by statute to be determined on the record after op-

---

1. In the Senate Comparative Print of June 1945, p. 2 (Sen. Doc. p. 13), it is stated: "It should be noted that the definition of agencies does not mean that all acts of such agencies are subject to the procedural requirements. * * * If an agency is subject to the proposal under this section, nevertheless it is subject thereto only to the extent that acts, rules, or orders are defined and not further excluded in the following sections and subsections."

41

portunity for an agency hearing". It has been pointed out that "Limiting application of the sections to those cases in which statutes require a hearing is particularly significant, because thereby are excluded the great mass of administrative routine as well as pensions, claims, and a variety of similar matters in which Congress has usually intentionally or traditionally refrained from requiring an administrative hearing." Senate Comparative Print of June 1945, p. 7 (Sen. Doc. p. 22).

It will be noted that the formal procedural requirements of the Act are invoked only where agency action "on the record after opportunity for an agency hearing" is required by some other *statute*. The legislative history makes clear that the word "statute" was used deliberately so as to make sections 5, 7 and 8 applicable only where the Congress has otherwise *specifically* required a hearing to be held. Senate Hearings (1941) pp. 453, 577; Senate Comparative Print of June 1945, p. 7 (Sen. Doc. p. 22); House Hearings (1945) p. 33 (Sen. Doc. p. 79); Sen. Rep. p. 40

(Sen. Doc. p. 226); 92 Cong. Rec. 5651 (Sen. Doc. p. 359). Mere statutory authorization to hold hearings (e.g., "such hearings as may be deemed necessary") does not constitute such a requirement. In cases where a hearing is held, although not required by statute, but as a matter of due process or agency policy or practice, sections 5, 7 and 8 do not apply. Senate Hearings (1941) p. 1456.

Under section 5 of the Federal Trade Commission Act, for example, it is clear that orders to cease and desist from unfair methods of competition must be issued on the basis of the record made in the hearing which is required by that Act (15 U.S.C. 45). See also section 10 of the National Labor Relations Act (29 U.S.C. 160). Licensing proceedings constitute adjudication by definition and where they are required by statute to be "determined on the record after opportunity for an agency hearing", sections 5, 7 and 8 are applicable. Thus, under section 15 of the Securities Exchange Act (15 U.S.C. 78o), the Securities and Exchange Commission may deny an application for broker-dealer registration or revoke such registration after notice and opportunity for hearing; while the Securities Exchange Act does not expressly require orders of denial or revocation of registration to be made "on the record", such a requirement is clearly implied in the provision for judicial review of these orders in the circuit courts of appeal. Upon such review, the Commission files "a transcript of the record upon which the order complained of was entered", and "The finding of the Commission as to the facts, if supported by substantial evidence, shall be conclusive." (15 U.S.C. 78y).

Other statutes authorizing agency action which is clearly adjudicatory in nature, such as the revocation of licenses, specifically require the agency to hold a hearing but contain no provision expressly requiring decision "on the record". For example, the Secretary of Agriculture may issue cease and desist orders under section 312 of the Packers and Stockyards Act, 1921 (7 U.S.C. 213), only after "notice and full hearing", and these orders are made reviewable under the Urgent Deficiencies Act. The Department of Agriculture has always assumed that these orders must be based upon the evidentiary record made in the hearing, and the courts have held that upon review the validity of an order issued under the Packers and Stockyards Act must be determined upon the administrative record. *Tagg Bros. & Moorhead v. United States,* 280 U.S. 420 (1930). It seems clear that administrative adjudication exercised in this context is subject to sections 5, 7 and 8.

A further group of statutes merely authorizes adjudicatory action after hearing, and contains no reference to decision "on the record" nor any specific provision for judicial review. Thus, under the United States Warehouse Act, the Secretary of Agriculture may suspend or revoke warehousemen's licenses "after opportunity for hearing" (7 U.S.C. 246). It is believed that with respect to adjudication the specific statutory requirement of a hearing, without anything more, carries with it the further requirement of decision on the basis of the evidence adduced at the hearing.[2] With respect to rule making, it was concluded, *supra*, that a statutory provision that rules be issued after a hearing, without more, should not be construed as requiring agency action "on the record", but rather as merely requiring an opportunity for the expression of views. That conclusion was based on the legislative nature of rule making, from which it was inferred, unless a statute requires otherwise, that an agency hearing on proposed rules would be similar to a hearing before a legislative committee, with neither the legislature nor the agency being limited to the material adduced at the hearing. No such rationale

---

2. It in clear that nothing in the Administrative Procedure Act precludes private parties from waiving their right to a hearing. Similarly. an agency is not prevented from requiring parties to indicate within a reasonable time their desire for a hearing.

applies to administrative adjudication. In fact, it is assumed that where a statute specifically provides for administrative adjudication (such as the suspension or revocation of a license) after opportunity for an agency hearing, such specific requirement for a hearing ordinarily implies the further requirement of decision in accordance with evidence adduced at the hearing. H.R. Rep. p. 51, fn. 9 (Sen. Doc. p. 285). Of course, the foregoing discussion is inapplicable to any situation in which the legislative history or the context of the pertinent statute indicates a contrary congressional intent.

Certain licensing statutes provide that an application for a license may be granted or become effective upon lapse of time without a hearing, but that there must be an opportunity for hearing prior to the denial of the application. See Securities Exchange Act of 1934, section 15 (b), (15 U.S.C. 78o (b)) and Communications Act of 1934, section 309 (47 U.S.C. 309). Nothing in section 5 of the Administrative Procedure Act is intended to require hearings where such statutes now permit the granting of licenses without a hearing.

Exempted adjudications. Section 5 specifically exempts from its provisions (and, accordingly, from the provisions of sections 7 and 8) six types of adjudicatory functions or proceedings which are discussed hereafter. It is important to note that these exemptions extend to all of the provisions of section 5. Furthermore, the exemption is applicable even where the exempted function is required by statute to be exercised "on the record after opportunity for an agency hearing". Sen. Rep. p. 16; H.R. Rep. p. 26 (Sen. Doc. pp. 202, 260).

1. "Any matter subject to a subsequent trial of the law and the facts de novo in any court". This exemption was explained in the reports of the Senate and House Committees on the Judiciary, as follows: "Where the adjudication is subject to a judicial trial de novo [it] is included because whatever judgment the agency makes is effective only in a prima facie sense at most and the party aggrieved is entitled to complete judicial retrial and decision." Sen. Rep. p. 16; H.R. Rep. p. 26 (Sen. Doc. pp. 202, 260). Exempt under this heading are certain proceedings which lead to reparation orders awarding damages, such as are issued by the Interstate Commerce Commission (49 U.S.C. 16) and the Secretary of Agriculture (7 U.S.C. 210). Senate Hearings (1941) pp. 75, 1389, 1508. In the Senate Comparative Print of June 1945

(p.8) (Sen. Doc. p. 22) the scope of the exemption was described as follows:

> This exception also exempts administrative reparation orders assessing damages, such as are issued by the Interstate Commerce Commission and the Secretary of Agriculture, since such orders are subject to trial de novo in court upon attempted enforcement.

2. "The selection or tenure of an officer or employee of the United States other than examiners appointed pursuant to section 11". This exemption of adjudications involving the selection and tenure of officers other than examiners was made "because the selection and control of public personnel has been traditionally regarded as a largely discretionary function". Sen. Rep. p. 16; H.R. Rep. p. 26 (Sen. Doc. pp. 202, 260). There is excluded from this exemption the selection or tenure of "examiners appointed pursuant to section 11"; this refers to the provision of section 11 that "Examiners shall be removable by the agency in which they are employed only for good cause established and determined by the Civil Service Commission * * * after opportunity for hearing and upon the record thereof." Proceedings for the removal of such examiners must be conducted in accordance with sections 5, 7 and 8.

3. "Proceedings in which decisions rest solely on inspections, tests, or elections". The reason for the exemption is that "those methods of determination do not lend themselves to the hearing process". Sen. Rep. p. 16; H.R. Rep. p. 27 (Sen. Doc. pp. 202, 261). This exemption is applicable even though a statute requires an opportunity for an agency hearing; thus the words "rest solely" do not mean that the exemption is available only where decisions are based solely upon inspections, tests, or elections, without opportunity for hearing or other proceedings. Rather, "rest solely" appears to mean that the exemption shall apply where all the issues involved in the decision are determined mainly on the basis of an inspection, test, or election. The legislative history of the Act, commencing with the Final Report of the Attorney General's Committee on Administrative Procedure, pp. 36-38, suggests the following as examples of "proceedings in which decisions rest solely on inspections, tests, or elections":

(a) the denial of airman certificates under section 602 of the Civil Aeronautics Act (49 U.S.C. 552) (statute provides for a hearing); Senate Hearings (1941) pp. 602-3;

(b) the denial or revocation of certificates of seaworthiness by local inspectors of the Coast Guard (46 U.S.C. 391); Senate

Hearings (1941) pp. 833-4;

(c) locomotive inspections by the Interstate Commerce Commission (45 U.S.C. 29) (statute provides for a hearing); Senate Hearings (1941) pp. 833-4;

(d) the grading of grain under the United States Grain Standards Act (7 U.S.C. 71 et seq.); Senate Hearings (1941) pp. 833-4.

The rationale for exempting such adjudications from formal procedural requirements was well stated by the Attorney General's Committee on Administrative Procedure in the following passage:

> In all these cases, as well as in others not here described, the most important element in the decision is the judgment of the man who saw ind tested the ship or grain or fruit or locomotive, or who examined the prospective airplane pilot, or seaman, or proposed periodical. Formal proceedings are not, of course, impossible. A trial examiner could be designated; the inspector could be summoned to testify, under oath, concerning his observations just as a traffic officer who gives a driving test to an applicant for a motor operator's permit could be required to describe the applicant's performance to a second officer who could, in turn, decide whether the permit should be issued. But resort to formal procedure in this type of administrative matter, although sometimes provided for as in certain of the instances noted above, is not desired or utilized by the person whose rights or privileges are being adjudicated, because it gives no added protection. The judgment of the inspector who examined the applicant or tested the article would necessarily remain the determining element in the decision, and, in any event, some immediate decision concerning the fitness of an applicant, or of in airplane, or a locomotive, or a ship, is necessary to protect the public interest. That cannot await a formal hearing. Nor would formal procedure give greater assurance of a correct decision. The surest way to ascertain what is the grade of grain is for a skilled inspector to test it; the best way to discover whether the radio equipment of a ship is in proper working order is for a radio mechanic to examine it and test it. (Final Report, p. 37)

For further legislative history relating to this exemption, see Senate Hearings (1941) pp. 590, 602, 833.

4. "The conduct of military, naval, or foreign affairs functions". Both Committee reports state that the section "exempts military, naval, and foreign affairs functions for the same reasons that they are exempted from section 4; and, in any event, rarely if ever do statutes require such functions to be exercised upon hearing." Sen. Rep. p. 16; H.R. Rep. p. 27 (Sen. Doc. pp. 202, 261). Thus, the exercise of adjudicatory functions by the War and Navy Departments or by any other agency is exempt to the extent that the conduct of military or naval affairs is involved. Senate Hearings (1941) pp. 502-3. The term "foreign affairs functions" appears to be eased in the same sense as in section 4. H.R. Rep. p. 27 (Sen. Doc. p. 261).

5. "Cases in which an agency is acting as an agent for a

court". This is self-explanatory. Senate Hearings (1941) pp. 422, 474, 1457.

6. "The certification of employee representatives". This exemption for "the certification of employee representatives such as the Labor Board operations under section 9 (c) of the National Labor Relations Act, is included because those determinations rest so largely upon an election or the availability of an election". Sen. Rep. p. 16; H.R. Rep. p. 27 (Sen. Doc. pp. 202, 261). And see Senate Hearings (1941) pp. 260, 271. It also exempts the certification of employee representatives by the National Mediation Board pursuant to section 2 (9) of the Railway Labor Act (45 U.S.C. 152).

SECTION 5 (A)—NOTICE

The first sentence of section 5 (a) provides that "Persons entitled to notice of an agency hearing shall be timely informed of—

(1) "the time, place, and nature thereof". The subsection does not specify the period of notice of hearing to be given by an agency, other than to require "timely" notice. Whether a given period of time constitutes timely notice will depend upon the circumstances, including the urgency of the situation and the complexity of the issues involved in the proceeding. It is clear that nothing in the subsection revokes the specific provisions of other statutes as to the amount of notice which must be given in various proceedings. See generally section 8 of the Federal Register Act (44 U.S.C. 308) and specific statutory provisions such as section 5 of the Federal Trade Commission Act, requiring 30 days' notice of hearing (15 U.S.C. 45). In addition to specifying the time and place of hearing, the notice should specify the nature of the hearing, e.g., whether a cease and desist order should issue.

The last sentence of section 5 (a) provides that "In fixing the times and places for hearings, due regard shall be had for the convenience and necessity of the parties or their representatives." This simply means that consistent with the public interest and the due execution of the agency's functions, each agency shall attempt to schedule hearings at times and places which will be convenient for the parties and their representatives. Sen. Rep. p. 17 (Sen. Doc. p. 203).

(2) "the legal authority and jurisdiction under which the hearing is to be held". The notice should contain reference to the

47

agency's authority sufficient to inform the parties of the legal powers and jurisdiction which the agency is invoking in the particular case, and thus enable the parties to raise any legal issues they consider relevant.

(3) "The matters of fact and law asserted". It is not required to set forth evidentiary facts or legal argument. All that is necessary is to advise the parties of the legal and factual issues involved.

Responsive pleading. The second sentence of section 5 (a) provides that "In instances in which private persons are the moving parties, other parties to the proceeding shall give prompt notice of issues controverted in fact or law; and in other instances agencies may by rule require responsive pleading." In the Committee reports, it is stated that "The second sentence of the subsection applies in those cases where the agency does not control the matter of notice because private persons are the moving parties; and in such cases the respondent parties must give notice of the issues of law and fact which they controvert so that the moving party will be apprised of the issues he must sustain." Sen. Rep. p. 17; H.R. Rep. p. 27 (Sen. Doc. pp. 203, 261). The first clause of this sentence is mandatory. This provision for responsive pleading appears to be applicable, for example, where the moving party is applying for a license and the agency admits as parties or intervenors competitors of the applicant who are opposing the application. Under section 5 (a), the agency should require such additional parties to disclose their position promptly. While the subsection does not specify the consequences to be attached to a party's failure so to plead, it would clearly support an agency rule requiring a party to answer specifically the allegations of the moving party, or be deemed to have admitted such allegations.

The second sentence of section 5 (a) also provides that "in other instances agencies may by rule require responsive pleading". "In other instances" apparently refers to cases in which the agency, rather than a private party, is the moving party. Thus, the quoted clause authorizes an agency, in adjudicatory proceedings which it has initiated, such as for the suspension or revocation of licenses, to require the respondent to plead responsively, i.e., to "give prompt notice of issues controverted in fact or law".

SECTION 5 (b)—PROCEDURE

Section 5 (b) provides that "The agency shall afford all interested parties opportunity for (1) the submission and consideration of facts, arguments, offers of settlement, or proposals of adjustment where time, the nature of the proceeding, and the public interest permit, and (2) to the extent that the parties are unable so to determine any controversy by consent, hearing,[3] and decision upon notice and in conformity with section 7 and 8." The settlement of cases and issues by informal methods is nothing new in Federal administrative procedure. In its Final Report, the Attorney General's Committee on Administrative Procedure pointed out (p. 35) that "even where formal proceedings are fully available, informal procedures constitute the vast bulk of administrative adjudication and are truly the lifeblood of the administrative process".

Like section 5 generally, subsection 5 (b) applies only to cases of adjudication required by statute to be determined on the record after opportunity for an agency hearing". The purpose of this subsection is to provide, so far as practicable, for the informal settlement or adjustment of controversies in lieu of formal adjudicatory proceedings. Section 5 (b), however, does not require agencies to settle informally all cases which the parties desire to settle. Rather it requires the agencies to make available opportunities for such settlements, "where time, the nature of the proceeding, and the public interest permit".

Agencies must in some way provide opportunities for informal disposition of controversies. However, the precise manner in which such opportunities are to be afforded has been deliberately left by Congress to development by the agencies themselves. See Senate Comparative Print of June 1945, p. 9 (Sen. Doc. p. 24). The subsection apparently leaves the agencies free to provide such opportunity either before or after the initiation of a formal proceeding (e.g., the issuance of a complaint). If the opportunity is to be made available prior to the issuance of a complaint or notice, the agency must in some way advise the parties that formal proceedings are contemplated. In such a situation, the agency should advise the party at some preliminary stage (investigatory or otherwise) that it is contemplating the initiation of a formal proceeding and that it is giving him an opportunity to settle or adjust the matter. Where the opportunity is made available after the issuance of a notice or complaint, it is sufficient if the agency's published procedures

---

3. The comma after "hearing" in section 5(b) is a printer's error.

49

advise parties as to how an informal settlement or adjustment may be sought.

Whether such opportunity is provided before or after the initiation of the formal proceeding, it should enable parties to present their proposals for settlement to responsible officers or employees of the agency. Since section 5 (b) does not prescribe adjustment procedures, they may consist entirely of oral conferences or agencies may require proposals for adjustment or settlement to be submitted in writing. If proposals are submitted and they are unsatisfactory, the agency should consider the advisability of informing the parties involved of the conditions, if any, on which the agency is willing to settle the controversy or accept compliance without formal proceedings. It is clear that section 5 (b) does not require an agency to defer formal proceedings indefinitely while parties submit a series of proposals for the purpose of delay.

In the settlement of cables pursuant to section 5 (b), agencies may, as heretofore, require to enter into consent decrees or orders or stipulations to cease and desist as a part of the settlement. As Representative Walter stated: "The settlement by consent provision is extremely important because agencies ought not to engage in formal proceedings where the parties are perfectly willing to *consent to judgments* or adjust situations informally." [Italics supplied] 92 Cong. Rec. 5651 (Sen. Doc. p. 361). Final Report, pp. 41-42.

The requirement of section 5 (b) that agencies provide opportunity for informal settlement is limited to cases "where time, the nature of the proceeding, and the public interest permit". The quoted language is to be treated in the alternative. Where an agency is confronted with the necessity for emergency action or where a statute requires that ,t hearing be held within a limited period of time, the agency may be obliged to limit or refuse opportunity for informal settlement. The "nature of the proceeding" may be said to preclude negotiation in situations where the party has declared that he does not intend to comply with a known requirement of the agency or where statutes require that hearings be held in any event.[4] Senate Hearings (1941) p. 1474. Where an agency believes that the informal settlement of an alleged violation or certain classes of violations will not insure future compliance with law, it would be justified in concluding that

---

4. For example, the Civil Aeronautics Board is required to hold hearings before granting a certificate of public convenience and necessity for a new route (49 U.S.C. 481).

such settlement by consent would not be in the public interest.

Each agency should make public, pursuant to section 3 (a), the manner in which it will provide interested parties an opportunity for the informal settlement or adjustment of the matters in issue. H.R. Rep. p. 27 (Sen. Doc. p. 261).

SECTION 5 (c)—SEPARATION OF FUNCTIONS

Section 5 (c) generally requires each agency, in the adjudication of cases subject to section 5, to establish an internal separation of functions between the officials who hear and decide and those who investigate or prosecute. The discussion will be simplified if the exceptions from the requirements of section 5 (c) are considered first.

Exceptions. Section 5 (c), like the rest of section 5, applies only to cases of adjudication "required by statute to be determined on the record after opportunity for an agency hearing", and if the subject matter of the proceeding is not exempted by the first paragraph of section 5. Rule making, of course, is not subject to section 5 (c). Section 5 (c), in addition, provides that the provisions of that subsection "shall not apply in determining applications for initial licenses or to proceedings involving the validity or application of rates, facilities, or practices of public utilities or carriers".

Section 5 (c) does not apply to agency proceedings to determine applications for initial licenses—regardless of whether the agency grants or denies the license. "License" is defined in section 2 (d). The phrase "initial license" must be interpreted from the context and legislative history.

The Administrative Procedure Act is based upon a broad and logical dichotomy between rule making and adjudication, i.e., between the legislative and judicial functions. See Chapter I. The legislative history of section 5 (c) reveals that "determining applications for initial licenses" was exempted from the requirements of the subsection on the ground that such proceedings are similar to rule making. In the Committee reports, it is explained that "The exemption of applications for initial licenses frees from the requirements of the section such matters as the granting of certificates of convenience and necessity, upon the theory that in most licensing cases the original application may be much like rule making. The latter, of course, is not subject to any provision of section 5." Sen. Rep. p. 17; H.R. Rep. p.

51

30 (Sen. Doc. pp. 203, 262). The rationale for the exemption was further developed by Representative Walter on the floor of the House, as follows: "However, the subsection does not apply in determining applications for initial licenses, because it is felt that the determination of such matters is much like rule making and hence the parties will be better served if the proposed decision—later required by section 8—reflects the views of the responsible officers in the agencies whether or not they have actually taken the evidence." 92 Cong. Rec. 5651 (Sen. Doc. p. 361).

In view of the function of the exemption, the phrase "application for initial licences" must be construed to include applications by the licensee for modifications of his original license. In effect, this gives full meaning to the broad definition of "license" in section 2 (e), i.e., "the whole or part of any agency *permit,* certificate, *approval,* registration, charter, membership, statutory exemption *or other form of permission"*. [Italics supplied] In other words, the definition clearly suggests that any agency "approval" or "permission" is a license, regardless of whether it is in addition to or related to an earlier license.[5] Only by such a construction can the appropriate procedures be made applicable to those aspects of licensing which are dominated by policy making considerations and in which accusatory and disciplinary factors are absent. Senate Hearings (1941) p. 1451. In this way, the basic dichotomy of the feet between rule making and adjudication is preserved, because section 5 (c) will remain applicable to licensing proceedings involving renewal, revocation, suspension, annulment, withdrawal or the *agency-initiated* modification or amendment of licenses—i.e., all those phases of licensing in which the accusatory or disciplinary factors are, or are likely to be, present.

This interpretation of the scope of the exemption is consistent with the remainder of its legislative history. When the ad-

---

5. Any other interpretation of the exemption will largely destroy it and will result in an erratic application of section 5 (c). For example. the function of the Civil Aeronautics Board with respect to certificates of public convenience and necessity increasingly relates to applications for modifications or extensions of existing routes rather than to original applications for entirely new routes. Thus, A, with a certificate for a route from New York to Chicago with a stop at Cleveland for a modification of the certificate to permit an additional stop at Pittsburgh. The considerations involved in determining such an application for modification of A's certificate are the same as those involved in his original application—traffic flow, availability of facilities effect on competing carriers, etc. The accusatory and disciplinary elements are entirely lacking. Another example clearly illustrates the inconsistent results of such a narrow construction of the exemption for initial licensing: A has a certificate for a route from New York to St. Louis and he applies for a modification which will authorize extension of the route to Omaha; B applies for a new certificate authorizing him to operate a route between St. Louis and Omaha. Under the narrow construction of the exemption, section 5 (c)would apply to the Board's determination of A's application, but would not be applicable with respect to B's application. Similar anomalies would exist under the Federal Power Act, the Communications Act and the Natural Gas Act, particularly the latter.

ministrative procedure bill (S. 7) was introduced by Senator McCarran in January 1945, the provision that was then section 5 (b) contained an exemption for "determining applications for licenses". When S. 7 was reported by the Senate Committee on the Judiciary in November 1945, section 5 (c) contained the present language exempting "determining applications for initial licenses". In the discussion of the definitions of "adjudication" and "licensing" in the Committee reports, it is stated that "Licensing is specifically included [in adjudication] to remove any question, since licenses involve a pronouncement of present rights of named parties although they may also prescribe terms and conditions for future observance. Licensing as such is later exempted from some of the provisions of sections 5, 7 and 8 relating to hearings and decisions. * * * *Later provisions of the bill distinguish between initial licensing and renewals or other licensing proceedings."* [Italics supplied] Sen. Rep. p. 11; H.R. Rep. p. 20 (Sen. Doc. pp. 197, 254). It is apparent from the legislative history that the word "initial" was inserted in the exception to distinguish original applications for licenses, i.e., any agency "approval" or "permission", from applications for renewals of licenses. This is entirely consistent with the underlying analogy of initial licensing to rule making, because renewal proceedings frequently involve a review of the licensee's past conduct and thus resemble adjudication rather than rule making.

The insertion of "initial" similarly distinguishes applications for licenses from modifications or limitations imposed by an agency upon an existing license. Thus, the Senate Committee Report also contains a memorandum from the Attorney General in which it is stated that "The section does apply, however, to licensing, with the exception that section 5 (c), relating to the separation of functions, does not apply in determining applications for initial licenses, i.e., original licenses as contradistinguished from renewals or amendments of existing licenses." Sen. Rep. p. 40 (Sen. Doc. p. 226). In referring to "amendments", the quoted language contemplated amendments or modifications imposed by the agency on the ground that in such proceedings, as in renewal proceedings, the issues would often relate to the licensee's past conduct.

It is concluded, therefore, that the exemption from the provisions of section 5 (c) of proceedings to determine "applications for initial licenses" extends not only to applications for original

53

licenses but also to applications by licensees, for modification of licenses.

The exception of "proceedings involving the validity or application of rates, facilities, or practices of public utilities or carriers" originally read "in determining * * * the past reasonableness of rates". See S. 7, 79th Cong. 2nd sess., as passed by the Senate on March 12, 1946. H.R. Rep. p. 52 (Sen. Doc. p. 286). The exemption was apparently created on the ground that questions as to the past reasonableness of rates are sometimes consolidated with the making of future rates—a rule making function—and that the exception would encourage such consolidation. In the House, the exemption was broadened to include the validity or application of facilities and practices on the theory that such matters also are often consolidated with rule making. H.R. Rep. pp. 30, 52 (Sen. Doc. pp. 262, 286). However, it should be noted that the Act itself does not limit the exception to cases where there is consolidation with rule making proceedings.

Hearing officers. The first sentence of section 5 (c) provides that "The same officers who preside at the reception of evidence pursuant to section 7 shall make the recommended decision or initial decision required by section 8 except where such officers become unavailable to the agency." Section 8 (a) provides that in cases in which the agency has not presided at the reception of the evidence, the officer who presided (or, in cases not subject to section 5 (c), such as initial licensing, any other officer or officers qualified to preside at hearings pursuant to section 7) shall make the initial decision or recommended decision as the case may be. Thus, apart from the exceptions referred to above, the officer who presides at the adjudicatory hearing and hears the evidence must prepare the initial or recommended decision, as the case may be, unless he becomes unavailable (as by illness or leaving the agency). Where the hearing officer becomes unavailable to the agency, the agency may itself complete the hearing or substitute another hearing officer to do so.

The second and third sentences of section 5 (c) make provision for the separation of the functions of hearing and decision from the functions of investigation and prosecution. The second sentence of section 5 (c) provides that:

> Save to the extent required for the disposition of ex parte matters as authorized by law, no such officer shall consult any person or party on any fact in issue unless upon notice and opportunity for all parties to participate; nor shall such officer be responsible to or subject to the supervision or direction of any officer, employee, or agent engaged in the performance of investigative or prosecuting functions for any agency.

The third sentence provides:

> No officer, employee, or agent engaged in the performance of investigative or prosecuting functions for any agency in any case shall, in that or a factually related case, participate or advise in the decision, recommended decision, or agency review pursuant to section 8 except as witness or counsel in public proceedings.

It is thus apparent that the second sentence applies generally to the hearing process or the making of the record; the third, to the decisional process or the making of the initial or recommended decision by the hearing officer. The broad purpose of the second sentence is to assure that hearings be conducted by hearing officers who have not received or obtained factual information outside the record and who are neither supervised nor directed in the conduct of the hearing by agency officials engaged in the performance of investigative or prosecuting functions. To achieve fairness and independence in the hearing process it is first provided that (except for ex parte matters) no hearing officer "shall consult any person or party on any fact in issue unless upon notice and opportunity for all parties to participate". That is, the officer is prohibited from obtaining or receiving evidentiary or factual information bearing on the issues unless, after notice, all parties are permitted to participate. This would apply as well to expert testimony; the officer may not informally obtain evidentiary material from such experts either during or after the hearing, any more than he may from other witnesses.

The broad purpose of the third sentence is to insure that hearing officers make initial or recommended decisions free from the participation or advice of agency personnel engaged in the performance of investigative or prosecuting functions in that or a factually related case.[6] As to the decisional process

---

6. The limitation of the prohibition against consultation to those who performed investigative or prosecuting functions "in that or a factually related case" should be construed literally. As this provision originally appeared in H.R. 1203, 79th Cong., 1st sess. (1945), it was a complete prohibition against consultation with investigative and prosecuting personnel, as follows: "No officer, employee, or agent engaged in the performance of investigative or prosecuting functions for any agency shall participate or advise in the decision, recommended decision, or agency review pursuant to section 8 except as witness or counsel in public proceedings." See Sen. Doc. p. 157.

The phrase "factually related case" connotes a situation in which a party, is faced with two different proceedings arising out of the same or a connected set of facts. For example, a particular investigation may result in the institution of a cease and desist proceeding against a party as well as a proceeding involving the revocation of his license. The employees of the agency, engaged in the investigation or prosecution of such a cease and desist proceeding would be precluded from rendering any assistance to the agency, not only in the decision of the cease and desist proceeding, but also in the decision of the revocation proceeding. However, they would not be prevented from assisting the agency in the decision of other cases (in which they had not engaged either as investigators or prosecutors) merely because the facts of these other cases may form a pattern similar to those which they had theretofore investigated or prosecuted.

55

it is clear that, to insure the separation of the functions of hearing and decision from the functions of investigation and prosecution and to insure the independence of the hearing officer, he may not consult or receive advice from any employee of the agency who is engaged in the performance of investigative or prosecuting functions in that or a factually related case. Likewise, under fundamental principles of due process, he may not receive advice or opinions from private parties or their counsel, unless, after notice, all parties are permitted to participate.

Further, it is manifest from the third sentence of section 5 (c) that the hearing officer may obtain advice from or consult with agency personnel not engaged in investigative or prosecuting functions in that or a factually related case. The agency personnel in question may include, for example, the agency heads, the supervisors of the hearing officers, and persons assigned to assist the hearing officer in analyzing the record. Permitting the hearing officer to engage with appropriate agency personnel in an analytical discussion of the record is thoroughly consistent with the purposes of the Act. A principal purpose is that the hearing be followed by an initial or recommended decision proposed by the hearing officer which will focus the parties' attention upon the issues and conclusions of law, fact and policy which, in the hearing officer's judgment, govern the case. The availability to the hearing officer of appropriate assistance and advice will result normally in a more accurate initial or recommended decision and one that better reflects the views of the agency on questions of law and policy. Thus, the parties are better advised on the real issues that must be met in the subsequent procedure before final decision. See Senate Hearings (1941) pp. 266, 465, 646, 662, 836, 1487.

The exemption for the "disposition of ex parte matters as authorized by law" would permit the hearing examiner to act without notice on such matters as requests for adjournments, continuances, and the filing of papers. Sen. Rep. p. 17; H.R. Rep. p. 30 (Sen. Doc. pp. 203, 262). Also, it would apparently permit an examiner to act *ex parte* on requests for subpenas.

The independence of hearing officers is further assured by the requirement that they shall not "be responsible to or subject to the supervision or direction of any officer, employee, or agent engaged in the performance of investigative functions for any agency". As a practical matter this means that an agency's hearing examiners should be placed in an organizational unit apart from those to which investigative and prosecuting personnel are assigned, and that the examiners' unit should be under the supervision only of the agency itself or of agency officers who exercise no investigative or prosecuting functions. For example, if the agency's general counsel supervises the investigation and prosecution activities of the agency, the examiners' unit should not be subject to his supervision or control. However, section 5 (c) would not prevent the trial examiners from being under the supervision of the general counsel where in fact the supervision of investigative and prosecuting functions is exercised by an associate or assistant general counsel who has no responsibility to the general counsel for such functions but is responsible therefor directly to the agency.

It is clear that nothing in the separation of functions requirements of section 5 (c) is intended to preclude agency officials, regardless of their functions, from participating in necessary administrative arrangements, such as the efficient scheduling of hearings.

The agency. The third sentence of section 5 (c) provides that "No officer, employee, or agent engaged in the performance of investigative or prosecuting functions for any agency in any case shall, in that or a factually related case, participate or advise in the decision, recommended decision, or agency review pursuant to section 8 except as witness or counsel in public proceedings." Thus, on "agency review", the agency heads, as well as the hearing examiner, will be precluded from consulting or obtaining advice from any officer or employee with respect to any case in which, or in a factually related case,[7] such officer or employee has participated in the investigation or prosecution. In other words, the views of officials who investigated and prosecuted the case (or a factually related case) must be presented to hearing examiners and to agency heads in the public proceedings, i.e., hearings or oral argument, or by requested findings, exceptions, and briefs which are served upon the parties. Before discussing the scope of these requirements, it will be useful to consider some aspects of the administrative process.

The expertise of an administrative agency is not limited to the heads of the agency; it includes also the staff of specialists through whom and with whose assistance most of the agency's functions are carried on. The issues in adjudicatory cases, while frequently less complex and with narrower

---

7. See discussion of "factually related case" in footnote 6.

policy implications than are often involved in rule making, present in many cases difficult questions of law and policy. The determination of whether an industry-wide trade practice violates the Federal Trade Commission Act, or whether a certain series of stock market transactions constitute unlawful manipulation, often involves important and difficult issues. In determining such issues, agency heads have consulted with their principal advisers and specialists. Indeed, it is clearly in the public interest that they continue to do so. Section 5 (c) does not purport to isolate the agency heads from their staffs. Rather, in the interest of fair procedure, it merely excludes from any such participation in the decision of a case those employees of the agency who have had such previous participation in an adversary capacity in that or a factually related case that they may be "disabled from bringing to its decision that dispassionate judgment which Anglo-American tradition demands of officials who decide questions". Final Report, p. 56.

An agency officer or employee may not participate or advise in the decision, recommended decision, or agency review of an examiner's initial decision if in that or a factually related case he performed investigative or prosecuting functions. For example, if the agency's general counsel or chief accountant engages in the performance of investigative or prosecuting functions in a case, he becomes unavailable to the agency for consultation on the decision of that or a factually related case. Of course, he could always present his views as witness or counsel in the public proceedings, including the filing of briefs.

Assuming that an agency will in many cases wish to consult with certain of its staff members, it may proceed in one of two ways. It may in a particular case consult with staff members who in fact have not performed investigative or prosecuting functions in that or a factually related case. In the alternative, the agency may find it feasible so to organize its staff assignments that the staff members whom it most frequently desires to consult will be free of all investigative and prosecuting functions. The latter method appears to offer two distinct advantages, particularly where the agency has a considerable volume of cases subject to section 5 (c).

First, using the agency's general counsel for an example: If the investigation and prosecution of adjudicatory cases are performed by the legal division under his supervision, it could be argued that his personal consideration of the routine cases has been so limited that he should be permitted to advise the agency in the decision of such cases. Even assuming that this is permitted by section 5 (c), it would seem to be immaterial since his counsel will not be particularly needed in the routine cases. It is in the difficult and novel cases that the agency most needs his advice, and it is in these cases that he is most likely to be consulted extensively by his subordinates. Thus, he becomes unavailable to advise the agency in the very cases in which his advice would be most useful. On the other hand, if the agency so organizes its staff that the general counsel is not responsible for the investigative and prosecuting functions, he would be regularly available to the agency for consultation on the decision of cases.[8]

Second, if an agency thus organizes its staff and, accordingly, identifies the officers with whom it is free to consult in the decision of cases subject to section 5 (c), these matters can be spelled out in the agency's published rules of procedure. Such publication would, in effect, inform the public of the identity (by title or group) of the staff members who advise in the decision of such cases. In any litigation on the issue of compliance with section 5 (c), the published rules, embodying an organization and division of functions in the light of section 5 (c), would assist in establishing proof of compliance with the separation of functions requirements.

The last sentence of section 5 (c) sets forth certain exemptions from the requirements of the subsection. These have already been discussed, except the provision that "nor shall it be applicable in any manner to the agency or any member or members of the body comprising the agency". It was pointed out that this exemption "of the agency itself or the members of the board who comprise it is required by the very nature of administrative agencies, where the same authority is responsible for both the investigation-prosecution and the hearing and decision of cases". Sen. Rep. p. 18; H.R. Rep. p. 30 (Sen. Doc. pp. 204, 262). Thus, if a member of the Interstate Commerce Commission actively participates in or directs the investigation of an adjudicatory case, he will not be precluded from participating with his colleagues in the decision of that case. Sen. Rep. p. 41 (Sen. Doc. p. 227).

---

8. The general counsel's participation in rule making and in court litigation would be entirely compatible with his role in advising the agency in the decision of adjudicatory cases subject to section 5(c).

59

SECTION 5 (d)—DECLARATORY ORDERS

Section 5 (d) provides that "The agency is authorized in its sound discretion, with like effect as in the case of other orders, to issue a declaratory order to terminate a controversy or remove uncertainty." The purpose of section 5 (d), like that of the Declaratory Judgment Act (28 U.S.C. 400), is to develop predictability in the law by authorizing binding determinations "which dispose of legal controversies without the necessity of any party's acting at his peril upon his own view". Final Report, p. 30.

This grant of authority to the agencies to issue declaratory orders is limited by the introductory clause of section 5 so that such declaratory orders are authorized only with respect to matters which are required by statute to be determined "on the record after opportunity for an agency hearing". In addition, if the subject matter falls within one of the numbered exceptions in the introductory clause of section 5, such as a matter in which an agency is acting as an agent for a court, section 5 (d) does not apply. Sen. Rep. p. 18; H.R. Rep. p. 31 (Sen. Doc. pp. 204, 263). For example, where an agency is authorized after hearing to issue orders to cease and desist from specified illegal conduct, it may, under section 5 (d), if it otherwise has jurisdiction, issue a declaratory order declaring whether or not specified facts constitute illegal conduct. On the other hand, while the Securities and Exchange Commission has long issued informal advisory interpretations through its principal officers as to whether a proposed issue of securities would be exempt from the registration requirements of the Securities Act, there is no statutory agency hearing procedure in which this question can be determined; if securities are sold without registration and the Commission believes that registration was required, it can only institute civil or criminal proceedings. Accordingly, section 5 (d) does not authorize the Commission to issue declaratory orders as to whether particular securities must be registered under the Securities Act.[9]

Agencies are authorized in their "sound discretion" to issue declaratory orders. They are not required to issue such orders merely because request is made therefor. Sen. Rep. p. 18; H.R. Rep. p. 31 (Sen. Doc. pp. 204, 263). By "sound dis-

---

9. Of course, this does not affect the Securities and Exchange Commission's advisory service described above.

cretion", it is meant that agencies shall issue declaratory orders only under such circumstances that both the public interest and the interest of the party are protected. Thus, "a necessary condition of its [declaratory order] ready use is that it be employed only in situations where the critical facts can be explicitly stated, without possibility that subsequent events will alter them. This is necessary to avoid later litigation concerning the applicability of a declaratory ruling which an agency may seek to disregard because, in its opinion, the facts to which it related have changed". Final Report, p. 32. Again, since the issuance of declaratory orders is a matter of sound discretion, it is clear that an agency need not issue such orders where it appears that the questions involved will be determined in a pending administrative or judicial proceeding, or where there is available some other statutory proceeding which will be more appropriate or effective under the circumstances. More broadly, it appears that "The administrative issuance of declaratory orders would be governed by the same basic principles that govern declaratory judgments in the courts." Sen. Rep. p. 18; H.R. Rep. p. 31 (Sen. Doc. pp. 204, 263).

61

V
SECTION 6—ANCILLARY MATTERS

Section 6 defines various procedural rights of private parties which may be incidental to rule making, adjudication, or the exercise of any other agency authority. The introductory words of section 6, "Except as otherwise provided in this Act," are intended to assure that its provisions do not override contrary provisions in other parts of the act. Thus, the opportunity for informal appearance contemplated by section 6 (a) is not to be construed so as to authorize *ex parte* conferences during formal proceedings when such conferences are forbidden by other sections of the act. Sen. Rep. p. 18, H.R. Rep. p. 31 (Sen. Doc. pp. 204, 263).

Governing Definitions. The provisions of section 6 hinge to a considerable extent upon the definition of the terms "party", "person" and "agency proceeding". These terms are defined in section 2 of the act as follows:

> (b) "Person" includes individuals, partnerships, corporations, associations, or public or private organizations of any character other than agencies. "Party" includes any person or agency named or admitted as a party, or properly seeking and entitled as of right to be admitted as a party, in any agency proceeding; but nothing herein shall be construed to prevent an agency from admitting any person or agency as a party for limited purposes.
>
> * * * *
>
> (g) "Agency proceeding" means any agency process as defined in subsections (c), (d), and (e) of this section. [Defining rule making, adjudication and licensing, respectively.]

SECTION 6 (a)—APPEARANCE

Formal Appearance. The first sentence of section 6 (a) provides that "Any person compelled to appear in person before any agency or representative thereof shall be accorded the right to be accompanied, represented, and advised by counsel or, if permitted by the agency, by other qualified representative." This restates existing law and practice that persons compelled to appear in person before an agency or its representative must be accorded the right to be accompanied by counsel and to consult with or be advised by such counsel. Such persons are also entitled to have counsel act as their spokesmen in argument and where otherwise appropriate. Senate Comparative Print of June 1945, p. 10 (Sen. Doc. p. 26). It is clear, of course, that this provision relates only to persons whose appearance is compelled or commanded, and does not extend to persons who appear voluntarily or in response to mere request by an agency. Where appearance is compelled, whether as a party or as a witness, the right to counsel exists.

The phrase "or, if permitted by the agency, by other qualified representative" refers to the present practice of some agencies of permitting appearance or representation in certain matters by non-lawyers, such as accountants. The phrasing of this clause, together with the last sentence of the subsection, makes it clear that nothing in the first sentence was intended to change the existing powers of agencies in this respect. See discussion, *infra* at pp. 65-6.

The second sentence of the subsection relates to the rights of "parties" to "agency proceedings". It provides that every "party" shall have the right to appear in any agency proceeding "in person or by or with counsel or other duly qualified representative."[1]

The right of a party to appear personally or by or with counsel extends, in view of the definition of "agency proceeding", to proceedings involving rule making, adjudication or licensing. The identity of the "parties" is usually clear in adjudication, licensing and formal rule making proceedings. However, since the provision is not limited to formal proceedings (those governed by sections 7 and 8), but extends to informal rule making proceedings, the term "party", in the latter type of proceeding, means any person showing the requisite interest in the matters involved. Sen. Rep. p. 19; H.R. Rep. p. 31 (Sen. Doc. pp. 205, 263). It is entirely clear that this right to appear in informal rule making proceedings is limited by the nature of the procedure adopted by an agency, pursuant to section 4 (b). If the agency, under section 4 (b), provides interested persons an opportunity to present their views orally, the agency must allow any person with the requisite interest to appear personally or by counsel or other qualified representative. On the other hand, if the agency desires to hold informal rule making proceedings consisting of the submission of written data, views, or arguments, nothing in section 6 (a) requires the agency to provide in addition for personal appearance. In other words, the second sentence of section 6 (a) is not intended to limit an agency's discretion as to the type of rule making proceedings to be held in a particular case. (See opening clause of section 6: "Except as otherwise provided in this Act").

---

1. The phrase "qualified representative", as used in the second sentence of subsection 6 (a), relates to non-lawyers whose appearance as representatives for others is left, as under the first sentence of the subsection, to the control of the agencies. See *infra*, pp. 65-6.

Informal Appearance. The third sentence of section 6 (a) provides that "So far as the orderly conduct of public business permits, any interested person may appear before any agency or its responsible officers or employees for the presentation, adjustment, or determination of any issue, request, or controversy in any proceeding (interlocutory, summary, or otherwise) or in connection with any agency function." This sentence contemplates that interested persons may appear not only in matters involving rule making, adjudication, and licensing, but also in connection with other agency functions. This provision is not to be construed as requiring an agency to give notice of its proposed action and to invite appearances by interested persons; an agency is not required to provide an opportunity for appearance and adjustment to interested persons unless they request it. Sen. Rep. p. 19 (Sen. Doc. p. 205).

The opportunity for informal appearance contemplated by the third sentence of section 6 (a) means that any person should be given an opportunity to confer or discuss with responsible officers or employees of the agency matters in which he is properly interested. This opportunity should be with a responsible officer or employee—one who can decide the matter or whose function it is to make recommendations on such matters—rather than officers or employees whose duties are merely mechanical or formal. Sen. Rep. p. 19; H.R. Rep. p. 32 (Sen. Doc. pp. 205, 264).

This provision for informal appearance is expressly limited by the subsection to "so far as the orderly conduct of public business permits." Clearly, both the right and its limitation should be construed to achieve practical and fair results. Appearance should be allowed except where it would be inconsistent with the orderly conduct of public business. A properly interested person who is permitted to appear should be accorded an opportunity to present his case or proposals to a responsible officer or employee as defined above. Repeated opportunities to present the same arguments or proposals are not required. Further, the act does not require that every interested person be permitted to follow the chain of command to the head of the agency. It was not intended to require the directors of the Reconstruction Finance Corporation, for example, to confer personally with every applicant for a loan. It is sufficient if the opportunity to confer is with an official of such status that he knows the agency's policy, and is able to bring unusual or meritorious cases to the attention of the officials who shape the policy or make final decisions.

The opportunity thus to appear "for the presentation, adjustment, or determination of any issue, request, or controversy in any proceeding"—or "in connection with any agency function" relates not only to "agency proceedings" as defined in section 2 (g), but also to all other agency functions. It means, for example, that upon request any person should be allowed, where this is feasible, to present his reasons as to why a particular loan or benefit should be made or granted to him. It would also seem to mean that he can present his reasons as to why a particular controversy should be settled informally rather than in formal proceedings with attendant publicity. However, there is no requirement that the agency accept such proposals for informal settlement; if, for example, the agency believes that formal public proceedings will best serve the public interest, it is free to conduct such proceedings.

The reference to "interlocutory" or "summary" proceedings appears to be intended to provide an opportunity for informal appearance and discussion in those situations where an agency takes significant action without prior formal proceedings. H.R. Rep. p. 32 (Sen. Doc. p. 264). For example, section 609 of the Civil Aeronautics Act of 1938 (49 U.S.C. 559) provides that "In cases of emergency, any such certificate [airworthiness certificate, airman certificate, etc.] may be suspended, in whole or in part, for a period not in excess of thirty days, without regard to any requirement as to notice and hearing." Under section 6 (a) of the Administrative Procedure Act, the persons who would be affected by such summary action should, if feasible, be allowed to appear and present their views on the proposed action. It is absolutely clear, however, that nothing in this subsection was intended to interfere with the primary objective of assuring safety in air travel. To the extent that the timely execution of the Administrator's duties, i.e., the "orderly conduct of public business," precludes discussion and negotiation, he need not hold such discussions.

There will doubtless be many cases in which an agency will find it necessary to notice a matter for public hearing without preliminary discussion because a statute or the subject matter or the special circumstances so require. Sen. Rep. p. 41 (Sen. Doc. p. 227).

65

The fourth sentence of section 6 (a) provides that "Every agency shall proceed with reasonable dispatch to conclude any matter presented to it except that due regard shall be had for the convenience and necessity of the parties or their representatives." This provision merely restates a principle of good administration.

Practice Before Agencies. The last sentence of section 6 (a) provides that "Nothing herein shall be construed either to grant or to deny to any person who is not a lawyer the right to appear for or represent others before any agency or in any agency proceeding." The question of the extent to which non-lawyers should be permitted to practice before administrative agencies was deliberately left to the determination of the various agencies, as, heretofore. House Hearings (1945) p. 34 (Sen. Doc. p. 80); H. R. Rep. p. 32 (Sen. Doc. p. 264).

More broadly, section 6 (a) leaves intact the agencies' control over both lawyers and non-lawyers who practice before them. The reports of the Senate and House Judiciary Committees contain expressions of opinion to the effect that, as to lawyers desiring to practice before an agency, the agency should normally require no more than a statement from a lawyer that he is in good standing before the courts. Sen. Rep. p. 19; H.R. Rep. p. 39. (Sen. Doc. pp. 205, 264). However, the legislative history leaves no doubt that the Congress intended to keep unchanged the agencies' existing powers to regulate practice before them. When the House Committee on the Judiciary held hearings in 1945 on H.R. 1203 (79th Cong., lst sess.) which, under the title of S. 7, was enacted as the Administrative Procedure Act, the Committee was specifically aware of the fact that H.R. 1203 contained no provision relating to attorneys practicing before agencies, while H.R. 339, and H.R. 1117, also pending before the Committee, contained such provisions. House Hearings (1945) p. 34 (Sen. Doc. p. 80). Finally, during the House debate on S. 7, Representative Kefauver offered the following amendment to section 6:

> Any member of the bar who is in good standing and who has been admitted to the bar of the Supreme Court of the United States or of the highest court of the State of his or her residence shall be eligible to practice before any agency: Provided, however, That an agency shall for good cause be authorized by order to suspend or deny the right to practice before such agency.

The amendment was rejected by the House, apparently on the ground that the subject should be covered by separate legislation. 92 Cong. Rec. 5666-8 (Sen. Doc. pp. 401-405).

It is clear, therefore, that the existing powers of the agencies to control practice before them are not changed by the Administrative Procedure Act. For example, an agency may exclude, after notice and opportunity for hearing, persons of improper character from practice before it, *Goldsmith* v. *Board of Tax Appeals,* 270 U.S. 117 (1926), or exclude parties or counsel from participation in proceedings by reason of unruly conduct, *Okin* v. *Securities and Exchange Commission,* 137 F. (2d) 398 (C.C.A. 2, 1943), or impose reasonable time limits during which former employees may not practice before the agency.

SECTION 6 (b)—INVESTIGATIONS

The first sentence of section 6 (b) provides that "No process, requirement of a report, inspection, or other investigative act or demand shall be issued, made, or enforced in any manner or for any purpose except as authorized by law." This is a restatement of existing law. Senate Comparative Print of June 1945, p. 11, Sen. Rep. p. 41 (Sen. Doc. pp. 27, 227).

The second sentence of subsection 6 (b) provides that "Every person compelled to submit data or evidence shall be entitled to retain or, on payment of lawfully prescribed costs, procure a copy or transcript thereof, except that in a nonpublic investigatory proceeding the witness may for good cause be limited to inspection of the official transcript of his testimony." Under this, any person compelled to submit data or evidence, either as a party or as a witness, must be accorded the right to retain copies of written data submitted in response to a *subpena duces tecum* or other demand, or, upon payment of lawfully prescribed costs, to procure from the agency a copy of the data thus submitted or a transcript of the oral testimony which he was required to give. This right, it will be noted, is limited to the data and evidence submitted by the particular witness, and does not entitle him to copies or transcripts of the data and evidence submitted by other persons. Moreover, it extends only to persons "compelled" to testify or to submit data, and not to those who are merely requested to do so or who do so voluntarily.

The right defined in the second sentence of section 6 (b) is subject to the limitation "That in a nonpublic investigatory proceeding the witness may for good cause be limited to inspection of the official transcript of his testimony." In the Committee reports, it is stated that this limitation was deemed necessary "where

67

evidence is taken in a case in which prosecutions may be brought later and it is obviously detrimental to the due execution of the laws to permit copies to be circulated." Sen. Rep. p. 19, H.R. Rep. p. 33 (Sen. Doc. pp. 205, 265). Thus, the phrase "nonpublic investigatory proceeding" covers all confidential phases of investigations, formal or informal, conducted by agencies to determine whether there have been violations of law. In such situations, the witness may be limited to inspection of such portions of the transcript of investigation as contain his own testimony. This right to inspect the transcript extends only to persons who have been compelled to testify.

SECTION 6 (c)—SUBPENAS

The first sentence of section 6 (c) provides that "Agency subpenas authorized by law shall be issued to any party upon request and, as may be required by rules of procedure, upon a statement or showing of general relevance and reasonable scope of the evidence sought." The purpose of this provision is to make agency subpenas available to private parties to the same extent as to agency representatives. Sen. Rep. p. 20, H.R. Rep. p. 33 (Sen. Doc. pp. 206, 265); 92 Cong. Rec. 5652 (Sen. Doc. p. 363). It applies to both subpenas *ad testificandum* and subpenas *duces tecum*. It should be emphasized that section 6 (c) relates only to existing subpena powers conferred upon agencies; it does not grant power to issue subpenas to agencies which are not so empowered by other statutes. Senate Comparative Print of June 1945, p. 14 (Sen. Doc. pp. 29-30).

The subsection requires the issuance of subpenas to any party "upon request and, as may be required by rules of procedure, upon a statement or showing of general relevance and reasonable scope of the evidence sought." It may be argued from the quoted language that agency subpenas must be issued merely upon request of a party unless the agency requires, by its published procedural rules, a "statement or showing of general relevance and reasonable scope of the evidence sought"; accordingly, each agency which is empowered to issue subpenas should issue rules of procedure stating the manner in which parties are to request subpenas and the contents of such requests. The standard of "general relevance and reasonable scope" should be interpreted and applied in the light of the statutory purpose of making administrative subpenas equally available to private parties and agency representatives. (See the second sentence of section 12. On the other hand, agencies should consider that subpenas which it may issue to aid private parties, like subpenas issued to assist the agencies themselves, are subject to the legal requirements and limitations restated in the second sentence of section 6(c). Thus, agencies may refuse to issue to private parties subpenas which appear to be so irrelevant or unreasonable that a court would refuse to enforce them.

The right to subpenas stated in section 6 (c) is limited to "parties", as defined in section 2 (b). Accordingly, the right to administrative subpenas is applicable to parties to rule making, adjudication and licensing proceedings.

The Act is silent as to the responsibility for payment of fees to witnesses called by private parties pursuant to subpenas issued by an agency.[2] It was apparently thought that such a provision should be the subject of separate legislation. Senate Comparative Print of June 1945, p. 11 (Sen. Doc. p. 28). In view of this, it appears that the question of payment of witness fees may be dealt with by reasonable administrative regulations such as many agencies have already adopted.[3]

The second sentence of section 6 (c) provides that "Upon contest the court shall sustain any such subpena or similar process or demand to the extent that it is found to be in accordance with law and, in any proceeding for enforcement, shall issue an order requiring the appearance of the witness or the production of the evidence or data within a reasonable time under penalty of punishment for contempt in case of contumacious failure to comply." Upon its face, the subsection in requiring judicial enforcement of subpenas "found to be in accordance with law" is a reference to and an adoption of the existing law with respect to subpenas. For example, nothing in section 6 (c) seems intended

---

2. Section 10 of the Act of August 2, 1946 (Public Law 600, 79th Cong., 2d sess.) provides that "Whenever a department is authorized by law to hold hearings and to subpena witnesses for appearance at said hearings, witnesses summoned to and attending such hearings shall be entitled to the same fees and mileage, or expenses in the case of Government officers and employees, as provided by law for witnesses attending in the United States courts."

3. The following examples appear to be reasonable and appropriate:
Federal Power Commission—Rules of Practice Under the Federal Power Act.
Rule 1.131. "Fees of witnesses.—Witnesses who are summoned are entitled to the same fees as are paid for like services in the courts of the United States, such fees to be paid by the party at whose instance the testimony is taken, and the Commission before issuing subpoena may require a deposit of an amount adequate to cover the fees and milage involved." [16 U.S.C. 825f].
Interstate Commerce Commission—Rules of Practice.
Rule 66(e). "Witness fees. A witness who is summoned and responds thereto is entitled to the same fee as is paid for like service in the courts of the United States, such fee to be paid by the party at whose instance the testimony is taken at the time the subpena is served." [49 U.S.C. 18].

69

to change existing law as to the reasonableness and scope of subpenas. Similarly, the subsection leaves unchanged existing law as to the scope of judicial inquiry where enforcement of a subpena is sought. In *Endicott Johnson Corp.* v. *Perkins,* 317 U.S. 501 (1943), the Supreme Court held that where the Secretary of Labor sought judicial enforcement of a subpena issued in a proceeding under the Walsh-Healey Public Contracts Act, the District Court was not authorized to determine whether the respondent was subject to that act, as a condition precedent to enforcement of the subpena. Accord, under the Fair Labor Standards Act, *Oklahoma Press Publishing Company* v. *Walling,* 327 U.S. 186 (1946). Nothing in the language of section 6 (c) suggests any purpose to change this established rule. It is said only that the court shall enforce a subpena "to the extent that it is found to be in accordance with law." "Law" refers to the statutes which a particular agency administers, together with relevant judicial decisions.

This natural and literal construction of the second sentence of section 6 (c) finds conclusive support in the legislative history of the provision. When S. 7 was introduced by Senator McCarran on January 6, 1945, section 6 (c) provided that "Upon any contest of the validity of a subpena or similar process or demand, the court shall determine all relevant questions of law raised by the parties, *including the authority or jurisdiction of the agency.*" (Italics supplied). Clearly this language could be construed as intended to change the rule stated in *Endicott Johnson Corp.* v. *Perkins, supra.* However, when S. 7 was reported by the Senate Committee on the Judiciary on November 19, 1945 (Sen. Rep. p. 34 (Sen. Doc. p. 220)), section 6 was rephrased in its present form. This significant change in language, as well as the natural and literal reading of section 6 (c), is persuasive that the subsection leaves unchanged the scope of judicial inquiry upon an application for the enforcement of a subpena. See also Sen. Rep. p. 41 (Sen. Doc. p. 227); 92 Cong. Rec. A2988 (Sen. Doc. p. 415).

SECTION 6 (d)—DENIALS

Section 6 (d) provides that "prompt notice shall be given of the denial in whole or in part of any written application, petition, or other request of any interested person made in connection with any agency proceeding. Except in affirming a prior denial or where the denial is self-explanatory, such notice shall be accompanied by a simple statement of procedural or other grounds." This requirement relates to applications, petitions and requests made by "interested persons" in connection with any "agency proceeding", i.e., rule making, adjudication and licensing proceedings. It applies to such proceedings regardless of whether they are formal or informal. Sen. Rep. p. 20, H.R. Rep. p. 33 (Sen. Doc. pp. 206, 265). As in the case of section 4 (d), an "interested person" may be defined generally as one whose interests are or will be affected by the agency action which may result from the proceeding. It is clear that with respect to formal proceedings, the only interested persons are those who are "parties" to such proceedings within the meaning of section 2 (b).

Section 6 (d) has no application to matters which do not relate to rule making, adjudication or licensing. Generally, it is not applicable to the mass of administrative routine unrelated to those proceedings.

The prompt notice of denial required by section 6 (d) may be given in writing, addressed to the applicant, or orally (e.g., in the case of a proceeding conducted by an examiner). The required statement of grounds for denial, while simple in nature, must be sufficient to advise the party of the general basis of the denial.

Where the denial is self-explanatory or affirms a previous denial, it need not be accompanied by a statement of reasons; in such cases, it is assumed that the applicant has knowledge of the grounds for denial.

71

VI
SECTION 7—HEARINGS

The provisions of section 7 govern the conduct of hearings in those cases of rule making and adjudication which are required by sections 4 and 5 to be conducted in accordance with sections 7 and 8. The requirements of section 7 are closely integrated with those of sections 5 (c) (as to certain types of adjudication) and 8. Section 7, together with sections 5 (c) and 8, became effective on December 11, 1946, and is applicable to proceedings commenced on and after that date. See section 12.

SECTION 7 (a)—PRESIDING OFFICERS

The first sentence of section 7 (a) provides that "There shall preside at the taking of evidence (1) the agency, (2) one or more members of the body which comprises the agency or (3) one or more examiners appointed as provided in this Act; but nothing in this Act shall be deemed to supersede the conduct of specified classes of proceedings in whole or part by or before boards or other officers specially provided for by or designated pursuant to statute."

Inasmuch as the provisions of section 11 relating to the selection and status of hearing examiners did not become effective until June 11, 1947 (see section 12), it is obvious that until then the agencies could continue to utilize their usual hearing examiners or officers, in compliance, of course, with the other requirements of sections 5 (c), 7 and 8.

The last clause of the sentence is designed to permit agencies to continue to utilize hearing officers or boards "specially provided for by or designated pursuant to statute." An earlier draft referred to "other officers specially designated by statute." See Senate Comparative Print, June 1945 pp. 12-13 (Sen. Doc. p. 28). Under the original language, it might have been necessary for such an officer to be designated specifically by a statute to conduct a particular hearing, e.g., in the manner that 19 U.S.C. 1641 requires that hearings to determine whether a customhouse broker's license should be suspended or revoked must be held by the collector or chief officer of the customs. Under the present broader language, the exception will also apply if a statute authorizes the agency to designate a specific officer or employee or one of a specific class of officers or employees to conduct the hearing. Examples of statutory provisions for hearing officers who may be utilized without regard to section 11 are: (1) joint hearings before officers of Federal agencies and persons designated by one or more States (e.g., section 13(3) of the Interstate Commerce Act, 49 U.S.C. 13(3)), as well as hearings before joint State boards under section 209(a) of the Federal Power Act (16 U.S.C. 824h), (2) where officers of more than one agency sit, as joint boards composed of members of the Interstate Commerce Commission and the Civil Aeronautics Board pursuant to section 1003 of the Civil Aeronautics Act (49 U.S.C. 643), (3) quota review committees under the Agricultural Adjustment Act of 1938 (7 U.S.C. 1363), and (4) boards of employees under the Interstate Commerce Act (49 U.S.C. 17 (2)). Sen. Rep. pp. 41-42, (Sen. Doc. pp. 227-228). A statutory provision which merely provides for the conduct of hearings by any officers or employees the agency may designate, does not come within the exception so as to authorize the agency to dispense with hearing examiners appointed in accordance with section 11. H.R. Rep. p. 34 (Sen. Doc. p. 268).

Generally, whoever presides at the hearing (whether an examiner appointed pursuant to section 11, a member of the agency or a special statutory board or hearing officer) is subject to the remaining provisions of the Act. Sen. Rep. p. 21; H.R. Rep. p. 34 (Sen. Doc. pp. 207, 268). However, where a member of the agency acts as presiding officer, the exception in the last clause of section 5 (c) applies, with the result that he is not disqualified, as an examiner would be, by previous participation in the investigation of the case. Similarly, a statute requiring or authorizing a hearing to be conducted by a particular board or officer may have the further effect of requiring such board or officer to participate in the investigation or prosecution or of placing the board or officer under the supervision or direction of investigating or prosecuting officials. See 19 U.S.C. 1641. In the latter case, it would seem that to the extent the general requirements of section 5 (c) are inconsistent they are inapplicable.

The second sentence of section 7 (a) provides that "The functions of all presiding officers and of officers participating in decisions in conformity with section 8 shall be conducted in an impartial manner." This means, of course, that "They must conduct the hearing in a strictly impartial manner, rather than as the representative of an investigative or prosecuting authority, but this does not mean that they do not have the authority and duty—as a court does—to make sure that all necessary evidence is adduced and to keep the hearing orderly and efficient." Sen. Rep. p. 21, H.R. Rep. p. 34 (Sen. Doc. pp. 207, 268). This is not intended to prohibit a hearing officer from questioning witnesses and otherwise encouraging the making of a complete record.

The third sentence of section 7 (a) provides that "Any such officer may at any time withdraw if he deems himself disqualified; and, upon the filing in good faith of a timely and sufficient affidavit of personal bias or disqualification of any such officer, the agency shall determine the matter as a part of the record and decision in the case." This provision authorizes any presiding officer to withdraw from a proceeding if he considers himself disqualified, for example, as being related to a party. In addition, a party may, by the "filing in good faith of a timely and sufficient affidavit", present to the agency the issue of the "personal bias or disqualification of any such officer"; thereupon "the agency shall determine the matter as a part of the record and decision in the case". Hearings are not required on every charge of bias or disqualification of a presiding officer.[1] If the affidavit is insufficient upon its face, it may be dismissed summarily. In other cases, the agency may consider it appropriate to investigate the charge itself or by another hearing officer. In any event, the agency's decision and the proceedings upon such an affidavit must be made a part of the record of the case in which the affidavit is filed. Sen. Rep. pp. 21, 42, H.R. Rep. p. 35 (Sen. Doc. pp. 207, 228, 269).

If a court in reviewing the agency's final action finds, contrary to the agency, that the hearing officer was biased or disqualified, the agency action based upon the recommended or initial decision made by such officer is not thereby automatically void; rather, the question is whether the private party was prejudiced by such error. See last sentence of section 10 (e). The consequences of such bias or disqualification on the part of a presiding officer are alluded to in the reports of the Senate and House Committees on the Judiciary as follows: "The effect which bias or disqualification shown upon the record might have would be determined by the ordinary rules of law and the other provisions of this bill. If it appeared or were discovered late, it would have the effect where issues of fact or discretion were important and the con-

---

1. This is emphasized by the fact that an earlier draft of the bill required such hearings. See Senate Comparative Print, June 1945, p. 13 (Sen. Doc. p. 158).

duct and demeanor of witnesses relevant in determining them of rendering the recommended decisions or initial decisions of such officers invalid." Sen. Rep. p. 21, H.R. Rep. p. 35 (Sen. Doc. pp. 207, 269).

SECTION 7 (b)—HEARING POWERS

Section 7 (b) provides that "Officers presiding at hearings shall have authority, subject to the published rules of the agency and within its powers, to (1) administer oaths and affirmations, (2) issue subpenas authorized by law, (3) rule upon offers of proof and receive relevant evidence, (4) take or cause depositions to be taken whenever the ends of justice would be served thereby, (5) regulate the course of the hearing, (6) hold conferences for the settlement or simplification of the issues by consent of the parties, (7) dispose of procedural requests or similar matters, (8) make decisions or recommend decisions in conformity with section 8, and (9) take any other action authorized by agency rule consistent with this Act."

The quoted language automatically vests[2] in hearing officers the enumerated powers to the extent that such powers have been given to the agency itself, i.e., "within its powers." In other words, not only are the enumerated powers thus given to hearing officers by section 7 (b) without the necessity of express agency delegation, but an agency is without power to withhold such powers from its hearing officers. This follows not only from the statutory language, "shall have authority", but from the general statutory purpose of enhancing the status and role of hearing officers. Thus, in the Senate Comparative Print of June 1945, p. 14 (Sen. Doc. p. 29), it is stated that "The statement of the powers of administrative hearing officers is designed to secure that responsibility and status which the Attorney General's Committee stressed as essential (Final Report, pp. 43-53 particularly at pp. 45-46 and 50)." See also Sen. Rep. p. 21, H.R. Rep. p. 35, 92 Cong. Rec. 2157 (Sen. Doc. pp. 207, 269, 319-320); cf. Sen. Rep. p. 42 (Sen. Doc. p. 228).

As noted above, the subsection vests in hearing officers only such of the enumerated powers as the agency itself possesses. If an agency lacks the authority to issue subpenas, subsection 7 (b) does not grant the subpena power to that agency's hearing

---

2. Since section 7 (b) itself vests these powers (including the subpena power) in hearing officers, *Cudahy Packing Co.* v. *Holland*, 315 U.S. 357 (1942), and *Fleming* v. *Mohawk Co.*, 331 U. S. 111 (1947), dealing with the authority of agencies to delegate such powers, have no application here.

officers. Senate Comparative Print, June 1945, p. 14 (Sen. Doc. pp. 29-30). The phrase "subject to the published rules of the agency" is intended to make clear the authority of the agency to lay down policies and procedural rules which will govern the exercise of such powers by presiding officers. Senate Hearings (1941) pp. 653, 1457-1458. For example, if an agency provides by rule that the fact of citizenship must be established in a prescribed manner, the hearing officer must conform to such rule in exercising his power to "rule upon offers of proof and receive relevant evidence". Similarly, if an agency provides that subpenas duces tecum shall be issued only upon written application specifying the documents desired and their relevance, the hearing officer is bound to comply.

Agencies remain free to provide for appeals to the agency heads from rulings of hearing officers in the exercise of the powers enumerated in section 7 (b). For example, when a ruling excluding certain evidence, if reversed by the agency, would necessitate reopening of the hearing and recalling witnesses, it may be desirable to permit an immediate appeal from the ruling.

SECTION 7 (c)—EVIDENCE

Burden of proof. The first sentence of section 7 (c) provides that "Except as statutes otherwise provide, the proponent of a rule or order shall have the burden of proof." In the Senate Comparative Print, June 1945, p. 15 (Sen. Doc. p. 31), it is stated that "The provision relating to burden of proof is the standard rule." There is some indication that the term "burden of proof" was not employed in any strict sense, but rather as synonymous with the "burden of going forward".[3] In either case, it is clear from the introductory clause that this general statement was not intended to repeal specific provisions of other statutes which, as by establishing presumptions, alter what would otherwise be the "burden of proof" or the "burden of going forward". Sen. Rep. p. 42 (Sen. Doc. p. 228).

Evidence. The second sentence of section 7 (c) provides that "Any oral or documentary evidence may be received, but every agency

---

3. Thus, In Sen. Rep. p. 22 (Sen. Doc. p. 208), it is stated: "That the proponent of a rule or order has the burden of proof means not only that the party initiating the proceeding has the general burden of coming forward with a prima facie case but that other parties, who are proponents of some different result, also for that purpose have a burden to maintain." See also H.R. Rep. p. 36 (Sen. Doc. p. 270).

shall as a matter of policy provide for the exclusion of irrelevant, immaterial, or unduly repetitious evidence and no sanction shall be imposed or rule or order be issued except upon consideration of the whole record or such portions thereof as may be cited by any party and as supported by and in accordance with the reliable, probative, and substantial evidence."

Under section 7 (c) it is clear that, as heretofore, the technical rules of evidence will not be applicable to administrative hearings. See also Final Report, p. 70. Thus, it is stated that "the mere admission of evidence is not to be taken as prejudicial error (there being no lay jury to be protected from improper influence) although irrelevant, immaterial, and unduly repetitious evidence is useless and is to be excluded as a matter of efficiency and good practice." H.R. Rep. p. 36, Sen. Rep. p. 22 (Sen. Doc. pp. 270, 208). To carry out this policy, it is advisable that each agency direct its hearing officers to exclude from the record so far as practicable irrelevant, immaterial or unduly repetitious evidence.

Agency action must be supported by "reliable, probative, and substantial evidence." It is said that "These are standards or principles usually applied tacitly and resting mainly upon common sense which people engaged in the conduct of responsible affairs instinctively understand." H.R. Rep. p. 36, Sen. Rep. p. 22 (Sen. Doc. pp. 270, 208). This restates the present law. H.R. Rep. p. 53, fn. 18 (Sen. Doc. p. 287); *Consolidated Edison Co. v. National Labor Relations Board,* 305 U.S. 197, 230 (1938); Senate Comparative Print, p. 14 (Sen. Doc. p. 31). It is clear that nothing in section 7 (c) is intended to change the standard or scope of judicial review; section 10 (e) (5) specifically restates the "substantial evidence rule", as developed by the Congress and the courts, under which the reviewing court ascertains whether the agency's findings of fact are supported by substantial evidence.

Nothing in section 7 (c) is intended to preclude an agency from imposing reasonable requirements as to how particular facts must be established—such as age, citizenship, marital status, etc. Nor is an agency forbidden to draw such inferences or presumptions as the courts customarily employ, such as the failure to explain by a party in exclusive possession of the facts, or the presumption of continuance of a state of facts once shown to exist.

77

Furthermore, section 7 (c) does not repeal provisions of other statutes which establish certain presumptions of fact.[4]

Presentation of evidence. Section 7 (c) provides further that "Every party shall have the right to present his case or defense by oral or documentary evidence, to submit rebuttal evidence, and to conduct such cross-examination as may be required for a full and true disclosure of the facts." It is concluded that the provision is intended to emphasize the right of parties in cases of adjudication (other than determining claims for money or benefits or applications for initial licenses) to present their evidence orally, and in addition to present such "documentary evidence" as would be admissible in judicial proceedings, such as writings and records made in regular course of business. 28 U.S.C. 695. As here used "documentary evidence" does not mean affidavits and written evidence of any kind. Such a construction would flood agency proceedings with hearsay evidence. In the last sentence of the subsection, there appears the phrase "evidence in written form," thus indicating that the Congress distinguished between "written evidence" and "documentary evidence." See also section 203 (c) of the Emergency Price Control Act. Again, the subsection expressly states the right to adequate cross-examination. Against this background, it is clear that the "right to present his case or defense by oral or documentary evidence" does not extend to presenting evidence in affidavit or other written form so as to deprive the agency or opposing parties of opportunity for cross-examination, nor so as to force them to assume the expense of calling the affiants for cross-examination. See *Powhatan Mining Co. v. Ickes,* 118 F. 2d 105, 109 (C.C.A. 6, 1941).

Of course, the agency may, if it desires, receive such written evidence as it determines would tend to be reliable and probative and the admission of which would not prejudicially deprive other parties or the agency of opportunity for cross-examination. Thus, technical and statistical data may be introduced in convenient written form subject to adequate opportunity for cross-examination and rebuttal. Sen. Rep. p. 42, H.R. Rep. p. 37 (Sen. Doc. pp. 228, 271). Any evidence may be admitted by agreement or if no

---

4. For example, section 20 (d) of the Longshoremen's and Harbor Workers' Compensation Act (33 U.S.C. 920 (d)), provides that "In any proceedings for the enforcement of a claim for compensation it shall be presumed, in the absence of substantial evidence to the contrary—(d) that the Injury was not occasioned by the willful intention of the injured employee to injure or kill himself or another." See *Del Vecchio v. Bowers,* 296 U.S. 280 (1935). See also section 2 (a) 9 of the Investment Company Act of 1940 (15 U.S.C. 80a-2 (9)).

objection is made. *Opp Cotton Mills, Inc.* v. *Administrator*, 312 U.S. 126, 155 (1941).

The provision for "such cross-examination as may be required for a full and true disclosure of the facts" does not, according to the House Committee Report, "confer a right of so-called 'unlimited' cross-examination. Presiding officers will have to make the necessary initial determination whether the cross-examination is pressed to unreasonable lengths by a party or whether it is required for the 'full and true disclosure of the facts' stated in the provision. Nor is it the intention to eliminate the authority of agencies to confer sound discretion upon presiding officers in the matter of its extent. The test is—as the section states—whether it is required 'for a full and true disclosure of the facts.' In many rule making proceedings where the subject matter and evidence are broadly economic or statistical in character and the parties or witnesses numerous, the direct or rebuttal evidence may be of such a nature that cross-examination adds nothing substantial to the record and unnecessarily prolongs the hearings." H.R. Rep. p. 37 (Sen. Doc. p. 271).

In proceedings involving rule making or determining claims for money or benefits or applications for initial licenses, an agency may adopt procedures for the submission of all or part of the evidence in written form. Thus, in rate making and licensing proceedings, which frequently involve extensive technical or statistical data, the agency may require that the mass of such material be submitted in orderly exhibit form rather than be read into the record by witnesses. Similarly, in determining claims for money or benefits, the agency may require that the papers filed in support of the application contain the factual material. Such procedures may be required only "where the interest of any party will not be prejudiced thereby." Typically, in these cases, the veracity and demeanor of witnesses are not important. It is difficult to see how any party's interests would be prejudiced by such procedures where sufficient opportunity for rebuttal exists. However, "To the extent that cross-examination is necessary to bring out the truth, the party should have it." Sen. Rep. p. 23, H.R. Rep. p. 37 (Sen. Doc. pp. 209, 271). Such is the present practice of such agencies as the Civil Aeronautics Board, which has made extensive use of written evidence procedures to simplify records and shorten formal hearings.

SECTION 7 (d)—RECORD

Record. The first sentence of section 7 (d) provides that "The transcript of testimony and exhibits, together with all papers and requests filed in the proceeding, shall constitute the exclusive record for decision in accordance with section 8 and, upon payment of lawfully prescribed costs, shall be made available to the parties." The record must include any agency proceedings upon an affidavit of personal bias or disqualification of a hearing officer pursuant to section 7 (a). All decisions (initial, recommended or tentative) are required by section 8 (b) to be made a part of the record. It is believed, by analogy to judicial practice, that the subsection does not require the transcription of oral arguments for inclusion in the record.

In the interests of economy, certain agencies have followed the practice of not transcribing the stenographic record of the hearing unless there is an appeal from the decision of the officer presiding at the hearing. Section 7 (d) does not require an agency to have the record transcribed automatically in every case, but it does require transcription in any case where a party demands a copy of the record, so that it will be available to him "upon payment of lawfully prescribed costs." This requirement is satisfied by the present agency practice of contracting with private stenographic agencies for reporting service on terms that enable parties to obtain copies at a reasonable price.

Official notice. The second sentence of section 7 (d) provides that "Where any agency decision rests on official notice of a material fact not appearing in the evidence in the record, any party shall on timely request be afforded an opportunity to show the contrary." In the Senate Comparative Print, June 1945, p. 15 (Sen. Doc. p. 32), it is stated that "The rule of official notice is that recommended by the Attorney General's Committee, particularly the safeguard that parties be apprised of matters so noticed and accorded an 'opportunity for reopening of the hearing in order to allow the parties to come forward to meet the facts intended to be noticed.' (Final Report pp. 71-73)." The recommendation of the Attorney General's Committee, which is thus apparently adopted was that "the permissible area of official notice be extended" so as to avoid "laborious proof of what is obvious and notorious," subject to opportunity for rebuttal or explanation, as provided in section 7 (d). See the excellent discussion in Final Report, pp. 71-73, pointing out that the process of official notice should not be limited to the traditional matters of judicial notice but extends properly to all matters as to which the agency by reason of its functions is presumed to be expert, such as technical or scientific facts within its specialized knowledge. Cf. H.R. Rep. p. 38 (Sen. Doc. p. 272).

Agencies may take official notice of facts at any stage in a proceeding—even in the final decision[5]—but the matters thus noticed should be specified and "any party shall on timely request be afforded an opportunity to show the contrary." The matters thus noticed become a part of the record and, unless successfully controverted, furnish the same basis for findings of fact as does "evidence" in the usual sense.

---

5. "Where agencies take such notice they must so state on the record or in their decisions and then afford the parties an opportunity to show the contrary." Sen. Rep. p. 23, H.R. Rep. pp. 37-38 (Sen. Doc. pp. 209, 271). If official notice is taken of facts in the course of the final decision, the proceeding need not be reopened automatically, but the parties will be entitled to request reopening for the purpose of contesting the facts thus officially noticed by the agency.

VII
SECTION 8—DECISIONS

The provisions of section 8, together with those of section 5 (c), govern the procedure subsequent to hearing. Section 8 applies to cases of rule making and adjudication which are required by sections 4 and 5 to be conducted in accordance with sections 7 and 8. It became effective on December 11, 1946, and is applicable to proceedings commenced on and after that date. See section 12.

SECTION 8 (a)—WHO DECIDES

Section 8 (a) provides for intermediate and final decisions, prescribes who shall make them, and defines the decisional relationship between the agency heads and presiding officers.[1] The subsection reads as follows:

> *Action by subordinates.* In cases in which the agency has not presided at the reception of the evidence, the officer who presided (or, in cases not subject to subsection (c) of section 5, any other officer or officers qualified to preside at hearings pursuant to section 7) shall initially decide the case or the agency shall require (in specific cases or by general rule) the entire record to be certified to it for initial decision. Whenever such officers make the initial decision and in the absence of either an appeal to the agency or review upon motion of the agency within time provided by rule, such decision shall without further proceedings then become the decision of the agency. On appeal from or review of the initial decisions of such officers the agency shall, except as it may limit the issues upon notice or by rule, have all the powers which it would have in making the initial decision. Whenever the agency makes the initial decision without having presided at the reception of the evidence, such officers shall first recommend a decision except that in rule making or determining applications for initial licenses (1) in lieu thereof the agency may issue a tentative decision or any of its responsible officers may recommend a decision or (2) any such procedure may be omitted in any case in which the agency finds upon the record that due and timely execution of its functions imperatively and unavoidably so requires.

At the outset, it should be noted that section 8 (a) has no application to cases in which the agency itself has presided at the reception of the evidence. The procedures required by this subsection are intended "to bridge the gap between the officials who hear and those who decide cases." H.R. Rep. p. 38 (Sen. Doc. p. 272). If the agency itself, e.g., the Interstate Commerce Commission, hears the evidence, it may decide the case without the use of any intermediate decision. In such cases, however, the agency may, if it desires, preface its final decision with a tentative decision to which the parties may file exceptions.

---

1. Any of the requirements of section 8 may be waived by the parties. Sen. Rep. p. 23 (Sen. Doc. p. 209).

In cases of adjudication subject to section 5 (c) and in which the agency itself has not presided at the reception of evidence, the presiding officer[2] must "initially decide the case or the agency shall require (in specific cases or by general rule) the entire record to be certified to it for initial decision." It is further provided that "Whenever the agency makes the initial decision without having presided at the reception of the evidence [the presiding officer] shall first recommend a decision." That is, in cases of adjudication subject to section 5 (c), the presiding officer must make either (a) an "initial" decision which will become the agency's final decision in the absence of an appeal to or review by the agency, or (b) a "recommended" decision which will be followed by an "initial" decision by the agency.

Under the terms of the subsection, the presiding officer's decision will constitute an initial decision unless the agency provides otherwise either by general rule published in the Federal Register or by order in the particular case. Accordingly, each agency should determine whether it desires the decisions of its presiding officers to be "initial" decisions or recommended decisions.

In cases not subject to section 5 (c), the agency may provide for the making of initial decisions by "any other officer or officers qualified to preside at hearings pursuant to section 7." That is, in rule making, in "determining applications for initial licenses," and in "proceedings involving the validity or application of rates, facilities, or practices of public utilities or carriers," an "initial" decision may be made, for example, by a hearing examiner other than the one who heard the evidence. Further, the fourth sentence of section 8 (a) provides that in rule making and in determining applications for initial licenses the agency may issue a tentative decision or *any* of its responsible officers may recommend a decision in lieu of a recommended decision by the hearing examiner who conducted the hearing. This last clause permits, in rule making and determining applications for initial licenses, "the continuation of the widespread agency practice of serving upon the parties, as a substitute for either an examiner's report or a tentative agency report, a report prepared by the staff of specialists and technicians normally engaged in that portion of

---

2. As here used, presiding officer means the member of the agency, the examiner appointed pursuant to section 11, or the special statutory board or hearing officer who conducted the hearing. See section 7 (a). Where the presiding officer becomes unavailable as by illness or leaving the agency, the agency may direct another hearing officer to make an initial or recommended decision, or it may issue a tentative decision, or it may order a rehearing.

83

the agency's operations to which the proceeding in question relates." Sen. Rep. p. 43[3] (Sen. Doc. p. 229).

Finally, in rule making or determining applications for initial licenses the agency may itself decide the case without any prior initial, recommended or tentative decision, even though it has not presided at the reception of the evidence, "in any case in which the agency finds upon the record that due and timely execution of its functions imperatively and unavoidably so requires."

Appeals and review. Where the agency permits a hearing officer to make an "initial" decision, "in the absence of either an appeal to the agency or review upon motion of the agency within time provided by rule, such decision shall without further proceedings then become the decision of the agency." Parties may appeal from the hearing officer's initial decision to the agency, which must thereupon itself consider and decide the case. Also, the agency may review the hearing officer's initial decision even though the parties fail to appeal. Each agency should publish a rule prescribing the time within which parties may appeal or the agency may call up the case for review.[4] Where the hearing examiner (or other officer where permitted by the subsection makes a recommended decision, the agency must always make an "initial" or final decision.

In making its decision, whether following an initial or recommended decision, the agency is in no way bound by the decision of its subordinate officer; it retains complete freedom of decision—as though it had heard the evidence itself. This follows from the fact that a recommended decision is advisory in nature. See *National Labor Relations Board* v. *Elkland Leather Co.,* 114 F. 2d 221, 225 (C.C.A. 3, 1940), certiorari denied, 311 U.S. 705. Similarly, the third sentence of section 8 (a) provides that "On appeal from or review of the initial decisions of such [hearing] officers the agency shall, except as it may limit the issues upon notice or by rule, have all the powers which it would have in making the initial decision." This is not to say that hearing

---

3. It is to be noted that in "proceedings involving the validity or application of rates, facilities, or practices of public utilities or carriers" (if they do not constitute either rule making or the determination of an application for an initial license), an intermediate (i.e., "initial" or "recommended") decision must be made by the hearing examiner who conducted the hearing or by some other officer or officers qualified to preside at hearings pursuant to section 7 (a).

4. It is important to note that section 10 (c) permits an agency to require parties to appeal from hearing officers' initial decisions to the agency as a prerequisite to obtaining judicial review. Such a requirement must be set forth in a published rule which must further provide that the hearing officer's initial decision shall be inoperative pending the agency's review of the case. Sen. Rep. p. 27, H.R. Rep. pp. 43, 55, fn. 21 (Sen. Doc. p. 213, 277, 289).

examiners' initial or recommended decisions are without effect. "They become a part of the record [as required by subsection 8 (b)] and are of consequence, for example, to the extent that material facts in any case depend on the determination of credibility of witnesses as shown by their demeanor or conduct at the hearing." Sen. Rep. p. 24, H.R. Rep. p. 38 (Sen. Doc. pp. 210, 272). In such cases, it is apparently assumed that agencies will attach considerable weight to the findings of the examiner who saw and heard the witnesses. However, in cases where the credibility of witnesses is not a material factor, or cases where the recommended or initial decision is made by an officer other than the one who heard the evidence, the function of such decision will be, rather, the sharpening of the issues for subsequent proceedings.

Section 8 (a) empowers agencies to "limit the issues upon notice or by rule" on appeal from or review of the *initial* decisions of hearing officers. That is, an agency may limit the issues which it will consider in such cases by notice in a particular case or by a general rule published in the Federal Register. It may restrict its review to questions of law and policy or, where it is alleged that erroneous findings of fact have been made by the hearing officer, to determining whether cited portions of the record disclose that the findings are clearly wrong. Final Report, p. 51. See also Sen. Rep. p. 43 (Sen. Doc. p. 229).

Where the hearing officer makes a recommended decision, the agency must itself consider and determine all issues properly presented. However, it may provide that it will consider only such objections to its subordinates' decisions (recommended or initial) as are presented to it as exceptions to such decisions. See *Marshall Field & Co.* v. *National Labor Relations Board,* 318 U.S. 253, 255 (1943); *National Labor Relations Board* v. *Cheney California Lumber Co.*, 327 U.S. 385, 387-88 (1946). It may also require that exceptions be precise and supported by specific citations, to the record.[5] The agency in reviewing either initial or recommended decisions may adopt in whole or in part the findings, conclusions, and basis therefor stated by the presiding

---

5. See Final Report, p. 52: "The Committee strongly urges that the agencies abandon the notion that no matter how unspecified or unconvincing the grounds set out for appeal, there is yet a duty to reexamine the record minutely and reach fresh conclusions without reference to the hearing commissioner's decision. Agencies should insist upon meaningful content and exactness in the appeal from the hearing commissioner's decision and in the subsequent oral argument before the agency. Too often, at present, exceptions are blanket in character, without reference to pages in the record and without in any way narrowing the issues. They simply seek to impose upon the agency the burden of complete reexamination. Review of the hearing commissioner's decision should in general and in the absence of clear error be limited to grounds specified in the appeal."

85

officer. On the other hand, it may make entirely new findings either upon the record or upon new evidence which it takes. Also, it may remand the case to the hearing officer for any appropriate further proceedings. Sen. Rep. p. 43, H.R. Rep. pp. 38-39 (Sen. Doc. pp. 229, 272-273).

SECTION 8 (b)—SUBMITTALS AND DECISIONS

Submittals. The first sentence of section 8 (b) provides that "Prior to each recommended, initial, or tentative decision, or decision upon agency review of the decision of subordinate officers the parties shall be afforded a reasonable opportunity to submit for the consideration of the officers participating in such decisions (1) proposed findings and conclusions, *or* (2) exceptions to the decisions or recommended decisions of subordinate officers or to tentative agency decisions, and (3) supporting reasons for such exceptions or proposed findings or conclusions." [Italics supplied]. The procedure thus prescribed for the focusing of issues and arguments is a codification of the present general practice. Senate Comparative Print, June 1945, p. 16 (Sen. Doc. p. 33). "Ordinarily proposed findings and conclusions are submitted only to the officers making the initial [or recommended] decision, and the parties present exceptions thereafter if they contest the result. However, such exceptions may in form or effect include proposed findings or conclusions for the reviewing authority to consider as part of the exceptions." Sen. Rep. pp. 24, 43 (Sen. Doc. pp. 210, 229).

Agencies may require that proposed findings and conclusions and exceptions be supported by precise citation of the record or legal authorities as the case may be. Reasonable time limits for the submission of such materials may be imposed. The opportunity to submit supporting reasons means that briefs on the law and facts which are filed by parties in support of their proposed findings and conclusions and exceptions must be received and considered. Sen. Rep. p. 24, H.R. Rep. p. 39 (Sen. Doc. pp. 210, 273). Section 8 (b) does not purport to prescribe opportunities for oral argument. Accordingly, subject to the provisions of particular statutes, each agency must itself determine in what cases oral argument before hearing officers or the agency is necessary or appropriate.[6]

---

6. See *Morgan v. United States*, 298 U.S. 468, 481 (1936): "Argument may be oral or written."

Decisions. Section 8 (b) further provides: "The record shall show the ruling upon each such finding, conclusion, or exception presented. All decisions (including initial, recommended, or tentative decisions) shall become a part of the record and include a statement of (1) findings and conclusions, as well as the reasons or basis therefor, upon all the material issues of fact, law, or discretion presented on the record; and (2) the appropriate rule, order, sanction, relief, or denial thereof."

Since all decisions, whether made by the agency or by a subordinate officer, become a part of the record, the requirement of the first quoted sentence will be satisfied if such decisions in some way indicate the ruling of the agency or such officer upon each requested finding or conclusion or exception presented to the agency or to such officer. The purpose of this requirement is "to preclude later controversy as to what the agency had done." H.R. Rep. p. 54, fn. 19 (Sen. Doc. p. 288).

The form and content of decisions, as prescribed in the last sentence of section 8 (b), are discussed in the Committee reports as follows:

> The requirement that the agency must state the basis for its findings and conclusions means that such findings and conclusions must be sufficiently related to the record as to advise the parties of their record basis. Most agencies will do so by opinions which reason and relate the issues of fact, law, and discretion. Statements of reasons, however, may be long or short as the nature of the case and the novelty or complexity of the issues may require.
>
> Findings and conclusions must include all the relevant issues presented by the record in the light of the law involved. They may be few or many. A particular conclusion of law may render certain issues and findings immaterial, or vice versa. Where oral testimony is conflicting or subject to doubt of its credibility, the credibility of witnesses would be a necessary finding if the facts are material. It should also be noted that the relevant issues extend to matters of administrative discretion as well as of law and fact. This is important because agencies often determine whether they have power to act rather than whether their discretion should be exercised or how it should be exercised. Furthermore, without a disclosure of the basis for the exercise of, or failure to exercise, discretion, the parties are unable to determine what other or additional facts they might offer by way of rehearing or reconsideration of decisions. Sen. Rep. pp. 24-25, H.R. Rep. p. 39. (Sen. Doc. pp. 210-211, 273).

An agency which issues opinions in narrative and expository form may continue to do so without making separate findings of fact and conclusions of law. However, such opinions must indicate the agency's findings and conclusions on material issues of fact, law or discretion with such specificity "as to advise the parties and any reviewing court of their record and legal basis."[7] The

---

7. Agencies should keep in mind that pursuant to section 3 (b) they may cite as precedents only such previous orders and opinions as have been published or made available for public inspection.

87

requirement that such decisions indicate the reasons for the exercise of discretionary power is a codification of existing good practice. See *Phelps Dodge Corp.* v. *National Labor Relations Board,* 313 U.S. 177, 194-197 (1941).

Nothing in the Act is intended to preclude agency heads from utilizing the services of agency employees as assistants for analysis and drafting. *Morgan* v. *United States,* 298 U.S. 468, 481 (1936). Of course, in adjudicatory cases subject to section 5 (c), such assistants could not have performed investigative or prosecuting functions in the cases (or in factually related cases) in which they are so employed. Also, the agency heads are free to employ the hearing officer who heard a particular case as the draftsman of their final decision and otherwise to assist in its formulation. Compare generally section 4 (a) of the National Labor Relations Act, as amended.

Appeals to superior agency. Nothing in section 8 is intended to cut off any rights which parties may have for appeal to or review by a superior agency. Sen. Rep. p. 23 (Sen. Doc. p. 209). The requirements of subsection 8 (b) as to the form and content of decisions do not apply to decisions of a superior agency upon such appeal from or review of the agency's decision.

VIII
SECTION 9—SANCTIONS AND POWERS

Section 9 generally prohibits unauthorized action by agencies and prescribes certain rules to govern licensing proceedings. The provisions of section 9 apply to all relevant cases (other than the agencies and functions exempted by section 2 (a)) regardless of the applicability of the other sections of the Act.

SECTION 9 (a)—SANCTIONS

Section 9 (a) provides that "in the exercise of any power or authority no sanction shall be imposed or substantive rule or order be issued except within jurisdiction delegated to the agency and as authorized by law." The term sanction is broadly defined in section 2 (f) to include the whole or part of any agency prohibition, requirement, limitation, or other condition affecting the freedom of any person; (2) withholding of relief; (3) imposition of any form of penalty or fine; (4) destruction, taking, seizure, or withholding of property; (5) assessment of damages, reimbursement, restitution, compensation, costs, charges, or fees; (6) requirement, revocation, or suspension of a license;[1] or (7) taking of other compulsory or restrictive action."

The original draft of section 9 (a) limited the imposition of sanctions to those "as specified and authorized by statute." Senate Comparative Print, June 1945, p. 17 (Sen. Doc. p. 159). The change of the word "statute" to "law" was intentional so as to recognize that an agency may impose a sanction or issue a substantive rule or order if such power is authorized not only by statutes but by treaties, court decisions, commonly recognized administrative practices, or other law. See *United States* v. *MacDaniel*, 7 Pet. (32 U.S.) 1, 13-14 (1833). Both the Senate and House reports recognize that the source of authority for the imposition of a sanction or the issuance of a substantive rule or order may be either specific or general, as the case may be. Sen. Rep. p. 25, H.R. Rep. p. 40 (Sen. Doc. pp. 211, 274).

The purpose of section 9 (a) is, evidently, to assure that agencies will not appropriate to themselves powers Congress has not intended them to exercise. Section 9 (a) merely restates existing law. Sen. Rep. p. 43 (Sen. Doc. p. 229). Many agencies' powers

---

1. The denial of an application for a renewal of a license is not a penal measure. *Federal Communications Commission* v. *WOKO*. 329 U.S. 223 (1946). It is, by definition in section 2 (f), a form of agency sanction.

89

are very clear; they are set forth specifically in the act creating the agency. Still other powers may be readily inferred from the framework of the act creating the agency or may be logically necessary for the conduct of the powers granted to the agency. But whether an agency's powers are express or implied, in either case they may be exercised. Particularly pertinent in this connection is the language of the Supreme Court in *Phelps Dodge Corp.* v. *National Labor Relations Board,* 313 U.S. 177, 194 (1941):

> A statute expressive of such large public policy as that on which the National Labor Relations Board is based must be broadly phrased and necessarily carries with it the task of administrative application. There is an area plainly covered by the language of the Act and an area no less plainly without it. *But in the nature of things Congress could not catalogue all the devices and strategems for circumventing the policies of the Act. Nor could it define the whole gamut of remedies to effectuate these policies in an infinite variety of specific situations.* Congress met these difficulties by leaving the adaptation of means to end to the empiric process of administration.*** the relation of remedy to policy is peculiarly a matter for administrative competence. [*Italics* supplied].

SECTION 9 (b)—LICENSES

Section 9 (b) is composed of three sentences, each of which is mutually exclusive of the others. The first sentence applies specifically to applications for licenses, the second to suspension or revocation of licenses, and the third to renewals. Each of these will be considered separately.

Applications for licenses. The first sentence of section 9 (b) provides: "In any case in which application is made for a license required by law the agency, with due regard to the rights or privileges of all the interested parties or adversely affected persons and with reasonable dispatch, shall set and complete any proceedings required to be conducted pursuant to sections 7 and 8 of this Act or other proceedings required by law and shall make its decision." The import of this sentence is that an agency shall hear and decide licensing proceedings as quickly as possible. Should the licensing proceedings be required by statute to be determined upon the record after opportunity for an agency hearing, an agency will be required to follow the provisions as to hearing and decision contained in sections 7 and 8 of the Act. As to other types of licensing proceedings, the Act does not formulate any fixed procedure (just as no fixed procedure has been formulated for adjudications other than those that are required by statute to be determined on the record after opportunity for an agency hearing).

The requirement that licensing proceedings be completed with reasonable dispatch is merely a statement of fair administrative procedure. Congress decided not to set any maximum period of time for agency consideration of applications for licenses. In the first draft of S. 7 there was a provision to the effect that an application for a license would be deemed granted unless the agency within 60 days after the application was made, rendered its decision or set the matter down for hearing. Senate Comparative Print, June 1945, p. 17 (Sen. Doc. p. 159). This provision was dropped in later drafts and replaced with the phrase "with reasonable dispatch."

The term "reasonable dispatch" is not an absolute one and cannot be described in precise terms. What is reasonable for one agency may not be reasonable for another agency. The time necessary to consider license applications for certificates of public convenience and necessity is much greater, as a rule, than that needed for issuing warehousemen's licenses under 7 U.S.C. 244. Similarly, variations in an agency's work-load, reflecting developments in an industry, may result in unavoidable temporary backlogs. Of course, where another statute prescribes a specific period of time for agency consideration of an application for a license, such specific provision will be controlling. For example, under section 355 (c) of Title 21, U.S.C., an application for a license for the sale of new drugs becomes effective on the sixtieth day after the filing of the application unless the Federal Security Administrator takes appropriate action.

Suspension or revocation of licenses. The second sentence of section 9 (b) provides: "Except in cases of willfulness or those in which public health, interest, or safety requires otherwise, no withdrawal, suspension, revocation, or annulment of any license shall be lawful unless, prior to the institution of agency proceedings therefor, facts or conduct which may warrant such action shall have been called to the attention of the licensee by the agency in writing and the licensee shall have been accorded opportunity to demonstrate or achieve compliance with all lawful requirements." This sentence requires an agency to give a licensee an opportunity to change his conduct before his license can be revoked by the agency unless the licensee's conduct is willful or the public health, interest or safety requires otherwise.

91

Thus, if a particular licensee should under ordinary circumstances transcend the bounds of the privilege granted to him, the agency which has granted him the license must inform him in writing of such conduct and afford him an opportunity to comply with the requirements of the agency before it can revoke, withdraw, suspend or annul his license. While the warning must be in writing, it need not take any special form.

No prior notice need be given if the licensee's conduct is willful. In such a situation the license may be revoked immediately without "another chance." Also, "another chance" need not be given where "the public health, interest, or safety requires otherwise." The latter phrase refers to a situation where immediate cancellation of a license is necessary in the public interest irrespective "of the equities or injuries to the licensee." Sen. Rep. p. 26 (Sen. Doc. p. 212). For example, in case of an accident involving aircraft, the Administrator of Civil Aeronautics may suspend the license of the pilot pending investigation. The public safety and interest require such immediate suspension. 49 U.S.C. 559.

It is clear that the provisions of this second sentence do not apply to temporary permits or temporary licenses. Sen. Rep. p. 26, H.R. Rep. p. 41 (Sen. Doc. pp. 212, 275). Such permits or licenses may be revoked without "another chance" and regardless of whether there is willfulness or whether the public health, interest, or safety is involved. And it is clear, too, that the provisions of this sentence do not apply to renewal of licenses. Renewals are treated specifically in the next sentence.

Renewal of licenses. The last sentence of section 9 (b) provides: "In any case in which the licensee has, in accordance with agency rules, made timely and sufficient application for a renewal or a new license, no license with reference to any activity of a continuing nature shall expire until such application shall have been finally determined by the agency." This sentence states the best existing law and practice. Sen. Rep. p. 43 (Sen. Doc. p. 229). It is only fair where a licensee has filed his application for a renewal or a new license in ample time prior to the expiration of his license, and where the application itself is sufficient, that his license should not expire until his application shall have been determined by the agency. In such a case the licensee has done everything that is within his power to do and he should not suffer if the agency has failed, for one reason or another, to consider his application prior to the lapse of his license. Agencies, of course, may make reasonable rules requiring sufficient advance application.[2]

---

2. The Office of Alien Property of the Department of Justice has adopted such a rule with reference to renewal of licenses. 11 F.R. 177A-629.

93

IX
Section 10—Judicial Review

The provisions of section 10 constitute a general restatement of the principles of judicial review embodied in many statutes and judicial decisions.[1] Section 10, it must be emphasized, deals largely with principles. It not only does not supersede special statutory review proceedings, but also generally leaves the mechanics of judicial review to be governed by other statutes and by judicial rules. For example, many statutes provide that where the reviewing court finds that the taking of new evidence would be warranted, such evidence must be presented to the agency with opportunity to modify its findings. See section 9 of the Securities Act (15 U.S.C. 77i). Such provisions continue in effect. Similarly, the time within which review must be sought will be governed, as in the past, by relevant statutory provisions or by judicial application of the doctrine of laches. See Section 5 (c) of the Federal Trade Commission Act (15 U.S.C. 45 (c)) and *U.S. ex rel. Arant* v. *Lane*, 249 U.S. 367 (1919). Accordingly, the general principles stated in section 10 must be carefully coordinated with existing statutory provisions and case law.[2]

Section 10 is applicable irrespective of whether the agency action for which review is sought was governed by the procedural provisions of sections 4, 5, 7 and 8. However, section 10 does not apply to those agencies and functions which are excepted by section 2 (a) from all provisions of the Act except section 3. For example, the provisions of section 10 are in no way applicable to the review of agency action taken pursuant to the Housing and Rent Act of 1947.

Section 10 became effective on September 11, 1946, and is applicable from that date to the judicial review of agency action.[3] However, the Department of Justice, in briefs filed in the Supreme Court, has taken the position that section 10 does not apply to cases which were pending in the courts on September 11, 1946. While these cases were decided by the Supreme Court without

---

1. See statements of Carl McFarland, Chairman of the Committee on Administrative Procedure of the American Bar Association, in House Hearings (1945) pp. 37-38 (Sen. Doc. pp. 83-84), and of the Attorney General in Sen. Rep. pp. 38, 43 (Sen. Doc. pp. 224, 229). 92 Cong. Rec. A2982 (Sen. Doc. pp. 406-407).

2. Recognizing the delicacy of this problem and the obligation of Government counsel to render every assistance to the courts in this task, the Attorney General has established a committee within the Department of Justice to assist in developing a uniform approach to the problems which arise in litigation.

3. See section 12 of the Act as to the effective dates of the various provisions of the Act.

any express reference to section 10, it seems fair to infer that the Court has accepted this construction. *United States* v. *Ruzicka,* 329 U.S. 287 (19-46); *Board of Governors of the Federal Reserve System* v. *Agnew,* 329 U.S. 441 (1947); *Krug* v. *Santa Fe Pacific Rd. Co.,* 329 U.S. 591 (1947); *Patterson* v. *Lamb,* 329 U.S. 539 (1947).

SCOPE OF SECTION 10

Section 10 applies "Except so far as (1) statutes preclude judicial review or (2) agency action is by law committed to agency discretion". The intended result of the introductory clause of section 10 is to restate the existing law as to the area of reviewable agency action. House Hearings (1945) p. 38 (Sen. Doc. p. 84).

A statute may in terms preclude, or be interpreted as intended to preclude, judicial review altogether. An example of a statute expressly precluding any judicial review is the Act of March 20, 1933 (38 U.S.C. 705) providing that "All decisions rendered by the Administrator of Veterans' Affairs under the provisions [of designated statutory sections] shall be final and conclusive on all questions of law and fact, and no other official or court of the United States shall have jurisdiction to review by mandamus or otherwise any such decision." Senate Hearings (1941) p. 1358. *Switchmen's Union of North America* v. *National Mediation Board,* 320 U.S. 297 (1943), illustrates the interpretation of a statute as intended to preclude judicial review although the statute does not expressly so provide.[4] Sen. Rep. pp. 43-44 (Sen. Doc. pp. 229-230).

The provisions of section 10 are applicable "Except so far as agency action is by law committed to agency discretion." For an example of such unreviewable agency action, see *United States* v. *George S. Bush & Co.,* 310 U.S. 371 (1940) (reaction by the President under section 336 (c) of the Tariff Act "if in his judgment" such action is necessary). More broadly, there are many statutory provisions which merely authorize agencies to make loans; under such statutes, the agencies' discretion is usually so complete that the refusal to make a loan is not reviewable under section 10 or

---

4. As S. 7 was introduced in the Senate in January 1945, the introductory phrase of section 10 read "Except (1) so far as statutes *expressly* preclude judicial review". [Italics supplied]. As reported in its present form by the Senate Committee on the Judiciary, the word "expressly" was omitted. This omission provides strong support for the conclusion that the courts remain free to deduce from the statutory context of particular agency action that the Congress intended to preclude judicial review of such action.

95

any other statute. Also, the refusal by the National Labor Relations Board to issue a complaint is, as heretofore, an exercise of discretion unreviewable by the courts. See *Jacobsen* v. *National Labor Relations Board,* 120 F. 2d 96 (C.C.A. 3, 1941), and Senate Comparative Print of June 1945, p. 19, para. (3) (Sen. Doc. p.38). For the same reason, the denial of a petition pursuant to section 4 (d) of this Act for the issuance, amendment or repeal of a rule is not subject to judicial review. Sen. Rep. p. 44 (Sen. Doc. p. 230).

In addition, the introductory clause of section 10 provides a most important principle of construction for reconciling the provisions of the section with other statutory provisions relating to judicial review. All of the provisions of section 10 are qualified by the introductory clause, *"Except so far as* (1) statutes preclude judicial review or (2) agency action is by law committed to agency discretion"* [Emphasis supplied]. The emphasized phrase does not mean that every provision of section 10 is applicable except where statutes preclude judicial review altogether. Instead, it reads *"Except so far as* (1) statutes preclude judicial review"*, with the clear result that some other statute, while not precluding review altogether, will have the effect of preventing the application of some of the provisions of section 10. The net effect, clearly intended by the Congress, is to provide for a dovetailing of the general provisions of the Administrative Procedure Act with the particular statutory provisions which the Congress has moulded for special situations.[5] Thus, a civil service employee of the Federal Government who alleges unlawful removal from office, can obtain judicial review only of the question of whether the procedures of the Civil Service Act were followed. *Levine* v. *Farley,* 107 F. 2d 186 (App. D.C., 1939), certiorari denied, 308 U.S. 622. In such a case, the provisions of section 10 (e), for example, relating to substantial evidence and to review of abuses of discretion, will not apply.

SECTION 10 (a)—RIGHT OF REVIEW

Section 10 (a) provides that "Any person suffering legal wrong because of any agency action, or adversely affected or aggrieved by such action within the meaning of any relevant

---

5. This conclusion is supported by the following statement in the Senate Comparative Print, p. 18 (Sen. Doc. p. 36): "The introductory exceptions state the two present general or basic situations in which judicial review is precluded—where (1) the matter is discretionary or (2) statutes withhold *judicial powers.*" [Italics supplied].

statute, shall be entitled to judicial review thereof." This statement of the persons entitled to judicial review has occasioned considerable comment because of the use of the phrase "any person suffering legal wrong". This phrase was used as one of limitation and not for the purpose of making judicial review available to anyone adversely affected by governmental action.[6] The delicate problem of the draftsmen was to identify in general terms the persons who are entitled to judicial review. As so used, "legal wrong" means such wrong as particular statutes and the courts have recognized as constituting ground for judicial review. "Adversely affected or aggrieved" has frequently been used in statutes to designate the persons who can obtain judicial review of administrative action.[7] The determination of who is "adversely affected or aggrieved * * * within the meaning of any relevant statute" has "been marked out largely by the gradual judicial process of inclusion and exclusion, aided at times by the courts' judgment as to the probable legislative intent derived from the spirit of the statutory scheme". Final Report, p. 83; see also pp. 84-85. The Attorney General advised the Senate Committee on the Judiciary of his understanding that section 10 (a) was a restatement of existing law. More specifically he indicated his understanding that section 10 (a) preserved the rules developed by the courts in such cases as *Alabama Power Co. v. Ickes,* 302 U.S. 464 (1938); *Massachusetts* v. *Mellon,* 262 U.S. 447 (1923) *The Chicago Junction Case,* 264 U.S. 258 (1924); *Sprunt & Son* v. *U.S.,* 281 U.S. 249 (1930); *Perkins* v. *Lukens Steel Co.,* 310 U.S. 113 (1940); and *Federal Communications Commission* v. *Sanders Brs. Radio Station,* 309 U.S. 470 (1940). Sen. Rep. p. 44 (Sen. Doc. p. 230). This construction of section 10 (a) was not questioned or contradicted in the legislative history.[8] Also implied is the continuing role of the courts in determining, in the context of constitutional requirements and the particular statutory pattern, who is entitled to judicial review.

SECTION 10 (b)—FORM AND VENUE OF ACTION

Section 10 (b) provides that "The form of proceeding for judicial review shall be any special statutory review proceeding

---

6. Compare original provision of S. 7 as introduced in the Senate: "Any person adversely affected by any agency action shall be entitled to judicial review thereof in accordance with this section."

7. See section 9 of the Securities Act (15 U.S.C. 77i), "any person aggrieved"; section 402 (b) (2) of the Communications Act (46 U.S.C. 402), "person aggrieved or whose interests are adversely affected"; section 1006 of the Civil Aeronautics Act (49 U.S.C. 649), "person disclosing a substantial interest in such order".

8. See *American Stevedores, Inc.* v. *Porello,* 339 U.S. 446 (1947).

97

relevant to the subject matter in any court specified by statute or, in the absence or inadequacy thereof, any applicable form of legal action (including actions for declaratory judgments or writs of prohibitory or mandatory injunction or habeas corpus) in any court of competent jurisdiction. Agency action shall be subject to judicial review in civil or criminal proceedings for judicial enforcement except to the extent that prior, adequate, and exclusive opportunity for such review is provided by law."

Form of action. Many regulatory statutes provide for judicial review of agency action by requiring the complaining party to file with a circuit court of appeals (or with a district court) a written petition praying that the agency action be modified or set aside; thereafter, the agency files with the reviewing court a transcript of the record.[9] Under such statutory provisions, the filing of a petition to modify or set aside agency action will continue to be the required form of proceeding for judicial review. Similarly, where agency action is now reviewable pursuant to the Urgent Deficiencies Act of 1913 (28 U.S.C. 47), the form of proceeding will consist of suits to enjoin[10] in accordance with the provisions of that Act.

In the absence of any special statutory review proceedings, other forms of action, as heretofore found by the courts to be appropriate in particular situations, will be used. Thus, habeas corpus proceedings should be used to obtain review of exclusion and deportation orders. *U.S. ex rel. Vajtauer* v. *Commissioner of Immigration*, 273 U.S. 103 (1927). Likewise, an order of the Postmaster General suspending second-class mailing privileges may, as before, be tested by a suit to enjoin such action. *Hannegan* v. *Esquire, Inc.,* 327 U.S. 146 (1946). In brief, where agency action is reviewable, but the Congress has not specified the form of review, the courts will continue to select the appropriate form of action.

Also, where a special statutory review proceeding is not legally adequate, the form of proceeding for judicial review will be "any applicable form of legal action * * * in any court of competent jurisdiction". The Act does not purport to define "inadequate",

---

9. See section 5 (c) of the Federal Trade Commission Act (15 U.S.C. 45 (c)); section 9 of the Securities Act (15 U.S.C. 77i); and section 701 of the Federal Food, Drug and Cosmetic Act (21 U.S.C. 371 (f)).

10. "The expression 'special statutory review' means not only special review proceedings wholly created by statute, but so-called common-law forms referred to and adopted by other statutes as the appropriate mode of review in given cases." Sen. Rep. p. 26; H.R. Rep. p. 42 (Sen. Doc. pp. 212, 276).

and thus leaves to the courts the determination of whether a particular statutory review proceeding is legally adequate. As stated by the Attorney General: "if the procedure is inadequate *(i.e., where under existing law a court would regard the special statutory procedure as inadequate and would grant another form of relief)*, then any applicable procedure, such as prohibitory or mandatory injunction, declaratory judgment, or habeas corpus, is available". [Emphasis supplied]. Sen. Rep. p. 44 (Sen. Doc. p. 230). Thus, the Act does not provide any new definition of "adequate", but rather assumes that the courts will determine the adequacy of statutory review procedures by the legal standards which the courts themselves have already developed. See *Myers* v. *Bethlehem Shipbuilding Corp.,* 303 U.S. 41, 48 (1938).

Venue. Section 10 (b) does rot purport to change existing venue requirements for judicial review. In fact, it specifically refers to review "in any court specified by statute,", or "in any court of competent jurisdiction". In the report of the House Committee, it is stated that "The section does not alter venue provisions under existing law, whether in connection with specially provided statutory review or the so-called nonstatutory or commonlaw action variety." H.R. Rep. p. 42 (Sen. Doc. p. 276). See also Representative Walter's statement to the House, 92 Cong. Rec. 5654 (Sen. Doc. p. 369). Thus, for example, station and construction licensing orders issued by the Federal Communications Commission remain reviewable only by the Court of Appeals for the District of Columbia (47 U.S.C. 402 (b)). More generally, statutes specifically providing for judicial review in a circuit court of appeals or a district court often designate the venue by relation to the matters involved, such as "any circuit court of appeals of the United States in the circuit wherein the unfair labor practice in question was alleged to have been engaged in or wherein [the person aggrieved] resides or transacts business, or in the Court of Appeals of the District of Columbia". (Section 10 (f) of the National Labor Relations Act).[11] Such provisions are continued in effect. So also are the general statutory provisions concerning venue, such as 28 U.S.C. 112 that "no civil suit shall be brought in any district court against any person by any original process or proceeding in any other district than that whereof he is an inhabitant". For the application of this section to suits against

---

11. For other examples, see 28 U.S.C. 43 for venue of suits to enjoin orders of the Interstate Commerce Commission, section 1006 (b) of the Civil Aeronautics Act (49 U.S.C. 646 (b)), and section 21 of the Longshoremen's and Harbor Workers' Compensation Act (33 U.S.C. 921).

99

Government agencies, see *Kentucky Natural Gas Corp.* v. *Public Service Comm.*, 28 F. Supp. 509, affirmed 119 F. 2d 417 (C.C.A. 6, 1941); and *Scientific Mfg. Co.* v. *Walker,* 40 F. Supp. 465 (M.D. Pa. 1941).

Review in enforcement proceedings. Section 10 (b) also provides that "Agency action shall be subject to judicial review in civil or criminal proceedings for judicial enforcement except to the extent that prior, adequate, and exclusive opportunity for such review is provided by law". In the Committee reports it is stated that "The provision respecting 'prior, adequate, and exclusive * * * review' in the second sentence is operative only where statutes, *either expressly or as they are interpreted,* require parties to resort to some special statutory form of judicial review which is prior in time and adequate to the case." [Emphasis supplied]. Sen. Rep. p. 27; H.R. Rep. p. 42 (Sen. Doc. pp. 213, 276). So interpreted, this provision restates existing law.[12] Thus, a statute may either expressly provide for an exclusive method of judicial review which precludes challenge of agency action in enforcement proceedings,[13] or a court may conclude from the statutory context that such was the legislative intention. *United States* v. *Ruzicka,* 329 U.S. 287 (1946), interpreting the Agricultural Marketing Agreement Act of 1937, is an excellent example of the latter situation.[14] Similarly, section 10 (b) leaves intact the doctrine of primary jurisdiction developed by the courts in cases involving the reasonableness of the charges of carriers and public utilities. See *Ambassador, Inc.* v. *United States,* 325 U.S. 317 (1945). It also leaves intact the requirements of the doctrine of exhaustion of administrative remedies. In many situations, however, an appropriate method of attacking the validity of agency action is to set up the alleged invalidity as a defense in a civil or criminal enforcement proceeding.

The adequacy of an exclusive method for judicial review would appear to be governed by the same considerations as the courts would apply in determining the adequacy or inadequacy of a

---

12. The Senate Committee changed the last phrase of the provision from "provided by statute" to "provided by law". See also Senate Comparative Print, June 1945, p. 18 (Sen. Doc. P. 37), stating that "The second sentence states the present rule as to enforcement proceedings." See Representative Walter's statement to the House, 92 Cong. Rec. 5654 (Sen. Doc. p. 369): "These provisions summarize the situation as it is now generally understood. The section does not disturb special proceedings which Congress has provided, nor does it disturb the venue arrangements under existing law."

13. See section 204 (d) of the Emergency Price Control Act of 1942.

14. See also *Walling* v. *Cohen.* 48 F. Supp. 859 (E.D. Pa. 1943), affirmed 140 F. 2d 453 (C.C.A. 3, 1944) under the Fair Labor Standards Act, and *Piuma* v. *United States,* 126 F. 2d 601 (C.C.A. 9, 1942). certiorari denied, 317 U.S. 637, under the Federal Trade Commission Act.

statutory review proceeding for the purposes of the first sentence of section 10 (b). Thus, the use of the word "prior" in the last sentence of section 10 (b) does not mean that the validity of agency action may always be challenged collaterally by way of defense in enforcement proceedings whenever the method of review specified by the Congress does not result in a judicial determination as to the validity of such action prior to the commencement of enforcement proceedings. As indicated above, the Congress intended section 10 as a whole to be integrated and reconciled with existing statutory provisions for judicial review. Specifically, the general principle stated in the last sentence of section 10 (b) was not regarded by the Congress as an innovation. Rather, it was said that "The second sentence states the present rule as to enforcement proceedings." Senate Comparative Print, p. 18 (Sen. Doc. p. 37). And further: "These provisions summarize the situation as it is now generally understood. The section [10 (b)] does not disturb special proceedings which Congress has provided, nor does it disturb the venue arrangements under existing law." Representative Walter, 92 Cong. Rec. 5654 (Sen. Doc. p. 369).

There are many situations in which the invalidity of agency action may be set up as a defense in enforcement proceedings. On the other hand, there are special statutory arrangements under which the Congress has provided for immediate and continuous enforcement while the exclusive route to judicial review is by first exhausting an administrative procedure; in such an agency proceeding, the agency and the parties make a record with a view toward (a) reconsideration by the agency itself, and (b) providing an adequate factual record as the basis for judicial review by a specified court. See *United States* v. *Ruzicka, supra*. There is nothing to indicate that the Congress intended to repeal by implication such special statutory arrangements for compliance pending orderly judicial review, or to preclude itself from making similar arrangements in the future. Similarly, it is believed that the courts are left free to apply the primary jurisdiction doctrine in enforcement proceedings so as to require issues relating to the alleged unreasonableness of filed tariffs to be first presented to the appropriate administrative agency rather than to an enforcement court. See *Ambassador, Inc.* v. *United States, supra*. In brief, the courts must determine in each case whether the Congress, by establishing a special review procedure,

101

intended to preclude or to permit judicial review of agency action in enforcement proceedings. And, the extent to which the "opportunity" for judicial review prior to the enforcement proceedings has been waived or disregarded by the defendant in those proceedings must also be considered.

SECTION 10 (c)—REVIEWABLE ACTS

The provisions of this subsection defining agency action subject to judicial review are said to "involve no departure from the usual and well understood rules of procedure in this field". Representative Walter, 92 Cong. Rec. 5654 (Sen. Doc. p. 369); Sen. Rep. p. 44 (Sen. Doc. p. 230).

First, it is provided that "Every agency action made reviewable by statute and every final agency action for which there is no other adequate remedy in any court shall be subject to judicial review." Many statutes specifically provide for judicial review of particular agency action, and such action will continue to be reviewable. The second category, "and every final agency action for which there is no other adequate remedy in any court", must be interpreted in the light of other statutory and case law. To begin with, of course, it does not make reviewable agency action as to which "(1) statutes preclude judicial review or (2) agency action is by law committed to agency discretion." Furthermore, this provision does not provide additional judicial remedies in situations where the Congress has provided special and adequate review procedures. See the first clause of section 10 (b). Thus, the Customs Court and the Court of Customs and Patent Appeals retain their present exclusive jurisdictions.[15]

"Agency action", as used in section 10, is defined in section 2 (g) as including "the whole or part of every agency rule, order, license, sanction, relief, or the equivalent or denial thereof, or failure to act." Sen. Rep. p. 11; H.R. Rep. p. 21 (Sen. Doc. pp. 197, 255). While "final", as used to designate reviewable agency action, is not defined in the Act, its meaning may be gleaned from the second and third sentences of section 10 (c). Moreover, many regulatory statutes, either expressly or as they are interpreted, have provided for review of (and only of) "final" agency orders, with the result that the judicial construction of such provisions

---

15. The Attorney General's memorandum to the Senate Committee, he stated that "'Courts' includes the Tax Court, Court of Customs and Patent Appeals, the Court of Claims, and similar courts. This act does not apply to their procedure nor affect the requirement of resort thereto." Sen. Rep. p. 38 (Sen. Doc. p. 224).

will carry over to the interpretation of "final" as used in section 10 (b). See *Rochester Telephone Corp. v. United States,* 307 U.S. 125 (1939).

Since "agency action" is defined to include "rule", the question arises as to whether the phrase, "final agency action for which there is no other adequate remedy in any court", provides for direct judicial review of all rules. Many statutes which give rule making powers (particularly rules of general applicability) to agencies make no provision for judicial review of such rules. The validity of such rules has generally been open to challenge in proceedings for their enforcement. In addition, it has been suggested that in appropriate circumstances, review could be obtained in proceedings under the Declaratory Judgment Act (28 U.S.C. 400). It is clear from the legislative history that section 10 (c) was not intended to provide for judicial review in the abstract of all rules. Representative Walter stated to the House that "The provisions of this [sub] section are technical but involve no departure from the usual and well understood rules of procedure in this field." 92 Cong. Rec. 5654 (Sen. Doc. p. 369). Also, during the Senate Hearings in 1941, the subject of judicial review of rules was thoroughly discussed. Two of the bills then pending provided for direct judicial review of rules by declaratory judgment proceedings. (See S. 674 and S. 918). The inclusion of such a provision was strongly advocated by a minority of the Attorney General's Committee on Administrative Procedure who stated that their purpose was—

> to adapt declaratory judgment procedure to this special subject. The minority feels that it is unnecessary and unwise to provide for court review (except where otherwise required by particular statutes) of rules in the abstract. On the other hand, such review upon the application of the rule to a particular person, or upon accepted principles of declaratory judgment, should be expressly recognized. In his letter accompanying the veto of the Logan-Walter bill, the Attorney General stated that—
>
>> under the Declaratory Judgments Act of 1934, any person may now obtain a judgment as to the validity of such administrative rules, if he can show such an interest and present injury therefrom as to constitute a "case or controversy."
>
> However, the Declaratory Judgments Act does not altogether fit the subject and needs some limitation (not, it may be noted, extension) to care for the determination of fact issues, since under the Declaratory Judgments Act juries determine the facts under instructions from the presiding judge. In adapting declaratory judgment procedure to this field, some special provision must be made for the determination of facts, for otherwise the facts in the first instance would be determined through judicial rather than administrative process. (Senate Hearings (1941) pp. 1344, 1386.)

In other words, even the proponents of detailed provisions for judicial review of rules did not intend to prescribe an abstract form of review going far beyond the limitations of the Declaratory Judgment Act. Thus, it is fair to conclude that the general statement in the first sentence of section 10 (c) was not intended to achieve such a result.

The second sentence of section 10 (c) provides that "Any preliminary, procedural, or intermediate agency action or ruling not directly reviewable shall be subject to review upon the review of the final agency action." This language was designed "to negative any intention to make reviewable merely preliminary or procedural orders where there is a subsequent and adequate remedy at law available, as is presently the rule." Senate Comparative Print, June 1945, p. 19[16] (Sen. Doc. p. 37). For example, intermediate orders such as orders setting matters for hearing are not reviewable either directly *(Federal Power Commission* v. *Metropolitan Edison Co.,* 304 U.S. 375 (1938)) or collaterally, as by suits for injunction (*Myers* v. *Bethlehem Shipbuilding Corp.,* 303 U.S. 41 (1938)) or declaratory judgment (*Macauley* v. *Waterman S. S. Co.,* 327 U.S. 540 (1946); *Federal Power Commission* v. *Arkansas Power & Light Co., per curiam,* 330 U. S. 802 (1947)). The provision for review of such questions as a part of the review of final agency action restates existing practice. See section 10 (e) (4).

Section 10 (c) further provides that "Except as otherwise expressly required by statute, agency action otherwise final shall be final for the purposes of this subsection whether or not there has been presented or determined any application for a declaratory order, for any form of reconsideration, or (unless the agency otherwise requires by rule and provides that the action meanwhile shall be inoperative) for an appeal to superior agency authority." This provision, together with the preceding sentence of the subsection, embodies the doctrine of exhaustion of administrative remedies. H.R. Rep. p. 55, fn. 21 (Sen. Doc. p. 289). Agency action which is finally operative and decisive is reviewable. On the other hand, "Action which is automatically stayable on further proceedings invoked by a party is not final." H.R. Rep. p. 43 (Sen. Doc. p. 277).

It is specifically provided that agency action otherwise final is final for the purposes of the subsection notwithstanding a party's failure to apply for any form of agency reconsideration (reopening, rehearing, etc.), unless a statute expressly requires

---

16. See Final Report, pp. 85-86.

an application for such reconsideration as a prerequisite to judicial review. Under statutes such as the Federal Power Act (16 U.S.C. 791, 825l) and the Natural Gas Act (15 U.S.C. 717r) which expressly require that such reconsideration be sought, the filing of an application for reconsideration will continue to be a condition precedent to judicial review. In addition, it would seem that under the common statutory provision that no objection to agency action not urged before the agency shall be considered by the courts, an application for agency reconsideration remains a prerequisite to obtaining judicial review of such an objection. See 15 U.S.C. 77 (I) and 49 U.S.C. 646 (e). However, under a statute which merely confers upon parties the right to apply for rehearing, it is now clear that an application for such reconsideration need not precede judicial review. See generally, as to the effect of agency rules in this field, *Levers* v. *Anderson,* 326 U.S. 219 (1945).

The last clause of section 10 (c) relates to two situations. First, pursuant to section 8 (a), an agency may permit its hearing examiners to make initial decisions which will become the agency's final decisions in the absence of an appeal to or review by the agency. The last clause of section 10 (c) permits an agency to require *by rule* that in such cases parties who are dissatisfied with the "initial" decisions of hearing officers must appeal to the agency before seeking judicial review, but only if the agency further provides that the hearing, officers' decisions shall be inoperative pending such administrative appeals. Thus, an agency with licensing powers may by rule require a party to appeal to it from an initial decision of a hearing officer only if, for example, the license suspension or revocation determined upon by the hearing officer is held in abeyance pending the agency's action on the appeal. Sen. Rep. p. 27; H.R. Rep. pp. 43, 55, fn. 21 (Sen. Doc. pp. 213, 277, 289).

The second and similar application of the last clause of section 10 (c) relates to appeals from agency decisions to a superior agency authority. For example, under some circumstances, it would seem that a bureau or other subdivision within an agency may itself be the agency with respect to a particular function. In such a situation, it may be desired to require appeal from the bureau's decision to the department head or other "superior agency authority" as a prerequisite to judicial review. Under section 10 (c), such a requirement may be imposed, but only, as in the case of required appeals from hearing officers' initial decisions, if the agency's decision is inopera-

105

tive pending such appeal. Sen. Rep. p. 27; H.R. Rep. p. 43 (Sen. Doc. pp. 213, 277).

The requirement that agency action be inoperative pending required appeals to the agency or to superior agency authority does not require the agency to take positive action for the benefit of an applicant. It was not intended to require the issuance of licenses or the payment of benefits in any case where an agency requires that the denial of licenses or benefits be appealed to it or to superior agency authority as a prerequisite to judicial review.[17]

SECTION 10 (d)—INTERIM RELIEF

Section 10 (d) provides that "Pending judicial review any agency is authorized, where it finds that justice so requires, to postpone the effective date of any action taken by it. Upon such conditions as may be required and to the extent necessary to prevent irreparable injury, every reviewing court (including every court to which a case may be taken on appeal from or upon application for certiorari or other writ to a reviewing court) is authorized to issue all necessary and appropriate process to postpone the effective date of any agency action or to preserve status or rights pending conclusion of the review proceedings." The first sentence of the subsection is a restatement of existing law.

The second sentence of section 10 (d) confers upon every "reviewing court" discretionary authority to stay agency action pending judicial review "to the extent necessary to prevent irreparable injury." The function of such a power is, as heretofore, to make judicial review effective. Sen. Rep. p. 27; H.R. Rep. p. 43 (Sen. Doc. pp. 213, 277). *Scripps-Howard Radio, Inc. v. Federal Communications Commission*, 316 U.S. 4 (1942). The subsection does not permit a court to order the grant of an initial license pending judicial review of an agency's denial of such a license. Sen. Rep. p. 27; H.R. Rep. p. 43 (Sen. Doc. pp. 213, 277). By the same logic, the subsection does not give to reviewing courts the power to order interim payment of grants or benefits the denial of which is the subject of review.

---

17. This conclusion is corollary to the following statement made with respect to section 10 (d): This section permits either agencies or courts, if the proper showing be made, to maintain the status quo. While it would not permit a court to grant an initial license, it provides intermediate judicial relief for every other situation in order to make judicial review effective." Sen. Rep. p. 27, H.R. Rep. p. 43 (Sen. Doc. pp. 213, 277).

The stay power conferred upon reviewing courts is to be exercised only "to the extent necessary to prevent irreparable injury." In other words, irreparable injury, the historic condition of equity jurisdiction, is the indispensable condition to the exercise of the power conferred by section 10 (d) upon reviewing courts. Sen. Rep. p. 44 (Sen. Doc. p. 230). Mere maintenance of the status quo for the convenience of parties pending judicial review of agency action will not be adequate ground for the exercise of this stay power.[18]

This power to stay agency action is an equitable power, to be exercised "upon such conditions as may be required." Section 10 (d) does not require the issuance of stay orders automatically upon a showing of irreparable damage. As in the past, reviewing courts may "balance the equities" in determining whether to postpone the effective date of agency action. Thus, "in determining whether agency action should be postponed, the court should take into account that persons other than parties may be adversely affected by such postponement and in such cases the party seeking postponement may be required to furnish security to protect such other persons from loss resulting from postponement." H.R. Rep. p. 43 (Sen. Doc. p. 277). More broadly, it is clear that a reviewing court in exercising this power may do so under such conditions as the equities of the situation may require.

The "reviewing court" in which section 10 (d) vests the power to stay agency action is the court, and only that court, which has obtained jurisdiction to review the final agency action in accordance with subsections (b) and (c) and the applicable provisions of particular statutes.[19] Section 10 (d) confers no power upon a court in advance of the submission to it of final agency action for review on the merits. See *Federal Power Commission* v. *Metropolitan Edison Co.,* 304 U.S. 375, 383 (1938). This is the only logical conclusion to be drawn from the employment of the phrase "reviewing court", rather than "any court." Any other construction would twist section 10 (d) into a general grant of power to the Federal courts to review all kinds of questions presented by preliminary and intermediate agency action. The specific provisions of section 10 (c) defining reviewable action negate such a result. The legislative history of section 10 (d) is

---

18. This distinction and the Congressional intent with respect to it are clearly illustrated by the fact that when S. 7 was introduced in the Senate, it read: "to the extent necessary to preserve status or rights, afford an opportunity for judicial review of any question of law *or prevent irreparable injury.*" [Emphasis supplied)

19. This was the holding in *Avon Dairy Company* v. *Eisaman,* 69 F Supp. 500 (N. D. Ohio, 1946).

107

equally persuasive; as S. 7 was introduced in the Senate, section 10 (d) provided for its exercise "to the extent necessary to afford an opportunity for *judicial review of any question of law* or prevent irreparable injury." The italicized language was dropped by the Senate Committee, which reported the subsection in its present form. Finally, section 10 (d) provides that the reviewing court may "issue all necessary and appropriate process to postpone the effective date of any agency action or to preserve status or rights pending conclusion *of the review proceedings.*" [Emphasis supplied]. The italicized language is conclusive that the stay power conferred by the subsection is only ancillary to review proceedings—proceedings in which the court is reviewing final agency action within the meaning of section 10 (c).

Section 10 (d) prescribes no procedure for the exercise of the power which it confers upon reviewing courts to postpone the effective date of agency action. Section 381 of Title 28, U.S. Code,[20] contains general procedural provisions governing the issuance of preliminary injunctions and restraining orders. Since these procedural provisions are in no way inconsistent with section 10 (d), they appear to be applicable to the exercise of the power conferred by that subsection. Similarly, the provisions of the Urgent Deficiencies Act (28 U.S.C. 47), governing the procedure for the issuance of interlocutory injunctions and temporary stays, remain applicable in proceedings for judicial review under that Act.

SECTION 10(e)—SCOPE OF REVIEW

The scope of judicial review is defined in section 10 (e) as follows:

> So far as necessary to decision and where presented the reviewing court shall decide all relevant questions of law, interpret constitutional and statutory provisions, and determine the meaning or applicability of the terms of any agency action. It shall (A) compel agency action unlawfully withheld or unreasonably delayed; and (B) hold unlawful and set aside agency action, findings, and conclusions found to be (1) arbitrary, capricious, an abuse of discretion, or otherwise not in accordance with law; (2) contrary to constitutional right, power, privilege, or immunity; (3) in excess of statutory jurisdiction, authority, or limitations, or short of statutory right; (4) without observance of procedure required by law; (5) unsupported by substantial evidence in any case subject to the requirements of sections 7 and 8 or otherwise reviewed on the record of an agency hearing provided by statute; or (6) unwarranted by the facts to the extent that the facts are subject to trial de novo by the reviewing court. In making the foregoing determinations the court shall review the whole record or such portions thereof as may be cited by any party, and due account shall be taken of the rule of prejudicial error.

---

20. See also Rule 65 of the Federal Rules of Civil Procedure.

This restates the present law as to the scope of judicial review. Senate Comparative Print, June 1945, p. 20[21] (Sen. Doc. p. 39); House Hearings (1945) pp. 37-38 (Sen. Doc. pp. 83-84); Sen. Rep. pp. 38, 43, 44 (Sen. Doc. pp. 224, 229, 230).

Clause (A) authorizing a reviewing court to "compel agency action unlawfully withheld or unreasonably delayed", appears to be a particularized restatement of existing judicial practice under section 262 of the Judicial Code (28 U.S.C. 377). *Safeway Stores, Inc.* v. *Brown*, 138 F. 2d 278 (E.C.A., 1943), certiorari denied, 320 U.S. 797. The power thus stated is vested in "the reviewing court", which, in this context, would seem to be the court which has or would have jurisdiction to review the final agency action. See *Roche* v. *Evaporated Milk Ass'n.*, 319 U.S. 21, 25 (1943). Orders in the nature of a writ of mandamus have been employed to compel an administrative agency to act, *Safeway Stores, Inc.* v. *Brown*, supra, or to assume jurisdiction, *Interstate Commerce Commission* v. *United States ex rel. Humboldt Steamship Co.*, U.S. 474 (1912), or to compel an agency or officer to perform a ministerial or non-discretionary act. Clause (A) of section 10 (e) was apparently intended to codify these judicial functions.

Obviously, the clause does not purport to empower a court to substitute its discretion for that of an administrative agency and thus exercise administrative duties. In fact, with respect to constitutional courts, it could not do so. *Keller* v. *Potomac Electric Power Co.*, 261 U.S. 428 (1923)); *Postum Cereal Co.* v. *California Fig Nut Co.*, 272 U.S. 693 (1927); *Federal Radio Commission* v. *General Electric Co.*, U.S. 464 (1930). However, as in *Safeway Stores* v. *Brown*, supra, a court may require an agency to take action upon a matter, without directing how it shall act.

The numbered clauses of section 10 (e) (B) restate the scope of the judicial function in reviewing final agency action. Sen. Rep. p. 44 (Sen. Doc. p. 230); Senate Hearings (1941) pp. 1150, 1351, 1400, 1437. Courts having jurisdiction have always exercised the power in appropriate cases to set aside agency action which they found to be "(1) arbitrary, capricious, an abuse of discretion, or otherwise not in accordance with law; (2) contrary to constitutional right, power, privilege, or immunity; (3) in excess of statutory jurisdiction, authority, or limitations, or

---

21. Subsection (e), therefore, seeks merely to restate the several categories of law subject to judicial review."

109

short of statutory right; (4) without observance of procedure required by law."

Clause (5) directs reviewing courts to "hold unlawful and set aside agency action, findings, and conclusions found to be * * * unsupported by substantial evidence in any case subject to the requirements of sections 7 and 8 or otherwise reviewed on the record of an agency hearing provided by statute." This is a general codification of the substantial evidence rule which, either by statute or judicial rule, has long been applied to the review of Federal administrative action. *Consolidated Edison Co. v. National Labor Relations Board,* 305 U.S. 197 (1938); *National Labor Relations Board v. Remington Rand,* 94 F. 2d 862 (C.C.A. 2, 1938). It will be noted that this codified substantial evidence rule is made applicable not only to cases governed by sections 7 and 8, but also to those types of cases in which statutes provide for agency hearings, but which are exempted from sections 7 and 8 by the introductory clause of section 5.

As to clause (6), the legislative history has resulted in misunderstanding. As S. 7 was introduced in the Senate, clause (6) was followed by a provision that "The relevant facts shall be tried and determined de novo by the original court of review in all cases in which adjudications are not required by statute to be made upon agency hearing." When S. 7 was reported by the Senate Committee, the quoted provision was omitted. Notwithstanding, the subsequent legislative history contains repeated statements to the effect that clause (6) embodies the "established rule * * * [which requires a judicial] trial de novo to establish the relevant facts as to the applicability of any rule and as to the propriety of adjudications where there is no statutory administrative hearing." Senate Comparative Print, June 1945, p. 20 (Sen. Doc. pp. 39-40); H.R. Rep. p. 45 (Sen. Doc. p. 279).

To the contrary, the language of clause (6), "to the extent that the facts are subject to trial de novo by the reviewing court", obviously refers only to those existing situations in which judicial review has consisted of a trial de novo. For example, reparation orders under the Interstate Commerce Act and the Packers and Stockyards Act have only prima facie weight and are thus reviewable *de novo*. In addition, there is no "established rule" requiring a judicial trial *de novo* wherever statutes fail to require an agency hearing. Thus, in deportation (8 U.S.C. 155) and mail fraud (39 U.S.C. 259) cases, hearings are held as a matter of due process although the statutes do not require agency hearings. In both types of cases, the judicial review of agency action has consisted of a review of the record made in the agency proceeding to determine whether the agency action is supported by evidence.[22]

Accordingly, since clause (6) of section 10(e) prescribes a judicial trial *de novo* only in situations where other statutes or the courts have prescribed such review, it is clear that deportation and mail fraud orders will continue to be reviewable on the record made in the agency hearing, even though such hearing is not required by statute. Also, in *National Broadcasting Company* v. *United States,* 319 U.S. 190, 227 (1943), it was held that a trial *de novo* was not appropriate where, prior to the issuance of general regulations, the agency conducted a formal hearing although not required by statute to do so.

Finally, section 10 (e) provides that "In making the foregoing determinations the court shall review the whole record or such portions thereof as may be cited by any party, and due account shall be taken of the rule of prejudicial error." This appears to restate existing law. Specifically, the phrase "whole record" was not intended to require reviewing courts to weigh the evidence and make independent findings of fact; rather, it means that in determining whether agency action is supported by substantial evidence, the reviewing court should consider all of the evidence and not merely the evidence favoring one side. Senate Hearings (1941) p. 1359.

The last phrase of section 10 (e) sums up in succinct fashion the "harmless error" rule applied by the courts in the review of lower court decisions as well as of administrative bodies, namely, that errors which have no substantial bearing on the ultimate rights of the parties will be disregarded. *Market Street Ry.* v. *Comm'n.,* 324 U.S. 548, 561-2 (1945).

---

22. *Vajtauer* v. *Commissioner,* 273 U.S. 103, 106 (1927) and *Bridges* v. *Wixon,* 326 U.S. 135, 149 (1945) (deportation). In deportation proceedings, a judicial trial *de novo* may be had on the issue of citizenship. *Kessler* v. *Strecker,* 307 U.S. 22, 35 (1939). See *Farley* v. *Simmons,* 99 F. 2d 343, 347 (App. D.C. 1938) certiorari denied, 305 U.S. 651, for review of mail fraud orders; also Senate Hearings, (1941) p. 59.

APPENDIX A

[PUBLIC LAW 404—79TH CONGRESS]
[CHAPTER 324—2D SESSION]
[S. 7]

AN ACT

To improve the administration of justice by prescribing fair administrative procedure.

Be it enacted by the Senate and House of Representatives of the United States of America in Congress assembled,

TITLE

SECTION 1. This Act may be cited as the "Administrative Procedure Act".

DEFINITIONS

SEC. 2. As used in this Act—

(a) AGENCY.—"Agency" means each authority (whether or not within or subject to review by another agency) of the Government of the United States other than Congress, the courts, or the governments of the possessions, Territories, or the District of Columbia. Nothing in this Act shall be construed to repeal delegations of authority as provided by law. Except as to the requirements of section 3, there shall be excluded from the operation of this Act (1) agencies composed of representatives of the parties or of representatives of organizations of the parties to the disputes determined by them, (2) courts martial and military commissions, (3) military or naval authority exercised in the field in time of war or in occupied territory, or (4) functions which by law expire on the termination of present hostilities, within any fixed period thereafter, or before July 1, 1947, and the functions conferred by the following statutes: Selective Training and Service Act of 1940; Contract Settlement Act of 1944; Surplus Property Act of 1944.

(b) PERSON AND PARTY.—"Person" includes individuals, partnerships, corporations, associations, or public or private organizations of any character other than agencies. "Party" includes any person or agency named or admitted as a party, or properly seeking and entitled as of right to be admitted as a party, in any agency proceeding; but nothing herein shall be construed to prevent an agency from admitting any person or agency as a party for limited purposes.

(c) RULE AND RULE MAKING.—"Rule" means the whole or any part of any agency statement of general or particular applicability and future effect designed to implement, interpret, or prescribe law or policy or to describe the organization, procedure, or practice requirements of any agency and includes the approval or perscription for the future of rates, wages, corporate or financial structures or reorganizations thereof, prices, facilities, appliances, services or allowances therefor or of valuations, costs, or accounting, or practices bearing upon any of the foregoing. "Rule making" means agency process for the formulation, amendment, or repeal of a rule.

(d) ORDER AND ADJUDICATION.—"Order" means the whole or any part of the final disposition (whether affirmative, negative, injunctive, or declaratory in form) of any agency in any matter other than rule making but including licensing. "Adjudication" means agency process for the formulation of an order.

(e) LICENSE AND LICENSING.—"License" includes the whole or part of any agency permit, certificate, approval, registration, charter, membership, statutory exemption or other form of permission. "Licensing" includes agency process respecting the grant, renewal, denial, revocation, suspension, annulment, withdrawal, limitation amendment, modification, or conditioning of a license.

(f) SANCTION AND RELIEF.—"Sanction" includes the whole or part of any agency (1) prohibition, requirement, limitation, or other condition affecting the freedom of any person; (2) withholding of relief; (3) imposition of any form of penalty or fine; (4) destruction, taking, seizure, or withholding of property; (5) assessment of damages, reimbursement, restitution, compensation, costs, charges, or fees; (6) requirement, revocation, or suspension of a license; or (7) taking of other compulsory or restrictive action. "Relief" includes the whole or part of any agency (1) grant of money, assistance, license, authority, exemption, exception, privilege, or remedy; (2) recognition of any claim, right, immunity, privilege, exemption, or exception; or (3) taking of any other action upon the application or petition of, and beneficial to, any person.

(g) AGENCY PROCEEDING AND ACTION.—"Agency proceeding" means any agency process as defined in subsections (c), (d), and

(e) of this section. "Agency action" includes the whole or part of every agency rule, order, license, sanction, relief, or the equivalent or denial thereof, or failure to act.

PUBLIC INFORMATION

SEC. 3. Except to the extent that there is involved (1) any function of the United States requiring secrecy in the public interest or (2) any matter relating solely to the internal management of an agency—

(a) RULES.—Every agency shall separately state and currently publish in the Federal Register (1) descriptions of its central and field organization including delegations by the agency of final authority and the established places at which, and methods whereby, the public may secure information or make submittals or requests; (2) statements of the general course and method by which its functions are channeled and determined, including the nature and requirements of all formal or informal procedures available as well as forms and instructions as to the scope and contents of all papers, reports, or examinations; and (3) substantive rules adopted as authorized by law and statements of general policy or interpretations formulated and adopted by the agency for the guidance of the public, but not rules addressed to and served upon named persons in accordance with law. No person shall in any manner be required to resort to organization or procedure not so published.

(b) OPINIONS AND ORDERS.—Every agency shall publish or, in accordance with published rule, make available to public inspection all final opinions or orders in the adjudication of cases (except those required for good cause to be held confidential and not cited as precedents) and all rules.

(c) PUBLIC RECORDS.—Save as otherwise required by statute, matters of official record shall in accordance with published rule be made available to persons properly and directly concerned except information held confidential for good cause found.

RULE MAKING

SEC. 4. Except to the extent that there is involved (1) any military, naval, or foreign affairs function of the United States or (2) any matter relating to agency management or personnel or to public property, loans, grants, benefits, or contracts—

(a) NOTICE.—General notice of proposed rule making shall be published in the Federal Register (unless all persons subject thereto are named and either personally served or otherwise have actual notice thereof in accordance with law) and shall include (1) a statement of the time, place, and nature of public rule making proceedings; (2) reference to the authority under which the rule is proposed; and (3) either the terms or substance of the proposed rule or a description of the subjects and issues involved. Except where notice or hearing is required by statute, this subsection shall not apply to interpretative rules, general statements of policy, rules of agency organization, procedure, or practice, or in any situation in which the agency for good cause finds (and incorporates the finding and a brief statement of the reasons therefor in rules issued) that notice and public procedure thereon are impracticable, unnecessary, or contrary to the public interest.

(b) PROCEDURES.—After notice required by this section, the agency shall afford interested persons an opportunity to participate in the rule making through submission of written data, views, or arguments with or without opportunity to present the same orally in any manner; and, after consideration of all relevant matter presented, the agency shall incorporate in any rules adopted a concise general statement of their basis and purpose. Where rules are required by statute to be made on the record after opportunity for an agency hearing, the requirements of sections 7 and 8 shall apply in place of the provisions of this subsection.

(c) EFFECTIVE DATES.—The required publication or service of any substantive rule (other than one granting or recognizing exemption or relieving restriction or interpretative rules and statements of policy) shall be made not less than thirty days prior to the effective date thereof except as otherwise provided by the agency upon good cause found and published with the rule.

(d) PETITIONS.—Every agency shall accord any interested person the right to petition for the issuance, amendment, or repeal of a rule.

ADJUDICATION

SEC. 5. In every case of adjudication required by statute to be determined on the record after opportunity for an agency hearing, except to the extent that there is involved (1) any matter subject to a subsequent trial of the law and the facts de novo in any court; (2) the selection or tenure of an officer or employee

115

of the United States other than examiners appointed pursuant to section 11; (3) proceedings in which decisions rest solely on inspections, tests, or elections; (4) the conduct of military, naval, or foreign affairs functions; (5) cases in which an agency is acting as an agent for a court; and (6) the certification of employee representatives—

(a) NOTICE.—Persons entitled to notice of an agency hearing shall be timely informed of (1) the time, place, and nature thereof; (2) the legal authority and jurisdiction under which the hearing is to be held; and (3) the matters of fact and law asserted. In instances in which private persons are the moving parties, other parties to the proceeding shall give prompt notice of issues controverted in fact or law; and in other instances agencies may by rule require responsive pleading. In fixing the times and places for hearings, due regard shall be had for the convenience and necessity of the parties or their representatives.

(b) PROCEDURE.—The agency shall afford all interested parties opportunity for (1) the submission and consideration of facts, arguments, offers of settlement, or proposals of adjustment where time, the nature of the proceeding, and the public interest permit, and (2) to the extent that the parties are unable so to determine any controversy by consent, hearing, and decision upon notice and in conformity with sections 7 and 8.

(c) SEPARATION OF FUNCTIONS.—The same officers who preside at the reception of evidence pursuant to section 7 shall make the recommended decision or initial decision required by section 8 except where such officers become unavailable to the agency. Save to the extent required for the disposition of ex parte matters as authorized by law, no such officer shall consult any person or party on any fact in issue unless upon notice and opportunity for all parties to participate; nor shall such officer be responsible to or subject to the supervision or direction of any officer, employee, or agent engaged in the performance of investigative or prosecuting functions for any agency. No officer, employee, or agent engaged in the performance of investigative or prosecuting functions for any agency in any case shall, in that or a factually related case, participate or advise in the decision, recommended decision, or agency review pursuant to section 8 except as witness or counsel in public proceedings. This subsection shall not apply in determining applications for initial licenses or to proceedings involving the validity or application of rates, facilities, or practices of public utilities or carriers; nor shall it be applicable in any manner to the agency or any member or members of the body comprising the agency.

(d) DECLARATORY ORDERS.—The agency is authorized in its sound discretion, with like effect as in the case of other orders, to issue a declaratory order to terminate a controversy or remove uncertainty.

ANCILLARY MATTERS

SEC. 6. Except as otherwise provided in this Act—

(a) APPEARANCE—Any person compelled to appear in person before any agency or representative thereof shall be accorded the right to be accompanied, represented, and advised by counsel or, if permitted by the agency, by other qualified representative. Every party shall be accorded the right to appear in person or by or with counsel or other duly qualified representative in any agency proceeding. So far as the orderly conduct of public business permits, any interested person may appear before any agency or its responsible officers or employees for the presentation, adjustment, or determination of any issue, request, or controversy in any proceeding (interlocutory, summary, or otherwise) or in connection with any agency function. Every agency shall proceed with reasonable dispatch to conclude any matter presented to it except that due regard shall be had for the convenience and necessity of the parties or their representatives. Nothing herein shall be construed either to grant or to deny to any person who is not a lawyer the right to appear for or represent others before any agency or in any agency proceeding.

(b) INVESTIGATIONS—No process, requirement of a report, inspection, or other investigative act or demand shall be issued, made, or enforced in any manner or for any purpose except as authorized by law. Every person compelled to submit data or evidence shall be entitled to retain or, on payment of lawfully prescribed costs, procure a copy or transcript thereof, except that in a nonpublic investigatory proceeding the witness may for good cause be limited to inspection of the official transcript of his testimony.

(c) SUBPENAS.—Agency subpenas authorized by law shall be issued to any party upon request and, as may be required by rules of procedure, upon a statement or showing of general relevance and reasonable scope of the evidence sought. Upon contest the court shall sustain any such subpena or similar process or demand, to the extent that it is found to be in accordance with law and, in any

117

proceeding for enforcement, shall issue an order requiring the appearance of the witness or the production of the evidence or data within a reasonable time under penalty of punishment for contempt in case of contumacious failure to comply.

(d) DENIALS.—Prompt notice shall be given of the denial in whole or in part of any written application, petition, or other request of any interested person made in connection with any agency proceeding. Except in affirming a prior denial or where the denial is self-explanatory, such notice shall be accompanied by a simple statement of procedural or other grounds.

HEARINGS

SEC. 7. In hearings which section 4 or 5 requires to be conducted pursuant to this section—

(a) PRESIDING OFFICERS.—There shall preside at the taking of evidence (1) the agency, (2) one or more members of the body which comprises the agency, or (3) one or more examiners appointed as provided in this Act; but nothing in this Act shall be deemed to supersede the conduct of specified classes of proceedings in whole or part by or before boards or other officers specially provided for by or designated pursuant to statute. The functions of all presiding officers and of officers participating in decisions in conformity with section 8 shall be conducted in an impartial manner. Any such officer may at any time withdraw if he deems himself disqualified; and, upon the filing in good faith of a timely and sufficient affidavit of personal bias or disqualification of any such officer, the agency shall determine the matter as a part of the record and decision in the case.

(b) HEARING POWERS.—Officers presiding at hearings shall have authority, subject to the published rules of the agency and within its powers, to (1) administer oaths and affirmations, (2) issue subpenas authorized by law, (3) rule upon offers of proof and receive relevant evidence, (4) take or cause depositions to be taken whenever the ends of justice would be served thereby, (5) regulate the course of the hearing, (6) hold conferences for the settlement or simplification of the issues by consent of the parties, (7) dispose of procedural requests or similar matters, (8) make decisions or recommend decisions in conformity with section 8, and (9) take any other action authorized by agency rule consistent with this Act.

118

(c) EVIDENCE.—Except as statutes otherwise provide, the proponent of a rule or order shall have the burden of proof. Any oral or documentary evidence may be received, but every agency shall as a matter of policy provide for the exclusion of irrelevant immaterial, or unduly repetitious evidence and no sanction shall be imposed or rule or order be issued except upon consideration of the whole record or such portions thereof as may be cited by any party and as supported by and in accordance with the reliable, probative, and substantial evidence. Every party shall have the right to present his case or defense by oral or documentary evidence, to submit rebuttal evidence, and to conduct such crossexamination as may be required for a full and true disclosure of the facts. In rule making or determining claims for money or benefits or applications for initial licenses any agency may, where the interest of any party will not be prejudiced thereby, adopt procedures for the submission of all or part of the evidence in written form.

(d) RECORD.—The transcript of testimony and exhibits, together with all papers and requests filed in the proceeding, shall constitute the exclusive record for decision in accordance with section 8 and, upon payment of lawfully prescribed costs, shall be made available to the parties. Where any agency decision rests on official notice of a material fact not appearing in the evidence in the record, any party shall on timely request be afforded an opportunity to show the contrary.

DECISIONS

SEC. 8. In cases in which a hearing is required to be conducted in conformity with section 7—

(a) ACTION BY SUBORDINATES.—In cases in which the agency has not presided at the reception of the evidence, the officer who presided (or, in cases not subect to subsection (c) of section 5, any other officer or officers qualified to preside at hearings pursuant to section 7) shall initially decide the case or the agency shall require (in specific cases or by general rule) the entire record to be certified to it for initial decision. Whenever such officers make the initial decision and in the absence of either an appeal to the agency or review upon motion of the agency within time provided by rule, such decision shall without further proceedings then become the decision of the agency. On appeal from or review of the initial decisions of such officers the agency shall, except as it may limit

119

the issues upon notice or by rule, have all the powers which it would have in making the initial decision. Whenever the agency makes the initial decision without having presided at the reception of the evidence, such officers shall first recommend a decision except that in rule making or determining applications for initial licenses (1) in lieu thereof the agency may issue a tentative decision or any of its responsible officers may recommend a decision or (2) any such procedure may be omitted in any case in which the agency finds upon the record that due and timely execution of its functions imperatively and unavoidably so requires.

(b) SUBMITTALS AM DECISIONS.—Prior to each recommended, initial, or tentative decision, or decision upon agency review of the decision of subordinate officers the parties shall be afforded a reasonable opportunity to submit for the consideration of the officers participating in such decisions (1) proposed findings and conclusions, or (2) exceptions to the decisions or recommended decisions of subordinate officers or to tentative agency decisions, and (3) supporting reasons for such exceptions or proposed findings or conclusions. The record shall show the ruling upon each such finding, conclusion, or exception presented. All decisions (including initial, recommended, or tentative decisions) shall become a part of the record and include a statement of (1) findings and conclusions, as well as the reasons or basis therefor, upon all the material issues of fact, law, or discretion presented on the record; and (2) the appropriate rule, order, sanction, relief, or denial thereof.

SANCTIONS AND POWERS

SEC. 9. In the exercise of any power or authority—

(a) IN GENERAL.—No sanction shall be imposed or substantive rule or order be issued except within jurisdiction delegated to the agency and as authorized by law.

(b) LICENSES.—In any case in which application is made for a license required by law the agency, with due regard to the rights or privileges of all the interested parties or adversely affected persons and with reasonable dispatch, shall set and complete any proceedings required to be conducted pursuant to sections 7 and 8 of this Act or other proceedings required by law and shall make its decision. Except in cases of willfulness or those in which public health, interest, or safety requires otherwise, no withdrawal, suspension, revocation, or annulment of any license shall be lawful unless, prior to the institution of agency proceedings therefor, facts or conduct which may warrant such action shall have been called to the attention of the licensee by the agency in writing and the licensee shall have been accorded opportunity to demonstrate or achieve compliance with all lawful requirements. In any case in which the licensee has, in accordance with agency rules, made timely and sufficient application for a renewal or a new license, no license with reference to any activity of a continuing nature shall expire until such application shall have been finally determined by the agency.

JUDICIAL REVIEW

SEC. 10. Except so far as (1) statutes preclude judicial review or (2) agency action is by law committed to agency discretion—

(a) RIGHT OF REVIEW.—Any person suffering legal wrong because of any action, or adversely affected or aggrieved by such action within the meaning of any relevant statute, shall be entitled to judicial review thereof.

(b) FORM AND VENUE OF ACTION.—The form of proceeding, for judicial review shall be any special statutory review proceeding, relevant to the subject matter in any court specified by statute or, in the absence or inadequacy thereof, any applicable form of legal action (including actions for declaratory judgments or writs of prohibitory or mandatory injunction or habeas corpus) in any court of competent jurisdiction. Agency action shall be subject to judicial review in civil or criminal proceedings for judicial enforcement except to the extent that prior, adequate, and exclusive opportunity for such review is provided by law.

(c) REVIEWABLE ACTS.—Every agency action made reviewable by statute and every final agency action for which there is no other adequate remedy in any court shall be subject to judicial review. Any preliminary, procedural, or intermediate agency action or ruling not directly reviewable shall be subject to review upon the review of the final agency action. Except as otherwise expressly required by statute, agency action otherwise final shall be final for the purposes of this subsection whether or not there has been presented or determined any application for a declaratory order, for any form of reconsideration, or (unless the agency otherwise requires by rule and provides that the action meanwhile shall be inoperative) for an appeal to superior agency authority.

121

(d) INTERIM RELIEF.—Pending judicial review any agency is authorized, where it finds that justice so requires, to postpone the effective date of any action taken by it. Upon such conditions as may be required and to the extent necessary to prevent irreparable injury, every reviewing court (including every court to which a case may be taken on appeal from or upon application for certiorari or other writ to a reviewing court) is authorized to issue all necessary and appropriate process to postpone the effective date of any agency action or to preserve status or rights pending conclusion of the review proceedings.

(e) SCOPE OF REVIEW.—So far as necessary to decision and where presented the reviewing court shall decide all relevant questions of law, interpret constitutional and statutory provisions, and determine the meaning or applicability of the terms of any agency action. It shall (A) compel agency action unlawfully withheld or unreasonably delayed; and (B) hold unlawful and set aside agency action, findings, and conclusions found to be (1) arbitrary, capricious, an abuse of discretion, or otherwise not in accordance with law; (2) contrary to constitutional right, power, privilege, or immunity; (3) in excess of statutory jurisdiction, authority, or limitations, or short of statutory right; (4) without observance of procedure required by law; (5) unsupported by substantial evidence in any case subject to the requirements of sections 7 and 8 or otherwise reviewed on the record of an agency hearing provided by statute; or (6) unwarranted by the facts to the extent that the facts are subject to trail de novo by the reviewing court. In making the foregoing determinations the court shall review the whole record or such portions thereof as may be cited by any party, and due account shall be taken of the rule of prejudicial error.

EXAMINERS

SEC. 11. Subject to the civil-service and other laws to the extent not inconsistent with this Act, there shall be appointed by and for each agency as many qualified and competent examiners as may be necessary for proceedings pursuant to sections 7 and 8, who shall be assigned to cases in rotation so far as practicable and shall perform no duties inconsistent with their duties and responsibilities as examiners. Examiners shall be removable by the agency in which they are employed only for good cause established and determined by the Civil Service Commission (hereinafter called the Commission) after opportunity for hearing and upon the record thereof. Examiners shall receive compensation prescribed by the Commission independently of agency recommendations or ratings and in accordance with the Classification Act of 1923, as amended, except that the provisions of paragraphs (2) and (3) of subsection (b) of section 7 of said Act, as amended, and the provisions of section 9 of said Act, as amended, shall not be applicable. Agencies occasionally or temporarily insufficiently staffed may utilize examiners selected by the Commission from and with the consent of other agencies. For the purposes of this section, the Commission is authorized to make investigations, require reports by agencies, issue reports, including an annual report to the Congress, promulgate rules, appoint such advisory committees as may be deemed necessary, recommend legislation, subpena witnesses or records, and pay witness fees as established for the United States courts.

CONSTRUCTION AND EFFECT

SEC. 12. Nothing in this Act shall be held to diminish the constitutional rights of any person or to limit or repeal additional requirements imposed by statute or otherwise recognized by law. Except as otherwise required by law, all requirements or privileges relating to evidence or procedure shall apply equally to agencies and persons. If any provision of this Act or the application thereof is held invalid, the remainder of this Act or other applications of such provision shall not be affected. Every agency is granted all authority necessary to comply with the requirements of this Act through the issuance of rules or otherwise. No subsequent legislation shall be held to supersede or modify the provisions of this Act except to the extent that such legislation shall do so expressly. This Act shall take effect three months after its approval except that sections 7 and 8 shall take effect six months after such approval, the requirement of the selection of examiners pursuant to section 11 shall not become effective until one year after such approval, and no procedural requirement shall be mandatory as to any agency proceeding initiated prior to the effective date of such requirement.

Approved June 11, 1946.

123

APPENDIX B

OFFICE OF THE ATTORNEY GENERAL,
Washington, D.C., October 19, 1945.

Hon. Pat McCarran,
    Chairman, Senate Judiciary Committee,
        United State Senate, Washington, D.C.

My Dear Senator: You have asked me to comment on S. 7, a bill to improve the administration of justice by prescribing fair administrative procedure, in the form in which it appears in the revised committee print issued October 5, 1945.

I appreciate the opportunity to comment on this proposed legislation.

For more than a decade there has been pending in the Congress legislation in one form or another designed to deal horizontally with the subject of administrative procedure, so as to overcome the confusion which inevitably has resulted from leaving to basic agency statutes the prescription of the procedures to be followed or, in many instances, the delegation of authority to agencies to prescribe their own procedures. Previous attempts to enact general procedural legislation have been unsuccessful generally because they failed to recognize the significant and inherent differences between the tasks of courts and those of administrative agencies or because, in their zeal for simplicity and uniformity, they propose too narrow and rigid a mold.

Nevertheless, the goal toward which these efforts have been directed is, in my opinion, worth while. Despite difficulties of draftsmanship, I believe that over-all procedural legislation is possible and desirable. The administrative process is now well developed. It has been subject in recent years to the most intensive and informed study—by various congressional committees, by the Attorney General's Committee on Administrative Procedure, by organizations such as the American Bar Association, and by many individual practitioners and legal scholars. We have in general—as we did not have until fairly recently—the materials and facts at hand. I think the time is ripe for some measure of control and prescription by legislation. I cannot agree that there is anything inherent in the subject of administrative procedure, however complex it may be, which defies workable codification.

124

Since the original introduction of S. 7, I understand that opportunity has been afforded to public and private interests to study its provisions and to suggest amendments. The agencies of the Government primarily concerned have been consulted and their views considered. In particular, I am happy to note that your committee and the House Committee on the Judiciary, in an effort to reconcile the views of the interested parties, have consulted officers of this Department and experts in administrative law made available by this Department.

The revised committee print issued October 5, 1945, seems to me to achieve a considerable degree of reconciliation between the views expressed by the various Government agencies and the views of the proponents of the legislation. The bill in its present form requires administrative agencies to publish or make available to the public an increased measure of information concerning their organization, functions, and procedures. It gives to that portion of the public which is to be affected by administrative regulations an opportunity to express its views before the regulations become effective. It prescribes, in instances in which existing statutes afford opportunity for hearing in connection with the formulation and issuance of administrative rules and orders, the procedures which shall govern such hearings. It provides for the selection of hearing officers on a basis designed to obtain highly qualified and impartial personnel and to insure their security of tenure. It also restates the law governing judicial review of administrative action.

The bill appears to offer a hopeful prospect of achieving reasonable uniformity and fairness in administrative procedures without at the same time interfering unduly with the efficient and economical operation of the Government. Insofar as possible, the bill recognizes the needs of individual agencies by appropriate exemption of certain of their functions.

After reviewing the committee print, therefore, I have concluded that this Department should recommend its enactment.

My conclusion as to the workability of the proposed legislation rest on my belief that the provisions of the bill can and should be construed reasonably and in a sense which will fairly balance the requirements and interests of private persons and governmental agencies. I think it may be advisable for me to attach to this report an appendix discussing the principle provisions of the bill. This may serve to clarify some of the essential issues, and may

125

assist the committee in evaluating the impact of the bill on public and private interests.

I am advised by the Acting Director of the Bureau of the Budget that while there would be no objection to the submission of this report, he questions the appropriateness of the inclusion of the words "independently of agency recommendations or ratings," appearing after the words "Examiners shall receive compensation prescribed by the [Civil Service] Commission" in section 11 of the bill, inasmuch as he deems it highly desirable that agency recommendations and ratings be fully considered by the Commission.

With kind personal regards.

Sincerely yours,
TOM C. CLARK,
Attorney General

126

APPENDIX TO ATTORNEY GENERAL'S STATEMENT REGARDING REVISED COMMITTEE PRINT OF OCTOBER 5, 1945

Section 2: The definitions given in section 2 are of very broad character. It is believed, however, that this scope of definition will not be found to have any unexpected or unfortunate consequences in particular cases, inasmuch as the operative sections of the act are themselves carefully limited.

"Courts" includes the Tax Court, Court of Customs and Patent Appeals, the Court of Claims, and similar courts. This act does not apply to their procedure nor affect the requirement of resort thereto.

In section 2 (a) the words "agencies composed of representatives of the parties or of representatives of organizations of the parties to the disputes determined by them" are intended to refer to the following, among others: National War Labor Board and the National Railroad Adjustment Board.

In section 2 (c) the phrase "the approval or prescription for the future of rates, wages, corporate or financial structures or reorganizations thereof, prices, facilities, appliances," etc., is not, of course, intended to be an exhaustive enumeration of the types of subject matter of rule making. Specification of these particular subjects is deemed desirable, however, because there is no unanimity of recognition that they are, in fact, rule making. The phrase "for the future" is designed to differentiate, for example, between the process of prescribing rates for the future and the process of determining the lawfulness of rates charged in the past. The latter, of course, is "adjudication" and not "rule making." (*Arizona Grocery Co.* v. *Atchison, Topeka, and Santa Fe Railway Co.* (284 U.S. 370).)

The definitions of "rule making" and "adjudication," set forth in subsections (c) and (d) of section 2, are especially significant. The basic scheme underlying this legislation is to classify all administrative proceedings into these two categories. The pattern is familiar to those who have examined the various proposals for administrative procedure legislation which have been introduced during the past few years; it appears also in the recommendations of the Attorney General's Committee on Administrative Procedure. Proceedings are classed as rule making under this act not merely because, like the legislative process, they result in regulations of

127

general applicability but also because they involve subject matter demanding judgments based on technical knowledge and experience. As defined in subsection (c), for example, rule making includes not only the formulation of rules of general applicability, but also the formulation of agency action whether of general or particular applicability, relating to the types of subject matter enumerated in subsection (c). In many instances of adjudication, on the other hand, the accusatory element is strong, and individual compliance or behavior is challenged; in such cases, special procedural safeguards should be provided to insure fair judgments on the facts as they may properly appear of record. The statute carefully differentiates between these two basically different classes of proceedings so as to avoid, on the one hand, too cumbersome a procedure and to require, on the other hand, an adequate procedure.

Section 3: This section applies to all agencies covered by the act, including war agencies and war functions. The exception of any function of the United States requiring secrecy in the public interest is intended to cover (in addition to military, naval, and foreign affairs functions) the confidential operations of the Secret Service, the Federal Bureau of Investigation, United States attorneys, and other prosecuting agencies, as well as the confidential functions of any other agency.

Section 3 (a), by requiring publication of certain classes of information in the Federal Register, is not intended to repeal the Federal Register Act (44 U.S.C. 301 et seq.) but simply to require the publication of certain additional material.

Section 3 (a) (4) is intended to include (in addition to substantive rules) only such statements of general policy or interpretations as the agency believes may be formulated with a sufficient degree of definiteness and completeness to warrant their publication for the guidance of the public.

Section 3 (b) is designed to make available all final opinions or orders in the adjudication of cases. Even here material may be held confidential if the agency finds good cause. This confidential material, however, should not be cited as a precedent. If it is desired to rely upon the citation of confidential material, the agency should first make available some abstract of the confidential material in such form as will show the principles relied upon without revealing the confidential facts.

Section 3 (c) is not intended to open up Government files for general inspection. What is intended is that the agencies, to the degree of specificity practicable, shall classify its material in terms of whether or not it is confidential in character and shall set forth in published rules the information or type of material which is confidential and that which is not.

Section 4. The term "naval" in the first exception clause is intended to include the defense functions of the Coast Guard and the Bureau of Marine Inspection and Navigation.

Section 4 (b), in requiring the publication of a concise general statement of the basis and purpose of rules made without formal hearing, is not intended to require an elaborate analysis of rules or of the detailed considerations upon which they are based, but it is designed to enable the public to obtain a general idea of the purpose of, and a statement of the basic justification for, the rules. The requirement would also serve much the same as the whereas clauses which are now customarily found in the preambles of Executive orders.

Section 4 (c): This subsection is not intended to hamper the agencies in cases in which there is good cause for putting a rule into effect immediately, or at some time earlier than 30 days. The section requires, however, that where an earlier effective date is desired the agency should make a finding of good cause therefor and publish its finding along with rule.

Section 4 (d) simply permits any interested person to petition an agency for the issuance, amendment, or repeal of a rule. It requires the reception and consideration of petitions, but does not compel an agency to undertake any rule-making procedure merely because a petition is filed.

SEC. 5. Subject to the six exceptions set forth at the commencement of the section, section 5 to administrative adjudications "required by statute to be determined on the record after opportunity for an agency hearing." It is thus limited to cases in which the Congress has specifically required a certain type of hearing. The section has no application to rule making, as defined in section 2 (c). The section does apply, however, to licensing with the exception that section 5 (c), relating to the separation of functions, does not apply in determining applications for initial licenses, i.e., original licenses as contradistinguished from renewals or amendments of existing licenses.

If a case falls within one of the six exceptions at the opening of section 5, no provision of section 5 has any application

129

to that case; such a case would be governed by the requirements of other existing statutes.

The first exception is intended to exempt, among other matters, certain types of reparation orders assessing damages, such as are issued by the Interstate Commerce Commission and the Secretary of Agriculture, since such orders are admissible only as prima facie evidence in court upon attempted enforcement proceedings or (at least in the case of reparation orders issued by the Secretary of Agriculture under the Perishable Agricultural Commodities Act) on the appeal of the losing party. Reparation orders involving in part an administrative determination of the reasonableness of rates in the past so far as they are not subject to trial de novo would be subject to the provisions of section 5 generally but they have been specifically exempted from the segregation provisions of section 5 (c). In the fourth exception the term "naval" is intended to include adjudicative defense functions of the Coast Guard and the Bureau of Marine Inspection and Navigation, where such functions pertain to national defense.

Section 5 (a) is intended to state minimum requirements for the giving of notice to persons who under existing law are entitled to notice of an agency hearing in a statutory adjudication. While in most types of proceedings all of the information required to be given in clauses (1), (2), and (3) may be included in the "notice of hearing" or other moving paper, in many instances the agency or other moving party may not be in position to set forth all of such information in the moving paper, or perhaps not even in advance of the hearing, especially the "matters of fact and law asserted." The first sentence of this subsection merely requires that the information specified should be given as soon as it can be set forth and, in any event, in a sufficiently timely manner as to afford those entitled to the information an adequate opportunity to meet it. The second sentence complements the first and requires agencies and other parties promptly to reply to moving papers of private persons or permits agencies to require responsive pleading in any proceedings.

Section 5 (c) applies only to the class of adjudicatory proceedings included within the scope of section 5, i. e., cases of adjudication required by statute to be determined after opportunity for an agency hearing, and then not falling within one of the six excepted situations listed at the opening of section 5. As explained in the comments with respect to section 5 generally, this subsection does not apply either in proceedings to determine applications for initial licenses or in those to determine the reasonableness of rates in the past.

In the cases to which this subsection is applicable, if the informal procedures described in section 5 (b) (1) are not appropriate or have failed, a hearing is to be held as provided in sections 7 and 8. At such hearings the same officers who preside at the reception of evidence pursuant to section 7 shall make the recommended decision or initial decision "required by section 8" except where such officers become unavailable to the agency. The reference to section 8 is significant. Section 8 (a) provides that, in cases in which the agency has not presided at the reception of the evidence, the officer who presided (or, in cases not subject to subsection (c) of section 5, an officer or officers qualified to preside at hearings pursuant to section 7) shall make the initial or recommended decision, as the case may be. It is plain, therefore, that in cases subject to section 5 (c) only the officer who presided at the hearing (unless he is unavailable for reasons beyond the agency's control) is eligible to make the initial or recommended decision, as the case may be.

This subsection further provides that in the adjudicatory hearings covered by it no presiding officer shall consult any person or party on any fact in issue unless upon notice and opportunity for all parties to participate (except to the extent required for the disposition of ex parte matters as authorized by law). The term "fact in issue" is used in its technical, litigious sense.

In most of the agencies which conduct adjudicative proceedings of the types subject to this subsection, the examiners are placed in organizational units apart from those to which the investigative or prosecuting personnel are assigned. Under this subsection such an arrangement will become operative in all such agencies. Further, in the adjudicatory cases covered by section 5 (c), no officer, employee, or agent engaged in the performance of investigative or prosecuting functions for any agency in any case shall, in that or a factually related case, participate or advise in the decision, recommended decision or agency review pursuant to section 8 except as witness or counsel in public proceedings. However, section 5 (c) does not apply to the agency itself or, in the case of a multiheaded agency, any member thereof. It would not preclude, for example, a member of the Interstate Commerce Commission personally conducting or supervising an investigation and subsequently participating in the determination of the agency action arising out of such investigation.

Section 5 (c), applying as it does only to cases of adjudication (except determining applications for initial licenses or determining reasonableness of rates in the past) within the scope of section 5 generally, has no application whatever to rule making, as defined in section 2 (c). As explained in the comment on section 2 (c), rule making includes a wide variety of subject matters, and within the scope of those matters it is not limited to the formulation of rules of general applicability but includes also the formulation of agency action whether of general or particular application, for example, the reorganization of a particular company.

Section 5 (d): Within the scope of section 5 (i.e., in cases of adjudication required by statute to be determined on the record after opportunity for an agency hearing, subject to certain exceptions) the agency is authorized to issue a declaratory order to terminate a controversy or remove uncertainty. Where declaratory orders are found inappropriate to the subject matter, no agency is required to issue them.

Section 6: Subsection (a), in stating a right of appearance for the purpose of settling or informally determining the matter in controversy, would not obtain if the agency properly determines that the responsible conduct of public business does not permit. It may be necessary, for example, to set the matter down for public hearing without preliminary discussion because a statute or the subject matter or the special circumstances so require.

It is not intended by this provision to require the agency to give notice to all interested persons, unless such notice is otherwise required by law.

This subsection does not deal with, or in any way qualify, the present power of an agency to regulate practice at its bar. It expressly provides, moreover, that nothing in the act shall be construed either to grant or to deny the right of nonlawyers to appear before agencies in a representative capacity. Control over this matter remains in the respective agencies.

Section 6 (b): The first sentence states existing law. The second sentence is new.

Section 6 (c): The first sentence entitles a party to a subpena upon a statement or showing of general relevance and reasonable scope of the evidence sought. The second sentence is intended to

132

state the existing law with respect to the judicial enforcement of subpenas.

Section 6 (d): The statement of grounds required herein will be very simple, as contrasted with the more elaborate findings which are customarily issued to support an order.

Section 7: This section applies in those cases of statutory hearing which are required by sections 4 and 5 to be conducted pursuant to section 7. Subject to the numerous exceptions contained in sections 4 and 5, they are cases in which an order or rule is to be made upon the basis of the record in a statutory hearing.

Section 7 (a): The subsection is not intended to disturb presently existing statutory provisions which explicitly provide for certain types of hearing officers. Among such are (1) joint hearings before officers of the Federal agencies and persons designated by one or more States, (2) where officers of more than one agency sit, (3) quota allotment cases under the Agricultural Adjustment Act of 1938, (4) Marine Casualty Investigation Boards, (5) registers of the General Land Office, (6) special boards set up to review the rights of disconnected servicemen (38 U.S.C. 693h) and the rights of veterans to special unemployment compensation (38 U.S.C. 696h), and (7) boards of employees authorized under the Interstate Commerce Act (49 U.S.C. 17 (2)).

Subject to this qualification, section 7 (a) requires that there shall preside at the taking of evidence one or more examiners appointed as provided in this act, unless the agency itself or one or more of its members presides. This provision is one of the most important provisions in the act. In many agencies of the Government this provision may mean the appointment of a substantial number of hearing officers having no other duties. The resulting expense to the Government may be increased, particularly in agencies where hearings are now conducted by employees of a subordinate status or by employees having duties in addition to presiding at hearings. On the other hand, it is contemplated that the Civil service Commission, which is empowered under the provisions of section 11 to prescribe salaries for hearing officers, will establish various salary grades in accordance with the nature and importance of the duties performed, and will assign those in the lower grades to duties now performed by employees in the lower brackets. It may also be possible for the agencies to reorganize their staffs so as to permit the appointment of full-time hearing officers by reducing the number of employees engaged on other duties.

This subsection further provides for withdrawal or removal of examiners disqualified in a particular proceeding. Some of the agencies have voiced concern that this provision would permit undue delay in the conduct of their proceedings because of unnecessary hearings or other procedure to determine whether affidavits of bias are well founded. The provision does not require hearings in every instance but simply requires such procedure, formal or otherwise, as would be necessary to establish the merits of the allegations of bias. If it is manifest that the charge is groundless, there may be prompt disposition of the matter. On the other hand, if the affidavit appears to have substance, it should be inquired into. In any event, whatever procedure the agency deems appropriate must be made a part of the record in the proceeding in which the affidavit is filed.

Section 7 (b): The agency may delegate to a hearing officer any of the enumerated powers with which it is vested. The enumeration of the powers of hearing officers is not intended to be exclusive.

Section 7 (c): The first sentence states the customary rule that the proponent of a rule or order shall have the burden of proof. Statutory exceptions to the rule are preserved. Parties shall have the right to conduct such cross-examination as may be required for a full and true disclosure of the facts. This is not intended to disturb the existing practice of submitting technical written reports, summaries, and analyses of material gathered in field surveys, and other devices appropriately adapted to the particular issues involved in specialized proceedings. Whether the agency must in such cases produce the maker of the report depends, as it does under the present law, on what is reasonable in all the circumstances.

It may be noted that agencies are empowered, in this subsection, to dispense with oral evidence only in the types of proceedings enumerated; that is, in instances in which normally it is not necessary to see and hear the witnesses in order properly to appraise the evidence. While there may be types of proceedings other than those enumerated in which the oral testimony of the witnesses is not essential, in such instances the parties generally consent to submission of the evidence in written form so that the inability of the agency to compel submission of written evidence would not be burdensome.

The provision regarding "evidence in written form" does not limit the generality of the prevailing principle that "any evidence may be received"; that is, that the rules of evidence as such are not applicable in administrative proceedings, and that all types of pertinent evidentiary material may be considered. It is assumed, of course, that agencies will, in the words of the Attorney General's Committee on Administrative Procedure, rely only on such evidence (whether written or oral) as is "relevant, reliable, and probative." This is meant as a guide, but the courts in reviewing an order are governed by the provisions of section 10 (e), which states the "substantial evidence" rule.

Section 7 (d): The transcript of testimony and exhibits, together with all papers and requests filed in the proceeding, shall constitute the exclusive record for decision, in the cases covered by section 7. This follows from the proposition that sections 7 and 8 deal only with cases where by statute the decision is to be based on the record of hearing. Further, section 7 is limited by the exceptions contained in the opening sentences of sections 4 and 5; accordingly, certain special classes of cases, such as those where decisions rest solely on inspections, tests, or elections, are not covered. The second sentence of the subsection enables the agency to take official notice of material facts which do not appear in the record, provided the taking of such notice is stated in the record or decision, but in such cases any party affected shall, on timely request, be afforded an opportunity to show the contrary.

Section 8: This section applies to all hearings held under section 7.

Section 8 (a): Under this subsection either the agency or a subordinate hearing officer may make the initial decision. As previously observed with respect to subsection (c) of section 5, in cases to which that subsection is applicable the same officer who personally presided over the hearing shall make such decision if it is to be made by a subordinate hearing officer. The agency may provide that in all cases the agency itself is to make the initial decision, or after the hearing it may remove a particular case from a subordinate hearing officer and thereupon make the initial decision. The initial decision of the hearing officer, in the absence of appeal to or review by the agency, is (or becomes) the decision of the agency. Upon review the agency may restrict its decision to ques-

135

tions of law, or to the question of whether the findings are supported by substantial evidence or the weight of evidence, as the nature of the case may be. On the other hand, it may make entirely new findings either upon the record or upon new evidence which it takes. It may remand the matter to the hearing officer for any appropriate further proceedings.

The intention underlying the last sentence of this subsection is to require the adoption of a procedure which will give the parties an opportunity to make their contentions to the agency before the issuance of a final agency decision. This sentence states as a general requirement that, whenever the agency makes the initial decision without having presided at the reception of the evidence, a recommended decision shall be filed by the officer who presided at the hearing (or, in cases not subject to section 5 (c), by any other officer qualified to preside at section 7 hearings). However, this procedure need not be followed in rule making or in determining applications for initial licenses (1) if, in lieu of a recommended decision by such hearing officer, the agency issues a tentative decision; (2) if, in lieu of a recommended decision by such hearing officer, a recommended decision is submitted by any of the agency's responsible officers; or (3) if, in any event, the agency makes a record finding that "due and timely execution of its function imperatively and unavoidably so requires."

Subsection (c) of section 5, as explained in the comments on that subsection, does not apply to rule making. The broad scope of rule making is explained in the notes to subsection (c) of section 2.

The second exception permits, in proceedings to make rules and to determine applications for initial licenses, the continuation of the widespread agency practice of serving upon the parties, as a substitute for either an examiner's report or a tentative agency report, a report prepared by the staff of specialists and technicians normally engaged in that portion of the agency's operations to which the proceeding in question relates. The third exception permits, in lieu of any sort of preliminary report, the agency to issue forthwith its final rule or its order granting or denying an initial license in the emergent instances indicated. The subsection, however, requires that an examiner issue either an initial or a recommended decision, as the case may be, in all cases subject to section 7 except rule making and determining applications for initial licenses. The act permits no deviation from this requirement, unless, of course, the parties waive such procedure.

Section 8 (b): Prior to each recommended, initial, or tentative decision, parties shall have a timely opportunity to submit proposed findings and conclusions, and, prior to each decision upon agency review of either the decision of subordinate officers or of the agency's tentative decision, to submit exceptions to the initial, recommended, or tentative decision, as the case may be. Subject to the agency's rules, either the proposed findings or the exceptions may be oral in form where such mode of presentation is adequate.

Section 9: Subsection (a) is intended to declare the existing law. Subsection (b) is intended to codify the best existing law and practice. The second sentence of subsection (b) is not intended to apply to temporary licenses which may be issued pending the determination of applications for licenses.

Section 10: This section, in general, declares the existing law concerning judicial review. It provides for judicial review except insofar as statutes preclude it, or insofar as agency action is by law committed to agency discretion. A statute may in terms preclude judicial review or be interpreted as manifesting a congressional intention to preclude judicial review. Examples of such interpretation are: *Switchmen's Union of North America* v. *National Mediation Board* (320 U. S. 297); *American Federation of Labor* v. *National Labor Relations Board* (308 U. S. 401); *Butte, Anaconda & Pacific Railway Co.* v. *United States* (290 U. S. 127). Many matters are committed partly or wholly to agency discretion. Thus, the courts have held that the refusal by the National Labor Relations Board to issue a complaint is an exercise of discretion unreviewable by the courts *(Jacobsen* v. *National Labor Relations Board,* 120 F. (2d) 96 (C. C. A. 3d); *Marine Engineers' Beneficial Assn.* v. *National Labor Relations Board,* decided April 8, 1943 (C. C. A. 2d). certiorari denied, 320 U.S. 777). In this act, for example, the failure to grant a petition filed under section 4 (d) would be similarly unreviewable.

Section 10 (a) : Any person suffering legal wrong because of any agency action, or adversely affected or aggrieved by such action within the meaning of any relevant statute, shall be entitled to judicial review of such action. This reflects existing law. In *Alabama Power Co.* v. *Ickes* (302 U.S. 464), the Supreme Court stated the rule concerning persons entitled to judicial review. Other cases having an important bearing on this subject are

137

Massachusetts v. *Mellon* (262 U.S. 447), *The Chicago Junction Case* (264 U.S. 258), *Sprunt & Son* v. *United States* (281 U.S. 249), and *Perkins* v. *Lukens Steel Co.* (310 U.S. 113). An important decision interpreting the meaning of the terms "aggrieved" and "adversely affected" is *Federal Communications Commission* v. *Sanders Bros. Radio Station* (309 U. S. 470).

Section 10 (b): This subsection requires that, where a specific statutory method is provided for reviewing a given type of case in the courts, that procedure shall be used. If there is no such procedure, or if the procedure is inadequate (i.e., where under existing law a court would regard the special statutory procedure as inadequate and would grant another form of relief), then any applicable procedure, such as prohibitory or mandatory injunction, declaratory judgment, or habeas corpus, is available. The final sentence of the subsection indicates that the question of the validity of an agency action may arise in a court proceeding to enforce the agency action. The statutes presently provide various procedures for judicial enforcement of agency action, and nothing in this act is intended to disturb those procedures. In such a proceeding the defendant may contest the validity of the agency action unless a prior, adequate, and exclusive opportunity to contest or review validity has been provided by law.

Section 10 (c): This subsection states (subject to the provisions of section 10 (a)) the acts which are reviewable under section 10. It is intended to state existing law. The last sentence makes it clear that the doctrine of exhaustion of administrative remedies with respect to finality of agency action is intended to be applicable only (1) where expressly required by statute (as, for example, is provided in 49 U.S.C. 17 (9)) or (2) where the agency's rules require that decisions by subordinate officers must be appealed to superior agency authority before the decision may be regarded as final for purposes of judicial review.

Section 10 (d): The first sentence states existing law. The second sentence may be said to change existing law only to the extent that the language of the opinion in *Scripps-Howard Radio, Inc.* v. *Federal Communications Commission* (316 U.S. 4,14), may be interpreted to deny to reviewing courts the power to permit an applicant for a renewal of a license to continue to operate as if the original license had not expired, pending conclusion of the judicial review proceedings. In any event, the court must find, of course, that granting of interim relief is necessary to prevent irreparable injury.

Section 10 (e): This declares the existing law concerning the scope of judicial review. The power of the court to direct or compel agency action unlawfully withheld or unreasonably delayed is not intended to confer any nonjudicial functions or to narrow the principle of continuous administrative control enunciated by the Supreme Court in *Federal Communications Commission v. Pottsville Broadcasting Co.* (309 U.S. 134). Clause (5) is intended to embody the law as declared, for example, in *Consolidated Edison Co. v. National Labor Relations Board* (305 U.S. 197). There the Chief Justice said: "Substantial evidence is more than a mere scintilla. It means such relevant evidence as a reasonable mind might accept as adequate to support a conclusion (p. 229) * * * assurance of a desirable flexibility in administrative procedure does not go so far as to justify orders without a basis in evidence having rational probative force" (p. 230).

The last sentence of this section makes it clear that not every failure to observe the requirements of this statute or of the law is ipso facto fatal to the validity of an order. The statute adopts the rule now well established as a matter of common law in all jurisdictions that error is not fatal unless prejudicial.

Sec. 11: This section provides for the appointment, compensation, and tenure of examiners who will preside over hearings and render decisions pursuant to section 7 and 8. The section provides that appointments shall be made "subject to the civil service and other laws to the extent not inconsistent with this act". Appointments are to be made by the respective employing agencies of personnel determined by the Civil Service Commission to be qualified and competent examiners. The examiners appointed are to serve only as examiners except that, in particular instances (especially where the volume of hearings under a given statute or in a given agency is not very great), examiners may be assigned additional duties which are not inconsistent with or which do not interfere with their duties as examiners. To insure equality of participation among examiners in the hearing and decision of cases, the agencies are required to use them in rotation so far as may be practicable.

Examiners are subject to removal only for good cause "established and determined" by the Commission. The Commission must afford the examiner a hearing, if requested, and must rest its

139

decision solely upon the basis of the record of such hearing. It should be noted that the hearing and the decision are to be conducted and made pursuant to the provisions of section 7 and 8.

Section 11 provides further that the Commission shall prescribe the compensation of examiners, in accordance with the compensation schedules provided in the Classification Act, except that the efficiency rating system set forth in that act shall not be applicable to examiners.

Sec. 12: The first sentence of section 12 is intended simply to indicate that the act will be interpreted as supplementing constitutional and legal requirements imposed by existing law.

The section further provides that "no subsequent legislation shall be held to supersede or modify the provisions of this act except to the extent that such legislation shall do so expressly". It is recognized that no congressional legislation can bind subsequent sessions of the Congress. The present act can be repealed in whole or in part at any time after its passage. However, the act is intended to express general standards of wide applicability. it is believed that the courts should as a rule of construction interpret the act as applicable on a broad basis, unless some subsequent act clearly provides to the contrary.

Judicial Review of Agency Action

Citations:

5 U.S.C. §§701-706 (2000), originally enacted as Administrative Procedure Act §10; significantly amended by Pub. L. No. 94-574, 90 Stat. 2721; 28 U.S.C. §§1331, 1631, 2112, 2341-51 (2000).

Overview:

APA Provisions. The principal statutory authority governing judicial review of agency action is 5 U.S.C. §§701-706, which codify section 10 of the Administrative Procedure Act. (The APA's text may be found in the Appendix to Chapter 1.) Sections 701-706 constitute a general restatement of the principles of judicial review embodied in many statutes and judicial decisions; however, they leave the mechanics regarding judicial review to be governed by other statutes or court rules.[1] For a thorough discussion of cases concerning both availability and scope of judicial review, see *A Guide to Judicial and Political Review of Federal Agencies*, 1-210 (John F. Duffy & Michael Herz eds., ABA. 2005). For a summary of the law, see Section of Administrative Law and Regulatory Practice, American Bar Association, *A Blackletter Statement of Federal Administrative Law*, 54 Admin. L. Rev. 1, 36-59 (2002).

Section 701 embodies the basic presumption that judicial review is available as long as no statute precludes such relief or the action is not one committed by law to agency discretion. *(Abbott Laboratories v. Gardner*, 387 U.S. 136, 140 (1967); *Citizens To Preserve Overton Park, Inc. v. Volpe*,

---

[1] *Attorney General's Manual on the Administrative Procedure Act* 93 (1947).

401 U.S. 402, 410 (1971); *Heckler v. Chaney*, 470 U.S. 821, 826 (1985)). Preliminary or interlocutory actions are ordinarily reviewable only on review of the final agency action. (*See, e.g., Association of National Advertisers, Inc. v. FTC*, 565 F.2d 237 (2d Cir. 1977)). In those situations where preliminary or interlocutory actions are immediately reviewable, any suit seeking such relief that might affect a court of appeals' jurisdiction over a final agency decision is subject to exclusive review in the court of appeals rather than district court. (See *Telecommunications Research & Action Center v. FCC*, 750 F.2d 70 (D.C. Cir. 1984).)

Section 702 is designed to govern the issue of who has standing to challenge agency action. It sets forth the general principle that a person suffering legal wrong or adversely affected or aggrieved by agency action is entitled to judicial review of that action. The phrase "legal wrong" merely connotes such wrong as statutes or court decisions identify as constituting grounds for judicial review. The determination of who is "adversely affected or aggrieved" reflects judicial evolution of the law of standing; the courts make their determination based on constitutional and statutory requirements.[2]

Section 703 deals with the form and venue of the judicial review proceeding. Briefly, there are three types of review proceedings:

- "Statutory review," a review proceeding specifically provided by statute for the agency action in question (e.g., a proceeding to review a rule of the Federal Trade Commission under 15 U.S.C. §57a(e));
- "Nonstatutory review," a review through a suit against the agency or its officers for declaratory or injunctive relief or habeas corpus in a court of competent jurisdiction;
- A civil or criminal enforcement proceeding instituted by the government or possibly by a private party that involves the validity of agency action.

Where a statutory proceeding is provided, such review is frequently, though not always, in the courts of appeals. Nonstatutory review proceedings and enforcement proceedings are almost invariably brought in the U.S. district courts. Where there is an adequate statutory review provided, a

---

[2] *Id.* at 96.

party may not seek nonstatutory review. However, review is available in an enforcement proceeding except where a prior opportunity for judicial review was adequate and expressly or impliedly exclusive.[3]

Section 704 provides that "agency action made reviewable by statute and final agency action for which there is no other adequate remedy in a court are subject to judicial review." The Supreme Court's summary of the law of finality in *Bennett v. Spear*, 520 U.S. 154, 177-78 (1997), is now the widely cited test: "As a general matter, two conditions must be satisfied for agency action to be 'final': First, the action must mark the 'consummation' of the agency's decisionmaking process—it must not be of a merely tentative or interlocutory nature. And second, the action must be one by which "rights or obligations have been determined, or from which 'legal consequences will flow.'"

For suits brought under the APA, the exhaustion-of-administrative-remedies requirement is largely subsumed within the finality requirement of § 704. Where agency action is final for purposes of § 704, nonstatutory exhaustion requirements do not preclude review. Section 704 makes clear that unless expressly required by statute, a party seeking review of otherwise final agency action pursuant to the APA need not pursue (1) any process for agency reconsideration of its decision or (2) any intra-agency appeals (except where the agency has, by rule, required exhaustion of the appeal and provided that the agency action is inoperative during the time of the appeal). See *Darby v. Cisneros*, 509 U.S. 137 (1993).

Agency action under the APA "includes the whole or a part of any agency rule, order, license, sanction, relief, or the equivalent or denial thereof, or failure to act." 5 U.S.C. §551(13).

Section 705 authorizes a reviewing court to postpone the effectiveness of agency action or preserve the status or rights affected by an agency's order pending completion of judicial review proceedings. The standards for deciding requests for stays of agency action are set out in *Virginia Petroleum Jobbers Ass'n v. FPC*, 259 F.2d 921 (D.C. Cir. 1958), as elaborated by the court's decisions in *Washington Metropolitan Area Transit Commission v. Holiday Tours, Inc.*, 559 F.2d 841 (D.C. Cir. 1977), *Wisconsin Gas Co. v. FERC*, 758 F.2d 669 (D.C. Cir. 1985), and *Cuomo v. NRC*, 772 F.2d 972 (D.C. Cir. 1985).

---

[3] *Id.* at 99-100.

Section 706 sets forth the scope of review of agency actions. The case law on the subject of scope of review is rich and varied and cannot easily be summed up. In general, the scope of review depends on the nature of the agency determination under challenge. Agency conclusions on questions of law are reviewed *de novo*. When a court reviews an agency's construction of the statute it administers the court is required to uphold Congress's intent where Congress has directly spoken to the precise statutory question at issue. If the statute is silent or ambiguous with respect to the specific issue, however, the agency's interpretation of the statute must be upheld if the agency's construction of the statute is permissible. See *Chevron U.S.A. Inc. v. Natural Resources Defense Council, Inc.*, 467 U.S. 837 (1984). But whether the Chevron test applies at all depends on the type of proceeding in which the agency made the interpretation. Where the agency's statutory interpretation is made in an informal adjudication or in a policy statement or interpretative rule that was not subject to notice and comment, the interpretation will receive lesser deference. See *Christensen v. Harris County*, 529 U.S. 576 (2000), *United States v. Mead Corp.*, 533 U.S. 218 (2001).

Agency exercises of judgment or discretion are reviewed under the "arbitrary, capricious, abuse of discretion" standard. Under this standard, an agency determination will by upheld if it is rational, based on consideration of the relevant factors, and within the scope of the authority delegated to the agency by statute. The agency must examine the relevant data and articulate a satisfactory explanation for its action, including a rational connection between the facts found and the choices made. A court is not to substitute its judgment for that of the agency. (See *Motor Vehicle Manufacturers Ass'n v. State Farm Mutual Automobile Insurance Co.*, 463 U.S. 29, 42-43 (1983)). In applying the arbitrary-and-capricious test, the courts have reversed agency actions on the following bases: (1) reliance on impermissible factors, (2) no reasonable relationship to statutory purposes or requirements, (3) inadequate factual premises, (4) unsupported by any reasoning or based on seriously flawed reasoning, (5) failure to consider key aspects of the issue presented, unexplained inconsistency with prior actions, (6) failure to consider alternative solutions, (7) failure to respond to relevant arguments or comments, or disproportionate sanctions. See *A Guide to Judicial and Political Review of Federal Agencies* at 181-195.

Agency determinations of fact are reviewed under the "substantial evidence" test when the agency determination is reviewed on the record of an agency hearing required by statute. See *Consolo v. FMC*, 383 U.S. 607,

618-21 (1966), citing *Universal Camera Corp. v. NLRB,* 340 U.S. 474 (1951). Otherwise, factual determinations are also subject to the arbitrary or capricious standard, except for the unusual situation in which the facts are subject to trial *de novo* by the reviewing court. However, the courts themselves have difficulty in applying the fine distinction between the arbitrary or capricious and the substantial evidence tests. The tests converge where an agency's determination is based on a mix of factual and judgmental conclusions (see, e.g., *Amoco Oil Co. v. EPA,* 501 F.2d 722, 739-41 (D.C. Cir. 1974)) and may be identical where an agency's factual support is concerned. (See *Ass'n of Data Processing Service Organizations, Inc. v. Board Governors of the Federal Reserve System,* 745 F.2d 677 (D.C. Cir. 1984).)

Section 706 contains a rule of harmless error. A court will not overturn an agency's decision even if the agency committed some error unless the error was genuinely harmful or prejudicial. (See *Dolcin Corp. v. FTC,* 219 F.2d 742 (D.C. Cir. 1954), *cert. denied* 348 U.S. 981 (1955).)

Illustrative Statutory Provision. The Administrative Orders Review Act (28 U.S.C. §§2341-2351) is a special statutory provision governing review of the actions of several different agencies. It provides for review in the courts of appeals for final orders of the Federal Communications Commission Federal Maritime Commission, Maritime Administration, and Surface Transportation Board, and certain final orders of the Secretaries of Agriculture, Energy, Housing and Urban Development and Transportation, and it specifies the procedure for instituting such review proceedings. Venue of the proceedings is in the judicial circuit where the petitioner resides or has its principal office or in the Court of Appeals for the District of Columbia Circuit (28 U.S.C. §2343).

The "orders" that may be reviewed under the Administrative Orders Review Act include not only final orders in adjudicative proceedings, but also orders promulgating agency rules of general applicability (see *Gage v. U.S. Atomic Energy Commission,* 479 F.2d 1214, 1218-19 (D.C. Cir. 1973); *United States v. Storer Broadcasting Co.,* 351 U.S. 192 (1956)). However, because under 28 U.S.C. §2344, a review proceeding may be initiated by "any party aggrieved by the final order," some courts have held that one who did not participate in the administrative proceeding resulting in the order may not seek review under the Act *(Gage v. U.S. Atomic Energy Commission,* 479 F.2d at 1217-18).

Section 2344 provides that review must be sought within 60 days of the entry of the agency order about which a person complains. Failure to seek judicial review within 60 days renders a request for review untimely. (See *B.J. McAdams, Inc. v. ICC,* 551 F.2d 1112 (8th Cir. 1977).) This requirement may create problems with respect to persons seeking relief from a rule some time after its issuance. Where a dispute over a rule arises after its issuance, some courts will deem the 60-day period to run from the agency's denial of the party's request for amendment or waiver of the rule, rather than from the issuance date (see *Public Citizen v. Nuclear Regulatory Commission,* 901 F.2d 147, 152, 53 & n.1 (D.C. Cir. 1990)).

Sovereign Immunity. For many years proceedings for nonstatutory review were subject to possible dismissal on the ground that the government had not consented to be sued. The case law on the availability of the sovereign immunity defense was in hopeless disarray, but a careful pleader could usually bring his case within one of the recognized exceptions to the doctrine. In 1976, in response to recommendations from the Administrative Conference and the American Bar Association, Congress enacted Pub. L. No. 94-574, which amended 5 U.S.C. §702 to abolish the defense of sovereign immunity in any action in a court of the United States seeking relief other than money damages and based on a claim that an agency or officer acted or failed to act in an official capacity or under color of legal authority. It is important to emphasize that the purpose of Pub. L. No. 94-574 was to abolish the technical defense of sovereign immunity in proceedings for nonstatutory review *(Food Town Stores, Inc. v. EEOC,* 708 F.2d 920, 922 (4th Cir. 1983), *cert. denied* 465 U.S. 1005 (1984)), and not to eliminate other more substantive limitations on judicial review such as the plaintiff's lack of standing or failure to exhaust administrative remedies, or that the action in question is not ripe for review. Pub. L. No. 94-574 also eliminated several other technical obstacles to suits for judicial review.[4]

---

[4] In addition to amending section 702 to abolish the defense of sovereign immunity, Pub. L. No. 94-574 amended section 703 to deal with the problem of misnomer of government defendants, amended 28 U.S.C. §1331(a) to permit nonstatutory review cases to be brought in district courts on the basis of federal jurisdiction without regard to the amount of controversy, and amended 28 U.S.C. §1391(e) to permit a plaintiff to use the section's provisions for broad venue and extraterritorial service of process against government defendants despite the presence in the action of a nonfederal defendant. These changes had all been recommended by the Administrative Conference. See S. Rep. No. 94-996 and H.R. Rep. No. 94-1656, 94th Cong. 2d Sess., 1976 U.S. Code Cong. & Ad. News 6121.

Jurisdiction. Where the relevant statute expressly provides for judicial review in a particular court or courts, the statute itself operates as a grant of subject matter jurisdiction to the courts specified. In 1977 the Supreme Court, resolving a longstanding conflict of views, held that the Administrative Procedure Act, section 702, was not itself a grant to the federal district courts of jurisdiction over review proceedings (*Califano v. Sanders*, 430 U.S. 99 (1977)). Consequently, the jurisdictional basis for proceedings for review other than those expressly provided for by statute must be found elsewhere, such as chapter 85 of title 28, U.S.C., which describes the jurisdiction of United States district courts. But this is not a problem, because section 1331 of title 28, which grants the district courts original jurisdiction of all civil actions arising under the Constitution, laws, or treaties of the United States, provides an adequate jurisdictional basis for substantially any review proceeding challenging agency action. Prior to 1976, section 1331 could be invoked only when the amount in controversy was at least $10,000. However, Pub. L. No. 94-574, the statute that abolished the sovereign immunity defense, also eliminated the jurisdictional amount in actions against the United States or its officers; in 1980 the jurisdictional amount was deleted in all cases under section 1331.

In the Federal Courts Improvement Act of 1982, Congress authorized any federal court without jurisdiction over a civil action that is filed with it (including a petition for review of agency action) to transfer the action to a court where such cases could have been brought in the first instance, if it is in the interest of justice to do so. 28 U.S.C. §1631. See generally *Air Line Pilots Ass'n, Int'l v. CAB*, 750 F.2d 81, 84-85 (D.C. Cir. 1984).

Forum Selection. 28 U.S.C. §2112 governs the procedures for filing the record on review by the agency in the courts of appeals and the resolution of conflicts where proceedings have been instituted in two or more courts of appeals with respect to the same agency order. Section 2112(a) provides that the agency shall file the record (or, if local court rules permit, a certified list of the materials comprising the record) in a designated court of appeals. If only a single petition for review is filed within 10 days after issuance of an agency's order, the agency shall file the record in that court of appeals notwithstanding the subsequent institution of any other court proceedings for review of the same order. If two or more petitions for review of the same agency order are filed in different courts of appeals within ten days after issuance of the agency's order, the agency shall notify the judicial panel on multidistrict litigation, which shall by means of random selection designate one court of appeals from among the courts in which petitions were filed to hear the case; the panel shall consolidate all petitions for review in that court and the agency shall thereafter file the record in the designated court. In all other circumstances, the agency shall file the record in the court of appeals in which proceedings with respect to the order were first instituted. The random selection provisions in section 2112(a)(3) were established by Pub. L. No. 100-236, 101 Stat. 1731 (1988), to implement the Conference's recommendation to eliminate so-called "races to the courthouse" (Administrative Conference Recommendation 80-5, *Eliminating or Simplifying the "Race to the Courthouse" in Appeals from Agency Action*[5]).

Section 2112(a)(5) requires all courts in which proceedings are instituted, other than the court in which the record is filed, to transfer those proceedings to the court in which the record is filed. The section nonetheless authorizes the court in which the record is filed to transfer all proceedings to any other court of appeals for the convenience of the parties and in the interest of justice.

Bibliography:

I. Legislative History

1. See Chapter 1 on Administrative Procedure Act.
2. *Report to Accompany H.R. 1162*, House Committee on the Judiciary, H.R. Rep. No. 100-72, 100th Cong., 1st Sess. (1987).
3. *Report to Accompany S. 1134*, Senate Committee on the Judiciary, S. Rep. No. 100-263, 100th Cong., 1st Sess. (1987).

II. Book

1. *A Guide to Judicial and Political Review of Federal Agencies* 1-210 (John F. Duffy & Michael Herz eds., A.B.A. 2005).

---

[5] 45 Fed. Reg. 84,954 (Dec. 24, 1980). *See generally* McGarity, *Multi-Party Forum Shopping for Appellate Review of Administrative Action*, Report to the Administrative Conference of the U.S., 129 U. Pa. L. Rev. 302 (1980); 1980 ACUS 437.

Appendix:

1. 5 U.S.C. §§701-706 (2000) (See Chapter 1 Appendix).
2. 28 U.S.C. §§1331, 1631, 2112, 2341-51 (2000).

Judicial Review of Agency Action

Title 28, U.S. Code

§1331. Federal question

The district courts shall have original jurisdiction of all civil actions arising under the Constitution, laws, or treaties of the United States.

(June 25, 1948, ch. 646, 62 Stat. 930; Pub. L. No. 85-554, Sec. 1, July 25, 1958, 72 Stat. 415; Pub. L. No. 94-574, Sec. 2, Oct. 21, 1976, 90 Stat. 2721; Pub. L. No. 96-486, Sec. 2(a), Dec. 1, 1980, 94 Stat. 2369.)

Amendments

1980—Pub. L. No. 96-486 struck out "; amount in controversy; costs" in section catchline, struck out minimum amount in controversy requirement of $10,000 for original jurisdiction in federal question cases which necessitated striking the exception to such required minimum amount that authorized original jurisdiction in actions brought against the United States, any agency thereof, or any officer or employee thereof in an official capacity, struck out provision authorizing the district court except where express provision therefore was made in a federal statute to deny costs to a plaintiff and in fact impose such costs upon such plaintiff where plaintiff was adjudged to be entitled to recover less than the required amount in controversy, computed without regard to set-off or counterclaim and exclusive of interests and costs, and struck out existing subsection designations.

1976—Subsec. (a). Pub. L. No. 94-574 struck out $10,000 jurisdictional amount where action is brought against the United States, any agency thereof, or any officer or employee thereof in his official capacity.

1958—Pub. L. No. 85-554 included costs in section catchline, designated existing provisions as subsec. (a), substituted "$10,000" for "$3,000", and added subsec. (b).

§1631. Transfer to cure want of jurisdiction

Whenever a civil action is filed in a court as defined in section 610 of this title or an appeal, including a petition for review of administrative action, is noticed for or filed with such a court and that court finds that there is a want of jurisdiction, the court shall, if it is in the interest of justice, transfer such action or appeal to any other such court in which the action or appeal could have been brought at the time it was filed or noticed, and the action or appeal shall proceed as if it had been filed in or noticed for the court to which it is transferred on the date upon which it was actually filed in or noticed for the court from which it is transferred.

(Added Pub. L. No. 97-164, title III, Sec. 301(a), Apr. 2, 1982, 96 Stat. 55.)

§2112. Record on review and enforcement of agency orders

(a) The rules prescribed under the authority of section 2072 of this title may provide for the time and manner of filing and the contents of the record in all proceedings instituted in the courts of appeals to enjoin, set aside, suspend, modify, or otherwise review or enforce orders of administrative agencies, boards, commissions, and officers. Such rules may authorize the agency, board, commission, or officer to file in the court a certified list of the materials comprising the record and retain and hold for the court all such materials and transmit the same or any part thereof to the court, when and as required by it, at any time prior to the final determination of the proceeding, and such filing of such certified list of the materials comprising the record and such subsequent transmittal of any such materials when and as required shall be deemed full compliance with any provision of law requiring the filing of the record in the court. The record in such proceedings shall be certified and filed in or held for and transmitted to the court of appeals by the agency, board, commission, or officer concerned within the time and in the manner prescribed by such rules. If proceedings are instituted in two or more courts of appeals with respect to the same order, the following shall apply:

(1) If within ten days after issuance of the order the agency, board, commission, or officer concerned receives, from the persons instituting the proceedings, the petition for review with respect to proceedings in at least two courts of appeals, the agency, board, commission, or officer shall proceed in accordance with paragraph (3) of this subsection. If within ten days after the issuance of the order the agency, board, commission, or officer concerned receives, from the persons instituting the proceedings, the petition for review with respect to proceedings in only one court of appeals, the agency, board, commission, or officer shall file the record in that court notwithstanding the institution in any other court of appeals of proceedings for review of that order. In all other cases in which proceedings have been instituted in two or more courts of appeals with respect to the same order, the agency, board,

commission, or officer concerned shall file the record in the court in which proceedings with respect to the order were first instituted.

(2) For purposes of paragraph (1) of this subsection, a copy of the petition or other pleading which institutes proceedings in a court of appeals and which is stamped by the court with the date of filing shall constitute the petition for review. Each agency, board, commission, or officer, as the case may be, shall designate by rule the office and the officer who must receive petitions for review under paragraph (1).

(3) If an agency, board, commission, or officer receives two or more petitions for review of an order in accordance with the first sentence of paragraph (1) of this subsection, the agency, board, commission, or officer shall, promptly after the expiration of the ten-day period specified in that sentence, so notify the judicial panel on multidistrict litigation authorized by section 1407 of this title, in such form as that panel shall prescribe. The judicial panel on multidistrict litigation shall, by means of random selection, designate one court of appeals, from among the courts of appeals in which petitions for review have been filed and received within the ten-day period specified in the first sentence of paragraph (1), in which the record is to be filed, and shall issue an order consolidating the petitions for review in that court of appeals. The judicial panel on multidistrict litigation shall, after providing notice to the public and an opportunity for the submission of comments, prescribe rules with respect to the consolidation of proceedings under this paragraph. The agency, board, commission, or officer concerned shall file the record in the court of appeals designated pursuant to this paragraph.

(4) Any court of appeals in which proceedings with respect to an order of an agency, board, commission, or officer have been instituted may, to the extent authorized by law, stay the effective date of the order. Any such stay may thereafter be modified, revoked, or extended by a court of appeals designated pursuant to paragraph (3) with respect to that order or by any other court of appeals to which the proceedings are transferred.

(5) All courts in which proceedings are instituted with respect to the same order, other than the court in which the record is filed pursuant to this subsection, shall transfer those proceedings to the court in which the record is so filed. For the convenience of the parties in the interest of justice, the court in which the record is filed may hereafter transfer all the proceedings with respect to that order to any other court ofappeals.

(b) The record to be filed in the court of appeals in such a proceeding shall consist of the order sought to be reviewed or enforced, the findings or report upon which it is based, and the pleadings, evidence, and proceedings before the agency, board, commission, or officer concerned, or such portions thereof (1) as the rules prescribed under the authority of section 2072 of this title may require to be included therein, or (2) as the agency, board, commission, or officer concerned, the petitioner for review or respondent in enforcement, as the case may be, and any intervenor in the court proceeding by written stipulation filed with the agency, board, commission, or officer concerned or in the court in any such proceeding may consistently with the rules prescribed under the authority of section 2072 of this title designate to be included therein, or (3) as the court upon motion of a party or, after a prehearing conference, upon its own motion may by order in any such proceeding designate to be included therein. Such a stipulation or order may provide in an appropriate case that no record need be filed in the court of appeals. If, however, the correctness of a finding of fact by the agency, board, commission, or officer is in question all of the evidence before the agency, board, commission, or officer shall be included in the record except such as the agency, board, commission, or officer concerned, the petitioner for review or respondent in enforcement, as the case may be, and any intervenor in the court proceeding by written stipulation filed with the agency, board, commission, or officer concerned or in the court agree to omit as wholly immaterial to the questioned finding. If there is omitted from the record any portion of the proceedings before the agency, board, commission, or officer which the court subsequently determines to be proper for it to consider to enable it to review or enforce the order in question the court may direct that such additional portion of the proceedings be filed as a supplement to the record. The agency, board, commission, or officer concerned may, at its option and without regard to the foregoing provisions of this subsection, and if so requested by the petitioner for review or respondent in enforcement shall, file in the court the entire record of the proceedings before it without abbreviation.

(c) The agency, board, commission, or officer concerned may transmit to the court of appeals the original papers comprising the whole or any part of the record or any supplemental record, otherwise true copies of such papers certified by an authorized officer or deputy of the agency, board, commission, or officer concerned shall be transmitted. Any original papers thus transmitted to the court of appeals shall be returned to the agency, board, commission, or officer concerned upon the final determination of the review or enforcement proceeding. Pending such final determination any such papers may be returned by the court temporarily to the custody of the agency, board, commission, or officer concerned if needed for the transaction of the public business. Certified copies of any papers included in the record or any supplemental record may also be returned to the agency, board, commission, or officer concerned upon the final determination of review or enforcement proceedings.

(d) The provisions of this section are not applicable to proceedings to review decisions of the Tax Court of the United States or to proceedings to review or enforce those orders of administrative agencies, boards, commissions, or officers which are by law reviewable or enforceable by the district courts.

(Added Pub. L. No. 85-791, Sec. 2, Aug. 28, 1958, 72 Stat. 941; amended Pub. L. No. 89-773, Sec. 5(a), (b), Nov. 6, 1966, 80 Stat. 1323; Pub. L. No. 100-236, Sec. 1, Jan. 8, 1988, 101 Stat. 1731.)

Amendments

1988—Subsec. (a). Pub. L. No. 100-236 substituted "If proceedings are instituted in two or more courts of appeals with respect to the same order, the following shall apply:" and pars. (1) to (5) for "If proceedings have been instituted in two or more courts of appeals with respect to the same order the agency, board, commission, or officer concerned shall file the record in that one of such courts in which a proceeding with respect to such order was first instituted. The other courts in which such proceedings are pending shall thereupon transfer them to the court of appeals in which the record has been filed. For the convenience of the parties in the interest of justice such court may thereafter transfer all the proceedings with respect to such order to any other court of appeals."

1966—Subsec. (a). Pub. L. No. 89-773, Sec. 5(a), substituted "The rules prescribed under the authority of section 2072 of this title may provide for the time and manner of filing" for "The several courts of appeal shall have power to adopt, with the approval of the Judicial Conference of the United States, rules, which so far as practicable shall be uniform in all such courts prescribing the time and manner of filing." See section 2072 of this title. Subsec. (b). Pub. L. No. 89-773, Sec. 5(b), substituted "the rules prescribed under the authority of section 2072 of this title" for "the said rules of the court of appeals" and for "the rules of such court".

§2341. Definitions

As used in this chapter—

(1) "clerk" means the clerk of the court in which the petition for the review of an order, reviewable under this chapter, is filed;

(2) "petitioner" means the party or parties by whom a petition to review an order, reviewable under this chapter, is filed; and

(3) "agency" means—

(A) the Commission, when the order sought to be reviewed was entered by the Federal Communications Commission, the Federal Maritime Commission, or the Atomic Energy Commission, as the case may be;

(B) the Secretary, when the order was entered by the Secretary of Agriculture or the Secretary of Transportation;

(C) the Administration, when the order was entered by the Maritime Administration;

(D) the Secretary, when the order is under section 812 of the Fair Housing Act; and

(E) the Board, when the order was entered by the Surface Transportation Board.

(Added Pub. L. No. 89-554, Sec. 4(e), Sept. 6, 1966, 80 Stat. 622; amended Pub. L. No. 93-584, Sec. 3, Jan. 2, 1975, 88 Stat. 1917; Pub. L. No. 100-430, Sec. 11(b), Sept. 13, 1988, 102 Stat. 1635; Pub. L. No. 102-365, Sec. 5(c)(1), Sept. 3, 1992, 106 Stat. 975; Pub. L. No. 104-88, title III, Sec. 305(d)(1)-(4), Dec. 29, 1995, 109 Stat. 945.)

AMENDMENTS

1995—Par. (3)(A). Pub. L. No. 104-88, Sec. 305(d)(1), struck out "the Interstate Commerce Commission," after "Maritime Commission,". Par. (3)(E). Pub. L. No. 104-88, Sec. 305(d)(2)-(4), added subpar. (E).

1992—Par. (3)(B). Pub. L. No. 102-365 inserted "or the Secretary of Transportation" after "Secretary of Agriculture".

1988—Par. (3)(D). Pub. L. No. 100-430 added subpar. (D).

1975—Par. (3)(A). Pub. L. No. 93-584 inserted reference to the Interstate Commerce Commission.

§2342. Jurisdiction of court of appeals

The court of appeals (other than the United States Court of Appeals for the Federal Circuit) has exclusive jurisdiction to enjoin, set aside, suspend (in whole or in part), or to determine the validity of—

(1) all final orders of the Federal Communication Commission made reviewable by section 402(a) of title 47;

(2) all final orders of the Secretary of Agriculture made under chapters 9 and 20A of title 7, except orders issued under sections 210(e), 217a, and 499g(a) of title 7;

(3) all rules, regulations, or final orders of—
   (A) the Secretary of Transportation issued pursuant to section 50501, 50502, 56101-56104 or 57109 of title 46 or pursuant to part B or C of subtitle IV, subchapter III of chapter 311, chapter 313, or chapter 315 of title 49; and
   (B) the Federal Maritime Commission issued pursuant to section 305, 41304, 41308, or 41309 or chapter 421 or 441 of title 46;
(4) all final orders of the Atomic Energy Commission made reviewable by section 2239 of title 42;
(5) all rules, regulations, or final orders of the Surface Transportation Board made reviewable by section 2321 of this title;
(6) all final orders under section 812 of the Fair Housing Act; and
(7) all final agency actions described in section 20114(c) of title 49.
Jurisdiction is invoked by filing a petition as provided by section 2344 of this title.

(Added Pub. L. No. 89-554, Sec. 4(e), Sept. 6, 1966, 80 Stat. 622; amended Pub. L. No. 93-584, Sec. 4, Jan. 2, 1975, 88 Stat. 1917; Pub. L. No. 95-454, title II, Sec. 206, Oct. 13, 1978, 92 Stat. 1144; Pub. L. No. 96-454, Sec. 8(b)(2), Oct. 15, 1980, 94 Stat. 2021; Pub. L. No. 97-164, title I, Sec. 137, Apr. 2, 1982, 96 Stat. 41; Pub. L. No. 98-554, title II, Sec. 227(a)(4), Oct. 30, 1984, 98 Stat. 2852; Pub. L. No. 99-336, Sec. 5(a), June 19, 1986, 100 Stat. 638; Pub. L. No. 100-430, Sec. 11(a), Sept. 13, 1988, 102 Stat. 1635; Pub. L. No. 102-365, Sec. 5(c)(2), Sept. 3, 1992, 106 Stat. 975; Pub. L. No. 103-272, Sec. 5(h), July 5, 1994, 108 Stat. 1375; Pub. L. No. 104-88, title III, Sec. 305(d)(5)-(8), Dec. 29, 1995, 109 Stat. 945; Pub. L. No. 104-287, Sec. 6(f)(2), Oct. 11, 1996, 110 Stat. 3399; Pub. L. No. 109-59, Title IV, § 4125(a), Aug. 10, 2005, 119 Stat. 1738; Pub. L. No. 109-304, § 17(f)(3), Oct. 6, 2006, 120 Stat. 1708.)

Amendments

2006—Subsec. (3)(A). Pub.L. 109-304, § 17(f)(3)(A), struck out "section 2, 9, 37, or 41 of the Shipping Act, 1916 (46 U.S.C. App. 802, 803, 808, 835, 839, and 841a)" and inserted "section 50501, 50502, 56101-56104, or 57109 of title 46". Subsec. (3)(B). Pub.L. 109-304, § 17(f)(3)(B), rewrote subpar. (B), which formerly read:

"(B) the Federal Maritime Commission issued pursuant to—

"(i) section 19 of the Merchant Marine Act, 1920 (46 U.S.C. App. 876);

"(ii) section 14 or 17 of the Shipping Act of 1984 (46 U.S.C. App.1713 or 1716); or

"(iii) section 2(d) or 3(d) of the Act of November 6, 1966 (46 U.S.C. App. 817d(d) or 817e(d);

"[(iv) and (v) Redesignated (ii) and (iii)]".

2005—Par. (3)(A). Pub.L. 109-59, § 4125(a), in subpar. (A), inserted ", subchapter III of chapter 311, chapter 313, or chapter 315" before "of title 49".

1996—Par. (3)(A). Pub. L. No. 104-287 amended Pub. L. No. 104-88, Sec. 305(d)(6). See 1995 Amendment note below.

1995—Par. (3)(A). Pub. L. No. 104-88, Sec. 305(d)(6), as amended by Pub. L. No. 104-287, inserted "or pursuant to part B or C of subtitle IV of title 49" before the semicolon. Pub. L. No. 104-88, Sec. 305(d)(5), substituted "or 41" for "41, or 43". Par. (3)(B). Pub. L. No. 104-88, Sec. 305(d)(7), redesignated cls. (ii), (iv), and (v) as (i), (ii), and (iii), respectively, and struck out former cls. (i) and (iii) which read as follows: "(i) section 23, 25, or 43 of the Shipping Act, 1916 (46 U.S.C. App. 822, 824, or 841a); "(iii) section 2, 3, 4, or 5 of the Intercoastal Shipping Act, 1933 (46 U.S.C. App. 844, 845, 845a, or 845b);". Par. (5). Pub. L. No. 104-88, Sec. 305(d)(8), added par. (5) and struck out former par. (5) which read as follows: "all rules, regulations, or final orders of the Interstate Commerce Commission made reviewable by section 2321 of this title and all final orders of such Commission made reviewable under section 11901(j)(2) of title 49, United States Code;".

1994—Par. (7). Pub. L. No. 103-272 substituted "section 20114(c) of title 49" for "section 202(f) of the Federal Railroad Safety Act of 1970".

1992—Par. (7). Pub. L. No. 102-365, which directed the addition of par. (7) at end, was executed by adding par. (7) after par. (6) and before concluding provisions, to reflect the probable intent of Congress.

1988—Par. (6). Pub. L. No. 100-430 added par. (6).

1986—Par. (3). Pub. L. No. 99-336 amended par. (3) generally. Prior to amendment, par. (3) read as follows: "such final orders of the Federal Maritime Commission or the Maritime Administration entered under chapters 23 and 23A of title 46 as are subject to judicial review under section 830 of title 46;".

1984—Par. (5). Pub. L. No. 98-554 substituted "11901(j)(2)" for "11901(i)(2)".

1982—Pub. L. No. 97-164 inserted "(other than the United States Court of Appeals for the Federal Circuit)" after "court of appeals" in provisions preceding par. (1), and struck out par. (6) which had given the court of appeals jurisdiction in cases involving all final orders of the Merit Systems Protection Board except as provided for in section 7703(b) of title 5. See section 1295(a)(9) of this title.

1980—Par. (5). Pub. L. No. 96-454 inserted "and all final orders of such Commission made reviewable under section 11901(i)(2) of title 49, United States Code" after "section 2321 of this title".

1978—Par. (6). Pub. L. No. 95-454 added par. (6).

1975—Par. (5). Pub. L. No. 93-584 added par. (5).

§2343. Venue

The venue of a proceeding under this chapter is in the judicial circuit in which the petitioner resides or has its principal office, or in the United States Court of Appeals for the District of Columbia Circuit.

(Added Pub. L. No. 89-554, Sec. 4(e), Sept. 6, 1966, 80 Stat. 622.)

§2344. Review of orders; time; notice; contents of petition; service

On the entry of a final order reviewable under this chapter, the agency shall promptly give notice thereof by service or publication in accordance with its rules. Any party aggrieved by the final order may, within 60 days after its entry, file a petition to review the order in the court of appeals wherein venue lies. The action shall be against the United States. The petition shall contain a concise statement of—
(1) the nature of the proceedings as to which review is sought;
(2) the facts on which venue is based;
(3) the grounds on which relief sought; and
(4) the relief prayed.

The petitioner shall attach to the petition, as exhibits, copies of the order, report, or decision of the agency. The clerk shall serve a true copy of the petition on the agency and on the Attorney General by registered mail, with request for a return receipt.

(Added Pub. L. No. 89-554, Sec. 4(e), Sept. 6, 1966, 80 Stat. 622.)

§2345. Prehearing conference

The court of appeals may hold a prehearing conference or direct a judge of the court to hold a prehearing conference.

(Added Pub. L. No. 89-554, Sec. 4(e), Sept. 6, 1966, 80 Stat. 622.)

§2346. Certification of record on review

Unless the proceeding has been terminated on a motion to dismiss the petition, the agency shall file in the office of the clerk the record on review as provided by section 2112 of this title.

(Added Pub. L. No. 89-554, Sec. 4(e), Sept. 6, 1966, 80 Stat. 623.)

§2347. Petitions to review; proceedings

(a) Unless determined on a motion to dismiss, petitions to review orders reviewable under this chapter are heard in the court of appeals on the record of the pleadings, evidence adduced and proceedings before the agency, when the agency has held a hearing whether or not required to do so by law.

(b) When the agency has not held a hearing before taking the action of which review is sought by the petition, the court of appeals shall determine whether a hearing is required by law. After that determination, the court shall—

(1) remand the proceedings to the agency to hold a hearing, when a hearing is required by law;

(2) pass on the issues presented, when a hearing is not required by law and it appears from the pleadings and affidavits filed by the parties that no genuine issue of material fact is presented; or

(3) transfer the proceedings to a district court for the district in which the petitioner resides or has its principal office for a hearing and determination as if the proceedings were originally initiated in the district court, when a hearing is not required by law and a genuine issue of material fact is presented. The procedure in these cases in the district court is governed by the Federal Rules of Civil Procedure.

(c) If a party to a proceeding to review applies to the court of appeals in which the proceeding is pending for leave to adduce additional evidence and shows to the satisfaction of the court that—

(1) the additional evidence is material; and

(2) there were reasonable grounds for failure to adduce the evidence before the agency; the court may order the additional evidence and any counterevidence the opposite party desires to offer to be taken by the agency. The agency may modify its findings of fact, or make new findings, by reason of the additional evidence so taken, and may modify or set aside its order, and shall file in the court the additional evidence, the modified findings or new findings, and the modified order or the order setting aside the original order.

(Added Pub. L. No. 89-554, Sec. 4(e), Sept. 6, 1966, 80 Stat. 623.)

§2348. Representation in proceeding; intervention

The Attorney General is responsible for and has control of the interests of the Government in all court proceedings under this chapter. The agency, and any party in interest in the proceeding before the agency whose interests will be affected if an order of the agency is or is not enjoined, set aside, or suspended, may appear as parties thereto of their own motion and as of right, and be represented by counsel in any proceeding to review the order. Communities, associations, corporations, firms, and individuals, whose interests are affected by the order of the agency, may intervene in any proceeding to review the order. The Attorney General may not dispose of or discontinue the proceeding to review over the objection of any party or intervenor, but any intervenor may prosecute, defend, or continue the proceeding unaffected by the action or inaction of the Attorney General.

(Added Pub. L. No. 89-554, Sec. 4(e), Sept. 6, 1966, 80 Stat. 623.)

§2349. Jurisdiction of the proceeding

(a) The court of appeals has jurisdiction of the proceeding on the filing and service of a petition to review. The court of appeals in which the record on review is filed, on the filing, has jurisdiction to vacate stay orders or interlocutory injunctions previously granted by any court, and has exclusive jurisdiction to make and enter, on the petition, evidence, and proceedings set forth in the record on review, a judgment determining the validity of, and enjoining, setting aside, or suspending, in whole or in part, the order of the agency.

(b) The filing of the petition to review does not of itself stay or suspend the operation of the order of the agency, but the court of appeals in its discretion may restrain or suspend, in whole or in part, the operation of the order pending the final hearing and determination of the petition. When the petitioner makes application for an interlocutory injunction restraining or suspending the enforcement, operation, or execution of, or setting aside, in whole or in part, any order reviewable under this chapter, at least 5 days' notice of the hearing thereon shall be given to the agency and to the Attorney General. In a case in which irreparable damage would otherwise result to the petitioner, the court of appeals may, on hearing, after reasonable notice to the agency and to the Attorney General, order a temporary stay or suspension, in whole or in part, of the operation of the order of the agency for not more than 60 days from the date of the order pending the hearing on the application for the interlocutory injunction, in which case the order of the court of appeals shall contain a specific finding, based on evidence submitted to the court of appeals, and identified by reference thereto, that irreparable damage would result to the petitioner and specifying the nature of the damage. The court of appeals, at the time of hearing the application for an interlocutory injunction, on a like finding, may continue the temporary stay or suspension, in whole or in part, until decision on the application.

(Added Pub. L. No. 89-554, Sec. 4(e), Sept. 6, 1966, 80 Stat. 624; amended Pub. L. No. 98-620, title IV, Sec. 402(29)(F), Nov. 8, 1984, 98 Stat. 3359.)

Amendments

1984—Subsec. (b). Pub. L. No. 98-620 struck out provisions that the hearing on an application for an interlocutory injunction be given preference and expedited and heard at the earliest practicable date after the expiration of the notice of hearing on the application, and that on the final hearing of any proceeding to review any order under this chapter, the same requirements as to precedence and expedition was to apply.

§2350. Review in Supreme Court on certiorari or certification

(a) An order granting or denying an interlocutory injunction under section 2349(b) of this title and a final judgment of the court of appeals in a proceeding to review under this chapter are subject to review by the Supreme Court on a writ of certiorari as provided by section 1254(1) of this title. Application for the writ shall be made within 45 days after entry of the order and within 90 days after entry of the judgment, as the case may be. The United States, the agency, or an aggrieved party may file a petition for a writ of certiorari.

(b) The provisions of section 1254(2) of this title, regarding certification, and of section 2101(f) of this title, regarding stays, also apply to proceedings under this chapter.

(Added Pub. L. No. 89-554, Sec. 4(e), Sept. 6, 1966, 80 Stat. 624; amended Pub. L. No. 100-352, Sec. 5(e), June 27, 1988, 102 Stat. 663.)

Amendments

1988—Subsec. (b). Pub. L. No. 100-352 substituted "1254(2)" for "1254(3)".

§2351. Enforcement of orders by district courts

The several district courts have jurisdiction specifically to enforce, and to enjoin and restrain any person from violating any order issued under section 193 of title 7.

(Added Pub. L. No. 89-554, Sec. 4(e), Sept. 6, 1966, 80 Stat. 624.)

Congressional Review of Agency Rulemaking

Citations:

5. U.S.C. §§801-808 (2000); enacted March 29, 1996 by Pub. L. No. 104-121, §251, 110 Stat. 847, 868-74.

Lead Agencies:

No one single agency is charged with overseeing the Act. Various executive and legislative branch agencies have responsibilities: The Office of Information and Regulatory Affairs (OIRA) in the Office of Management and Budget, Eisenhower Executive Office Building, 1650 Pennsylvania Avenue NW, Washington, DC 20502, (202) 395-4852, determines which rules are "major" rules.

Agencies must submit rules to both Houses of Congress: House Clerk, Room H-154, the Capitol, Washington, DC 20515-6601, (202) 225-7000 and the Secretary of the Senate, Room S-312, the Capitol, Washington, DC 20510-7100, (202) 224-3622; and to the General Counsel, Government Accountability Office, Room 7167, 441 G Street, NW, Washington, DC 20548, (202) 512-5400.

Overview:

The Small Business Regulatory Enforcement Fairness Act of 1996, enacted as Title II of the Contract with America Advancement Act (Pub. L. No. 104-121), included a Subtitle E that created a process for Congressional review of agency rulemaking. It added a new chapter 8 to title 5 of the U.S.C. In an effort to increase accountability for costly rules, this Act mandates that agencies must submit a copy to Congress which then has the opportunity to use expedited procedures to pass a joint resolution of disapproval of the rule. It was effective upon enactment (March 29, 1996).

Summary of procedure. The principal provisions of section 801 may be summarized briefly. Subsection (a)(1)(A) defines the basic procedure that the agency must follow. Before a rule can take effect, the agency must submit a report to each House of Congress and to the Comptroller General (GAO) containing a copy of the rule and indicating whether it is a major rule or not. A copy of any cost-benefit analysis of the rule, and the agency statements made under any other acts (such as the Unfunded Mandates Reform Act, the Paperwork Reduction Act, or the Regulatory Flexibility Act) must also be submitted. For major rules, the Comptroller has 15 days after submission to provide a report to the committees of jurisdiction in each House of Congress.

Major and non-major rules. The term "rule" as used in the Congressional Review Act follows the definition found in the Administrative Procedure Act. Section 804(1). The term "rule," therefore, includes rules that may be exempt from the APA's notice-and-comment procedures such as, statements of general policy, interpretive rules, and rules relating to government grants, benefits, contracts, etc. A "major rule" is defined as a rule that has resulted in, or is likely to result in, an annual effect on the economy of one million dollars or more, a major increase in cost of prices for consumers or industry, or significant adverse effects on competition, employment, investment, productivity, or competition of prices in foreign markets. Section 804(2). The effective date of non-major rules is not delayed by the Act, but the effective date of major rules is delayed at least 60 days from the date the rule is published in the *Federal Register* or from the date the agency's report on the rule is submitted (whichever is later) (unless a resolution of disapproval is defeated during that time). Section 801(3). However all rules for which the agency has invoked the "good cause" exemption in the APA from notice and comment procedures are effective immediately, as are rules concerning hunting, fishing and camping. Section 808.

Exemptions. The following types of rules are exempted from congressional review: (1) rules of particular applicability (including rules that approve or prescribes for future rates, wages, prices, etc.); (2) rules relating to agency management or personnel; and (3) rules of agency organization, procedure, or practice that do not substantially affect the rights or obligations of non-agency parties. Section 804(3).[1] Also excluded are rules pro-

---

[1] *See, e.g.,* U.S. Gen. Accounting Office, Letter B-292045 to Rep. Lane Evans (May 19, 2003) (concluding that a DVA memorandum terminating a discretionary loan program was not a covered "rule" under the CRA because it was a "rule relating to 'agency management' or 'agency organization, procedure, or practice that does not substantially affect the rights or obligations of non-agency parties'").

mulgated by the FCC under the Telecommunications Act of 1996, and Federal Reserve Board monetary rules.

Congressional Procedures. The Act allows for any Member of Congress to introduce a resolution of disapproval. The disapproval takes effect with agreement of both Houses and presentment to the President. If the President vetoes the joint resolution, Congress then has the opportunity to override the veto.

The CRA also contains complicated provisions in section 802 on how days are counted for the purposes of the expedited legislative process for considering joint resolutions of disapproval.[2] For example, as long as a resolution of disapproval is introduced within 60 calendar days (but not counting periods when either house is adjourned for longer than three days) of receipt of the rule and report, there is no time limit on congressional action on that resolution during that Congress.

There are also procedures, primarily designed to prevent Senate filibusters, that require a discharge from committee and floor debate on the resolution when at least 30 Members so petition. Expedited consideration of resolutions already approved by one House are also included.

Under section 801(f), once a resolution of disapproval is enacted, a new rule that had already gone into effect is "treated as though such rule had never taken effect." Moreover when a rule is disapproved, a new rule that is "substantially the same" as the disapproved rule may not be issued unless authorized by subsequent law.

Judicial Review. The judicial review provision is found in section 805, and states that no action or omission in this chapter is subject to judicial review. Section 801(g) provides that if the Congress does not enact a joint resolution of disapproval, "no court or agency may infer any intent of the Congress from any action or inaction...."

Impact of the Law. While a large number of rules are sent to Congress each week, the impact of the CRA on the rulemaking process has been slight. So far, only one rule has been disapproved and few resolutions of disapproval have even been introduced. The disapproval occurred in March 2001 when the Congressional leadership, supported by the Bush Administration, successfully used the Congressional Review Act to overturn OSHA's controversial ergonomic regulations. President Clinton had issued final er-

---

[2] The CRA's drafters met the dictates of *INS v. Chadha*, 462 U.S. 919 (1983), by requiring that rules could only be rejected through joint resolutions, which require passage by both Houses and "presentment" to the President for signature or veto.

gonomic regulations in November 2000, but the rules did not take effect until January 16, 2001, four days before Clinton left office. *See* 65 Fed. Reg. 68,262 (Nov. 14, 2000). After the inauguration of President Bush, the Republican-controlled Senate and House voted to approve the Joint Resolution of disapproval and President Bush signed it into law.[3]

This was an unusual circumstance because the rule in question was a rule approved by a previous administration and, due to the holdover provision in the law, was subject to review by a Congress and new President controlled by the other party. It should be remembered that enactment requires either signing (normally) by the same President whose OMB has already cleared the rule or a very rare veto override—so the number of rules to be overturned through this mechanism will likely be low.[4]

Legislative History:

The legislation that was to become the Congressional Review Act was included in several Senate "comprehensive regulatory reform bills" considered in the 104th Congress. The Judiciary Committee's bill, S. 343, introduced by Majority Leader Dole (R-KS) on February 2, 1995 did not contain this provision originally. Subcommittee hearings were held on February 22, and full Committee hearings on March 17. On May 26 it was jointly reported to the Senate by both the Judiciary and Governmental Affairs Committee and contained a simplified version of the Congressional Review Act. Ultimately S. 343 failed to achieve cloture in floor votes and was not passed. Other bills which did not reach a floor vote included a similar provision: the Governmental Affairs Committee bill, S. 291, introduced by Sen. Roth (R-DE) which was reported by that Committee on May 25, 1995, and an alternative bill introduced in June by the ranking member of that Committee, Senator Glenn (D-OH), S. 1001.

---

[3] For House and Senate votes on Pub L. 107-5, see CONG. REC. H684, Mar. 7, 2001, roll call no. 33, CONG. REC. S51888, CONG. REC. H684, roll call no. 33. (Mar. 7, 2001), and CONG. REC. S51888, vote no. 15 (Mar. 6, 2001).

[4] Of course, the rules of independent agencies are not reviewed by OMB and are less controllable by the President. So it is more likely perhaps that a rule from such an agency might be made subject to such a resolution. *See e.g.*, H. J. Res. 72 & S. J. Res. 17, 108th Cong., 1st Sess. (disapproving a rule submitted by the Federal Communications Commission with respect to broadcast media ownership). The matter was subsequently addressed in an appropriations rider instead.

Although these comprehensive bills lacked enough bipartisan support to be enacted, the Congressional review provisions attracted support from both parties. In the next session, Rep. Archer (R-TX) introduced H.R. 3136 (the bill that ultimately was enacted as Pub. L. No. 104-21), on March 29, 1996. Its title at the time of introduction was "A bill to provide for enactment of the Senior Citizens' Right to Work Act of 1996, the Line Item Veto Act, and the Small Business Growth and Fairness Act of 1996, and to provide for a permanent increase in the public debt limit." Subtitle E contained the more complicated version of the Congressional Review Act that was subsequently enacted. The bill was subsequently reported for floor action by the Rules Committee as the "Contract With America Advancement Act of 1996." (See H. Res. 392, approved by recorded vote in the House on March 28, 1996.)

The bill was amended to add several other "regulatory reform" provisions acceptable to the White House—some of which derived from H.R. 9, the "Job Creation and Wage Enhancement Act of 1995" (the legislation introduced at the beginning of the 104th Congress to implement the original "Contract With America."). As passed by the House, H.R. 3136 was quickly sent to the Senate and was approved by unanimous consent. It was signed into law by President Clinton the next day.

Bibliography:

I. Legislative History

1. *Regulatory Reform*, hearings before the Senate Committee on Governmental Affairs, 104th Cong. 1st Sess. (Feb. 7, 8, 15, Mar. 8, 1995).

2. *Comprehensive Regulatory Reform Act of 1995*, hearings before the Subcommittee on Administrative Oversight and the Courts, Senate Committee on the Judiciary, 104th Cong. 1st Sess. (Feb. 22, 24, 1995).

3. *Regulatory Reform*, hearings before the Senate Committee on the Judiciary, 104th Cong. 1st Sess. (Mar. 17, 1995).

4. *S. 291, Regulatory Reform Act of 1995*, Senate Committee on Governmental Affairs, Sen. Rep. 104-88, 104th Cong. 1st Sess. (May 25, 1995).

5. *Comprehensive Regulatory Reform Act of 1995: S.343*, Senate Committee on the Judiciary, Sen. Rep. 104-89, 104th Cong. 1st Sess. (May 26, 1995).

6. *Comprehensive Regulatory Reform Act of 1995: S.343*, Senate Committee on the Judiciary, Sen. Rep. 104-90, 104th Cong. 1st Sess. (May 26, 1995).

7. *H. Res 391, Providing for the Consideration of H.R. 3136, the Contract With America Advancement Act of 1996*, House Rules Committee, House Rep. 104-500 (Mar. 27, 1996).

II. Other Government Documents

1. Administrator, Office of Information and Regulatory Affairs, Office of Management and Budget, Memorandum for Heads of Executive Departments, Agencies, and Independent Establishments, *New Statutory Procedures for Regulations* (April 2, 1996).

2. *Oversight Hearings on the Congressional Review Act*, Hearings before the Subcommittee on Commercial and Administrative Law of the House Committee on the Judiciary, 105th Congress, 1st Sess. (March 6, 1997).

3. U.S. General Accounting Office, *Regulatory Reform: Major Rules Submitted for Congressional Review During the First 2 Years*, (letter to Members of Congress), GAO/GGD-98-102R (April 24, 1998).

4. U.S. General Accounting Office, *Congressional Review Act: Update on Implementation and Coordination*, T-OGC-98-55 (June 17, 1998).

5. U.S. General Accounting Office, *Comments on Whether EPA Interim Guidance Is a Rule Under the Congressional Review Act*, B-281575 (Jan. 20, 1999).

6. Office of Information and Regulatory Affairs, Office of Management and Budget, *Form for Submission of Federal Rules Under the Congressional Review Act* (March 23, 1999).

7. Morton Rosenberg, *Congressional Review of Agency Rulemaking: An Update and Assessment of the Congressional Review Act After Ten Years* (CRS Report for Congress, American Law Division) (RL30116) (March 29, 2006), available at http://www.opencrs.com/rpts/RL30116_20060329.pdf.

8. Richard S. Beth, *Disapproval of Regulations by Congress: Procedure Under the Congressional Review Act* (CRS Report for Congress Oct. 10, 2001), available at http://www.senate.gov/reference/resources/pdf/RL31160.pdf.

9. U.S. Government Accountability Office, *Federal Rulemaking: Perspectives on 10 Years of Congressional Review Act Implementation*, GAO-06-601T (Mar. 30, 2006).

10. U.S. Government Accountability Office, *Congressional Review Act*, Statement of Gary Kepplinger, General Counsel. Before the Subcommittee on Commercial and Adminsitrative Law, Committee on the Judiciary, House of Representatives, GAO-08-268T (Nov. 6, 2007). *[For a full list of GAO "opinions and testimonies" concerning the Congressional Review Act, see http://www.gao.gov/decisions/cra/index.html.]*

III. Books and Articles

1. Daniel Cohen & Peter L. Strauss, *Congressional Review of Agency Regulations*, 49 Admin. L. Rev. 95 (1997).
2. James T. O'Reilly, *FDA Rulemaking After the 104th Congress: Major Rules Enter the Twilight Zone of Review*, 51 Food & Drug L.J. 677 (1996).
3. Peter A. Pfohl, *Congressional Review of Agency Rulemaking: The 104th Congress and the Salvage Timber Directive*, 14 J. L. & Politics 1 (1998).
4. Morton Rosenberg, *Whatever Happened to Congressional Review of Rulemaking?: A Brief Overview, Assessment, and Proposal for Reform*, 51 Admin. L. Rev. 1051 (1999).
5. Steven J. Balla, *Legislative Organization and Congressional Review of Agency Regulations*, 16 J.L. Econ. & Org. 424 (2000).
6. Julie A. Parks, *Comment, Lessons In Politics: Initial Use Of The Congressional Review Act*, 55 Admin. L. Rev. 187 (2003).

Appendix:

1. 5 U.S.C. Chapter 8 (§§801-808) (2000) ("Congressional Review of Agency Rulemaking").
2. Office of Information and Regulatory Affairs, Office of Management and Budget, *Form for Submission of Federal Rules Under the Congressional Review Act* (Mar. 23, 1999).

Congressional Review of Agency Rulemaking

Title 5, U. S. Code

§801. Congressional review

(a)(1)(A) Before a rule can take effect, the Federal agency promulgating such rule shall submit to each House of the Congress and to the Comptroller General a report containing—
>(i) a copy of the rule
>(ii) a concise general statement relating to the rule, including whether it is a major rule; and
>(iii) the proposed effective date of the rule.

(B) On the date of the submission of the report under subparagraph (A), the Federal agency promulgating the rule shall submit to the Comptroller General and make available to each House of Congress—
>(i) a complete copy of the cost-benefit analysis of the rule, if any;
>(ii) the agency's actions relevant to sections 603, 604, 605, 607, and 609;
>(iii) the agency's actions relevant to sections 202, 203, 204, and 205 of the Unfunded Mandates Reform Act of 1995; and
>(iv) any other relevant information or requirements under any other Act and any relevant Executive orders.

(C) Upon receipt of a report submitted under subparagraph (A), each House shall provide copies of the report to the chairman and ranking member of each standing committee with jurisdiction under the rules of the House of Representatives or the Senate to report a bill to amend the provision of law under which the rule is issued.

(2)(A) The Comptroller General shall provide a report on each major rule to the committees of jurisdiction in each House of the Congress by the end of 15 calendar days after the submission or publication date as provided in section 802(b)(2). The report of the Comptroller General shall include an assessment of the agency's compliance with procedural steps required by paragraph (1)(B).

(B) Federal agencies shall cooperate with the Comptroller General by providing information relevant to the Comptroller General's report under subparagraph (A).

(3) A major rule relating to a report submitted under paragraph (1) shall take effect on the latest of—

(A) the later of the date occurring 60 days after the date on which—
> (i) Congress receives the report submitted under paragraph (1); or
> (ii) rule is published in the *Federal Register*, if so published;

(B) the Congress passes a joint resolution of disapproval described in section 802 relating to the rule, and the President signs a veto of such resolution, the earlier date—
> (i) on which either House of Congress votes and fails to override the veto of the President; or
> (ii) occurring 30 session days after the date on which the Congress received the veto and objections of the President; or

(C) the date the rule would have otherwise taken effect, if not for this section (unless a joint resolution of disapproval under section 802 is enacted).

(4) Except for a major rule, a rule shall take effect as otherwise provided by law after submission to Congress under paragraph (1).

(5) Notwithstanding paragraph (3), the effective date of a rule shall not be delayed by operation of this chapter beyond the date on which either House of Congress votes to reject a joint resolution of disapproval under section 802.

(b)(1) A rule shall not take effect (or continue), if the Congress enacts a joint resolution of disapproval, described under section 802, of the rule.

(2) A rule that does not take effect (or does not continue) under paragraph (1) may not be reissued in substantially the same form, and a new rule that is substantially the same as such a rule may not be issued, unless the reissued or new rule is specifically authorized by a law enacted after the date of the joint resolution disapproving the original rule.

(c)(1) Notwithstanding any other provision of this section (except subject to paragraph (3)), a rule that would not take effect by reason of subsection (a)(3) may take effect, if the President makes a determination under paragraph (2) and submits written notice of such determination to the Congress.

(2) Paragraph (1) applies to a determination made by the President by Executive order that the rule should take effect because such rule is –
> (A) necessary because of an imminent threat to health or safety or other emergency;
> (B) necessary for the enforcement of criminal laws;
> (C) necessary for national security; or
> (D) issued pursuant to any statute implementing an international trade agreement.

(3) An exercise by the President of the authority under this subsection shall have no effect on the procedures under section 802 or the effect of a joint resolution of disapproval under this section.

(d)(1) In addition to the opportunity for review otherwise provided under this chapter, in the case of any rule for which a report was submitted in accordance with subsection (a)(1)(A) during the period beginning on the date occurring—
    (A) in the case of the Senate, 60 session days, or
    (B) in the case of the House of Representatives, 60 legislative days, before the date the Congress adjourns a session of Congress through the date on which the same or succeeding Congress first convenes its next session, section 802 shall apply to such rule in the succeeding session of Congress.

(2)(A) In applying section 802 for purposes of such additional review, a rule described under paragraph (1) shall be treated as though—
    (i) such rule were published in the *Federal Register* (as a rule that shall take effect) on—
        (I) in the case of the Senate, the 15th session day, or
        (II) in the case of the House of Representatives, the 15th legislative day, after the succeeding session of Congress first convenes; and
    (ii) a report on such rule were submitted to Congress under subsection (a)(1) on such date.
    (B) Nothing in this paragraph shall be construed to affect the requirement under subsection (a)(1) that a report shall be submitted to Congress before a rule can take effect.

(3) A rule described under paragraph (1) shall take effect as otherwise provided by law (including other subsections of this section).

(e)(1) For purposes of this subsection, section 802 shall also apply to any major rule promulgated between March 1, 1996, and the date of the enactment of this chapter.

(2) In applying section 802 for purposes of Congressional review, a rule described under paragraph (1) shall be treated as though—
    (A) such rule were published in the *Federal Register* on the date of enactment of this chapter; and
    (B) a report on such rule were submitted to Congress under subsection (a)(1) on such date.

(3) The effectiveness of a rule described under paragraph (1) shall be as otherwise provided by law, unless the rule is made of no force or effect under section 802.

(f) Any rule that takes effect and later is made of no force or effect by enactment of a joint resolution under section 802 shall be treated as though such rule had never taken effect.

(g) If the Congress does not enact a joint resolution of disapproval under section 802 respecting a rule, no court or agency may infer any intent of the Congress from any action or inaction of the Congress with regard to such rule, related statute, or joint resolution of disapproval.

§802. Congressional disapproval procedure

(a) For purposes of this section, the term "joint resolution" means only a joint resolution introduced in the period beginning on the date on which the report referred to in section 801(a)(1)(A) is received by Congress and ending 60 days thereafter (excluding days either House of Congress is adjourned for more than 3 days during a session of Congress), the matter after the resolving clause of which is as follows: "That Congress disapproves the rule submitted by the _____ relating to _____ , and such rule shall have no force or effect." (The blank spaces being appropriately filled in).

(b)(1) A joint resolution described in subsection (a) shall be referred to the committees in each House of Congress with jurisdiction.

(2) For purposes of this section, the term "submission or publication date" means the later of the date on which—

(A) the Congress receives the report submitted under section 801(a)(1); or

(B) the rule is published in the *Federal Register*, if so published.

(c) In the Senate, if the committee to which is referred a joint resolution described in subsection (a) has not reported such joint resolution (or an identical joint resolution) at the end of 20 calendar days after the submission or publication date defined under subsection (b)(2), such committee may be discharged from further consideration of such joint resolution upon a petition supported in writing by 30 Members of the Senate, and such joint resolution shall be placed on the calendar.

(d)(1) In the Senate, when the committee to which a joint resolution is referred has reported, or when a committee is discharged (under subsection (c)) from further consideration of a joint resolution described in subsection (a), it is at any time thereafter in order (even though a previous motion to the same effect has been disagreed to) for a motion to proceed to the consideration of the joint resolution, and all points of order against the joint resolution (and against consideration of the joint resolution) are waived. The motion is not subject to amendment, or to a motion to postpone, or to a motion to proceed to the consideration of other business. A motion to reconsider the vote by which the motion is agreed to or disagreed to shall not be in order. If a motion to proceed to the consideration of the joint resolution is agreed to, the joint resolution shall remain the unfinished business of the Senate until disposed of.

(2) In the Senate, debate on the joint resolution, and on all debatable motions and appeals in connection therewith, shall be limited to not more than 10 hours, which shall be divided equally between those favoring and those opposing the joint resolution. A motion further to limit debate is in order and not debatable. An amendment to, or a motion to postpone, or a motion to proceed to the consideration of other business, or a motion to recommit the joint resolution is not in order.

(3) In the Senate, immediately following the conclusion of the debate on a joint resolution described in subsection (a), and a single quorum call at the conclusion of the debate if requested in accordance with the rules of the Senate, the vote on final passage of the joint resolution shall occur.

(4) Appeals from the decisions of the Chair relating to the application of the rules of the Senate to the procedure relating to a joint resolution described in subsection (a) shall be decided without debate.

(e) In the Senate the procedure specified in subsection (c) or (d) shall not apply to the consideration of a joint resolution respecting a rule—

(1) after the expiration of the 60 session days beginning with the applicable submission or publication date, or

(2) if the report under section 801(a)(1)(A) was submitted during the period referred to in section 801(d)(1), after the expiration of the 60 session days beginning on the 15th session day after the succeeding session of Congress first convenes.

(f) If, before the passage by one House of a joint resolution of that House described in subsection (a), that House receives from the other House a joint resolution described in subsection (a), then the following procedures shall apply:

(1) The joint resolution of the other House shall not be referred to a committee.

(2) With respect to a joint resolution described in subsection (a) of the House receiving the joint resolution—

(A) The procedure in that House shall be the same as if no joint resolution had been received from the other House; but

(B) the vote on final passage shall be on the joint resolution of the other House.

(g) This section is enacted by Congress—

(1) as an exercise of the rulemaking power of the Senate and House of Representatives, respectively, and as such it is deemed a part of the rules of each House, respectively, but applicable only with respect to

the procedure to be followed in that House in the case of a joint resolution described in subsection (a), and it supersedes other rules only to the extent that it is inconsistent with such rules; and

(2) with full recognition of the constitutional right of either House to change the rules (so far as relating to the procedure of that House) at any time, in the same manner, and to the same extent as in the case of any other rule of that House.

§803. Special rule on statutory, regulatory, and judicial deadlines

(a) In the case of any deadline for, relating to, or involving any rule which does not take effect (or the effectiveness of which is terminated) because of enactment of a joint resolution under section 802, that deadline is extended until the date 1 year after the date of enactment of the joint resolution. Nothing in this subsection shall be construed to affect a deadline merely by reason of the postponement of a rule's effective date under section 801(a).

(b) The term "deadline" means any date certain for fulfilling any obligation or exercising any authority established by or under any Federal statute or regulation, or by or under any court order implementing any Federal statute or regulation.

§804. Definitions

For purposes of this chapter—
>(1) The term "Federal agency" means any agency as that term is defined in section 551(1).
>(2) The term "major rule" means any rule that the Administrator of the Office of Information and Regulatory Affairs of the Office of Management and Budget finds has resulted in or is likely to result in—
>>(A) an annual effect on the economy of $100,000,000 or more;
>>(B) a major increase in costs or prices for consumers, individual industries, Federal, State, or local government agencies, or geographic regions; or
>>(C) significant adverse effects on competition, employment, investment, productivity, innovation, or on the ability of United States-based enterprises to compete with foreign-based enterprises in domestic and export markets.

The term does not include any rule promulgated under the Telecommunications Act of 1996 and the amendments made by that Act.

(3) The term "rule" has the meaning given such term in section 551, except that such term does not include—

(A) any rule of particular applicability, including a rule that approves or prescribes for the future rates, wages, prices, services, or allowances therefor, corporate or financial structures, reorganizations, mergers, or acquisitions thereof, or accounting practices or disclosures bearing on any of the foregoing;
(B) any rule relating to agency management or personnel; or
(C) any rule of agency organization, procedure, or practice that does not substantially affect the rights or obligations of non-agency parties.

§805. Judicial review

No determination, finding, action, or omission under this chapter shall be subject to judicial review.

§806. Applicability; severability

(a) This chapter shall apply notwithstanding any other provision of law.
(b) If any provision of this chapter or the application of any provision of this chapter to any person or circumstance, is held invalid, the application of such provision to other persons or circumstances, and the remainder of this chapter, shall not be affected thereby.

§807. Exemption for monetary policy

Nothing in this chapter shall apply to rules that concern monetary policy proposed or implemented by the Board of Governors of the Federal Reserve System or the Federal Open Market Committee.

§808. Effective date of certain rules

Notwithstanding section 801—
(1) any rule that establishes, modifies, opens, closes, or conducts a regulatory program for a commercial, recreational, or subsistence activity related to hunting, fishing, or camping, or
(2) any rule which an agency for good cause finds (and incorporates the finding and a brief statement of reasons therefor in the rule issued) that notice and public procedure thereon are impracticable, unnecessary, or contrary to the public interest, shall take effect at such time as the Federal agency promulgating

CONGRESSIONAL REVIEW OF AGENCY RULEMAKING   215

24722

Submission of Federal Rules
Under the Congressional Review Act

☐ President of the Senate   ☐ Speaker of the House of Representatives   ☐ GAO

Please fill the circles electronically or with black pen or #2 pencil.

1. Name of Department or Agency	2. Subdivision or Office

3. Rule Title

4. Regulation Identifier Number (RIN) or Other Unique Identifier (if applicable)

5.   Major Rule   Non-major Rule

6.   Final Rule   Other _____

7. With respect to this rule, did your agency solicit public comments?   Yes ○   No   N/A

8. Priority of Regulation (fill in one)

    Economically Significant; or   Routine and Frequent or
    Significant; or   Informational/Administrative/Other
    Substantive, Nonsignificant   (Do not complete the other side of this form
                                                     if filled in above.)

9. Effective Date (if applicable)

10. Concise Summary of Rule (fill in one or both)   attached   stated in rule

Submitted by: _____ (signature)

Name: _____

Title: _____

For Congressional Use Only:

Date Received: _____

Committee of Jurisdiction: _____

3/23/99

216   CONGRESSIONAL REVIEW OF AGENCY RULEMAKING

24722

		Yes	No	N/A

A. With respect to this rule, did your agency prepare an analysis of costs and benefits?

B. With respect to this rule, by the final rulemaking stage, did your agency

    1. certify that the rule would not have a significant economic impact on a substantial number of small entities under 5 U.S.C. § 605(b)?

    2. prepare a final Regulatory Flexibility Analysis under 5 U.S.C. § 604(a)?

C. With respect to this rule, did your agency prepare a written statement under § 202 of the Unfunded Mandates Reform Act of 1995?

D. With respect to this rule, did your agency prepare an Environmental Assessment or an Environmental Impact Statement under the National Environmental Policy Act (NEPA)?

E. Does this rule contain a collection of information requiring OMB approval under the Paperwork Reduction Act of 1995?

F. Did you discuss any of the following in the preamble to the rule?

- E.O. 12612, Federalism
- E.O. 12630, Government Actions and Interference with Constitutionally Protected Property Rights
- E.O. 12866, Regulatory Planning and Review
- E.O. 12875, Enhancing the Intergovernmental Partnership
- E.O. 12988, Civil Justice Reform
- E.O. 13045, Protection of Children from Environmental Health Risks and Safety Risks
- Other statutes or executive orders discussed in the preamble concerning the rulemaking process (please specify)

3/23/99

White House Orders, Bulletins, and Memoranda on Regulation

4

Citations:

This section contains the text of the most significant presidential Executive Orders, Bulletins, and Memoranda, effective as of May 1, 2007, which pertain to the rulemaking process or federal regulation. Other executive orders and memoranda may be found in other sections of this book, e.g., those relating to the Federal Advisory Committee Act.

It contains the texts of the following Bush II and Clinton Administration Orders (and Orders from previous administrations) in chronological order—that have remained in effect.

More information on many of these matters can be found on the website of OMB's Office of Information and Regulatory Affairs (OIRA), at:
http://www.whitehouse.gov/omb/inforeg/regpol.html.

I. Bush II and Clinton Administration Executive Orders

A. Executive Order 12,866: Regulatory Planning and Review (1993) (as amended by Executive Orders 13,258 (2002) and 13,422 (2007)).
B. Executive Order 12,889: Implementation of the North American Free Trade Agreement (1993).
C. Executive Order 12,898: Federal Actions to Address Environmental Justice in Minority Populations and Low-Income Populations (1994).
D. Executive Order 12,988: Civil Justice Reform (1996).
E. Executive Order 13,045: Protection of Children From Environmental Health Risks and Safety Risks (1997).
F. Executive Order 13,132: Federalism (1999).
G. Executive Order 13,175: Consultation and Coordination with Indian Tribal Governments (2000).

H. Executive Order 13,211: Actions Concerning Regulations That Significantly Affect Energy Supply, Distribution, or Use (2001).
I. Executive Order 13,272: Proper Consideration of Small Entities in Agency Rulemaking (2002).

II. Pre-1992 Executive Orders Still in Effect

A. Executive Order 12,372: Intergovernmental Review of Federal Programs.
B. Executive Order 12,630: Governmental Actions and Interference with Constitutionally Protected Property Rights (1988).

III. Other White House Bulletins and Memoranda

A. Presidential Memorandum: "Regulatory Reform—Waiver of Penalties and Reduction of Reports" (1995).
B. OMB Director's Memorandum: "Federal Participation in the Development and Use of Voluntary Standards" (1998).
C. Presidential Memorandum: "Designation of Interagency Committees to Facilitate and Encourage Agency Use of Alternate Means of Dispute Resolution and Negotiated Rulemaking" (1998).
D. Presidential Memorandum: "Plain Language in Government Writing" (1998).
E. OIRA Guidance on Presidential Review of Agency Rulemaking (2001).
F. OIRA Memorandum: "OMB's Circular No. A-4, New Guidelines for the Conduct of Regulatory Analysis" (2004).
G. OMB's Peer Review Bulletin (2004).
H. Final Bulletin for Agency Good Guidance Practices (and associated OMB/OIRA Memorandum on "Implementation of Executive Order 13,422 (amending Executive Order 12,866) and the OMB Bulletin on Good Guidance Practices") (2007).
I. Updated Principles for Risk Analysis (2007).

Lead Agency:

The Office of Information and Regulatory Affairs (OIRA) in the Office of Management and Budget (OMB), Eisenhower Executive Office Building, 1650 Pennsylvania Avenue NW, Washington, DC 20502, (202) 395-4852.

Overview:

History of Presidential Oversight of Rulemaking and Regulation

Presidential oversight of regulation is not a recent innovation. It has been in effect, in one form or another, since 1971, and it accompanied a major expansion in the scope and complexity of federal regulation that occurred in the 1960s and 1970s when a number of important social and environmental regulatory statutes were enacted.

In June 1971, President Nixon established a "Quality of Life Review" program, under which all "significant" draft proposed and final rules were submitted to the Office of Management and Budget (OMB), which circulated them to other agencies for comment. Agencies were required to submit a summary of their proposals, a description of the alternatives that had been considered, and a cost comparison of alternatives. In practice, this program applied to rules pertaining to environmental quality, consumer protection and occupational health and safety.

In 1974, President Ford issued an executive order requiring executive branch agencies to prepare an "inflation impact statement" for each "major" federal action.[1] The order empowered the Director of OMB to administer the program, with authority to delegate functions to other agencies, including the Council on Wage and Price Stability (COWPS). Under the Inflation Impact Statement program, agencies were required to prepare an inflation impact statement (IIS) for "major" rules[2] prior to publication of the notice of pro-

---

[1] Executive. Order 11,821, 3 C.F.R. 203 (1971-1975). When the Executive Order was later extended, the "inflation impact statement" (IIS) was replaced by an "economic impact statement" to better reflect the required analysis, which could be characterized as a loose cost-benefit analysis. *See* OMB Circular No. A-107, §4(d) (Jan. 28, 1975), *cited in* Note, *The Inflation Impact Statement Program: An Assessment of the First Two Years*, 26 AM. U. L. REV. 1138, 1141 n.28 (1977).

[2] Originally, agencies were left to develop their own criteria for determining what was a "major" proposal, subject to OMB approval; eventually COWPS adopted a list of suggested criteria that essentially defined "major" proposal as entailing a cost of $100 million or more in one year, or $150 million or more in two years. *See* Note, *Regulation Analyses and Judicial Review of Informal Rulemaking*, 91 YALE L.J. 739, 746 n.51 (1982).

posed rulemaking (NPRM), and then to forward a summary of the IIS to COWPS upon publication of the NPRM. COWPS would review the IIS and, in its discretion, offer informal criticism of the proposal or participate in the public proceedings on the rule.[3]

President Carter continued presidential review of agency rules by means of Executive Order 12,044, issued in 1978.[4] Under the order, executive agencies were required to: (1) publish semi-annual agendas, describing and giving the legal bases for, any "significant" regulations under development by the agency; (2) establish procedures to identify "significant" rules, to evaluate their need, and to have the agency head assure that the "least burdensome of the acceptable alternatives" was proposed; and (3) prepare a "regulatory analysis" that examined the cost-effectiveness of alternative regulatory approaches for "major rules."

President Carter also established a Regulatory Analysis Review Group to review the regulatory analyses prepared for a limited number of proposed "major" rules and to submit comments on the proposed rules during the public comment period.[5] He created another rulemaking review body, the Regulatory Council, which was charged with coordinating agency rulemaking to avoid duplication of effort or conflicting policy in regulation of any area.[6] These efforts to coordinate agency rulemaking were challenged unsuccessfully in several lawsuits.

President Reagan acted quickly after taking office to increase control over executive branch rulemaking. On February 17, 1981, the President issued an executive order on federal regulations designed "to reduce the burdens of existing and future regulations, increase agency accountability for regulatory actions, provide for presidential oversight of the regulatory process, minimize duplication and conflict of regulations, and insure well-reasoned regulations."[7] The new Executive Order 12,291 replaced Executive Order 12,044, which President Reagan said had "proven ineffective."[8]

---

[3] *Id.*

[4] 3 C.F.R. 152 (1979).

[5] 43 Fed. Reg. 12,668 (1978).

[6] Memorandum from President Carter to Executive Departments and Agencies, entitled "Strengthening Regulatory Management" (Oct. 13, 1978). The Regulatory Council included the heads of all executive branch agencies and the heads of any independent agencies who chose to participate on a voluntary basis.

[7] Executive Order 12,291, 3 C.F.R. 127 (1982), *reprinted* as note to 5 U.S.C. §601.

[8] Office of the Vice President, *Fact Sheet Accompanying Executive Order on Regulatory Management* 2 (1981).

Executive Order 12,291 contained both substantive requirements and procedural steps to be followed in the development and promulgation of new rules. The Office of Information and Regulatory Affairs (OIRA) in the Office of Management and Budget was given responsibility for implementing Executive Order 12,291. OMB's rulemaking review function is supplemented by the powers it was given in the Paperwork Reduction Act of 1980, by which Congress statutorily established OIRA to, among other things, review and approve or disapprove agency "information collection requests."

The Office of Legal Counsel in the U.S. Department of Justice issued an opinion supporting the validity of Executive Order 12,291. The opinion stated that the President's authority to issue the order was based on his constitutional power to "take care that the laws be faithfully executed." While concluding that any inquiry into Congressional intent in enacting specific rulemaking statutes "will usually support the legality of presidential supervision of rulemaking by Executive Branch agencies," the opinion stated that presidential supervision of agency rulemaking "is more readily justified when it does not purport wholly to displace, but only to guide and limit, discretion which Congress had allocated to a particular subordinate official."

Despite criticism of this new form of presidential review, President Reagan began his second term by expanding the program through Executive Order 12,498, which established a "regulatory planning process" with the purpose of helping to "ensure that each major step in the process of rule development is consistent with Administration policy."[9]

According to OMB, the problem with regulatory review under Executive Order 12,291 was that such review "often came late in the regulatory process, after huge investments of agency time and resources, and often after agency staff commitments to constituents had made it extremely difficult to consider any legally acceptable, but previously ignored, regulatory alternative."[10] This resulted, OMB said, in the "bureaucracy often present[ing] agency heads with *faits accompli*."[11]

Executive Order 12,498's regulatory planning process was designed to avoid this problem.[12] Under this procedure, the head of each agency was required to determine at the beginning of the regulatory process whether a proposed regulatory venture was "consistent with the goals of the Administra-

---

[9] Office of Management and Budget, *Regulatory Program of the United States Government* xiv (1987-1988).

[10] *Id.* at xliii.

[11] *Id.*

[12] President's Memorandum for the Heads of Executive Departments and Agencies, 21 Weekly Comp. Pres. Doc. 13 (1985).

tion."[13] At the beginning of the year, Agency heads were to develop a plan for managing the agency's most significant regulatory actions. OMB then reviewed the plan for consistency with the administration's program and published the coordinated agency plans in a government-wide document.[14] This document, entitled *Regulatory Program of the United States Government,* governs more than 20 major rulemaking agencies and was published each year during the second Reagan term and the Bush administration to inform Congress and the public of the government's regulatory plans.

President Reagan, in 1987 and 1988, issued three additional executive orders, dealing with federalism,[15] interference with property rights,[16] (which is still in effect) and the family.[17] OMB was given a role in ensuring coordination of regulatory policy in these areas. President Bush basically continued the program of presidential review of agency rulemaking established by President Reagan, although due to Congressional opposition to OIRA actions, President Bush's nominee to head OIRA was not confirmed. To counter this weakening of OIRA's authority, President Bush created the Council on Competitiveness, headed by Vice President Quayle, and gave it authority to intervene in major agency rulemakings.[18] Several of the Council's interventions provoked intense criticisms leading up to the 1992 elections.

The Clinton Executive Order—Executive Order 12,866

With the election of President Clinton, one of his first actions was an attempt to reestablish some bipartisan consensus on rulemaking review. His nominee as OIRA Administrator was the first subcabinet nominee to be appointed. Following the example of the Reagan Administration, the President Clinton then set out to redraft the extant Executive Order, and produced Executive Order 12,866 on September 30, 1993.[19] This Order, which remains operative in 2007 (with two sets of amendments by President George W. Bush),

---

[13] *Id.*

[14] Executive Order 12,498, §§2, 3.

[15] Executive Order 12,612, 3 C.F.R. 252 (1988) (ensuring that executive departments are guided by "principles of federalism"). This Order was repealed by E.O. 13,132 in 1999.

[16] Executive Order 12,630, 3 C.F.R. 554 (1989) (relating to "Governmental Actions and Interference with Constitutionally Protected Property Rights").

[17] Executive Order 12,606, 3 C.F.R. 241 (1988) (intending to "ensure that the autonomy and rights of the family are considered" in formulation of government policy). This Order was repealed by Executive Order 13,045, 62 Fed. Reg. 36,965.

[18] The Council was created by a press release from the Vice President's office.

[19] Executive Order 12,866, 58 Fed. Reg. 51,735 (1993).

carries over many of the principles of E.O. 12,291 (and E.O. 12,498) which it superseded, but it also made some significant modifications that simplified the process, made it more selective, and introduced more transparency into the OMB/agency consultations. In drafting this Order, the Clinton Administration followed many of the suggestions of the Administrative Conference in its Recommendation 88-9, "Presidential Review of Agency Rulemaking."[20]

The Order begins with a lengthy "Statement of Regulatory Philosophy and Principles," that are quite similar to those in Executive Order 12,291 except that it takes pains to specify that measurement of costs and benefits should include both quantifiable and qualitative measures. As with previous Orders, Executive Order12,866 retains the traditional (since 1978) level of $100 million annual effect on the economy for those major rules (now referred to as "economically significant" rules) that must be accompanied by cost-benefit assessments when forwarded to OIRA as proposed and final rules.

Executive Order 12,866 also retains the OIRA review process for other rules, although it only requires that "significant regulatory actions" be subject to review. This includes those $100 million rules plus others that have material adverse effects on "the economy, a sector of the economy, productivity, competition, jobs, the environment, public health or safety, or State, local, or tribal governments or communities." It also include rules that may materially alter the budgetary impact of benefit programs or the rights of recipients, that raise "novel legal or policy issues" or are inconsistent or interfere with actions taken by another agency. The process established for identifying such "significant regulatory actions" relies on agency identification of them in the first instance, vetted by OIRA. Rules that are not so identified may be issued without OIRA review. This selectivity has streamlined the review process considerably, and has made it possible to include, for the first time, a firm deadline (of 90 days, with one 30-day extension allowed) for completion of OIRA review. In the event of an unresolved dispute between OIRA and the agency, the President's Chief of Staff is directed to make the decision (or recommend one to the President).

The review process set forth in the Order is quite transparent. Following an ACUS recommendation closely, the Order provides that after the agency has concluded its rulemaking it should make available to the public all submissions to OIRA, and identify all changes made in the rule, noting those made at the behest of OIRA. In addition OIRA, for its part, must

---

[20] ACUS Recommendation 88-9, 54 Fed. Reg. 5,207 (Feb. 2, 1989).

regularize the way it receives any outside communications concerning an agency rule that is subject to review. Only the Administrator or her designee may receive such communications. OIRA must forward any such communications to the agency within ten days, invite agency officials to any meetings held with outsiders, and maintain a public log of all such contacts. At the end of the proceeding OIRA must also make available all documents exchanged with the agency.

In place of the Reagan E.O. 12,498 on regulatory planning, the Clinton Order establishes its own yearly planning mechanism. It continues the semi-annual publication of the Unified Regulatory Agenda, which lists all proposed, pending and completed regulatory and deregulatory actions. And it requires that the October Agenda contain each agency's annual Regulatory Plans, which must be approved by agency's Regulatory Policy Officer (who must be a presidential appointee) and the President's Regulatory Advisors designated under the Order. These plans must be forwarded to OIRA (and then on to Advisors and affected agencies) by June 1 of each year. The Plans are supposed to also include agency determinations on which existing rules are to be reviewed and reconsidered during the ensuing year, and "preliminary estimates of the anticipated costs and benefits of each rule as well as the agency's best estimate of the combined aggregate costs and benefits of all its regulations planned for that calendar year." With the exception of the aggregate cost estimate requirement, added by President Bush in 2007, these actions do not represent any sharp break from the practices of previous administrations. However, Executive Order 12,866 is a departure in one regard—for the first time the *independent regulatory agencies* are specifically directed to comply with the planning and agenda provisions (though *not* with the rule-review process).

The Clinton Executive Order was generally well received by most observers of the regulatory scene. Its basic approach has remained fundamentally unchanged since its issuance, and OIRA has worked out a stable and workable relationship with the agencies in administering it. The once rather vibrant legal and policy debate over the pros and cons of presidential review has gradually evolved into a fairly broad agreement that it is not only legal, but that if properly administered, it is essential to effective executive branch management.

It should be pointed out that President Bush has made some significant changes of some significance. In 2002, he made some small changes in Executive Order 13,258, basically removing the Vice-President from the process. In January 2007, in Executive Order 13,422, he made more fundamental changes. Most significantly he added a requirement that "significant guidance documents" also be reviewed by OIRA in a way similar to significant regulatory actions. He also required that agencies identify in writing specific "market failures" that necessitate a rulemaking, that agency Regulatory Policy Officers be presidential appointees, that these Officers must approve the Regulatory Plan, that aggregate costs and benefits for all rules must be included in the Regulatory Plan, (and that agencies consider whether to use "formal" (on the record") rulemaking for "complex determinations."

President Clinton also issued a presidential directive on plain language, and number of other executive orders that remain in effect, concerning: environmental justice in minority populations and low-income populations (E.O. 12,898), civil justice reform (E.O. 12,988), protection of children from environmental risks (E.O. 13,045), federalism (E.O. 13,132), and consultation with Indian Tribal Governments (E.O. 13,175).

The Bush Administration did continue to use Executive Order 12,866, and it also issued a memorandum placing its own stamp on the review process and announcing several new initiatives in its review process. First, it made extensive use of its website to publish its guidelines and other information pertaining to the process and to specific rule reviews. Second, it began the practice of issuing public "return letters" that send rules back to the agency for reconsideration, "post-review letters" that comment on aspects of a particular rule review, and "prompt letters," which are sent on OMB's initiative and contain suggestions for new or stronger regulations.

President Bush has also issued two executive orders concerning regulations that significantly affect energy supply, distribution, or use (E.O. 13,211) and proper consideration of small entities in agency rulemaking (E.O. 13,272). OMB also issued a more far-reaching and controversial "Peer Review Bulletin" in December 2004, which requires administrative agencies to conduct a peer review on all "influential regulatory information that the agency intends to disseminate." Finally, in 2007, OMB issued an important new government-wide "Bulletin on Good Guidance Practices."

Bibliography:

I. Government Documents

A. OMB Reports to Congress on the Costs and Benefits of Regulations[21]

1. *Report to Congress on the Costs and Benefits of Federal Regulations* (Sept. 30, 1997), http://www.whitehouse.gov/omb/inforeg/rcongress.html. Notice of availability of draft report and request for comments, 62 Fed. Reg. 39,352 (July 22, 1997).

2. *Report to Congress on the Costs and Benefits of Federal Regulations* (January 1999), http://www.whitehouse.gov/omb/inforeg/costbenefitreport 1998.pdf. Notice of availability of draft report and request for comments, 63 Fed. Reg. 44,034 (Aug. 17, 1998), extended 63 Fed. Reg. 49,935 (Sept. 18, 1998).

3. *Report to Congress on the Costs and Benefits of Federal Regulations* (June 2000), http://www.whitehouse.gov/omb/inforeg/2000fedreg-report.pdf. Notice of availability of draft report and request for comments, 65 Fed. Reg. 1296 (Jan. 7, 2000); extended 65 Fed. Reg. 4447 (Jan. 27, 2000) and 65 Fed. Reg. 7198 (Feb. 7, 2000).

4. *Making Sense of Regulation, 2001 Report to Congress on the Costs and Benefits of Federal Regulations and Unfunded Mandates on State, Local, and Tribal Entities* (December 2001), http://www.whitehouse.gov/omb/inforeg/costbenefitreport.pdf. Notice of availability of draft report and request for comments, 66 Fed. Reg. 22,041 (May 2, 2001); extended 66 Fed. Reg. 34,963 (July 2, 2001).

5. *Stimulating Smarter Regulation, 2002 Report to Congress on the Costs and Benefits of Federal Regulations and Unfunded Mandates on State, Local, and Tribal Entities* (December 2002), http://www.whitehouse.gov/omb/inforeg/2002_report_to_congress.pdf. Notice of availability of draft report and request for comments, 67 Fed. Reg. 15,014 (March 28, 2002).

6. *Informing Regulatory Decisions, 2003 Report to Congress on the Costs and Benefits of Federal Regulations and Unfunded Mandates on State, Local, and Tribal Entities* (September 2003), http://www.whitehouse.gov/

---

[21] These reports are required by the Regulatory Right to Know Act, 31 U.S.C. § 1105 note, Pub. L. No. 106-554, §1(a)(3) [Title VI, §624], Dec. 21, 2000, 114 Stat. 2763, 2763A-161, and the Unfunded Mandates Reform Act, Pub. L. No. 104-4, Title II. (Prior to the 2002 Report, they were required by various riders in annual appropriations acts.)

omb/inforeg/2003_cost-ben_final_rpt.pdf. Notice of availability of draft report and request for comments, 68 Fed. Reg. 15,772 (April 1, 2003).

7. *Progress in Regulatory Reform, 2004 Report to Congress on the Costs and Benefits of Federal Regulations and Unfunded Mandates on State, Local, and Tribal Entities* (December 2004), http://www.whitehouse.gov/omb/inforeg/2004_cb_final.pdf. Notice of availability of draft report and request for comments, 69 Fed. Reg. 7987 (Feb. 20, 2004).

8. *Validating Regulatory Analysis, 2005 Report to Congress on the Costs and Benefits of Federal Regulations and Unfunded Mandates on State, Local, and Tribal Entities* (December 2005), http://www.whitehouse.gov/omb/inforeg/2005_cb/final_2005_cb_report.pdf. Notice of availability of draft report and request for comments, 70 Fed. Reg. 14,735 (March 23, 2005).

9. *2006 Report to Congress on the Costs and Benefits of Federal Regulations and Unfunded Mandates on State, Local, and Tribal Entities* (January 2007), http://www.whitehouse.gov/omb/inforeg/2006_cb/2006_cb_final_report.pdf. Notice of availability of draft report and request for comments, 71 Fed. Reg. 19,213 (April 13, 2006).

10. *2007 Draft Report to Congress on the Costs and Benefits of Federal Regulations*, http://www.whitehouse.gov/omb/inforeg/2007_cb/2007_draft_cb_report.pdf. Notice of availability of draft report and request for comments, 72 Fed. Reg. 11,061 (March 12, 2007).

B. Other Government Documents

1. *Additional Procedures Concerning OIRA Reviews Under Executive Order Nos. 12,291 and 12,498*, Op. Off. of Legal Counsel, *reprinted in* Office of Management and Budget, Regulatory Program of the United States Government 532-36 (1988-1989).

2. ACUS Recommendation 88-9, "Presidential Review of Agency Rulemaking, 54 Fed. Reg. 5207 (Feb. 2, 1989).

3. Copeland, Congressional Research Service, *Changes to the OMB Regulatory Review Process by Executive Order 13422* (RL33862) (Feb. 5, 2007), http://www.fas.org/sgp/crs/misc/RL33862.pdf.

4. Copeland, Congressional Research Service, *The Federal Rulemaking Process: An Overview* (RL32240) (Feb. 7, 2007), http://www.opencrs.com/rpts/RL32240_20050207.pdf.

5. Copeland, Congressional Research Service, *Federal Rulemaking: The Role of the Office of Information and Regulatory Affairs* (RL32397) (May 28, 2004), http://www.opencrs.com/rpts/RL32397_20040528.pdf.

6. Council on Environmental Quality, *Environmental Justice Guidance Under the National Environmental Policy Act* (Dec. 10, 1997), http://ceq.eh.doe.gov/nepa/nepanet.htm.

Ninth Annual Report on Federal Agency Use of Voluntary Consensus Standards and Conformity Assessment, prepared by the National Institute of Standards and Technology (NIST) at the Department of Commerce, transmitted by the Administrator of OIRA, (Jan. 25, 2007), http://www.whitehouse.gov/omb/inforeg/regpol-reports_congress.html. [Eighth and Seventh Annual Reports also available on same website.]

7. Office of Management and Budget, *Regulatory Program of the United States Government (1987-1988)* (and through 1990-91).

8. Office of Management and Budget, *Report on Executive Order No. 12,866,* 59 Fed. Reg. 24,293 (1994).

9. Office of Management and Budget, Office of Information and Regulatory Affairs, *More Benefits Fewer Burdens—Creating a Regulatory System that Works For the American People, A Report to the President on the Third Anniversary of Executive Order 12,866* (1996), http://www.whitehouse.gov/OMB/inforeg/3_year_report.html.

10. Office of Management and Budget, Office of Information and Regulatory Affairs, *Progress in Regulatory Reform: 2004 Report to Congress on the Costs and Benefits of Federal Regulations and Unfunded Mandates on State, Local, and Tribal Entities* (Dec. 2004), http://www.whitehouse.gov/omb/inforeg/2004_cb_final.pdf.

11. Office of Management and Budget, Office of Information and Regulatory Affairs, *Stimulating Smarter Regulation: 2002 Report to Congress on the Costs and Benefits of Regulation and Unfunded Mandates on State, Local and Tribal Entities* (2002), http://www.whitehouse.gov/omb/inforeg/2002_report_to_congress.pdf.

12. Office of the Vice President, *Creating a Government That Works Better and Costs Less, Improving Regulatory Systems*, National Performance Review (1993).

13. Oversight Hearing on: "Amending Executive Order 12866: Good Governance or Regulatory Usurpation?" House Subcommittee on Commercial and Administrative Law, Committee of the Judiciary (Feb 13, 2007).

14. Regulatory Information Service Center, *Unified Agenda of Federal Regulatory and Deregulatory Action*, published in May and October each year in the *Federal Register.*

15. *Regulatory Reform, Hearing before the House Subcomm. on Energy Policy, Natural Resources and Regulatory Affairs*, 108th Cong. (Nov. 17, 2004) (statement of John D. Graham, Administrator of OIRA), http://

www.whitehouse.gov/omb/legislative/testimony/graham/111704_graham_reg_reform.html.

16. U.S., Environmental Protection Agency. *The Benefits and Costs of the Clean Air Act, 1970-1992—Draft Report for Congress* (April 1997).

17. U.S. General Accounting Office, *Cost-Benefit Analysis Can Be Useful in Assessing Environmental Regulations, Despite Limitations* (GAO/RCED-84-62) (Apr. 6, 1984).

18. U.S. General Accounting Office, *Federalism: Implementation of Executive Order 12612 in the Rulemaking Process* (T-GGD-99-93) (May 5, 1999).

19. U.S. Gen. Accounting Office, *Federalism: Previous Initiatives Have Had Little Effect on Agency Rulemaking* (GAO/T-GGD-99-31) (June 30, 1999).

20. U.S. General Accounting Office, *Regulatory Accounting—Analysis of OMB's Reports on the Costs and Benefits of Federal Regulation* (GAO/GGD-99-59) (Apr. 1999).

21. U.S. General Accounting Office, *Regulatory Reform Agencies Could Improve Development, Documentation and Clarity of Regulatory Economic Analysis* (GAO/RCED-98-142) (May 26, 1998).

22. U.S. General Accounting Office, *Regulatory Burden: Recent Studies, Industry Issues, and Agency Initiatives* (GAO/GGD-94-28) (Dec. 13, 1993).

23. U.S. General Accounting Office, *Regulatory Burden: Measurement Challenges Raised by Selected Companies* (GAO/GGD-97-2) (Nov. 18, 1996).

24. U.S. General Accounting Office, *Regulatory Reform: Changes Made to Agencies' Rules Are Not Always Clearly Documented* (GAO/GGD-98-31) (Jan. 1998).

25. U.S. General Accounting Office, *Regulatory Reform: Information on Costs, Cost-Effectiveness, and Mandated Deadlines for Regulations* (GAO/PEMD-95-18BR) (Mar. 8, 1995).

26. U.S. General Accounting Office, *Regulatory Takings: Implementation of Executive Order on Government Actions Affecting Private Property Use* (GAO-03-1015) (Sept. 2003).

27. U.S. General Accounting Office, *Rulemaking: OMB's Role in Reviews of Agencies' Draft Rules and the Transparency of Those Reviews* (GAO-03-929) (Sept. 2003).

28. U.S. Government Accountability Office, *Environmental Justice: EPA Should Devote More Attention to Environmental Justice When Developing Clean Air Rules* (GAO-05-289) (July 25, 2005).

II. Selected Books and Articles

1. Adams, *Regulating the Rule-Makers: John Graham at OIRA*, CQ Weekly 520 (Feb. 23, 2002).
2. Anthony, *Executive Order, OMB Bulletin Focus on Guidances*, 32 Admin. L. & Reg. News 10 (Spring 2007).
3. Bagley & Revesz, *Centralized Oversight of the Regulatory State*, 106 Colum. L. Rev. 1260 (2006).
4. Blumstein, *Regulatory Review by the Executive Office of the President: An Overview and Policy Analysis of Current Issues*, 51 Duke L. J. 851 (2001).
5. Bressman & Vandenbergh, *Inside the Administrative State: A Critical Look at the Practice of Presidential Control*, 105 Mich. L. Rev. 47 (2006).
6. Bruff, *Presidential Management of Agency Rulemaking*, 57 Geo. Wash. L. Rev. 533 (1989).
7. *Clinton Regulation Will Be "Rational": Interview with Sally Katzen, the New OIRA Administrator*, Regulation Magazine No. 3, at 36 (1993), http://www.cato.org/pubs/regulation/reg16n3b.html.
8. Craig, *The Bush Administration's Use and Abuse of Rulemaking. Part I: The Rise of OIRA*, 28 Admin. & Reg. L. News 8 (Summer 2003).
9. Croley, *White House Review of Agency Rulemaking: An Empirical Investigation*, 70 U. Chi. L. Rev. 821 (2003).
10. DeMuth & Ginsburg, *White House Review of Agency Rulemaking*, 99 Harv. L. Rev. 1075 (1986).
11. DeWitt, Comment, *The Council on Competitiveness: Undermining the Administrative Procedure Act with Regulatory Review*, 6 Admin. L. J. Am. U. 759 (1993).
12. Farina, *Undoing the New Deal Through the New Presidentialism*, 22 Harv. J. L. & Pub. Pol'y 227 (1998).
13. Farrow, *Improving Regulatory Performance: Does Executive Office Oversight Matter?*, AEI Publication (Dec. 2001), http://www.aei.brook.edu/admin/authorpdfs/page.php?id=123.
14. Graham, Noe & Branch, *Managing the Regulatory State: The Experience of the Bush Administration*, 33 Fordham Urb. L. J. 953 (2006).
15. Greene, *Checks and Balances in an Era of Presidential Lawmaking*, 61 U. Chi. L. Rev. 123 (1994).
16. Grimmer, Note, *Public Controversy Over Peer Review*, 57 Admin. L. Rev. 275 (2005).
17. Hahn, *Risks, Costs, and Lives Saved: Getting Better Results From Regulation* (New York: Oxford University Press and AEI Press, 1996).

18. Hahn & Hird, *The Costs and Benefits of Regulation: Review and Synthesis*, Yale J. on Reg. (Vol. 8, No. 1, Winter 1991).
19. Heinzerling, *Statutory Interpretation in the Era of OIRA*, 33 Fordham Urb. L. J. 1097 (2006).
20. Kagan, *Presidential Administration*, 114 Harv. L. Rev. 2245 (2001).
21. Kerwin, *Rulemaking: How Government Agencies Write Law and Make Policy* (3d ed. 2003).
22. Litan & Nordhaus, *Reforming Federal Regulation* (New Haven, Ct.: Yale University Press, 1983).
23. Lubbers, *A Guide to Federal Agency Rulemaking*, (4th ed.) (American Bar Association) (2006).
24. Lubbers, *OMB to Require Peer Review for Regulatory Science Documents*, 29 Admin. L. & Reg. News 3 (Fall 2003).
25. Mahon, Note, *Proceed With Caution: The Implications of the OMB Peer Review Guidelines on Precautionary Legislation*, 84 Wash. U. L. Rev. 461(2006).
26. May, *OMB's Peer Review Proposal—Swamped by Science?* 29 Admin. & Reg. L. News 4 (Spring 2004).
27. McGarity, *Presidential Control of Regulatory Agency Decisionmaking*, 36 Am. U. L. Rev. 443, 454-62 (1987).
28. Morrison, *OMB Interference with Agency Rulemaking: The Wrong Way to Write a Regulation*, 99 Harv. L. Rev. 1059 (1986).
29. Noah, *Peer Review and Regulatory Reform*, 30 Envtl. L. Rep. (Envtl. L. Inst.) 10,606 (2000).
30. Note, *Regulation Analyses and Judicial Review of Informal Rulemaking*, 91 Yale L. J. 739, 746 n.51 (1982).
31. Note, *The Inflation Impact Statement Program: An Assessment of the First Two Years*, 26 Am. U. L. Rev. 1138, 1141 n.28 (1977).
32. Olson, *The Quiet Shift of Power: Office of Management & Budget Supervision of Environmental Protection Agency Rulemaking Under Executive Order 12,291*, 4 Va. J. Nat. Resources 1, 75-77 (1984).
33. Percival, *Presidential Management of the Administrative State: The Not-So-Unitary Executive*, 51 Duke L. J. 963 (2001).
34. Rabin, *Federal Regulation in Historical Perspective*, 38 Stan L. Rev. 1189 (1986).
35. Ridgway et al., *The Council on Competitiveness and Regulatory Review: A "Kinder, Gentler" Approach to Regulation?*, 6 Admin. L. J. Am. U. 691, 698 & n.196 (1993).
36. Rivkin, *The Unitary Executive and Presidential Control of Executive Branch Rulemaking*, 7 Admin. L. J. Am. U. 309 (1993).

37. Rosenberg, *Beyond the Limits of Executive Power: Presidential Control of Agency Rulemaking Under Executive Order 12,291*, 80 Mich. L. Rev. 193 (1981).

38. Sargentich, *The Emphasis on the Presidency in U.S. Public Law: An Essay Critiquing Presidential Administration*, 59 Admin. L. Rev. 1 (2007).

39. Section on Administrative Law and Regulatory Practice, *A Guide to Judicial and Political Review of Federal Agencies* 211-50, 275-82 (John F. Duffy & Michael Herz eds., 2005).

40. Shane, *Political Accountability in a System of Checks and Balances: The Case of Presidential Review of Rulemaking*, 48 Ark. L. Rev. 161 (1995).

41. Sidney A. Shapiro, *OMB's Dubious Peer Review Procedures*, 34 Envtl. L. Rep. (Envtl. L. Inst.) 10,064 (2004).

42. Sidney A. Shapiro, *OMB's Revised Peer Review Bulletin*, 29 Admin. L. & Reg. News 10 (Summer 2004).

43. Strauss & Sunstein, *The Role of the President and OMB in Informal Rulemaking*, 38 Admin. L. Rev. 181, 202-205 (1986).

44. Verkuil, *Jawboning Administrative Agencies: Ex Parte Contacts by the White House*, 80 Colum. L. Rev. 943, 944-47 (1980).

45. Warber, *Executive Orders and the Modern Presidency: Legislating from the Oval Office* (Lynne Reiner Publishers 2006).

46. Wilson, Comment: *Not Good Enough for Government Work: How OMB's Good Guidance Practices May Unintentionally Complicate Administrative Law*, 59 Admin. L. Rev. 177 (2007).

III. Miscellaneous

1. National Academy of Public Administration, *Presidential Management of Rulemaking in Regulatory Agencies* 23 (1987).

I. Bush II and Clinton Administration Executive Orders:

A. Executive Order 12,866

Regulatory Planning and Review

September 30, 1993

58 Fed. Reg. 51,735 (Oct. 4, 1993) [President Clinton]

As amended by Executive Order 13,258, February 26, 2002, 67 Fed. Reg. 9385 (Feb. 28, 2002) [President Bush]

And by Executive Order 13,422, January 18, 2007, 72 Fed. Reg. 2763 (Jan. 23, 2007 [President Bush]

The American people deserve a regulatory system that works for them, not against them: a regulatory system that protects and improves their health, safety, environment, and well-being and improves the performance of the economy without imposing unacceptable or unreasonable costs on society; regulatory policies that recognize that the private sector and private markets are the best engine for economic growth; regulatory approaches that respect the role of State, local, and tribal governments; and regulations that are effective, consistent, sensible, and understandable. We do not have such a regulatory system today. With this Executive order, the Federal Government begins a program to reform and make more efficient the regulatory process. The objectives of this Executive order are to enhance planning and coordination with respect to both new and existing regulations; to reaffirm the primacy of Federal agencies in the regulatory decision-making process; to restore the integrity and legitimacy of regulatory review and oversight; and to make the process more accessible and open to the public. In pursuing these objectives, the regulatory process shall be conducted so as to meet applicable statutory requirements and with due regard to the discretion that has been entrusted to the Federal agencies. Accordingly, by the authority vested in me as President by the Constitution and the laws of the United States of America, it is hereby ordered as follows:

Section 1. *Statement of Regulatory Philosophy and Principles.*
(a) *The Regulatory Philosophy.* Federal agencies should promulgate only such regulations as are required by law, are necessary to interpret the law, or are made necessary by compelling public need, such as material failures of pri-

vate markets to protect or improve the health and safety of the public, the environment, or the well-being of the American people. In deciding whether and how to regulate, agencies should assess all costs and benefits of available regulatory alternatives, including the alternative of not regulating. Costs and benefits shall be understood to include both quantifiable measures (to the fullest extent that these can be usefully estimated) and qualitative measures of costs and benefits that are difficult to quantify, but nevertheless essential to consider. Further, in choosing among alternative regulatory approaches, agencies should select those approaches that maximize net benefits (including potential economic, environmental, public health and safety, and other advantages; distributive impacts; and equity), unless a statute requires another regulatory approach.

(b) *The Principles of Regulation.* To ensure that the agencies' regulatory programs are consistent with the philosophy set forth above, agencies should adhere to the following principles, to the extent permitted by law and where applicable:

(1) Each agency shall identify in writing the specific market failure (such as externalities, market power, lack of information) or other specific problem that it intends to address (including, where applicable, the failures of public institutions) that warrant new agency action, as well as assess the significance of that problem, to enable assessment of whether any new regulation is warranted.

(2) Each agency shall examine whether existing regulations (or other law) have created, or contributed to, the problem that a new regulation is intended to correct and whether those regulations (or other law) should be modified to achieve the intended goal of regulation more effectively.

(3) Each agency shall identify and assess available alternatives to direct regulation, including providing economic incentives to encourage the desired behavior, such as user fees or marketable permits, or providing information upon which choices can be made by the public.

(4) In setting regulatory priorities, each agency shall consider, to the extent reasonable, the degree and nature of the risks posed by various substances or activities within its jurisdiction.

(5) When an agency determines that a regulation is the best available method of achieving the regulatory objective, it shall design its regulations in the most cost-effective manner to achieve the regulatory objective. In doing so, each agency shall consider incentives for innovation, consistency, predictability, the costs of enforcement and compliance (to the government, regulated entities, and the public), flexibility, distributive impacts, and equity.

(6) Each agency shall assess both the costs and the benefits of the intended regulation and, recognizing that some costs and benefits are difficult to quantify, propose or adopt a regulation only upon a reasoned determination that the benefits of the intended regulation justify its costs.
(7) Each agency shall base its decisions on the best reasonably obtainable scientific, technical, economic, and other information concerning the need for, and consequences of, the intended regulation or guidance document.
(8) Each agency shall identify and assess alternative forms of regulation and shall, to the extent feasible, specify performance objectives, rather than specifying the behavior or manner of compliance that regulated entities must adopt.
(9) Wherever feasible, agencies shall seek views of appropriate State, local, and tribal officials before imposing regulatory requirements that might significantly or uniquely affect those governmental entities. Each agency shall assess the effects of Federal regulations on State, local, and tribal governments, including specifically the availability of resources to carry out those mandates, and seek to minimize those burdens that uniquely or significantly affect such governmental entities, consistent with achieving regulatory objectives. In addition, as appropriate, agencies shall seek to harmonize Federal regulatory actions with related State, local, and tribal regulatory and other governmental functions.
(10) Each agency shall avoid regulations and guidance documents that are inconsistent, incompatible, or duplicative with its other regulations and guidance documents or those of other Federal agencies.
(11) Each agency shall tailor its regulations and guidance documents to impose the least burden on society, including individuals, businesses of differing sizes, and other entities (including small communities and governmental entities), consistent with obtaining the regulatory objectives, taking into account, among other things, and to the extent practicable, the costs of cumulative regulations.
(12) Each agency shall draft its regulations and guidance documents to be simple and easy to understand, with the goal of minimizing the potential for uncertainty and litigation arising from such uncertainty.

Section 2. *Organization.*
An efficient regulatory planning and review process is vital to ensure that the Federal Government's regulatory system best serves the American people.

(a) *The Agencies.* Because Federal agencies are the repositories of significant substantive expertise and experience, they are responsible for developing regulations and guidance documents and assuring that the regulations and guidance documents are consistent with applicable law, the President's priorities, and the principles set forth in this Executive order.

(b) *The Office of Management and Budget.* Coordinated review of agency rulemaking is necessary to ensure that regulations and guidance documents are consistent with applicable law, the President's priorities, and the principles set forth in this Executive order, and that decisions made by one agency do not conflict with the policies or actions taken or planned by another agency. The Office of Management and Budget (OMB) shall carry out that review function. Within OMB, the Office of Information and Regulatory Affairs (OIRA) is the repository of expertise concerning regulatory issues, including methodologies and procedures that affect more than one agency, this Executive order, and the President's regulatory policies. To the extent permitted by law, OMB shall provide guidance to agencies and assist the President and regulatory policy advisors to the President in regulatory planning and shall be the entity that reviews individual regulations and guidance documents, as provided by this Executive order.

(c) *Assistance.* In fulfilling his responsibilities under this Executive order, the President shall be assisted by the regulatory policy advisors within the Executive Office of the President and by such agency officials and personnel as the President may, from time to time, consult.

Section 3. *Definitions.*

For purposes of this Executive order:

(a) "Advisors" refers to such regulatory policy advisors to the President as the President may from time to time consult, including, among others: (1) the Director of OMB; (2) the Chair (or another member) of the Council of Economic Advisers; (3) the Assistant to the President for Economic Policy; (4) the Assistant to the President for Domestic Policy; (5) the Assistant to the President for National Security Affairs; (6) the Director of the Office of Science and Technology Policy ; (7) the Deputy Assistant to the President and Director for Intergovernmental Affairs; (8) the Assistant to the President and Staff Secretary; (9) the Assistant to the President and Chief of Staff to the Vice President; (10) the Assistant to the President and Counsel to the President; (11) the Chairman of the Council on Environmental Quality and Director of the Office of Environmental Quality; (12) the Assistant to the President for Homeland Security; and (13) the Administrator of OIRA, who also shall coordinate communications relating to this Executive order among the agencies, OMB, the other Advisors, and the Office of the Vice President.

(b) "Agency," unless otherwise indicated, means any authority of the United States that is an "agency" under 44 U.S.C. 3502(1), other than those considered to be independent regulatory agencies, as defined in 44 U.S.C. 3502(10).
(c) "Director" means the Director of OMB.
(d) "Regulation" means an agency statement of general applicability and future effect, which the agency intends to have the force and effect of law, that is designed to implement, interpret, or prescribe law or policy or to describe the procedure or practice requirements of an agency. It does not, however, include:
> (1) Regulations issued in accordance with the formal rulemaking provisions of 5 U.S.C. 556, 557;
> (2) Regulations that pertain to a military or foreign affairs function of the United States, other than procurement regulations and regulations involving the import or export of non-defense articles and services;
> (3) Regulations that are limited to agency organization, management, or personnel matters; or
> (4) Any other category of regulations exempted by the Administrator of OIRA.

(e) "Regulatory action" means any substantive action by an agency (normally published in the *Federal Register*) that promulgates or is expected to lead to the promulgation of a final regulation, including notices of inquiry, advance notices of proposed rulemaking, and notices of proposed rulemaking.
(f) "Significant regulatory action" means any regulatory action that is likely to result in a regulation that may:
> (1) Have an annual effect on the economy of $100 million or more or adversely affect in a material way the economy, a sector of the economy, productivity, competition, jobs, the environment, public health or safety, or State, local, or tribal governments or communities;
> (2) Create a serious inconsistency or otherwise interfere with an action taken or planned by another agency;
> (3) Materially alter the budgetary impact of entitlements, grants, user fees, or loan programs or the rights and obligations of recipients thereof; or
> (4) Raise novel legal or policy issues arising out of legal mandates, the President's priorities, or the principles set forth in this Executive order.

(g) "Guidance document" means an agency statement of general applicability and future effect other than a regulatory action, that sets forth a policy on a statutory, regulatory, or technical issue or an interpretation of a statutory or regulatory issue.

(h) "Significant guidance document"—

(1) Means a guidance document disseminated to regulated entities or the general public that, for purposes of this order, may reasonably be anticipated to:

(A) Lead to an annual effect of $100 million or more or adversely affect in a material way the economy, a sector of the economy, productivity, competition, jobs, the environment, public health or safety, or State, local, or tribal governments or communities;

(B) Create a serious inconsistency or otherwise interfere with an action taken or planned by another agency;

(C) Materially alter the budgetary impact of entitlements, grants, user fees, or loan programs or the rights or obligations of recipients thereof; or

(D) Raise novel legal or policy issues arising out of legal mandates, the President's priorities, or the principles set forth in this Executive order; and

(2) Does not include:

(A) Guidance documents on regulations issued in accordance with the formal rulemaking provisions of 5 U.S.C. 556, 557;

(B) Guidance documents that pertain to a military or foreign affairs function of the United States, other than procurement regulations and regulations involving the import or export of non-defense articles and services;

(C) Guidance documents on regulations that are limited to agency organization, management, or personnel matters; or

(D) Any other category of guidance documents exempted by the Administrator of OIRA.

Section 4. *Planning Mechanism.*

In order to have an effective regulatory program, to provide for coordination of regulations, to maximize consultation and the resolution of potential conflicts at an early stage, to involve the public and its State, local, and tribal officials in regulatory planning, and to ensure that new or revised regulations promote the President's priorities and the principles set forth in this Executive order, these procedures shall be followed, to the extent permitted by law:

(a) The Director may convene a meeting of agency heads and other government personnel as appropriate to seek a common understanding of priorities and to coordinate regulatory efforts to be accomplished in the upcoming year.

(b) *Unified Regulatory Agenda.* For purposes of this subsection, the term "agency" or "agencies" shall also include those considered to be independent regulatory agencies, as defined in 44 U.S.C. 3502(10). Each agency shall prepare an agenda of all regulations under development or review, at a time and in a manner specified by the Administrator of OIRA. The description of each regulatory action shall contain, at a minimum, a regulation identifier number, a brief summary of the action, the legal authority for the action, any legal deadline for the action, and the name and telephone number of a knowledgeable agency official. Agencies may incorporate the information required under 5 U.S.C. 602 and 41 U.S.C. 402 into these agendas.

(c) *The Regulatory Plan.* For purposes of this subsection, the term "agency" or "agencies" shall also include those considered to be independent regulatory agencies, as defined in 44 U.S.C. 3502(10).

(1) As part of the Unified Regulatory Agenda, beginning in 1994, each agency shall prepare a Regulatory Plan (Plan) of the most important significant regulatory actions that the agency reasonably expects to issue in proposed or final form in that fiscal year or thereafter. Unless specifically authorized by the head of the agency, no rulemaking shall commence nor be included on the Plan without the approval of the agency's Regulatory Policy Office[r], and the Plan shall contain at a minimum:

(A) A statement of the agency's regulatory objectives and priorities and how they relate to the President's priorities;

(B) A summary of each planned significant regulatory action including, to the extent possible, alternatives to be considered and preliminary estimates of the anticipated costs and benefits of each rule as well as the agency's best estimate of the combined aggregate costs and benefits of all its regulations planned for that calendar year to assist with the identification of priorities;

(C) A summary of the legal basis for each such action, including whether any aspect of the action is required by statute or court order, and specific citation to such statute, order, or other legal authority;

(D) A statement of the need for each such action and, if applicable, how the action will reduce risks to public health, safety, or the environment, as well as how the magnitude of the risk addressed by the action relates to other risks within the jurisdiction of the agency;

(E) The agency's schedule for action, including a statement of any applicable statutory or judicial deadlines; and

(F) The name, address, and telephone number of a person the public may contact for additional information about the planned regulatory action.

(2) Each agency shall forward its Plan to OIRA by June 1st of each year.

(3) Within 10 calendar days after OIRA has received an agency's Plan, OIRA shall circulate it to other affected agencies and the Advisors.

(4) An agency head who believes that a planned regulatory action of another agency may conflict with its own policy or action taken or planned shall promptly notify, in writing, the Administrator of OIRA, who shall forward that communication to the issuing agency and the Advisors.

(5) If the Administrator of OIRA believes that a planned regulatory action of an agency may be inconsistent with the President's priorities or the principles set forth in this Executive order or may be in conflict with any policy or action taken or planned by another agency, the Administrator of OIRA shall promptly notify, in writing, the affected agencies and the Advisors.

(6) The Director may consult with the heads of agencies with respect to their Plans and, in appropriate instances, request further consideration or inter-agency coordination.

(7) The Plans developed by the issuing agency shall be published annually in the October publication of the Unified Regulatory Agenda. This publication shall be made available to the Congress; State, local, and tribal governments; and the public. Any views on any aspect of any agency Plan, including whether any planned regulatory action might conflict with any other planned or existing regulation, impose any unintended consequences on the public, or confer any unclaimed benefits on the public, should be directed to the issuing agency, with a copy to OIRA.

(d) *Regulatory Working Group.* Within 30 days of the date of this Executive order, the Administrator of OIRA shall convene a Regulatory Working Group ("Working Group"), which shall consist of representatives of the heads of each agency that the Administrator determines to have significant domestic regulatory responsibility and the Advisors. The Administrator of OIRA shall chair the Working Group and shall periodically advise the Director on the activities of the Working Group. The Working Group shall serve as a forum to assist agencies in identifying and analyzing important regulatory issues (including, among others (1) the development of innovative regulatory techniques, (2) the methods, efficacy, and utility of comparative risk assessment in regulatory decision-making, and (3) the development of short forms and other streamlined regulatory approaches for small businesses and other entities). The Working Group shall meet at least quarterly and may meet as a whole or in subgroups of agencies with an interest in particular issues or subject areas. To inform its discussions, the Working Group may commission analytical studies and reports by OIRA, the Administrative Conference of the United States, or any other agency.

(e) *Conferences.* The Administrator of OIRA shall meet quarterly with representatives of State, local, and tribal governments to identify both existing and proposed regulations that may uniquely or significantly affect those governmental entities. The Administrator of OIRA shall also convene, from time to time, conferences with representatives of businesses, nongovernmental organizations, and the public to discuss regulatory issues of common concern.

Section 5. *Existing Regulations.*
In order to reduce the regulatory burden on the American people, their families, their communities, their State, local, and tribal governments, and their industries; to determine whether regulations promulgated by the executive branch of the Federal Government have become unjustified or unnecessary as a result of changed circumstances; to confirm that regulations are both compatible with each other and not duplicative or inappropriately burdensome in the aggregate; to ensure that all regulations are consistent with the President's priorities and the principles set forth in this Executive order, within applicable law; and to otherwise improve the effectiveness of existing regulations:

(a) Within 90 days of the date of this Executive order, each agency shall submit to OIRA a program, consistent with its resources and regulatory priorities, under which the agency will periodically review its existing significant regulations to determine whether any such regulations should be modified or eliminated so as to make the agency's regulatory program more effective in achieving the regulatory objectives, less burdensome, or in greater alignment with the President's priorities and the principles set forth in this Executive order. Any significant regulations selected for review shall be included in the agency's annual Plan. The agency shall also identify any legislative mandates that require the agency to promulgate or continue to impose regulations that the agency believes are unnecessary or outdated by reason of changed circumstances.

(b) The Administrator of OIRA shall work with the Regulatory Working Group and other interested entities to pursue the objectives of this section. State, local, and tribal governments are specifically encouraged to assist in the identification of regulations that impose significant or unique burdens on those governmental entities and that appear to have outlived their justification or be otherwise inconsistent with the public interest.

(c) The Director, in consultation with the Advisors, may identify for review by the appropriate agency or agencies other existing regulations of an agency or groups of regulations of more than one agency that affect a particular group, industry, or sector of the economy, or may identify legislative mandates that may be appropriate for reconsideration by the Congress.

Section 6. *Centralized Review of Regulations.*

The guidelines set forth below shall apply to all regulatory actions, for both new and existing regulations, by agencies other than those agencies specifically exempted by the Administrator of OIRA:

(a) *Agency Responsibilities.*

(1) Each agency shall (consistent with its own rules, regulations, or procedures) provide the public with meaningful participation in the regulatory process. In particular, before issuing a notice of proposed rulemaking, each agency should, where appropriate, seek the involvement of those who are intended to benefit from and those expected to be burdened by any regulation (including, specifically, State, local, and tribal officials). In addition, each agency should afford the public a meaningful opportunity to comment on any proposed regulation, which in most cases should include a comment period of not less than 60 days. In consultation with OIRA, each agency may also consider whether to utilize formal rulemaking procedures under 5 U.S.C. 556 and 557 for the resolution of complex determinations. Each agency also is directed to explore and, where appropriate, use consensual mechanisms for developing regulations, including negotiated rulemaking.

(2) Within 60 days of the date of this Executive order, each agency head shall designate one of the agency's Presidential Appointees to be its Regulatory Policy Officer, advise OMB of such designation, and annually update OMB on the status of this designation. The Regulatory Policy Officer shall be involved at each stage of the regulatory

process to foster the development of effective, innovative, and least burdensome regulations and to further the principles set forth in this Executive order.

(3) In addition to adhering to its own rules and procedures and to the requirements of the Administrative Procedure Act, the Regulatory Flexibility Act, the Paperwork Reduction Act, and other applicable law, each agency shall develop its regulatory actions in a timely fashion and adhere to the following procedures with respect to a regulatory action:

> (A) Each agency shall provide OIRA, at such times and in the manner specified by the Administrator of OIRA, with a list of its planned regulatory actions, indicating those which the agency believes are significant regulatory actions within the meaning of this Executive order. Absent a material change in the development of the planned regulatory action, those not designated as significant will not be subject to review under this section unless, within 10 working days of receipt of the list, the Administrator of OIRA notifies the agency that OIRA has determined that a planned regulation is a significant regulatory action within the meaning of this Executive order. The Administrator of OIRA may waive review of any planned regulatory action designated by the agency as significant, in which case the agency need not further comply with subsection (a)(3)(B) or subsection (a)(3)(C) of this section.
>
> (B) For each matter identified as, or determined by the Administrator of OIRA to be, a significant regulatory action, the issuing agency shall provide to OIRA:
>
> > (i) The text of the draft regulatory action, together with a reasonably detailed description of the need for the regulatory action and an explanation of how the regulatory action will meet that need; and
> >
> > (ii) An assessment of the potential costs and benefits of the regulatory action, including an explanation of the manner in which the regulatory action is consistent with a statutory mandate and, to the extent permitted by law, promotes the President's priorities and avoids undue interference with State, local, and tribal governments in the exercise of their governmental functions.
>
> (C) For those matters identified as, or determined by the Administrator of OIRA to be, a significant regulatory action within

the scope of section 3(f)(1), the agency shall also provide to OIRA the following additional information developed as part of the agency's decision-making process (unless prohibited by law):

(i) An assessment, including the underlying analysis, of benefits anticipated from the regulatory action (such as, but not limited to, the promotion of the efficient functioning of the economy and private markets, the enhancement of health and safety, the protection of the natural environment, and the elimination or reduction of discrimination or bias) together with, to the extent feasible, a quantification of those benefits;

(ii) An assessment, including the underlying analysis, of costs anticipated from the regulatory action (such as, but not limited to, the direct cost both to the government in administering the regulation and to businesses and others in complying with the regulation, and any adverse effects on the efficient functioning of the economy, private markets (including productivity, employment, and competitiveness), health, safety, and the natural environment), together with, to the extent feasible, a quantification of those costs; and

(iii) An assessment, including the underlying analysis, of costs and benefits of potentially effective and reasonably feasible alternatives to the planned regulation, identified by the agencies or the public (including improving the current regulation and reasonably viable nonregulatory actions), and an explanation why the planned regulatory action is preferable to the identified potential alternatives.

(D) In emergency situations or when an agency is obligated by law to act more quickly than normal review procedures allow, the agency shall notify OIRA as soon as possible and, to the extent practicable, comply with subsections (a)(3)(B) and (C) of this section. For those regulatory actions that are governed by a statutory or court-imposed deadline, the agency shall, to the extent practicable, schedule rulemaking proceedings so as to permit sufficient time for OIRA to conduct its review, as set forth below in subsection (b)(2) through (4) of this section.

(E) After the regulatory action has been published in the *Federal Register* or otherwise issued to the public, the agency shall:

(i) Make available to the public the information set forth in subsections (a)(3)(B) and (C);

(ii) Identify for the public, in a complete, clear, and simple manner, the substantive changes between the draft submitted to OIRA for review and the action subsequently announced; and

(iii) Identify for the public those changes in the regulatory action that were made at the suggestion or recommendation of OIRA.

(F) All information provided to the public by the agency shall be in plain, understandable language.

(b) *OIRA Responsibilities*. The Administrator of OIRA shall provide meaningful guidance and oversight so that each agency's regulatory actions are consistent with applicable law, the President's priorities, and the principles set forth in this Executive order and do not conflict with the policies or actions of another agency. OIRA shall, to the extent permitted by law, adhere to the following guidelines:

(1) OIRA may review only actions identified by the agency or by OIRA as significant regulatory actions under subsection (a)(3)(A) of this section.

(2) OIRA shall waive review or notify the agency in writing of the results of its review within the following time periods:

(A) For any notices of inquiry, advance notices of proposed rulemaking, or other preliminary regulatory actions prior to a Notice of Proposed Rulemaking, within 10 working days after the date of submission of the draft action to OIRA;

(B) For all other regulatory actions, within 90 calendar days after the date of submission of the information set forth in subsections (a)(3)(B) and (C) of this section, unless OIRA has previously reviewed this information and, since that review, there has been no material change in the facts and circumstances upon which the regulatory action is based, in which case, OIRA shall complete its review within 45 days; and

(C) The review process may be extended (1) once by no more than 30 calendar days upon the written approval of the Director and (2) at the request of the agency head.

(3) For each regulatory action that the Administrator of OIRA returns to an agency for further consideration of some or all of its provisions, the Administrator of OIRA shall provide the issuing agency a written explanation for such return, setting forth the pertinent provision of this Executive order on which OIRA is relying. If the agency head disagrees with some or all of the bases for the return, the agency

head shall so inform the Administrator of OIRA in writing.

(4) Except as otherwise provided by law or required by a Court, in order to ensure greater openness, accessibility, and accountability in the regulatory review process, OIRA shall be governed by the following disclosure requirements:

(A) Only the Administrator of OIRA (or a particular designee) shall receive oral communications initiated by persons not employed by the executive branch of the Federal Government regarding the substance of a regulatory action under OIRA review;

(B) All substantive communications between OIRA personnel and persons not employed by the executive branch of the Federal Government regarding a regulatory action under review shall be governed by the following guidelines:

(i) A representative from the issuing agency shall be invited to any meeting between OIRA personnel and such person(s);

(ii) OIRA shall forward to the issuing agency, within 10 working days of receipt of the communication(s), all written communications, regardless of format, between OIRA personnel and any person who is not employed by the executive branch of the Federal Government, and the dates and names of individuals involved in all substantive oral communications (including meetings to which an agency representative was invited, but did not attend, and telephone conversations between OIRA personnel and any such persons); and

(iii) OIRA shall publicly disclose relevant information about such communication(s), as set forth below in subsection (b)(4)(C) of this section.

(C) OIRA shall maintain a publicly available log that shall contain, at a minimum, the following information pertinent to regulatory actions under review:

(i) The status of all regulatory actions, including if (and if so, when and by whom) Presidential consideration was requested;

(ii) A notation of all written communications forwarded to an issuing agency under subsection (b)(4)(B)(ii) of this section; and

(iii) The dates and names of individuals involved in all substantive oral communications, including meetings and telephone conversations, between OIRA personnel and any person not employed by the executive branch of the Federal Government, and the subject matter discussed during such communications.

(D) After the regulatory action has been published in the *Federal Register* or otherwise issued to the public, or after the agency has announced its decision not to publish or issue the regulatory action, OIRA shall make available to the public all documents exchanged between OIRA and the agency during the review by OIRA under this section.

(5) All information provided to the public by OIRA shall be in plain, understandable language.

Section 7. *Resolution of Conflicts.*

(a) To the extent permitted by law, disagreements or conflicts between or among agency heads or between OMB and any agency that cannot be resolved by the Administrator of OIRA shall be resolved by the President, with the assistance of the Chief of Staff to the President ("Chief of Staff"), with the relevant agency head (and, as appropriate, other interested government officials). Presidential consideration of such disagreements may be initiated only by the Director, by the head of the issuing agency, or by the head of an agency that has a significant interest in the regulatory action at issue. Such review will not be undertaken at the request of other persons, entities, or their agents.

(b) Resolution of such conflicts shall be informed by recommendations developed by the Chief of Staff, after consultation with the Advisors (and other executive branch officials or personnel whose responsibilities to the President include the subject matter at issue). The development of these recommendations shall be concluded within 60 days after review has been requested.

(c) During the Presidential review period, communications with any person not employed by the Federal Government relating to the substance of the regulatory action under review and directed to the Advisors or their staffs or to the staff of the Chief of Staff shall be in writing and shall be forwarded by the recipient to the affected agency(ies) for inclusion in the public docket(s). When the communication is not in writing, such Advisors or staff members shall inform the outside party that the matter is under review and that any comments should be submitted in writing.

(d) At the end of this review process, the President, or the Chief of Staff acting at the request of the President, shall notify the affected agency and the Administrator of OIRA of the President's decision with respect to the matter.

Section 8. *Publication.*
Except to the extent required by law, an agency shall not publish in the *Federal Register* or otherwise issue to the public any regulatory action that is subject to review under section 6 of this Executive order until (1) the Administrator of OIRA notifies the agency that OIRA has waived its review of the action or has completed its review without any requests for further consideration, or (2) the applicable time period in section 6(b)(2) expires without OIRA having notified the agency that it is returning the regulatory action for further consideration under section 6(b)(3), whichever occurs first. If the terms of the preceding sentence have not been satisfied and an agency wants to publish or otherwise issue a regulatory action, the head of that agency may request Presidential consideration through the Director, as provided under section 7 of this order. Upon receipt of this request, the Director shall notify OIRA and the Advisors. The guidelines and time period set forth in section 7 shall apply to the publication of regulatory actions for which Presidential consideration has been sought.

Section 9. *Significant Guidance Documents.*
Each agency shall provide OIRA, at such times and in the manner specified by the Administrator of OIRA, with advance notification of any significant guidance documents. Each agency shall take such steps as are necessary for its Regulatory Policy Officer to ensure the agency's compliance with the requirements of this section. Upon the request of the Administrator, for each matter identified as, or determined by the Administrator to be, a significant guidance document, the issuing agency shall provide to OIRA the content of the draft guidance document, together with a brief explanation of the need for the guidance document and how it will meet that need. The OIRA Administrator shall notify the agency when additional consultation will be required before the issuance of the significant guidance document.

Section 10. *Preservation of Agency Authority.* Nothing in this order shall be construed to impair or otherwise affect the authority vested by law in an agency or the head thereof, including the authority of the Attorney General relating to litigation.

Section 11. *Judicial Review.*
Nothing in this Executive order shall affect any otherwise available judicial review of agency action. This Executive order is intended only to improve the internal management of the Federal Government and does not create any right or benefit, substantive or procedural, enforceable at law or equity by a party against the United States, its agencies or instrumentalities, its officers or employees, or any other person.

Section 12. *Revocations.*
Executive Orders Nos. 12291 and 12498; all amendments to those Executive orders; all guidelines issued under those orders; and any exemptions from those orders heretofore granted for any category of rule are revoked.

WILLIAM CLINTON [Amendments by George W. Bush]

EXECUTIVE ORDER 12866 SUBMISSION

Important

Please read the instructions on the reverse side before completing this form.

For additional forms or assistance in completing this form, contact the OIRA Docket Library, 202-395-6880, or your OIRA Desk Officer.

Send three copies of both this form and supporting material (four copies if Economically Significant or an Unfunded Mandate) to:

Office of Information and Regulatory Affairs
Office of Management and Budget
Attention: Docket Library, Room 10102
725 17th Street, N.W.
Washington, D. C. 20503

1. Agency/Subagency originating request

2. Regulation Identifier Number (RIN)

3. Title

4. Stage of Development
   - [ ] Prerule
   - [ ] Proposed Rule
   - [ ] Interim Final Rule
   - [ ] Final Rule
   - [ ] Final Rule - No material change
   - [ ] Notice
   - [ ] Other

   Description of Other

5. Legal Deadline for this submission
   a) [ ] Yes   [ ] No
   b) Date __/__/__ (DD/MM/YYYY)
   c) [ ] Statutory   [ ] Judicial

6. Designations
   a) Economically Significant (E.O. 12866)
      [ ] Yes   [ ] No
   b) Unfunded mandate (2 U.S.C 1532)
      [ ] Yes   [ ] No

   If either of the above is "Yes", submit four (4) complete packages to OIRA

7. Agency Contact (person who can best answer questions regarding the content of this submission)

   Phone

Certification for Executive Order 12866 Submissions

The authorized regulatory contact and the program official certify that the agency has complied with the requirements of E. O. 12866 and any applicable policy directives.

Signature of Program Official	Date
Signature of Authorized Regulatory Contact	Date

OMB 83-R   Revision: 12/97 (Previous versions obsolete)

Reset Form

INSTRUCTIONS FOR REQUESTING OMB REVIEW UNDER EXECUTIVE ORDER 12866

GENERAL

Please make sure to answer all questions and have the appropriate officials sign the form.

If you check "Yes" in question 6a or 6b, you must submit four copies of both this form and the supporting material. Otherwise, you only need to submit three copies.

1. Agency/Subagency

Provide the name of the agency or subagency originating the request. For most Cabinet-level agencies, a subagency designation is also necessary. For non-Cabinet agencies, the subagency designation is generally unnecessary. For example, if you are at the National Park Service, put "Department of the Interior/National Park Service."

2. Regulation Identifier Number (RIN)

Fill in the RIN for this rulemaking. RINs are assigned by the Regulatory Information Service Center (RISC) and are a means of linking rules listed in the Unified Agenda of Federal Regulatory and Deregulatory Actions, The Regulatory Plan, and E.O. 12866 reviews. The RIN is a four-digit agency/subagency code followed by two letters and two numbers, e.g., 1024-AA01. If you do not have a RIN for this action, contact RISC at (202) 482-7340 before you submit it to OIRA.

3. Title

Please provide a brief title that describes, as specifically as you can, the subject of this rulemaking. Avoid using general headings or the title of the CFR part for your rulemaking. To the extent possible, you should keep the title the same as in the Agenda. Also, you should use the same title for all stages of a rulemaking.

4. Stage of Development

Check the stage of development for this action:

Check "Prerule" when the action submitted for review seeks to determine whether or how to initiate rulemaking. Examples include ANPRMs and reviews of existing regulations.

Check "Proposed Rule" when the action submitted will be published in the Proposed Rules section of the Federal Register (for example, an NPRM).

Check "Interim Final Rule" when the action submitted will be published in the Rules and Regulations section of the Federal Register with an Action caption of Interim Rule or Interim Final Rule.

Check "Final Rule" when the action submitted will be published in the Rules an Regulations section of the Federal Register and there have been material changes in the facts and circumstances upon which the previous action was based.

Check "Final Rule -- No material change" when the action submitted is associated with a previous request (for example, an NPRM) and there has been no material change in the facts and circumstances upon which the previous action was based.

Check "Notice" when the action submitted will be published in the Notices section of the Federal Register.

Check "Other" when the action does not meet the criteria of any of any of the above categories. (Indicate on the line provided what type of action you are submitting; for example, a policy statement.)

5. Legal Deadline for This Submission

This question refers to deadlines for this specific action only, not deadlines which may exist for future or past actions in the same rulemaking.

a) Indicate whether the action submitted is subject to any specific legal deadline. For example, if this submission is for an NPRM and the Final Rule stage has a deadline, check No. If this submission is for the Final Rule, check Yes.

b) If 5a is Yes, provide the day, month, and year of the deadline for this action (whether past or future).

c) If 5a is Yes, indicate whether the deadline is statutory or judicial.

6. Designations

a) Economically Significant - Check "Yes" if the action submitted is likely to have an annual effect on the economy of $100 million or more or adversely affect in a material way the economy, a sector of the economy, productivity, competition, jobs, the environment, public health and safety, or State, local, or tribal governments or communities. (Section 3(f)(1) of E.O. 12866.)

b) Unfunded Mandate - Check "Yes" if the agency believes the rule may constitute an unfunded mandate under 2 U.S.C. 1532(a).

7. Agency Contact

Provide the name and telephone number of agency person best able to answer questions regarding the content of this submission.

12/97

B. Executive Order 12,889

Implementation of the North American Free Trade Agreement

December 27, 1993

58 Fed. Reg. 69,681 (Dec. 30, 1993)

By the authority vested in me as President by the Constitution and the laws of the United States of America, including the North American Free Trade Agreement Implementation Act (Public Law 103-182, 107 Stat. 2057) (the NAFTA Implementation Act) and section 302 of title 3, United States Code, and in order to implement the North American Free Trade Agreement (NAFTA), it is hereby ordered:

****

Section 4. *Publication of Proposed Rules regarding Technical Regulations and Sanitary and Phytosanitary Measures.*

    a. In accordance with Articles 718 and 909 of the NAFTA, each agency subject to the provisions of the Administrative Procedure Act, as amended (5 U.S.C. 551 et seq.), shall, in applying section 553 of title 5, United States Code, with respect to any proposed Federal technical regulation or any Federal sanitary or phytosanitary measure of general application, other than a regulation issued pursuant to section 104(a) of the NAFTA Implementation Act, publish or serve notice of such regulation or measure not less than 75 days before the comment due date, except:

    1. in the case of a technical regulation relating to perishable goods, in which case the agency shall, to the greatest extent practicable, publish or serve notice at least 30 days prior to adoption of such regulation;

    2. in the case of a technical regulation, where the United States considers it necessary to address an urgent problem relating to safety or to protection of human, animal or plant life or health, the environment or consumers; or

    3. in the case of a sanitary or phytosanitary measure, where the United States considers it necessary to address an urgent problem relating to sanitary or phytosanitary protection.

    b. For purposes of this section, the term "sanitary or phytosanitary measure" shall be defined in accordance with section 463 of the Trade Agreements Act of 1979, and "technical regulation" shall be defined in accordance with section 473 of the Trade Agreements Act of 1979.

c. This section supersedes section 1 of Executive Order No. 12662 of December 31, 1988.

****

Section 7. *Judicial Review.* This order does not create any right or benefit, substantive or procedural, enforceable at law by a party against the United States, its agencies, its officers, or any person.

Section 8. *Effective Date.* This order shall take effect upon the date of entry into force of the NAFTA for the United States.

WILLIAM J. CLINTON

C. Executive Order 12,898

Federal Actions to Address Environmental Justice in Minority Populations and Low-Income Populations

February 11, 1994

59 Fed. Reg. 7629 (Feb.16, 1994)

By the authority vested in me as President by the Constitution and the laws of the United States of America, it is hereby ordered as follows:

Section 1-1. *Implementation.*

1-101. Agency Responsibilities. To the greatest extent practicable and permitted by law, and consistent with the principles set forth in the report on the National Performance Review, each Federal agency shall make achieving environmental justice part of its mission by identifying and addressing, as appropriate, disproportionately high and adverse human health or environmental effects of its programs, policies, and activities on minority populations and low-income populations in the United States and its territories and possessions, the District of Columbia, the Commonwealth of Puerto Rico, and the Commonwealth of the Mariana Islands.

1-102. *Creation of an Interagency Working Group on Environmental Justice.*

(a) Within 3 months of the date of this order, the Administrator of the Environmental Protection Agency ("Administrator") or the Administrator's designee shall convene an interagency Federal Working Group on Environmental Justice ("Working Group"). The Working Group shall comprise the heads of the following executive agencies and offices, or their designees: (a) Department of Defense; (b) Department of Health and Human Services; (c) Department of Housing and Urban Development; (d) Department of Labor; (e) Department of Agriculture; (f) Department of Transportation; (g) Department of Justice; (h) Department of the Interior; (i) Department of Commerce; (j) Department of Energy; (k) Environmental Protection Agency; (l) Office of Management and Budget; (m) Office of Science and Technology Policy; (n) Office of the Deputy Assistant to the President for Environmental Policy; (o) Office of the Assistant to the President for Domestic Policy; (p) National Economic Council; (q) Council of Economic Advisers; and (r) such other Government officials as the President may designate. The Working Group shall report to the President through the Deputy Assistant to the President for

Environmental Policy and the Assistant to the President for Domestic Policy.

(b) The Working Group shall: (1) provide guidance to Federal agencies on criteria for identifying disproportionately high and adverse human health or environmental effects on minority populations and low-income populations; (2) coordinate with, provide guidance to, and serve as a clearinghouse for, each Federal agency as it develops an environmental justice strategy as required by section 1-103 of this order, in order to ensure that the administration, interpretation and enforcement of programs, activities and policies are undertaken in a consistent manner; (3) assist in coordinating research by, and stimulating cooperation among, the Environmental Protection Agency, the Department of Health and Human Services, the Department of Housing and Urban Development, and other agencies conducting research or other activities in accordance with section 3-3 of this order; (4) assist in coordinating data collection, required by this order; (5) examine existing data and studies on environmental justice; (6) hold public meetings as required in section 5-502(d) of this order; and (7) develop interagency model projects on environmental justice that evidence cooperation among Federal agencies.

1-103. *Development of Agency Strategies.*

(a) Except as provided in section 6-605 of this order, each Federal agency shall develop an agency-wide environmental justice strategy, as set forth in subsections (b)-(e) of this section that identifies and addresses disproportionately high and adverse human health or environmental effects of its programs, policies, and activities on minority populations and low-income populations. The environmental justice strategy shall list programs, policies, planning and public participation processes, enforcement, and/or rulemakings related to human health or the environment that should be revised to, at a minimum: (1) promote enforcement of all health and environmental statutes in areas with minority populations and low-income populations; (2) ensure greater public participation; (3) improve research and data collection relating to the health of and environment of minority populations and low-income populations; and (4) identify differential patterns of consumption of natural resources among minority populations and low-income populations. In addition, the environmental justice strategy shall include, where appropriate, a timetable for undertaking identified revisions and consideration of economic and social implications of the revisions.

(b) Within 4 months of the date of this order, each Federal agency shall identify an internal administrative process for developing its environmental justice strategy, and shall inform the Working Group of the process.

(c) Within 6 months of the date of this order, each Federal agency shall provide the Working Group with an outline of its proposed environmental justice strategy.

(d) Within 10 months of the date of this order, each Federal agency shall provide the Working Group with its proposed environmental justice strategy.

(e) [Within 12 months of the date of this order]* each Federal agency shall finalize its environmental justice strategy and provide a copy and written description of its strategy to the Working Group. [During the 12 month period from the date of this order,]** each Federal agency, as part of its environmental justice strategy, shall identify several specific projects that can be promptly undertaken to address particular concerns identified during the development of the proposed environmental justice strategy, and a schedule for implementing those projects.

(f) Within 24 months of the date of this order, each Federal agency shall report to the Working Group on its progress in implementing its agency-wide environmental justice strategy.

(g) Federal agencies shall provide additional periodic reports to the Working Group as requested by the Working Group.

1-104. Reports to the President. Within 14 months of the date of this order, the Working Group shall submit to the President, through the Office of the Deputy Assistant to the President for Environmental Policy and the Office of the Assistant to the President for Domestic Policy, a report that describes the implementation of this order, and includes the final environmental justice strategies described in section 1-103(e) of this order.

Section 2-2. *Federal Agency Responsibilities for Federal Programs.*

Each Federal agency shall conduct its programs, policies, and activities that substantially affect human health or the environment, in a manner that ensures that such programs, policies, and activities do not have the effect of excluding persons (including populations) from participation in, denying persons (including populations) the benefits of, or subjecting persons (in-

---

* Amended by Executive Order 12948 to read "By March 24, 1995," (January 30, 1995).

** Amended by Executive Order 12948 to read, "From the date of this order through March 24, 1995," (January 30, 1995).

cluding populations) to discrimination under, such programs, policies, and activities, because of their race, color, or national origin.

Section 3-3. *Research, Data Collection, and Analysis.*

3-301. *Human Health and Environmental Research and Analysis.*

(a) Environmental human health research, whenever practicable and appropriate, shall include diverse segments of the population in epidemiological and clinical studies, including segments at high risk from environmental hazards, such as minority populations, low-income populations and workers who may be exposed to substantial environmental hazards.

(b) Environmental human health analyses, whenever practicable and appropriate, shall identify multiple and cumulative exposures.

(c) Federal agencies shall provide minority populations and low-income populations the opportunity to comment on the development and design of research strategies undertaken pursuant to this order.

3-302. *Human Health and Environmental Data Collection and Analysis.* To the extent permitted by existing law, including the Privacy Act, as amended (5 U.S.C. § 552a):

(a) Each Federal agency, whenever practicable and appropriate, shall collect, maintain, and analyze information assessing and comparing environmental and human health risks borne by populations identified by race, national origin, or income. To the extent practical and appropriate, Federal agencies shall use this information to determine whether their programs, policies, and activities have disproportionately high and adverse human health or environmental effects on minority populations and low-income populations;

(b) In connection with the development and implementation of agency strategies in section 1-103 of this order, each Federal agency, whenever practicable and appropriate, shall collect, maintain and analyze information on the race, national origin, income level, and other readily accessible and appropriate information for areas surrounding facilities or sites expected to have a substantial environmental, human health, or economic effect on the surrounding populations, when such facilities or sites become the subject of a substantial Federal environmental administrative or judicial action. Such information shall be made available to the public, unless prohibited by law; and

(c) Each Federal agency, whenever practicable and appropriate, shall collect, maintain, and analyze information on the race, national origin, income level, and other readily accessible and appropriate information for areas surrounding Federal facilities that are: (1) subject to the reporting requirements under the Emergency Planning and Community Right-to-Know Act, 42 U.S.C. § 11001-11050 as mandated in Executive Order No. 12856; and (2) expected to have a substantial environmental, human health, or economic effect on surrounding populations. Such information shall be made available to the public, unless prohibited by law.

(d) In carrying out the responsibilities in this section, each Federal agency, whenever practicable and appropriate, shall share information and eliminate unnecessary duplication of efforts through the use of existing data systems and cooperative agreements among Federal agencies and with States, local, and tribal governments.

Section 4-4. *Subsistence Consumption of Fish and Wildlife.*

4-401. Consumption Patterns. In order to assist in identifying the need for ensuring protection of populations with differential patterns of subsistence consumption of fish and wildlife, Federal agencies, whenever practicable and appropriate, shall collect, maintain, and analyze information on the consumption patterns of populations who principally rely on fish and/or wildlife for subsistence. Federal agencies shall communicate to the public the risks of those consumption patterns.

4-402. Guidance. Federal agencies, whenever practicable and appropriate, shall work in a coordinated manner to publish guidance reflecting the latest scientific information available concerning methods for evaluating the human health risks associated with the consumption of pollutant-bearing fish or wildlife. Agencies shall consider such guidance in developing their policies and rules.

Section 5-5. *Public Participation and Access to Information.*

(a) The public may submit recommendations to Federal agencies relating to the incorporation of environmental justice principles into Federal agency programs or policies. Each Federal agency shall convey such recommendations to the Working Group.

(b) Each Federal agency may, whenever practicable and appropriate, translate crucial public documents, notices, and hearings relating to human health or the environment for limited English speaking populations.

(c) Each Federal agency shall work to ensure that public documents, notices, and hearings relating to human health or the environment are concise, understandable, and readily accessible to the public.

(d) The Working Group shall hold public meetings, as appropriate, for the purpose of fact-finding, receiving public comments, and conducting inquiries concerning environmental justice. The Working Group shall prepare for public review a summary of the comments and recommendations discussed at the public meetings.

Section 6-6. *General Provisions.*

6-601. Responsibility for Agency Implementation. The head of each Federal agency shall be responsible for ensuring compliance with this order. Each Federal agency shall conduct internal reviews and take such other steps as may be necessary to monitor compliance with this order.

6-602. Executive Order No. 12250. This Executive order is intended to supplement but not supersede Executive Order No. 12250, which requires consistent and effective implementation of various laws prohibiting discriminatory practices in programs receiving Federal financial assistance. Nothing herein shall limit the effect or mandate of Executive Order No. 12250.

6-603. Executive Order No. 12875. This Executive order is not intended to limit the effect or mandate of Executive Order No. 12875.

6-604. Scope. For purposes of this order, Federal agency means any agency on the Working Group, and such other agencies as may be designated by the President, that conducts any Federal program or activity that substantially affects human health or the environment. Independent agencies are requested to comply with the provisions of this order.

6-605. Petitions for Exemptions. The head of a Federal agency may petition the President for an exemption from the requirements of this order on the grounds that all or some of the petitioning agency's programs or activities should not be subject to the requirements of this order.

6-606. Native American Programs. Each Federal agency responsibility set forth under this order shall apply equally to Native American programs. In addition, the Department of the Interior, in coordination with the Working Group, and, after consultation with tribal leaders, shall coordinate steps to be taken pursuant to this order that address Federally-recognized Indian Tribes.

6-607. Costs. Unless otherwise provided by law, Federal agencies shall assume the financial costs of complying with this order.

6-608. General. Federal agencies shall implement this order consistent with, and to the extent permitted by, existing law.

6-609. Judicial Review. This order is intended only to improve the internal management of the executive branch and is not intended to, nor does it create any right, benefit, or trust responsibility, substantive or procedural, enforceable at law or equity by a party against the United States, its agencies, its officers, or any person. This order shall not be construed to create any right to judicial review involving the compliance or noncompliance of the United States, its agencies, its officers, or any other person with this order.

WILLIAM J. CLINTON

D. Executive Order 12,988

Civil Justice Reform

February 5, 1996

61 Fed. Reg. 4729 (Feb. 7, 1996)

By the authority vested in me as President by the Constitution and the laws of the United States of America, including section 301 of title 3, United States Code, and in order to improve access to justice for all persons who wish to avail themselves of court and administrative adjudicatory tribunals to resolve disputes, to facilitate the just and efficient resolution of civil claims involving the United States Government, to encourage the filing of only meritorious civil claims, to improve legislative and regulatory drafting to reduce needless litigation, to promote fair and prompt adjudication before administrative tribunals, and to provide a model for similar reforms of litigation practices in the private sector and in various states, it is hereby ordered as follows:

Section 1. *Guidelines to Promote Just and Efficient Government Civil Litigation.*

To promote the just and efficient resolution of civil claims, those Federal agencies and litigation counsel that conduct or otherwise participate in civil litigation on behalf of the United States Government in Federal court shall respect and adhere to the following guidelines during the conduct of such litigation:

(a) Pre-filing Notice of a Complaint. No litigation counsel shall file a complaint initiating civil litigation without first making a reasonable effort to notify all disputants about the nature of the dispute and to attempt to achieve a settlement, or confirming that the referring agency that previously handled the dispute has made a reasonable effort to notify the disputants and to achieve a settlement or has used its conciliation processes.

(b) Settlement Conferences. As soon as practicable after ascertaining the nature of a dispute in litigation, and throughout the litigation, litigation counsel shall evaluate settlement possibilities and make reasonable efforts to settle the litigation. Such efforts shall include offering to participate in a settlement conference or moving the court for a conference pursuant to Rule 16 of the Federal Rules of Civil Procedure in an attempt to resolve the dispute without additional civil litigation.

(c) Alternative Methods of Resolving the Dispute in Litigation. Litigation counsel shall make reasonable attempts to resolve a dispute expeditiously and properly before proceeding to trial.

(1) Whenever feasible, claims should be resolved through informal discussions, negotiations, and settlements rather than through utilization of any formal court proceeding. Where the benefits of Alternative Dispute Resolution ("ADR") may be derived, and after consultation with the agency referring the matter, litigation counsel should suggest the use of an appropriate ADR technique to the parties.

(2) It is appropriate to use ADR techniques or processes to resolve claims of or against the United States or its agencies, after litigation counsel determines that the use of a particular technique is warranted in the context of a particular claim or claims, and that such use will materially contribute to the prompt, fair, and efficient resolution of the claims.

(3) To facilitate broader and effective use of informal and formal ADR methods, litigation counsel should be trained in ADR techniques.

(d) Discovery. To the extent practical, litigation counsel shall make every reasonable effort to streamline and expedite discovery in cases under counsel's supervision and control.

(1) Review of Proposed Document Requests. Each agency within the executive branch shall establish a coordinated procedure for the conduct and review of document discovery undertaken in litigation directly by that agency when that agency is litigation counsel. The procedure shall include, but is not necessarily limited to, review by a senior lawyer prior to service or filing of the request in litigation to determine that the request is not cumulative or duplicative, unreasonable, oppressive, unduly burdensome or expensive, taking into account the requirements of the litigation, the amount in controversy, the importance of the issues at stake in the litigation, and whether the documents can be obtained from some other source that is more convenient, less burdensome, or less expensive.

(2) Discovery Motions. Before petitioning a court to resolve a discovery motion or petitioning a court to impose sanctions for discovery abuses, litigation counsel shall attempt to resolve the dispute with opposing counsel. If litigation counsel makes a discovery motion concerning the dispute, he or she shall represent in that motion that any attempt at resolution was unsuccessful or impracticable under the circumstances.

(e) Sanctions. Litigation counsel shall take steps to seek sanctions against opposing counsel and opposing parties where appropriate.

(1) Litigation counsel shall evaluate filings made by opposing parties and, where appropriate, shall petition the court to impose sanctions against those responsible for abusive practices.

(2) Prior to filing a motion for sanctions, litigation counsel shall submit the motion for review to the sanctions officer, or his or her designee, within the litigation counsel's agency. Such officer or designee shall be a senior supervising attorney within the agency, and shall be licensed to practice law before a State court, courts of the District of Columbia, or courts of any territory or Commonwealth of the United States. The sanctions officer or designee shall also review motions for sanctions that are filed against litigation counsel, the United States, its agencies, or its officers.

(f) Improved Use of Litigation Resources. Litigation counsel shall employ efficient case management techniques and shall make reasonable efforts to expedite civil litigation in cases under that counsel's supervision and control. This includes but is not limited to: (1) making reasonable efforts to negotiate with other parties about, and stipulate to, facts that are not in dispute; (2) reviewing and revising pleadings and other filings to ensure that they are accurate and that they reflect a narrowing of issues, if any, that has resulted from discovery; (3) requesting early trial dates where practicable; (4) moving for summary judgment in every case where the movant would be likely to prevail, or where the motion is likely to narrow the issues to be tried; and (5) reviewing and revising pleadings and other filings to ensure that unmeritorious threshold defenses and jurisdictional arguments, resulting in unnecessary delay, are not raised.

Section 2. *Government Pro Bono and Volunteer Service.*

All Federal agencies should develop appropriate programs to encourage and facilitate pro bono legal and other volunteer service by government employees to be performed on their own time, including attorneys, as permitted by statute, regulation, or other rule or guideline.

Section 3. *Principles to Enact Legislation and Promulgate Regulations Which Do Not Unduly Burden the Federal Court System.*

(a) General Duty to Review Legislation and Regulations. Within current budgetary constraints and existing executive branch coordination mechanisms and procedures established in OMB Circular A-19 and Executive Order No. 12866, each agency promulgating new regulations, reviewing existing regulations, developing legislative proposals concerning regulations, and developing new legislation shall adhere to the following requirements: (1) The agency's proposed legislation and regulations shall be reviewed by the agency to eliminate drafting errors and ambiguity; (2) The agency's proposed legislation and regulations shall be written to minimize litigation; and (3) The agency's proposed legislation and regulations shall provide a clear legal standard for affected conduct rather than a general standard, and shall promote simplification and burden reduction.

(b) Specific Issues for Review. In conducting the reviews required by subsection (a), each agency formulating proposed legislation and regulations shall make every reasonable effort to ensure:

(1) that the legislation, as appropriate—(A) specifies whether all causes of action arising under the law are subject to statutes of limitations; (B) specifies in clear language the preemptive effect, if any, to be given to the law; (C) specifies in clear language the effect on existing Federal law, if any, including all provisions repealed, circumscribed, displaced, impaired, or modified; (D) provides a clear legal standard for affected conduct; (E) specifies whether private arbitration and other forms of private dispute resolution are appropriate under enforcement and relief provisions; subject to constitutional requirements; (F) specifies whether the provisions of the law are severable if one or more of them is found to be unconstitutional; (G) specifies in clear language the retroactive effect, if any, to be given to the law; (H) specifies in clear language the applicable burdens of proof; (I) specifies in clear language whether it grants private parties a right to sue and, if so, the relief available and the conditions and terms for authorized awards of attorney's fees, if any; (J) specifies whether State courts have jurisdiction under the law and, if so, whether and under what conditions an action would be removable to Federal court; (K) specifies whether administrative proceedings are to be required before parties may file suit in court and, if so, describes those proceedings and requires the exhaustion of administrative remedies; (L) sets forth the standards governing the assertion of personal jurisdiction, if any; (M) defines key statutory terms, either explicitly or by reference to other statutes that explicitly define those terms; (N) specifies whether the legislation applies to the Federal Government or its agencies; (O) specifies whether the legislation applies to States, territories, the District of Columbia, and the Commonwealths of Puerto Rico and of the Northern Mariana Islands; (P) specifies what remedies are available such as money

damages, civil penalties, injunctive relief, and attorney's fees; and (Q) addresses other important issues affecting clarity and general draftsmanship of legislation set forth by the Attorney General, with the concurrence of the Director of the Office of Management and Budget ("OMB") and after consultation with affected agencies, that are determined to be in accordance with the purposes of this order.
(2) that the regulation, as appropriate—(A) specifies in clear language the preemptive effect, if any, to be given to the regulation; (B) specifies in clear language the effect on existing Federal law or regulation, if any, including all provisions repealed, circumscribed, displaced, impaired, or modified; (C) provides a clear legal standard for affected conduct rather than a general standard, while promoting simplification and burden reduction; (D) specifies in clear language the retroactive effect, if any, to be given to the regulation; (E) specifies whether administrative proceedings are to be required before parties may file suit in court and, if so, describes those proceedings and requires the exhaustion of administrative remedies; (F) defines key terms, either explicitly or by reference to other regulations or statutes that explicitly define those items; and (G) addresses other important issues affecting clarity and general draftsmanship of regulations set forth by the Attorney General, with the concurrence of the Director of OMB and after consultation with affected agencies, that are determined to be in accordance with the purposes of this order.

(c) Agency Review. The agencies shall review such draft legislation or regulation to determine that either the draft legislation or regulation meets the applicable standards provided in subsections (a) and (b) of this section, or it is unreasonable to require the particular piece of draft legislation or regulation to meet one or more of those standards.

Section 4. *Principles to Promote Just and Efficient Administrative Adjudications.*

(a) Implementation of Administrative Conference Recommendations. In order to promote just and efficient resolution of disputes, an agency that adjudicates administrative claims shall, to the extent reasonable and practicable, and when not in conflict with other sections of this order, implement the recommendations of the Administrative Conference of the United States, entitled "Case Management as a Tool for Improving Agency Adjudication," as contained in 1 C.F.R. 305.86-7 (1991).

(b) Improvements in Administrative Adjudication. All Federal agencies should review their administrative adjudicatory processes and develop specific procedures to reduce delay in decision-making, to facilitate self-representation where appropriate, to expand non-lawyer counseling and representation where appropriate, and to invest maximum discretion in fact-finding officers to encourage appropriate settlement of claims as early as possible.

(c) Bias. All Federal agencies should review their administrative adjudicatory processes to identify any type of bias on the part of the decision-makers that results in an injustice to persons who appear before administrative adjudicatory tribunals; regularly train all fact-finders, administrative law judges, and other decision-makers to eliminate such bias; and establish appropriate mechanisms to receive and resolve complaints of such bias from persons who appear before administrative adjudicatory tribunals.

(d) Public Education. All Federal agencies should develop effective and simple methods, including the use of electronic technology, to educate the public about its claims/benefits policies and procedures.

Section 5. *Coordination by the Department of Justice.*

(a) The Attorney General shall coordinate efforts by Federal agencies to implement sections 1, 2 and 4 of this order.

(b) To implement the principles and purposes announced by this order, the Attorney General is authorized to issue guidelines implementing sections 1 and 4 of this order for the Department of Justice. Such guidelines shall serve as models for internal guidelines that may be issued by other agencies pursuant to this order.

Section 6. *Definitions.*

For purposes of this order:

(a) The term "agency" shall be defined as that term is defined in section 105 of title 5, United States Code.

(b) The term "litigation counsel" shall be defined as the trial counsel or the office in which such trial counsel is employed, such as the United States Attorney's Office for the district in which the litigation is pending or a litigating division of the Department of Justice. Special Assistant United States Attorneys are included within this definition. Those agencies authorized by law to represent themselves in court without assistance from the Department of Justice are also included in this definition, as are private counsel hired by any Federal agency to conduct litigation on behalf of the agency or the United States.

Section 7. *No Private Rights Created.*

This order is intended only to improve the internal management of the executive branch in resolving disputes, conducting litigation in a reasonable and just manner, and reviewing legislation and regulations. This order shall not be construed as creating any right or benefit, substantive or procedural, enforceable at law or in equity by a party against the United States, its agencies, its officers, or any other person. This order shall not be construed to create any right to judicial review involving the compliance or noncompliance of the United States, its agencies, its officers, or any other person with this order. Nothing in this order shall be construed to obligate the United States to accept a particular settlement or resolution of a dispute, to alter its standards for accepting settlements, to forego seeking a consent decree or other relief, or to alter any existing delegation of settlement or litigating authority.

Section 8. *Scope.*

(a) No Applicability to Criminal Matters or Proceedings in Foreign Courts. This order is applicable to civil matters only. It is not intended to affect criminal matters, including enforcement of criminal fines or judgments of criminal forfeiture. This order does not apply to litigation brought by or against the United States in foreign courts or tribunals.

(b) Application of Notice Provision. Notice pursuant to subsection (a) of section 1 is not required (1) in any action to seize or forfeit assets subject to forfeiture or in any action to seize property; (2) in any bankruptcy, insolvency, conservatorship, receivership, or liquidation proceeding; (3) when the assets that are the subject of the action or that would satisfy the judgment are subject to flight, dissipation, or destruction; (4) when the defendant is subject to flight; (5) when, as determined by litigation counsel, exigent circumstances make providing such notice impracticable or such notice would otherwise defeat the purpose of the litigation, such as in actions seeking temporary restraining orders or preliminary injunctive relief; or (6) in those limited classes of cases where the Attorney General determines that providing such notice would defeat the purpose of the litigation.

(c) Additional Guidance as to Scope. The Attorney General shall have the authority to issue further guidance as to the scope of this order, except section 3, consistent with the purposes of this order.

Section 9. *Conflicts with Other Rules.*

Nothing in this order shall be construed to require litigation counsel or any agency to act in a manner contrary to the Federal Rules of Civil Procedure, Tax Court Rules of Practice and Procedure, State or Federal law, other applicable rules of practice or procedure, or court order.

Section 10. *Privileged Information.*

Nothing in this order shall compel or authorize the disclosure of privileged information, sensitive law enforcement information, information affecting national security, or information the disclosure of which is prohibited by law.

Section 11. *Effective Date.* This order shall become effective 90 days after the date of signature. This order shall not apply to litigation commenced prior to the effective date.

Section 12. *Revocation.*
Executive Order No. 12778 is hereby revoked.

WILLIAM J. CLINTON

E. Executive Order 13,045

Protection of Children From Environmental Health Risks and Safety Risks

April 21, 1997

62 Fed. Reg. 19,885 (April 23, 1997)

By the authority vested in me as President by the Constitution and the laws of the United States of America, it is hereby ordered as follows:
Section 1. *Policy.*
(1-101) A growing body of scientific knowledge demonstrates that children may suffer disproportionately from environmental health risks and safety risks. These risks arise because: children's neurological, immunological, digestive, and other bodily systems are still developing; children eat more food, drink more fluids, and breathe more air in proportion to their body weight than adults; children's size and weight may diminish their protection from standard safety features; and children's behavior patterns may make them more susceptible to accidents because they are less able to protect themselves. Therefore, to the extent permitted by law and appropriate, and consistent with the agency's mission, each Federal agency:

    (a) shall make it a high priority to identify and assess environmental health risks and safety risks that may disproportionately affect children; and

    (b) shall ensure that its policies, programs, activities, and standards address disproportionate risks to children that result from environmental health risks or safety risks.

(1-102) Each independent regulatory agency is encouraged to participate in the implementation of this order and comply with its provisions.
Section 2. *Definitions.*
The following definitions shall apply to this order.
(2-201) "Federal agency" means any authority of the United States that is an agency under 44 U.S.C. 3502(1) other than those considered to be independent regulatory agencies under 44 U.S.C. 3502(5). For purposes of this order, "military departments," as defined in 5 U.S.C. 102, are covered under the auspices of the Department of Defense.
(2-202) "Covered regulatory action" means any substantive action in a rulemaking, initiated after the date of this order or for which a Notice of

Proposed Rulemaking is published 1 year after the date of this order, that is likely to result in a rule that may:

(a) be "economically significant" under Executive Order 12866 (a rulemaking that has an annual effect on the economy of $100 million or more or would adversely affect in a material way the economy, a sector of the economy, productivity, competition, jobs, the environment, public health or safety, or State, local, or tribal governments or communities); and

(b) concern an environmental health risk or safety risk that an agency has reason to believe may disproportionately affect children.

(2-203) "Environmental health risks and safety risks" mean risks to health or to safety that are attributable to products or substances that the child is likely to come in contact with or ingest (such as the air we breath, the food we eat, the water we drink or use for recreation, the soil we live on, and the products we use or are exposed to).

Section 3. *Task Force on Environmental Health Risks and Safety Risks to Children.*

(3-301) There is hereby established the Task Force on Environmental Health Risks and Safety Risks to Children ("Task Force").

(3-302) The Task Force will report to the President in consultation with the Domestic Policy Council, the National Science and Technology Council, the Council on Environmental Quality, and the Office of Management and Budget (OMB).

(3-303) Membership. The Task Force shall be composed of the: (a) Secretary of Health and Human Services, who shall serve as a Co-Chair of the Council; (b) Administrator of the Environmental Protection Agency, who shall serve as a Co-Chair of the Council; (c) Secretary of Education; (d) Secretary of Labor; (e) Attorney General; (f) Secretary of Energy; (g) Secretary of Housing and Urban Development; (h) Secretary of Agriculture; (i) Secretary of Transportation; (j) Director of the Office of Management and Budget; (k) Chair of the Council on Environmental Quality; (l) Chair of the Consumer Product Safety Commission; (m) Assistant to the President for Economic Policy; (n) Assistant to the President for Domestic Policy; (o) Assistant to the President and Director of the Office of Science and Technology Policy; (p) Chair of the Council of Economic Advisers; and (q) Such other officials of executive departments and agencies as the President may, from time to time, designate. Members of the Task Force may delegate their responsibilities under this order to subordinates.

(3-304) Functions. The Task Force shall recommend to the President Federal strategies for children's environmental health and safety, within the limits of the Administration's budget, to include the following elements: (a) statements of principles, general policy, and targeted annual priorities to guide the Federal approach to achieving the goals of this order; (b) a coordinated research agenda for the Federal Government, including steps to implement the review of research databases described in section 4 of this order; (c) recommendations for appropriate partnerships among Federal, State, local, and tribal governments and the private, academic, and nonprofit sectors; (d) proposals to enhance public outreach and communication to assist families in evaluating risks to children and in making informed consumer choices; (e) an identification of high-priority initiatives that the Federal Government has undertaken or will undertake in advancing protection of children's environmental health and safety; and (f) a statement regarding the desirability of new legislation to fulfill or promote the purposes of this order.

(3-305) The Task Force shall prepare a biennial report on research, data, or other information that would enhance our ability to understand, analyze, and respond to environmental health risks and safety risks to children. For purposes of this report, cabinet agencies and other agencies identified by the Task Force shall identify and specifically describe for the Task Force key data needs related to environmental health risks and safety risks to children that have arisen in the course of the agency's programs and activities. The Task Force shall incorporate agency submissions into its report and ensure that this report is publicly available and widely disseminated. The Office of Science and Technology Policy and the National Science and Technology Council shall ensure that this report is fully considered in establishing research priorities.

(3-306) The Task Force shall exist for a period of 4 years from the first meeting. At least 6 months prior to the expiration of that period, the member agencies shall assess the need for continuation of the Task Force or its functions, and make appropriate recommendations to the President.

Section 4. *Research Coordination and Integration.*

(4-401) Within 6 months of the date of this order, the Task Force shall develop or direct to be developed a review of existing and planned data resources and a proposed plan for ensuring that researchers and Federal research agencies have access to information on all research conducted or funded by the Federal Government that is related to adverse health risks in children resulting from exposure to environmental health risks or safety risks. The National Science and Technology Council shall review the plan.

(4-402) The plan shall promote the sharing of information on academic and private research. It shall include recommendations to encourage that such data, to the extent permitted by law, is available to the public, the scientific and academic communities, and all Federal agencies.

Section 5. *Agency Environmental Health Risk or Safety Risk Regulations.*

(5-501) For each covered regulatory action submitted to OMB's Office of Information and Regulatory Affairs (OIRA) for review pursuant to Executive Order 12866, the issuing agency shall provide to OIRA the following information developed as part of the agency's decisionmaking process, unless prohibited by law:

(a) an evaluation of the environmental health or safety effects of the planned regulation on children; and

(b) an explanation of why the planned regulation is preferable to other potentially effective and reasonably feasible alternatives considered by the agency.

(5-502) In emergency situations, or when an agency is obligated by law to act more quickly than normal review procedures allow, the agency shall comply with the provisions of this section to the extent practicable. For those covered regulatory actions that are governed by a court-imposed or statutory deadline, the agency shall, to the extent practicable, schedule any rulemaking proceedings so as to permit sufficient time for completing the analysis required by this section.

(5-503) The analysis required by this section may be included as part of any other required analysis, and shall be made part of the administrative record for the covered regulatory action or otherwise made available to the public, to the extent permitted by law.

Section 6. *Interagency Forum on Child and Family Statistics.*

(6-601) The Director of the OMB ("Director") shall convene an Interagency Forum on Child and Family Statistics ("Forum"), which will include representatives from the appropriate Federal statistics and research agencies. The Forum shall produce an annual compendium ("Report") of the most important indicators of the well-being of the Nation's children.

(6-602) The Forum shall determine the indicators to be included in each Report and identify the sources of data to be used for each indicator. The Forum shall provide an ongoing review of Federal collection and dissemination of data on children and families, and shall make recommendations to improve the coverage and coordination of data collection and to reduce duplication and overlap.

(6-603) The Report shall be published by the Forum in collaboration with the National Institute of Child Health and Human Development. The Forum shall present the first annual Report to the President, through the Director, by

July 31, 1997. The Report shall be submitted annually thereafter, using the most recently available data.

Section 7. *General Provisions.*

(7-701) This order is intended only for internal management of the executive branch. This order is not intended, and should not be construed to create, any right, benefit, or trust responsibility, substantive or procedural, enforceable at law or equity by a party against the United States, its agencies, its officers, or its employees. This order shall not be construed to create any right to judicial review involving the compliance or noncompliance with this order by the United States, its agencies, its officers, or any other person.

(7-702) Executive Order 12606 of September 2, 1987 is revoked.

WILLIAM J. CLINTON

F. Executive Order 13,132

Federalism

August 4, 1999

64 Fed. Reg. 43,255 (Aug. 10, 1999)

By the authority vested in me as President by the Constitution and the laws of the United States of America, and in order to guarantee the division of governmental responsibilities between the national government and the States that was intended by the Framers of the Constitution, to ensure that the principles of federalism established by the Framers guide the executive departments and agencies in the formulation and implementation of policies, and to further the policies of the Unfunded Mandates Reform Act, it is hereby ordered as follows:

Section 1. *Definitions.*

For purposes of this order:

(a) "Policies that have federalism implications" refers to regulations, legislative comments or proposed legislation, and other policy statements or actions that have substantial direct effects on the States, on the relationship between the national government and the States, or on the distribution of power and responsibilities among the various levels of government.

(b) "State" or "States" refer to the States of the United States of America, individually or collectively, and, where relevant, to State governments, including units of local government and other political subdivisions established by the States.

(c) "Agency" means any authority of the United States that is an "agency" under 44 U.S.C. 3502(1), other than those considered to be independent regulatory agencies, as defined in 44 U.S.C. 3502(5).

(d) "State and local officials" means elected officials of State and local governments or their representative national organizations.

Section 2. *Fundamental Federalism Principles.*

In formulating and implementing policies that have federalism implications, agencies shall be guided by the following fundamental federalism principles:

(a) Federalism is rooted in the belief that issues that are not national in scope or significance are most appropriately addressed by the level of government closest to the people.

(b) The people of the States created the national government and delegated to it enumerated governmental powers. All other sovereign powers, save those expressly prohibited the States by the Constitution, are reserved to the States or to the people.

(c) The constitutional relationship among sovereign governments, State and national, is inherent in the very structure of the Constitution and is formalized in and protected by the Tenth Amendment to the Constitution.

(d) The people of the States are free, subject only to restrictions in the Constitution itself or in constitutionally authorized Acts of Congress, to define the moral, political, and legal character of their lives.

(e) The Framers recognized that the States possess unique authorities, qualities, and abilities to meet the needs of the people and should function as laboratories of democracy.

(f) The nature of our constitutional system encourages a healthy diversity in the public policies adopted by the people of the several States according to their own conditions, needs, and desires. In the search for enlightened public policy, individual States and communities are free to experiment with a variety of approaches to public issues. One-size-fits-all approaches to public policy problems can inhibit the creation of effective solutions to those problems.

(g) Acts of the national government—whether legislative, executive, or judicial in nature—that exceed the enumerated powers of that government under the Constitution violate the principle of federalism established by the Framers.

(h) Policies of the national government should recognize the responsibility of—and should encourage opportunities for—individuals, families, neighborhoods, local governments, and private associations to achieve their personal, social, and economic objectives through cooperative effort.

(i) The national government should be deferential to the States when taking action that affects the policymaking discretion of the States and should act only with the greatest caution where State or local governments have identified uncertainties regarding the constitutional or statutory authority of the national government.

Section 3. *Federalism Policymaking Criteria.*

In addition to adhering to the fundamental federalism principles set forth in section 2, agencies shall adhere, to the extent permitted by law, to the following criteria when formulating and implementing policies that have federalism implications:

(a) There shall be strict adherence to constitutional principles. Agencies shall closely examine the constitutional and statutory authority supporting any action that would limit the policymaking discretion of the States and shall carefully assess the necessity for such action. To the extent practicable, State and local officials shall be consulted before any such action is implemented. Executive Order 12372 of July 14, 1982 ("Intergovernmental Review of Federal Programs") remains in effect for the programs and activities to which it is applicable.

(b) National action limiting the policymaking discretion of the States shall be taken only where there is constitutional and statutory authority for the action and the national activity is appropriate in light of the presence of a problem of national significance. Where there are significant uncertainties as to whether national action is authorized or appropriate, agencies shall consult with appropriate State and local officials to determine whether Federal objectives can be attained by other means.

(c) With respect to Federal statutes and regulations administered by the States, the national government shall grant the States the maximum administrative discretion possible. Intrusive Federal oversight of State administration is neither necessary nor desirable.

(d) When undertaking to formulate and implement policies that have federalism implications, agencies shall:

> (1) encourage States to develop their own policies to achieve program objectives and to work with appropriate officials in other States;
>
> (2) where possible, defer to the States to establish standards;
>
> (3) in determining whether to establish uniform national standards, consult with appropriate State and local officials as to the need for national standards and any alternatives that would limit the scope of national standards or otherwise preserve State prerogatives and authority; and
>
> (4) where national standards are required by Federal statutes, consult with appropriate State and local officials in developing those standards.

Section 4. *Special Requirements for Preemption.*
Agencies, in taking action that preempts State law, shall act in strict accordance with governing law.

> (a) Agencies shall construe, in regulations and otherwise, a Federal statute to preempt State law only where the statute contains an express preemption provision or there is some other clear evidence that the Congress intended preemption of State law, or where the exercise of State authority conflicts with the exercise of Federal authority under the Federal statute.

(b) Where a Federal statute does not preempt State law (as addressed in subsection (a) of this section), agencies shall construe any authorization in the statute for the issuance of regulations as authorizing preemption of State law by rulemaking only when the exercise of State authority directly conflicts with the exercise of Federal authority under the Federal statute or there is clear evidence to conclude that the Congress intended the agency to have the authority to preempt State law.

(c) Any regulatory preemption of State law shall be restricted to the minimum level necessary to achieve the objectives of the statute pursuant to which the regulations are promulgated.

(d) When an agency foresees the possibility of a conflict between State law and Federally protected interests within its area of regulatory responsibility, the agency shall consult, to the extent practicable, with appropriate State and local officials in an effort to avoid such a conflict.

(e) When an agency proposes to act through adjudication or rulemaking to preempt State law, the agency shall provide all affected State and local officials notice and an opportunity for appropriate participation in the proceedings.

Section 5. *Special Requirements for Legislative Proposals.*
Agencies shall not submit to the Congress legislation that would:

(a) directly regulate the States in ways that would either interfere with functions essential to the States' separate and independent existence or be inconsistent with the fundamental federalism principles in section 2;

(b) attach to Federal grants conditions that are not reasonably related to the purpose of the grant; or

(c) preempt State law, unless preemption is consistent with the fundamental federalism principles set forth in section 2, and unless a clearly legitimate national purpose, consistent with the federalism policymaking criteria set forth in section 3, cannot otherwise be met.

Section 6. *Consultation.*

(a) Each agency shall have an accountable process to ensure meaningful and timely input by State and local officials in the development of regulatory policies that have federalism implications. Within 90 days after the effective date of this order, the head of each agency shall designate an official with principal responsibility for the agency's implementation of this order and that designated official shall submit to the Office of Management and Budget a description of the agency's consultation process.

(b) To the extent practicable and permitted by law, no agency shall promulgate any regulation that has federalism implications, that imposes substantial direct compliance costs on State and local governments, and

that is not required by statute, unless:
>   (1) funds necessary to pay the direct costs incurred by the State and local governments in complying with the regulation are provided by the Federal Government; or
>   (2) the agency, prior to the formal promulgation of the regulation,
>   >   (A) consulted with State and local officials early in the process of developing the proposed regulation;
>   >   (B) in a separately identified portion of the preamble to the regulation as it is to be issued in the *Federal Register*, provides to the Director of the Office of Management and Budget a federalism summary impact statement, which consists of a description of the extent of the agency's prior consultation with State and local officials, a summary of the nature of their concerns and the agency's position supporting the need to issue the regulation, and a statement of the extent to which the concerns of State and local officials have been met; and
>   >   (C) makes available to the Director of the Office of Management and Budget any written communications submitted to the agency by State and local officials.

(c) To the extent practicable and permitted by law, no agency shall promulgate any regulation that has federalism implications and that preempts State law, unless the agency, prior to the formal promulgation of the regulation,
>   (1) consulted with State and local officials early in the process of developing the proposed regulation;
>   (2) in a separately identified portion of the preamble to the regulation as it is to be issued in the *Federal Register*, provides to the Director of the Office of Management and Budget a federalism summary impact statement, which consists of a description of the extent of the agency's prior consultation with State and local officials, a summary of the nature of their concerns and the agency's position supporting the need to issue the regulation, and a statement of the extent to which the concerns of State and local officials have been met; and
>   (3) makes available to the Director of the Office of Management and Budget any written communications submitted to the agency by State and local officials.

Section 7. *Increasing Flexibility for State and Local Waivers.*
>   (a) Agencies shall review the processes under which State and local governments apply for waivers of statutory and regulatory requirements and

take appropriate steps to streamline those processes.

(b) Each agency shall, to the extent practicable and permitted by law, consider any application by a State for a waiver of statutory or regulatory requirements in connection with any program administered by that agency with a general view toward increasing opportunities for utilizing flexible policy approaches at the State or local level in cases in which the proposed waiver is consistent with applicable Federal policy objectives and is otherwise appropriate.

(c) Each agency shall, to the extent practicable and permitted by law, render a decision upon a complete application for a waiver within 120 days of receipt of such application by the agency. If the application for a waiver is not granted, the agency shall provide the applicant with timely written notice of the decision and the reasons therefor.

(d) This section applies only to statutory or regulatory requirements that are discretionary and subject to waiver by the agency.

Section 8. *Accountability.*

(a) In transmitting any draft final regulation that has federalism implications to the Office of Management and Budget pursuant to Executive Order 12866 of September 30, 1993, each agency shall include a certification from the official designated to ensure compliance with this order stating that the requirements of this order have been met in a meaningful and timely manner.

(b) In transmitting proposed legislation that has federalism implications to the Office of Management and Budget, each agency shall include a certification from the official designated to ensure compliance with this order that all relevant requirements of this order have been met.

(c) Within 180 days after the effective date of this order, the Director of the Office of Management and Budget and the Assistant to the President for Intergovernmental Affairs shall confer with State and local officials to ensure that this order is being properly and effectively implemented.

Section 9. *Independent Agencies.*

Independent regulatory agencies are encouraged to comply with the provisions of this order.

Section 10. *General Provisions.*

(a) This order shall supplement but not supersede the requirements contained in Executive Order 12372 ("Intergovernmental Review of Federal Programs"), Executive Order 12866 ("Regulatory Planning and Review"), Executive Order 12988 ("Civil Justice Reform"), and OMB Circular A-19.

(b) Executive Order 12612 ("Federalism"), Executive Order 12875 ("Enhancing the Intergovernmental Partnership"), Executive Order 13083 ("Federalism"), and Executive Order 13095 ("Suspension of Executive Order 13083") are revoked.

(c) This order shall be effective 90 days after the date of this order.

Section 11. *Judicial Review.*
This order is intended only to improve the internal management of the executive branch, and is not intended to create any right or benefit, substantive or procedural, enforceable at law by a party against the United States, its agencies, its officers, or any person.

WILLIAM J. CLINTON

[Note: For Guidance for Implementing E.O. 13,132, "Federalism," see Memorandum For Heads Of Executive Departments And Agencies, And Independent Regulatory Agencies (Oct. 28, 1999), from Jacob J. Lew, Director, OMB, *available at* http://www.whitehouse.gov/omb/memoranda/m00-02.pdf]

G Executive Order 13,175

Consultation and Coordination With Indian Tribal Governments

November 6, 2000

65 Fed. Reg. 67,249 (Nov.9, 2000)

By the authority vested in me as President by the Constitution and the laws of the United States of America, and in order to establish regular and meaningful consultation and collaboration with tribal officials in the development of Federal policies that have tribal implications, to strengthen the United States government-to-government relationships with Indian tribes, and to reduce the imposition of unfunded mandates upon Indian tribes; it is hereby ordered as follows:

Section 1. *Definitions.*

For purposes of this order:

(a) "Policies that have tribal implications" refers to regulations, legislative comments or proposed legislation, and other policy statements or actions that have substantial direct effects on one or more Indian tribes, on the relationship between the Federal Government and Indian tribes, or on the distribution of power and responsibilities between the Federal Government and Indian tribes.

(b) "Indian tribe" means an Indian or Alaska Native tribe, band, nation, pueblo, village, or community that the Secretary of the Interior acknowledges to exist as an Indian tribe pursuant to the Federally Recognized Indian Tribe List Act of 1994, 25 U.S.C. 479a.

(c) "Agency" means any authority of the United States that is an "agency" under 44 U.S.C. 3502(1), other than those considered to be independent regulatory agencies, as defined in 44 U.S.C. 3502(5).

(d) "Tribal officials" means elected or duly appointed officials of Indian tribal governments or authorized intertribal organizations.

Section 2. *Fundamental Principles.*

In formulating or implementing policies that have tribal implications, agencies shall be guided by the following fundamental principles:

(a) The United States has a unique legal relationship with Indian tribal governments as set forth in the Constitution of the United States, treaties, statutes, Executive Orders, and court decisions. Since the formation of the Union, the United States has recognized Indian tribes as domestic dependent nations under its protection. The Federal Government has enacted numerous statutes and promulgated numerous regulations that establish and define a trust relationship with Indian tribes.

(b) Our Nation, under the law of the United States, in accordance with treaties, statutes, Executive Orders, and judicial decisions, has recognized the right of Indian tribes to self-government. As domestic dependent nations, Indian tribes exercise inherent sovereign powers over their members and territory. The United States continues to work with Indian tribes on a government-to-government basis to address issues concerning Indian tribal self-government, tribal trust resources, and Indian tribal treaty and other rights.

(c) The United States recognizes the right of Indian tribes to self- government and supports tribal sovereignty and self-determination.

Section 3. *Policymaking Criteria.*
In addition to adhering to the fundamental principles set forth in section 2, agencies shall adhere, to the extent permitted by law, to the following criteria when formulating and implementing policies that have tribal implications:

(a) Agencies shall respect Indian tribal self-government and sovereignty, honor tribal treaty and other rights, and strive to meet the responsibilities that arise from the unique legal relationship between the Federal Government and Indian tribal governments.

(b) With respect to Federal statutes and regulations administered by Indian tribal governments, the Federal Government shall grant Indian tribal governments the maximum administrative discretion possible.

(c) When undertaking to formulate and implement policies that have tribal implications, agencies shall:

(1) encourage Indian tribes to develop their own policies to achieve program objectives;

(2) where possible, defer to Indian tribes to establish standards; and

(3) in determining whether to establish Federal standards, consult with tribal officials as to the need for Federal standards and any alternatives that would limit the scope of Federal standards or otherwise preserve the prerogatives and authority of Indian tribes.

Section 4. *Special Requirements for Legislative Proposals.*
Agencies shall not submit to the Congress legislation that would be inconsistent with the policymaking criteria in Section 3.

Section 5. *Consultation.*

(a) Each agency shall have an accountable process to ensure meaningful and timely input by tribal officials in the development of regulatory policies that have tribal implications. Within 30 days after the effective date of this order, the head of each agency shall designate an official with principal responsibility for the agency's implementation of this order. Within 60 days of the effective date of this order, the designated official shall submit to the Office of Management and Budget (OMB) a description of the agency's consultation process.

(b) To the extent practicable and permitted by law, no agency shall promulgate any regulation that has tribal implications, that imposes substantial direct compliance costs on Indian tribal governments, and that is not required by statute, unless:

(1) funds necessary to pay the direct costs incurred by the Indian tribal government or the tribe in complying with the regulation are provided by the Federal Government; or

(2) the agency, prior to the formal promulgation of the regulation,

(A) consulted with tribal officials early in the process of developing the proposed regulation;

(B) in a separately identified portion of the preamble to the regulation as it is to be issued in the *Federal Register*, provides to the Director of OMB a tribal summary impact statement, which consists of a description of the extent of the agency's prior consultation with tribal officials, a summary of the nature of their concerns and the agency's position supporting the need to issue the regulation, and a statement of the extent to which the concerns of tribal officials have been met; and

(C) makes available to the Director of OMB any written communications submitted to the agency by tribal officials.

(c) To the extent practicable and permitted by law, no agency shall promulgate any regulation that has tribal implications and that preempts tribal law unless the agency, prior to the formal promulgation of the regulation,

(1) consulted with tribal officials early in the process of developing the proposed regulation;

(2) in a separately identified portion of the preamble to the regulation as it is to be issued in the *Federal Register*, provides to the Director of OMB a tribal summary impact statement, which consists of a description of the extent of the agency's prior consultation with tribal officials, a summary of the nature of their concerns and the agency's position supporting the need to issue the regulation, and a statement of the extent to which the concerns of tribal officials have been met; and

(3) makes available to the Director of OMB any written communications submitted to the agency by tribal officials.

(d) On issues relating to tribal self-government, tribal trust resources, or Indian tribal treaty and other rights, each agency should explore and, where appropriate, use consensual mechanisms for developing regulations, including negotiated rulemaking.

Section 6. *Increasing Flexibility for Indian Tribal Waivers.*

(a) Agencies shall review the processes under which Indian tribes apply for waivers of statutory and regulatory requirements and take appropriate steps to streamline those processes.

(b) Each agency shall, to the extent practicable and permitted by law, consider any application by an Indian tribe for a waiver of statutory or regulatory requirements in connection with any program administered by the agency with a general view toward increasing opportunities for utilizing flexible policy approaches at the Indian tribal level in cases in which the proposed waiver is consistent with the applicable Federal policy objectives and is otherwise appropriate.

(c) Each agency shall, to the extent practicable and permitted by law, render a decision upon a complete application for a waiver within 120 days of receipt of such application by the agency, or as otherwise provided by law or regulation. If the application for waiver is not granted, the agency shall provide the applicant with timely written notice of the decision and the reasons therefor.

(d) This section applies only to statutory or regulatory requirements that are discretionary and subject to waiver by the agency.

Section 7. *Accountability.*

(a) In transmitting any draft final regulation that has tribal implications to OMB pursuant to Executive Order 12866 of September 30, 1993, each agency shall include a certification from the official designated to ensure compliance with this order stating that the requirements of this order have been met in a meaningful and timely manner.

(b) In transmitting proposed legislation that has tribal implications to OMB, each agency shall include a certification from the official designated to ensure compliance with this order that all relevant requirements of this order have been met.

(c) Within 180 days after the effective date of this order the Director of OMB and the Assistant to the President for Intergovernmental Affairs shall confer with tribal officials to ensure that this order is being properly and effectively implemented.

Section 8. *Independent Agencies.*

Independent regulatory agencies are encouraged to comply with the provisions of this order.

Section 9. *General Provisions.*

(a) This order shall supplement but not supersede the requirements contained in Executive Order 12866 (Regulatory Planning and Review), Executive Order 12988 (Civil Justice Reform), OMB Circular A-19, and the Executive Memorandum of April 29, 1994, on Government-to-Government Relations with Native American Tribal Governments.

(b) This order shall complement the consultation and waiver provisions in sections 6 and 7 of Executive Order 13132 (Federalism).

(c) Executive Order 13084 (Consultation and Coordination with Indian Tribal Governments) is revoked at the time this order takes effect.

(d) This order shall be effective 60 days after the date of this order.

Section 10. *Judicial Review.*

This order is intended only to improve the internal management of the executive branch, and is not intended to create any right, benefit, or trust responsibility, substantive or procedural, enforceable at law by a party against the United States, its agencies, or any person.

WILLIAM J. CLINTON

H. Executive Order 13,211

Actions Concerning Regulations That Significantly Affect Energy Supply, Distribution, or Use

May 18, 2001

66 Fed. Reg. 28,355 (May 22, 2001)

By the authority vested in me as President by the Constitution and the laws of the United States of America, and in order to appropriately weigh and consider the effects of the Federal Government's regulations on the supply, distribution, and use of energy, it is hereby ordered as follows:

Section 1. *Policy.*
The Federal Government can significantly affect the supply, distribution, and use of energy. Yet there is often too little information regarding the effects that governmental regulatory action can have on energy. In order to provide more useful energy-related information and hence improve the quality of agency decisionmaking, I am requiring that agencies shall prepare a Statement of Energy Effects when undertaking certain agency actions. As described more fully below, such Statements of Energy Effects shall describe the effects of certain regulatory actions on energy supply, distribution, or use.

Section 2. *Preparation of a Statement of Energy Effects.*

(a) To the extent permitted by law, agencies shall prepare and submit a Statement of Energy Effects to the Administrator of the Office of Information and Regulatory Affairs, Office of Management and Budget, for those matters identified as significant energy actions.

(b) A Statement of Energy Effects shall consist of a detailed statement by the agency responsible for the significant energy action relating to:

(i) any adverse effects on energy supply, distribution, or use (including a shortfall in supply, price increases, and increased use of foreign supplies) should the proposal be implemented, and

(ii) reasonable alternatives to the action with adverse energy effects and the expected effects of such alternatives on energy supply, distribution, and use.

(c) The Administrator of the Office of Information and Regulatory Affairs shall provide guidance to the agencies on the implementation of this order and shall consult with other agencies as appropriate in the implementation of this order.

Section 3. *Submission and Publication of Statements.*

(a) Agencies shall submit their Statements of Energy Effects to the Administrator of the Office of Information and Regulatory Affairs, Office of Management and Budget, when-ever they present the related submission under Executive Order 12866 of September 30, 1993, or any successor order.

(b) Agencies shall publish their Statements of Energy Effects, or a summary thereof, in each related Notice of Proposed Rulemaking and in any resulting Final Rule.

Section 4. *Definitions.*

For purposes of this order:

(a) "Regulation" and "rule" have the same meaning as they do in Executive Order 12866 or any successor order.

(b) "Significant energy action" means any action by an agency (normally published in the *Federal Register*) that promulgates or is expected to lead to the promulgation of a final rule or regulation, including notices of inquiry, advance notices of proposed rulemaking, and notices of proposed rulemaking:

(1)(i) that is a significant regulatory action under Executive Order 12866 or any successor order, and

(ii) is likely to have a significant adverse effect on the supply, distribution, or use of energy; or

(2) that is designated by the Administrator of the Office of Information and Regulatory Affairs as a significant energy action.

(c) "Agency" means any authority of the United States that is an "agency" under 44 U.S.C. 3502(l), other than those considered to be independent regulatory agencies, as defined in 44 U.S.C. 3502(5).

Section 5. *Judicial Review.*

Nothing in this order shall affect any otherwise available judicial review of agency action. This order is intended only to improve the internal management of the Federal Government and does not create any right or benefit, substantive or procedural, enforceable at law or equity by a party against the United States, its agencies or instrumentalities, its officers or employees, or any other person.

GEORGE W. BUSH

I. Executive Order 13,272

Proper Consideration of Small Entities in Agency Rulemaking

August 13, 2002

67 Fed. Reg. 53,461 (Aug. 16, 2002)

By the authority vested in me as President by the Constitution and the laws of the United States of America, it is hereby ordered as follows:

Section 1. *General Requirements.*
Each agency shall establish procedures and policies to promote compliance with the Regulatory Flexibility Act, as amended (5 U.S.C. 601 et seq.) (the "Act"). Agencies shall thoroughly review draft rules to assess and take appropriate account of the potential impact on small businesses, small governmental jurisdictions, and small organizations, as provided by the Act. The Chief Counsel for Advocacy of the Small Business Administration (Advocacy) shall remain available to advise agencies in performing that review consistent with the provisions of the Act.

Section 2. *Responsibilities of Advocacy.*
Consistent with the requirements of the Act, other applicable law, and Executive Order 12866 of September 30, 1993, as amended, Advocacy:

(a) shall notify agency heads from time to time of the requirements of the Act, including by issuing notifications with respect to the basic requirements of the Act within 90 days of the date of this order;

(b) shall provide training to agencies on compliance with the Act; and

(c) may provide comment on draft rules to the agency that has proposed or intends to propose the rules and to the Office of Information and Regulatory Affairs of the Office of Management and Budget (OIRA).

Section 3. *Responsibilities of Federal Agencies.*
Consistent with the requirements of the Act and applicable law, agencies shall:

(a) Within 180 days of the date of this order, issue written procedures and policies, consistent with the Act, to ensure that the potential impacts of agencies' draft rules on small businesses, small governmental jurisdictions, and small organizations are properly considered during the rulemaking process. Agency heads shall submit, no later than 90 days from the date of this order, their written procedures and policies to Advocacy for comment. Prior to issuing final procedures and policies, agencies shall consider any such comments received within 60 days from the date of the submission of the agencies' procedures and policies to Advocacy. Except to the extent otherwise specifically provided by statute or Executive Order, agencies shall make the final procedures and policies available to the public through the Internet or other easily accessible means;

(b) Notify Advocacy of any draft rules that may have a significant economic impact on a substantial number of small entities under the Act. Such notifications shall be made (i) when the agency submits a draft rule to OIRA under Executive Order 12866 if that order requires such submission, or (ii) if no submission to OIRA is so required, at a reasonable time prior to publication of the rule by the agency; and

(c) Give every appropriate consideration to any comments provided by Advocacy regarding a draft rule. Consistent with applicable law and appropriate protection of executive deliberations and legal privileges, an agency shall include, in any explanation or discussion accompanying publication in the *Federal Register* of a final rule, the agency's response to any written comments submitted by Advocacy on the proposed rule that preceded the final rule; provided, however, that such inclusion is not required if the head of the agency certifies that the public interest is not served thereby. Agencies and Advocacy may, to the extent permitted by law, engage in an exchange of data and research, as appropriate, to foster the purposes of the Act.

Section 4. *Definitions.*

Terms defined in section 601 of title 5, United States Code, including the term "agency," shall have the same meaning in this order.

Section 5. *Preservation of Authority.*

Nothing in this order shall be construed to impair or affect the authority of the Administrator of the Small Business Administration to supervise the Small Business Administration as provided in the first sentence of section 2(b)(1) of Public Law 85-09536 (15 U.S.C. 633(b)(1)).

Section 6. *Reporting.*

For the purpose of promoting compliance with this order, Advocacy shall submit a report not less than annually to the Director of the Office of Management and Budget on the extent of compliance with this order by agencies.

Section 7. *Confidentiality.*

Consistent with existing law, Advocacy may publicly disclose information that it receives from the agencies in the course of carrying out this order only to the extent that such information already has been lawfully and publicly disclosed by OIRA or the relevant rulemaking agency.

Section. 8. *Judicial Review.*
This order is intended only to improve the internal management of the Federal Government. This order is not intended to, and does not, create any right or benefit, substantive or procedural, enforceable at law or equity, against the United States, its departments, agencies, or other entities, its officers or employees, or any other person.

GEORGE W. BUSH

[Note: For A Memorandum of Understanding Between the Office of Advocacy U.S. Small Business Administration and the Office of Information and Regulatory Affairs, OMB, concerning review of rules affecting small entities, signed March 19, 2002, see http://www.whitehouse.gov/omb/inforeg/oira.pdf.]

II. Pre-1992 Executive Orders—still in effect

A. Executive Order 12,372

Intergovernmental Review of Federal Programs

July 14, 1982

47 Fed. Reg. 30,959 (July 16, 1982)

By the authority vested in me as President by the Constitution and laws of the United States of America, including Section 401(a) of the Intergovernmental Cooperation Act of 1968 (42 U.S.C. 4231(a)) and Section 301 of Title 3 of the United States Code, and in order to foster an intergovernmental partnership and a strengthened federalism by relying on State and local processes for the State and local government coordination and review of proposed Federal financial assistance and direct Federal development, it is hereby ordered as follows:

Section 1. Federal agencies shall provide opportunities for consultation by elected officials of those State and local governments that would provide the non-Federal funds for, or that would be directly affected by, proposed Federal financial assistance or direct Federal development.

Section 2. To the extent the States, in consultation with local general purpose governments, and local special purpose governments they consider appropriate, develop their own processes or refine existing processes for State and local elected officials to review and coordinate proposed Federal financial assistance and direct Federal development, the Federal agencies shall, to the extent permitted by law:

(a) Utilize the State process to determine official views of State and local elected officials.

(b) Communicate with State and local elected officials as early in the program planning cycle as is reasonably feasible to explain specific plans and actions.

(c) Make efforts to accommodate State and local elected officials' concerns with proposed Federal financial assistance and direct Federal development that are communicated through the designated State process. For those cases where the concerns cannot be accommodated, Federal officials shall explain the bases for their decision in a timely manner.

(d) Allow the States to simplify and consolidate existing Federally required State plan submissions. Where State planning and budgeting systems are sufficient and where permitted by law, the substitution of State plans for Federally required State plans shall be encouraged by the agencies.

(e) Seek the coordination of views of affected State and local elected officials in one State with those of another State when proposed Federal financial assistance or direct Federal development has an impact on interstate metropolitan urban centers or other interstate areas. Existing interstate mechanisms that are redesignated as part of the State process may be used for this purpose.

(f) Support State and local governments by discouraging the reauthorization or creation of any planning organization which is Federally-funded, which has a Federally-prescribed membership, which is established for a limited purpose, and which is not adequately representative of, or accountable to, State or local elected officials.

Section 3.

(a) The State process referred to in Section 2 shall include those where States delegate, in specific instances, to local elected officials the review, coordination, and communication with Federal agencies.

(b) At the discretion of the State and local elected officials, the State process may exclude certain Federal programs from review and comment.

Section 4. The Office of Management and Budget (OMB) shall maintain a list of official State entities designated by the States to review and coordinate proposed Federal financial assistance and direct Federal development. The Office of Management and Budget shall disseminate such lists to the Federal agencies.

Section 5.

(a) Agencies shall propose rules and regulations governing the formulation, evaluation, and review of proposed Federal financial assistance and direct Federal development pursuant to this Order, to be submitted to the Office of Management and Budget for approval.

(b) The rules and regulations which result from the process indicated in Section 5(a) above shall replace any current rules and regulations and become effective April 30, 1983.

Section 6. The Director of the Office of Management and Budget is authorized to prescribe such rules and regulations, if any, as he deems appropriate for the effective implementation and administration of this Order and the Intergovernmental Cooperation Act of 1968. The Director is also authorized to exercise the authority vested in the President by Section 401(a) of that Act (42 U.S.C. 4231(a)), in a manner consistent with this Order.

Section 7. The Memorandum of November 8, 1968, is terminated (33 Fed. Reg. 16487, November 13, 1968). The Director of the Office of Management and Budget shall revoke OMB Circular A-95, which was issued pursuant to that Memorandum. However, Federal agencies shall continue to comply with the rules and regulations issued pursuant to that Memorandum, including those issued by the Office of Management and Budget, until new rules and regulations have been issued in accord with this Order.

Section 8. The Director of the Office of Management and Budget shall report to the President within two years on Federal agency compliance with this Order. The views of State and local elected officials on their experiences with these policies, along with any suggestions for improvement, will be included in the Director's report.

RONALD REAGAN

B. Executive Order 12,630

Governmental Actions and Interference with Constitutionally Protected Property Rights

March 15, 1988

53 Fed. Reg. 8859 (March 18, 1988)

By the authority vested in me as President by the Constitution and laws of the United States of America, and in order to ensure that government actions are undertaken on a well-reasoned basis with due regard for fiscal accountability, for the financial impact of the obligations imposed on the Federal government by the Just Compensation Clause of the Fifth Amendment, and for the Constitution, it is hereby ordered as follows:

Section 1. (a) The Fifth Amendment of the United States Constitution provides that private property shall not be taken for public use without just compensation. Government historically has used the formal exercise of the power of eminent domain, which provides orderly processes for paying just compensation, to acquire private property for public use. Recent Supreme Court decisions, however, in reaffirming the fundamental protection of private property rights provided by the Fifth Amendment and in assessing the nature of governmental actions that have an impact on constitutionally protected property rights, have also reaffirmed that governmental actions that do not formally invoke the condemnation power, including regulations, may result in a taking for which just compensation is required.

(b) Responsible fiscal management and fundamental principles of good government require that government decision-makers evaluate carefully the effect of their administrative, regulatory, and legislative actions on constitutionally protected property rights. Executive departments and agencies should review their actions carefully to prevent unnecessary takings and should account in decision-making for those takings that are necessitated by statutory mandate.

(c) The purpose of this Order is to assist Federal departments and agencies in undertaking such reviews and in proposing, planning, and implementing actions with due regard for the constitutional protections provided by the Fifth Amendment and to reduce the risk of undue or inadvertent burdens on the public fisc resulting from lawful governmental action. In furtherance of the purpose of this Order, the Attorney General shall, consistent with the principles stated herein and in consultation with the Executive departments and agencies, promulgate Guidelines for the Evaluation of Risk and Avoidance of Unanticipated Takings to which each Executive department or agency shall refer in making the evaluations required by this Order or in otherwise taking any action that is the subject of this Order. The Guidelines shall be promulgated no later than May 1, 1988, and shall be disseminated to all units of each Executive department and agency no later than July 1, 1988. The Attorney General shall, as necessary, update these guidelines to reflect fundamental changes in takings law occurring as a result of Supreme Court decisions.

Section 2. For the purpose of this Order:

(a) "Policies that have takings implications" refers to Federal regulations, proposed Federal regulations, proposed Federal legislation, comments on proposed Federal legislation, or other Federal policy statements that, if implemented or enacted, could effect a taking, such as rules and regulations that propose or implement licensing, permitting, or other condition requirements or limitations on private property use, or that require dedications or exactions from owners of private property. "Policies that have takings implications" does not include:

(1) Actions abolishing regulations, discontinuing governmental programs, or modifying regulations in a manner that lessens interference with the use of private property;

(2) Actions taken with respect to properties held in trust by the United States or in preparation for or during treaty negotiations with foreign nations;

(3) Law enforcement actions involving seizure, for violations of law, of property for forfeiture or as evidence in criminal proceedings;

(4) Studies or similar efforts or planning activities;

(5) Communications between Federal agencies or departments and State or local land-use planning agencies regarding planned or proposed State or local actions regulating private property regardless of whether such communications are initiated by a Federal agency or department or are undertaken in response to an invitation by the State or local authority;

(6) The placement of military facilities or military activities involving the use of Federal property alone; or

(7) Any military or foreign affairs functions (including procurement functions thereunder) but not including the U.S. Army Corps of Engineers civil works program.

(b) Private property refers to all property protected by the Just Compensation Clause of the Fifth Amendment.

(c) "Actions" refers to proposed Federal regulations, proposed Federal legislation, comments on proposed Federal legislation, applications of Federal regulations to specific property, or Federal governmental actions physically invading or occupying private property, or other policy statements or actions related to Federal regulation or direct physical invasion or occupancy, but does not include:

(1) Actions in which the power of eminent domain is formally exercised;

(2) Actions taken with respect to properties held in trust by the United States or in preparation for or during treaty negotiations with foreign nations;

(3) Law enforcement actions involving seizure, for violations of law, of property for forfeiture or as evidence in criminal proceedings;

(4) Studies or similar efforts or planning activities;

(5) Communications between Federal agencies or departments and State or local land-use planning agencies regarding planned or proposed State or local actions regulating private property regardless of whether such communications are initiated by a Federal agency or department or are undertaken in response to an invitation by the State or local authority;

(6) The placement of military facilities or military activities involving the use of Federal property alone; or

(7) Any military or foreign affairs functions (including procurement functions thereunder), but not including the U.S. Army Corps of Engineers civil works program.

Section 3. In formulating or implementing policies that have takings implications, each Executive department and agency shall be guided by the following general principles:

(a) Governmental officials should be sensitive to, anticipate, and account for, the obligations imposed by the Just Compensation Clause of the Fifth Amendment in planning and carrying out governmental actions so that they do not result in the imposition of unanticipated or undue additional burdens on the public fisc.

(b) Actions undertaken by governmental officials that result in a physical invasion or occupancy of private property, and regulations imposed on private property that substantially affect its value or use, may constitute a taking of property. Further, governmental action may amount to a taking even though the action results in less than a complete deprivation of all use or value, or of all separate and distinct interests in the same private property and even if the action constituting a taking is temporary in nature.

(c) Government officials whose actions are taken specifically for purposes of protecting public health and safety are ordinarily given broader latitude by courts before their actions are considered to be takings. However, the mere assertion of a public health and safety purpose is insufficient to avoid a taking. Actions to which this Order applies asserted to be for the protection of public health and safety, therefore, should be undertaken only in response to real and substantial threats to public health and safety, be designed to advance significantly the health and safety purpose, and be no greater than is necessary to achieve the health and safety purpose.

(d) While normal governmental processes do not ordinarily effect takings, undue delays in decision-making during which private property use if interfered with carry a risk of being held to be takings. Additionally, a delay in processing may increase significantly the size of compensation due if a taking is later found to have occurred.

(e) The Just Compensation Clause is self-actuating, requiring that compensation be paid whenever governmental action results in a taking of private property regardless of whether the underlying authority for the action contemplated a taking or authorized the payment of compensation. Accordingly, governmental actions that may have a significant impact on the use or value of private property should be scrutinized to avoid undue or unplanned burdens on the public fisc.

Section 4. *Department and Agency Action.*

In addition to the fundamental principles set forth in Section 3, Executive departments and agencies shall adhere, to the extent permitted by law, to the following criteria when implementing policies that have takings implications:

(a) When an Executive department or agency requires a private party to obtain a permit in order to undertake a specific use of, or action with respect to, private property, any conditions imposed on the granting of a permit shall:

(1) Serve the same purpose that would have been served by a prohibition of the use or action; and

(2) Substantially advance that purpose.

(b) When a proposed action would place a restriction on a use of private property, the restriction imposed on the use shall not be disproportionate to the extent to which the use contributes to the overall problem that the restriction is imposed to redress.

(c) When a proposed action involves a permitting process or any other decision-making process that will interfere with, or otherwise prohibit, the use of private property pending the completion of the process, the duration of the process shall be kept to the minimum necessary.

(d) Before undertaking any proposed action regulating private property use for the protection of public health or safety, the Executive department or agency involved shall, in internal deliberative documents and any submissions to the Director of the Office of Management and Budget that are required:

(1) Identify clearly, with as much specificity as possible, the public health or safety risk created by the private property use that is the subject of the proposed action;

(2) Establish that such proposed action substantially advances the purpose of protecting public health and safety against the specifically identified risk;

(3) Establish to the extent possible that the restrictions imposed on the private property are not disproportionate to the extent to which the use contributes to the overall risk; and

(4) Estimate, to the extent possible, the potential cost to the government in the event that a court later determines that the action constituted a taking. In instances in which there is an immediate threat to health and safety that constitutes an emergency requiring immediate response, this analysis may be done upon completion of the emergency action.

Section 5. *Executive Department and Agency Implementation*

(a) The head of each Executive department and agency shall designate an official to be responsible for ensuring compliance with this Order with respect to the actions of the department or agency.

(b) Executive departments and agencies shall, to the extent permitted by law, identify the takings implications of proposed regulatory actions and address the merits of those actions in light of the identified takings implications, if any, in all required submissions made to the Office of Management and Budget. Significant takings implications should also be identified and discussed in notices of proposed rule-making and messages transmitting legislative proposals to the Congress stating the departments' and agencies' conclusions on the takings issues.

(c) Executive departments and agencies shall identify each existing Federal rule and regulation against which a takings award has been made or against which a takings claim is pending including the amount of each claim or award. A "takings" award has been made or a "takings" claim pending if the award was made, or the pending claim brought, pursuant to the Just Compensation Clause of the Fifth Amendment. An itemized compilation of all such awards made in Fiscal Years 1985, 1986, and 1987 and all such pending claims shall be submitted to the Director, Office of Management and Budget, on or before May 16, 1988.

(d) Each Executive department and agency shall submit annually to the Director, Office of Management and Budget, and to the Attorney General an itemized compilation of all awards of just compensation entered against the United States for takings, including awards of interest as well as monies paid pursuant to the provisions of the Uniform Relocation Assistance and Real Property Acquisition Policies Act of 1970, 42 U.S.C. 4601.

(e)(1) The Director, Office of Management and Budget, and the Attorney General shall each, to the extent permitted by law, take action to ensure that the policies of the Executive departments and agencies are consistent with the principles, criteria, and requirements stated in Sections 1 through 5 of this Order, and the Office of Management and Budget shall take action to ensure that all takings awards levied against agencies are properly accounted for in agency budget submissions.

(2) In addition to the guidelines required by Section 1 of this Order, the Attorney General shall, in consultation with each Executive department and agency to which this Order applies, promulgate such supplemental guidelines as may be appropriate to the specific obligations of that department or agency.

Section 6. This Order is intended only to improve the internal management of the Executive branch and is not intended to create any right or benefit, substantive or procedural, enforceable at law by a party against the United States, its agencies, its officers, or any person.

RONALD REAGAN.

III. Other White House Memoranda

A. Presidential Memorandum: "Regulatory Reform—Waiver of Penalties and Reduction of Reports"

Memorandum of President of the United States

April 21, 1995

60 Fed. Reg. 20,621 (April 26, 1995)

Memorandum for The Secretary of State, The Secretary of the Treasury, The Secretary of Defense, The Attorney General, The Secretary of the Interior, The Secretary of Agriculture, The Secretary of Commerce, The Secretary of Labor, The Secretary of Health and Human Services, The Secretary of Housing and Urban Development, The Secretary of Transportation, The Secretary of Energy, The Secretary of Education, The Secretary of Veterans Affairs, The Administrator, Environmental Protection Agency, The Administrator, Small Business Administration, The Secretary of the Army, The Secretary of the Navy, The Secretary of the Air Force, The Director, Federal Emergency Management Agency, The Administrator, National Aeronautics and Space Administration, The Director, National Science Foundation, The Acting Archivist of the United States, The Administrator of General Services, The Chair, Railroad Retirement Board, The Chairperson, Architectural and Transportation Barriers, Compliance Board, The Executive Director, Pension Benefit Guaranty Corporation,

On March 16, I announced that the Administration would implement, new policies to give compliance officials more flexibility in dealing with small business and to cut back on paperwork. These Governmentwide policies, as well as the specific agency actions I announced, are part of this Administration's continuing commitment to sensible regulatory reform. With your help and cooperation, we hope to move the Government toward a more flexible, effective, and user friendly approach to regulation.

A. Actions: This memorandum directs the designated department and agency heads to implement the policies set forth below.

1. Authority to Waive Penalties.

(a) To the extent permitted by law, each agency shall use its discretion to modify the penalties for small businesses in the following situations. Agencies shall exercise their enforcement discretion to waive the imposition of all or a portion of a penalty when the violation is corrected within a time period appropriate to the violation in question. For those violations that may take longer to correct than the period set by the agency, the agency shall use its enforcement discretion to waive up to 100 percent of the financial penalties if the amounts waived are used to bring the entity into compliance. The provisions in paragraph 1(a) of this memorandum shall apply only where there has been a good faith effort to comply with applicable regulations and the violation does not involve criminal wrongdoing or significant threat to health, safety, or the environment.

(b) Each agency shall, by June 15, 1995, submit a plan to the Director of the Office of Management and Budget ("Director") describing the actions it will take to implement the policies in paragraph 1(a) of this memorandum. The plan shall provide that the agency will implement the policies described in paragraph 1(a) of this memorandum on or before July 14, 1995. Plans should include information on how notification will be given to frontline workers and small businesses.

2. Cutting Frequency of Reports.

(a) Each agency shall reduce by one-half the frequency of the regularly scheduled reports that the public is required, by rule or by policy, to provide to the Government (from quarterly to semiannually, from semiannually to annually, etc.), unless the department or agency head determines that such action is not legally permissible; would not adequately protect health, safety, or the environment; would be inconsistent with achieving regulatory flexibility or reducing regulatory burdens; or would impede the effective administration of the agency's program. The duty to make such determinations shall be nondelegable.

(b) Each agency shall, by June 15, 1995, submit a plan to the Director describing the actions it will take to implement the policies in paragraph 2(a), including a copy of any determination that certain reports are excluded.

B. Application and Scope:

1. The Director may issue further guidance as necessary to carry out the purposes of this memorandum.
2. This memorandum does not apply to matters related to law enforcement, national security, or foreign affairs, the importation or exportation of prohibited or restricted items, Government taxes, duties, fees, revenues, or receipts; nor does it apply to agencies (or components thereof) whose principal purpose is the collection, analysis, and dissemination of statistical information.
3. This memorandum is not intended, and should not be construed, to create any right or benefit, substantive or procedural, enforceable at law by a party against the United States, its agencies, its officers, or its employees.
4. The Director of the Office of Management and Budget is authorized and directed to publish this memorandum in the *Federal Register*.

WILLIAM J. CLINTON

B. OMB Director's Memorandum: "Federal Participation in the Development and Use of Voluntary Consensus Standards and in Conformity Assessment Activities"

OFFICE OF MANAGEMENT AND BUDGET
WASHINGTON, D.C.

THE DIRECTOR

February 10, 1998

TO THE HEADS OF EXECUTIVE DEPARTMENTS AND ESTABLISHMENTS

SUBJECT: Federal Participation in the Development and Use of Voluntary Consensus Standards and in Conformity Assessment Activities

Revised OMB Circular A-119 establishes policies on Federal use and development of voluntary consensus standards and on conformity assessment activities. Pub. L. 104-113, the "National Technology Transfer and Advancement Act of 1995," codified existing policies in A-119, established reporting requirements, and authorized the National Institute of Standards and Technology to coordinate conformity assessment activities of the agencies. OMB is issuing this revision of the Circular in order to make the terminology of the Circular consistent with the National Technology Transfer and Advancement Act of 1995, to issue guidance to the agencies on making their reports to OMB, to direct the Secretary of Commerce to issue policy guidance for conformity assessment, and to make changes for clarity.

Franklin D. Raines

Director

[Editors' Note: See OMB Circular No. A-119, "Federal Participation in the Development and Use of Voluntary Consensus Standards and in Conformity Assessment Activities," (revised Feb. 10, 1998), 63 Fed. Reg. 8546 (Feb. 19, 1998). *See also* NATIONAL INSTITUTE OF STANDARDS AND TECHNOLOGY, EIGHTH ANNUAL REPORT ON FEDERAL AGENCY USE OF VOLUNTARY CONSENSUS STANDARDS AND CONFORMITY ASSESSMENT (Fiscal Year 2004 annual report on Federal participation in the development and use of voluntary consensus standards, in accordance with OMB Circular A-119 and as required by Section 12(d) of the National Technology Transfer and Advancement Act Amendments of 1996. Letter from OMB transmitting report to Congress (Aug. 12, 2005), *available at* http://www.whitehouse.gov/omb/inforeg/regpol-reports_congress.html.]

TO THE HEADS OF EXECUTIVE DEPARTMENTS AND ESTABLISHMENTS

SUBJECT: Federal Participation in the Development and Use of Voluntary Consensus Standards and in Conformity Assessment Activities

TABLE OF CONTENTS
BACKGROUND
1. What Is The Purpose Of This Circular?
2. What Are The Goals Of The Government Using Voluntary Consensus Standards?
DEFINITIONS OF STANDARDS
3. What Is A Standard?
4. What Are Voluntary, Consensus Standards?
a. Definition of voluntary, consensus standard.
(1) Definition of voluntary, consensus standards body.
b. Other types of standards.
(1) Non-consensus standards, industry standards, company standards, or de facto standards.
(2) Government-unique standards.
(3) Standards mandated by law.
POLICY
5. Who Does This Policy Apply To?
6. What Is The Policy For Federal Use Of Standards?
a. When must my agency use voluntary consensus standards?
(1) Definition of "Use."
(2) Definition of "Impractical."
b. What must my agency do when such use is determined by my agency to be inconsistent with applicable law or otherwise impractical?
c. How does this policy affect my agency's regulatory authorities and responsibilities?
d. How does this policy affect my agency's procurement authority?

e. What are the goals of agency use of voluntary consensus standards?
f. What considerations should my agency make when it is considering using a standard?
g. Does this policy establish a preference between consensus and non-consensus standards that are developed in the private sector?
h. Does this policy establish a preference between domestic and international voluntary consensus standards?
i. Should my agency give preference to performance standards?
j. How should my agency reference voluntary consensus standards?
k. What if no voluntary consensus standard exists?
l. How may my agency identify voluntary consensus standards?
7. What Is The Policy For Federal Participation In Voluntary Consensus Standards Bodies?
a. What are the purposes of agency participation?
b. What are the general principles that apply to agency support?
c. What forms of support may my agency provide?
d. Must agency participants be authorized?
e. Does agency participation indicate endorsement of any decisions reached by voluntary consensus standards bodies?
f. Do agency representatives participate equally with other members?
g. Are there any limitations on participation by agency representatives?
h. Are there any limits on the number of federal participants in voluntary consensus standards bodies?
i. Is there anything else agency representatives should know?
j. What if a voluntary consensus standards body is likely to develop an acceptable, needed standard in a timely fashion?
8. What Is The Policy On Conformity Assessment?

MANAGEMENT AND REPORTING OF STANDARDS USE
9. What Is My Agency Required To Report?
10. How Does My Agency Manage And Report On Its Development and Use Of Standards?
11. What Are The Procedures For Reporting My Agency's Use Of Standards In Regulations?
12. What Are The Procedures For Reporting My Agency's Use Of Standards In Procurements?
a. How does my agency report the use of standards in procurements on a categorical basis?
b. How does my agency report the use of standards in procurements on a transaction basis?

AGENCY RESPONSIBILITIES
13. What Are The Responsibilities Of The Secretary Of Commerce?
14. What Are The Responsibilities Of The Heads Of Agencies?
15. What Are The Responsibilities Of Agency Standards Executives?
SUPPLEMENTARY INFORMATION
16. When Will This Circular Be Reviewed?
17. What Is The Legal Effect Of This Circular?
18. Do You Have Further Questions?

BACKGROUND
1. What Is The Purpose Of This Circular?
This Circular establishes policies to improve the internal management of the Executive Branch. Consistent with Section 12(d) of P.L. 104-113, the "National Technology Transfer and Advancement Act of 1995" (hereinafter "the Act"), this Circular directs agencies to use voluntary consensus standards in lieu of government-unique standards except where inconsistent with law or otherwise impractical. It also provides guidance for agencies participating in voluntary consensus standards bodies and describes procedures for satisfying the reporting requirements in the Act. The policies in this Circular are intended to reduce to a minimum the reliance by agencies on government-unique standards. These policies do not create the bases for discrimination in agency procurement or regulatory activities among standards developed in the private sector, whether or not they are developed by voluntary consensus standards bodies. Consistent with Section 12(b) of the Act, this Circular directs the Secretary of Commerce to issue guidance to the agencies in order to coordinate conformity assessment activities. This Circular replaces OMB Circular No. A-119, dated October 20, 1993.

2. What Are The Goals Of The Government In Using Voluntary Consensus Standards?
Many voluntary consensus standards are appropriate or adaptable for the Government's purposes. The use of such standards, whenever practicable and appropriate, is intended to achieve the following goals:

    a. Eliminate the cost to the Government of developing its own standards and decrease the cost of goods procured and the burden of complying with agency regulation.

    b. Provide incentives and opportunities to establish standards that serve national needs.

    c. Encourage long-term growth for U.S. enterprises and promote efficiency and economic competition through harmonization of standards.

d. Further the policy of reliance upon the private sector to supply Government needs for goods and services.

DEFINITIONS OF STANDARDS
3. What Is A Standard?
   a. The term "standard," or "technical standard" as cited in the Act, includes all of the following:
      (1) Common and repeated use of rules, conditions, guidelines or characteristics for products or related processes and production methods, and related management systems practices.
      (2) The definition of terms; classification of components; delineation of procedures; specification of dimensions, materials, performance, designs, or operations; measurement of quality and quantity in describing materials, processes, products, systems, services, or practices; test methods and sampling procedures; or descriptions of fit and measurements of size or strength.
   b. The term "standard" does not include the following:
      (1) Professional standards of personal conduct.
      (2) Institutional codes of ethics.
   c. "Performance standard" is a standard as defined above that states requirements in terms of required results with criteria for verifying compliance but without stating the methods for achieving required results. A performance standard may define the functional requirements for the item, operational requirements, and/or interface and interchangeability characteristics. A performance standard may be viewed in juxtaposition to a prescriptive standard which may specify design requirements, such as materials to be used, how a requirement is to be achieved, or how an item is to be fabricated or constructed.
   d. "Non-government standard" is a standard as defined above that is in the form of a standardization document developed by a private sector association, organization or technical society which plans, develops, establishes or coordinates standards, specifications, handbooks, or related documents.

4. What Are Voluntary Consensus Standards?
   a. For purposes of this policy, "voluntary consensus standards" are standards developed or adopted by voluntary consensus standards bodies, both domestic and international. These standards include provisions requiring that owners of relevant intellectual property have agreed to make that intellectual property available on a non-discriminatory, royalty-free or reasonable royalty basis to all interested parties. For purposes of this

Circular, "technical standards that are developed or adopted by voluntary consensus standard bodies" is an equivalent term.

(1) "Voluntary consensus standards bodies" are domestic or international organizations which plan, develop, establish, or coordinate voluntary consensus standards using agreed-upon procedures. For purposes of this Circular, "voluntary, private sector, consensus standards bodies," as cited in Act, is an equivalent term. The Act and the Circular encourage the participation of federal representatives in these bodies to increase the likelihood that the standards they develop will meet both public and private sector needs. A voluntary consensus standards body is defined by the following attributes:

(i) Openness.

(ii) Balance of interest.

(iii) Due process.

(vi) An appeals process.

(v) Consensus, which is defined as general agreement, but not necessarily unanimity, and includes a process for attempting to resolve objections by interested parties, as long as all comments have been fairly considered, each objector is advised of the disposition of his or her objection(s) and the reasons why, and the consensus body members are given an opportunity to change their votes after reviewing the comments.

b. Other types of standards, which are distinct from voluntary consensus standards, are the following:

(1) "Non-consensus standards," "Industry standards," "Company standards," or "de facto standards," which are developed in the private sector but not in the full consensus process.

(2) "Government-unique standards," which are developed by the government for its own uses.

(3) Standards mandated by law, such as those contained in the United States Pharmacopeia and the National Formulary, as referenced in 21 U.S.C. 351.

POLICY

5. Who Does This Policy Apply To?

This Circular applies to all agencies and agency employees who use standards and participate in voluntary consensus standards activities, domestic and international, except for activities carried out pursuant to treaties. "Agency" means any executive department, independent commission, board, bureau, office, agency, Government-owned or controlled corporation or other establishment of the Federal Government. It also includes any regulatory commission or board, except for independent regulatory commissions insofar as they are subject to separate statutory requirements regarding the use of voluntary consensus standards. It does not include the legislative or judicial branches of the Federal Government.

6. What Is The Policy For Federal Use Of Standards?

All federal agencies must use voluntary consensus standards in lieu of government-unique standards in their procurement and regulatory activities, except where inconsistent with law or otherwise impractical. In these circumstances, your agency must submit a report describing the reason(s) for its use of government-unique standards in lieu of voluntary consensus standards to the Office of Management and Budget (OMB) through the National Institute of Standards and Technology (NIST).

a. When must my agency use voluntary consensus standards?

Your agency must use voluntary consensus standards, both domestic and international, in its regulatory and procurement activities in lieu of government-unique standards, unless use of such standards would be inconsistent with applicable law or otherwise impractical. In all cases, your agency has the discretion to decline to use existing voluntary consensus standards if your agency determines that such standards are inconsistent with applicable law or otherwise impractical.

(1) "Use" means incorporation of a standard in whole, in part, or by reference for procurement purposes, and the inclusion of a standard in whole, in part, or by reference in regulation(s).

(2) "Impractical" includes circumstances in which such use would fail to serve the agency's program needs; would be infeasible; would be inadequate, ineffectual, inefficient, or inconsistent with agency mission; or would impose more burdens, or would be less useful, than the use of another standard.

b. What must my agency do when such use is determined by my agency to be inconsistent with applicable law or otherwise impractical?

The head of your agency must transmit to the Office of Management and Budget (OMB), through the National Institute of Standards and Technology (NIST), an explanation of the reason(s) for using government-unique standards in lieu of voluntary consensus standards. For more information on reporting, see section 9.

c. How does this policy affect my agency's regulatory authorities and responsibilities?

This policy does not preempt or restrict agencies' authorities and responsibilities to make regulatory decisions authorized by statute. Such regulatory authorities and responsibilities include determining the level of acceptable risk; setting the level of protection; and balancing risk, cost, and availability of technology in establishing regulatory standards. However, to determine whether established regulatory limits or targets have been met, agencies should use voluntary consensus standards for test methods, sampling procedures, or protocols.

d. How does this policy affect my agency's procurement authority?
This policy does not preempt or restrict agencies' authorities and responsibilities to identify the capabilities that they need to obtain through procurements. Rather, this policy limits an agency's authority to pursue an identified capability through reliance on a government-unique standard when a voluntary consensus standard exists (see Section 6a).

e. What are the goals of agency use of voluntary consensus standards?
Agencies should recognize the positive contribution of standards development and related activities. When properly conducted, standards development can increase productivity and efficiency in Government and industry, expand opportunities for international trade, conserve resources, improve health and safety, and protect the environment.

f. What considerations should my agency make when it is considering using a standard?
When considering using a standard, your agency should take full account of the effect of using the standard on the economy, and of applicable federal laws and policies, including laws and regulations relating to antitrust, national security, small business, product safety, environment, metrication, technology development, and conflicts of interest. Your agency should also recognize that use of standards, if improperly conducted, can suppress free and fair competition; impede innovation and technical progress; exclude safer or less expensive products; or otherwise adversely affect trade, commerce, health, or safety. If your agency is proposing to incorporate a standard into a proposed or final rulemaking, your agency must comply with the "Principles of Regulation" (enumerated in Section 1(b)) and with the other analytical requirements of Executive Order 12866, "Regulatory Planning and Review."

g. Does this policy establish a preference between consensus and non-consensus standards that are developed in the private sector?
This policy does not establish a preference among standards developed in the private sector. Specifically, agencies that promulgate regulations referencing non-consensus standards developed in the private sector are not required to report on these actions, and agencies that procure products or services based on non-consensus standards are not required to report on

such procurements. For example, this policy allows agencies to select a non-consensus standard developed in the private sector as a means of establishing testing methods in a regulation and to choose among commercial-off-the-shelf products, regardless of whether the underlying standards are developed by voluntary consensus standards bodies or not.

h. Does this policy establish a preference between domestic and international voluntary consensus standards?

This policy does not establish a preference between domestic and international voluntary consensus standards. However, in the interests of promoting trade and implementing the provisions of international treaty agreements, your agency should consider international standards in procurement and regulatory applications.

i. Should my agency give preference to performance standards?

In using voluntary consensus standards, your agency should give preference to performance standards when such standards may reasonably be used in lieu of prescriptive standards.

j. How should my agency reference voluntary consensus standards?

Your agency should reference voluntary consensus standards, along with sources of availability, in appropriate publications, regulatory orders, and related internal documents. In regulations, the reference must include the date of issuance. For all other uses, your agency must determine the most appropriate form of reference, which may exclude the date of issuance as long as users are elsewhere directed to the latest issue. If a voluntary standard is used and published in an agency document, your agency must observe and protect the rights of the copyright holder and any other similar obligations.

k. What if no voluntary consensus standard exists?

In cases where no voluntary consensus standards exist, an agency may use government-unique standards (in addition to other standards, see Section 6g) and is not required to file a report on its use of government-unique standards. As explained above (see Section 6a), an agency may use government-unique standards in lieu of voluntary consensus standards if the use of such standards would be inconsistent with applicable law or otherwise impractical; in such cases, the agency must file a report under Section 9a regarding its use of government-unique standards.

l. How may my agency identify voluntary consensus standards?

Your agency may identify voluntary consensus standards through databases of standards maintained by the National Institute of Standards and Technology (NIST), or by other organizations including voluntary consensus standards bodies, other federal agencies, or standards publishing companies.

7. *What Is The Policy For Federal Participation In Voluntary Consensus Standards Bodies?*

Agencies must consult with voluntary consensus standards bodies, both domestic and international, and must participate with such bodies in the development of voluntary consensus standards when consultation and participation is in the public interest and is compatible with their missions, authorities, priorities, and budget resources.

a. What are the purposes of agency participation?

Agency representatives should participate in voluntary consensus standards activities in order to accomplish the following purposes:

>(1) Eliminate the necessity for development or maintenance of separate Government-unique standards.
>
>(2) Further such national goals and objectives as increased use of the metric system of measurement; use of environmentally sound and energy efficient materials, products, systems, services, or practices; and improvement of public health and safety.

b. What are the general principles that apply to agency support?

Agency support provided to a voluntary consensus standards activity must be limited to that which clearly furthers agency and departmental missions, authorities, priorities, and is consistent with budget resources. Agency support must not be contingent upon the outcome of the standards activity. Normally, the total amount of federal support should be no greater than that of other participants in that activity, except when it is in the direct and predominant interest of the Government to develop or revise a standard, and its timely development or revision appears unlikely in the absence of such support.

c. What forms of support may my agency provide?

The form of agency support, may include the following:

>(1) Direct financial support; e.g., grants, memberships, and contracts.
>
>(2) Administrative support; e.g., travel costs, hosting of meetings, and secretarial functions.
>
>(3) Technical support; e.g., cooperative testing for standards evaluation and participation of agency personnel in the activities of voluntary consensus standards bodies.
>
>(4) Joint planning with voluntary consensus standards bodies to promote the identification and development of needed standards.
>
>(5) Participation of agency personnel.

d. Must agency participants be authorized?
Agency employees who, at Government expense, participate in standards activities of voluntary consensus standards bodies on behalf of the agency must do so as specifically authorized agency representatives. Agency support for, and participation by agency personnel in, voluntary consensus standards bodies must be in compliance with applicable laws and regulations. For example, agency support is subject to legal and budgetary authority and availability of funds. Similarly, participation by agency employees (whether or not on behalf of the agency) in the activities of voluntary consensus standards bodies is subject to the laws and regulations that apply to participation by federal employees in the activities of outside organizations. While we anticipate that participation in a committee that is developing a standard would generally not raise significant issues, participation as an officer, director, or trustee of an organization would raise more significant issues. An agency should involve its agency ethics officer, as appropriate, before authorizing support for or participation in a voluntary consensus standards body.

e. Does agency participation indicate endorsement of any decisions reached by voluntary consensus standards bodies?
Agency participation in voluntary consensus standards bodies does not necessarily connote agency agreement with, or endorsement of, decisions reached by such organizations.

f. Do agency representatives participate equally with other members?
Agency representatives serving as members of voluntary consensus standards bodies should participate actively and on an equal basis with other members, consistent with the procedures of those bodies, particularly in matters such as establishing priorities, developing procedures for preparing, reviewing, and approving standards, and developing or adopting new standards. Active participation includes full involvement in discussions and technical debates, registering of opinions and, if selected, serving as chairpersons or in other official capacities. Agency representatives may vote, in accordance with the procedures of the voluntary consensus standards body, at each stage of the standards development process unless prohibited from doing so by law or their agencies.

g. Are there any limitations on participation by agency representatives?
In order to maintain the independence of voluntary consensus standards bodies, agency representatives must refrain from involvement in the internal management of such organizations (e.g., selection of salaried officers and employees, establishment of staff salaries, and administrative policies). Agency representatives must not dominate such bodies, and in

any case are bound by voluntary consensus standards bodies' rules and procedures, including those regarding domination of proceedings by any individual. Regardless, such agency employees must avoid the practice or the appearance of undue influence relating to their agency representation and activities in voluntary consensus standards bodies.

h. Are there any limits on the number of federal participants in voluntary consensus standards bodies?

The number of individual agency participants in a given voluntary standards activity should be kept to the minimum required for effective representation of the various program, technical, or other concerns of federal agencies.

i. Is there anything else agency representatives should know?

This Circular does not provide guidance concerning the internal operating procedures that may be applicable to voluntary consensus standards bodies because of their relationships to agencies under this Circular. Agencies should, however, carefully consider what laws or rules may apply in a particular instance because of these relationships. For example, these relationships may involve the Federal Advisory Committee Act, as amended (5 U.S.C. App. I), or a provision of an authorizing statute for a particular agency.

j. What if a voluntary consensus standards body is likely to develop an acceptable, needed standard in a timely fashion?

If a voluntary consensus standards body is in the process of developing or adopting a voluntary consensus standard that would likely be lawful and practical for an agency to use, and would likely be developed or adopted on a timely basis, an agency should not be developing its own government-unique standard and instead should be participating in the activities of the voluntary consensus standards body.

8. What Is The Policy On Conformity Assessment?

Section 12(b) of the Act requires NIST to coordinate Federal, State, and local standards activities and conformity assessment activities with private sector standards activities and conformity assessment activities, with the goal of eliminating unnecessary duplication and complexity in the development and promulgation of conformity assessment requirements and measures. To ensure effective coordination, the Secretary of Commerce must issue guidance to the agencies.

MANAGEMENT AND REPORTING OF STANDARDS USE
9. What Is My Agency Required to Report?

a. As required by the Act, your agency must report to NIST, no later than December 31 of each year, the decisions by your agency in the previous fiscal year to use government-unique standards in lieu of voluntary consensus standards. If no voluntary consensus standard exists, your agency does not need to report its use of government-unique standards. (In addition, an agency is not required to report on its use of other standards. See Section 6g.) Your agency must include an explanation of the reason(s) why use of such voluntary consensus standard would be inconsistent with applicable law or otherwise impractical, as described in Sections 11b(2), 12a(3), and 12b(2) of this Circular. Your agency must report in accordance with format instructions issued by NIST.

b. Your agency must report to NIST, no later than December 31 of each year, information on the nature and extent of agency participation in the development and use of voluntary consensus standards from the previous fiscal year. Your agency must report in accordance with format instructions issued by NIST. Such reporting must include the following:

(1) The number of voluntary consensus standards bodies in which there is agency participation, as well as the number of agency employees participating.

(2) The number of voluntary consensus standards the agency has used since the last report, based on the procedures set forth in sections 11 and 12 of this Circular.

(3) Identification of voluntary consensus standards that have been substituted for government-unique standards as a result of an agency review under section 15b(7) of this Circular.

(4) An evaluation of the effectiveness of this policy and recommendations for any changes.

c. No later than the following January 31, NIST must transmit to OMB a summary report of the information received.

10. How Does My Agency Manage And Report Its Development and Use Of Standards?

Your agency must establish a process to identify, manage, and review your agency's development and use of standards. At minimum, your agency must have the ability to (1) report to OMB through NIST on the agency's use of government-unique standards in lieu of voluntary consensus standards, along with an explanation of the reasons for such non-usage, as described in section 9a, and (2) report on your agency's participation in the development and use of voluntary consensus standards, as described in section 9b. This policy establishes two ways, category based reporting and transaction based reporting, for agencies to manage and report their use of standards. Your agency must report all uses of standards in one or both ways.

11. What Are The Procedures For Reporting My Agency's Use Of Standards In Regulations?

Your agency should use transaction based reporting if your agency issues regulations that use or reference standards. If your agency is issuing or revising a regulation that contains a standard, your agency must follow these procedures:

    a. Publish a request for comment within the preamble of a Notice of Proposed Rulemaking (NPRM) or Interim Final Rule (IFR). Such request must provide the appropriate information, as follows:

        (1) When your agency is proposing to use a voluntary consensus standard, provide a statement which identifies such standard.

        (2) When your agency is proposing to use a government-unique standard in lieu of a voluntary consensus standard, provide a statement which identifies such standards and provides a preliminary explanation for the proposed use of a government-unique standard in lieu of a voluntary consensus standard.

        (3) When your agency is proposing to use a government-unique standard, and no voluntary consensus standard has been identified, a statement to that effect and an invitation to identify any such standard and to explain why such standard should be used.

    b. Publish a discussion in the preamble of a Final Rulemaking that restates the statement in the NPRM or IFR, acknowledges and summarizes any comments received and responds to them, and explains the agency's final decision. This discussion must provide the appropriate information, as follows:

        (1) When a voluntary consensus standard is being used, provide a statement that identifies such standard and any alternative voluntary consensus standards which have been identified.

        (2) When a government-unique standard is being used in lieu of a voluntary consensus standard, provide a statement that identifies the standards and explains why using the voluntary consensus standard would be inconsistent with applicable law or otherwise impractical. Such explanation must be transmitted in accordance with the requirements of Section 9a.

        (3) When a government-unique standard is being used, and no voluntary consensus standard has been identified, provide a statement to that effect.

12. What Are The Procedures For Reporting My Agency's Use Of Standards In Procurements?

To identify, manage, and review the standards used in your agency's procurements, your agency must either report on a categorical basis or on a transaction basis.

a. How does my agency report the use of standards in procurements on a categorical basis?

Your agency must report on a category basis when your agency identifies, manages, and reviews the use of standards by group or category. Category based reporting is especially useful when your agency either conducts large procurements or large numbers of procurements using government-unique standards, or is involved in long-term procurement contracts which require replacement parts based on government-unique standards. To report use of government-unique standards on a categorical basis, your agency must:

(1) Maintain a centralized standards management system that identifies how your agency uses both government-unique and voluntary consensus standards.

(2) Systematically review your agency's use of government-unique standards for conversion to voluntary consensus standards.

(3) Maintain records on the groups or categories in which your agency uses government-unique standards in lieu of voluntary consensus standards, including an explanation of the reasons for such use, which must be transmitted according to Section 9a.

(4) Enable potential offerors to suggest voluntary consensus standards that can replace government-unique standards.

b. How does my agency report the use of standards in procurements on a transaction basis?

Your agency should report on a transaction basis when your agency identifies, manages, and reviews the use of standards on a transaction basis rather than a category basis. Transaction based reporting is especially useful when your agency conducts procurement mostly through commercial products and services, but is occasionally involved in a procurement involving government-unique standards. To report use of government-unique standards on a transaction basis, your agency must follow the following procedures:

(1) In each solicitation which references government-unique standards, the solicitation must:

(i) Identify such standards.

(ii) Provide potential offerors an opportunity to suggest alternative voluntary consensus standards that meet the agency's requirements.

(2) If such suggestions are made and the agency decides to use government-unique standards in lieu of voluntary consensus standards, the agency must explain in its report to OMB as described in Section 9a why using such voluntary consensus standards is inconsistent with applicable law or otherwise impractical.

c. For those solicitations that are for commercial-off-the-shelf products (COTS), or for products or services that rely on voluntary consensus standards or non-consensus standards developed in the private sector, or for products that otherwise do not rely on government-unique standards, the requirements in this section do not apply.

AGENCY RESPONSIBILITIES

13. What Are The Responsibilities Of The Secretary Of Commerce?
The Secretary of Commerce:
a. Coordinates and fosters executive branch implementation of this Circular and, as appropriate, provides administrative guidance to assist agencies in implementing this Circular including guidance on identifying voluntary consensus standards bodies and voluntary consensus standards.
b. Sponsors and supports the Interagency Committee on Standards Policy (ICSP), chaired by the National Institute of Standards and Technology, which considers agency views and advises the Secretary and agency heads on the Circular.
c. Reports to the Director of OMB concerning the implementation of the policy provisions of this Circular.
d. Establishes procedures for agencies to use when developing directories described in Section 15b(5) and establish procedures to make these directories available to the public.
e. Issues guidance to the agencies to improve coordination on conformity assessment in accordance with section 8.

14. What Are The Responsibilities Of The Heads Of Agencies?
The Heads of Agencies:
a. Implement the policies of this Circular in accordance with procedures described.
b. Ensure agency compliance with the policies of the Circular.
c. In the case of an agency with significant interest in the use of standards, designate a senior level official as the Standards Executive who will be responsible for the agency's implementation of this Circular and who will represent the agency on the ICSP.
d. Transmit the annual report prepared by the Agency Standards Executive as described in Sections 9 and 15b(6).

15. What Are The Responsibilities Of Agency Standards Executives?
An Agency Standards Executive:
    a. Promotes the following goals:
        (1) Effective use of agency resources and participation.
        (2) The development of agency positions that are in the public interest and that do not conflict with each other.
        (3) The development of agency positions that are consistent with administration policy.
        (4) The development of agency technical and policy positions that are clearly defined and known in advance to all federal participants on a given committee.
    b. Coordinates his or her agency's participation in voluntary consensus standards bodies by:
        (1) Establishing procedures to ensure that agency representatives who participate in voluntary consensus standards bodies will, to the extent possible, ascertain the views of the agency on matters of paramount interest and will, at a minimum, express views that are not inconsistent or in conflict with established agency views.
        (2) To the extent possible, ensuring that the agency's participation in voluntary consensus standards bodies is consistent with agency missions, authorities, priorities, and budget resources.
        (3) Ensuring, when two or more agencies participate in a given voluntary consensus standards activity, that they coordinate their views on matters of paramount importance so as to present, whenever feasible, a single, unified position and, where not feasible, a mutual recognition of differences.
        (4) Cooperating with the Secretary in carrying out his or her responsibilities under this Circular.
        (5) Consulting with the Secretary, as necessary, in the development and issuance of internal agency procedures and guidance implementing this Circular, including the development and implementation of an agency-wide directory identifying agency employees participating in voluntary consensus standards bodies and the identification of voluntary consensus standards bodies.
        (6) Preparing, as described in Section 9, a report on uses of government-unique standards in lieu of voluntary consensus standards and a report on the status of agency standards policy activities.
        (7) Establishing a process for ongoing review of the agency's use of standards for purposes of updating such use.

(8) Coordinating with appropriate agency offices (e.g., budget and legal offices) to ensure that effective processes exist for the review of proposed agency support for, and participation in, voluntary consensus standards bodies, so that agency support and participation will comply with applicable laws and regulations.

SUPPLEMENTARY INFORMATION

16. When Will This Circular Be Reviewed?
This Circular will be reviewed for effectiveness by the OMB three years from the date of issuance.

17. What Is The Legal Effect Of This Circular?
Authority for this Circular is based on 31 U.S.C. 1111, which gives OMB broad authority to establish policies for the improved management of the Executive Branch. This Circular is intended to implement Section 12(d) of P.L. 104-113 and to establish policies that will improve the internal management of the Executive Branch. This Circular is not intended to create delay in the administrative process, provide new grounds for judicial review, or create new rights or benefits, substantive or procedural, enforceable at law or equity by a party against the United States, its agencies or instrumentalities, or its officers or employees.

18. Do You Have Further Questions?
For information concerning this Circular, contact the Office of Management and Budget, Office of Information and Regulatory Affairs: Telephone 202/ 395-3785.

C. Presidential Memorandum: "Plain Language in Government Writing"

MEMORANDUM FOR THE HEADS OF EXECUTIVE DEPARTMENTS AND AGENCIES

SUBJECT: Plain Language in Government Writing

DATE: June 1, 1998 [63 Fed. Reg. 31,885 (June 10, 1998)]

The Vice President and I have made reinventing the Federal Government a top priority of my Administration. We are determined to make the Government more responsive, accessible, and understandable in its communications with the public.

The Federal Government's writing must be in plain language. By using plain language, we send a clear message about what the Government is doing, what it requires, and what services it offers. Plain language saves the Government and the private sector time, effort, and money.

Plain language requirements vary from one document to another, depending on the intended audience. Plain language documents have logical organization, easy-to-read design features, and use:
- common, everyday words, except for necessary technical terms;
- "you" and other pronouns;
- the active voice; and
- short sentences.

To ensure the use of plain language, I direct you to do the following:

- By October 1, 1998, use plain language in all new documents, other than regulations, that explain how to obtain a benefit or service or how to comply with a requirement you administer or enforce. For example, these documents may include letters, forms, notices, and instructions. By January 1, 2002, all such documents created prior to October 1, 1998 must also be in plain language.
- By January 1, 1999, use plain language in all proposed and final rulemakings published in the *Federal Register*, unless you proposed the rule before that date. You should consider rewriting existing regu-

lations in plain language when you have the opportunity and resources to do so.

The National Partnership for Reinventing Government will issue guidance to help you comply with these directives and to explain more fully the elements of plain language. You should also use customer feedback and common sense to guide your plain language efforts.

I ask the independent agencies to comply with these directives.

This memorandum does not confer any right or benefit enforceable by law against the United States or its representatives. The Director of the Office of Management and Budget will publish this memorandum in the *Federal Register*.

WILLIAM J. CLINTON

D. OIRA Guidance on Presidential Review of Agency Rulemaking

September 20, 2001

MEMORANDUM FOR THE PRESIDENT'S MANAGEMENT COUNCIL

FROM: John D. Graham, [OIRA] Administrator

SUBJECT: Presidential Review of Agency Rulemaking by OIRA

Federal regulations can provide cost-effective solutions to many problems. If not properly developed, regulations can lead to an enormous burden on the economy.

In this context, I call your attention to Executive Order No. 12866, "Regulatory Planning and Review." Under this Executive Order, the Administrator of the Office of Information and Regulatory Affairs (OIRA) carries out a regulatory review process on behalf of the President. The President's Chief of Staff, Andrew H. Card, Jr., has directed me to work with the agencies to implement vigorously the principles and procedures in E.O. 12866 until a modified or new Executive order is issued.

I want to stress that it is my goal to work with you to carry out OIRA's regulatory reviews thoroughly and cooperatively. To help us work together more effectively, I have attached a detailed description of how OIRA carries out this regulatory review, summarizing the principles we follow and the procedures we use. I request that you send this attachment to the appropriate officials in your agency that are responsible for regulatory development.

Working together to apply the regulatory principles in E.O. 12866, I believe we will strengthen the country's regulatory structure. I look forward to working with all of you and your staff.

Attachment

****

OMB REGULATORY REVIEW: PRINCIPLES AND PROCEDURES

This attachment describes the general principles and procedures that will be applied by OMB in the implementation of E.O. 12866 and related statutory and executive authority.

OIRA Review of Significant Regulations

E.O. 12866, "Regulatory Planning and Review,"[1] governs OIRA's oversight of agency rulemaking, requiring OIRA review of "significant" agency regulatory actions before they are proposed for public comment, and again before they are issued in final form. The Order defines "regulatory action" broadly to include all substantive action by an agency that is expected to lead to the issuance of a final rule. Over the past several years, OIRA staff have worked with agencies to develop a common understanding of what is meant by a "significant" regulatory action (see section 3(f)). While OIRA does not formally review non-significant regulatory actions, agencies are expected to ensure that they are consistent with the Order's regulatory principles (section 1).

Following agency transmittal to OIRA of a draft rule, OIRA reviews the draft rule for consistency with the regulatory principles stated in the Order, and with the President's policies and priorities. The review determines whether the agency has, in deciding whether and how to regulate, assessed the costs and benefits of available regulatory alternatives (including the alternative of not regulating). Specifically, E.O. 12866 states that, "in choosing among alternative regulatory approaches, agencies should select those approaches that maximize net benefits... ." E.O. 12866 further states that, "Each agency shall assess both the costs and the benefits of the intended regulation and, recognizing that some costs and benefits are difficult to quantify, propose or adopt a regulation only upon a reasoned determination that the benefits of the intended regulation justify its costs."

Regulatory Impact Analysis

Agencies must prepare a Regulatory Impact Analysis (RIA) for each regulation that OIRA or the agency designates as "economically significant." Section 3(f)(1) of the Order defines an "economically significant" rule as one likely to "have an annual effect on the economy of $100 million or more or adversely affect in a material way the economy, a sector of the economy, productivity, competition, jobs, the environment, public health or safety, or State, local, or tribal governments or communities." This definition is functionally equivalent to the definition of a "major" rule as that term is used in the Congressional Review Act.[2]

The RIA must provide an assessment of benefits, costs, and potentially effective and reasonably feasible alternatives to the planned regulatory action (see section 6(a)(3)(C)). This is submitted to OIRA along with the applicable draft regulatory action. Preparing RIAs helps agencies evaluate the need for and consequences of possible Federal action. By analyzing alternate ways to structure a rule, agencies can select the best option while providing OIRA and the public a broader understanding of the ranges of issues that may be involved. Accordingly, it is important that a draft RIA be reviewed by agency economists, engineers, and scientists, as well as by agency attorneys, prior to submission to OIRA.

OIRA also relies on RIAs to meet its obligations (1) under the Congressional Review Act, which directs the OIRA Administrator to determine if final rules are "major"[3] and (2) under another law,[4] which requires the OMB Director to submit an annual report to Congress on the costs and benefits of Federal regulation.[5] As a result, agency submissions to OIRA of economically significant rules shall include RIAs, regardless of the extent to which an agency is permitted by law to consider risks, costs, or benefits in issuing a regulation. RIAs should be prepared in a way consistent with OMB Memorandum M-00-08.[6]

Risk Assessments

OIRA's review also evaluates, on occasion in consultation with the Office of Science and Technology Policy, whether the agency has, in assessing exposure to a risk or environmental hazard, conducted an adequate risk assessment. The risk assessment should be an objective, realistic, and scientifically balanced analysis.

We note that in 1996 the Congress, for health decisions under the Safe Drinking Water Act, adopted a basic standard of quality for the use of science in agency decisionmaking. Congress directed an agency, "to the degree that an [a]gency action is based on science," to use "(i) the best available, peer-reviewed science and supporting studies conducted in accordance with sound and objective scientific practices; and (ii) data collected by accepted methods or best available methods (if the reliability of the method and the nature of the decision justifies use of the data)."[7] We further note that, in 1996 the Congress adopted a basic quality standard for the dissemination of public information involving risk effects. Congress directed the agency, "to ensure that the presentation of information [risk] effects is comprehensive, informative, and understandable." Congress further directed the agency, "in a document made available to the public in support of a regulation [to] specify, to the extent practicable - (i) each population addressed by any estimate [of applicable risk effects]; (ii) the expected risk or central estimate of risk for the specific populations [affected]; (iii) each appropriate upper-bound or lower-bound estimate of risk; (iv) each significant uncertainty identified in the process of the assessment of [risk] effects and the studies that would assist in resolving the uncertainty; and (v) peer-reviewed studies known to the [agency] that support, are directly relevant to, or fail to support any estimate of [risk] effects and the methodology used to reconcile inconsistencies in the scientific data."[8] OMB recommends that each agency consider adopting or adapting these basic Congressional standards for judging the quality of scientific information about risk it uses and disseminates.

Peer Review

For economically significant and major rulemakings, OMB recommends that agencies subject RIAs and supporting technical documents to independent, external peer review by qualified specialists. Given the growing public interest in peer review at agencies, OMB recommends that (a) peer reviewers be selected primarily on the basis of necessary technical expertise, (b) peer reviewers be expected to disclose to agencies prior technical/policy positions they may have taken on the issues at hand, (c) peer reviewers be expected to disclose to agencies their sources of personal and institutional funding (private or public sector), and (d) peer reviews be conducted in an open and rigorous manner. OIRA will be giving a measure of deference to agency analysis that has been developed in conjunction with such peer review procedures.

Impact on State and Local Governments and Indian Tribal Governments

As part of OIRA's regulatory review, OIRA staff will ensure that regulatory clearance packages include, if applicable, the agency certification required by two Executive orders, E.O. 13132, "Federalism,"[9] and E.O. 13175, "Consultation and Coordination with Indian Tribal Governments."[10] As OMB Director Daniels has pledged to Congress, rulemaking proposals that were not subjected to adequate State and local consultation will be returned to agencies for reconsideration.

Impact on Energy Supply, Production, and Consumption

OIRA will also be reviewing agency "Statements of Energy Effects" and determining whether the agency should have submitted one with its regulatory clearance package. In order to ensure that agencies appropriately weigh and consider the effects of the Federal Government's regulations on the supply, distribution, and use of energy, E.O. 13211, "Actions Concerning Regulations That Significantly Affect Energy Supply, Distribution, or Use,"[11] requires agencies to prepare and submit to OIRA a "Statement of Energy

Effects" whenever they submit a significant energy action for OIRA review under E.O. 12866.

Impacts on Other Federal Agencies

An important aspect of OIRA's review of a draft rule is an evaluation of its possible impact on the programs of other Federal agencies. This evaluation often involves an interagency review by specialists from affected agencies and the coordination of agency positions, as necessary.

Impacts on Small Business

In particular, as in the past, OIRA often seeks the views of the Small Business Administration and the SBA Chief Counsel for Advocacy. We do this for two reasons. First, E.O. 12866 directs each agency to "tailor its regulations to impose the least burden on ... businesses of different sizes ..." (section 1(11)). Second, the Regulatory Flexibility Act[12] sets forth the regulatory principle that Federal agencies endeavor, consistent with applicable statutes, to fit regulatory requirements to the scale of entities subject to the regulation, and designates the SBA Chief Counsel for Advocacy as the official responsible for overseeing agency compliance with that Act.

Clearance of Significant Regulatory Actions

In the course of OIRA's review of a draft regulatory action (and accompanying RIA and risk assessment, where applicable), the OIRA Desk Officer will work closely with agency staff. When OIRA has completed its review of a regulatory action, OIRA notifies the agency by telephone that it has concluded review. After receiving notification from OIRA that it has concluded review, the agency may issue the regulatory action.

In the case of a proposed rule, we encourage each agency to provide the public with at least 60 days to comment on proposals (section 6(a)(1)). In the case of a rule subject to statutory or judicial deadlines, OMB will not unilaterally delay publication beyond the deadline. In such cases, the agency must submit the rule to OIRA in a timely fashion, so as to provide a meaningful opportunity for Executive Office review. In cases where time frames are particularly tight due to a statutory or judicial deadline, agencies should consider submitting the draft rule to OIRA for preliminary review at the same time that it is being reviewed by senior agency policymakers.

Public Disclosure of OIRA Communications with Outside Parties

On occasion, parties outside the Executive branch will meet with the OIRA Administrator or his or her designee regarding a rule under review. OIRA will invite representatives of relevant agencies to such meetings and OIRA appreciates having agencies make senior regulatory policy officials available to attend such meetings. In addition, written materials received from those outside the Executive branch are retained for public inspection in OIRA's public docket room and forwarded to the rulemaking agency. It is the responsibility of each agency to place these in the rulemaking docket. These communications are disclosed to the public as described in E.O. 12866, section 6(b)(4).

The "Return" Letter

During the course of OIRA's review of a draft regulation, the Administrator may decide to send a letter to the agency that returns the rule for reconsideration. Such a return may occur if the quality of the agency's analyses is inadequate, if the regulatory standards adopted are not justified by the analyses, if the rule is not consistent with the regulatory principles stated in the Order or with the President's policies and priorities, or if the rule is not compatible with other Executive orders or statutes. As Director Daniels stated in an earlier memorandum,"if OMB determines that more substantial work is needed, OMB will return the draft rule to the agency for improved analysis."[13] Since that memo was issued, OIRA has returned two agency draft rules, in both cases due to analytical problems.

It is important to understand that such a return does not necessarily imply that either OIRA or OMB is opposed to the draft rule. Rather, the return letter will explain why OIRA believes that the rulemaking would benefit from further consideration by the agency.

The "Prompt" Letter

The agencies prepare semi-annual regulatory agendas under E.O. 12866, section 4(b), outlining the agencies foreseeable regulatory priorities. OIRA plans to send, as occasion arises, what will be referred to as "prompt" letters. The purpose of a prompt letter is to suggest an issue that OMB believes is worthy of agency priority. Rather than being sent in response to the agency's submission of a draft rule for OIRA review, a "prompt" letter will be sent on OMB's initiative and will contain a suggestion for how the agency could improve its regulations. For example, the suggestion might be that an agency explore a promising regulatory issue for agency action, accelerate its efforts on an ongoing regulatory matter, or consider rescinding or modifying an existing rule. We will request prompt agency response to "prompt" letters, normally within 30 days.

OMB's Related Statutory and Executive Obligations

OIRA has related statutory and executive obligations that directly affect OIRA's responsibility to review agency regulatory actions under E.O. 12866.

- Under the Congressional Review Act,[14] the OIRA Administrator determines if an agency final rule is "major" (in general, having an annual economic effect of over $100,000,000), and thus subject to special provisions of that Act.[15]
- Under another law,[16] the OMB Director must submit an annual report to Congress on the costs and benefits of Federal regulation; OIRA prepares that report, based largely on the regulatory impact analyses that agencies prepare in compliance with E.O. 12866.
- Under the Unfunded Mandates Reform Act,[17] each agency must prepare a specific kind of benefit-cost analysis for any proposed and final rule "that may result in the expenditure by State, local, and tribal governments, in the aggregate, or by the private sector, of $100,000,000 or more (adjusted annually for inflation) in any one year." When preparing such an analysis, the agency must also "identify and consider a reasonable number of regulatory alternatives and from those alternatives select the least costly, most cost-effective or least burdensome alternative that achieves the objectives of the rule ...". OMB reports annually to Congress on agency compliance with these requirements.
- Under an appropriations rider,[18] OMB is to issue government-wide guidelines that provide policy and procedural guidance to Federal agencies for ensuring and maximizing the quality, objectivity, utility, and integrity of information (including statistical information) disseminated by Federal agencies. Under these OMB guidelines, agencies are to issue their own implementing guidelines that include administrative mechanisms allowing affected persons to seek and obtain correction of the information. This law affects the regulatory development process because Federal regulations may be based on the findings of scientific or other research studies disseminated by a Federal agency in the course of the rulemaking.

- Under the Paperwork Reduction Act,[19] OIRA reviews and approves (or disapproves) each collection of information by a Federal agency. This includes information collections contained in agency regulations.

We are looking forward to working cooperatively with you and your staff to meet our respective statutory obligations and to move the President's programs forward.

If there are any questions concerning OIRA's regulatory review process, agency staff should contact the appropriate OIRA Desk Officer, the OIRA Deputy Administrator, Donald R. Arbuckle (395-5897), or the OIRA Administrator, John D. Graham (395-4852).

1. 58 Fed. Reg. 51735 (October 4, 1993).
2. 5 U.S.C. 804(2).
3. 5 U.S.C. 804(2).
4. Consolidated Appropriations Act of 2001 (H.R. 5658, section 624, P.L. 106-554).
5. See, OMB Memorandum M-00-08, "Guidelines to Standardize Measures of Costs and Benefits and the Format of Accounting Statements" (March 22, 2000).
6. See, OMB Memorandum M-01-23, "Improving Regulatory Impact Analyses" (June 19, 2001).
7. 42 U.S.C. 300g-1(b)(3)(A).
8. 42 U.S.C. 300g-1(b)(3)(B).
9. 64 Fed. Reg. 43255 (August 10, 1999). See, OMB Memorandum M-00-02, "Guidance for Implementing E.O. 13132, 'Federalism.' "
10. 65 Fed. Reg. 67249 (November 9, 2000). See, OMB Memorandum M-01-07, "Guidance for Implementing E.O. 13175, 'Consultation and Coordination with Indian Tribal Governments.' "
11. E.O. 13211 of May 18, 2001 (66 Fed. Reg. 28355 (May 22, 2001)). See, OMB Memorandum M-01-27, "Guidance for Implementing E.O. 13211" (July 13, 2001).
12. 5 U.S.C. chapter 6.
13. OMB Memorandum M-01-23, "Improving Regulatory Impact Analyses" (June 19, 2001).
14. 5 U.S.C. chapter 8.
15. See, OMB Memorandum M-99-13, "Guidance for Implementing the Congressional Review Act" (March 30, 1999).

16. The Consolidated Appropriations Act of 2001, H.R. 5658, section 624, P.L. 106-554.
17. P.L. 104-4, section 202 (March 22, 1995).
18. Section 515 of the Treasury and General Government Appropriations Act for Fiscal Year 2001 (P.L. 106-554).
19. 44 U.S.C. chapter 35.

E. OIRA Memorandum: "OMB's Circular No. A-4, New Guidelines for the Conduct of Regulatory Analysis"

March 2, 2004

MEMORANDUM FOR THE PRESIDENT'S MANAGEMENT COUNCIL

FROM: John D. Graham, Ph.D., Administrator of OIRA

SUBJECT: OMB's Circular No. A-4, New Guidelines for the Conduct of Regulatory Analysis

On January 1, 2004, the Office of Management and Budget's (OMB's) new Guidelines for the Conduct of Regulatory Analysis, which was issued as OMB Circular No. A-4 on September 17, 2003, became effective for economically significant proposed rules. It becomes effective for economically significant final rules on January 1, 2005. Economically significant rules generally are rules that have an annual effect on the economy of $100 million of more. OMB developed the guidelines pursuant to the Regulatory Right-to-Know Act and in collaboration with the President's Council of Economic Advisors. After publishing proposed guidelines in the *Federal Register*, OMB revised the guidelines based on substantial public comments and peer review. OMB also convened a group of agency experts and practitioners to review and offer suggestions to improve the guidelines. The final guidelines are designed to help analysts in the regulatory agencies by encouraging good regulatory impact analysis and standardizing the way that benefits and costs of Federal regulations are measured and reported. They include several significant changes from previous OMB guidance. For example, they include (1) more emphasis on cost-effectiveness analysis, (2) formal probability analysis for rules with more than a billion dollar impact on the economy, and (3) more systematic evaluation of qualitative as well as quantified benefits and costs. OMB analysts are now reviewing for compliance with Circular No. A-4 the regulatory analyses prepared under Executive Order No. 12866. OMB may return a rule to an agency if its regulatory analysis does not conform to Circular No. A-4. We request that you remind the rulemaking offices in your Department or agency of the new Guidelines. If you have any questions about implementation of the Guidance, please feel free to contact me

[NOTE: OMB Circular A-4, "Regulatory Analysis" (Sept. 17, 2003) is available at: http://www.whitehouse.gov/omb/circulars/a004/a-4.pdf]

F. OMB's Peer Review Bulletin

December 16, 2004 [70 Fed. Reg. 2664 (Jan. 14, 2005)]

MEMORANDUM FOR HEADS OF DEPARTMENTS AND AGENCIES

FROM: Joshua B. Bolten, Director, OMB

SUBJECT: Issuance of OMB's "Final Information Quality Bulletin for Peer Review"

OMB has today issued a bulletin applicable to all departments and agencies entitled "Final Information Quality Bulletin for Peer Review." This Bulletin establishes government-wide guidance aimed at enhancing the practice of peer review of government science documents. Peer review is an important procedure used by the scientific community to ensure that the quality of published information. Peer review can increase the quality and credibility of the scientific information generated across the federal government. This Bulletin is one aspect of a larger OMB effort to improve the quality of the scientific information upon which policy decisions are based.

The bulletin has benefited from extensive public and agency comments received on two prior draft versions, which were released by OMB in September 15, 2003 and April 28, 2004. The bulletin includes guidance to federal agencies on what information is subject to peer review, the selection of appropriate peer reviewers, opportunities for public participation, and related issues. The bulletin also defines a peer review planning process that will permit the public and scientific societies to contribute to agency dialogue about which scientific reports merit especially rigorous peer review.

If your staff has questions about this guidance, please contact Margo Schwab at (202) 395-5647 or mschwab@omb.eop.govIf gov.

[Note: the Bulletin is reprinted in the Appendix to Chapter 16, Information Quality Act, *supra* at pages 792-830 and is available at http://www.whitehouse.gov/omb/memoranda/fy2005/m05-03.pdf.]

G. Final Bulletin for Agency Good Guidance Practices [and related OMB Memo on Implementation]

January 18, 2007 [Fed. Reg. 3432 (Jan. 25, 2007)]

MEMORANDUM FOR THE HEADS OF EXECUTIVE DEPARTMENTS AND AGENCIES

FROM: Rob Portman

SUBJECT: Issuance of OMB's "Final Bulletin for Agency Good Guidance Practices"

The Office of Management and Budget (OMB) today issued a bulletin applicable to all departments and agencies entitled "Final Bulletin for Agency Good Guidance Practices." This Bulletin establishes policies and procedures for the development, issuance, and use of significant guidance documents by Executive Branch departments and agencies and is intended to increase the quality and transparency of agency guidance practices and the significant guidance documents produced through them.

This Bulletin is one aspect of a larger OMB effort to ensure and maximize the quality, utility, objectivity and integrity of information disseminated by Federal agencies, pursuant to the Information Quality Act.

This Bulletin has benefited from extensive public and agency comments received on a draft released by OMB on November 23, 2005.

OFFICE OF MANAGEMENT AND BUDGET
Final Bulletin for Agency Good Guidance Practices

AGENCY: Office of Management and Budget, Executive Office of the President.

ACTION: Final Bulletin.

SUMMARY: The Office of Management and Budget (OMB) is publishing a final Bulletin entitled, "Agency Good Guidance Practices," which establishes policies and procedures for the development, issuance, and use of significant guidance documents by Executive Branch departments and agencies. This Bulletin is intended to increase the quality and transparency of agency guidance practices and the significant guidance documents produced through them.

On November 23, 2005, OMB proposed a draft Bulletin for public comment. 70 Fed. Reg. 71,866 (November 30, 2005). Upon request, OMB extended the public comment period from December 23, 2005 to January 9, 2006. 70 Fed. Reg. 76,333 (December 23, 2005). OMB received 31 comments on the proposal from diverse public and private stakeholders (see http://www.whitehouse.gov/omb/inforeg/good_guid/c-index.html) and input from Federal agencies. The final Bulletin includes refinements developed through the public comment process and interagency deliberations.

DATE: The effective date of this Bulletin is 180 days after its publication in the *Federal Register*.

FOR FURTHER INFORMATION CONTACT: Margaret Malanoski, Office of Information and Regulatory Affairs, Office of Management and Budget, 725 17th Street, N.W., New Executive Office Building, Room 10202, Washington, DC, 20503. Telephone (202) 395-3122.

SUPPLEMENTARY INFORMATION:

Introduction

As the scope and complexity of regulatory programs have grown, agencies increasingly have relied on guidance documents to inform the public and to provide direction to their staffs. As the impact of guidance documents on the public has grown, so too, has the need for good guidance practices — clear and consistent agency practices for developing, issuing, and using guidance documents.

OMB is responsible both for promoting good management practices and for overseeing and coordinating the Administration's regulatory policy. Since early in the Bush Administration, OMB has been concerned about the proper development and use of agency guidance documents. In its 2002 draft annual Report to Congress on the Costs and Benefits of Regulations,

OMB discussed this issue and solicited public comments regarding problematic guidance practices and specific examples of guidance documents in need of reform.[1] OMB has been particularly concerned that agency guidance practices should be more transparent, consistent and accountable. Such concerns also have been raised by other authorities, including Congress and the courts.[2]

---

[1] U.S. Office of Management and Budget, *Draft Report to Congress on the Costs and Benefits of Federal Regulations*, 67 FR 15,014, 15,034-35 (March 28, 2002).

[2] *See, e.g.*, Food and Drug Administration Modernization Act of 1997, 21 U.S.C. § 371(h) (establishing FDA good guidance practices as law); "Food and Drug Administration Modernization and Accountability Act of 1997," S. Rep. 105-43, at 26 (1997) (raising concerns about public knowledge of, and access to, FDA guidance documents, lack of a systematic process for adoption of guidance documents and for allowing public input, and inconsistency in the use of guidance documents); House Committee on Government Reform, "Non-Binding Legal Effect of Agency Guidance Documents," H. Rep. 106-1009 (106th Cong., 2d Sess. 2000) (criticizing "back-door" regulation); the Congressional Accountability for Regulatory Information Act, H.R. 3521, 106th Cong., § 4 (2000) (proposing to require agencies to notify the public of the non-binding effect of guidance documents); *Gen. Elec. Co. v. EPA*, 290 F.3d 377 (D.C. Cir. 2002) (striking down PCB risk assessment guidance as legislative rule requiring notice and comment); *Appalachian Power Co. v. EPA*, 208 F.3d 1015 (D.C. Cir. 2000) (striking down emissions monitoring guidance as legislative rule requiring notice and comment); *Chamber of Commerce v. Dep't of Labor*, 174 F.3d 206 (D.C. Cir. 1999) (striking down OSHA Directive as legislative rule requiring notice and comment); Administrative Conference of the United States, Rec. 92-2, 1 C.F.R. 305.92-2 (1992) (agencies should afford the public a fair opportunity to challenge the legality or wisdom of policy statements and to suggest alternative choices); American Bar Association, *Annual Report Including Proceedings of the Fifty-Eighth Annual Meeting*, August 10-11, 1993, Vol. 118, No. 2, at 57 ("the American Bar Association recommends that: Before an agency adopts a nonlegislative rule that is likely to have a significant impact on the public, the agency provide an opportunity for members of the public to comment on the proposed rule and to recommend alternative policies or interpretations, provided that it is practical to do so; when nonlegislative rules are adopted without prior public participation, immediately following adoption, the agency afford the public an opportunity for post-adoption comment and give notice of this opportunity."); 3 American Bar Association, "Recommendation on Federal Agency Web Pages" (August 2001) (agencies should maximize the availability and searchability of existing law and policy on their websites and include their governing statutes, rules and regulations, and all important policies, interpretations, and other like matters on which members of the public are likely to request).

In its 2002 Report to Congress, OMB recognized the enormous value of agency guidance documents in general. Well-designed guidance documents serve many important or even critical functions in regulatory programs.[3] Agencies may provide helpful guidance to interpret existing law through an interpretive rule or to clarify how they tentatively will treat or enforce a governing legal norm through a policy statement. Guidance documents, used properly, can channel the discretion of agency employees, increase efficiency, and enhance fairness by providing the public clear notice of the line between permissible and impermissible conduct while ensuring equal treatment of similarly situated parties.

Experience has shown, however, that guidance documents also may be poorly designed or improperly implemented. At the same time, guidance documents may not receive the benefit of careful consideration accorded under the procedures for regulatory development and review.[4] These procedures include: (1) internal agency review by a senior agency official; (2) public participation, including notice and comment under the Administrative Procedure Act (APA); (3) justification for the rule, including a statement of basis and purpose under the APA and various analyses under Executive Order 12866 (as further amended), the Regulatory Flexibility Act, and the Unfunded Mandates Reform Act; (4) interagency review through OMB; (5) Congressional oversight; and (6) judicial review. Because it is procedurally easier to issue guidance documents, there also may be an incentive for regulators to issue guidance documents in lieu of regulations. As the D.C. Circuit observed in *Appalachian Power*:

> The phenomenon we see in this case is familiar. Congress passes a broadly worded statute. The agency follows with regulations containing broad language, open-ended phrases, ambiguous standards and the like. Then as years pass, the agency issues circulars or guidance or memoranda, explaining, interpreting, defining and often expanding the commands in regulations. One guidance document may yield another and then another and so on. Several words in a regulation may spawn hundreds of pages of text as the agency offers more and more detail regarding what its regulations demand of regulated entities. Law is made, without notice and comment, without

---

[3] *See* U.S. Office of Management and Budget, *Stimulating Smarter Regulation: 2002 Report to Congress on the Costs and Benefits of Regulations and Unfunded Mandates on State, Local and Tribal Entities*, 72-74 (2002) (hereinafter "2002 Report to Congress").

[4] *Id.*, at 72.

public participation, and without publication in the *Federal Register* or the Code of Federal Regulations.[5]

Concern about whether agencies are properly observing the notice-and-comment requirements of the APA has received significant attention. The courts, Congress, and other authorities have emphasized that rules which do not merely interpret existing law or announce tentative policy positions but which establish new policy positions that the agency treats as binding must comply with the APA's notice-and-comment requirements, regardless of how they initially are labeled.[6] More general concerns also have been raised that agency guidance practices should be better informed and more transparent, fair and accountable.[7] Poorly designed or misused guidance documents can impose significant costs or limit the freedom of the public. OMB has received comments raising these concerns and providing specific examples in response to its proposed Bulletin,[8] its 2002 request for comments on problematic guidance[9] and its other requests for regulatory reform nominations in 2001[10] and 2004.[11] This Bulletin and recent amendments to Executive Order 12866 respond to these problems.[12]

---

[5] *Appalachian Power*, 208 F.3d at 1019.

[6] *See, e.g., Appalachian Power; Gen. Elec. Co.; Chamber of Commerce*; House Committee on Government Reform, "Non-Binding Legal Effect of Agency Guidance Documents"; ACUS Rec. 92-2, *supra* note 2; Robert A. Anthony, "Interpretive Rules, Policy Statements, Guidances, Manuals and the Like – Should Federal Agencies Use Them to Bind the Public?" 41 Duke L.J. 1311 (1992).

[7] *See, e.g.,* note 2, *supra*.

[8] U.S. Office of Management and Budget, "Proposed Bulletin for Good Guidance Practices," 70 FR 76,333 (Dec. 23, 2005).

[9] *See* note 1, *supra*.

[10] U.S. Office of Management and Budget, *Draft Report to Congress on the Costs and Benefits of Federal Regulations*, 66 FR 22,041 (May 2, 2001).

[11] U.S. Office of Management and Budget, *Draft Report to Congress on the Costs and Benefits of Federal Regulations*, 69 FR 7,987 (Feb. 20, 2004); *see also* U.S. Office of Management and Budget, *Validating Regulatory Analysis: 2005 Report to Congress on the Costs and Benefits of Federal Regulations and Unfunded Mandates on State, Local and Tribal Entities* 107-125 (2005).

[12] President Bush recently signed Executive Order 13422, "Further Amendment to Executive Order 12866 on Regulatory Planning and Review." Among other things, E.O. 13422 addresses the potential need for interagency review of certain significant guidance documents by clarifying OMB's authority to have advance notice of, and to review, agency guidance documents.

This Bulletin on "Agency Good Guidance Practices" sets forth general policies and procedures for developing, issuing and using guidance documents. The purpose of Good Guidance Practices (GGP) is to ensure that guidance documents of Executive Branch departments and agencies are: developed with appropriate review and public participation, accessible and transparent to the public, of high quality, and not improperly treated as legally binding requirements. Moreover, GGP clarify what does and does not constitute a guidance document to provide greater clarity to the public. All offices in an agency should follow these policies and procedures.

There is a strong foundation for establishing standards for the initiation, development, and issuance of guidance documents to raise their quality and transparency. The former Administrative Conference of the United States (ACUS), for example, developed recommendations for the development and use of agency guidance documents.[13] In 1997, the Food and Drug Administration (FDA) created a guidance document distilling its good guidance practices (GGP).[14] Congress then established certain aspects of the 1997 GGP document as the law in the Food and Drug Administration Modernization Act of 1997 (FDAMA; Public Law No. 105-115).[15] The FDAMA also directed FDA to evaluate the effectiveness of the 1997 GGP document and then to develop and issue regulations specifying FDA's policies and procedures for the development, issuance, and use of guidance documents. FDA conducted an internal evaluation soliciting FDA employees' views on the effectiveness of GGP and asking whether FDA employees had received complaints regarding the agency's development, issuance, and use of guidance documents since the development of GGP. FDA found that its GGP had been beneficial and effective in standardizing the agency's procedures for development, issuance, and use of guidance documents, and that FDA employees had generally been following GGP.[16] FDA then made some changes to its existing procedures to clarify its GGP.[17] The provisions of the FDAMA and FDA's implementing regulations, as well as the ACUS recommendations, informed the development of this government-wide Bulletin.

---

[13] See, e.g., note 2, *supra*.

[14] Notice, "The Food and Drug Administration's Development, Issuance, and Use of Guidance Documents," 62 FR 8961 (Feb. 27, 1997).

[15] 21 U.S.C. § 371(h).

[16] See FDA, "Administrative Practices and Procedures; Good Guidance Practices," 65 FR 7321, 7322-23 (proposed Feb. 14, 2000).

[17] 21 C.F.R. § 10.115; 65 FR 56,468 (Sept. 19, 2000).

Legal Authority for This Bulletin

This Bulletin is issued under statutory authority, Executive Order, and OMB's general authorities to oversee and coordinate the rulemaking process. In what is commonly known as the Information Quality Act, Congress directed OMB to issue guidelines to "provide policy and procedural guidance to Federal agencies for ensuring and maximizing the quality, utility, objectivity and integrity of information disseminated by Federal agencies."[18] Moreover, Executive Order 13422, "Further Amendment to Executive Order 12866 on Regulatory Planning and Review," recently clarified OMB's authority to oversee agency guidance documents. As further amended, Executive Order 12866 affirms that "[c]oordinated review of agency rulemaking is necessary to ensure that regulations and guidance documents are consistent with applicable law, the President's priorities, and the principles set forth in this Executive order," and the Order assigns that responsibility to OMB.[19] E.O. 12866 also establishes OMB's Office of Information and Regulatory Affairs as "the repository of expertise concerning regulatory issues, including methodologies and procedures that affect more than one agency."[20] Finally, OMB has additional authorities to oversee the agencies in the administration of their programs.

The Requirements of the Final Bulletin and Response to Public Comments

A. Overview

This Bulletin establishes: a definition of a significant guidance document; standard elements for significant guidance documents; practices for developing and using significant guidance documents; requirements for agencies to enable the public to comment on significant guidance documents or request that they be created, reconsidered, modified or rescinded; and ways

---

[18] Pub. L. No. 106-554, § 515(a) (2000). The Information Quality Act was developed as a supplement to the Paperwork Reduction Act, 44 U.S.C. § 3501 et seq., which requires OMB, among other things, to "develop and oversee implementation of policies, principles, standards, and guidelines to — (1) apply to Federal agency dissemination of public information, regardless of the form or format in which such information is disseminated; and (2) promote public access to public information and fulfill the purposes of this subchapter, including through the effective use of information technology." 44 U.S.C. § 3504(d).

[19] Executive Order 12866, as further amended, § 2(b).

[20] *Id.*

for making guidance documents available to the public. These requirements should be interpreted and implemented in a manner that, consistent with the goals of improving the quality, accountability and transparency of agency guidance documents, provides sufficient flexibility for agencies to take those actions necessary to accomplish their essential missions.

B. Definitions

Section I provides definitions for the purposes of this Bulletin. Several terms are identical to or based on those in FDA's GGP regulations, 21 C.F.R. § 10.115; the Paperwork Reduction Act, 44 U.S.C. § 3501 et seq.; Executive Order 12866, as further amended; and OMB's Government-wide Information Quality Guidelines, 67 FR 8452 (Feb. 22, 2002).

Section I(1) provides that the term "Administrator" means the Administrator of the Office of Information and Regulatory Affairs (OIRA) in the Office of Management and Budget.

Section I(2) provides that the term "agency" has the same meaning as it has under the Paperwork Reduction Act, 44 U.S.C. § 3502(1), other than those entities considered to be independent agencies, as defined in 44 U.S.C. § 3502(5).

Section I(3) defines the term "guidance document" as an agency statement of general applicability and future effect, other than a regulatory action (as defined in Executive Order 12866, as further amended), that sets forth a policy on a statutory, regulatory, or technical issue or an interpretation of a statutory or regulatory issue. This definition is used to comport with definitions used in Executive Order 12866, as further amended. Nothing in this Bulletin is intended to indicate that a guidance document can impose a legally binding requirement.

Guidance documents often come in a variety of formats and names, including interpretive memoranda, policy statements, guidances, manuals, circulars, memoranda, bulletins, advisories, and the like. Guidance documents include, but are not limited to, agency interpretations or policies that relate to: the design, production, manufacturing, control, remediation, testing, analysis or assessment of products and substances, and the processing, content, and evaluation/approval of submissions or applications, as well as compliance guides. Guidance documents do not include solely scientific research. Although a document that simply summarizes the protocol and conclusions of a specific research project (such as a clinical trial funded by the National Institutes of Health) would not qualify as a guidance document, such research may be the basis of a guidance document (such as the

HHS/USDA "Dietary Guidelines for Americans," which provides guidance to Americans on what constitutes a healthy diet).

Some commenters raised the concern that the term "guidance document" reflected too narrow a focus on written materials alone. While the final Bulletin adopts the commonly used term "guidance document," the definition is not limited only to written guidance materials and should not be so construed. OMB recognizes that agencies are experimenting with offering guidance in new and innovative formats, such as video or audio tapes, or interactive web-based software. The definition of "guidance document" encompasses all guidance materials, regardless of format. It is not the intent of this Bulletin to discourage the development of promising alternative means to offer guidance to the public and regulated entities.

A number of commenters raised concerns that the definition of "significant guidance document" in the proposed Bulletin was too broad in some respects. In particular, the proposed definition included guidance that set forth initial interpretations of statutory and regulatory requirements and changes in interpretation or policy. The definition in the proposed Bulletin was adapted from the definition of "Level 1 guidance documents" in FDA's GGP regulations.

Upon consideration of the comments, the need for clarity, and the broad application of this Bulletin to diverse agencies, the definition of "significant guidance document" has been changed. Section I(4) defines the term "significant guidance document" as a guidance document disseminated to regulated entities or the general public that may reasonably be anticipated to: (i) Lead to an annual effect on the economy of $100 million or more or adversely affect in a material way the economy, a sector of the economy, productivity, competition, jobs, the environment, public health or safety, or State, local, or tribal governments or communities; or (ii) Create a serious inconsistency or otherwise interfere with an action taken or planned by another agency; or (iii) Materially alter the budgetary impact of entitlements, grants, user fees, or loan programs or the rights and obligations of recipients thereof; or (iv) Raise novel legal or policy issues arising out of legal mandates, the President's priorities, or the principles set forth in Executive Order 12866, as further amended. Under the Bulletin, significant guidance documents include interpretive rules of general applicability and statements of general policy that have the effects described in Section I(4)(i) – (iv).

The general definition of "significant guidance document" in the final Bulletin adopts the definition in Executive Order 13422, which recently amended Executive Order 12866 to clarify OMB's role in overseeing and coordinating significant guidance documents. This definition, in turn, closely tracks the general definition of "significant regulatory action" in E.O. 12866, as further amended. One advantage of this definition is that agencies have years of experience in the regulatory context applying the parallel definition of "significant regulatory action" under E.O. 12866, as further amended. However, a few important changes were made to the definition used in E.O. 12866, as further amended, to make it better suited for guidance. For example, in recognition of the non-binding nature of guidance the words "may reasonably be anticipated to" preface all four prongs of the "significant guidance document" definition. This prefatory language makes clear that the impacts of guidance often will be more indirect and attenuated than binding legislative rules.

Section I(4) also clarifies what is not a "significant guidance document" under this Bulletin. For purposes of this Bulletin, documents that would not be considered significant guidance documents include: legal advisory opinions for internal Executive Branch use and not for release (such as Department of Justice Office of Legal Counsel opinions); briefs and other positions taken by agencies in investigations, pre-litigation, litigation, or other enforcement proceedings; speeches; editorials; media interviews; press materials; Congressional correspondence; guidances that pertain to a military or foreign affairs function of the United States (other than guidance on procurement or the import or export of non-defense articles and services); grant solicitations; warning letters; case or investigatory letters responding to complaints involving fact-specific determinations; purely internal agency policies; guidances that pertain to the use, operation or control of a government facility; and internal operational guidances directed solely to other federal agencies (including Office of Personnel Management personnel issuances, General Services Administration Federal Travel Regulation bulletins, and most of the National Archives and Records Administration's records management bulletins). The Bulletin also exempts speeches of agency officials.

Information collections, discretionary grant application packages, and compliance monitoring reports also are not significant guidance documents. Though the Bulletin does not cover guidance documents that pertain to the use, operation, or control of a Federal facility, it does cover generally applicable instructions to contractors. Section I(4) also provides that an agency head, in consultation and concurrence with the OIRA Administrator, may exempt one or more categories of significant guidance documents from the requirements of the Bulletin.

The definition of guidance document covers agency statements of "general applicability" and "future effect," and accordingly, the Bulletin does not cover documents that result from an adjudicative decision. We construe "future effects" as intended (and likely beneficial) impacts due to voluntary compliance with a guidance document. Moreover, since a significant guidance document is an agency statement of "general applicability," correspondence such as opinion letters or letters of interpretation prepared for or in response to an inquiry from an individual person or entity would not be considered a significant guidance document, unless the correspondence is reasonably anticipated to have precedential effect and a substantial impact on regulated entities or the public. Thus, this Bulletin should not inhibit the beneficial practice of agencies providing informal guidance to help specific parties. If the agency compiles and publishes informal determinations to provide guidance to, and with a substantial impact on, regulated industries, then this Bulletin would apply. Guidance documents are considered "significant" when they have a broad and substantial impact on regulated entities, the public or other Federal agencies. For example, a guidance document that had a substantial impact on another Federal agency, by interfering with its ability to carry out its mission or imposing substantial burdens, would be significant under Section I(4)(ii) and perhaps could trigger Section I(5) as well.

In general, guidance documents that concern routine matters would not be "significant." Among an agency's internal guidance documents, there are many categories that would not constitute significant guidance documents. There is a broad category of documents that may describe the agency's day-to-day business. Though such documents might be of interest to the public, they do not fall within the definition of significant guidance documents for the purposes of this Bulletin. More generally, there are internal guidance documents that bind agency employees with respect to matters that do not directly or substantially impact regulated entities. For example, an agency may issue guidance to field offices directing them to maintain electronic data files of complaints regarding regulated entities.

Section I(5) states that the term "economically significant guidance document" means a significant guidance document that "may reasonably be anticipated to lead to" an annual effect on the economy of $100 million or more or adversely affect in a material way the economy or a sector of the economy. The relevant economic impacts include those that may be imposed by Federal agencies, state, or local governments, or foreign governments that affect the U.S. economy, as well as impacts that could arise from private sector conduct. The definition of economically significant guidance document tracks only the part of the definition of significant guidance document in Section I(4)(i) related to substantial economic impacts. This clarifies that the definition of "economically significant guidance document" includes only a relatively narrow category of significant guidance documents. This definition enables agencies to determine which interpretive rules of general applicability or statements of general policy might be so consequential as to merit advance notice-and-comment and a response-to-comments document – and which do not. Accordingly, the definition of economically significant guidance document includes economic impacts that rise to $100 million in any one year or adversely affect the economy or a sector of the economy.

The definition of economically significant guidance document also departs in other ways from the language describing an economically significant regulatory action in Section 3(f)(1) of E.O. 12866, as further amended. A number of commenters on the proposed Bulletin raised questions about how a guidance document – which is not legally binding — could have an annual effect on the economy of $100 million or more or adversely affect in a material way the economy or a sector of the economy. As other commenters recognized, although guidance may not be legally binding, there are situations in which it may reasonably be anticipated that a guidance document could lead parties to alter their conduct in a manner that would have such an economically significant impact.

Guidance can have coercive effects or lead parties to alter their conduct. For example, under a statute or regulation that would allow a range of actions to be eligible for a permit or other desired agency action, a guidance document might specify fast track treatment for a particular narrow form of behavior but subject other behavior to a burdensome application process with an uncertain likelihood of success. Even if not legally binding, such guidance could affect behavior in a way that might lead to an economically significant impact. Similarly, an agency might make a pronouncement about the conditions under which it believes a particular substance or product is unsafe. While not legally binding, such a statement could reasonably be anticipated to lead to changes in behavior by the private sector or governmental authorities such that it would lead to a significant economic effect. Unless the guidance document is exempted due to an emergency or other appropriate consideration, the agency should observe the notice-and-comment procedures of § IV.

In recognition of the non-binding nature of guidance documents, the Bulletin's definition of economically significant guidance document differs in key respects from the definition of an economically significant regulatory action in § 3(f)(1) of E.O. 12866, as further amended. First, as described above, the words "may reasonably be anticipated to" are included in the definition. Second, the definition of economically significant guidance document contemplates that the guidance document could "lead to" (as opposed to "have") an economically significant effect. This language makes clear that the impacts of guidance documents often will be more indirect and dependent on third-party decisions and conduct than is the case with binding legislative rules. This language also reflects a recognition that, as various commenters noted, guidance documents often will not be amenable to formal economic analysis of the kind that is prepared for an economically significant regulatory action. Accordingly, this Bulletin does not require agencies to conduct a formal regulatory impact analysis to guide their judgments about whether a guidance document is economically significant.

The definition of "economically significant guidance document" excludes guidance documents on Federal expenditures and receipts. Therefore, guidance documents on Federal budget expenditures (e.g., entitlement programs) and taxes (the administration or collection of taxes, tax credits, or duties) are not subject to the requirements for notice and comment and a response to comments document in § IV. However, if such guidance documents are "significant," then they are subject to the other requirements of this Bulletin, including the transparency and approval provisions.

Section I(6) states that the term "disseminated" means prepared by the agency and distributed to the public or regulated entities. Dissemination does not include distribution limited to government employees; intra- or interagency use or sharing of government information; and responses to requests for agency records under the Freedom of Information Act, the Privacy Act, the Federal Advisory Committee Act or other similar law.[21]

Consistent with Executive Order 12866, as further amended, Section I(7) defines the term "regulatory action" as any substantive action by an agency (normally published in the *Federal Register*) that promulgates or is expected to lead to the promulgation of a final regulation, including notices of inquiry, advance notices of inquiry and notices of proposed rulemaking.

---

[21] *See* U.S. Office of Management and Budget's Government-wide Information Quality Guidelines, 67 FR 8452, 8454, 8460 (Feb. 22, 2002).

Section I(8) defines the term "regulation," consistent with Executive Order 12866, as further amended, as an agency statement of general applicability and future effect, which the agency intends to have the force and effect of law, that is designed to implement, interpret, or prescribe law or policy or to describe the procedure or practice requirements of an agency.

C. Basic Agency Standards

Section II describes basic agency standards for significant guidance documents.

1. Agency Approval Procedures

Section II(1)(a) directs each agency to develop or have written procedures for the internal clearance of significant guidance documents no later than the effective date of this Bulletin. Those procedures should ensure that issuance of significant guidance documents is approved by appropriate agency officials. Currently at FDA the Director in a Center or an Office of Regulatory Affairs equivalent or higher approves a significant guidance document before it is distributed to the public in draft or final form. Depending on the nature of specific agency guidance documents, these procedures may require approval or concurrence by other components within an agency. For example, if guidance is provided on compliance with an agency regulation, we would anticipate that the agency's approval procedures would ensure appropriate coordination with other agency components that have a stake in the regulation's implementation, such as the General Counsel's office and the component responsible for development and issuance of the regulation.

Section II(1)(b) states that agency employees should not depart from significant agency guidance documents without appropriate justification and supervisory concurrence. It is not the intent of this Bulletin to inhibit the flexibility needed by agency officials to depart appropriately from significant guidance documents by rigidly requiring concurrence only by very high-level officials. Section II(1)(a) also is not intended to bind an agency to exercise its discretion only in accordance with a general policy where the agency is within the range of discretion contemplated by the significant guidance document.

Agencies are to follow GGP when providing important policy direction on a broad scale. This includes when an agency communicates, informally or indirectly, new or different regulatory expectations to a broad public audience for the first time, including regulatory expectations different from guidance issued prior to this Bulletin. [22] This does not limit the agency's ability to respond to questions as to how an established policy applies to a specific situation or to answer questions about areas that may lack established policy (although such questions may signal the need to develop guidance in that area). This requirement also does not apply to positions taken by agencies in litigation, pre-litigation, or investigations, or in any way affect their authority to communicate their views in court or other enforcement proceedings. This requirement also is not intended to restrict the authority of agency General Counsels or the Department of Justice Office of Legal Counsel to provide legal interpretations of statutory and regulatory requirements.

Agencies also should ensure consistent application of GGP. Employees involved in the development, issuance, or application of significant guidance documents should be trained regarding the agency's GGP, particularly the principles of Section II(2). In addition, agency offices should monitor the development, issuance and use of significant guidance documents to ensure that employees are following GGP.

2. Standard Elements

Section II(2) establishes basic requirements for significant guidance documents. They must: (i) Include the term "guidance" or its functional equivalent; (ii) Identify the agenc(ies) or office(s) issuing the document; (iii) Identify the activity to which and the persons to whom the document applies; (iv) Include the date of issuance; (v) Note if it is a revision to a previously issued guidance document and, if so, identify the guidance that it replaces; (vi) Provide the title of the guidance and any document identification number, if one exists; and (vii) include the citation to the statutory provision or regulation (in Code of Federal Regulations format) which it applies to or interprets.

In implementing this Bulletin, particularly Section II(2)(e), agencies should be diligent to identify for the public whether there is previous guid-

---

[22] *See* FDA's Good Guidance Practices, 21 C.F.R. § 10.115(e): *"Can FDA use means other than a guidance document to communicate new agency policy or a new regulatory approach to a broad public audience?* The agency must not use documents or other means of communication that are excluded from the definition of guidance document to informally communicate new or different regulatory expectations to a broad public audience for the first time. These GGPs must be followed whenever regulatory expectations that are not readily apparent from the statute or regulations are first communicated to a broad public audience."

ance on an issue, and, if so, to clarify whether that guidance document is repealed by the new significant guidance document completely, and if not, to specify what provisions in the previous guidance document remain in effect. Superseded guidance documents that remain available for historical purposes should be stamped or otherwise prominently identified as superseded. Draft significant guidance documents that are being made available for pre-adoption notice and comment should include a prominent "draft" notation. As existing significant guidance documents are revised, they should be updated to comply with this Bulletin.

Finally, § II(2)(h) clarifies that, given their legally nonbinding nature, significant guidance documents should not include mandatory language such as "shall," "must," "required" or "requirement," unless the agency is using these words to describe a statutory or regulatory requirement, or the language is addressed to agency staff and will not foreclose consideration by the agency of positions advanced by affected private parties.[23] For example, a guidance document may explain how the agency believes a statute or regulation applies to certain regulated activities. Before a significant guidance document is issued or revised, it should be reviewed to ensure that improper mandatory language has not been used. As some commenters noted, while a guidance document cannot legally bind, agencies can appropriately bind their employees to abide by agency policy as a matter of their supervisory powers over such employees without undertaking pre-adoption notice and comment rulemaking. As a practical matter, agencies also may describe laws of nature, scientific principles, and technical requirements in mandatory terms so long as it is clear that the guidance document itself does not impose legally enforceable rights or obligations.

A significant guidance document should aim to communicate effectively to the public about the legal effect of the guidance and the consequences for the public of adopting an alternative approach. For example, a significant guidance document could be captioned with the following disclaimer under appropriate circumstances:

"This [draft] guidance, [when finalized, will] represent[s] the [Agency's] current thinking on this topic. It does not create or

---

[23] As the courts have held, *see supra* note 2, agencies need to follow statutory rulemaking requirements, such as those of the APA, to issue documents with legally binding effect, i.e., legislative rules. One benefit of GGP for an agency is that the agency's review process will help to identify any draft guidance documents that instead should be promulgated through the rulemaking process.

confer any rights for or on any person or operate to bind the public. You can use an alternative approach if the approach satisfies the requirements of the applicable statutes and regulations. If you want to discuss an alternative approach (you are not required to do so), you may contact the [Agency] staff responsible for implementing this guidance. If you cannot identify the appropriate [Agency] staff, call the appropriate number listed on the title page of this guidance."

When an agency determines it would be appropriate, the agency should use this or a similar disclaimer. Agency staff should similarly describe the legal effect of significant guidance documents when speaking to the public about them.

D. Public Access and Feedback

Section III describes public access procedures related to the development and issuance of significant guidance documents.

1. Internet Access

Section III directs agencies to ensure that information about the existence of significant guidance documents and the significant guidance documents themselves are made available to the public in electronic form. Section III(1) enables the public to obtain from an agency's website a list of all of an agency's significant guidance documents. Under § III(1)(a), agencies will maintain a current electronic list of all significant guidance documents on their websites in a manner consistent with OMB policies for agency public websites and information dissemination.[24] To assist the public in locating such electronic lists, they should be maintained on an agency's website – or as a link on an agency's website to the electronic list posted on a component or subagency's website — in a quickly and easily identifiable manner (e.g., as part of or in close visual proximity to the agency's list of regulations and proposed regulations). New documents will be added to

---

[24] U.S. Office of Management and Budget, Memorandum M-05-04, "Policies for Federal Agency Public Websites" (Dec. 17, 2004), available at: *http://www.whitehouse.gov/omb/memoranda/fy2005/m05-04.pdf*; U.S. Office of Management and Budget, Memorandum M-06-02, "Improving Public Access to and Dissemination of Government Information and Using the Federal Enterprise Architecture Data Reference Model" (Dec. 16, 2005), available at: *http://www.whitehouse.gov/omb/memoranda/fy2006/m06-02.pdf*

this list within 30 days from the date of issuance. The agency list of significant guidance documents will include: the name of the significant guidance document, any docket number, and issuance and revision dates. As agencies develop or revise significant guidance documents, they should organize and catalogue their significant guidance documents to ensure users can easily browse, search for, and retrieve significant guidance documents on their websites.

The agency shall provide a link from the list to each significant guidance document (including any appendices or attachments) that currently is in effect. Many recently issued guidance documents have been made available on the Internet, but there are some documents that are not now available in this way. Agencies should begin posting those significant guidance documents on their websites with the goal of making all of their significant guidance documents currently in effect publicly available on their websites by the effective date of this Bulletin.[25] Other requirements of this Bulletin, such as § II(2) (Standard Elements), apply only to significant guidance documents issued or amended after the effective date of the Bulletin. For such significant guidance documents (including economically significant guidance documents), agencies should provide, to the extent appropriate and feasible, a website link from the significant guidance document to the public comments filed on it. This would enable interested stakeholders and the general public to understand the various viewpoints on the significant guidance documents.

Under § III(1)(b), the significant guidance list will identify those significant guidance documents that were issued, revised or withdrawn within the past year. Agencies are encouraged, to the extent appropriate and feasible, to offer a listserve or similar mechanism for members of the public who would like to be notified by email each time an agency issues its annual update of significant guidance documents. To further assist users in better understanding agency guidance and its relationship to current or proposed Federal regulations, agencies also should link their significant guidance document lists to Regulations.gov.[26]

---

[25] In this regard, we note that under the Electronic Freedom of Information Act Amendments of 1996, agencies have been posting on their websites statements of general policy and interpretations of general applicability. *See* 5 U.S.C. § 552(a)(2).

[26] Regulations.gov is available at *http://www.Regulations.gov/fdmspublic/component/main*.

2. Public Feedback

Section III(2) requires each agency to have adequate procedures for public comments on significant guidance documents and to address complaints regarding the development and use of significant guidance documents. Not later than 180 days from the publication of this Bulletin, each agency shall establish and clearly advertise on its website a means for the public to submit electronically comments on significant guidance documents, and to request electronically that significant guidance documents be issued, reconsidered, modified or rescinded. The public may state their view that specific guidance documents are "significant" or "economically significant" and therefore are subject to the applicable requirements of this Bulletin. At any time, the public also may request that an agency modify or rescind an existing significant guidance document. Such requests should specify why and how the significant guidance document should be rescinded or revised.

Public comments submitted under these procedures on significant guidance documents are for the benefit of the agency, and this Bulletin does not require a formal response to comments (of course, agencies must comply with any applicable statutory requirements to respond, and this Bulletin does not alter those requirements). In some cases, the agency, in consultation with the Administrator of OMB's Office of Information and Regulatory Affairs, may in its discretion decide to address public comments by updating or altering the significant guidance document.

Although this Bulletin does not require agencies to provide notice and an opportunity for public comment on all significant guidance documents before they are adopted, it is often beneficial for an agency to do so when they determine that it is practical. Pre-adoption notice-and-comment can be most helpful for significant guidance documents that are particularly complex, novel, consequential, or controversial. Agencies also are encouraged to consider observing notice-and-comment procedures for interpretive significant guidance documents that effectively would extend the scope of the jurisdiction the agency will exercise, alter the obligations or liabilities of private parties, or modify the terms under which the agency will grant entitlements. As it does for legislative rules, providing pre-adoption opportunity for comment on significant guidance documents can increase the quality of the guidance and provide for greater public confidence in and acceptance of the ultimate agency judgments. For these reasons, agencies sometimes follow the notice-and-comment procedures of the APA even when doing so is not legally required.[27] Of course, where an agency provides for notice and comment before adoption, it need not do so again upon issuance of the significant guidance document.[28]

Many commenters expressed the desire for a better way to resolve concerns about agency guidance documents and adherence to good guidance practices. To help resolve public concerns over problematic guidance documents, § III(2)(b) requires each agency to designate an office (or offices) to receive and address complaints by the public that the agency is not following the procedures in this Bulletin or is improperly treating a guidance document as a binding requirement. The public also could turn to this office to request that the agency classify a guidance as "significant" or "economically significant" for purposes of this Bulletin. The agency shall provide the name and contact information for the office(s) on its website.

E. Notice and Comment on Economically Significant Guidance Documents

Under § IV, after the agency prepares a draft of an economically significant guidance document, the agency must publish a notice in the *Federal Register* announcing that the draft guidance document is available for comment. In a manner consistent with OMB policies for agency public websites and information dissemination, the agency must post the draft on its website, make it publicly available in hard copy, and ensure that persons with disabilities can reasonably access and comment on the guidance development process.[29] If the guidance document is not in a format that permits such electronic posting with reasonable efforts, the agency should notify the public how they can review the guidance document. When inviting public comments on the draft guidance document, the agency will propose

---

[27] For example, in developing its guidelines for self-evaluation of compensation practices regarding systemic compensation discrimination, the Department of Labor provided for pre-adoption notice and opportunity for comment. *See* Office of Federal Contract Compliance Programs, "Guidelines for Self-Evaluation of Compensation Practices for Compliance with Nondiscrimination Requirements of Executive Order 11246 with Respect to Systemic Compensation Discrimination," 69 FR 67,252 (Nov. 16, 2004).

[28] *See, e.g.*, Office of Federal Procurement Policy Act, 41 U.S.C. § 418(b) (providing for pre-adoption notice and comment for procurement policies with a significant effect or cost).

[29] Federal agency public websites must be designed to make information and services fully available to individuals with disabilities. For additional information, see: *http://www.access-board.gov/index.htm*; *see also* Rehabilitation Act, 29 U.S.C. § 701, 794, 794d.

a period of time for the receipt of comments and make the comments available to the public for review. The agency also may hold public meetings or workshops on a draft guidance document, or present it for review to an advisory committee or, as required or appropriate, to a peer review committee.[30] In some cases, the agency may, in its discretion, seek early public input even before it prepares the draft of an economically significant guidance document. For example, the agency could convene or participate in meetings or workshops.

After reviewing comments on a draft, the agency should incorporate suggested changes, when appropriate, into the final version of the economically significant guidance document. The agency then should publish a notice in the *Federal Register* announcing that the significant guidance document is available. The agency must post the significant guidance document on the Internet and make it available in hard copy. The agency also must prepare a robust response-to-comments document and make it publicly available. Though these procedures are similar to APA notice-and-comment requirements, this Bulletin in no way alters (nor is it intended to interpret) the APA requirements for legislative rules under 5 U.S.C. § 553.

Prior to or upon announcing the availability of the draft guidance document, the agency should establish a public docket. Public comments submitted on an economically significant guidance document should be sent to the agency's docket. The comments submitted should identify the docket number on the guidance document (if such a docket number exists), as well as the title of the document. Comments should be available to the public at the docket and, when feasible, on the Internet. Agencies should provide a link on their website from the guidance document to the public comments as well as the response to comments document.

After providing an opportunity for comment, an agency may decide, in its discretion, that it is appropriate to issue another draft of the significant guidance document. The agency may again solicit comment by publishing a notice in the *Federal Register*, posting a draft on the Internet and making the draft available in hard copy. The agency then would proceed to issue a final version of the guidance document in the manner described above. Copies of the *Federal Register* notices of availability should be available on the agency's website. In addition, the response-to-comments document should address the additional comments received on the revised draft.

---

[30] *See* U.S. Office of Management and Budget, "Final Information Quality Bulletin for Peer Review," 70 FR 2664 (Jan. 14, 2005).

An agency head, in consultation and concurrence with the OIRA Administrator, may identify a particular significant guidance document or class of guidance documents for which the procedures of this Section are not feasible and appropriate. Under § IV, the agency is not required to seek public comment before it implements an economically significant guidance document if prior public participation is not feasible or appropriate. It may not be feasible or appropriate for an agency to seek public comment before issuing an economically significant guidance document if there is a public health, safety, environmental or other emergency requiring immediate issuance of the guidance document, or there is a statutory requirement or court order that requires immediate issuance. Another type of situation is presented by guidance documents that, while important, are issued in a routine and frequent manner. For example, one commenter raised concerns that the National Weather Service not only frequently reports on weather and air conditions but also gives consumers guidance, such as heat advisories, on the best course of action to take in severe weather conditions. Even if such notices or advisories had an economically significant impact, subjecting them to the notice-and-comment procedures of Section IV would not be feasible or appropriate. An agency may discuss with OMB other exceptions that are consistent with § IV(2).

Though economically significant guidance documents that fall under the exemption in § IV(2) are not required to undergo the full notice-and-comment procedures, the agency should: (a) publish a notice in the *Federal Register* announcing that the guidance document is available; (b) post the guidance document on the Internet and make it available in hard copy (or notify the public how they can review the guidance document if it is not in a format that permits such electronic posting with reasonable efforts); and (c) seek public comment when it issues or publishes the guidance document. If the agency receives comments on an excepted guidance document, the agency should review those comments and revise the guidance document when appropriate. However, the agency is not required to provide post-promulgation notice-and-comment if such procedures are not feasible or appropriate.

F. Emergencies

In emergency situations or when an agency is obligated by law to act more quickly than normal review procedures allow, the agency shall notify OIRA as soon as possible and, to the extent practicable, comply with this Bulletin. For those significant guidance documents that are governed by a statutory or court-imposed deadlines, the agency shall, to the extent practicable, schedule its proceedings so as to permit sufficient time to comply with this Bulletin.

G. *Judicial Review*

This Bulletin is intended to improve the internal management of the Executive Branch and is not intended to, and does not, create any right or benefit, substantive or procedural, enforceable at law or in equity, against the United States, its agencies or other entities, its officers or employees, or any other person.[31]

H. *Effective Date*

The requirements of this Bulletin shall take effect 180 days after publication in the *Federal Register* except that agencies will have 210 days to comply with requirements for significant guidance documents promulgated on or before the date of publication of this Bulletin.

Bulletin for Agency Good Guidance Practices

I. *Definitions.*

For purposes of this Bulletin—

1. The term "Administrator" means the Administrator of the Office of Information and Regulatory Affairs in the Office of Management and Budget (OIRA).

2. The term "agency" has the same meaning it has under the Paperwork Reduction Act, 44 U.S.C. § 3502(1), other than those considered to be independent regulatory agencies, as defined in 44 U.S.C. § 3502(5).

3. The term "guidance document" means an agency statement of general applicability and future effect, other than a regulatory action (as defined in Executive Order 12866, as further amended, § 3(g)), that sets forth a policy on a statutory, regulatory or technical issue or an interpretation of a statutory or regulatory issue.

4. The term "significant guidance document" —

a. means (as defined in Executive Order 12866, as further amended, § 3(h)) a guidance document disseminated to regulated entities or the general public that may reasonably be anticipated to:

---

[31] The provisions of this Bulletin, and an agency's compliance or noncompliance with the Bulletin's requirements, are not intended to, and should not, alter the deference that agency interpretations of laws and regulations should appropriately be given.

(i) Lead to an annual effect on the economy of $100 million or more or adversely affect in a material way the economy, a sector of the economy, productivity, competition, jobs, the environment, public health or safety, or State, local, or tribal governments or communities;

(ii) Create a serious inconsistency or otherwise interfere with an action taken or planned by another agency;

(iii) Materially alter the budgetary impact of entitlements, grants, user fees, or loan programs or the rights and obligations of recipients thereof; or

(iv) Raise novel legal or policy issues arising out of legal mandates, the President's priorities, or the principles set forth in Executive Order 12866, as further amended.

b. does not include legal advisory opinions for internal Executive Branch use and not for release (such as Department of Justice Office of Legal Counsel opinions); briefs and other positions taken by agencies in investigations, pre-litigation, litigation, or other enforcement proceedings (nor does this Bulletin in any other way affect an agency's authority to communicate its views in court or in other enforcement proceedings); speeches; editorials; media interviews; press materials; Congressional correspondence; guidance documents that pertain to a military or foreign affairs function of the United States (other than guidance on procurement or the import or export of non-defense articles and services); grant solicitations; warning letters; case or investigatory letters responding to complaints involving fact-specific determinations; purely internal agency policies; guidance documents that pertain to the use, operation or control of a government facility; internal guidance documents directed solely to other Federal agencies; and any other category of significant guidance documents exempted by an agency head in consultation with the OIRA Administrator.

5. The term "economically significant guidance document" means a significant guidance document that may reasonably be anticipated to lead to an annual effect on the economy of $100 million or more or adversely affect in a material way the economy or a sector of the economy, except that economically significant guidance documents do not include guidance documents on Federal expenditures and receipts.

6. The term "disseminated" means prepared by the agency and distributed to the public or regulated entities. Dissemination does not include distribution limited to government employees; intra- or interagency use or sharing of government information; and responses to requests for agency records under the Freedom of Information Act, the Privacy Act, the Federal Advisory Committee Act or other similar laws.

7. The term "regulatory action" means any substantive action by an agency (normally published in the *Federal Register*) that promulgates or is expected to lead to the promulgation of a final regulation, including notices of inquiry, advance notices of inquiry and notices of proposed rulemaking (see Executive Order 12866, as further amended, § 3).

8. The term "regulation" means an agency statement of general applicability and future effect, which the agency intends to have the force and effect of law, that is designed to implement, interpret, or prescribe law or policy or to describe the procedure or practice requirements of an agency (see Executive Order 12866, as further amended, § 3).

II. *Basic Agency Standards for Significant Guidance Documents.*
   1. *Approval Procedures*:
   a. Each agency shall develop or have written procedures for the approval of significant guidance documents. Those procedures shall ensure that the issuance of significant guidance documents is approved by appropriate senior agency officials.
   b. Agency employees should not depart from significant guidance documents without appropriate justification and supervisory concurrence.
   2. *Standard Elements*: Each significant guidance document shall:
   a. Include the term "guidance" or its functional equivalent;
   b. Identify the agenc(ies) or office(s) issuing the document;
   c. Identify the activity to which and the persons to whom the significant guidance document applies;
   d. Include the date of issuance;
   e. Note if it is a revision to a previously issued guidance document and, if so, identify the document that it replaces;
   f. Provide the title of the document, and any document identification number, if one exists;
   g. Include the citation to the statutory provision or regulation (in Code of Federal Regulations format) which it applies to or interprets; and
   h. Not include mandatory language such as "shall," "must," "required" or "requirement," unless the agency is using these words to describe a statutory or regulatory requirement, or the language is addressed to agency staff and will not foreclose agency consideration of positions advanced by affected private parties.

III. *Public Access and Feedback for Significant Guidance Documents.*
   1. *Internet Access*:
   a. Each agency shall maintain on its website — or as a link on an agency's website to the electronic list posted on a component or subagency's website — a current list of its significant guidance documents in effect. The list shall include the name of each significant guidance document, any document identification number, and issuance and revision dates. The agency shall provide a link from the current list to each significant guidance document that is in effect. New significant guidance documents and their website links shall be added promptly to this list, no later than 30 days from the date of issuance.
   b. The list shall identify significant guidance documents that have been added, revised or withdrawn in the past year.
   2. *Public Feedback*:
   a. Each agency shall establish and clearly advertise on its website a means for the public to submit comments electronically on significant guidance documents, and to submit a request electronically for issuance, reconsideration, modification, or rescission of significant guidance documents. Public comments under these procedures are for the benefit of the agency, and no formal response to comments by the agency is required by this Bulletin.
   b. Each agency shall designate an office (or offices) to receive and address complaints by the public that the agency is not following the procedures in this Bulletin or is improperly treating a significant guidance document as a binding requirement. The agency shall provide, on its website, the name and contact information for the office(s).

IV. *Notice and Public Comment for Economically Significant Guidance Documents.*
   1. *In General*: Except as provided in Section IV(2), when an agency prepares a draft of an economically significant guidance document, the agency shall:
   a. Publish a notice in the *Federal Register* announcing that the draft document is available;
   b. Post the draft document on the Internet and make it publicly available in hard copy (or notify the public how they can review the guidance document if it is not in a format that permits such electronic posting with reasonable efforts);
   c. Invite public comment on the draft document; and

d. Prepare and post on the agency's website a response-to-comments document.

2. *Exemptions*: An agency head, in consultation with the OIRA Administrator, may identify a particular economically significant guidance document or category of such documents for which the procedures of this Section are not feasible or appropriate.

V. *Emergencies*.

In emergency situations or when an agency is obligated by law to act more quickly than normal review procedures allow, the agency shall notify OIRA as soon as possible and, to the extent practicable, comply with this Bulletin. For those significant guidance documents that are governed by a statutory or court-imposed deadline, the agency shall, to the extent practicable, schedule its proceedings so as to permit sufficient time to comply with this Bulletin.

VI. *Judicial Review*.

This Bulletin is intended to improve the internal management of the Executive Branch and is not intended to, and does not, create any right or benefit, substantive or procedural, enforceable at law or in equity, against the United States, its agencies or other entities, its officers or employees, or any other person.

VII. *Effective Date*.

The requirements of this Bulletin shall take effect 180 days after its publication in the *Federal Register* except that agencies will have 210 days to comply with requirements for significant guidance documents promulgated on or before the date of publication of this Bulletin.

Dated: January 16, 2007

Stephen D. Aitken,

Acting administrator, Office of Information and Regulatory Affairs [FR Doc. E7-1055 Filed 1-24-07; 8:45 am]

BILLING CODE 3110-01-P

EXECUTIVE OFFICE OF THE PRESIDENT
OFFICE OF MANAGEMENT AND BUDGET
WASHINGTON, D.C. 20503

THE DIRECTOR

April 25, 2007

M-07-13

MEMORANDUM FOR HEADS OF EXECUTIVE DEPARTMENTS AND AGENCIES, AND INDEPENDENT REGULATORY AGENCIES

FROM: Rob Portman

SUBJECT: Implementation of Executive Order 13422 (amending Executive Order 12866) and the OMB Bulletin on Good Guidance Practices

On January 18, 2007, the President issued Executive Order (EO) 13422, "Further Amendment to Executive Order 12866 on Regulatory Planning and Review." On the same day, and in connection with EO 13422, I issued an Office of Management and Budget (OMB) Bulletin on Agency Good Guidance Practices (Bulletin).

The primary focus of EO 13422 and the Bulletin is on improving the way the Federal government does business with respect to guidance documents -- by increasing their quality, transparency, accountability, and coordination. Guidance documents, used properly, can have important benefits. These include, for example, advising and assisting individuals, small businesses and other regulated entities in their compliance with agency regulations. When an agency issues a guidance document that has a significant impact on society, the guidance document should be subject to an appropriate level of review – by the public, within an agency, and by other Federal agencies.

Within OMB, the Office of Information and Regulatory Affairs (OIRA) has primary responsibility for implementing EO 12866, as amended by EO 13422, and the Bulletin. To assist your agencies in implementing EO 13422 and Bulletin, OIRA has prepared the attached compliance assistance memorandum which describes what agencies should do to comply with the EO and the Bulletin. Please circulate this memorandum to the appropriate officials within your agency for immediate attention.

OMB looks forward to working with your agencies in the implementation of EO 12866, as amended, and the Bulletin.

Attachment

EXECUTIVE OFFICE OF THE PRESIDENT
OFFICE OF MANAGEMENT AND BUDGET
WASHINGTON, D.C. 20503

ADMINISTRATOR
OFFICE OF
INFORMATION AND
REGULATORY AFFAIRS

April 25, 2007

MEMORANDUM FOR REGULATORY POLICY OFFICERS

FROM: Susan E. Dudley SED
          Administrator
          Office of Information and Regulatory Affairs

SUBJECT: Implementation of the OMB Bulletin on Good Guidance Practices and Executive Order 13422 (amending Executive Order 12866)

On January 18, 2007, the President issued Executive Order (EO) 13422, "Amendment to Executive Order 12866 for Regulatory Planning and Review." On that same day, the OMB Director issued a related document, the OMB Bulletin on Agency Good Guidance Practices (the Bulletin). The primary focus of the Executive Order and the Bulletin is on improving the way the Federal government does business with respect to guidance documents – by increasing their quality, transparency, accountability, and coordination.

The Bulletin, which OMB issued after seeking public comment on a proposed version, establishes policies and procedures for agencies to apply in their development and issuance of "significant" and "economically significant" guidance documents. The Bulletin will ensure that guidance documents are of high quality, developed with appropriate agency review and public participation, and readily accessible by the public.

The principal change made by EO 13422 is that it amends EO 12866 to establish a process that will provide an opportunity for interagency coordination and review of significant guidance documents prior to their issuance. EO 13422 also amends EO 12866 in several other ways. To ensure appropriate accountability, the EO modifies the procedures for an agency's adoption of its annual Regulatory Plan and requires that an agency's Regulatory Policy Officer be a Presidential appointee. The EO also updates the Principles of Regulation in EO 12866 to reflect the guidance-coordination provisions that are added by EO 13422 as well as pre-existing OMB guidance. Finally, the EO invites agencies to consider whether they would want to rely on formal rulemaking procedures for resolving complex determinations.

Within OMB, the Office of Information and Regulatory Affairs (OIRA) has primary responsibility for implementing EO 12866, as amended, and the Bulletin. To assist agencies in their implementation of the EO and Bulletin, OIRA has prepared and is now issuing this memorandum that provides answers to a number of questions. Agencies should also consult the preamble to the Bulletin for additional implementation assistance.

If your agencies have any questions about the attached implementation assistance, or about the EO or the Bulletin, they may contact Margaret Malanoski at (202) 395-3122 or Margaret_A._Malanoski@omb.eop.gov.

OIRA looks forward to working with your agencies in implementing the EO and Bulletin.

Attachment

A. General Information 1

    1. When do Executive Order 13422 and the Agency Good Guidance Practices Bulletin take effect? 1
    2. What agencies are covered by the Executive Order and the Bulletin? 1

B. Guidance Questions -- Applicable to Both the Bulletin and the Executive Order 1

    3. What types of guidance documents are covered by the Bulletin and by the Executive Order? 1
    4. What types of guidance documents are not covered by the Bulletin and by the Executive Order? 2
    5. What is a "significant" guidance document? 2
    6. What is an "economically significant" guidance document and how is it related to a "significant" guidance document? 2
    7. Does either the Executive Order or the Bulletin require agencies to prepare a benefit-cost analysis for guidance documents as agencies are required to do for regulations? 3

C. Guidance Questions -- Applicable to Requirements specific to the Bulletin 3

    8. Under the Bulletin, what are the requirements for the content of "significant" guidance documents? 3
    9. Under the Bulletin, what information are agencies required to post on their Web sites? 4
    10. Can a subcomponent of an agency establish a separate Web site listing guidance documents and/or designate more than one office to receive and address complaints from the public on the guidance documents? 4
    11. What requirements does the Bulletin establish -- for public comments and for Agency responses to those comments -- for "economically significant" guidance documents? 5
    12. What requirements does the Bulletin establish -- for public comments and for Agency responses to those comments -- for "significant" guidance documents? .. 5
    13. Should agencies use Regulations.gov to process public comments for guidance documents? 6
    14. Under the Bulletin, what should an agency do if it believes that it would not be feasible or appropriate for the agency to provide the public with advance notice of, and an opportunity to comment on, an economically significant guidance document before the agency issues the guidance in final form? 6
    15. Under the Bulletin, what should an agency do if it needs to issue a significant guidance document to address an emergency situation? 6
    16. What are the timelines for meeting the requirements of the Bulletin? 6

D. Guidance Questions – Applicable to Requirements specific to the Executive Order... 7

17. Under the Executive Order, what is an agency required to do when it wants to issue a "significant" guidance document? 7
18. Under the Executive Order, how should an agency provide advance notification to OIRA of a significant guidance document? 8
19. What is the next step when the OIRA Administrator determines that additional consultation under the Executive Order is warranted? 8
20. How will the OIRA Administrator determine which significant guidance documents are exempt from review under the Executive Order? 9
21. What is the time period for consultation with OIRA on significant guidance documents under the Executive Order? 9
22. What should an agency do, under the Executive Order, if the agency needs to issue a significant guidance document to address an emergency situation? 9
23. How were the Regulatory Principles of Executive Order 12866 amended to apply to guidance documents? 9

E. Non-Guidance provisions in Executive Order 13422 10

24. When does an agency head need to designate its Regulatory Policy Officer? 10
25. What changes does the Executive Order make to the appointment of the Regulatory Policy Officer? 10
26. Can the agency head designate as the Regulatory Policy Officer an agency employee who serves in a position for which the agency head (not the President) is the appointing official? 10
27. If there is a vacancy in the Presidentially-appointed position that the agency head has designated as the Regulatory Policy Officer, may the person who is serving in an "acting" capacity in that position be the Regulatory Policy Officer? 11
28. Are independent regulatory agencies required to designate a Presidential appointee as a Regulatory Policy Officer? 11
29. Will the Regulatory Policy Officers continue to report to their agency heads, as they did under Executive Order 12866 prior to its recent amendment? 11
30. Does the agency need to establish a Regulatory Policy Office, in addition to the agency head designating a Regulatory Policy Officer? 11
31. What changes does the Executive Order make to the responsibilities of the Regulatory Policy Officer? 11
32. When does a rulemaking "commence" for the purpose of meeting the new requirement for the Regulatory Policy Officer's (or the agency head's) authorization of the agency's "commencement of a rulemaking"? 12
33. What are the new requirements for the Regulatory Plan? 12
34. Do the revisions to the Principles of Regulation, specifically those in Section 1(b)(1) related to "market failure," require agencies to provide more or different information to OIRA when submitting a regulation for review? 12
35. Does the Executive Order require an agency to consider the use of formal rulemaking? 13

ii

A. General Information

1. When do Executive Order 13422 and the Agency Good Guidance Practices Bulletin take effect?

Executive Order 13422 (Executive Order) became effective when it was signed by the President, on January 18, 2007.

The requirements of the Agency Good Guidance Practices Bulletin (Bulletin) will take effect on July 24, 2007. However, for significant guidance documents promulgated prior to January 25, 2007, agencies have until August 23, 2007 to comply with the requirements of Section III of the Bulletin. For documents promulgated after January 25, 2007, agencies should comply with the requirements of Section III of the Bulletin by July 24, 2007 or within thirty (30) days of issuance of the guidance document, whichever is later.

Agencies are encouraged to comply with the provisions of the Bulletin sooner if possible.

2. What agencies are covered by the Executive Order and the Bulletin?

The Executive Order and the Bulletin as a whole apply to all Federal agencies, except for the independent regulatory agencies as defined in 44 U.S.C. § 3502. (Sec. 3(b) of the Executive Order). The scope of agencies covered by the Bulletin and the Executive Order does not differ from the scope of agencies covered by Executive Order 12866.

The independent regulatory agencies are included in provisions concerning the "Unified Regulatory Agenda" (Sec. 4(b) of the Executive Order) and "The Regulatory Plan" (Sec. 4(c) of the Executive Order) and they must comply with the new requirements for the "Unified Regulatory Agenda" (Sec. 4(b) of the Executive Order) contained in the Executive Order. As OMB requested in 1993 following the issuance of Executive Order 12866, the independent agencies are requested on a voluntary basis to adhere to the provisions of the Executive Order that may be pertinent to their activities.

B. Guidance Questions -- Applicable to <u>Both the Bulletin and the Executive Order</u>

3. What types of guidance documents are covered by the Bulletin and by the Executive Order?

Both the Executive Order and the Bulletin define "guidance documents" as "an agency statement of general applicability and future effect, other than a regulatory action, that sets forth a policy on a statutory, regulatory, or technical issue or an interpretation of a statutory or regulatory issue."

The definition is not limited to written guidance materials; it encompasses all guidance materials regardless of format, including guidance offered through video, audio tapes, interactive web-based software, or other innovative formats. Guidance documents may be currently referred to by a variety of names, such as interpretive memoranda, policy statements, guidances, manuals, circulars, memoranda, bulletins, or advisories.

4. **What types of guidance documents are not covered by the Bulletin and by the Executive Order?**

Guidance documents that are not significant are not covered by the Bulletin or the Executive Order. Further, Section I(4) of the Bulletin clarifies what is not a significant guidance document.

5. **What is a "significant" guidance document?**

Both the Bulletin (Sec. I(4)) and the Executive Order (Sec. 3(h)) define a "significant" guidance document as a guidance document disseminated to regulated entities or the general public that may reasonably be anticipated to:

   (1) lead to an annual effect of $100 million or more or adversely affect in a material way the economy, a sector of the economy, productivity, competition, jobs, the environment, public health or safety, or State, local, or tribal governments or communities;
   (2) create a serious inconsistency or otherwise interfere with an action taken or planned by another agency;
   (3) materially alter the budgetary impacts of entitlements, grants, user fees or loan programs or the rights or obligations of recipients thereof; or
   (4) raise novel legal or policy issues arising out of legal mandates, the President's priorities, or the principles set forth in this Executive order.

OIRA will work with agencies in applying the definition of "significant guidance" to the agency's guidance documents.

6. **What is an "economically significant" guidance document and how is it related to a "significant" guidance document?**

The Bulletin defines an "economically significant guidance document" as a "significant guidance document that may reasonably be anticipated to lead to an annual effect on the economy of $100 million or more or adversely affect in a material way the economy or a sector of the economy, except that economically significant documents do not include guidance documents on Federal expenditures and receipts." Therefore, economically significant guidance documents are a subset of significant guidance documents.

The Executive Order does not define "economically significant" guidance documents nor does it impose a separate process for "economically significant" guidance documents. Therefore, guidance documents that meet the definition of "economically significant" in the Bulletin will be a "significant" guidance document for the purposes of the Executive Order.

If agency staff are uncertain about whether a guidance document should be classified as economically significant, they may contact OIRA for assistance.

7. **Does either the Executive Order or the Bulletin require agencies to prepare a benefit-cost analysis for guidance documents as agencies are required to do for regulations?**

No. The amendments to Executive Order 12866 did not alter the Section 6 requirements for analysis of regulations – specifically Sec. 6 (a)(3)(B)-(C) – to include guidance documents. The requirements for significant guidance documents (Sec. 9 of the Executive Order) do not impose similar analytical requirements.

In determining whether a guidance document is economically significant, agencies are not expected to complete a benefit-cost analysis or to do more than they currently do when they make preliminary recommendations to OIRA about the designation of regulations under Executive Order 12866. Rather, we expect agencies to use common-sense principles and readily available facts and assumptions in making their evaluation of whether a guidance document is reasonably likely to have an impact of $100 million or more annually. We recommend that the agency as part of its determination, consider both the expected adoption rate of guidance, in whole or in part, and the potential benefits that would occur with such adoption. If information to make reasonable assumptions is not available, we suggest that the agency consider the effect of the guidance as if it were adopted widely by all affected parties.

C. **Guidance Questions -- Applicable to Requirements specific to the Bulletin**

8. **Under the Bulletin, what are the requirements for the content of "significant" guidance documents?**

The Bulletin requires that significant guidance documents: (i) include the term "guidance" or its functional equivalent; (ii) identify the agenc(ies) or office(s) issuing the document; (iii) identify the activity to which and the persons to whom the document applies; (iv) include the date of issuance; (v) note if it is a revision to a previously issued guidance document and, if so, identify the guidance that it revises or replaces; (vi) provide the title of the guidance and any document identification number, if one exists; and (vii) include the citation to the statutory provision or regulation (in Code of Federal Regulations format) which it applies to or interprets.

9. **Under the Bulletin, what information are agencies required to post on their Web sites?**

The Bulletin requires each agency to maintain a current electronic list of all significant guidance documents in effect on its Web site – or as a link on an agency's Web site to the electronic list posted on a component or subagency's Web site. The agency must provide a link from the current list to each significant guidance document that is in effect.

The agency list of significant guidance documents must include: the name of the significant guidance document, any document identification number, and issuance and revision dates and must identify significant guidance documents that have been added, revised or withdrawn in the past year. New significant guidance documents and their links should be added to this list within 30 days from the date of their issuance, but ideally as soon as possible. (Sec. III(1) of the Bulletin).

The lists should be maintained in a manner consistent with OMB policies for agency public Web sites and information dissemination. As agencies develop or revise significant guidance documents, they should organize and catalogue their significant guidance documents to ensure users can easily browse, search for, and retrieve significant guidance documents on agency Web sites. To further assist users in understanding agency guidance documents and the relationship of the guidance documents to current or proposed Federal regulations, agencies should also link their significant guidance document lists to Regulations.gov.

The agency must also provide, on its Web site, the name and contact information for the office or offices designated by the agency to receive and address complaints by the public that the agency is not following the procedures in the Bulletin or is improperly treating a significant guidance document as a binding requirement. (Sec. III(2)(b) of the Bulletin). The agency's Regulatory Policy Officer should ensure that these individuals respond promptly and appropriately to any such complaints

10. **Can a subcomponent of an agency establish a separate Web site listing guidance documents and/or designate more than one office to receive and address complaints from the public on the guidance documents?**

The Bulletin allows for an electronic list of significant guidance documents to be posted on a component or subagency Web site as long as the agency maintains a link to this list on its Web site. In this case, both the component or subagency Web site and the agency Web site must be maintained in a manner consistent with OMB policies for public Web sites and information dissemination.

The Bulletin requires the agency to designate an office (or offices) to receive and address complaints by the public that the agency is not following the procedures in the Bulletin or is improperly treating a guidance document as a binding requirement. Accordingly, the Bulletin permits an agency to establish one or more such offices, at its discretion. The agency shall provide the name and contact information for the office(s) on its Web site.

11. What requirements does the Bulletin establish -- for public comments and for Agency responses to those comments -- for "economically significant" guidance documents?

When the agency prepares a draft of an economically significant guidance document, the agency must publish a notice in the Federal Register announcing that the draft guidance document is available for comment and otherwise make it publicly available (e.g., by maintaining a hard copy, posting the draft on its Web site and ensuring that persons with disabilities can reasonably access and comment on the guidance). The Federal Register notice should explain how to submit comments and establish a period of time for the receipt of comments. Prior to or upon announcing availability of the draft guidance document, the agency should establish a public docket. Agencies should provide a link on their Web site from the guidance document to the public comments. In response to comments received on economically significant guidance documents, the agency also must prepare a response-to-comments document and make it publicly available in hard copy and on its Web site. (Sec. IV of the Bulletin). Further, in their requests for public comment, agencies should state that the guidance document does not have the force and effect of law.

12. What requirements does the Bulletin establish -- for public comments and for Agency responses to those comments -- for "significant" guidance documents?

The Bulletin does not require agencies to publish draft significant guidance documents for public comment prior to final issuance. However, each agency should have adequate procedures for handling public comments on significant guidance documents after they are published. Each agency must establish and clearly advertise on its Web site a means for the public to submit comments electronically and to provide a way for the public to request electronically that significant guidance documents be issued, reconsidered, modified or rescinded. However, unlike for economically significant guidance documents, the agency is not required to prepare a formal response-to-comments document. (Sec. III(2)(a) of the Bulletin).

The agency should provide, to the extent appropriate and feasible, a Web site link from the significant guidance document to the public comments filed on it. While agencies must comply with the Federal Records Act, agencies are not required to display public comments on their Web sites indefinitely. Accordingly, it would be appropriate for agencies to develop procedures for posting and maintaining the comments on the agency's Web site for a specified and reasonable period of time so as to enable interested members of the public to view the comments (and perhaps to offer their own comments in reply), and then to withdraw the comments from the Web site.

Should an agency determine that publishing a draft for public comment would be beneficial, they should provide a link from the significant guidance document to the public comments filed on it.

13. Should agencies use Regulations.gov to process public comments for guidance documents?

Yes. Agencies must use Regulations.gov to process public comments for economically significant guidance documents. Regulations.gov may also be used to process public comments for significant guidance documents. If your agency has not yet migrated to Regulations.gov, your agency can utilize existing processing capabilities. Your agency's Chief Information Officer can assist in scheduling and obtaining this service.

14. Under the Bulletin, what should an agency do if it believes that it would not be feasible or appropriate for the agency to provide the public with advance notice of, and an opportunity to comment on, an economically significant guidance document before the agency issues the guidance in final form?

An agency head or the Regulatory Policy Officer, in consultation with the OIRA Administrator, may identify a particular economically significant guidance document or class of economically significant guidance documents for which the procedures of Section IV of the Bulletin are not feasible and appropriate. In these circumstances, the agency should nonetheless: (a) publish a notice in the Federal Register announcing that the guidance document is available; (b) post the guidance document on its Web site and make it available in hard copy (or notify the public how they can review the guidance document if it is not in a format that permits such electronic posting with reasonable efforts); and (c) seek public comment when it issues or publishes the guidance document. If the agency receives comments on an excepted guidance document, the agency should review those comments and revise the guidance document as appropriate.

15. Under the Bulletin, what should an agency do if it needs to issue a significant guidance document to address an emergency situation?

The Bulletin expressly provides for emergency situations or when an agency is obligated by law to act more quickly than would occur under normal review procedures. In those cases, the agency shall notify OIRA as soon as possible and, to the extent practicable, comply with the Bulletin. (See also the question in D(22) below concerning how the agency should proceed under the Executive Order when issuing guidance to address an emergency situation.)

16. What are the timelines for meeting the requirements of the Bulletin?

No later than July 24, 2007, agencies must:

- Have developed procedures for the approval of significant guidance documents. Those procedures should ensure that the issuance of a significant guidance document is approved by appropriate senior agency officials (Sec. II(1) of the Bulletin);

- Comply with the standards for guidance documents contained in Section II(2) of the Bulletin;
- Provide for public comment on new economically significant guidance documents and otherwise meet the requirements of Section IV of the Bulletin.
- In accordance with Section III(1) of the Bulletin, provide on their Web sites a list of significant guidance documents promulgated after January 25, 2007.
- Advertise on the Web site a means for public feedback (Sec. III(2)(a) of the Bulletin); and
- Designate an office (or offices) to receive and address complaints by the public. The designated office should be clearly identified on the agency Web site, along with the contact information for the office. (Sec. III(2)(b) of the Bulletin)

No later than August 23, 2007, agencies must:

- Provide a list of significant guidance documents currently in effect and promulgated on or before January 25, 2007 on their agency Web site in accordance with Section III(1) of the Bulletin (and new significant guidance documents and their Web site links shall be added promptly to this list, no later than 30 days from the date of issuance); and
- Identify (and update at the beginning of each calendar year) significant guidance documents on the list that have been added, revised, or withdrawn within the past year, in accordance with Sec. III(1)(b) of the Bulletin.

We encourage the agencies to implement the requirements of the Bulletin sooner, if practicable.

D. Guidance Questions – Applicable to Requirements specific to the Executive Order

17. Under the Executive Order, what is an agency required to do when it wants to issue a "significant" guidance document?

Before an agency promulgates a significant guidance document, the agency must:

(1) Provide to OIRA advance notification of any significant guidance documents; and
(2) Upon the Administrator's request, provide to OIRA the content of the draft guidance, together with a brief explanation of the need for the guidance document and how it will meet that need.

Within ten (10) days of providing such notice to OIRA, OIRA will notify the agency if additional consultation will be required before issuing the guidance. (Sec. 9 of the Executive Order)

The Executive Order assigns responsibility for ensuring compliance with these requirements to the Regulatory Policy Officer.

18. Under the Executive Order, how should an agency provide advance notification to OIRA of a significant guidance document?

As a general rule, no less than 10 days prior to intended dissemination of a significant guidance document, including draft documents that an agency may disseminate for public comment, the appropriate personnel at the agency should work with the OIRA desk officer who handles review of that agency's rules pursuant to Executive Order 12866. At a minimum, for each significant guidance document, the agency should provide the following information to OIRA:

- DEPARTMENT/Subcomponent;
- Title;
- Planned Publication Date;
- Name and Telephone number of the agency official who can answer detailed questions about the guidance document and;
- A brief description of what the agency is intending to do and why, issues associated with the guidance, time pressures, and why the action is important. If the agency received comment on a draft guidance document, include a brief statement of the nature and extent of public comment and the nature and extent of changes made in response to the public comment.

Lengthy or detailed descriptions of the issues listed above are not necessary. Based on these descriptions, OIRA will determine whether the agency should submit the content of the draft guidance.

Please note that these summaries are required only for "significant" guidance documents, which includes "economically significant" guidance documents.

An agency should provide this information to OIRA using the same process that the agency uses to request significance determinations for regulations.

19. What is the next step when the OIRA Administrator determines that additional consultation under the Executive Order is warranted?

If the Administrator determines that additional consultation is warranted, OIRA will review the guidance to ensure that it is consistent with the philosophy and principles of Executive Order 12866, as amended, and will also coordinate review among appropriate Executive branch departments and agencies. Additionally, OIRA will discuss with the agency its compliance with the requirements in the Bulletin that apply to "significant" and/or "economically significant" guidance documents. OIRA will remain in close consultation with the agency until the review is completed and will conduct the review in as expedited a manner as is possible. OIRA will complete its consultative process within 30 days or, at that time, advise the agency when consultation will be complete.

20. How will the OIRA Administrator determine which significant guidance documents are exempt from review under the Executive Order?

The Executive Order gives the OIRA Administrator the authority to exempt any category of agency guidance documents from centralized review. If an agency wishes to request an exemption, it should make such a request to the Administrator who will consider the request in consultation with the agency.

21. What is the time period for consultation with OIRA on significant guidance documents under the Executive Order?

The Executive Order does not specify a time period for review of significant guidance documents. However, as noted above, OIRA will remain in close consultation with the agency until the review is completed and will conduct the review in as expedited a manner as is possible. OIRA will complete its consultative process within 30 days or, at that time, advise the agency when consultation will be complete.

22. What should an agency do, under the Executive Order, if the agency needs to issue a significant guidance document to address an emergency situation?

If an agency needs to issue a significant guidance document to address an emergency situation, the agency should notify OIRA as soon as possible. After the emergency has been addressed, OIRA and the agency will consult on whether further review, including interagency review, is warranted under the Executive Order.

23. How were the Regulatory Principles of Executive Order 12866 amended to apply to guidance documents?

The Executive Order amends the Principles of Regulation (Sec. (1)(b) of the Executive Order) to ensure guidance documents are consistent with the philosophy of Executive Order 12866. Four of the principles are revised to clarify that they apply to guidance. Specifically, the principles, as amended, state [changes in italics]:

- Each agency shall base its decisions on the best reasonably obtainable scientific, technical, economic, and other information concerning the need for, and consequences of the intended regulation *or guidance document* (Sec. (1)(b)(7) of the Executive Order);
- Each agency shall avoid regulations *or guidance documents* that are inconsistent, incompatible, or duplicative with its other regulations *or guidance documents* or those of other Federal agencies (Sec. (1)(b)(10) of the Executive Order);

- Each agency shall tailor its regulations *and guidance documents* to impose the least burden on society, including individuals, businesses of differing sizes, and other entities (including small communities and governmental entities), consistent with obtaining regulatory objectives, taking into account, among other things, and to the extent practicable, the cost of cumulative regulations (Sec. (1)(b)(11) of the Executive Order); and
- Each agency shall draft its regulations *and guidance documents* to be simple and easy to understand with the goal of minimizing the potential for uncertainty and litigation arising from such uncertainty (Sec. (1)(b)(12) of the Executive Order).

E. Non-Guidance provisions in Executive Order 13422

24. When does an agency head need to designate its Regulatory Policy Officer?

Under the Order, each agency head was required to designate the agency's Regulatory Policy Officer no later than March 19, 2007. If your agency has not done so, please notify Margaret Malanoski at (202) 395-3122 or mmalanos@omb.eop.gov of this designation immediately. Further, the agency head must annually update OMB on the status of this designation.

Independent agencies are encouraged to appoint a Regulatory Policy Officer.

25. What changes does the Executive Order make to the appointment of the Regulatory Policy Officer?

The Order requires the Regulatory Policy Officer to be one of the agency's Presidential appointees. (Sec.6(a)(2) of the Executive Order) For many agencies, this will not be a change, because their Regulatory Policy Officers have already been Presidential appointees. These Presidential appointees will report to the heads of their agencies in carrying out their role as the agency's Regulatory Policy Officer, as they do when carrying out their other responsibilities and as the Regulatory Policy Officers have previously done.

26. Can the agency head designate as the Regulatory Policy Officer an agency employee who serves in a position for which the agency head (not the President) is the appointing official?

No. The agency head may designate the agency's Regulatory Policy Officer from among those agency positions whose appointment is vested by law in the President. Such "political appointees" as Schedule C and non-career SES employees are appointed by the agency head, not by the President, and thus they may not be designated as the agency's Regulatory Policy Officer.

27. **If there is a vacancy in the Presidentially-appointed position that the agency head has designated as the Regulatory Policy Officer, may the person who is serving in an "acting" capacity in that position be the Regulatory Policy Officer?**

Yes. If a person who is not a Presidential appointee is serving in the acting capacity in a position that is Presidentially-appointed (PA), the amended Executive Order does not require an agency head to designate another official to serve as the Regulatory Policy Officer when a vacancy exists in the PA position that is designated as the Regulatory Policy Officer. Such a requirement to change the designation would be disruptive of agency operations.

28. **Are independent regulatory agencies required to designate a Presidential appointee as a Regulatory Policy Officer?**

No. Independent regulatory agencies are not subject to the requirement in Section 6(a)(2) of the Executive Order regarding the designation of Regulatory Policy Officers. However, the heads of independent regulatory agencies may decide to designate a Regulatory Policy Officer in order to meet the requirements for the Regulatory Plan (Sec. 4(c) of the Executive Order). We encourage independent agencies to do so.

29. **Will the Regulatory Policy Officers continue to report to their agency heads, as they did under Executive Order 12866 prior to its recent amendment?**

Yes. The deletion of the "report to the agency head" language by the recent Executive Order does not change the fact that the Regulatory Policy Officer reports to the agency head. As before, the agency head continues to be the official who designates the agency's Regulatory Policy Officer. The Regulatory Policy Officer will continue to report to the agency head in performing that role, as well as in performing his or her other responsibilities.

30. **Does the agency need to establish a Regulatory Policy Office, in addition to the agency head designating a Regulatory Policy Officer?**

No. The reference in Executive Order 13442 to a Regulatory Policy "Office" was a typographical error. This is in fact another reference to the Regulatory Policy Officer.

31. **What changes does the Executive Order make to the responsibilities of the Regulatory Policy Officer?**

Under the Executive Order, the Regulatory Policy Officer must:

- Personally authorize the commencement of rulemakings and the inclusion of rulemakings on the Regulatory Plan, unless they are otherwise authorized by the head of the agency. (Sec. 4(c) of the Executive Order); and

- Ensure that the agency provides OIRA with advance notification of and an opportunity to review any significant guidance documents prior to their promulgation. (Sec. 9 of the Executive Order).

Of course, it is assumed that these requirements will be implemented in a way that complies with all applicable laws.

32. When does a rulemaking "commence" for the purpose of meeting the new requirement for the Regulatory Policy Officer's (or the agency head's) authorization of the agency's "commencement of a rulemaking"?

The point at which a rulemaking commences may vary from one agency to the next, depending on each agency's procedures and practices, and may vary from rulemaking to rulemaking. As a general matter, a rulemaking commences when the agency has decided as an institutional matter that it will engage in a rulemaking. At the latest, the rulemaking will commence when the rulemaking receives a Regulation Identification Number (RIN).

33. What are the new requirements for the Regulatory Plan?

As noted above, the Executive Order requires the Regulatory Policy Officer (or the head of the agency) personally to authorize the commencement of rulemakings and the inclusion of rulemakings on the *Regulatory Plan*.

As has always been the case under Executive Order 12866, regulations identified in Part II of the *Plan* should, to the extent possible, include preliminary estimates of the anticipated costs and benefits of each rule. The change made by Executive Order 13422 is that each agency providing such estimates must sum-up these individual rule-by-rule estimates into a combined aggregate estimate of the costs and benefits of all its regulations planned for each calendar year or thereafter. (Sec. 4(c) of the Executive Order). The summation methodology should be internally consistent and transparent. The aggregate figures should be provided in a manner that allows for the public to easily understand the overall impact of the planned regulatory actions.

In summarizing the legal basis for each action, agencies must provide a specific citation for the statute, order, or other legal authority for each planned regulation. In particular, with regard to legal deadlines for completion of rulemakings, it will be necessary for agencies to provide full and specific information sufficient to identify in detail the source of any deadline requirements.

34. Do the revisions to the Principles of Regulation, specifically those in Section 1(b)(1) related to "market failure," require agencies to provide more or different information to OIRA when submitting a regulation for review?

The Executive Order clarifies in the Principles of Regulation (Sec. 1(b)(1) of the Executive Order) that: "Each agency shall identify in writing the specific market failure (such as externalities, market power, lack of information) or other specific problem that it intends to address (including, where applicable, the failures of public institutions) that warrant new agency action, as well as assess the significance of that problem."

This is not a substantive change to the Regulatory Principles of Executive Order 12866. Rather, this change makes clear that agencies must state "in writing" the problem the regulation seeks to address. Many agencies already provide this information in their preambles and, for those agencies, this should not represent any change.

Please note that the revision to the principle does not prescribe or limit the agencies' written rationale exclusively to "market failure, though that issue should be addressed where it is applicable. The language from the principle explicitly recognizes that there may be other "specific problems that [an agency] intends to address…that warrant new agency action." In addition, the language that expressly directs Federal agencies to "promulgate . . . such regulations as are required by law, [or] are necessary to interpret the law" has not been amended and so it continues to apply. Agencies should continue to set forth the appropriate basis for any proposed regulatory action.

35. Does the Executive Order require an agency to consider the use of formal rulemaking?

No. The Executive Order instead reminds agencies that they may, in consultation with OIRA, consider whether to use formal rulemaking procedures under the Administrative Procedure Act (APA) for the resolution of complex determinations. This is a reminder to agencies of an authority that they have long had, and that remains available to them, under the APA. Some agencies have utilized this authority and may want to consider doing so in the future, and other agencies may identify situations in which it could be beneficial.

* * * *

Further Questions

With whom should agency staff consult about questions concerning the Executive Order and the Bulletin?

If your staff has questions concerning the Executive Order or the Bulletin, please contact Margaret Malanoski in OIRA ((202) 395-3122 and mmalanos@omb.eop.gov.)

H. Updated Principles for Risk Analysis

Executive Office of the President Executive Office of the President

Office of Management and Budget Office of Science and Technology Policy

September 19, 2007

M-07-24

MEMORANDUM FOR THE HEADS OF EXECUTIVE DEPARTMENTS AND AGENCIES

FROM: Susan E. Dudley

Administrator, Office of Information and Regulatory Affairs,

Office of Management and Budget

Sharon L. Hays

Associate Director and Deputy Director for Science,

Office of Science and Technology Policy

SUBJECT: Updated Principles for Risk Analysis

Federal agencies take a variety of actions to improve public health, safety, and the environment. Agency activities designed to reduce risks are influenced by numerous factors, including Congressional priorities, information on the degree of risk faced by different populations, entities, or individuals, resources available, and the ease of implementing chosen priorities. Development of these actions often begins with an assessment of the risks posed under certain conditions, as well as assessments of the potential changes in risk achievable due to different policy options.

In 1995, an interagency working group, co-chaired by the Office of Management and Budget (OMB) and the Office of Science and Technology Policy (OSTP), developed a set of principles to guide policymakers in assessing, managing, and communicating policies to address environmental, health, and safety risks (the 1995 Principles).[1] The 1995 Principles, shared

---

[1] U.S. Office of Mgmt. and Budget (OMB), Memorandum for the Regulatory Working Group, *Principles for Risk Analysis* (1995), *available at* http://www.whitehouse.gov/omb/inforeg/regpol/jan1995_risk_analysis_principles.pdf.

with regulatory agencies in a memorandum from Sally Katzen, then Administrator of OMB's Office of Information and Regulatory Affairs (OIRA), remain valid today.

This Memorandum reinforces the 1995 Principles with reference to more recent guidance from the scientific community, the Congress, and the Executive Branch. This Memorandum also benefits from feedback received on OMB's Proposed Risk Assessment Bulletin issued in 2006 (Proposed Risk Assessment Bulletin).[2]

In January 2006, OIRA, in consultation with OSTP, released the Proposed Risk Assessment Bulletin for public comment and asked the National Academy of Sciences (NAS) to conduct an expert peer review.[3] The NAS issued its report on the Proposed Risk Assessment Bulletin in 2007 (the 2007 NAS Report on the Proposed Risk Assessment Bulletin).[4] While supportive of the goal of "increasing the quality and objectivity of risk assessment in the federal government," the NAS recommended an approach that would "outline goals and general principles of risk assessment."[5] After carefully evaluating these constructive recommendations from the NAS, as well as feedback from a rigorous interagency review, and public comments,[6] we have decided not to issue the bulletin in final form. Rather, we are issuing this Memorandum to reinforce generally-accepted principles for risk analysis upon which a wide consensus now exists.

Recognizing the diversity of documents that stem from risk analysis techniques, this Memorandum reinforces generally-accepted principles for risk

---

[2] OMB, *Proposed Risk Assessment Bulletin*, (2006) [hereinafter Proposed Risk Assessment Bulletin], *available at* http://www.whitehouse.gov/omb/inforeg/proposed_risk_assessment_bulletin_010906.pdf.

[3] *ee* Press Release, OMB, OMB Requests Peer Review of Proposed Risk Assessment Bulletin (Jan. 9, 2006), *available at* http://www.whitehouse.gov/omb/pubpress/2006/2006-01.pdf.

[4] National Research Council, National Academy of Sciences, *Scientific Review of the Proposed Risk Assessment Bulletin from the Office of Management and Budget* (2007) [hereinafter 2007 NAS Report on the Proposed Risk Assessment Bulletin].

[5] *Id.* at 6 - 7.

[6] OMB received 79 public comments on the Proposed Risk Assessment Bulletin. These comments are posted on OMB's website, *available at* http://www.whitehouse.gov/omb/inforeg/comments_rab/list_rab2006.html.

analysis related to environmental, health, and safety risks.[7] As a whole, the Memorandum endeavors to enhance the scientific quality, objectivity, and utility of Agency risk analyses and the complementary objectives of improving efficiency and consistency among the Federal family.[8] The general principles presented here should continue to assist and guide agencies as they conduct risk analyses, and thereby should enhance the multiple decisions that are based upon these analyses.

The 1995 Principles were divided into five parts: general principles, principles for risk assessment, principles for risk management, principles for risk communication, and priority setting.[9] This Memorandum reiterates each of these principles (in bold text) and, where appropriate, highlights and references more recent guidance (in plain text). OMB and OSTP will work with Federal agencies to ensure consistency with the principles in this memo-

---

[7] While many of the principles presented in this Memorandum may be relevant to other fields, such as financial or information technology risk analyses, the focus of this Memorandum is on those risk analyses related to environmental, health, and safety risks.

[8] The enhancement of information quality, objectivity, transparency, and reproducibility is addressed in other OMB guidance as well. See OMB, Circular A-4 for Regulatory Review (2003) [hereinafter Circular A-4] (includes requirements for regulatory analysis as it relates to risk management decisions, particularly those required under Executive Order 12866), *available at* http://www.whitehouse.gov/omb/circulars/a004/a-4.pdf. In addition, pursuant to what is commonly referred to as the Information Quality Act (Sec. 515 of the Treasury and General Government Appropriations Act for FY 2001, Pub. L. No. 106-554), OMB issued government-wide Guidelines for Ensuring and Maximizing the Quality, Objectivity, Utility, and Integrity of Information Disseminated by Federal Agencies (2002), 67 Fed. Reg. 8452 (Feb. 22, 2002) [hereinafter Information Quality Guidelines], *available at* http://www.whitehouse.gov/omb/fedreg/reproducible2.pdf; and its Final Information Quality Bulletin for Peer Review (2004), 70 Fed. Reg. 2664 (Jan. 14, 2005) [hereinafter Peer Review Bulletin], *available at* http://www.whitehouse.gov/omb/memoranda/fy2005/m05-03.pdf. These documents were each issued first as a proposal for public comment. In addition, the Information Quality Guidelines were then implemented by agencies in their own agency-specific information quality guidelines. This Memorandum is intended to complement and support the Information Quality Guidelines.

[9] This framework is consistent with the long-standing distinction between risk assessment, risk management, and risk communication. See National Research Council, National Academy of Sciences, *Risk Assessment in the Federal Government: Managing the Process* (1983).

randum. Agencies should review their current risk analysis practices and guidelines and incorporate these principles as they develop, update, and issue risk analyses and guidelines.

Should you have any questions regarding this Memorandum, or would like to discuss it, please do not hesitate to contact either of us or our staff at 202-395-4852 (OIRA) or 202-456-7116 (OSTP).

General Principles

1. **These Principles are intended to be goals for agency activities with respect to the assessment, management, and communication of environmental, health, and safety risks. Agencies should recognize that risk analysis is a tool—one of many, but nonetheless an important tool—in the regulatory tool kit. These Principles are intended to provide a general policy framework for evaluating and reducing risk, while recognizing that risk analysis is an evolving process and agencies must retain sufficient flexibility to incorporate scientific advances.**

The 2007 NAS Report on the Proposed Risk Assessment Bulletin recommended that OMB "develop goals for risk assessment that emphasize the central objective of enhanced scientific quality and the complementary objectives of efficiency and consistency among agencies evaluating the same or similar risks."[10] Recognizing that "[r]isk assessment is not a monolithic process or a single method," and that "[a]ll risk assessments share some common principles, but their application varies widely among domains," the NAS recommended that "affected federal agencies develop their own technical risk assessment guidelines that are consistent with the OMB general principles."[11]

2. **The Principles in this document are intended to be applied and interpreted in the context of statutory policies and requirements, and Administration priorities.**

3. **As stated in Executive Order No. 12866, "In setting regulatory priorities, each agency shall consider, to the extent reasonable, the degree and nature of the risks posed by various substances or ac-**

---

[10] 2007 NAS Report on the Proposed Risk Assessment Bulletin, *supra* note 4, at 110.
[11] *Id.* at 106, 110-11.

tivities within its jurisdiction" [Section 1(b)(4)]. Further, in developing regulations, federal agencies should consider "... how the action will reduce risks to public health, safety, or the environment, as well as how the magnitude of the risk addressed by the action relates to other risks within the jurisdiction of the agency" [Section 4(c)(1)(D)].[12]

Agencies should refer to Circular A-4 for expanded and updated guidance regarding best practices for agency regulatory analysis.[13]

4. In undertaking risk analyses, agencies should establish and maintain a clear distinction between the identification, quantification, and characterization of risks, and the selection of methods or mechanisms for managing risks. Such a distinction, however, does not mean separation. Risk management policies may induce changes in human behaviors that can alter risks (i.e., reduce, increase, or change their character), and these linkages must be incorporated into evaluations of the effectiveness of such policies.

5. The depth or extent of the analysis of the risks, benefits and costs associated with a decision should be commensurate with the nature and significance of the decision.

Subsequent reports have reaffirmed this principal. The 1997 Presidential/Congressional Commission on Risk Assessment and Risk Management (re-

---

[12] *See* Exec. Order No. 12866, 58 Fed. Reg. 51,735 (Oct. 4, 1993), *available at* http://www.whitehouse.gov/omb/inforeg/eo12866.pdf. *See also* Exec. Order No. 13132, 72 Fed. Reg. 2763 (Jan. 23, 2007), *available at* http://www.whitehouse. gov/omb/inforeg/eo12866/index_eo12866.html.

[13] *See* footnote 8. Circular A-4 refined OMB's "Economic Analysis of Federal Regulations Under Executive Order 12866" (1996) (a "best practices" guide to preparing a regulatory analysis), *available at* http://www.whitehouse.gov/omb/inforeg/riaguide.html. The "best practices" guide was issued as guidance in 2000, OMB's Memorandum for the Heads of Departments and Agencies on Guidelines to Standardize Measures of Costs and Benefits and the Format of Accounting Statements (2000), *available at* http://www.whitehouse.gov/omb/memoranda/m00-08.pdf; and reaffirmed in 2001, OMB's Memorandum for the President's Management Council on Presidential Review of Agency Rulemaking (2001), *available at* http://www.whitehouse.gov/omb/inforeg/oira_review-process.html. Before finalization, Circular A-4 went through public comment, interagency review, and peer review.

ferred to as the Presidential Commission on Risk) issued a two-volume report that stated as follows:

> The level of detail considered in a risk assessment and included in a risk characterization should be commensurate with the problem's importance, expected health or environmental impact, expected economic or social impact, urgency, and level of controversy, as well as with the expected impact and cost of protective measures.[14]

A 2007 NAS report on global change assessments evaluated lessons learned from relevant past global change assessments.[15] The NAS, drawing on its analysis and the relevant literature, identified essential elements of effective assessments and included elements relating to the adequacy of funding and the balance between benefits of the assessment and the opportunity costs of producing it.[16]

Principles for Risk Assessment

1. Agencies should employ the best reasonably obtainable scientific information to assess risks to health, safety, and the environment.

Risk analyses should be based upon the best available scientific methodologies, information, data, and weight of the available scientific evidence.[17] The Presidential Commission on Risk observed:

> Because so many judgments must be based on limited information, it is critical that all reliable information be considered. Risk assessors and economists are responsible for providing decision-makers

---

[14] Presidential/Congressional Commission on Risk Assessment and Risk Management, *Framework for Environmental Health Risk Management*, 1 Final Report 25 (1997) [hereinafter Risk Commission Report I].

[15] *See* National Research Council, National Academy of Sciences, *Analysis of Global Change Assessments: Lessons Learned* (in press 2007) [hereinafter 2007 NAS Report on Global Change Assessments].

[16] *Id., supra* note 15, at 4 (two essential elements of effective assessments are "[a]dequate funding that is both commensurate with the mandate and effectively managed to ensure an efficient assessment process" and a "balance between the benefits of a particular assessment and the opportunity costs (e.g., commitments of time and effort) to the scientific community").

[17] In this Memorandum, "scientific" information includes information related to applied sciences (such as engineering) and technical information related to these fields.

with the best technical information available or reasonably attainable, including evaluations of the weight of the evidence that supports different assumptions and conclusions.[18]

Congress emphasized using the best available scientific evidence for risk information in the 1996 amendments to the Safe Drinking Water Act (SDWA).[19] Pursuant to the SDWA, an agency is directed "to the degree that an agency action is based on science," to use:

(i) the best available, peer-reviewed science and supporting studies conducted in accordance with sound and objective scientific practices; and (ii) data collected by accepted methods or best available methods (if the reliability of the method and the nature of the decision justifies use of the data).[20]

Agencies have adopted or adapted this SDWA standard in their Information Quality Guidelines with regard to the analysis of risks to human health, safety, and the environment.[21]

2. **Characterizations of risks and of changes in the nature or magnitude of risks should be both qualitative and quantitative, consistent with available data. The characterizations should be broad enough to inform the range of policies to reduce risks.**

In the 1996 SDWA amendments, Congress adopted a basic quality standard for the dissemination of public information about risks of adverse health

---

[18] Risk Commission Report I, *supra* note 14, at 38. The Risk Commission Report I provides examples of the kinds of considerations entailed in making judgments on the basis of the weight of the scientific evidence in a toxicity study: quality of the toxicity study, appropriateness of the toxicity study methods, consistency of results across studies, biological plausibility of statistical associations, and similarity of results to responses and effects in humans.

[19] 42 U.S.C. § 300g-1(b)(3)(A,B).

[20] 42 U.S.C. § 300g–1(b)(3)(A).

[21] Links to agency specific information quality guidelines can be found in the OMB Draft 2007 Report to Congress on the Costs and Benefits of Federal Regulations, Appendix C, *available at* http://www.whitehouse.gov/omb/inforeg/2007_cb/2007_draft_cb_report.pdf. For specific examples of agency guidelines, *see* http://dms.dot.gov/submit/DataQualityGuidelines.pdf (Department of Transportation guidelines), http://aspe.hhs.gov/infoquality/Guidelines/index.shtml (Department of Health and Human Services guidelines), http://www.sti.nasa.gov/qualinfo.html (National Aeronautics and Space Administration guidelines), http://www.dol.gov/informationquality.htm (Department of Labor guidelines).

effects. Under the 1996 SDWA amendments, the Environmental Protection Agency is directed "to ensure that the presentation of information on public health effects is comprehensive, informative, and understandable."[22] The Information Quality Guidelines adapt this language and further direct the agencies to:

> in a document made available to the public in support of a regulation [to] specify, to the extent practicable— (i) each population addressed by any estimate [of applicable risk effects]; (ii) the expected risk or central estimate of risk for the specific populations [affected]; (iii) each appropriate upper-bound or lower-bound estimate of risk; (iv) each significant uncertainty identified in the process of the assessment of [risk] effects and the studies that would assist in resolving the uncertainty; and (v) peer-reviewed studies known to the [agency] that support, are directly relevant to, or fail to support any estimate of [risk] effects and the methodology used to reconcile inconsistencies in the scientific data.[23]

Agencies have adopted or adapted this standard in their Information Quality Guidelines with regard to analysis of risks to human health, safety, and the environment.[24]

In addition, the Information Quality Guidelines state that agency disseminations should be objective; these guidelines, as well as individual agency information quality guidelines, provide further discussion of objectivity and its application in agency disseminations.[25] While risks should not be minimized nor exaggerated, the 2007 NAS Report on the Proposed Risk Assessment Bulletin stated that "[i]nformation on the variability of effects across potentially affected populations is essential to decision-making."[26]

---

[22] 42 U.S.C. § 300g-1(b)(3)(B).
[23] *See* Information Quality Guidelines, *supra* note 8.
[24] *See* footnote 21.
[25] *See* Information Quality Guidelines, *supra* note 8. On a substantive level, objectivity ensures accurate, reliable and unbiased information.
[26] *See* 2007 NAS Report on the Proposed Risk Assessment Bulletin, *supra* note 4, at 63 (in referring to the Proposed Risk Assessment Bulletin's statement that risk assessments should be presented such that they are "neither minimizing nor exaggerating the nature and magnitude of risks," the NAS stated that this "could, however, degrade risk analysis if it were interpreted so as to deprive decision-makers of important information on sensitive subpopulations on the grounds that such information may generate risk estimates considerably higher than a central tendency or general population estimates.").

When characterizing risk in its 1996 report on understanding risk and how it informs decisions, the NAS stated that "quantitative models to organize and interpret data are particularly important to risk characterization."[27] When a risk analysis is influential,[28] increased efforts to provide useful quantitative estimates of risk are particularly important. Due to the inherent uncertainties associated with estimates of risk, presentation of a single estimate may be misleading and provide a false sense of precision.[29] Expert panels agree that when a quantitative characterization of risk is provided, a range of plausible risk estimates should be provided.[30] When something more than a superficial analysis can be conducted, quantitative uncertainty analy-

---

[27] National Research Council, National Academy of Sciences, *Understanding Risk: Informing Decisions in a Democratic Society* 99-100 (1996) [hereinafter 1996 NAS Report on Understanding Risk and Informing Decisions].

[28] In this Memorandum, the term "influential" is defined in the same way as it is defined in the Information Quality Guidelines. Influential means that "the agency can reasonably determine that dissemination of the information will have or does have a clear and substantial impact on important public policies or important private sector decisions." In their information quality guidelines, agencies have defined "influential" in ways appropriate for them given the nature and multiplicity of issues for which the agencies are responsible.

[29] *See* National Research Council, National Academy of Sciences, *Models in Environmental Regulatory Decision Making* 136 (2007) [hereinafter 2007 NAS Report on Environmental Decision Making] ("there are substantial problems in reducing the results of a large-scale study with many sources of uncertainty to a single number or even a single probability distribution. We contend that such an approach draws the line between the role of analysts and the role of policy makers in decision making at the wrong place."); *Id.* at 7 ("Effective decision making will require providing policy makers with more than a single probability distribution for a model result (and certainly more than just a single number, such as the expected net benefit, with no indication of uncertainty). Such summaries obscure the sensitivities of the outcome to individual sources of uncertainty, thus undermining the ability of policy makers to make informed decisions and constraining the efforts of stakeholders to understand the basis for the decisions."). *See also* 1996 NAS Report on Understanding Risk and Informing Decisions, *supra* note 27, at 66 ("Risk characterizations often fail because they attribute meaning to scientific estimates in ways that mislead participants in the risk decision process or are incomprehensible to them.").

[30] *See* 2007 NAS Report on the Proposed Risk Assessment Bulletin, *supra* note 4, at 37 ("The committee agrees with OMB that in some cases 'presentation of single estimates of risk is misleading' and that ranges of 'plausible risk' should be presented; however, the challenge is in the operational definitions of such words as *central, expected,* and *plausible*.") (emphasis in original).

sis, sensitivity analysis, and a discussion of model uncertainty can greatly inform risk management decisions.[31]

Experts have recognized that when presenting risk information qualitatively, or quantitatively, agencies' methodological approaches will likely vary and will depend upon the context for which the analysis is used.[32] These methodologies are continuing to develop as the science associated with quantitative uncertainty analysis advances. As technical guidance continues to develop, so too should agencies' presentation of quantitative risk information.

3. **Judgments used in developing a risk assessment, such as assumptions, defaults, and uncertainties, should be stated explicitly.** The

---

[31] *See* 2007 NAS Report on Environmental Decision Making, *supra* note 29, at 6 ("A wide range of possibilities is available for performing model uncertainty analysis. At one extreme, all model uncertainties could be represented probabilistically, and the probability distribution of any model outcome of interest could be calculated. However, in assessing environmental regulatory issues, these analyses generally would be quite complicated to carry out convincingly, especially when some of the uncertainties in critical parameters have broad ranges or when the parameter uncertainties are difficult to quantify. Thus, although probabilistic uncertainty analysis is an important tool, requiring EPA to do complete probabilistic regulatory analyses on a routine basis would probably result in superficial treatments of many sources of uncertainty. The practical problems of performing a complete probabilistic analysis stem from models that have large numbers of parameters whose uncertainties must be estimated in a cursory fashion. Such problems are compounded when models are linked into a highly complex system, for example, when emissions and meteorological model results are used as inputs into an air quality model."); *Id.* at 7 ("It is not necessary to choose between purely probabilistic approaches and deterministic approaches. Hybrid analyses combining aspects of probabilistic and deterministic approaches might provide the best solution for quantifying uncertainties, given the finite resources available for any analysis. For example, a sensitivity analysis might be used to determine which model parameters are most likely to have the largest impacts on the conclusions, and then a probabilistic analysis could be used to quantify bounds on the conclusions due to uncertainties in those parameters.").

[32] *Id.* at 7-8 ("In some cases, presenting results from a small number of model scenarios will provide an adequate uncertainty analysis (for example, cases in which the stakes are low, modeling resources are limited, or insufficient information is available). In many instances, however, probabilistic methods will be necessary to characterize properly at least some uncertainties and to communicate clearly the overall uncertainties.").

rationale for these judgments and their influence on the risk assessment should be articulated.

If important judgments are supported by, or conflict with, empirical data, that information should be discussed. The discussion should address the range of scientific and/or technical opinions regarding the likelihood of plausible alternate judgments and the direction and magnitude of any resulting changes that might arise in the analysis due to changes in key judgments.[33] Every effort should be made to perform a quantitative evaluation of reasonable alternative assumptions.[34] When an analysis combines multiple assumptions, the basis and rationale for combining the assumptions should be explicitly described.[35]

Critical judgments are often made when choosing and presenting study results. Results based on different effects and/or different studies should be presented to convey how the choice of effect and/or study influences the analysis. The presentation of information regarding different scientifically plausible endpoints should allow for a robust discussion of the available data, associated uncertainties, and underlying science. In its 2007 report evaluating global change assessments, the NAS recommended that "[t]here should be a deliberate effort to clarify the importance of alternative assumptions and to illustrate the impacts of uncertainties."[36] When relying on data from one study over others, the agency should provide a clear rationale and/or scientific basis for its choice.[37]

---

[33] *See* 1996 NAS Report on Understanding Risk and Informing Decisions, *supra* note 27, at 53 ("Simplifying assumptions generate especially serious problems when some of the assumptions are unreasonable in the face of information available to people outside the analytical process.").

[34] *Id.* at 99 ("Without good analysis, deliberative processes can arrive at agreements that are unwise or not feasible."). *See also* National Research Council, National Academy of Sciences, *Health Risks from Dioxin and Related Compounds* 7 (2006) ("Although EPA [in its dioxin assessment] addressed many sources of variability and uncertainty qualitatively, the committee noted that the Reassessment would be substantially improved if its risk characterization included more quantitative approaches. Failure to characterize variability and uncertainty thoroughly can convey a false sense of precision in the conclusions of the risk assessment.").

[35] *See* Circular A-4, *supra* note 8, at 39 ("Inferences and assumptions used in your analysis should be identified, and your analytical choices should be explicitly evaluated and adequately justified.").

[36] *See* 2007 NAS Report on Global Change Assessments, *supra* note 15, at 126.

[37] *See* Circular A-4, *supra* note 8, at 39.

4. **Risk assessments should encompass all appropriate hazards (e.g., acute and chronic risks, including cancer and non-cancer risks, to human health and the environment). In addition to considering the full population at risk, attention should be directed to subpopulations that may be particularly susceptible to such risks and/or may be more highly exposed.**

A good risk analysis should clearly summarize the scope of the assessment, including a description of: the agent, technology and/or activity that is the subject of the analysis; the hazard of concern; the affected entities (populations, subpopulations, individuals, natural resources, ecosystems, critical infrastructure, or other) that are the subject of the assessment; the exposure/event scenarios relevant to the objectives of the assessment; and the type of event-consequence or dose-response relationship for the hazard of concern.[38] In the 2007 NAS Report on the Proposed Risk Assessment Bulletin, the NAS reaffirmed that including this information would improve the clarity of a risk analysis and is consistent with the recommendations of previous expert reports.[39]

More recent reports have reaffirmed that, in addition to considering the full population or entities at risk, the risk analysis should also consider subpopulations or sub-entities that may be particularly susceptible to such risks and/or may experience greater exposures.[40] If a risk analysis is to address only specific subpopulations, the scope should be very clear about this limitation.

Where there are known differences in risk for different individuals, subpopulations or ecosystems, analysts should characterize this variability. Risk managers will be better informed when an understanding of variability and the key contributors to the cause of this variability are presented in the risk

---

[38] *See* Risk Commission Report I, *supra* note 14, at 24 (a list of questions should be addressed in a risk characterization).

[39] *See* 2007 NAS Report on the Proposed Risk Assessment Bulletin, *supra* note 4, at 62.

[40] *See* Risk Commission Report I, *supra* note 14, at 24 (a list of questions that includes asking about individuals or groups that are at risk and if some people are more likely to be at risk than others).

analysis.[41] As guidance on the presentation of risk information to the public continues to develop, so too will agencies' presentation and discussion of variability.

The President's Commission on Risk stated: "A good risk management decision is based on a careful analysis of the weight of scientific evidence that supports conclusions about a problem's potential risks to human health and the environment."[42] This may include consideration of both positive and negative studies, in light of each study's technical quality. Agencies and the risk assessment community are continuing to develop techniques for weight of evidence evaluations.

Agencies should consider confounding and/or synergistic factors. The scientific process of considering these elements may assist policy makers in developing a broader sense of how risk can be reduced significantly and the range of decision options that need to be considered in developing risk management approaches.[43]

5. **Peer review of risk assessments can ensure that the highest professional standards are maintained. Therefore, agencies should develop policies to maximize its use.**

Agencies should refer to the Peer Review Bulletin for updated guidance regarding agency best practices for peer review.[44]

6. **Agencies should strive to adopt consistent approaches to evaluating the risks posed by hazardous agents or events.**

---

[41] *See* 2007 NAS Report on the Proposed Risk Assessment Bulletin, *supra* note 4, at 80 ("information on the variability of effects across potentially affected populations—due to differences in sensitivity, exposure, or both—is essential to decision-making.").

[42] *See* Risk Commission Report I, *supra* note 14, at 23; *Id.* at 23-24 ("It is important that risk assessors respect the objective scientific basis of risks and procedures for making inferences in the absence of adequate data. Risk assessors should provide risk managers and other stakeholders with plausible conclusions about risk that can be made on the basis of the available information, along with evaluations of the scientific weight of evidence supporting those conclusions and descriptions of major sources of uncertainty and alternative views.").

[43] *Id.* at 24 (a list of questions that includes asking about "[w]hat other sources cause the same type of effects or risks.").

[44] *See* Peer Review Bulletin, *supra* note 8.

Principles for Risk Management

1. In making significant risk management decisions, agencies should analyze the distribution of the risks and the benefits and costs (both direct and indirect, both quantifiable and non-quantifiable) associated with the selection or implementation of risk management strategies. Reasonably feasible risk management strategies, including regulation, positive and negative economic incentives, and other ways to encourage behavioral changes to reduce risks (e.g., information dissemination), should be evaluated. Agencies should employ the best available scientific, economic and policy analysis, and such analyses should include explanations of significant assumptions, uncertainties, and methods of data development.

Agencies should refer to Circular A-4 for updated guidance regarding agency best practices for regulatory analysis.[45]

2. In choosing among alternative approaches to reducing risk, agencies should seek to offer the greatest net improvement in total societal welfare, accounting for a broad range of relevant social and economic considerations such as equity, quality of life, individual preferences, and the magnitude and distribution of benefits and costs (both direct and indirect, both quantifiable and non-quantifiable).

Agencies should refer to Circular A-4 for updated guidance regarding agency best practices for regulatory analysis.[46]

Principles for Risk Communication

1. Risk communication should involve the open, two-way exchange of information between professionals, including both policy makers and "experts" in relevant disciplines, and the public.

In describing its approach to risk characterization in the 1996 NAS Report on Understanding Risk and Informing Decisions, NAS stated that "[t]he responsible organization's staff should describe the stated and implicit purposes of the decision-making activity, the type of decision and general aims

---

[45] *See* Circular A-4, *supra* note 8.
[46] *Id.*

furthered by the activity, and the intended users of the risk characterization."[47]

Agencies should provide this information as it will assist the readers and users in better understanding the questions that the analysis sought to answer and will help to ensure that the risk analyses are used for their intended purposes. This information is particularly important in cases where likely users of the risk analyses are not the original intended audience for the document.

2. **Risk management goals should be stated clearly, and risk assessments and risk management decisions should be communicated accurately and objectively in a meaningful manner.**

An executive summary that discloses the objectives and scope, the key findings of the analysis, and the key scientific limitations and uncertainties can be an important part of risk communication.[48] In the 2007 NAS Report on the Proposed Risk Bulletin, the NAS commented that the inclusion of an executive summary could improve the clarity of risk assessments.[49] Presentation of information in a helpful and concise introductory section of the report will not only foster improved communication of the findings, but will also help ensure that the risk analysis is appropriately interpreted by diverse end users.

To maximize public understanding and participation in risk-related decisions, agencies should:

a. **explain the basis for significant assumptions, data, models, and inferences used or relied upon in the assessment or decision;**

---

[47] *See* 1996 NAS Report on Understanding Risk and Informing Decisions, *supra* note 27, at 146; *Id.* ("Different types of decisions may require different types of knowledge and perspectives and hence require different participants in the analytic-deliberative process—both inside and outside the organization.").

[48] Key limitations are those that are most likely to affect significantly the determinations and/or estimates of risk presented in the analysis.

[49] *See* 2007 NAS Report on the Proposed Risk Assessment Bulletin, *supra* note 4, at 64 ("These qualitative standards . . . [presented in an executive summary] could improve the clarity of risk assessment in the federal government if risk assessments do not implement them already (although the existence of such problems is not established by the bulletin).").

A high degree of transparency with respect to data, assumptions, and methods will increase the credibility of the risk analysis, and will allow interested individuals, internal and external to the agency, to understand better the technical basis of the analysis.[50]

b. describe the sources, extent and magnitude of significant uncertainties associated with the assessment or decision;

In the 1996 NAS Report on Understanding Risk and Informing Decisions, the NAS observed that "[t]here is strong agreement that risk analysts should explicitly summarize uncertainty, and there are methods for doing so."[51] In the 2007 NAS Report on Global Change Assessments, when referring to critical elements of a credible, legitimate and salient assessment, the NAS included as one of four central elements:

> Deliberative and consistent methods of treating and communicating uncertainties add credibility and salience. Regardless of method (statistics, sensitivity analysis, scenario development, or expert judg-

---

[50] *See* 1996 NAS Report on Understanding Risk and Informing Decisions, *supra* note 27, at 67; *Id.* at 100 (in a good quantitative analysis, "[a]ny assumptions used are clearly explained, used consistently, and tested for reasonableness," "[c]alculations are presented in such a form that they can be checked by others interested in verifying the results," and "[u]ncertainties are indicated, including those in data, models, parameters, and calculations."). *See* 2007 NAS Report on Global Change Assessments, *supra* note 15, at 126 (NAS recommends that "[t]here should be a deliberate effort to clarify the importance of alternative assumptions and to illustrate the impacts of uncertainties."). *See also* U.S. Environmental Protection Agency, *Science Policy Council Handbook, Risk Characterization* 15 (2000) [hereinafter EPA Risk Characterization Handbook] ("[Transparency] ensures that any reader understands all the steps, logic, key assumptions, limitations, and decisions in the risk assessment, and comprehends the supporting rationale that lead to the outcome."). In the EPA Risk Characterization Handbook, EPA lists 10 elements of full disclosure. *Id.* at 15-16.

[51] *See* 1996 NAS Report on Understanding Risk and Informing Decisions, *supra* note 27, at 107 ("When uncertainty is recognizable and quantifiable, the language of probability can be used to describe it."). *See also* EPA Risk Characterization Handbook, *supra* note 50, at 41 ("While it is generally preferred that quantitative uncertainty analyses are used in each risk characterization, there is no single recognized guidance that currently exists on how to conduct an uncertainty analysis. Nonetheless, risk assessors should perform an uncertainty analysis . . . . Uncertainty analysis should not be restricted to discussion of precision and accuracy, but should include such issues as data gaps and models.").

ment), each measure must be defined and communicated in a consistent manner.[52]

In the same report the NAS also stated:

> An effective characterization of uncertainty in assessments requires determining what sorts of uncertainty information would be useful for decision makers as well as developing quantitative or qualitative measures of uncertainty .... The manner in which uncertainties are acknowledged and characterized will affect both the salience and credibility of the assessment."[53]

The agency also should identify the sources of the underlying information (consistent with sensitive information and confidentiality protections) and the supporting data and models, so that the public can evaluate whether there may be some reason to question objectivity.[54] Data should be accurately documented, and error sources affecting data quality should be identified and disclosed.[55]

c. make appropriate risk comparisons, taking into account, for example, public attitudes with respect to voluntary versus involuntary risk; and,

When making risk comparisons, agencies should be careful to consider the perspectives, assumptions, attitudes and context that the public associates with each risk. Agencies may want to consult the risk communication literature when considering appropriate comparisons. Although the risk assessor has considerable latitude in making risk comparisons, the fundamental point is that risk should be placed in a context that is useful and relevant for the intended audience.[56] Furthermore, effective communication of risk in-

---

[52] *See* 2007 NAS Report on Global Change Assessments, *supra* note 15, at 60.

[53] *Id.* at 126.

[54] *See* Information Quality Guidelines, *supra* note 8.

[55] *See* OMB, Statistical Policy Working Paper No. 31, *Measuring and Reporting Sources of Error in Surveys,* 1-5 (2001) ("The measurement and reporting of error sources is important for everyone who uses statistical data. For the analyst, this information helps data analyses through an awareness of the limitations of the data."), *available at* http://www.fcsm.gov/01papers/SPWP31_ final.pdf.

[56] *See* National Research Council, National Academy of Sciences, *Improving Risk Communication* 165-79 (1989). *See also* Risk Commission Report I, *supra* note 14, at 4 (the problems a regulation is intended to address should be placed in their "public health and ecological context.").

formation can assist the public in balancing benefits and risks.[57] As our understanding regarding the presentation of risk information to policy makers and the public continues to develop, so too will agencies' presentation and discussion of risk comparison information.

d. provide timely, public access to relevant supporting documents and a reasonable opportunity for public comment.

Agencies should refer to OMB's Final Bulletin for Agency Good Guidance Practices, as well as the Peer Review Bulletin, for updated guidance regarding best practices for increasing public access and public comment concerning guidance documents and influential scientific information.[58] In addition, as noted in the OMB Information Quality Guidelines, influential risk analyses should be reproducible.[59] For guidance on how to provide the public with timely access to government information, Agencies should refer to OMB's Circular A-130, which addresses the management of Federal information resources, and OMB Memorandum 06-02, which addresses improving public access to Federal information.[60]

---

[57] *See* Institute of Medicine, National Academy of Sciences, *Seafood Choices: Balancing Benefits and Risks* 207 (2006) ("In the committee's judgment, it is important to conduct substitution analyses of the potential impacts of changes in consumption despite the uncertainties about the underlying nutrient and contamination levels."). *Id.* at 231 (in referring to guidance and information that can simplify such tradeoffs, the NAS lists considerations for guidance development).

[58] *See* OMB, *Final Bulletin for Agency Good Guidance Practices* (2007), *available at* http://www.whitehouse.gov/omb/fedreg/2007/012507_good_395395guidance.pdf, and Peer Review Bulletin, *supra* note 8.

[59] *See* Information Quality Guidelines, *supra* note 8, 67 Fed. Reg. at 8460 (independent reanalysis of the original or supporting data using the same methods would generate similar analytical results, subject to an acceptable degree of precision).

[60] *See* OMB, Circular A-130, *Management of Federal Information Resources* (2000), *available at* http://www.whitehouse.gov/omb/circulars/a130/a130trans4.pdf; OMB Memorandum No. 06-02, *Improving Public Access to and Dissemination of Government Information and Using the Federal Enterprise Architecture Data Reference Model* (2005), *available at* http://www.whitehouse.gov/omb/memoranda/fy2006/m06-02.pdf.

Principles for Priority Setting Using Risk Analysis

1. To inform priority setting, agencies should seek to compare risks, grouping them in broad categories of concern (e.g., high, moderate, and low).

2. Agencies should set priorities for managing risks so that those actions resulting in the greatest net improvement in societal welfare are taken first, accounting for relevant management and social considerations such as different types of health or environmental impacts; individual preferences; the feasibility of reducing or avoiding risks; quality of life; environmental justice; and the magnitude and distribution of both short- and long-term benefits and costs.

3. The setting of priorities should be informed by internal agency experts and a broad range of individuals in state and local government, industry, academia, and nongovernmental organizations, as well as the public at large. Where possible, consensus views should be reflected in the setting of priorities.

4. Agencies should attempt to coordinate risk reduction efforts wherever feasible and appropriate.

Administrative Dispute Resolution Act

Citations:

5 U.S.C. §§571-584 (2000) (general provisions, confidentiality, administrative arbitration); 5 U.S.C. §556(c) (2000) (ALJ authority); 9 U.S.C. §10 (2000) (arbitration, judicial review); 41 U.S.C. §§604-607 (contract disputes); 29 U.S.C. §173 (2000) (FMCS authority); 28 U.S.C. §2672 (2000) (tort claims); and 31 U.S.C. §3711(a)(2) (2000) (government claims); enacted November 15, 1990 by Pub. L. No. 101-552, 104 Stat. 2736; significantly amended August 6, 1992 by Pub. L. No. 102-354, 106 Stat. 944, and October 19, 1996 by Pub. L. No. 104-320, 110 Stat. 3870.

Lead Agency:

U.S. Department of Justice, Office of Alternative Dispute Resolution, Office of the Associate Attorney General, 10th Street and Constitution Avenue, NW, Room 5238, Washington, DC 20530 (202) 616-9471.

Overview:

Background of the Act. The Administrative Dispute Resolution Act of 1990 established a statutory framework for federal agency use of ADR. Based largely on reforms advocated by many observers, including the Administrative Conference of the U.S. in numerous formal recommendations to Congress and agencies, the Act recognized the value of, and encouraged federal agencies to employ, alternative means of dispute resolution. These methods—which have been used increasingly by states, courts and private entities in recent years—enable parties to bring to bear their experience to foster creative, acceptable solutions and to produce expeditious decisions requiring fewer resources than litigation and adjudicative processes. Mediation, conciliation, arbitration, minitrials, factfinding, early neutral evaluation, settlement judges, ombuds, and similar methods have begun to prove increasingly useful in resolving administrative disputes.

It became evident to many experts that legislation was needed to resolve legal questions regarding agency authority to employ ADR, to define procedural safeguards, and to prompt agencies to experiment. The 1990 Act was the response. It authorized and encouraged all federal agencies to use consensual processes to enhance the possibility of reaching agreements expeditiously within the confines of agency authority. It was premised on Congress' findings that ADR can lead to more creative, efficient, stable and sensible outcomes. In 1996, the Congress amended and permanently reauthorized the Act. By eliminating further sunset dates and special reporting requirements, Congress recognized ADR methods' permanent place in agency decisionmaking activities.

Agency Implementation. Section 3 of the Administrative Dispute Resolution Act of 1990 provides for agency action to put the legislation's provisions into effect. The Act calls for an internal review process for agencies to consider whether, and under what circumstances, ADR techniques may benefit the public and help it to fulfill statutory duties more effectively.

An agency is required to consider if ADR can be useful to each of its "administrative programs." Section 571 of this subchapter defines an agency's "administrative program" broadly to include all activities involving "protection of the public interest and the determination of rights. . . ." Agency review is directed to all manner of agency actions including actions involving entitlement programs, grants, contracts, insurance, loans, guarantees, licensing, inspections, taxes, fees, enforcement, postal services, economic regulation, management, claims, or private party complaints. Following review of its administrative programs, an agency is directed to adopt policies on use of ADR. Section 572(b) lists factors an agency should use to determine if the dispute a agency has identified lends itself to ADR, especially binding arbitration.

Section 3 assigns responsibility to implement the provisions of the Act. Each agency head is expected to designate a senior official to be the dispute resolution specialist (DRS) of the agency. This official generally works at a departmental or comparable level to oversee the implementation of ADR activities and development of the agency policy on ADR. Ideally, the specialist or a designee would also seek to interact with counsel and program officers in helping these colleagues make full and effective use of the wide range of available dispute resolution options and in keeping them apprised of relevant developments in the public and private sectors. Each agency is expected to make training available to its specialist and other employees involved in implementing the Act. The agency specialist is expected to recommend to the agency head a list of other agency employees for similar training to be conducted by the specialist within the agency.

Section 3(d)(1) provides that each agency with significant grant or contract functions review its standard contract or assistance agreements to determine if a need exists for amendments to those agreements to authorize or encourage ADR use. Section 3(d)(2) provides that the Federal Acquisition Regulation be amended to reflect the amendments made by the Act, and FAR amendments became effective on December 29, 1998. 63 Fed. Reg.58,594 (Oct. 30, 1998).

ADR Methods. *Arbitration.* Arbitration is closely akin to adjudication in that a neutral third party decides the submitted issue after reviewing evidence and hearing argument from the parties. It may be binding on the parties either through agreement or operation of law, or it may be nonbinding in that the decision is only advisory. Arbitration may be voluntary, where the parties agree to resolve the issues by means of arbitration, or it may be mandatory, where the process is the exclusive means provided. Under the Act, it must always be voluntary.

Minitrial. A minitrial is a structured settlement process in which each side presents a highly abbreviated summary of its case before senior officials of each party authorized to settle the case. A neutral adviser sometimes presides over the proceeding and will render an advisory opinion if asked to do so. Following the presentations, the officials seek to negotiate a settlement.

Mediation. Mediation involves a neutral third party trained to assist the parties in negotiating an agreement. The mediator has no independent authority and does not render a decision; any decision must be reached by the parties themselves.

Facilitation. Facilitation helps parties reach a decision or a satisfactory resolution of the matter to be addressed. While often used interchangeably with "mediator," a facilitator generally conducts meetings and coordinates discussions, but does not become as involved in the resolution of substantive issues as does a mediator.

Convening or Conflict Assessment. Convening helps identify issues in controversy and affected interests. The convenor is generally called upon to determine whether direct negotiations among the parties would be a suitable means of resolving the issues, and if so to bring the parties together for that purpose. Convening has proved valuable in negotiated rulemaking and environmental disputes.

Negotiated Rulemaking. This formal process (covered separately by the Negotiated Rulemaking Act) is initiated by an agency promulgating a regulation. If a convenor recommends negotiation, neutral-led discussions including interested parties seek to effect an acceptable solution. It is used when an agency issues or revises a rule, especially when controversy is expected. The result is a proposed rule.

Summary Jury Trial. Disputants present evidence at a brief mock trial with a mock jury. After an advisory verdict, the presiding official may assist disputants negotiate.

Neutral Evaluation/Factfinding. Unbiased input on technical aspects of a dispute is provided by a subject matter specialist. These methods are apt where parties are willing to share pertinent data, desire perspective on strengths and weaknesses, or want prompt resolution by real decisionmakers. Following the findings, the parties may then negotiate a settlement, hold further proceedings, or conduct more research or discovery.

Settlement Judge. This process involves mediation or discussions by disputants before a neutral, generally a judge other than the presiding one. It is generally voluntary. The settlement judge may give an informal advisory opinion.

ADR Definitions and Authority. The Act, section 572(a), authorizes agencies to use any ADR method to resolve any controversy relating to an administrative program. The term "alternative means of dispute resolution," a key one in the legislation, is defined in section 571(3) as including any procedure that is used to resolve issues in controversy, including, but not limited to, conciliation, facilitation, mediation, factfinding, minitrials, arbitration, and use of ombuds, or any combination thereof.

The original version of the Act enacted in 1990 also referred to "ADR" as any procedure "used in lieu of an adjudication" as defined in to section 551(7) of title 5. Section 551(7) defines "adjudication" to include "agency process for the formulation of an order," and an "order" under section 551(6) is the "final disposition. . . . of an agency in a matter other than rule making. . . ." Thus, "order" and "rule" encompass almost everything agencies do. Consequently, the term "alternative means of dispute resolution," when used in the body of the legislation, was intended to include any procedure an agency may use to resolve any issue in controversy in any federal program activity.

"Issue in controversy" and "administrative program" (sections 571(8) and (2)) are similarly inclusive.

The Act explicitly gives agencies broad discretion as to when and how to use ADR methods. Agency decisions on using or not using ADR are unreviewable (section 581(b)(1). The sole exception allows any nonparty adversely affected by an arbitral award to seek review of an agency decision to arbitrate under the Act. In such an action, a United States district court would decide whether the agency's decision to use arbitration was clearly inconsistent with section 572(b)'s criteria for appropriate use of ADR.

Recognizing that ADR may be inappropriate in certain settings, 572(b) states that agencies should "consider not using" ADR when:

(1) a definitive or authoritative resolution of the matter is required for precedential value and such a proceeding is not likely to be accepted generally as an authoritative precedent;
(2) the matter involves or may bear upon significant questions of Government policy that require additional procedures before a final resolution may be made, and such a proceeding would not likely serve to develop a recommended policy for the agency;
(3) maintaining established policies is of special importance, so that variations among individual decisions are not increased and such a proceeding would not likely reach consistent results among individual decisions;
(4) the matter significantly affects persons or organizations who are not parties to the proceeding;
(5) a full public record of the proceeding is important, and a dispute resolution proceeding cannot provide such a record; and
(6) the agency must maintain continuing jurisdiction over the matter with authority to alter the disposition of the matter in the light of changed circumstances, and a dispute resolution proceeding would interfere with the agency's fulfilling that requirement.

This does not simply mean that the agency should not use ADR in a case involving public policy. A subtler balancing will be needed. The Act sets forth some situations in which an agency might decide not to employ ADR. In many cases, mediation, negotiated rulemaking, and similar methods will be very useful even if policy issues are implicated. On the other hand, agencies should not ordinarily use arbitration to decide a major policy issue. This approach was intended to afford agencies maximum discretion, reinforced by the general nonreviewability of almost all decisions on use of ADR. The voluntary use of ADR is never specifically forbidden. Section 572(b)'s structure indicates that ADR is generally presumed appropriate. (Note that the provision does not state that the agency "shall not consider," and the conjunctive "and" is employed in this section.) In exercising their very broad discretion, agencies should take into account all factors and qualifiers as to when, and what kind, of ADR methods to use. In no case need a formal finding or justification accompany an agency decision on employing ADR.

Administrative Arbitration. One ADR process—binding arbitration—has evoked significant controversy in the public sector. After Congress passed the U.S. Arbitration Act in 1925, binding arbitration in private sector disputes became a widely accepted alternative to litigation. *Shearson/American Express, Inc. v. McMahon*, 484 U.S. 220 (1987), and numerous other Supreme Court decisions have been encouraging to arbitration. For nearly a century, however, the Comptroller General took the view that unless a federal agency had explicit statutory authorization, it was prohibited from using a private arbitrator to decide the validity of virtually any claim involving the government.[1] The ADR Act underscores the growing modern acceptance of arbitration by reversing this presumption. Section 4, 5 U.S.C. §§575-581, now authorizes parties to administrative proceedings, including agencies, to agree to binding arbitration.

The Act stipulates, in section 579, that the arbitrator shall set a time and place for the hearing and that an arbitration proceeding shall be conducted expeditiously and in an informal manner. The parties may present evidence and cross-examine witnesses, but the arbitrator may exclude evidence that is irrelevant, immaterial, unduly repetitious, or privileged. The arbitrator may interpret and apply relevant statutory and regulatory requirements, legal precedents, and policy directives. The arbitrator shall make the award within 30 days of the hearing unless the parties agree to some other time limit or are bound by a rule providing otherwise. Arbitral awards generally have no precedential value, and are subject to review under the U.S. Arbitration Act.

While the 1990 Act provided that the arbitral award did not become final and binding on an agency party for 30 days and allowed the agency head to vacate the arbitral award during that period, the 1996 amendments eliminated this one-sided "opt-out" provision. The amendments authorize, for the first time, "true" binding arbitration—or something very similar to it—for all federal agencies, though agency arbitration is still subject to some constraints. The Act now requires federal agencies entering into binding arbitration to specify a maximum award that may be issued in that case by the arbitrator. It also requires agency heads, prior to an agency's initial use of arbitration under the 1996 Act, to issue guidance on the appropriate use of arbitration after consulting with the Attorney General. Following the 1996 amendments, Phyllis Hanfling and Martha McClellan, on behalf of the federal Interagency Dispute Resolution Working Group, prepared a document with advice for agencies on implementing the Act's arbitral procedures, *De-*

---

[1] *See* Richard Berg, *Legal and Structural Obstacles to the Use of ADR in Federal Programs, Agency Arbitration,* Administrative Conference of the U.S. (1987).

veloping Guidance for Binding Arbitration: A Handbook for Federal Agencies (distributed by the Department of Justice 1999).

Confidentiality. Section 4, 5 U.S.C. §574, fosters agency use of ADR by ensuring appropriate protection of parties' and neutrals' "dispute resolution communications." In doing so, the Act seeks a balance between the openness required for legitimacy and the confidentiality that is critical if many sensitive negotiations are to yield agreements. In legislating, Congress defined these protections in detail. The Act forbids neutrals from disclosing such communications, and also states that they shall not "be compelled to disclose" such communications. As the Senate report for the original Act stated, the Act's confidentiality "protections are created to enable parties to ADR proceedings to be forthcoming and candid, without fear that frank statements may be used later against them. Thus, documents produced during an ADR proceeding, such as proposals to resolve the dispute, are immune to discovery unless certain specific conditions are met." (S. Rep. No. 1005, 101st Congress, 2d Sess., p. 11)

The legislation intends to provide a definite measure of confidentiality for neutrals and parties. In addition to Conference Recommendations 88-11, *Encouraging Settlements by Protecting Mediator Confidentiality*, and 95-6, *The Freedom of Information Act and Confidentiality under the Administrative Dispute Resolution Act*, two other sources are important in determining the Act's approach to confidentiality. These are the Federal Rules of Evidence and the Federal Rules of Civil Procedure. Each of these offers limited and, at times, contradictory protection to parties and neutrals in settlement negotiations. The protections of section 574 are generally consistent with case law under those authorities, but are clearer and surer in their application, especially as regards neutrals.

Section 574 generally prohibits disclosure of most settlement communications. Protected communications include the verbal exchange of information in caucus between a party and the neutral facilitator. They also include a "settlement document," which is any written material that is provided in confidence to or generated by the neutral or generated by the parties for the purpose of a settlement proceeding, including memoranda, notes, and work product. Section 574 covers documents that are created specifically for the negotiations and that are furnished in confidence to the neutral by a participant in the negotiation.

Section 574(a)(4) has a few narrow, clearly stated exceptions to confidentiality, most notably for information that could prevent harm to the public health and welfare, prevent a manifest injustice, or reveal a violation of law. When such disclosures are sought, the Act requires prior notice to parties, an opportunity to contest disclosure, and judicial balancing subject to stated criteria. A judge who is asked to order disclosure of confidential communications would be expected to assure that parties have been given a chance to object to disclosure and then undertake a careful balancing using the Act's criteria. This would require some meaningful consideration of the evidence sought and an explicit weighing of competing needs (including those of future parties and mediators). Disclosure or testimony can in those situations be ordered when the court finds the magnitude in a particular case sufficient to outweigh the integrity of dispute resolution, in general. The mere issuance of a subpoena would not be sufficient.

Section 574(j) provides that the Act is a statute specifically exempting disclosure under section 552(b)(3) of the Freedom of Information Act. Applicability of FOIA under the 1990 Act arose at the last minute and was not fully resolved. In a floor colloquy at the time of that Act's Senate passage, Senators Grassley and Levin expressed concern that the Act's current provisions did not adequately protect settlement communications. Senator Leahy, who chaired the Judiciary Subcommittee with jurisdiction over FOIA, pledged "to the sponsor of the bill, Senator Grassley, . . . to work with him next year on this issue and try to determine whether certain dispute resolution communications should be exempt from FOIA." 136 Cong. Rec. S18088 (daily ed. Oct. 24, 1990). The Administrative Conference's subsequent 1995 study and recommendation (see Bibliography) called on Congress to reverse the 1990 proviso by providing that a dispute resolution communication between a party and a neutral that is confidential under section 574 be exempt from disclosure under FOIA. The 1996 Act effectively accomplished this recommendation. Similarly, a dispute resolution communication originating with a neutral and provided to all parties (such as a neutral evaluation or a settlement proposal) is now protected from disclosure, including disclosure under FOIA.

The Act also requires that anyone seeking confidential information try initially to obtain it from parties before looking to the neutral. Neutrals who are requested to disclose protected documents must make an effort to notify the parties of demands for disclosure, and a party that does not offer to defend a neutral's refusal to disclose is considered to have waived any objection. The Act gives parties authority to vary the confidentiality provisions if all parties and the neutral agree to alternate provisions in advance, although that agreement cannot provide for less disclosure under FOIA than the Act's basic provisions do.

The confidentiality provisions of the Act have been a subject of considerable attention and some controversy since the Act's passage. An ABA Ad Hoc Confidentiality Committee completed a collaborative effort in 2005, publishing a *Guide to Confidentiality under the Administrative Dispute Resolution Act*. This volume offers analysis and tips to assist program administrators, neutrals, and others on dealing with federal ADR confidentiality. The *Guide* contains analyses, policy recommendations, and advice on dealing with day-to-day issues like intake, convening, confidentiality agreements, document handling, access requests, evaluation, and training. Recent advice has also been issued by interagency entities charged with overseeing federal ADR activities; this advice complements and elaborates on the ABA's *Guide*; see *Protecting the Confidentiality of Dispute Resolution Proceedings: A Guide for Federal Workplace ADR Program Administrators*, posted on the IADRWG website at http://www.adr.gov/guidance.html; *see also* Federal ADR Council/ U.S. Department of Justice, Confidentiality in Federal Alternative Dispute Resolution Programs, Questions & Answers on Confidentiality, 65 Fed. Reg. 83,085 (Dec. 29, 2000).

Neutrals. Section 4, adding 5 U.S.C. §573, provides that any person acceptable to both parties may serve as an arbitrator, mediator, convenor, facilitator, settlement judge, or other ADR neutral under the Act. The "neutral" is defined as an individual who functions specifically in aiding the parties to resolve an issue in controversy. Services of a neutral may be obtained by such methods as purchase orders, contracts, basic ordering agreements, interagency agreements, and under some circumstances, via requirement contracts.

The 1996 Act sought to expedite agency acquisition of neutrals' services. It amended the competitive bidding and award requirements generally applicable to federal agencies to authorize an agency to use less than full and open competition to acquire the services of a neutral or an expert in a negotiated rulemaking and any other alternative dispute resolution proceeding. In particular, 5 U.S.C. §569(c) amended federal procurement statutes (including 41 U.S.C. §253(c)(3)(C) for civilian agencies and 10 U.S.C. §2304(c)(3)(C) for defense agencies) to authorize agencies to use expedited procedures to acquire the services of experts and neutrals in connection with any part of any dispute.

Amendments to Existing Legislation. The Administrative Dispute Resolution Act was crafted to be "built into" existing agency processes. Section 4 amends the primary law governing federal agency administrative actions, the Administrative Procedure Act. The Act endeavors, through the APA amendments, to achieve its goals without disruption to any existing authority or dispute resolution system. Section 4 authorizes agencies and parties to administrative proceedings to use neutrals, including mediators, facilitators, and arbitrators. The Act authorizes agencies to use the full range of alternative means of dispute resolution for their programs. The Act removes any doubt an agency official may have had about the authority to use ADR techniques, and expands arbitration authority. The only conditions are that the agreement to use an ADR technique be voluntary and—in the case of arbitration—not inappropriate under the standards set forth in section 572(b).

Section 6 amends 41 U.S.C. §§604-607, the Contract Disputes Act, to make it clear that government contracting officers and boards of contract appeals are encouraged to resolve claims by ADR and have the authority to do so. This includes the authority to make use of arbitration in appropriate cases. Judicial review is available as in existing law. The amendments to the Contract Disputes Act are supplemental to existing arbitration authority in a few agencies.

Section 7 amends section 203 of the Labor Management Relations Act to authorize the Federal Mediation and Conciliation Service to make its mediators' and trainers' services available to other agencies.

Section 8 amends the Federal Tort Claims Act (28 U.S.C. §2672) to grant the Attorney General the authority to delegate additional tort claim compromise or settlement authority to agency heads without the necessity of prior Attorney General approval. Such delegations have been fixed at $25,000 for almost all agencies since 1966. They now can be raised as high as, but cannot exceed, the dollar amount of delegated approval authority given to United States attorneys to settle claims against the United States (at present $500,000).

Section 9 amends 31 U.S.C. §3711(a)(2) to raise agency claims compromise authority without prior Attorney General approval from $20,000 to $100,000, or even higher at the direction of the Attorney General.

Administrative Procedure Technical Amendments Act. When initially enacted, both the ADR Act and the Negotiated Rulemaking Act of 1990, Pub. L. No. 101-648, occupied sections in title 5 of the U.S. Code numbered 581-590. The Technical Amendments Act remedied this situation in 1992. The post-amendment section numbers are used herein.

Legislative History:

Administrative Dispute Resolution Act of 1990. The Act reflects numerous Administrative Conference recommendation (see Bibliography for a complete list). Recommendation 86-3, *Agencies' Use of Alternative Means of Dispute Resolution*, 1 CFR §305.86-3 (1992), urged Congress to authorize agencies to use ADR processes, including arbitration, to resolve matters that would otherwise be decided formally. This 1986 recommendation also set out other features that became part of the final legislation, including the criteria for appropriate use of ADR, judicial review, enforcement standards, and suggestions related to the general nature of Congressional action designed to foster, rather than inhibit, the use of ADR. Other Conference recommendations incorporated into the legislation include 88-11, *Encouraging Settlements by Protecting Mediator Confidentiality*, 1 CFR §305.88-11 (1992); 86-8, *Acquiring the Services of "Neutrals" for Alternative Means of Dispute Resolution*, 1 CFR §305.86-8 (1992); and 87-5, *Arbitration in Federal Programs*, 1 CFR §305.87-5 (1992).

On April 12, 1988, S. 2274, the Administrative Dispute Resolution Act of 1988, was introduced in the Senate by Senator Charles Grassley and referred to the Committee on Governmental Affairs. Introductory information is found at 134 Cong. Rec. S3803 (daily ed. April 12, 1988). Hearings were held on May 25, 1988, before the Judiciary Subcommittee on Courts and Administrative Practice. A virtually identical bill was introduced in the House of Representatives by Representative Donald Pease on July 27, 1988. The House bill, H.R. 5101, was referred to the Subcommittee on Administrative Law and Governmental Relations of the House Committee on the Judiciary. Introductory information is found at 134 Cong. Rec. H5990 (daily ed. July 27, 1988). Hearings were held before the Subcommittee on June 16, 1988. Neither bill was reported to the floor for House or Senate action.

The bill that became the Administrative Dispute Resolution Act was again introduced by Senator Grassley on May 11, 1989 as S. 971 and referred to the Senate Committee on Governmental Affairs. 135 Cong. Rec. S5166 (daily ed. May 11, 1988). The bill was the subject of hearings by the Subcommittee on Oversight of Government Management on September 19, 1989. The Senate Committee on Governmental Affairs reported the bill to the floor of the Senate for action on October 19, 1990. S. Rep. No. 1005, 101st Cong., 2d Sess. (1990). The Senate passed the bill by voice vote on October 24, 1990. 136 Cong. Rec. S18082-18091 (daily ed. October 24, 1990). Several of the Act's provisions were discussed at that time, including the meaning of the confidentiality protections; their relation to FOIA disclosure provisions; and operation of the administrative arbitration attorneys fee section. The Senate bill was reported to the House on October 24, 1990.

On May 25, 1989, a comparable bill was introduced in the House by Congressmen Glickman and Pease as H.R. 2497. The bill was referred to the House Committee on the Judiciary. 135 Cong. Rec. H2206 (daily ed. May 25, 1989). Hearings were held by the Subcommittee on Administrative Law and Governmental Relations on January 31, 1990. On April 25, 1990, Subcommittee markup was completed and the bill, as amended, was forwarded to the full Committee. *Administrative Dispute Resolution Act, 1990: Hearings on H.R. 2497 Before the Subcommittee on Administrative Law and Governmental Relations of the Committee on the Judiciary*, 101st Cong., 2d Sess. (1990). The Judiciary Committee completed consideration and markup on May 22, 1990 and the amended bill was reported to the House floor on June 1, 1990. See H.R. Rep. No. 101-513, 101st Cong., 2d Sess. (1990). The bill passed by voice vote on June 5, 1990. 136 Cong. Rec. H3152 (daily ed. June 5, 1990). Following Senate passage of H.R. 2497 in comparable form, the House passed the Senate version on October 26, 1990. The President signed the bill into law on November 15, 1990.

Several changes were made to resolve differences in the House and Senate bills and to deal with concerns raised, including those mentioned. One major change made to both bills prior to passage involved arbitration awards. At the instigation of the respective House and Senate Committees, the Department of Justice, the Administrative Conference, and the American Bar Association developed amendments to permit arbitration in federal programs under a unique 30-day delayed finality provision that required payment of attorneys fees in most cases for which an award was vacated by the agency head.

Administrative Dispute Resolution Act of 1996. The 1996 Act amended and permanently reauthorized the 1990 Act. It reflected numerous suggestions made in the Administrative Conference's 1995 reports to Congress on implementation of the ADR Act and the Negotiated Rulemaking Act, as well as post-1990 Conference recommendations. A valuable commentary on the 1996 Act's legislative history, intent, and effect has been prepared by Diane R. Liff, Special Counsel at the Federal Highway Administration. (It can be obtained by requesting *Pub. Law 104-320, Administrative Dispute Resolution Act and Negotiated Rulemaking Act of 1996: Text and Commentary*, from the Federal Mediation and Conciliation Service Resource Center.) The Administrative Dispute Resolution Act of 1995, S. 1224, was initially prepared by staff at the Administrative Conference and was introduced in the Senate by Senator Grassley on September 5, 1995. It was referred to the Committee on Governmental Affairs, where hearings were held on November 29, 1995 before the Subcommittee on Oversight of Government Management and the District of Columbia. The full committee marked up the bill on December 12, 1995, and subsequently reported it to the Senate floor along with a March 27, 1996 report, S. Rep. No. 104-245.

The House Judiciary Subcommittee on Commercial and Administrative Law held oversight hearings on December 12, 1995 on federal agencies' use of ADR. On February 27, 1996, a bill similar to the Grassley bill—H.R.

2977, entitled the Administrative Dispute Resolution Act of 1996—was introduced to the Judiciary Committee. The Subcommittee on Commercial and Administrative Law marked up this bill on February 29, 1996; the full Committee did so on March 12, 1996, and then ordered it reported to the House floor. The House report, H. Rep. No. 104-597, was filed on May 26, 1996. The Act was approved by the House on June 4, 1996. 142 Cong. Rec. H5786-5789 (daily ed. June 4, 1996).

The Senate considered the House bill, incorporated H.R. 2977 into S. 1224 with some amendments, and passed the bill on June 12, 1996. 142 Cong. Rec. S6155-6163 (daily ed. June 12, 1996). A conference committee negotiated differences between the two chambers' bills, which dealt primarily with binding arbitration, confidentiality provisions, and permanent reauthorization of the Negotiated Rulemaking Act. The Conference Report resolving these differences, H. Rep. 104-841, was filed on September 25, 1996 (142 Cong. Rec. H11108-11111 (daily ed. September 25, 1996)). The House approved a substitute bill embodying the conferees' agreement, H.R.4194, on September 27, 1996. 142 Cong. Rec. H11446-11452 (daily ed. May 11, 1988). The Senate further amended the bill and approved it on September 30, 1996. The House accepted these amendments on October 4, 1996. 142 Cong. Rec. H12276-12281 (daily ed. Oct. 4, 1996). The 1996 amendments were signed by President Clinton on October 19, 1996.

Source Note:

Literature on ADR is immense and growing, and this Bibliography focuses on a small selection of items dealing specifically with issues raised by the ADR Act for federal agencies. In addition, in recent years numerous federal agencies have developed brochures, training materials, videos, and other materials on using ADR methods. Much of this material is available from agencies' dispute resolution specialists.

Several sources regularly publish useful short news articles relevant to federal agencies. These include Dispute Resolution (published by the ABA Section of Dispute Resolution) and Alternatives to the High Cost of Litigation (published by the CPR Institute for Dispute Resolution). Administrative Conference recommendations and reports are available at American University in Washington, DC and many federal depository libraries. Administrative Conference recommendations, which underpinned much of the 1990 and 1996 acts, were, upon adoption, published in the *Federal Register* and, until 1993, codified in 1 CFR Part 305. The final listing of ACUS recommendations was published in 60 Fed. Reg. 56,312 (Nov. 8, 1995). *See also* http://www.law.fsu.edu/library/admin/acus/acustoc.html.

Other potential resources include the Ohio State Journal of Dispute Resolution, which publishes an annual bibliography of articles relating to ADR. The US Air Force maintains a very useful ADR web site, http://www.adr.af.mil. That site, among other things, provides links to other sites relating to government agency ADR, including the site of the Interagency Alternative Dispute Resolution Working Group, http://adr.gov.

Bibliography:

I. Legislative History

1. See Legislative History above.

II. Administrative Conference Recommendations Relating to the ADR Act

1. Administrative Conference of the U.S., Recommendation 95-6, *The Freedom of Information Act and Confidentiality under the Administrative Dispute Resolution Act*, 60 Fed. Reg. 43,115 (Aug. 18, 1995).
2. Administrative Conference of the U.S., Recommendation 90-2, *The Ombudsman in Federal Agencies*, 55 Fed. Reg. 34,211 (Aug. 22, 1990).
3. Administrative Conference of the U.S., Recommendation 89-2, *Contracting Officers' Management of Disputes*, 54 Fed. Reg. 28,967 (July 10, 1989).
4. Administrative Conference of the U.S., Recommendation 88-11, *Encouraging Settlements by Protecting Mediator Confidentiality*, 54 Fed. Reg. 5212 (Feb. 2, 1989).
5. Administrative Conference of the U.S., Recommendation 88-5, *Agency Use of Settlement Judges*, 53 Fed. Reg. 260 (July 11, 1988).
6. Administrative Conference of the U.S., Recommendation 87-11, *Alternatives for Resolving Government Contract Disputes*, 52 Fed. Reg. 49,148 (Dec. 30, 1987).
7. Administrative Conference of the U.S., Recommendation 87-9, *Dispute Procedures in Federal Debt Collection*, 52 Fed. Reg. 49,146 (Dec. 30, 1987).
8. Administrative Conference of the U.S., Recommendation 87-5, *Arbitration in Federal Programs*, 52 Fed. Reg. 23,635 (June 24, 1987).

9. Administrative Conference of the U.S., Recommendation 86-8, *Acquiring the Services of "Neutrals" for Alternative Means of Dispute Resolution*, 51 Fed. Reg. 46,990 (Dec. 30, 1986).

10. Administrative Conference of the U.S., Recommendation 86-7, *Case Management as a Tool for Improving Agency Adjudication*, 51 Fed. Reg. 46,989 (Dec. 30, 1986).

11. Administrative Conference of the U.S., Recommendation 86-3, *Agencies' Use of Alternative Means of Dispute Resolution*, 51 Fed. Reg. 25,641 (July 16, 1986).

12. Administrative Conference of the U.S., Recommendation 86-1, *Nonlawyer Assistance and Representation*, 51 Fed. Reg. 25,643 (July 16, 1986).

13. Administration Conference of the U.S., Recommendation 84-7, *Administrative Settlement of Tort and Other Monetary Claims Against the Government*, 49 Fed. Reg. 49,840 (Dec. 24, 1984).

14. Administrative Conference of the U.S., Recommendation 84-4, *Negotiated Cleanup of Hazardous Waste Sites Under CERCLA*, 49 Fed. Reg. 29,442 (July 25, 1984).

15. Administrative Conference of the U.S., Recommendation 82-2, *Resolving Disputes Under Federal Grant Programs*, 47 Fed. Reg. 30,704 (July 15, 1982).

III. Administrative Conference and Other Publications Relating to the ADR Act

1. ABA Ad Hoc Committee on Federal Government Confidentiality, *Guide to Confidentiality under the Administrative Dispute Resolution Act* (2005), *available at* http://meetings.abanet.org/webupload/commupload/DR030450/relatedresources/CopyofGuideFinalJul05.pdf.

2. Administrative Conference of the U.S., *Agency Arbitration* (1988).

3. Administrative Conference of the U.S., *Implementing the ADR Act: Guidance for Agency Dispute Resolution Specialists* (1992).

4. Administrative Conference of the U.S., *Mediation: A Primer for Federal Agencies* (1993).

5. Administrative Conference of the U.S., *The Ombudsman: A Primer for Federal Agencies* (1991).

6. Administrative Conference of the U.S., *Sourcebook: Federal Agency Use of Alternative Means of Dispute Resolution* (Marguerite Millhauser and Charles Pou, eds.) (Office of the Chairman, 1987).

7. Administrative Conference of the U.S., *Toward Improved Agency Dispute Resolution: Implementing the ADR Act*, Report to the Congress (1995).

8. Anderson, David and Diane Stockton, *Ombudsmen in Federal Agencies: The Theory and the Practice*, Report to the Administrative Conference of the U.S., 1990 ACUS 105, *reprinted in* 5 Admin. L. J. 275 (1991).

9. F. Anderson, *Negotiation and Informal Agency Action: The Case of Superfund*, Report to the Administrative Conference of the U.S., 1984 ACUS 263, *reprinted in* 1985 Duke L. J. 261.

10. Richard J Bednar, *Government Contracting Officers Should Make Greater Use of ADR Techniques in Resolving Contract Disputes*, Report to the Administrative Conference of the U.S., 1989 ACUS 149.

11. George A. Bermann, *Administrative Handling of Monetary Claims: Tort Claims at the Agency Level*, Report to the Administrative Conference of the U.S., 1984 ACUS 639, *portions reprinted in Federal Tort Claims at the Agency Level: The FTCA Administrative Process*, 35 Case W. Res. L. Rev. 509 (1984-85).

12. Marshall Breger (ed.), *Federal Administrative Dispute Resolution Deskbook* (ABA Section of Administrative Law & Regulatory Practice, 2001).

13. Harold Bruff, *Public Decisions, Private Deciders: The Constitutionality of Arbitration in Federal Programs*, Report to the Administrative Conference of the U.S., 1987 ACUS 533, *reprinted in* 67 Tex. L. Rev. 441 (1989).

14. M. Clagett, *Environmental ADR and Negotiated Rule and Policy Making: Criticisms of the Institute for Environmental Conflict Resolution and the U.S. Environmental Protection Agency*, 15 Tul. Envtl. L. J. 409 (2002).

15. Eldon Crowell & Charles Pou, *Appealing Government Contract Decisions: Reducing the Cost and Delay of Procurement Litigation*, Report to the Administrative Conference of the U.S., 1987 ACUS 1139 (Vol. II), *reprinted in* 49 Md. L. Rev. 183 (1989).

16. Federal ADR Council/U.S. Department of Justice, *Confidentiality in Federal Alternative Dispute Resolution Programs, Questions & Answers on Confidentiality*, 65 Fed. Reg. 83,085 (Dec. 29, 2000).

17. Federal Interagency ADR Working Group Steering Committee, *Protecting the Confidentiality of Dispute Resolution Proceedings: A Guide for Federal Workplace ADR Program Administrators* (2006), available at http://www.adr.gov/guidance.html.

18. R. Gomez, *Mediating Government Contract Claims: How It Is Different*, 32 Pub. Contract L. J. 63 (2002).

19. Mark Grunewald, *The Freedom of Information Act and Confidentiality under the Administrative Dispute Resolution Act*, Report to the Administrative Conference of the U.S., 1994-95 ACUS 557, *reprinted in* 9 Admin. L. J. 985 (1996).

20. Phyllis Hanfling & Martha McClellan, *Developing Guidance for Binding Arbitration: A Handbook for Federal Agencies* (Distributed by the Department of Justice 1999).

21. Philip J. Harter, *Neither Cop Nor Collection Agent: Encouraging Administrative Settlements by Ensuring Mediator Confidentiality*, Report to the Administrative Conference of the U.S., 1988 ACUS 839, *reprinted in* 1 Admin. L. J. 315 (1989).

22. Philip J. Harter, *Points on a Continuum: Dispute Resolution Procedures and the Administrative Process*, Report to the Administrative Conference of the U.S., 1986 ACUS 165, *reprinted in* 1 Admin. L. J. 141 (1987).

23. Daniel Joseph & Michelle Gilbert, *Breaking the Settlement Ice: The Use of Settlement Judges in Administrative Proceedings*, Report to the Administrative Conference of the U.S., 1988 ACUS 281, *reprinted in* 3 Admin. L. J. 571 (1990).

24. D. Lacy, *Alternative Dispute Resolution or Appropriate Dispute Resolution: Will ADR Help or Hurt the EEO Complaint Process?*, 80 Univ. Detroit Mercy L. Rev. 31 (2002).

25. Diane R. Liff, *Pub. L. 104-320 (1996), The Administrative Dispute Resolution Act of 1996/Negotiated Rulemaking Act of 1996: Text and Commentary* (FMCS 1997).

26. Peter Marksteiner, *How Confidential Are Federal Employment-Related Dispute Mediations?*, 14 Ohio St. J. Dis. Res. 89 (1998).

27. G. Mathews, *Using Negotiation, Mediation, and Arbitration to Resolve IRS-Taxpayer Disputes*, 19 Ohio St. J. Dis. Res. 709 (2004).

28. Leah Meltzer, *The Federal Workplace Ombuds*, Report to the Administrative Conference of the U.S., *reprinted in* 13(2) Ohio St. J. Dis. Res. 549 (1998).

29. J. Niermann, *Alternative Dispute Resolution in CERCLA Settlement*, 17 J. Envtl. L. & Litig. 389 (2002).

30. Charles Pou, *Gandhi Meets Elliott Ness: 5th Circuit Ruling Raises Concerns about Confidentiality in Federal Agency ADR*, Dispute Resolution 9 (Winter 1998); *reprinted in* Admin. L. & Reg. News 5 (Spring 1999).

31. George D. Ruttinger, *Acquiring the Services of Neutrals for Alternative Means of Dispute Resolution and Negotiated Rulemaking*, Report to the Administrative Conference of the U.S., 1986 ACUS 863.

32. Jeffrey M. Senger, *Federal Dispute Resolution: Using ADR with the United States Government* (Jossey-Bass 2004).

33. Marianne K. Smythe, *The Reparations Program at the Commodity Futures Trading Commission: Reducing Formality in Agency Adjudication*,

Report to the Administrative Conference of the U.S., 1988 ACUS 873, *reprinted in* 2 Admin. L. J. 39 (1988).

34. R. Talbot, *A Practical Guide to Representing Parties in EEOC Mediations*, 37 *Univ. S. Fran. L. Rev.* 627 (2003).

Appendix:

1. Administrative Dispute Resolution Act, 5 U.S.C. §§556(c), 581-593 (2000); 9 U.S.C. §10 (2000); 41 U.S.C. §§604-608 (2000); 29 U.S.C. §173 (2000); 28 U.S.C. §2672 (2000); 31 U.S.C. §3711(a)(2)(2000).

2. Memorandum for Heads of Executive Departments and Agencies, Designation of Interagency Committees to Facilitate and Encourage Agency Use of Alternative Means of Dispute Resolution, May 1, 1998.

Administrative Dispute Resolution Act
Title 5, U.S. Code
Sec. 1. Short Title

This Act may be cited as the "Administrative Dispute Resolution Act of 1996." (Pub. Law No. 104-320, §1, Oct. 19, 1996, 110 Stat. 3870)

Sec. 2. Congressional Findings

Section 2 of Pub. L. 101-552 provided that "The Congress finds that–

(1) administrative procedure, as embodied in chapter 5 of title 5, United States Code, and other statutes, is intended to offer a prompt, expert, and inexpensive means of resolving disputes as an alternative to litigation in the Federal courts;

(2) administrative proceedings have become increasingly formal, costly, and lengthy resulting in unnecessary expenditures of time and in a decreased likelihood of achieving consensual resolution of disputes;

(3) alternative means of dispute resolution have been used in the private sector for many years and, in appropriate circumstances, have yielded decisions that are faster, less expensive, and less contentious;

(4) such alternative means can lead to more creative, efficient, and sensible outcomes;

(5) such alternative means may be used advantageously in a wide variety of administrative programs

(6) explicit authorization of the use of well-tested dispute resolution techniques will eliminate ambiguity of agency authority under existing law;

(7) Federal agencies may not only receive the benefit of techniques that were developed in the private sector, but may also take the lead in the further development and refinement of such techniques; and

(8) the availability of a wide range of dispute resolution procedures, and an increased understanding of the most effective use of such procedures, will enhance the operation of the Government and better serve the public."
(Pub. Law. No. 101-552, §2, Nov. 15, 1990, 104 Stat. 2738)

Sec. 3. Promotion of Alternative Means of Dispute Resolution

(a) Promulgation of Agency Policy. Each agency shall adopt a policy that addresses the use of alternative means of dispute resolution and case management. In developing such a policy, each agency shall—

(1) consult with the agency designated by, or the interagency committee designated or established by, the President under section 573 of title 5, United States Code, to facilitate and encourage agency use of alternative dispute resolution under subchapter IV of chapter 5 of such title; and

(2) examine alternative means of resolving disputes in connection with—
  (A) formal and informal adjudications;
  (B) rulemakings;
  (C) enforcement actions;
  (D) issuing and revoking licenses or permits;
  (E) contract administration;
  (F) litigation brought by or against the agency; and
  (G) other agency actions.

(b) Dispute Resolution Specialists. The head of each agency shall designate a senior official to be the dispute resolution specialist of the agency. Such official shall be responsible for the implementation of—

(1) the provisions of this Act and the amendments made by this Act; and

(2) the agency policy developed under subsection (a).

(c) Training. Each agency shall provide for training on a regular basis for the dispute resolution specialist of the agency and other employees involved in implementing the policy of the agency developed under subsection (a). Such training should encompass the theory and practice of negotiation, mediation, arbitration, or related techniques. The dispute resolution specialist shall periodically recommend to the agency head agency employees who would benefit from similar training.

(d) Procedures for Grants and Contracts

(1) Each agency shall review each of its standard agreements for contracts, grants, and other assistance and shall determine whether to amend any such standard agreements to authorize and encourage the use of alternative means of dispute resolution.

(2) (A) Within 1 year after the date of the enactment of this Act, the Federal Acquisition Regulation shall be amended, as necessary, to carry out this Act and the amendments made by this Act.

(B) For purposes of this section, the term 'Federal Acquisition Regulation' means the single system of Government-wide procurement regulation referred to in section 6(a) of the Office of Federal Procurement Policy Act (41 U.S.C. 405(a)).

(Pub. L No. 101-552, §3, as amended Pub. L. No. 104-320, § 4(a), Oct. 19, 1996, 110 Stat. 3871)

Sec. 4. Administrative Procedures

(a) Administrative Hearings.—Section 556(c) of title 5, United States Code, is amended—

(1) in paragraph (6) by inserting before the semicolon at the end thereof the following: "or by the use of alternative means of dispute resolution as provided in subchapter IV of this chapter"; and

(2) by redesignating paragraphs (7) through (9) as paragraphs (9) through (11), respectively, and inserting after paragraph (6) the following new paragraphs:

"(7) inform the parties as to the availability of one or more alternative means of dispute resolution, and encourage use of such methods;

"(8) require the attendance at any conference held pursuant to paragraph (6) of at least one representative of each party who has authority to negotiate concerning resolution of issues in controversy;".

(b) Alternative Means of Dispute Resolution.—Chapter 5 of title 5, United States Code, is amended by adding at the end the following new subchapter:

Subchapter IV Alternative Means of Dispute Resolution in the Administrative Process[2]

   §571. Definitions.
   §572. General authority.
   §573. Neutrals.
   §574. Confidentiality.
   §575. Authorization of arbitration.
   §576. Enforcement of arbitration agreements.
   §577. Arbitrators.
   §578. Authority of the arbitrator.
   §579. Arbitration proceedings.
   §580. Arbitration awards.
   §581. Judicial review.
   §582. ~~Compilation of Information~~ (Repealed).
   §583. Support services.
   §584. Authorization of appropriations (New).

---

[2] In Pub. L. No. 101-552, Nov. 15, 1990, 104 Stat. 2736, Congress enacted two subchapters IV and two §§581-590. The sections of this subchapter were renumbered as §§571 *et seq.* by Pub. L. 102-354, Aug. 26, 1992, 106 Stat. 944.

§571. Definitions[3]

For the purposes of this subchapter, the term—

(1) "agency" has the same meaning as in section 551(1) of this title;

(2) "administrative program" includes a Federal function which involves protection of the public interest and the determination of rights, privileges, and obligations of private persons through rule making, adjudication, licensing, or investigation, as those terms are used in subchapter II of this chapter;

(3) "alternative means of dispute resolution" means any procedure that is used to resolve issues in controversy, including, but not limited to, conciliation, facilitation, mediation, fact finding, minitrials, arbitration, and use of ombuds, or any combination thereof;

(4) "award" means any decision by an arbitrator resolving the issues in controversy;

(5) "dispute resolution communication" means any oral or written communication prepared for the purposes of a dispute resolution proceeding, including any memoranda, notes or work product of the neutral, parties or nonparty participant; except that a written agreement to enter into a dispute resolution proceeding, or final written agreement or arbitral award reached as a result of a dispute resolution proceeding, is not a dispute resolution communication;

(6) "dispute resolution proceeding" means any process in which an alternative means of dispute resolution is used to resolve an issue in controversy in which a neutral is appointed and specified parties participate;

(7) "in confidence" means, with respect to information, that the information is provided—

> (A) with the expressed intent of the source that it not be disclosed; or
> (B) under circumstances that would create the reasonable expectation on behalf of the source that the information will not be disclosed;

(8) "issue in controversy" means an issue which is material to a decision concerning an administrative program of an agency, and with which there is disagreement—

---

[3] Sunset Provisions: the termination of authority to use dispute resolution proceedings on and after Oct. 1, 1995, provided by §11 of Pub. L. No. 101-552, set out as a note under section 571 of this title, was repealed by Pub. L. No. 104-320, §9, Oct. 19, 1996, 110 Stat. 3872.

(A) between an agency and persons who would be substantially affected by the decision; or

(B) between persons who would be substantially affected by the decision;

(9) "neutral" means an individual who, with respect to an issue in controversy, functions specifically to aid the parties in resolving the controversy;

(10) "party" means—

(A) for a proceeding with named parties, the same as in section 551(3) of this title; and

(B) for a proceeding without named parties, a person who will be significantly affected by the decision in the proceeding and who participates in the proceeding;

(11) "person" has the same meaning as in section 551(2) of this title; and

(12) "roster" means a list of persons qualified to provide services as neutrals.

(Added Pub. L. No. 101-552, §4(b), Nov. 15, 1990, 104 Stat. 2738, and amended Pub. L. No. 102-354, §§3(b)(2), 5(b)(1), (2), Aug. 26, 1992, 106 Stat. 944, 946, as amended Pub. L. No. 104-320, §2, Oct. 19, 1996, 110 Stat. 3870)

§572. General authority

(a) An agency may use a dispute resolution proceeding for the resolution of an issue in controversy that relates to an administrative program, if the parties agree to such proceeding.

(b) An agency shall consider not using a dispute resolution proceeding if—

(1) a definitive or authoritative resolution of the matter is required for precedential value, and such a proceeding is not likely to be accepted generally as an authoritative precedent;

(2) the matter involves or may bear upon significant questions of Government policy that require additional procedures before a final resolution may be made, and such a proceeding would not likely serve to develop a recommended policy for the agency;

(3) maintaining established policies is of special importance, so that variations among individual decisions are not increased and such a proceeding would not likely reach consistent results among individual decisions;

(4) the matter significantly affects persons or organizations who are not parties to the proceeding;

(5) a full public record of the proceeding is important, and a dispute resolution proceeding cannot provide such a record; and

(6) the agency must maintain continuing jurisdiction over the matter with authority to alter the disposition of the matter in the light of changed circumstances, and a dispute resolution proceeding would interfere with the agency's fulfilling that requirement.

(c) Alternative means of dispute resolution authorized under this subchapter are voluntary procedures which supplement rather than limit other available agency dispute resolution techniques.

(Added Pub. L. No. No. 101-552, §4(b), Nov. 15, 104 Stat. 2739)

§573. Neutrals

(a) A neutral may be a permanent or temporary officer or employee of the Federal Government or any other individual who is acceptable to the parties to a dispute resolution proceeding. A neutral shall have no official, financial, or personal conflict of interest with respect to the issues in controversy, unless such interest is fully disclosed in writing to all parties and all parties agree that the neutral may serve.

(b) A neutral who serves as a conciliator, facilitator, or mediator serves at the will of the parties.

(c) The President shall designate an agency or designate or establish an interagency committee to facilitate and encourage agency use of dispute resolution under this subchapter. Such agency or interagency committee, in consultation with other appropriate Federal agencies and professional organizations experienced in matters concerning dispute resolution, shall—

(1) encourage and facilitate agency use of alternative means of dispute resolution; and

(2) develop procedures that permit agencies to obtain the services of neutrals on an expedited basis.[4]

---

[4] To expedite the hiring of neutrals, §7 of Pub. L. No. 104-320, Oct 19, 1996, 110 Stat. 3872, amends the competitive requirements for defense agency (10 U.S.C. §2304(c)(3)(C)) and federal civilian agency (41 U.S.C. §253(c)(3)(C)) contracts to provide, in relevant part: "(c) The head of an agency may use procedures other than competitive ones only when . . . (3) it is necessary to award the contract to a particular source or sources in order . . . (C) to procure the services of an expert for use, in any litigation or dispute (including any reasonably foreseeable litigation or dispute) involving the Federal Government, in any trial, hearing or proceeding before any court, administrative tribunal, or agency, or to procure the services of an expert or neutral for use in any part of an alternative dispute resolution or negotiated rulemaking process, whether or not the expert is expected to testify."

(d) An agency may use the services of one or more employees of other agencies to serve as neutrals in dispute resolution proceedings. The agencies may enter into an interagency agreement that provides for the reimbursement by the user agency or the parties of the full or partial cost of the services of such an employee.
(e) Any agency may enter into a contract with any person for services as a neutral, or for training in connection with alternative means of dispute resolution. The parties in a dispute resolution proceeding shall agree on compensation for the neutral that is fair and reasonable to the Government.
(Added Pub. L. No. 101-552, §4(b), Nov. 15, 1990, 104 Stat. 2739, as amended Pub. L. No. 104-320, §7(b), Oct. 19, 1996, 110 Stat. 3872)

§574. Confidentiality

(a) Except as provided in subsections (d) and (e), a neutral in a dispute resolution proceeding shall not voluntarily disclose or through discovery or compulsory process be required to disclose any dispute resolution communication or any communication provided in confidence to the neutral, unless—
   (1) all parties to the dispute resolution proceeding and the neutral consent in writing, and, if the dispute resolution communication was provided by a nonparty participant, that participant also consents in writing;
   (2) the dispute resolution communication has already been made public;
   (3) the dispute resolution communication is required by statute to be made public, but a neutral should make such communication public only if no other person is reasonably available to disclose the communication; or
   (4) a court determines that such testimony or disclosure is necessary to—
      (A) prevent a manifest injustice;
      (B) help establish a violation of law; or
      (C) prevent harm to the public health or safety, of sufficient magnitude in the particular case to outweigh the integrity of dispute resolution proceedings in general by reducing the confidence of parties in future cases that their communications will remain confidential;
(b) A party to a dispute resolution proceeding shall not voluntarily disclose or through discovery or compulsory process be required to disclose any dispute resolution communication, unless—
   (1) the communication was prepared by the party seeking disclosure;
   (2) all parties to the dispute resolution proceeding consent in writing;
   (3) the dispute resolution communication has already been made public;
   (4) the dispute resolution communication is required by statute to be made public;

(5) a court determines that such testimony or disclosure is necessary to—
(A) prevent a manifest injustice;
(B) help establish a violation of law; or
(C) prevent harm to the public health and safety, of sufficient magnitude in the particular case to outweigh the integrity of dispute resolution proceedings in general by reducing the confidence of parties in future cases that their communications will remain confidential;

(6) the dispute resolution communication is relevant to determining the existence or meaning of an agreement or award that resulted from the dispute resolution proceeding or to the enforcement of such an agreement or award; or

(7) except for dispute resolution communications generated by the neutral, the dispute resolution communication was provided to or was available to all parties to the dispute resolution proceeding.

(c) Any dispute resolution communication that is disclosed in violation of subsection (a) or (b), shall not be admissible in any proceeding relating to the issues in controversy with respect to which the communication was made.

(d) (1) The parties may agree to alternative confidential procedures for disclosures by a neutral. Upon such agreement the parties shall inform the neutral before the commencement of the dispute resolution proceeding of any modifications to the provisions of subsection (a) that will govern the confidentiality of the dispute resolution proceeding. If the parties do not so inform the neutral, subsection (a) shall apply.

(2) To qualify for the exemption established under subsection (j), an alternative confidential procedure under this subsection may not provide for less disclosure than the confidential procedures otherwise provided under this section.

(e) If a demand for disclosure, by way of discovery request or other legal process, is made upon a neutral regarding a dispute resolution communication, the neutral shall make reasonable efforts to notify the parties and any affected nonparty participants of the demand. Any party or affected nonparty participant who receives such notice and within 15 calendar days does not offer to defend a refusal of the neutral to disclose the requested information shall have waived any objection to such disclosure.

(f) Nothing in this section shall prevent the discovery or admissibility of any evidence that is otherwise discoverable, merely because the evidence was presented in the course of a dispute resolution proceeding.

(g) Subsections (a) and (b) shall have no effect on the information and data that are necessary to document an agreement reached or order issued pursuant to a dispute resolution proceeding.

(h) Subsections (a) and (b) shall not prevent the gathering of information for research or educational purposes, in cooperation with other agencies, governmental entities, or dispute resolution programs, so long as the parties and the specific issues in controversy are not identifiable.

(i) Subsections (a) and (b) shall not prevent use of a dispute resolution communication to resolve a dispute between the neutral in a dispute resolution proceeding and a party to or participant in such proceeding, so long as such dispute resolution communication is disclosed only to the extent necessary to resolve such dispute.

(j) A dispute resolution communication which is between a neutral and a party and which may not be disclosed under this section shall also be exempt from disclosure under section 552(b)(3).

(Added Pub. L. No. 101-552, §4(b), Nov. 15, 1990, 104 Stat. 2740, as amended Pub. L. No. 104-320, §3, Oct. 19, 1996, 110 Stat. 3870)

§575. Authorization of arbitration

(a) (1) Arbitration may be used as an alternative means of dispute resolution whenever all parties consent. Consent may be obtained either before or after an issue in controversy has arisen. A party may agree to—

    (A) submit only certain issues in controversy to arbitration; or

    (B) arbitration on the condition that the award must be within a range of possible outcomes.

    (2) The arbitration agreement that sets forth the subject matter submitted to the arbitrator shall be in writing. Each such arbitration agreement shall specify a maximum award that may be issued by the arbitrator and may specify other conditions limiting the range of possible outcomes.

    (3) An agency may not require any person to consent to arbitration as a condition of entering into a contract or obtaining a benefit.

(b) An officer or employee of an agency shall not offer to use arbitration for the resolution of issues in controversy unless such officer or employee—

    (1) would otherwise have authority to enter into a settlement concerning the matter; or

    (2) is otherwise specifically authorized by the agency to consent to the use of arbitration.

(c) Prior to using binding arbitration under this subchapter, the head of an agency, in consultation with the Attorney General and after taking into account the factors in section 572(b), shall issue guidance on the appropriate use of binding arbitration and when an officer or employee of the agency has authority to settle an issue in controversy through binding arbitration.

(Added Pub. L. No. 101-552, §4(b), Nov. 15, 1990, 104 Stat. 2742, as amended Pub. L. No. 104-320, §8(c), Oct. 19, 1996, 110 stat. 3872)

§576. Enforcement of arbitration agreements

An agreement to arbitrate a matter to which this subchapter applies is enforceable pursuant to section 4 of title 9, and no action brought to enforce such an agreement shall be dismissed nor shall relief therein be denied on the grounds that it is against the United States or that the United States is an indispensable party.

(Added Pub. L. No. 101-552, §4(b), Nov. 15, 1990, 104 Stat. 2742)

§577. Arbitrators

(a) The parties to an arbitration proceeding shall be entitled to participate in the selection of the arbitrator.
(b) The arbitrator shall be a neutral who meets the criteria of section 573 of this title.

(Added Pub. L. No. 101-552, §4(b), Nov. 15, 1990, and amended Pub. L. No. 102-354, §3(b)(3), Aug. 26, 1992, 106 Stat. 945)

§578. Authority of the arbitrator

An arbitrator to whom a dispute is referred under this subchapter may—
    (1) regulate the course of and conduct arbitral hearings;
    (2) administer oaths and affirmations;
    (3) compel the attendance of witnesses and production of evidence at the hearing under the provisions of section 7 of title 9 only to the extent the agency involved is otherwise authorized by law to do so; and
    (4) make awards.

(Added Pub. L. No. 101-552, §4(b), Nov. 15, 1990, 104 Stat. 2742)

§579. Arbitration proceedings

(a) The arbitrator shall set a time and place for the hearing on the dispute and shall notify the parties not less than 5 days before the hearing.
(b) Any party wishing a record of the hearing shall—
    (1) be responsible for the preparation of such record;

(2) notify the other parties and the arbitrator of the preparation of such record;

(3) furnish copies to all identified parties and the arbitrator; and

(4) pay all costs for such record, unless the parties agree otherwise or the arbitrator determines that the costs should be apportioned.

(c) (1) The parties to the arbitration are entitled to be heard, to present evidence material to the controversy, and to cross-examine witnesses appearing at the hearing.

(2) The arbitrator may, with the consent of the parties, conduct all or part of the hearing by telephone, television, computer, or other electronic means, if each party has an opportunity to participate.

(3) The hearing shall be conducted expeditiously and in an informal manner.

(4) The arbitrator may receive any oral or documentary evidence, except that irrelevant, immaterial, unduly repetitious, or privileged evidence may be excluded by the arbitrator.

(5) The arbitrator shall interpret and apply relevant statutory and regulatory requirements, legal precedents, and policy directives.

(d) No interested person shall make or knowingly cause to be made to the arbitrator an unauthorized ex parte communication relevant to the merits of the proceeding, unless the parties agree otherwise. If a communication is made in violation of this subsection, the arbitrator shall ensure that a memorandum of the communication is prepared and made a part of the record, and that an opportunity for rebuttal is allowed. Upon receipt of a communication made in violation of this subsection, the arbitrator may, to the extent consistent with the interests of justice and the policies underlying this subchapter, require the offending party to show cause why the claim of such party should not be resolved against such party as a result of the improper conduct.

(e) The arbitrator shall make the award within 30 days after the close of the hearing, or the date of the filing of any briefs authorized by the arbitrator, whichever date is later, unless—

(1) the parties agree to some other time limit; or

(2) the agency provides by rule for some other time limit.

(Added Pub. L. No. 101-552, §4(b), Nov. 15, 1990, 104 Stat. 2742)

§580. Arbitration awards

(a) (1) Unless the agency provides otherwise by rule, the award in an arbitration proceeding under this subchapter shall include a brief, informal discussion of the factual and legal basis for the award, but formal findings of fact or conclusions of law shall not be required.

(2) The prevailing parties shall file the award with all relevant agencies, along with proof of service on all parties.

(b) The award in an arbitration proceeding shall become final 30 days after it is served on all parties. Any agency that is a party to the proceeding may extend this 30-day period for an additional 30-day period by serving a notice of such extension on all other parties before the end of the first 30-day period.

(c) A final award is binding on the parties to the arbitration proceeding, and may be enforced pursuant to sections 9 through 13 of title 9. No action brought to enforce such an award shall be dismissed nor shall relief therein be denied on the grounds that it is against the United States or that the United States is an indispensable party.

(d) An award entered under this subchapter in an arbitration proceeding may not serve as an estoppel in any other proceeding for any issue that was resolved in the proceeding. Such an award also may not be used as precedent or otherwise be considered in any factually unrelated proceeding, whether conducted under this subchapter, by an agency, or in a court, or in any other arbitration proceeding.[5]

(Added Pub. L. No. 101-552, §4(b), Nov. 15, 1990, 104 Stat. 2743, and amended Pub. L. No. 102-354, §5(b)(3), Aug. 26, 1992, 106 Stat. 946, as amended Pub. L. No. 104-320, §8(a), Oct. 19, 1996, 110 Stat. 3872)

§581. Judicial Review

(a) Notwithstanding any other provision of law, any person adversely affected or aggrieved by an award made in an arbitration proceeding conducted under this subchapter may bring an action for review of such award only pursuant to the provisions of sections 9 through 13 of title 9.

(b) A decision by an agency to use or not to use a dispute resolution proceeding under this subchapter shall be committed to the discretion of the agency and shall not be subject to judicial review, except that arbitration shall be subject to judicial review under section 10(b) of title 9.

(Added Pub L. 101-552, §4(b), Nov. 15, 1990, 104 Stat. 2744, and amended Pub. L. No. 102-354, §3(b)(4), Aug. 26, 1992, 106 Stat. 945, as amended Pub. L. No. 104-320, §8(b), Oct. 19, 1996, 110 Stat. 3872)

---

[5] (e) redesignated (d) and (f) and (g) repealed. Pub. L. 104-320, §8(a)(1), Oct. 19, 1996, 110 Stat. 3872.

§582. ~~Compilation of information~~ (Repealed)

§583. Support services

For the purposes of this subchapter, an agency may use (with or without reimbursement) the services and facilities of other Federal agencies, State, local, and tribal governments, public and private organizations and agencies, and individuals, with the consent of such agencies, organizations, and individuals. An agency may accept voluntary and uncompensated services for purposes of this subchapter without regard to the provisions of section 1342 of title 31.

(Added Pub. L. No. 101-552, §4(b), Nov. 15, 1990, as amended Pub. L. No. 104-320, §5, Oct. 19, 1996, 110 Stat. 3871)

§584. Authorization of appropriations

There are authorized to be appropriated such sums as may be necessary to carry out the purposes of this subchapter.

Sec. 5. Judicial Review of Arbitration Awards

Section 10 of title 9, United States Code, is amended—
   (1) by designating subsections (a) through (e) as paragraphs (1) through (5), respectively;
   (2) by striking out "In either" and inserting in lieu thereof "(a) in any"; and
   (3) by adding at the end thereof the following:

> "(b) The United States district court for the district wherein an award was made that was issued pursuant to section 580 of title 5 may make an order vacating the award upon the application of a person, other than a party to the arbitration, who is adversely affected or aggrieved by the award, if the use of arbitration or the award is clearly inconsistent with the factors set forth in section 572 of title 5."

Sec. 6. Government Contract Claims

(a) Alternative Means of Dispute Resolution.—Section 6 of the Contract Disputes Act of 1978 (41 U.S.C. 606) is amended by adding at the end the following new subsections:

"(d) Notwithstanding any other provision of this Act, a contractor and a contracting officer may use any alternative means of dispute resolution under subchapter IV of chapter 5 of title 5, United States Code, or other mutually agreeable procedures, for resolving claims. The contractor shall certify the claim when required to do so as provided under subsection (c)(1) or as otherwise required by law. All provisions of subchapter IV of chapter 5 of title 5, United States Code, shall apply to such alternative means of dispute resolution."

(b) Judicial Review of Arbitral Awards.—Section 8(g) of the Contract Disputes Act of 1978 (41 U.S.C. 607(g)) is amended by adding at the end the following new paragraph:

"(3) An award by an arbitrator under this Act shall be reviewed pursuant to sections 9 through 13 of title 9, United States Code, except that the court may set aside or limit any award that is found to violate limitations imposed by Federal statute."

Sec. 7. Federal Mediation and Conciliation Service

Section 203 of the Labor Management Relations Act, 1947 (29 U.S.C. 173) is amended by adding at the end the following new subsection:

"(f) The Service may make its services available to Federal agencies to aid in the resolution of disputes under the provisions of subchapter IV of chapter 5 of title 5, United States Code. Functions performed by the Service may include assisting parties to disputes related to administrative programs, training persons in skills and procedures employed in alternative means of dispute resolution, and furnishing officers and employees of the Service to act as neutrals. Only officers and employees who are qualified in accordance with section 573 of title 5, United States Code, may be assigned to act as neutrals. The Service shall consult with the agency designated by, or the interagency committee designated or established by, the President under section 573 of title 5, United States Code, in maintaining rosters of neutrals and arbitrators, and to adopt such procedures and rules as are necessary to carry out the services authorized in this subsection."

Sec. 8. Government Tort and Other Claims

(a) Federal Tort Claims.—Section 2672 of title 28, United States Code, is amended by adding at the end of the first paragraph the following: "Notwithstanding the proviso contained in the preceding sentence, any award, compromise, or settlement may be effected without the prior written approval of the Attorney General or his or her designee, to the extent that the Attorney General delegates to the head of the agency the authority to make such award, compromise, or settlement. Such delegations may not exceed the authority delegated by the Attorney General to the United States attorneys to settle claims for money damages against the United States. Each Federal agency may use arbitration, or other alternative means of dispute resolution under the provisions of subchapter IV of chapter 5 of title 5, to settle any tort claim against the United States, to the extent of the agency's authority to award, compromise, or settle such claim without the prior written approval of the Attorney General or his or her designee."

(b) Claims of the Government.—Section 3711(a)(2) of title 31, United States Code, is amended by striking out "$20,000 (excluding interest)" and inserting in lieu thereof "$100,000 (excluding interest) or such higher amount as the Attorney General may from time to time prescribe."

Sec. 9. Use of Nonattorneys

Section 9 of Pub. L. 101-552 provided that:
(a) Representation of Parties.—Each agency, in developing a policy on the use of alternative means of dispute resolution under this Act, shall develop a policy with regard to the representation by persons other than attorneys of parties in alternative dispute resolution proceedings and shall identify any of its administrative programs with numerous claims or disputes before the agency and determine—

(1) the extent to which individuals are represented or assisted by attorneys or by persons who are not attorneys; and

(2) whether the subject areas of the applicable proceedings or the procedures are so complex or specialized that only attorneys may adequately provide such representation or assistance.

(b) Representation and Assistance by Nonattorneys.—A person who is not an attorney may provide representation or assistance to any individual in a claim or dispute with an agency, if-

(1) such claim or dispute concerns an administrative program identified under subsection (a);

(2) such agency determines that the proceeding or procedure does not necessitate representation or assistance by an attorney under subsection (a)(2); and

(3) such person meets any requirement of the agency to provide representation or assistance in such a claim or dispute.

(c) Disqualification of Representation or Assistance.—Any agency that adopts regulations under subchapter IV of chapter 5 of title 5, United States Code, to permit representation or assistance by persons who are not attorneys shall review the rules of practice before such agency to—

(1) ensure that any rules pertaining to disqualification of attorneys from practicing before the agency shall also apply, as appropriate, to other persons who provide representation or assistance; and

(2) establish effective agency procedures for enforcing such rules of practice and for receiving complaints from affected persons.

Sec. 10. Definitions

As used in this Act, the terms 'agency', 'administrative program', and 'alternative means of dispute resolution' have the meanings given such terms in section 571 of title 5, United States Code (enacted as section 581 of title 5, United States Code, by section 4(b) of this Act, and redesignated as section 571 of such title by section 3(b) of the Administrative Procedure Technical Amendments Act of 1991).

Sec. 11. Reauthorization of Negotiated Rulemaking Act of 1990

(a) Permanent Reauthorization. Section 5 of the Negotiated Rulemaking Act of 1990 (Public Law 101-648; 5 U.S.C. 561 note) is repealed.

THE WHITE HOUSE

May 1, 1998

MEMORANDUM FOR HEADS OF EXECUTIVE DEPARTMENTS AND AGENCIES

SUBJECT: Designation of Interagency Committees to Facilitate and Encourage Agency Use of Alternate Means of Dispute Resolution and Negotiated Rulemaking

As part of an effort to make the Federal Government operate in a more efficient and effective manner, and to encourage, where possible, consensual resolution of disputes and issues in controversy involving the United States, including the prevention and avoidance of disputes, I have determined that each Federal agency must take steps to:

1. promote greater use of mediation, arbitration, early neutral evaluation, agency ombuds, and other alternative dispute resolution techniques, and

2. promote greater use of negotiated rulemaking.

By the authority vested in me as President by the Constitution and laws of the United States including sections 569(a) and 573(c) of title 5, United States Code, as amended by the Administrative Dispute Resolution Act of 1996 (Public Law 104320), I hereby direct as follows:

An Alternative Dispute Resolution Working Group, comprised of the Cabinet Departments and, as determined by the Attorney General, such other agencies with a significant interest in dispute resolution, shall be convened and is designated under 5 U.S.C. 573(c) as the interagency committee to facilitate and encourage agency use of alternative means of dispute resolution. The Working Group shall consist of representatives of the heads of all participating agencies, and may meet as a whole or in subgroups of agencies with an interest in particular issues or subject areas, such as disputes involving personnel, procurement, and claims. The Working Group shall be convened by the Attorney General, who may designate a representative to convene and facilitate meetings of the subgroups. The Working Group shall facilitate, encourage, and provide coordination for agencies in such areas as:

1. development of programs that employ alternative means of dispute resolution,

2. training of agency personnel to recognize when and how to use alternative means of dispute resolution,

3. development of procedures that permit agencies to obtain the services of neutrals on an expedited basis, and

4. recordkeeping to ascertain the benefits of alternative means of dispute resolution.

The Working Group shall also periodically advise the President, through the Director of the Office of Management and Budget, on its activities.

The Regulatory Working Group established under section 4(d) of Executive Order 12866 is designated under 5 U.S.C. 569(a) as the interagency committee to facilitate and encourage agency use of negotiated rulemaking.

This directive is for the internal management of the executive branch and does not create any right or benefit, substantive or procedural, enforceable by a party against the United States, its agencies or instrumentalities, its officers or employees, or any other person.

WILLIAM J. CLINTON

Agency Practice Act

Citations:

5 U.S.C. §500 (2000); enacted November 8, 1965, by Pub. L. No. 89332, 79 Stat. 1281; incorporated into the U.S. Code by Pub. L. No. 9083, 81 Stat. 195 (September 11, 1967) (with minor stylistic changes); amended by Pub. L. No. 106-113, Div. B, §1000(a)(9) [Title IV, §4732(b)(2)], Nov. 29, 1999, 113 Stat. 1536, 1501A-583.

Overview:

The Agency Practice Act provides that an attorney in good standing in any state may represent persons before federal agencies. An agency may require an attorney to file a written declaration of current qualification and to state that he is authorized to represent the particular person before the agency. Similarly, a duly qualified certified public accountant may represent persons before the Internal Revenue Service. The Act was intended to prohibit agency-established admission requirements for licensed attorneys and special enrollment requirements for CPAs. (Note: The Patent and Trademark Office is exempted from the Act.[1]) The Act expressly neither grants nor denies other persons the right to practice before an agency, nor does it authorize or limit an agency's right to discipline or disbar persons practicing before it.[2]

---

[1] *See* 37 CFR Part 11 (2006) for the regulations of the Patent and Trademark Office concerning recognition of individuals to practice in patent cases. The PTO's rules were extensively revised in 2004, see 69 Fed. Reg. 35,428 (June 24, 2004).

[2] For discussion of admission and discipline of attorneys under the Agency Practice Act, see Michael P. Cox, *Regulation of Attorneys Practicing Before Federal Agencies*, Report to the Administrative Conference of the U.S., 1982 ACUS (Vol. II) 491, *reprinted in* 34 Case W. Res. L. Rev. 173, 186-193 (1984).

434   AGENCY PRACTICE ACT

In 1982, the Administrative Conference adopted a statement on discipline of attorneys practicing before federal agencies.[3] After studying agency concerns and existing disciplinary procedures,[4] the Conference concluded that any current problems concerning attorney discipline before federal agencies were not of such magnitude or so widespread as to require legislative action or the adoption of uniform federal standards.

Legislative History:

In 1957 the Department of Justice recommended discontinuing the practice of many agencies whereby attorneys were required to apply for acceptance by the agency as practitioners. Several bills were introduced in the early 1960s to abolish agency admission requirements. By 1965 few agencies retained admission requirements, and only the Treasury Department and the Patent Office objected to discontinuing them. (See House Judiciary Committee Report, cited below.) Pub. L. No. 89-32 was enacted in 1965 with the passage of S.1758.

In 1999, the Act was amended to substitute the "Patent and Trademark Office" for "Patent Office."

Source Note:

The House report on S.1758 is reprinted in U.S. Code Congressional and Administrative News. Professor Michael Cox's 1982 report to the Administrative Conference discusses federal agency attorney discipline and contains an extensive bibliography. See also the statement of the Administrative Conference cited in footnote 3 of this chapter and the reports of the Administrative Conference and American Bar Association committees cited below.

Also relevant is section 9 ("Use of Nonattorneys") of the Administrative Dispute Resolution Act (see Chapter 5).

---

[3] "Statement of the Administrative Conference on Discipline of Attorneys Practicing Before Federal Agencies," 47 Fed. Reg. 58,210 (Dec. 30, 1982).

[4] See Cox, *supra* note 2.

Bibliography:

I. Legislative History

1. *Report to Accompany S.1758,* Senate Committee on the Judiciary, S. Rep. No. 755, 89th Cong., 1st Sess. (1965).
2. *Report to Accompany S.1758*, House Committee on the Judiciary, H.R. Rep. No. 1141, 89th Cong., 1st Sess. (1965), *reprinted in* 1965 U.S. Code Cong. & Admin. News, 89th Cong., 1st Sess. at 4170.

II. Other Government Documents

1. Administrative Conference Committee on Governmental Processes, *Report Concerning Discipline of Attorneys Practicing Before Federal Agencies*, 1982 ACUS (Vol. II) 488.
2. Administrative Conference of the U.S., Recommendation 79-7, *Appropriate Restrictions on Participation by a Former Agency Official in Matters Involving the Agency*, 45 Fed. Reg. 2,309 (Jan. 11, 1980).
3. Administrative Conference of the U.S., Recommendation 86-1, *Nonlawyer Assistance and Representation*, 51 Fed. Reg. 25,641 (July 16, 1986).
4. Administrative Conference of the U.S., *Statement on Discipline of Attorneys Practicing Before Federal Agencies*, 47 Fed. Reg. 58,210 (Dec. 30, 1982).

III. Books and Articles

1. C. Allen, *Attorney Ethics and Agency Practice: Representing Clients in Coast Guard Marine Casualty Investigations*, 22 J. Mar. L. & Comm. 225 (1991).
2. American Bar Association, *Report to the House of Delegates on Federal Agency Attorney Discipline* (August 1982).
3. Comment, *Determining Secondary Liability under Securities Laws: Attorney Beware!*, 11 Hamline L. Rev. 61, 96-104 (1988).
4. M. Cox, *Regulation of Attorneys Practicing Before Federal Agencies,* Report to the Administrative Conference of the U.S., 1982 ACUS (Vol. II) 491, *reprinted in* 34 Case W. Res. L. Rev. 173 (1984).
5. R. Karmel, *Rule 2(e)—A Reprise*, 210 N.Y.L.J. 3 (1993).

Agency Regulations:

Agriculture .... 7 C.F.R. §1.26
Commodity Futures Trading Commission ..... 17 CFR §§10.11, 14.1-.10
Consumer Product Safety Commission .... 16 CFR §§1025.61-.67
Drug Enforcement Administration (Justice) ..... 21 CFR §§1316.50-.51
Energy .... 10 CFR §1003.3
Environmental Protection Agency .... 40 CFR §§22.10, 305.10
Farm Credit Administration .... 12 CFR §§622.3, 623
Federal Aviation Administration (Transportation) .... 14 CFR § 13.33
Federal Communications Commission .... 47 CFR §§1.22-.24
Federal Deposit Insurance Corporation .... 12 CFR §308.6
Federal Energy Regulatory Commission ..... 18 CFR §§385.2101-.2103
Federal Housing Finance Board .... 12 CFR §908.72
Federal Maritime Commission .... 46 CFR §§502.21-.32
Federal Mine Safety and Health Review Commission . 29 CFR §§2700.3, 2700.80
Federal Reserve Board .... 12 CFR §263.6
Federal Trade Commission .... 16 CFR §4.1
Food and Drug Administration .... 21 CFR §12.40-.41
General Services Administration (Board of Contract Appeals) .... 48 CFR §6101.6
Homeland Security (Immigration cases) .... 8 CFR Part 292
Housing and Urban Development .... 24 CFR §§26.7-.8
Interstate Land Sales Program .... 24 CFR §§1720.120, .130, .135
Interior .... 43 CFR Part 1
Internal Revenue Service .... 26 CFR 601.502; 31 CFR Part 10
Justice (Immigration cases) .... 28 CFR §68.33(c)
Labor .... 29 CFR §§18.34, 417.8
Benefits Review Board .... 20 CFR §802.202
Employees' Compensation Appeals Board .... 20 CFR §501.11
Longshoremen's and Harbor Workers' Compensation
    Act .... 29 CFR § 1921.10
Maritime Administration (Transportation) .... 46 CFR §§201.15-.26
Merit Systems Protection Board .... 5 CFR §1201.31
National Highway Traffic Safety Administration
    (Transportation) .... 49 CFR §511.71-.76
National Labor Relations Board .... 29 CFR §102.177

National Oceanic and Atmospheric Administration
  (Commerce) .... 15 CFR §904.5
National Science Foundation .... 45 CFR §672.6
National Transportation Safety Board .... 49 CFR §821.6
Navy (JAG cases) .... 32 CFR Part 776
Nuclear Regulatory Commission .... 10 CFR §2.314
Occupational Safety & Health Review Commission . . 29 CFR §§2200.22-.23
Office of Thrift Supervision (Treasury) .... 12 CFR §509.6
Postal Regulatory Commission .... 39 CFR §3001.6
Postal Service .... 39 CFR Part 951
Securities and Exchange
  Commission .... 17 CFR §201.102; 17 CFR Part 205
Small Business Administration .... 13 CFR §134.208
Social Security Administration .... 20 CFR §§404.1700-.1799
Surface Transportation Board (Transportation) .... 49 CFR Part 1103
Transportation, Office of the Secretary
  (Aviation proceedings) .... 14 CFR §302.416
Treasury (Bureau of Alcohol, Tobacco, and Firearms) .... 31 CFR Part 8
United States International Trade Commission .... 19 CFR §201.15
Veterans Affairs (Board of Veterans' Appeals) .... 38 CFR § Part 20

Appendix:

1. Agency Practice Act, 5 U.S.C. §500 (2000).

6

Agency Practice Act

Title 5, U.S. Code

Subchapter I –General Provisions

§500. Administrative practice; general provisions

(a) For the purpose of this section—
(1) "agency" has the meaning given it by section 551 of this title; and
(2) "State" means a State, a territory or possession of the United States including a Commonwealth, or the District of Columbia.
(b) An individual who is a member in good standing of the bar of the highest court of a State may represent a person before an agency on filing with the agency a written declaration that he is currently qualified as provided by this subsection and is authorized to represent the particular person in whose behalf he acts.
(c) An individual who is duly qualified to practice as a certified public accountant in a State may represent a person before the Internal Revenue Service of the Treasury Department on filing with that agency a written declaration that he is currently qualified as provided by this subsection and is authorized to represent the particular person in whose behalf he acts.
(d) This section does not—
(1) grant or deny to an individual who is not qualified as provided by subsection (b) or (c) of this section the right to appear for or represent a person before an agency or in an agency proceeding;
(2) authorize or limit the discipline, including disbarment, of individuals who appear in a representative capacity before an agency;
(3) authorize an individual who is a former employee of an agency to represent a person before an agency when the representation is prohibited by statute or regulation; or
(4) prevent an agency from requiring a power of attorney as a condition to the settlement of a controversy involving the payment of money.
(e) Subsections (b)-(d) of this section do not apply to practice before the Untied States Patent and Trademark Office with respect to patent matters that continue to be covered by chapter 3 (sections 31-33) of title 35.
(f) When a participant in a matter before an agency is represented by an

individual qualified under subsection (b) or (c) of this section, a notice or other written communication required or permitted to be given the participant in the matter shall be given to the representative in addition to any other service specifically required by statute. When a participant is represented by more than one such qualified representative, service on any one of the representatives is sufficient.

Contract Disputes Act

Citations:

41 U.S.C.A. §§601-613 (2007); 28 U.S.C. §§1346(a)(2), 1491(a)(2), 2401(a), 2414, 2510, 2517 (2000); 31 U.S.C. §1304(a)(3)(C)(2000); enacted November 1, 1978 by Pub. L. No. 95-563, 92 Stat. 2383; significantly amended April 2, 1982 by Pub. L. No. 97-164, title I, §§156-157, 161, 96 Stat. 25, 47-49, November 5, 1990 by Pub. L. No. 101-509, Sec. 104, 104 Stat. 1447, and November 15, 1990 by Pub. L. No. 101-552, 104 Stat. 273; October 29, 1992 by Pub. L. No. 102-572, title IX, Sec. 907(a)(1),106 Stat. 4518; October 13, 1994 by Pub. L. No. 103-355, title II, Sec. 2351(a)((1)), (b), (e), 2352, 108 Stat. 3322; February 10, 1996 by Pub. L. No. 104-106, div. D, title XLIII, Sec. 4321(a)(6), (7), 4322(b)(6), 110 Stat. 671, 677; October 19, 1996 by Pub. L. No. 104-320, Sec. 6, 110 Stat. 3871; November 18, 1997 by Pub. L. No. 105-85, div. A, title X, Sec. 1073(g)(3), 111 Stat. 1906; January 6, 2006 by Pub. L. No. 109-163, div A, title VIII, subtitle E, §847(d)(1)-(4), 119 Stat. 3393; October 17, 2006 by Pub. L. No. 109-364, div. A, title VIII, subtitle E, §857, 120 Stat. 2394.

Lead Agency:

Office of Federal Procurement Policy, Office of Management and Budget, Washington, DC 20503 (202) 395-5802.

Overview:

Background. The Contract Disputes Act of 1978 was intended to bring greater consistency, fairness, and efficiency to the resolution of disputes arising out of government contracts. Before the Act's passage, this process was governed by various contract clauses, agency regulations, judicial decisions, and statutory provisions; procedures varied depending on the nature of the dispute and the agency involved. The legislation reflected in large part the recommendations of the Commission on Government Procurement, created by Congress in 1969 to recommend improvements in the procurement process.

Coverage. The Act and its procedures apply to claims arising under or relating to express or implied contracts made by executive branch agencies for the procurement of property other than real property, services, construction, alteration, repair, or maintenance of real property, or for the disposal of personal property. The Act does not reach bid protests or proceedings for the debarment or suspension of government contractors.

The term "claim" is not defined by the Act; however, the Federal Acquisition Regulation (FAR), a detailed regulation establishing uniform procedures and policies for procurement by federal executive agencies, defines it as:

> Claim, as used in this clause, means a written demand or written assertion by one of the contracting parties seeking, as a matter of right, the payment of money in a sum certain, the adjustment or interpretation of contract terms, or other relief arising under or relating to this contract. . . . A voucher, invoice, or other routine request for payment that is not in dispute when submitted is not a claim under the Act.[1]

Cognizable claims, include disputes arising under specific contract clauses (for example, when the parties cannot agree on an amount of compensation owed under clauses authorizing equitable adjustment for contract changes or for site conditions different from those anticipated when the contract was formed) as well as claims for breach of contract. Terminations for default are considered claims by the government under the Act.

Agency Procedures. The system established by the Contract Disputes Act begins with the contracting officer, an agency official authorized to enter into, administer, and terminate contracts on behalf of the government. The contracting officer plays a dual role in the disputes process, both representing the government as a party to the contract and rendering decisions on claims arising out of disputes between the parties. If a dispute arises during contract performance that cannot be amicably resolved (e.g., through exchange of

---

[1] 48 C.F.R. §52.233-1(c) (2007).

correspondence or negotiation), the contractor can invoke the procedures of the Contract Disputes Act by presenting a claim to the contracting officer. The claim must be in writing, provide adequate notice to the government of the basis for the demand and the relief sought, and clearly indicate the contractor's intent to seek a decision from the contracting officer.

If the essence of the dispute is money (for example, a claim for increased costs or for payment of the contract balance), the contractor must quantify the claim. In addition, for any claim over $100,000, the contractor must certify that "the claim is made in good faith, that the supporting data are accurate and complete to the best of [the contractor's] knowledge and belief, [and] that the amount requests accurately reflects the contract adjustment for which the contractor believes the government is liable." 41 U.S.C. §605(c)(1). The certification also must state that the person who is certifying is "duly authorized to certify the claim on behalf of the contractor."

The certification provision, incorporated into the Act to discourage inflated contractor claims, has proven to be one of the more controversial aspects of the law.[2] Much of this controversy was reduced by a recent change in the Act stating that a defective certification does not deprive a court or an agency board of contract appeals of jurisdiction over the claim. §605(c)(6). Prior to entry of a final judgment by a court or decision by a board of contract appeals, though, the court or board must obtain correction of a defective certification. A contracting officer has no duty to render a final decision on any claim over $100,000 that is not certified in accordance with §605(c)(1) if, within 60 days, the contracting officer notifies the contractor in writing of the reasons why an attempted certification was found to be defective.

If a claim cannot be settled by mutual agreement, the contracting officer must issue a written decision on the claim, stating the reasons for the decision and informing the contractor of available appeal rights. The Act requires the contracting officer to issue this decision within 60 days of receipt of a claim for $100,000 or less, and within a reasonable time after receipt of a larger claim (in which case the contracting officer must notify the contractor within 60 days as to when the decision will issue). If these deadlines are not met, the contractor may petition the relevant tribunal to direct the contracting officer to issue a decision. In any event, if the contracting officer fails to issue a

---

[2] *See* Administrative Conference Recommendation 83-1, *The Certification Requirement in the Contract Disputes Act*, 48 Fed. Reg. 31,179 (July 17, 1983); Madden, *Certification Requirements Under the Contract Disputes Act*, Report to the Administrative Conference of the U.S., 1983 ACUS 23.

timely decision, the claim will be deemed denied under the statute, permitting the contractor to pursue an appeal.

If the contracting officer issues an adverse decision on a contractor's claim or issues a decision asserting a government claim against the contractor (e.g., terminating the contract for default, asserting a right to excess reprocurement costs, or demanding payment to recover the costs or repairing or replacing defective work), the contractor has two avenues of appeal to choose from. The contractor may file an appeal at the appropriate agency board of contract appeals within 90 days after receiving the contracting officer's decision. Alternatively, the contractor may file suit directly in the U.S. Court of Federal Claims within 12 months from the date it received the contracting officer's decision. In either forum, proceedings on the claim will be *de novo*; any findings of fact made by the contracting officer in his or her final decision will not be binding. Only the contractor has the right to initiate litigation and to select the forum; if the contractor neither appeals nor files suit in the Court of Federal Claims, the contracting officer's decision becomes final.

The boards of contract appeals are quasi-judicial tribunals within the executive branch, composed of administrative judges with at least 5 years of public contract law experience who are authorized to adjudicate contract disputes on behalf of the heads of their respective agencies.[3] Congress intended the boards to be informal, expeditious, and inexpensive. In spirit, if not always in practice, the procedures of the boards reflect this intention. For example, under uniform rules of procedure developed by the Office of Federal Procurement Policy (see below), hearings are to be "as informal as may be reasonable and appropriate under the circumstances." Contractors may appear *pro se*—without the aid of counsel. Boards offer accelerated disposition of appeals involving claims of $100,000 or less (providing resolution within 180 days of the contractor's election) and expedited disposition for disputes of $50,000 or less (with a 120-day resolution period). The boards have taken some steps to encourage parties to consider alternatives to full-scale litigation (so-called alternative dispute resolution, or "ADR"). For instance, the Armed Services Board of Contract Appeals distributes a notice regarding ADR to its litigants, which describes various alternatives to litigation.

In contrast to the boards, which deal exclusively with government contracting, the Court of Federal Claims' docket includes a broad range of litigation involving the federal government in addition to government procurement.

---

[3] A U.S. District Court may request a board of contract appeals with jurisdiction to provide it with an advisory opinion on matters of contract interpretation. 41 U.S.C. §605(f).

Its proceedings are somewhat more formalized than those of the boards. For instance, use of the Federal Rules of Evidence is mandatory and corporations must be represented by attorneys. Despite its formalities, the court has implemented an ADR program featuring settlement judges and minitrials. Although the Court of Federal Claims does not offer accelerated or expedited procedures, it can (unlike the boards) adjudicate disputes alleging fraud and grant injunctive relief. In contrast to board decisions, which are collegial, Claims Court decisions are issued by a single judge. The contractor may appeal the decision of either tribunal to the U.S. Court of Appeals for the Federal Circuit. In addition, the Act permits the government (with the Attorney General's approval) to appeal adverse decisions; previously, the government could not appeal contract appeals board decisions. The standard of review for findings of fact by contract appeals boards is one of substantial evidence (this standard was retained from preexisting law); for Court of Federal Claims decisions, the Federal Circuit will apply a "clearly erroneous" standard to rulings on questions of fact. Practically speaking, the decision of the Federal Circuit ends the litigation. A party may not seek review by the Supreme Court as a matter of right, and the Supreme Court rarely agrees to consider government contract cases.

Consolidation of Boards of Contract Appeals. Section 847 of the National Defense Authorization Act for Fiscal Year 2006, Pub. L. No. 109-163, established the Civilian Board of Contract Appeals (CBCA) within the General Services Administration to hear contract disputes under the Contract Disputes Act. Effective January 6, 2007, contract disputes involving most non-defense executive agencies will be heard and decided by the CBCA. Most of the previously existing boards of contract appeals (e.g., those at the General Services Administration and the departments of Agriculture, Energy, Housing and Urban Development, Interior, Labor, Transportation, and Veterans Affairs) no longer exist, and board judges and other personnel at those entities were transferred to the new Civilian Board. See 71 Fed. Reg. 65825 (Nov. 9, 2006). (The CBCA's website will be located at http://www.cbca.gsa.gov.)

Appeals on contract decisions involving the Departments of Defense, Army, Navy, and Air Force as well as NASA will continue to be heard at the Armed Services Board of Contract Appeals. Contract disputes from other non-defense federal agencies will be heard by the new CBCA, except that the Postal Service and Tennessee Valley Authority will continue to operate their own boards.

Alternative Dispute Resolution. A contracting officer is specifically authorized to use ADR under the provisions of the Administrative Dispute

Resolution Act for a contract claim at any time that he or she has authority to resolve the issue in controversy. Also, if a contracting officer rejects a small business contractor's request to use ADR, he or she must provide a written explanation that cites one or more conditions in 5 U.S.C. §572(b) or other specific reasons why ADR is not appropriate for that dispute. Conversely, a contractor that rejects an agency offer to use ADR must inform the agency in writing of its specific reasons.

OFPP Guidance. The Act directed the Office of Federal Procurement Policy to issue guidelines for the establishment and procedures of contract appeals boards. The model rules developed pursuant to this mandate appear in the Appendix to this chapter. In addition, the Office of Federal Procurement Policy issued, and subsequently rescinded, a policy directive (OFPP Policy Letter 80-3) setting forth procedures for handling claims by agency contracting officers and the text of a disputes clause to be included in government contracts.

Other Provisions. In addition to establishing a single comprehensive law covering the contract disputes process for almost all government contracts (some, such as procurements by the Tennessee Valley Authority, remain outside the scope of the law), the Contract Disputes Act made several other important changes in existing law. The Act strengthened contract appeals boards, giving them subpoena power and authorizing them to grant any relief within the authority of the Court of Federal Claims.[4] Moreover, appeals boards can now hear breach of contract claims as well as those "arising under" a contract. The law also added new requirements for selecting appeals board members, intended to enhance quality and independence.

Legislative History:

Efforts to pass contract disputes legislation began after the Commission on Government Procurement issued its final report and recommendations in 1973 and reached fruition in October 1978. H.R. 11002 was introduced by Representatives Harris (D-VA.) and Kindness (R-OH) on February 20, 1978 and reported favorably by the House Judiciary Committee without hearings. (The Commission had held hearings on similar legislation the previous year.) The House passed the bill on September 26, 1978. A similar bill, S. 3178, was introduced by Senators Chiles (D-FL), Packwood (R-OR), Heinz (R-

---

[4] Amendments to the Equal Access to Justice Act in 1985 authorized the boards to award attorneys fees and expenses under the Equal Access to Justice Act, eliminating one of the distinctions between the two fora.

PA), and DeConcini (D-AZ) on June 7, 1978 and favorably reported, with amendments, by the Committees on Government Affairs and the Judiciary. The Senate took up floor consideration of the bill on October 12, 1978, agreeing to amendments that exempted the Tennessee Valley Authority from certain of the Act's requirements, added the certification requirement, deleted a requirement that an informal settlement conference be afforded contractors, and changed the standard of judicial review of contract appeals board decisions from "clearly erroneous" to "substantial evidence," among other things. The Senate then passed H.R. 11002, amended to contain the amended provisions of S. 3178 and the House agreed to the Senate-passed version the next day.

Perhaps because it was passed quickly, at the end of the legislative session, the Contract Disputes Act (including the Senate amendments to it) was not the subject of extensive debate. However, the Congressional Record for October 12 does include a brief explanation of the amendments agreed to on the floor (95 Cong. Rec. 36,261-68).

Source Note:

There are considerable materials available on federal contract law generally and on contract claims and the Contract Disputes Act specifically. Most of these materials are aimed at practicing attorneys specializing in government contract law. The items listed here are representative of the types of materials available; the list is by no means complete. Of these materials the services published by CCH (*Government Contracts Reporter* and *Contract Appeals Board Decisions*) are the most comprehensive and, because they are frequently updated, the most current. *The Government Contractor* (Thomson West) also provides up-to-date information and analysis.

Government Contract Disputes and *Government Contract Claims* include extensive historical material and information on other aspects of government contract law as well as the Contract Disputes Act. Crowell and Pou's *Appealing Government Contract Decisions* (1990) examines agency experience with, and gives advice on, using ADR in contract claims.

Note that pre-1983 publications do not reflect amendments to the Act made by the Federal Courts Improvement Act of 1982, which (among other things) created the Court of Appeals for the Federal Circuit and gave it jurisdiction over appeals from decisions of contract appeals boards and decisions of the Court of Federal Claims.

Bibliography:

I. Legislative History

1. *Hearings on H.R. 664 and Related Bills before the Subcommittee on Administrative Law and Government Relations of the House Committee on the Judiciary*, 95th Cong., 1st Sess. (1977).
2. House of Representatives Committee on the Judiciary, *Report to Accompany H.R. 11002*, H.R. Rep. 95-1556 95th Cong., 2d Sess. (1978).
3. *Joint Hearings before the Subcommittee on Federal Spending Practices and Open Government Senate Governmental Affairs Committee, and the Subcommittee on Citizens and Shareholders Rights and Remedies, Senate Judiciary Committee, on S. 3178 and S. 2787*, 95th Cong. 2d Sess. (1978).
4. Senate Comms. on Governmental Affairs and the Judiciary, *Report to Accompany S. 3178*, S. Rep. No. 95-1118, 95th Cong., 2d Sess. (1978), *reprinted in* 1978 U.S. Code Cong. & Ad. News 5235.

II. Other Government Documents

1. Commission on Government Procurement, *Report of the Commission on Government Procurement*, Vol. 4 (Washington, DC 1972).
2. Office of Federal Procurement Policy, Proposed Uniform Rules of Procedure for Boards of Contract Appeals, 44 Fed. Reg. 5210 (Jan. 25, 1979).
3. Office of Federal Procurement Policy, Interim Final Uniform Rules of Procedure for Boards of Contract Appeals and Related Regulations, 44 Fed. Reg. 12,519 (March 7, 1979).
4. Office of Federal Procurement Policy, Final Uniform Rules of Procedure for Boards of Contract Appeals Under the Contract Disputes Act of 1978, 44 Fed. Reg. 34,227 (June 14, 1979).
5. T. Madden, *Certification Requirements under the Contract Disputes Act*, Report to the Administrative Conference of the U.S, 1983 ACUS 23.
6. Administrative Conference of the U.S., Recommendation 83-1, *The Certification Requirement in the Contract Disputes Act*, 48 Fed. Reg. 31,179 (July 17, 1983).
7. Government Accounting Office, *The Armed Services Board of Contract Appeals Has Operated Independently*, GAO/NSIAD-85-102, B-198620 (1985).
8. E. Crowell & C. Pou, *Appealing Government Contract Decisions: Reducing the Cost and Delay of Procurement Litigation*, Report to the Administrative Conference of the U.S., 1987 ACUS 1139, *portions reprinted in* 49 Maryland L. Rev. 183 (1990).

9. Administrative Conference of the U.S., Recommendation 87-11, *Alternatives for Resolving Government Contract Disputes*, 52 Fed. Reg. 49,148 (Dec. 30, 1987).

10. R. Bednar, *Government Contracting Officers Should Make Greater Use of ADR Techniques in Resolving Contract Disputes*, Report to the Administrative Conference of the U.S., 1989 ACUS 149.

11. Administrative Conference of the U.S., Recommendation 89-2, *Contracting Officers' Management of Disputes*, 54 Fed. Reg. 28,967 (July 10, 1989).

12. General Services Administration, Board of Contract Appeals; BCA Case 2006–61-1; Rules of Procedure of the Civilian Board of Contract Appeals, Interim rule, 72 Fed. Reg. 36,794, (July 5, 2007).

III. Reports and Periodicals

1. BNA, *Federal Contracts Report* (published weekly; reports major developments in government contracting, including legislation, regulations, administrative policies, court and board decisions).

2. CCH, *Contract Appeals Decisions* (published periodically; includes the full text of decisions by boards of contract appeals).

3. CCH, *Government Contracts Reporter* (published periodically; includes current information and new developments related to statutes, regulations, cases, and legislation, as well as the Federal Acquisition Regulation and agency supplements; current edition available only in electronic format).

4. Federal Publications, *Briefing Papers* (published periodically; practical, topical papers on government contracting issues—includes an annual "Procurement Review," surveying significant developments of the preceding year, and an annual "Procurement Bibliography," citing most procurement articles published during the previous year).

5. Federal Publications, *Federal Court Procurement Decisions* (published periodically; provides government contract decisions issued by the Court of Federal Claims, the Court of Appeals for the Federal Circuit, and the Supreme Court, including decisions by the Federal Circuit that are designated not to be cited as precedent because they do not contribute significantly to the body of law).

6. Federal Publications, *The Government Contractor* (published periodically; reports on and analyzes legal rulings and other significant developments, such as new and proposed laws and regulations).

7. Federal Publications, *Yearbook of Procurement Articles* (published in annual volumes from 1940-1990; no longer published; contains photo-reproductions of significant procurement articles written during the prior year).

8. Management Concepts, *Federal Acquisition Report* (published periodically; highlights contract news, including legislation, regulatory changes, and legal decisions).

9. Thomson West, *The Nash & Cibinic Report* (published monthly; provides opinion and advice on current government contract issues).

10. National Contract Management Association, *Journal of Contract Management* (published annually; contains articles on issues of government contract administration and highlights legislative and regulatory developments).

11. Section of Public Contract Law, American Bar Association, *Public Contract Law Journal* (published quarterly; a law review with a public contract focus).

12. Section of Public Contract Law, American Bar Association, *An Ounce of Prevention: Best Practices in Dispute Avoidance for Government Contracting* (ABA, 2002).

IV. Texts, Articles, and Instructional Materials

1. Anthony & Smith, *The Federal Courts Improvement Act of 1982: Its Impact on the Resolution of Federal Contract Disputes*, 13 Pub. Cont. L.J. 201 (1983).

2. Arnavas & Ferrell, *Motions Before Contract Appeals Boards*, Briefing Papers No. 86-9 (Fed. Pubs., 1986).

3. D. Arnavas & W. Ruberry, *Government Contract Guidebook* (Fed. Pubs., 1992 with supplements).

4. Blum, *Government Contract Guidebook Workbook* (Fed. Pubs., 3rd ed. 1990).

5. Board of Contract Appeals Committee, Federal Bar Association, *Manual for Practice before Boards of Contract Appeals* (Fed. B.A., 1981).

6. Cibinic, *What's a "Claim": Is Prior Disagreement Necessary?*, 2 N&CR ¶25 (Keiser Pubs., 1988).

7. J. Cibinic & R. Nash, *Administration of Government Contracts* (Government Contracts Program, Geo. Wash. U., 3rd ed. 1995).

8. J. Cibinic & R. Nash, *Government Contract Claims* (Government Contracts Program, Geo. Wash. U., 1981).

9. Coburn, *The Contract Disputes Act of 1978* (Practicing Law Institute, 1982).

10. Dees & Churchill, *Government Contract Disputes and Remedies: Corrective Legislation is Required*, 14 Pub. Cont. L.J. 201 (1984).

11. Dover & Polack, *Invoking the Contract Disputes Act—Potential Pitfalls*, Briefing Papers No. 90-8 (Fed. Pubs., 1990).

12. Fugh & Nagle, *The Disputes Process—A Management Tool: Advice for Contracting Personnel*, The Army Lawyer, Oct. 1989, at 4.

13. Ganther, *Representing the Federal Government Contractor*, 70 Florida B. J. 58 (April 1996).

14. Hinton, *Post-Contract Disputes Act Jurisdiction over Nonmonetary Contract Disputes: A Critique of Malone v. United States*, 19 Pub. Cont. L. J. 174 (1989).

15. J. Howell, *The Role of the Office of Federal Procurement Policy in the Management of the Boards of Contract Appeals: From Great Expectations to Paradise Lost?*, 28 Pub. Cont. L. J. 559 (1999).

16. Janik & Rhodes, *Contractor Claims for Relief under Illegal Contracts with the Government*, 45 Am. U. L. Rev. 1949 (1996).

17. Keyes, *Government Contracts in a Nutshell* (4th ed. Thomson West, 2004).

18. F. Lees. *Consolidation of Boards of Contract Appeals: An Old Idea Whose Time Has Come?*, 33 Pub. Contract L. J. (2004).

19. Lipman, *Basics of Government Contracting* (audio cassettes) (Fed. Pubs., 1990).

20. J. McBride & T. Touhey, *Government Contracts: Cyclopedic Guide to Law Administration and Procedure* (Matthew Bender, 1996 with periodic updates).

21. J. Nagle, *A History of Government Contracting* (Geo. Wash. Univ., 1999).

22. Nash, *Litigating Contract Disputes: Expediting Appeals Board Cases*, 4 N&CR ¶39 (Keiser Pubs., 1990).

23. Nash, *The Contract Disputes Act: A Prescription for Wheelspinning*, 4 N&CR ¶29 (Keiser Pubs., 1990).

24. R. Nash, S. Schooner, & K. O'Brien, *The Government Contracts Reference Book: A Comprehensive Guide to the Language of Procurement* (Government Contracts Program, Geo. Wash. U., 1998).

25. Peacock, *Discovery Before Boards of Contracts Appeals*, 13 Pub. Cont. L. J. 1 (1982).

26. Pettit, Anthony, Joseph & Vacketta, *Contract Disputes Act of 1978: Explanation and Analysis*, Briefing Papers No. 79-2 (Fed. Pubs., 1979).

27. Pettit, Vacketta, & Anthony, *Government Contract Default Termination* (Fed. Pubs. 1993).

28. Reifel & Bastianelli, *Contracting Officer Authority*, Briefing Papers No. 86-4 (Fed. Pubs., 1986).

29. D. Riley, *Federal Contracts Grants & Assistance* (McGraw-Hill, 1983 & supplements).

30. S. Schooner, *Pondering the Decline of Federal Government Contract Litigation in the United States*, 8 Pub. Procurement L. Rev. 242 (1999).

31. S. Schooner & K. Coleman, *The CDA at Twenty: A Brief Assessment of BCA Activity*, 34 Procurement Law 10 (1999).

32. Section of Public Contract Law, American Bar Association, *Current Issues in Disputes Litigation* (ABA, 1987).

33. Section of Public Contract Law, American Bar Association, *An Ounce of Prevention: Best Practices in Dispute Avoidance for Government Contracting* (2002).

34. Section of Public Contract Law, American Bar Association, *Alternative Dispute Resolution: A Practical Guide for Resolving Government Contract Controversies*, (2nd ed. 2006).

35. Shea & Shaengold, *A Guide to the Court of Appeals for the Federal Circuit*, Briefing Papers No. 90-13 (Fed. Pubs., 1990).

36. Williams, *A Brief Look at the Armed Services Board of Contract Appeals*, Pub Cont. Newsl. at 3) (Fall 1986).

Board of Contract Appeals Regulations:

Armed Services . . . . 48 C.F.R. Chap.2, Subch. 1, Appendix A
Civilian (General Services
   Administration) . . . . 48 C.F.R. §§ 6101-05 (2007)[5]
Postal Service . . . . 39 C.F.R. Part 955
Tennessee Valley Authority . . . . 18 C.F.R. Part 1308

Appendix:

1. Contract Disputes Act of 1978, 41 U.S.C. §§601-613; 28 U.S.C. §§1346(a)(2), 1491(a)(2), 2401(a), 2414, 2510, 2517; 31 U.S.C. §1304(a)(3)(C).

---

[5] The Civilian Board of Contract Appeals published interim-final rules of procedure in the *Federal Register* on July 5, 2007 (72 Fed. Reg. 36,794); these rules are published in the Code of Federal Regulations at 48 C.F.R. §§6101.1-.54 (2007). Rules for other proceedings are at §§6102-05. The Board announced that it will operate under these rules until final rules are issued.

Contract Disputes Act

Title 41, U.S. Code

§601. Definitions

As used in this chapter—

(1) the term "agency head" means the head and any assistant head of an executive agency, and may "upon the designation by" the head of an executive agency include the chief official of any principal division of the agency;

(2) the term "executive agency" means an executive department as defined in section 101 of title 5, an independent establishment as defined by section 104 of title 5 (except that it shall not include the Government Accountability Office), a military department as defined by section 102 of title 5, and a wholly owned Government corporation as defined by section 9101(3) of title 31;

(3) the term "contracting officer" means any person who, by appointment in accordance with applicable regulations, has the authority to enter into and administer contracts and make determinations and findings with respect thereto. The term also includes the authorized representative of the contracting officer, acting within the limits of his authority;

(4) the term "contractor" means a party to a Government contract other than the Government;

(5) the term "Administrator" means the Administrator for Federal Procurement Policy appointed pursuant to the Office of Federal Procurement Policy Act (41 U.S.C. 401 et seq.);

(6) the terms "agency board" or "agency board of contract appeals" mean—

(A) the Armed Services Board of Contract Appeals established under section 8(a)(1) of this Act;

(B) the Civilian Board of Contract Appeals established under section 42 of the Office of Federal Procurement Policy Act (41 U.S.C. 403 et seq.);

(C) the board of contract appeals of the Tennessee Valley Authority; or

(D) the Postal Service Board of Contract Appeals established under section 8(c) of this Act;

(7) the term "Armed Services Board" means the Armed Services Board of Contract Appeals established under section 8(a)(1) of this Act;

(8) the term "Civilian Board" means the Civilian Board of Contract Appeals established under section 42 of the Office of Federal Procurement Policy Act (41 U.S.C. 403 et seq.); and

(9) the term "misrepresentation of fact" means a false statement of substantive fact, or any conduct which leads to a belief of a substantive fact material to proper understanding of the matter in hand, made with intent to deceive or mislead.

(Pub. L. No. 95-563, Sec. 2, Nov. 1, 1978, 92 Stat. 2383; Pub. L. No. 104-106, div. D, title XLIII, Sec. 4322(b)(5), Feb. 10, 1996, 110 Stat. 677; Pub. L. No. 109-163, div. A, title VIII, subtitle E, Sec. 847(d)(1), Jan. 6, 2006, 119 Stat. 3393.)

§602. Applicability of law

(a) Executive agency contracts
Unless otherwise specifically provided herein, this chapter applies to any express or implied contract (including those of the nonappropriated fund activities described in sections 1346 and 1491 of title 28) entered into by an executive agency for—
    (1) the procurement of property, other than real property in being;
    (2) the procurement of services;
    (3) the procurement of construction, alteration, repair or maintenance of real property; or,
    (4) the disposal of personal property.
(b) Tennessee Valley Authority contracts
With respect to contracts of the Tennessee Valley Authority, the provisions of this chapter shall apply only to those contracts which contain a disputes clause requiring that a contract dispute be resolved through an agency administrative process. Notwithstanding any other provision of this chapter, contracts of the Tennessee Valley Authority for the sale of fertilizer or electric power or related to the conduct or operation of the electric power system shall be excluded from the chapter.
(c) Foreign government or international organization contracts
This chapter does not apply to a contract with a foreign government, or agency thereof, or international organization, or subsidiary body thereof, if the head of the agency determines that the application of the chapter to the contract would not be in the public interest.

(Pub. L. No. 95-563, Sec. 3, Nov. 1, 1978, 92 Stat. 2383.)

§603. Maritime contracts

Appeals under paragraph (g) of section 607 of this title and suits under section 609 of this title, arising out of maritime contracts, shall be governed by chapter 20 or 22 of title 46, Appendix, as applicable, to the extent that those chapters are not inconsistent with this chapter.

(Pub. L. No. 95-563, Sec. 4, Nov. 1, 1978, 92 Stat. 2384.)

§604. Fraudulent claims

If a contractor is unable to support any part of his claim and it is determined that such inability is attributable to misrepresentation of fact or fraud on the part of the contractor, he shall be liable to the Government for an amount equal to such unsupported part of the claim in addition to all costs to the Government attributable to the cost of reviewing said part of his claim. Liability under this subsection[6] shall be determined within six years of the commission of such misrepresentation of fact or fraud.

(Pub. L. No. 95-563, Sec. 5, Nov. 1, 1978, 92 Stat. 2384.)

§605. Decision by contracting officer

(a) Contractor claims
All claims by a contractor against the government relating to a contract shall be in writing and shall be submitted to the contracting officer for a decision. All claims by the government against a contractor relating to a contract shall be the subject of a decision by the contracting officer. Each claim by a contractor against the government relating to a contract and each claim by the government against a contractor relating to a contract shall be submitted within 6 years after the accrual of the claim. The preceding sentence does not apply to a claim by the government against a contractor that is based on a claim by the contractor involving fraud. The contracting officer shall issue his decisions in writing, and shall mail or otherwise furnish a copy of the decision to the contractor. The decision shall state the reasons for the decision reached, and shall inform the contractor of his rights as provided in this chapter. Specific findings of fact are not required, but, if made, shall not be binding in any subsequent proceeding. The authority of this subsection shall not extend to a claim or dispute for penalties or forfeitures prescribed by statute or regulation which another Federal agency is specifically authorized to administer, settle, or determine. This section shall not authorize any agency head to settle, compromise, pay, or otherwise adjust any claim involving fraud.

(b) Review; performance of contract pending appeal
The contracting officer's decision on the claim shall be final and conclusive and not subject to review by any forum, tribunal, or Government agency,

---

[6] So in original. Probably should be "section."

unless an appeal or suit is timely commenced as authorized by this chapter. Nothing in this chapter shall prohibit executive agencies from including a clause in government contracts requiring that pending final decision of an appeal, action, or final settlement, a contractor shall proceed diligently with performance of the contract in accordance with the contracting officer's decision.

(c) Amount of claim; certification; notification; time of issuance; presumption; authorization of certifier

(1) A contracting officer shall issue a decision on any submitted claim of $100,000 or less within sixty days from his receipt of a written request from the contractor that a decision be rendered within that period. For claims of more than $100,000, the contractor shall certify that the claim is made in good faith, that the supporting data are accurate and complete to the best of his knowledge and belief, that the amount requested accurately reflects the contract adjustment for which the contractor believes the government is liable, and that the certifier is duly authorized to certify the claim on behalf of the contractor.

(2) A contracting officer shall, within sixty days of receipt of a submitted certified claim over $100,000—

    (A) issue a decision; or

    (B) notify the contractor of the time within which a decision will be issued.

(3) The decision of a contracting officer on submitted claims shall be issued within a reasonable time, in accordance with regulations promulgated by the agency, taking into account such factors as the size and complexity of the claim and the adequacy of the information in support of the claim provided by the contractor.

(4) A contractor may request the tribunal concerned to direct a contracting officer to issue a decision in a specified period of time, as determined by the tribunal concerned, in the event of undue delay on the part of the contracting officer.

(5) Any failure by the contracting officer to issue a decision on a contract claim within the period required will be deemed to be a decision by the contracting officer denying the claim and will authorize the commencement of the appeal or suit on the claim as otherwise provided in this chapter. However, in the event an appeal or suit is so commenced in the absence of a prior decision by the contracting officer, the tribunal concerned may, at its option, stay the proceedings to obtain a decision on the claim by the contracting officer.

(6) The contracting officer shall have no obligation to render a final decision on any claim of more than $100,000 that is not certified in accordance with paragraph (1) if, within 60 days after receipt of the claim, the contracting

officer notifies the contractor in writing of the reasons why any attempted certification was found to be defective. A defect in the certification of a claim shall not deprive a court or an agency board of contract appeals of jurisdiction over that claim. Prior to the entry of a final judgment by a court or a decision by an agency board of contract appeals, the court or agency board shall require a defective certification to be corrected.

(7) The certification required by paragraph (1) may be executed by any person duly authorized to bind the contractor with respect to the claim.

(d) Alternative means of dispute resolution

Notwithstanding any other provision of this chapter, a contractor and a contracting officer may use any alternative means of dispute resolution under subchapter IV of chapter 5 of title 5, or other mutually agreeable procedures, for resolving claims. The contractor shall certify the claim when required to do so as provided under subsection (c)(1) of this section or as otherwise required by law. All provisions of subchapter IV of chapter 5 of title 5 shall apply to such alternative means of dispute resolution.

(e) Termination of authority to engage in alternative means of dispute resolution; savings provision

In any case in which the contracting officer rejects a contractor's request for alternative dispute resolution proceedings, the contracting officer shall provide the contractor with a written explanation, citing one or more of the conditions in section 572(b) of title 5 or such other specific reasons that alternative dispute resolution procedures are inappropriate for the resolution of the dispute. In any case in which a contractor rejects a request of an agency for alternative dispute resolution proceedings, the contractor shall inform the agency in writing of the contractor's specific reasons for rejecting the request.

(Pub. L. No. 95-563, Sec. 6, Nov. 1, 1978, 92 Stat. 2384; as amended Pub. L. No. 101-552, Sec. 6(a), Nov. 15, 1990, 104 Stat. 2745; Pub. L. No. 102-572, title IX, Sec. 907(a)(1), Oct. 29, 1992, 106 Stat. 4518; Pub. L. No. 103-355, title II, Sec. 2351(a)((1)), (b), (e), 2352, Oct. 13, 1994, 108 Stat. 3322; Pub. L. No. 104-106, div. D, title XLIII, Sec. 4321(a)(6), (7), 4322(b)(6), Feb. 10, 1996, 110 Stat. 671, 677; Pub. L. No.104-320, Sec. 6, Oct. 19, 1996, 110 Stat. 3871; Pub. L. No. 105-85, div. A, title X, Sec. 1073(g)(3), Nov. 18, 1997, 111 Stat. 1906.)

§606. Contractor's right of appeal to board of contract appeals

Within ninety days from the date of receipt of a contracting officer's decision under section 605 of this title, the contractor may appeal such decision to an agency board of contract appeals, as provided in section 607 of this title.

(Pub. L. No. 95-563, Sec. 7, Nov. 1, 1978, 92 Stat. 2385.)

§607. Agency boards of contracts appeals

(a) Establishment; consultation; Tennessee Valley Authority

(1) An Armed Services Board of Contract Appeals may be established within the Department of Defense when the Secretary of Defense, after consultation with the Administrator, determines from a workload study that the volume of contract claims justifies the establishment of a full-time agency board of at least three members who shall have no other inconsistent duties. Workload studies will be updated at least once every three years and submitted to the Administrator.

(2) The Board of Directors of the Tennessee Valley Authority may establish a board of contract appeals for the Authority of an indeterminate number of members.

(b) Appointment of members; chairman; compensation

(1) The members of the Armed Services Board of Contract Appeals shall be selected and appointed to serve in the same manner as administrative law judges appointed pursuant to section 3105 of title 5, with an additional requirement that such members shall have had not fewer than five years' experience in public contract law. Full-time members of such Board serving as such on the effective date of this chapter shall be considered qualified. The chairman and vice chairman of such Board shall be designated by the Secretary of Defense from members so appointed. Compensation for the chairman, the vice chairman, and all other members of such Board shall be determined under section 5372a of title 5.

(2) The Board of Directors of the Tennessee Valley Authority shall establish criteria for the appointment of members to its agency board of contract appeals established in subsection (a)(2) of this section, and shall designate a chairman of such board. The chairman and all other members of such board shall receive compensation, at the daily equivalent of the rates determined under section 5372a of title 5, for each day they are engaged in the actual performance of their duties as members of the board.

(c) Appeals; inter-agency arrangements

There is established an agency board of contract appeals to be known as the "Postal Service Board of Contract Appeals". Such board shall have jurisdiction to decide any appeal from a decision of a contracting officer of the United States Postal Service or the Postal Rate Commission relative to a contract made by either agency. Such board shall consist of judges appointed by the Postmaster General who shall meet the qualifications of and serve in the same manner as members of the Civilian Board of Contract Appeals. This Act shall apply to contract disputes before the Postal Service Board of Contract Appeals in the same manner as they apply to contract disputes before the Civilian Board.

(d) Jurisdiction

The Armed Services Board shall have jurisdiction to decide any appeal from a decision of a contracting officer of the Department of Defense, the Department of the Army, the Department of the Navy, the Department of the Air Force, or the National Aeronautics and Space Administration relative to a contract made by that department or agency. The Civilian Board shall have jurisdiction to decide any appeal from a decision of a contracting officer of any executive agency (other than the Department of Defense, the Department of the Army, the Department of the Navy, the Department of the Air Force, the National Aeronautics and Space Administration, the United States Postal Service, the Postal Rate Commission, or the Tennessee Valley Authority) relative to a contract made by that agency. Each other agency board shall have jurisdiction to decide any appeal from a decision of a contracting officer relative to a contract made by its agency. In exercising this jurisdiction, the agency board is authorized to grant any relief that would be available to a litigant asserting a contract claim in the United States Court of Federal Claims.

(e) Decisions

An agency board shall provide to the fullest extent practicable, informal, expeditious, and inexpensive resolution of disputes, and shall issue a decision in writing or take other appropriate action on each appeal submitted, and shall mail or otherwise furnish a copy of the decision to the contractor and the contracting officer.

(f) Accelerated appeal disposition

The rules of each agency board shall include a procedure for the accelerated disposition of any appeal from a decision of a contracting officer where the amount in dispute is $100,000 or less. The accelerated procedure shall be applicable at the sole election of only the contractor. Appeals under the accelerated procedure shall be resolved, whenever possible, within one hundred and eighty days from the date the contractor elects to utilize such procedure.

(g) Review

(1) The decision of an agency board of contract appeals shall be final, except that—

(A) a contractor may appeal such a decision to the United States Court of Appeals for the Federal Circuit within one hundred twenty days after the date of receipt of a copy of such decision, or

(B) the agency head, if he determines that an appeal should be taken, and with the prior approval of the Attorney General, transmits the decision of the board of contract appeals to the Court of Appeals for the Federal Circuit for judicial review under section 1295 of title 28, within one hundred and twenty days from the date of the agency's receipt of a copy of the board's decision.

(2) Notwithstanding the provisions of paragraph (1), the decision of the board of contract appeals of the Tennessee Valley Authority shall be final, except that—

(A) a contractor may appeal such a decision to a United States district court pursuant to the provisions of section 1337 of title 28, within one hundred twenty days after the date of receipt of a copy of such decision, or

(B) The Tennessee Valley Authority may appeal the decision to a United States district court pursuant to the provisions of section 1337 of title 28, within one hundred twenty days after the date of the decision in any case.

(3) An award by an arbitrator under this chapter shall be reviewed pursuant to sections 9 through 13 of title 9, except that the court may set aside or limit any award that is found to violate limitations imposed by Federal statute.

(Pub. L. No. 95-563, Sec. 8, Nov. 1, 1978, 92 Stat. 2385; Pub. L. No. 97-164, title I, Sec. 156, 160(a)(15), Apr. 2, 1982, 96 Stat. 47, 48; as amended Pub. L. No. 101-509, title V, Sec. 529 (title I, Sec. 104(d)(4)), Nov. 5, 1990, 104 Stat. 1427, 1447; Pub. L. No. 101-552, Sec. 6(b), Nov. 15, 1990, 104 Stat. 2746; Pub. L. No. 102-572, title IX, Sec. 902(b)(1), Oct. 29, 1992, 106 Stat. 4516; Pub. L. No. 103-355, title II, Sec. 2351(c), Oct. 13, 1994, 108 Stat. 3322, Pub. L. No. 109-163, div. A, title VIII, subtitle E, Sec. 847(d)(2)-(4), Jan. 6, 2006, 119 Stat. 3393.)

§608. Small claims

(a) Accelerated disposition of appeals

The rules of each agency board shall include a procedure for the expedited disposition of any appeal from a decision of a contracting officer where the amount in dispute is $50,000 or less or, in the case of a small business concern (as defined in the Small Business Act and regulations under that Act), $150,000 or less. The small claims procedure shall be applicable at the sole election of the contractor.

(b) Simplified rules of procedure

The small claims procedure shall provide for simplified rules of procedure to facilitate the decision of any appeal thereunder. Such appeals may be decided by a single member of the agency board with such concurrences as may be provided by rule or regulation.

(c) Time of decision

Appeals under the small claims procedure shall be resolved, whenever possible, within one hundred twenty days from the date on which the contractor elects to utilize such procedure.

(d) Finality of decision
A decision against the Government or the contractor reached under the small claims procedure shall be final and conclusive and shall not be set aside except in cases of fraud.

(e) Effect of decision
Administrative determinations and final decisions under this section shall have no value as precedent for future cases under this chapter.

(f) Review of requisite amount in controversy
The Administrator is authorized to review at least every three years, beginning with the third year after November 1, 1978, the dollar amount defined in subsection (a) of this section as a small claim, and based upon economic indexes selected by the Administrator adjust that level accordingly.

(Pub. L. No. 95-563, Sec. 9, Nov. 1, 1978, 92 Stat. 2387; as amended Pub. L. No. 103-355, title II, Sec. 2351(d), Oct. 13, 1994, 108 Stat. 3322; Pub. L. No. 109-364, div. A, title VIII, subtitle E, Sec. 857, Oct. 17, 2006, 120 Stat. 2349.)

§609. Judicial review of board decisions

(a) Actions in United States Court of Federal Claims; district court actions; time for filing

(1) Except as provided in paragraph (2), and in lieu of appealing the decision of the contracting officer under section 605 of this title to an agency board, a contractor may bring an action directly on the claim in the United States Court of Federal Claims, notwithstanding any contract provision, regulation, or rule of law to the contrary.

(2) In the case of an action against the Tennessee Valley Authority, the contractor may only bring an action directly on the claim in a United States district court pursuant to section 1337 of title 28, notwithstanding any contract provision, regulation, or rule of law to the contrary.

(3) Any action under paragraph (1) or (2) shall be filed within twelve months from the date of the receipt by the contractor of the decision of the contracting officer concerning the claim, and shall proceed de novo in accordance with the rules of the appropriate court.

(b) Finality of board decision
In the event of an appeal by a contractor or the Government from a decision of any agency board pursuant to section 607 of this title, notwithstanding any contract provision, regulation, or rules of law to the contrary, the decision of the agency board on any question of law shall not be final or conclusive, but the decision on any question of fact shall be final and conclusive and shall not be set aside unless the decision is fraudulent, or arbitrary, or capricious, or so

grossly erroneous as to necessarily imply bad faith, or if such decision is not supported by substantial evidence.

(c) Remand or retention of case

In any appeal by a contractor or the Government from a decision of an agency board pursuant to section 607 of this title, the court may render an opinion and judgment and remand the case for further action by the agency board or by the executive agency as appropriate, with such direction as the court considers just and proper.

(d) Consolidation

If two or more suits arising from one contract are filed in the United States Court of Federal Claims and one or more agency boards, for the convenience of parties or witnesses or in the interest of justice, the United States Court of Federal Claims may order the consolidation of such suits in that court or transfer any suits to or among the agency boards involved.

(e) Judgments as to fewer than all claims

In any suit filed pursuant to this chapter involving two or more claims, counterclaims, cross-claims, or third-party claims, and where a portion of one such claim can be divided for purposes of decision or judgment, and in any such suit where multiple parties are involved, the court, whenever such action is appropriate, may enter a judgment as to one or more but fewer than all of the claims, portions thereof, or parties.

(f) Advisory opinions

(1) Whenever an action involving an issue described in paragraph (2) is pending in a district court of the United States, the district court may request a board of contract appeals to provide the court with an advisory opinion on the matters of contract interpretation at issue.

(2) An issue referred to in paragraph (1) is any issue that could be the proper subject of a final decision of a contracting officer appealable under this chapter.

(3) A district court shall direct any request under paragraph (1) to the board of contract appeals having jurisdiction under this chapter to adjudicate appeals of contract claims under the contract or contracts being interpreted by the court.

(4) After receiving a request for an advisory opinion under paragraph (1), a board of contract appeals shall provide the advisory opinion in a timely manner to the district court making the request.

(Pub. L. No. 95-563, Sec. 10, Nov. 1, 1978, 92 Stat. 2388; Pub. L. No. 97-164, title I, Sec. 157, 160(a)(15), 161(10), Apr. 2, 1982, 96 Stat. 47-49; as amended Pub. L. No. 102-572, title IX, Sec. 902(b)(1), Oct. 29, 1992, 106 Stat. 4516; Pub. L. No. 103-355, title II, Sec. 2354, Oct. 13, 1994, 108 Stat. 3323.)

§610. Subpena, discovery, and deposition

A member of an agency board of contract appeals may administer oaths to witnesses, authorize depositions and discovery proceedings, and require by subpena the attendance of witnesses, and production of books and papers, for the taking of testimony or evidence by deposition or in the hearing of an appeal by the agency board. In case of contumacy or refusal to obey a subpena by a person who resides, is found, or transacts business within the jurisdiction of a United States district court, the court, upon application of the agency board through the Attorney General; or upon application by the board of contract appeals of the Tennessee Valley Authority, shall have jurisdiction to issue the person an order requiring him to appear before the agency board or a member thereof, to produce evidence or to give testimony, or both. Any failure of any such person to obey the order of the court may be punished by the court as a contempt thereof.

(Pub. L. No. 95-563, Sec. 11, Nov. 1, 1978, 92 Stat. 2388.)

§611. Interest

Interest on amounts found due contractors on claims shall be paid to the contractor from the date the contracting officer receives the claim pursuant to section 605(a) of this title from the contractor until payment thereof. The interest provided for in this section shall be paid at the rate established by the Secretary of the Treasury pursuant to Public Law 92-41 (85 Stat. 97) for the Renegotiation Board.

(Pub. L. No. 95-563, Sec. 12, Nov. 1, 1978, 92 Stat. 2389.)

§612. Payment of claims

(a) Judgments
Any judgment against the United States on a claim under this chapter shall be paid promptly in accordance with the procedures provided by section 1304 of title 31.
(b) Monetary awards
Any monetary award to a contractor by an agency board of contract appeals shall be paid promptly in accordance with the procedures contained in subsection (a) of this section.
(c) Reimbursement
Payments made pursuant to subsections (a) and (b) of this section shall be reimbursed to the fund provided by section 1304 of title 31 by the agency

whose appropriations were used for the contract out of available funds or by obtaining additional appropriations for such purposes.

(d) Tennessee Valley Authority

(1) Notwithstanding the provisions of subsection (a) through (c) of this section, any judgment against the Tennessee Valley Authority on a claim under this chapter shall be paid promptly in accordance with the provisions of section 831h(b) of title 16.

(2) Notwithstanding the provisions of subsection (a) through (c), any monetary award to a contractor by the board of contract appeals for the Tennessee Valley Authority shall be paid in accordance with the provisions of section 831h(b) of title 16.

(Pub. L. No. 95-563, Sec. 13, Nov. 1, 1978, 92 Stat. 2389; as amended Pub. L. No. 104-106, div. D, title XLIII, Sec. 4322(b)(7), Feb. 10, 1996, 110 Stat. 677.)

§613. Separability

If any provision of this chapter, or the application of such provision to any persons or circumstances, is held invalid, the remainder of this chapter, or the application of such provision to persons or circumstances other than those to which it is held invalid, shall not be affected thereby.

(Pub. L. No. 95-563, Sec. 15, Nov. 1, 1978, 92 Stat. 2391.)

* * * *

Title 28, U.S. Code

§1346. United States as defendant

(a) The district courts shall have original jurisdiction, concurrent with the United States Court of Federal Claims, of:

(1) · · · ·

(2) Any other civil action or claim against the United States, not exceeding $10,000 in amount, founded either upon the Constitution, or any Act of Congress, or any regulation of an executive department, or upon any express or implied contract with the United States, or for liquidated or unliquidated damages in cases not sounding in tort, except that the district courts shall not have jurisdiction of any civil action or claim against the United States founded upon any express or implied contract with the United States or for liquidated or unliquidated damages in cases not sounding in tort which are subject to

sections 8(g)(1) and 10(a)(1) of the Contract Disputes Act of 1978. For the purpose of this paragraph, an express or implied contract with the Army and Air Force Exchange Service, Navy Exchanges, Marine Corps Exchanges, Coast Guard Exchanges, or Exchange Councils of the National Aeronautics and Space Administration shall be considered an express or implied contract with the United States.

(June 25, 1948, ch. 646, 62 Stat. 933; Apr. 25, 1949, ch. 92, Sec. 2(a), 63 Stat. 62; May 24, 1949, ch. 139, Sec. 80(a), (b), 63 Stat. 101; Oct. 31, 1951, ch. 655, Sec. 50(b), 65 Stat. 727; July 30, 1954, ch. 648, Sec. 1, 68 Stat. 589; Pub. L. No. 85-508, Sec. 12(e), July 7, 1958, 72 Stat. 348; Pub. L. No. 88-519, Aug. 30, 1964, 78 Stat. 699; Pub. L. No. 89-719, title II, Sec. 202(a), Nov. 2, 1966, 80 Stat.1148; Pub. L. No. 91-350, Sec. 1(a), July 23, 1970, 84 Stat. 449; Pub. L. No. 92-562, Sec. 1, Oct. 25, 1972, 86 Stat. 1176; Pub. L. No. 94-455, title XII, Sec. 1204(c)(1), title XIII, Sec. 1306(b)(7), Oct. 4, 1976, 90 Stat. 1697, 1719; Pub. L. No. 95-563, Sec. 14(a), Nov. 1, 1978, 92 Stat. 2389; Pub. L. No. 97-164, title I, Sec. 129, Apr. 2, 1982, 96 Stat. 39; Pub. L. No. 97-248, title IV, Sec. 402(c)(17), Sept. 3, 1982, 96 Stat. 669; Pub. L. No. 99-514, Sec. 2, Oct. 22, 1986, 100 Stat. 2095; Pub. L. No. 102-572, title IX, Sec.902(b)(1), Oct. 29, 1992, 106 Stat. 4516; Pub. L. No. 104-134, title I, Sec. 101((a)) (title VIII, Sec.806), Apr. 26, 1996, 110 Stat. 1321, 1321-75; renumbered title I, Pub. L. No. 104-140, Sec. 1(a), May 2, 1996, 110 Stat. 1327; Pub. L. No. 104-331, Sec. 3(b)(1), Oct. 26, 1996, 110 Stat. 4069.)

§1491. Claims against United States generally; actions involving Tennessee Valley Authority

(a)

(1) · · · ·

(2) To provide an entire remedy and to complete the relief afforded by the judgment, the court may, as an incident of and collateral to any such judgment, issue orders directing restoration to office or position, placement in appropriate duty or retirement status, and correction of applicable records, and such orders may be issued to any appropriate official of the United States. In any case within its jurisdiction, the court shall have the power to remand appropriate matters to any administrative or executive body or official with such direction as it may deem proper and just. The Court of Federal Claims shall have jurisdiction to render judgment upon any claim by or against, or dispute with, a contractor arising under section 10(a)(1) of the Contract Disputes Act of 1978, including a dispute concerning termination of a contract, rights in tangible or intangible property, compliance with cost accounting standards, and other nonmonetary disputes on which a decision of the contracting officer has been issued under section 6 of that Act.

(June 25, 1948, ch. 646, 62 Stat. 940; July 28, 1953, ch. 253, Sec. 7, 67 Stat. 226; Sept. 3, 1954, ch. 1263, Sec. 44(a), (b), 68 Stat. 1241; Pub. L. No. 91-350, Sec. 1(b), July 23, 1970, 84 Stat. 449; Pub. L. No. 92-415, Sec. 1, Aug. 29, 1972, 86 Stat. 652; Pub. L. No. 95-563, Sec. 14(i), Nov. 1, 1978, 92 Stat. 2391; Pub. L. No. 96-417, title V, Sec. 509, Oct. 10, 1980, 94 Stat. 1743; Pub. L. No. 97-164, title I, Sec. 133(a), Apr. 2, 1982, 96 Stat. 39; Pub. L. No. 102-572, title IX, Sec. 902(a), 907(b)(1), Oct. 29, 1992, 106 Stat. 4516, 4519; Pub. L. No. 104-320, Sec. 12(a), Oct. 19, 1996, 110 Stat. 3874.)

§2401. Time for commencing action against United States

(a) Except as provided by the Contract Disputes Act of 1978, every civil action commenced against the United States shall be barred unless the complaint is filed within six years after the right of action first accrues. The action of any person under legal disability or beyond the seas at the time the claim accrues may be commenced within three years after the disability ceases.

(June 25, 1948, ch. 646, 62 Stat. 971; Apr. 25, 1949, ch. 92, Sec. 1, 63 Stat. 62; Pub. L. No. 86-238, Sec. 1(3), Sept. 8, 1959, 73 Stat. 472; Pub. L. No. 89-506, Sec. 7, July 18, 1966, 80 Stat. 307; Pub. L. No. 95-563, Sec. 14(b), Nov. 1, 1978, 92 Stat. 2389.)

§2414. Payment of judgments and compromise settlements

(a) Except as provided by the Contract Disputes Act of 1978, payment of final judgments rendered by a district court or the Court of International Trade against the United States shall be made on settlements by the Secretary of the Treasury. Payment of final judgments rendered by a State or foreign court or tribunal against the United States, or against its agencies or officials upon obligations or liabilities of the United States, shall be made on settlements by the Secretary of the Treasury after certification by the Attorney General that it is in the interest of the United States to pay the same.
(b) Whenever the Attorney General determines that no appeal shall be taken from a judgment or that no further review will be sought from a decision affirming the same, he shall so certify and the judgment shall be deemed final.
(c) Except as otherwise provided by law, compromise settlements of claims referred to the Attorney General for defense of imminent litigation or suits against the United States, or against its agencies or officials upon obligations or liabilities of the United States, made by the Attorney General or any person authorized by him, shall be settled and paid in a manner similar to judgments in like causes and appropriations or funds available for the payment of

such judgments are hereby made available for the payment of such compromise settlements.

(June 25, 1948, ch. 646, 62 Stat. 974; Pub. L. No. 87-187, Sec. 1, Aug. 30, 1961, 75 Stat. 415; Pub. L. No. 95-563, Sec. 14(d), Nov. 1, 1978, 92 Stat. 2390; Pub. L. No. 96-417, title V, Sec. 512, Oct. 10, 1980, 94 Stat. 1744; Pub. L. No. 104-316, title II, Sec. 202(k), Oct. 19, 1996, 110 Stat. 3843.)

§2510. Referral of cases by Comptroller General

(a) The Comptroller General may transmit to the United States Court of Federal Claims for trial and adjudication any claim or matter of which the Court of Federal Claims might take jurisdiction on the voluntary action of the claimant, together with all vouchers, papers, documents, and proofs pertaining thereto.

(b) The Court of Federal Claims shall proceed with the claims or matters so referred as in other cases pending in such Court and shall render judgment thereon.

(June 25, 1948, ch. 646, 62 Stat. 977; July 28, 1953, ch. 253, Sec. 11, 67 Stat. 227; Sept. 3, 1954, ch. 1263, Sec. 47(b), 68 Stat. 1243; Pub. L. No. 95-563, Sec. 14(h)(1), (2)(A), Nov. 1, 1978, 92 Stat. 2390; Pub. L. No. 97-164, title I, Sec. 139(i)(1), Apr. 2, 1982, 96 Stat. 43; Pub. L. No. 102-572, title IX, Sec. 902(a), Oct. 29, 1992, 106 Stat. 4516.)

§2517. Payment of judgments

(a) Except as provided by the Contract Disputes Act of 1978, every final judgment rendered by the United States Court of Federal Claims against the United States shall be paid out of any general appropriation therefor, on presentation to the Secretary of the Treasury of a certification of the judgment by the clerk and chief judge of the court.

(b) Payment of any such judgment and of interest thereon shall be a full discharge to the United States of all claims and demands arising out of the matters involved in the case or controversy, unless the judgment is designated a partial judgment, in which event only the matters described therein shall be discharged.

(June 25, 1948, ch. 646, 62 Stat. 979; Pub. L. No. 95-563, Sec. 14(e), (f), Nov. 1, 1978, 92 Stat. 2390; Pub. L. No. 97-164, title I, Sec. 139(k), Apr. 2, 1982, 96 Stat. 43; Pub. L. No. 102-572, title IX, Sec. 902(a)(1), Oct. 29, 1992, 106 Stat. 4516; Pub. L. No. 104-316, title II, Sec. 202(l), Oct. 19, 1996, 110 Stat. 3843.)

****

Title 31, U.S. Code

§1304. Judgments, awards, and compromise settlements

(a) Necessary amounts are appropriated to pay final judgments, awards, compromise settlements, and interest and costs specified in the judgments or otherwise authorized by law when—
- (1) · · · ·
- (2) · · · ·
- (3) the judgment, award, or settlement is payable—
  - (A) · · · ·
  - (B) · · · ·
  - (C) under a decision of a board of contract appeals; or
  - (D) · · · ·

(Pub. L. No. 97-258, Sec. 1, 2(m)(2), Sept. 13, 1982, 96 Stat. 917, 1062; Pub. L. No. 102-572, title IX, Sec. 902(b)(1), Oct. 29, 1992, 106 Stat. 4516; Pub. L. No. 104-316, title II, Sec. 202(m), Oct. 19, 1996, 110 Stat. 3843.)

E-Government Act of 2002

Citations:

Pub. L. No. 107-347, 116 Stat. 2899, (Dec. 17, 2002), codified *inter alia* at 44 U.S.C.A. §§3601-3606 (2007), 40 U.S.C. §305 (Supp IV 2004), and 44 U.S.C.A. §3501 note (2007).

Lead Agency:

The Office of E-Government and Information Technology, Office of Management and Budget, Eisenhower Executive Office Building, 1650 Pennsylvania Avenue NW, Washington, DC 20502, (202) 395-1181.

Overview:

The E-Government Act of 2002 (H.R. 2458/S. 803) was signed by the President on December 17, 2002, with an effective date for most provisions of April 17, 2003. It was intended to further the federal government's approach to information dissemination in the Internet Age. It contains many requirements for the government, but the main provisions of interest to administrative lawyers are those that require:

- *Public Information.* To the extent practicable, agencies must provide a website that includes all "information about that agency" required to be published in the *Federal Register* under 5 U.S.C. §552(a)(1) and (2).[1]

---

[1] *Id.* at §206(b). But note that subsection 552(a)(2) of Title 5 does not, by its terms, require publication of any documents, only making specified documents available for public inspection and copying. Of course many agencies now publish these materials on their websites.

- *Electronic Submission.* To the extent practicable, agencies must accept electronically those submissions made in rulemaking under 5 U.S.C. §553(c).[2]
- *Electronic Dockets.* To the extent practicable, agencies must have an internet-accessible rulemaking docket that includes all public comments and other materials that by agency rule or practice are included in the agency docket, whether or not electronically submitted.[3]
- *Privacy Impact Assessments.* OMB is required to develop guidelines for privacy notices on agency websites, and agencies must conduct "privacy impact assessments" before collecting information that will be collected, maintained, or disseminated using information technology and that "includes any information in an identifiable form permitting the physical or online contacting of a specific individual, if identical questions have been posed to, or identical reporting requirements imposed on, 10 or more persons, other than" federal agencies or employees.[4] It should be noted here that a number of agencies are also required by a recent appropriations act to do a special privacy assessment for proposed rules "on the privacy of information in an identifiable form, including the type of personally identifiable information collected and the number of people affected."[5]

The Act also served to codify many of the White House's E-Government Initiatives. It codifies OMB's role by creating an E-Administrator and Office of E-Government in OMB. It endorses and requires agencies to support cross agency initiatives such as E-Rulemaking, Geospatial One-Stop, E-Records Management, E-Authentication (especially E-signatures) and Disaster Management; FirstGov (now USA.gov); and enterprise architecture). And it authorizes funds for these activities.

The Act also created new responsibilities for OMB to:

- File an annual report to Congress

---

[2] *Id.* at §206(c).
[3] *Id.* at §206(d).
[4] *Id.* at §208.
[5] Consolidated Appropriations Act, 2005 Pub. L. No. 108-447, 118 Stat. 2809, 3268 division H, §522(a)(5) (codified at 5 U.S.C.A. §552a note) (2004) (covering agencies within the Transportation, Treasury, Independent Agencies, and General Government Appropriations Act).

- Sponsor ongoing dialogue with state, local, and tribal governments, as well as the general public, the private, and the non-profit sectors to find innovative ways to improve the performance of governments in collaborating on the use of information technology to improve the delivery of Government information and services
- Set standards for categorizing and indexing government information
- Set standards for agency web sites
- Create a public directory for agency web sites
- Select agencies to engage in pilot projects on data integration
- Improve access for people with and without computers

Title I and much of Title II of this lengthy Act, covering the above e-government provisions are reproduced in this Sourcebook. Other provisions in Title II authorize agencies to award "share-in-savings" contracts under which contractors share in the savings achieved by agencies through the provision of technologies that improve or accelerate their work. Under these provisions, the executive branch is supposed to ensure, consistent with applicable law, that these contracts are operated according to sound fiscal policy and limit authorized waivers for funding of potential termination costs to appropriate circumstances, so as to minimize the financial risk to the Government.

Title III of this Act is the Federal Information Security Management Act of 2002. It is very similar to Title X of the Homeland Security Act of 2002, also known as the Federal Information Security Management Act of 2002 (codified principally at 44 U.S.C. §§3541-49). Title IV contains an authorization of appropriations and effective dates. Title V contains a series of section devoted to Confidential Information Protection and Statistical Efficiency.

Legislative History:

Rep Jim Turner (D-TX) introduced H.R. 2458 with 40 co-sponsors on July 11, 2001. It was referred to the Subcommittee on Technology and Procurement Policy on September 18, 2002. The Subcommittee held hearings on October 1, 2002. The bill was forwarded by the Subcommittee to the full Committee by voice vote on October 8, 2002. It was reported to the House Floor Committee on Government Reform, on November 14, 2002 (with substitute language), H. Rep. No. 107-787 (Part I), 107th Cong. 2d Sess. After being referred sequentially to the House Judiciary Committee, it was discharged by that Committee on November 14, 2002. It passed the House (Committee of the Whole) by unanimous consent on November 15, 2002.

On the Senate side, a companion bill S. 803 had been introduced on May 1, 2001 by Senator Joe Lieberman (D-CT). After a Hearing on July 11, 2001 before the Committee on Governmental Affairs, the Committee reported the bill to the Senate floor on June 24, 2002 with an amendment in the nature of a substitute and an amendment to the title. S. Rep. No 107-172. On June 27, 2002, S. 803 passed the Senate with an amendment and an amendment to the title by unanimous consent. On November 15, 2002, the Senate received and agreed to H.R. 2458 as passed by the House, sending it to the President. President Bush signed it on December 17, 2002 as Public Law 107-347.

Bibliography:

I. Legislative History

1. H.R. 2458 and S. 803, To Enhance the Management and Promotion of Electronic Government Services and Processes by Establishing an Office of Electronic Government Within the Office of Management and Budget, and by Establishing a Broad Framework of Measures That Require Using Internet-Based Information Technology to Enhance Citizen Access to Government Information and Services, and for Other Purposes, Hearing before the Subcommittee on Technology and Procurement Policy of the House Committee on Government Reform, 107th Cong., 2d Sess, on, Sept. 18, 2002, (Serial No. 107-184), *available at* http://frwebgate.access.gpo.gov/cgi-bin/getdoc.cgi?dbname=107_house_hearings&docid=f:86062.wais.

2. *Ensuring Coordination, Reducing Redundancy: A Review of OMB's Freeze on IT Spending at Homeland Security Agencies*, Hearing before the Subcommittee on Technology and Procurement Policy of the House Committee on Government Reform House of Representatives, 107th Cong., 2d Sess., Oct. 1, 2002 (Serial No. 107-186), *available at* http://frwebgate.access.gpo.gov/cgi-bin/getdoc.cgi?dbname=107_house_hearings&docid=f:86064.wais.

II. Other Government Documents

1. General Services Administration, *E-Authentication Policy for Federal Agencies*, Request for Comments, 68 Fed. Reg. 41,370 (July 11, 2003) (issued in cooperation with OMB).

2. U.S. General Accounting Office, *Electronic Rulemaking: Efforts to Facilitate Public Participation Can Be Improved* (GAO-03-901) (Sept. 2003).

3. Office of Management and Budget, *Guidance for Implementing the Privacy Provisions of the E-Government Act of 2002* (September 26, 2003) (M-03-22).

4. Office of Management and Budget, *FY 2003 Report to Congress on Implementation of the E-Government Act* (2004).

5. U.S. General Accounting Office, *Electronic Government: Initiatives Sponsored by the Office of Management and Budget Have Made Mixed Progress* (GAO-04-561T) (Mar. 24 2004).

6. National Archives & Records Administration, *FY 2004 Implementation of the E-Government Act* (Dec. 6, 2004), *available at* http://www.archives.gov/about/plans-reports/e-gov.

7. U.S. Government Accountability Office, *Electronic Government: Federal Agencies Have Made Progress Implementing the E-Government Act of 2002* (GAO-05-12) (Dec. 10, 2004).

8. U.S. Government Accountability Office, *Electronic Government: Funding of the Office of Management and Budget's Initiatives* (GAO-05-420) (April 25, 2005).

9. U.S. Government Accountability Office, *Electronic Rulemaking: Progress Made in Developing Centralized E-Rulemaking System* (GAO-05-777) (Sept. 9, 2005).

10. Office of Management and Budget, *Expanding E-Government: Improved Service Delivery for the American People Using Information Technology* (Dec. 2005), *available at* http://www.whitehouse.gov/omb/budintegration/expanding_egov_2005.pdf.

11. Office of Management and Budget, *Expanding E-Government: Making a Difference for the American People Using Information Technology* (Dec. 2006), *available at* http://www.whitehouse.gov/omb/egov/documents/expanding_egov_2006.pdf.

12. Office of Management and Budget, *FY 2007 Report to Congress on the Benefits of the E-Government Initiatives* (Feb. 2007), *available at* http://www.whitehouse.gov/omb/egov/documents/FY07_Benefits_Report.pdf.

III. Books and Articles

1. Stephen M. Johnson, *The Internet Changes Everything: Revolutionizing Public Participation and Access to Government Information Through the Internet*, 50 Admin. L. Rev. 277 (1998).

2. Barbara H. Brandon & Robert D. Carlitz, *Online Rulemaking and Other Tools for Strengthening Our Civil Infrastructure*, 54 Admin. L. Rev. 1421 (2002).

3. Jeffrey S. Lubbers, *The Future of Electronic Rulemaking: A Research Agenda*, Regulatory Policy Program Paper RPP-2002-04 (Mar. 2002), Kennedy School of Government, Harvard University, *available at* http://www.ksg.harvard.edu/cbg/research/rpp/RPP-2002-04.pdf, *reprinted in* 27 Admin. & Reg. L. News 6 (Summer 2002).

4. Stephen Zavestoski & Stuart W. Shulman, *The Internet and Environmental Decision Making: An Introduction*, 15 Org. & Env't 323 (2002).

5. Thomas C. Beierle, *Discussing the Rules: Electronic Rulemaking and Democratic Deliberation* (2003) (Resources for the Future Discussion Paper 03-22), *available at* http://www.rff.org/rff/Documents/RFF-DP-03-2.pdf.

6. Barbara H. Brandon, *An Update on the E-Government Act and Electronic Rulemaking*, 29 Admin. & Reg. L. News 7 (Fall, 2003).

7. Jaime Klima, *The E-Government Act: Promoting E-Quality or Exaggerating the Digital Divide?*, 2003 Duke L. & Tech. Rev. 9 (2003).

8. Beth Simone Noveck, *Designing Deliberative Democracy in Cyberspace: the Role of the Cyberlawyer*, 9 B.U. J. Sci. & Tech. L. 1 (2003).

9. Cary Coglianese, *E-Rulemaking: Information Technology and the Regulatory Process*, 56 Admin. L. Rev. 353 (2004).

10. John Morison, *e-Democracy: On-Line Civic Space and the Renewal of Democracy?*, 17 Can. J. L. & Juris. 129 (2004).

11. Beth Simone Noveck, *The Electronic Revolution in Rulemaking*, 53 Emory L.J. 433 (2004).

12. Peter M. Shane, ed., *Democracy Online: the Prospects for Political Renewal through the Internet* (2004).

13. Stuart W. Shulman, *The Internet Still Might (but Probably Won't) Change Everything: Stakeholder Views on the Future of Electronic Rulemaking* (2004), *available at* http://erulemaking.ucsur.pitt.edu/doc/reports/e-rulemaking_final.pdf.

14. Michael Tonsing, *Two Arms! Two Arms! E-Government is Coming!*, 51 Fed. Law. 18 (July, 2004).

15. Cary Coglianese, Stuart Shapiro & Steven J. Balla, *Unifying Rulemaking Information: Recommendations For The New Federal Docket Management System*, 57 Admin. L. Rev. 621 (2005).

16. David Schlosberg, Stephen Zavetoski & Stuart Shulman, *To Submit a Form or Not to Submit a Form, That Is the (Real) Question: Deliberation*

and Mass Participation in U.S. Regulatory Rulemaking (2005), *available at* http://erulemaking.ucsur.pitt.edu/doc/papers/SDEST_stanford_precon. pdf.

17. Hui Yang & Jamie Callen, *Near Duplicate Detection for eRulemaking*, in Proceedings of the Fifth National Conference on Digital Government Research (2005), *available at* http://erulemaking.ucsur.pitt.edu /doc/papers/dgo05-huiyang.pdf.

18. Stuart W. Shulman, *E-Rulemaking: Issues in Current Research and Practice*, 28 Int'l J. Pub. Admin. 621 (2005).

19. Peter M. Shane, *Turning GOLD into EPG: Lessons from Low-Tech Democratic Experimentalism for Electronic Rulemaking and Other Ventures in Cyberdemocracy*, 1 Journal of Law and Policy for the Information Society 147 (2005).

20. John C. Reitz, *Section VI: Computers and Law, E-Government*, 54 Am. J. Comp. L. 733 (2006).

21. Oscar Morales & John Moses, *eRulemaking's Federal Docket Management System*, (May 24, 2006), *available at* http://erulemaking.ucsur.pitt.edu/doc/Crossroads.pdf.

22. Stuart Shapiro & Cary Coglianese, *First Generation E-Rulemaking: An Assessment of Regulatory Agency Websites*, U of Penn. Law School, Public Law Research Paper No. 07-15 (April 11, 2007), *available at* http://papers.ssrn.com/abstract=980247.

Agency Regulations:

1. Office of Personnel Management, 5 C.F.R. Part 370 (2007), *Information Technology Exchange Program* (implementing sections 209(b)(6) and (c) of the E-Government Act of 2002 (Pub. L. 107-347).

Appendix:

1. E-Government Act of 2002, 40 U.S.C. §305 (Supp IV 2004); 44 U.S.C.A. §§3601-3606 (2007), and 44 U.S.C.A. §3501 note (2007).

E-Government Act of 2002

Title 40 U.S. Code

§305. Electronic Government and information technologies

The Administrator of General Services shall consult with the Administrator of the Office of Electronic Government on programs undertaken by the General Services Administration to promote electronic Government and the efficient use of information technologies by Federal agencies.
(Added Pub. L. No. 107-347, title I, Sec. 102(a)(1), Dec. 17, 2002, 116 Stat. 2910.)

Title 44 U.S. Code

§3601. Definitions

In this chapter, the definitions under section 3502 shall apply, and the term—
    (1) "Administrator" means the Administrator of the Office of Electronic Government established under section 3602;
    (2) "Council" means the Chief Information Officers Council established under section 3603;
    (3) "electronic Government" means the use by the Government of web-based Internet applications and other information technologies, combined with processes that implement these technologies, to—
        (A) enhance the access to and delivery of Government information and services to the public, other agencies, and other Government entities; or
        (B) bring about improvements in Government operations that may include effectiveness, efficiency, service quality, or transformation;
    (4) "enterprise architecture"—
        (A) means—
            (i) a strategic information asset base, which defines the mission;
            (ii) the information necessary to perform the mission;
            (iii) the technologies necessary to perform the mission; and
            (iv) the transitional processes for implementing new technologies in response to changing mission needs; and
        (B) includes—

(i) a baseline architecture;
(ii) a target architecture; and
(iii) a sequencing plan;

(5) "Fund" means the E-Government Fund established under section 3604;

(6) "interoperability" means the ability of different operating and software systems, applications, and services to communicate and exchange data in an accurate, effective, and consistent manner;

(7) "integrated service delivery" means the provision of Internet-based Federal Government information or services integrated according to function or topic rather than separated according to the boundaries of agency jurisdiction; and

(8) "tribal government" means—
(A) the governing body of any Indian tribe, band, nation, or other organized group or community located in the continental United States (excluding the State of Alaska) that is recognized as eligible for the special programs and services provided by the United States to Indians because of their status as Indians, and
(B) any Alaska Native regional or village corporation established pursuant to the Alaska Native Claims Settlement Act (43 U.S.C. 1601 et seq.).

(Added Pub. L. No. 107-347, title I, Sec. 101(a), Dec. 17, 2002, 116 Stat. 2901.)

FINDINGS AND PURPOSES

Pub. L . No. 107-347, Sec. 2, Dec. 17, 2002, 116 Stat. 2900, provided that:
"(a) Findings.—Congress finds the following:
"(1) The use of computers and the Internet is rapidly transforming societal interactions and the relationships among citizens, private businesses, and the Government.
"(2) The Federal Government has had uneven success in applying advances in information technology to enhance governmental functions and services, achieve more efficient performance, increase access to Government information, and increase citizen participation in Government.
"(3) Most Internet-based services of the Federal Government are developed and presented separately, according to the jurisdictional boundaries of an individual department or agency, rather than being integrated cooperatively according to function or topic.
"(4) Internet-based Government services involving interagency cooperation are especially difficult to develop and promote, in part because of a

lack of sufficient funding mechanisms to support such interagency cooperation.

"(5) Electronic Government has its impact through improved Government performance and outcomes within and across agencies.

"(6) Electronic Government is a critical element in the management of Government, to be implemented as part of a management framework that also addresses finance, procurement, human capital, and other challenges to improve the performance of Government.

"(7) To take full advantage of the improved Government performance that can be achieved through the use of Internet-based technology requires strong leadership, better organization, improved interagency collaboration, and more focused oversight of agency compliance with statutes related to information resource management.

"(b) Purposes.—The purposes of this Act [see Tables for classification] are the following:

"(1) To provide effective leadership of Federal Government efforts to develop and promote electronic Government services and processes by establishing an Administrator of a new Office of Electronic Government within the Office of Management and Budget.

"(2) To promote use of the Internet and other information technologies to provide increased opportunities for citizen participation in Government.

"(3) To promote interagency collaboration in providing electronic Government services, where this collaboration would improve the service to citizens by integrating related functions, and in the use of internal electronic Government processes, where this collaboration would improve the efficiency and effectiveness of the processes.

"(4) To improve the ability of the Government to achieve agency missions and program performance goals.

"(5) To promote the use of the Internet and emerging technologies within and across Government agencies to provide citizen-centric Government information and services.

"(6) To reduce costs and burdens for businesses and other Government entities.

"(7) To promote better informed decisionmaking by policymakers.

"(8) To promote access to high quality Government information and services across multiple channels.

"(9) To make the Federal Government more transparent and accountable.

"(10) To transform agency operations by utilizing, where appropriate, best practices from public and private sector organizations.

"(11) To provide enhanced access to Government information and services in a manner consistent with laws regarding protection of personal privacy, national security, records retention, access for persons with disabilities, and other relevant laws."

§3602. Office of Electronic Government

(a) There is established in the Office of Management and Budget an Office of Electronic Government.

(b) There shall be at the head of the Office an Administrator who shall be appointed by the President.

(c) The Administrator shall assist the Director in carrying out—

(1) all functions under this chapter;

(2) all of the functions assigned to the Director under title II of the E-Government Act of 2002; and

(3) other electronic government initiatives, consistent with other statutes.

(d) The Administrator shall assist the Director and the Deputy Director for Management and work with the Administrator of the Office of Information and Regulatory Affairs in setting strategic direction for implementing electronic Government, under relevant statutes, including—

(1) chapter 35;

(2) subtitle III of title 40, United States Code;

(3) section 552a of title 5 (commonly referred to as the "Privacy Act");

(4) the Government Paperwork Elimination Act (44 U.S.C. 3504 note); and

(5) the Federal Information Security Management Act of 2002.

(e) The Administrator shall work with the Administrator of the Office of Information and Regulatory Affairs and with other offices within the Office of Management and Budget to oversee implementation of electronic Government under this chapter, chapter 35, the E-Government Act of 2002, and other relevant statutes, in a manner consistent with law, relating to—

(1) capital planning and investment control for information technology;

(2) the development of enterprise architectures;

(3) information security;

(4) privacy;

(5) access to, dissemination of, and preservation of Government information;

(6) accessibility of information technology for persons with disabilities; and

(7) other areas of electronic Government.

(f) Subject to requirements of this chapter, the Administrator shall assist the Director by performing electronic Government functions as follows:

(1) Advise the Director on the resources required to develop and effectively administer electronic Government initiatives.

(2) Recommend to the Director changes relating to Governmentwide strategies and priorities for electronic Government.

(3) Provide overall leadership and direction to the executive branch on electronic Government.

(4) Promote innovative uses of information technology by agencies, particularly initiatives involving multiagency collaboration, through support of pilot projects, research, experimentation, and the use of innovative technologies.

(5) Oversee the distribution of funds from, and ensure appropriate administration and coordination of, the E-Government Fund established under section 3604.

(6) Coordinate with the Administrator of General Services regarding programs undertaken by the General Services Administration to promote electronic government and the efficient use of information technologies by agencies.

(7) Lead the activities of the Chief Information Officers Council established under section 3603 on behalf of the Deputy Director for Management, who shall chair the council.

(8) Assist the Director in establishing policies which shall set the framework for information technology standards for the Federal Government developed by the National Institute of Standards and Technology and promulgated by the Secretary of Commerce under section 11331 of title 40, taking into account, if appropriate, recommendations of the Chief Information Officers Council, experts, and interested parties from the private and nonprofit sectors and State, local, and tribal governments, and maximizing the use of commercial standards as appropriate, including the following:

(A) Standards and guidelines for interconnectivity and interoperability as described under section 3504.

(B) Consistent with the process under section 207(d) of the E-Government Act of 2002, standards and guidelines for categorizing Federal Government electronic information to enable efficient use of technologies, such as through the use of extensible markup language.

(C) Standards and guidelines for Federal Government computer system efficiency and security.

(9) Sponsor ongoing dialogue that—

(A) shall be conducted among Federal, State, local, and tribal government leaders on electronic Government in the executive, legislative, and judicial branches, as well as leaders in the private and nonprofit sectors, to encourage collaboration and enhance understanding of best practices and innovative approaches in acquiring, using, and managing information resources;

(B) is intended to improve the performance of governments in collaborating on the use of information technology to improve the delivery of Government information and services; and

(C) may include—

(i) development of innovative models—

(I) for electronic Government management and Government information technology contracts; and

(II) that may be developed through focused discussions or using separately sponsored research;

(ii) identification of opportunities for public-private collaboration in using Internet-based technology to increase the efficiency of Government-to-business transactions;

(iii) identification of mechanisms for providing incentives to program managers and other Government employees to develop and implement innovative uses of information technologies; and

(iv) identification of opportunities for public, private, and intergovernmental collaboration in addressing the disparities in access to the Internet and information technology.

(10) Sponsor activities to engage the general public in the development and implementation of policies and programs, particularly activities aimed at fulfilling the goal of using the most effective citizen-centered strategies and those activities which engage multiple agencies providing similar or related information and services.

(11) Oversee the work of the General Services Administration and other agencies in developing the integrated Internet-based system under section 204 of the E-Government Act of 2002.

(12) Coordinate with the Administrator for Federal Procurement Policy to ensure effective implementation of electronic procurement initiatives.

(13) Assist Federal agencies, including the General Services Administration, the Department of Justice, and the United States Access Board in—

(A) implementing accessibility standards under section 508 of the Rehabilitation Act of 1973 (29 U.S.C. 794d); and

(B) ensuring compliance with those standards through the budget review process and other means.

(14) Oversee the development of enterprise architectures within and across agencies.

(15) Assist the Director and the Deputy Director for Management in overseeing agency efforts to ensure that electronic Government activities incorporate adequate, risk-based, and cost-effective security compatible with business processes.

(16) Administer the Office of Electronic Government established under this section.

(17) Assist the Director in preparing the E-Government report established under section 3606.

(g) The Director shall ensure that the Office of Management and Budget, including the Office of Electronic Government, the Office of Information and Regulatory Affairs, and other relevant offices, have adequate staff and resources to properly fulfill all functions under the E-Government Act of 2002.

(Added Pub. L. No. 107-347, title I, Sec. 101(a), Dec. 17, 2002, 116 Stat. 2902.)

§3603. Chief Information Officers Council

(a) There is established in the executive branch a Chief Information Officers Council.

(b) The members of the Council shall be as follows:

(1) The Deputy Director for Management of the Office of Management and Budget, who shall act as chairperson of the Council.

(2) The Administrator of the Office of Electronic Government.

(3) The Administrator of the Office of Information and Regulatory Affairs.

(4) The chief information officer of each agency described under section 901(b) of title 31.

(5) The chief information officer of the Central Intelligence Agency.

(6) The chief information officer of the Department of the Army, the Department of the Navy, and the Department of the Air Force, if chief information officers have been designated for such departments under section 3506(a)(2)(B).

(7) Any other officer or employee of the United States designated by the chairperson.

(c)(1) The Administrator of the Office of Electronic Government shall lead the activities of the Council on behalf of the Deputy Director for Management.

(2)(A) The Vice Chairman of the Council shall be selected by the Council from among its members.

(B) The Vice Chairman shall serve a 1-year term, and may serve multiple terms.

(3) The Administrator of General Services shall provide administrative and other support for the Council.

(d) The Council is designated the principal interagency forum for improving agency practices related to the design, acquisition, development, modernization, use, operation, sharing, and performance of Federal Government information resources.

(e) In performing its duties, the Council shall consult regularly with representatives of State, local, and tribal governments.

(f) The Council shall perform functions that include the following:

(1) Develop recommendations for the Director on Government information resources management policies and requirements.

(2) Share experiences, ideas, best practices, and innovative approaches related to information resources management.

(3) Assist the Administrator in the identification, development, and coordination of multiagency projects and other innovative initiatives to improve Government performance through the use of information technology.

(4) Promote the development and use of common performance measures for agency information resources management under this chapter and title II of the E-Government Act of 2002.

(5) Work as appropriate with the National Institute of Standards and Technology and the Administrator to develop recommendations on information technology standards developed under section 20 of the National Institute of Standards and Technology Act (15 U.S.C. 278g-3) and promulgated under section 11331 of title 40, and maximize the use of commercial standards as appropriate, including the following:

(A) Standards and guidelines for interconnectivity and interoperability as described under section 3504.

(B) Consistent with the process under section 207(d) of the E-Government Act of 2002, standards and guidelines for categorizing Federal Government electronic information to enable efficient use of technologies, such as through the use of extensible markup language.

(C) Standards and guidelines for Federal Government computer system efficiency and security.

(6) Work with the Office of Personnel Management to assess and address the hiring, training, classification, and professional development needs of the Government related to information resources management.

(7) Work with the Archivist of the United States to assess how the Federal Records Act can be addressed effectively by Federal information resources management activities.

(Added Pub. L. No.107-347, title I, Sec. 101(a), Dec. 17, 2002, 116 Stat. 2905.)

§3604. E-Government Fund

(a)(1) There is established in the Treasury of the United States the E-Government Fund.

(2) The Fund shall be administered by the Administrator of the General Services Administration to support projects approved by the Director, assisted by the Administrator of the Office of Electronic Government, that enable the Federal Government to expand its ability, through the development and implementation of innovative uses of the Internet or other electronic methods, to conduct activities electronically.

(3) Projects under this subsection may include efforts to—

(A) make Federal Government information and services more readily available to members of the public (including individuals, businesses, grantees, and State and local governments);

(B) make it easier for the public to apply for benefits, receive services, pursue business opportunities, submit information, and otherwise conduct transactions with the Federal Government; and

(C) enable Federal agencies to take advantage of information technology in sharing information and conducting transactions with each other and with State and local governments.

(b)(1) The Administrator shall—

(A) establish procedures for accepting and reviewing proposals for funding;

(B) consult with interagency councils, including the Chief Information Officers Council, the Chief Financial Officers Council, and other interagency management councils, in establishing procedures and reviewing proposals; and

(C) assist the Director in coordinating resources that agencies receive from the Fund with other resources available to agencies for similar purposes.

(2) When reviewing proposals and managing the Fund, the Administrator shall observe and incorporate the following procedures:

(A) A project requiring substantial involvement or funding from an agency shall be approved by a senior official with agencywide authority on behalf of the head of the agency, who shall report directly to the head of the agency.

(B) Projects shall adhere to fundamental capital planning and investment control processes.

(C) Agencies shall identify in their proposals resource commitments from the agencies involved and how these resources would be coordinated with support from the Fund, and include plans for potential continuation of projects after all funds made available from the Fund are expended.

(D) After considering the recommendations of the interagency councils, the Director, assisted by the Administrator, shall have final authority to determine which of the candidate projects shall be funded from the Fund.

(E) Agencies shall assess the results of funded projects.

(c) In determining which proposals to recommend for funding, the Administrator—

(1) shall consider criteria that include whether a proposal—

(A) identifies the group to be served, including citizens, businesses, the Federal Government, or other governments;

(B) indicates what service or information the project will provide that meets needs of groups identified under subparagraph (A);

(C) ensures proper security and protects privacy;

(D) is interagency in scope, including projects implemented by a primary or single agency that—

(i) could confer benefits on multiple agencies; and

(ii) have the support of other agencies; and

(E) has performance objectives that tie to agency missions and strategic goals, and interim results that relate to the objectives; and

(2) may also rank proposals based on criteria that include whether a proposal—

(A) has Governmentwide application or implications;

(B) has demonstrated support by the public to be served;

(C) integrates Federal with State, local, or tribal approaches to service delivery;

(D) identifies resource commitments from nongovernmental sectors;

(E) identifies resource commitments from the agencies involved;

(F) uses web-based technologies to achieve objectives;

(G) identifies records management and records access strategies;

(H) supports more effective citizen participation in and interaction with agency activities that further progress toward a more citizen-centered Government;

(I) directly delivers Government information and services to the public or provides the infrastructure for delivery;

(J) supports integrated service delivery;

(K) describes how business processes across agencies will reflect appropriate transformation simultaneous to technology implementation; and

(L) is new or innovative and does not supplant existing funding streams within agencies.

(d) The Fund may be used to fund the integrated Internet-based system under section 204 of the E-Government Act of 2002.

(e) None of the funds provided from the Fund may be transferred to any agency until 15 days after the Administrator of the General Services Administration has submitted to the Committees on Appropriations of the Senate and the House of Representatives, the Committee on Governmental Affairs of the Senate, the Committee on Government Reform of the House of Representatives, and the appropriate authorizing committees of the Senate and the House of Representatives, a notification and description of how the funds are to be allocated and how the expenditure will further the purposes of this chapter.

(f)(1) The Director shall report annually to Congress on the operation of the Fund, through the report established under section 3606.

(2) The report under paragraph (1) shall describe—

(A) all projects which the Director has approved for funding from the Fund; and

(B) the results that have been achieved to date for these funded projects.

(g)(1) There are authorized to be appropriated to the Fund—

(A) $45,000,000 for fiscal year 2003;

(B) $50,000,000 for fiscal year 2004;

(C) $100,000,000 for fiscal year 2005;

(D) $150,000,000 for fiscal year 2006; and

(E) such sums as are necessary for fiscal year 2007.

(2) Funds appropriated under this subsection shall remain available until expended.

(Added Pub. L. No. 107-347, title I, Sec. 101(a), Dec. 17, 2002, 116 Stat. 2906.)

CHANGE OF NAME

Committee on Governmental Affairs of Senate changed to Committee on Homeland Security and Governmental Affairs of Senate, effective Jan. 4, 2005, by Senate Resolution No. 445, One Hundred Eighth Congress, Oct. 9, 2004.

§3605. Program to encourage innovative solutions to enhance electronic Government services and processes

(a) Establishment of Program.—The Administrator shall establish and promote a Governmentwide program to encourage contractor innovation and excellence in facilitating the development and enhancement of electronic Government services and processes.

(b) Issuance of Announcements Seeking Innovative Solutions.—Under the program, the Administrator, in consultation with the Council and the Administrator for Federal Procurement Policy, shall issue announcements seeking unique and innovative solutions to facilitate the development and enhancement of electronic Government services and processes.

(c) Multiagency Technical Assistance Team.—

(1) The Administrator, in consultation with the Council and the Administrator for Federal Procurement Policy, shall convene a multiagency technical assistance team to assist in screening proposals submitted to the Administrator to provide unique and innovative solutions to facilitate the development and enhancement of electronic Government services and processes. The team shall be composed of employees of the agencies represented on the Council who have expertise in scientific and technical disciplines that would facilitate the assessment of the feasibility of the proposals.

(2) The technical assistance team shall—

(A) assess the feasibility, scientific and technical merits, and estimated cost of each proposal; and

(B) submit each proposal, and the assessment of the proposal, to the Administrator.

(3) The technical assistance team shall not consider or evaluate proposals submitted in response to a solicitation for offers for a pending procurement or for a specific agency requirement.

(4) After receiving proposals and assessments from the technical assistance team, the Administrator shall consider recommending appropriate proposals for funding under the E-Government Fund established under section 3604 or, if appropriate, forward the proposal and the assessment of it to the executive agency whose mission most coincides with the subject matter of the proposal.

(Added Pub. L. No. 107-347, title I, Sec. 101(a), Dec. 17, 2002, 116 Stat. 2909.)

§3606. E-Government report

(a) Not later than March 1 of each year, the Director shall submit an E-Government status report to the Committee on Governmental Affairs of the Senate and the Committee on Government Reform of the House of Representatives.

(b) The report under subsection (a) shall contain—

(1) a summary of the information reported by agencies under section 202(f) of the E-Government Act of 2002;

(2) the information required to be reported by section 3604(f); and

(3) a description of compliance by the Federal Government with other goals and provisions of the E-Government Act of 2002.

(Added Pub. L. No. 107-347, title I, Sec. 101(a), Dec. 17, 2002, 116 Stat. 2909.)

CHANGE OF NAME

Committee on Governmental Affairs of Senate changed to Committee on Homeland Security and Governmental Affairs of Senate, effective Jan. 4, 2005, by Senate Resolution No. 445, One Hundred Eighth Congress, Oct. 9, 2004.

44 U.S.C. §3501 note.

Pub. L. No. 107-347, Title II, §§201-216, 116 Stat. 2910 (Dec. 17, 2002), as amended by Pub. L. No. 108-271, §8(b), 118 Stat. 814 (July 7, 2004); and Pub. L. No. 108-281, §1, 118 Stat. 889 (Aug. 2, 2004):

TITLE II—FEDERAL MANAGEMENT AND PROMOTION OF ELECTRONIC GOVERNMENT SERVICES

SEC. 201. DEFINITIONS.

Except as otherwise provided, in this title the definitions under sections 3502 and 3601 of title 44, United States Code, shall apply.

SEC. 202. FEDERAL AGENCY RESPONSIBILITIES.

(a) IN GENERAL.—The head of each agency shall be responsible for—

(1) complying with the requirements of this Act (including the amendments made by this Act), the related information resource management poli-

cies and guidance established by the Director of the Office of Management and Budget, and the related information technology standards promulgated by the Secretary of Commerce;

(2) ensuring that the information resource management policies and guidance established under this Act by the Director, and the related information technology standards promulgated by the Secretary of Commerce are communicated promptly and effectively to all relevant officials within their agency; and

(3) supporting the efforts of the Director and the Administrator of the General Services Administration to develop, maintain, and promote an integrated Internet-based system of delivering Federal Government information and services to the public under section 204.

(b) PERFORMANCE INTEGRATION.—

(1) Agencies shall develop performance measures that demonstrate how electronic government enables progress toward agency objectives, strategic goals, and statutory mandates.

(2) In measuring performance under this section, agencies shall rely on existing data collections to the extent practicable.

(3) Areas of performance measurement that agencies should consider include—

(A) customer service;

(B) agency productivity; and

(C) adoption of innovative information technology, including the appropriate use of commercial best practices.

(4) Agencies shall link their performance goals, as appropriate, to key groups, including citizens, businesses, and other governments, and to internal Federal Government operations.

(5) As appropriate, agencies shall work collectively in linking their performance goals to groups identified under paragraph (4) and shall use information technology in delivering Government information and services to those groups.

(c) AVOIDING DIMINISHED ACCESS.—When promulgating policies and implementing programs regarding the provision of Government information and services over the Internet, agency heads shall consider the impact on persons without access to the Internet, and shall, to the extent practicable—

(1) ensure that the availability of Government information and services has not been diminished for individuals who lack access to the Internet; and

(2) pursue alternate modes of delivery that make Government information and services more accessible to individuals who do not own computers or lack access to the Internet.

(d) ACCESSIBILITY TO PEOPLE WITH DISABILITIES.—All actions taken by Federal departments and agencies under this Act shall be in compliance with section 508 of the Rehabilitation Act of 1973 (29 U.S.C. 794d).

(e) SPONSORED ACTIVITIES.—Agencies shall sponsor activities that use information technology to engage the public in the development and implementation of policies and programs.

(f) CHIEF INFORMATION OFFICERS.—The Chief Information Officer of each of the agencies designated under chapter 36 of title 44, United States Code (as added by this Act) shall be responsible for—

(1) participating in the functions of the Chief Information Officers Council; and

(2) monitoring the implementation, within their respective agencies, of information technology standards promulgated by the Secretary of Commerce, including common standards for interconnectivity and interoperability, categorization of Federal Government electronic information, and computer system efficiency and security.

(g) E-GOVERNMENT STATUS REPORT.—

(1) IN GENERAL.—Each agency shall compile and submit to the Director an annual E-Government Status Report on—

(A) the status of the implementation by the agency of electronic government initiatives;

(B) compliance by the agency with this Act; and

(C) how electronic Government initiatives of the agency improve performance in delivering programs to constituencies.

(2) SUBMISSION.—Each agency shall submit an annual report under this subsection—

(A) to the Director at such time and in such manner as the Director requires;

(B) consistent with related reporting requirements; and

(C) which addresses any section in this title relevant to that agency.

(h) USE OF TECHNOLOGY.—Nothing in this Act supersedes the responsibility of an agency to use or manage information technology to deliver Government information and services that fulfill the statutory mission and programs of the agency.

(i) NATIONAL SECURITY SYSTEMS.—

(1) INAPPLICABILITY.—Except as provided under paragraph (2), this title does not apply to national security systems as defined in section 11103 of title 40, United States Code.

(2) APPLICABILITY.—This section, section 203, and section 214 do

apply to national security systems to the extent practicable and consistent with law.

SEC. 203. COMPATIBILITY OF EXECUTIVE AGENCY METHODS FOR USE AND ACCEPTANCE OF ELECTRONIC SIGNATURES.

(a) PURPOSE.—The purpose of this section is to achieve interoperable implementation of electronic signatures for appropriately secure electronic transactions with Government.

(b) ELECTRONIC SIGNATURES.—In order to fulfill the objectives of the Government Paperwork Elimination Act (Public Law 105– 277; 112 Stat. 2681–749 through 2681–751), each Executive agency (as defined under section 105 of title 5, United States Code) shall ensure that its methods for use and acceptance of electronic signatures are compatible with the relevant policies and procedures issued by the Director.

(c) AUTHORITY FOR ELECTRONIC SIGNATURES.—The Administrator of General Services shall support the Director by establishing a framework to allow efficient interoperability among Executive agencies when using electronic signatures, including processing of digital signatures.

(d) AUTHORIZATION OF APPROPRIATIONS.—There are authorized to be appropriated to the General Services Administration, to ensure the development and operation of a Federal bridge certification authority for digital signature compatibility, and for other activities consistent with this section, $8,000,000 or such sums as are necessary in fiscal year 2003, and such sums as are necessary for each fiscal year thereafter.

SEC. 204. FEDERAL INTERNET PORTAL.

(a) IN GENERAL.—

(1) PUBLIC ACCESS.—The Director shall work with the Administrator of the General Services Administration and other agencies to maintain and promote an integrated Internet-based system of providing the public with access to Government information and services.

(2) CRITERIA.—To the extent practicable, the integrated system shall be designed and operated according to the following criteria:

(A) The provision of Internet-based Government information and services directed to key groups, including citizens, business, and other governments, and integrated according to function or topic rather than separated according to the boundaries of agency jurisdiction.

(B) An ongoing effort to ensure that Internet-based Government services relevant to a given citizen activity are available from a single point.

(C) Access to Federal Government information and services consolidated, as appropriate, with Internet-based information and services provided by State, local, and tribal governments.

(D) Access to Federal Government information held by 1 or more agencies shall be made available in a manner that protects privacy, consistent with law.

(b) AUTHORIZATION OF APPROPRIATIONS.—There are authorized to be appropriated to the General Services Administration $15,000,000 for the maintenance, improvement, and promotion of the integrated Internet-based system for fiscal year 2003, and such sums as are necessary for fiscal years 2004 through 2007.

SEC. 205. FEDERAL COURTS.

(a) INDIVIDUAL COURT WEBSITES.—The Chief Justice of the United States, the chief judge of each circuit and district and of the Court of Federal Claims, and the chief bankruptcy judge of each district shall cause to be established and maintained, for the court of which the judge is chief justice or judge, a website that contains the following information or links to websites with the following information:

(1) Location and contact information for the courthouse, including the telephone numbers and contact names for the clerk's office and justices' or judges' chambers.

(2) Local rules and standing or general orders of the court.

(3) Individual rules, if in existence, of each justice or judge in that court.

(4) Access to docket information for each case.

(5) Access to the substance of all written opinions issued by the court, regardless of whether such opinions are to be published in the official court reporter, in a text searchable format.

(6) Access to documents filed with the courthouse in electronic form, to the extent provided under subsection (c).

(7) Any other information (including forms in a format that can be downloaded) that the court determines useful to the public.

(b) MAINTENANCE OF DATA ONLINE.—

(1) UPDATE OF INFORMATION.—The information and rules on each website shall be updated regularly and kept reasonably current.

(2) CLOSED CASES.—Electronic files and docket information for cases closed for more than 1 year are not required to be made available online, except all written opinions with a date of issuance after the effective date of this section shall remain available online.

(c) ELECTRONIC FILINGS.—

(1) IN GENERAL.—Except as provided under paragraph (2) or in the rules prescribed under paragraph (3), each court shall make any document that is filed electronically publicly available online. A court may convert any document that is filed in paper form to electronic form. To the extent such conversions are made, all such electronic versions of the document shall be made available online.

(2) EXCEPTIONS.—Documents that are filed that are not otherwise available to the public, such as documents filed under seal, shall not be made available online.

(3) PRIVACY AND SECURITY CONCERNS.—

(A)(i) The Supreme Court shall prescribe rules, in accordance with sections 2072 and 2075 of title 28, United States Code, to protect privacy and security concerns relating to electronic filing of documents and the public availability under this subsection of documents filed electronically.

(ii) Such rules shall provide to the extent practicable for uniform treatment of privacy and security issues throughout the Federal courts.

(iii) Such rules shall take into consideration best practices in Federal and State courts to protect private information or otherwise maintain necessary information security.

(iv) To the extent that such rules provide for the redaction of certain categories of information in order to protect privacy and security concerns, such rules shall provide that a party that wishes to file an otherwise proper document containing such information may file an unredacted document under seal, which shall be retained by the court as part of the record, and which, at the discretion of the court and subject to any applicable rules issued in accordance with chapter 131 of title 28, United States Code, shall be either in lieu of, or in addition to, a redacted copy in the public file.

(B)(i) Subject to clause (ii), the Judicial Conference of the United States may issue interim rules, and interpretive statements relating to the application of such rules, which conform to the requirements of this paragraph and which shall cease to have effect upon the effective date of the rules required under subparagraph (A).

(ii) Pending issuance of the rules required under subparagraph (A), any rule or order of any court, or of the Judicial Conference, providing for the redaction of certain categories of information in order to protect privacy and security concerns arising from electronic filing shall comply with, and be construed in conformity with, subparagraph (A)(iv).

(C) Not later than 1 year after the rules prescribed under subparagraph (A) take effect, and every 2 years thereafter, the Judicial Conference shall submit to Congress a report on the adequacy of those rules to protect privacy and security.

(d) DOCKETS WITH LINKS TO DOCUMENTS.—The Judicial Conference of the United States shall explore the feasibility of technology to post online dockets with links allowing all filings, decisions, and rulings in each case to be obtained from the docket sheet of that case.

(e) COST OF PROVIDING ELECTRONIC DOCKETING INFORMATION.—

Section 303(a) of the Judiciary Appropriations Act, 1992 (28 U.S.C. 1913 note) is amended in the first sentence by striking "shall hereafter" and inserting "may, only to the extent necessary,".

(f) TIME REQUIREMENTS.—Not later than 2 years after the effective date of this title, the websites under subsection (a) shall be established, except that access to documents filed in electronic form shall be established not later than 4 years after that effective date.

(g) DEFERRAL.—

(1) IN GENERAL.—

(A) ELECTION.—

(i) NOTIFICATION.—The Chief Justice of the United States, a chief judge, or chief bankruptcy judge may submit a notification to the Administrative Office of the United States Courts to defer compliance with any requirement of this section with respect to the Supreme Court, a court of appeals, district, or the bankruptcy court of a district.

(ii) CONTENTS.—A notification submitted under this subparagraph shall state—

(I) the reasons for the deferral; and

(II) the online methods, if any, or any alternative methods, such court or district is using to provide greater public access to information.

(B) EXCEPTION.—To the extent that the Supreme Court, a court of appeals, district, or bankruptcy court of a district maintains a website under subsection (a), the Supreme Court or that court of appeals or district shall comply with subsection (b)(1).

(2) REPORT.—Not later than 1 year after the effective date of this title, and every year thereafter, the Judicial Conference of the United States shall submit a report to the Committees on Governmental Affairs and the Judiciary of the Senate and the Committees on Government Reform and the Judiciary of the House of Representatives that—

(A) contains all notifications submitted to the Administrative Office of the United States Courts under this subsection; and

(B) summarizes and evaluates all notifications.

SEC. 206. REGULATORY AGENCIES.

(a) PURPOSES.—The purposes of this section are to—

(1) improve performance in the development and issuance of agency regulations by using information technology to increase access, accountability, and transparency; and

(2) enhance public participation in Government by electronic means, consistent with requirements under subchapter II of chapter 5 of title 5, United States Code, (commonly referred to as the "Administrative Procedures [sic] Act").

(b) INFORMATION PROVIDED BY AGENCIES ONLINE.—To the extent practicable as determined by the agency in consultation with the Director, each agency (as defined under section 551 of title 5, United States Code) shall ensure that a publicly accessible Federal Government website includes all information about that agency required to be published in the Federal Register under paragraphs (1) and (2) of section 552(a) of title 5, United States Code.

(c) SUBMISSIONS BY ELECTRONIC MEANS.—To the extent practicable, agencies shall accept submissions under section 553(c) of title 5, United States Code, by electronic means.

(d) ELECTRONIC DOCKETING.—

(1) IN GENERAL.—To the extent practicable, as determined by the agency in consultation with the Director, agencies shall ensure that a publicly accessible Federal Government website contains electronic dockets for rulemakings under section 553 of title 5, United States Code.

(2) INFORMATION AVAILABLE.—Agency electronic dockets shall make publicly available online to the extent practicable, as determined by the agency in consultation with the Director—

(A) all submissions under section 553(c) of title 5, United States Code; and

(B) other materials that by agency rule or practice are included in the rulemaking docket under section 553(c) of title 5, United States Code, whether or not submitted electronically.

(e) TIME LIMITATION.—Agencies shall implement the requirements of this section consistent with a timetable established by the Director and reported to Congress in the first annual report under section 3606 of title 44 (as added by this Act).

SEC. 207. ACCESSIBILITY, USABILITY, AND PRESERVATION OF GOVERNMENT INFORMATION.

(a) PURPOSE.—The purpose of this section is to improve the methods by which Government information, including information on the Internet, is organized, preserved, and made accessible to the public.

(b) DEFINITIONS.—In this section, the term—

(1) "Committee" means the Interagency Committee on Government Information established under subsection (c); and

(2) "directory" means a taxonomy of subjects linked to websites that—

(A) organizes Government information on the Internet according to subject matter; and

(B) may be created with the participation of human editors.

(c) INTERAGENCY COMMITTEE.—

(1) ESTABLISHMENT.—Not later than 180 days after the date of enactment of this title, the Director shall establish the Interagency Committee on Government Information.

(2) MEMBERSHIP.—The Committee shall be chaired by the Director or the designee of the Director and—

(A) shall include representatives from—

(i) the National Archives and Records Administration;

(ii) the offices of the Chief Information Officers from Federal agencies; and

(iii) other relevant officers from the executive branch; and

(B) may include representatives from the Federal legislative and judicial branches.

(3) FUNCTIONS.—The Committee shall—

(A) engage in public consultation to the maximum extent feasible, including consultation with interested communities such as public advocacy organizations;

(B) conduct studies and submit recommendations, as provided under this section, to the Director and Congress; and

(C) share effective practices for access to, dissemination of, and retention of Federal information.

(4) TERMINATION.—The Committee may be terminated on a date determined by the Director, except the Committee may not terminate before the Committee submits all recommendations required under this section.

(d) CATEGORIZING OF INFORMATION.—

(1) COMMITTEE FUNCTIONS.—Not later than 2 years after the date of enactment of this Act, the Committee shall submit recommendations to the

Director on—

(A) the adoption of standards, which are open to the maximum extent feasible, to enable the organization and categorization of Government information—

(i) in a way that is searchable electronically, including by searchable identifiers; and

(ii) in ways that are interoperable across agencies;

(B) the definition of categories of Government information which should be classified under the standards; and

(C) determining priorities and developing schedules for the initial implementation of the standards by agencies.

(2) FUNCTIONS OF THE DIRECTOR.—Not later than 1 year after the submission of recommendations under paragraph (1), the Director shall issue policies—

(A) requiring that agencies use standards, which are open to the maximum extent feasible, to enable the organization and categorization of Government information—

(i) in a way that is searchable electronically, including by searchable identifiers;

(ii) in ways that are interoperable across agencies; and

(iii) that are, as appropriate, consistent with the provisions under section 3602(f)(8) of title 44, United States Code;

(B) defining categories of Government information which shall be required to be classified under the standards; and

(C) determining priorities and developing schedules for the initial implementation of the standards by agencies.

(3) MODIFICATION OF POLICIES.—After the submission of agency reports under paragraph (4), the Director shall modify the policies, as needed, in consultation with the Committee and interested parties.

(4) AGENCY FUNCTIONS.—Each agency shall report annually to the Director, in the report established under section 202(g), on compliance of that agency with the policies issued under paragraph (2)(A).

(e) PUBLIC ACCESS TO ELECTRONIC INFORMATION.—

(1) COMMITTEE FUNCTIONS.—Not later than 2 years after the date of enactment of this Act, the Committee shall submit recommendations to the Director and the Archivist of the United States on—

(A) the adoption by agencies of policies and procedures to ensure that chapters 21, 25, 27, 29, and 31 of title 44, United States Code, are applied effectively and comprehensively to Government information on the Internet and to other electronic records; and

(B) the imposition of timetables for the implementation of the policies and procedures by agencies.

(2) FUNCTIONS OF THE ARCHIVIST.—Not later than 1 year after the submission of recommendations by the Committee under paragraph (1), the Archivist of the United States shall issue policies—

(A) requiring the adoption by agencies of policies and procedures to ensure that chapters 21, 25, 27, 29, and 31 of title 44, United States Code, are applied effectively and comprehensively to Government information on the Internet and to other electronic records; and (B) imposing timetables for the implementation of the policies, procedures, and technologies by agencies.

(3) MODIFICATION OF POLICIES.—After the submission of agency reports under paragraph (4), the Archivist of the United States shall modify the policies, as needed, in consultation with the Committee and interested parties.

(4) AGENCY FUNCTIONS.—Each agency shall report annually to the Director, in the report established under section 202(g), on compliance of that agency with the policies issued under paragraph (2)(A).

(f) AGENCY WEBSITES.—

(1) STANDARDS FOR AGENCY WEBSITES.—Not later than 2 years after the effective date of this title, the Director shall promulgate guidance for agency websites that includes—

(A) requirements that websites include direct links to—

(i) descriptions of the mission and statutory authority of the agency;

(ii) information made available to the public under subsections (a)(1) and (b) of section 552 of title 5, United States Code (commonly referred to as the "Freedom of Information Act");

(iii) information about the organizational structure of the agency; and

(iv) the strategic plan of the agency developed under section 306 of title 5, United States Code; and

(B) minimum agency goals to assist public users to navigate agency websites, including—

(i) speed of retrieval of search results;

(ii) the relevance of the results;

(iii) tools to aggregate and disaggregate data; and

(iv) security protocols to protect information.

(2) AGENCY REQUIREMENTS.—

(A) Not later than 2 years after the date of enactment of this Act, each agency shall—

(i) consult with the Committee and solicit public comment;

(ii) establish a process for determining which Government information the agency intends to make available and accessible to the public on the Internet and by other means;

(iii) develop priorities and schedules for making Government information available and accessible;

(iv) make such final determinations, priorities, and schedules available for public comment;

(v) post such final determinations, priorities, and schedules on the Internet; and

(vi) submit such final determinations, priorities, and schedules to the Director, in the report established under section 202(g).

(B) Each agency shall update determinations, priorities, and schedules of the agency, as needed, after consulting with the Committee and soliciting public comment, if appropriate.

(3) PUBLIC DOMAIN DIRECTORY OF PUBLIC FEDERAL GOVERNMENT WEBSITES.—

(A) ESTABLISHMENT.—Not later than 2 years after the effective date of this title, the Director and each agency shall—

(i) develop and establish a public domain directory of public Federal Government websites; and

(ii) post the directory on the Internet with a link to the integrated Internet-based system established under section 204.

(B) DEVELOPMENT.—With the assistance of each agency, the Director shall—

(i) direct the development of the directory through a collaborative effort, including input from—

(I) agency librarians;

(II) information technology managers;

(III) program managers;

(IV) records managers;

(V) Federal depository librarians; and

(VI) other interested parties; and

(ii) develop a public domain taxonomy of subjects used to review and categorize public Federal Government websites.

(C) UPDATE.—With the assistance of each agency, the Administrator of the Office of Electronic Government shall—

(i) update the directory as necessary, but not less than every 6 months; and

(ii) solicit interested persons for improvements to the directory.

(g) ACCESS TO FEDERALLY FUNDED RESEARCH AND DEVELOPMENT.—

(1) DEVELOPMENT AND MAINTENANCE OF GOVERNMENT-WIDE REPOSITORY AND WEBSITE.—

(A) REPOSITORY AND WEBSITE.—The Director of the Office of Management and Budget (or the Director's delegate), in consultation with the Director of the Office of Science and Technology Policy and other relevant agencies, shall ensure the development and maintenance of—

(i) a repository that fully integrates, to the maximum extent feasible, information about research and development funded by the Federal Government, and the repository shall—

(I) include information about research and development funded by the Federal Government, consistent with any relevant protections for the information under section 552 of title 5, United States Code, and performed by—

(aa) institutions not a part of the Federal Government, including State, local, and foreign governments; industrial firms; educational institutions; not-for-profit organizations; federally funded research and development centers; and private individuals; and

(bb) entities of the Federal Government, including research and development laboratories, centers, and offices; and

(II) integrate information about each separate research and development task or award, including—

(aa) the dates upon which the task or award is expected to start and end;

(bb) a brief summary describing the objective and the scientific and technical focus of the task or award;

(cc) the entity or institution performing the task or award and its contact information;

(dd) the total amount of Federal funds expected to be provided to the task or award over its lifetime and the amount of funds expected to be provided in each fiscal year in which the work of the task or award is ongoing;

(ee) any restrictions attached to the task or award that would prevent the sharing with the general public of any or all of the information required by this subsection, and the reasons for such restrictions; and

(ff) such other information as may be determined to be appropriate; and

(ii) 1 or more websites upon which all or part of the repository of Federal research and development shall be made available to and searchable by Federal agencies and non-Federal entities, including the general public, to facilitate—

(I) the coordination of Federal research and development activities;

(II) collaboration among those conducting Federal research and development;

(III) the transfer of technology among Federal agencies and between Federal agencies and non- Federal entities; and

(IV) access by policymakers and the public to information concerning Federal research and development activities.

(B) OVERSIGHT.—The Director of the Office of Management and Budget shall issue any guidance determined necessary to ensure that agencies provide all information requested under this subsection.

(2) AGENCY FUNCTIONS.—Any agency that funds Federal research and development under this subsection shall provide the information required to populate the repository in the manner prescribed by the Director of the Office of Management and Budget.

(3) COMMITTEE FUNCTIONS.—Not later than 18 months after the date of enactment of this Act, working with the Director of the Office of Science and Technology Policy, and after consultation with interested parties, the Committee shall submit recommendations to the Director on—

(A) policies to improve agency reporting of information for the repository established under this subsection; and

(B) policies to improve dissemination of the results of research performed by Federal agencies and federally funded research and development centers.

(4) FUNCTIONS OF THE DIRECTOR.—After submission of recommendations by the Committee under paragraph (3), the Director shall report on the recommendations of the Committee and Director to Congress, in the E-Government report under section 3606 of title 44 (as added by this Act).

(5) AUTHORIZATION OF APPROPRIATIONS.—There are authorized to be appropriated for the development, maintenance, and operation of the Governmentwide repository and website under this subsection—

(A) $2,000,000 in each of the fiscal years 2003 through 2005; and

(B) such sums as are necessary in each of the fiscal years 2006 and 2007.

SEC. 208. PRIVACY PROVISIONS.

(a) PURPOSE.—The purpose of this section is to ensure sufficient protections for the privacy of personal information as agencies implement citizen-centered electronic Government.

(b) PRIVACY IMPACT ASSESSMENTS.—

(1) RESPONSIBILITIES OF AGENCIES.—

(A) IN GENERAL.—An agency shall take actions described under subparagraph (B) before—

(i) developing or procuring information technology that collects, maintains, or disseminates information that is in an identifiable form; or

(ii) initiating a new collection of information that—

(I) will be collected, maintained, or disseminated using information technology; and

(II) includes any information in an identifiable form permitting the physical or online contacting of a specific individual, if identical questions have been posed to, or identical reporting requirements imposed on, 10 or more persons, other than agencies, instrumentalities, or employees of the Federal Government.

(B) AGENCY ACTIVITIES.—To the extent required under subparagraph (A), each agency shall—

(i) conduct a privacy impact assessment;

(ii) ensure the review of the privacy impact assessment by the Chief Information Officer, or equivalent official, as determined by the head of the agency; and

(iii) if practicable, after completion of the review under clause (ii), make the privacy impact assessment publicly available through the website of the agency, publication in the Federal Register, or other means.

(C) SENSITIVE INFORMATION.—Subparagraph (B)(iii) may be modified or waived for security reasons, or to protect classified, sensitive, or private information contained in an assessment.

(D) COPY TO DIRECTOR.—Agencies shall provide the Director with a copy of the privacy impact assessment for each system for which funding is requested.

(2) CONTENTS OF A PRIVACY IMPACT ASSESSMENT.—

(A) IN GENERAL.—The Director shall issue guidance to agencies specifying the required contents of a privacy impact assessment.

(B) GUIDANCE.—The guidance shall—

(i) ensure that a privacy impact assessment is commensurate with the size of the information system being assessed, the sensitivity of information that is in an identifiable form in that system, and the risk of harm from unauthorized release of that information; and

   (ii) require that a privacy impact assessment address—
    (I) what information is to be collected;
    (II) why the information is being collected;
    (III) the intended use of the agency of the information;
    (IV) with whom the information will be shared;
    (V) what notice or opportunities for consent would be provided to individuals regarding what information is collected and how that information is shared;
    (VI) how the information will be secured; and
    (VII) whether a system of records is being created under section 552a of title 5, United States Code, (commonly referred to as the "Privacy Act").

 (3) RESPONSIBILITIES OF THE DIRECTOR.—The Director shall—
  (A) develop policies and guidelines for agencies on the conduct of privacy impact assessments;
  (B) oversee the implementation of the privacy impact assessment process throughout the Government; and
  (C) require agencies to conduct privacy impact assessments of existing information systems or ongoing collections of information that is in an identifiable form as the Director determines appropriate.

(c) PRIVACY PROTECTIONS ON AGENCY WEBSITES.—
 (1) PRIVACY POLICIES ON WEBSITES.—
  (A) GUIDELINES FOR NOTICES.—The Director shall develop guidance for privacy notices on agency websites used by the public.
  (B) CONTENTS.—The guidance shall require that a privacy notice address, consistent with section 552a of title 5, United States Code—
   (i) what information is to be collected;
   (ii) why the information is being collected;
   (iii) the intended use of the agency of the information;
   (iv) with whom the information will be shared;
   (v) what notice or opportunities for consent would be provided to individuals regarding what information is collected and how that information is shared;
   (vi) how the information will be secured; and
   (vii) the rights of the individual under section 552a of title 5, United States Code (commonly referred to as the "Privacy Act"), and other laws relevant to the protection of the privacy of an individual.

(2) PRIVACY POLICIES IN MACHINE-READABLE FORMATS.—
The Director shall issue guidance requiring agencies to translate privacy policies into a standardized machine-readable format.

(d) DEFINITION.—In this section, the term "identifiable form" means any representation of information that permits the identity of an individual to whom the information applies to be reasonably inferred by either direct or indirect means.

SEC. 209. FEDERAL INFORMATION TECHNOLOGY WORKFORCE DEVELOPMENT.

(a) PURPOSE.—The purpose of this section is to improve the skills of the Federal workforce in using information technology to deliver Government information and services.

(b) WORKFORCE DEVELOPMENT.—

(1) IN GENERAL.—In consultation with the Director of the Office of Management and Budget, the Chief Information Officers Council, and the Administrator of General Services, the Director of the Office of Personnel Management shall—

(A) analyze, on an ongoing basis, the personnel needs of the Federal Government related to information technology and information resource management;

(B) identify where current information technology and information resource management training do not satisfy the personnel needs described in subparagraph (A);

(C) oversee the development of curricula, training methods, and training priorities that correspond to the projected personnel needs of the Federal Government related to information technology and information resource management; and

(D) assess the training of Federal employees in information technology disciplines in order to ensure that the information resource management needs of the Federal Government are addressed.

(2) INFORMATION TECHNOLOGY TRAINING PROGRAMS.—The head of each Executive agency, after consultation with the Director of the Office of Personnel Management, the Chief Information Officers Council, and the Administrator of General Services, shall establish and operate information technology training programs consistent with the requirements of this subsection. Such programs shall—

(A) have curricula covering a broad range of information technology disciplines corresponding to the specific information technology and information resource management needs of the agency involved;

(B) be developed and applied according to rigorous standards; and

(C) be designed to maximize efficiency, through the use of self-paced courses, online courses, on-the-job training, and the use of remote instructors, wherever such features can be applied without reducing the effectiveness of the training or negatively impacting academic standards.

(3) GOVERNMENTWIDE POLICIES AND EVALUATION.—The Director of the Office of Personnel Management, in coordination with the Director of the Office of Management and Budget, shall issue policies to promote the development of performance standards for training and uniform implementation of this subsection by Executive agencies, with due regard for differences in program requirements among agencies that may be appropriate and warranted in view of the agency mission. The Director of the Office of Personnel Management shall evaluate the implementation of the provisions of this subsection by Executive agencies.

(4) CHIEF INFORMATION OFFICER AUTHORITIES AND RESPONSIBILITIES.—Subject to the authority, direction, and control of the head of an Executive agency, the chief information officer of such agency shall carry out all powers, functions, and duties of the head of the agency with respect to implementation of this subsection. The chief information officer shall ensure that the policies of the agency head established in accordance with this subsection are implemented throughout the agency.

(5) INFORMATION TECHNOLOGY TRAINING REPORTING.—The Director of the Office of Management and Budget shall ensure that the heads of Executive agencies collect and maintain standardized information on the information technology and information resources management workforce related to the implementation of this subsection.

(6) AUTHORITY TO DETAIL EMPLOYEES TO NON-FEDERAL EMPLOYERS.—In carrying out the preceding provisions of this subsection, the Director of the Office of Personnel Management may provide for a program under which a Federal employee may be detailed to a non-Federal employer. The Director of the Office of Personnel Management shall prescribe regulations for such program, including the conditions for service and duties as the Director considers necessary.

(7) COORDINATION PROVISION.—An assignment described in section 3703 of title 5, United States Code, may not be made unless a program under paragraph (6) is established, and the assignment is made in accordance with the requirements of such program.

(8) EMPLOYEE PARTICIPATION.—Subject to information resource management needs and the limitations imposed by resource needs in other occupational areas, and consistent with their overall workforce development

strategies, agencies shall encourage employees to participate in occupational information technology training.

(9) AUTHORIZATION OF APPROPRIATIONS.—There are authorized to be appropriated to the Office of Personnel Management for the implementation of this subsection, $15,000,000 in fiscal year 2003, and such sums as are necessary for each fiscal year thereafter.

(10) EXECUTIVE AGENCY DEFINED.—For purposes of this subsection, the term "Executive agency" has the meaning given the term "agency" under section 3701 of title 5, United States Code (as added by subsection (c)).

(c) INFORMATION TECHNOLOGY EXCHANGE PROGRAM.—

(1) IN GENERAL.—Subpart B of part III of title 5, United States Code, is amended by adding at the end the following:

"CHAPTER 37—INFORMATION TECHNOLOGY EXCHANGE PROGRAM
"Sec.
"3701. Definitions.
"3702. General provisions.
"3703. Assignment of employees to private sector organizations.
"3704. Assignment of employees from private sector organizations.
"3705. Application to Office of the Chief Technology Officer of the District of Columbia.
"3706. Reporting requirement.
"3707. Regulations

[OMITTED]

SEC. 209(d)-(f)

(d) ETHICS PROVISIONS.—
(e) REPORT ON EXISTING EXCHANGE PROGRAMS.—
(f) REPORT ON THE ESTABLISHMENT OF A GOVERNMENTWIDE INFORMATION TECHNOLOGY TRAINING PROGRAM.—

[OMITTED]

SEC. 210-216 OMITTED]:

Sec. 210. Share-in-savings initiatives.

Sec. 211. Authorization for acquisition of information technology by State and local governments through Federal supply schedules.

Sec. 212. Integrated reporting study and pilot projects.

Sec. 213. Community technology centers.

Sec. 214. Enhancing crisis management through advanced information technology.

Sec. 215. Disparities in access to the Internet.

Sec. 216. Common protocols for geographic information systems.

[ALSO OMITTED: Pub. L. No. 107-347, Title V, §§501 to 526—Confidential Information Protection and Statistical Efficiency]

Equal Access to Justice Act

Citations:

5 U.S.C. §504, 504 note (2000) and 28 U.S.C. §2412, 2412 note (2000); enacted October 21, 1980 as title II of the Small Business Export Expansion Act of 1980, Pub. L. No. 96-481, 94 Stat. 2325; amended September 3, 1982, by Pub. L. No. 97-248, title II, §292, 96 Stat. 574; August 5, 1985, by Pub. L. No. 99-80, 99 Stat. 183; October 21, 1986 by Pub. L. No. 99-509, title VI, §6103(c), 100 Stat. 1948; November 10, 1988 by Pub. L. No. 100-647, title VI, §6239(b), 102 Stat. 3746; October 29, 1992 by Pub. L. No. 102-572, §506, 106 Stat. 4506, 4513; November 16, 1993 by Pub. L. No. 103-141, 107 Stat. 1489; December 21, 1995 by Pub. L. 104-66, title I, Sec. 1091(b), 109 Stat. 722; March 29, 1996 by Pub. L. No. 104-121, 110 Stat. 862.

Lead Agencies:

General oversight: Office of the Chief Counsel for Advocacy, U.S. Small Business Administration, 409 Third Street SW, Washington, DC 20416 (202) 205-6533. [Note: the Administrative Conference of the United States, which was given reporting responsibility for administrative proceedings, was terminated in 1995. The Administrative Office of the United States Courts was originally given reporting responsibility for judicial proceedings. The Attorney General was substituted in 1992, but this provision (28 U.S.C. §2412(d)(5)) was deleted in 1995.]

Overview:

Eligibility and Coverage. The Equal Access to Justice Act provides that certain parties who prevail over the federal government in covered litigation are entitled to an award of attorneys' fees and other expenses unless the government can demonstrate that its position was substantially justified or that special circumstance would make an award unjust. The parties eligible to receive such awards include individuals whose net worth (at the time the adjudication was initiated) is not more than $2 million; businesses, organizations, associations or units of local government with a net worth of no more than $7 million and with no more than 500 employees; and tax exempt organizations and agricultural cooperatives with no more than 500 employees, regardless of net worth. This must be shown by adequate affidavits. *See Al Ghanim Combined Group Co. Gen. Trad. & Cont. W.L.L. v. United States*, 67 Fed. Cl. 494 (Fed. Cl. 2005). *See also Tri-State Steel Construction Co. v. Herman*, 164 F.3d 973 (6th Cir. 1999) (corporate subsidiary may qualify for recovery under the EAJA, even if it is owned by a parent far too substantial to fit below the net worth limitations). The 1996 Amendments also allow "a small entity" (as defined in the Regulatory Flexibility Act, 5 U.S.C. §601(6)) to utilize the new "excessive demand" avenue of relief, see discussion below in "showing required."

The Act covers two groups of proceedings: (1) adversary administrative adjudications, which are defined to include formal hearing proceedings under 5 U.S.C. §554 (other than licensing and ratemaking proceedings, but including license suspension or revocation proceedings) in which the agency takes a position as a party at the proceeding, government contract appeals adjudicated under the Contract Disputes Act of 1978 (41 U.S.C. §§601-613), administrative civil penalty proceedings under the Program Fraud Civil Remedies Act (31 U.S.C. Chapter 38), and hearings under the Religious Freedom Restoration Act of 1993; and (2) civil court actions other than tort cases (not including tax cases, which are covered by a separate attorneys fee provision[1]). The Act also authorizes the award of attorneys' fees against the United States in those limited situations in which fees could be awarded against any other party under existing common law and statutory provisions, unless a statute expressly prohibits such an award.

Determining what constitutes an administrative proceeding "under" section 554 has created some controversy, particularly with respect to deportation and other administrative immigration proceedings, which are conducted with procedures equivalent to those required by section 554, even though they are expressly exempted from the Administrative Procedure Act's re-

---

[1] 26 U.S.C. §7430. This provision applies to cases commenced after February 28, 1983. Tax cases (other than those in the Tax Court) pending on October 1, 1981, or commenced between that date and March 1, 1983, are covered by the Equal Access to Justice Act.

quirements. The U.S. Supreme Court resolved this issue, ruling that proceedings must be "subject to" section 554 to fall within the Act's coverage (and thus that administrative deportation proceedings are not covered). *Ardestani v. INS*, 502 U.S. 129 (1991). In other contexts, many courts had already reached a similar conclusion. *See, e.g., Friends of the Earth v. Reilly*, 966 F.2d 690 (D.C. Cir 1992) (EPA proceeding leading to withdrawal of authorization for state hazardous waste program authorization not an adversary adjudication where formal hearing was provided voluntarily under agency regulations, rather than required by statute); *Dart v. United States*, 961 F.2d 284 (D.C. Cir. 1992) (Export Control Act proceedings not covered by EAJA because exempt from §554 of APA); *St. Louis Fuel & Supply Co. v. FERC*, 890 F.2d 446 (D.C. Cir. 1989) (Department of Energy proceedings not covered by EAJA where formal hearing was provided voluntarily); *Haire v. United States*, 869 F.2d 531 (9th Cir. 1989) (Department of Commerce enforcement proceedings under the Export Administration Act not covered by EAJA because specifically exempted from §554 by statute); *Owens v. Brock*, 860 F.2d 1363 (6th Cir. 1988) (Department of Labor proceedings under the Federal Employees Compensation Act not covered by EAJA); *Olsen v. Dep't of Commerce, Census Bureau*, 735 F.2d 558 (Fed. Cir. 1984) (Merit Systems Protection Board proceeding concerning employee tenure not covered by EAJA); *Smedberg Machine & Tool, Inc. v. Donovan*, 730 F.2d 1089 (7th Cir. 1984) (labor certification review at Department of Labor not covered by EAJA). But see *Lane v. USDA*, 120 F.3d 106 (8th Cir. 1997) (adjudications conducted by hearing officers in the USDA's National Appeals Division are "adversary adjudications" covered by EAJA), and *Collard v. U.S. Department of Interior*, 154 F.3d 933 (9th Cir. 1998) (although statute governing extinguishing of mining patent did not expressly call for formal APA adjudication, an APA hearing was constitutionally required; thus under *Wong Yang Sung v. McGrath*, 339 U.S. 33 (1950) the hearing was governed by §554 for the APA, making plaintiffs eligible for EAJA reimbursement).

The Supreme Court has significantly narrowed the definition of "prevailing party" in federal fee shifting statutes. In *Buckhannon Board & Care Home, Inc. v. West Virginia Department of Health & Human Resources*, 532 U.S. 598, 600 (2001), the Court held that a "party that has failed to secure a judgment on the merits or a court-ordered consent decree, but has nonetheless achieved the desired result because the lawsuit brought about a voluntary change in the defendant's conduct" is *not* a "prevailing party" under federal statutes allowing courts to award attorney's fees and costs to the "prevailing party." Six circuit courts have found that *Buckhannon* applies to the EAJA. See *Morillo-Cedron v. Dist. Dir. for The U.S. Citizenship & Immigration*

Servs., 452 F.3d 1254, 1258 (11th Cir. 2006); *Goldstein v. Moatz*, 445 F.3d 747, 751 (4th Cir.2006); *Marshall v. Comm'r of Soc. Sec.*, 444 F.3d 837, 840 (6th Cir. 2006); *Vacchio v. Ashcroft*, 404 F.3d 663, 673 (2d Cir. 2005); *Thomas v. NSF*, 330 F.3d 486, 492-93 (D.C. Cir. 2003); *Brickwood Contractors, Inc.*, 288 F.3d at 1379-80; *Perez-Arellano v. Smith*, 279 F.3d 791, 795 (9th Cir. 2002). However, a district court recently disagreed, finding that those courts did so with cursory or no analysis. *Kholyavskiy v. Schlecht*, 479 F. Supp. 2d 897, 906, n.8 (E.D. Wis. 2007).

Applicability. The Equal Access to Justice Act, as amended in 1985, applies to all covered cases and proceedings pending on, or commenced on or after, August 5, 1985. The original Act, which expired under a sunset provision on September 30, 1984, applied to cases and proceedings commenced between October 1, 1981, and September 30, 1984, as well as those pending on October 1, 1981. The 1996 Amendments are applicable to civil actions and adversary adjudications commenced on or after March 29, 1996.

In 2002, the Supreme Court resolved the question of the possible overlap of the EAJA and the Social Security Act's attorney fee provisions. *Gisbrecht v. Barnhart*, 535 U.S. 789 (2002), held that EAJA fees for claimants prevailing in court supplement the fees payable to attorneys out of the claimants past-due benefits under § 406(b) of the Social Security Act.

Showing Required. A party seeking an award of fees must submit an application to the court or agency adjudicative officer within 30 days of the final judgment (for civil actions) or final disposition (for administrative adjudications) of the underlying proceeding.[2] The application must demonstrate the party's eligibility and include itemized statements from attorneys and expert witnesses for whose services an award is sought. The party must also allege that the position of the United States was not substantially justified, but need not provide supporting evidence; based on the Act's legislative history, the courts have concluded that the federal government bears the burden of showing that its position was substantially justified.

The "position" that must be substantially justified under the Act includes both the government's litigation position and the underlying government action or failure to act leading up to the litigation. The determination of whether the government's position was substantially justified is to be made on the record of the proceeding; discovery on that issue is not permitted. To show

---

[2] In *Melkonyan v. Sullivan*, 501 U.S. 89 (1991), the Supreme Court ruled that when fees are sought under the provisions of the Act applicable to civil actions, the "final judgment" that triggers the 30-day deadline must be rendered by a court rather than by an agency in proceedings on remand from a court.

that its position was substantially justified, the government must demonstrate that it had a reasonable basis in law and fact. *Pierce v. Underwood*, 487 U.S. 552 (1988). See also *Meinhold v. United States Dep't of Defense*, 123 F.3d 1275, 1277 (9th Cir. 1997), *modified by* 131 F.3d 842 (1997), providing that the government bears the burden to show that its position was substantially justified. The 1996 amendments also allow a party to collect even if it does not prevail in litigation if the government's demand is found to be excessive or is unreasonable when compared with the ultimate decision (unless the party has acted willfully or in bad faith). The D.C. Circuit granted a partial fee award under this provision in *American Wrecking Corp. v. Secretary of Labor*, 364 F.3d 321 (D.C. Cir. 2004), in a case where the agency had sought $126,000 in penalties but was allowed to assess only $7,000.

United States v. Hallmark Construction Co., 200 F.3d 1076, 1080 (7th Cir. 2000) outlined a three-part test for determining whether an agency's position was substantially justified. The agency's decision is substantially justified if "its position was grounded in (1) a reasonable basis in truth for the facts alleged; (2) a reasonable basis in law for the theory propounded; and (3) a reasonable connection between the facts alleged and the legal theory advanced" (internal quotation omitted). The test was applied in the EPA's favor in *Bricks, Inc. v. EPA*, 426 F.3d 918 (7th Cir. 2005).

However, even if the government quickly improved its policies in response to the initiation of litigation, its pre-litigation conduct can be sufficiently "unreasonable" to render "the entire Government position not 'substantially justified.'" *Healey v. Leavitt*, 485 F.3d 63, 68 (2d Cir. 2007).

Amount of Awards. Before 1996, the Act allowed the prevailing party to be awarded attorneys' fees and expenses, including expert witness fees and the cost of studies or tests necessary for case preparation. Under the 1996 Act, attorneys' fee awards were increased from $75 an hour to $125 an hour. This is the awarded rate unless special factors, such as cost-of-living increases or a shortage of qualified attorneys, justify a higher rate. For administrative proceedings, agencies must make any determination that special factors justify a higher rate by regulation. Some agencies have done so.[3] Higher rates may be authorized on a case-by-case basis in court proceedings, and many courts have used the provision to award higher rates based on cost-of-living in-

---

[3] *See, e.g.*, National Transportation Safety Board rule, 49 CFR §826.6 (2006). *See also* Operative Plasterers and Cement Masons International Association, 91-2 BCA 23, 782 (CCH 1991) (DOL Board of Contract Appeals allowed attorneys' fees at a rate in excess of the then-statutory limit of $75 per hour in the absence of a regulation).

creases. See *Kerin v. U.S.P.S.*, 218 F.3d 185 (2d Cir. 2000); *Masters v. Nelson*, 105 F.3d 708 (D.C. Cir. 1997); *Dewalt v. Sullivan*, 963 F.2d 27 (3d Cir. 1992); *Russell v. Sullivan*, 930 F.2d 1443 (9th Cir. 1991); *Phillips v. GSA*, 924 F.2d 1577 (Fed. Cir. 1991); *Johnson v. Sullivan*, 919 F.2d 503 (8th Cir. 1990); *Trichilo v. Secretary, HHS*, 823 F.2d 702 (2d Cir. 1987); *Allen v. Bowen*, 821 F.2d 963 (3d Cir. 1987); *Sierra Club v. Secretary of the Army*, 820 F.2d 513 (1st Cir. 1987); *Hirschey v. FERC*, 777 F.2d 1 (D.C. Cir. 1985); *Greenidge v. Barnhart*, 2005 WL 357318 (N.D.N.Y. 2005); *Former Employees of Tyco Electronics Fiber Optics Division v. U.S. Department of Labor*, 350 F. Supp. 2d 1075, 1093 (C.I.T. 2004); *United States v. Eleven Vehicles*, 937 F. Supp. 1143 (E.D. Pa. 1996); *Kimball v. Shalala*, 826 F. Supp. 573 (D. Me. 1993). But see *Masonry Masters, Inc. v. Nelson*, 105 F.3d 708 (D.C. Cir. 1997) (cost-of-living adjustments must be calculated separately for each year services performed); *May v. Sullivan*, 936 F.2d 176 (4th Cir. 1991) (affirming denial of upward adjustment); *Spencer v. Apfel*, 1998 WL 264843 (E.D. La. 1998) (cost-of-living adjustment not automatic).

Rate increases based on other special factors have been less frequent. The Supreme Court has ruled that traditional attorneys' fee calculation principles, such as lodestar rates or risk multipliers, cannot be used to award rates about the statutory maximum, and that the exception for "limited availability of qualified attorneys" refers to attorneys with specialized knowledge or skills. *Pierce v. Underwood, supra.* Lower courts have allowed rates above the pre-1996 rate of $75 per hour for specialists in areas such as environmental law, *National Wildlife Federation v. FERC*, 870 F.2d 542 (9th Cir. 1989), *Portland Audubon Society v. Lujan*, 865 F. Supp. 1464 (D. Or 1994); social security law, *Pirus v. Bowen*, 869 F.2d 536 (9th Cir. 1989) (but see *Stewart v. Sullivan*, 810 F. Supp. 1102 (D. Haw. 1993) (no adjustment upward due to limited availability of social security disability lawyers)); tax law, *Howards' Yellow Cabs, Inc. v. United States*, 1998 WL 62485 (W.D.N.C. 1998) and immigration law. Judge Posner has opined that "immigration lawyers who bring relevant expertise to a case, such as knowledge of foreign cultures or of particular, esoteric nooks and crannies of immigration law, in which such expertise is needed to give the alien a fair shot at prevailing," *Muhur v. Ashcroft*, 382 F.3d 653, 656 (7th Cir. 2004). See also *Nadler v. INS*, 737 F. Supp. 658 (D.D.C. 1989), but see *Singh v. INS*, 1998 WL 101742 (N.D. Cal. 1998) (immigration law not recognized as a specialty warranting adjustment). The Second Circuit also recently narrowly construed the concept of "specialized expertise," refusing to grant it to lawyers specializing in the practice of Medicare law. *Healey v. Leavitt*, 485 F.3d 63 (2d Cir. 2007). The court stated: "[A] case requires 'specialized expertise' within the meaning of the EAJA only when it requires some knowledge or skill that cannot be obtained by a competent practicing attorney through routine research or legal experience." *Id.* at 70. Indeed, the *Healey* court also affirmed the district court's decision to reduce the fee award "given the considerable amount of time plaintiffs devoted to [an] unsuccessful [related] claim." *Id.* at 72.

The Supreme Court has also ruled that attorneys' fee awards should ordinarily include fees for the portion of the litigation concerning the fee award itself. In *Commissioner, INS v. Jean*, 496 U.S. 154 (1990), the Court rejected the argument that a separate determination must be made as to whether the government's position on the fee issues was substantially justified before fees could be awarded for fee litigation.

While paralegal expenses may be recoverable under EAJA, see *Role Models Am., Inc. v. Brownlee*, 353 F.3d 962, 974 (D.C. Cir. 2004); *Hyatt v. Barnhart*, 315 F.3d 239, 255 (4th Cir. 2002); *Jean v. Nelson*, 863 F.2d 759, 778 (11th Cir. 1988), the Federal Circuit recently held that they could only be recovered as "expenses" (allowable only at cost) and not "fees." *Richlin Security Service Co. v. Chertoff*, 482 F.3d 1358, 1359 (Fed. Cir. 2007).

Authority of Agencies and Courts. Ordinarily, awards for administrative proceedings are to be made by the presiding agency (which is usually, but not always, the agency that will have to pay any award) and awards for court cases by the court. The Act provides, however, that where a court reviews the decision on the merits in an adversary adjudication, the court shall make any award for the administrative stage as well as the judicial review stage of the proceeding. In some cases, moreover, the courts may make fee awards for administrative proceedings that are not independently covered by the Equal Access to Justice Act. In *Sullivan v. Hudson*, 490 U.S. 877 (1989), the Supreme Court rule that a court could award EAJA fees for the portion of a Social Security disability proceeding occurring after a court remand, even though the proceeding was not "adversarial" within the meaning of the EAJA. In this case, the party seeking fees did not become a prevailing party under the EAJA until completion of the agency proceeding on remand. The remand proceedings was "intimately tied to the resolution of the judicial action and necessary to the attainment of the results Congress sought to promote by providing for fees," 490 U.S. at 888, and so should be considered an integral part of the "civil action." Lower courts interpreting the *Sullivan v. Hudson* ruling have disagreed on its breadth. See *Full Gospel Portland Church v. Thornburgh*, 927 F.2d 628 (D.C. Cir. 1991) (fees available only where there is a remand under a detailed statutory scheme providing for greater interaction between the agency and the reviewing court than is usual in traditional review of agency action); *Pollgreen v. Morris*, 911 F.2d 527 (11th Cir. 1990) (fees available where there is an "intimate interrelationship" between judicial and agency proceedings, including where initial administrative hearing was provided pursuant to court order). *See also In re Armstead*, 106 BR 405, 2 Ad. L. Rep. 3d 1068 (P & F) (E.D. Pa. 1989) (fees available for HUD administrative proceeding on remand from bankruptcy court).

Agency Procedures. The Act requires agencies to adopt procedures for processing applications for awards in administrative proceedings. More than 30 agencies have issued final procedures for handling applications for attorneys' fee awards in their administrative proceedings. Most of these agencies have generally followed model rules prepared by the Administrative Conference in furtherance of its statutory responsibility to consult with agencies in the development of these procedures. The Conference's model rules for implementation of the Act are located in the Appendix to this chapter, and citations to the agencies' individual rules are included below.

Legislative History:

Viewed by Congress both as a small business relief measure and as a regulatory reform bill, the Equal Access to Justice Act was originally passed in 1980 as part of a small business assistance act, to which it was added by amendment on the floor of the Senate. The conference committee accepted the Senate version over a House version of the legislation that did not contain the Equal Access provisions. A substantially identical bill, S. 265, had passed the Senate overwhelmingly in 1979 and had been reported favorably (with a few amendments) by the House Judiciary Committee the day before Senate passage of H.R. 5612. Thus, courts and others interpreting the Act have frequently referred to the Congressional reports on S. 265 (cited below) as well as the Conference Report on H.R. 5612. The measure was probably tacked on to H.R. 5612 both to ensure passage before adjournment of the 96th Congress and to forestall a possible presidential veto.

Significant changes from the Senate version made in the House Judiciary Committee (and explained briefly in that Committee's report on S. 265) include the addition of the 500-employee eligibility requirement, the exemption of certain nonprofit organizations from the net worth eligibility requirements, the limitation of covered administrative proceedings to formal adversary adjudications (and the exclusion thereby of most Social Security administrative proceedings) and assignment of the responsibility for fee determinations in administrative proceedings to agency adjudicative officers.

The Act was the subject of continuing legislative attention, in part because of its 3-year sunset provision. A 1982 amendment excluded tax cases from the Act's coverage, and created a separate provision for those cases with different standards and burdens of proof (26 U.S.C. §7430). A House Judiciary Subcommittee held oversight hearings on the Equal Access to Justice Act in April 1982, and similar hearings were held by the Senate Judiciary Subcommittee in December of that year.

A Senate bill to amend the Act and make it permanent, S. 919, was reported favorably by the Senate Judiciary Committee in August 1984; a similar House bill, H.R. 5470, was passed by both houses of Congress on October 3, 1984. H.R. 5479 included several important changes to the law. In addition to repealing the sunset provision, it added contract appeals board proceedings (and appeals from board decisions) to those covered by the Act, raised the net worth limits on eligibility for fee awards, and specified that the position of the United States that must be substantially justified to avoid an award included its underlying position as well as its litigation position. In addition, it required the payment of awards from agency funds, deleting an earlier statutory provision that permitted awards to be paid from the general judgment fund of the United States when not paid by the agency.[4]

This legislation was vetoed by President Reagan after Congress had adjourned. The President supported reauthorization of the Act, but objected to two provisions of H.R. 5479: the one that would require consideration of the government's underlying position as well as its litigation position, and another that would have required the payment of interest by the United States on awards not paid within 60 days.

Legislation to extend and amend the Act was reintroduced in the 99th Congress, passed by both Houses of Congress (H.R. 2378), and signed by the President August 5, 1985. In a compromise designed to avoid another veto, the final legislation retained the provision requiring consideration of the government's underlying position, but added a provision that substantial justification determinations are to be made on the record, rather than on the basis of discovery; the provision for the payment of interest was dropped, except where the United States appeals an award of costs or fees in court and the award is later upheld. Two other changes from the 1984 bill appeared in the final legislation. First, while H.R. 5479 would have made the adjudicative officer's decision on a fee application in an administrative proceeding the final decision of the agency, Pub. L. No. 99-80 gave final authority to the

---

[4] An additional provision of the original Act, section 207, forbade payment from the judgment fund in administrative proceedings unless a special appropriation were made for that purpose; no such special appropriation was ever made.

agency itself. Also, because the original Act had expired before passage of the new law, a savings provision was included to cover proceedings both commenced and completed during the gap from October 1, 1984 to August 5, 1985.

The Equal Access to Justice Act has been amended several times since then. In 1986, the amendment clarified that the administrative provisions of the Act do not apply to tax cases, and in 1988 an amendment added civil penalty proceedings under the Program Fraud Civil Remedies Act to the Act's coverage. In 1992, Congress enacted section 506 of the Federal Courts Administration Act, which made EAJA applicable to the Court of Veterans Appeals (now the Court of Appeals for Veterans Claims),[5] for cases pending as of October 29, 1992 and subsequent cases. In 1993, coverage of administrative proceedings under the Religious Freedom Protection Act was added.

More major changes were made in 1996. In March, 1995, Senator Feingold introduced S. 554, the Equal Access to Justice Reform Amendments of 1995. A modified version of S. 554 was subsequently inserted into S. 942, the Small Business Regulatory Fairness Act of 1995, introduced by Senator Bond. The Senate Committee on Small Business held a hearing on this bill on February 28, 1996. The bill was passed by the Senate 100-0 on March 19, 1996. The bill was ultimately incorporated into H.R. 3136, The Contract With America Advancement Act of 1996, Pub. L. No. 104-121, Title III, Subtitle C, 110 Stat. 862.[6] The amendments increased the maximum hourly rate from $75 to $125, allowed for an award of fees even if the party lost in litigation if the government's demand was deemed excessive, and increased the class of parties entitled to fees. These amendments were controversial. Supporters expressed concern that the Act as originally enacted was not allowing as many parties to collect as originally intended, and had not provided enough

---

[5] According to testimony of the Chief Judge of that court, since Congress extended the EAJA to the Court in 1992, there has been a substantial number of EAJA applications. He gave the following figures for recent years: the court acted on 1048 EAJA applications in FY 2004; 1339 in FY 2003; 1104 in FY 2002; 801 in FY 2001; and 770 in FY 2000. Testimony of Donald L. Ivers, Chief Judge United States Court of Appeals for Veterans Claims, House Appropriations Committee, Subcommittee on Military Quality of Life and Veterans Affairs, *Fiscal 2006 Appropriations: Military Quality of Life and VA* (April 6, 2005).

[6] There was no House or Senate Report submitted with this legislation. Title III, the Small Business Regulatory Enforcement Act, was added by an amendment to H.R. 3136 by Rep. Hyde on March 26, 1996, see 142 Cong. Rec. H2870-74 (daily ed. Mar. 26, 1996).

of a brake on unsupportable government litigation. On the other hand some members expressed the concern that the government is now open to an increased liability every time they choose to litigate. See discussion in Kramer, *Equal Access to Justice Act Amendments of 1996: A New Avenue for Recovering Fees from the Government*, 51 Admin. L. Rev. 363, 373-76 (1999).

Source Note:

There is no truly comprehensive, up-to-date source of information on the Equal Access to Justice Act. No publication deals exclusively with Equal Access cases. *Monitoring the Federal Government's Conduct Through Fee Shifting Under the Equal Access to Justice Act—An Inconclusive Experiment*, prepared by Harold J. Krent for the Administrative Conference in 1992, offers case analysis as well as insight into how the Act worked in practice up to then; Recommendation 92-5, *Streamlining Attorney's Fee Litigation Under the Equal Access to Justice Act*, based in part on Professor Krent's study, suggested legislative improvements to the Act. Judith Kramer's 1999 article focusing on the 1996 amendments is still the most up-to-date analysis.

The Bibliography that follows is not intended to be comprehensive, particularly with respect to books and articles about the Act, but to offer a selection of potentially useful publications. Sources before 1985, when the Act was significantly amended, are listed for their background value as well as for their discussion of provisions that remain unchanged. In particular, the preambles to the Conference's proposed and final rules for agency implementation of the original Act (as well as the 1985 amendments) contain extensive discussion of many questions concerning interpretation of the Equal Access to Justice Act, as does the Justice Department's 1985 publication, *Award of Attorney's Fees and Other Expenses in Judicial Proceedings Under the Equal Access to Justice Act*.

Statistical information on the amount of fees and expenses awarded under the Act in many administrative proceedings and court cases appeared in annual reports (until 1994) by the Chairman of the Administrative Conference of the United States and (until 1992) by the Director of the Administrative Office of the U.S. Courts, respectively. Because these reports depend on the accuracy and completeness of the information provided by the agencies and the courts, they are not necessarily comprehensive.

Bibliography:

I. Legislative History

1. *Hearings on S. 265 before the Subcommittee on Improvements in Judicial Machinery of the Senate Committee on the Judiciary*, 96th Cong., 1st Sess. (1979).
2. *Report to Accompany S. 265*, Senate Committee on the Judiciary, S. Rep. No. 96-253, 96th Cong., 1st Sess. (1979).
3. *Report to Accompany S. 265,* House Committee on the Judiciary, H.R. Rep. No. 96-1418, 96th Cong., 2d Sess. (1980).
4. *S.265, Award of Attorneys' Fees Against the Federal Government,* Hearings before the Subcommittee on Courts, Civil Liberties, and the Administration of Justice of the House Committee of the Judiciary, 96th Cong., 2d Sess. (1980).
5. *Conference Report to Accompany H.R. 5612*, Committee of the Conference, H.R. Rep. No. 96-1434, 96th Cong., 2d Sess. (1980).
6. *Implementation of the Equal Access to Justice Act,* Hearings before the Subcommittee on Courts, Civil Liberties, and the Administration of Justice of the House Committee on the Judiciary, 97th Cong., 2d Sess. (March 1, April 1, 1982).
7. *Equal Access to Justice,* Hearings before the Subcommittee on Agency Administration of the Senate Committee on the Judiciary, 97th Cong., 2d Sess. (Dec. 9, 1982).
8. *S. 919, Reauthorization of the Equal Access to Justice Act,* Hearings before the Subcommittee on Administrative Practice and Procedure of the Senate Committee on the Judiciary, 98th Cong., 1st Sess. (April 14, 1983).
9. *S. 919, Equal Access to Justice Act, S. 993,* Senate Committee on the Judiciary, S. Rep. No. 98-586, 98th Cong., 2d Sess. (1984) (Aug. 8, 1984).
10. *Hearings on H.R. 5059* before the Subcommittee on Courts, Civil Liberties, and the Administration of Justice of the House Committee on the Judiciary, 98th Cong., 2d Sess. (March 14, 1984).
11. *H.R. 5479, Equal Access to Justice Act Amendments*, House Committee on the Judiciary, H.R. Rep. No. 98-992, 98th Cong., 2d Sess. (Sept. 6, 1984).
12. *H.R. 2223, Equal Access to Justice Act Amendments,* Hearings before the Subcommittee on Courts, Civil Liberties and the Administration of Justice of the House Committee on the Judiciary, 99th Cong., 1st Sess. (1985).

13. *H.R. 2378, Equal Access to Justice Act Amendments*, House Committee on the Judiciary, H.R. Rep. No. 99-120, 99th Cong., 1st Sess. Part 1 (May 15, 1985), Part 2 (June 13, 1985).

14. *S. 917 and S. 942: Implementing the White House Conference on Small Business—Recommendations on Regulation and Paperwork*, Hearings before the Senate Committee on Small Business, 104th Cong., 2d Sess. (Feb. 28, 1996).

15. *Legislation Relating to Compensation COLA, Court of Veterans Appeals, and Other Matters*, Hearing before the Senate Committee on Veterans' Affairs, 104th Cong., 2d Sess. (May 23, 1996). (See pages 173-97 for a discussion of EAJA Awards in Court of Veterans Appeals cases.)

16. *Legislative Hearing on H.R. 435, the "Equal Access to Justice Reform Act of 2005."* Subcommittee on Courts, the Internet, and Intellectual Property, House Committee on the Judiciary, 109th Cong., 2d Sess. (May 23, 2006).

II. Other Government Documents

1. Administrative Conference of the U.S., Recommendation 92-5, *Streamlining Attorney's Fee Litigation Under the Equal Access to Justice Act*, 57 Fed. Reg. 30,108 (July 8, 1992).

2. Administrative Conference of the U.S., *Report of the Chairman of the Administrative Conference of the United States on Agency Activities Under the Equal Access to Justice Act, October 1, 1989–September 30, 1990* (1991). (See also reports for the fiscal years 1982 through 1989.)

3. Administrative Conference of the U.S., *Draft Model Rules for Implementation of the Equal Access to Justice Act*, 46 Fed. Reg. 15,895 (March 10, 1981).

4. Administrative Conference of the U.S., *Model Rules for Agency Implementation of the Equal Access to Justice Act*, 46 Fed. Reg. 32,900 (June 25, 1981).

5. Administrative Conference of the U.S., *Draft Revised Model Rules for Implementation of the Equal Access to Justice Act*, 50 Fed. Reg. 46,250 (Nov. 6, 1985).

6. Administrative Conference of the U.S., *Model Rules for Implementation of the Equal Access to Justice Act in Agency Proceedings*, 1 C.F.R. Part 315 (1993).

7. Administrative Office of the United States Courts, *Report by the Director of the Administrative Office of the United States Courts of Requests for Fees and Expenses Under the Equal Access to Justice Act of 1980, July 1,*

1991–June 30, 1992, reprinted in Annual Report of the Director of the Administrative Office of the United States Courts 1992, at 92. (See also annual reports for 1982 through 1991.)

8. U.S. General Accounting Office, *Equal Access to Justice Act: Its Use in Selected Agencies*, GAO-HEHS-98-58R (Jan. 14, 1998).

9. U.S. Small Business Administration, Office of Advocacy, *Small Business Attorneys' Fee Recovery: Report on the Equal Access to Justice Act* (1984).

10. U.S. Small Business Administration, Office of Advocacy, *The Equal Access to Justice Act and Small Business—Analysis and Critique* (Aug. 10, 2001), *available at* http://www.sba.gov/advo/laws/eaja01_0810.html.

11. U.S. Department of Justice, Office of Legal Policy, *Award of Attorneys' Fees and Other Expenses in Judicial Proceedings Under the Equal Access to Justice* Act (Rev. ed. 1985).

III. Books and Articles

1. Bennett, *Winning Attorneys' Fees from the U.S. Government* (Chapter 1) (Law Journal Seminars Press, 1984 (looseleaf, updated periodically).

2. Blankinship, *Washington Equal Access to Justice Act: A Substantial Proposal for Reform*, 77 Wash. L. Rev. 169 (2002).

3. Carbone, *The Misguided Application of Traditional Fee Doctrine to the Equal Access to Justice Act*, 26 B.C. L. Rev. 843 (1985).

4. Comment, *The Waiver of Immunity in the Equal Access to Justice Act: Clarifying Opaque Language*, 61 Wash. L. Rev. 217 (1986).

5. Dobbs, *The Market Test for Attorney Fee Awards: Is the Hourly Rate Test Mandatory?*, 28 Ariz. L. Rev. 1 (1986).

6. Enlow, *International Law—Protecting National Security Substantially Justifies U.S. Position and Makes an Award of Fees Under the Equal Access to Justice Act Unjust—Kiareldeen v. Ashcroft, 273 F. 3d 542 (3d Cir. 2001)*, 26 Suffolk Transnat'l L. Rev. 231 (2002).

7. Finley, *Note, Unjust Access to the Equal Access to Justice Act: A Proposal to the Act's Eligibility Loophole for Members of Trade Associations*, 53 Wash. U. J. Urb. & Contemp. L. 243 (1998).

8. Fischer, *The Equal Access to Justice Act—Are the Bankruptcy Courts Less Equal than Others?*, 92 Mich. L. Rev, 2248 (1994).

9. Geer, *Making Uncle Sam Pay: A Review of Equal Access to Justice Act Cases in the Sixth Circuit, 1983-1987*, 19 U. Tol. L. Rev. 301 (1988).

10. Hill, *An Analysis and Explanation of the Equal Access to Justice Act*, 19 Ariz. St. L.J. 229 (1987).

11. Hill, *Equal Access to Justice Act—Paving the Way for Legislative Change*, 36 Case W. Res. L. Rev. 50 (1985-86).

12. Kelly, *Attorney's Fee Awards For Unreasonable Government Conduct: Notes on the Equal Access to Justice Act*, Ark. L. Notes 65 (2004).

13. Kim, Better Access to Justice, *Better Access to Attorneys' Fees—the Procedural Implications of* Scarborough v. Principi, 25 J. Nat'l Ass'n Admin. L. Judges 583 (2005).

14. Kinlin and Kavanaugh, *A Current Guide to Recovery Under the Equal Access to Justice Act,* American Bar Association Section of Public Contract Law (1989).

15. Kramer, *Equal Access to Justice Act Amendments of 1996: A New Avenue for Recovering Fees from the Government*, 51 Admin. L. Rev 363 (1999).

16. Krent, *Monitoring the Federal Government's Conduct Through Fee Shifting Under the Equal Access to Justice Act—An Inconclusive Experiment*, Report to the Administrative Conference of the U.S. 1992 ACUS 331 (Vol. 1). Portions reprinted in *Fee Shifting Under the Equal Access to Justice Act: A Qualified Success*, 11 Yale L. & Pol'y Rev. 458 (1993).

17. Lee, *Sovereign Immunity, Holding the Federal Government Liable for Current Basis Fee Enhancements Requires an Explicit Waiver of Sovereign Immunity from Interest*, 66 Geo. Wash. L. Rev. 1066 (1997).

18. A. Miller, *Calling Sierra Club for Help?: Attorney Fees Under the Equal Access to Justice Act and its Effects on Litigation Involving Large Environmental Groups*, 9 Dick. J. Envtl. L. & Pol'y 553 (2001).

19. M. Miller, *Catalysts as Prevailing Parties under the Equal Access to Justice Act*, 69 U. Chi. L. Rev. 1347 (2002).

20. Note, *Aliens' Alienation From Justice: The Equal Access to Justice Act Should Apply to Deportation Proceedings*, 75 Minn. L. Rev. 1185 (1991).

21. Note, *Determining Fees for Fees Under the Equal Access to Justice Act: Accomplishing the Act's Goals*, 9 Card. L. Rev. 1091 (1988).

22. Note, Gavette v. Office of Personnel Management: *The Right to Attorney Fees Under the Equal Access to Justice Act*, 36 Am. U. L. Rev. 1013 (1987).

23. Note, *Reenacting the Equal Access to Justice Act: A Proposal for Automatic Attorneys' Fee Awards*, 94 Yale L. J. 1207 (1985).

24. Note, *The Equal Access to Justice Act in the Federal Courts*, 84 Colum. L. Rev. 1089 (1984).

25. R. Rossi, *Attorneys' Fees* (3d ed. 2001) (West Group) § 10:5.

26. Sabino, *"And Unequal Justice for All"—Bankruptcy Court Jurisdiction Under the Equal Access to Justice Act*, 22 Mem. St. U. L. Rev. 453 (1992).

27. Sisk, *A Primer on Awards of Attorney's Fees against the Federal Government*, 25 Ariz. St. L.J. 733 (1993).

28. Sisk, *The Essentials of the Equal Access to Justice Act: Court Awards of Attorney's Fees for Unreasonable Government Conduct (Part One)*, 55 La. L. Rev. 217 (1994); *(Part Two)*, 56 La. L. Rev. 1 (1995).

29. Sullivan, *The Equal Access to Justice Act in the Federal Courts*, 84 Colum. L. Rev 1089 (1984).

30. Winold, *Institutionalizing an Experiment: The Extension of the Equal Access to Justice Act—Questions Resolved, Questions Remaining*, 14 Fla. St. U. L. Rev. 925 (1987).

IV. Miscellaneous

1. *What constitutes "adversary adjudication" by administrative agencies entitling prevailing parties to award of attorneys' fees under the Equal Access to Justice Act?*, 96 ALR Fed. 336.

2. *Who Is "Party" Entitled to Recover Attorneys' Fees Under Equal Access to Justice Act (28 U.S.C.A. § 2412(D))?*, 107 ALR Fed. 827.

3. *Who Is "Prevailing Party" So as to be Entitled to Award of Attorneys' Fees by Court Under Equal Access to Justice Act (28 U.S.C.A. § 2412(D))?*, 105 ALR Fed. 110.

4. *Recoupment by Pro Se Litigant of Attorney's Fees Under Equal Access to Justice Act (28 U.S.C.A. § 2412)*, 107 ALR Fed. 888.

5. *Award of Attorneys' Fees in Excess of $75 Per Hour Under Equal Access to Justice Act (EAJA) Provision (28 U.S.C.A. § 2412(D)(2)(A)(ii)) Authorizing Higher Awards—Cases Involving Law Other Than Social Security*, 119 ALR Fed. 1.

6. *Recoupment of Attorney Fees, Under Equal Access to Justice Act (EAJA) (28 U.S.C.A. § 2412), by Litigant Represented by Counsel to Whom No Fee Is Paid by Litigant*, 121 ALR Fed. 291.

Agency Regulations:

Agriculture	7 C.F.R. §§1.180-1.203
Commerce	5 C.F.R. Part 18
Commodity Futures Trading Commission	17 C.F.R. Part 148
Consumer Product Safety Commission	16 C.F.R. §§1025.70-1025.72
Education	34 C.F.R. Part 21
Environmental Protection Agency	40 C.F.R. Part 17
Federal Communications Commission	47 C.F.R. §§1.1501-1.1530
Federal Deposit Insurance Corporation	12 C.F.R. §§308.169-308.183
Federal Labor Relations Authority	5 C.F.R. Part 2430
Federal Maritime Commission	46 C.F.R. §§502.501-502.503
Federal Mine Safety and Health Review Commission	29 C.F.R. Part 2704
Federal Reserve System	12 C.F.R. §§ 263.100-263.111
Federal Trade Commission	16 C.F.R. §§3.81-3.83
Health and Human Services	45 C.F.R. Part 13
Housing and Urban Development	24 C.F.R. Part 14
Interior	43 C.F.R. §§4.601-4.619
International Trade Commission	19 C.F.R. Part 212
Justice	28 C.F.R. Part 24
Labor	29 C.F.R. Part 16
Merit Systems Protection Board	5 C.F.R. 1201.203
National Aeronautics and Space Administration	14 C.F.R. Part 1262
National Credit Union Administration	12 C.F.R. §§747.601-747.616
National Labor Relations Board	29 C.F.R. §§102.143-102.155
National Transportation Safety Board	.49 C.F.R. Part 826
Nuclear Regulatory Commission	10 C.F.R. Part 12
Occupational Safety and Health Review Commission	29 C.F.R. Part 2204
Office of Government Ethics	5.C.F.R. 2610
Postal Service	39 C.F.R. Part 960
Securities and Exchange Commission	17 C.F.R. §§201.31-201.60
Small Business Administration	13 C.F.R. §§134.601-134.618
State	22 C.F.R. Part 134
Transportation	49 C.F.R. Part 6
FAA	14 C.F.R. Part 14
Surface Transportation Board	49 C.F.R. Part 1016
Treasury	31 C.F.R. Part 6
Comptroller of the Currency	12 C.F.R. § 19.210

Appendix:

1. Equal Access to Justice Act, 5 U.S.C. §504, 504 note (2000); 28 U.S.C. §2412, 2412 note (2000).

2. Administrative Conference of the U.S., *Model Rules for Implementation of the Equal Access to Justice Act*, 1 C.F.R. Part 315 (1993).

Equal Access to Justice Act

Title 5, U.S. Code

Administrative Proceedings

§504. Costs and fees of parties

(a)(1) An agency that conducts an adversary adjudication shall award, to a prevailing party other than the United States, fees and other expenses incurred by that party in connection with that proceeding, unless the adjudicative officer of the agency finds that the position of the agency was substantially justified or that special circumstances make an award unjust. Whether or not the position of the agency was substantially justified shall be determined on the basis of the administrative record, as a whole, which is made in the adversary adjudication for which fees and other expenses are sought.

(2) A party seeking an award of fees and other expenses shall, within thirty days of a final disposition in the adversary adjudication, submit to the agency an application which shows that the party is a prevailing party and is eligible to receive an award under this section, and the amount sought, including an itemized statement from any attorney, agent, or expert witness representing or appearing in behalf of the party stating the actual time expended and the rate at which fees and other expenses were computed. The party shall also allege that the position of the agency was not substantially justified. When the United States appeals the underlying merits of an adversary adjudication, no decision on an application for fees and other expenses in connection with that adversary adjudication shall be made under this section until a final and unreviewable decision is rendered by the court on the appeal or until the underlying merits of the case have been finally determined pursuant to the appeal.

(3) The adjudicative officer of the agency may reduce the amount to be awarded, or deny an award, to the extent that the party during the course of the proceedings engaged in conduct which unduly and unreasonably protracted the final resolution of the matter in controversy. The decision of the adjudicative officer of the agency under this section shall be made a part of the record containing the final decision of the agency and shall include written findings and conclusions and the reason or basis therefor. The decision of the agency on the application for fees and other expenses

shall be the final administrative decision under this section.

(4) If, in an adversary adjudication arising from an agency action to enforce a party's compliance with a statutory or regulatory requirement, the demand by the agency is substantially in excess of the decision of the adjudicative officer and is unreasonable when compared with such decision, under the facts and circumstances of the case, the adjudicative officer shall award to the party the fees and other expenses related to defending against the excessive demand, unless the party has committed a willful violation of law or otherwise acted in bad faith, or special circumstances make an award unjust. Fees and expenses awarded under this paragraph shall be paid only as a consequence of appropriations provided in advance.

(b)(1) For the purposes of this section -

    (A) "fees and other expenses" includes the reasonable expenses of expert witnesses, the reasonable cost of any study, analysis, engineering report, test, or project which is found by the agency to be necessary for the preparation of the party's case, and reasonable attorney or agent fees (The amount of fees awarded under this section shall be based upon prevailing market rates for the kind and quality of the services furnished, except that

        (i) no expert witness shall be compensated at a rate in excess of the highest rate of compensation for expert witnesses paid by the agency involved, and

        (ii) attorney or agent fees shall not be awarded in excess of $125 per hour unless the agency determines by regulation that an increase in the cost of living or a special factor, such as the limited availability of qualified attorneys or agents for the proceedings involved, justifies a higher fee.);

(B) "party" means a party, as defined in section 551(3) of this title, who is (i) an individual whose net worth did not exceed $2,000,000 at the time the adversary adjudication was initiated, or (ii) any owner of an unincorporated business, or any partnership, corporation, association, unit of local government, or organization, the net worth of which did not exceed $7,000,000 at the time the adversary adjudication was initiated, and which had not more than 500 employees at the time the adversary adjudication was initiated; except that an organization described in section 501(c)(3) of the Internal Revenue Code of 1986 (26 U.S.C. 501(c)(3)) exempt from taxation under section 501(a) of such Code, or a cooperative association as defined in section 15(a) of the Agricultural Marketing Act (12 U.S.C.

1141j(a)), may be a party regardless of the net worth of such organization or cooperative association or for purposes of subsection (a)(4), a small entity as defined in section 601;

(C) "adversary adjudication" means (i) an adjudication under section 554 of this title in which the position of the United States is represented by counsel or otherwise, but excludes an adjudication for the purpose of establishing or fixing a rate or for the purpose of granting or renewing a license, (ii) any appeal of a decision made pursuant to section 6 of the Contract Disputes Act of 1978 (41 U.S.C. 605) before an agency board of contract appeals as provided in section 8 of that Act (41 U.S.C. 607), (iii) any hearing conducted under chapter 38 of title 31, and (iv) the Religious Freedom Restoration Act of 1993;

(D) "adjudicative officer" means the deciding official, without regard to whether the official is designated as an administrative law judge, a hearing officer or examiner, or otherwise, who presided at the adversary adjudication;

(E) "position of the agency" means, in addition to the position taken by the agency in the adversary adjudication, the action or failure to act by the agency upon which the adversary adjudication is based; except that fees and other expenses may not be awarded to a party for any portion of the adversary adjudication in which the party has unreasonably protracted the proceedings; and

(F) "demand" means the express demand of the agency which led to the adversary adjudication, but does not include a recitation by the agency of the maximum statutory penalty (i) in the administrative complaint, or (ii) elsewhere when accompanied by an express demand for a lesser amount.

(2) Except as otherwise provided in paragraph (1), the definitions provided in section 551 of this title apply to this section.

(c)(1) After consultation with the Chairman of the Administrative Conference of the United States, each agency shall by rule establish uniform procedures for the submission and consideration of applications for an award of fees and other expenses. If a court reviews the underlying decision of the adversary adjudication, an award for fees and other expenses may be made only pursuant to section 2412(d)(3) of title 28, United States Code.

(2) If a party other than the United States is dissatisfied with a determination of fees and other expenses made under subsection (a), that party may, within 30 days after the determination is made, appeal the determination to the court of the United States having jurisdiction to review the

merits of the underlying decision of the agency adversary adjudication. The court's determination on any appeal heard under this paragraph shall be based solely on the factual record made before the agency. The court may modify the determination of fee and other expenses only if the court finds that the failure to make an award of fees and other expenses, or the calculation of the amount of the award, was unsupported by substantial evidence.

(d) Fees and other expenses awarded under this subsection shall be paid by any agency over which the party prevails from any funds made available to the agency by appropriation or otherwise.

(e) The Chairman of the Administrative Conference of the United States, after consultation with the Chief Counsel for Advocacy of the Small Business Administration, shall report annually to the Congress on the amount of fees and other expenses awarded during the preceding fiscal year pursuant to this section. The report shall describe the number, nature, and amount of the awards, the claims involved in the controversy, and any other relevant information which may aid the Congress in evaluating the scope and impact of such awards. Each agency shall provide the Chairman with such information as is necessary for the Chairman to comply with the requirements of this subsection.

(f) No award may be made under this section for costs, fees, or other expenses which may be awarded under section 7430 of the Internal Revenue Code of 1986.

(Added Pub. L. No. 96-481, title II, Sec. 203(a)(1), (c), Oct. 21, 1980, 94 Stat. 2325, 2327; revived and amended Pub. L. No. 99-80, Sec. 1, 6, Aug. 5, 1985, 99 Stat. 183, 186; Pub. L. No. 99-509, title VI, Sec. 6103(c), Oct. 21, 1986, 100 Stat. 1948; Pub. L. No. 99-514, Sec. 2, Oct. 22, 1986, 100 Stat. 2095; Pub. L. No. 100-647, title VI, Sec. 6239(b), Nov. 10, 1988, 102 Stat. 3746; Pub. L. No. 103-141, Sec. 4(b), Nov. 16, 1993, 107 Stat. 1489; Pub. L. No. 104-121, title II, Sec. 231, Mar. 29, 1996, 110 Stat. 862.)

CONGRESSIONAL FINDINGS AND PURPOSES

Section 202 of title II of Pub. L. No. 96-481 provided that:

"(a) The Congress finds that certain individuals, partnerships, corporations, and labor and other organizations may be deterred from seeking review of, or defending against, unreasonable governmental action because of the expense involved in securing the vindication of their rights in civil actions and in administrative proceedings.

"(b) The Congress further finds that because of the greater resources and expertise of the United States the standard for an award of fees against the United States should be different from the standard governing an award against a private litigant, in certain situations.

"(c) It is the purpose of this title

"(1) to diminish the deterrent effect of seeking review of, or defending against, governmental action by providing in specified situations an award of attorney fees, expert witness fees, and other costs against the United States; and

"(2) to insure the applicability in actions by or against the United States of the common law and statutory exceptions to the 'American rule' respecting the award of attorney fees."

Amendments

1996—Subsec. (a)(4). Pub. L. No. 104-121, Sec. 231(a), added par. (4). Subsec. (b)(1)(A)(ii). Pub. L. No. 104-121, Sec. 231(b)(1), substituted "$125" for "$75".

Subsec. (b)(1)(B). Pub. L. No. 104-121, Sec. 231(b)(2), inserted before semicolon at end "or for purposes of subsection (a)(4), a small entity as defined in section 601".

Subsec. (b)(1)(F). Pub. L. No. 104-121, Sec. 231(b)(3)-(5), added subpar. (F).

1993—Subsec. (b)(1)(C). Pub. L. No. 103-141 added cl. (iv).

1988—Subsec. (f). Pub. L. No. 100-647 added subsec. (f).

1986—Subsec. (b)(1)(B). Pub. L. No. 99-514 substituted "Internal Revenue Code of 1986" for "Internal Revenue Code of 1954".

Subsec. (b)(1)(C)(iii). Pub. L. No. 99-509 added cl. (iii).

1985—Subsec. (a)(1). Pub. L. No. 99-80, Sec. 1(a)(1), (2), struck out "as a party to the proceeding" after "the position of the agency", and inserted "Whether or not the position of the agency was substantially justified shall be determined on the basis of the administrative record, as a whole, which is made in the adversary adjudication for which fees and other expenses are sought."

Subsec. (a)(2). Pub. L. No. 99-80, Sec. 1(b), inserted "When the United States appeals the underlying merits of an adversary adjudication, no decision on an application for fees and other expenses in connection with that adversary adjudication shall be made under this section until a final and unreviewable decision is rendered by the court on the appeal or until the underlying merits of the case have been finally determined pursuant to the appeal."

Subsec. (a)(3). Pub. L. No. 99-80, Sec. 1(a)(3), inserted "The decision of the agency on the application for fees and other expenses shall be the final administrative decision under this section."

Subsec. (b)(1)(B). Pub. L. No. 99-80, Sec. 1(c)(1), amended subpar. (B) generally. Prior to amendment, subpar. (B) read as follows: "'party' means a party, as defined in section 551(3) of this title, which is an individual, partnership, corporation, association, or public or private organization other than an agency, but excludes (i) any individual whose net worth exceeded $1,000,000 at the time the adversary adjudication was initiated, and any sole owner of an unincorporated business, or any partnership, corporation, association, or organization whose net worth exceeded $5,000,000 at the time the adversary adjudication was initiated, except that an organization described in section 501(c)(3) of the Internal Revenue Code of 1954 (26 U.S.C. 501(c)(3)) exempt from taxation under section 501(a) of the Code and a cooperative association as defined in section 15(a) of the Agricultural Marketing Act (12 U.S.C. 1141j(a)), may be a party regardless of the net worth of such organization or cooperative association, and (ii) any sole owner of an unincorporated business, or any partnership, corporation, association, or organization, having more than 500 employees at the time the adversary adjudication was initiated;".

Subsec. (b)(1)(C). Pub. L. No. 99-80, Sec. 1(c)(2), designated existing provisions of subpar. (C) as cl. (i) thereof by inserting "(i)" before "an adjudication under", added cl. (ii), and struck out "and" after the semicolon at the end.

Subsec. (b)(1)(D), (E). Pub. L. No. 99-80, Sec. 1(c)(3), substituted "; and" for the period at end of subpar. (D), and added subpar. (E).

Subsec. (c)(2). Pub. L. No. 99-80, Sec. 1(d), amended par. (2) generally. Prior to amendment, par. (2) read as follows: "A party dissatisfied with the fee determination made under subsection (a) may petition for leave to appeal to the court of the United States having jurisdiction to review the merits of the underlying decision of the agency adversary adjudication. If the court denies the petition for leave to appeal, no appeal may be taken from the denial. If the court grants the petition, it may modify the determination only if it finds that the failure to make an award, or the calculation of the amount of the award, was an abuse of discretion."

Subsec. (d). Pub. L. No. 99-80, Sec. 1(e), amended subsec. (d) generally. Prior to amendment, subsec. (d) read as follows: "(1) Fees and other expenses awarded under this section may be paid by any agency over which the party prevails from any funds made available to the agency, by appropriation or otherwise, for such purpose. If not paid by any agency, the fees and other expenses shall be paid in the same manner as the payment of final judgments is made pursuant to section 2414 of title 28, United States Code. "(2) There is authorized to be appropriated to each agency for each of the fiscal years 1982, 1983, and 1984, such sums as may be necessary to pay fees and other expenses awarded under this section in such fiscal years."

1980—Pub. L. No. 96-481, Sec. 203(c), which provided for the repeal of this section effective Oct. 1, 1984, was itself repealed and this section was revived by section 6 of Pub. L. No. 99-80, set out as a note below.

Effective Date of 1996 Amendment

Section 233 of Pub. L. No. 104-121 provided that: "The amendments made by sections 331 and 332 (probably means sections 231 and 232, amending this section and section 2412 of Title 28, Judiciary and Judicial Procedure) shall apply to civil actions and adversary adjudications commenced on or after the date of the enactment of this subtitle (Mar. 29, 1996)."

Termination of Administrative Conference of United States

For termination of Administrative Conference of United States, see provision of title IV of Pub. L. No. 104-52, set out as a note preceding section 591 of this title.

Prohibition on Use of Energy and Water Development Appropriations to Pay Intervening Parties in Regulatory or Adjudicatory Proceedings

Pub. L. No. 102-377, title V, Sec. 502, Oct. 2, 1992, 106 Stat. 1342, provided that: "None of the funds in this Act or subsequent Energy and Water Development Appropriations Acts shall be used to pay the expenses of, or otherwise compensate, parties intervening in regulatory or adjudicatory proceedings funded in such Acts."

Limitation on Payments

Section 207 of title II of Pub. L. No. 96-481, which provided that the payment of judgments, fees and other expenses in the same manner as the payment of final judgments as provided in this Act would be effective only to the extent and in such amounts as are provided in advance in appropriation Acts, was repealed by Pub. L. No. 99-80, Sec. 4, Aug. 5, 1985, 99 Stat. 186.

Title 28, U.S. Code

Judicial Proceedings

§2412. Costs and fees

(a)(1) Except as otherwise specifically provided by statute, a judgment for costs, as enumerated in section 1920 of this title, but not including the fees and expenses of attorneys, may be awarded to the prevailing party in any civil action brought by or against the United States or any agency or any official of the United States acting in his or her official capacity in any court having jurisdiction of such action. A judgment for costs when taxed against the United States shall, in an amount established by statute, court rule, or order, be limited to reimbursing in whole or in part the prevailing party for the costs incurred by such party in the litigation.

(2) A judgment for costs, when awarded in favor of the United States in an action brought by the United States, may include an amount equal to the filing fee prescribed under section 1914(a) of this title. The preceding sentence shall not be construed as requiring the United States to pay any filing fee.

(b) Unless expressly prohibited by statute, a court may award reasonable fees and expenses of attorneys, in addition to the costs which may be awarded pursuant to subsection (a), to the prevailing party in any civil action brought by or against the United States or any agency or any official of the United States acting in his or her official capacity in any court having jurisdiction of such action. The United States shall be liable for such fees and expenses to the same extent that any other party would be liable under the common law or under the terms of any statute which specifically provides for such an award.

(c)(1) Any judgment against the United States or any agency and any official of the United States acting in his or her official capacity for costs pursuant to subsection (a) shall be paid as provided in sections 2414 and 2517 of this title and shall be in addition to any relief provided in the judgment.

(2) Any judgment against the United States or any agency and any official of the United States acting in his or her official capacity for fees and expenses of attorneys pursuant to subsection (b) shall be paid as provided in sections 2414 and 2517 of this title, except that if the basis for the award is a finding that the United States acted in bad faith, then the

award shall be paid by any agency found to have acted in bad faith and shall be in addition to any relief provided in the judgment.

(d)(1)(A) Except as otherwise specifically provided by statute, a court shall award to a prevailing party other than the United States fees and other expenses, in addition to any costs awarded pursuant to subsection (a), incurred by that party in any civil action (other than cases sounding in tort), including proceedings for judicial review of agency action, brought by or against the United States in any court having jurisdiction of that action, unless the court finds that the position of the United States was substantially justified or that special circumstances make an award unjust.

(B) A party seeking an award of fees and other expenses shall, within thirty days of final judgment in the action, submit to the court an application for fees and other expenses which shows that the party is a prevailing party and is eligible to receive an award under this subsection, and the amount sought, including an itemized statement from any attorney or expert witness representing or appearing in behalf of the party stating the actual time expended and the rate at which fees and other expenses were computed. The party shall also allege that the position of the United States was not substantially justified. Whether or not the position of the United States was substantially justified shall be determined on the basis of the record (including the record with respect to the action or failure to act by the agency upon which the civil action is based) which is made in the civil action for which fees and other expenses are sought.

(C) The court, in its discretion, may reduce the amount to be awarded pursuant to this subsection, or deny an award, to the extent that the prevailing party during the course of the proceedings engaged in conduct which unduly and unreasonably protracted the final resolution of the matter in controversy.

(D) If, in a civil action brought by the United States or a proceeding for judicial review of an adversary adjudication described in section 504(a)(4) of title 5, the demand by the United States is substantially in excess of the judgment finally obtained by the United States and is unreasonable when compared with such judgment, under the facts and circumstances of the case, the court shall award to the party the fees and other expenses related to defending against the excessive demand, unless the party has committed a willful violation of law or otherwise acted in bad faith, or special circumstances make an award unjust. Fees and expenses awarded under this subparagraph shall be paid only as a consequence of appropriations provided in advance.

(2) For the purposes of this subsection –

(A) "fees and other expenses" includes the reasonable expenses of expert witnesses, the reasonable cost of any study, analysis, engineering report, test, or project which is found by the court to be necessary for the preparation of the party's case, and reasonable attorney fees (The amount of fees awarded under this subsection shall be based upon prevailing market rates for the kind and quality of the services furnished, except that (i) no expert witness shall be compensated at a rate in excess of the highest rate of compensation for expert witnesses paid by the United States; and (ii) attorney fees shall not be awarded in excess of $125 per hour unless the court determines that an increase in the cost of living or a special factor, such as the limited availability of qualified attorneys for the proceedings involved, justifies a higher fee.);

(B) "party" means (i) an individual whose net worth did not exceed $2,000,000 at the time the civil action was filed, or (ii) any owner of an unincorporated business, or any partnership, corporation, association, unit of local government, or organization, the net worth of which did not exceed $7,000,000 at the time the civil action was filed, and which had not more than 500 employees at the time the civil action was filed; except that an organization described in section 501(c)(3) of the Internal Revenue Code of 1986 (26 U.S.C. 501(c)(3)) exempt from taxation under section 501(a) of such Code, or a cooperative association as defined in section 15(a) of the Agricultural Marketing Act (12 U.S.C. 1141j(a)), may be a party regardless of the net worth of such organization or cooperative association or for purposes of subsection (d)(1)(D), a small entity as defined in section 601 of title 5;

(C) "United States" includes any agency and any official of the United States acting in his or her official capacity;

(D) "position of the United States" means, in addition to the position taken by the United States in the civil action, the action or failure to act by the agency upon which the civil action is based; except that fees and expenses may not be awarded to a party for any portion of the litigation in which the party has unreasonably protracted the proceedings;

(E) "civil action brought by or against the United States" includes an appeal by a party, other than the United States, from a decision of a contracting officer rendered pursuant to a disputes clause in a contract with the Government or pursuant to the Contract Disputes Act of 1978;

(F) "court" includes the United States Court of Federal Claims and the United States Court of Appeals for Veterans Claims;

(G) "final judgment" means a judgment that is final and not appealable, and includes an order of settlement;

(H) "prevailing party", in the case of eminent domain proceedings, means a party who obtains a final judgment (other than by settlement), exclusive of interest, the amount of which is at least as close to the highest valuation of the property involved that is attested to at trial on behalf of the property owner as it is to the highest valuation of the property involved that is attested to at trial on behalf of the Government; and

(I) "demand" means the express demand of the United States which led to the adversary adjudication, but shall not include a recitation of the maximum statutory penalty (i) in the complaint, or (ii) elsewhere when accompanied by an express demand for a lesser amount.

(3) In awarding fees and other expenses under this subsection to a prevailing party in any action for judicial review of an adversary adjudication, as defined in subsection (b)(1)(C) of section 504 of title 5, United States Code, or an adversary adjudication subject to the Contract Disputes Act of 1978, the court shall include in that award fees and other expenses to the same extent authorized in subsection (a) of such section, unless the court finds that during such adversary adjudication the position of the United States was substantially justified, or that special circumstances make an award unjust.

(4) Fees and other expenses awarded under this subsection to a party shall be paid by any agency over which the party prevails from any funds made available to the agency by appropriation or otherwise.

(e) The provisions of this section shall not apply to any costs, fees, and other expenses in connection with any proceeding to which section 7430 of the Internal Revenue Code of 1986 applies (determined without regard to subsections (b) and (f) of such section). Nothing in the preceding sentence shall prevent the awarding under subsection (a) of section 2412 of title 28, United States Code, of costs enumerated in section 1920 of such title (as in effect on October 1, 1981).

(f) If the United States appeals an award of costs or fees and other expenses made against the United States under this section and the award is affirmed in whole or in part, interest shall be paid on the amount of the award as affirmed. Such interest shall be computed at the rate determined under section

1961(a) of this title, and shall run from the date of the award through the day before the date of the mandate of affirmance.

(Added June 25, 1948, ch. 646, 62 Stat. 973; Pub. L. No. 89-507, Sec. 1, July 18, 1966, 80 Stat. 308; Pub. L. No. 96-481, title II, Sec. 204(a), (c), Oct. 21, 1980, 94 Stat. 2327, 2329; Pub. L. No. 97-248, title II, Sec. 292(c), Sept. 3, 1982, 96 Stat. 574; Pub. L. No. 99-80, Sec. 2, 6, Aug. 5, 1985, 99 Stat. 184, 186; Pub. L. No. 99-514, Sec. 2, Oct. 22, 1986, 100 Stat. 2095; Pub. L. No. 102-572, title III, Sec. 301(a), title V, Sec. 502(b), 506(a), title IX, Sec. 902(b)(1), Oct. 29, 1992, 106 Stat. 4511-4513, 4516; Pub. L. No. 104-66, title I, Sec. 1091(b), Dec. 21, 1995, 109 Stat. 722; Pub. L. No. 104-121, title II, Sec. 232, Mar. 29, 1996, 110 Stat. 863; Pub. L. No. 105-368, Title V, § 512(b)(1)(B), Nov. 11, 1998, 112 Stat. 3342.)

Amendments

1998—Subsec. (d)(2)(F). Pub. L. No. 105-368, Sec. 512(b)(1)(B), struck "Court of Veterans Appeals" and inserted "Court of Appeals for Veterans Claims."
1996—Subsec. (d)(1)(D). Pub. L. No. 104-121, Sec. 232(a), added subpar. (D).
 Subsec. (d)(2)(A)(ii). Pub. L. No. 104-121, Sec. 232(b)(1), substituted "$125" for "$75".
 Subsec. (d)(2)(B). Pub. L. No. 104-121, Sec. 232(b)(2), inserted before semicolon at end "or for purposes of subsection (d)(1)(D), a small entity as defined in section 601 of title 5".
 Subsec. (d)(2)(I). Pub. L. No. 104-121, Sec. 232(b)(3)-(5), added subpar. (I).
1995—Subsec. (d)(5). Pub. L. No. 104-66 struck out par. (5) which read as follows: "The Attorney General shall report annually to the Congress on the amount of fees and other expenses awarded during the preceding fiscal year pursuant to this subsection. The report shall describe the number, nature, and amount of the awards, the claims involved in the controversy, and any other relevant information which may aid the Congress in evaluating the scope and impact of such awards."
1992—Subsec. (a). Pub. L. No. 102-572, Sec. 301(a), designated existing provisions as par. (1) and added par. (2).
 Subsec. (d)(2)(F). Pub. L. No. 102-572, Sec. 902(b)(1), substituted "United States Court of Federal Claims" for "United States Claims Court".
 Pub. L. No. 102-573, Sec. 506(a), inserted before semicolon at end "and the United States Court of Veterans Appeals".
 Subsec. (d)(5). Pub. L. No. 102-572, Sec. 502(b), substituted "The Attorney General shall report annually to the Congress on" for "The Director of the Administrative Office of the United States Courts shall include in the annual report prepared pursuant to section 604 of this title,".
1986—Subsecs. (d)(2)(B), (e). Pub. L. No. 99-514 substituted "Internal Revenue Code of 1986" for "Internal Revenue Code of 1954".

1985—Subsecs. (a), (b). Pub. L. No. 99-80, Sec. 2(a)(1), substituted "or any agency or any official of the United States" for "or any agency and any official of the United States".

Subsec. (d). Pub. L. No. 99-80, Sec. 6, repealed amendment made by Pub. L. No. 96-481, Sec. 204(c), and provided that subsec. (d) was effective on or after Aug. 5, 1985, as if it had not been repealed by section 204(c). See 1980 Amendment note below.

Subsec. (d)(1)(A). Pub. L. No. 99-80, Sec. 2(a)(2), inserted ", including proceedings for judicial review of agency actions," after "in tort)".

Subsec. (d)(1)(B). Pub. L. No. 99-80, Sec. 2(b), inserted provisions directing that whether or not the position of the United States was substantially justified must be determined on the basis of the record (including the record with respect to the action or failure to act by the agency upon which the civil action was based) which is made in the civil action for which fees and other expenses are sought.

Subsec. (d)(2)(B). Pub. L. No. 99-80, Sec. 2(c)(1), substituted "$2,000,000" for "$1,000,000" in cl. (i), and substituted "or (ii) any owner of an unincorporated business, or any partnership, corporation, association, unit of local government, or organization, the net worth of which did not exceed $7,000,000 at the time the civil action was filed, and which had not more than 500 employees at the time the civil action was filed; except that an organization described in section 501(c)(3) of the Internal Revenue Code of 1954 (26 U.S.C. 501(c)(3)) exempt from taxation under section 501(a) of such Code, or a cooperative association as defined in section 15(a) of the Agricultural Marketing Act (12 U.S.C. 1141j(a)), may be a party regardless of the net worth of such organization or cooperative association;" for "(ii) a sole owner of an unincorporated business, or a partnership, corporation, association, or organization whose net worth did not exceed $5,000,000 at the time the civil action was filed, except that an organization described in section 501(c)(3) of the Internal Revenue Code of 1954 (26 U.S.C. 501(c)(3)) exempt from taxation under section 501(a) of the Code and a cooperative association as defined in section 15(a) of the Agricultural Marketing Act (12 U.S.C. 1141j(a)), may be a party regardless of the net worth of such organization or cooperative association, or (iii) a sole owner of an unincorporated business, or a partnership, corporation, association, or organization, having not more than 500 employees at the time the civil action was filed; and".

Subsec. (d)(2)(D) to (H). Pub. L. No. 99-80, Sec. 2(c)(2), added subpars. (D) to (H).

Subsec. (d)(4). Pub. L. No. 99-80, Sec. 2(d), amended par. (4) generally. Prior to amendment, par. (4) read as follows: "(A) Fees and other expenses awarded under this subsection may be paid by any agency over which the party prevails from any funds made available to the agency, by appropriation or otherwise, for such purpose. If not paid by any agency, the fees and other expenses shall be paid in the same manner as the payment of final judgments is made in accordance with sections 2414 and 2517 of this title." (B) There is authorized to be appropriated to each agency for each of the fiscal years 1982, 1983, and 1984, such sums as may be necessary to pay fees and other expenses awarded pursuant to this subsection in such fiscal years."

Subsec. (f). Pub. L. No. 99-80, Sec. 2(e), added subsec. (f).

1982—Subsec (e). Pub. L. No. 97-248 added subsec. (e).

1980—Pub. L. No. 96-481, Sec. 204(a), designated existing provisions as subsec. (a), struck out provision that payment of a judgment for costs shall be as provided in section 2414 and section 2517 of this title for the payment of judgments against the United States, and added subsecs. (b) to (d). Pub. L. No. 96-481, Sec. 204(c), repealed subsec. (d) eff. Oct. 1, 1984.

1966—Pub L. No. 89-507 empowered a court having jurisdiction to award judgment for costs, except as otherwise specifically provided by statute, to the prevailing party in any action brought by or against the United States or any agency or official of the United States acting in his official capacity, limited the judgment for costs when taxed against the Government to reimbursing in whole or in part the prevailing party for costs incurred by him in the litigation, required the payment of a judgment for costs to be as provided in section 2414 and section 2517 of this title for the payment of judgments against the United States and eliminated provisions which limited the liability of the United States for fees and costs to those cases in which liability was expressed provided for by Act of Congress, permitted the district court or the Court of Claims, in an action under section 1346(a) or 1491 of this title if the United States put in issue plaintiff's right to recover, to allow costs to the prevailing party from the time of joining such issue, and which authorized the allowance of costs to the successful claimant in an action under section 1346(b) of this title.

Effective Date of 1996 Amendment

Amendment by Pub. L. No. 104-121 applicable to civil actions and adversary adjudications commenced on or after March 29, 1996; see section 233 of Pub. L. No. 104-121, set out as a note under section 504 of Title 5, Government Organization and Employees.

Savings Provisions

Section 206 of Pub. L. No. 96-481, as amended by Pub. L. No. 99-80, Sec. 3, Aug. 5, 1985, 99 Stat. 186, provided that: "(a) Except as provided in subsection (b), nothing in section 2412(d) of title 28, United States Code, as added by section 204(a) of this title, alters, modifies, repeals, invalidates, or supersedes any other provision of Federal law which authorizes an award of such fees and other expenses to any party other than the United States that prevails in any civil action brought by or against the United States.

"(b) Section 206(b) of the Social Security Act (42 U.S.C. 406(b)(1)) shall not prevent an award of fees and other expenses under section 2412(d) of title 28, United States Code. Section 206(b)(2) of the Social Security Act shall not apply with respect to any such award but only if, where the claimant's attorney receives fees for the same work under both section 206(b) of that Act and section 2412(d) of title 28, United States Code, the claimant's attorney refunds to the claimant the amount of the smaller fee."

Nonliability of Judicial Officers for Costs

Pub. L. No. 104-317, title III, Sec. 309(a), Oct. 19, 1996, 110 Stat. 3853, provided that: "Notwithstanding any other provision of law, no judicial officer shall be held liable for any costs, including attorney's fees, in any action brought against such officer for an act or omission taken in such officer's judicial capacity, unless such action was clearly in excess of such officer's jurisdiction."

Fee Agreements

Section 506(c) of Pub. L. No. 102-572 provided that: "Section 5904(d) of title 38, United States Code, shall not prevent an award of fees and other expenses under section 2412(d) of title 28, United States Code. Section 5904(d) of title 38, United States Code, shall not apply with respect to any such award but only if, where the claimant's attorney receives fees for the same work under both section 5904 of title 38, United States Code, and section 2412(d) of title 28, United States Code, the claimant's attorney refunds to the claimant the amount of the smaller fee."

Admin. Conference of the United States

PART 315—MODEL RULES FOR IMPLEMENTATION OF THE EQUAL ACCESS TO JUSTICE ACT IN AGENCY PROCEEDINGS

Subpart A—General Provisions

Sec.
315.101 Purpose of these rules.
315.102 When the Act applies.
315.103 Proceedings covered.
315.104 Eligibility of applicants.
315.105 Standards for awards.
315.106 Allowable fees and expenses.
315.107 Rulemaking on maximum rates for attorney fees.
315.108 Awards against other agencies.
315.109 Delegations of authority.

Sec.
Subpart B—Information Required From Applicants

315.201 Contents of application.
315.202 Net worth exhibit.
315.203 Documentation of fees and expenses.
315.204 When an application may be filed.

Subpart C—Procedures for Considering Applications

315.301 Filing and service of documents.
315.302 Answer to application.
315.303 Reply.
315.304 Comments by other parties.
315.305 Settlement.
315.306 Further proceedings.
315.307 Decision.
315.308 Agency review.
315.309 Judicial review.
315.310 Payment of award.

AUTHORITY: Sec. 203(a)(1), Pub. L. 96-481, 94 Stat. 2325 (5 U.S.C. 504(c)(1)); Pub. L. 99-80, 99 Stat. 183.

SOURCE: 51 FR 16665, May 6, 1986, unless otherwise noted.

Subpart A—General Provisions

§ 315.101 Purpose of these rules.

The Equal Access to Justice Act, 5 U.S.C. 504 (called "the Act" in this part), provides for the award of attorney fees and other expenses to eligible individuals and entities who are parties to certain administrative proceedings (called "adversary adjudications") before this agency. An eligible party may receive an award when it prevails over an agency, unless the agency's position was substantially justified or special circumstances make an award unjust. The rules in this part describe the parties eligible for awards and the proceedings that are covered. They also explain how to apply for awards, and the procedures and standards that this agency will use to make them.

§ 315.102 When the Act applies.

The Act applies to any adversary adjudication pending or commenced before this agency on or after August 5, 1985. It also applies to any adversary adjudication commenced on or after October 1, 1984, and finally disposed of before August 5, 1985, provided that an application for fees and expenses, as described in Subpart B of these rules, has been filed with the agency within 30 days after August 5, 1985, and to any adversary adjudication pending on or commenced on or after October 1, 1981, in which an application for fees and other expenses was timely filed and was dismissed for lack of jurisdiction.

§ 315.103 Proceedings covered.

(a) The Act applies to adversary adjudications conducted by this agency. These are (1) adjudications under 5 U.S.C. 554 in which the position of this or any other agency of the United States, or any component of an agency, is presented by an attorney or other representative who enters an appearance and participates in the proceeding, and (2) appeals of decisions of contracting officers made pursuant to section 6 of the Contract Disputes Act of 1978 (41 U.S.C. 605) before agency boards of contract appeals as provided in section 8 of that Act (41 U.S.C. 607). Any proceeding in which this agency may prescribe a lawful present or future rate is not covered by the Act. Proceedings to grant or renew licenses are also excluded, but proceedings to modify, suspend, or revoke licenses are covered if they are otherwise "adversary adjudications." For this agency, the types of proceedings generally covered include: [to be supplied by the agency]

Alt. 315.103(a): [for use by contract appeals boards] The Act applies to appeals of decisions of contracting officers made pursuant to section 6 of the Contract Disputes Act of 1978 (41 U.S.C. 605) before this board as provided in section 8 of that Act (41 U.S.C. 607).

(b) This agency's failure to identify a type of proceeding as an adversary adjudication shall not preclude the filing of an application by a party who believes the proceeding is covered by the Act; whether the proceeding is covered will then be an issue for resolution in proceedings on the application.

(c) If a proceeding includes both matters covered by the Act and matters specifically excluded from coverage, any award made will include only fees and expenses related to covered issues.

ACUS Model Rules for Implementing EAJA

§ 315.104 Eligibility of applicants.

(a) To be eligible for an award of attorney fees and other expenses under the Act, the applicant must be a party to the adversary adjudication for which it seeks an award. The term "party" is defined in 5 U.S.C. 551(3). The applicant must show that it meets all conditions of eligibility set out in this subpart and in subpart B.

(b) The types of eligible applicants are as follows:

(1) An individual with a net worth of not more than $2 million;

(2) The sole owner of an unincorporated business who has a net worth of not more than $7 million, including both personal and business interests, and not more than 500 employees;

(3) A charitable or other tax-exempt organization described in section 501(c)(3) of the Internal Revenue Code (26 U.S.C. 501(c)(3)) with not more than 500 employees;

(4) A cooperative association as defined in section 15(a) of the Agricultural Marketing Act (12 U.S.C. 1141j(a)) with not more than 500 employees; and

(5) Any other partnership, corporation, association, unit of local government, or organization with a net worth of not more than $7 million and not more than 500 employees.

(c) For the purpose of eligibility, the net worth and number of employees of an applicant shall be determined as of the date the proceeding was initiated.

Alt. 315.104(c): [for use by contract appeals boards] For the purpose of eligibility, the net worth and number of employees of an applicant shall be determined as of the date the applicant filed its appeal under 41 U.S.C. 606.

(d) An applicant who owns an unincorporated business will be considered as an "individual" rather than a "sole owner of an unincorporated business" if the issues on which the applicant prevails are related primarily to personal interests rather than to business interests.

(e) The employees of an applicant include all persons who regularly perform services for renumeration for the applicant, under the applicant's direction and control. Part-time employees shall be included on a proportional basis.

(f) The net worth and number of employees of the applicant and all of its affiliates shall be aggregated to determine eligibility. Any individual, corporation or other entity that directly or indirectly controls or owns a majority of the voting shares or other interests of the applicant, or any corporation or other entity of which the applicant directly or indirectly owns or controls a majority of the voting shares or other interest, will be considered an affiliate for purposes of this part, unless the adjudicative officer determines that such treatment would be unjust and contrary to the purposes of the Act in light of the actual relationship between the affiliated entities. In addition, the adjudicative officer may determine that financial relationships of the applicant other than those described in this paragraph constitute special circumstances that would make an award unjust.

(g) An applicant that participates in a proceeding primarily on behalf of one or more other persons or entities that would be ineligible is not itself eligible for an award.

§ 315.105 Standards for awards.

(a) A prevailing applicant may receive an award for fees and expenses incurred in connection with a proceeding or in a significant and discrete substantive portion of the proceeding, unless the position of the agency over which the applicant has prevailed was substantially justified. The position of the agency includes, in addition to the position taken by the agency in the adversary adjudication, the action or failure to act by the agency upon which the adversary adjudication is based. The burden of proof that an award should not be made to an ineligible prevailing applicant because the agency's position was substantially justified is on the agency counsel.

(b) An award will be reduced or denied if the applicant has unduly or unreasonably protracted the proceeding or if special circumstances make the award sought unjust.

§ 315.106 Allowable fees and expenses.

(a) Awards will be based on rates customarily charged by persons en-

§ 315.107

gaged in the business of acting as attorneys, agents and expert witnesses, even if the services were made available without charge or at reduced rate to the applicant.

(b) No award for the fee of an attorney or agent under these rules may exceed $75.00 per hour. No award to compensate an expert witness may exceed the highest rate at which this agency pays expert witnesses, which is [to be supplied by the agency]. However, an award may also include the reasonable expenses of the attorney, agent, or witness as a separate item, if the attorney, agent or witness ordinarily charges clients separately for such expenses.

(c) In determining the reasonableness of the fee sought for an attorney, agent or expert witness, the adjudicative officer shall consider the following:

(1) If the attorney, agent or witness is in private practice, his or her customary fees for similar services, or, if an employee of the applicant, the fully allocated costs of the services;

(2) The prevailing rate for similar services in the community in which the attorney, agent or witness ordinarily performs services;

(3) The time actually spent in the representation of the applicant;

(4) The time reasonably spent in light of the difficulty or complexity of the issues in the proceeding; and

(5) Such other factors as may bear on the value of the services provided.

(d) The reasonable cost of any study, analysis, engineering report, test, project or similar matter prepared on behalf of a party may be awarded, to the extent that the charge for the services does not exceed the prevailing rate for similar services, and the study or other matter was necessary for preparation of applicant's case.

§ 315.107 **Rulemaking on maximum rates for attorney fees.**

(a) If warranted by an increase in the cost of living or by special circumstances (such as limited availability of attorneys qualified to handle certain types of proceedings), this agency may adopt regulations providing that attorney fees may be awarded at a rate higher than $75 per hour in some or all of the types of proceedings covered by this part. This agency will conduct any rulemaking proceedings for this purpose under the informal rulemaking procedures of the Administrative Procedure Act.

(b) Any person may file with this agency a petition for rulemaking to increase the maximum rate for attorney fees, in accordance with [cross-reference to, or description of, standard agency procedure for rulemaking petitions.] The petition should identify the rate the petitioner believes this agency should establish and the types of proceedings in which the rate should be used. It should also explain fully the reasons why the higher rate is warranted. This agency will respond to the petition within 60 days after it is filed, by initiating a rulemaking proceeding, denying the petition, or taking other appropriate action.

§ 315.108 **Awards against other agencies.**

If an applicant is entitled to an award because it prevails over another agency of the United States that participates in a proceeding before this agency and takes a position that is not substantially justified, the award or appropriate portion of the award shall be made against that agency.

§ 315.109 **Delegations of authority.**

This agency delegates to [identify appropriate agency unit or officer] authority to take final action on matters pertaining to the Equal Access to Justice Act, 5 U.S.C. 504, in actions arising under [list statutes or types of proceedings.] This agency may by order delegate authority to take final action on matters pertaining to the Equal Access to Justice Act in particular cases to other subordinate officials of bodies.

Alt. 315.109: [Contract appeals boards may omit this section.]

Subpart B—Information Required From Applicants

§ 315.201 **Contents of application.**

(a) An application for an award of fees and expenses under the Act shall identify the applicant and the proceeding for which an award is sought

The application shall show that the applicant has prevailed and identify the position of an agency or agencies that the applicant alleges was not substantially justified. Unless the applicant is an individual, the application shall also state the number of employees of the applicant and describe briefly the type and purpose of its organization or business.

(b) The application shall also include a statement that the applicant's net worth does not exceed $2 million (if an individual) or $7 million (for all other applicants, including their affiliates). However, an applicant may omit this statement if:

(1) It attaches a copy of a ruling by the Internal Revenue Service that it qualifies as an organization described in section 501(c)(3) of the Internal Revenue Code (26 U.S.C. 501(c)(3)) or, in the case of a tax-exempt organization not required to obtain a ruling from the Internal Revenue Service on its exempt status, a statement that describes the basis for the applicant's belief that it qualifies under such section; or

(2) It states that it is a cooperative association as defined in section 15(a) of the Agricultural Marketing Act (12 U.S.C. 1141j(a)).

(c) The application shall state the amount of fees and expenses for which an award is sought.

(d) The application may also include any other matters that the applicant wishes this agency to consider in determining whether and in what amount an award should be made.

(e) The application shall be signed by the applicant or an authorized officer or attorney of the applicant. It shall also contain or be accompanied by a written verification under oath or under penalty of perjury that the information provided in the application is true and correct.

§ 315.202 Net worth exhibit.

(a) Each applicant except a qualified tax-exempt organization or cooperative association must provide with its application a detailed exhibit showing the new worth of the applicant and any affiliates (as defined in § 315.104(f) of this part) when the proceeding was initiated. The exhibit may be in any form convenient to the applicant that provides full disclosure of the applicant's and its affiliates' assets and liabilities and is sufficient to determine whether the applicant qualifies under the standards in this part. The adjudicative officer may require an applicant to file additional information to determine its eligibility for an award.

(b) Ordinarily, the net worth exhibit will be included in the public record of the proceeding. However, an applicant that objects to public disclosure of information in any portion of the exhibit and believes there are legal grounds for withholding it from disclosure may submit that portion of the exhibit directly to the adjudicative officer in a sealed envelope labeled "Confidential Financial Information," accompanied by a motion to withhold the information from public disclosure. The motion shall describe the information sought to be withheld and explain, in detail, why it falls within one or more of the specific exemptions from mandatory disclosure under the Freedom of Information Act, 5 U.S.C. 552(b)(1)-(9), why public disclosure of the information would adversely affect the applicant, and why disclosure is not required in the public interest. The material in question shall be served on counsel representing the agency against which the applicant seeks an award, but need not be served on any other party to the proceeding. If the adjudicative officer finds that the information should not be withheld from disclosure, it shall be placed in the public record of the proceeding. Otherwise, any request to inspect or copy the exhibit shall be disposed of in accordance with this agency's established procedures under the Freedom of Information Act [insert cross reference to agency FOIA rules].

§ 315.203 Documentation of fees and expenses.

The application shall be accompanied by full documentation of the fees and expenses, including the cost of any study, analysis, engineering report, test, project or similar matter for which an award is sought. A separate itemized statement shall be sub

§ 315.204

mitted for each professional firm or individual whose services are covered by the application, showing the hours spent in connection with the proceeding by each individual, a description of the specific services performed, the rates at which each fee has been computed, any expenses for which reimbursement is sought, the total amount claimed, and the total amount paid or payable by the applicant or by any other person or entity for the services provided. The adjudicative officer may require the applicant to provide vouchers, receipts, logs, or other substantiation for any fees or expenses claimed, pursuant to § 315.306 of these rules.

§ 315.204 When an application may be filed.

(a) An application may be filed whenever the applicant has prevailed in the proceeding or in a significant and discrete substantive portion of the proceeding, but in no case later than 30 days after this agency's final disposition of the proceeding.

(b) For purposes of this rule, final disposition means the date on which a decision or order disposing of the merits of the proceeding or any other complete resolution of the proceeding, such as a settlement or voluntary dismissal, become a final and unappealable, both within the agency and to the courts.

(c) If review or reconsideration is sought or taken of a decision as to which an applicant believes it has prevailed, proceedings for the award of fees shall be stayed pending final disposition of the underlying controversy. When the United States appeals the underlying merits of an adversary adjudication to a court, no decision on an application for fees and other expenses in connection with that adversary adjudication shall be made until a final and unreviewable decision is rendered by the court on the appeal or until the underlying merits of the case have been finally determined pursuant to the appeal.

Subpart C—Procedures for Considering Applications

§ 315.301 Filing and service of documents.

Any application for an award or other pleading or document related to an application shall be filed and served on all parties to the proceeding in the same manner as other pleadings in the proceeding, except as provided in § 315.202(b) for confidential financial information.

§ 315.302 Answer to application.

(a) Within 30 days after service of an application, counsel representing the agency against which an award is sought may file an answer to the application. Unless agency counsel requests an extension of time for filing or files a statement of intent to negotiate under paragraph (b) of this section, failure to file an answer within the 30-day period may be treated as a consent to the award requested.

(b) If agency counsel and the applicant believe that the issues in the fee application can be settled, they may jointly file a statement of their intent to negotiate a settlement. The filing of this statement shall extend the time for filing an answer for an additional 30 days, and further extensions may be granted by the adjudicative officer upon request by agency counsel and the applicant.

(c) The answer shall explain in detail any objections to the award requested and identify the facts relied on in support of agency counsel's position. If the answer is based on any alleged facts not already in the record of the proceeding, agency counsel shall include with the answer either supporting affidavits or a request for further proceedings under § 315.306.

§ 315.303 Reply.

Within 15 days after service of an answer, the applicant may file a reply. If the reply is based on any alleged facts not already in the record of the proceeding, the applicant shall include with the reply either supporting affidavits or a request for further proceedings under § 315.306.

§ 315.304 Comments by other parties.

Any party to a proceeding other than the applicant and agency counsel may file comments on an application within 30 days after it is served or on an answer within 15 days after it is served. A commenting party may not participate further in proceedings on the application unless the adjudicative officer determines that the public interest requires such participation in order to permit full exploration of matters raised in the comments.

§ 315.305 Settlement.

The application and agency counsel may agree on a proposed settlement of the award before final action on the application, either in connection with a settlement of the underlying proceeding, or after the underlying proceeding has been concluded, in accordance with the agency's standard settlement procedure. If a prevailing party and agency counsel agree on a proposed settlement of an award before an application has been filed, the application shall be filed with the proposed settlement.

§ 315.306 Further proceedings.

(a) Ordinarily, the determination of an award will be made on the basis of the written record. However, on request of either the applicant or agency counsel, or on his or her own initiative, the adjudicative officer may order further proceedings, such as an informal conference, oral argument, additional written submissions or, as to issues other than substantial justification (such as the applicant's eligibility or substantiation of fees and expenses), pertinent discovery or an evidentiary hearing. Such further proceedings shall be held only when necessary for full and fair resolution of the issues arising from the application, and shall be conducted as promptly as possible. Whether or not the position of the agency was substantially justified shall be determined on the basis of the administrative record, as a whole, which is made in the adversary adjudication for which fees and other expenses are sought.

(b) A request that the adjudicative officer order further proceedings under this section shall specifically identify the information sought or the disputed issues and shall explain why the additional proceedings are necessary to resolve the issues.

§ 315.307 Decision.

The adjudicative officer shall issue an initial decision on the application within [to be supplied by the agency] days after completion of proceedings on the application. The decision shall include written findings and conclusions on the applicant's eligibility and status as a prevailing party, and an explanation of the reasons for any difference between the amount requested and the amount awarded. The decision shall also include, if at issue, findings on whether the agency's position was substantially justified, whether the applicant unduly protracted the proceedings, or whether special circumstances make an award unjust. If the applicant has sought an award against more than one agency, the decision shall allocate responsibility for payment of any award made among the agencies, and shall explain the reasons for the allocation made.

Alt. 315.307 [for use by contract appeals boards] The Board shall issue its decision on the application within [to be supplied by the agency] days after completion of proceedings on the application. Whenever possible, the decision shall be made by the same administrative judge or panel that decided the contract appeal for which fees are sought. The decision shall include written findings . . . . [Continue as in 315.307, from the second sentence to the end.]

§ 315.308 Agency review.

Either the applicant or agency counsel may seek review of the initial decision on the fee application, or the agency may decide to review the decision on its own initiative, in accordance with [cross-reference to agency's regular review procedures.] If neither the applicant nor agency counsel seeks review and the agency does not take review on its own initiative, the initial decision on the application shall become a final decision of the agency [30] days after it is issued. Whether to review a decision is a matter within the discretion of the agency. If review is taken, the agency will issue a final decision on the application or remand the application to the adjudicative officer for further proceedings.

Alt. 315.308: (for use by contract appeals board) Reconsideration. Either party may seek reconsideration of the decision on the fee application in accordance with [cross-reference to rule on reconsideration of contract appeals board decisions].

§ 315.309 Judicial review.

Judicial review of final agency decisions on awards may be sought as provided in 5 U.S.C. 504(c)(2).

§ 315.310 Payment of award.

An applicant seeking payment of an award shall submit to the [comptroller or other disbursing official] of the paying agency a copy of the agency's final decision granting the award, accompanied by a certification that the applicant will not seek review of the decision in the United States courts. [Include here address for submissions at specific agency.] The agency will pay the amount awarded to the applicant within 60 days.

Federal Advisory Committee Act

Citations:

5 U.S.C. App. 2 (2000), enacted October 6, 1972, by Pub. L. No. 92-463, 86 Stat. 770. Amended by Pub. L. No. 105-153, §1, Dec. 17, 1997, 111 Stat. 2689.

Lead Agency:

General Services Administration, Office of Administration, Committee Management Secretariat, 18th & F Streets NW, Washington, D.C. 20405 (202) 708-5082; http://www.gsa.gov

Overview:

The Federal Advisory Committee Act (FACA) regulates the formation and operation of advisory committees by federal agencies in the Executive Branch. "Advisory committee" is defined in section 3 to include any committee or similar group that is established by statute or organization plan, established or utilized by the President, or established or utilized by any agency in the interest of obtaining advice or recommendations for the President or one or more federal agencies or officers. Excepted from this definition are groups not wholly composed of full-time, or permanent part-time, federal officers or employees. In addition, the Act also exempts advisory committees of the National Academy of Sciences, the National Academy of Public Administration,[1] the Central Intelligence Agency, and the Federal Reserve System, any

---

[1] Although the advisory committees of the National Academy of Sciences and the National Academy of Public Administration are exempted from the definition, the Act prohibits agencies from using the advice or recommendations of committees created by these two national academies unless their creation and

local civic group whose primary function is to render a public service with respect to a federal program, and any State or local committee established to advise State or local officials or agencies. Finally, some other statutes specifically exempt certain activities from the Act.[2]

The Act requires in part that new advisory committees be established only after public notice and upon a determination that establishment is in the public interest (§9(a)); that each advisory committee have a clearly defined purpose and that its membership be fairly balanced in terms of the points of view represented and the functions to be performed (§5); that the status of and need for each committee be subject to periodic review (§§7, 14); and that meetings of advisory committees be open to public observation, subject to the same exemptions as those provided in the Government in the Sunshine Act (§10).

Section 7 of the Act places oversight and policy responsibility in the Administrator of the General Services Administration and directs the creation of a Committee Management Secretariat in GSA to fulfill those duties. That office maintains a web page about federal advisory committees. (http://www.gsa.gov/Portal/gsa/ep/channelView.do?pageTypeId=8203&channelId=-13170).

At the end of fiscal year 2005, there were 943 federal advisory committees. Of these, 515 were not mandated by statute, a 35% decrease since 1993, when Executive Order 12,838 (February 11, 1993) directed the elimination of at least one-third of all discretionary advisory committees. The Office of Management and Budget issued OMB Circular A-135 to implement this Executive Order.

The breadth of the definition of "advisory committee" has provoked uncertainty and litigation.[3] GSA regulations attempt to provide guidance in

---

meetings follow the specific procedures contained in section 15 of the Act. These procedures generally mirror the requirements applicable to normal advisory committees but are tailored to the particular needs of the academies.

[2] *See, e.g.*, 2 U.S.C. §1534(b) (exempting certain meetings between federal officials and elected officers of state, local, or tribal governments acting in their official capacity).

[3] *See, e.g., In re* Cheney, 406 F.3d 723 (D.C. Cir. 2005) (persons are not "members" of an "advisory committee" unless they have a vote in or, in the case of consensus decisions, a veto over the committee's decisions); Byrd v. U.S.E.P.A., 174 F.3d 239 (D.C. Cir. 1999) (a panel convened by a consultant pursuant to a contract with EPA requiring it to convene a panel to provide technical advice to EPA, whose members were subject to EPA approval, was neither "established" nor "utilized" by EPA); Judicial Watch v. Clinton, 76 F.3d 1232 (D.C. Cir. 1996)

this regard. See 41 C.F.R. 102-3.25, 102-3.40. The requirement for committees to be balanced in terms of their composition and the procedures applicable to "meetings" have also been the subject of litigation.[4] Most of the litigation under FACA has arisen pursuant to the judicial review provisions of the APA; it is an open question whether FACA itself creates a private cause of action for a violation of its terms.[5]

The statute itself prescribes no conflict-of-interest requirements for advisory committee members. However, chapter 11 of title 18 of the U.S. Code, particularly section 208, is applicable to federal employees generally, includ-

---

(President's legal expense trust not an advisory committee); California Forestry Assn. v. U.S. Forest Service, 102 F.3d 609 (D.C. Cir. 1996) (committee established by agency to provide advice to Congress was "advisory committee" under the Act because it also advised the agency).

In *Public Citizen v. U.S. Dep't of Justice*, 109 S. Ct. 2558 (1989), the Supreme Court held that FACA did not apply to the "special advisory relationship" between the President and the American Bar Association Standing Committee on Federal Judiciary on matters of judicial nomination. The opinion turned on the court's conclusion that the ABA group was not a "utilized" committee within the meaning intended by Congress and, thus, the ABA committee did not fall under the statutory definition of "advisory committee" under FACA. Subsequent cases have further refined the definition of what constitutes a "utilized" advisory committee. *See, e.g.*, Sofamor Danek Group, Inc. v. Gaus, 61 F.3d 929 (D.C. Cir. 1995), *cert. denied* 116 S. Ct. 910 (1996); Washington Legal Found. v. U.S. Sentencing Comm'n, 17 F.3d 1446 (D.C. Cir. 1994); Huron Env. Activist League v. EPA, 917 F. Supp. 34 (D.D.C. 1996); Food Chemical News v. Young, 900 F.2d 328 (D.C. Cir. 1990); and Ctr. for Auto Safety v. Fed. Highway Admin., unpub. mem. opin. (Civ. Action No. 89-1045) (D.D.C. Oct.12, 1990).

[4] *See, e.g.*, Cargill, Inc. v. United States, 173 F.3d 323 (D.C. Cir. 1996) (what constitutes fair balance); Ass'n of Am. Physicians & Surgeons, Inc. v. Clinton, 997 F.2d 898 (D.C. Cir. 1993) (the First Lady should be considered a full-time federal employee for purposes of FACA); Public Citizen v. Dep't of HHS, Civ. Action, 795 F. Supp. 1212 (D.D.C. 1992) (what constitutes fair balance); Wash. Post v. National Council on the Arts, Civ. Action No. 92-0955 (D.D.C. April 29, 1992) (grounds for closure); Bureau of Nat'l Affairs v. President's Council of Advisors on Science and Technology, Civ. Action No. 92-1088 (D.D.C. May 7, 1992) (grounds for closure); and Natural Resources Def. Council v. EPA, 806 F. Supp. 275 (D.D.C. 1992) (grounds for closure); Nader v. Baroody, 396 F. Supp. 1231 (D.D.C. 1975); Ctr. for Auto Safety v. Cox, 580 F.2d 689 (D.C. Cir. 1978); Lombardo v. Handler, 397 F. Supp. 792 (D.D.C. 1975), *aff'd*, 546 F.2d 1043 (D.C. Cir. 1976); Food Chemical News, Inc. v. Davis, 378 F. Supp. 1048 (DDC 1974).

[5] *See* Manshardt v. Fed. Judicial Qualifications Comm., 408 F.3d 1154, 1155 n.3 (9th Cir. 2005) (collecting cases).

ing the category of "special government employees." Unless an advisory committee member is appointed as a representative of a particular interest, and is thus not considered a government employee, he or she is likely to be a special government employee, whether or not compensated. Section 208(b)(3) authorizes an official who appoints an advisory committee member to exempt a special government employee where the need for the individual's services outweighs the potential for a conflict of interest. See generally, Memorandum Opinion for the Chief Counsel, Food and Drug Administration, 2 Op. O.L.C. 151 (1978).

Special government employees are subject to disclosure requirements. See 57 Fed. Reg. 11,800 (April 7, 1992).

Section 219(a) of title 18 of the U.S. Code makes it a criminal offense for a public official to be or to act as an agent of a foreign principal required to register under the Foreign Agents Registration Act of 1938. The Department of Justice has concluded that members of federal advisory committees governed by the Federal Advisory Committee Act come within the definition of "public official." Letter of Deputy Assistant Attorney General, Office of Legal Counsel to Deputy Counsel to the President (Apr. 29, 1991). Section 219(b) allows the head of an agency to exempt from section 219(a) those individuals who serve on advisory committees as "special government employees" but not those who serve as representatives. In addition, the Department took the position that the Emoluments Clause of the U.S. Constitution, Article 1, §9, cl. 8, prohibits an individual who is an agency of a foreign government from serving on an advisory committee absent specific congressional consent. The Department concluded that Congress has not consented to such service by enacting the Federal Advisory Committee Act.

Legislative History:

Congress considered legislation to establish minimum standards for the organization and operation of federal advisory committees intermittently since the mid-1950s. After oversight hearings in the 91st Congress (1969-70), legislation was introduced in both houses in the 92d Congress, and both the Senate Committee on Governmental Affairs and the House Committee on Government Operations held hearings. The House Committee on Government Operations reported out H.R. 4383, the Federal Advisory Committee Standards Act in April 1972 (H.R. Rep. No. 92-1017), which was considered and passed by the House on May 9, 1972. The Senate Committee on Governmental Affairs, having considered three separate bills, reported a clean bill, S. 3529, the Federal Advisory Committee Act, on September 7, 1972 (S.

Rep. No. 92-1098). The Senate approved this bill on September 12, 1972 and substituted its text for that in the House-passed bill. The relatively minor differences between the two bills were resolved in a Conference Report (H.R. Rep. No. 92-1403), which the Senate adopted on September 20, 1972. FACA became effective on January 4, 1973.

In 1976, the Congress applied to advisory committees the grounds for closure of meetings found in the Government in the Sunshine Act (5 U.S.C. §552b, Pub. L. No. 94-409, Sept. 13, 1976).

On November 9, 1997, Representative Horn, Chairman of the House Subcommittee on Government Management, Information, and Technology, introduced H.R. 2977, the Federal Advisory Committee Act Amendments of 1997 to the 105th Congress. The proposed legislation sought to clarify public disclosure requirements applicable to the National Academy of Sciences and the National Academy of Public Administration and to overrule legislatively the decision of *Animal Legal Defense Fund v. Shalala*, 104 F.3d 424 (D.C. Cir. 1997). The bill was marked with few revisions and passed the same day. (*See* Cong. Rec. H 10578). On November 13, 1997, the Senate introduced and passed H.R.2977 with no revisions. (*See* Cong. Rec. S. 12515). The Federal Advisory Committee Act Amendments of 1997 became Public Law 105-153 on December 17, 1997.

Source Note:

The relevant legislative history materials of the original Act are collected in *Federal Advisory Committee Act (Public Law 92-463), Source Book.- Legislative History, Texts, and Other Documents* (1978), prepared for the Senate Committee on Governmental Affairs.

Bibliography:

I. Legislative History

1. See discussion above.
2. Congressional Research Service, *Federal Advisory Committee* Act (Pub. L. No. 92-463), *Source Book: Legislative History, Texts and Other Documents* (July 1978).
3. *Hearings on Bills to Amend the Federal Advisory Committee Act, Pub. L. No. 92-463, 86 Stat. 770 (1972) before Subcommittee on Reports, Accounting, and Management of the Senate Committee on Governmental Affairs*, 94th Cong., 2d Sess. (1976).

4. Senate Committee on Governmental Affairs, *Oversight of the Federal Advisory Committee Act*, S. Hrg. No. 98-1037, 98th Cong., 2d Sess. (June 21, 1984).

5. Senate Committee on Governmental Affairs, *Federal Advisory Committee Act and the President's AIDS Commission*, S. Hrg. No. 100-538, 100th Cong., 1st Sess. (Dec. 3, 1987).

6. Senate Committee on Governmental Affairs, *Department of Defense Strategic Defense Initiative Organization Compliance With the Federal Advisory Committee Act*, S. Hrg. 100-681, 100th Cong., 2d Sess. (Apr. 19, 1988).

7. Senate Committee on Governmental Affairs, *Federal Advisory Committee Amendments of 1988*, S. Hrg. 100-945, 100th Cong., 2d Sess. (Oct. 5, 1988).

8. Senate Committee on Governmental Affairs, *Federal Advisory Committee Act Amendments of 1989*, S. Hrg. 101-38, 101st Cong., 1st Sess. (Mar. 15, 1989).

9. Senate Committee on Governmental Affairs, *Federal Advisory Committee Act Amendments of 1992*, S. Rep. No. 102-281, 102d Cong., 2d Sess. (1992).

10. *Hearing on the Federal Advisory Committee Act before the Subcommittee on Government Management, Information, and Technology*, House Government Reform and Oversight Committee, 105th Cong., 1st Sess. (Nov. 5, 1997).

II. Other Government Documents

1. Administrative Conference of the U.S., Recommendation 80-3, *Interpretation and Implementation of the Federal Advisory Committee Act*, 45 Fed. Reg. 46,775 (July 11, 1980).

2. Administrative Conference of the U.S., Recommendation 82-4, *Procedures for Negotiating Proposed Regulations*, 47 Fed. Reg. 30,708 (July 15, 1982).

3. Administrative Conference of the U.S., Recommendation 85-5, *Procedures for Negotiating Proposed Regulations*, 50 Fed. Reg. 52,894 (Dec. 27, 1985).

4. Administrative Conference of the U.S., Recommendation 89-3, *Conflict-of-Interest Requirements for Federal Advisory Committees*, 54 Fed. Reg. 28,969 (July 10, 1989).

5. *Annual Report of the President on Federal Advisory Committees* (1972-1998), *available at* http://www.fido.gov/facadatabase/PrintedAnnual

Reports.asp). (The annual report was discontinued in favor of providing the information online, *at*: http://www.fido.gov/facadatabase/public.asp.

6. Executive Order 12,838, Termination and Limitation of Federal Advisory Committees, 58 Fed. Reg. 8,207 (Feb. 10, 1993).

7. General Accounting Office, *Federal Advisory Committee Act: Advisory Committee Process Appears to Be Working, but Some Concerns Exist* (T-GGD-98-163. July 14, 1998), *available at* (http://www.gao.gov/archive/1998/gg98163t.pdf)

8. General Accounting Office, *Federal Advisory Committees: Additional Guidance Could Help Agencies Better Ensure Independence and Balance* (GAO-04-328 April 16, 2004), *available at* http://www.gao.gov/new.items/d04328.pdf.

III. Books and Articles

1. A. Adler, *Litigation Under the Federal Open Government Laws: The Privacy Act, The Freedom of Information Act, The Federal Advisory Committee Act, The Government in the Sunshine Act* (American Civil Liberties Union Foundation, 20th ed. 1997)

2. J. Bybee, *Advising the President: Separation of Powers and the Federal Advisory Committee Act*, 104 Yale L.J. 51 (1994).

3. M. Cardozo, *The Federal Advisory Committee Act in Operation*, 33 Admin. L. Rev. 1 (1981).

4. J. Chung, *Federal Advisory Committee Act* (part of annual D.C. Circuit Review), 65 Geo. Wash. L. Rev. 786 (1997).

5. S. Croley, *Practical Guidance on the Applicability of the Federal Advisory Committee Act*, 10 Admin. L.J. Am. U. 111 (1996).

6. S. Croley & W. Funk, *The Federal Advisory Committee Act and Good Government*, 14 Yale J. on Reg. 451 (1997).

7. G. Edles. *Service on Federal Advisory Committees: A Case Study of OLC's Little-Known Emoluments Clause Jurisprudence*, 58 Admin. L. Rev. 1 (2006).

8. D. Marblestone, *The Coverage of the Federal Advisory Committee Act*, 35 Fed. B. J. 119 (1976).

9. B. Murphy, *Implementation of the Federal Advisory Committee Act: An Overview*, 9 Gov't Publications Rev. 3 (1982).

10. M. Palladino, *Ensuring Coverage, Balance, Openness, and Ethical Conduct for Advisory Committee Members Under the Federal Advisory Committee Act*, 5 Admin. L.J. 231 (1991).

11. R. Wegman, *The Utilization and Management of Federal Advisory Committees* (Kettering Foundation, 1983).

Appendix:

1. Federal Advisory Committee Act, 5 U.S.C. App. 2 (2000).
2. General Services Administration, Federal Advisory Committee Management Regulations, 41 C.F.R. Part 102-3 (2006).
3. Office of Management and Budget, Circular A-135, Management of Federal Advisory Committees, 59 Fed. Reg. 53,856 (Oct 26, 1994).

Federal Advisory Committee Act

Title 5 Appendix 2, U.S. Code

§1. Short title

This Act may be cited as the "Federal Advisory Committee Act."
(Pub. L. No. 92-463, §1, Oct. 6, 1972, 86 Stat. 770.)

§2. Findings and purpose

(a) The Congress finds that there are numerous committees, boards, commissions, councils, and similar groups which have been established to advise officers and agencies in the executive branch of the Federal Government and that they are frequently a useful and beneficial means of furnishing expert advice, ideas, and diverse opinions to the Federal Government.
(b) The Congress further finds and declares that—

(1) the need for many existing advisory committees has not been adequately reviewed;

(2) new advisory committees should be established only when they are determined to be essential and their number should be kept to the minimum necessary;

(3) advisory committees should be terminated when they are no longer carrying out the purposes for which they were established;

(4) standards and uniform procedures should govern the establishment, operation, administration, and duration of advisory committees;

(5) the Congress and the public should be kept informed with respect to the number, purpose, membership, activities, and cost of advisory committees; and

(6) the function of advisory committees should be advisory only, and that all matters under their consideration should be determined, in accordance with law, by the official, agency, or officer involved.

(Pub. L. No. 92-463, §2, Oct. 6, 1972, 86 Stat. 770.)

EXECUTIVE ORDER NO. 11,686

Ex. Ord. No. 11,686, Oct. 7, 1972, 37 F.R. 21,421, formerly set out as a note under this section, which related to committee management, was superseded by Ex. Ord. No. 11,769, Feb. 21, 1974, 39 F.R. 7,125, formerly set out as a note under this section.

EXECUTIVE ORDER NO. 11,769

Ex. Ord. No. 11,769, Feb. 21, 1974, 39 F.R. 7,125, formerly set out as a note under this section, which related to committee management, was revoked by Ex. Ord. No. 12,024, Dec. 1, 1977, 42 F.R. 61,445, set out as a note under this section.

EXECUTIVE ORDER NO. 12,024
TRANSFER OF CERTAIN ADVISORY COMMITTEE FUNCTIONS
Dec. 1, 1977, 42 F.R. 61,445

By virtue of the authority vested in me by the Constitution and statutes of the United States of America, including the Federal Advisory Committee Act, as amended (5 U.S.C. App. 2) [this Appendix], Section 301 of Title 3 of the United States Code [section 301 of Title 3, The President], Section 202 of the Budget and Accounting Procedures Act of 1950 (31 U.S.C. 581c) [now section 1531 of Title 31, Money and Finance], and Section 7 of Reorganization Plan No. 1 of 1977 (42 FR 56,101 (October 21, 1977)), and as President of the United States of America, in accord with the transfer of advisory committee functions from the Office of Management and Budget to the General Services Administration provided by Reorganization Plan No. 1 of 1977, it is hereby ordered as follows:

Section 1. The transfer, provided by Section 5F of Reorganization Plan No. 1 of 1977 (42 FR 56,101), of certain functions under the Federal Advisory Committee Act, as amended (5 U.S.C. App. 2) [this Appendix], from the Office of Management and Budget and its Director to the Administrator of General Services is hereby effective.

Sec. 2. There is hereby delegated to the Administrator of General Services all the functions vested in the President by the Federal Advisory Committee Act, as amended, except that, the annual report to the Congress required by Section 6(c) of that Act [section 6(c) of this Appendix] shall be prepared by the Administrator for the President's consideration and transmittal to the Congress.

Sec. 3. The Director of the Office of Management and Budget shall take all actions necessary or appropriate to effectuate the transfer of functions provided in this Order, including the transfer of funds, personnel and positions, assets, liabilities, contracts, property, records, and other items related to the functions transferred.

Sec. 4. Executive Order No. 11,769 of February 21, 1974 [formerly set out as a note under this section] is hereby revoked.

Sec. 5. Any rules, regulations, orders, directives, circulars, or other actions taken pursuant to the functions transferred or reassigned as provided in this Order from the Office of Management and Budget to the Administrator of General Services, shall remain in effect as if issued by the Administrator until amended, modified, or revoked.

Sec. 6. This Order shall be effective November 20, 1977.

Jimmy Carter

§3. Definitions

For the purpose of this Act—

(1) The term "Administrator" means the Administrator of General Services.

(2) The term "advisory committee" means any committee, board, commission, council, conference, panel, task force, or other similar group, or any subcommittee or other subgroup thereof (hereafter in this paragraph referred to as "committee"), which is—

(A) established by statute or reorganization plan, or

(B) established or utilized by the President, or

(C) established or utilized by one or more agencies,

in the interest of obtaining advice or recommendations for the President or one or more agencies or officers of the Federal Government, except that such term excludes (i) any committee that is composed wholly of full-time, or permanent part-time, officers or employees of the Federal Government, and (ii) any committee that is created by the National Academy of Sciences or the National Academy of Public Administration.

(3) The term "agency" has the same meaning as in section 551(1) of title 5, United States Code.

(4) The term "Presidential advisory committee" means an advisory committee which advises the President.

(Pub. L. No. 92-463, §3, Oct. 6, 1972, 86 Stat. 770; 1977 Reorg. Plan No. 1, § 5F, eff. Nov. 20, 1977, 42 F.R. 56,101, 91 Stat. 1,634.)

TRANSFER OF FUNCTIONS

"'Administrator' means Administrator of General Services" was substituted for " 'Director' means Director of the Office of Management and Budget" in par. (1), pursuant to Reorg. Plan No. 1 of 1977, §5F, 42 F.R. 56,101, 91 Stat. 1,634, set out in Appendix 1 of this title, which transferred all functions of the Office of Management and Budget and its Director relating to the Committee Management Secretariat, which is responsible pursuant to section 7(a) of this Act for all matters relating to advisory committees, to the Administrator of General Services, effective Nov. 20, 1977, as provided by section 1 of Ex. Ord. No. 12,024, Dec. 1, 1977, 42 Fed. Reg. 61,445, set out under section 2 of this Act in this Appendix.

COMMISSION ON GOVERNMENT PROCUREMENT

The Commission on Government Procurement, referred to in par. (2)(ii), terminated Apr. 30, 1973, pursuant to Pub. L. No. 91-129, formerly set out as a note under section 251 of Title 41, Public Contracts.

§4. Applicability; restrictions

(a) The provisions of this Act or of any rule, order, or regulation promulgated under this Act shall apply to each advisory committee except to the extent that any Act of Congress establishing any such advisory committee specifically provides otherwise.

(b) Nothing in this Act shall be construed to apply to any advisory committee established or utilized by—

    (1) the Central Intelligence Agency; or

    (2) the Federal Reserve System.

(c) Nothing in this Act shall be construed to apply to any local civic group whose primary function is that of rendering a public service with respect to a Federal program, or any State or local committee, council, board, commission, or similar group established to advise or make recommendations to State or local officials or agencies.

(Pub. L. No. 92-463, §4, Oct. 6, 1972, 86 Stat. 771.)

§5. Responsibilities of Congressional committees; review; guidelines

    (a) In the exercise of its legislative review function, each standing committee of the Senate and the House of Representatives shall make a continuing review of the activities of each advisory committee under its jurisdiction to determine whether such advisory committee should be abolished or merged with any other advisory committee, whether the responsibilities of such advisory committee should be revised, and whether such advisory committee performs a necessary function not already being performed. Each such standing committee shall take appropriate action to obtain the enactment of legislation necessary to carry out the purpose of this subsection.

    (b) In considering legislation establishing, or authorizing the establishment of any advisory committee, each standing committee of the Senate and of the House of Representatives shall determine, and report such determination to the Senate or to the House of Representatives, as the case may be, whether the functions of the proposed advisory committee are being or could be performed by one or more agencies or by an advisory committee already in existence, or by enlarging the mandate of an existing advisory committee. Any such legislation shall—

    (1) contain a clearly defined purpose for the advisory committee;

    (2) require the membership of the advisory committee to be fairly balanced in terms of the points of view represented and the functions to be performed by the advisory committee;

(3) contain appropriate provisions to assure that the advice and recommendations of the advisory committee will not be inappropriately influenced by the appointing authority or by any special interest, but will instead be the result of the advisory committee's independent judgment;

(4) contain provisions dealing with authorization of appropriations, the date for submission of reports (if any), the duration of the advisory committee, and the publication of reports and other materials, to the extent that the standing committee determines the provisions of section 10 of this Act to be inadequate; and

(5) contain provisions which will assure that the advisory committee will have adequate staff (either supplied by an agency or employed by it), will be provided adequate quarters, and will have funds available to meet its other necessary expenses.

(c) To the extent they are applicable, the guidelines set out in subsection (b) of this section shall be followed by the President, agency heads, or other Federal officials in creating an advisory committee.

(Pub. L. No. 92-463, §5, Oct. 6, 1972, 86 Stat. 771.)

§6. Responsibilities of the President; report to Congress; annual report to Congress; exclusion

(a) The President may delegate responsibility for evaluating and taking action, where appropriate, with respect to all public recommendations made to him by Presidential advisory committees.

(b) Within one year after a Presidential advisory committee has submitted a public report to the President, the President or his delegate shall make a report to the Congress stating either his proposals for action or his reasons for inaction, with respect to the recommendations contained in the public report.

(c) The President shall, not later than December 31 of each year, make an annual report to the Congress on the activities, status, and changes in the composition of advisory committees in existence during the preceding fiscal year. The report shall contain the name of every advisory committee, the date of and authority for its creation, its termination date or the date it is to make a report, its functions, a reference to the reports it has submitted, a statement of whether it is an ad hoc or continuing body, the dates of its meetings, the names and occupations of its current members, and the total estimated annual cost to the United States to fund, service, supply, and maintain such committee. Such report shall include a list of those advisory committees abolished by the President, and in the case of advisory committees established by statute, a list of those advisory committees which the President recommends be abolished together with his reasons therefor. The President shall exclude from this report any information which, in his judgment, should be withheld for reasons of national security, and he shall include in such report a statement that such information is excluded.

(Pub. L. No. 92-463, §6, Oct. 6, 1972, 86 Stat. 772; Pub. L. No. 97-375, Title II, § 201(c), Dec. 21, 1982, 96 Stat. 1,822.)

§7. Responsibilities of the Administrator of General Services; Committee Management Secretariat, establishment; review; recommendations to President and Congress; agency cooperation; performance guidelines; uniform pay guidelines; travel expenses; expense recommendations

(a) The Administrator shall establish and maintain within the General Services Administration a Committee Management Secretariat, which shall be responsible for all matters relating to advisory committees.

(b) The Administrator shall, immediately after October 6, 1972, institute a comprehensive review of the activities and responsibilities of each advisory committee to determine—

(1) whether such committee is carrying out its purpose;

(2) whether, consistent with the provisions of applicable statutes, the responsibilities assigned to it should be revised;

(3) whether it should be merged with other advisory committees; or

(4) whether is[6] should be abolished.

The Administrator may from time to time request such information as he deems necessary to carry out his functions under this subsection. Upon the completion of the Administrator's review he shall make recommendations to the President and to either the agency head or the Congress with respect to action he believes should be taken. Thereafter, the Administrator shall carry out a similar review annually. Agency heads shall cooperate with the Administrator in making the reviews required by this subsection.

(c) The Administrator shall prescribe administrative guidelines and management controls applicable to advisory committees, and, to the maximum extent feasible, provide advice, assistance, and guidance to advisory committees to improve their performance. In carrying out his functions under this subsection, the Administrator shall consider the recommendations of each agency head with respect to means of improving the performance of advisory committees whose duties are related to such agency.

---

[6] So in original.

(d)(1) The Administrator, after study and consultation with the Director of the Office of Personnel Management, shall establish guidelines with respect to uniform fair rates of pay for comparable services of members, staffs, and consultants of advisory committees in a manner which gives appropriate recognition to the responsibilities and qualifications required and other relevant factors. Such regulations shall provide that—

(A) no member of any advisory committee or of the staff of any advisory committee shall receive compensation at a rate in excess of the rate specified for GS-18 of the General Schedule under section 5332 of title 5, United States Code;

(B) such members, while engaged in the performance of their duties away from their homes or regular places of business, may be allowed travel expenses, including per diem in lieu of subsistence, as authorized by section 5703 of title 5, United States Code, for persons employed intermittently in the Government service; and

(C) such members—

(i) who are blind or deaf or who otherwise qualify as handicapped individuals (within the meaning of section 501 of the Rehabilitation Act of 1973 (29 U.S.C. 794)), and

(ii) who do not otherwise qualify for assistance under section 3102 of title 5, United States Code, by reason of being an employee of an agency (within the meaning of section 3102(a)(1) of such title 5), may be provided services pursuant to section 3102 of such title 5 while in performance of their advisory committee duties.

(2) Nothing in this subsection shall prevent—

(A) an individual who (without regard to his service with an advisory committee) is a full-time employee of the United States, or

(B) an individual who immediately before his service with an advisory committee was such an employee,

from receiving compensation at the rate at which he otherwise would be compensated (or was compensated) as a full-time employee of the United States.

(e) The Administrator shall include in budget recommendations a summary of the amounts he deems necessary for the expenses of advisory committees, including the expenses for publication of reports where appropriate.

(Pub. L. No. 92-463, §7, Oct. 6, 1972, 86 Stat. 772; 1977 Reorg. Plan No. 1, §5F, eff. Nov. 20, 1977, 42 F.R. 56,101, 91 Stat. 1,634; 1978 Reorg. Plan No. 2, §102, eff. Jan. 1, 1979, 43 Fed. Reg. 36,067, 92 Stat. 3,783; Pub. L. No.96-523, §2, Dec. 12, 1980, 94 Stat. 3,040.)

§8. Responsibilities of agency heads; Advisory Committee Management Officer, designation

(a) Each agency head shall establish uniform administrative guidelines and management controls for advisory committees established by that agency, which shall be consistent with directives of the Administrator under section 7 and section 10. Each agency shall maintain systematic information on the nature, functions, and operations of each advisory committee within its jurisdiction.

(b) The head of each agency which has an advisory committee shall designate an Advisory Committee Management Officer who shall—

(1) exercise control and supervision over the establishment, procedures, and accomplishments of advisory committees established by that agency;

(2) assemble and maintain the reports, records, and other papers of any such committee during its existence; and

(3) carry out, on behalf of that agency, the provisions of section 552 of title 5, United States Code, with respect to such reports, records, and other papers.

(Pub. L. No. 92-463, §8, Oct. 6, 1972, 86 Stat. 773; 1977 Reorg. Plan No. 1, §5F, eff. Nov. 20, 1977, 42 F.R. 56,101, 91 Stat. 1,634.)

§9. Establishment and purpose of advisory committees; publication in Federal Register; charter: filing, contents, copy

(a) No advisory committee shall be established unless such establishment is—

(1) specifically authorized by statute or by the President; or

(2) determined as a matter of formal record, by the head of the agency involved after consultation with the Administrator with timely notice published in the Federal Register, to be in the public interest in connection with the performance of duties imposed on that agency by law.

(b) Unless otherwise specifically provided by statute or Presidential directive, advisory committees shall be utilized solely for advisory functions. Determinations of action to be taken and policy to be expressed with respect to matters upon which an advisory committee reports or makes recommendations shall be made solely by the President or an officer of the Federal Government.

(c) No advisory committee shall meet or take any action until an advisory committee charter has been filed with (1) the Administrator, in the case of Presidential advisory committees, or (2) with the head of the agency to whom any advisory committee reports and with the standing committees of the Senate and of the House of Representatives having legislative jurisdiction of such agency. Such charter shall contain the following information:

(A) the committee's official designation;

(B) the committee's objectives and the scope of its activity;

(C) the period of time necessary for the committee to carry out its purposes;

(D) the agency or official to whom the committee reports;

(E) the agency responsible for providing the necessary support for the committee;

(F) a description of the duties for which the committee is responsible, and, if such duties are not solely advisory, a specification of the authority for such functions;

(G) the estimated annual operating costs in dollars and man-years for such committee;

(H) the estimated number and frequency of committee meetings;

(I) the committee's termination date, if less than two years from the date of the committee's establishment; and

(J) the date the charter is filed.

A copy of any such charter shall also be furnished to the Library of Congress.

(Pub. L. No. 92-463, §9, Oct. 6, 1972, 86 Stat. 773; 1977 Reorg. Plan No. 1, §5F, eff. Nov. 20, 1977, 42 Fed. Reg. 56,101, 91 Stat. 1,634.)

§10. Advisory committee procedures; meetings; notice, publication in Federal Register; regulations; minutes; certification; annual report; Federal officer or employee, attendance

(a)(1) Each advisory committee meeting shall be open to the public.

(2) Except when the President determines otherwise for reasons of national security, timely notice of each such meeting shall be published in the Federal Register, and the Administrator shall prescribe regulations to provide for other types of public notice to insure that all interested persons are notified of such meeting prior thereto.

(3) Interested persons shall be permitted to attend, appear before, or file statements with any advisory committee, subject to such reasonable rules or regulations as the Administrator may prescribe.

(b) Subject to section 552 of title 5, United States Code, the records, reports, transcripts, minutes, appendixes, working papers, drafts, studies, agenda, or other documents which were made available to or prepared for or by each advisory committee shall be available for public inspection and copying at a single location in the offices of the advisory committee or the agency to which the advisory committee reports until the advisory committee ceases to exist.

(c) Detailed minutes of each meeting of each advisory committee shall be kept and shall contain a record of the persons present, a complete and accurate description of matters discussed and conclusions reached, and copies of all reports received, issued, or approved by the advisory committee. The accuracy of all minutes shall be certified to by the chairman of the advisory committee.

(d) Subsections (a)(1) and (a)(3) of this section shall not apply to any portion of an advisory committee meeting where the President, or the head of the agency to which the advisory committee reports, determines that such portion of such meeting may be closed to the public in accordance with subsection (c) of section 552b of title 5, United States Code. Any such determination shall be in writing and shall contain the reasons for such determination. If such a determination is made, the advisory committee shall issue a report at least annually setting forth a summary of its activities and such related matters as would be informative to the public consistent with the policy of section 552(b) of title 5, United States Code.

(e) There shall be designated an officer or employee of the Federal Government to chair or attend each meeting of each advisory committee. The officer or employee so designated is authorized, whenever he determines it to be in the public interest, to adjourn any such meeting. No advisory committee shall conduct any meeting in the absence of that officer or employee.

(f) Advisory committees shall not hold any meetings except at the call of, or with the advance approval of, a designated officer or employee of the Federal Government, and in the case of advisory committees (other than Presidential advisory committees), with an agenda approved by such officer or employee.

(Pub. L. No. 92-463, §10, Oct. 6, 1972, 86 Stat. 774; Pub. L. No. 94-409, § 5(c), Sept. 13, 1976, 90 Stat. 1,247; 1977 Reorg. Plan No. 1, §5F, eff. Nov. 20, 1977, 42 Fed. Reg. 56,101, 91 Stat. 1,634.)

§11. Availability of transcripts; "agency proceeding"

(a) Except where prohibited by contractual agreements entered into prior to the effective date of this Act, agencies and advisory committees shall make available to any person, at actual cost of duplication, copies of transcripts of agency proceedings or advisory committee meetings.

(b) As used in this section "agency proceeding" means any proceeding as defined in section 551(12) of title 5, United States Code.

(Pub. L. No. 92-463, §11, Oct. 6, 1972, 86 Stat. 775.)

§12. Fiscal and administrative provisions; recordkeeping; audit; agency support services

(a) Each agency shall keep records as will fully disclose the disposition of any funds which may be at the disposal of its advisory committees and the nature and extent of their activities. The General Services Administration, or such other agency as the President may designate, shall maintain financial records with respect to Presidential advisory committees. The Comptroller General of the United States, or any of his authorized representatives, shall have access, for the purpose of audit and examination, to any such records.

(b) Each agency shall be responsible for providing support services for each advisory committee established by or reporting to it unless the establishing authority provides otherwise. Where any such advisory committee reports to more than one agency, only one agency shall be responsible for support services at any one time. In the case of Presidential advisory committees, such services may be provided by the General Services Administration.

(Pub. L. No. 92-463, §12, Oct. 6, 1972, 86 Stat. 775.)

§13. Responsibilities of Library of Congress; reports and background papers; depository

Subject to section 552 of title 5, United States Code, the Administrator shall provide for the filing with the Library of Congress of at least eight copies of each report made by every advisory committee and, where appropriate, background papers prepared by consultants. The Librarian of Congress shall establish a depository for such reports and papers where they shall be available to public inspection and use.

(Pub. L. No. 92-463, §13, Oct. 6, 1972, 86 Stat. 775; 1977 Reorg. Plan No. 1, §5F, eff. Nov. 20, 1977, 42 Fed. Reg. 56,101, 91 Stat. 1,634.)

§14. Termination of advisory committees; renewal; continuation

(a)(1) Each advisory committee which is in existence on the effective date of this Act shall terminate not later than the expiration of the two-year period following such effective date unless—

(A) in the case of an advisory committee established by the President or an officer of the Federal Government, such advisory committee is renewed by the President or that officer by appropriate action prior to the expiration of such two-year period; or

(B) in the case of an advisory committee established by an Act of Congress, its duration is otherwise provided for by law.

(2) Each advisory committee established after such effective date shall terminate not later than the expiration of the two-year period beginning on the date of its establishment unless—

(A) in the case of an advisory committee established by the President or an officer of the Federal Government such advisory committee is renewed by the President or such officer by appropriate action prior to the end of such period; or

(B) in the case of an advisory committee established by an Act of Congress, its duration is otherwise provided for by law.

(b)(1) Upon the renewal of any advisory committee, such advisory committee shall file a charter in accordance with section 9(c).

(2) Any advisory committee established by an Act of Congress shall file a charter in accordance with such section upon the expiration of each successive two-year period following the date of enactment of the Act establishing such advisory committee.

(3) No advisory committee required under this subsection to file a charter shall take any action (other than preparation and filing of such charter) prior to the date on which such charter is filed.

(c) Any advisory committee which is renewed by the President or any officer of the Federal Government may be continued only for successive two-year periods by appropriate action taken by the President or such officer prior to the date on which such advisory committee would otherwise terminate.

(Pub. L. No. 92-463, §14, Oct. 6, 1972, 86 Stat. 776.)

EXECUTIVE ORDER NO. 12,838
TERMINATION AND LIMITATION OF FEDERAL ADVISORY COMMITTEES
Feb. 10, 1993, 58 F.R. 8,207

By the authority vested in me as President by the Constitution and the laws of the United States of America, including the Federal Advisory Committee Act ("FACA"), as amended (5 U.S.C. App.), it is hereby ordered as follows:

Section 1. Each executive department and agency shall terminate not less than one-third of the advisory committees subject to FACA (and not required by statute) that are sponsored by the department or agency by no later than the end of fiscal year 1993.

Sec. 2. Within 90 days, the head of each executive department and agency shall submit to the Director of the Office of Management and Budget, for each advisory committee subject to FACA sponsored by that department or agency: (a) a detailed justification for the continued existence, or a brief description in support of the termination, of any advisory committee not required by statute; and (b) a detailed recommendation for submission to the Congress to continue or to terminate any advisory committee required by statute. The Administrator of General Services shall prepare such justifications and recommendations for each advisory committee subject to FACA and not sponsored by a department or agency.

Sec. 3. Effective immediately, executive departments and agencies shall not create or sponsor a new advisory committee subject to FACA unless the committee is required by statute or the agency head (a) finds that compelling considerations necessitate creation of such a committee, and (b) receives the approval of the Director of the Office of Management and Budget. Such approval shall be granted only sparingly and only if compelled by considerations of national security, health or safety, or similar national interests. These requirements shall apply in addition to the notice and other approval requirements of FACA.

Sec. 4. The Director of the Office of Management and Budget shall issue detailed instructions regarding the implementation of this order, including exemptions necessary for the delivery of essential services and compliance with applicable law.

Sec. 5. All independent regulatory commissions and agencies are requested to comply with the provisions of this order.

William J. Clinton

§15. Requirements relating to the National Academy of Sciences and the National Academy of Public Administration

(a) In general.—An agency may not use any advice or recommendation provided by the National Academy of Sciences or National Academy of Public Administration that was developed by use of a committee created by that academy under an agreement with an agency, unless—

(1) the committee was not subject to any actual management or control by an agency or an officer of the Federal Government;

(2) in the case of a committee created after the date of the enactment of the Federal Advisory Committee Act Amendments of 1997, the membership of the committee was appointed in accordance with the requirements described in subsection (b)(1); and

(3) in developing the advice or recommendation, the academy complied with—

(A) subsection (b)(2) through (6), in the case of any advice or recommendation provided by the National Academy of Sciences; or

(B) subsection (b)(2) and (5), in the case of any advice or recommendation provided by the National Academy of Public Administration.

(b) Requirements.—The requirements referred to in subsection (a) are as follows:

(1) The Academy shall determine and provide public notice of the names and brief biographies of individuals that the Academy appoints or intends to appoint to serve on the committee. The Academy shall determine and provide a reasonable opportunity for the public to comment on such appointments before they are made or, if the Academy determines such prior comment is not practicable, in the period immediately following the appointments. The Academy shall make its best efforts to ensure that (A) no individual appointed to serve on the committee has a conflict of interest that is relevant to the functions to be performed, unless such conflict is promptly and publicly disclosed and the Academy determines that the conflict is unavoidable, (B) the committee membership is fairly balanced as determined by the Academy to be appropriate for the functions to be performed, and (C) the final report of the Academy will be the result of the Academy's independent judgment. The Academy shall require that individuals that the Academy appoints or intends to appoint to serve on the committee inform the Academy of the individual's conflicts of interest that are relevant to the functions to be performed.

(2) The Academy shall determine and provide public notice of committee meetings that will be open to the public.

(3) The Academy shall ensure that meetings of the committee to gather data from individuals who are not officials, agents, or employees of the Academy are open to the public, unless the Academy determines that a meeting would disclose matters described in section 552(b) of title 5, United States Code. The Academy shall make available to the public, at reasonable charge if appropriate, written materials presented to the committee by individuals who are not officials, agents, or employees of the Academy, unless the Academy determines that making material available would disclose matters described in that section.

(4) The Academy shall make available to the public as soon as practicable, at reasonable charge if appropriate, a brief summary of any committee meeting that is not a data gathering meeting, unless the Academy determines that the summary would disclose matters described in section 552(b) of title

5, United States Code. The summary shall identify the committee members present, the topics discussed, materials made available to the committee, and such other matters that the Academy determines should be included.

(5) The Academy shall make available to the public its final report, at reasonable charge if appropriate, unless the Academy determines that the report would disclose matters described in section 552(b) of title 5, United States Code. If the Academy determines that the report would disclose matters described in that section, the Academy shall make public an abbreviated version of the report that does not disclose those matters.

(6) After publication of the final report, the Academy shall make publicly available the names of the principal reviewers who reviewed the report in draft form and who are not officials, agents, or employees of the Academy.

(c) Regulations.—The Administrator of General Services may issue regulations implementing this section.

(Pub. L. No. 92-463, §15, as added Pub. L. No. 105-153, §2(b), Dec. 17, 1997, 111 Stat. 2,689.)

§16. Effective date

Except as provided in section 7(b), this Act shall become effective upon the expiration of ninety days following October 6, 1972.

(Pub. L. No. 92-463, formerly §15, Oct. 6, 1972, 86 Stat. 776; renumbered §16, Pub. L. No. 105-153, §2(b), Dec. 17, 1997, 111 Stat. 2,689.)

10

General Services Administration
Federal Advisory Committee Management Regulations

Code of Federal Regulations
Title 41—Public Contracts and Property Management
Subtitle C—Federal Property Management Regulations System
Chapter 102—Federal Management Regulation
Subchapter A—General
Part 102-3—Federal Advisory Committee Management

AUTHORITY: Sec. 205(c), 63 Stat. 390 (40 U.S.C. 486(c)); sec. 7, 5 U.S.C., App.; and E.O. 12,024; 3 CFR, 1977 Comp., p.158.

SOURCE: 66 Fed. Reg. 37,733, July 19, 2001, unless otherwise noted.

SUBPART A-WHAT POLICIES APPLY TO ADVISORY COMMITTEES ESTABLISHED WITHIN THE EXECUTIVE BRANCH?

§102-3.5 What does this subpart cover and how does it apply?

This subpart provides the policy framework that must be used by agency heads in applying the Federal Advisory Committee Act (FACA), as amended (or "the Act"), 5 U.S.C., App., to advisory committees they establish and operate. In addition to listing key definitions underlying the interpretation of the Act, this subpart establishes the scope and applicability of the Act, and outlines specific exclusions from its coverage.

§102-3.10 What is the purpose of the Federal Advisory Committee Act?

FACA governs the establishment, operation, and termination of advisory committees within the executive branch of the Federal Government. The Act defines what constitutes a Federal advisory committee and provides general procedures for the executive branch to follow for the operation of these advisory committees. In addition, the Act is designed to assure that the Congress and the public are kept informed with respect to the number, purpose, membership, activities, and cost of advisory committees.

§102-3.15 Who are the intended users of this part?

(a) The primary users of this Federal Advisory Committee Management part are:

(1) Executive branch officials and others outside Government currently involved with an established advisory committee;

(2) Executive branch officials who seek to establish or utilize an advisory committee;

(3) Executive branch officials and others outside Government who have decided to pursue, or who are already engaged in, a form of public involvement or consultation and want to avoid inadvertently violating the Act; and

(4) Field personnel of Federal agencies who are increasingly involved with the public as part of their efforts to increase collaboration and improve customer service.

(b) Other types of end-users of this part include individuals and organizations outside of the executive branch who seek to understand and interpret the Act, or are seeking additional guidance.

§102-3.20 How does this part meet the needs of its audience?

This Federal Advisory Committee Management part meets the general and specific needs of its audience by addressing the following issues and related topics:

(a) Scope and applicability. This part provides guidance on the threshold issue of what constitutes an advisory committee and clarifies the limits of coverage by the Act for the benefit of the intended users of this part.

(b) Policies and guidelines. This part defines the policies, establishes minimum requirements, and provides guidance to Federal officers and agencies for the establishment, operation, administration, and duration of advisory committees subject to the Act. This includes reporting requirements that keep Congress and the public informed of the number, purpose, membership, activities, benefits, and costs of these advisory committees. These requirements form the basis for implementing the Act at both the agency and Governmentwide levels.

(c) Examples and principles. This part provides summary-level key points and principles at the end of each subpart that provide more clarification on the role of Federal advisory committees in the larger context of public involvement in Federal decisions and activities. This includes a discussion of the applicability of the Act to different decisionmaking scenarios.

§102-3.25 What definitions apply to this part?

The following definitions apply to this Federal Advisory Committee Management part:

Act means the Federal Advisory Committee Act, as amended, 5 U.S.C., App.

Administrator means the Administrator of General Services.

Advisory committee subject to the Act, except as specifically exempted by the Act or by other statutes, or as not covered by this part, means any committee, board, commission, council, conference, panel, task force, or other similar group, which is established by statute, or established or utilized by the President or by an agency official, for the purpose of obtaining advice or recommendations for the President or on issues or policies within the scope of an agency official's responsibilities.

Agency has the same meaning as in 5 U.S.C. 551(1).

Committee Management Officer ("CMO"), means the individual designated by the agency head to implement the provisions of section 8(b) of the Act and any delegated responsibilities of the agency head under the Act.

Committee Management Secretariat ("Secretariat"), means the organization established pursuant to section 7(a) of the Act, which is responsible for all matters relating to advisory committees, and carries out the responsibilities of the Administrator under the Act and Executive Order 12024 (3 C.F.R., 1977 Comp., p. 158).

Committee meeting means any gathering of advisory committee members (whether in person or through electronic means) held with the approval of an agency for the purpose of deliberating on the substantive matters upon which the advisory committee provides advice or recommendations.

Committee member means an individual who serves by appointment or invitation on an advisory committee or subcommittee.

Committee staff means any Federal employee, private individual, or other party (whether under contract or not) who is not a committee member, and who serves in a support capacity to an advisory committee or subcommittee.

Designated Federal Officer ("DFO"), means an individual designated by the agency head, for each advisory committee for which the agency head is responsible, to implement the provisions of sections 10(e) and (f) of the Act and any advisory committee procedures of the agency under the control and supervision of the CMO.

Discretionary advisory committee means any advisory committee that is established under the authority of an agency head or authorized by statute. An advisory committee referenced in general (non-specific) authorizing language or Congressional committee report language is discretionary, and its establishment or termination is within the legal discretion of an agency head.

Independent Presidential advisory committee means any Presidential advisory committee not assigned by the Congress in law, or by President or the President's delegate, to an agency for administrative and other support.

Non-discretionary advisory committee means any advisory committee either required by statute or by Presidential directive. A non-discretionary advisory committee required by statute generally is identified specifically in a statute by name, purpose, or functions, and its establishment or termination is beyond the legal discretion of an agency head.

Presidential advisory committee means any advisory committee authorized by the Congress or directed by the President to advise the President.

Subcommittee means a group, generally not subject to the Act, that reports to an advisory committee and not directly to a Federal officer or agency, whether or not its members are drawn in whole or in part from the parent advisory committee.

Utilized for the purposes of the Act, does not have its ordinary meaning. A committee that is not established by the Federal Government is utilized within the meaning of the Act when the President or a Federal office or agency exercises actual management or control over its operation.

§102-3.30 What policies govern the use of advisory committees?

The policies to be followed by Federal departments and agencies in establishing and operating advisory committees consistent with the Act are as follows:

(a) Determination of need in the public interest. A discretionary advisory committee may be established only when it is essential to the conduct of agency business and when the information to be obtained is not already available through another advisory committee or source within the Federal Government. Reasons for deciding that an advisory committee is needed may include whether:

(1) Advisory committee deliberations will result in the creation or elimination of (or change in) regulations, policies, or guidelines affecting agency business;

(2) The advisory committee will make recommendations resulting in significant improvements in service or reductions in cost; or

(3) The advisory committee's recommendations will provide an important additional perspective or viewpoint affecting agency operations.

(b) Termination. An advisory committee must be terminated when:

(1) The stated objectives of the committee have been accomplished;

(2) The subject matter or work of the committee has become obsolete by the passing of time or the assumption of the committee's functions by another entity;

(3) The agency determines that the cost of operation is excessive in relation to the benefits accruing to the Federal Government;

(4) In the case of a discretionary advisory committee, upon the expiration of a period not to exceed two years, unless renewed;

(5) In the case of a non-discretionary advisory committee required by Presidential directive, upon the expiration of a period not to exceed two years, unless renewed by authority of the President; or

(6) In the case of a non-discretionary advisory committee required by statute, upon the expiration of the time explicitly specified in the statute, or implied by operation of the statute.

(c) Balanced membership. An advisory committee must be fairly balanced in its membership in terms of the points of view represented and the functions to be performed.

(d) Open meetings. Advisory committee meetings must be open to the public except where a closed or partially-closed meeting has been determined proper and consistent with the exemption(s) of the Government in the Sunshine Act, 5 U.S.C. 552b(c), as the basis for closure.

(e) Advisory functions only. The function of advisory committees is advisory only, unless specifically provided by statute or Presidential directive.

§102-3.35 What policies govern the use of subcommittees?

(a) In general, the requirements of the Act and the policies of this Federal Advisory Committee Management part do not apply to subcommittees of advisory committees that report to a parent advisory committee and not directly to a Federal officer or agency. However, this section does not preclude an agency from applying any provision of the Act and this part to any subcommittee of an advisory committee in any particular instance.

(b) The creation and operation of subcommittees must be approved by the agency establishing the parent advisory committee.

§102-3.40 What types of committees or groups are not covered by the Act and this part?

The following are examples of committees or groups that are not covered by the Act or this Federal Advisory Committee Management part:

(a) Committees created by the National Academy of Sciences (NAS) or the National Academy of Public Administration (NAPA). Any committee created by NAS or NAPA in accordance with section 15 of the Act, except as otherwise covered by subpart E of this part;

(b) Advisory committees of the Central Intelligence Agency and the Federal Reserve System. Any advisory committee established or utilized by the Central Intelligence Agency or the Federal Reserve System;

(c) Committees exempted by statute. Any committee specifically exempted from the Act by law;

(d) Committees not actually managed or controlled by the executive branch.

Any committee or group created by non-Federal entities (such as a contractor or private organization), provided that these committees or groups are not actually managed or controlled by the executive branch;

(e) Groups assembled to provide individual advice. Any group that meets with a Federal official(s), including a public meeting, where advice is sought from the attendees on an individual basis and not from the group as a whole;

(f) Groups assembled to exchange facts or information. Any group that meets with a Federal official(s) for the purpose of exchanging facts or information;

(g) Intergovernmental committees. Any committee composed wholly of full-time or permanent part-time officers or employees of the Federal Government and elected officers of State, local and tribal governments (or their designated employees with authority to act on their behalf), acting in their official capacities. However, the purpose of such a committee must be solely to exchange views, information, or advice relating to the management or implementation of Federal programs established pursuant to statute, that explicitly or inherently share intergovernmental responsibilities or administration (see guidelines issued by the Office of Management and Budget (OMB) on section 204(b) of the Unfunded Mandates Reform Act of 1995, 2 U.S.C. 1534(b), OMB Memorandum M-95-20, dated September 21, 1995, available from the Committee Management Secretariat (MC), General Services Administration, 1800 F Street, NW., Washington, DC 20405-0002);

(h) Intragovernmental committees. Any committee composed wholly of full-time or permanent part-time officers or employees of the Federal Government;

(i) Local civic groups. Any local civic group whose primary function is that of rendering a public service with respect to a Federal program;

(j) Groups established to advise State or local officials. Any State or local committee, council, board, commission, or similar group established to advise or make recommendations to State or local officials or agencies; and

(k) Operational committees. Any committee established to perform primarily operational as opposed to advisory functions. Operational functions are those specifically authorized by statute or Presidential directive, such as making or implementing Government decisions or policy. A committee designated operational may be covered by the Act if it becomes primarily advisory in nature. It is the responsibility of the administering agency to determine whether a committee is primarily operational. If so, it does not fall under the requirements of the Act and this part.

Appendix A to Subpart A of Part 102-3— Key Points and Principles

This appendix provides additional guidance in the form of answers to frequently asked questions and identifies key points and principles that may be applied to situations not covered elsewhere in this subpart. The guidance follows:

Key points and principles
  I. FACA applies to advisory committees that are either "established" or "utilized" by an agency

Section(s)
102-3.25, 102-3.40(d), 102-3.40(f)

Question(s)
  1. A local citizens group wants to meet with a Federal official(s) to help improve the condition of a forest's trails and quality of concessions. May the Government meet with the group without chartering the group under the Act?
  2. May an agency official attend meetings of external groups where advice may be offered to the Government during the course of discussions?
  3. May an agency official participate in meetings of groups or organizations as a member without chartering the group under the Act?
  4. Is the Act applicable to meetings between agency officials and their contractors, licensees, or other "private sector program partners?"

Guidance
  A. The answer to questions 1, 2, and 3 is yes, if the agency does not either "establish" or "utilize" (exercise "actual management or control" over) the group. (i) Although there is no precise legal definition of "actual management or control," the following factors may be used by an agency to determine whether or not a group is "utilized" within the meaning of the Act: (a) Does the agency manage or control the group's membership or otherwise determine its composition? (b) Does the agency manage or control the group's agenda? (c) Does the agency fund the group's activities? (ii) Answering "yes" to any or all of questions 1, 2, or 3 does not automatically mean the

group is "utilized" within the meaning of the Act. However, an agency may need to reconsider the status of the group under the Act if the relationship in question essentially is indistinguishable from an advisory committee established by the agency.

B. The answer to question 4 is no. Agencies often meet with contractors and licensees, individually and as a group, to discuss specific matters involving a contract's solicitation, issuance, and implementation, or an agency's efforts to ensure compliance with its regulations. Such interactions are not subject to the Act because these groups are not "established" or "utilized "for the purpose of obtaining advice or recommendations.

Key points and principles
    II. The development of consensus among all or some of the attendees at a public meeting or similar forum does not automatically invoke FACA

Section(s)
102-3.25, 102-3.40(d), 102-3.40(f)

Question
    1. If, during a public meeting of the "town hall" type called by an agency, it appears that the audience is achieving consensus, or a common point of view, is this an indication that the meeting is subject to the Act and must be stopped?

Guidance
    A. No, the public meeting need not be stopped. (i) A group must either be "established" or "utilized" by the executive branch in order for the Act to apply. (ii) Public meetings represent a chance for individuals to voice their opinions and/or share information. In that sense, agencies do not either "establish" the assemblage of individuals as an advisory committee or "utilize" the attendees as an advisory committee because there are no elements of either "management" or "control" present or intended.

Key points and principles
III. Meetings between a Federal official(s) and a collection of individuals where advice is sought from the attendees on an individual basis are not subject to the Act

Section
102-3.40(e)

Question(s)
1. May an agency official meet with a number of persons collectively to obtain their individual views without violating the Act?
2. Does the concept of an "individual" apply only to "natural persons?"

Guidance
A. The answer to questions 1 and 2 is yes. The Act applies only where a group is established or utilized to provide advice or recommendations "as a group." (i) A mere assemblage or collection of individuals where the attendees are providing individual advice is not acting "as a group" under the Act. (ii) In this respect, "individual" is not limited to "natural persons." Where the group consists of representatives of various existing organizations, each representative individually may provide advice on behalf of that person's organization without violating the Act, if those organizations themselves are not "managed or controlled" by the agency.

Key points and principles
IV. Meetings between Federal, State, local, and tribal elected officials are not subject to the Act

Section
102-3.40(g)

Question
1. Is the exclusion from the Act covering elected officials of State, local, and tribal governments acting in their official capacities also applicable to associations of State officials?

Guidance

A. Yes. The scope of activities covered by the exclusion from the Act for intergovernmental activities should be construed broadly to facilitate Federal/State/local/tribal discussions on shared intergovernmental program responsibilities or administration. Pursuant to a Presidential delegation, the Office of Management and Budget (OMB) issued guidelines for this exemption, authorized by section 204(b) of the Unfunded Mandates Reform Act of 1995, 2 U.S.C. 1534(b). (See OMB Memorandum M-95-20, dated September 21, 1995, published at 60 FR 50651 (September 29, 1995), and which is available from the Committee Management Secretariat (MC), General Services Administration, 1800 F Street, NW, Washington, DC 20405-0002).

Key points and principles

V. Advisory committees established under the Act may perform advisory functions only, unless authorized to perform "operational" duties by the Congress or by Presidential directive

Section

102-3.30(e), 102-3.40(k)

Question

1. Are "operational committees" subject to the Act, even if they may engage in some advisory activities?

Guidance

A. No, so long as the operational functions performed by the committee constitute the "primary" mission of the committee. Only committees established or utilized by the executive branch in the interest of obtaining advice or recommendations are subject to the Act. However, without specific authorization by the Congress or direction by the President, Federal functions (decisionmaking or operations) cannot be delegated to, or assumed by, non-Federal individuals or entities.

Key points and principles

VI. Committees authorized by the Congress in law or by Presidential directive to perform primarily "operational" functions are not subject to the Act

Section

102-3.40(k)

Questions
1. What characteristics are common to "operational committees?"
2. A committee created by the Congress by statute is responsible, for example, for developing plans and events to commemorate the contributions of wildlife to the enjoyment of the Nation's parks. Part of the committee's role includes providing advice to certain Federal agencies as may be necessary to coordinate these events. Is this committee subject to FACA?

Guidance
A. In answer to question 1, non-advisory, or "operational" committees generally have the following characteristics: (i) Specific functions and/or authorities provided by the Congress in law or by Presidential directive; (ii) The ability to make and implement traditionally Governmental decisions; and (iii) The authority to perform specific tasks to implement a Federal program.
B. Agencies are responsible for determining whether or not a committee primarily provides advice or recommendations and is, therefore, subject to the Act, or is primarily "operational" and not covered by FACA.
C. The answer to question 2 is no. The committee is not subject to the Act because:
   (i) Its functions are to plan and implement specific tasks;
   (ii) The committee has been granted the express authority by the Congress to perform its statutorily required functions; and (iii) Its incidental role of providing advice to other Federal agencies is secondary to its primarily operational role of planning and implementing specific tasks and performing statutory functions.

Subpart B. How Are Advisory Committees Established, Renewed, Reestablished, and Terminated?

§102-3.45 What does this subpart cover and how does it apply?

Requirements for establishing and terminating advisory committees vary depending on the establishing entity and the source of authority for the advisory committee. This subpart covers the procedures associated with the establishment, renewal, reestablishment, and termination of advisory committees. These procedures include consulting with the Secretariat, preparing and filing an advisory committee charter, publishing notice in the Federal Register, and amending an advisory committee charter.

§102-3.50 What are the authorities for establishing advisory committees?

FACA identifies four sources of authority for establishing an advisory committee:

(a) Required by statute. By law where the Congress establishes an advisory committee, or specifically directs the President or an agency to establish it (non-discretionary);
(b) Presidential authority. By Executive order of the President or other Presidential directive (non-discretionary);
(c) Authorized by statute. By law where the Congress authorizes, but does not direct the President or an agency to establish it (discretionary); or
(d) Agency authority. By an agency under general authority in title 5 of the United States Code or under other general agency-authorizing statutes (discretionary).

§102-3.55 What rules apply to the duration of an advisory committee?

(a) An advisory committee automatically terminates two years after its date of establishment unless:
(1) The statutory authority used to establish the advisory committee provides a different duration;
(2) The President or agency head determines that the advisory committee has fulfilled the purpose for which it was established and terminates the advisory committee earlier;
(3) The President or agency head determines that the advisory committee is no longer carrying out the purpose for which it was established and terminates the advisory committee earlier; or
(4) The President or agency head renews the committee not later than two years after its date of establishment in accordance with §102-3.60. If an advisory committee needed by the President or an agency terminates because it was not renewed in a timely manner, or if the advisory committee has been terminated under the provisions of §102-3.30(b), it can be reestablished in accordance with §102-3.60.

(b) When an advisory committee terminates, the agency shall notify the Secretariat of the effective date of the termination.

§102-3.60 What procedures are required to establish, renew, or reestablish a discretionary advisory committee?

(a) Consult with the Secretariat. Before establishing, renewing, or reestablishing a discretionary advisory committee and filing the charter as addressed later in §102-3.70, the agency head must consult with the Secretariat. As part of this consultation, agency heads are encouraged to engage in constructive dialogue with the Secretariat. With a full understanding of the background and purpose behind the proposed advisory committee, the Secretariat may share its knowledge and experience with the agency on how best to make use of the proposed advisory committee, suggest alternate methods of attaining its purpose that the agency may wish to consider, or inform the agency of a pre-existing advisory committee performing similar functions.

(b) Include required information in the consultation. Consultations covering the establishment, renewal, and reestablishment of advisory committees must, as a minimum, contain the following information:
   (1) Explanation of need. An explanation stating why the advisory committee is essential to the conduct of agency business and in the public interest;
   (2) Lack of duplication of resources. An explanation stating why the advisory committee's functions cannot be performed by the agency, another existing committee, or other means such as a public hearing; and
   (3) Fairly balanced membership. A description of the agency's plan to attain fairly balanced membership. The plan will ensure that, in the selection of members for the advisory committee, the agency will consider a cross-section of those directly affected, interested, and qualified, as appropriate to the nature and functions of the advisory committee. Advisory committees requiring technical expertise should include persons with demonstrated professional or personal qualifications and experience relevant to the functions and tasks to be performed.

§102-3.65 What are the public notification requirements for discretionary advisory committees?

A notice to the public in the Federal Register is required when a discretionary advisory committee is established, renewed, or reestablished.

(a) Procedure. Upon receiving notice from the Secretariat that its review is complete in accordance with §102-3.60(a), the agency must publish a notice in the Federal Register announcing that the advisory committee is being established, renewed, or reestablished. For the establishment of a new advisory committee, the notice also must describe the nature and purpose of the advisory committee and affirm that the advisory committee is necessary and in the public interest.

(b) Time required for notices. Notices of establishment and reestablishment of advisory committees must appear at least 15 calendar days before the charter is filed, except that the Secretariat may approve less than 15 calendar days when requested by the agency for good cause. This requirement for advance notice does not apply to advisory committee renewals, notices of which may be published concurrently with the filing of the charter.

§102-3.70 What are the charter filing requirements?

No advisory committee may meet or take any action until a charter has been filed by the Committee Management Officer (CMO) designated in accordance with section 8(b) of the Act, or by another agency official designated by the agency head.

(a) Requirement for discretionary advisory committees. To establish, renew, or reestablish a discretionary advisory committee, a charter must be filed with:
(1) The agency head;
(2) The standing committees of the Senate and the House of Representatives having legislative jurisdiction of the agency, the date of filing with which constitutes the official date of establishment for the advisory committee;
(3) The Library of Congress, Anglo-American Acquisitions Division, Government Documents Section, Federal Advisory Committee Desk, 101 Independence Avenue, SE., Washington, DC 20540-4172; and
(4) The Secretariat, indicating the date the charter was filed in accordance with paragraph (a)(2) of this section.

(b) Requirement for non-discretionary advisory committees. Charter filing requirements for non-discretionary advisory committees are the same as those in paragraph (a) of this section, except the date of establishment for a Presidential advisory committee is the date the charter is filed with the Secretariat.

(c) Requirement for subcommittees that report directly to the Government. Subcommittees that report directly to a Federal officer or agency must comply with this subpart and include in a charter the information required by §102-3.75.

§102-3.75 What information must be included in the charter of an advisory committee?

(a) Purpose and contents of an advisory committee charter. An advisory committee charter is intended to provide a description of an advisory committee's mission, goals, and objectives. It also provides a basis for evaluating an advisory committee's progress and effectiveness. The charter must contain the following information:
   (1) The advisory committee's official designation;
   (2) The objectives and the scope of the advisory committee's activity;
   (3) The period of time necessary to carry out the advisory committee's purpose(s);
   (4) The agency or Federal officer to whom the advisory committee reports;
   (5) The agency responsible for providing the necessary support to the advisory committee;
   (6) A description of the duties for which the advisory committee is responsible and specification of the authority for any non-advisory functions;
   (7) The estimated annual costs to operate the advisory committee in dollars and person years;
   (8) The estimated number and frequency of the advisory committee's meetings;
   (9) The planned termination date, if less than two years from the date of establishment of the advisory committee;
   (10) The name of the President's delegate, agency, or organization responsible for fulfilling the reporting requirements of section 6(b) of the Act, if appropriate; and
   (11) The date the charter is filed in accordance with §102-3.70.

(b) The provisions of paragraphs (a)(1) through (11) of this section apply to all subcommittees that report directly to a Federal officer or agency.

§102-3.80 How are minor charter amendments accomplished?

(a) Responsibility and limitation. The agency head is responsible for amending the charter of an advisory committee. Amendments may be either minor or major. The procedures for making changes and filing amended charters will depend upon the authority basis for the advisory committee. Amending any existing advisory committee charter does not constitute renewal of the advisory committee under §102-3.60.

(b) Procedures for minor amendments. To make a minor amendment to an advisory committee charter, such as changing the name of the advisory committee or modifying the estimated number or frequency of meetings, the following procedures must be followed:

(1) Non-discretionary advisory committees. The agency head must ensure that any minor technical changes made to current charters are consistent with the relevant authority. When the Congress by law, or the President by Executive order, changes the authorizing language that has been the basis for establishing an advisory committee, the agency head or the chairperson of an independent Presidential advisory committee must amend those sections of the current charter affected by the new statute or Executive order, and file the amended charter as specified in §102-3.70.

(2) Discretionary advisory committees. The charter of a discretionary advisory committee may be amended when an agency head determines that technical provisions of a filed charter are inaccurate, or specific provisions have changed or become obsolete with the passing of time, and that these amendments will not alter the advisory committee's objectives and scope substantially. The agency must amend the charter language as necessary and file the amended charter as specified in §102-3.70.

§102-3.85 How are major charter amendments accomplished?

Procedures for making major amendments to advisory committee charters, such as substantial changes in objectives and scope, duties, and estimated costs, are the same as in §102-3.80, except that for discretionary advisory committees an agency must:

(a) Consult with the Secretariat on the amended language, and explain the purpose of the changes and why they are necessary; and

(b) File the amended charter as specified in §102-3.70.

Appendix A to Subpart B of Part 102-3
Key Points and Principles

This appendix provides additional guidance in the form of answers to frequently asked questions and identifies key points and principles that may be applied to situations not covered elsewhere in this subpart. The guidance follows:

Key points and principles
I. Agency heads must consult with the Secretariat prior to establishing a discretionary advisory committee.

Section(s)
102-3.60, 102-3.115

Question(s)
1. Can an agency head delegate to the Committee Management Officer (CMO) responsibility for consulting with the Secretariat regarding the establishment, renewal, or reestablishment of discretionary advisory committees?

Guidance
A. Yes. Many administrative functions performed to implement the Act may be delegated. However, those functions related to approving the final establishment, renewal, or reestablishment of discretionary advisory committees are reserved for the agency head. Each agency CMO should assure that their internal processes for managing advisory committees include appropriate certifications by the agency head.

Key points and principles
II. Agency heads are responsible for complying with the Act, including determining which discretionary advisory committees should be established and renewed.

Section(s)
102-3.60(a), 102-3.105

Question
1. Who retains final authority for establishing or renewing a discretionary advisory committee?

Guidance
A. Although agency heads retain final authority for establishing or renewing discretionary advisory committees, these decisions should be consistent with § 102-3.105(e) and reflect consultation with the Secretariat under § 102-3.60(a).

Key points and principles
> III. An advisory committee must be fairly balanced in its membership in terms of the points of view represented and the functions to be performed.

Section(s)
102-3.30(c), 102-3.60(b)(3)

Question
> 1. What factors should be considered in achieving a "balanced" advisory committee membership?

Guidance
> A. The composition of an advisory committee's membership will depend upon several factors, including: (i) The advisory committee's mission; (ii) The geographic, ethnic, social, economic, or scientific impact of the advisory committee's recommendations; (iii) The types of specific perspectives required, for example, such as those of consumers, technical experts, the public at-large, academia, business, or other sectors; (iv) The need to obtain divergent points of view on the issues before the advisory committee; and (v) The relevance of State, local, or tribal governments to the development of the advisory committee's recommendations.

Key points and principles
> IV. Charters for advisory committees required by statute must be filed every two years regardless of the duration provided in the statute.

Section
102-3.70(b)

Question(s)
> 1. If an advisory committee's duration exceeds two years, must a charter be filed with the Congress and GSA every two years?

Guidance
> A. Yes. Section 14(b)(2) of the Act provides that: Any advisory committee established by an Act of Congress shall file a charter upon the expiration of each successive two-year period following the date of enactment of the Act establishing such advisory committee.

Subpart C—How Are Advisory Committees Managed?

§102-3.90 What does this subpart cover and how does it apply?

This subpart outlines specific responsibilities and functions to be carried out by the General Services Administration (GSA), the agency head, the Committee Management Officer (CMO), and the Designated Federal Officer (DFO) under the Act.

§102-3.95 What principles apply to the management of advisory committees?

Agencies are encouraged to apply the following principles to the management of their advisory committees:

(a) Provide adequate support. Before establishing an advisory committee, agencies should identify requirements and assure that adequate resources are available to support anticipated activities. Considerations related to support include office space, necessary supplies and equipment, Federal staff support, and access to key decisionmakers.

(b) Focus on mission. Advisory committee members and staff should be fully aware of the advisory committee's mission, limitations, if any, on its duties, and the agency's goals and objectives. In general, the more specific an advisory committee's tasks and the more focused its activities are, the higher the likelihood will be that the advisory committee will fulfill its mission.

(c) Follow plans and procedures. Advisory committee members and their agency sponsors should work together to assure that a plan and necessary procedures covering implementation are in place to support an advisory committee's mission. In particular, agencies should be clear regarding what functions an advisory committee can perform legally and those that it cannot perform.

(d) Practice openness. In addition to achieving the minimum standards of public access established by the Act and this part, agencies should seek to be as inclusive as possible. For example, agencies may wish to explore the use of the Internet to post advisory committee information and seek broader input from the public.

(e) Seek feedback. Agencies continually should seek feedback from advisory committee members and the public regarding the effectiveness of the advisory committee's activities. At regular intervals, agencies should communicate to the members how their advice has affected agency programs and decisionmaking.

§102-3.100 What are the responsibilities and functions of GSA?

(a) Under section 7 of the Act, the General Services Administration (GSA) prepares regulations on Federal advisory committees to be prescribed by the Administrator of General Services, issues other administrative guidelines and management controls for advisory committees, and assists other agencies in implementing and interpreting the Act. Responsibility for these activities has been delegated by the Administrator to the GSA Committee Management Secretariat.

(b) The Secretariat carries out its responsibilities by:

(1) Conducting an annual comprehensive review of Governmentwide advisory committee accomplishments, costs, benefits, and other indicators to measure performance;

(2) Developing and distributing Governmentwide training regarding the Act and related statutes and principles;

(3) Supporting the Interagency Committee on Federal Advisory Committee Management in its efforts to improve compliance with the Act;

(4) Designing and maintaining a Governmentwide shared Internet-based system to facilitate collection and use of information required by the Act;

(5) Identifying performance measures that may be used to evaluate advisory committee accomplishments; and

(6) Providing recommendations for transmittal by the Administrator to the Congress and the President regarding proposals to improve accomplishment of the objectives of the Act.

§102-3.105 What are the responsibilities of an agency head?

The head of each agency that establishes or utilizes one or more advisory committees must:

(a) Comply with the Act and this Federal Advisory Committee Management part;

(b) Issue administrative guidelines and management controls that apply to all of the agency's advisory committees subject to the Act;

(c) Designate a Committee Management Officer (CMO);

(d) Provide a written determination stating the reasons for closing any advisory committee meeting to the public, in whole or in part, in accordance with the exemption(s) of the Government in the Sunshine Act, 5 U.S.C. 552b(c), as the basis for closure;

(e) Review, at least annually, the need to continue each existing advisory committee, consistent with the public interest and the purpose or functions of each advisory committee;

(f) Determine that rates of compensation for members (if they are paid for their services) and staff of, and experts and consultants to advisory committees are justified and that levels of agency support are adequate;

(g) Develop procedures to assure that the advice or recommendations of advisory committees will not be inappropriately influenced by the appointing authority or by any special interest, but will instead be the result of the advisory committee's independent judgment;

(h) Assure that the interests and affiliations of advisory committee members are reviewed for conformance with applicable conflict of interest statutes, regulations issued by the U.S. Office of Government Ethics (OGE) including any supplemental agency requirements, and other Federal ethics rules;

(i) Designate a Designated Federal Officer (DFO) for each advisory committee and its subcommittees; and

(j) Provide the opportunity for reasonable participation by the public in advisory committee activities, subject to §102-3.140 and the agency's guidelines.

§102-3.110 What are the responsibilities of a chairperson of an independent Presidential advisory committee?

The chairperson of an independent Presidential advisory committee must:

(a) Comply with the Act and this Federal Advisory Committee Management part;

(b) Consult with the Secretariat concerning the designation of a Committee Management Officer (CMO) and Designated Federal Officer (DFO); and

(c) Consult with the Secretariat in advance regarding any proposal to close any meeting in whole or in part.

§102-3.115 What are the responsibilities and functions of an agency Committee Management Officer (CMO)?

In addition to implementing the provisions of section 8(b) of the Act, the CMO will carry out all responsibilities delegated by the agency head. The

CMO also should ensure that sections 10(b), 12(a), and 13 of the Act are implemented by the agency to provide for appropriate recordkeeping. Records to be kept by the CMO include, but are not limited to:

(a) Charter and membership documentation. A set of filed charters for each advisory committee and membership lists for each advisory committee and subcommittee;

(b) Annual comprehensive review. Copies of the information provided as the agency's portion of the annual comprehensive review of Federal advisory committees, prepared according to §102-3.175(b);

(c) Agency guidelines. Agency guidelines maintained and updated on committee management operations and procedures; and

(d) Closed meeting determinations. Agency determinations to close or partially close advisory committee meetings required by §102-3.105.

§102-3.120 What are the responsibilities and functions of a Designated Federal Officer (DFO)?

The agency head or, in the case of an independent Presidential advisory committee, the Secretariat, must designate a Federal officer or employee who must be either full-time or permanent part-time, to be the DFO for each advisory committee and its subcommittees, who must:

(a) Approve or call the meeting of the advisory committee or subcommittee;

(b) Approve the agenda, except that this requirement does not apply to a Presidential advisory committee;

(c) Attend the meetings;

(d) Adjourn any meeting when he or she determines it to be in the public interest; and

(e) Chair the meeting when so directed by the agency head.

§102-3.125 How should agencies consider the roles of advisory committee members and staff?

FACA does not assign any specific responsibilities to members of advisory committees and staff, although both perform critical roles in achieving the goals and objectives assigned to advisory committees. Agency heads, Committee Management Officers (CMOs), and Designated Federal Officers (DFOs) should consider the distinctions between these roles and how they relate to each other in the development of agency guidelines implementing the Act and this Federal Advisory Committee Management part. In general, these guidelines should reflect:

(a) Clear operating procedures. Clear operating procedures should provide for the conduct of advisory committee meetings and other activities, and specify the relationship among the advisory committee members, the DFO, and advisory committee or agency staff;

(b) Agency operating policies. In addition to compliance with the Act, advisory committee members and staff may be required to adhere to additional agency operating policies; and

(c) Other applicable statutes. Other agency-specific statutes and regulations may affect the agency's advisory committees directly or indirectly. Agencies should ensure that advisory committee members and staff understand these requirements.

§102-3.130 What policies apply to the appointment, and compensation or reimbursement of advisory committee members, staff, and experts and consultants?

In developing guidelines to implement the Act and this Federal Advisory Committee Management part at the agency level, agency heads must address the following issues concerning advisory committee member and staff appointments, and considerations with respect to uniform fair rates of compensation for comparable services, or expense reimbursement of members, staff, and experts and consultants:

(a) Appointment and terms of advisory committee members. Unless otherwise provided by statute, Presidential directive, or other establishment authority, advisory committee members serve at the pleasure of the appointing or inviting authority. Membership terms are at the sole discretion of the appointing or inviting authority.

(b) Compensation guidelines. Each agency head must establish uniform compensation guidelines for members and staff of, and experts and consultants to an advisory committee.

(c) Compensation of advisory committee members not required. Nothing in this subpart requires an agency head to provide compensation to any member of an advisory committee, unless otherwise required by a specific statute.

(d) Compensation of advisory committee members. When an agency has authority to set pay administratively for advisory committee members, it may establish appropriate rates of pay (including any applicable locality pay authorized by the President's Pay Agent under 5 U.S.C. 5304(h)), not to exceed the rate for level IV of the Executive Schedule under 5 U.S.C. 5315, unless a higher rate expressly is allowed by another statute. However, the agency head personally must authorize a rate of basic pay in excess of the maximum rate of basic pay established for the General Schedule under 5 U.S.C. 5332, or alternative similar agency compensation system. This maximum rate includes any applicable locality payment under 5 U.S.C. 5304. The agency may pay advisory committee members on either an hourly or a daily rate basis. The agency may not provide additional compensation in any form, such as bonuses or premium pay.

(e) Compensation of staff. When an agency has authority to set pay administratively for advisory committee staff, it may establish appropriate rates of pay (including any applicable locality pay authorized by the President's Pay Agent under 5 U.S.C. 5304(h)), not to exceed the rate for level IV of the Executive Schedule under 5 U.S.C. 5315, unless a higher rate expressly is allowed by another statute. However, the agency head personally must authorize a rate of basic pay in excess of the maximum rate of basic pay established for the General Schedule under 5 U.S.C. 5332, or alternative similar agency compensation system. This maximum rate includes any applicable locality payment under 5 U.S.C. 5304. The agency must pay advisory committee staff on an hourly rate basis. The agency may provide additional compensation, such as bonuses or premium pay, so long as aggregate compensation paid in a calendar year does not exceed the rate for level IV of the Executive Schedule, with appropriate proration for a partial calendar year.

(f) Other compensation considerations. In establishing rates of pay for advisory committee members and staff, the agency must comply with any applicable statutes, Executive orders, regulations, or administrative guidelines. In determining an appropriate rate of basic pay for advisory committee members and staff, an agency must give consideration to the significance, scope, and technical complexity of the matters with which the advisory committee is concerned, and the qualifications required for the work involved. The agency also should take into account the rates of pay applicable to Federal employees who have duties that are similar in terms of difficulty and responsibility. An agency may establish rates of pay for advisory committee staff based on the pay these persons would receive if they were covered by the General Schedule in 5 U.S.C. Chapter 51 and Chapter 53, subchapter III, or by an alternative similar agency compensation system.

(g) Compensation of experts and consultants. Whether or not an agency has other authority to appoint and compensate advisory committee members or staff, it also may employ experts and consultants under 5 U.S.C. 3109 to perform work for an advisory committee. Compensation of experts and consultants may not exceed the maximum rate of basic pay established for the General Schedule under 5 U.S.C. 5332 (that is, the GS-15, step 10 rate, excluding locality pay or any other supplement), unless a higher rate expressly is allowed by another statute. The appointment and compensation of experts and consultants by an agency must be in conformance with applicable regulations issued by the U. S. Office of Personnel Management (OPM) (See 5 CFR part 304.).

(h) Federal employees assigned to an advisory committee. Any advisory committee member or staff person who is a Federal employee when assigned duties to an advisory committee remains covered during the assignment by the compensation system that currently applies to that employee, unless that person's current Federal appointment is terminated. Any staff person who is a Federal employee must serve with the knowledge of the Designated Federal Officer (DFO) for the advisory committee to which that person is assigned duties, and the approval of the employee's direct supervisor.

(i) Other appointment considerations. An individual who is appointed as an advisory committee member or staff person immediately following termination of another Federal appointment with a full-time work schedule may receive compensation at the rate applicable to the former appointment, if otherwise allowed by applicable law (without regard to the limitations on pay established in paragraphs (d) and (e) of this section). Any advisory committee staff person who is not a current Federal employee serving under an assignment must be appointed in accordance with applicable agency procedures, and in consultation with the DFO and the members of the advisory committee involved.

(j) Gratuitous services. In the absence of any special limitations applicable to a specific agency, nothing in this subpart prevents an agency from accepting the gratuitous services of an advisory committee member or staff person who is not a Federal employee, or expert or consultant, who agrees in advance and in writing to serve without compensation.

(k) Travel expenses. Advisory committee members and staff, while engaged in the performance of their duties away from their homes or regular places of business, may be allowed reimbursement for travel expenses, including per diem in lieu of subsistence, as authorized by 5 U.S.C. 5703, for persons employed intermittently in the Government service.

(l) Services for advisory committee members with disabilities. While performing advisory committee duties, an advisory committee member with disabilities may be provided services by a personal assistant for employees with disabilities, if the member qualifies as an individual with disabilities as provided in section 501 of the Rehabilitation Act of 1973, as amended, 29 U.S.C. 791, and does not otherwise qualify for assistance under 5 U.S.C. 3102 by reason of being a Federal employee.

Appendix A to Subpart C of Part 102-3— Key Points and Principles

This appendix provides additional guidance in the form of answers to frequently asked questions and identifies key points and principles that may be applied to situations not covered elsewhere in this subpart. The guidance follows:

Key points and principles
    I.   FACA does not specify the manner in which advisory committee members and staff must be appointed

Section(s)
102-3.105, 102-3.130(a)

Question(s)
    1.   Does the appointment of an advisory committee member necessarily result in a lengthy process?

Guidance
    A.   No. Each agency head may specify those policies and procedures, consistent with the Act and this part, or other specific authorizing statute, governing the appointment of advisory committee members and staff.

    B.   Some factors that affect how long the appointment process takes include: (i) Solicitation of nominations; (ii) Conflict of interest clearances; (iii) Security or background evaluations; (iv) Availability of candidates; and (v) Other statutory or administrative requirements.

    C.   In addition, the extent to which agency heads have delegated responsibility for selecting members varies from agency to agency and may become an important factor in the time it takes to finalize the advisory committee's membership.

Key points and principles
II. Agency heads retain the final authority for selecting advisory committee members, unless otherwise provided for by a specific statute or Presidential directive

Section
102-3.130(a)

Question(s)
1. Can an agency head select for membership on an advisory committee from among nominations submitted by an organization?
2. If so, can different persons represent the organization at different meetings?

Guidance
A. The answer to question 1 is yes. Organizations may propose for membership individuals to represent them on an advisory committee. However, the agency head establishing the advisory committee, or other appointing authority, retains the final authority for selecting all members.
B. The answer to question 2 also is yes. Alternates may represent an appointed member with the approval of the establishing agency, where the agency head is the appointing authority.

Key points and principles
III. An agency may compensate advisory committee members and staff, and also employ experts and consultants

Section(s)
102-3.130(d), 102-3.130(e), 102-3.130(g)

Question(s)
1. May members and staff be compensated for their service or duties on an advisory committee?
2. Are the guidelines the same for compensating both members and staff?
3. May experts and consultants be employed to perform other advisory committee work?

Guidance

A. The answer to question 1 is yes. (i) However, FACA limits compensation for advisory committee members and staff to the rate for level IV of the Executive Schedule, unless higher rates expressly are allowed by other statutes. (ii) Although FACA provides for compensation guidelines, the Act does not require an agency to compensate its advisory committee members.

B. The answer to question 2 is no. The guidelines for compensating members and staff are similar, but not identical. For example, the differences are that: (i) An agency "may" pay members on either an hourly or a daily rate basis, and "may not" provide additional compensation in any form, such as bonuses or premium pay; while (ii) An agency "must" pay staff on an hourly rate basis only, and "may" provide additional compensation, so long as aggregate compensation paid in a calendar year does not exceed the rate for level IV of the Executive Schedule, with appropriate proration for a partial calendar year.

C. The answer to question 3 is yes. Other work not part of the duties of advisory committee members or staff may be performed by experts and consultants. For additional guidance on the employment of experts and consultants, agencies should consult the applicable regulations issued by the U. S. Office of Personnel Management (OPM). (See 5 CFR part 304.)

Key points and principles

IV. Agency heads are responsible for ensuring that the interests and affiliations of advisory committee members are reviewed for conformance with applicable conflict of interest statutes and other Federal ethics rules.

Section(s)
102-3.105(h)

Question(s)
1. Are all advisory committee members subject to conflict of interest statutes and other Federal ethics rules?
2. Who should be consulted for guidance on the proper application of Federal ethics rules to advisory committee members?

Guidance

A. The answer to question 1 is no. Whether an advisory committee member is subject to Federal ethics rules is dependent on the member's status. The determination of a member's status on an advisory committee is largely a personnel classification matter for the appointing agency. Most advisory committee members will serve either as a "representative" or a "special Government employee" (SGE), based on the role the member will play. In general, SGEs are covered by regulations issued by the U. S. Office of Government Ethics (OGE) and certain conflict of interest statutes, while representatives are not subject to these ethics requirements.

B. The answer to question 2 is the agency's Designated Agency Ethics Official (DAEO), who should be consulted prior to appointing members to an advisory committee in order to apply Federal ethics rules properly.

Key points and principles

V. An agency head may delegate responsibility for appointing a Committee Management Officer (CMO) or Designated Federal Officer (DFO); however, there may be only one CMO for each agency.

Section(s)

102-3.105(c), 102-3.105(i)

Question(s)

1. Must an agency's CMO and each advisory committee DFO be appointed by the agency head?
2. May an agency have more than one CMO?

Guidance

A. The answer to question 1 is no. The agency head may delegate responsibility for appointing the CMO and DFOs. However, these appointments, including alternate selections, should be documented consistent with the agency's policies and procedures.

B. The answer to question 2 also is no. The functions of the CMO are specified in the Act and include oversight responsibility for all advisory committees within the agency. Accordingly, only one CMO may be appointed to perform these functions. The agency may, however, create additional positions, including those in its subcomponents, which are subordinate to the CMO's agencywide responsibilities and functions.

Key points and principles
VI. FACA is the principal statute pertaining to advisory committees. However, other statutes may impact their use and operations.

Section(s)
102-3.125(c)

Question(s)
1. Do other statutes or regulations affect the way an agency carries out its advisory committee management program?

Guidance
A. Yes. While the Act provides a general framework for managing advisory committees Governmentwide, other factors may affect how advisory committees are managed. These include: (i) The statutory or Presidential authority used to establish an advisory committee; (ii) A statutory limitation placed on an agency regarding its annual expenditures for advisory committees; (iii) Presidential or agency management directives; (iv) The applicability of conflict of interest statutes and other Federal ethics rules; (v) Agency regulations affecting advisory committees; and (vi) Other requirements imposed by statute or regulation on an agency or its programs, such as those governing the employment of experts and consultants or the management of Federal records.

Subpart D—
Advisory Committee Meeting And Recordkeeping Procedures

§102-3.135 What does this subpart cover and how does it apply?

This subpart establishes policies and procedures relating to meetings and other activities undertaken by advisory committees and their subcommittees. This subpart also outlines what records must be kept by Federal agencies and what other documentation, including advisory committee minutes and reports, must be prepared and made available to the public.

§102-3.140 What policies apply to advisory committee meetings?

The agency head, or the chairperson of an independent Presidential advisory committee, must ensure that:

(a) Each advisory committee meeting is held at a reasonable time and in a manner or place reasonably accessible to the public, to include facilities that are readily accessible to and usable by persons with disabilities, consistent with the goals of section 504 of the Rehabilitation Act of 1973, as amended, 29 U.S.C. 794;

(b) The meeting room or other forum selected is sufficient to accommodate advisory committee members, advisory committee or agency staff, and a reasonable number of interested members of the public;

(c) Any member of the public is permitted to file a written statement with the advisory committee;

(d) Any member of the public may speak to or otherwise address the advisory committee if the agency's guidelines so permit; and

(e) Any advisory committee meeting conducted in whole or part by a teleconference, video conference, the Internet, or other electronic medium meets the requirements of this subpart.

§102-3.145 What policies apply to subcommittee meetings?

If a subcommittee makes recommendations directly to a Federal officer or agency, or if its recommendations will be adopted by the parent advisory committee without further deliberations by the parent advisory committee, then the subcommittee's meetings must be conducted in accordance with all openness requirements of this subpart.

§102-3.150 How are advisory committee meetings announced to the public?

(a) A notice in the Federal Register must be published at least 15 calendar days prior to an advisory committee meeting, which includes:
  (1) The name of the advisory committee (or subcommittee, if applicable);
  (2) The time, date, place, and purpose of the meeting;
  (3) A summary of the agenda, and/or topics to be discussed;
  (4) A statement whether all or part of the meeting is open to the public or closed; if the meeting is closed state the reasons why, citing the

specific exemption(s) of the Government in the Sunshine Act, 5 U.S.C. 552b(c), as the basis for closure; and

(5) The name and telephone number of the Designated Federal Officer (DFO) or other responsible agency official who may be contacted for additional information concerning the meeting.

(b) In exceptional circumstances, the agency or an independent Presidential advisory committee may give less than 15 calendar days notice, provided that the reasons for doing so are included in the advisory committee meeting notice published in the Federal Register.

§102-3.155 How are advisory committee meetings closed to the public?

To close all or part of an advisory committee meeting, the Designated Federal Officer (DFO) must:

(a) Obtain prior approval. Submit a request to the agency head, or in the case of an independent Presidential advisory committee, the Secretariat, citing the specific exemption(s) of the Government in the Sunshine Act, 5 U.S.C. 552b(c), that justify the closure. The request must provide the agency head or the Secretariat sufficient time (generally, 30 calendar days) to review the matter in order to make a determination before publication of the meeting notice required by §102-3.150.

(b) Seek General Counsel review. The General Counsel of the agency or, in the case of an independent Presidential advisory committee, the General Counsel of GSA should review all requests to close meetings.

(c) Obtain agency determination. If the agency head, or in the case of an independent Presidential advisory committee, the Secretariat, finds that the request is consistent with the provisions in the Government in the Sunshine Act and FACA, the appropriate agency official must issue a determination that all or part of the meeting be closed.

(d) Assure public access to determination. The agency head or the chairperson of an independent Presidential advisory committee must make a copy of the determination available to the public upon request.

§102-3.160 What activities of an advisory committee are not subject to the notice and open meeting requirements of the Act?

The following activities of an advisory committee are excluded from the procedural requirements contained in this subpart:

(a) Preparatory work. Meetings of two or more advisory committee or subcommittee members convened solely to gather information, conduct research, or analyze relevant issues and facts in preparation for a meeting of the advisory committee, or to draft position papers for deliberation by the advisory committee; and

(b) Administrative work. Meetings of two or more advisory committee or subcommittee members convened solely to discuss administrative matters of the advisory committee or to receive administrative information from a Federal officer or agency.

§102-3.165 How are advisory committee meetings documented?

(a) The agency head or, in the case of an independent Presidential advisory committee, the chairperson must ensure that detailed minutes of each advisory committee meeting, including one that is closed or partially closed to the public, are kept. The chairperson of each advisory committee must certify the accuracy of all minutes of advisory committee meetings.

(b) The minutes must include:
(1) The time, date, and place of the advisory committee meeting;
(2) A list of the persons who were present at the meeting, including advisory committee members and staff, agency employees, and members of the public who presented oral or written statements;
(3) An accurate description of each matter discussed and the resolution, if any, made by the advisory committee regarding such matter; and
(4) Copies of each report or other document received, issued, or approved by the advisory committee at the meeting.

(c) The Designated Federal Officer (DFO) must ensure that minutes are certified within 90 calendar days of the meeting to which they relate.

§102-3.170 How does an interested party obtain access to advisory committee records?

Timely access to advisory committee records is an important element of the public access requirements of the Act. Section 10(b) of the Act provides for the contemporaneous availability of advisory committee records that, when taken in conjunction with the ability to attend committee meetings, provide a meaningful opportunity to comprehend fully the work undertaken by the advisory committee. Although advisory committee records may be withheld under the provisions of the Freedom of Information Act (FOIA), as amended, if there is a reasonable expectation that the records sought fall within the exemptions contained in section 552(b) of FOIA, agencies may not require members of the public or other interested parties to file requests for non-exempt advisory committee records under the request and review process established by section 552(a)(3) of FOIA.

§102-3.175 What are the reporting and recordkeeping requirements for an advisory committee?

(a) Presidential advisory committee follow-up report. Within one year after a Presidential advisory committee has submitted a public report to the President, a follow-up report required by section 6(b) of the Act must be prepared and transmitted to the Congress detailing the disposition of the advisory committee's recommendations. The Secretariat shall assure that these reports are prepared and transmitted to the Congress as directed by the President, either by the President's delegate, by the agency responsible for providing support to a Presidential advisory committee, or by the responsible agency or organization designated in the charter of the Presidential advisory committee pursuant to §102-3.75(a)(10). In performing this function, GSA may solicit the assistance of the President's delegate, the Office of Management and Budget (OMB), or the responsible agency Committee Management Officer (CMO), as appropriate. Reports shall be consistent with specific guidance provided periodically by the Secretariat.

(b) Annual comprehensive review of Federal advisory committees. To conduct an annual comprehensive review of each advisory committee as specified in section 7(b) of the Act, GSA requires Federal agencies to report information on each advisory committee for which a charter has been filed in accordance with §102-3.70, and which is in existence during any part of a Federal fiscal year. Committee Management Officers (CMOs), Designated Federal Officers (DFOs), and other responsible agency officials will provide this information by data filed electronically with GSA on a fiscal year basis, using a Governmentwide shared Internet-based system that GSA maintains. This information shall be consistent with specific guidance provided periodically by the Secretariat. The preparation of these electronic submissions by agencies has been assigned interagency report control number (IRCN) 0304-GSA-AN.

(c) Annual report of closed or partially-closed meetings. In accordance with section 10(d) of the Act, advisory committees holding closed or partially-closed meetings must issue reports at least annually, setting forth a summary of activities and such related matters as would be informative to the public consistent with the policy of 5 U.S.C. 552(b).

(d) Advisory committee reports. Subject to 5 U.S.C. 552, 8 copies of each report made by an advisory committee, including any report of closed or partially-closed meetings as specified in paragraph (c) of this section and, where appropriate, background papers prepared by experts or consultants, must be filed with the Library of Congress as required by section 13 of the Act for public inspection and use at the location specified §102-3.70(a)(3).

(e) Advisory committee records. Official records generated by or for an advisory committee must be retained for the duration of the advisory committee. Upon termination of the advisory committee, the records must be processed in accordance with the Federal Records Act (FRA), 44 U.S.C. Chapters 21, 29-33, and regulations issued by the National Archives and Records Administration (NARA) (see 36 CFR parts 1220, 1222, 1228, and 1234), or in accordance with the Presidential Records Act (PRA), 44 U.S.C. Chapter 22.

Appendix A to Subpart D of Part 102-3— Key Points and Principles

This appendix provides additional guidance in the form of answers to frequently asked questions and identifies key points and principles that may be applied to situations not covered elsewhere in this subpart. The guidance follows:

Key points and principles
  I. With some exceptions, advisory committee meetings are open to the public

Section(s)
102-3.140, 102-3.145(a), 102-3.155

Question
  1. Must all advisory committee and subcommittee meetings be open to the public?

Guidance
  A. No. Advisory committee meetings may be closed when appropriate, in accordance with the exemption(s) for closure contained in the Government in the Sunshine Act, 5 U.S.C. 552b(c). (i) Subcommittees that report to a parent advisory committee, and not directly to a Federal officer or agency, are not required to open their meetings to

the public or comply with the procedures in the Act for announcing meetings. (ii) However, agencies are cautioned to avoid excluding the public from attending any meeting where a subcommittee develops advice or recommendations that are not expected to be reviewed and considered by the parent advisory committee before being submitted to a Federal officer or agency. These exclusions may run counter to the provisions of the Act requiring contemporaneous access to the advisory committee deliberative process.

Key points and principles

II. Notices must be published in the Federal Register announcing advisory committee meetings

Section(s)
102-3.150

Question
1. Can agencies publish a single Federal Register notice announcing multiple advisory committee meetings?

Guidance
A. Yes, agencies may publish a single notice announcing multiple meetings so long as these notices contain all of the information required by § 102-3.150. (i) "Blanket notices" should not announce meetings so far in advance as to prevent the public from adequately being informed of an advisory committee's schedule. (ii) An agency's Office of General Counsel should be consulted where these notices include meetings that are either closed or partially closed to the public.

Key points and principles

III. Although certain advisory committee records may be withheld under the Freedom of Information Act (FOIA), as amended, 5 U.S.C. 552, agencies may not require the use of FOIA procedures for records available under section 10(b) of FACA

Section(s)
102-3.170

Question

1. May an agency require the use of its internal FOIA procedures for access to advisory committee records that are not exempt from release under FOIA?

Guidance

A. No. Section 10(b) of FACA provides that: Subject to section 552 of title 5, United States Code, the records, reports, transcripts, minutes, appendixes, working papers, drafts, studies, agenda, or other documents which were made available to or prepared for or by each advisory committee shall be available for public inspection and copying at a single location in the offices of the advisory committee or the agency to which the advisory committee reports until the advisory committee ceases to exist. (i) The purpose of section 10(b) of the Act is to provide for the contemporaneous availability of advisory committee records that, when taken in conjunction with the ability to attend advisory committee meetings, provide a meaningful opportunity to comprehend fully the work undertaken by the advisory committee. (ii) Although advisory section 552(b) of FOIA may be withheld. An opinion of the Office of Legal Counsel (OLC), U.S. Department of Justice concludes that: FACA requires disclosure of written advisory committee documents, including predecisional materials such as drafts, working papers, and studies. The disclosure exemption available to agencies under exemption 5 of FOIA for predecisional documents and other privileged materials is narrowly limited in the context of FACA to privileged "inter-agency or intra-agency" documents prepared by an agency and transmitted to an advisory committee. The language of the FACA statute and its legislative history support this restrictive application of exemption 5 to requests for public access to advisory committee documents. Moreover, since an advisory committee is not itself an agency, this construction is supported by the express language of exemption 5 which applies only to inter-agency or intra-agency materials. (iv) Agencies first should determine, however, whether or not records being sought by the public fall within the scope of FACA in general, and section 10(b) of the Act in particular, prior to applying the available exemptions under FOIA. (See OLC Opinion 12 Op. O.L.C. 73, dated April 29, 1988, which is available from the Committee Management Secretariat (MC), General Services Administration, 1800 F Street, NW., Washington, DC 20405-0002.)

Key points and principles

IV. Advisory committee records must be managed in accordance with the Federal Records Act (FRA), 44 U.S.C. Chapters 21, 29-33, and regulations issued by the National Archives and Records Administration (NARA) (see 36 CFR parts 1220, 1222, 1228, and 1234), or the Presidential Records Act (PRA), 44 U.S.C. Chapter 22

Section(s)
102-175(e)

Question
1. How must advisory committee records be treated and preserved?

Guidance

A. In order to ensure proper records management, the Committee Management Officer (CMO), Designated Federal Officer (DFO), or other representative of the advisory committee, in coordination with the agency's Records Management Officer, should clarify upon the establishment of the advisory committee whether its records will be managed in accordance with the FRA or the PRA.

B. Official records generated by or for an advisory committee must be retained for the duration of the advisory committee. Responsible agency officials are encouraged to contact their agency's Records Management Officer or NARA as soon as possible after the establishment of the advisory committee to receive guidance on how to establish effective records management practices. Upon termination of the advisory committee, the records must be processed in accordance with the FRA and regulations issued by NARA, or in accordance with the PRA.

C. The CMO, DFO, or other representative of an advisory committee governed by the FRA, in coordination with the agency's Records Management Officer, must contact NARA in sufficient time to review the process for submitting any necessary disposition schedules of the advisory committee's records, disposition schedules need to be submitted to NARA no later than 6 months before the termination of the advisory committee.

D. For Presidential advisory committees governed by the PRA, the CMO, DFO, or other representative of the advisory committee should consult with the White House Counsel on the preservation of any records subject to the PRA, and may also confer with NARA officials.

Subpart E—
How Does This Subpart Apply to Advice or Recommendations Provided to Agencies by the National Academy of Sciences or the National Academy of Public Administration?

§102-3.180 What does this subpart cover and how does it apply?

This subpart provides guidance to agencies on compliance with section 15 of the Act. Section 15 establishes requirements that apply only in connection with a funding or other written agreement involving an agency's use of advice or recommendations provided to the agency by the National Academy of Sciences (NAS) or the National Academy of Public Administration (NAPA), if such advice or recommendations were developed by use of a committee created by either academy. For purposes of this subpart, NAS also includes the National Academy of Engineering, the Institute of Medicine, and the National Research Council. Except with respect to NAS committees that were the subject of judicial actions filed before December 17, 1997, no part of the Act other than section 15 applies to any committee created by NAS or NAPA.

§102-3.185 What does this subpart require agencies to do?

(a) Section 15 requirements. An agency may not use any advice or recommendation provided to an agency by the National Academy of Sciences (NAS) or the National Academy of Public Administration (NAPA) under an agreement between the agency and an academy, if such advice or recommendation was developed by use of a committee created by either academy, unless:
(1) The committee was not subject to any actual management or control by an agency or officer of the Federal Government; and
(2) In the case of NAS, the academy certifies that it has complied substantially with the requirements of section 15(b) of the Act; or
(3) In the case of NAPA, the academy certifies that it has complied substantially with the requirements of sections 15(b) (1), (2), and (5) of the Act.
(b) No agency management or control. Agencies must not manage or control the specific procedures adopted by each academy to comply with the requirements of section 15 of the Act that are applicable to that academy. In addition, however, any committee created and used by an academy in the development of any advice or recommendation to be provided by the academy to an agency must be subject to both actual management and control by that academy and not by the agency.

(c) Funding agreements. Agencies may enter into contracts, grants, and cooperative agreements with NAS or NAPA that are consistent with the requirements of this subpart to obtain advice or recommendations from such academy. These funding agreements require, and agencies may rely upon, a written certification by an authorized representative of the academy provided to the agency upon delivery to the agency of each report containing advice or recommendations required under the agreement that:

(1) The academy has adopted policies and procedures that comply with the applicable requirements of section 15 of the Act; and

(2) To the best of the authorized representative's knowledge and belief, these policies and procedures substantially have been complied with in performing the work required under the agreement.

Appendix A to Subpart E of Part 102-3— Key Points and Principles

This appendix provides additional guidance in the form of answers to frequently asked questions and identifies key points and principles that may be applied to situations not covered elsewhere in this subpart. The guidance follows:

Key points and principles

I. Section 15 of the Act allows the National Academy of Sciences (NAS) and the National Academy of Public Administration (NAPA) to adopt separate procedures for complying with FACA

Section(s)
102-3.185(a)

Question

1. May agencies rely upon an academy certification regarding compliance with section 15 of the Act if different policies and procedures are adopted by NAS and NAPA?

Guidance

A. Yes. NAS and NAPA are completely separate organizations. Each is independently chartered by the Congress for different purposes, and Congress has recognized that the two organizations are structured and operate differently. Agencies should defer to the discretion of each academy to adopt policies and procedures that will enable it to comply substantially with the provisions of section 15 of the Act that apply to that academy.

Key points and principles
II. Section 15 of the Act allows agencies to enter into funding agreements with NAS and NAPA without the academies' committees being "managed" or" controlled"

Section(s)
102-3.185(c)

Question
1. Can an agency enter into a funding agreement with an academy which provides for the preparation of one or more academy reports containing advice or recommendations to the agency, to be developed by the academy by use of a committee created by the academy, without subjecting an academy to "actual management or control" by the agency?

Guidance
A. Yes, if the members of the committee are selected by the academy and if the committee's meetings, deliberations, and the preparation of reports are all controlled by the academy. Under these circumstances, neither the existence of the funding agreement nor the fact that it contemplates use by the academy of an academy committee would constitute actual management or control of the committee by the agency.

Office of Management and Budget
Circular A-135, "Management of Federal Advisory Committees"

59 Fed. Reg. 53,856 (October 26, 1994)

AGENCY: Office of Management and Budget, Federal Services Branch.

ACTION: Issuance of OMB Circular A-135, "Management of Federal Advisory Committees" dated October 5, 1994.

SUMMARY: This Circular outlines the Administration's policy of controlling the growth of Federal advisory committees through an annual agency review and planning process.

The Circular requires agencies to report annually to OMB and the General Services Administration's (GSA) Committee Management Secretariat on initiatives to reduce existing committees, terminate statutory committees and plans to establish new advisory committees during the next fiscal year.

OMB and GSA are responsible for reviewing and approving agency plans and setting agency advisory committee ceilings that maintain the President's government-wide advisory committee reduction goal established through Executive Order 12,838.

FOR FURTHER INFORMATION CONTACT: Steve Mertens, Federal Services Branch, Office of Management and Budget, (202) 395-5090.

To the Heads of Executive Departments and Establishments
Subject: Management of Federal Advisory Committees

1. Purpose. This Circular provides guidance and instructions on the management of Federal advisory committees and requires Executive Departments and agencies to establish a committee planning and review process.

2. Background. On February 10, 1993, the President signed Executive Order 12,838, "Termination and Limitation of Federal Advisory Committees," which requires each Executive Department and agency to reduce the number of discretionary committees by one-third. New discretionary advisory committees are subject to review and approval by the Director of OMB.

On June 28, 1994, the Vice President issued a memorandum reiterating Administration policy regarding the maintenance of the reduction targets mandated by Executive Order 12,838, as well as new guidance relating to Executive Branch action on advisory committees proposed by statute. The

Vice President's memorandum also called for additional savings in committee costs over and above those achieved under E.O. 12,838, as recommended by the National Performance Review (NPR).

3. Policy. The Administration is committed to maintaining advisory committees as a way of ensuring public and expert involvement and advice in Federal decision-making. At the same time, the number and cost of advisory committees must be carefully managed. Advisory committees should get down to the public's business, complete it and then go out of business. Agencies should review and eliminate advisory committees that are obsolete, duplicative, low priority or serve a special, rather than national interest. New advisory committees should be established only when essential to the attainment of clearly defined Executive Branch priorities, as defined by E.O. 12,838, and when they will not exceed an agency's advisory committee ceiling as established by the Executive order's reduction requirement.

The Administration will generally not support the establishment of new statutory committees or legislative language that exempts advisory committees from coverage under the Federal Advisory Committee Act (FACA). In addition, each agency should make a concerted effort to work with its Congressional oversight committees to reduce the number of existing committees required by statute.

4. Definitions. For purposes of this Circular, definitions for "advisory committee," "agency," and other terms are the same as defined in GSA's implementation regulations for the Federal Advisory Committee Act (41 CFR Part 101-6). In addition:

A "non-discretionary advisory committee" is an advisory committee either mandated by Presidential directive or by statute and is subject to the Federal Advisory Committee Act. A "non- discretionary advisory committee" mandated by statute is: (1) specifically identified by name, specific purpose or function in statute, and (2) a committee whose creation or termination is beyond an agency's legal discretion. Advisory committees referenced by general (non-specific) authorizing language or committee report language will not be considered "non-discretionary." In addition, where a statute requires an advisory committee as defined above, but allows for one or more committees, only one committee shall be considered to be required by statute.

5. Required Action. Each Executive Department and agency shall report to OMB annually on the results of its efforts to maintain discretionary committee levels required by E.O. 12,838, and other actions to reduce its inventory of non-discretionary statutory committees. This submission will be used by the Director of OMB as the basis for approving requests to establish new committees.

(1) Agency advisory committee management plans will be submitted to OMB and GSA each year and include:

(a) performance measures used to evaluate each committee's progress in achieving its stated goals or mission;

(b) plans for the establishment of any new advisory committees during the coming fiscal year;

(c) a summary of actions taken to ensure the advisory committee reduction goal is maintained; and

(d) the results of a review of non-discretionary advisory committees and plans to continue, terminate or merge these groups through legislation. This will include a list of those committees established by specific statutory authority during the current fiscal year regardless of their coverage under the Federal Advisory Committee Act.

(2) With regard to non-discretionary advisory committees mandated by statute, the agency will notify GSA of plans to establish such committees prior to filing the charter required by section 9(c) of the Federal Advisory Committee Act. Such notification will provide GSA with at least 10 working days to review the proposed committee charter and advise the agency of its recommendations.

6. OMB Responsibilities. The Office of Management and Budget shall:

(a) review and approve agency advisory committee management plans pursuant to Section 5 and in accordance with the Executive order;

(b) set advisory committee ceilings for each agency within the government-wide advisory committee reduction goal established by the Executive order;

(c) work with agencies to control the establishment of statutory advisory committees and develop legislation to terminate those non- discretionary committees which are no longer necessary;

(d) ensure that relevant legislation is reviewed consistent with OMB Circular A-19; and

(e) ensure agencies meet the cost reduction target recommended by the Vice President's National Performance Review.

7. GSA Responsibilities. The General Services Administration shall (in addition to its responsibilities under the FACA and as an agency under Section 5 above):

(a) prepare required justifications and recommendations specified in Section 5 for each advisory committee subject to the FACA and not sponsored by another department or agency;

(b) assist OMB in its management and oversight of advisory committees, including tracking agency compliance with the reduction goals specified by E.O. 12,838;

(c) develop guidance, specific reporting formats and instructions to implement Section 5 of this Circular. To the extent practicable, new reporting requirements will be limited to information not readily available through existing sources of data;

(d) provide recommendations to OMB and each agency regarding the continuance or management of advisory committees as required by Section 7(b) of FACA, which mandates an annual comprehensive review of all advisory committees; and

(e) implement section 5(2) of this Circular.

8. Information Contact. Questions about this Circular should be addressed to the Federal Services Branch (202) 395-5090. Questions concerning the role of GSA should be directed to the Committee Management Secretariat (202) 273-3556.

9. Termination Review Date. This Circular will be subject to review two years after issuance.

10. Effective Date. This Circular is effective upon issuance.

/s/ Alice M. Rivlin, Acting Director

Federal Register Act

Citations:

44 U.S. Code §§1501-1511 (2000), enacted July 25, 1935 by Pub. L. No. 74-220, 49 Stat. 500; significantly amended June 19, 1937 by Pub. L. No. 75-158, 56 Stat. 304; September 23, 1950 by Pub. L. No. 81-821, 61 Stat. 636; October 22, 1968 by Pub. L. No. 90-620, 82 Stat. 1273, October 10, 1978 by Pub. L. No. 95-440, 92 Stat. 1063; October 19, 1984 by title I, Pub. L. No. 98-497, 98 Stat. 2280, 2286.

Lead Agency:

Office of the Federal Register, National Archives and Records Administration, 800 North Capitol Street, NW, Washington, DC 20002 (mailing address: 700 Pennsylvania Ave NW, Washington DC 20408-0001), (202) 523-4534.

Overview:

Background. Recognizing the need for a uniform system for publication of federal regulations and other important documents, Congress approved the Federal Register Act in 1935. Prior to establishment of the Federal Register, there were no facilities for filing and publication of rules, executive orders, and similar documents having general applicability and legal effect. This made it extremely difficult, and sometimes impossible, for interested persons to learn about rules and orders that had the force of law. Indeed, passage of this legislation ended what many sponsors of the bill described as "the twilight zone of government regulations."

The Federal Register Act requires the filing of certain documents with the Office of the Federal Register, availability of these documents for public inspection, publication of documents in the Federal Register, and the permanent codification of rules in the Code of Federal Regulations. Agencies must file proclamations and executive orders and documents having general applicability and legal effect. Publication of documents in the Federal Register provides "constructive" notice legally sufficient to give anyone affected legal notice of document's existence and contents and is deemed legally sufficient to give affected persons notice of the document's contents. In addition, the Administrative Procedure Act requires publication in the Federal Register of agency statements of organization, procedural rules, and the public notices required for agency rulemaking.

Office of the Federal Register. The Archivist of the United States, acting through the Office of the Federal Register, is charged with the custody and, together with the Public Printer, with the prompt and uniform printing and distribution of the documents required or authorized to be published in the Federal Register. The Government Printing Office (GPO) is responsible for actual publication of the Federal Register.

Through its Office of the Federal Register (OFR), the National Archives and Records Administration (NARA) provides ready access to regulations by filing them for public inspection, publishing them in the daily Federal Register, preparing indexes and tables of contents, and codifying them in the Code of Federal Regulations (CFR). It provides access to federal public laws by publishing slip laws and compiling them as the U.S. Statutes at Large. Presidential documents appear in the daily Federal Register, the Weekly Compilation of Presidential Documents, the semiannual volumes of Public Papers of the President, in Title 3 of the Code of Federal Regulations, and in the Codification of Proclamations and Executive Orders.

The Federal Register. The Federal Register is an official gazette published every business day. It contains federal agency regulations; proposed rules and notices; and executive orders, proclamations and other Presidential documents. The Federal Register informs citizens of their rights and obligations and provides access to a wide range of federal benefits and opportunities for funding. NARA's OFR prepares the Federal Register for publication in partnership with the GPO, which distributes it in paper, on microfiche and on the World Wide Web.

The Federal Register is intended to provide potentially useful information about government activities to people who need to know about the day-to-day operations of the federal government; those whose business is regulated by a federal agency; attorneys practicing before a regulatory agency; organizations wishing to attend public hearings or meetings or apply for grants; and others concerned with government actions that affect the environment, health care, financial services, exports, education, or other major public policy issues.

Organization of the Register. Each issue of the Federal Register is organized into four categories:

- Presidential Documents, including Executive orders and proclamations;
- Rules and Regulations, including policy statements and interpretations of rules;
- Proposed Rules, including petitions for rulemaking and other advance proposals; and
- Notices, including scheduled hearings and meetings open to the public, grant applications, and administrative orders.

The Code of Federal Regulations. Documents published in the Federal Register as rules and proposed rules include citations to the Code of Federal Regulations to refer readers to the CFR parts affected. The CFR contains the complete and official text of agency regulations organized into fifty titles covering broad subject areas. The CFR is updated and published once a year in print, fiche and online formats.

Obtaining Federal Register Information. Free access to the online Federal Register and CFR can be had at GPO Access: http://www.access.gpo.gov/nara. Depository Library locations and Federal Register services can be located at http://www.nara.gov/fedreg. Mail orders may be placed to the Superintendent of Documents, P.O. Box 371954, Pittsburgh, PA 15250-7954. E-mail questions and comments on Federal Register services may be directed to info@fedreg.nara.gov.

The daily Federal Register has a table of contents organized alphabetically by agency, which lists each document. Two monthly publications provide information on documents that appeared in past issues of the Federal Register: the LSA (List of CFR Sections Affected) is a numerical listing that helps readers track changes to the CFR; and the Federal Register Index is a cumulative subject index of documents published in the Federal Register. The online edition has the same table of contents as the paper edition with hypertext links to take users directly to each document in the current issue. Tables of contents with these hypertext links provide access to Federal Register documents published since January 1, 1998. Online users also can search by category, subject matter and date to retrieve documents in current or past issues from 1994 through the present day.

Role of the Administrative Committee. The Administrative Committee of the Federal Register consists of the Archivist of the United States or

Acting Archivist, an officer of the Department of Justice designated by the Attorney General, and the Public Printer or Acting Public Printer. This Committee is responsible for prescribing, with the approval of the President, regulations for carrying out the Federal Register Act. These regulations appear in 1 C.F.R. Chapter 1 (parts 1-22), and deal with format and distribution of the Federal Register and preparation and transmittal of documents.

Legislative History:

For years prior to passage of the Federal Register Act, many people had advocated legislation that would establish a means for systematic publication and availability of important government documents. Until the Act's passage, though, the United States was one of very few large nations without an official gazette. In 1934, the American Bar Association formally recommended that rules and "other exercises of legislative power by executive or administrative officials" be made readily available at some central office and be subject to requirements that they be published "as prerequisite to their going into force and effect." Later that year, the need for such a system was evidenced when, in the "Hot Oil" case (*Panama Refining Co. v. Ryan*, 293 U.S. 388 (1935)), the Attorney General, arguing in the Supreme Court, admitted that the trial below had proceeded in ignorance of a technical, though inadvertent, revocation of the regulation on which prosecution had rested. This last minute discovery—of an executive order that accomplished the unintended amendment and had been overlooked for over a year, to the detriment of the defendant—highlighted the need for systematic publication. An interagency committee examined the problem of making administrative law readily available and recommended a legislative solution that would centralize custody and publication of agency rules and orders.

Several bills establishing a central office to collect and publish agency rules and orders were introduced during the first session of the 74th Congress in early 1935. These included H.R. 1403, H.R. 2884, H.R. 4015, H.R. 5154, and H.R. 6323. Most of these were referred to the Committee on the Judiciary, which held hearings on February 6, 1935, concerning H.R. 5154 and H.R. 2884 (introduced by Congressman Celler). *Hearings before Subcommittee of Committee on the Judiciary, House of Representatives, on H.R. 5154 and H.R. 2884, February 6, 1935*. On March 4, 1935, Mr. Celler submitted a report, to accompany H.R. 6323, on *Publication of Governmental Rules and Regulations* (Report No. 280), that synopsized the bill and recommended its passage by the full House. The Committee on the Library also reported H.R.

4015, a bill for filing and indexing government publications, on May 13, 1935. *Filing and Indexing Service for Useful Government Publications* (Report No. 885). The full House approved H.R. 6323 on April 1, 1935. (Bound volume, pp. 4785-4791)

A bill similar to H.R. 6323, was introduced in the Senate by Mr. Ashurst on March 13, 1935. Both this bill, S. 2236, and H.R. 6323 were initially referred to the Senate Judiciary Committee; H.R. 6323 was subsequently referred to the Committee on the Library. The full Senate approved H.R. 6323, with several amendments, on June 10, 1935. (Bound volume, pp. 8963-8964)

On July 11, 1935, a conference report (House Report No. 1502) was submitted by the Committee of Conference. The Senate agreed to the report that day (Bound volume, p. 10,998), and the House did the same on July 22. The bill was signed into law on July 25, 1935.

Source Note:

NARA's OFR has prepared a useful guide, *The Federal Register: What It Is and How to Use It*. This office also publishes a *Document Drafting Handbook* that explains in detail how to prepare documents for the Federal Register. These publications are available online. As stated above, the regulations for carrying out FRA are located at 1 C.F.R. Chapter 1 (Parts 1-22). NARA has a list of Federal Register Research Tools, also available online, that can provide page numbers or citations to help with use of GPO Access.

Bibliography:

I. Legislative History

1. See Legislative History above.

II. Other Publications

1. E. Griswold, *Government in Ignorance of the Law: A Plea for Better Publication of Executive Legislation*, 48 Harv. L. Rev. 197 (1934).
2. R. McKinney, *A Research Guide to the Federal Register and the Code of Federal Regulations* (Law Librarians Society of Washington, DC, 2002), *available at* http://www.llsdc.org/sourcebook/fed-reg-cfr.htm.
3. National Archives of the United States, Office of the Federal Regis-

ter, *Document Drafting Handbook* (1999), *available at* http//www.nara.gov/fedreg/ddh/ddhfaq.html.

4. National Archives of the United States, Office of the Federal Register, *The Federal Register: What It Is and How to Use It* (GPO).

5. Note, *The Federal Register and the Code of Federal Regulations—A Reappraisal*, 20 Harv. L. Rev. 439 (1966).

6. A. Proulx, *Federal Register*, Law Notes (Vol. XLVI, p. 15) (1942).

7. J. Wigmore, *Federal Administrative Agencies: How to Locate Their Rules of Practice and Their Rulings with Special Reference to their Rules of Evidence*, A.B.A. J. 25 (1939).

Appendix:

1. Federal Register Act, 44 U.S. Code §§1501-1511 (2000).

Federal Register Act

Title 44, U.S. Code

Title 44—Public printing and Documents
Chapter 15—Federal Register and Code of Federal Regulations

§1501. Definitions

As used in this chapter, unless the context otherwise requires—

"document" means a Presidential proclamation or Executive order and an order, regulation, rule, certificate, code of fair competition, license, notice, or similar instrument, issued, prescribed, or promulgated by a Federal agency;
"Federal agency" or "agency" means the President of the United States, or an executive department, independent board, establishment, bureau, agency, institution, commission, or separate office of the administrative branch of the Government of the United States but not the legislative or judicial branches of the Government;
"person" means an individual, partnership, association, or corporation; and
"National Archives of the United States" has the same meaning as in section 2901(11) of this title.

(Pub. L. No. 90-620, Oct. 22, 1968, 82 Stat. 1273; Pub. L. No. 98-497, Title I, §107(b)(2), Oct. 19, 1984, 98 Stat. 2286.)

§1502. Custody and printing of Federal documents; appointment of Director

The Archivist of the United States, acting through the Office of the Federal Register, is charged with the custody and, together with the Public Printer, with the prompt and uniform printing and distribution of the documents required or authorized to be published by section 1505 of this title. There shall be at the head of the Office a director, appointed by, and who shall act under the general direction of, the Archivist of the United States in carrying out this chapter and the regulations prescribed under it.

(Pub. L. No. 90-620, Oct. 22, 1968, 82 Stat. 1273; Pub. L. No. 98-497, Title I, §107(b)(3), Oct. 19, 1984, 98 Stat. 2287.)

§1503. Filing documents with Office; notation of time; public inspection; transmission for printing

The original and two duplicate originals or certified copies of a document required or authorized to be published by section 1505 of this title shall be filed with the Office of the Federal Register, which shall be open for that purpose during all hours of the working days when the National Archives Building is open for official business. The Archivist of the United States shall cause to be noted on the original and duplicate originals or certified copies of each document the day and hour of filing. When the original is issued, prescribed, or promulgated outside the District of Columbia, and certified copies are filed before the filing of the original, the notation shall be of the day and hour of filing of the certified copies. Upon filing, at least one copy shall be immediately available for public inspection in the Office. The original shall be retained by the National Archives and Records Administration and shall be available for inspection under regulations prescribed by the Archivist, unless such original is disposed of in accordance with disposal schedules submitted by the Administrative Committee of the Federal Register and authorized by the Archivist pursuant to regulations issued under chapter 33 of this title; however, originals of proclamations of the President and Executive orders shall be permanently retained by the Administration as part of the National Archives of the United States. The Office shall transmit immediately to the Government Printing Office for printing, as provided by this chapter, one duplicate original or certified copy of each document required or authorized to be published by section 1505 of this title. Every Federal agency shall cause to be transmitted for filing the original and the duplicate originals or certified copies of all such documents issued, prescribed, or promulgated by the agency.

(Pub. L. No. 90-620, Oct. 22, 1968, 82 Stat. 1274; Pub. L. No. 95-440, §2, Oct. 10, 1978, 92 Stat. 1063; Pub. L. No. 98-497, Title I, §107(b)(4), Oct. 19, 1984, 98 Stat. 2287.)

§1504. "Federal Register"; printing; contents; distribution; price

Documents required or authorized to be published by section 1505 of this title shall be printed and distributed immediately by the Government Printing Office in a serial publication designated the "Federal Register." The Public Printer shall make available the facilities of the Government Printing Office for the prompt printing and distribution of the Federal Register in the manner and at the times required by this chapter and the regulations prescribed under it. The contents of the daily issues shall be indexed and shall comprise all documents, required or authorized to be published, filed with the Office of the Federal Register up to the time of the day immediately preceding the day of distribution fixed by regulations under this chapter. There shall be printed with each document a copy of the notation, required to be made by section 1503 of this title, of the day and hour when, upon filing with the Office, the document was made available for public inspection. Distribution shall be made by delivery or by deposit at a post office at a time in the morning of the day of distribution fixed by regulations prescribed under this chapter. The prices to be charged for the Federal Register may be fixed by the Administrative Committee of the Federal Register established by section 1506 of this title without reference to the restrictions placed upon and fixed for the sale of Government publications by sections 1705 and 1708 of this title.

(Pub. L. No. 90-620, Oct. 22, 1968, 82 Stat. 1274.)

§1505. Documents to be published in Federal Register

(a) Proclamations and Executive Orders; Documents Having General Applicability and Legal Effect; Documents Required To Be Published by Congress. There shall be published in the Federal Register—

(1) Presidential proclamations and Executive orders, except those not having general applicability and legal effect or effective only against Federal agencies or persons in their capacity as officers, agents, or employees thereof;

(2) documents or classes of documents that the President may determine from time to time have general applicability and legal effect; and

(3) documents or classes of documents that may be required so to be published by Act of Congress.

For the purposes of this chapter every document or order which prescribes a penalty has general applicability and legal effect.

(b) Documents Authorized To Be Published by Regulations; Comments and News Items Excluded. In addition to the foregoing there shall also be published in the Federal Register other documents or classes of documents authorized to be published by regulations prescribed under this chapter with the approval of the President, but comments or news items of any character may not be published in the Federal Register.

(c) Suspension of Requirements for Filing of Documents; Alternate Systems for Promulgating, Filing, or Publishing Documents; Preservation of Originals. In the event of an attack or threatened attack upon the continental United States and a determination by the President that as a result of an attack or threatened attack—

(1) publication of the Federal Register or filing of documents with the Office of the Federal Register is impracticable, or

(2) under existing conditions publication in the Federal Register would not serve to give appropriate notice to the public of the contents of documents, the President may, without regard to any other provision of law, suspend all or part of the requirements of law or regulation for filing with the Office or publication in the Federal Register of documents or classes of documents.

The suspensions shall remain in effect until revoked by the President, or by concurrent resolution of the Congress. The President shall establish alternate systems for promulgating, filing, or publishing documents or classes of documents affected by such suspensions, including requirements relating to their effectiveness or validity, that may be considered under the then existing circumstances practicable to provide public notice of the issuance and of the contents of the documents. The alternate systems may, without limitation, provide for the use of regional or specialized publications or depositories for documents, or of the press, the radio, or similar mediums of general communication. Compliance with alternate systems of filing or publication shall have the same effect as filing with the Office or publication in the Federal Register under this chapter or other law or regulation. With respect to documents promulgated under alternate systems, each agency shall preserve the original and two duplicate originals or two certified copies for filing with the Office when the President determines that it is practicable.

(Pub. L. No. 90-620, Oct. 22, 1968, 82 Stat. 1274.)

§1506. Administrative Committee of the Federal Register; establishment and composition; powers and duties

The Administrative Committee of the Federal Register shall consist of the Archivist of the United States or Acting Archivist, who shall be chairman, an officer of the Department of Justice designated by the Attorney General, and the Public Printer or Acting Public Printer. The Director of the Federal Register shall act as secretary of the committee. The committee shall prescribe, with the approval of the President, regulations for carrying out this chapter. The regulations shall provide, among other things—

(1) the manner of certification of copies required to be certified under section 1503 of this title, which certification may be permitted to be based upon confirmed communications from outside the District of Columbia;

(2) the documents which shall be authorized under section 1505(b) of this title to be published in the Federal Register;

(3) the manner and form in which the Federal Register shall be printed, reprinted, and compiled, indexed, bound, and distributed;

(4) the number of copies of the Federal Register, which shall be printed, reprinted, and compiled, the number which shall be distributed without charge to Members of Congress, officers and employees, of the United States, or Federal agency, for official use, and the number which shall be available for distribution to the public; and

(5) the prices to be charged for individual copies of, and subscriptions to, the Federal Register and reprints and bound volumes of it.

(Pub. L. No. 90-620, Oct. 22, 1968, 82 Stat. 1275; Pub. L. No. 98-497, Title I, §107(b)(5), Oct. 19, 1984, 98 Stat. 2287.)

§1507. Filing document as constructive notice; publication in Federal Register as presumption of validity; judicial notice; citation

A document required by section 1505(a) of this title to be published in the Federal Register is not valid as against a person who has not had actual knowledge of it until the duplicate originals or certified copies of the document have been filed with the Office of the Federal Register and a copy made available for public inspection as provided by section 1503 of this title. Unless otherwise specifically provided by statute, filing of a document, required or authorized to be published by section 1505 of this title, except in cases where notice by publication is insufficient in law, is sufficient to give notice of the contents of the document to a person subject to or affected by it. The publication in the Federal Register of a document creates a rebuttable presumption—

(1) that it was duly issued, prescribed, or promulgated;

(2) that it was filed with the Office of the Federal Register and made available for public inspection at the day and hour stated in the printed notation;

(3) that the copy contained in the Federal Register is a true copy of the original; and

(4) that all requirements of this chapter and the regulations prescribed under it relative to the document have been complied with.

The contents of the Federal Register shall be judicially noticed and without prejudice to any other mode of citation, may be cited by volume and page number.

(Pub. L. No. 90-620, Oct. 22, 1968, 82 Stat. 1276.)

§1508. Publication in Federal Register as notice of hearing

A notice of hearing or of opportunity to be heard, required or authorized to be given by an Act of Congress, or which may otherwise properly be given, shall be deemed to have been given to all persons residing within the States of the Union and the District of Columbia, except in cases where notice by publication is insufficient in law, when the notice is published in the Federal Register at such a time that the period between the publication and the date fixed in the notice for the hearing or for the termination of the opportunity to be heard is—

(1) not less than the time specifically prescribed for the publication of the notice by the appropriate Act of Congress; or

(2) not less than fifteen days when time for publication is not specifically prescribed by the Act, without prejudice, however, to the effectiveness of a notice of less than fifteen days where
the shorter period is reasonable.

(Pub. L. No. 90-620, Oct. 22, 1968, 82 Stat. 1276.)

§1509. Costs of publication, etc.

(a) The cost of printing, reprinting, wrapping, binding, and distributing the Federal Register and the Code of Federal Regulations, and, except as provided in subsection (b), other expenses incurred by the Government Printing Office in carrying out the duties placed upon it by this chapter shall be charged to the revolving fund provided in section 309. Reimbursements for such costs and expenses shall be made by the Federal agencies and credited, together with all receipts, as provided in section 309(b).

(b) The cost of printing, reprinting, wrapping, binding, and distributing all other publications of the Federal Register program, and other expenses incurred by the Government Printing Office in connection with such publications, shall be borne by the appropriations to the Government Printing Office and the appropriations are made available, and are authorized to be increased by additional sums necessary for the purposes, the increases to be based upon estimates submitted by the Public Printer.

(Pub. L. No. 90-620, Oct. 22, 1968, 82 Stat. 1277; Pub. L. No. 95-94, Title IV, §408(a)(1), Aug. 5, 1977, 91 Stat. 683.)

§1510. Code of Federal Regulations

(a) The Administrative Committee of the Federal Register, with the approval of the President, may require, from time to time as it considers necessary, the preparation and publication in special or supplemental editions of the Federal Register of complete codifications of the documents of each agency of the Government having general applicability and legal effect, issued or promulgated by the agency by publication in the Federal Register or by filing with the Administrative Committee, and are relied upon by the agency as authority for, or are invoked or used by it in the discharge of, its activities or functions, and are in effect as to facts arising on or after dates specified by the Administrative Committee.

(b) A codification published under subsection (a) of this section shall be printed and bound in permanent form and shall be designated as the "Code of Federal Regulations." The Administrative Committee shall regulate the binding of the printed codifications into separate books with a view to practical usefulness and economical manufacture. Each book shall contain an explanation of its coverage and other aids to users that the Administrative Committee may require. A general index to the entire Code of Federal Regulations shall be separately printed and bound.

(c) The Administrative Committee shall regulate the supplementation and the collation and republication of the printed codifications with a view to keeping the Code of Federal Regulations as current as practicable. Each book shall be either supplemented or collated and republished at least once each calendar year.

(d) The Office of the Federal Register shall prepare and publish the codifications, supplements, collations, and indexes authorized by this section.

(e) The codified documents of the several agencies published in the supplemental edition of the Federal Register under this section, as amended by documents subsequently filed with the Office and published in the daily issues of the Federal Register shall be prima facie evidence of the text of the documents and of the fact that they are in effect on and after the date of publication.

(f) The Administrative Committee shall prescribe, with the approval of the President, regulations for carrying out this section.

(g) This section does not require codification of the text of Presidential documents published and periodically compiled in supplements to Title 3 of the Code of Federal Regulations.

(Pub. L. No. 90-620, Oct. 22, 1968, 82 Stat. 1277.)

§1511. International agreements excluded from provisions of chapter

This chapter does not apply to treaties, conventions, protocols, and other international agreements, or proclamations thereof by the President.

(Pub. L. No. 90-620, Oct. 22, 1968, 82 Stat. 1278)

Federal Tort Claims Act

Citations:

28 U.S. Code §§1291, 1346, 1402, 2401, 2402, 2411, 2412, 2671-80 (2000 & Supp. I 2001) (originally 28 U.S.C. §§921-946); enacted August 2, 1946 as title IV of the Legislative Reorganization Act of 1946 by Pub. L. No. 79-601, 60 Stat. 812-44; significantly amended July 18, 1966 by Pub. L. No. 89-506, 80 Stat. 306; March 16, 1974 by Pub. L. No. 93-253, 88 Stat. 50; November 18, 1988 by Pub. L. No. 100-694, 102 Stat. 4563-67; November 15, 1990 by Pub. L. No. 101-552, 104 Stat. 2736; October 29, 1992 by Pub. L. No. 102-572, 106 Stat. 4511; March 29, 1996 by Pub. L. No. 104-121, 110 Stat. 863; April 26, 1996 by Pub. L. No. 104-134, 110 Stat. 1321-75; and Apr. 25, 2000 by Pub. L. No. 106-185, §3(a), 114 Stat. 211; Oct. 30, 2000 by Pub. L. No. 106-398, §1 [[div. A], title VI, §665(b)], 114 Stat. 1654, 1654A–169; Nov. 13, 2000 by Pub. L. No. 106-518, title IV, §401, 114 Stat. 2421.

Lead Agency:

Department of Justice, Civil Division, Torts Branch, Tenth Street and Constitution Avenue NW, Room 3649, Washington, DC 20530 (202) 514-3045.

Overview:

Before 1946, the doctrine of sovereign immunity obliged almost all victims of government wrongdoing to seek relief via congressional enactment of a private bill. The Federal Tort Claims Act (FTCA) waived this defense to permit damage actions against the United States for injury, loss of property or death caused by the negligent or wrongful acts or omissions of federal employees acting within the scope of their employment. The Act provides that the United States shall be liable in the same manner and to the same extent as a private individual under like circumstances in accordance with the law of the place where the negligent or wrongful conduct occurred.

Administrative Claims. As first drafted, the FTCA sought to transfer to the federal courts primary responsibility for determining what redress was warranted, but amendments enacted in 1966 shifted much of that burden to the agencies. Claims must now be presented to the responsible agency as a prerequisite for suit (§2675(a)). The claim must be presented in writing within 2 years after it accrued and the agency has a minimum of 6 months in which to act. If the agency fails to make a final disposition of the claim within that period, the claimant, at anytime thereafter, may treat that as a denial and file suit.

Agencies may settle claims under the Act in any amount, subject, however, to prior written approval by the Attorney General or his or her designee for settlements in excess of a specified level (§2672),[1] and must exercise their settlement authority "in accordance with regulations prescribed by the Attorney General." These regulations are fairly short, and are set forth in the Appendix.

As a result of the 1966 amendments, many agencies have established relatively elaborate procedures for the presentation, investigation, and administrative adjustment of tort claims. Today thousands of claims are disposed of at the agency level. Considerable litigation has occurred involving the statute of limitations and the sufficiency of claimants' administrative filings, particularly over agencies' authority to demand extensive information substantiating a claim and to regard a claim as invalid for all purposes when such data are not provided. A widely cited case, *Adams v. United States*, 615 F. 2d 284, *on reh.,* 622 F. 2d 197 (5th Cir. 1980), holds that §2675(a)'s mandate that a claim be filed initially with the agency requires only that the claimant place a monetary value

---

[1] In 1990, the Administrative Dispute Resolution Act of 1990 amended the FTCA to encourage agency use of arbitration and other alterative means of dispute resolution to resolve administrative tort claims. That act, discussed above, also provided that the Department of Justice could raise any agency's authority to settle tort claims without prior Department of Justice approval from $25,000 to an amount not to exceed "the authority delegated by the Attorney General to the United States attorneys to settle claims for monetary damages against the United States." Pursuant to an analogous provision of another law, the Department of Veterans Affairs previously obtained authority to settle tort claims for up to $100,000; the 1990 amendment was intended to enable other agencies to obtain similar authority.

on the claim and give sufficient written notice of the claim to enable the agency to conduct an investigation. Several prior decisions (e.g., *Swift v. United States*, 614 F. 2d 812 (1st Cir. 1980)) had required considerably more of claimants. To make the agency-level process more open and less adversarial, the Administrative Conference in 1984 recommended a number of changes and called for some amendments to the FTCA and the Attorney General's rules (Recommendation 84-7, see Bibliography). The Administrative Dispute Resolution Act of 1990 implemented some of these changes.

Court Claims. If administrative settlement efforts fail, the claimant may sue either in the federal district court for the district in which the alleged negligent or wrongful act occurred or where he or she resides (§1402(b)), provided that the administrative claim was properly presented within 2 years after it accrued and suit is brought within 6 months after the agency's final denial (§2401(b)). Suit may be brought only against the Untied States, not against the federal agency. The only remedy under the FTCA is money damages; the Act does not authorize equitable remedies. The sum demanded in the lawsuit generally cannot exceed the amount of the claim presented to the agency (§2675(b)). Liability and damage standards, in most instances, are based on the law of the place where the negligent or wrongful act occurred, except that the United States is not liable for punitive damages or prejudgment interest (§2674). Jury trials are not authorized under the FTCA, and attorneys' fees are subject to a ceiling of 20 percent of the amount recovered in agency-level settlements and 25 percent of judgments and litigation settlements (§2678).

Coverage. The FTCA contains more than a dozen exceptions (§2680). It does not apply, for example, to the following:

- Claims arising in a foreign country;
- Claims based upon the performance of a discretionary function;
- Claims arising out of the assessment or collection of any tax or customs duty;
- Claims covered by certain other statutes;
- Claims arising out of libel, slander, deceit, or interference with contract; and
- Claims arising out of assault, battery, false imprisonment, false arrest, malicious prosecution or abuse of process, except where based upon acts or omissions of federal investigative or law enforcement officers occurring after 1974.

In addition, the FTCA does not apply to claims of members of the armed forces arising out of activity incident to their service (*Feres v. United States*,

340 U.S. 135 (1950)). Nor does it apply to injury claims of civilian federal employees arising in the performance of duty (their exclusive remedy against the government is under the Federal Employees' Compensation Act).

Congress considered several bills during the 1980s that would have expanded the Act to cover agency employees' actions that violate constitutional or statutory rights. Another subject of considerable commentary and legislative interest has been the scope of the discretionary function exception. None of the bills relating to these matters has received approval; and federal employees remain subject to personal damage suits for so-called constitutional torts.

In 1988, Congress did modify the FTCA to render it the exclusive remedy for common law torts—as opposed to actions that violate constitutional or statutory rights—committed by federal employees within the scope of their employment. This legislation was necessitated by the Supreme Court's decision in *Westfall v. Erwin*, 484 U.S. 292 (1988), which dramatically expanded the personal tort liability of federal employees. The 1988 amendments also made explicit that activities of officials of the judicial and legislative branches are covered by the FTCA, and preserved for the United States any defenses based upon judicial or legislative immunity that could have been asserted by the official individually.

Related Statutes. Besides the FTCA, more than 40 "meritorious claims" and other ancillary statutes afford an administrative or judicial remedy for certain additional kinds of losses occasioned by governmental action. These statutes vary considerably as to kinds of claims covered, claimants eligible, remedies available, proof required, and procedures followed. They include the Military and Foreign Claims Act, Coast Guard and National Guard Claims Acts, Small Claims Act, Copyright Infringement Act, Trading with the Enemy Act, Public Vessels Act, Suits in Admiralty Act, and statutes covering some actions of the Departments of State, Agriculture, HHS, and Justice, NASA, the NRC, the Peace Corps, and the Postal Service. They are catalogued and discussed in Lester Jayson's *Handling Federal Tort Claims* and George Bermann's *Administrative Handling of Monetary Claims*.

Legislative History:

Efforts at passage of legislation similar to the FTCA began in the 1920s; a measure with similar purposes was passed by the 70th Congress, but met with a pocket veto by President Coolidge. Twin bills in many respects identical to the present Act, H.R. 7236 and S. 2690, were introduced in the 76th Congress in 1940. H.R. 7236 passed the House, but after hearings the Senate Judiciary Committee did not report S. 2690 and the measure died. In the 77th

Congress, the Senate passed S. 2221. The House Committee on the Judiciary, after hearings on similar measures introduced by Representative Celler, H.R. 5373 and H.R. 6463, reported the Senate measure favorably, with amendments, but it was not considered by the full House. (All these bills are reprinted in the reports of the committee hearings.)As thus amended, S. 2221 is a virtual duplicate of the Act finally passed by the 79th Congress in 1946.

Because of this similarity, the hearings and reports on the 1940 and 1942 measures are valuable source material in analyzing the FTCA, especially as the hearings and reports on the 1946 Act are relatively sparse. As Lester Jayson noted in discussing the more then 30 prior bills introduced in this area, "[S]ince many of the provisions of the Federal Tort Claims Act as it exists today have their genesis in these proposals, and since many of these provisions were the subjects of discussion and explanation at committee hearings and in committee reports, it often may prove to be fruitful, if not crucial to [the practitioner's] presentation and preparation of a case involving the meaning or interpretation of some part of the existing law to examine its legislative history, and to review these earlier bills and hearings and reports."

Source Note:

The two most comprehensive FTCA sources are Jayson and Longstreth's multi-volume *Handling Federal Tort Claims* (2007), treating FTCA litigation exhaustively, and George Bermann's *Administrative Handling of Monetary Claims* (1984), examining at length the operation of agencies' settlement processes and basic legal and procedural questions thereunder. Donald Zillman (1983) gives valuable information on presenting a claim. A useful Yale Law Journal note entitled *The Federal Tort Claims Act* (1947) examines the tort claims bills introduced between 1925 and 1946 (pages 2-55) along with significant committee reports and hearings relating to them.

The literature on officials' constitutional tort liability (especially from the 1970's and 1980's) is vast, and Thomas Madden and Nicholas Allard's *Advice on Official Liability and Immunity* (1982) contains an extensive annotated bibliography. *Suing Government* (1983) offers an overview of issues relating to constitutional tort liability. Several more recent articles on the subject are listed in the Bibliography.

Numerous articles, only a few of which are listed below, deal with the government's potential liability in a variety of specific situations, including negligent occupational, mine or airplane safety inspections, improper customs seizures, weather forecasts, parole of dangerous criminals, atomic testing, and medical or other cases involving the military.

Bibliography:

I. Legislative History

1. *Hearings before the House Committee on the Judiciary on H.R. 5373 and H.R. 6463*, 77th Cong., 2d Sess. (1942).
2. *Hearings before the House Committee on the Judiciary on H.R. 7236*, 76th Cong., 3d Sess. (1940).
3. *Hearings before the Joint Committee on the Organization of Congress Pursuant to H. Con. Res. 18*, 79th Cong., 1st Sess. (1945).
4. *Hearings before the Senate Committee on the Judiciary on S. 2690*, 76th Cong., 3d Sess. (1940).
5. *Hearings on Improvement of Procedures in Claims Settlement and Government Litigation before Subcommittee No. 2 of the House Committee on the Judiciary*, 89th Cong., 2d Sess. (1966).
6. House of Representatives Committee on the Judiciary, *Report to Accompany H.R. 13650*, H.R. Rep. No. 1532, 89th Cong., 2d Sess. (1966).
7. House of Representatives Committee on the Judiciary, *H.R. Rep. No. 100-700*, 100th Cong., 2d Sess. (1988), *reprinted in* 1988 U.S. Code Cong. & Ad. News 5945.
8. *H.R. Rep. No. 1287*, 79th Cong., 1st Sess. (1945).
9. *H.R. Rep. No. 2245*, 77th Cong., 2d Sess (1942).
10. Joint Committee on the Organization of Congress, *Report to Accompany S. 2177*, S. Rep. No. 1400, 79th Cong., 2d Sess. (1941).
11. *S. Rep. No. 1196*, 77th Cong., 2d Sess. (1941).
12. *S. Rep. No. 1327*, 89th Cong., 2d Sess. (1966), *reprinted in* 1966 U.S. Code Cong. & Ad. News 2515.

II. Other Government Documents

1. Administrative Conference of the U.S., Recommendation 84-7, *Administrative Settlement of Tort and Other Monetary Claims Against the Government*, 49 Fed. Reg. 49,840 (Dec. 24, 1984).
2. Administrative Conference of the U.S., Recommendation 82-6, *Federal Officials' Liability for Constitutional Violations*, 47 Fed. Reg. 58,208 (Dec. 30, 1982).
3. G. Bermann, *Administrative Handling of Monetary Claims: Tort Claims at the Agency Level*, Report to the Administrative Conference of the U.S., 1984 ACUS 639, *portions reprinted in* 35 Case W. Res. L. Rev. 509 (1985).

4. R. Cass, *The Discretionary Function Exception to the Federal Tort Claims Act*, Report to the Administrative Conference of the U.S. (1988).

5. Congressional Research Service, *Homeland Security Act of 2002: Tort Liability Provisions* (Sept. 23, 2005) (Reference No. RL31649).

6. Department of Justice, *Torts Branch Monographs* (1981-2006). (This is a series of monographs presenting the Department of Justice's views on administrative claims, statute of limitations, the scope and effect of the discretionary function and other exceptions, and other significant substantive and procedural issues arising under the FTCA.)

7. T. Madden and N. Allard, *Advice on Official Liability and Immunity*, Report to the Administrative Conference of the U.S., 1982 ACUS 201 (Vol. 2), *portions reprinted in Bedtime for Bivens*, 20 Harv. J. on Legis. 469 (1983).

8. U.S. General Accounting Office, *Principles of Federal Appropriations Law* (3 vols. 1994), *available at* http://www. gao. gov/special. pubs/ publist. htm.

III. Books and Articles

1. Astley, *United States v. Johnson: Feres Doctrine Gets New Life and Continues to Grow*, 38 Am. U. L. Rev. 185 (1989).

2. Axelrad, *Federal Tort Claims Act Administrative Claims: Better Than Third-Party ADR for Resolving Federal Tort Claims*, 52 Admin. L. Rev. 1331 (2000).

3. Axelrad, *Litigation Under the Federal Tort Claims Act*, 8 Litigation 22 (ABA Section on Litigation 1981).

4. Baer & Broder, *How to Prepare and Negotiate Claims for Settlement* (1973).

5. Barash, *The Discretionary Function Exception and Mandatory Regulations*, 54 U. Chi. L. Rev. 1300 (1987).

6. Block, *Suits Against Government Officers and the Sovereign Immunity Doctrine*, 59 Harv. L. Rev. 1060 (1946).

7. Borchard, *The Federal Tort Claims Bill*, 1 U. Chi. L. Rev. 1 (1933).

8. Brown, *Letting Statutory Tails Wag Constitutional Dogs: Have the* Bivens *Dissenters Prevailed?*, 64 Ind. L. J. 263 (1989).

9. *Civil Actions Against the United States, Its Agencies, Officers and Employees* (Shepard's/McGraw-Hill, 2d edition, 1993).

10. H. Cohen, *Federal Tort Claims Act: Current Legislative and Judicial Issues* (Congressional Research Service, 2001).

11. U. Colella & A. Bain, *The Burden of Proving Jurisdiction under the Federal Tort Claims Act: A Uniform Approach to Allocation*, 67 Fordham L. Rev. 2859 (1999).

12. U. Colella, *Revisiting Equitable Tolling and the Federal Tort Claims Act: Putting the Legislative History in Proper Perspective*, 31 Seton Hall L. Rev. 174 (2000).

13. Comment, *In Defense of the Government Contractor Defense*, 36 Cath. U.L. Rev. 219 (1986).

14. Comment, *The Art of Claimsmanship: What Constitutes Sufficient Notice of a Claim under the Federal Tort Claims Act?*, 52 U. Cin. L. Rev. 149 (1983).

15. K. Davis, *Constitutional Torts* (1984).

16. Gellhorn & Lauer, *Federal Liability for Personal and Property Damage*, 29 N.Y.U.L. Rev. 1325 (1954).

17. Gottlieb, *A New Approach to the Handling of Tort Claims against the Sovereign* (1967).

18. Gottlieb, *The Federal Tort Claims Act: A Statutory Interpretation*, 35 Geo. L.J. 1 (1946).

19. C. Haig, *Discretionary Activities of Federal Agents vis-a-vis the Federal Tort Claims Act and the Military Claims Act: Are Discretionary Activities Protected at the Administrative Adjudication Level, and to What Extent Should They Be Protected?*, 183 Mil. L. Rev. 110 (2005).

20. L. Jayson and R. Longstreth, *Handling Federal Tort Claims* (multiple vols., updated periodically) (New York: Matthew Bender, 2007).

21. D. Kilduff, *Tort, Taking, or Both?*, 42 Fed. Law 25 (1995).

22. Kratzke, *The Convergence of the Discretionary Function Exception to the Federal Tort Claims Act with Limitations of Liability in Common Law Negligence*, 60 St. Johns L. Rev. 221 (1986).

23. R. Lundberg, *Discovery of Internal Governmental Agency Guidelines for the Purpose of Evading the Discretionary Function Exception to the Federal Tort Claims Act*, 70 Geo. Wash. L. Rev. 429 (2002).

24. J. Massey, *A Proposal to Narrow the Assault and Battery Exception to the Federal Tort Claims Act*, 82 Tex. L. Rev. 1621 (2004).

25. McChesney, *Problems in Calculating and Awarding Compensatory Damages for Wrongful Death under the Federal Tort Claims Act*, 36 Emory L. J. 149 (1987).

26. M. Niles, *"Nothing but Mischief": The Federal Tort Claims Act and the Scope of Discretionary Immunity*, 54 Admin. L. Rev. 1275 (2002).

27. Note, *Administrative Exhaustion under the Federal Tort Claims Act: The Impact on Class Actions*, 58 B.U. L. Rev. 627 (1978).

28. Note, *Claim Requirements of the Federal Tort Claims Act: Minimal Notice or Substantial Documentation?*, 81 Mich. L. Rev. 1641 (1983).

29. Note, *Federal Tort Claims Act: Administrative Claim Prerequisite*, 1983 Ariz. St. L.J. 173 (1983).

30. Note, *Federal Tort Claims Act: Notice of Claim Requirement*, 67 Minn. L. Rev. 513 (1982).

31. Note, *Federal Tort Claims Act: The Development and Application of the Discretionary Function Exemption*, 13 Cumb. L. Rev. 535 (1982/83).

32. Note, *Joinder of the Government Under the Federal Tort Claims Act*, 59 Yale L.J. 1515 (1950).

33. Note, *Notice of Claims Provisions: an Equal Protection Perspective*, 60 Cornell L. Rev. 417 (1975).

34. Note, Prescott v. United States: *Discretionary Function Exception Strikes Again*, 74 Or. L. Rev. 365 (1995).

35. Note, *The Federal Tort Claims Act*, 56 Yale L.J. 534 (1947).

36. K. Pearson, Departing from the Routine: Application of Indian Tribal Law Under the Federal Tort Claims Act, 32 Ariz. St. L. J. 695 (2000).

37. H. Perlstein, *TDRL and the Feres Doctrine*, 43 A.F.L. Rev. 259 (1997).

38. C. Pillard, *Taking Fiction Seriously: The Strange Results of Public Officials' Individual Liability Under* Bivens, 88 Geo. L. J. 65 (1999).

39. Pitard, *Procedural Aspects of the Federal Tort Claims Act*, 21 Loy. L. Rev. 899 (1975).

40. D. Read, *The Courts' Difficult Balancing Act To Be Fair to Both Plaintiff and Government under the FTCA's Administrative Claims Process*, 57 Baylor L. Rev. 785 (2005).

41. Rosen, *The* Bivens *Constitutional Tort: An Unfulfilled Promise*, 67 N.C. L. Rev. 337 (1989).

42. S. Schooner, *The Quality of Mercy Is Not Strained: Interpreting the Notice Requirement of the Federal Tort Claims Act*, 97 Mich. L. Rev. 1034 (1999).

43. P. Schuck, *Suing Government: Citizen Remedies for Official Wrongs* (1983).

44. R. Seaman, *Causation and the Discretionary Function Exception to the Federal Tort Claims Act*, 30 U.C. Davis L. Rev. 691 (1997).

45. Seidelson, *From* Feres v. United States *to* Boyle v. United Technologies Corp. *: An Examination of Supreme Court Jurisprudence and a Couple of Suggestions*, 32 Duq. L. Rev. 219 (1994).

46. Shimomura, *The History of Claims Against the United States: The Evolution from a Legislative Toward a Judicial Model of Payment*, 45 La. L. Rev. 625 (1985).

47. Silverman, *The Ins and Outs of Filing a Claim Under the FTCA*, 45 Air L. & Com. 41 (1980).

48. J. Snyder, *The Requirement of Scope of Employment under the Federal Tort Claims Act: Where Is the Line? Scrutinizing* Primeaux v. United States, 33 Creighton L. Rev. 465 (2000).

49. Symposium, *Government Tort Liability*, 9 Law & Contemp. Prob. No. 2 (1942).

50. M. Van der Weide, *Susceptible to Faulty Analysis:* U.S. v. Gaubert *and the Resurrection of Federal Sovereign Immunity*, 72 Notre Dame L. Rev. 447 (1997).

51. J. Towe, *Is the IRS Above the Law?: Potential Remedies for Taxpayers Damaged by Unlawful IRS Conduct*, 55 Mont. L. Rev. 469 (1994).

52. J. Viders, *Negligent Hiring, Supervision and Training—The Scope of the Assault and Battery Exception:* Senger v. United States, 39 B. C. L. Rev. 452 (1998).

53. S. Watts, Boyle v. United Technologies Corp. *and the Government Contractor Defense: An Analysis Based on the Current Circuit Split Regarding the Scope of the Defense*, 40 Wm. and Mary L. Rev. 687 (1999).

54. D. Zillman, *Presenting a Claim under the Federal Tort Claims Act*, 43 La. L. Rev. 961 (1983).

55. D. Zillman, *Congress, Courts, and Government Tort Liability: Reflections on the Discretionary Function Exception to the Federal Tort Claims Act*, 1989 Utah L. Rev. 687 (1987).

56. D. Zillman, *Judicial Interpretation of the Discretionary Function Exception to the Federal Tort Claims Act*, 47 Me. L. Rev. 366 (1995).

Agency Regulations:

Agriculture	7 C.F.R. §1.51
Air Force (Defense)	32 C.F.R. §§842.0-.150
Army (Defense)	32 C.F.R. §§536.50, 536.83-.89
Broadcasting Board of Governors	22 C.F.R. §§511.1-.12
Bureau of Prisons (Justice)	28 C.F.R. §§543.30-.32
Commerce	15 C.F.R. §§2.1-.8
Defense Logistics Agency (Defense)	32 C.F.R. §§1280.1-.5
Education	34 C.F.R. §§35.1-.10
Energy	10 C.F.R. §§1014.1-.11
Environmental Protection Agency	40 C.F.R. §§10.1-.11
Health & Human Services	45 C.F.R. §§35.1-.10
Housing and Urban Development	24 C.F.R. §§17.1-.12
Interior	43 C.F.R. §§22.1-.6
Internal Revenue Service (Treasury)	26 C.F.R. §§601.201-.205
Justice	28 C.F.R. §§14.1-.11
Labor	29 C.F.R. §§15.1-.10
NASA	14 C.F.R. §§1261.300-.315
National Credit Union Administration	12 C.F.R. §§793.1-.10
National Gallery of Art	36 C.F.R. §530.1
Navy (Defense)	32 C.F.R. §§750.21-.36
Nuclear Regulatory Commission	10 C.F.R. §§14.1-.57
Office of Personnel Management	5 C.F.R. §§177.101-.110
Peace Corps	22 C.F.R. §§304.1-.12
Postal Service	39 C.F.R. §§912.1-.14
Small Business Administration	13 C.F.R. §§114.100-.111
Smithsonian Institution	36 C.F.R. §§530.1-.23
Transportation	28 C.F.R. §14.1-14.11
Treasury	31 C.F.R. §§3.1-.8
U.S. Chemical Safety and Hazard Investigation Board	40 C.F.R. Part 1620
Veterans Affairs	38 C.F.R. §§14.600-.615

Appendix:

1. Federal Tort Claims Act, 28 U.S.C. §§1291, 1346, 1402, 2401, 2402, 2411, 2412, 2671-80 (2000 & Supp. I 2001).

2. Department of Justice, Administrative Claims under Federal Tort Claims Act Regulations, 28 C.F.R. §§14.1-.11 (2006).

12

Federal Tort Claims Act

Title 28, U.S. Code

§1291. Final decisions of district courts

The courts of appeals (other than the United States Court of Appeals for the Federal Circuit) shall have jurisdiction of appeals from all final decisions of the district courts of the United States, the United States District Court for the District of the Canal Zone, the District Court of Guam, and the District Court of the Virgin Islands, except where a direct review may be had in the Supreme Court. The jurisdiction of the United States Court of Appeals for the Federal Circuit shall be limited to the jurisdiction described in sections 1292(c) and (d) and 1295 of this title.

(June 25, 1948, ch. 646, 62 Stat. 929; Oct. 31, 1951, ch. 655, §48, 65 Stat. 726; July 7, 1958, Pub. L. No. 85-508, §12(e), 72 Stat. 348; Apr. 2, 1982, Pub. L. No. 97-164, Title I, §124, 96 Stat. 36.)

* * * *

§1346. United States as defendant

(a) The district courts shall have original jurisdiction, concurrent with the United States Court of Federal Claims, of:

(1) Any civil action against the United States for the recovery of any internalrevenue tax alleged to have been erroneously or illegally assessed or collected, or any penalty claimed to have been collected without authority or any sum alleged to have been excessive or in any manner wrongfully collected under the internal revenue laws;

(2) Any other civil action or claim against the United States, not exceeding $10,000 in amount, founded either upon the Constitution, or any Act of Congress, or any regulation of an executive department, or upon any express or implied contract with the United States, or for liquidated or unliquidated damages in cases not sounding in tort, except that the district courts shall not have jurisdiction of any civil action or claim against the United States founded upon any express or implied contract with the United States or for liquidated or unliquidated damagesin cases not sounding in tort which are subject to sections 8(g)(1) and 10(a)(1) of the Contract Disputes Act of 1978. For the purpose of this paragraph, an express or implied contract with the Army and

Air Force Exchange Service, Navy Exchanges, Marine Corps Exchanges, Coast Guard Exchanges, or Exchange Councils of the National Aeronautics and Space Administration shall be considered an express or implied contract with the United States.

(b) (1) Subject to the provisions of chapter 171 of this title, the district courts, together with the United States District Court for the District of the Canal Zone and the District Court of the Virgin Islands, shall have exclusive jurisdiction of civil actions on claims against the United States, for money damages, accruing on and after January 1, 1945, for injury or loss of property, or personal injury or death caused by the negligent or wrongful act or omission of any employee of the Government while acting within the scope of his office or employment, under circumstances where the United States, if a private person, would be liable to the claimant in accordance with the law of the place where the act or omission occurred.

(2) No person convicted of a felony who is incarcerated while awaiting sentencing orwhile serving a sentence may bring a civil action against the United States or an agency, officer, or employee of the Government, for mental or emotional injury suffered while in custody without a prior showing of physical injury.

(c) The jurisdiction conferred by this section includes jurisdiction of any setoff, counterclaim, or other claim or demand whatever on the part of the United States against any plaintiff commencing an action under this section.

(d) The district courts shall not have jurisdiction under this section of any civil action or claim for a pension.

(e) The district courts shall have original jurisdiction of any civil action against the United States provided in section 6226, 6228(a), 7426, or 7428 (in the case of the United States district court for the District of Columbia) or section 7429 of the Internal Revenue Code of 1986.

(f) The district courts shall have exclusive original jurisdiction of civil actions under section 2409a to quiet title to an estate or interest in real property in which an interest is claimed by the United States.

(g) Subject to the provisions of chapter 179, the district courts of the United States shall have exclusive jurisdiction over any civil action commenced under section 453(2) of title 3, by a covered employee under chapter 5 of such title.

(June 25, 1948, ch. 646, 62 Stat. 933; Apr. 25, 1949, ch. 92, §2(a), 63 Stat. 62; May 24, 1949, ch. 139, §80(a), (b), 63 Stat. 101; Oct. 31, 1951, ch. 655, §50(b), 65 Stat. 727; July 30, 1954, ch. 648, §1, 68 Stat. 589; July 7, 1958, Pub. L. No. 85-508, §12(e), 72 Stat. 348; Aug. 30, 1964, Pub. L. No. 88-519, 78 Stat. 699; Nov. 2, 1966, Pub. L. No. 89-719, Title II, §202(a), 80 Stat. 1148; July 23, 1970, Pub. L.

No. 91-390, §1(a), 84 Stat. 449; Oct. 25, 1972, Pub. L. No. 92-562, §1, 86 Stat. 1176; Oct. 4, 1976, Pub. L. No. 94-455, Title XII, §1204(c)(1), Title XIII, §1306(b)(7), 90 Stat. 1697, 1719; Nov. 1, 1978, Pub. L. No. 95-563, §14(a), 92 Stat. 2389; Apr. 2, 1982, Pub. L. No. 97-164, Title I, §129, 96 Stat. 39; Sept. 3, 1982, Pub. L. No. 97-248, Title IV, §402(c)(17), 96 Stat. 669; Oct. 22, 1986, Pub. L. No. 99-514, §2, 100 Stat. 2095; Oct. 29, 1992, Pub. L. No. 102-572, Title IX, §902(b)(1), 106 Stat. 4516; as amended Apr. 26, 1996, Pub. L. No. 104-134, Title I, §101[(a)] [Title VIII, §806], 110 Stat. 1321-75; renumbered Title I, May 2, 1996, Pub. L. No. 104-140, §1(a), 110 Stat. 1327; Oct. 26, 1996, Pub. L. No. 104-331, §3(b)(1), 110 Stat. 4069.)

* * * *

§1402. United States as defendant

(a) Any civil action in a district court against the United States under subsection (a) of section 1346 of this title may be prosecuted only:

(1) Except as provided in paragraph (2), in the judicial district where the plaintiff resides;

(2) In the case of a civil action by a corporation under paragraph (1) of subsection (a) of section 1346, in the judicial district in which is located the principal place of business or principal office or agency of the corporation; or if it has no principal place of business or principal office or agency in any judicial district

(A) in the judicial district in which is located the office to which was made the return of the tax in respect of which the claim is made, or

(B) if no return was made, in the judicial district in which lies the District of Columbia. Notwithstanding the foregoing provisions of this paragraph a district court, for the convenience of the parties and witnesses, in the interest of justice, may transfer any such action to any other district or division.

(b) Any civil action on a tort claim against the United States under subsection (b) of section 1346 of this title may be prosecuted only in the judicial district where the plaintiff resides or wherein the act or omission complained of occurred.

(c) Any civil action against the United States under subsection (e) of section 1346 of this title may be prosecuted only in the judicial district where the property is situated at the time of levy, or if no levy is made, in the judicial district in which the event occurred which gave rise to the cause of action.

(d) Any civil action under section 2409a to quiet title to an estate or interest in real property in which an interest is claimed by the United States shall be brought in the district court of the district where the property is located or, if located in different districts, in any of such districts.

(June 25, 1948, ch. 646, 62 Stat. 937; Sept. 2, 1958, Pub. L. No. 85-920, 72 Stat. 1770; Nov. 2, 1966, Pub. L. No. 89-719, Title II, §202(b), 80 Stat. 1149; Oct. 25, 1972, Pub. L. No. 92-562, §2, 86 Stat. 1176; Apr. 2, 1982, Pub. L. No. 97-164, Title I, §131, 96 Stat. 39.)

* * * *

§2401. Time for commencing action against United States

(a) Except as provided by the Contract Disputes Act of 1978, every civil action commenced against the United States shall be barred unless the complaint is filed within six years after the right of action first accrues. The action of any person under legal disability or beyond the seas at the time the claim accrues may be commenced within three years after the disability ceases. (b) A tort claim against the United States shall be forever barred unless it is presented in writing to the appropriate Federal agency within two years after such claim accrues or unless action is begun within six months after the date of mailing, by certified or registered mail, of notice of final denial of the claim by the agency to which it was presented.

(June 25, 1948, ch. 646, 62 Stat. 971; Apr. 25, 1949, ch. 92 §1, 63 Stat. 62; Sept. 8, 1959, Pub. L. No. 86-238, §1(3), 73 Stat. 472; July 18, 1996, Pub. L. No. 89-506, §7, 80 Stat. 307; Nov. 1, 1978, Pub. L. No. 95-563, §14(b), 92 Stat. 2389.)

§2402. Jury trial in actions against United States

Subject to chapter 179 of this title, any action against the United States under section 1346 shall be tried by the court without a jury, except that any action against the United States under section 1346(a)(1) shall, at the request of either party to such action, be tried by the court with a jury.

(June 25, 1948, ch. 646, 62 Stat. 971; July 30, 1954, ch. 648, §2(a), 68 Stat. 589; as amended Oct. 26, 1996, Pub. L. No. 104-331, §3(b)(3), 110 Stat. 4069.)

§2411. Interest

In any judgment of any court rendered (whether against the United States, a collector or deputy collector of internal revenue, a former collector or deputy collector, or the personal representative in case of death) for any overpayment in respect of any internal revenue tax, interest shall be allowed at the overpayment rate established under section 6621 of the Internal Revenue Code of 1986 upon the amount of the overpayment, from the date of the payment or collection thereof to a date preceding the date of the refund check by not more than thirty days, such date to be determined by the Commissioner of Internal Revenue. The Commissioner is authorized to tender by check payment of any such judgment, with interest as herein provided, at any time after such judgment becomes final, whether or not a claim for such payment has been duly filed, and such tender shall stop the running of interest, whether or not such refund check is accepted by the judgment creditor.

(June 25, 1948, ch. 646, 62 Stat. 973; May 24, 1949, ch. 139, §120, 63 Stat. 106; Jan. 3, 1975, Pub. L. No. 93-625, §7(a)(2), 88 Stat. 2115; Apr. 2, 1982, Pub. L. No. 97-164, Title III, §302(b), 96 Stat. 56; Oct. 22, 1986, Pub. L. No. 99-514, §2, title XV, §1511(c)(18), 100 Stat. 2095, 2746.)

§2412. Costs and fees

(a)(1) Except as otherwise specifically provided by statute, a judgment for costs, as enumerated in section 1920 of this title, but not including the fees and expenses of attorneys, may be awarded to the prevailing party in any civil action brought by or against the United States or any agency or any official of the United States acting in his or her official capacity in any court having jurisdiction of such action. A judgment for costs when taxed against the United States shall, in an amount established by statute, court rule, or order, be limited to reimbursing in whole or in part the prevailing party for the costs incurred by such party in the litigation.

(2) A judgment for costs, when awarded in favor of the United States in an action brought by the United States, may include an amount equal to the filing fee prescribed under section 1914(a) of this title. The preceding sentence shall not be construed as requiring the United States to pay any filing fee.

(b) Unless expressly prohibited by statute, a court may award reasonable fees and expenses of attorneys, in addition to the costs which may be awarded pursuant to subsection (a), to the prevailing party in any civil action brought by or against the United States or any agency or any official of the United States acting in his or her official capacity in any court having jurisdiction of such action. The United States shall be liable for such fees and expenses to the same extent that any other party would be liable under the common law or under the terms of any statute which specifically provides for such an award.

(c)(1) Any judgment against the United States or any agency and any official of the United States acting in his or her official capacity for costs pursuant to subsection (a) shall be paid as provided in sections 2414 and 2517 of this title and shall be in addition to any relief provided in the judgment.

(2) Any judgment against the United States or any agency and any official of the United States acting in his or her official capacity for fees and expenses of attorneys pursuant to subsection (b) shall be paid as provided in sections 2414 and 2517 of this title, except that if the basis for the award is a finding that the United States acted in bad faith, then the award shall be paid by any agency found to have acted in bad faith and shall be in addition to any relief provided in the judgment.

(d)(1)(A) Except as otherwise specifically provided by statute, a court shall award to a prevailing party other than the United States fees and other expenses, in addition to any costs awarded pursuant to subsection (a), incurred by that party in any civil action (other than cases sounding in tort), including proceedings for judicial review of agency action, brought by or against the United States in any court having jurisdiction of that action, unless the court finds that the position of the United States was substantially justified or that special circumstances make an award unjust.

(B) A party seeking an award of fees and other expenses shall, within thirty days of final judgment in the action, submit to the court an application for fees and other expenses which shows that the party is a prevailing party and is eligible to receive an award under this subsection, and the amount sought, including an itemized statement from any attorney or expert witness representing or appearing in behalf of the party stating the actual time expended and the rate at which fees and other expenses were computed. The party shall also allege that the position of the United States was not substantially justified. Whether or not the position of the United States was substantially justified shall be determined on the basis of the record (including the record with respect to the action or failure to act by the agency upon which the civil action is based) which is made in the civil action for which fees and other expenses are sought.

(C) The court, in its discretion, may reduce the amount to be awarded pursuant to this subsection, or deny an award, to the extent that the prevailing party during the course of the proceedings engaged in conduct which unduly and unreasonably protracted the final resolution of the matter in controversy.

(D) If, in a civil action brought by the United States or a proceeding for judicial review of an adversary adjudication described in section 504(a)(4) of title 5, the demand by the United States is substantially in excess of the judgment finally obtained by the United States and is unreasonable when compared with such judgment, under the facts and circumstances of the case, the court shall award to the party the fees and other expenses related to defending against the excessive demand, unless the party has committed a willful violation of law or otherwise acted in bad faith, or special circumstances make an award unjust. Fees and expenses awarded under this subparagraph shall be paid only as a consequence of appropriations provided in advance.

(2) For the purposes of this subsection—

(A) "fees and other expenses" includes the reasonable expenses of expert witnesses, the reasonable cost of any study, analysis, engineering report, test, or project which is found by the court to be necessary for the preparation of the party's case, and reasonable attorney fees (The amount of fees awarded under this subsection shall be based upon prevailing market rates for the kind and quality of the services furnished, except that (i) no expert witness shall be compensated at a rate in excess of the highest rate of compensation for expert witnesses paid by the United States; and (ii) attorney fees shall not be awarded in excess of $125 per hour unless the court determines that an increase in the cost of living or a special factor, such as the limited availability of qualified attorneys for the proceedings involved, justifies a higher fee.);

(B) "party" means (i) an individual whose net worth did not exceed $2,000,000 at the time the civil action was filed, or (ii) any owner of an unincorporated business, or any partnership, corporation, association, unit of local government, or organization, the net worth of which did not exceed $7,000,000 at the time the civil action was filed, and which had not more than 500 employees at the time the civil action was filed; except that an organization described in section 501(c)(3) of the Internal Revenue Code of 1986 (26 U.S.C. 501(c)(3)) exempt from taxation under section 501(a) of such Code, or a cooperative association as defined in section 15(a) of the Agricultural Marketing Act (12 U.S.C. 1141j(a)), may be a party regardless of the net worth of such organization or cooperative association or for purposes of subsection (d)(1)(D), a small entity as defined in section 601 of title 5;

(C) "United States" includes any agency and any official of the United States acting in his or her official capacity;

(D) "position of the United States" means, in addition to the position taken by the United States in the civil action, the action or failure to act by the agency upon which the civilaction is based; except that fees and expenses may not be awarded to a party for any portion of the litigation in which the party has unreasonably protracted the proceedings;

(E) "civil action brought by or against the United States" includes an appeal by a party, other than the United States, from a decision of a contracting officer rendered pursuant to a disputes clause in a contract with the Government or pursuant to the Contract Disputes Act of 1978;

(F) "court" includes the United States Court of Federal Claims and the United States Court of Veterans Appeals;

(G) "final judgment" means a judgment that is final and not appealable, and includes an order of settlement;

(H) "prevailing party", in the case of eminent domain proceedings, means a party who obtains a final judgment (other than by settlement), exclusive of interest, the amount of which is at least as close to the highest valuation of the property involved that is attested to at trial on behalf of the property owner as it is to the highest valuation of the property involved that is attested to at trial on behalf of the Government; and

(I) "demand" means the express demand of the United States which led to the adversary adjudication, but shall not include a recitation of the maximum statutory penalty (i) in the complaint, or (ii) elsewhere when accompanied by an express demand for a lesser amount.

(3) In awarding fees and other expenses under this subsection to a prevailing party in any action for judicial review of an adversary adjudication, as defined in subsection (b)(1)(C) of section 504 of title 5, United States Code, or an adversary adjudication subject to the Contract Disputes Act of 1978, the court shall include in that award fees and other expenses to the same extent authorized in subsection (a) of such section, unless the court finds that during such adversary adjudication the position of the United States was substantially justified, or that special circumstances make an award unjust.

(4) Fees and other expenses awarded under this subsection to a party shall be paid by any agency over which the party prevails from any funds made available to the agency by appropriation or otherwise.

[(5) Repealed. Pub. L. No. 104-66, Title I, §1091(b), Dec. 21, 1995, 109 Stat. 722]

(e) The provisions of this section shall not apply to any costs, fees, and other expenses in connection with any proceeding to which section 7430 of the Internal Revenue Code of 1986 applies (determined without regard to subsections (b) and (f) of such section). Nothing in the preceding sentence shall prevent the awarding under subsection (a) of section 2412 of title 28, United States Code, of costs enumerated in section 1920 of such title (as in effect on October 1, 1981).

(f) If the United States appeals an award of costs or fees and other expenses made against the United States under this section and the award is affirmed in whole or in part, interest shall be paid on the amount of the award as affirmed. Such interest shall be computed at the rate determined under section

1961(a) of this title, and shall run from the date of the award through the day before the date of the mandate of affirmance.

(June 25, 1948, ch. 646, 62 Stat. 973; July 18, 1966, Pub. L. No. 89-507, §1, 80 Stat. 308; Oct. 21, 1980, Pub. L. No. 96-481, Title II, §204(a), (c), 94 Stat. 2327, 2329; Sept. 3, 1982, Pub. L. No. 97-248, Title II, §292(c), 96 Stat. 574; Aug 5, 1985, Pub. L. No. 99-80, §§2, 6(a), (b)(2), 99 Stat. 184, 186; Oct. 22, 1986, Pub. L. No. 99-514, §2, 100 Stat. 2095; Oct. 29, 1992, Pub. L. No. 102-572, Title III, §301(a), Title V, §§502(b), 506(a), Title IX, §902(b)(1), 106 Stat. 4511-4513, 4516; as amended Dec. 21, 1995, Pub. L. No. 104-66, Title I, §1091(b), 109 Stat. 722; Mar. 29, 1996, Pub. L. No. 104-121, Title II, §232, 110 Stat. 863; Nov. 10, 1998, Pub. L. No. 105-368, Title V, §512(b)(1)(B), 112 Stat. 3342.)

Chapter 171—Tort Claims Procedures

§2671. Definitions.
§2672. Administrative adjustment of claims.
§2673. Reports to Congress.
§2674. Liability of United States.
§2675. Disposition by federal agency as prerequisite; evidence.
§2676. Judgment as bar.
§2677. Compromise.
§2678. Attorney fees; penalty.
§2679. Exclusiveness of remedy.
§2680. Exceptions.

§2671. Definitions

As used in this chapter and sections 1346(b) and 2401(b) of this title, the term "Federal agency" includes the executive departments, the judicial and legislative branches, the military departments, independent establishments of the United States, and corporations primarily acting as instrumentalities or agencies of the United States, but does not include any contractor with the United States.

"Employee of the government" includes:

(1) officers or employees of any federal agency, members of the military or naval forces of the United States, members of the National Guard while engaged in training or duty under section 115, 316, 502, 503, 504, or 505 of title 32, and persons acting on behalf of a federal agency in an official capacity, temporarily or perma-

nently in the service of the United States, whether with or without compensation, and

(2) any officer or employee of a Federal public defender organization, except when such officer or employee performs professional services in the course of providing representation under section 3006A of title 18.

"Acting within the scope of his office or employment", in the case of a member of the military or naval forces of the United States or a member of the National Guard as defined in section 101(3) of title 32, means acting in line of duty.

(June 25, 1948, ch. 646, 62 Stat. 982; May 24, 1949, ch. 139, §124, 63 Stat. 106; July 18, 1966, Pub L. 89-506, §8, 80 Stat. 307; Dec. 29, 1981, Pub. L. No. 97-124, §1, 95 Stat. 1666; Nov. 18, 1988, Pub. L. No. 100-649, §3, 102 Stat. 4564; Oct. 30, 2000, Pub. L. No. 106-398, §1 [[div. A], title VI, §665(b)], 114 Stat. 1654, 1654A–169; Nov. 13, 2000, Pub. L. No. 106-518, title IV, §401, 114 Stat. 2421.)

§2672. Administrative adjustment of claims

The head of each Federal agency or his designee, in accordance with regulations prescribed by the Attorney General, may consider, ascertain, adjust, determine, compromise, and settle any claim for money damages against the United States for injury or loss of property or personal injury or death caused by the negligent or wrongful act or omission of any employee of the agency while acting within the scope of his office or employment, under circumstances where the United States, if a private person, would be liable to the claimant in accordance with the law of the place where the act or omission occurred: Provided, That any award, compromise, or settlement in excess of $25,000 shall be effected only with the prior written approval of the Attorney General or his designee. Notwithstanding the proviso contained in the preceding sentence, any award, compromise, or settlement may be effected without the prior written approval of the Attorney General or his or her designee, to the extent that the Attorney General delegates to the head of the agency the authority to make such award, compromise, or settlement. Such delegations may not exceed the authority delegated by the Attorney General to the United States attorneys to settle claims for money damages against the United States. Each Federal agency may use arbitration, or other alternative means of dispute resolution under the provisions of subchapter IV of chapter 5 of title 5, to settle any tort claim against the United States, to the extent of the agency's authority to award, compromise, or settle such claim without the prior written approval of the Attorney General or his or her designee.

Subject to the provisions of this title relating to civil actions on tort claims against the United States, any such award, compromise, settlement, or determination shall be final and conclusive on all offices of the Government, except when procured by means of fraud.

Any award, compromise, or settlement in an amount of $2,500 or less made pursuant to this section shall be paid by the head of the Federal agency concerned out of appropriations available to that agency. Payment of any award, compromise, or settlement in an amount in excess of $2,500 made pursuant to this section or made by the Attorney General in any amount pursuant to section 2677 of this title shall be paid in a manner similar to judgments and compromises in like causes and appropriations or funds available for the payment of such judgments and compromises are hereby made available for the payment of awards, compromises, or settlements under this chapter.

The acceptance by the claimant of any such award, compromise, or settlement shall be final and conclusive on the claimant, and shall constitute a complete release of any claim against the United States and against the employee of the government whose act or omission gave rise to the claim, by reason of the same subject matter.

(June 25, 1948, ch. 646, 62 Stat. 983; Apr. 25, 1949, ch. 92, §2(b), 63 Stat. 62; May 24, 1949, ch. 139, §125, 63 Stat. 106; Sept. 23, 1950, ch. 1010, §9, 64 Stat. 987; Sept. 8, 1959, Pub. L. No. 86-238, §1(1), 73 Stat. 471; July 18, 1966, Pub L. 89-506, §§1, 9(a), 80 Stat. 306, 308; Nov. 15, 1990, Pub. L. No. 101-552, §8(a), 104 Stat. 2746.)

§2673. Reports to Congress

The head of each federal agency shall report annually to Congress all claims paid by it under section 2672 of this title, stating the name of each claimant, the amount claimed, the amount awarded, and a brief description of the claim.

(June 25, 1948, ch. 646, 62 Stat. 983.)

§2674. Liability of United States

The United States shall be liable, respecting the provisions of this title relating to tort claims, in the same manner and to the same extent as a private individual under like circumstances, but shall not be liable for interest prior to judgment or for punitive damages.

If, however, in any case wherein death was caused, the law of the place where the act or omission complained of occurred provides, or has been construed to provide, for damages only punitive in nature, the United States shall be liable for actual or compensatory damages, measured by the pecuniary injuries resulting from such death to the persons respectively, for whose benefit the action was brought, in lieu thereof.

With respect to any claim under this chapter, the United States shall be entitled to assert any defense based upon judicial or legislative immunity which otherwise would have been available to the employee of the United States whose act or omission gave rise to the claim, as well as any other defenses to which the United States is entitled.

With respect to any claim to which this section applies, the Tennessee Valley Authority shall be entitled to assert any defense which otherwise would have been available to the employee based upon judicial or legislative immunity, which otherwise would have been available to the employee of the Tennessee Valley Authority whose act or omission gave rise to the claim as well as any other defenses to which the Tennessee Valley Authority is entitled under this chapter.

(June 25, 1948, ch. 646, 62 Stat. 983; Nov. 18, 1988, Pub. L. No. 100-694, §§4, 9(c), 102 Stat. 4564, 4567.)

§2675. Disposition by federal agency as prerequisite; evidence

(a) An action shall not be instituted upon a claim against the United States for money damages for injury or loss of property or personal injury or death caused by the negligent or wrongful act or omission of any employee of the Government while acting within the scope of his office or employment, unless the claimant shall have first presented the claim to the appropriate Federal agency and his claim shall have been finally denied by the agency in writing and sent by certified or registered mail. The failure of an agency to make final disposition of a claim within six months after it is filed shall, at the option of the claimant any time thereafter, be deemed a final denial of the claim for purposes of this section. The provisions of this subsection shall not apply to such claims as may be asserted under the Federal Rules of Civil Procedure by third party complaint, crossclaim, or counterclaim.

(b) Action under this section shall not be instituted for any sum in excess of the amount of the claim presented to the federal agency, except where the increased amount is based upon newly discovered evidence not reasonably discoverable at the time or presenting the claim to the federal agency, or upon allegation and proof of intervening facts, relating to the amount of the claim.

(c) Disposition of any claim by the Attorney General or other head of a federal agency shall not be competent evidence of liability or amount of damages.

(June 25, 1948, ch. 646, 62 Stat. 983; May 24, 1949, ch. 139, §126, 63 Stat. 107; July 18, 1966, Pub. L. No. 89-506, §2, 80 Stat. 306.)

§2676. Judgment as bar

The judgment in an action under section 1346 (b) of this title shall constitute a complete bar to any action by the claimant, by reason of the same subject matter, against the employee of the government whose act or omission gave rise to the claim.

(June 25, 1948, ch. 646, 62 Stat. 984.)

§2677. Compromise

The Attorney General or his designee may arbitrate, compromise, or settle any claim cognizable under section 1346(b) of this title, after the commencement of an action thereon.

(June 25, 1948, ch. 646, 62 Stat. 984; July 18, 1966, Pub. L. No. 89-506, §3, 80 Stat. 307.)

§2678. Attorney fees; penalty

No attorney shall charge, demand, receive, or collect for services rendered, fees in excess of 25 per centum of any judgment rendered pursuant to section 1346(b) of this title or any settlement made pursuant to section 2677 of this title, or in excess of 20 per centum of any award, compromise, or settlement made pursuant to section 2672 of this title.

Any attorney who charges, demands, receives, or collects for services rendered in connection with such claim any amount in excess of that allowed under this section, if recovery be had, shall be fined not more than $2,000 or imprisoned not more than one year, or both.

(June 25, 1948, ch. 646, 62 Stat. 984; July 18, 1966, Pub. L. No. 89-506, §4, 80 Stat. 307.)

§2679. Exclusiveness of remedy

(a) The authority of any federal agency to sue and be sued in its own name shall not be construed to authorize suits against such federal agency on claims which are cognizable under section 1346(b) of this title, and the remedies provided by this title in such cases shall be exclusive.

(b)(1) The remedy against the United States provided by sections 1346(b) and 2672 of this title for injury or loss of property, or personal injury or death arising or resulting from the negligent or wrongful act or omission of any employee of the Government while acting within the scope of his office or employment is exclusive of any other civil action or proceeding for money damages by reason of the same subject matter against the employee whose act or omission gave rise to the claim or against the estate of such employee. Any other civil action or proceeding for money damages arising out of or relating to the same subject matter against the employee or the employee's estate is precluded without regard to when the act or omission occurred.

(2) Paragraph (1) does not extend or apply to a civil action against an employee of the Government—

    (A) which is brought for a violation of the Constitution of the United States, or

    (B) which is brought for a violation of a statute of the United States under which such action against an individual is otherwise authorized.

(c) The Attorney General shall defend any civil action or proceeding brought in any court against any employee of the Government or his estate for any such damage or injury. The employee against whom such civil action or proceeding is brought shall deliver within such time after date of service or knowledge of service as determined by the Attorney General, all process served upon him or an attested true copy thereof to his immediate superior or to whomever was designated by the head of his department to receive such papers and such person shall promptly furnish copies of the pleadings and process therein to the United States attorney for the district embracing the place wherein the proceeding is brought, to the Attorney General, and to the head of his employing Federal agency.

(d)(1) Upon certification by the Attorney General that the defendant employee was acting within the scope of his office or employment at the time of the incident out of which the claim arose, any civil action or proceeding commenced upon such claim in a United States district court shall be deemed an action against the United States under the provisions of this title and all references thereto, and the United States shall be substituted as the party defendant.

(2) Upon certification by the Attorney General that the defendant employee was acting within the scope of his office or employment at the time of the incident out of which the claim arose, any civil action or proceeding commenced upon such claim in a State court shall be removed without bond at any time before trial by the Attorney General to the district court of the United States for the district and division embracing the place in which the action or proceeding is pending. Such action or proceeding shall be deemed to be an action or proceeding brought against the United States under the provisions of this title and all references thereto, and the United States shall be substituted as the party defendant. This certification of the Attorney General shall conclusively establish scope of office or employment for purposes of removal.

(3) In the event that the Attorney General has refused to certify scope of office or employment under this section, the employee may at any time before trial petition the court to find and certify that the employee was acting within the scope of his office or employment. Upon such certification by the court, such action or proceeding shall be deemed to be an action or proceeding brought against the United States under the provisions of this title and all references thereto, and the United States shall be substituted as the party defendant. A copy of the petition shall be served upon the United States in accordance with the provisions of Rule 4(d)(4) of the Federal Rules of Civil Procedure. In the event the petition is filed in a civil action or proceeding pending in a State court, the action or proceeding may be removed without bond by the Attorney General to the district court of the United States for the district and division embracing the place in which it is pending. If, in considering the petition, the district court determines that the employee was not acting within the scope of his office or employment, the action or proceeding shall be remanded to the State court.

(4) Upon certification, any action or proceeding subject to paragraph (1), (2), or (3) shall proceed in the same manner as any action against the United States filed pursuant to section 1346(b) of this title and shall be subject to the limitations and exceptions applicable to those actions.

(5) Whenever an action or proceeding in which the United States is substituted as the party defendant under this subsection is dismissed for failure first to present a claim pursuant to section 2675(a) of this title, such a claim shall be deemed to be timely presented under section 2401(b) of this title if—

(A) the claim would have been timely had it been filed on the date the underlying civil action was commenced, and

(B) the claim is presented to the appropriate Federal agency within 60 days after dismissal of the civil action.

(e) The Attorney General may compromise or settle any claim asserted in such civil action or proceeding in the manner provided in section 2677, and with the same effect.

(June 25, 1948, ch. 646, 62 Stat. 984; Sept. 21, 1961, Pub. L. No. 87-258, §1, 75 Stat. 539; July 18, 1966, Pub. L. No. 89-506, §5(a), 80 stat. 307; Nov. 18, 1988, Pub. L. No. 100-694, §§5, 6, 102 Stat. 4564.)

§2680. Exceptions

The provisions of this chapter and section 1346(b) of this title shall not apply to—

(a) Any claim based upon an act or omission of an employee of the Government, exercising due care, in the execution of a statute or regulation, whether or not such statute or regulation be valid, or based upon the exercise or performance or the failure to exercise or perform a discretionary function or duty on the part of a federal agency or an employee of the Government, whether or not the discretion involved be abused.

(b) Any claim arising out of the loss, miscarriage, or negligent transmission of letters or postal matter.

(c) Any claim arising in respect of the assessment or collection of any tax or customs duty, or the detention of any goods, merchandise, or other property by any officer of customs or excise or any other law enforcement officer, except that the provisions of this chapter and section 1346 (b) of this title apply to any claim based on injury or loss of goods, merchandise, or other property, while in the possession of any officer of customs or excise or any other law enforcement officer, if—

(1) the property was seized for the purpose of forfeiture under any provision of Federal law providing for the forfeiture of property other than as a sentence imposed upon conviction of a criminal offense;

(2) the interest of the claimant was not forfeited;

(3) the interest of the claimant was not remitted or mitigated (if the property was subject to forfeiture); and

(4) the claimant was not convicted of a crime for which the interest of the claimant in the property was subject to forfeiture under a Federal criminal forfeiture law.

(d) Any claim for which a remedy is provided by sections 741-752, 781-790 of Title 46, relating to claims or suits in admiralty against the United States.

(e) Any claim arising out of an act or omission of any employee of the Government in administering the provisions of sections 1-31 of Title 50, Appendix.

(f) Any claim for damages caused by the imposition or establishment of a quarantine by the United States.

[(g) Repealed. Sept. 26, 1950, ch. 1049, §13(5), 64 Stat. 1043.]

(h) Any claim arising out of assault, battery, false imprisonment, false arrest, malicious prosecution, abuse of process, libel, slander, misrepresentation, deceit, or interference with contract rights: Provided, That, with regard to acts or omissions of investigative or law enforcement officers of the United States Government, the provisions of this chapter and section 1346(b) of this title shall apply to any claim arising, on or after the date of the enactment of this proviso, out of assault, battery, false imprisonment, false arrest, abuse of process, or malicious prosecution. For the purpose of this subsection, "investigative or law enforcement officer" means any officer of the United States who is empowered by law to execute searches, to seize evidence, or to make arrests for violations of Federal law.

(i) Any claim for damages caused by the fiscal operations of the Treasury or by the regulation of the monetary system.

(j) Any claim arising out of the combatant activities of the military or naval forces, or the Coast Guard, during time of war.

(k) Any claim arising in a foreign country.

(l) Any claim arising from the activities of the Tennessee Valley Authority.

(m) Any claim arising from the activities of the Panama Canal Company.

(n) Any claim arising from the activities of a Federal land bank, a Federal intermediate credit bank, or a bank for cooperatives.

(June 25, 1948, ch. 646, 62 Stat. 984; July 16, 1949, ch. 340, 63 Stat. 444; Sept. 26, 1950, ch. 1049, §§2(a)(2), 13(5), 64 Stat. 1038; Aug. 18, 1959, Pub. L. No. 86-168, Title II, §202(b), 73 Stat. 389; Mar. 16, 1974, Pub. L. No. 93-253, §2, 88 Stat. 50; Apr. 25, 2000, Pub. L. No. 106–185, § 3(a), 114 Stat. 211.)

Department of Justice Regulations
28 C.F.R. Part 14—Administrative Claims
Under Federal Tort Claims Act

Contents

§14.1 Scope of regulations.
§14.2 Administrative claim; when presented.
§14.3 Administrative claim; who may file.
§14.4 Administrative claims; evidence and information to be submitted.
§14.5 Review by legal officers.
§14.6 Dispute resolution techniques and limitations on agency authority.
§14.7 [Reserved]
§14.8 Investigation and examination.
§14.9 Final denial of claim.
§14.10 Action on approved claims.
§14.11 Supplementing regulations.

Appendix to Part 14—Delegations of Settlement Authority

Authority: 5 U.S.C. 301; 28 U.S.C. 509, 510, 2672; 38 U.S.C. 224(a).

Source: Order No. 371-66, 31 Fed. Reg. 16,616, Dec. 29, 1966, unless otherwise noted.

§14.1 Scope of regulations.

These regulations shall apply only to claims asserted under the Federal Tort Claims Act. The terms *Federal agency* and *agency,* as used in this part, include the executive departments, the military departments, independent establishments of the United States, and corporations primarily acting as instrumentalities or agencies of the United States but do not include any contractor with the United States.

[Order No. 960-81, 46 Fed. Reg. 52,355, Oct. 27, 1981]

§14.2 Administrative claim; when presented.

(a) For purposes of the provisions of 28 U.S.C. 2401(b), 2672, and 2675, a claim shall be deemed to have been presented when a Federal agency receives from a claimant, his duly authorized agent or legal representative, an executed Standard Form 95 or other written notification of an incident, accompanied by a claim for money damages in a sum certain for injury to or loss of property, personal injury, or death alleged to have occurred by reason of the incident; and the title or legal capacity of the person signing, and is accompanied by evidence of his authority to present a claim on behalf of the claimant as agent, executor, administrator, parent, guardian, or other representative.

(b)(1) A claim shall be presented to the Federal agency whose activities gave rise to the claim. When a claim is presented to any other Federal agency, that agency shall transfer it forthwith to the appropriate agency, if the proper agency can be identified from the claim, and advise the claimant of the transfer. If transfer is not feasible the claim shall be returned to the claimant. The fact of transfer shall not, in itself, preclude further transfer, return of the claim to the claimant or other appropriate disposition of the claim. A claim shall be presented as required by 28 U.S.C. 2401(b) as of the date it is received by the appropriate agency.

(2) When more than one Federal agency is or may be involved in the events giving rise to the claim, an agency with which the claim is filed shall contact all other affected agencies in order to designate the single agency which will thereafter investigate and decide the merits of the claim. In the event that an agreed upon designation cannot be made by the affected agencies, the Department of Justice shall be consulted and will thereafter designate an agency to investigate and decide the merits of the claim. Once a determination has been made, the designated agency shall notify the claimant that all future correspondence concerning the claim shall be directed to that Federal agency. All involved Federal agencies may agree either to conduct their own administrative reviews and to coordinate the results or to have the investigations conducted by the designated Federal agency, but, in either event, the designated Federal agency will be responsible for the final determination of the claim.

(3) A claimant presenting a claim arising from an incident to more than one agency should identify each agency to which the claim is submitted at the time each claim is presented. Where a claim arising from an incident is presented to more than one Federal agency without any indication that more than one agency is involved, and any one of the concerned Federal agencies takes final action on that claim, the final action thus taken is conclusive on the claims presented to the other agencies in regard to the time required for filing suit set forth in 28 U.S.C. 2401(b). However, if a second involved Federal agency subsequently desires to take further action with a view towards settling the claim the second Federal agency may treat the matter as a request for reconsideration of the final denial under 28 C.F.R. 14.9(b), unless suit has been filed in the interim, and so advise the claimant.

(4) If, after an agency final denial, the claimant files a claim arising out of the same incident with a different Federal agency, the new submission of the

claim will not toll the requirement of 28 U.S.C. 2401(b) that suit must be filed within six months of the final denial by the first agency, unless the second agency specifically and explicitly treats the second submission as a request for reconsideration under 28 C.F.R. 14.9(b) and so advises the claimant.

(c) A claim presented in compliance with paragraph (a) of this section may be amended by the claimant at any time prior to final agency action or prior to the exercise of the claimant's option under 28 U.S.C. 2675(a). Amendments shall be submitted in writing and signed by the claimant or his duly authorized agent or legal representative. Upon the timely filing of an amendment to a pending claim, the agency shall have six months in which to make a final disposition of the claim as amended and the claimant's option under 28 U.S.C. 2675(a) shall not accrue until six months after the filing of an amendment.

[Order No. 870-79, 45 Fed. Reg. 2650, Jan. 14, 1980, as amended by Order No. 960-81, 46 Fed. Reg. 52,355, Oct. 27, 1981; Order No. 1179-87, 52 Fed. Reg. 7411, March 11, 1987]

§14.3 Administrative claim; who may file.

(a) A claim for injury to or loss of property may be presented by the owner of the property, his duly authorized agent or legal representative.

(b) A claim for personal injury may be presented by the injured person, his duly authorized agent, or legal representative.

(c) A claim based on death may be presented by the executor or administrator of the decedent's estate, or by any other person legally entitled to assert such a claim in accordance with applicable State law.

(d) A claim for loss wholly compensated by an insurer with the rights of a subrogee may be presented by the insurer. A claim for loss partially compensated by an insurer with the rights of a subrogee may be presented by the parties individually as their respective interests appear, or jointly.

[Order No. 371-66, 31 Fed. Reg. 16,616, Dec. 29, 1966, as amended by Order No. 1179-87, 52 Fed. Reg. 7412, March 11, 1987]

§14.4 Administrative claims; evidence and information to be submitted.

(a) *Death.* In support of a claim based on death, the claimant may be required to submit the following evidence or information:

(1) An authenticated death certificate or other competent evidence showing cause of death, date of death, and age of the decedent.

(2) Decedent's employment or occupation at time of death, including his monthly or yearly salary or earnings (if any), and the duration of his last employment or occupation.

(3) Full names, addresses, birth dates, kinship, and marital status of the decedent's survivors, including identification of those survivors who were dependent for support upon the decedent at the time of his death.

(4) Degree of support afforded by the decedent to each survivor dependent upon him for support at the time of his death.

(5) Decedent's general physical and mental condition before death.

(6) Itemized bills for medical and burial expenses incurred by reason of the incident causing death, or itemized receipts of payment for such expenses.

(7) If damages for pain and suffering prior to death are claimed, a physician's detailed statement specifying the injuries suffered, duration of pain and suffering, any drugs administered for pain, and the decedent's physical condition in the interval between injury and death.

(8) Any other evidence or information which may have a bearing on either the responsibility of the United States for the death or the damages claimed.

(b) *Personal injury.* In support of a claim for personal injury, including pain and suffering, the claimant may be required to submit the following evidence or information:

(1) A written report by his attending physician or dentist setting forth the nature and extent of the injury, nature and extent of treatment, any degree of temporary or permanent disability, the prognosis, period of hospitalization, and any diminished earning capacity. In addition, the claimant may be required to submit to a physical or mental examination by a physician employed by the agency or another Federal agency. A copy of the report of the examining physician shall be made available to the claimant upon the claimant's written request provided that he has, upon request, furnished the report referred to in the first sentence of this paragraph and has made or agrees to make available to the agency any other physician's reports previously or thereafter made of the physical or mental condition which is the subject matter of his claim.

(2) Itemized bills for medical, dental, and hospital expenses incurred, or itemized receipts of payment for such expenses.

(3) If the prognosis reveals the necessity for future treatment, a statement of expected expenses for such treatment.

(4) If a claim is made for loss of time from employment, a written statement from his employer showing actual time lost from employment, whether he is a full or part-time employee, and wages or salary actually lost.

(5) If a claim is made for loss of income and the claimant is self-employed, documentary evidence showing the amounts of earnings actually lost.

(6) Any other evidence or information which may have a bearing on either the responsibility of the United States for the personal injury or the damages claimed.

(c) *Property damage.* In support of a claim for injury to or loss of property, real or personal, the claimant may be required to submit the following evidence or information:

(1) Proof of ownership.

(2) A detailed statement of the amount claimed with respect to each item of property.

(3) An itemized receipt of payment for necessary repairs or itemized written estimates of the cost of such repairs.

(4) A statement listing date of purchase, purchase price and salvage value, where repair is not economical.

(5) Any other evidence or information which may have a bearing on either the responsibility of the United States for the injury to or loss of property or the damages claimed.

§14.5 Review by legal officers.

The authority to adjust, determine, compromise, and settle a claim under the provisions of section 2672 of title 28, United States Code, shall, if the amount of a proposed compromise, settlement, or award exceeds $5,000, be exercised by the head of an agency or his designee only after review by a legal officer of the agency.

[Order No. 371-66, 31 Fed. Reg. 16,616, Dec. 29, 1966, as amended by Order No. 757-77, 42 Fed. Reg. 62,001, Dec. 8, 1977; Order No. 960–81, 46 Fed. Reg. 52,355, Oct. 27, 1981]

§14.6 Dispute resolution techniques and limitations on agency authority

(a) *Guidance regarding dispute resolution.* The administrative process established pursuant to 28 U.S.C. 2672 and this part 14 is intended to serve as an efficient effective forum for rapidly resolving tort claims with low costs to all participants. This guidance is provided to agencies to improve their use of this administrative process and to maximize the benefit achieved through application of prompt, fair, and efficient techniques that achieve an informal resolution of administrative tort claims without burdening claimants or the agency. This section provides guidance to agencies only and does not create or establish any right to enforce any provision of this part on behalf of any claimant against the United States, its agencies, its officers, or any other person. This section also does not require any agency to use any dispute resolution technique or process.

(1) Whenever feasible, administrative claims should be resolved through informal discussions, negotiations, and settlements rather than through the use of any formal or structured process. At the same time, agency personnel processing administrative tort claims should be trained in dispute resolution techniques and skills that can contribute to the prompt, fair, and efficient resolution of administrative claims.

(2) An agency may resolve disputed factual questions regarding claims against the United States under the FTCA, including 28 U.S.C. 2671-2680, through the use of any alternative dispute resolution technique or process if the agency specifically agrees to employ the technique or process, and reserves to itself the discretion to accept or reject the determinations made through the use of such technique or process.

(3) Alternative dispute resolution techniques or processes should not be adopted arbitrarily but rather should be based upon a determination that use of a particular technique is warranted in the context of a particular claim or claims, and that such use will materially contribute to the prompt, fair, and efficient resolution of the claims. If alternative dispute resolution techniques will not materially contribute to the prompt, fair, and efficient resolution of claims, the dispute resolution processes otherwise used pursuant to these regulations shall be the preferred means of seeking resolution of such claims.

(b) *Alternative dispute resolution*—(1) *Case-by-case.* In order to use, and before using, any alternative dispute resolution technique or process to facilitate the prompt resolution of disputes that are in excess of the agency's delegated authority, an agency may use the following procedure to obtain written approval from the Attorney General, or his or her designee, to compromise a claim or series of related claims.

(i) A request for settlement authority under paragraph (b)(1) of this section shall be directed to the Director, Torts Branch, Civil Division, Department of Justice, ("Director") and shall contain information justifying the request, including:

(A) The basis for concluding that liability exists under the FTCA;

(B) A description of the proposed alternative dispute resolution technique or process and a statement regarding why this proposed form of alternative dispute resolution is suitable for the claim or claims;

(C) A statement reflecting the claimant's or claimants' consent to use of the proposed form of alternative dispute resolution, indicating the proportion of any additional cost to the United States from use of the proposed alternative dispute resolution technique or process that shall be borne by the claimant or claimants, and specifying the manner and timing of payment of that proportion to be borne by the claimant or claimants;

(D) A statement of how the requested action would facilitate use of an alternative dispute resolution technique or process;

(E) An explanation of the extent to which the decision rendered in the alternative dispute resolution proceeding would be made binding upon claimants; and,

(F) An estimate of the potential range of possible settlements resulting from use of the proposed alternative dispute resolution technique.

(ii) The Director shall forward a request for expedited settlement action under paragraph (b)(1)(i) of this section, along with the Director's recommendation as to what action should be taken, to the Department of Justice official who has authority to authorize settlement of the claim or related claims. If that official approves the request, a written authorization shall be promptly forwarded to the requesting agency.

(2) *Delegation of authority.* Pursuant to, and within the limits of, 28 U.S.C. 2672, the head of an agency or his or her designee may request delegations of authority to make any award, compromise, or settlement without the prior written approval of the Attorney General or his or her designee in excess of the agency's authority. In considering whether to delegate authority pursuant to 28 U.S.C. 2672 in excess of previous authority conferred upon the agency, consideration shall be given to:

(i) The extent to which the agency has established an office whose responsibilities expressly include the administrative resolution of claims presented pursuant to the Federal Tort Claims Act;

(ii) The agency's experience with the resolution of administrative claims presented pursuant to 28 U.S.C. 2672;

(iii) The Department of Justice's experiences with regard to administrative resolution of tort claims arising out of the agency's activities.

(c) *Monetary authority.* An award, compromise, or settlement of a claim by an agency under 28 U.S.C. 2672, in excess of $25,000 or in excess of the authority delegated to the agency by the Attorney General pursuant to 28 U.S.C. 2672, whichever is greater, shall be effected only with the prior written approval of the Attorney General or his or her designee. For purposes of this paragraph, a principal claim and any derivative or subrogated claim shall be treated as a single claim.

(d) *Limitations on settlement authority*—(1) *Policy.* An administrative claim may be adjusted, determined, compromised, or settled by an agency under 28 U.S.C. 2672 only after consultation with the Department of Justice when, in the opinion of the agency:

(i) A new precedent or a new point of law is involved; or

(ii) A question of policy is or may be involved; or

(iii) The United States is or may be entitled to indemnity or contribution from a third party and the agency is unable to adjust the third party claim; or

(iv) The compromise of a particular claim, as a practical matter, will or may control the disposition of a related claim in which the amount to be paid may exceed $25,000 or may exceed the authority delegated to the agency by the Attorney General pursuant to 28 U.S.C. 2672, whichever is greater.

(2) *Litigation arising from the same incident.* An administrative claim may be adjusted, determined, compromised, or settled by an agency under 28 U.S.C. 2672 only after consultation with the Department of Justice when the agency is informed or is otherwise aware that the United States or an employee, agent, or cost-plus contractor of the United States is involved in litigation based on a claim arising out of the same incident or transaction.

(e) *Procedure.* When Department of Justice approval or consultation is required, or the advice of the Department of Justice is otherwise to be requested, under this section, the written referral or request of the Federal agency shall be directed to the Director at any time after presentment of a claim to the Federal agency, and shall contain:

(1) A short and concise statement of the facts and of the reasons for the referral or request;

(2) Copies of relevant portions of the agency's claim file; and

(3) A statement of the recommendations or views of the agency.

[Order No. 1591-92, 57 Fed. Reg. 21,738, May 22, 1992]

§14.7 [Reserved]

§14.8 Investigation and examination.

A Federal agency may request any other Federal agency to investigate a claim filed under section 2672, title 28, U.S. Code, or to conduct a physical examination of a claimant and provide a report of the physical examination. Compliance with such requests may be conditioned by a Federal agency upon reimbursement by the requesting agency of the expense of investigation or examination where reimbursement is authorized, as well as where it is required, by statute or regulation.

§14.9 Final denial of claim.

(a) Final denial of an administrative claim shall be in writing and sent to the claimant, his attorney, or legal representative by certified or registered mail. The notification of final denial may include a statement of the reasons for the denial and shall include a statement that, if the claimant is dissatisfied with the agency action, he may file suit in an appropriate U.S. District Court not later than 6 months after the date of mailing of the notification.

(b) Prior to the commencement of suit and prior to the expiration of the 6-month period provided in 28 U.S.C. 2401(b), a claimant, his duly authorized agent, or legal representative, may file a written request with the agency for reconsideration of a final denial of a claim under paragraph (a) of this section. Upon the timely filing of a request for reconsideration the agency shall have 6 months from the date of filing in which to make a final disposition of the claim and the claimant's option under 28 U.S.C. 2675(a) shall not accrue until 6 months after the filing of a request for reconsideration. Final agency action on a request for reconsideration shall be effected in accordance with the provisions of paragraph (a) of this section.

[Order No. 371-66, 31 Fed. Reg. 16,616, Dec. 29, 1966, as amended by Order No. 422-69, 35 Fed. Reg. 315, Jan. 8, 1970]

§14.10 Action on approved claims.

(a) Any award, compromise, or settlement in an amount of $2,500 or less made pursuant to 28 U.S.C. 2672 shall be paid by the head of the Federal agency concerned out of the appropriations available to that agency. Payment of an award, compromise, or settlement in excess of $2,500 shall be obtained by the agency by forwarding Standard Form 1145 to the Claims Division, General Accounting Office. When an award is in excess of $25,000, or in excess of the authority delegated to the agency by the Attorney General pursuant to 28 U.S.C. 2672, whichever is greater, Standard Form 1145 must be accompanied by evidence that the award, compromise, or settlement has been approved by the Attorney General or his designee. When the use of Standard Form 1145 is required, it shall be executed by the claimant, or it shall be accompanied by either a claims settlement agreement or a Standard Form 95 executed by the claimant. When a claimant is represented by an attorney, the voucher for payment shall designate both the claimant and his attorney as payees; the check shall be delivered to the attorney, whose address shall appear on the voucher.

(b) Acceptance by the claimant, his agent, or legal representative, of any award, compromise or settlement made pursuant to the provisions of section 2672 or 2677 of title 28, United States Code, shall be final and conclusive on the claimant, his agent or legal representative and any other person on whose behalf or for whose benefit the claim has been presented, and shall constitute a complete release of any claim against the United States and against any employee of the Government whose act or omission gave rise to the claim, by reason of the same subject matter.

[Order No. 371-66, 31 Fed. Reg. 16,616, Dec. 29, 1966, as amended by Order No. 834-79, 44 Fed. Reg. 33,399, June 11, 1979; Order No. 1591-92, 57 Fed. Reg. 21,740, May 22, 1992]

§14.11 Supplementing regulations.

Each agency is authorized to issue regulations and establish procedures consistent with the regulations in this part.

Appendix to Part 14—Delegations of Settlement Authority
Delegation of Authority to the Secretary of Veterans Affairs
Section 1. Authority to compromise tort claims.

(a) The Secretary of Veterans Affairs shall have the authority to adjust, determine, compromise and settle a claim involving the United States Department of Veterans Affairs under section 2672 of title 28, United States Code, relating to the administrative settlement of federal tort claims, if the amount of the proposed adjustment, compromise, or award does not exceed $200,000. When the Secretary of Veterans Affairs believes a claim pending before him presents a novel question of law or of policy, he shall obtain the advice of the Assistant Attorney General in charge of the Civil Division.

(b) The Secretary of Veterans Affairs may redelegate in writing the settlement authority delegated to him under this section.

Section 2. Memorandum.

Whenever the Secretary of Veterans Affairs settles any administrative claim pursuant to the authority granted by section 1 for an amount in excess of $100,000 and within the amount delegated to him under section 1, a memorandum fully explaining the basis for the action taken shall be executed. A copy of this memorandum shall be sent to the Director, FTC Staff, Torts Branch of the Civil Division.

Delegation of Authority to the Postmaster General
Section 1. Authority to compromise tort claims.

(a) The Postmaster General shall have the authority to adjust, determine, compromise and settle a claim involving the Postal Service under section 2672 of title 28, United States Code, relating to the administrative settlement of federal tort claims, if the amount of the proposed adjustment, compromise, or award does not exceed $200,000. When the Postmaster General believes a claim pending before him presents a novel question of law or of policy, he shall obtain the advice of the Assistant Attorney General in charge of the Civil Division.

(b) The Postmaster General may redelegate in writing the settlement authority delegated to him under this section.

Section 2. Memorandum.

Whenever the Postmaster General settles any administrative claim pursuant to the authority granted by section 1 for an amount in excess of $100,000 and within the amount delegated to him under section 1, a memorandum fully explaining the basis for the action taken shall be executed. A copy of this memorandum shall be sent to the Director, FTCA Staff, Torts Branch of the Civil Division.

Delegation of Authority to the Secretary of Defense
Section 1. Authority to compromise tort claims.

(a) The Secretary of Defense shall have the authority to adjust, determine, compromise and settle a claim involving the United States Department of Defense under section 2672 of title 28, United States Code, relating to the administrative settlement of federal tort claims, if the amount of the proposed adjustment, compromise, or award does not exceed $200,000. When the Secretary of Defense believes a claim pending before him presents a novel question of law or of policy, he shall obtain the advice of the Assistant Attorney General in charge of the Civil Division.

(b) The Secretary of Defense may redelegate in writing the settlement authority delegated to him under this section.

Section 2. Memorandum.

Whenever the Secretary of Defense settles any administrative claim pursuant to the authority granted by section 1 for an amount in excess of $100,000 and within the amount delegated to him under section 1, a memorandum fully explaining the basis for the action taken shall be executed. A copy of this memorandum shall be sent to the Director, FTCA Staff, Torts Branch of the Civil Division.

Delegation of Authority to the Secretary of Transportation
Section 1. Authority to compromise tort claims.

(a) The Secretary of Transportation shall have the authority to adjust, determine, compromise and settle a claim involving the United States Department of Transportation under section 2672 of title 28, United States Code, relating to the administrative settlement of federal tort claims, if the amount of the proposed adjustment, compromise, or award does not exceed $100,000. When the Secretary of Transportation believes a claim pending before him presents a novel question of law or of policy, he shall obtain the advice of the

Assistant Attorney General in charge of the Civil Division.

(b) The Secretary of Transportation may redelegate in writing the settlement authority delegated to him under this section.

Section 2. Memorandum.

Whenever the Secretary of Transportation settles any administrative claim pursuant to the authority granted by section 1 for an amount in excess of $50,000 and within the amount delegated to him under section 1, a memorandum fully explaining the basis for the action taken shall be executed. A copy of this memorandum shall be sent to the Director, FTCA Staff, Torts Branch of the Civil Division.

Delegation of Authority to the Secretary of Health and Human Services
Section 1. Authority To Compromise Tort Claims.

(a) The Secretary of Health and Human Services shall have the authority to adjust, determine, compromise, and settle a claim involving the Department of Health and Human Services under section 2672 of title 28, United States Code, relating to the administrative settlement of federal tort claims, if the amount of the proposed adjustment, compromise, or award does not exceed $200,000. When the Secretary of Health and Human Services believes a claim pending before him presents a novel question of law or policy, he shall obtain the advice of the Assistant Attorney General in charge of the Civil Division.

(b) The Secretary of Health and Human Services may redelegate, in writing, the settlement authority delegated to him under this section.

Section 2. Memorandum.

Whenever the Secretary of Health and Human Services settles any administrative claim pursuant to the authority granted by section 1 for an amount in excess of $100,000 and within the amount delegated to him under section 1, a memorandum fully explaining the basis for the action taken shall be executed. A copy of this memorandum shall be sent to the Director, FTCA Staff, Torts Branch of the Civil Division.

[Order No. 1302-88, 53 Fed. Reg. 37,753, Sept. 28, 1988, as amended by Order No. 1471-91, 56 Fed. Reg. 4943, Feb. 7, 1991; Order No. 1482-91, 56 Fed. Reg. 12,846, Mar. 28, 1991; Order No. 1583-92, 57 Fed. Reg. 13,320, April 16, 1992; 58 Fed. Reg. 36,867, July 9, 1993; 61 Fed. Reg. 66,220, Dec. 17, 1996; 68 Fed. Reg. 62,517, Nov. 5, 2003]

Freedom of Information Act

Citations:

5 U.S.C. §552 (Supp. II 2002); enacted September 6, 1966, by Pub. L. No. 89-554, 80 Stat. 383; amended by Pub. L. No. 90-23, §1, June 5, 1967, 81 Stat. 54; Pub. L. No. 93-502, §§1-3, November 21, 1974, 88 Stat. 1,561-64; Pub. L. No. 94-409, §5(b), September 13, 1976, 90 Stat. 1,247; Pub. L. No. 95-454, title IX, §906(a)(10), October 13, 1978, 92 Stat. 1,225; Pub. L. No. 98-620, title IV, §402(2), November 8, 1984, 98 Stat. 3,357; Pub. L. No. 99-570, title I, §§1801-04, October 27, 1986, 100 Stat. 3,207; Pub. L. No. 104-231, §§3-11, Oct. 2, 1996, 110 Stat. 3,049; Pub. L. No. 107-306, Title III, §312, November 27, 2002, 116 Stat. 2390.

Note: As this book went to press, the Congress on December 19, 2007 passed the "Openness Promotes Effectiveness in our National Government Act of 2007" or the "OPEN Government Act of 2007," and the President signed it on December 31, Pub. L. No 110-___, which extensively amended the Freedom of Information Act.

The Act made important changes in the fee provisions, especially concerning requests from "news media," and in situations where the agency missed applicable deadlines; attorney fee provisions; disciplinary proceedings by the Office of Special Counsel, the 20-day time limit for processing and tracking requests, annual agency reports to the Attorney General. It also extended coverage to records "maintained for an agency by an entity under Government contract, for the purposes of records management." It also established the Office of Government Information Services within the National Archives and Records Administration to (1) review agency FOIA policies and procedures and compliance with the Act, (2) recommend policy changes to Congress and the President to improve the administration of the Act and offer mediation services to resolve disputes between requestors and agencies as a "non-exclusive alternative to litigation."

The text in this volume includes the Act as modified.

Lead Agency:

Department of Justice, Office of Information and Privacy, 1425 New York Avenue, NW, Suite 11050, Washington, DC 20530 (202) 514-3642; http://www.usdoj.gov/oip/oip.html. Freedom of Information Act (FOIA) information page: http://www.usdoj.gov/04foia.

Overview:

The Freedom of Information Act requires all agencies (1) to publish certain items of information in the Federal Register, (2) to make available for public inspection and copying certain other items of information, and (3) to make certain agency records available to any members of the public upon request for such records.

Federal Register Publication. Each agency is required (5 U.S.C. §552(a)(1)) to publish in the *Federal Register*:

- Descriptions of its central and field organization and the established places at which, the employees (and in the case of a uniformed service, the members) from whom, and the methods whereby, the public may obtain information, make submittals or requests, or obtain decisions;
- Statements of the general course and method by which its functions are determined and assigned, including the nature and requirements of all formal and informal procedures available;
- Rules of procedure, descriptions of forms available or the places at which forms may be obtained, and instructions as to the scope and contents of all papers, reports, or examinations;
- Substantive rules of general applicability adopted as authorized by law, and statements of general policy or interpretations of general applicability formulated and adopted by the agency; and
- Each amendment, revision, or repeal of the foregoing.

If any listed item is not so published, persons without actual and timely notice of the substance of the items may not be required to conform their behavior to, or be adversely affected by, the item.

Opinions, Orders, Interpretations, Manuals, Previously Requested Records. Adjudicative orders and opinions, statements of policy and interpretations not published in the Federal Register, and staff manuals and instructions to staff must either be made available for inspection and copying or be promptly published and made available for sale (5 U.S.C. §552(a)(2)). Agency records of this type created on or after November 1, 1996 must be accessible to the public in two ways: (1) through the "paper reading rooms," available for public inspection and copying or be published; and (2) through the "electronic reading rooms," accessible through computer telecommunications, i.e., the Internet and World Wide Web (§552(a)(2)). This latter requirement is just one of many changes made to the FOIA in the Electronic Freedom of Information Act Amendments of 1996 (hereafter 1996 FOIA Amendments) to take account of new information technology.

The 1996 FOIA Amendments also require that the public have access to copies of agency records previously processed for disclosure under the Act that, "because of the nature of their subject matter, the agency determines have become or are likely to become the subject of subsequent requests for substantially the same records" as well as a general index of those records (§552(a)(2)(D), (E)). An agency may, with a full written explanation, delete identifying items that would constitute a clear invasion of personal privacy. Note also that agencies may "withhold" (i.e., not make available) a subsection (a)(2) record (or portion of such a record) if it falls within other FOIA exemptions, just as they can do in response to FOIA requests. See *FOMC v. Merrill*, 443 U.S. 340, 360 n.23 (1979) (applying commercial privilege to subsection (a)(1) record and recognizing that subsection (a)(2) records likewise may be protected by FOIA exemptions).

Requests for Other Records. All other agency records must promptly be made available upon a request that reasonably describes the records and is made in accordance with published procedures (5 U.S.C. §552(a)(3)-(4)(A)). Agencies must honor the requester's choice of format and make reasonable efforts to produce records in that form if readily reproducible in that form (§552(a)(3)(B)). To constitute an "agency record," a document must be either created or obtained by an agency and under agency control at the time of the request. See *Department of Justice v. Tax Analysts*, 492 U.S. 136, 144-45 (1989); see also *Wolfe v. HHS*, 711 F.2d 1077, 1079-82 (D.C. Cir. 1983).

A record is "reasonably describe[d]" if the description of the requested agency document is sufficient to enable a professional agency employee familiar with the subject area to locate the record with a reasonable amount of effort (H.R. Rep. No. 876, 93d Cong., 2d Sess. 6 (1974)). Requests must be made in accordance with the agency's published rules regarding the time, place, filing fees, and required procedures. 5 U.S.C. §552(a)(3).

The agency must use reasonable efforts to search for the requested records using electronic methods, except in cases where it would significantly interfere with the operation of the agency's automated information system (5 U.S.C. §552(a)(3)(C)). "Search" is now defined explicitly to include both manual and electronic methods (§ 552(a)(3)(D)).

Time Limits. An agency must inform a FOIA requester within 20 days of receiving a request as to the agency's intent to fulfill or deny the request (5 U.S.C. §552(a)(6)(A)(i)). The requester may appeal a denial to the agency head. The agency head must decide appeals within 20 working days (5 U.S.C. §552(a)(6)(A)(i)). Either time limit may be extended for 10 working days in unusual circumstances upon written notice to the requester. Section 552(a)(6)(B) specifies the circumstances permitting the extension of the time limits. If an agency anticipates that the request may take more than the extended time period, it must provide the requester an opportunity to either: (i) limit the scope of the request or (ii) arrange with the agency a new or alternative time limit or a modified request (§ 552(a)(6)(B)(ii)). See also judicial review discussion, below.

Agencies may promulgate regulations providing for multitrack processing of requests for records. (§552(a)(6)(D)(i)). This allows for processing of requests on a "first-in, first-out" basis within each track, but also permits agencies to bypass agency backlogs by responding to relatively simple requests before requests for complex and/or voluminous records.

Agencies also must provide for expedited processing of requests for records (§552(a)(6)(E)). If a FOIA requester can show "compelling need" (defined in §552(a)(6)(E)(v)) the agency may expedite the request and process it out of sequence. Compelling need is explicitly defined as either an imminent threat to life or public safety or an urgency to inform the public concerning actual or alleged Federal Government activity (§552(a)(6)(E)(v)(I), (II)). Within 10 calendar days after its receipt of a request for expedited treatment, the agency must notify the requester if it will expedite the process, and the requester must be given an opportunity to appeal the agency's determination.

Fees and Fee Waivers. As amended by the FOIA Reform Act of 1986, the FOIA sets forth three levels of fees that may be assessed for FOIA requests, depending on the category of the requester:

> (1) An agency may charge a requester for document search time, duplication, and review costs if the request is made for a "commercial use" (§552(a)(4)(A)(ii)(I)). A search includes both manual and electronic means (§552(a)(3)(D)).

(2) An agency may only charge a requester for document duplication if the request is made by an educational or noncommercial scientific institution, whose purpose is scholarly or scientific research, or by a representative of the news media, provided that the records are not sought for a commercial use (§552(a)(4)(A)(ii)(II)).

(3) An agency may charge requesters not covered by categories (1) and (2) above for the costs of document search and duplication (§552(a)(4)(A)(ii)(III)).

These three categories of fees are further modified by several general limitations that were added to the FOIA by the 1986 amendments. These limitations are: (1) no fee may be charged if the costs of collecting and processing the fee are likely to equal or exceed the amount of the fee; (2) a noncommercial requester may not be charged for the first 2 hours of search time or the first 100 pages of document duplication; (3) no agency may require advance payment of fees unless the requester has previously failed to pay a fee in a timely fashion or the agency has determined that the fee will exceed $250; and (4) review costs may not be charged for review related to appeals or the resolution of issues of law or policy raised by the request (§552(a)(4)(A)(iv), (v)).

The 1986 amendments also directed the Office of Management and Budget to develop guidelines, following notice-and-comment procedures, to provide a "uniform schedule of fees for all agencies," and each federal agency was directed to promulgate regulations conforming to those guidelines (§552(a)(4)(A)(i)). OMB published its guidelines on March 27, 1987 (52 Fed. Reg. 10,012). See http://www.whitehouse.gov/omb/inforeg/foia_fee_schedule_1987.pdf.

Notwithstanding the fee schedules, the FOIA provides for waivers of fees in particular cases. As amended by the FOIA Reform Act in 1986, the fee waiver provision states that "[d]ocuments shall be furnished without any charge or at a [reduced] charge . . . if disclosure of the information is in the public interest because it is likely to contribute significantly to public understanding of the operations or activities of the government and is not primarily in the commercial interest of the requester" (§552(a)(4)(A)(iii)).

The Department of Justice issued a fee waiver policy statement in April 1987 to reflect the change in the fee waiver provision made by the FOIA Reform Act (Memorandum, Stephen J. Markman, Assistant Attorney General, Office of Legal Policy, to Agency Heads, Apr. 2, 1987). The guidance was intended for use by agencies adopting new fee waiver regulations. The memorandum includes a six-factor test for deciding to grant or deny a request for waiver or reduction of FOIA fees (see discussion in the Justice Department's FOIA Guide (http://www.usdoj.gov/oip/foia_guide07/fees_feewaivers.pdf)).

Exemptions. Nine categories of records (or portions of records) are exempt under 5 U.S.C. §552(b) from mandatory disclosure under the FOIA. However, any reasonably segregable, non-exempt portions of requested records must be released to the requester, even if the material falls under one of the nine categories below. The record must also indicate the amount of information deleted (unless that indication is itself protected from disclosure by an exemption) and, if technically feasible, the place in the record where the deletion is made (§552(b), concluding paragraphs). While not considered "exempt" records, the 2002 amendments provided that intelligence agencies are not to make any record available to foreign governments (§552(a)(3)(E)). In addition, there are a number of other statutes that specifically exclude records described therein from the FOIA. For example, the Critical Infrastructure Information Act exempts critical infrastructure information voluntarily submitted to an agency from the FOIA. See 6 U.S.C. § 133(a)(1)(A). In addition, in 1984 Congress amended the National Security Act of 1947 to exempt from the FOIA's search and review requirements certain operational files of the Central Intelligence Agency. The CIA Information Act (Pub. L. No. 98-477, 98 Stat. 2,209) did not broaden the CIA's authority to withhold information, but it relieves the CIA of the administrative burden of searching and reviewing files that almost always are classified or otherwise not releasable under the FOIA.

Because the FOIA is a disclosure statute only, it does not prohibit agencies from disclosing records merely because they are exempt from mandatory disclosure (although in some cases other statutes may prohibit disclosure). Under President Jimmy Carter the Justice Department informed heads of agencies that the Department would not defend an agency in a suit seeking disclosure under the FOIA unless the agency found not only that a particular exemption was applicable but also that disclosure would be contrary to the public interest. This memorandum was revoked by the Attorney General appointed by President Ronald Reagan, who informed heads of agencies that the Department would defend any withholding of a record that was subject to a FOIA exemption. This policy was continued by President George H.W. Bush, but President William Clinton's Attorney General reinstituted the Carter-era policy. George W. Bush's Attorney General subsequently rescinded the Clinton-era policy and assured heads of agencies that their withholdings would be defended by the Department unless they lacked a sound basis in the law.

(1) Records that are specifically authorized under criteria established by an executive order to be kept secret in the interest of national defense or foreign policy, and are in fact properly classified pursuant to such executive order.

The applicable executive order is Executive Order 12,958, which became effective on October 17, 1995, 3 C.F.R. 333 (1996), 60 Fed. Reg. 19,825, *reprinted in* 50 U.S.C.A. §435 note. This original executive order has been supplemented from time to time, most notably by President Clinton in 1997, and by President Bush in 2003. See id. See Justice Department's FOIA Guide (2007 ed.) (http://www.usdoj.gov/oip/foia_guide07/exemption1.pdf) for discussion of litigation under this exemption, including issues of deference to agency classification, court review, Executive Order 12,958's provisions, and other issues.

(2) Records that are related solely to the internal personnel rules and practices of an agency.

The case law on this exemption initially was divided, reflecting the manner in which the House and Senate reports addressed Exemption 2 when the FOIA was enacted. Compare S. Rep. No. 813, 89th Cong., 1st Sess. 8 (1965) (exemption relates only to internal personnel rules and practices within an agency) with H.R. Rep. No. 1497, 89th Cong., 2d Sess. 10 (1966) (exemption does not cover all matters of internal management). The Supreme Court, however, in *Department of the Air Force v. Rose*, 425 U.S. 352 (1976), accepted the Senate report as authoritative for routine personnel matters.

The exemption, as interpreted by the courts, encompasses two distinct categories of information: (i) that related to internal agency matters of a relatively trivial nature, and (ii) that related to more substantial internal agency matters, the disclosure of which would enable persons to circumvent a legal requirement. A request for the former type of information is sometimes referred to as a "low 2" matter, while a request for the latter type of information is referred to as "high 2."

Leading cases interpreting Exemption 2 are *Founding Church of Scientology v. Smith*, 721 F.2d 828, 830-31 & n.4 (D.C. Cir. 1983), and *Crooker v. Bureau of Alcohol, Tobacco & Firearms*, 670 F.2d 1051, 1073 (D.C. Cir. 1981) (en banc). See also *Schwaner v. Department of the Air Force*, 898 F.2d 793, 795-97 (D.C. Cir. 1990).

(3) Records that are specifically exempted from disclosure by statute (other than section 552b), provided that such statute (A) requires that the matters be withheld from the public in such a manner as to leave no discretion on the issue, or (B) establishes particular criteria for withholding or refers to particular types of matters to be withheld.

Exemption 3 is triggered only by federal statutes, and not, for instance, by executive orders or regulations (*Washington Post Co. v. HHS*, 690 F.2d 252, 273 (D.C. Cir. 1982)) or by rules of the Supreme Court (*Founding Church of Scientology v. Bell*, 603 F.2d 945, 952 (D.C. Cir. 1979)). In *Reporters Committee for Freedom of the Press v. Department of Justice*, 816 F.2d 730, 735 (D.C. Cir. 1987), *rev'd on other grounds*, 489 U.S. 749 (1989), the Court of Appeals for the D.C. Circuit held that congressional intent to exempt matters from disclosure must be found "in the actual words of the statute . . . or at least in the legislative history of FOIA" and not merely in the legislative history of a claimed withholding statute (citation omitted). The Privacy Act does not qualify as an Exemption 3 statute (5 U.S.C. §552a(t)(2), as added by Pub. L. No. 98-477, §2(c), Oct. 15, 1984, 98 Stat. 2209). The Trade Secrets Act, 18 U.S.C. §1905, also does not qualify as an Exemption 3 statute, see *CNA Financial Corp. v. Donovan*, 830 F.2d 1132, 1137-43 (D.C. Cir. 1987), *cert. denied*, 485 U.S. 977 (1988).

Exemption 3 statutes enacted while a FOIA request is pending or being litigated may apply retroactively to exempt the requested records from disclosure. See *City of Chicago v. U.S. Dep't of Treasury, BATF*, 423 F.3d 777 (7th Cir. 2005); *Project on Nuclear Arms Control v. U.S. Dep't of Commerce*, 317 F.3d 275 (D.C. Cir. 2003); *Southwest Center for Biological Diversity v. USDA*, 314 F.3d 1060 (9th Cir. 2002).

(4) Trade secrets and commercial or financial information obtained from a person and privileged or confidential.

This category relates only to records that have been supplied to the government by a "person" (i.e., someone other than the government itself). "Trade secrets" has been defined narrowly by the D.C. Circuit instead of applying the broad common law meaning, see *Public Citizen Health Research Group v. FDA*, 704 F.2d 1280, 1288 (D.C. Cir. 1983). "Trade secrets" are limited to information regarding the "productive process itself." *Ctr. for Auto Safety v. Nat'l Highway Traffic Safety Admin.*, 244 F.3d 144, 150-51 (D.C. Cir. 2001). However, if information relates to business or trade, most courts have little difficulty in finding it "commercial or financial." Most litigation of Exemption 4 issues has turned on the meaning of "confidential."

The D.C. Circuit, in *Critical Mass Energy Project v. NRC*, 975 F.2d 871 (D.C. Cir. 1992) (en banc), established two standards for determining confidentiality. If the information is "required" by the government, and if disclosure is likely to either (i) impair the government's ability to obtain information in the future, or (ii) to cause substantial harm to the competitive position of the submitter of the information, then the information is confidential (*National Parks and Conservation Ass'n v. Morton*, 498 F.2d 765 (D.C. Cir. 1974)). However, if a person "voluntarily" submits the information to the government, then that information is categorically protected, provided that it is not customarily released by the submitter to the public. *Critical Mass*, 975 F.2d at 879. See *Ctr. for Auto Safety v. NHTSA*, 244 F.3d 144, 149 (D.C. Cir. 2001), for an extensive analysis of *Critical Mass*. Some courts have held that harm to governmental programs unrelated to the government's ability to obtain information might be grounds for protecting such information. See, e.g., *9 to 5 Organization for Women Office Workers v. Board of Governors of the Federal Reserve System*, 721 F.2d 1, 10 (1st Cir. 1983). For a discussion of these tests, the distinction between "required" and "voluntary," and what constitutes "customarily," see the Justice Department's FOIA Guide at http://www.usdoj.gov/oip/foia_guide07/exemption4.pdf.

The Trade Secrets Act, 18 U.S.C. §1905, imposes criminal penalties on agency employees who wrongfully disclose trade secrets. In *Chrysler Corp. v. Brown*, 441 U.S. 281, 319, n.49 (1979), the Supreme Court held that Exemption 4 and the Trade Secrets Act are essentially congruent, limiting an agency's ability to make a discretionary release of material exempt under Exemption 4, because to do so in violation of the Trade Secrets Act would constitute an action inconsistent with law. See also *CNA Financial Corp. v. Donovan*, 830 F.2d 1132, 1144-52 (D.C. Cir. 1987)

A "reverse FOIA" case is one in which the submitter of information seeks to enjoin the agency from releasing that information in response to a third party's FOIA request. In *Chrysler Corp. v. Brown*, above, the Supreme Court held that submitters could not sue under the FOIA or the Trade Secrets Act, but only under the Administrative Procedure Act (5 U.S.C. §701, et seq.), claiming illegal agency action. A leading case on the scope of review in "reverse FOIA" cases is *NOW, Washington, D.C. Chapter v. Social Security Administration*, 736 F.2d 727, 745-47 (D.C. Cir. 1984). In 1987 the President issued an executive order that requires agencies to establish and follow procedures with respect to requests for records potentially subject to this exemption. Executive Order 12,600, Predisclosure Notification Procedures for Confidential Commercial Information, 52 Fed. Reg. 23,781.

(5) Interagency or intra-agency memorandums or letters which would not be available by law to a party other than an agency in litigation with the agency.

Exemption 5 applies to documents normally privileged in the civil discovery context and is not limited to those privileges mentioned in the legislative history *(United States v. Weber Aircraft Co.,* 465 U.S. 792, 800 (1984)). See also *FTC v. Grolier Inc.,* 462 U.S. 19, 26 (1983); *Martin v. Office of Special Counsel,* 819 F.2d 1181, 1184 (D.C. Cir. 1987). But see B*urka v. HHS,* 87 F.3d 508, 517 (D.C. Cir. 1996) (before certain material may be found privileged, the agency must show that it is protected in discovery for reasons similar to those used by agency in FOIA context). The most frequently invoked privileges under Exemption 5 are the deliberative process privilege ("executive privilege"), the attorney work-product privilege, and the attorney-client privilege *(NRLB v. Sears, Roebuck & Co.,* 421 U.S. 132, 149 (1975)). Initially, however, the record must be an "interagency or intraagency memorandum or letter." This language has been construed to extend the exemption to recommendations and advice made by a number of persons outside agencies, such as members of Congress and agency consultants. See *Department of the Interior v. Klamath Water Users Protective Ass'n,* 532 U.S. 1, 12-16 & n.4 (2001). It does not extend to outside consultants who have a direct interest in the matter that is adverse to others. Id. For a discussion of the cases, see Justice Department's FOIA Guide at http://www.usdoj.gov/oip/foia_guide07/exemption5.pdf.

(6) Personnel and medical files and similar files the disclosure of which would constitute a clearly unwarranted invasion of personal privacy.

In 1982 the Supreme Court defined "similar files" broadly, holding that any information that "applies to a particular individual" may qualify for consideration under Exemption 6. *Department of State v. Washington Post Co.,* 456 U.S. 595, 599-603 (1982). The exemption may only be invoked to protect individuals; neither corporations nor associations possess protectable "personal privacy" interests. See, e.g., *Sims v. CIA,* 642 F.2d 562, 572 n.47 (D.C. Cir. 1980); *National Parks and Conservation Ass'n v. Kleppe,* 547 F.2d 673, 685 n.44 (D.C. Cir. 1976).

In deciding to grant or deny a request for information under Exemption 6, the decisionmaker must balance the severity of the threat to an individual's privacy interest by disclosure against the public interest, if any, in disclosure. *Department of the Air Force v. Rose,* 425 U.S. 352, 372 (1976). The FOIA's words "clearly unwarranted," modifying the phrase "invasion of personal privacy," tilts the balance in favor of disclosure. Id. at 378 n.16. However, where no public interest in disclosure exists, the information should be protected. *National Association of Retired Federal Employees v. Horner*, 879 F.2d 873, 879 (D.C. Cir. 1989). The Supreme Court's decision in *Department of Justice v. Reporters Committee for Freedom of the Press*, 489 U.S. 749 (1989), enunciates principles that guide privacy/public interest balancing under both Exemptions 6 and 7(C) (below). In *National Archives and Records Administration v. Favish*, 541 U.S 157 (2004), the Court held that the privacy interests protected by this exemption include the privacy interests of surviving family members in information concerning a decedent. For a discussion of the cases and the balancing test, see Justice Department's FOIA Guide at http://www.usdoj.gov/oip/foia_guide/exemption6.pdf. For a U.S. Supreme Court decision on the effect of redaction on release of files containing personal information about individuals, see *Department of State v. Ray*, 502 U.S. 164 (1991).

(7) Records or information compiled for law enforcement purposes, but only to the extent that the production of such records or information (A) could reasonably be expected to interfere with enforcement proceedings, (B) would deprive a person of a right to a fair trial or an impartial adjudication, (C) could reasonably be expected to constitute an unwarranted invasion of personal privacy, (D) could reasonably be expected to disclose the identity of a confidential source, including a State, local, or foreign agency or authority or any private institution which furnished information on a confidential basis, and in the case of a record or information compiled by a criminal law enforcement authority in the course of criminal investigation or by an agency conducting a lawful national security intelligence investigation, information furnished by a confidential source, (E) would disclose investigative techniques and procedures for law enforcement investigations or prosecutions if such disclosure could reasonably be expected to risk circumvention of the law, or (F) could reasonably be expected to endanger the life or physical safety of any individual.

When the FOIA was amended in 1974, Exemption 7 was narrowed to allow withholding of investigatory records compiled for law enforcement purposes, but only to the extent that disclosure of the records would cause one of six enumerated harms. Government agencies subsequently complained that the 1974 language provided inadequate protection for confidential sources, ongoing investigations, and law enforcement manuals and other materials.

The FOIA Reform Act of 1986 (Pub. L. No. 99-570, §1802) amended the exemption again to significantly broaden the protection given to law enforcement records.

The FOIA Reform Act removed the requirement that records or information be "investigatory" in character. Thus, the protections listed in Exemption 7's six subparts now apply to all records or information compiled for law enforcement purposes regardless of the format in which it is maintained. The Reform Act also substituted "could reasonably be expected to" for "would" as the standard for the risk of harm with respect to subparagraphs (A) interference with enforcement proceedings, (C) unwarranted invasion of personal privacy, (D) disclosure of the identity of a confidential source, and (F) endangering the life or physical safety of any individual. This change eases a federal law enforcement agency's burden in invoking the exemption (*Department of Justice v. Reporters Committee for Freedom of the Press*, 489 U.S. 749, 756 n.9 (1989). The Act also provided that the term "confidential source" includes state, local and foreign agencies and private institutions. The courts have made clear that "law enforcement purposes" includes records involved in national security and homeland security. See, e.g., *Center for National Security Studies v. United States Department of Justice*, 331 F.3d 918, 926 (D.C. Cir. 2003). For a further discussion of this exemption, see Justice Department's FOIA Guide at http://www.usdoj.gov/oip/foia_guide/exemption7.pdf.

(8) Records that are contained in or related to examination, operating, or condition reports prepared by, on behalf of, or for the use of an agency responsible for the regulation or supervision of financial institutions.

Although the legislative history of this broad exemption is not extensive, it was included to (i) protect the security of financial institutions by withholding reports from the public that contain frank evaluation of an institution's stability and (ii) promote cooperation and communication between financial institution employees and regulatory institution examiners. *Consumers Union of the United States v. Heimann*, 589 F.2d 531 (D.C. Cir. 1978).

(9) Geological or geophysical information and data, including, maps, concerning wells.

Exemption 9 is infrequently invoked. According to the House Report on the 1966 Act, the provision was added after witnesses contended that disclosure of seismic reports and other exploratory findings of oil companies would give speculators an unfair advantage over the companies that had invested heavily in exploration. H.R. Rep. No. 1497, 89th Cong., 2d Sess. 11 (1966).

Judicial Review. A requester may bring suit in district court to compel the production of records wrongfully withheld by an agency (§552(a)(4)(B)-(G)). In addition, an agency's failure to comply with the time limits for either the initial request or the administrative appeal may be treated as a constructive exhaustion of administrative remedies, and a requester may immediately seek judicial review. A court, however, may withhold action if exceptional circumstances exist (defined in §552(a)(6)(C)(ii) and (iii)).

The 1996 FOIA Amendments have substantially limited the circumstances under which agencies may claim exceptional circumstances in responding to the backlog of FOIA requests. Instead of "due diligence," the FOIA now states that agencies must demonstrate "reasonable progress" in reducing its backlog of pending requests before this delay may qualify as an exceptional circumstance (§552 (a)(6)(C)(ii)).

This effect may be moderated by §552(a)(6)(C)(iii), which states that a requester's refusal to modify a request (under §552(a)(6)(B)(ii)) may be considered in determining whether exceptional circumstances exist.

A reviewing court will decide the case de novo and can examine agency records as necessary. The defending agency bears the burden of sustaining its action of withholding records. The agency may be required to prepare a "Vaughn" index (from *Vaughn v. Rosen*, 484 F.2d 820 (D.C. Cir. 1973), *cert. denied*, 415 U.S. 977 (1974)), an itemized index that correlates each withheld document (or portion) with a specific FOIA exemption and the relevant part of the agency's nondisclosure justification.

A plaintiff who has "substantially prevailed" may recover attorneys' fees from the government (§552(a)(4)(E)). The plaintiff must show that prosecution of the suit was reasonably necessary to obtain the information and that a causal connection exists between the suit and the agency's production of the documents (see, e.g., *Weisberg v. Department of Justice*, 745 F.2d 1476, 1448 (D.C. Cir. 1984); *Vermont Low Income Advocacy Council, Inc. v. Usery*, 546 F.2d 509, 513 (2d Cir. 1976)). A fee award is discretionary with the court and is based on four criteria: (1) the public benefit derived from the case; (2) the commercial benefit to the complainant; (3) the nature of the complainant's interest in the records sought; and (4) whether the government's withholding had a reasonable basis in law (*Fenster v. Brown*, 617 F.2d 740, 742 (D.C. Cir. 1979)). But see also *Buckhannon Board & Care Home, Inc. v. West Virginia Dept. of Health and Human Resources*, 532 U.S. 598 (2001), limiting the definition of "prevailing parties."

Agency employees who act arbitrarily or capriciously in withholding information may be subject to disciplinary action (under §552(a)(4)(F)) when the court (i) orders production of records improperly withheld; (ii) awards attorney fees and litigation costs against the government; and (iii) issues specific "written findings" of suspected arbitrary or capricious conduct.

Reports. Each agency must submit electronically an annual report to the Attorney General containing both summaries and details of matters related to the FOIA §552(e). The reports are made available to the public and Congress. This section was considerably beefed up in the 2007 Amendments. The Attorney General must submit an annual report to Congress on litigation and policy activity related to the FOIA.

Legislative History:

Federal laws bearing on public access to government information date to 1789 (see 1 Stat. 28, 49, 65, 68 (1789)). Under the Housekeeping Statute (5 U.S.C. §301) agency heads have long had the authority to control the dissemination of information from the files of their departments. Section 3 of the Administrative Procedure Act of 1946 (the "public disclosure" section, 5 U.S.C. §1002 (1964 ed.)), provided that the public could obtain agency information if (1) the matter was of official public record, (2) no other statute barred release of the information, (3) persons seeking access followed published agency rules, (4) persons seeking access could show a "proper" and "direct" concern, and (5) the agency did not otherwise find good cause to deem the information confidential.

The Freedom of Information Act evolved after a decade of debate among agency officials, legislators, and public interest group representatives (most notably, members of the press). The FOIA, which was shaped largely by the efforts of Representative John Moss, revised the public disclosure section of the Administrative Procedure Act, which had come to be looked upon as falling far short of its disclosure goals. See S. Rep. No. 813, 89th Cong., 1st Sess. 5 (1965).

The FOIA was enacted in 1966 as new section 552 of title 5, United States Code (Pub. L. No. 89-554, Sept. 6, 1966, 80 Stat. 383). The Act provided access to "any person" without requiring a showing of need, ensured the right to go to court to enforce its provisions, and left the agencies no discretion to sidestep its mandatory disclosure requirements. Despite these changes to the APA, the FOIA contained, in the views of many, both procedural and substantive weaknesses. Courts responded to some of the Act's weaknesses by fashioning procedural aids or interpretations, such as the requirement for an agency to provide a detailed index of withheld documents (established in *Vaughn v Rosen*, above) and the requirement that agencies release segregable, nonexempt portions of a partially exempt record (established in *EPA v. Mink*, 410 U.S. 73 (1973)).

Representative Moorhead's House hearings in 1972-73 (see, for example, Administration of the Freedom of Information Act, H.R. Rep. No. 1419, 92d Cong., 2d Sess. (1972)) identified four problems with the 1966 Act:

- Agency refusal to supply information by use of an exemption in the Act was commonplace;
- Long delays in responding to requests often made the information useless once provided;
- Delaying tactics during litigation unreasonably extended both the time and the costs to the requester; and
- Lack of technical compliance with the requirements of the Act, as interpreted by the agency, often led to a refusal to supply requested information.

The FOIA was substantially amended in 1974 to address these problems and also in reaction to the abuses of the Watergate era. The 1974 amendments (Pub. L. No. 93-502, §§1-3, Nov. 21, 1974, 88 Stat. 1561-64) substantially narrowed the scope of the FOIA's law enforcement and national security exemptions, and broadened the procedural provisions relating to fees, time limits, segregability, and in camera inspection of withheld information by the courts.

In 1976 Congress, by means of a rider to the Government in the Sunshine Act (Pub. L. No. 94-409, §5(b), Sept. 13, 1976, 90 Stat. 1241), again limited the agencies' ability to withhold information, this time by narrowing Exemption 3 relating to the incorporation of the non-disclosure provisions of other statutes.

In 1984 Congress eliminated the requirement that FOIA proceedings have precedence over all cases on federal court dockets (Pub. L. No. 98-620, title IV, §402(2), Nov. 8, 1984, 98 Stat. 3357). In 1984 Congress also passed the CIA Information Act (Pub. L. No. 98-477, 98 Stat. 2209), which amended the National Security Act of 1947 to exempt certain operational files of the Central Intelligence Agency from FOIA's search and review requirements. The Act was intended to relieve the CIA of the administrative burden of searching and reviewing files that are almost always classified or otherwise not releasable under FOIA. See H.R. Rep. No. 726, Part 1, 98th Cong., 2d Sess. 4 (1984) (Permanent Select Committee on Intelligence).

In 1986, Congress included FOIA amendments in the Anti-Drug Abuse Act of 1986 (Pub. L. No. 99-570, §§1801-1804, Oct. 27, 1986, 100 Stat. 3207-48–3207-50). The FOIA amendments are in subtitle N, the "Freedom of Information Reform Act of 1986." The Act broadened Exemption 7's applicability to records compiled for law enforcement purposes, established new FOIA fee standards, and required each agency to adopt a schedule of fees that conforms to guidelines promulgated by the Director of the Office of Management and Budget.

In 1996, Congress passed the Electronic Freedom of Information Act Amendments (Pub. L. No. 104-231, Oct. 2, 1996, 110 Stat. 3049-54). These amendments were the fruit of several years' consideration on how to apply the FOIA to electronic records. The legislation required that certain types of agency records be accessible and maintained via electronic formats. It also included several procedural requirements that sought to address agency backlog of FOIA requests and provided for the expedited processing of FOIA requests in certain situations.

In 2002, Congress included an FOIA amendment in the Intelligence Authorization Act (Pub. L. No. 107-306, 116 Stat. 2383, §312). This amendment precludes intelligence agencies from disclosing any records to foreign governments or their representatives.

As noted above, a major amendment was enacted in December 2007 in the OPEN Government Act.

Source Note:

The Justice Department maintains a website devoted to the FOIA. See http://www.usdoj.gov/04foia/index.html. Documents the Department previously published can now be found linked to this site. Among these is the Department's Freedom of Information Act Guide, published biennially, which contains a detailed discussion of the Act's exemptions and procedural requirements. It also elaborates on many of the terms used in the Act and points the reader to significant cases bearing on the various provisions of the FOIA. The Guide is available either in book format or through the DOJ's FOIA website at: http://www.usdoj.gov/oip/foia_guide07.htm. A number of other documents, including the Freedom of Information Case List, which was published biennially until 2002 (last published in May 2002) and containing an extensive bibliography of FOIA-related materials and relevant case law on the FOIA, can be found online at: http://www.usdoj.gov/oip/cl-tofc.html.

Another valuable source of practical information about, and interpretation of, the FOIA is Litigation Under the Federal Open Government Laws: the Freedom of Information Act, the Privacy Act, the Government in the Sunshine Act, and the Federal Advisory Committee Act. The most recent edition, by Harry Hammit, David Sobel, and Tiffany Stedman, was published in 2004 by the Electronic Privacy Information Center.

Bibliography:

I. Legislative History

1. House of Representatives Committee on Government Operations, A Citizen's Guide on How to Use the Freedom of Information Act and the Privacy Act of 1974 to Request Government Records, H.R. Rep. No. 50, 106th Cong., 1st Sess. (1999). The 1997 version is available at http://www.tncrimlaw.com/foia/I.html.
2. House of Representatives Committee on Government Operations, Clarifying and Protecting the Right of the Public to Information, H.R. Rep. No. 1497, 89th Cong., 2d Sess. (1966).
3. House of Representatives Committee on Government Reform and Oversight, Electronic Freedom of Information Amendments of 1996, H.R. Rep. No. 795, 104th Cong., 2d Sess. (1996).
4. House of Representatives Committee on Government Reform and Oversight, Implementation of the Electronic Freedom of Information Act Amendments of 1996: Is Access to Government Information Improving? Hearing, 105th Cong., 2d Sess. (1998). (Unpublished at time of printing.)
5. House of Representatives Committee on Government Operations, Freedom of Information Act Requests for Business Data and Reverse FOIA Lawsuits, H.R. Rep. No. 1382, 95th Cong., 2d Sess. (1978).
6. Senate Committee on the Judiciary, Clarifying and Protecting the Right of the Public to Information, and Other Purposes, S. Rep. No. 813, 89th Cong., 1st Sess. (1965).
7. Senate Committee on the Judiciary, Electronic Freedom of Information Improvement Act of 1995, S. Rep. No. 272, 104th Cong., 2d Sess. (1996).
8. Senate Committee in the Judiciary, Freedom of Information Reform Act, S. Rep. No. 221, 98th Cong., 1st Sess. (1983).
9. Senate Committee on the Judiciary, Freedom of Information Act Source Book: Legislative Materials, Cases, Articles, S. Doc. No. 82, 93d Cong., 2d Sess. (1974).

10. Staffs of House of Representatives Committee on Government Operations and Senate Committee on the Judiciary, Freedom of Information Act, 94th Cong., 1st Sess. (Joint Committee Print 1975).

II. Other Government Documents

1. Attorney General's Memorandum on the Public Information Section of the Administrative Procedure Act (FOIA) (June 1967, 40 pages) (Out of print; reprinted in Prentice-Hall, Inc., Government Disclosure Service, vol. 1 ¶300,601).
2. Attorney General's Memorandum on the 1974 Amendments to the Freedom of Information Act (Feb. 1975).
3. Attorney General's Memorandum on the 1986 Amendments to the Freedom of Information Act (Dec. 1987).
4. Attorney General's Memorandum for Heads of All Federal Departments and Agencies Regarding the FOIA (October 2001).
5. U.S. Department of Justice, FOIA Update, a newsletter of information and guidance for federal agencies, that was published quarterly by the Office of Information and Privacy during the period 1979-2000, can be found at http://www.usdoj.gov/oip/foi-upd.htm.
6. U.S. Department of Justice, Freedom of Information Case List, an alphabetical compilation of judicial decisions addressing access issues under the Freedom of Information Act and Privacy Act, published biennially until 2002 by the Office of Information and Privacy. Includes a topical index to the cases, texts of the acts, and a comprehensive FOIA bibliography. (Available from the Superintendent of Documents, U.S. Government Printing Office, Washington, DC 20402, or at http://www.usdoj.gov/oip/cl-tofc.html.)
7. Citizen's Guide on Using the Freedom of Information Act and the Privacy Act of 1974 to Request Government Records, Second Report by the Committee on Government Reform, H. Report 109-226, 109th Cong. 1st Sess., available at http://www.fas.org/sgp/foia/citizen.html.
8. General Services Administration and the U.S. Department of Justice, Your Right to Federal Records (2006). (Available from the Consumer Information Center, Department 319E, Pueblo, CO 81009, publication number: 320N, or online at: http://www.pueblo.gsa.gov/cic_text/fed_prog/foia/foia.htm.)
9. U.S. Department of Justice, Freedom of Information Act Guide, March 2007. (Available from the Superintendent of Documents, U.S. Government Printing Office, Washington, DC 20402, or at http://www.usdoj.gov/oip/foia_guide07.htm.)

10. Executive Order 13,392, Improving Agency Disclosure of Information, December 14, 2005.

11. Executive Order 13,392 Implementation Guidance, April 27, 2006.

III. Nongovernment Publications

1. Access Reports, a biweekly newsletter published by Access Reports, Inc., Lynchburg, Va.

2. Litigation under the Federal Open Government Laws: the Freedom of Information Act, the Privacy Act, the Government in the Sunshine Act, the Federal Advisory Committee Act, 22d edition (Electronic Privacy Information Center, 2004).

3. J.T. O'Reilly, Federal Information Disclosure (West Group, Rochester, N.Y. 14694) (3d ed. 2000, annual supplements).

IV. Other FOIA Articles

Several hundred articles dealing with the Freedom of Information Act have been published in law reviews and other journals and periodicals. An extensive listing may be found in the Freedom of Information Case List, published biennially by the Department of Justice, through 2002, cited above.

Agency Regulations:

Pursuant to E.O. 13,392, Improving Agency Disclosure of Information, all agencies maintain websites providing information on how the agency complies with that executive order and the FOIA. Links to all of these websites can be found at the Department of Justice FOIA website: http://www.usdoj.gov/04foia/other_age.htm.

Appendix:

1. Freedom of Information Act, 5 U.S.C. §552 (Supp. II 2000) & Supp. IV 2004.

2. Executive Order No. 12,600, Predisclosure Notification Procedures for Confidential Commercial Information (52 Fed. Reg. 23,781, June 23, 1987).

3. Executive Order No. 13,392, Improving Agency Disclosure of Information (70 Fed. Reg. 75,373, December 19, 2005).

Freedom of Information Act
Title 5, U.S. Code

§552. Public information; agency rules, opinions, orders, records, and proceedings

(a) Each agency shall make available to the public information as follows:

(1) Each agency shall separately state and currently publish in the Federal Register for the guidance of the public—

(A) descriptions of its central and field organization and the established places at which, the employees (and in the case of a uniformed service, the members) from whom, and the methods whereby, the public may obtain information, make submittals or requests, or obtain decisions;

(B) statements of the general course and method by which its functions are channeled and determined, including the nature and requirements of all formal and informal procedures available;

(C) rules of procedure, descriptions of forms available or the places at which forms may be obtained, and instructions as to the scope and contents of all papers, reports, or examinations;

(D) substantive rules of general applicability adopted as authorized by law, and statements of general policy or interpretations of general applicability formulated and adopted by the agency; and

(E) each amendment, revision, or repeal of the foregoing. Except to the extent that a person has actual and timely notice of the terms thereof, a person may not in any manner be required to resort to, or be adversely affected by, a matter required to be published in the Federal Register and not so published. For the purpose of this paragraph, matter reasonably available to the class of persons affected thereby is deemed published in the Federal Register when incorporated by reference therein with the approval of the Director of the Federal Register.

(2) Each agency, in accordance with published rules, shall make available for public inspection and copying—

(A) final opinions, including concurring and dissenting opinions, as well as orders, made in the adjudication of cases;

(B) those statements of policy and interpretations which have been adopted by the agency and are not published in the Federal Register;

(C) administrative staff manuals and instructions to staff that affect a member of the public;

(D) copies of all records, regardless of form or format, which have been released to any person under paragraph (3) and which, because of the nature of their subject matter, the agency determines have become or are likely to become the subject of subsequent requests for substantially the same records; and

(E) a general index of the records referred to under subparagraph (D); unless the materials are promptly published and copies offered for sale. For records created on or after November 1, 1996, within one year after such date, each agency shall make such records available, including by computer telecommunications or, if computer telecommunications means have not been established by the agency, by other electronic means. To the extent required to prevent a clearly unwarranted invasion of personal privacy, an agency may delete identifying details when it makes available or publishes an opinion, statement of policy, interpretation, staff manual, instruction, or copies of records referred to in subparagraph (D). However, in each case the justification for the deletion shall be explained fully in writing, and the extent of such deletion shall be indicated on the portion of the record which is made available or published, unless including that indication would harm an interest protected by the exemption in subsection (b) under which the deletion is made. If technically feasible, the extent of the deletion shall be indicated at the place in the record where the deletion was made. Each agency shall also maintain and make available for public inspection and copying current indexes providing identifying information for the public as to any matter issued, adopted, or promulgated after July 4, 1967, and required by this paragraph to be made available or published. Each agency shall promptly publish, quarterly or more frequently, and distribute (by sale or otherwise) copies of each index or supplements thereto unless it determines by order published in the Federal Register that the publication would be unnecessary and impracticable, in which case the agency shall nonetheless provide copies of such index on request at a cost not to exceed the direct cost of duplication. Each agency shall make the index referred to in subparagraph (E) available by computer telecommunications by December 31, 1999. A final order, opinion, statement of policy, interpretation, or staff manual or instruction that affects a member of the public may be relied on, used, or cited as precedent by an agency against a party other than an agency only if—

(i) it has been indexed and either made available or published as provided by this paragraph; or

(ii) the party has actual and timely notice of the terms thereof.

(3)(A) Except with respect to the records made available under paragraphs (1) and (2) of this subsection, and except as provided in subparagraph (E), each agency, upon any request for records which (i) reasonably describes such records and (ii) is made in accordance with published rules stating the time, place, fees (if any), and procedures to be followed, shall make the records promptly available to any person.

(B) In making any record available to a person under this paragraph, an agency shall provide the record in any form or format requested by the person if the record is readily reproducible by the agency in that form or format. Each agency shall make reasonable efforts to maintain its records in forms or formats that are reproducible for purposes of this section.

(C) In responding under this paragraph to a request for records, an agency shall make reasonable efforts to search for the records in electronic form or format, except when such efforts would significantly interfere with the operation of the agency's automated information system.

(D) For purposes of this paragraph, the term "search" means to review, manually or by automated means, agency records for the purpose of locating those records which are responsive to a request.

(E) An agency, or part of an agency, that is an element of the intelligence community (as that term is defined in section 3(4) of the National Security Act of 1947 (50 U.S.C. 401a(4))) shall not make any record available under this paragraph to—

(i) any government entity, other than a State, territory, commonwealth, or district of the United States, or any subdivision thereof; or

(ii) a representative of a government entity described in clause (i).

(4)(A)(i) In order to carry out the provisions of this section, each agency shall promulgate regulations, pursuant to notice and receipt of public comment, specifying the schedule of fees applicable to the processing of requests under this section and establishing procedures and guidelines for determining when such fees should be waived or reduced. Such schedule shall conform to the guidelines which shall be promulgated, pursuant to notice and receipt of public comment, by the Director of the Office of Management and Budget and which shall provide for a uniform schedule of fees for all agencies.

(ii) Such agency regulations shall provide that—

(I) fees shall be limited to reasonable standard charges for document search, duplication, and review, when records are requested for commercial use;

(II) fees shall be limited to reasonable standard charges for document duplication when records are not sought for commercial use and the request is made by an educational or noncommercial scientific institution, whose purpose is scholarly or scientific research; or a representative of the news media; and

(III) for any request not described in (I) or (II), fees shall be limited to reasonable standard charges for document search and duplication.

In this clause, the term "a representative of the news media" means any person or entity that gathers information of potential interest to a segment of the public, uses its editorial skills to turn the raw materials into a distinct work, and distributes that work to an audience. In this clause, the term "news" means information that is about current events or that would be of current interest to the public. Examples of news-media entities are television or radio stations broadcasting to the public at large and publishers of periodicals (but only if such entities qualify as disseminators of "news") who make their products available for purchase by or subscription by or free distribution to the general public. These examples are not all-inclusive. Moreover, as methods of news delivery evolve (for example, the adoption of the electronic dissemination of newspapers through telecommunications services), such alternative media shall be considered to be news-media entities. A freelance journalist shall be regarded as working for a news-media entity if the journalist can demonstrate a solid basis for expecting publication through that entity, whether or not the journalist is actually employed by the entity. A publication contract would present a solid basis for such an expectation; the Government may also consider the past publication record of the requester in making such a determination.

(iii) Documents shall be furnished without any charge or at a charge reduced below the fees established under clause (ii) if disclosure of the information is in the public interest because it is likely to contribute significantly to public understanding of the operations or activities of the government and is not primarily in the commercial interest of the requester.

(iv) Fee schedules shall provide for the recovery of only the direct costs of search, duplication, or review. Review costs shall include only the direct costs incurred during the initial examination of a document for the purposes of determining whether the documents must be disclosed under this section and for the purposes of withholding any portions exempt from disclosure under this section. Review costs may not include any costs incurred in resolving issues of law or policy that may be raised in the course of processing a request under this section. No fee may be charged by any agency under this section—

(I) if the costs of routine collection and processing of the fee are likely to equal or exceed the amount of the fee; or

(II) for any request described in clause (ii) (II) or (III) of this subparagraph for the first two hours of search time or for the first one hundred pages of duplication.

(v) No agency may require advance payment of any fee unless the requester has previously failed to pay fees in a timely fashion, or the agency has determined that the fee will exceed $250.

(vi) Nothing in this subparagraph shall supersede fees chargeable under a statute specifically providing for setting the level of fees for particular types of records.

(vii) In any action by a requester regarding the waiver of fees under this section, the court shall determine the matter de novo: Provided, That the court's review of the matter shall be limited to the record before the agency.

(viii) An agency shall not assess search fees (or in the case of a requester described under clause (ii)(II), duplication fees) under this subparagraph if the agency fails to comply with any time limit under paragraph (6), if no unusual or exceptional circumstances (as those terms are defined for purposes of paragraphs (6)(B) and (C), respectively) apply to the processing of the request.

(B) On complaint, the district court of the United States in the district in which the complainant resides, or has his principal place of business, or in which the agency records are situated, or in the District of Columbia, has jurisdiction to enjoin the agency from withholding agency records and to order the production of any agency records improperly withheld from the complainant. In such a case the court shall determine the matter de novo, and may examine the contents of such agency records in camera to determine whether such records or any part thereof shall be withheld under any of the exemptions set forth in subsection (b) of this section, and the burden is on the agency to sustain its action. In addition to any other matters to which a court accords substantial weight, a court shall accord substantial weight to an affidavit of an agency concerning the agency's determination as to technical feasibility under paragraph (2)(C) and subsection (b) and reproducibility under paragraph (3)(B).

(C) Notwithstanding any other provision of law, the defendant shall serve an answer or otherwise plead to any complaint made under this subsection within thirty days after service upon the defendant of the pleading in which such complaint is made, unless the court otherwise directs for good cause shown.

(D) Repealed. Pub. L. 98-620, title IV, Sec. 402(2), Nov. 8, 1984, 98 Stat. 3357.

(E)*(i)*The court may assess against the United States reasonable attorney fees and other litigation costs reasonably incurred in any case under this section in which the complainant has substantially prevailed.

(ii) For purposes of this subparagraph, a complainant has substantially prevailed if the complainant has obtained relief through either—

(I) a judicial order, or an enforceable written agreement or consent decree; or

(II) a voluntary or unilateral change in position by the agency, if the complainant's claim is not insubstantial.[1]

(F)(*i*) Whenever the court orders the production of any agency records improperly withheld from the complainant and assesses against the United States reasonable attorney fees and other litigation costs, and the court additionally issues a written finding that the circumstances surrounding the withholding raise questions whether agency personnel acted arbitrarily or capriciously with respect to the withholding, the Special Counsel shall promptly initiate a proceeding to determine whether disciplinary action is warranted against the officer or employee who was primarily responsible for the withholding. The Special Counsel, after investigation and consideration of the evidence submitted, shall submit his findings and recommendations to the administrative authority of the agency concerned and shall send copies of the findings and recommendations to the officer or employee or his representative. The administrative authority shall take the corrective action that the Special Counsel recommends.

(ii) The Attorney General shall—

(I) notify the Special Counsel of each civil action described under the first sentence of clause (i); and

(II) annually submit a report to Congress on the number of such civil actions in the preceding year.

(iii) The Special Counsel shall annually submit a report to Congress on the actions taken by the Special Counsel under clause (i).

(G) In the event of noncompliance with the order of the court, the district court may punish for contempt the responsible employee, and in the case of a uniformed service, the responsible member.

---

[1] The OPEN Government Act of 2007, §4(b), contained the following restriction:

> Limitation—Notwithstanding section 1304 of title 31, United States Code, no amounts may be obligated or expended from the Claims and Judgment Fund of the United States Treasury to pay the costs resulting from fees assessed under section 552(a)(4)(E) of title 5, United States Code. Any such amounts shall be paid only from funds annually appropriated for any authorized purpose for the Federal agency against which a claim or judgment has been rendered.

(5) Each agency having more than one member shall maintain and make available for public inspection a record of the final votes of each member in every agency proceeding.

(6)(A) Each agency, upon any request for records made under paragraph (1), (2), or (3) of this subsection, shall—

(i) determine within 20 days (excepting Saturdays, Sundays, and legal public holidays) after the receipt of any such request whether to comply with such request and shall immediately notify the person making such request of such determination and the reasons therefor, and of the right of such person to appeal to the head of the agency any adverse determination; and

(ii) make a determination with respect to any appeal within twenty days (excepting Saturdays, Sundays, and legal public holidays) after the receipt of such appeal. If on appeal the denial of the request for records is in whole or in part upheld, the agency shall notify the person making such request of the provisions for judicial review of that determination under paragraph (4) of this subsection. *The 20-day period under clause (i) shall commence on the date on which the request is first received by the appropriate component of the agency, but in any event not later than ten days after the request is first received by any component of the agency that is designated in the agency's regulations under this section to receive requests under this section. The 20-day period shall not be tolled by the agency except—*

(I) that the agency may make one request to the requester for information and toll the 20-day period while it is awaiting such information that it has reasonably requested from the requester under this section; or

(II) if necessary to clarify with the requester issues regarding fee assessment. In either case, the agency's receipt of the requester's response to the agency's request for information or clarification ends the tolling period.[2]

(B)(i) In unusual circumstances as specified in this subparagraph, the time limits prescribed in either clause (i) or clause (ii) of subparagraph (A) may be extended by written notice to the person making such request setting forth the unusual circumstances for such extension and the date on which a determination is expected to be dispatched. No such notice shall specify a date that would result in an extension for more than ten working days, except as provided in clause (ii) of this subparagraph.

---

[2] The OPEN Government Act of 2007, §6(a)(2), provided that: "The amendment made by this subsection shall take effect 1 year after the date of enactment of this Act." This applies only to the portion of this provision beginning "The 20-day period under clause (i). . . ." The Act was enacted in late December 2007.

(ii) With respect to a request for which a written notice under clause (i) extends the time limits prescribed under clause (i) of subparagraph (A), the agency shall notify the person making the request if the request cannot be processed within the time limit specified in that clause and shall provide the person an opportunity to limit the scope of the request so that it may be processed within that time limit or an opportunity to arrange with the agency an alternative time frame for processing the request or a modified request. *To aid the requester, each agency shall make available its FOIA Public Liaison, who shall assist in the resolution of any disputes between the requester and the agency.*[3] Refusal by the person to reasonably modify the request or arrange such an alternative time frame shall be considered as a factor in determining whether exceptional circumstances exist for purposes of subparagraph (C).

(iii) As used in this subparagraph, "unusual circumstances" means, but only to the extent reasonably necessary to the proper processing of the particular requests—

(I) the need to search for and collect the requested records from field facilities or other establishments that are separate from the office processing the request;

(II) the need to search for, collect, and appropriately examine a voluminous amount of separate and distinct records which are demanded in a single request; or

(III) the need for consultation, which shall be conducted with all practicable speed, with another agency having a substantial interest in the determination of the request or among two or more components of the agency having substantial subject-matter interest therein.

(iv) Each agency may promulgate regulations, pursuant to notice and receipt of public comment, providing for the aggregation of certain requests by the same requestor, or by a group of requestors acting in concert, if the agency reasonably believes that such requests actually constitute a single request, which would otherwise satisfy the unusual circumstances specified in this subparagraph, and the requests involve clearly related matters. Multiple requests involving unrelated matters shall not be aggregated.

---

[3] The OPEN Government Act of 2007, §6(b)(1)(B), provided that: "The amendment made by this subsection shall take effect 1 year after the date of enactment of this Act and apply to requests for information under section 552 of title 5, United States Code, filed on or after that effective date." This applies to the footnoted sentence only. *See id.*

(C)(i) Any person making a request to any agency for records under paragraph (1), (2), or (3) of this subsection shall be deemed to have exhausted his administrative remedies with respect to such request if the agency fails to comply with the applicable time limit provisions of this paragraph. If the Government can show exceptional circumstances exist and that the agency is exercising due diligence in responding to the request, the court may retain jurisdiction and allow the agency additional time to complete its review of the records. Upon any determination by an agency to comply with a request for records, the records shall be made promptly available to such person making such request. Any notification of denial of any request for records under this subsection shall set forth the names and titles or positions of each person responsible for the denial of such request.

(ii) For purposes of this subparagraph, the term "exceptional circumstances" does not include a delay that results from a predictable agency workload of requests under this section, unless the agency demonstrates reasonable progress in reducing its backlog of pending requests.

(iii) Refusal by a person to reasonably modify the scope of a request or arrange an alternative time frame for processing a request (or a modified request) under clause (ii) after being given an opportunity to do so by the agency to whom the person made the request shall be considered as a factor in determining whether exceptional circumstances exist for purposes of this subparagraph.

(D)(i) Each agency may promulgate regulations, pursuant to notice and receipt of public comment, providing for multitrack processing of requests for records based on the amount of work or time (or both) involved in processing requests.

(ii) Regulations under this subparagraph may provide a person making a request that does not qualify for the fastest multitrack processing an opportunity to limit the scope of the request in order to qualify for faster processing.

(iii) This subparagraph shall not be considered to affect the requirement under subparagraph (C) to exercise due diligence.

(E)(i) Each agency shall promulgate regulations, pursuant to notice and receipt of public comment, providing for expedited processing of requests for records—

(I) in cases in which the person requesting the records demonstrates a compelling need; and

(II) in other cases determined by the agency.

(ii) Notwithstanding clause (i), regulations under this subparagraph must ensure—

(I) that a determination of whether to provide expedited processing shall be made, and notice of the determination shall be provided to the person making the request, within 10 days after the date of the request; and

(II) expeditious consideration of administrative appeals of such determinations of whether to provide expedited processing.

(iii) An agency shall process as soon as practicable any request for records to which the agency has granted expedited processing under this subparagraph. Agency action to deny or affirm denial of a request for expedited processing pursuant to this subparagraph, and failure by an agency to respond in a timely manner to such a request shall be subject to judicial review under paragraph (4), except that the judicial review shall be based on the record before the agency at the time of the determination.

(iv) A district court of the United States shall not have jurisdiction to review an agency denial of expedited processing of a request for records after the agency has provided a complete response to the request.

(v) For purposes of this subparagraph, the term "compelling need" means—

(I) that a failure to obtain requested records on an expedited basis under this paragraph could reasonably be expected to pose an imminent threat to the life or physical safety of an individual; or

(II) with respect to a request made by a person primarily engaged in disseminating information, urgency to inform the public concerning actual or alleged Federal Government activity.

(vi) A demonstration of a compelling need by a person making a request for expedited processing shall be made by a statement certified by such person to be true and correct to the best of such person's knowledge and belief.

(F) In denying a request for records, in whole or in part, an agency shall make a reasonable effort to estimate the volume of any requested matter the provision of which is denied, and shall provide any such estimate to the person making the request, unless providing such estimate would harm an interest protected by the exemption in subsection (b) pursuant to which the denial is made.

(7) Each agency shall—

(A) establish a system to assign an individualized tracking number for each request received that will take longer than ten days to process and provide to each person making a request the tracking number assigned to the request; and

(B) establish a telephone line or Internet service that provides information about the status of a request to the person making the request using the assigned tracking number, including—

(i) the date on which the agency originally received the request; and

(ii) an estimated date on which the agency will complete action on the request.[4]

(b) This section does not apply to matters that are—

(1)(A) specifically authorized under criteria established by an Executive order to be kept secret in the interest of national defense or foreign policy and (B) are in fact properly classified pursuant to such Executive order;

(2) related solely to the internal personnel rules and practices of an agency;

(3) specifically exempted from disclosure by statute (other than section 552b of this title), provided that such statute (A) requires that the matters be withheld from the public in such a manner as to leave no discretion on the issue, or (B) establishes particular criteria for withholding or refers to particular types of matters to be withheld;

(4) trade secrets and commercial or financial information obtained from a person and privileged or confidential;

(5) inter-agency or intra-agency memorandums or letters which would not be available by law to a party other than an agency in litigation with the agency;

(6) personnel and medical files and similar files the disclosure of which would constitute a clearly unwarranted invasion of personal privacy;

(7) records or information compiled for law enforcement purposes, but only to the extent that the production of such law enforcement records or information (A) could reasonably be expected to interfere with enforcement proceedings, (B) would deprive a person of a right to a fair trial or an impartial adjudication, (C) could reasonably be expected to constitute an unwarranted invasion of personal privacy, (D) could reasonably be expected to disclose the identity of a confidential source, including a State, local, or foreign agency or authority or any private institution which furnished information on a confidential basis, and, in the case of a record or information compiled by criminal law enforcement authority in the course of a criminal investigation or by an agency conducting a lawful national security intelligence investigation, information furnished by a confidential source, (E) would disclose techniques and procedures for law enforcement investigations or prosecutions, or would disclose guidelines for law enforcement investigations or

---

[4] The OPEN Government Act of 2007, §7(b), provided that: The amendment made by this section shall take effect 1 year after the date of enactment of this Act and apply to requests for information under section 552 of title 5, United States Code, filed on or after that effective date. This applies only to subsection (7). *See id.*

prosecutions if such disclosure could reasonably be expected to risk circumvention of the law, or (F) could reasonably be expected to endanger the life or physical safety of any individual;

(8) contained in or related to examination, operating, or condition reports prepared by, on behalf of, or for the use of an agency responsible for the regulation or supervision of financial institutions; or

(9) geological and geophysical information and data, including maps, concerning wells.

Any reasonably segregable portion of a record shall be provided to any person requesting such record after deletion of the portions which are exempt under this subsection. The amount of information deleted, *and the exemption under which the deletion is made,* shall be indicated on the released portion of the record, unless including that indication would harm an interest protected by the exemption in this subsection under which the deletion is made. If technically feasible, the amount of the information deleted, *and the exemption under which the deletion is made,* shall be indicated at the place in the record where such deletion is made.

(c)(1) Whenever a request is made which involves access to records described in subsection (b)(7)(A) and—

(A) the investigation or proceeding involves a possible violation of criminal law; and

(B) there is reason to believe that (i) the subject of the investigation or proceeding is not aware of its pendency, and (ii) disclosure of the existence of the records could reasonably be expected to interfere with enforcement proceedings, the agency may, during only such time as that circumstance continues, treat the records as not subject to the requirements of this section.

(2) Whenever informant records maintained by a criminal law enforcement agency under an informant's name or personal identifier are requested by a third party according to the informant's name or personal identifier, the agency may treat the records as not subject to the requirements of this section unless the informant's status as an informant has been officially confirmed.

(3) Whenever a request is made which involves access to records maintained by the Federal Bureau of Investigation pertaining to foreign intelligence or counterintelligence, or international terrorism, and the existence of the records is classified information as provided in subsection (b)(1), the Bureau may, as long as the existence of the records remains classified information, treat the records as not subject to the requirements of this section.

(d) This section does not authorize withholding of information or limit the availability of records to the public, except as specifically stated in this section. This section is not authority to withhold information from Congress.

(e)(1) On or before February 1 of each year, each agency shall submit to the Attorney General of the United States a report which shall cover the preceding fiscal year and which shall include—

(A) the number of determinations made by the agency not to comply with requests for records made to such agency under subsection (a) and the reasons for each such determination;

(B)(i) the number of appeals made by persons under subsection (a)(6), the result of such appeals, and the reason for the action upon each appeal that results in a denial of information; and

(ii) a complete list of all statutes that the agency relies upon to authorize the agency to withhold information under subsection (b)(3), the number of occasions on which each statute was relied upon, a description of whether a court has upheld the decision of the agency to withhold information under each such statute, and a concise description of the scope of any information withheld;

(C) the number of requests for records pending before the agency as of September 30 of the preceding year, and the median *and average* number of days that such requests had been pending before the agency as of that date;

(D) the number of requests for records received by the agency and the number of requests which the agency processed;

(E) the median number of days taken by the agency to process different types of requests, *based on the date on which the requests were received by the agency;*

(F) the average number of days for the agency to respond to a request beginning on the date on which the request was received by the agency, the median number of days for the agency to respond to such requests, and the range in number of days for the agency to respond to such requests;

(G) based on the number of business days that have elapsed since each request was originally received by the agency—

(i) the number of requests for records to which the agency has responded with a determination within a period up to and including 20 days, and in 20-day increments up to and including 200 days;

(ii) the number of requests for records to which the agency has responded with a determination within a period greater than 200 days and less than 301 days;

(iii) the number of requests for records to which the agency has responded with a determination within a period greater than 300 days and less than 401 days; and

(iv) the number of requests for records to which the agency has responded with a determination within a period greater than 400 days;

(H) *the average number of days for the agency to provide the granted information beginning on the date on which the request was originally filed, the median number of days for the agency to provide the granted information, and the range in number of days for the agency to provide the granted information;*

(I) the median and average number of days for the agency to respond to administrative appeals based on the date on which the appeals originally were received by the agency, the highest number of business days taken by the agency to respond to an administrative appeal, and the lowest number of business days taken by the agency to respond to an administrative appeal;

(J) data on the 10 active requests with the earliest filing dates pending at each agency, including the amount of time that has elapsed since each request was originally received by the agency;

(K) data on the 10 active administrative appeals with the earliest filing dates pending before the agency as of September 30 of the preceding year, including the number of business days that have elapsed since the requests were originally received by the agency;

(L) the number of expedited review requests that are granted and denied, the average and median number of days for adjudicating expedited review requests, and the number adjudicated within the required 10 days;

(M) the number of fee waiver requests that are granted and denied, and the average and median number of days for adjudicating fee waiver determinations;

(FN) the total amount of fees collected by the agency for processing requests; and

(GO) the number of full-time staff of the agency devoted to processing requests for records under this section, and the total amount expended by the agency for processing such requests.

(2) Information in each report submitted under paragraph (1) shall be expressed in terms of each principal component of the agency and for the agency overall.

(23) Each agency shall make each such report available to the public including by computer telecommunications, or if computer telecommunications means have not been established by the agency, by other electronic means. In addition, each agency shall make the raw statistical data used in its reports available electronically to the public upon request.

(34) The Attorney General of the United States shall make each report which has been made available by electronic means available at a single electronic access point. The Attorney General of the United States shall notify the Chairman and ranking minority member of the Committee on Government

Reform and Oversight of the House of Representatives and the Chairman and ranking minority member of the Committees on Governmental Affairs and the Judiciary of the Senate, no later than April 1 of the year in which each such report is issued, that such reports are available by electronic means.

(45) The Attorney General of the United States, in consultation with the Director of the Office of Management and Budget, shall develop reporting and performance guidelines in connection with reports required by this subsection by October 1, 1997, and may establish additional requirements for such reports as the Attorney General determines may be useful.

(56) The Attorney General of the United States shall submit an annual report on or before April 1 of each calendar year which shall include for the prior calendar year a listing of the number of cases arising under this section, the exemption involved in each case, the disposition of such case, and the cost, fees, and penalties assessed under subparagraphs (E), (F), and (G) of subsection (a)(4). Such report shall also include a description of the efforts undertaken by the Department of Justice to encourage agency compliance with this section.

(f) For purposes of this section, the term—

(1) "agency" as defined in section 551(1) of this title includes any executive department, military department, Government corporation, Government controlled corporation, or other establishment in the executive branch of the Government (including the Executive Office of the President), or any independent regulatory agency; and

(2) ~~"record" and any other term used in this section in reference to information includes any information that would be an agency record subject to the requirements of this section when maintained by an agency in any format, including an electronic format.~~

"record" and any other term used in this section in reference to information includes—

(A) any information that would be an agency record subject to the requirements of this section when maintained by an agency in any format, including an electronic format; and

(B) any information described under subparagraph (A) that is maintained for an agency by an entity under Government contract, for the purposes of records management.

(g) The head of each agency shall prepare and make publicly available upon request, reference material or a guide for requesting records or information from the agency, subject to the exemptions in subsection (b), including—

(1) an index of all major information systems of the agency;

(2) a description of major information and record locator systems maintained by the agency; and

(3) a handbook for obtaining various types and categories of public information from the agency pursuant to chapter 35 of title 44, and under this section.

(h)(1) There is established the Office of Government Information Services within the National Archives and Records Administration.

(2) The Office of Government Information Services shall—

(A) review policies and procedures of administrative agencies under this section;

(B) review compliance with this section by administrative agencies; and

(C) recommend policy changes to Congress and the President to improve the administration of this section.

(3) The Office of Government Information Services shall offer mediation services to resolve disputes between persons making requests under this section and administrative agencies as a non-exclusive alternative to litigation and, at the discretion of the Office, may issue advisory opinions if mediation has not resolved the dispute.

(i) The Government Accountability Office shall conduct audits of administrative agencies on the implementation of this section and issue reports detailing the results of such audits.

(j) Each agency shall designate a Chief FOIA Officer who shall be a senior official of such agency (at the Assistant Secretary or equivalent level).

(k) The Chief FOIA Officer of each agency shall, subject to the authority of the head of the agency—

(1) have agency-wide responsibility for efficient and appropriate compliance with this section;

(2) monitor implementation of this section throughout the agency and keep the head of the agency, the chief legal officer of the agency, and the Attorney General appropriately informed of the agency's performance in implementing this section;

(3) recommend to the head of the agency such adjustments to agency practices, policies, personnel, and funding as may be necessary to improve its implementation of this section;

(4) review and report to the Attorney General, through the head of the agency, at such times and in such formats as the Attorney General may direct, on the agency's performance in implementing this section;

(5) facilitate public understanding of the purposes of the statutory exemptions of this section by including concise descriptions of the exemptions in both the agency's handbook issued under subsection (g), and the agency's

annual report on this section, and by providing an overview, where appropriate, of certain general categories of agency records to which those exemptions apply; and

(6) designate one or more FOIA Public Liaisons.

(l) FOIA Public Liaisons shall report to the agency Chief FOIA Officer and shall serve as supervisory officials to whom a requester under this section can raise concerns about the service the requester has received from the FOIA Requester Center, following an initial response from the FOIA Requester Center Staff. FOIA Public Liaisons shall be responsible for assisting in reducing delays, increasing transparency and understanding of the status of requests, and assisting in the resolution of disputes.

* * * *

The following findings were made in enacting The OPEN Government Act of 2007, §2.

Congress finds that—

(1) the Freedom of Information Act was signed into law on July 4, 1966, because the American people believe that—

(A) our constitutional democracy, our system of selfgovernment, and our commitment to popular sovereignty depends upon the consent of the governed;

(B) such consent is not meaningful unless it is informed consent; and

(C) as Justice Black noted in his concurring opinion in Barr v. Matteo (360 U.S. 564 (1959)), "The effective functioning of a free government like ours depends largely on the force of an informed public opinion. This calls for the widest possible understanding of the quality of government service rendered by all elective or appointed public officials or employees.";

(2) the American people firmly believe that our system of government must itself be governed by a presumption of openness;

(3) the Freedom of Information Act establishes a "strong presumption in favor of disclosure" as noted by the United States Supreme Court in United States Department of State v. Ray (502 U.S. 164 (1991)), a presumption that applies to all agencies governed by that Act;

(4) "disclosure, not secrecy, is the dominant objective of the Act," as noted by the United States Supreme Court in Department of Air Force v. Rose (425 U.S. 352 (1976));

(5) in practice, the Freedom of Information Act has not always lived up to the ideals of that Act; and

(6) Congress should regularly review section 552 of title 5, United States Code (commonly referred to as the Freedom of Information Act), in order to determine whether further changes and improvements are necessary to ensure that the Government remains open and accessible to the American people and is always based not upon the "need to know" but upon the fundamental "right to know".

The following provision was part of The OPEN Government Act of 2007, §11, and will likely be found at §5 U.S.C. 552 (note).

Not later than 1 year after the date of enactment of this Act, the Office of Personnel Management shall submit to Congress a report that examines—

(1) whether changes to executive branch personnel policies could be made that would—

(A) provide greater encouragement to all Federal employees to fulfill their duties under section 552 of title 5, United States Code; and

(B) enhance the stature of officials administering that section within the executive branch;

(2) whether performance of compliance with section 552 of title 5, United States Code, should be included as a factor in personnel performance evaluations for any or all categories of Federal employees and officers;

(3) whether an employment classification series specific to compliance with sections 552 and 552a of title 5, United States Code, should be established;

(4) whether the highest level officials in particular agencies administering such sections should be paid at a rate of pay equal to or greater than a particular minimum rate; and

(5) whether other changes to personnel policies can be made to ensure that there is a clear career advancement track for individuals interested in devoting themselves to a career in compliance with such sections; and

(6) whether the executive branch should require any or all categories of Federal employees to undertake awareness training of such sections.

Executive Order No. 12,600
Predisclosure Notification Procedures for Confidential Commercial Information

June 23, 1987

52 Fed. Reg. 23,781

By the authority vested in me as President by the Constitution and statutes of the United States of America, and in order to provide predisclosure notification procedures under the Freedom of Information Act (5 U.S.C. 552) concerning confidential commercial information, and to make existing agency notification provisions more uniform, it is hereby ordered as follows:

Section 1. The head of each Executive department and agency subject to the Freedom of Information Act (5 U.S.C. 552) shall, to the extent permitted by law, establish procedures to notify submitters of records containing confidential commercial information as described in section 3 of this Order, when those records are requested under the Freedom of Information Act (FOIA), 5 U.S.C. 552, as amended, if after reviewing the request, the responsive records, and any appeal by the requester, the department or agency determines that it may be required to disclose the records. Such notice requires that an agency use good-faith efforts to advise submitters of confidential commercial information of the procedures established under this Order. Further, where notification of a voluminous number of submitters is required, such notification may be accomplished by posting or publishing the notice in a place reasonably calculated to accomplish notification.

Section 2. For purposes of this Order, the following definitions apply:

(a) "Confidential commercial information" means records provided to the government by a submitter that arguably contain material exempt from release under Exemption 4 of the Freedom of Information Act, 5 U.S.C. 552(b)(4), because disclosure could reasonably be expected to cause substantial competitive harm.

(b) "Submitter" means any person or entity who provides confidential commercial information to the government. The term "submitter" includes, but is not limited to, corporations, state governments, and foreign governments.

Section 3. (a) For confidential commercial information submitted prior to January 1, 1988, the head of each Executive department or agency shall, to the extent permitted by law, provide a submitter with notice pursuant to section 1 whenever:

(i) the records are less than 10 years old and the information has been designated by the submitter as confidential commercial information; or

(ii) the department or agency has reason to believe that disclosure of the information could reasonably be expected to cause substantial competitive harm.

(b) For confidential commercial information submitted on or after January 1, 1988, the head of each Executive department or agency shall, to the extent permitted by law, establish procedures to permit submitters of confidential commercial information to designate, at the time the information is submitted to the Federal government or a reasonable time thereafter, any information the disclosure of which the submitter claims could reasonably be expected to cause substantial competitive harm. Such agency procedures may provide for the expiration, after a specified period of time or changes in circumstances, of designations of competitive harm made by submitters. Additionally, such procedures may permit the agency to designate specific classes of information that will be treated by the agency as if the information had been so designated by the submitter. The head of each Executive department or agency shall, to the extent permitted by law, provide the submitter notice in accordance with section 1 of this Order whenever the department or agency determines that it may be required to disclose records:

(i) designated pursuant to this subsection; or

(ii) the disclosure of which the department or agency has reason to believe could reasonably be expected to cause substantial competitive harm.

Section 4. When notification is made pursuant to section 1, each agency's procedures shall, to the extent permitted by law, afford the submitter a reasonable period of time in which the submitter or its designee may object to the disclosure of any specified portion of the information and to state all grounds upon which disclosure is opposed.

Section 5. Each agency shall give careful consideration to all such specified grounds for nondisclosure prior to making an administrative determination of the issue. In all instances when the agency determines to disclose the requested records, its procedures shall provide that the agency give the submitter a written statement briefly explaining why the submitter's objections are not sustained. Such statement shall, to the extent permitted by law, be provided a reasonable number of days prior to a specified disclosure date.

Section 6. Whenever a FOIA requester brings suit seeking to compel disclosure of confidential commercial information, each agency's procedures shall require that the submitter be promptly notified.

Section 7. The designation and notification procedures required by this Order shall be established by regulations, after notice and public comment. If similar procedures or regulations already exist, they should be reviewed for conformity and revised where necessary. Existing procedures or regulations need not be modified if they are in compliance with this Order.

Section 8. The notice requirements of this Order need not be followed if:

(a) The agency determines that the information should not be disclosed;

(b) The information has been published or has been officially made available to the public;

(c) Disclosure of the information is required by law (other than 5 U.S.C. 552);

(d) The disclosure is required by an agency rule that (1) was adopted pursuant to notice and public comment, (2) specifies narrow classes of records submitted to the agency that are to be released under the Freedom of Information Act (5 U.S.C. 552), and (3) provides in exceptional circumstances for notice when the submitter provides written justification, at the time the information is submitted or a reasonable time thereafter, that disclosure of the information could reasonably be expected to cause substantial competitive harm;

(e) The information requested is not designated by the submitter as exempt from disclosure in accordance with agency regulations promulgated pursuant to section 7, when the submitter had an opportunity to do so at the time of submission of the information or a reasonable time thereafter, unless the agency has substantial reason to believe that disclosure of the information would result in competitive harm; or

(f) The designation made by the submitter in accordance with agency regulations promulgated pursuant to section 7 appears obviously frivolous; except that, in such case, the agency must provide the submitter with written notice of any final administrative disclosure determination within a reasonable number of days prior to the specified disclosure date.

Section 9. Whenever an agency notifies a submitter that it may be required to disclose information pursuant to section 1 of this Order, the agency shall also notify the requester that notice and an opportunity to comment are being provided the submitter. Whenever an agency notifies a submitter of a final decision pursuant to section 5 of this Order, the agency shall also notify the requester.

Section 10. This Order is intended only to improve the internal management of the Federal government, and is not intended to create any right or benefit, substantive or procedural, enforceable at law by a party against the United States, its agencies, its officers, or any person.

RONALD REAGAN
Oct. 4, 1993

Executive Order No. 13,392
Improving Agency Disclosure of Information

December 14, 2005

70 Fed. Reg. 75,373 (December 19, 2005)

By the authority vested in me as President by the Constitution and the laws of the United States of America, and to ensure appropriate agency disclosure of information, and consistent with the goals of section 552 of title 5, United States Code, it is hereby ordered as follows:

Section 1. *Policy.*
(a) The effective functioning of our constitutional democracy depends upon the participation in public life of a citizenry that is well informed. For nearly four decades, the Freedom of Information Act (FOIA) has provided an important means through which the public can obtain information regarding the activities of Federal agencies. Under the FOIA, the public can obtain records from any Federal agency, subject to the exemptions enacted by the Congress to protect information that must be held in confidence for the Government to function effectively or for other purposes.
(b) FOIA requesters are seeking a service from the Federal Government and should be treated as such. Accordingly, in responding to a FOIA request, agencies shall respond courteously and appropriately. Moreover, agencies shall provide FOIA requesters, and the public in general, with citizen-centered ways to learn about the FOIA process, about agency records that are publicly available (e.g., on the agency's website), and about the status of a person's FOIA request and appropriate information about the agency's response.
(c) Agency FOIA operations shall be both results-oriented and produce results. Accordingly, agencies shall process requests under the FOIA in an efficient and appropriate manner and achieve tangible, measurable improvements in FOIA processing. When an agency's FOIA program does not produce such results, it should be reformed, consistent with available resources appropriated by the Congress and applicable law, to increase efficiency and better reflect the policy goals and objectives of this order.
(d) A citizen-centered and results-oriented approach will improve service and performance, thereby strengthening compliance with the FOIA, and will help avoid disputes and related litigation.

Sec. 2. *Agency Chief FOIA Officers.*

(a) Designation. The head of each agency shall designate within 30 days of the date of this order a senior official of such agency (at the Assistant Secretary or equivalent level), to serve as the Chief FOIA Officer of that agency. The head of the agency shall promptly notify the Director of the Office of Management and Budget (OMB Director) and the Attorney General of such designation and of any changes thereafter in such designation.

(b) General Duties. The Chief FOIA Officer of each agency shall, subject to the authority of the head of the agency:

    (i) have agency-wide responsibility for efficient and appropriate compliance with the FOIA;

    (ii) monitor FOIA implementation throughout the agency, including through the use of meetings with the public to the extent deemed appropriate by the agency's Chief FOIA Officer, and keep the head of the agency, the chief legal officer of the agency, and the Attorney General appropriately informed of the agency's performance in implementing the FOIA, including the extent to which the agency meets the milestones in the agency's plan under section 3(b) of this order and training and reporting standards established consistent with applicable law and this order;

    (iii) recommend to the head of the agency such adjustments to agency practices, policies, personnel, and funding as may be necessary to carry out the policy set forth in section 1 of this order;

    (iv) review and report, through the head of the agency, at such times and in such formats as the Attorney General may direct, on the agency's performance in implementing the FOIA; and

    (v) facilitate public understanding of the purposes of the FOIA's statutory exemptions by including concise descriptions of the exemptions in both the agency's FOIA handbook issued under section 552(g) of title 5, United States Code, and the agency's annual FOIA report, and by providing an overview, where appropriate, of certain general categories of agency records to which those exemptions apply.

(c) FOIA Requester Service Center and FOIA Public Liaisons. In order to ensure appropriate communication with FOIA requesters:

    (i) Each agency shall establish one or more FOIA Requester Service Centers (Center), as appropriate, which shall serve as the first place that a FOIA requester can contact to seek information concerning the status of the person's FOIA request and appropriate information about the agency's FOIA response. The Center shall include appropriate staff to receive and respond to inquiries from FOIA requesters;

(ii) The agency Chief FOIA Officer shall designate one or more agency officials, as appropriate, as FOIA Public Liaisons, who may serve in the Center or who may serve in a separate office. FOIA Public Liaisons shall serve as supervisory officials to whom a FOIA requester can raise concerns about the service the FOIA requester has received from the Center, following an initial response from the Center staff. FOIA Public Liaisons shall seek to ensure a service-oriented response to FOIA requests and FOIA-related inquiries. For example, the FOIA Public Liaison shall assist, as appropriate, in reducing delays, increasing transparency and understanding of the status of requests, and resolving disputes. FOIA Public Liaisons shall report to the agency Chief FOIA Officer on their activities and shall perform their duties consistent with applicable law and agency regulations;

(iii) In addition to the services to FOIA requesters provided by the Center and FOIA Public Liaisons, the agency Chief FOIA Officer shall also consider what other FOIA-related assistance to the public should appropriately be provided by the agency;

(iv) In establishing the Centers and designating FOIA Public Liaisons, the agency shall use, as appropriate, existing agency staff and resources. A Center shall have appropriate staff to receive and respond to inquiries from FOIA requesters;

(v) As determined by the agency Chief FOIA Officer, in consultation with the FOIA Public Liaisons, each agency shall post appropriate information about its Center or Centers on the agency's website, including contact information for its FOIA Public Liaisons. In the case of an agency without a website, the agency shall publish the information on the Firstgov.gov website or, in the case of any agency with neither a website nor the capability to post on the Firstgov.gov website, in the Federal Register; and

(vi) The agency Chief FOIA Officer shall ensure that the agency has in place a method (or methods), including through the use of the Center, to receive and respond promptly and appropriately to inquiries from FOIA requesters about the status of their requests. The Chief FOIA Officer shall also consider, in consultation with the FOIA Public Liaisons, as appropriate, whether the agency's implementation of other means (such as tracking numbers for requests, or an agency telephone or Internet hotline) would be appropriate for responding to status inquiries.

Sec. 3. *Review, Plan, and Report.*

(a) Review. Each agency's Chief FOIA Officer shall conduct a review of the agency's FOIA operations to determine whether agency practices are consistent with the policies set forth in section 1 of this order. In conducting this review, the Chief FOIA Officer shall:

> (i) evaluate, with reference to numerical and statistical benchmarks where appropriate, the agency's administration of the FOIA, including the agency's expenditure of resources on FOIA compliance and the extent to which, if any, requests for records have not been responded to within the statutory time limit (backlog);
>
> (ii) review the processes and practices by which the agency assists and informs the public regarding the FOIA process;
>
> (iii) examine the agency's:
>
>> (A) use of information technology in responding to FOIA requests, including without limitation the tracking of FOIA requests and communication with requesters;
>>
>> (B) practices with respect to requests for expedited processing; and
>>
>> (C) implementation of multi-track processing if used by such agency;
>
> (iv) review the agency's policies and practices relating to the availability of public information through websites and other means, including the use of websites to make available the records described in section 552(a)(2) of title 5, United States Code; and
>
> (v) identify ways to eliminate or reduce its FOIA backlog, consistent with available resources and taking into consideration the volume and complexity of the FOIA requests pending with the agency.

(b) Plan.

> (i) Each agency's Chief FOIA Officer shall develop, in consultation as appropriate with the staff of the agency (including the FOIA Public Liaisons), the Attorney General, and the OMB Director, an agency-specific plan to ensure that the agency's administration of the FOIA is in accordance with applicable law and the policies set forth in section 1 of this order. The plan, which shall be submitted to the head of the agency for approval, shall address the agency's implementation of the FOIA during fiscal years 2006 and 2007.
>
> (ii) The plan shall include specific activities that the agency will implement to eliminate or reduce the agency's FOIA backlog, including (as applicable) changes that will make the processing of FOIA requests more streamlined and effective, as well as increased reli-

ance on the dissemination of records that can be made available to the public through a website or other means that do not require the public to make a request for the records under the FOIA.

(iii) The plan shall also include activities to increase public awareness of FOIA processing, including as appropriate, expanded use of the agency's Center and its FOIA Public Liaisons.

(iv) The plan shall also include, taking appropriate account of the resources available to the agency and the mission of the agency, concrete milestones, with specific timetables and outcomes to be achieved, by which the head of the agency, after consultation with the OMB Director, shall measure and evaluate the agency's success in the implementation of the plan.

(c) Agency Reports to the Attorney General and OMB Director.

(i) The head of each agency shall submit a report, no later than 6 months from the date of this order, to the Attorney General and the OMB Director that summarizes the results of the review under section 3(a) of this order and encloses a copy of the agency's plan under section 3(b) of this order. The agency shall publish a copy of the agency's report on the agency's website or, in the case of an agency without a website, on the Firstgov.gov website, or, in the case of any agency with neither a website nor the capability to publish on the Firstgov.gov website, in the Federal Register.

(ii) The head of each agency shall include in the agency's annual FOIA reports for fiscal years 2006 and 2007 a report on the agency's development and implementation of its plan under section 3(b) of this order and on the agency's performance in meeting the milestones set forth in that plan, consistent with any related guidelines the Attorney General may issue under section 552(e) of title 5, United States Code.

(iii) If the agency does not meet a milestone in its plan, the head of the agency shall:

(A) identify this deficiency in the annual FOIA report to the Attorney General;

(B) explain in the annual report the reasons for the agency's failure to meet the milestone;

(C) outline in the annual report the steps that the agency has already taken, and will be taking, to address the deficiency; and

(D) report this deficiency to the President's Management Council.

Sec. 4. *Attorney General.*

(a) Report. The Attorney General, using the reports submitted by the agencies under subsection 3(c)(i) of this order and the information submitted by agencies in their annual FOIA reports for fiscal year 2005, shall submit to the President, no later than 10 months from the date of this order, a report on agency FOIA implementation. The Attorney General shall consult the OMB Director in the preparation of the report and shall include in the report appropriate recommendations on administrative or other agency actions for continued agency dissemination and release of public information. The Attorney General shall thereafter submit two further annual reports, by June 1, 2007, and June 1, 2008, that provide the President with an update on the agencies' implementation of the FOIA and of their plans under section 3(b) of this order.

(b) Guidance. The Attorney General shall issue such instructions and guidance to the heads of departments and agencies as may be appropriate to implement sections 3(b) and 3(c) of this order.

Sec. 5. OMB Director. The OMB Director may issue such instructions to the heads of agencies as are necessary to implement this order, other than sections 3(b) and 3(c) of this order.

Sec. 6. Definitions. As used in this order:

(a) the term "agency" has the same meaning as the term "agency" under section 552(f)(1) of title 5, United States Code; and

(b) the term "record" has the same meaning as the term "record" under section 552(f)(2) of title 5, United States Code.

Sec. 7. General Provisions.

(a) The agency reviews under section 3(a) of this order and agency plans under section 3(b) of this order shall be conducted and developed in accordance with applicable law and applicable guidance issued by the President, the Attorney General, and the OMB Director, including the laws and guidance regarding information technology and the dissemination of information.

(b) This order:

> (i) shall be implemented in a manner consistent with applicable law and subject to the availability of appropriations;
>
> (ii) shall not be construed to impair or otherwise affect the functions of the OMB Director relating to budget, legislative, or administrative proposals; and
>
> (iii) is intended only to improve the internal management of the

executive branch and is not intended to, and does not, create any right or benefit, substantive or procedural, enforceable at law or in equity by a party against the United States, its departments, agencies, instrumentalities, or entities, its officers or employees, or any other person.

GEORGE W. BUSH

13

Government in the Sunshine Act

Citations:

5 U.S.C. §552b (2000); enacted September 13, 1976 by Pub. L. No. 94-409, 90 Stat. 1241; amended by Pub. L. No. 104-66, Title III §3002, 109 Stat. 707, 734 (Dec 21. 1995).

Overview:

The principal operative provision of the Government in the Sunshine Act, section 3, amended title 5 of the U.S. Code to add a new section 552b, entitled "Open Meetings."[1] Section 3 requires, in general, that meetings of each federal agency headed by a collegial body, a majority of whose members are appointed by the President with the advice and consent of the Senate, shall be open to public observation. (Approximately 50 federal agencies are subject to the Government in the Sunshine Act, including the major independent regulatory commissions, such as the Securities and Exchange Commission, Federal Trade Commission, Federal Communications Commission, Consumer Product Safety Commission, and National Labor Relations Board.) The right of observation provided by the Act does not include any right to participate in the agency's deliberations. The Act provides certain exemptions from the open meeting requirement and prescribes in detail the procedures that the agency must follow to invoke an exemption and close a meeting.

---

[1] Section 4 of Pub. L. No. 94-409 amended the Administrative Procedure Act, 5 U.S.C. §557, to forbid ex parte communications in certain agency proceedings (see Chapter 1, Administrative Procedure Act). Section 5 makes minor amendments in several other statutes. Neither section relates directly to the subject of agency open meetings.

Summary. The principal provisions of the Act may be summarized briefly. Subsection (a) defines the basic terms "agency," "meeting," and "member." Subsection (b) declares a presumption in favor of open meetings. Subsection (c) allows an agency to close a meeting or portion of a meeting or to withhold information about a meeting or portion of a meeting if the agency determines that the meeting or portion, if opened, or the information, if released, would be likely to disclose information protected from disclosure under one or more of the ten exemptions of subsection (c). These exemptions are permissive, not mandatory, and subsection (c) also provides that agency meetings otherwise exempt shall be open "where the agency finds that the public interest [so] requires."

Exemptions. The exemptions in subsection (c) generally parallel those in the Freedom of Information Act (5 U.S.C. §552). There is, however, an important exception. There is no exemption in the Sunshine Act that parallels the fifth exemption in the Freedom of Information Act for interagency and intra-agency memoranda and letters. This is because, while the FOIA recognizes the legitimate government interest in protecting the agency deliberative process as such, the Sunshine Act aims at maximum exposure of that process, at least at the collegial level. See R. Berg and S. Klitzman, *An Interpretive Guide to the Government in the Sunshine Act* (2d ed.) 67 (2005). This *Guide*, recently updated for the ABA, is the authoritative source on the Act, and this *Sourcebook* chapter relied heavily on its bibliography and list of agency regulations.

On the other hand, the Sunshine Act does have two important exemptions that lack counterparts in the FOIA and that protect the deliberative process in certain defined circumstances. Exemption 9 permits those agencies that regulate securities, commodities, or financial institutions to close meetings to protect information, the disclosure of which would lead to speculation or endanger the stability of financial institutions. More broadly, it permits any agency to close a meeting to protect information the disclosure of which would be likely to frustrate the implementation of a proposed agency action. Exemption 10 permits closure of meetings that concern agency participation in pending or anticipated litigation or the disposition by the agency of particular cases involving formal (but not "informal") adjudication.

Procedures for Closing Meetings. Subsections (d), (e), and (f) prescribe the procedures agencies must follow in closing meetings, announcing and changing meetings, and withholding and/or releasing substantive information regarding such meetings. Under subsection (d)(1), agencies may decide to close meetings or withhold information about meetings only by recorded majority vote of the entire membership of the agency. Subsection (d)(2) allows a "person whose interests may be directly affected by a portion of a meeting" to request closure based on exemptions (5), (6), or (7). The agency must vote on the request only "upon request of any one of its members." Subsection (d)(3) requires that, within 1 day of any vote to close or to withhold information about a meeting taken under subsections (d)(1) or (d)(2), the agency must "make publicly available" a written copy of the vote of each member. If the vote is to close or to withhold information, the agency must also make available "a full written explanation" of the closing and a list of all expected attendees and their affiliations. Subsection (d)(4) allows an agency, a majority of whose meetings may be closed under exemptions (4), (8), (9)(A), or (10), to close its meetings by expedited procedures and to dispense with some of the procedural requirements of subsections (d)(1), (d)(3), and (e).

Publicizing Meetings. Subsection (e)(1) requires that the agency publicly announce, at least one week prior to the meeting, its time, place, and subject matter, whether it is to be open or closed, and the name and telephone number of an agency contact person to provide additional information. The subsection also permits the agency to provide less than seven days notice of a meeting, provided a majority of the membership determines by recorded vote "that agency business requires" less notice, and the agency makes the requisite public announcement "at the earliest practicable time" and, in the case of a change in subject matter or open or closed status, a majority recorded vote is cast. Subsection (e)(1) and (e)(2) requires that information about the time, place, and subject matter of meetings, as well as changes in the time or place of meetings, must also be submitted for publication in the Federal Register. Furthermore, agencies are urged to use other means to ensure that the public is fully informed of public announcements, including posting notices on agency websites or distributing them to a listserv or mailing list. (See *An Interpretive Guide to the Government in the Sunshine Act* 121-22 (2005).)

Recordkeeping. Subsection (f)(1) requires that, for every meeting closed under one or more of the exemptions of subsection (c), the general counsel or chief legal officer of the agency must certify that the meeting may properly be closed. The agency must retain a copy of the certification and a statement from the presiding officer of the meeting stating the time and place of the meeting and listing the persons actually present. The agency must also maintain a complete verbatim transcript or electronic recording of all closed meetings, except that it may instead maintain detailed minutes of any meeting closed under exemptions (8), (9)(A), or (10). Subsection (f)(2) requires the agency to make "promptly available" for public inspection and copying a copy of the transcript, recording, or minutes, except for information exempted and withheld pursuant to subsection (c). The agency is also required under subsection (f)(2) to maintain for at least two years a complete verbatim copy of the transcript, recording or minutes.

Judicial Review. Subsection (g) provides for the issuance of agency rules to implement the Act. The Administrative Conference of the United States (ACUS) was originally given the responsibility for consulting with agencies prior to their issuance of regulations to implement the Act. (No successor to ACUS has been designated.) Subsection (h) provides for judicial review of agency decisions to close meetings. Such decisions may be challenged either in a separate proceeding in district court (subsection (h)(l)), or as part of a proceeding for review of the agency action taken at the meeting (subsection (h)(2)). However, the courts are discouraged from reversing the agency action simply because it was taken at a meeting that was improperly closed. Thus, whether the proceeding is under subsection (h)(1) or subsection (h)(2), the relief available is likely to be limited to allowing access to the transcript of the meeting and providing injunctive relief against future violations. In addition, under subsection (i) a successful plaintiff may be entitled to an award of attorneys' fees.

Reporting. Subsection (j) details the reporting requirements to Congress. Each agency under this subsection must report annually to Congress (1) the changes in policy and procedure that the agency has implemented the year prior, (2) the number of meetings held, the exemptions applied to closed meetings, and the days of public notice given concerning those closed meetings, (3) a description of litigation or complaints received concerning the implementation of section 552(b), and (4) an explanation of any changes in law that have affected the responsibilities of the agency under this section. The reporting requirements were changed by Pub. L. No. 104-66, which terminated certain reporting requirements in the area of substantive and time-related provisions. See the note following the Act's current text, below.

Legislative History:

Senate. The legislation that was to become the Government in the Sunshine Act was first introduced in the 92d Congress on August 4, 1972 by Senator Lawton Chiles (D-FL) as S. 3881 (118 Cong. Rec. 26902-19). No action was taken on the bill, and Senator Chiles reintroduced the bill, in the 93d Congress on January 9, 1973, as S. 260 (119 Cong. Rec. 646-651).

The bill was referred to the Subcommittee on Reorganization, Research and International Organizations of the Senate Committee on Government Operations, where it underwent several revisions. In 1974 the subcommittee held 3 days of hearings on Committee Print No. 3 (*Hearings on S. 260 before the Subcommittee on Reorganizations, Research and International Organizations of the Senate Committee on Government Operations*, 93d Cong., 2d Sess., May 21 and 22, October 15, 1974).

Subsequent to the October 1974 hearing the Subcommittee prepared Committee Print No. 4 of S. 260, which was introduced by Senator Chiles on January 15, 1975 in the 94th Congress as S.5 (121 Cong. Rec. 241-246).

On July 31, 1975, without further hearings, the Committee on Government Operations reported S. 5 with amendments (S. Rep. No. 94-354, 94th Cong., 1st Sess. (1975)). As reported, the bill consisted of two titles, title I, meetings of Congressional committees, and title II, agency meetings and *ex parte* communications.

Title I was referred to the Senate Committee on Rules and Administration, which on September 18, 1975 reported out S. 5 and recommended that title I be deleted from the bill (S. Rep. No. 94-381, 94th Cong., 1st Sess. (1975)).

On November 5, 1975, title I was deleted on the floor of the Senate (121 Cong. Rec. 35218). On November 6, 1975 S. 5 as amended was considered and passed without significant further amendment by a vote of 94-0 (121 Cong. Rec. 35321-36).

House. A bill identical to title II of S. 5, as reported by the Senate Committee on Government Operations, was introduced in the House of Representatives by Representative Dante Fascell (D-FL) on September 26, 1975, as H.R. 9868. (121 Cong. Rec. H 921). On October 22, 1975, Representative Bella Abzug (D-NY) introduced H.R. 10315, an amended version of title II of S.5 (121 Cong. Rec. H10242). The House versions were referred sequentially to the Committees on Government Operations and the Judiciary. On November 6 and 12, 1975, the Subcommittee on Government Operations Committee held hearings on H.R. 10315 and H.R. 9868.

On February 3, 1976, a clean bill was introduced in the House by Representatives Abzug, Fascell, and others as H.R. 11656 (122 Cong. Rec. H670), and it was reported out by the House Government Operations Committee on March 8, 1976 (H.R. Rep. No. 94-880, Pt. I, 94th Cong., 2d Sess. (1976)). On March 24 and 25, 1976, the Subcommittee on Administrative Law and Governmental Relations of the House Judiciary Committee held hearings on H.R. 11656, and on April 8, 1976, the House Judiciary Committee reported H.R. 11656 with amendments (H.R. Rep. No. 94-880, Pt. II, 94th Cong., 2d Sess. (1976)). On July 28, 1976, the House considered and passed H.R. 11656, with floor amendments, and then took up S. 5 and amended it to substitute the text of the House bill. S. 5 was then passed by a vote of 390-5 and sent to a Senate-House Conference (122 Cong. Rec. H7863-902).

Conference Committee and Enactment. On August 26 and 27, 1976, the report of the conference committee was filed, respectively, in the House and Senate (H.R. Rep. No. 94-1441; S. Rep. No. 94-1178, 94th Cong., 2d Sess. (1976)). On August 31, 1976, the report was adopted by voice vote in the Senate (122 Cong. Rec. 15043-45) and by a vote of 384-0 in the House (122 Cong. Rec. H9258-62). On September 13, 1976, President Ford signed the bill into law, to go into effect March 12, 1977 (Pub. L. No. 94-409, 90 Stat. 124, 12 Weekly Compilation of Presidential Documents 1233 (September 20, 1976)).

On May 11, 1995, the Federal Reports Elimination and Sunset Act of 1995 was introduced in the Senate by Senator John McCain (R-AZ). It provides for a modification or elimination of certain federal reporting requirements of specified federal departments and agencies. It also terminates certain periodic reporting requirements. It was signed into law as Pub. L. No. 104-66 on December 21, 1995, and amended subsection (j) of the Act.

Significant Case Law:

FCC v. ITT World Communications, 466 U.S. 463 (1984), held that the definition of "meeting" under the Act did not include gatherings of agency members to receive information and that international consultative sessions were not covered by the Act.

Natural Resources Defense Council, Inc. v. Nuclear Regulatory Commission, 216 F.3d 1180 (D.C. Cir. 2000), held that the NRC's definition of "meeting" adopted by regulation for purposes of the Government in the Sunshine Act, as deliberations of a quorum of Commissioners where such deliberations "are sufficiently focused on discrete proposals or issues as to cause or to be likely to cause the individual participating members to form reasonably firm positions regarding matters pending or likely to arise before the agency," being that of the Supreme Court in the *ITT* case, was not invalid as contrary to the Act or as fatally undermining it. The court further opined that the Supreme Court's definition was authoritative and not dictum even though there was an independent basis for its decision.

Natural Resources Defense Council v. Defense Nuclear Facilities Safety Board, 969 F.2d 1248 (D.C. Cir. 1992), upheld agency regulation under the Act that interpreted agency statute as permitting closure of meetings under exemption 3.

Energy Research Foundation v. Defense Nuclear Facilities Safety Board, 917 F.2d 581 (D.C. Cir. 1990), held that the Board in question is an "agency" for purposes of the Government in the Sunshine Act (and the FOIA).

Clark-Cowlitz Joint Operating Agency v. FERC, 798 F.2d 499 (D.C. Cir. 1986), held that where a meeting is closed pursuant to exemption 10 of the Sunshine Act, the need for confidentiality may survive the termination of the proceedings that were the subject of agency discussion and that the agency's determination that the public interest does not require the opening of a meeting eligible for closure is not subject to judicial review.

Rushforth v. Council of Economic Advisers, 762 F.2d 1038, 1039 n.3, 1043 (D.C. Cir. 1985) held that although plaintiff has standing to allege Sunshine Act violation, Council of Economic Advisers is not an "agency" for purposes of the Act, since it does not qualify as an agency under FOIA.

Common Cause v. Nuclear Regulatory Commission, 674 F.2d 921 (D.C. Cir. 1982), held that exemption 9(b) does not cover meetings to consider the agency's budget proposals.

Pacific Legal Foundation v. Council on Environmental Quality, 636 F.2d 1259 (D.C. Cir. 1980) held that the CEQ is covered by the Sunshine Act.

Communications Systems v. FCC, 595 F.2d 797 (D.C. Cir. 1978), held that agencies are not precluded by the Act from disposing of matters through notation voting rather than at meetings.

Public Citizen v. National Economic Commission, 703 F. Supp. 113 (D.D.C. 1989), held that exemption 9(b) was not available as the basis for closing a meeting to facilitate candid discussion (the case involves comparable exemptions under the Federal Advisory Committee Act, 5 U.S.C. App. II, §10(d) (1988)).

Bibliography:

I. Legislative History

1. The relevant legislative history materials are collected in *Government in the Sunshine Act—S. 5 (Public Law 94-409—Source Book: Legislative History, Texts and Other Documents* (94th Cong., 2d Sess. (1976)), published jointly by the Committees on Government Operations of the House of Representatives and the Senate.

2. The provisions of the Act were analyzed and the legislative history discussed in an Administrative Conference publication, Richard Berg and Stephen Klitzman, *An Interpretive Guide to the Government in the Sunshine Act* (1978). The *Guide* has been cited in many of the judicial decisions under

the Act. Recently Messrs. Berg and Klitzman (with former ACUS General Counsel, Gary J. Edles) have revised and updated the Guide for the ABA's Section of Administrative Law and Regulatory Practice, in *An Interpretive Guide to the Government in the Sunshine Act* (2d. ed. 2005).

3. *Government in the Sunshine Act: History and Recent Issues*, Senate Committee on Governmental Affairs, 101st Cong. 1st Sess. (November 1989) (reviews legislative history of the Act, recent issues and court rulings affecting the Act, and selected federal agencies' compliance with the Act).

II. Other Government Documents

1. Administrative Conference of the United States, *Report and Recommendation by the Special Committee to Review the Government in the Sunshine Act*, reprinted in 49 Admin. L. Rev. 421 (1997). [Transcript of public hearing held on September 19, 1995, on file in ACUS Archives, Washington College of Law, American University.]

2. Administrative Conference of the U.S., Recommendation 84-3, *Improvements in the Administration of the Government in the Sunshine Act*, 49 Fed. Reg. 29,942 (July 25, 1984).

3. R. Berg and S. Klitzman, *An Interpretive Guide to the Government in the Sunshine Act* (Administrative Conference of the U.S., 1978).

4. *Hearing on Federal Information Policy Oversight*, Before Subcommittee on Government Management, Information, and Technology, of the House Committee on Government Reform and Oversight, 104th Cong., 2d Sess. (June 13, 1996) at 121, 137-54, 184-89, 232-54.

5. *Hearing on Government in the Sunshine Act Implementation*, Before Subcommittee on Administrative Law and Governmental Relations, of the House Committee on the Judiciary, 95th Cong., 1st Sess. (1977).

6. Hearing on Nuclear Regulatory Commission Sunshine Act Regulations, Before Subcommittee on Energy Conservation and Power, of the House Committee on Energy and Commerce, 99th Cong., 1st Sess (May 21, 1985) (Serial No. 99-39).

7. *Hearings on Oversight of the Government in the Sunshine Act, Pub. L. No. 94-409,* Before Subcommittee on Federal Spending Practices and Open Government of the Senate Committee on Governmental Affairs, 95th Cong., 2d Sess. (1978).

8. *Hearings on Oversight of the Government in the Sunshine Act, Pub. L. No. 94-409,* Before the Subcommittee on Federal Spending Practices and Open Government, 95th Cong. 1st and 2d. Sess. (November 29, 1977, June 13, August 4, 1978).

9. *Hearings on Oversight of the Government in the Sunshine Act*, Before the Subcommittee on Federal Spending Budget and Accounting, 100th Cong. 2d. Sess. (April 19, 1988).

10. Senate Committee on Governmental Affairs, *Government in the Sunshine Act: History and Recent Issues*, S. Rep. No. 101-54, 101st Cong., 1st Sess. (1989).

11. D. Welborn, W. Lyons, and L. Thomas, Implementation and Effects of the Federal Government in the Sunshine Act, Report to the Administrative Conference of the U.S., 1984 ACUS 199. Abridged: The Federal Government in the Sunshine Act and Agency Decision Making, 20 Admin. & Soc'y 465 (1989).

III. Books and Articles

1. Barrett, *Facilitating Government Decision Making: Distinguishing Between Meetings and Nonmeetings Under the Federal Sunshine Act*, 66 Tex. L. Rev. 1195 (1988).

2. Bensch, *Seventeen Years Later: Has Government Let the Sun Shine In?*, 61 Geo. Wash. L. Rev. 1475 (1992).

3. R. Berg, S. Klitzman, & G. Edles, *An Interpretive Guide to the Government in the Sunshine Act* (American Bar Association., 2d ed. 2005).

4. Bradley, *Do You Feel the Sunshine? Government in the Sunshine Act: Its Objectives, Goals, and Effect on the FCC and You*, 49 Fed. Comm. L. J. 473 (1997).

5. Cawley, *Sunshine Law Overexposure and the Demise of Independent Agency Collegiality*, 1 Widener J. Pub. L. 43 (1992).

6. Lawrence, *Finding Shade From the Government in the Sunshine Act: A Proposal to Permit Private Informal Background Discussions at the United States International Trade Commission*, 45 Cath. U. L. Rev. 1 (1995).

7. Marblestone, *The Relationship Between the Government in the Sunshine Act and the Federal Advisory Committee Act*, 30 Fed. B. J. 65 (1977).

8. May, *Reforming the Sunshine Act*, 49 Admin L. Rev. 415 (1997).

9. O'Reilly & Berg, *Stealth Caused by Sunshine: How Sunshine Act Interpretation Results in Less Information for the Public About the Decision-Making Process of the International Trade Commission*, 36 Harv. Int'l L.J. 425 (1995).

10. Sloat, *Government in the Sunshine Act: A Danger of Overexposure*, 14 Harv. J. on Legis. 620 (1977).

11. Statler, *Let the Sunshine In?*, 67 A.B.A .J. 573 (1981).

12. Thomas, *The Courts and the Implementation of the Government in the Sunshine Act*, 37 Admin. L. Rev. 259 (1985).

13. Tucker, Commentary, *"Sunshine"—The Dubious New God*, 32 Admin. L. Rev. 537 (1980).

IV. Miscellaneous

1. Resolution approved by the American Bar Association House of Delegates, Report No. 100 (Feb. 16-17, 1987) (proposing guidelines to federal agencies and courts with respect to the interpretation of the term "meeting").

2. Availability of Judicial Review of Agency Compliance with Sunshine Act (5 U.S.C.A. § 552b(g) and (h)), 84 ALR Fed. 251.

3. Construction and Application of Exemptions Under 5 U.S.C.A. § 552b(c) to Open Meeting Requirements of Sunshine Act?, 82 ALR Fed. 465.

4. *What is an "Agency" Within the Meaning of Federal Sunshine Law (5 USC 552b)?*, 68 ALR Fed. 842.

Agency Regulations:[2]

African Development Foundation	22 C.F.R. §1500
Broadcasting Board of Governors	2 C.F.R. §507
Chemical Safety and Hazard Investigation Safety Board	40 C.F.R. §1603
Commission on Fine Arts	45 C.F.R. §2102
Commodity Credit Corporation	7 C.F.R. §1409
Commodity Futures Trading Commission	17 C.F.R. §147
Copyright Arbitration Royalty Panels (Library of Congress)	37 C.F.R. 251.11
Consumer Product Safety Commissioner	16 C.F.R. §1013
Copyright Office, Library of Congress	37 C.F.R. §251
Corporation for National and Community Service	45 C.F.R. §2505
Council on Environmental Quality	40 C.F.R. 1517
Defense Nuclear Facilities Safety Board	10 C.F.R. §1704
Equal Employment Opportunity Commission	29 C.F.R. §1612
Export-Import Bank	12 C.F.R. §407
Farm Credit Administration	12 C.F.R. §604

---

[2] Note: only agencies with regulations are listed; some other agencies meet the statutory definition but have no regulations. *See Interpretive Guide*, Appendix C (2005).

Federal Communications Commission	47 C.F.R. §0.601
Federal Deposit Insurance Corporation	12 C.F.R. §311
Federal Election Commission	11 C.F.R. §2
Federal Energy Regulatory Commission	18 C.F.R. §375.201
Federal Housing Finance Board	12 C.F.R. §912
Federal Labor Relations Authority	5 C.F.R. §2413
Federal Maritime Commission	46 C.F.R. §503.70
Federal Mine Safety and Health Review Commission	29 C.F.R. §2701
Federal Open Market Committee	12 C.F.R. §281.2
Federal Reserve System	12 C.F.R. §261b
Federal Retirement Thrift Investment Board	5 C.F.R. §1632
Federal Trade Commission	16 C.F.R. §§4.9.11, 4.14-15
Foreign Claims Settlement Commission	45 C.F.R. §503.20
Foreign Service Labor Relations Board	2 C.F.R. §1413
Harry S. Truman Scholarship Foundation	45 C.F.R. §1802
Inter-American Foundation	22 C.F.R. §1004
Legal Services Corporation	45 C.F.R. §1622
Marine Mammal Commission	50 C.F.R. §560
Merit Systems Protection Board	5 C.F.R. §1206
Mississippi River Commission	33 C.F.R. §209.50
National Commission on Libraries and Information Science	45 C.F.R. §1703.102
National Credit Union Administration	12 C.F.R. §791
National Labor Relations Board	29 C.F.R. §102.137
National Mediation Board	29 C.F.R. §1209.04
National Science Foundation	45 C.F.R. §614
National Transportation Safety Board	49 C.F.R. §804
Neighborhood Reinvestment Corporation	4 C.F.R. §4100.2
Nuclear Regulatory Commission	10 C.F.R. §§9, 9,100
Occupational Safety and Health Review Commission	29 C.F.R. §2203
Overseas Private Investment Corporation	22 C.F.R. §708
Postal Regulatory Commission	39 C.F.R. §3001.43
Railroad Retirement Board	20 C.F.R. §200.6
Rural Telephone Bank	7 C.F.R. §1600
Securities and Exchange Commission	17 C.F.R. §200.400
Surface Transportation Board	49 C.F.R. §1012
Tennessee Valley Authority	18 C.F.R. §1301.41
Uniformed Services University of the Health Services (Board of Regents)	32 C.F.R. §242a
U.S. Commission on Civil Rights	45 C.F.R. §702.50

U.S. International Trade Commission .... 19 C.F.R. §201.34
U.S. Parole Commission (Department of Justice) .... 28 C.F.R. §16
U.S. Postal Service .... 39 C.F.R. §7

Appendix:

   1. Government in the Sunshine Act, 5 U.S.C. §552b (2000).

Government in the Sunshine Act

Title 5, U.S. Code

§552b. Open meetings

(a) For purposes of this section—
    (1) the term "agency" means any agency, as defined in section 552(e) of this title, headed by a collegial body composed of two or more individual members, a majority of whom are appointed to such position by the President with the advice and consent of the Senate, and any subdivision thereof authorized to act on behalf of the agency;
    (2) the term "meeting" means the deliberations of at least the number of individual agency members required to take action on behalf of the agency where such deliberations determine or result in the joint conduct or disposition of official agency business, but does not include deliberations required or permitted by subsection (d) or (e); and
    (3) the term "member" means an individual who belongs to a collegial body heading an agency.

(b) Members shall not jointly conduct or dispose of agency business other than in accordance with this section. Except as provided in subsection (c), every portion of every meeting of an agency shall be open to public observation.

(c) Except in a case where the agency finds that the public interest requires otherwise, the second sentence of subsection (b) shall not apply to any portion of an agency meeting, and the requirements of subsections (d) and (e) shall not apply to any information pertaining to such meeting otherwise required by this section to be disclosed to the public, where the agency properly determines that such portion or portions of its meeting or the disclosure of such information is likely to—
    (1) disclose matters that are (A) specifically authorized under criteria established by an Executive order to be kept secret in the interests of national defense or foreign policy and (B) in fact properly classified pursuant to such Executive order;
    (2) relate solely to the internal personnel rules and practices of an agency;
    (3) disclose matters specifically exempted from disclosure by statute (other than section 552 of this title), provided that such statute (A) requires that the matters be withheld from the public in such a manner as to leave no discretion on the issue, or (B) establishes particular criteria for withholding or refers to particular types of matters to be withheld;

(4) disclose trade secrets and commercial or financial information obtained from a person and privileged or confidential;

(5) involve accusing any person of a crime, or formally censuring any person;

(6) disclose information of a personal nature where disclosure would constitute a clearly unwarranted invasion of personal privacy;

(7) disclose investigatory records compiled for law enforcement purposes, or information which if written would be contained in such records, but only to the extent that the production of such records or information would (A) interfere with enforcement proceedings, (B) deprive a person of a right to a fair trial or an impartial adjudication, (C) constitute an unwarranted invasion of personal privacy, (D) disclose the identity of a confidential source and, in the case of a record compiled by a criminal law enforcement authority in the course of a criminal investigation, or by an agency conducting a lawful national security intelligence investigation, confidential information furnished only by the confidential source, (E) disclose investigative techniques and procedures, or (F) endanger the life or physical safety of law enforcement personnel;

(8) disclose information contained in or related to examination, operating, or condition reports prepared by, on behalf of, or for the use of an agency responsible for the regulation or supervision of financial institutions;

(9) disclose information the premature disclosure of which would—

> (A) in the case of an agency which regulates currencies, securities, commodities, or financial institutions, be likely to (i) lead to significant financial speculation in currencies, securities, or commodities, or (ii) significantly endanger the stability of any financial institution; or
>
> (B) in the case of any agency, be likely to significantly frustrate implementation of a proposed agency action, except that subparagraph (B) shall not apply in any instance where the agency has already disclosed to the public the content or nature of its proposed action, or where the agency is required by law to make such disclosure on its own initiative prior to taking final agency action on such proposal; or

(10) specifically concern the agency's issuance of a subpena, or the agency's participation in a civil action or proceeding, an action in a foreign court or international tribunal, or an arbitration, or the initiation, conduct, or disposition by the agency of a particular case of formal agency adjudication pursuant to the procedures in section 554 of this title or

otherwise involving a determination on the record after opportunity for a hearing.

(d)(1) Action under subsection (c) shall be taken only when a majority of the entire membership of the agency (as defined in subsection (a)(1)) votes to take such action. A separate vote of the agency members shall be taken with respect to each agency meeting a portion or portions of which are proposed to be closed to the public pursuant to subsection (c), or with respect to any information which is proposed to be withheld under subsection (c). A single vote may be taken with respect to a series of meetings, a portion or portions of which are proposed to be closed to the public, or with respect to any information concerning such series of meetings, so long as each meeting in such series involves the same particular matters and is scheduled to be held no more than thirty days after the initial meeting in such series. The vote of each agency member participating in such vote shall be recorded and no proxies shall be allowed.

(2) Whenever any person whose interests may be directly affected by a portion of a meeting requests that the agency close such portion to the public for any of the reasons referred to in paragraph (5), (6), or (7) of subsection (c), the agency, upon request of any one of its members, shall vote by recorded vote whether to close such meeting.

(3) Within one day of any vote taken pursuant to paragraph (1) or (2), the agency shall make publicly available a written copy of such vote reflecting the vote of each member on the question. If a portion of a meeting is to be closed to the public, the agency shall, within one day of the vote taken pursuant to paragraph (1) or (2) of this subsection, make publicly available a full written explanation of its action closing the portion together with a list of all persons expected to attend the meeting and their affiliation.

(4) Any agency, a majority of whose meetings may properly be closed to the public pursuant to paragraph (4), (8), (9)(A), or (10) of subsection (c), or any combination thereof, may provide by regulation for the closing of such meetings or portions thereof in the event that a majority of the members of the agency votes by recorded vote at the beginning of such meeting, or portion thereof, to close the exempt portion or portions of the meeting, and a copy of such vote, reflecting the vote of each member on the question, is made available to the public. The provisions of paragraphs (1), (2), and (3) of this subsection and subsection (e) shall not apply to any portion of a meeting to which such regulations apply: Provided, That the agency shall, except to the extent that such information is exempt from disclosure under the provisions of subsection (c),

provide the public with public announcement of the time, place, and subject matter of the meeting and of each portion thereof at the earliest practicable time.

(e)(1) In the case of each meeting, the agency shall make public announcement, at least one week before the meeting, of the time, place, and subject matter of the meeting, whether it is to be open or closed to the public, and the name and phone number of the official designated by the agency to respond to requests for information about the meeting. Such announcement shall be made unless a majority of the members of the agency determines by a recorded vote that agency business requires that such meeting be called at an earlier date, in which case the agency shall make public announcement of the time, place, and subject matter of such meeting, and whether open or closed to the public, at the earliest practicable time.

(2) The time or place of a meeting may be changed following the public announcement required by paragraph (1) only if the agency publicly announces such change at the earliest practicable time. The subject matter of a meeting, or the determination of the agency to open or close a meeting, or portion of a meeting, to the public, may be changed following the public announcement required by this subsection only if (A) a majority of the entire membership of the agency determines by a recorded vote that agency business so requires and that no earlier announcement of the change was possible, and (B) the agency publicly announces such change and the vote of each member upon such change at the earliest practicable time.

(3) Immediately following each public announcement required by this subsection, notice of the time, place, and subject matter of a meeting, whether the meeting is open or closed, any change in one of the preceding, and the name and phone number of the official designated by the agency to respond to requests for information about the meeting, shall also be submitted for publication in the Federal Register.

(f)(1) For every meeting closed pursuant to paragraphs (1) through (10) of subsection (c), the General Counsel or chief legal officer of the agency shall publicly certify that, in his or her opinion, the meeting may be closed to the public and shall state each relevant exemptive provision. A copy of such certification, together with a statement from the presiding officer of the meeting setting forth the time and place of the meeting, and the persons present, shall be retained by the agency. The agency shall maintain a complete transcript or electronic recording adequate to record fully the proceedings of each meeting, or portion of a meeting, closed to the public, except that in the case of a meeting, or portion of a meeting, closed to the public pursuant to paragraph

(8), (9)(A), or (10) of subsection (c), the agency shall maintain either such a transcript or recording, or a set of minutes. Such minutes shall fully and clearly describe all matters discussed and shall provide a full and accurate summary of any actions taken, and the reasons therefor, including a description of each of the views expressed on any item and the record of any rollcall vote (reflecting the vote of each member on the question). All documents considered in connection with any action shall be identified in such minutes.

(2) The agency shall make promptly available to the public, in a place easily accessible to the public, the transcript, electronic recording, or minutes (as required by paragraph (1)) of the discussion of any item on the agenda, or of any item of the testimony of any witness received at the meeting, except for such item or items of such discussion or testimony as the agency determines to contain information which may be withheld under subsection (c). Copies of such transcript, or minutes, or a transcription of such recording disclosing the identity of each speaker, shall be furnished to any person at the actual cost of duplication or transcription. The agency shall maintain a complete verbatim copy of the transcript, a complete copy of the minutes, or a complete electronic recording of each meeting, or portion of a meeting, closed to the public, for a period of at least two years after such meeting, or until one year after the conclusion of any agency proceeding with respect to which the meeting or portion was held, whichever occurs later.

(g) Each agency subject to the requirements of this section shall, within 180 days after the date of enactment of this section, following consultation with the Office of the Chairman of the Administrative Conference of the United States and published notice in the Federal Register of at least thirty days and opportunity for written comment by any person, promulgate regulations to implement the requirements of subsections (b) through (f) of this section. Any person may bring a proceeding in the United States District Court for the District of Columbia to require an agency to promulgate such regulations if such agency has not promulgated such regulations within the time period specified herein. Subject to any limitations of time provided by law, any person may bring a proceeding in the United States Court of Appeals for the District of Columbia to set aside agency regulations issued pursuant to this subsection that are not in accord with the requirements of subsections (b) through (f) of this section and to require the promulgation of regulations that are in accord with such subsections.

(h)(1) The district courts of the United States shall have jurisdiction to enforce the requirements of subsections (b) through (f) of this section by declaratory judgment, injunctive relief, or other relief as may be appropriate.

Such actions may be brought by any person against an agency prior to, or within sixty days after, the meeting out of which the violation of this section arises, except that if public announcement of such meeting is not initially provided by the agency in accordance with the requirements of this section, such action may be instituted pursuant to this section at any time prior to sixty days after any public announcement of such meeting. Such actions may be brought in the district court of the United States for the district in which the agency meeting is held or in which the agency in question has its headquarters, or in the District Court for the District of Columbia. In such actions a defendant shall serve his answer within thirty days after the service of the complaint. The burden is on the defendant to sustain his action. In deciding such cases the court may examine in camera any portion of the transcript, electronic recording, or minutes of a meeting closed to the public, and may take such additional evidence as it deems necessary. The court, having due regard for orderly administration and the public interest, as well as the interests of the parties, may grant such equitable relief as it deems appropriate, including granting an injunction against future violations of this section or ordering the agency to make available to the public such portion of the transcript, recording, or minutes of a meeting as is not authorized to be withheld under subsection (c) of this section.

(2) Any Federal court otherwise authorized by law to review agency action may, at the application of any person properly participating in the proceeding pursuant to other applicable law, inquire into violations by the agency of the requirements of this section and afford such relief as it deems appropriate. Nothing in this section authorizes any Federal court having jurisdiction solely on the basis of paragraph (1) to set aside, enjoin, or invalidate any agency action (other than an action to close a meeting or to withhold information under this section) taken or discussed at any agency meeting out of which the violation of this section arose.

(i) The court may assess against any party reasonable attorney fees and other litigation costs reasonably incurred by any other party who substantially prevails in any action brought in accordance with the provisions of subsection (g) or (h) of this section, except that costs may be assessed against the plaintiff only where the court finds that the suit was initiated by the plaintiff primarily for frivolous or dilatory purposes. In the case of assessment of costs against an agency, the costs may be assessed by the court against the United States.

(j) Each agency subject to the requirements of this section shall annually report to the Congress regarding the following:

(1) The changes in the policies and procedures of the agency under this section that have occurred during the preceding 1-year period.

(2) A tabulation of the number of meetings held, the exemptions applied to close meetings, and the days of public notice provided to close meetings.

(3) A brief description of litigation or formal complaints concerning the implementation of this section by the agency.

(4) A brief explanation of any changes in law that have affected the responsibilities of the agency under this section.

(k) Nothing herein expands or limits the present rights of any person under section 552 of this title, except that the exemptions set forth in subsection (c) of this section shall govern in the case of any request made pursuant to section 552 to copy or inspect the transcripts, recordings, or minutes described in subsection (f) of this section. The requirements of chapter 33 of title 44, United States Code, shall not apply to the transcripts, recordings, and minutes described in subsection (f) of this section.

(l) This section does not constitute authority to withhold any information from Congress, and does not authorize the closing of any agency meeting or portion thereof required by any other provision of law to be open.

(m) Nothing in this section authorizes any agency to withhold from any individual any record, including transcripts, recordings, or minutes required by this section, which is otherwise accessible to such individual under section 552a of this title.

(Added Pub. L. No. 94-409, Sec. 3(a), Sept. 13, 1976, 90 Stat. 1241; amended Pub. L. No. 104-66, title III, Sec. 3002, Dec. 21, 1995, 109 Stat. 734.)

Declaration of Policy and Statement of Purpose

Section 2 of Pub. L. No. 94-409 provided that: "It is hereby declared to be the policy of the United States that the public is entitled to the fullest practicable information regarding the decisionmaking processes of the Federal Government. It is the purpose of this Act to provide the public with such information while protecting the rights of individuals and the ability of the Government to carry out its responsibilities."

Amendments

1995—Subsec. (j). Pub. L. No. 104-66 amended subsec. (j) generally. Prior to amendment, subsec. (j) read as follows: "Each agency subject to the requirements of this section shall annually report to Congress regarding its compliance with such requirements, including a tabulation of the total number of agency meetings open to the public, the total number of meetings closed to the public, the reasons for closing such meetings, and a description of any litigation brought against the agency under this section, including any costs assessed against the agency in such litigation (whether or not paid by the agency)."

Government Performance and Results Act

Citations:

5 U.S.C. §306; 31 U.S.C. §§1105(a)(29), 1115-1119, 3515(a), 9703-9704; 39 U.S. C. §§2801-2805 (2000); enacted August 3, 1993 by Pub. L. No. 103-62, 107 Stat. 286.

Lead Agencies:

Office of Management and Budget, Old Executive Office Building, 17th Street & Pennsylvania Avenue, NW, Washington, DC 20503; U.S. Government Accountability Office, General Government Division, 441 G Street, NW, Washington, DC 20548.

Overview:

Background. Concerns with government efficiency and shrinking dollars are stimulating federal agencies to improve the performance of their programs. The Government Performance and Results Act of 1993 (GPRA) provides a pathway for addressing these challenges, and is intended to bring about a fundamental transformation in the way government programs and operations are managed and administered. The change that GPRA seeks to bring about would place much greater emphasis within the government on what programs are actually accomplishing, and how well the accomplishments match programs' objectives.

The law requires federal agencies to develop strategic plans describing their overall goals and objectives, annual performance plans containing quantifiable measures of their progress, and performance reports describing their success in meeting those standards and measures. Enacted during the first year of the Clinton Administration, GPRA could loosely be viewed as part of the Administration's larger "Reinventing Government" initiative.

Coverage. Within the federal government, GPRA applies to all federal entities defined by 5 U.S.C. §105 as being an "agency," with a few exceptions. It covers 14 Cabinet departments, virtually all independent establishments (agencies), and all government corporations. The U.S. Postal Service is covered by the Act, but under a special provision designed to recognize its special status.

Main Features. The Act's features include:

- A requirement for federal departments and agencies to prepare strategic plans, beginning with an initial plan to be submitted to the Office of Management and Budget (OMB) and to Congress by September 30, 1997.
- A requirement that federal departments and agencies prepare annual performance plans, setting out specific performance goals for a fiscal year, starting with a performance plan for fiscal year 1999.
- A requirement that OMB prepare an annual government-wide performance plan based on the agency annual performance plans. The government-wide performance plan is to be a part of the President's budget and transmitted to Congress. In the agency and government-wide performance plans, the levels of program performance to be achieved is to correspond with the program funding level in the budget. The first of these plans was for the fiscal year 1999 budget.
- A requirement that federal departments and agencies submit an annual program performance report to the President and Congress, and which compares actual performance with the goal levels that were set in the annual performance plan. The annual report is due six months after the end of a fiscal year. The first report, covering fiscal year 1999, is to be submitted by March 31, 2000.
- Provisions giving managers greater flexibility in managing by allowing the waiver of various administrative controls and limitations. In return, managers are expected to be more accountable for the performance of their programs and operations.

Purposes. According to GPRA's proponents, it will help restore the public's confidence in government; agency management will be able to articulate and communicate missions, goals, and accomplishments better; and the President and Congress will be better able to decide which government efforts are worth continuing and/or expanding and which are best left to state and local government of the private or nonprofit sectors. GPRA's explicit goals are to:

- Initiate program performance reform by:
  - Requiring the creation of strategic plans with program goals,
  - Measuring program performance against those goals, and
  - Reporting publicly on progress.
- Improve federal program effectiveness and public accountability by promoting a new focus on reporting publicly on progress, helping federal managers improve service delivery by requiring the development of plans to meet program objectives, providing information about program results and service quality, and improving Congressional decision making and internal management of the federal government by providing more objective information.

Strategic plans. Strategic plans provide the foundation for carrying out all other GPRA requirements. The strategic plan states an agency purpose: why an agency and its programs exist, and what will be accomplished and when, and defines the long-range course of the agency with sufficient precision to guide the short-term actions of agency managers. Strategic plans cover a minimum of six years, and are to be revised and updated at least every three years. Development of strategic plans is intended to serve as an opportunity for broad discussion about the agency's future programmatic direction and priorities. Consultation with Congress is required during plan development, and agencies are also required to seek the views of other interested or potentially affected parties. Strategic plans were initially submitted to Congress in September 1997, and are required to be updated at least once every three years.

Annual performance plans. Performance plans are to be released annually by agencies. They are tools that discuss comparisons of actual performance achieved with performance level specified for each performance goal; explain why a goal was not met, and future plans for achieving the performance goal; offer summary findings of any program evaluations done that fiscal year; and explicate use of any waiver of administrative requirements and the effectiveness of these waivers in achieving performance goals.

Annual performance plans must contain one or more performance goals for each of the major programs and operations covered in the strategic plan. A performance goal is a target level of performance expressed as a tangible, measurable objective against which actual achievement can be compared, including a goal expressed as a quantitative standard, value, or rate. Plans must also contain performance indicators or values that will be used in measuring outputs and outcomes; a description of the means to be used to verify and validate measured values; and a description of operational processes, skills and technology, and human capital, information, or other resources required to meet the performance goals.

Annual performance reports. Annual program performance reports should contain a comparison of the actual performance achieved with the performance levels specified for each performance goal and performance indicator in the annual performance plan. If a performance goal was not met, it must have an explanation of why the goal was not met, along with either the plans and schedules for achieving the performance goal in the future or a statement that the performance goal as established is impractical or infeasible, and expressing the agency's intention to modify or discontinue the goal.

Waivers to promote management flexibility. In addition to strategic planning and performance measurement, GPRA is intended to promote greater flexibility for managers in return for greater accountability for results. This flexibility is introduced by permitting waiver of selected non-statutory requirements and controls, in return for achieving greater program results than would otherwise occur. These administrative and procedural requirements are prescribed by agency rules and directives, or are those imposed across the government by an agency which has a central management role, and cover areas such as financial management, personnel, supply, buildings, etc.

Pilot projects. Pilot projects have been employed under GPRA to demonstrate whether agencies can prepare annual performance plans that meet GPRA requirements, and to identify any difficulties agencies are encountering in plan preparation. Pilot projects were officially designated in all 14 Cabinet departments and an equivalent number of other agencies. Some agencies have more than one pilot project, and over 70 individual pilot projects have been so designated. In some instances, agencies have supplemented the designated list with their own informal or internal pilot projects. The pilot projects range from the very large—the entirety of the Social Security Administration and the Internal Revenue Service—to the very small.

Program Assessment Rating Tool. In 2001, OMB began developing a mechanism—the Program Assessment Rating Tool (PART)—to help budget examiners and federal managers measure program effectiveness. PART's stated objective is to build upon GPRA, obtain consistent and unbiased performance data from government programs, and use that information to link performance data and budget decisions.

PART was designed under the "Budget and Performance Integration Initiative," one of five Presidential management initiatives. OMB initially tested the tool on a limited number of programs in preparation for the FY 2003 budget. Each year since, PART has been used on 20 percent of all government programs/activities. All programs will have been reviewed once by 2007.

PART's six questionnaires are designed for different government activities—competitive grant programs, block/formula grant programs, regulatory-based programs, capital assets and service acquisition programs, credit programs, research and development programs, and direct federal programs. Programs are scored based on four areas (program purpose and design, strategic planning, program management, and program results). The final score is translated into one of five ratings, ranging from "effective" to "ineffective" (or "results not demonstrated").

The relationship between the PART and GPRA is not well defined. GAO has stated, "Many [agency officials] view PART's program-by-program focus and the substitution of program measures as detrimental to their GPRA planning and reporting processes." (GAO-04-174, January 2004) The official source for PART information is the 2006 PART guidance available at www.whitehouse.gov/omb/part/2006_part_guidance.pdf.

Legislative History:

GPRA's antecedents can be traced back over 30 years; most of its predecessors largely failed to take root. The first was the Program, Planning, and Budgeting System (PPBS), which was introduced in the 1960's and sought to extend the program management and budgeting scheme then being used by the Department of Defense to the government-at-large. PPBS was succeeded in the 1970's by Management by Objective (MBO) and then by Zero-Base-Budgeting (ZBB). Within the federal government, both MBO and ZBB soon became artifacts, although an evolved form of PPBS continues to be used in the Department of Defense. During the 1980's, several initiatives—including productivity improvement, quality management, and a short-lived resurrection of MBO—were featured.

GPRA, by comparison, was created as a law, unlike its predecessors, which were presidential directives. Its origin can primarily be traced to two separately conceived proposals. One proposal was described in the Management Report (January 1989) of then-President Reagan; his report contained a chapter, prepared by OMB staff, entitled "Government of the Future," which outlined the basic structure of what would become GPRA four years later. Another proposal came from Senator William Roth, who in 1990 first introduced the legislation that would eventually become the Government Performance and Results Act. In addition, the Chief Financial Officers Act (Pub. L. No. 101-576) became law in 1990. Several features of this Act also helped lay a foundation for GPRA.

On October 3, 1990 (101st Congress), Senator Roth (R-DE) introduced S. 3154, the "Federal Program Performance Standards and Goals Act of 1990," which was referred that same day to the Committee on Governmental Affairs. No hearings were held on the bill, but it was discussed by Senator Roth and witnesses at October 3 and 11 hearings on "OMB's Response to Government Management Failures" held by the Committee on Governmental Affairs.

On January 14, 1991 (102d Congress), Senator Roth introduced S. 20, the "Federal Program Performance Standards and Goals Act of 1991," which was referred that day to the Committee on Governmental Affairs. The legislation differed from the version introduced in October 1990 only by the addition of a Findings and Purposes section.

The Senate Committee on Governmental Affairs held hearings on S. 20 on May 23, 1991 and May 5, 1992. The Committee considered S. 20 on August 5, 1992. It adopted by voice vote an amendment in nature of a substitute offered by Senators Glenn, Roth, and Cohen, retitling the bill the "Government Performance and Results Act of 1992," providing for initiation of implementation with a set of 3-year pilot projects before government-wide application, and making other changes, and voted to report the bill favorably by voice vote.

The Committee on Governmental Affairs reported S. 20 (S. Rep. No. 102-429) as amended on September 29, 1992. The Senate passed the bill on October 1, 1992, under unanimous consent, but the House of Representatives took no action during that Congress.

On January 21, 1993 (103d Congress), Senator Roth (with Senators Glenn (D-OH), Graham (D-FL), Metzenbaum (D-OH), McCain (R-AZ), Akaka (D-HI), Robb (D-VA), and Lugar (R-IN)as cosponsors) reintroduced the bill as S.20, the "Government Performance and Results Act of 1993," which was referred that same day to the Committee on Governmental Affairs. The legislation was very similar to the version passed by the Senate the preceding year. In early 1993, newly-elected President Clinton gave early and strong support for the proposed legislation. The Administration expressly endorsed S. 20 at a hearing on March 11, 1993, before the Senate Committee on

Governmental Affairs. On March 24, 1993, the Committee on Governmental Affairs voted to report S. 20 as amended.

GPRA was subsequently passed by both the Senate and House of Representatives without objection, and was promoted and supported by members of both political parties.

Source Note:

Several executive branch documents lay out requirements for most federal agencies' activities to fulfill the Act's provisions. These include OMB Circular A-11 Part 2, Preparation and Submission of Strategic Plans and Annual Performance Plans (2006), and Congressional Consultations on the Implementation of the Government Performance and Results Act.

The Government Accountability Office has had a longstanding interest in improving government management through the use of strategic planning and performance measurement. Since 1973, GAO also has produced over 70 reports on performance measures and currently has nearly a dozen ongoing efforts to assess measurement in specific agencies. GAO has published an executive guide on implementing GPRA, as well as numerous reports discussing various aspects of agency implementation.

OPM has developed a comprehensive CD-ROM entitled *Government Performance & Results Act: A Multimedia Orientation & Toolkit*. A number of other sources have compiled guides, models, and descriptive materials to assist with implementing the Act. These include the Chief Financial Officers Council's Compilation of Reports and Guidance and GAO's Documents about the Results Act.

Several entities have established websites related to GPRA, strategic planning, and performance evaluation, including Fedworld's Results Library, OMB Watch's GPRA Report, NAPA's Center for Improving Government Performance, and the Congressional Institute Results Act Page.

Bibliography:

I. Legislative History

1. Senate Report No.103-58, Senate Committee on Governmental Affairs, 103d Congress, 1st Sess. (1993).
2. Senate Report No. 102-429, Senate Committee on Governmental Affairs, 102d Cong., 2d Sess. (1992).

3. Call up by Unanimous Consent in House of Representatives, Cong. Rec. H4734-4737 (July 15, 1993).

II. Other Government Documents

1. Chief Financial Officers Council, *Streamlining Governmentwide Statutory Reports* (1995).
2. Chief Financial Officers Council, *Implementation of the Government Performance and Results Act* (May 1995).
3. Chief Financial Officers Council, *Guiding Principles for Implementing GPRA* (May 1995).
4. Congressional Research Service, *Performance Measure Provisions in the 105th Congress: Analysis of a Selected Compilation* (December 1998).
5. U.S. Department of Energy, *Guidelines for Strategic Planning* (January 1996).
6. U.S. Department of Energy, *Guidelines for Performance Measurement* (June 1996).
7. Internal Revenue Service, Office of Economic Analysis, *Best Practices: The IRS Research Project on Integrating Strategic Planning, Budgeting, Investment and Review* (May 1996).
8. Department of the Navy, Total Quality Leadership Office, *A Handbook for Strategic Planning*.
9. Department of the Navy, Total Quality Leadership Office, *Strategic Planning: Selecting the Leadership Team* (May 1992).
10. Department of the Navy, *Total Quality Leadership Office, Strategic Management for Senior Leaders: A Handbook for Implementation*.
11. Department of the Navy, *Total Quality Leadership Office, In Their Own Words: Executive Summary of Strategic Management Interview Data*.
12. National Aeronautics and Space Administration, *Strategic Planning and Strategic Management within NASA: A Case Study* (June 1996).
13. National Aeronautics and Space Administration, *NASA Strategic Management Handbook* (October 1996).
14. National Aeronautics and Space Administration, *Strategic Planning: Charting a Course for the Future* (video) (Oct. 16, 1996).
15. National Highway Traffic Safety Administration, *The National Highway Traffic Safety Administration Case Study: Strategic Planning and Performance Measurement* (August 1996).
16. Office of Management and Budget, *Circular A-11, Preparation and Submission of Strategic Plans and Annual Performance Plans* (Revised, 2006).

17. Office of Management and Budget, *Government-wide Performance Plan for FY 1999* (February 1998).

18. Office of Management and Budget, *Primer on Performance Management* (February 1995).

19. Office of Management and Budget, *Guidance for Completing 2007 PARTs* (January 2007), *available at* www.whitehouse.gov/omb/part/2006_part_guidance.pdf.

20. Congressional Consultations on the Implementation of the Government Performance and Results Act (November 1996).

21. U.S. Government Accountability Office, *Executive Guide: Effectively Implementing the Government Performance and Results Act*, GAO/GGD-96-118 (June 1, 1996).

22. U.S. Government Accountability Office, *Managing for Results: Achieving GPRA's Objectives Requires Strong Congressional Role*, GAO/T-GGD-96-79 (March 6, 1996).

23. U.S. Government Accountability Office, *Managing for Results: Status of the Government Performance and Results Act*, GAO/T-GGD-95-193, (June 27, 1995).

24. U.S. Government Accountability Office, *Managing for Results: The Statutory Framework for Performance-Based Management and Accountability* (Jan. 28, 1998).

25. U.S. Office of Personnel Management, *Government Performance & Results Act: A Multimedia Orientation & Toolkit* (CD-Rom version 1.0, Sept. 1997).

III. Books, Reports, and Articles

1. A. Antonelli & G. Freeman, *Warning: Expect Bad Results from the Results Act Without Congressional Oversight* (Heritage Foundation, September 1997).

2. M. Heen, *Reinventing Tax Expenditure Reform: Improving Program Oversight Under the Government Performance and Results Act*, 35 Wake Forest L. Rev. 751 (2000).

3. National Academies, Committee on Science, Engineering, and Public Policy (COSEPUP), *Implementing the Government Performance and Results Act for Research: A Status Report* (2001).

4. OMB Watch, *GPRA Process Needs More Stakeholder Involvement* (September 1997).

5. OMB Watch, *A Nonprofit Assessment of the Government Performance and Results Act* (December 1998).

6. OMB Watch, *PART Backgrounder* (April 2005), *available at* http://www.ombwatch.org/regs/2005/performance/PARTbackgrounder.pdf.

Appendix:

1. Government Performance and Results Act, Provisions of Pub. L. No. 103-62. (Including 5 U.S.C. §§306 (2000); 31 U.S.C. §§1105(a)(29), 1115-1119, 3515(a), 9703-9704 (2000); 39 U.S.C. §§2801-2805 (2000).)

Government Performance and Results Act

Provisions of Pub. L. No. 103-62
Pub. L. 103-62, 107 Stat. 286 (August 3, 1993)

SHORT TITLE

Section 1 of Pub. L. No. 103-62 provided that: "This Act may be cited as the "Government Performance and Results Act of 1993."

FINDINGS AND PURPOSES

Section 2 of Pub. L. No. 103-62 provided that:
"(a) Findings—The Congress finds that—
(1) waste and inefficiency in Federal programs undermine the confidence of the American people in the Government and reduces the Federal Government's ability to address adequately vital public needs;
(2) Federal managers are seriously disadvantaged in their efforts to improve program efficiency and effectiveness, because of insufficient articulation of program goals and inadequate information on program performance; and
(3) congressional policymaking, spending decisions and program oversight are seriously handicapped by insufficient attention to program performance and results.
(b) Purposes—The purposes of this Act are to—
(1) improve the confidence of the American people in the capability of the Federal Government, by systematically holding Federal agencies accountable for achieving program results;
(2) initiate program performance reform with a series of pilot projects in setting program goals, measuring program performance against those goals, and reporting publicly on their progress;
(3) improve Federal program effectiveness and public accountability by promoting a new focus on results, service quality, and customer satisfaction;
(4) help Federal managers improve service delivery, by requiring that they plan for meeting program objectives and by providing them with information about program results and service quality;
(5) improve congressional decisionmaking by providing more objective information on achieving statutory objectives, and on the relative effectiveness and efficiency of Federal programs and spending; and
(6) improve internal management of the Federal Government."

CONGRESSIONAL OVERSIGHT

Section 8(a) of Pub. L. No. 103-62 provided that: "Nothing in this Act (see Short Title of 1993 Amendment note set out under section 1101 of this title) shall be construed as limiting the ability of Congress to establish, amend, suspend, or annul a performance goal. Any such action shallhave the effect of superseding that goal in the plan submitted under section 1105(a)(29) (now 1105(a)(28)) of title 31, United States Code."

GOVERNMENT ACCOUNTABILITY OFFICE REPORT

Section 8(b) of Pub. L. No. 103-62 provided that: "No later than June 1, 1997, the Comptroller General of the United States shall report to Congress on the implementation of this Act (see Short Title of 1993 Amendment note set out under section 1101 of this title), including the prospects for compliance by Federal agencies beyond those participating as pilot projects under sections 1118 and 9704 of title 31, United States Code."

STRATEGIC PLANNING AND PERFORMANCE MEASUREMENT TRAINING

Section 9 of Pub. L. No. 103-62 provided that: "The Office of Personnel Management shall, in consultation with the Director of the Office of Management and Budget and the Comptroller General of the United States, develop a strategic planning and performance measurement training component for its management training program and otherwise provide managers with an orientation on the development and use of strategic planning and program performance measurement."

APPLICATION OF ACT

No provision or amendment made by this Act may be construed as—

(1) creating any right, privilege, benefit, or entitlement for any person who is not an officer or employee of the United States acting in such capacity, and no person who is not an officer or employee of the United States acting in such capacity shall have standing to file any civil action in a court of the United States to enforce any provision or amendment made by this Act; or

(2) superseding any statutory requirement, including any requirement under section 553 of title 5, United States Code.

* * * *

Title 5, U.S. Code

Title 5—Government Organization and Employees
    Part 1—The Agencies Generally
        Chapter 3—Powers

§306. Strategic plans

(a) No later than September 30, 1997, the head of each agency shall submit to the Director of the Office of Management and Budget and to the Congress a strategic plan for program activities. Such plan shall contain—

(1) a comprehensive mission statement covering the major functions and operations of the agency;

(2) general goals and objectives, including outcome-related goals and objectives, for the major functions and operations of the agency;

(3) a description of how the goals and objectives are to be achieved, including a description of the operational processes, skills and technology, and the human, capital, information, and other resources required to meet those goals and objectives;

(4) a description of how the performance goals included in the plan required by section 1115(a) of title 31 shall be related to the general goals and objectives in the strategic plan;

(5) an identification of those key factors external to the agency and beyond its control that could significantly affect the achievement of the general goals and objectives; and

(6) a description of the program evaluations used in establishing or revising general goals and objectives, with a schedule for future program evaluations.

(b) The strategic plan shall cover a period of not less than five years forward from the fiscal year in which it is submitted, and shall be updated and revised at least every three years, except that the strategic plan for the Department of Defense shall be updated and revised at least every four years.[1]

(c) The performance plan required by section 1115 of title 31 shall be consistent with the agency's strategic plan. A performance plan may not be submitted for a fiscal year not covered by a current strategic plan under this section.

---

[1] The Act's 1999 amendment (Pub. L. No. 106-65) authorized the Department of Defense to update and revise its strategic plan every four, rather than three, years.

(d) When developing a strategic plan, the agency shall consult with the Congress, and shall solicit and consider the views and suggestions of those entities potentially affected by or interested in such a plan.

(e) The functions and activities of this section shall be considered to be inherently Governmental functions. The drafting of strategic plans under this section shall be performed only by Federal employees.

(f) For purposes of this section the term "agency" means an Executive agency defined under section 105, but does not include the Central Intelligence Agency, the Government Accountability Office, the Panama Canal Commission, the United States Postal Service, and the Postal Rate Commission.

(Aug. 3, 1993, added Pub. L. No. 103-62, §3, 107 Stat. 286; as amended Oct. 5, 1999, Pub. L. No. 106-65, Div. A, Title IX, §902, 113 Stat. 717 and July 7, 2004, Pub. L. No. 108-271, §8(b), 118 Stat. 814.).)

* * * *

Title 31, U.S. Code

Title 31—Money and Finance
    Subtitle II—The Budget Process
        Chapter 11—The Budget and Fiscal, Budget, and Program Information

§1105. Budget contents and submission to Congress

(a) On or after the first Monday in January but not later than the first Monday in February of each year, the President shall submit a budget of the United States Government for the following fiscal year. Each budget shall include a budget message and summary and supporting information. The President shall include in each budget the following:

. . . .

(29) beginning with fiscal year 1999, a Federal Government performance plan for the overall budget as provided for under section 1115.

. . . (Pub. L. No. 103-62, § 4(a), Aug. 3, 1993, 107 Stat. 286.)

§1115. Performance Plans

(a) In carrying out the provisions of section 1105(a)(29), the Director of the Office of Management and Budget shall require each agency to prepare an annual performance plan covering each program activity set forth in the budget of such agency. Such plan shall—

(1) establish performance goals to define the level of performance to be achieved by a program activity;

(2) express such goals in an objective, quantifiable, and measurable form unless authorized to be in an alternative form under subsection (b);

(3) provide a description of how the performance goals and objectives are to be achieved, including the operation processes, training, skills and technology, and the human, capital, information, and other resources and strategies required to meet those performance goals and objectives;

(4) establish performance indicators to be used in measuring or assessing the relevant outputs, service levels, and outcomes of each program activity;

(5) provide a basis for comparing actual program results with the established performance goals; and

(6) describe the means to be used to verify and validate measured values.

(b) If an agency, in consultation with the Director of the Office of Management and Budget, determines that it is not feasible to express the performance goals for a particular program activity in an objective, quantifiable, and measurable form, the Director of the Office of Management and Budget may authorize an alternative form. Such alternative form shall—

(1) include separate descriptive statements of—

(A)(i) a minimally effective program, and

(ii) a successful program, or

(B) such alternative as authorized by the Director of the Office of Management and Budget, with sufficient precision and in such terms that would allow for an accurate, independent determination of whether the program activity's performance meets the criteria of the description; or

(2) state why it is infeasible or impractical to express a performance goal in any form for the program activity.

(c) For the purpose of complying with this section, an agency may aggregate, disaggregate, or consolidate program activities, except that any aggregation or consolidation may not omit or minimize the significance of any program activity constituting a major function or operation for the agency.

(d) An agency may submit with its annual performance plan an appendix covering any portion of the plan that—

(1) is specifically authorized under criteria established by an Executive order to be kept secret in the interest of national defense or foreign policy; and

(2) is properly classified pursuant to such Executive order.

(e) The functions and activities of this section shall be considered to be inherently Governmental functions. The drafting of performance plans under this section shall be performed only by Federal employees.

(f) For purposes of this section and sections 1116 through 1119, and sections 9703 and 9704 the term—

(1) "agency" has the same meaning as such term is defined under section 306(f) of title 5;

(2) "outcome measure" means an assessment of the results of a program activity compared to its intended purpose;

(3) "output measure" means the tabulation, calculation, or recording of activity or effort and can be expressed in a quantitative or qualitative manner;

(4) "performance goal" means a target level of performance expressed as a tangible, measurable objective, against which actual achievement can be compared, including a goal expressed as a quantitative standard, value, or rate;

(5) "performance indicator" means a particular value or characteristic used to measure output or outcome;

(6) "program activity" means a specific activity or project as listed in the program and financing schedules of the annual budget of the United States Government; and

(7) "program evaluation" means an assessment, through objective measurement and systematic analysis, of the manner and extent to which Federal programs achieve intended objectives.

(Aug. 3, 1993, added Pub. L. No. 103-62, §4(b), 107 Stat. 287; amended Nov. 25, 2002 by Pub. L. No. 107-296, title XIII, §1311(a), 116 Stat. 2289 and Nov. 24, 2003 by Pub. L. No. 108-136, div. A, title XIV, §1421(b), 117 Stat. 1667.)

§1116. Program performance reports

(a) Not later than 150 days after the end of an agency's fiscal year, the head of each agency shall prepare and submit to the President and the Congress, a report on program performance for the previous fiscal year.

(b)(1) Each program performance report shall set forth the performance indicators established in the agency performance plan under section 1115, along with the actual program performance achieved compared with the performance goals expressed in the plan for that fiscal year.

(2) If performance goals are specified in an alternative form under section 1115(b), the results of such program shall be described in relation to such specifications, including whether the performance failed to meet the criteria of a minimally effective or successful program.

(c) The report for fiscal year 2000 shall include actual results for the preceding fiscal year, the report for fiscal year 2001 shall include actual results for the two preceding fiscal years, and the report for fiscal year 2002 and all subsequent reports shall include actual results for the three preceding fiscal years.

(d) Each report shall—

(1) review the success of achieving the performance goals of the fiscal year;

(2) evaluate the performance plan for the current fiscal year relative to the performance achieved toward the performance goals in the fiscal year covered by the report;

(3) explain and describe, where a performance goal has not been met (including when a program activity's performance is determined not to have met the criteria of a successful program activity under section 1115(b)(1)(A)(ii) or a corresponding level of achievement if another alternative form is used)—

(A) why the goal was not met;

(B) those plans and schedules for achieving the established performance goal; and

(C) if the performance goal is impractical or infeasible, why that is the case and what action is recommended;

(4) describe the use and assess the effectiveness in achieving performance goals of any waiver under section 9703 of this title; and

(5) include the summary findings of those program evaluations completed during the fiscal year covered by the report.

(e) (1) Except as provided in paragraph (2), each program performance report shall contain an assessment by the agency head of the completeness and reliability of the performance data included in the report. The assessment shall describe any material inadequacies in the completeness and reliability of the performance data, and the actions the agency can take and is taking to resolve such inadequacies.

(2) If a program performance report is incorporated into a report submitted under section 3516, the requirements of section 3516 (e) shall apply in lieu of paragraph (1).

(f) The functions and activities of this section shall be considered to be inherently Governmental functions. The drafting of program performance reports under this section shall be performed only by Federal employees.

(Aug. 3, 1993, added Pub. L. No. 103-62, §4(b), 107 Stat. 288; amended Nov. 22, 2000 by Pub. L. No. 106-531, §5(a)(1), (b), 114 Stat. 2539; and Nov. 25, 2002 by Pub. L. No. 107-296, title XIII, §1311(b), 116 Stat. 2290.)

§1117. Exemption

The Director of the Office of Management and Budget may exempt from the requirements of sections 1115 and 1116 of this title and section 306 of title 5, any agency with annual outlays of $20,000,000 or less.

(Aug. 3, 1993, added Pub. L. No. 103-62, §4(b), 107 Stat. 289.)

§1118. Pilot projects for performance goals

(a) The Director of the Office of Management and Budget, after consultation with the head of each agency, shall designate not less than ten agencies as pilot projects in performance measurement for fiscal years 1994, 1995, and 1996. The selected agencies shall reflect a representative range of Government functions and capabilities in measuring and reporting program performance.

(b) Pilot projects in the designated agencies shall undertake the preparation of performance plans under section 1115, and program performance reports under section 1116, other than section 1116(c), for one or more of the major functions and operations of the agency. A strategic plan shall be used when preparing agency performance plans during one or more years of the pilot period.

(c) No later than May 1, 1997, the Director of the Office of Management and Budget shall submit a report to the President and to the Congress which shall—

(1) assess the benefits, costs, and usefulness of the plans and reports prepared by the pilot agencies in meeting the purposes of the Government Performance and Results Act of 1993;

(2) identify any significant difficulties experienced by the pilot agencies in preparing plans and reports; and

(3) set forth any recommended changes in the requirements of the provisions of Government Performance and Results Act of 1993, section 306 of title 5, sections 1105, 1115, 1116, 1117, 1119 and 9703 of this title, and this section.

(Aug. 3, 1993, added Pub. L. No. 103-62, §6(a), 107 Stat. 290.)

§1119. Pilot projects for performance budgeting

(a) The Director of the Office of Management and Budget, after consultation with the head of each agency shall designate not less than five agencies as pilot projects in performance budgeting for fiscal years 1998 and 1999. At least three of the agencies shall be selected from those designated as pilot projects under section 1118, and shall also reflect a representative range of Government functions and capabilities in measuring and reporting program performance.

(b) Pilot projects in the designated agencies shall cover the preparation of performance budgets. Such budgets shall present, for one or more of the major functions and operations of the agency, the varying levels of performance, including outcome-related performance, that would result from different budgeted amounts.

(c) The Director of the Office of Management and Budget shall include, as an alternative budget presentation in the budget submitted under section 1105 for fiscal year 1999, the performance budgets of the designated agencies for this fiscal year.

(d) No later than March 31, 2001, the Director of the Office of Management and Budget shall transmit a report to the President and to the Congress on the performance budgeting pilot projects which shall—

(1) assess the feasibility and advisability of including a performance budget as part of the annual budget submitted under section 1105;

(2) describe any difficulties encountered by the pilot agencies in preparing a performance budget

(3) recommend whether legislation requiring performance budgets should be proposed and the general provisions of any legislation; and

(4) set forth any recommended changes in the other requirements of the Government Performance and Results Act of 1993, section 306 of title 5, sections 1105, 1115, 1116, 1117, and 9703 of this title, and this section.

(e) After receipt of the report required under subsection (d), the Congress may specify that a performance budget be submitted as part of the annual budget submitted under section 1105.

(Aug. 3, 1993, added Pub. L. No. 103-62, § 6(c), 107 Stat. 291.)

Title 31—Money and Finance

Subtitle III—Financial Management
   Chapter 35—Accounting and Collection

§3515. Financial statements of agencies

(a) Except as provided in subsection (e), not later than March 1 of 2003 and each year thereafter, the head of each covered executive agency shall prepare and submit to the Congress and the Director of the Office of Management and Budget an audited financial statement for the preceding fiscal year, covering all accounts and associated activities of each office, bureau, and activity of the agency.

(Nov. 15, 1990, added Pub. L. No. 101-576, Title III, §303(a)(1), 104 Stat. 2849, and amended Pub. L. No. 103-356, Title IV, §405(a), Oct. 13, 1994, 108 Stat. 3415.)

Subtitle VI—Miscellaneous
Chapter 97—Miscellaneous

§9703. Managerial accountability and flexibility

(a) Beginning with fiscal year 1999, the performance plans required under section 1115 may include proposals to waive administrative procedural requirements and controls, including specification of personnel staffing levels, limitations on compensation or remuneration, and prohibitions or restrictions on funding transfers among budget object classification 20 and subclassifications 11, 12, 31, and 32 of each annual budget submitted under section 1105, in return for specific individual or organization accountability to achieve a performance goal. In preparing and submitting the performance plan under section 1105(a)(28), the Director of the Office of Management and Budget shall review and may approve any proposed waivers. A waiver shall take effect at the beginning of the fiscal year for which the waiver is approved.

(b) Any such proposal under subsection (a) shall describe the anticipated effects on performance resulting from greater managerial or organizational flexibility, discretion, and authority, and shall quantify the expected improvements in performance resulting from any waiver. The expected improvements shall be compared to current actual performance, and to the projected level of performance that would be achieved independent of any waiver.

(c) Any proposal waiving limitations on compensation or remuneration shall precisely express the monetary change in compensation or remuneration amounts, such as bonuses or awards, that shall result from meeting, exceeding, or failing to meet performance goals.

(d) Any proposed waiver of procedural requirements or controls imposed by an agency (other than the proposing agency or the Office of Management and Budget) may not be included in a performance plan unless it is endorsed by the agency that established the requirement, and the endorsement included in the proposing agency's performance plan.

(e) A waiver shall be in effect for one or two years as specified by the Director of the Office of Management and Budget in approving the waiver. A waiver may be renewed for a subsequent year. After a waiver has been in effect for three consecutive years, the performance plan prepared under section 1115 may propose that a waiver, other than a waiver of limitations on compensation or remuneration, be made permanent.

(f) For purposes of this section, the definitions under section 1115(f) shall apply.

(Aug. 3, 1993, added Pub. L. No. 103-62, §6(c), 107 Stat. 291.)

§9704. Pilot projects for managerial accountability and flexibility

(a) The Director of the Office of Management and Budget shall designate not less than five agencies as pilot projects in managerial accountability and flexibility for fiscal years 1995 and 1996. Such agencies shall be selected from those designated as pilot projects under section 1118 and shall reflect a representative range of Government functions and capabilities in measuring and reporting program performance.

(b) Pilot projects in the designated agencies shall include proposed waivers in accordance with section 9703 for one or more of the major functions and operations of the agency.

(c) The Director of the Office of Management and Budget shall include in the report to the President and to the Congress required under section 1118(c)—

    (1) an assessment of the benefits, costs, and usefulness of increasing managerial and organizational flexibility, discretion, and authority in exchange for improved performance through a waiver; and

    (2) an identification of any significant difficulties experienced by the pilot agencies in preparing proposed waivers.

(d) For purposes of this section the definitions under section 1115(f) shall apply.

(Aug. 3, 1993, added Pub. L. No. 103-62, § 6(b), 107 Stat. 290.)

* * * *

Title 39, U.S. Code

Title 39—Postal Service
   Part III—Modernization and Fiscal Administration
      Chapter 28—Strategic Planning and Performance Management

§2801. Definitions

For purposes of this chapter the term—
   (1) "outcome measure" refers to an assessment of the results of a program activity compared to its intended purpose;
   (2) "output measure" refers to the tabulation, calculation, or recording of activity or effort and can be expressed in a quantitative or qualitative manner;
   (3) "performance goal" means a target level of performance expressed as a tangible, measurable objective, against which actual achievement shall be compared, including a goal expressed as a quantitative standard, value, or rate;
   (4) "performance indicator" refers to a particular value or characteristic used to measure output or outcome;
   (5) "program activity" means a specific activity related to the mission of the Postal Service; and
   (6) "program evaluation" means an assessment, through objective measurement and systematic analysis, of the manner and extent to which Postal Service programs achieve intended objectives.

(Aug. 3, 1993, added Pub. L. No. 103-62, §7, 107 Stat. 292.)

§2802. Strategic plans

(a) No later than September 30, 1997, the Postal Service shall submit to the President and the Congress a strategic plan for its program activities. Such plan shall contain—
   (1) a comprehensive mission statement covering the major functions and operations of the Postal Service;
   (2) general goals and objectives, including outcome-related goals and objectives, for the major functions and operations of the Postal Service;
   (3) a description of how the goals and objectives are to be achieved, including a description of the operational processes, skills and technology, and the human, capital, information, and other resources required to meet those goals and objectives;
   (4) a description of how the performance goals included in the plan required under section 2803 shall be related to the general goals and objectives in the strategic plan;

(5) an identification of those key factors external to the Postal Service and beyond its control that could significantly affect the achievement of the general goals and objectives; and

(6) a description of the program evaluations used in establishing or revising general goals and objectives, with a schedule for future program evaluations.

(b) The strategic plan shall cover a period of not less than five years forward from the fiscal year in which it is submitted, and shall be updated and revised at least every three years.

(c) The performance plan required under section 2803 shall be consistent with the Postal Service's strategic plan. A performance plan may not be submitted for a fiscal year not covered by a current strategic plan under this section.

(d) When developing a strategic plan, the Postal Service shall solicit and consider the views and suggestions of those entities potentially affected by or interested in such a plan, and shall advise the Congress of the contents of the plan.

(Aug. 3, 1993, added Pub. L. No. 103-62, §7,107 Stat. 292.)

§2803. Performance plans

(a) The Postal Service shall prepare an annual performance plan covering each program activity set forth in the Postal Service budget, which shall be included in the comprehensive statement presented under section 2401(g) of this title. Such plan shall—

(1) establish performance goals to define the level of performance to be achieved by a program activity;

(2) express such goals in an objective, quantifiable, and measurable form unless an alternative form is used under subsection (b);

(3) briefly describe the operational processes, skills and technology, and the human, capital, information, or other resources required to meet the performance goals;

(4) establish performance indicators to be used in measuring or assessing the relevant outputs, service levels, and outcomes of each program activity;

(5) provide a basis for comparing actual program results with the established performance goals; and

(6) describe the means to be used to verify and validate measured values.

(b) If the Postal Service determines that it is not feasible to express the performance goals for a particular program activity in an objective, quantifiable, and measurable form, the Postal Service may use an alternative form.

Such alternative form shall—
   (1) include separate descriptive statements of—
      (A) a minimally effective program, and
      (B) a successful program,
with sufficient precision and in such terms that would allow for an accurate, independent determination of whether the program activity's performance meets the criteria of either description; or
   (2) state why it is infeasible or impractical to express a performance goal in any form for the program activity.
(c) In preparing a comprehensive and informative plan under this section, the Postal Service may aggregate, disaggregate, or consolidate program activities, except that any aggregation or consolidation may not omit or minimize the significance of any program activity constituting a major function or operation.
(d) The Postal Service may prepare a non-public annex to its plan covering program activities or parts of program activities relating to—
   (1) the avoidance of interference with criminal prosecution; or
   (2) matters otherwise exempt from public disclosure under section 410(c) of this title.

(Aug. 3, 1993, added Pub. L. No. 103-62, §7, 107 Stat. 293.)

§2804. Program performance reports

(a) The Postal Service shall prepare a report on program performance for each fiscal year, which shall be included in the annual comprehensive statement presented under section 2401(g) of this title.
(b)(1) The program performance report shall set forth the performance indicators established in the Postal Service performance plan, along with the actual program performance achieved compared with the performance goals expressed in the plan for that fiscal year.
   (2) If performance goals are specified by descriptive statements of a minimally effective program activity and a successful program activity, the results of such program shall be described in relationship to those categories, including whether the performance failed to meet the criteria of either category.
(c) The report for fiscal year 2000 shall include actual results for the preceding fiscal year, the report for fiscal year 2001 shall include actual results for the two preceding fiscal years, and the report for fiscal year 2002 and all subsequent reports shall include actual results for the three preceding fiscal years.

(d) Each report shall—
 (1) review the success of achieving the performance goals of the fiscal year;
 (2) evaluate the performance plan for the current fiscal year relative to the performance achieved towards the performance goals in the fiscal year covered by the report;
 (3) explain and describe, where a performance goal has not been met (including when a program activity's performance is determined not to have met the criteria of a successful program activity under section 2803(b)(2))—
  (A) why the goal was not met;
  (B) those plans and schedules for achieving the established performance goal; and
  (C) if the performance goal is impractical or infeasible, why that is the case and what action is recommended; and
 (4) include the summary findings of those program evaluations completed during the fiscal year covered by the report.

(Aug. 3, 1993, added Pub. L. No. 103-62, §7, 107 Stat. 294.)

§2805. Inherently Governmental functions

The functions and activities of this chapter shall be considered to be inherently Governmental functions. The drafting of strategic plans, performance plans, and program performance reports under this section shall be performed only by employees of the Postal Service.

(Aug. 3, 1993, added Pub. L. No. 103-62, §7, 107 Stat. 294.)

Information Quality Act

Citations:

44 U.S.C. §3516 note (2000); enacted December 21, 2000 by Pub. L. No. 106-554 §515, 114 Stat. 2763, 2763A-153.

Lead Agency:

Office of Management and Budget, Office of Information and Regulatory Affairs, 725 17th Street NW, Washington, D.C. 20503, (202) 395-3785; informationquality@omb.eop.gov; http://www.whitehouse.gov/omb/inforeg/infopoltech.html.

Overview:

The Information Quality Act (IQA), also frequently termed the Data Quality Act, mandates the establishment of guidelines "ensuring and maximizing the quality, objectivity, utility, and integrity of information (including statistical information) disseminated" by agencies. The IQA consists of a two-sentence appropriations rider to the Treasury and General Government Appropriations Act for Fiscal Year 2001 (Pub. L. No. 106-554) and amends the 1995 Paperwork Reduction Act (PRA) 44 U.S.C. §§3501-3520 (2000). The amendment directs the Office of Management and Budget (OMB) to issue policy and procedural guidance to federal agencies that are subject to the PRA. The IQA requires OMB to guide agencies: (1) in issuing their own data quality guidelines to regulate agency use and dissemination of information; (2) in developing administrative mechanisms so that affected parties may seek correction of information that does not comply with information quality guidelines; and (3) in making periodic reports to OMB on the number, nature and resolution of any complaints the agencies receive concerning their failure to comply with either OMB or agency-specific information quality guidelines.

OMB published proposed guidelines pursuant to the IQA in the Federal Register on June 28, 2001 (66 Fed. Reg. 34,489). Following public comment, OMB published interim final guidelines on September 28, 2001 (66 Fed. Reg. 49,718), and then finalized guidelines, after additional public comment, on February 22, 2002 (67 Fed. Reg. 8452). On October 1, 2002, the OMB guidelines went into effect, thus requiring agencies to issue, by the same date, their own guidelines detailing their agency-specific information quality standards and outlining administrative mechanisms for affected parties to challenge the quality of agency-disseminated information. Any information disseminated by agencies on or after October 1, 2002, is subject to the OMB and agency specific information quality guidelines. Agency-specific guidelines may be found on the agency websites, in the Federal Register, or on the OMB website at http://www.whitehouse.gov /omb/inforeg/agency_info_quality_links.html.

Information Quality Guidelines. The IQA aims to regulate "the sharing by Federal agencies of, and access to, information disseminated by Federal agencies." The OMB guidelines define "information" as "any communication or representation of knowledge such as facts or data, in any medium or form, including textual, numerical, graphic, cartographic, narrative, or audiovisual forms" (§V.5). This definition includes information posted on an agency web page, but excludes hyperlinks to information disseminated by sources outside the agency. Similarly, if an agency presents information in a manner clearly indicating that the information reflects an opinion, not a fact or an agency view, the information is not subject to the same information quality standards. The guidelines define "dissemination" as "agency initiated or sponsored distribution of information to the public" (§V.8). The guidelines exclude from the definition of dissemination distribution that is limited to "government employees or agency contractors or grantees; intra- or interagency use or sharing of government information; and responses to requests for agency records under the Freedom of Information Act, the Privacy Act, the Federal Advisory Committee Act or other similar law." Further excluded are "correspondence with individuals or persons, press releases, archival records, public filings, [and] subpoenas or adjudicative processes" (§V.8).

The IQA addresses the "quality, objectivity, utility, and integrity" of agency information. The OMB guidelines provide definitions for these terms. "Quality" encompasses utility, objectivity, and integrity (§V.1). "Utility" contemplates the usefulness of information for both the agency and the public such that "when transparency of information is relevant for assessing the information's usefulness from the public's perspective, the agency must take care to ensure that transparency has been addressed in its review of the information" (§V.2). "Integrity" refers to the safeguarding of information from unauthorized access or revision (§V.4). "Objectivity" focuses on whether information is not only substantively, accurate, clear and complete, but also presented in an accurate, clear, complete, and unbiased manner (§§V.3.a-b).

To satisfy the presentation prong of the objectivity requirement, agencies must present information in context, which may—depending on the sort of information—require providing additional information, sources, supporting data, models, sources of errors and documentation. The substantive objectivity prong requires that scientific, financial, or statistical information be based on original and supporting data and analytic results produced using "sound statistical and research methods" (§V.3.b).

The guidelines provide that information presumptively satisfies the substantive objectivity requirement if the relevant data and analytic results have undergone formal, independent, external peer review (§V.3.b.i). A presumption of objectivity is rebuttable if a petitioner persuasively demonstrates a lack of objectivity. If peer review is agency-sponsored, certain transparency requirements are triggered to ensure the peer review is adequate. Agency-sponsored peer reviews must be open and rigorous, and peer reviewers must be selected primarily on the basis of necessary technical expertise, disclose to agencies any prior positions they may have taken on pertinent issues, and reveal sources of personal and institutional funding.

The objectivity standard—that information be "reproducible" to prove transparency—is more particular for information that falls into the category of not simply ordinary but "influential" information (§V.3.b.ii.B). Information is influential if "the agency can reasonably determine that dissemination of the information will have or does have a clear and substantial impact on important public policies or important private sector decisions" (§V. 9). Each agency may separately define "influential" to accord with "the nature and multiplicity of issues for which the agency is responsible" (§V.9). Agencies should consult with relevant scientific and technical communities on the feasibility of making certain categories of data subject to the reproducibility standard (§V.3.b.ii.A). Reproducibility in the analytic analysis context demands that "independent analysis of the original or supporting data using identical methods would generate similar analytic results, subject to an acceptable degree of imprecision or error" (§V.10). The acceptable degree of imprecision changes to reflect the impacts the information may have. The reproducibility standard for other categories of data is set forth by individual agencies in their guidelines whenever they identify specific categories of information as subject to the reproducibility standard (§V.10).

Compelling privacy interests, trade secrets, intellectual property, and other confidentiality protections take precedence over reproducibility and transparency requirements, in which case agencies must alternatively apply "especially rigorous robustness checks to analytic results and document what checks were undertaken" (§§V.3.b.ii.B.ii). Each agency determines the type and detail of robustness checks conducts. Privacy interests notwithstanding, "[a]gency guidelines shall ... in all cases, require a disclosure of the specific data sources that have been used and the specific quantitative methods and assumptions that have been employed" (§V.3.b.ii.B.ii).

Some categories of information are automatically subject to special information quality requirements under the OMB guidelines. Agencies disseminating vital health and medical information "shall interpret the reproducibility and peer-review standards in a manner appropriate to assuring the timely flow of vital information from agencies to medical providers, patients, health agencies, and the public" (§V.3.b.ii.C). Similarly, when agencies maintain and disseminate information with regard to analysis of risks to human health, safety, and the environment, they must "either adopt or adapt" the same information quality principle standards that apply to such information used and disseminated pursuant to the Safe Drinking Water Act Amendments of 1996 (42 U.S.C. §§300g-1(b)(3)(A) & (B) (2000)). The option to "adapt" rather than "adopt" these standards provides agencies flexibility in applying them (§V.3.b.ii.C).

In urgent situations involving imminent threats to public health or homeland security, for example, an agency my temporarily waive information quality standards according to standards set forth in the agency's own guidelines (§V.3.b.ii.C).

Administrative Mechanisms for Information Quality Challenges. The IQA and subsequent OMB guidelines require that in their guidelines agencies set forth an administrative process allowing affected parties to challenge agency-disseminated information that allegedly fails to meet the standards set forth in either the OMB guidelines or the disseminating agency's guidelines (§III.3). In establishing these processes, agencies must specify limits on the time an agency may take to consider a challenge and provide for notification to the affected party regarding the agency's decision (§III.3.i). Agency guidelines must also provide for an administrative appeal process to allow an affected party to seek reconsideration of an agency's initial decision (§III.3.ii). The appeals mechanism must similarly incorporate specific limits on the time allowed for reconsideration.

Agency Reporting Requirements. Pursuant to the OMB guidelines each agency was obligated to submit to OMB a report—following a draft report, public comment, and revisions—outlining its agency-specific information quality guidelines and how the guidelines ensure the quality of information, and also explaining the agency's administrative mechanisms for allowing affected persons to seek correction of agency information that allegedly does not meet information quality standards (§§IV.3-5). Following OMB review of the reports, agencies then had to post the reports on their respective web sites and publish notice of the availability of the final reports in the Federal Register by October 1, 2002 (§IV.5).

Since January 1, 2004, agencies must report annually to the director of OMB the number and nature of complaints received by the agency regarding agency compliance with information quality guidelines (§IV.6). The first reports are included in OMB's report to Congress, available online at: http://www.whitehouse.gov/omb/inforeg/fy03_info_quality_rpt.pdf.

Judicial Review. The U.S. Court of Appeals for the Fourth Circuit ruled, in *Salt Institute v. Leavitt*, 440 F.3d 156 (4th Cir. 2006), that the IQA does not create a legal right to information or information correctness. The Fourth Circuit's holding affirmed a decision of the U.S. District Court for the Eastern District of Virginia, *Salt Institute v. Thompson*, 345 F. Supp. 2d 589 (E.D. Va. 2004). The Salt Institute and the U.S. Chamber of Commerce sought judicial review of the National, Heart, Lung and Blood Institute's (NHLBI) denial of a petition under the IQA seeking correction of NHLBI statements that declared reducing salt consumption would lower blood pressure for all individuals, and seeking disclosure of the data and methods behind the statements. The Fourth Circuit affirmed the district court ruling that plaintiffs lacked standing to challenge the NHLBI's denial of the petition because the IQA did not provide the plaintiff with any legal right. Prior to the *Salt Institute* cases, the first and only court to have addressed the issue of judicial review under the IQA was the U.S. District Court for the District of Minnesota, which had similarly determined that the IQA does not provide for a private cause of action. *See In re: Operation of the Missouri River System Litigation*, 363 F. Supp. 2d 1145, 1174-75 (D. Minn. 2004).

Peer Review Bulletin. On January 14, 2005, OMB published notice in the Federal Register of its Final Information Quality Bulletin for Peer Review (Bulletin) (70 Fed. Reg. 2664) after having released and solicited public comment on two previous drafts dated September 15, 2003 (68 Fed. Reg. 54,023) and April 28, 2004 (69 Fed. Reg. 23,230). OMB issued the Bulletin under the IQA, Executive Order 12866 (58 Fed. Reg. 51,735, Oct. 4, 1993), and OMB's authority to manage agencies under the President's Constitutional authority to supervise the Executive Branch. The OMB's Office of Information and Regulatory Affairs (OIRA) oversees implementation of the Bulletin in consultation with the Office of Science and Technology Policy (OSTP). The Bulletin is available at http://www.whitehouse.gov/omb/inforeg/infopoltech.html#iq.

The Bulletin establishes government-wide guidance for peer review of agency scientific information that will be disseminated. "Scientific information" includes "factual inputs, data, models, analyses, technical information, or scientific assessments based on the behavioral and social sciences, public health and medical sciences, life and earth sciences, engineering, or physical sciences" (§I.5). Under the Bulletin the definition of "dissemination" encompasses the IQA definition, but further excludes both research produced by government-funded scientists that does not represent the views of an agency and displays a disclaimer to that effect; and information distributed for peer review bearing a disclaimer that the information's distribution is solely for the purpose of pre-dissemination peer review (§I.5).

Peer Review of Influential Scientific Information—Section II. Section II of the Bulletin mandates that agencies conduct peer reviews of influential scientific information intended for dissemination. The definition of "influential" is the same as that under the IQA. Section II grants agencies discretion to choose the reviewer selection process and the peer review mechanism. Reviewer selection must take into account reviewer expertise, the need for a balanced representation of perspectives, conflicts of interest, and the reviewers' independence from the work product under review (§II.3). In choosing a peer review mechanism, the agency must consider the information's novelty and complexity, importance to decision making, and prior peer review, as well as any benefits and costs of review (§II.4). Certain transparency requirements also apply to the peer review mechanism. The reviewers must have advance notice of how their comments will be conveyed. Reviewers must prepare a report describing their review, findings, and conclusions. The report must also provide the names and affiliations of the reviewers and "shall either (a) include a verbatim copy of each reviewer's comments (either with or without specific attributions) or (b) represent the views of the group as a whole, including any disparate and dissenting views" (§II.5). The agency is required to post the report on its website along with all related materials, discuss the report in the preamble to any related rulemaking, and include the report in the administrative record behind any related agency action (§II.5).

Agencies may commission independent entities to carry out reviewer selection and peer review (§II.6). Influential scientific information that has already undergone adequate peer review is exempt from the requirements of section II. Principal findings, recommendations, and conclusions in official reports of the National Academy of the Sciences are presumed to have undergone adequate peer review (§II.2).

Peer Review of Highly Influential Scientific Assessments-Section III. The Bulletin imposes requirements in addition to the section II requirements, for the peer review of highly influential scientific assessments. A "scientific assessment" is "an evaluation of a body of scientific or technical knowledge that typically synthesizes multiple factual inputs, data, models, assumptions, and/or applies best professional judgment to bridge uncertainties in the available information" (§I.7). The term "highly influential" means that the agency or the OIRA Administrator determines dissemination could have an impact of more than $500 million in any one year or will be "novel, controversial, or precedent-setting, or has significant interagency interest" (§III.1). The Bulletin provides that peer review of highly influential scientific assessments adhere to the following additional requirements:

- Scientists employed by the sponsoring agency (outside of the peer review context) may not function as reviewers. An exception may be made if the agency determines that an agency scientist employed by a different agency of the Cabinet-level department, possesses expertise essential to the review and does not hold a position of management or policy responsibility. The agency must obtain prior written approval on a non-delegable basis from the Secretary or Deputy Secretary to make such an exception (§III.3.c).
- Absent an essential need, the same reviewer should not participate in multiple peer reviews (§III.3.d).
- Reviewers must be provided information sufficient to enable them to understand the data, analytic procedures, and assumptions used to support the key findings or conclusions they are reviewing (§III.4).
- If feasible and appropriate, the agency must make the draft scientific assessment available for public comment and sponsor a public meeting attended by the reviewers. The reviewers should then have access to the public comments pertaining to significant scientific or technical issues (§III.5).
- "The peer review report shall include the charge to the reviewers and a short paragraph on both the credentials and relevant experiences of each peer reviewer" (§III.6). The agency must also write a response to the report to be posted on the agency's website, explaining the agency's agreement or disagreement with the report, the actions the agency has undertaken or will undertake in response to the report, and, if applicable, the reasoning behind the choice of those actions (§III.6).

Additional Peer Review Guidelines. Given a compelling rationale, the agency head may waive or defer the peer review requirements of sections II and III (§VIII.3). Additionally, instead of adhering to the requirements of sections II or III, an agency may ensure the quality of scientific information by relying on scientific information of the National Academy of Sciences; commissioning the National Academy of Sciences to conduct the peer review; or undertaking alternative procedures approved by the OIRA Administrator in consultation with OSTP (§IV).

"Peer review shall be conducted in a manner that respects (i) confidential business information and (ii) intellectual property" (§VIII.2). In disclosing information about a reviewer, the agency must comply with the requirements of the Privacy Act, 5 U.S.C. § 522a as amended, and OMB Circular A130 (Appendix I, 61 Fed. Reg. 6428 (Feb. 20, 1996)) (§VIII.1). Information relating to certain national security, foreign affairs, or negotiations involving international trade or treaties is exempt from the peer review requirements if adhering to the requirements would interfere with the need for secrecy or promptness. Similarly exempt is information disseminated in the course of an individual agency adjudication or permit proceeding (unless the agency determines that peer review is practical and appropriate and that the influential dissemination is scientifically or technically novel); time-sensitive health or safety information; regulatory impact analysis or regulatory flexibility analysis subject to interagency review under Executive Order 12866; routine statistical information released by federal statistical agencies; accounting, budget, actuarial, and financial information; and information disseminated in connection with routine rules that materially alter entitlements, grants, user fees, or loan programs, or the rights and obligations of recipients thereof (§IX).

If an agency supports a regulatory action using information subject to the Bulletin, it must include in the administrative record, along with relevant materials, a certification explaining how the agency complied with the Bulletin's requirements (§VII).

Agencies must post on their websites, and update at least biannually, an agenda providing descriptions of all planned and ongoing influential scientific information subject to the Bulletin, links to documents made public pursuant to the Bulletin, and a peer review plan for each entry (§V.2). Agencies must also establish a mechanism for allowing the public to comment on the adequacy of its peer review plans. Further each agency is required to provide to OIRA, by December 15 of each year, a summary of the peer reviews conducted by the agency during the fiscal year (§VI).

The Bulletin states that it "does not, create any right or benefit, substantive or procedural, enforceable at law or in equity, against the United States, its agencies or other entities, its officers or employees, or any other person" (§XII), thereby seeking to avoid judicial review of agency compliance with the Bulletin's requirements.

Proposed Risk Assessment Bulletin. On January 17, 2006, OMB posted notice in the Federal Register of its Proposed Risk Assessment Bulletin (Proposed Bulletin) and provided opportunity for public comment on the Proposed Bulletin until June 15, 2006 (71 Fed. Reg. 2600). The Proposed Bulletin sets forth potential uniform quality standards for agencies to adhere to in conducting risk assessments. A risk assessment "assembles and synthesizes scientific information to determine whether a potential hazard exists and/or the extent of possible risk to human health, safety or the environment" (§I.3). The Proposed Bulletin provides six standards that would apply to both influential and non-influential risk assessments; an additional standard for risk assessments that are likely to be used in regulatory analysis; and nine additional standards that would apply uniquely to influential risk assessments. If the Proposed Bulletin is published in final form, it is slated to govern agency risk assessments disseminated beginning twelve months after the final bulletin's publication and draft risk assessment disseminated beginning six months after publication of the final bulletin. The Proposed Bulletin is available at http://www.whitehouse.gov/omb/inforeg/infopoltech.html#iq.

Legislative History:

On December 21, 2000, Congress enacted the Information Quality Act requiring OMB to develop guidelines that establish quality standards for information disseminated by federal agencies, as a rider to Treasury and General Government Appropriations Act for Fiscal Year 2001 (Pub. L. No. 106-554; H.R. 4577). Congress accepted the rider to the appropriations bill without any hearings, floor debate, or legislative history specific to the IQA. However, the IQA amends the 1995 Paperwork Reduction Act's information dissemination requirements, which have some legislative history. Section 3504(d)(1) of the PRA provides: "With respect to information dissemination, the [OMB] Director shall develop and oversee the implementation of policies, principles, standards, and guidelines to (1) apply to Federal agency dissemination of public information, regardless of the form or format in which such information is disseminated" 44 U.S.C. § 3504(d)(1) (2000).

The legislative history, dated February 15, 1995, accompanying the 1995 PRA amendments explains that the amendments "promote[] the theme of improving the quality and use of information to strengthen agency decisionmaking and accountability and to maximize the benefit and utility of information created, collected, maintained, used, shared, disseminated, and retained by or for the Federal Government." (H.R. Rep. No. 104-37, at 35). Prior to the enactment of the IQA, OMB had not implemented the PRA's section 3504(d)(1) information dissemination requirements. On June 22, 1998, the House approved the FY 1999 Treasury, Postal Service, and General Government Appropriations Bill, which contained a non-binding provision that closely resembles the IQA in encouraging OMB to develop policy and procedural guidance to ensure information quality (H.R. Rep. No. 105-592 at 49-50). That provision provided that:

> The Committee urges the Office of Management and Budget (OMB) to develop, with public and Federal agency involvement, rules providing policy and procedural guidance to Federal agencies for ensuring and maximizing the quality, objectivity, utility, and integrity of information (including statistical information) disseminated by Federal agencies, and information disseminated by non-Federal entities with financial support from the Federal government, in fulfillment of the purposes and provisions of the Paperwork Reduction Act of 1995 (P.L. 104-13). The Committee expects issuance of these rules by September 30, 1999. The OMB rules shall also cover the sharing of, and access to, the aforementioned data and information, by members of the public. Such OMB rules shall require Federal agencies to develop, within one year and with public participation, their own rules consistent with the OMB rules. The OMB and agency rules shall contain administrative mechanisms allowing affected persons to petition for correction of information which does not comply with such rules; and the OMB rules shall contain provisions requiring the agencies to report to OMB periodically regarding the number and nature of petitions or complaints regarding Federal, or Federally-supported, information dissemination, and how such petitions and complaints were handled. OMB shall report to the Committee on the status of implementation of these directives no later than September 30, 1999.

Congresswoman Jo Ann Emerson of Missouri and Senator John Shelby of Alabama are recognized as the principal sponsors of the Information Quality Act.

Source Note:

The Office of Management and Budget maintains a website with links to government documents relevant to the Information Quality Act at http://

www.whitehouse.gov/omb/inforeg/infopoltech.html#iq. OMB also maintains a website providing links to many agencies information quality guidelines at http://www.whitehouse.gov/omb/inforeg/agency_info_quality_links.html. After receiving the first annual reports from agencies, OMB published them in a single OMB report to Congress along with OMB's summary of the data quality program. Office of Management and Budget, *Information Quality: A Report to Congress* (April 30, 2004), *available at* http://www.whitehouse.gov/omb/inforeg/fy03_info_quality_rpt.pdf. The organization OMB Watch maintains a website with links to the dockets of information quality petitions received by various agencies at http://www.ombwatch.org/article/articleview/2668/1/231?TopicID=7.

Bibliography:

I. Legislative History

1. See discussion above.

II. Other Government Documents

1. U.S. Government Accountability Office, *Information Quality Act: Expanded Oversight and Clearer Guidance by the Office of Management and Budget Could Improve Agencies' Implementation of the Act* (GAO-06-765) (Aug. 2006).
2. Office of Management and Budget, *Proposed Bulletin on Risk Assessment*, 71 Fed. Reg. 2600 (Jan. 17, 2006).
3. Office of Management and Budget. *Final Information Quality Bulletin for Peer Review*, 70 Fed. Reg. 2664-02 (Jan. 14, 2005).
4. Memorandum from OMB-OIRA Administrator to the President's Management Council, *Posting of Information Quality Correction Requests and Responses* (Aug. 30, 2004), *available at* http://www.whitehouse.gov/omb/inforeg/info_quality_posting_083004.pdf.
5. Office of Management and Budget, *Information Quality: A Report to Congress*, (April 30, 2004), *available at* http://www.whitehouse.gov/omb/inforeg/fy03_info_quality_rpt.pdf.
6. Memorandum from OMB-OIRA Administrator for the President's Management Council, *Guidance for the Information Quality Annual Agency Report to OMB* (Oct. 17, 2003), *available at* http://www.whitehouse.gov/omb/inforeg/pmc_oct03report.pdf.
7. Memorandum from OMB-OIRA Administrator for the President's

Management Council, *Executive Branch Information Quality Law* (Oct. 4, 2002), *available at* http://www.whitehouse.gov/omb/inforeg/pmc_graham_100402.pdf.

8. Memorandum from OMB-OIRA Administrator for the President's Management Council, *Agency Final Information Quality Guidelines* (Sept. 5, 2002).

9. Office of Information and Regulatory Affairs, *Administrator Speech: OMB'S Role In Overseeing Information Quality* (Remarks to Public Workshop on Information-Quality Guidelines, Sponsored by Committee on Data Quality, Science, Technology and Law Program, National Research Council/National Academy of Sciences, Washington, D.C. (March 21, 2002)), *available at* http://www.whitehouse.gov/omb/inforeg/info-quality_march21.pdf.

10. Office of Management and Budget, *Guidelines for Ensuring and Maximizing the Quality, Objectivity, Utility, and Integrity of Information Disseminated by Federal Agencies*, 67 Fed. Reg. 8451 (Feb. 22, 2002).

III. Articles

1. Ressmeyer, *The Information Quality Act: The Little Statute that Could (or Couldn't?) Applying the Safe Drinking Water Act Amendments of 1996 to the Federal Communications Commission*, 59 Fed. Comm. L.J. 215 (2006).

2. Bourdeau, *Information Quality Act Challenges to Flawed Use of Science*, 19-SPG Nat. Resources & Env't 41 (2005).

3. Conrad, *The Information Quality Act—Antiregulatory Costs of Mythic Proportions?*, 12-SPG Kan. J.L. & Pub. Pol'y 521 (2003).

4. Hecht, *Administrative Process in an Information Age: The Transformation of Agency Action Under the Data Quality Act*, 31 J. Legis. 233 (2005).

5. Johnson, *Junking the "Junk Science" Law: Reforming the Information Quality Act*, 58 Admin. L. Rev. 37 (2006).

6. Johnson, *Ruminations on Dissemination: Limits on Administrative and Judicial Review Under the Information Quality Act*, 55 Cath. U. L. Rev 59 (2005).

7. Lacko, Comment, *The Data Quality Act: Prologue to a Farce or a Tragedy?*, 53 Emory L.J. 305 (2004).

8. Magistrale, *An Introduction to the Information Quality Act and Its Application to Environmental Regulation*, 38 Urb. Law. 561 (2006).

9. Shapiro, *The Information Quality Act and Environmental Protection: The Perils of Reform by an Appropriations Rider*, 28 Wm. & Mary Envtl. L. & Pol'y Rev. 339 (2004).

10. Tideswell, *The Information Quality Act: An Environmental Primer*, 51 Naval L. Rev. 91 (2005).

11. Wagner, *Importing Daubert to Administrative Agencies Through the Information Quality Act*, 12 J. L. & Pol'y 589 (2004).

Appendix:

1. Information Quality Act, 44 U.S.C. §3516 note (2000).

2. Office of Management and Budget, *Guidelines for Ensuring and Maximizing the Quality, Objectivity, Utility, and Integrity of Information Disseminated by Federal Agencies*, 67 Fed. Reg. 8452 (Feb. 22, 2002).

3. Office of Management and Budget, *Final Information Quality Bulletin for Peer Review*, 70 Fed. Reg. 2664 (Jan. 14, 2005).

16

Information Quality Act

**Pub. L. No. 106-554, §1(a)(3) [Title V, § 515], Dec. 21, 2000,
114 Stat. 2763, 2763A-153
[set out as a note under 44 U.S.C. § 3516]**

(a) In general.—The Director of the Office of Management and Budget shall, by not later than September 30, 2001, and with public and Federal agency involvement, issue guidelines under sections 3504(d)(1) and 3516 [this section] of title 44, United States Code, that provide policy and procedural guidance to Federal agencies for ensuring and maximizing the quality, objectivity, utility, and integrity of information (including statistical information) disseminated by Federal agencies in fulfillment of the purposes and provisions of chapter 35 of title 44, United States Code [this chapter], commonly referred to as the Paperwork Reduction Act.

(b) Content of guidelines.—The guidelines under subsection (a) shall—

(1) apply to the sharing by Federal agencies of, and access to, information disseminated by Federal agencies; and

(2) Require that each Federal agency to which the guidelines apply—

(A) issue guidelines ensuring and maximizing the quality, objectivity, utility, and integrity of information (including statistical information) disseminated by the agency, by not later than 1 year after the date of issuance of the guidelines under subsection (a);

(B) establish administrative mechanisms allowing affected persons to seek and obtain correction of information maintained and disseminated by the agency that does not comply with the guidelines issued under subsection (a); and

(C) Report periodically to the director—

(i) the number and nature of complaints received by the agency regarding the accuracy of information disseminated by the agency; and

(ii) how such complaints were handled by the agency.

16

NOTICES

OFFICE OF MANAGEMENT AND BUDGET

Guidelines for Ensuring and Maximizing the Quality, Objectivity, Utility, and Integrity of Information Disseminated by Federal Agencies; Republication

Friday, February 22, 2002

Editorial Note [in original]: Due to numerous errors, this document was reprinted in its entirety. It was originally printed in the *Federal Register* on Thursday, January 3, 2002 at 67 F.R. 369-378 and was corrected on Tuesday, February 5, 2002 at 67 F.R. 5365.

AGENCY: Office of Management and Budget, Executive Office of the President.

ACTION: Final guidelines.

SUMMARY: These final guidelines implement section 515 of the Treasury and General Government Appropriations Act for Fiscal Year 2001 (Public Law 106-554; H.R. 5658). Section 515 directs the Office of Management and Budget (OMB) to issue government-wide guidelines that "provide policy and procedural guidance to Federal agencies for ensuring and maximizing the quality, objectivity, utility, and integrity of information (including statistical information) disseminated by Federal agencies." By October 1, 2002, agencies must issue their own implementing guidelines that include "administrative mechanisms allowing affected persons to seek and obtain correction of information maintained and disseminated by the agency" that does not comply with the OMB guidelines. These final guidelines also reflect the changes OMB made to the guidelines issued September 28, 2001, as a result of receiving additional comment on the "capable of being substantially reproduced" standard (paragraphs V.3.B, V.9, and V.10), which OMB previously issued on September 28, 2001, on an interim final basis.

DATES: Effective Date: January 3, 2002.

FOR FURTHER INFORMATION CONTACT: Brooke J. Dickson, Office of Information and Regulatory Affairs, Office of Management and Budget,

Washington, DC 20503. Telephone (202) 395-3785 or by e-mail to informationquality@omb.eop.gov.

SUPPLEMENTARY INFORMATION: In section 515(a) of the Treasury and General Government Appropriations Act for Fiscal Year 2001 (Public Law 106-554; H.R. 5658), Congress directed the Office of Management and Budget (OMB) to issue, by September 30, 2001, government-wide guidelines that "provide policy and procedural guidance to Federal agencies for ensuring and maximizing the quality, objectivity, utility, and integrity of information (including statistical information) disseminated by Federal agencies * * *" Section 515(b) goes on to state that the OMB guidelines shall:

"(1) apply to the sharing by Federal agencies of, and access to, information disseminated by Federal agencies; and

"(2) require that each Federal agency to which the guidelines apply—

"(A) issue guidelines ensuring and maximizing the quality, objectivity, utility, and integrity of information (including statistical information) disseminated by the agency, by not later than 1 year after the date of issuance of the guidelines under subsection (a);

"(B) establish administrative mechanisms allowing affected persons to seek and obtain correction of information maintained and disseminated by the agency that does not comply with the guidelines issued under subsection (a); and

"(C) report periodically to the Director—

"(i) the number and nature of complaints received by the agency regarding the accuracy of information disseminated by the agency and;

"(ii) how such complaints were handled by the agency."

Proposed guidelines were published in the Federal Register on June 28, 2001 (66 FR 34489). Final guidelines were published in the Federal Register on September 28, 2001 (66 FR 49718). The Supplementary Information to the final guidelines published in September 2001 provides background, the underlying principles OMB followed in issuing the final guidelines, and statements of intent concerning detailed provisions in the final guidelines.

In the final guidelines published in September 2001, OMB also requested additional comment on the "capable of being substantially reproduced" standard and the related definition of "influential scientific or statistical information" (paragraphs V.3.B, V.9, and V.10), which were issued on an interim final basis. The final guidelines published today discuss the public comments OMB received, the OMB response, and amendments to the final guidelines published in September 2001.

In developing agency-specific guidelines, agencies should refer both to the Supplementary Information to the final guidelines published in the Federal Register on September 28, 2001 (66 FR 49718), and also to the Supplementary Information published today. We stress that the three "Underlying Principles" that OMB followed in drafting the guidelines that we published on September 28, 2001 (66 FR 49719), are also applicable to the amended guidelines that we publish today.

In accordance with section 515, OMB has designed the guidelines to help agencies ensure and maximize the quality, utility, objectivity and integrity of the information that they disseminate (meaning to share with, or give access to, the public). It is crucial that information Federal agencies disseminate meets these guidelines. In this respect, the fact that the Internet enables agencies to communicate information quickly and easily to a wide audience not only offers great benefits to society, but also increases the potential harm that can result from the dissemination of information that does not meet basic information quality guidelines. Recognizing the wide variety of information Federal agencies disseminate and the wide variety of dissemination practices that agencies have, OMB developed the guidelines with several principles in mind.

First, OMB designed the guidelines to apply to a wide variety of government information dissemination activities that may range in importance and scope. OMB also designed the guidelines to be generic enough to fit all media, be they printed, electronic, or in other form. OMB sought to avoid the problems that would be inherent in developing detailed, prescriptive, "one-size-fits-all" government-wide guidelines that would artificially require different types of dissemination activities to be treated in the same manner. Through this flexibility, each agency will be able to incorporate the requirements of these OMB guidelines into the agency's own information resource management and administrative practices.

Second, OMB designed the guidelines so that agencies will meet basic information quality standards. Given the administrative mechanisms required by section 515 as well as the standards set forth in the Paperwork Reduction Act, it is clear that agencies should not disseminate substantive information that does not meet a basic level of quality. We recognize that some government information may need to meet higher or more specific information quality standards than those that would apply to other types of government information. The more important the information, the higher the quality standards to which it should be held, for example, in those situations involving "influential scientific, financial, or statistical information" (a phrase defined in these guidelines). The guidelines recognize, however, that information quality comes at a cost. Accordingly, the agencies should weigh the costs (for example, including costs attributable to agency processing effort, respondent burden, maintenance of needed privacy, and assurances of suitable confidentiality) and the benefits of higher information quality in the development of information, and the level of quality to which the information disseminated will be held.

Third, OMB designed the guidelines so that agencies can apply them in a common-sense and workable manner. It is important that these guidelines do not impose unnecessary administrative burdens that would inhibit agencies from continuing to take advantage of the Internet and other technologies to disseminate information that can be of great benefit and value to the public. In this regard, OMB encourages agencies to incorporate the standards and procedures required by these guidelines into their existing information resources management and administrative practices rather than create new and potentially duplicative or contradictory processes. The primary example of this is that the guidelines recognize that, in accordance with OMB Circular A-130, agencies already have in place well-established information quality standards and administrative mechanisms that allow persons to seek and obtain correction of information that is maintained and disseminated by the agency. Under the OMB guidelines, agencies need only ensure that their own guidelines are consistent with these OMB guidelines, and then ensure that their administrative mechanisms satisfy the standards and procedural requirements in the new agency guidelines. Similarly, agencies may rely on their implementation of the Federal Government's computer security laws (formerly, the Computer Security Act, and now the computer security provisions of the Paperwork Reduction Act) to establish appropriate security safeguards for ensuring the "integrity" of the information that the agencies disseminate.

In addition, in response to concerns expressed by some of the agencies, we want to emphasize that OMB recognizes that Federal agencies provide a wide variety of data and information. Accordingly, OMB understands that the guidelines discussed below cannot be implemented in the same way by each agency. In some cases, for example, the data disseminated by an agency are not collected by that agency; rather, the information the agency must provide in a timely manner is compiled from a variety of sources that are constantly updated and revised and may be confidential. In such cases, while agencies' implementation of the guidelines may differ, the essence of the guidelines will apply. That is, these agencies must make their methods transparent by providing documentation, ensure quality by reviewing the underlying methods used in developing the data and consulting (as appropriate) with experts and users, and keep users informed about corrections and revisions.

Summary of OMB Guidelines

These guidelines apply to Federal agencies subject to the Paperwork Reduction Act (44 U.S.C. chapter 35). Agencies are directed to develop information resources management procedures for reviewing and substantiating (by documentation or other means selected by the agency) the quality (including the objectivity, utility, and integrity) of information before it is disseminated. In addition, agencies are to establish administrative mechanisms allowing affected persons to seek and obtain, where appropriate, correction of information disseminated by the agency that does not comply with the OMB or agency guidelines. Consistent with the underlying principles described above, these guidelines stress the importance of having agencies apply these standards and develop their administrative mechanisms so they can be implemented in a common sense and workable manner. Moreover, agencies must apply these standards flexibly, and in a manner appropriate to the nature and timeliness of the information to be disseminated, and incorporate them into existing agency information resources management and administrative practices.

Section 515 denotes four substantive terms regarding information disseminated by Federal agencies: quality, utility, objectivity, and integrity. It is not always clear how each substantive term relates—or how the four terms in aggregate relate—to the widely divergent types of information that agencies disseminate. The guidelines provide definitions that attempt to establish a clear meaning so that both the agency and the public can readily judge whether a particular type of information to be disseminated does or does not meet these attributes.

In the guidelines, OMB defines "quality" as the encompassing term, of which "utility," "objectivity," and "integrity" are the constituents. "Utility" refers to the usefulness of the information to the intended users. "Objectivity" focuses on whether the disseminated information is being presented in an accurate, clear, complete, and unbiased manner, and as a matter of substance, is accurate, reliable, and unbiased. "Integrity" refers to security—the protection of information from unauthorized access or revision, to ensure that the information is not compromised through corruption or falsification. OMB modeled the definitions of "information," "government information," "information dissemination product," and "dissemination" on the longstanding definitions of those terms in OMB Circular A-130, but tailored them to fit into the context of these guidelines.

In addition, Section 515 imposes two reporting requirements on the agencies. The first report, to be promulgated no later than October 1, 2002, must provide the agency's information quality guidelines that describe administrative mechanisms allowing affected persons to seek and obtain, where appropriate, correction of disseminated information that does not comply with the OMB and agency guidelines. The second report is an annual fiscal year report to OMB (to be first submitted on January 1, 2004) providing information (both quantitative and qualitative, where appropriate) on the number, nature, and resolution of complaints received by the agency regarding its perceived or confirmed failure to comply with these OMB and agency guidelines.

Public Comments and OMB Response

Applicability of Guidelines. Some comments raised concerns about the applicability of these guidelines, particularly in the context of scientific research conducted by Federally employed scientists or Federal grantees who publish and communicate their research findings in the same manner as their academic colleagues. OMB believes that information generated and disseminated in these contexts is not covered by these guidelines unless the agency represents the information as, or uses the information in support of, an official position of the agency.

As a general matter, these guidelines apply to "information" that is "disseminated" by agencies subject to the Paperwork Reduction Act (44 U.S.C. 3502(1)). See paragraphs II, V.5 and V.8. The definitions of "information" and "dissemination" establish the scope of the applicability of these guidelines. "Information" means "any communication or representation of knowledge such as facts or data * * *" This definition of information in paragraph V.5 does "not include opinions, where the agency's presentation makes it clear that what is being offered is someone's opinion rather than fact or the agency's views."

"Dissemination" is defined to mean "agency initiated or sponsored distribution of information to the public." As used in paragraph V.8, "agency INITIATED * * * distribution of information to the public" refers to information that the agency disseminates, e.g., a risk assessment prepared by the agency to inform the agency's formulation of possible regulatory or other action. In addition, if an agency, as an institution, disseminates information prepared by an outside party in a manner that reasonably suggests that the agency agrees with the information, this appearance of having the information represent agency views makes agency dissemination of the information subject to these guidelines. By contrast, an agency does not "initiate" the dissemination of information when a Federally employed scientist or Federal grantee or contractor publishes and communicates his or her research findings in the same manner as his or her academic colleagues, even if the Federal agency retains ownership or other intellectual property rights because the Federal government paid for the research. To avoid confusion regarding whether the agency agrees with the information (and is therefore disseminating it through the employee or grantee), the researcher should include an appropriate disclaimer in the publication or speech to the effect that the "views are mine, and do not necessarily reflect the view" of the agency.

Similarly, as used in paragraph V.8., "agency * * * SPONSORED distribution of information to the public" refers to situations where an agency has directed a third-party to disseminate information, or where the agency has the authority to review and approve the information before release. Therefore, for example, if an agency through a procurement contract or a grant provides for a person to conduct research, and then the agency directs the person to disseminate the results (or the agency reviews and approves the results before they may be disseminated), then the agency has "sponsored" the dissemination of this information. By contrast, if the agency simply provides funding to support research, and it the researcher (not the agency) who decides whether to disseminate the results and—if the results are to be released—who determines the content and presentation of the dissemination, then the agency has not "sponsored" the dissemination even though it has funded the research and even if the Federal agency retains ownership or other intellectual property rights because the Federal government paid for the research. To avoid confusion regarding whether the agency is sponsoring the dissemination, the researcher should include an appropriate disclaimer in the publication or speech to the effect that the "views are mine, and do not necessarily reflect the view" of the agency. On the other hand, subsequent agency dissemination of such information requires that the information adhere to the agency's information quality guidelines. In sum, these guidelines govern an agency's dissemination of information, but generally do not govern a third-party's dissemination of information (the exception being where the agency is essentially using the third-party to disseminate information on the agency's behalf). Agencies, particularly those that fund scientific research, are encouraged to clarify the applicability of these guidelines to the various types of information they and their employees and grantees disseminate.

Paragraph V.8 also states that the definition of "dissemination" does not include "* * * distribution limited to correspondence with individuals or persons, press releases, archival records, public filings, subpoenas or adjudicative processes." The exemption from the definition of "dissemination" for "adjudicative processes" is intended to exclude, from the scope of these guidelines, the findings and determinations that an agency makes in the course of adjudications involving specific parties. There are well-established procedural safeguards and rights to address the quality of adjudicatory decisions and to provide persons with an opportunity to contest decisions. These guidelines do not impose any additional requirements on agencies during adjudicative proceedings and do not provide parties to such adjudicative proceedings any additional rights of challenge or appeal.

The Presumption Favoring Peer-Reviewed Information. As a general matter, in the scientific and research context, we regard technical information that has been subjected to formal, independent, external peer review as presumptively objective. As the guidelines state in paragraph V.3.b.i: "If data and analytic results have been subjected to formal, independent, external peer review, the information may generally be presumed to be of acceptable objectivity." An example of a formal, independent, external peer review is the review process used by scientific journals.

Most comments approved of the prominent role that peer review plays in the OMB guidelines. Some comments contended that peer review was not accepted as a universal standard that incorporates an established, practiced, and sufficient level of objectivity. Other comments stated that the guidelines would be better clarified by making peer review one of several factors that an agency should consider in assessing the objectivity (and quality in general) of original research. In addition, several comments noted that peer review does not establish whether analytic results are capable of being substantially reproduced. In light of the comments, the final guidelines in new paragraph V.3.b.i qualify the presumption in favor of peer-reviewed information as follows: "However, this presumption is rebuttable based on a persuasive showing by the petitioner in a particular instance."

We believe that transparency is important for peer review, and these guidelines set minimum standards for the transparency of agency-sponsored peer review. As we state in new paragraph V.3.b.i: "If data and analytic results have been subjected to formal, independent, external peer review, the information may generally be presumed to be of acceptable objectivity. However, this presumption is rebuttable based on a persuasive showing by the petitioner in a particular instance. If agency-sponsored peer review is employed to help satisfy the objectivity standard, the review process employed shall meet the general criteria for competent and credible peer review recommended by OMB-OIRA to the President's Management Council (9/20/01) (http://

www.whitehouse.gov/omb/inforeg/oira_review-process.html), namely, 'that (a) peer reviewers be selected primarily on the basis of necessary technical expertise, (b) peer reviewers be expected to disclose to agencies prior technical/policy positions they may have taken on the issues at hand, (c) peer reviewers be expected to disclose to agencies their sources of personal and institutional funding (private or public sector), and (d) peer reviews be conducted in an open and rigorous manner."'

The importance of these general criteria for competent and credible peer review has been supported by a number of expert bodies. For example, "the work of fully competent peer-review panels can be undermined by allegations of conflict of interest and bias. Therefore, the best interests of the Board are served by effective policies and procedures regarding potential conflicts of interest, impartiality, and panel balance." (EPA's Science Advisory Board Panels: Improved Policies and Procedures Needed to Ensure Independence and Balance, GAO-01-536, General Accounting Office, Washington, DC, June 2001, page 19.) As another example, "risk analyses should be peer-reviewed and accessible—both physically and intellectually—so that decision-makers at all levels will be able to respond critically to risk characterizations. The intensity of the peer reviews should be commensurate with the significance of the risk or its management implications." (Setting Priorities, Getting Results: A New Direction for EPA, Summary Report, National Academy of Public Administration, Washington, DC, April 1995, page 23.)

These criteria for peer reviewers are generally consistent with the practices now followed by the National Research Council of the National Academy of Sciences. In considering these criteria for peer reviewers, we note that there are many types of peer reviews and that agency guidelines concerning the use of peer review should tailor the rigor of peer review to the importance of the information involved. More generally, agencies should define their peer-review standards in appropriate ways, given the nature and importance of the information they disseminate.

Is Journal Peer Review Always Sufficient? Some comments argued that journal peer review should be adequate to demonstrate quality, even for influential information that can be expected to have major effects on public policy. OMB believes that this position overstates the effectiveness of journal peer review as a quality-control mechanism.

Although journal peer review is clearly valuable, there are cases where flawed science has been published in respected journals. For example, the NIH Office of Research Integrity recently reported the following case regarding environmental health research:

"Based on the report of an investigation conducted by [XX] University, dated July 16, 1999, and additional analysis conducted by ORI in its oversight review, the US Public Health Service found that Dr. [X] engaged in scientific misconduct. Dr. [X] committed scientific misconduct by intentionally falsifying the research results published in the journal SCIENCE and by providing falsified and fabricated materials to investigating officials at [XX] University in response to a request for original data to support the research results and conclusions report in the SCIENCE paper. In addition, PHS finds that there is no original data or other corroborating evidence to support the research results and conclusions reported in the SCIENCE paper as a whole." (66 FR 52137, October 12, 2001).

Although such cases of falsification are presumably rare, there is a significant scholarly literature documenting quality problems with articles published in peer-reviewed research. "In a [peer-reviewed] meta-analysis that surprised many—and some doubt—researchers found little evidence that peer review actually improves the quality of research papers." (See, e.g., *Science*, Vol. 293, page 2187 (September 21, 2001).) In part for this reason, many agencies have already adopted peer review and science advisory practices that go beyond journal peer review. See, e.g., Sheila Jasanoff, *The Fifth Branch: Science Advisers as Policy Makers,* Cambridge, MA, Harvard University Press, 1990; Mark R. Powell, *Science at EPA: Information in the Regulatory Process. Resources for the Future,* Washington, D.C., 1999, pages 138-139, 151-153; *Implementation of the Environmental Protection Agency's Peer Review Program: An SAB Evaluation of Three Reviews,* EPA-SAB-RSAC-01-009; *A Review of the Research Strategies Advisory Committee (RSAC) of the EPA Science Advisory Board (SAB)*, Washington, D.C., September 26, 2001. For information likely to have an important public policy or private sector impact, OMB believes that additional quality checks beyond peer review are appropriate.

Definition of "Influential." OMB guidelines apply stricter quality standards to the dissemination of information that is considered "influential." Comments noted that the breadth of the definition of "influential" in interim final paragraph V.9 requires much speculation on the part of agencies.

We believe that this criticism has merit and have therefore narrowed the definition. In this narrower definition, "influential," when used in the phrase "influential scientific, financial, or statistical information," is amended to mean that "the agency can reasonably determine that dissemination of the information will have or does have a clear and substantial impact on important public policies or important private sector decisions." The intent of the new phrase "clear and substantial" is to reduce the need for speculation on the part of agencies. We added the present tense—"or does have"—to this narrower definition because on occasion, an information dissemination may occur simultaneously with a particular policy change. In response to a public comment, we added an explicit reference to "financial" information as consistent with our original intent.

Given the differences in the many Federal agencies covered by these guidelines, and the differences in the nature of the information they disseminate, we also believe it will be helpful if agencies elaborate on this definition of "influential" in the context of their missions and duties, with due consideration of the nature of the information they disseminate. As we state in amended paragraph V.9, "Each agency is authorized to define 'influential' in ways appropriate for it given the nature and multiplicity of issues for which the agency is responsible."

Reproducibility. As we state in new paragraph V.3.b.ii: "If an agency is responsible for disseminating influential scientific, financial, or statistical information, agency guidelines shall include a high degree of transparency about data and methods to facilitate the reproducibility of such information by qualified third parties." OMB believes that a reproducibility standard is practical and appropriate for information that is considered "influential," as defined in paragraph V.9—that "will have or does have a clear and substantial impact on important public policies or important private sector decisions." The reproducibility standard applicable to influential scientific, financial, or statistical information is intended to ensure that information disseminated by agencies is sufficiently transparent in terms of data and methods of analysis that it would be feasible for a replication to be conducted. The fact that the use of original and supporting data and analytic results have been deemed "defensible" by peer-review procedures does not necessarily imply that the results are transparent and replicable.

Reproducibility of Original and Supporting Data. Several of the comments objected to the exclusion of original and supporting data from the reproducibility requirements. Comments instead suggested that OMB should apply the reproducibility standard to original data, and that OMB should provide flexibility to the agencies in determining what constitutes "original and supporting" data. OMB agrees and asks that agencies consider, in developing their own guidelines, which categories of original and supporting data should be subject to the reproducibility standard and which should not. To help in resolving this issue, we also ask agencies to consult directly with relevant scientific and technical communities on the feasibility of having the selected categories of original and supporting data subject to the reproducibility standard. Agencies are encouraged to address ethical, feasibility, and confidentiality issues with care. As we state in new paragraph V.3.b.ii.A, "Agencies may identify, in consultation with the relevant scientific and technical communities, those particular types of data that can practicably be subjected to a reproducibility requirement, given ethical, feasibility, or confidentiality constraints." Further, as we state in our expanded definition of "reproducibility" in paragraph V.10, "If agencies apply the reproducibility test to specific types of original or supporting data, the associated guidelines shall provide relevant definitions of reproducibility (e.g., standards for replication of laboratory data)." OMB urges caution in the treatment of original and supporting data because it may often be impractical or even impermissible or unethical to apply the reproducibility standard to such data. For example, it may not be ethical to repeat a "negative" (ineffective) clinical (therapeutic) experiment and it may not be feasible to replicate the radiation exposures studied after the Chernobyl accident. When agencies submit their draft agency guidelines for OMB review, agencies should include a description of the extent to which the reproducibility standard is applicable and reflect consultations with relevant scientific and technical communities that were used in developing guidelines related to applicability of the reproducibility standard to original and supporting data.

It is also important to emphasize that the reproducibility standard does not apply to all original and supporting data disseminated by agencies. As we state in new paragraph V.3.b.ii.A, "With regard to original and supporting data related [to influential scientific, financial, or statistical information], agency guidelines shall not require that all disseminated data be subjected to a reproducibility requirement." In addition, we encourage agencies to address how greater transparency can be achieved regarding original and supporting data. As we also state in new paragraph V.3.b.ii.A, "It is understood that reproducibility of data is an indication of transparency about research design and methods and thus a replication exercise (i.e., a new experiment, test, or sample) shall not be required prior to each dissemination." Agency guidelines need to achieve a high degree of transparency about data even when reproducibility is not required.

Reproducibility of Analytic Results. Many public comments were critical of the reproducibility standard and expressed concern that agencies would be required to reproduce each analytical result before it is disseminated. While several comments commended OMB for establishing an appropriate balance in the "capable of being substantially reproduced" standard, others considered this standard to be inherently subjective. There were also comments that suggested the standard would cause more burden for agencies.

It is not OMB's intent that each agency must reproduce each analytic result before it is disseminated. The purpose of the reproducibility standard is to cultivate a consistent agency commitment to transparency about how analytic results are generated: the specific data used, the various assumptions employed, the specific analytic methods applied, and the statistical procedures employed. If sufficient transparency is achieved on each of these matters, then an analytic result should meet the "capable of being substantially reproduced" standard.

While there is much variation in types of analytic results, OMB believes that reproducibility is a practical standard to apply to most types of analytic results. As we state in new paragraph V.3.b.ii.B, "With regard to analytic results related [to influential scientific, financial, or statistical information], agency guidelines shall generally require sufficient transparency about data and methods that an independent reanalysis could be undertaken by a qualified member of the public. These transparency standards apply to agency analysis of data from a single study as well as to analyses that combine information from multiple studies." We elaborate upon this principle in our expanded definition of "reproducibility" in paragraph V.10: "With respect to analytic results, 'capable of being substantially reproduced' means that independent analysis of the original or supporting data using identical methods would generate similar analytic results, subject to an acceptable degree of imprecision or error."

Even in a situation where the original and supporting data are protected by confidentiality concerns, or the analytic computer models or other research methods may be kept confidential to protect intellectual property, it may still be feasible to have the analytic results subject to the reproducibility standard. For example, a qualified party, operating under the same confidentiality protections as the original analysts, may be asked to use the same data, computer model or statistical methods to replicate the analytic results reported in the original study. See, e.g., *Reanalysis of the Harvard Six Cities Study and the American Cancer Society Study of Particulate Air Pollution and Mortality*, A Special Report of the Health Effects Institute's Particle Epidemiology Reanalysis Project, Cambridge, MA, 2000.

The primary benefit of public transparency is not necessarily that errors in analytic results will be detected, although error correction is clearly valuable. The more important benefit of transparency is that the public will be able to assess how much an agency's analytic result hinges on the specific analytic choices made by the agency. Concreteness about analytic choices allows, for example, the implications of alternative technical choices to be readily assessed. This type of sensitivity analysis is widely regarded as an essential feature of high-quality analysis, yet sensitivity analysis cannot be undertaken by outside parties unless a high degree of transparency is achieved. The OMB guidelines do not compel such sensitivity analysis as a necessary dimension of quality, but the transparency achieved by reproducibility will allow the public to undertake sensitivity studies of interest.

We acknowledge that confidentiality concerns will sometimes preclude public access as an approach to reproducibility. In response to public comment, we have clarified that such concerns do include interests in "intellectual property." To ensure that the OMB guidelines have sufficient flexibility with regard to analytic transparency, OMB has, in new paragraph V.3.b.ii.B.i, provided agencies an alternative approach for classes or types of analytic results that cannot practically be subject to the reproducibility standard. "[In those situations involving influential scientific, financial, or statistical information * * *] making the data and methods publicly available will assist in determining whether analytic results are reproducible. However, the objectivity standard does not override other compelling interests such as privacy, trade secrets, intellectual property, and other confidentiality protections. "Specifically, in cases where reproducibility will not occur due to other compelling interests, we expect agencies (1) to perform robustness checks appropriate to the importance of the information involved, e.g., determining whether a specific statistic is sensitive to the choice of analytic method, and, accompanying the information disseminated, to document their efforts to assure the needed robustness in information quality, and (2) address in their guidelines the degree to which they anticipate the opportunity for reproducibility to be limited by the confidentiality of underlying data. As we state in new paragraph V.3.b.ii.B.ii, "In situations where public access to data and methods will not occur due to other compelling interests, agencies shall apply especially rigorous robustness checks to analytic results and document what checks were undertaken. Agency guidelines shall, however, in all cases, require a disclosure of the specific data sources that have been used and the specific quantitative methods and assumptions that have been employed."

Given the differences in the many Federal agencies covered by these guidelines, and the differences in robustness checks and the level of detail for documentation thereof that might be appropriate for different agencies, we also believe it will be helpful if agencies elaborate on these matters in the context of their missions and duties, with due consideration of the nature of the information they disseminate. As we state in new paragraph V.3.b.ii.B.ii, "Each agency is authorized to define the type of robustness checks, and the level of detail for documentation thereof, in ways appropriate for it given the nature and multiplicity of issues for which the agency is responsible."

We leave the determination of the appropriate degree of rigor to the discretion of agencies and the relevant scientific and technical communities that work with the agencies. We do, however, establish a general standard for the appropriate degree of rigor in our expanded definition of "reproducibility" in paragraph V.10: "'Reproducibility' means that the information is capable of being substantially reproduced, subject to an acceptable degree of imprecision. For information judged to have more (less) important impacts, the degree of imprecision that is tolerated is reduced (increased)." OMB will review each agency's treatment of this issue when reviewing the agency guidelines as a whole.

Comments also expressed concerns regarding interim final paragraph V.3.B.iii, "making the data and models publicly available will assist in determining whether analytic results are capable of being substantially reproduced," and whether it could be interpreted to constitute public dissemination of these materials, rendering moot the reproducibility test. (For the equivalent provision, see new paragraph V.3.b.ii.B.i.) The OMB guidelines do not require agencies to reproduce each disseminated analytic result by independent re-analysis. Thus, public dissemination of data and models per se does not mean that the analytic result has been reproduced. It means only that the result should be *capable* of being reproduced. The transparency associated with this capability of reproduction is what the OMB guidelines are designed to achieve.

We also want to build on a general observation that we made in our final guidelines published in September 2001. In those guidelines we stated: "... in those situations involving influential scientific[, financial,] or statistical information, the substantial reproducibility standard is added as a quality standard above and beyond some peer review quality standards" (66 FR 49,722 (September 28, 2001)). A hypothetical example may serve to illustrate this point. Assume that two Federal agencies initiated or sponsored the dissemination of five scientific studies after October 1, 2002 (see paragraph III.4) that were, before dissemination, subjected to formal, independent, external peer review, i.e., that met the presumptive standard for "objectivity" under paragraph V.3.b.i. Further assume, at the time of dissemination, that neither agency reasonably expected that the dissemination of any of these studies would have "a clear and substantial impact" on important public policies, i.e., that these studies were not considered "influential" under paragraph V.9, and thus not subject to the reproducibility standards in paragraphs V.3.b.ii.A or B. Then assume, two years later, in 2005, that one of the agencies decides to issue an important and far-reaching regulation based clearly and substantially on the agency's evaluation of the analytic results set forth in these five studies and that such agency reliance on these five studies as published in the agency's notice of proposed rulemaking would constitute dissemination of these five studies. These guidelines would require the rulemaking agency, prior to publishing the notice of proposed rulemaking, to evaluate these five studies to determine if the analytic results stated therein would meet the "capable of being substantially reproduced" standards in paragraph V.3.b.ii.B and, if necessary, related standards governing original and supporting data in paragraph V.3.b.ii.A. If the agency were to decide that any of the five studies would not meet the reproducibility standard, the agency may still rely on them but only if they satisfy the transparency standard and—as applicable—the disclosure of robustness checks required by these guidelines. Otherwise, the agency should not disseminate any of the studies that did not meet the applicable standards in the guidelines at the time it publishes the notice of proposed rulemaking.

Some comments suggested that OMB consider replacing the reproducibility standard with a standard concerning "confirmation" of results for influential scientific and statistical information. Although we encourage agencies to consider "confirmation" as a relevant standard—at least in some cases—for assessing the objectivity of original and supporting data, we believe that "confirmation" is too stringent a standard to apply to analytic results. Often the regulatory impact analysis prepared by an agency for a major rule, for example, will be the only formal analysis of an important subject. It would be unlikely that the results of the regulatory impact analysis had already been confirmed by other analyses. The "capable of being substantially reproduced" standard is less stringent than a "confirmation" standard because it simply requires that an agency's analysis be sufficiently transparent that another qualified party could replicate it through reanalysis.

Health, Safety, and Environmental Information. We note, in the scientific context, that in 1996 the Congress, for health decisions under the Safe Drinking Water Act, adopted a basic standard of quality for the use of science in agency decisionmaking. Under 42 U.S.C. 300g-1(b)(3)(A), an agency is directed, "to the degree that an Agency action is based on science," to use "(i) the best available, peer-reviewed science and supporting studies conducted in accordance with sound and objective scientific practices; and (ii) data collected by accepted methods or best available methods (if the reliability of the method and the nature of the decision justifies use of the data)."

We further note that in the 1996 amendments to the Safe Drinking Water Act, Congress adopted a basic quality standard for the dissemination of public information about risks of adverse health effects. Under 42 U.S.C. 300g-1(b)(3)(B), the agency is directed, "to ensure that the presentation of information [risk] effects is comprehensive, informative, and understandable." The agency is further directed, "in a document made available to the public in support of a regulation [to] specify, to the extent practicable—(i) each population addressed by any estimate [of applicable risk effects]; (ii) the expected risk or central estimate of risk for the specific populations [affected]; (iii) each appropriate upper-bound or lower-bound estimate of risk; (iv) each significant uncertainty identified in the process of the assessment of [risk] effects and the studies that would assist in resolving the uncertainty; and (v) peer-reviewed studies known to the [agency] that support, are directly relevant to, or fail to support any estimate of [risk] effects and the methodology used to reconcile inconsistencies in the scientific data."

As suggested in several comments, we have included these congressional standards directly in new paragraph V.3.b.ii.C, and made them applicable to the information disseminated by all the agencies subject to these guidelines: "With regard to analysis of risks to human health, safety and the environment maintained or disseminated by the agencies, agencies shall either adopt or adapt the quality principles applied by Congress to risk information used and disseminated pursuant to the Safe Drinking Water Act Amendments of 1996 (42 U.S.C. 300g-1(b)(3)(A) & (B))." The word "adapt" is intended to provide agencies flexibility in applying these principles to various types of risk assessment.

Comments also argued that the continued flow of vital information from agencies responsible for disseminating health and medical information to medical providers, patients, and the public may be disrupted due to these peer review and reproducibility standards. OMB responded by adding to new paragraph V.3.b.ii.C: "Agencies responsible for dissemination of vital health and medical information shall interpret the reproducibility and peer-review standards in a manner appropriate to assuring the timely flow of vital information from agencies to medical providers, patients, health agencies, and the public. Information quality standards may be waived temporarily by agencies under urgent situations (e.g., imminent threats to public health or homeland security) in accordance with the latitude specified in agency-specific guidelines."

Administrative Correction Mechanisms. In addition to commenting on the substantive standards in these guidelines, many of the comments noted that the OMB guidelines on the administrative correction of information do not specify a time period in which the agency investigation and response must be made. OMB has added the following new paragraph III.3.i to direct agencies to specify appropriate time periods in which the investigation and response need to be made. "Agencies shall specify appropriate time periods for agency decisions on whether and how to correct the information, and agencies shall notify the affected persons of the corrections made."

Several comments stated that the OMB guidelines needed to direct agencies to consider incorporating an administrative appeal process into their administrative mechanisms for the correction of information. OMB agreed, and added the following new paragraph III.3.ii: "If the person who requested the correction does not agree with the agency's decision (including the corrective action, if any), the person may file for reconsideration within the agency. The agency shall establish an administrative appeal process to review the agency's initial decision, and specify appropriate time limits in which to resolve such requests for reconsideration." Recognizing that many agencies already have a process in place to respond to public concerns, it is not necessarily OMB's intent to require these agencies to establish a new or different process. Rather, our intent is to ensure that agency guidelines specify an objective administrative appeal process that, upon further complaint by the affected person, reviews an agency's decision to disagree with the correction request. An objective process will ensure that the office that originally disseminates the information does not have responsibility for both the initial response and resolution of a disagreement. In addition, the agency guidelines should specify that if the agency believes other agencies may have an interest in the resolution of any administrative appeal, the agency should consult with those other agencies about their possible interest.

Overall, OMB does not envision administrative mechanisms that would burden agencies with frivolous claims. Instead, the correction process should serve to address the genuine and valid needs of the agency and its constituents without disrupting agency processes. Agencies, in making their determination of whether or not to correct information, may reject claims made in bad faith or without justification, and are required to undertake only the degree of correction that they conclude is appropriate for the nature and timeliness of the information involved, and explain such practices in their annual fiscal year reports to OMB.

OMB's issuance of these final guidelines is the beginning of an evolutionary process that will include draft agency guidelines, public comment, final agency guidelines, development of experience with OMB and agency guidelines, and continued refinement of both OMB and agency guidelines. Just as OMB requested public comment before issuing these final guidelines, OMB will refine these guidelines as experience develops and further public comment is obtained.

Dated: December 21, 2001.

John D. Graham,
Administrator, Office of Information and Regulatory Affairs.

Guidelines for Ensuring and Maximizing the Quality, Objectivity, Utility, and Integrity of Information Disseminated by Federal Agencies

I. OMB Responsibilities

Section 515 of the Treasury and General Government Appropriations Act for FY2001 (Public Law 106-554) directs the Office of Management and Budget to issue government-wide guidelines that provide policy and procedural guidance to Federal agencies for ensuring and maximizing the quality, objectivity, utility, and integrity of information, including statistical information, disseminated by Federal agencies.

II. Agency Responsibilities

Section 515 directs agencies subject to the Paperwork Reduction Act (44 U.S.C. 3502(1)) to—

1. Issue their own information quality guidelines ensuring and maximizing the quality, objectivity, utility, and integrity of information, including statistical information, disseminated by the agency no later than one year after the date of issuance of the OMB guidelines;

2. Establish administrative mechanisms allowing affected persons to seek and obtain correction of information maintained and disseminated by the agency that does not comply with these OMB guidelines; and

3. Report to the Director of OMB the number and nature of complaints received by the agency regarding agency compliance with these OMB guidelines concerning the quality, objectivity, utility, and integrity of information and how such complaints were resolved.

III. Guidelines for Ensuring and Maximizing the Quality, Objectivity, Utility, and Integrity of Information Disseminated by Federal Agencies

1. Overall, agencies shall adopt a basic standard of quality (including objectivity, utility, and integrity) as a performance goal and should take appropriate steps to incorporate information quality criteria into agency information dissemination practices. Quality is to be ensured and established at levels appropriate to the nature and timeliness of the information to be disseminated. Agencies shall adopt specific standards of quality that are appropriate for the various categories of information they disseminate.

2. As a matter of good and effective agency information resources management, agencies shall develop a process for reviewing the quality (includ-

ing the objectivity, utility, and integrity) of information before it is disseminated. Agencies shall treat information quality as integral to every step of an agency's development of information, including creation, collection, maintenance, and dissemination. This process shall enable the agency to substantiate the quality of the information it has disseminated through documentation or other means appropriate to the information.

3. To facilitate public review, agencies shall establish administrative mechanisms allowing affected persons to seek and obtain, where appropriate, timely correction of information maintained and disseminated by the agency that does not comply with OMB or agency guidelines. These administrative mechanisms shall be flexible, appropriate to the nature and timeliness of the disseminated information, and incorporated into agency information resources management and administrative practices.

    i. Agencies shall specify appropriate time periods for agency decisions on whether and how to correct the information, and agencies shall notify the affected persons of the corrections made.

    ii. If the person who requested the correction does not agree with the agency's decision (including the corrective action, if any), the person may file for reconsideration within the agency. The agency shall establish an administrative appeal process to review the agency's initial decision, and specify appropriate time limits in which to resolve such requests for reconsideration.

4. The agency's pre-dissemination review, under paragraph III.2, shall apply to information that the agency first disseminates on or after October 1, 2002. The agency's administrative mechanisms, under paragraph III.3., shall apply to information that the agency disseminates on or after October 1, 2002, regardless of when the agency first disseminated the information.

IV. Agency Reporting Requirements

1. Agencies must designate the Chief Information Officer or another official to be responsible for agency compliance with these guidelines.

2. The agency shall respond to complaints in a manner appropriate to the nature and extent of the complaint. Examples of appropriate responses include personal contacts via letter or telephone, form letters, press releases or mass mailings that correct a widely disseminated error or address a frequently raised complaint.

3. Each agency must prepare a draft report, no later than April 1, 2002, providing the agency's information quality guidelines and explaining how such guidelines will ensure and maximize the quality, objectivity, utility, and

integrity of information, including statistical information, disseminated by the agency. This report must also detail the administrative mechanisms developed by that agency to allow affected persons to seek and obtain appropriate correction of information maintained and disseminated by the agency that does not comply with the OMB or the agency guidelines.

4. The agency must publish a notice of availability of this draft report in the Federal Register, and post this report on the agency's website, to provide an opportunity for public comment.

5. Upon consideration of public comment and after appropriate revision, the agency must submit this draft report to OMB for review regarding consistency with these OMB guidelines no later than July 1, 2002. Upon completion of that OMB review and completion of this report, agencies must publish notice of the availability of this report in its final form in the Federal Register, and post this report on the agency's web site no later than October 1, 2002.

6. On an annual fiscal-year basis, each agency must submit a report to the Director of OMB providing information (both quantitative and qualitative, where appropriate) on the number and nature of complaints received by the agency regarding agency compliance with these OMB guidelines and how such complaints were resolved. Agencies must submit these reports no later than January 1 of each following year, with the first report due January 1, 2004.

V. Definitions

1. "Quality" is an encompassing term comprising utility, objectivity, and integrity. Therefore, the guidelines sometimes refer to these four statutory terms, collectively, as "quality."

2. "Utility" refers to the usefulness of the information to its intended users, including the public. In assessing the usefulness of information that the agency disseminates to the public, the agency needs to consider the uses of the information not only from the perspective of the agency but also from the perspective of the public. As a result, when transparency of information is relevant for assessing the information's usefulness from the public's perspective, the agency must take care to ensure that transparency has been addressed in its review of the information.

3. "Objectivity" involves two distinct elements, presentation and substance.

    a. "Objectivity" includes whether disseminated information is being presented in an accurate, clear, complete, and unbiased manner. This involves whether the information is presented within a proper context. Sometimes, in disseminating certain types of information to the public, other information must also be disseminated in order to ensure an accurate, clear, complete, and unbiased presentation. Also, the agency needs to identify the sources of the disseminated information (to the extent possible, consistent with confidentiality protections) and, in a scientific, financial, or statistical context, the supporting data and models, so that the public can assess for itself whether there may be some reason to question the objectivity of the sources. Where appropriate, data should have full, accurate, transparent documentation, and error sources affecting data quality should be identified and disclosed to users.

b. In addition, "objectivity" involves a focus on ensuring accurate, reliable, and unbiased information. In a scientific, financial, or statistical context, the original and supporting data shall be generated, and the analytic results shall be developed, using sound statistical and research methods.

    i. If data and analytic results have been subjected to formal, independent, external peer review, the information may generally be presumed to be of acceptable objectivity. However, this presumption is rebuttable based on a persuasive showing by the petitioner in a particular instance. If agency-sponsored peer review is employed to help satisfy the objectivity standard, the review process employed shall meet the general criteria for competent and credible peer review recommended by OMB-OIRA to the President's Management Council (9/20/01) (http://www.whitehouse.gov/omb/inforeg/oira_review-process.html), namely, "that (a) peer reviewers be selected primarily on the basis of necessary technical expertise, (b) peer reviewers be expected to disclose to agencies prior technical/policy positions they may have taken on the issues at hand, (c) peer reviewers be expected to disclose to agencies their sources of personal and institutional funding (private or public sector), and (d) peer reviews be conducted in an open and rigorous manner."

    ii. If an agency is responsible for disseminating influential scientific, financial, or statistical information, agency guidelines shall include a high degree of transparency about data and methods to facilitate the reproducibility of such information by qualified third parties.

A. With regard to original and supporting data related thereto, agency guidelines shall not require that all disseminated data be subjected to a reproducibility requirement. Agencies may identify, in consultation with the relevant scientific and technical communities, those particular types of data that can practicable be subjected to a reproducibility requirement, given ethical, feasibility, or confidentiality constraints. It is understood that reproducibility of data is an indication of transparency about research design and methods and thus a replication exercise (i.e., a new experiment, test, or sample) shall not be required prior to each dissemination.
B. With regard to analytic results related thereto, agency guidelines shall generally require sufficient transparency about data and methods that an independent reanalysis could be undertaken by a qualified member of the public. These transparency standards apply to agency analysis of data from a single study as well as to analyses that combine information from multiple studies.
i. Making the data and methods publicly available will assist in determining whether analytic results are reproducible. However, the objectivity standard does not override other compelling interests such as privacy, trade secrets, intellectual property, and other confidentiality protections.
ii. In situations where public access to data and methods will not occur due to other compelling interests, agencies shall apply especially rigorous robustness checks to analytic results and document what checks were undertaken. Agency guidelines shall, however, in all cases, require a disclosure of the specific data sources that have been used and the specific quantitative methods and assumptions that have been employed. Each agency is authorized to define the type of robustness checks, and the level of detail for documentation thereof, in ways appropriate for it given the nature and multiplicity of issues for which the agency is responsible.
C. With regard to analysis of risks to human health, safety and the environment maintained or disseminated by the agencies, agencies shall either adopt or adapt the quality principles applied by Congress to risk information used and disseminated pursuant to the Safe Drinking Water Act Amendments of 1996 (42 U.S.C. 300g-1(b)(3)(A) & (B)). Agen-

cies responsible for dissemination of vital health and medical information shall interpret the reproducibility and peer-review standards in a manner appropriate to assuring the timely flow of vital information from agencies to medical providers, patients, health agencies, and the public. Information quality standards may be waived temporarily by agencies under urgent situations (e.g., imminent threats to public health or homeland security) in accordance with the latitude specified in agency-specific guidelines.

4. "Integrity" refers to the security of information—protection of the information from unauthorized access or revision, to ensure that the information is not compromised through corruption or falsification.

5. "Information" means any communication or representation of knowledge such as facts or data, in any medium or form, including textual, numerical, graphic, cartographic, narrative, or audiovisual forms. This definition includes information that an agency disseminates from a web page, but does not include the provision of hyperlinks to information that others disseminate. This definition does not include opinions, where the agency's presentation makes it clear that what is being offered is someone's opinion rather than fact or the agency's views.

6. "Government information" means information created, collected, processed, disseminated, or disposed of by or for the Federal Government.

7. "Information dissemination product" means any books, paper, map, machine-readable material, audiovisual production, or other documentary material, regardless of physical form or characteristic, an agency disseminates to the public. This definition includes any electronic document, CD-ROM, or web page.

8. "Dissemination" means agency initiated or sponsored distribution of information to the public (see 5 CFR 1320.3(d) (definition of "Conduct or Sponsor")). Dissemination does not include distribution limited to government employees or agency contractors or grantees; intra- or inter-agency use or sharing of government information; and responses to requests for agency records under the Freedom of Information Act, the Privacy Act, the Federal Advisory Committee Act or other similar law. This definition also does not include distribution limited to correspondence with individuals or persons, press releases, archival records, public filings, subpoenas or adjudicative processes.

9. "Influential," when used in the phrase "influential scientific, financial, or statistical information," means that the agency can reasonably determine that dissemination of the information will have or does have a clear and

substantial impact on important public policies or important private sector decisions. Each agency is authorized to define "influential" in ways appropriate for it given the nature and multiplicity of issues for which the agency is responsible.

10. "Reproducibility" means that the information is capable of being substantially reproduced, subject to an acceptable degree of imprecision. For information judged to have more (less) important impacts, the degree of imprecision that is tolerated is reduced (increased). If agencies apply the reproducibility test to specific types of original or supporting data, the associated guidelines shall provide relevant definitions of reproducibility (e.g., standards for replication of laboratory data). With respect to analytic results, "capable of being substantially reproduced" means that independent analysis of the original or supporting data using identical methods would generate similar analytic results, subject to an acceptable degree of imprecision or error.

Peer Review Bulletin
Office of Management and Budget
40 Fed. Reg. 2664 (January 14, 2005)

OFFICE OF MANAGEMENT AND BUDGET

Final Information Quality Bulletin for Peer Review

AGENCY: Office of Management and Budget, Executive Office of the President.

ACTION: Final bulletin.

SUMMARY: On December 16, 2004, the Office of Management and Budget (OMB), in consultation with the Office of Science and Technology Policy (OSTP), issued its Final Information Quality Bulletin for Peer Review to the heads of departments and agencies (available at *http://www.whitehouse.gov/omb/memoranda/fy2005/m05-03.html*). This new guidance is designed to realize the benefits of meaningful peer review of the most important science disseminated by the Federal Government. It is part of an ongoing effort to improve the quality, objectivity, utility, and integrity of information disseminated by the Federal Government to the public. This final bulletin has benefited from an extensive stakeholder process. OMB originally requested comment on its "Proposed Bulletin on Peer Review and Information Quality," published in the *Federal Register* on September 15, 2003. OMB received 187 public comments during the comment period (*available at* http://www.whitehouse.gov/omb/ inforeg/2003iq/iq_list.html). In addition, to improve the draft Bulletin, OMB encouraged federal agencies to sponsor a public workshop at the National Academy of Sciences (NAS). The NAS workshop (November 18, 2003, at the National Academies in Washington, DC) attracted several hundred participants, including leaders in the scientific community (*available at* http:/www7.nationalacademies.org/stl/ STL_Peer_ Review_ Agenda.html). OMB also participated in outreach activities with major scientific organizations and societies that had expressed specific interest in the draft Bulletin. A formal interagency review of the draft Bulletin, resulting in detailed comments from numerous Federal departments and agencies, was undertaken in collaboration with the White House Office of Science and Technology Policy. In light of the substantial interest in the Bulletin, including a wide range of constructive criticisms of the initial draft, OMB decided to issue a revised draft for further comment. This revised draft was published in the *Federal Register* on April 28, 2004, and solicited a second round of public comment. The revised draft stimulated a much smaller number of comments (57) (available at: *http://www.whitehouse.gov/omb/inforeg/peer2004/list_peer2004.html*). OMB's response to the additional criticisms, suggestions, and refinements offered for consideration is available at: *http://www.whitehouse.gov/omb inforeg/peer2004/peer_response.pdf*. The final Bulletin includes refinements that strike a balance among the diverse perspectives expressed during the comment period. Part I of the **SUPPLEMENTARY INFORMATION** below provides background. Part II provides the text of the final Bulletin.

DATES: The requirements of this Bulletin, with the exception of those in Section V (Peer Review Planning), apply to information disseminated on or after June 16, 2005. However, they do not apply to information for which an agency has already provided a draft report and an associated charge to peer reviewers. The requirements in Section V regarding "highly influential scientific assessments" are effective June 16, 2005. The requirements in Section V regarding "influential scientific information" are effective December 16, 2005.

FOR FURTHER INFORMATION CONTACT: Dr. Margo Schwab, Office of Information and Regulatory Affairs, Office of Management and Budget, 725 17th Street, NW., New Executive Office Building, Room 10201, Washington, DC 20503. Telephone (202) 395-5647 or email: *OMB_peer_review@omb.eop.gov*.

SUPPLEMENTARY INFORMATION:

Introduction

This Bulletin establishes that important scientific information shall be peer reviewed by qualified specialists before it is disseminated by the federal government. We published a proposed Bulletin on September 15, 2003. Based on public comments, we published a revised proposal for additional comment on April 28, 2004. We are now finalizing the April version, with minor revisions responsive to the public's comments.

The purpose of the Bulletin is to enhance the quality and credibility of the government's scientific information. We recognize that different types of peer review are appropriate for different types of information. Under this Bulletin, agencies are granted broad discretion to weigh the benefits and costs of using a particular peer review mechanism for a specific information product. The selection of an appropriate peer review mechanism for scientific information is left to the agency's discretion. Various types of information are exempted from the requirements of this Bulletin, including time-sensitive health and safety determinations, in order to ensure that peer review does not unduly delay the release of urgent findings.

This Bulletin also applies stricter minimum requirements for the peer review of highly influential scientific assessments, which are a subset of influential scientific information. A scientific assessment is an evaluation of a body of scientific or technical knowledge that typically synthesizes multiple factual inputs, data, models, assumptions, and/or applies best professional judgment to bridge uncertainties in the available information. To ensure that the Bulletin is not too costly or rigid, these requirements for more intensive peer review apply only to the more important scientific assessments disseminated by the federal government.

Even for these highly influential scientific assessments, the Bulletin leaves significant discretion to the agency formulating the peer review plan. In general, an agency conducting a peer review of a highly influential scientific assessment must ensure that the peer review process is transparent by making available to the public the written charge to the peer reviewers, the peer reviewers' names, the peer reviewers' report(s), and the agency's response to the peer reviewers' report(s). The agency selecting peer reviewers must ensure that the reviewers possess the necessary expertise. In addition, the agency must address reviewers' potential conflicts of interest (including those stemming from ties to regulated businesses and other stakeholders) and independence from the agency. This Bulletin requires agencies to adopt or adapt the committee selection policies employed by the National Academy of Sciences (NAS)[1] when selecting peer reviewers who are not government employees. Those that are government employees are subject to federal ethics requirements. The use of a transparent process, coupled with the selection of qualified and independent peer reviewers, should improve the quality of government science while promoting public confidence in the integrity of the government's scientific products.

---

[1] National Academy of Sciences, "Policy and Procedures on Committee Composition and Balance and Conflicts of Interest for Committees Used in the Development of Reports," May 2003, *available at:* http://www.nationalacademies.org/coi/index.html.

Peer Review

Peer review is one of the important procedures used to ensure that the quality of published information meets the standards of the scientific and technical community. It is a form of deliberation involving an exchange of judgments about the appropriateness of methods and the strength of the author's inferences.[2] Peer review involves the review of a draft product for quality by specialists in the field who were not involved in producing the draft.

The peer reviewer's report is an evaluation or critique that is used by the authors of the draft to improve the product. Peer review typically evaluates the clarity of hypotheses, the validity of the research design, the quality of data collection procedures, the robustness of the methods employed, the appropriateness of the methods for the hypotheses being tested, the extent to which the conclusions follow from the analysis, and the strengths and limitations of the overall product.

Peer review has diverse purposes. Editors of scientific journals use reviewer comments to help determine whether a draft scientific article is of sufficient quality, importance, and interest to a field of study to justify publication. Research funding organizations often use peer review to evaluate research proposals. In addition, some federal agencies make use of peer review to obtain evaluations of draft information that contains important scientific determinations.

Peer review should not be confused with public comment and other stakeholder processes. The selection of participants in a peer review is based on expertise, with due consideration of independence and conflict of interest. Furthermore, notice-and comment procedures for agency rulemaking do not provide an adequate substitute for peer review, as some experts—especially those most knowledgeable in a field—may not file public comments with federal agencies.

The critique provided by a peer review often suggests ways to clarify assumptions, findings, and conclusions. For instance, peer reviews can filter out biases and identify oversights, omissions, and inconsistencies.[3] Peer review also may encourage authors to more fully acknowledge limitations and uncertainties. In some cases, reviewers might recommend major changes to the draft, such as refinement of hypotheses, reconsideration of research de-

---

[2] CARNEGIE COMMISSION ON SCIENCE, TECHNOLOGY, AND GOVERNMENT, RISK AND THE ENVIRONMENT: IMPROVING REGULATORY DECISION MAKING 75 (New York, 1993).

[3] WILLIAM W. LOWRANCE, MODERN SCIENCE AND HUMAN VALUES 85 (New York: Oxford University Press, 1985).

sign, modifications of data collection or analysis methods, or alternative conclusions. However, peer review does not always lead to specific modifications in the draft product. In some cases, a draft is in excellent shape prior to being submitted for review. In others, the authors do not concur with changes suggested by one or more reviewers.

Peer review may take a variety of forms, depending upon the nature and importance of the product. For example, the reviewers may represent one scientific discipline or a variety of disciplines; the number of reviewers may range from a few to more than a dozen; the names of each reviewer may be disclosed publicly or may remain anonymous (e.g., to encourage candor); the reviewers may be blinded to the authors of the report or the names of the authors may be disclosed to the reviewers; the reviewers may prepare individual reports or a panel of reviewers may be constituted to produce a collaborative report; panels may do their work electronically or they may meet together in person to discuss and prepare their evaluations; and reviewers may be compensated for their work or they may donate their time as a contribution to science or public service.

For large, complex reports, different reviewers may be assigned to different chapters or topics. Such reports may be reviewed in stages, sometimes with confidential reviews that precede a public process of panel review. As part of government-sponsored peer review, there may be opportunity for written and/or oral public comments on the draft product.

The results of peer review are often only one of the criteria used to make decisions about journal publication, grant funding, and information dissemination. For instance, the editors of scientific journals (rather than the peer reviewers) make final decisions about a manuscript's appropriateness for publication based on a variety of considerations. In research-funding decisions, the reports of peer reviewers often play an important role, but the final decisions about funding are often made by accountable officials based on a variety of considerations. Similarly, when a government agency sponsors peer review of its own draft documents, the peer review reports are an important factor in information dissemination decisions but rarely are the sole consideration. Agencies are not expected to cede their discretion with regard to dissemination or use of information to peer reviewers; accountable agency officials must make the final decisions.

The Need for Stronger Peer Review Policies

There are a multiplicity of science advisory procedures used at federal agencies and across the wide variety of scientific products prepared by agencies.[4] In response to congressional inquiry, the U.S. General Accounting Office (now the Government Accountability Office) documented the variability in both the definition and implementation of peer review across agencies.[5] The Carnegie Commission on Science, Technology and Government[6] has highlighted the importance of "internal" scientific advice (within the agency) and "external" advice (through scientific advisory boards and other mechanisms).

A wide variety of authorities have argued that peer review practices at federal agencies need to be strengthened.[7] Some arguments focus on specific types of scientific products (e.g., assessments of health, safety and environmental hazards).[8] The Congressional/Presidential Commission on Risk Assessment and Risk Management suggests that "peer review of economic and social science information should have as high a priority as peer review of health, ecological, and engineering information."[9] Some agencies have for-

---

[4] SHEILA JASANOFF, THE FIFTH BRANCH: SCIENCE ADVISORS AS POLICY MAKERS, Harvard University Press, Boston, 1990.

[5] U.S. General Accounting Office, *Federal Research: Peer Review Practices at Federal Agencies Vary*, GAO/RCED-99-99, Washington, D.C., 1999.

[6] CARNEGIE COMMISSION ON SCIENCE, TECHNOLOGY, AND GOVERNMENT, RISK AND THE ENVIRONMENT: IMPROVING REGULATORY DECISION MAKING 90 (New York, 1993).

[7] National Academy of Sciences, *Peer Review in the Department of Energy—Office of Science and Technology*, Interim Report, National Academy Press, Washington, D.C., 1997; National Academy of Sciences, *Peer Review in Environmental Technology Development: The Department of Energy—Office of Science and Technology*, National Academy Press, Washington, D.C., 1998; National Academy of Sciences, *Strengthening Science at the U.S. Environmental Protection Agency: Research-Management and Peer-Review Practices*, National Academy Press, Washington, D.C., 2000; U.S. General Accounting Office, *EPA's Science Advisory Board Panels: Improved Policies and Procedures Needed to Ensure Independence and Balance*, GAO-01-536, Washington, D.C., 2001; U.S. Environmental Protection Agency, Office of Inspector General, *Pilot Study: Science in Support of Rulemaking 2003*-P-00003, Washington, D.C., 2002; Carnegie Commission on Science, Technology, and Government, *In the National Interest: The Federal Government in the Reform of K-12 Math and Science Education*, (New York, 1991); U.S. General Accounting Office, *Endangered Species Program: Information on How Funds Are Allocated and What Activities Are Emphasized*, GAO-02-581, Washington, D.C., 2002.

[8] National Research Council, *Science and Judgment in Risk Assessment*, National Academy Press, Washington, D.C., 1994.

[9] Presidential/Congressional Commission on Risk Assessment and Risk Management, Risk Commission Report, Volume 2, *Risk Assessment and Risk Management in Regulatory Decision-Making*, 1997:103.

mal peer review policies, while others do not. Even agencies that have such policies do not always follow them prior to the release of important scientific products.

Prior to the development of this Bulletin, there were no government-wide standards concerning when peer review is required and, if required, what type of peer review processes are appropriate. No formal interagency mechanism existed to foster crossagency sharing of experiences with peer review practices and policies. Despite the importance of peer review for the credibility of agency scientific products, the public lacked a consistent way to determine when an important scientific information product is being developed by an agency, the type of peer review planned for that product, or whether there would be an opportunity to provide comments and data to the reviewers.

This Bulletin establishes minimum standards for when peer review is required for scientific information and the types of peer review that should be considered by agencies in different circumstances. It also establishes a transparent process for public disclosure of peer review planning, including a web-accessible description of the peer review plan that the agency has developed for each of its forthcoming influential scientific disseminations.

Legal Authority for the Bulletin

This Bulletin is issued under the Information Quality Act and OMB's general authorities to oversee the quality of agency information, analyses, and regulatory actions. In the Information Quality Act, Congress directed OMB to issue guidelines to "provide policy and procedural guidance to Federal agencies for ensuring and maximizing the quality, objectivity, utility and integrity of information" disseminated by Federal agencies. Pub. No. 106-554, § 515(a). The Information Quality Act was developed as a supplement to the Paperwork Reduction Act, 44 U.S.C. § 3501 *et seq.,* which requires OMB, among other things, to "develop and oversee the implementation of policies, principles, standards, and guidelines to . . . apply to Federal agency dissemination of public information." In addition, Executive Order 12,866, 58 Fed. Reg. 51,735 (Oct. 4, 1993), establishes that OIRA is "the repository of expertise concerning regulatory issues," and it directs OMB to provide guidance to the agencies on regulatory planning. E.O. 12866, § 2(b). The Order also requires that "[e]ach agency shall base its decisions on the best reasonably obtainable scientific, technical, economic, or other information." E.O. 12866, § 1(b)(7). Finally, OMB has authority in certain circumstances to manage the agencies under the purview of the President's Constitutional authority to supervise the unitary Executive Branch. All of these authorities support this Bulletin.

The Requirements of this Bulletin

This Bulletin addresses peer review of scientific information disseminations that contain findings or conclusions that represent the official position of one or more agencies of the federal government.

Section I: Definitions

Section I provides definitions that are central to this Bulletin. Several terms are identical to or based on those used in OMB's government-wide information quality guidelines, 67 Fed. Reg. 8452 (Feb. 22, 2002), and the Paperwork Reduction Act, 44 U.S.C. § 3501 *et seq.*

The term "Administrator" means the Administrator of the Office of Information and Regulatory Affairs in the Office of Management and Budget (OIRA).

The term "agency" has the same meaning as in the Paperwork Reduction Act, 44 U.S.C. § 3502(1).

The term "Information Quality Act" means Section 515 of Public Law 106-554 (Pub. No. 106-554, § 515, 114 Stat. 2763, 2763A-153-154 (2000)).

The term "dissemination" means agency initiated or sponsored distribution of information to the public. Dissemination does not include distribution limited to government employees or agency contractors or grantees; intra- or inter-agency use or sharing of government information; or responses to requests for agency records under the Freedom of Information Act, the Privacy Act, the Federal Advisory Committee Act, the Government Performance and Results Act, or similar laws. This definition also excludes distribution limited to correspondence with individuals or persons, press releases, archival records, public filings, subpoenas and adjudicative processes. In the context of this Bulletin, the definition of "dissemination" modifies the definition in OMB's government-wide information quality guidelines to address the need for peer review prior to official dissemination of the information product. Accordingly, under this Bulletin, "dissemination" also excludes information distributed for peer review in compliance with this Bulletin or shared confidentially with scientific colleagues, provided that the distributing agency includes an appropriate and clear disclaimer on the information, as explained more fully below. Finally, the Bulletin does not directly cover information supplied to the government by third parties (e.g., studies by private consultants, companies and private, non-profit organizations, or research institutions such as universities). However, if an agency plans to disseminate information supplied by a third party (e.g., using this information as the basis for an agency's factual determination that a particular behavior causes a disease), the requirements of the Bulletin apply, if the dissemination is "influential."

In cases where a draft report or other information is released by an agency solely for purposes of peer review, a question may arise as to whether the draft report constitutes an official "dissemination" under information-quality guidelines. Section I instructs agencies to make this clear by presenting the following disclaimer in the report:

> "THIS INFORMATION IS DISTRIBUTED SOLELY FOR THE PURPOSE OF PREDISSEMINATION PEER REVIEW UNDER APPLICABLE INFORMATION QUALITY GUIDELINES. IT HAS NOT BEEN FORMALLY DISSEMINATED BY [THE AGENCY]. IT DOES NOT REPRESENT AND SHOULD NOT BE CONSTRUED TO REPRESENT ANY AGENCY DETERMINATION OR POLICY."

In cases where the information is highly relevant to specific policy or regulatory deliberations, this disclaimer shall appear on each page of a draft report. Agencies also shall discourage state, local, international and private organizations from using information in draft reports that are undergoing peer review. Draft influential scientific information presented at scientific meetings or shared confidentially with colleagues for scientific input prior to peer review shall include the disclaimer:

> "THE FINDINGS AND CONCLUSIONS IN THIS REPORT (PRESENTATION) HAVE NOT BEEN FORMALLY DISSEMINATED BY [THE AGENCY] AND SHOULD NOT BE CONSTRUED TO REPRESENT ANY AGENCY DETERMINATION OR POLICY."

An information product is not covered by the Bulletin unless it represents an official view of one or more departments or agencies of the federal government. Accordingly, for the purposes of this Bulletin, "dissemination" excludes research produced by government-funded scientists (e.g., those supported extramurally or intramurally by federal agencies or those working in state or local governments with federal support) if that information is not represented as the views of a department or agency (i.e., they are not official government disseminations). For influential scientific information that does not have the imprimatur of the federal government, scientists employed by the federal government are required to include in their information product a clear disclaimer that "the findings and conclusions in this report are those of the author(s) and do not necessarily represent the views of the funding agency." A similar disclaimer is advised for non-government employees who publish government-funded research.

For the purposes of the peer review Bulletin, the term "scientific information" means factual inputs, data, models, analyses, technical information, or scientific assessments related to such disciplines as the behavioral and social sciences, public health and medical sciences, life and earth sciences, engineering, or physical sciences. This includes any communication or representation of knowledge such as facts or data, in any medium or form, including textual, numerical, graphic, cartographic, narrative, or audiovisual forms. This definition includes information that an agency disseminates from a web page, but does not include the provision of hyperlinks on a web page to information that others disseminate. This definition excludes opinions, where the agency's presentation makes clear that an individual's opinion, rather than a statement of fact or of the agency's findings and conclusions, is being offered.

The term "influential scientific information" means scientific information the agency reasonably can determine will have or does have a clear and substantial impact on important public policies or private sector decisions. In the term "influential scientific information," the term "influential" should be interpreted consistently with OMB's government-wide information quality guidelines and the information quality guidelines of the agency. Information dissemination can have a significant economic impact even if it is not part of a rulemaking. For instance, the economic viability of a technology can be influenced by the government's characterization of its attributes. Alternatively, the federal government's assessment of risk can directly or indirectly influence the response actions of state and local agencies or international bodies.

One type of scientific information is a scientific assessment. For the purposes of this Bulletin, the term "scientific assessment" means an evaluation of a body of scientific or technical knowledge, which typically synthesizes multiple factual inputs, data, models, assumptions, and/or applies best professional judgment to bridge uncertainties in the available information. These assessments include, but are not limited to, state-of-science reports; technology assessments; weight-of-evidence analyses; meta-analyses; health, safety, or ecological risk assessments; toxicological characterizations of substances; integrated assessment models; hazard determinations; or exposure assessments. Such assessments often draw upon knowledge from multiple disciplines. Typically, the data and models used in scientific assessments have already been subject to some form of peer review (e.g., refereed journal peer review or peer review under Section II of this Bulletin).

Section II: Peer Review of Influential Scientific Information

Section II requires each agency to subject "influential" scientific information to peer review prior to dissemination. For dissemination of influential scientific information, Section II provides agencies broad discretion in determining what type of peer review is appropriate and what procedures should be employed to select appropriate reviewers. Agencies are directed to chose a peer review mechanism that is adequate, giving due consideration to the novelty and complexity of the science to be reviewed, the relevance of the information to decision making, the extent of prior peer reviews, and the expected benefits and costs of additional review.

The National Academy of Public Administration suggests that the intensity of peer review should be commensurate with the significance of the information being disseminated and the likely implications for policy decisions.[10] Furthermore, agencies need to consider tradeoffs between depth of peer review and timeliness.[11] More rigorous peer review is necessary for information that is based on novel methods or presents complex challenges for interpretation. Furthermore, the need for rigorous peer review is greater when the information contains precedent-setting methods or models, presents conclusions that are likely to change prevailing practices, or is likely to affect policy decisions that have a significant impact.

This tradeoff can be considered in a benefit-cost framework. The costs of peer review include both the direct costs of the peer review activity and those stemming from potential delay in government and private actions that can result from peer review. The benefits of peer review are equally clear: the insights offered by peer reviewers may lead to policy with more benefits and/or fewer costs. In addition to contributing to strong science, peer review, if performed fairly and rigorously, can build consensus among stakeholders and reduce the temptation for courts and legislators to second-guess or overturn

---

[10] National Academy of Public Administration, *Setting Priorities, Getting Results: A New Direction for EPA*, National Academy Press, Washington, D.C., 1995:23.

[11] Presidential/Congressional Commission on Risk Assessment and Risk Management, Risk Commission Report, 1997.

agency actions.[12] While it will not always be easy for agencies to quantify the benefits and costs of peer review, agencies are encouraged to approach peer review from a benefit-cost perspective.

Regardless of the peer review mechanism chosen, agencies should strive to ensure that their peer review practices are characterized by both scientific integrity and process integrity. "Scientific integrity," in the context of peer review, refers to such issues as "expertise and balance of the panel members; the identification of the scientific issues and clarity of the charge to the panel; the quality, focus and depth of the discussion of the issues by the panel; the rationale and supportability of the panel's findings; and the accuracy and clarity of the panel report." "Process integrity" includes such issues as "transparency and openness, avoidance of real or perceived conflicts of interest, a workable process for public comment and involvement," and adherence to defined procedures.[13]

When deciding what type of peer review mechanism is appropriate for a specific information product, agencies will need to consider at least the following issues: individual versus panel review; timing; scope of the review; selection of reviewers; disclosure and attribution; public participation; disposition of reviewer comments; and adequacy of prior peer review.

Individual versus Panel Review

Letter reviews by several experts generally will be more expeditious than convening a panel of experts. Individual letter reviews are more appropriate when a draft document covers only one discipline or when premature disclosure of a sensitive report to a public panel could cause harm to government or private interests. When time and resources warrant, panels are preferable, as they tend to be more deliberative than individual letter reviews and the reviewers can learn from each other. There are also multi-stage processes in which confidential letter reviews are conducted prior to release of a draft document for public notice and comment, followed by a formal panel review. These more rigorous and expensive processes are particularly valuable

---

[12] Mark R. Powell, *Science at EPA: Information in the Regulatory Process*, Resources for the Future, Washington, D.C., 1999: 148, 176; SHEILA JASANOFF, THE FIFTH BRANCH: SCIENCE ADVISORS AS POLICY MAKERS 242, Boston: Harvard University Press (1990).

[13] ILSI Risk Sciences Institute, *Policies and Procedures: Model Peer Review Center of Excellence* 4 (2002), *available at* http://rsi.ilsi.org/file/Policies&Procedures.pdf.

for highly complex, multidisciplinary, and more important documents, especially those that are novel or precedent-setting.

Timing of Peer Review

As a general rule, it is most useful to consult with peers early in the process of producing information. For example, in the context of risk assessments, it is valuable to have the choice of input data and the specification of the model reviewed by peers before the agency invests time and resources in implementing the model and interpreting the results. "Early" peer review occurs in time to "focus attention on data inadequacies in time for corrections.

When an information product is a critical component of rule-making, it is important to obtain peer review before the agency announces its regulatory options so that any technical corrections can be made before the agency becomes invested in a specific approach or the positions of interest groups have hardened. If review occurs too late, it is unlikely to contribute to the course of a rulemaking. Furthermore, investing in a more rigorous peer review early in the process "may provide net benefit by reducing the prospect of challenges to a regulation that later may trigger time consuming and resource-draining litigation."[14]

Scope of the Review

The "charge" contains the instructions to the peer reviewers regarding the objective of the peer review and the specific advice sought. The importance of the information, which shapes the goal of the peer review, influences the charge. For instance, the goal of the review might be to determine the utility of a body of literature for drawing certain conclusions about the feasibility of a technology or the safety of a product. In this context, an agency might ask reviewers to determine the relevance of conclusions drawn in one context for other contexts (e.g., different exposure conditions or patient populations).

The charge to the reviewers should be determined in advance of the selection of the reviewers. In drafting the charge, it is important to remember the strengths and limitations of peer review. Peer review is most powerful

---

[14] Fred Anderson, Mary Ann Chirba Martin, E. Donald Elliott, Cynthia Farina, Ernest Gellhorn, John D. Graham, C. Boyden Gray, Jeffrey Holmstead, Ronald M. Levin, Lars Noah, Katherine Rhyne, Jonathan Baert Wiener, *Regulatory Improvement Legislation: Risk Assessment, Cost-Benefit Analysis, and Judicial Review*, DUKE ENVTL. L. & POLICY FORUM, Fall 2000, vol. XI (1) at 132.

when the charge is specific and steers the reviewers to specific technical questions while also directing reviewers to offer a broad evaluation of the overall product.

Uncertainty is inherent in science, and in many cases individual studies do not produce conclusive evidence. Thus, when an agency generates a scientific assessment, it is presenting its scientific judgment about the accumulated evidence rather than scientific fact.[15] Specialists attempt to reach a consensus by weighing the accumulated evidence. Peer reviewers can make an important contribution by distinguishing scientific facts from professional judgments. Furthermore, where appropriate, reviewers should be asked to provide advice on the reasonableness of judgments made from the scientific evidence. However, the charge should make clear that the reviewers are not to provide advice on the policy (e.g., the amount of uncertainty that is acceptable or the amount of precaution that should be embedded in an analysis). Such considerations are the purview of the government.[16]

The charge should ask that peer reviewers ensure that scientific uncertainties are clearly identified and characterized. Since not all uncertainties have an equal effect on the conclusions drawn, reviewers should be asked to ensure that the potential implications of the uncertainties for the technical conclusions drawn are clear. In addition, peer reviewers might be asked to consider value-of-information analyses that identify whether more research is likely to decrease key uncertainties.[17] Value-of-information analysis was suggested for this purpose in the report of the Presidential/Congressional Commission on Risk Assessment and Risk Management.[18] A description of additional research that would appreciably influence the conclusions of the assessment can help an agency assess and target subsequent efforts.

Selection of Reviewers

Expertise. The most important factor in selecting reviewers is expertise: ensuring that the selected reviewer has the knowledge, experience, and skills

---

[15] Mark R. Powell, *Science at EPA: Information in the Regulatory Process*, Washington, D.C.: Resources for the Future (1999), at 139.

[16] *Id.*

[17] Granger Morgan & Max Henrion, *The Value of Knowing How Little You Know*, in Uncertainty: A Guide to Dealing with Uncertainty in Quantitative Risk and Policy Analysis, Cambridge University Press (1990) at 307.

[18] Presidential/Congressional Commission on Risk Assessment and Risk Management, Risk Commission Report, 1997, Volume 1: 39, Volume 2: 91.

necessary to perform the review. Agencies shall ensure that, in cases where the document being reviewed spans a variety of scientific disciplines or areas of technical expertise, reviewers who represent the necessary spectrum of knowledge are chosen. For instance, expertise in applied mathematics and statistics is essential in the review of models, thereby allowing an audit of calculations and claims of significance and robustness based on the numeric data.[19] For some reviews, evaluation of biological plausibility is as important as statistical modeling. Agencies shall consider requesting that the public, including scientific and professional societies, nominate potential reviewers.

Balance. While expertise is the primary consideration, reviewers should also be selected to represent a diversity of scientific perspectives relevant to the subject. On most controversial issues, there exists a range of respected scientific viewpoints regarding interpretation of the available literature. Inviting reviewers with competing views on the science may lead to a sharper, more focused peer review. Indeed, as a final layer of review, some organizations (e.g., the National Academy of Sciences) specifically recruit reviewers with strong opinions to test the scientific strength and balance of their reports. The NAS policy on committee composition and balance[20] highlights important considerations associated with perspective, bias, and objectivity.

Independence. In its narrowest sense, independence in a reviewer means that the reviewer was not involved in producing the draft document to be reviewed. However, for peer review of some documents, a broader view of independence is necessary to assure credibility of the process. Reviewers are generally not employed by the agency or office producing the document. As the National Academy of Sciences has stated, "external experts often can be more open, frank, and challenging to the status quo than internal reviewers, who may feel constrained by organizational concerns."[21] The Carnegie Commission on Science, Technology, and Government notes that "external science advisory boards serve a critically important function in providing regulatory agencies with ex-

---

[19] WILLIAM W. LOWRANCE, MODERN SCIENCE AND HUMAN VALUES, Oxford University Press, New York, NY 1985: 86.

[20] National Academy of Sciences, *Policy and Procedures on Committee Composition and Balance and Conflicts of Interest for Committees Used in the Development of Reports* (May 2003), *available at:* http://www.nationalacademies.org/coi/index.html.

[21] National Research Council, *Peer Review in Environmental Technology Development Programs: The Department of Energy's Office of Science and Technology* 3, Washington, D.C.: National Academy Press (1998).

pert advice on a range of issues."[22] However, the choice of reviewers requires a case-by-case analysis. Reviewers employed by other federal and state agencies may possess unique or indispensable expertise.

A related issue is whether government-funded scientists in universities and consulting firms have sufficient independence from the federal agencies that support their work to be appropriate peer reviewers for those agencies.[23] This concern can be mitigated in situations where the scientist initiates the hypothesis to be tested or the method to be developed, which effectively creates a buffer between the scientist and the agency. When an agency awards grants through a competitive process that includes peer review, the agency's potential to influence the scientist's research is limited. As such, when a scientist is awarded a government research grant through an investigator-initiated, peerreviewed competition, there generally should be no question as to that scientist's ability to offer independent scientific advice to the agency on other projects. This contrasts, for example, to a situation in which a scientist has a consulting or contractual arrangement with the agency or office sponsoring a peer review. Likewise, when the agency and a researcher work together (e.g., through a cooperative agreement) to design or implement a study, there is less independence from the agency. Furthermore, if a scientist has repeatedly served as a reviewer for the same agency, some may question whether that scientist is sufficiently independent from the agency to be employed as a peer reviewer on agency-sponsored projects.

As the foregoing suggests, independence poses a complex set of questions that must be considered by agencies when peer reviewers are selected. In general, agencies shall make an effort to rotate peer review responsibilities across the available pool of qualified reviewers, recognizing that in some cases repeated service by the same reviewer is needed because of essential expertise.

Some agencies have built entire organizations to provide independent scientific advice while other agencies tend to employ ad hoc scientific panels on specific issues. Respect for the independence of reviewers may be enhanced if an agency collects names of potential reviewers (based on considerations of expertise and reputation for objectivity) from the public, including scientific or professional societies. The Department of Energy's use of the American Society of Mechanical Engineers to identify potential peer reviewers from a variety

---

[22] Carnegie Commission on Science, Technology, and Government, *Risk and the Environment: Improving Regulatory Decision Making* 90 (New York 1993).

[23] Lars Noah, *Scientific "Republicanism": Expert Peer Review and the Quest for Regulatory Deliberation*, EMORY L. J., Atlanta, Fall 2000, at 1066.

of different scientific societies provides an example of how professional societies can assist in the development of an independent peer review panel.[24]

Conflict of Interest. The National Academy of Sciences defines "conflict of interest" as any financial or other interest that conflicts with the service of an individual on the review panel because it could impair the individual's objectivity or could create an unfair competitive advantage for a person or organization.[25] This standard provides a useful benchmark for agencies to consider in selecting peer reviewers. Agencies shall make a special effort to examine prospective reviewers' potential financial conflicts, including significant investments, consulting arrangements, employer affiliations and grants/contracts. Financial ties of potential reviewers to regulated entities (e.g., businesses), other stakeholders, and regulatory agencies shall be scrutinized when the information being reviewed is likely to be relevant to regulatory policy. The inquiry into potential conflicts goes beyond financial investments and business relationships and includes work as an expert witness, consulting arrangements, honoraria and sources of grants and contracts. To evaluate any real or perceived conflicts of interest with potential reviewers and questions regarding the independence of reviewers, agencies are referred to federal ethics requirements, applicable standards issued by the Office of Government Ethics, and the prevailing practices of the National Academy of Sciences. Specifically, peer reviewers who are federal employees (including special government employees) are subject to federal requirements governing conflicts of interest. See, e.g., 18 U.S.C. § 208; 5 C.F.R. Part 2635 (2004). With respect to reviewers who are not federal employees, agencies shall adopt or adapt the NAS policy for committee selection with respect to evaluating conflicts of interest.[26] Both the NAS and the federal government recognize that under certain circumstances some conflict may be unavoidable in order to obtain the necessary expertise. See, e.g., 18 U.S.C. §208(b)(3); 5 U.S.C. App. §15 (governing NAS committees). To improve the transparency of the process, when an agency determines that it is necessary to use a reviewer with

---

[24] American Society of Mechanical Engineers, *Assessment of Technologies Supported by the Office of Science and Technology, Department of Energy: Results of the Peer Review for Fiscal Year 2002*, ASME Technical Publishing, Danvers, Mass. (2003).

[25] National Academy of Sciences, *Policy and Procedures on Committee Composition and Balance and Conflicts of Interest for Committees Used in the Development of Reports*, May 2003, *available at:* http://www.nationalacademies.org/coi/index.html.

[26] *Id.*

a real or perceived conflict of interest, the agency should consider publicly disclosing those conflicts. In such situations, the agency shall inform potential reviewers of such disclosure at the time they are recruited.

Disclosure and Attribution: Anonymous versus Identified

Peer reviewers must have a clear understanding of how their comments will be conveyed to the authors of the document and to the public. When peer review of government reports is considered, the case for transparency is stronger, particularly when the report addresses an issue with significant ramifications for the public and private sectors. The public may not have confidence in the peer review process when the names and affiliations of the peer reviewers are unknown. Without access to the comments of reviewers, the public is incapable of determining whether the government has seriously considered the comments of reviewers and made appropriate revisions. Disclosure of the slate of reviewers and the substance of their comments can strengthen public confidence in the peer review process. It is common at many journals and research funding agencies to disclose annually the slate of reviewers. Moreover, the National Academy of Sciences now discloses the names of its peer reviewers, without disclosing the substance of their comments. The science advisory committees to regulatory agencies typically disclose at least a summary of the comments of reviewers as well as their names and affiliations.

For agency-sponsored peer review conducted under Sections II and III, this Bulletin strikes a compromise by requiring disclosure of the identity of the reviewers, but not public attribution of specific comments to specific reviewers. The agency has considerable discretion in the implementation of this compromise (e.g., summarizing the views of reviewers as a group or disclosing individual reviewer comments without attribution). Whatever approach is employed, the agency must inform reviewers in advance of how it intends to address this issue. Information about a reviewer retrieved from a record filed by the reviewer's name or other identifier may be disclosed only as permitted by the conditions of disclosure enumerated in the Privacy Act, 5 U.S.C. § 552a as amended, and as interpreted in OMB implementing guidance, 40 Fed. Reg. 28,948 (July 9, 1975).

Public Participation

Public comments can be important in shaping expert deliberations. Agencies may decide that peer review should precede an opportunity for public comment to ensure that the public receives the most scientifically strong product (rather than one that may change substantially as a result of peer reviewer suggestions). However, there are situations in which public participation in peer review is an important aspect of obtaining a high-quality product through a credible process. Agencies, however, should avoid open-ended comment periods, which may delay completion of peer reviews and complicate the completion of the final work product.

Public participation can take a variety of forms, including opportunities to provide oral comments before a peer review panel or requests to provide written comments to the peer reviewers. Another option is for agencies to publish a "request for comment" or other notice in which they solicit public comment before a panel of peer reviewers performs its work.

Disposition of Reviewer Comments

A peer review is considered completed once the agency considers and addresses the reviewers' comments. All reviewer comments should be given consideration and be incorporated where relevant and valid. For instance, in the context of risk assessments, the National Academy of Sciences recommends that peer review include a written evaluation made available for public inspection.[27] In cases where there is a public panel, the agency should plan publication of the peer review report(s) and the agency's response to peer reviewer comments.

In addition, the credibility of the final scientific report is likely to be enhanced if the public understands how the agency addressed the specific concerns raised by the peer reviewers. Accordingly, agencies should consider preparing a written response to the peer review report explaining: the agency's agreement or disagreement, the actions the agency has undertaken or will undertake in response to the report, and (if applicable) the reasons the agency believes those actions satisfy any key concerns or recommendations in the report.

Adequacy of Prior Peer Review

In light of the broad range of information covered by Section II, agencies are directed to choose a peer review mechanism that is adequate, giving due consideration to the novelty and complexity of the science to be reviewed, the relevance of the information to decision making, the extent of

---

[27] National Research Council, *Risk Assessment in the Federal Government: Managing the Process,* Washington, D.C., National Academy Press (1983).

prior peer reviews, and the expected benefits and costs of additional review.

Publication in a refereed scientific journal may mean that adequate peer review has been performed. However, the intensity of peer review is highly variable across journals. There will be cases in which an agency determines that a more rigorous or transparent review process is necessary. For instance, an agency may determine a particular journal review process did not address questions (e.g., the extent of uncertainty inherent in a finding) that the agency determines should be addressed before disseminating that information. As such, prior peer review and publication is not by itself sufficient grounds for determining that no further review is necessary.

Section III: Peer Review of Highly Influential Scientific Assessments

Whereas Section II leaves most of the considerations regarding the form of the peer review to the agency's discretion, Section III requires a more rigorous form of peer review for highly influential scientific assessments. The requirements of Section II of this Bulletin apply to Section III, but Section III has some additional requirements, which are discussed below. In planning a peer review under Section III, agencies typically will have to devote greater resources and attention to the issues discussed in Section II, i.e., individual versus panel review; timing; scope of the review; selection of reviewers; disclosure and attribution; public participation; and disposition of reviewer comments.

A scientific assessment is considered "highly influential" if the agency or the OIRA Administrator determines that the dissemination could have a potential impact of more than $500 million in any one year on either the public or private sector or that the dissemination is novel, controversial, or precedent-setting, or has significant interagency interest. One of the ways information can exert economic impact is through the costs or benefits of a regulation based on the disseminated information. The qualitative aspect of this definition may be most useful in cases where it is difficult for an agency to predict the potential economic effect of dissemination. In the context of this Bulletin, it may be either the approach used in the assessment or the interpretation of the information itself that is novel or precedent-setting. Peer review can be valuable in establishing the bounds of the scientific debate when methods or interpretations are a source of controversy among interested parties. If information is covered by Section III, an agency is required to adhere to the peer review procedures specified in Section III.

Section III (2) clarifies that the principal findings, conclusions and recommendations in official reports of the National Academy of Sciences that fall under this Section are generally presumed not to require additional peer review. All other highly influential scientific assessments require a review that meets the requirements of Section III of this Bulletin.

With regard to the selection of reviewers, Section III(3)(a) emphasizes consideration of expertise and balance. As discussed in Section II, expertise refers to the required knowledge, experience and skills required to perform the review whereas balance refers to the need for diversity in scientific perspective and disciplines. We emphasize that the term "balance" here refers not to balancing of stakeholder or political interests but rather to a broad and diverse representation of respected perspectives and intellectual traditions within the scientific community, as discussed in the NAS policy on committee composition and balance.[28]

Section III(3)(b) instructs agencies to consider barring participation by scientists with a conflict of interest. The conflict of interest standards for Sections II and III of the Bulletin are identical. As discussed under Section II, those peer reviewers who are federal employees, including Special Government Employees, are subject to applicable statutory and regulatory standards for federal employees. For non-government employees, agencies shall adopt or adapt the NAS policy for committee member selection with respect to evaluating conflicts of interest.

Section III(3)(c) instructs agencies to ensure that reviewers are independent of the agency sponsoring the review. Scientists employed by the sponsoring agency are not permitted to serve as reviewers for highly influential scientific assessments. This does not preclude Special Government Employees, such as academics appointed to advisory committees, from serving as peer reviewers. The only exception to this ban would be the rare situation in which a scientist from a different agency of a Cabinet-level department than the agency that is disseminating the scientific assessment has expertise, experience and skills that are essential but cannot be obtained elsewhere. In evaluating the need for this exception, agencies shall use the NAS criteria for assessing the appropriateness of using employees of sponsors (e.g., the government scientist must not have had any part in the development or prior review of the scientific information and must not hold a position of managerial or policy responsibility).

---

[28] National Academy of Sciences, *Policy and Procedures on Committee Composition and Balance and Conflicts of Interest for Committees Used in the Development of Reports* (May 2003), *available at:* http://www.nationalacademies.org/coi/index.html.

We also considered whether a reviewer can be independent of the agency if that reviewer receives a substantial amount of research funding from the agency sponsoring the review. Research grants that were awarded to the scientist based on investigator-initiated, competitive, peer-reviewed proposals do not generally raise issues of independence. However, significant consulting and contractual relationships with the agency may raise issues of independence or conflict, depending upon the situation.

Section III(3)(d) addresses concerns regarding repeated use of the same reviewer in multiple assessments. Such repeated use should be avoided unless a particular reviewer's expertise is essential. Agencies should rotate membership across the available pool of qualified reviewers. Similarly, when using standing panels of scientific advisors, it is suggested that the agency rotate membership among qualified scientists in order to obtain fresh perspectives and reinforce the reality and perception of independence from the agency.

Section III(4) requires agencies to provide reviewers with sufficient background information, including access to key studies, data and models, to perform their role as peer reviewers. In this respect, the peer review envisioned in Section III is more rigorous than some forms of journal peer review, where the reviewer is often not provided access to underlying data or models. Reviewers shall be informed of applicable access, objectivity, reproducibility and other quality standards under federal information quality laws.

Section III(5) addresses opportunity for public participation in peer review, and provides that the agency shall, wherever possible, provide for public participation. In some cases, an assessment may be so sensitive that it is critical that the agency's assessment achieve a high level of quality before it is publicized. In those situations, a rigorous yet confidential peer review process may be appropriate, prior to public release of the assessment. If an agency decides to make a draft assessment publicly available at the onset of a peer review process, the agency shall, whenever possible, provide a vehicle for the public to provide written comments, make an oral presentation before the peer reviewers, or both. When written public comments are received, the agency shall ensure that peer reviewers receive copies of comments that address significant scientific issues with ample time to consider them in their review. To avoid undue delay of agency activities, the agency shall specify time limits for public participation throughout the peer review process.

Section III(6) requires that agencies instruct reviewers to prepare a peer review report that describes the nature and scope of their review and their findings and conclusions. The report shall disclose the name of each peer reviewer and a brief description of his or her organizational affiliation, credentials and relevant experiences. The peer review report should either summarize the views of the group as a whole (including any dissenting views) or include a verbatim copy of the comments of the individual reviewers (with or without attribution of specific views to specific names). The agency shall also prepare a written response to the peer review report, indicating whether the agency agrees with the reviewers and what actions the agency has taken or plans to take to address the points made by reviewers. The agency is required to disseminate the peer review report and the agency's response to the report on the agency's website, including all the materials related to the peer review such as the charge statement, peer review report, and agency response to the review. If the scientific information is used to support a final rule then, where practicable, the peer review report shall be made available to the public with enough time for the public to consider the implications of the peer review report for the rule being considered.

Section III(7) authorizes but does not require an agency to commission an entity independent of the agency to select peer reviewers and/or manage the peer review process in accordance with this Bulletin. The entity may be a scientific or professional society, a firm specializing in peer review, or a nonprofit organization with experience in peer review.

Section IV: Alternative Procedures

Peer review as described in this Bulletin is only one of many procedures that agencies can employ to ensure an appropriate degree of pre-dissemination quality of influential scientific information. For example, Congress has assigned the NAS a special role in advising the federal government on scientific and technical issues. The procedures of the NAS are generally quite rigorous, and thus agencies should presume that major findings, conclusions, and recommendations of NAS reports meet the performance standards of this Bulletin.

As an alternative to complying with Sections II and III of this Bulletin, an agency may instead (1) rely on scientific information produced by the National Academy of Sciences, (2) commission the National Academy of Sciences to peer review an agency draft scientific information product, or (3) employ an alternative procedure or set of procedures, specifically approved by the OIRA Administrator in consultation with the Office of Science and Technology Policy (OSTP), that ensures that the scientific information product meets applicable information-quality standards.

An example of an alternative procedure is to commission a respected third party other than the NAS (e.g., the Health Effects Institute or the National Commission on Radiation Protection and Measurement) to conduct an assessment or series of related assessments. Another example of an alternative set of procedures is the three-part process used by the National Institutes of Health (NIH) to generate scientific guidance. Under that process, a scientific proposal or white paper is generated by a working group composed of external, independent scientific experts; that paper is then forwarded to a separate external scientific council, which then makes recommendations to the agency. The agency, in turn, decides whether to adopt and/or modify the proposal. For large science agencies that have diverse research portfolios and do not have significant regulatory responsibilities, such as NIH, an acceptable alternative would be to allow scientists from one part of the agency (for example, an NIH institute) to participate in the review of documents prepared by another part of the agency, as long as the head of the agency confirms in writing that each of the reviewers meets the NAS criteria relating to the appropriateness of using employees of sponsors (e.g., the government scientist must not have had any part in the development or prior review of the scientific information and must not hold a position of managerial or policy responsibility). The purpose of Section IV is to encourage these types of innovation in the methods used to ensure predissemination quality control of influential scientific information.

The mere existence of a public comment process (e.g., notice-and-comment procedures under the Administrative Procedure Act) does not constitute adequate peer review or an "alternative process," because it does not assure that qualified, impartial specialists in relevant fields have performed a critical evaluation of the agency's draft product.[29]

Section V: Peer Review Planning

Section V requires agencies to begin a systematic process of peer review planning for influential scientific information (including highly influential scientific assessments) that the agency plans to disseminate in the foreseeable future. A key feature of this planning process is a web-accessible listing of forthcoming influential scientific disseminations (i.e., an agenda) that is regularly updated by the agency. By making these plans publicly available, agencies will be able to gauge the extent of public interest in the peer review process for influential scientific information, including highly influential sci-

---

[29] WILLIAM W. LOWRANCE, MODERN SCIENCE AND HUMAN VALUES 86, New York: Oxford University Press (1985).

entific assessments. These web-accessible agendas can also be used by the public to monitor agency compliance with this Bulletin.

Each entry on the agenda shall include a preliminary title of the planned report, a short paragraph describing the subject and purpose of the planned report, and an agency contact person. The agency shall provide its prediction regarding whether the dissemination will be "influential scientific information" or a "highly influential scientific assessment," as the designation can influence the type of peer review to be undertaken. The agency shall discuss the timing of the peer review, as well as the use of any deferrals. Agencies shall include entries in the agenda for influential scientific information, including highly influential scientific assessments, for which the Bulletin's requirements have been deferred or waived. If the agency, in consultation with the OIRA Administrator, has determined that it is appropriate to use a Section IV "alternative procedure" for a specific dissemination, a description of that alternative procedure shall be included in the agenda.

Furthermore, for each entry on the agenda, the agency shall describe the peer review plan. Each peer review plan shall include: (i) a paragraph including the title, subject and purpose of the planned report, as well as an agency contact to whom inquiries may be directed to learn the specifics of the plan; (ii) whether the dissemination is likely to be influential scientific information or a highly influential scientific assessment; (iii) the timing of the review (including deferrals); (iv) whether the review will be conducted through a panel or individual letters (or whether an alternative procedure will be exercised); (v) whether there will be opportunities for the public to comment on the work product to be peer reviewed, and if so, how and when these opportunities will be provided; (vi) whether the agency will provide significant and relevant public comments to the peer reviewers before they conduct their review; (vii) the anticipated number of reviewers (3 or fewer; 4-10; or more than 10); (viii) a succinct description of the primary disciplines or expertise needed in the review; (ix) whether reviewers will be selected by the agency or by a designated outside organization; and (x) whether the public, including scientific or professional societies, will be asked to nominate potential peer reviewers. The agency shall provide a link from the agenda to each document made public pursuant to this Bulletin. Agencies shall link their peer review agendas to the U.S. Government's official web portal: *firstgov* at http://www.FirstGov.gov[30]

---

[30] Editors' note: This website has been renamed: http://www.usagov.gov.

Agencies should update their peer review agendas at least every six months. However, in some cases—particularly for highly influential scientific assessments and other particularly important information—more frequent updates of existing entries on the agenda, or the addition of new entries to the agenda, may be warranted. When new entries are added to the agenda of forthcoming reports and other information, the public should be provided with sufficient time to comment on the agency's peer review plan for that report or product. Agencies shall consider public comments on the peer review plan. Agencies are encouraged to offer a listserve or similar mechanism for members of the public who would like to be notified by email each time an agency's peer review agenda has been updated.

The peer review planning requirements of this Bulletin are designed to be implemented in phases. Specifically, the planning requirements of the Bulletin will go into effect for documents subject to Section III of the Bulletin (highly influential scientific assessments) six months after publication. However, the planning requirements for documents subject to Section II of the Bulletin do not go into effect until one year after publication. It is expected that agency experience with the planning requirements of the Bulletin for the smaller scope of documents encompassed in Section III will be used to inform implementation of these planning requirements for the larger scope of documents covered under Section II.

Section VI: Annual Report

Each agency shall prepare an annual report that summarizes key decisions made pursuant to this Bulletin. In particular, each agency should provide to OIRA the following: 1) the number of peer reviews conducted subject to the Bulletin (i.e., for influential scientific information and highly influential scientific assessments); 2) the number of times alternative procedures were invoked; 3) the number of times waivers or deferrals were invoked (and in the case of deferrals, the length of time elapsed between the deferral and the peer review); 4) any decision to appoint a reviewer pursuant to any exception to the applicable independence or conflict of interest standards of the Bulletin, including determinations by the Secretary or Deputy Secretary pursuant to Section III (3) (c); 5) the number of peer review panels that were conducted in public and the number that allowed public comment; 6) the number of public comments provided on the agency's peer review plans; and 7) the number of peer reviewers that the agency used that were recommended by professional societies.

Section VII: Certification in the Administrative Record

If an agency relies on influential scientific information or a highly influential scientific assessment subject to the requirements of this Bulletin in support of a regulatory action, the agency shall include in the administrative record for that action a certification that explains how the agency has complied with the requirements of this Bulletin and the Information Quality Act. Relevant materials are to be placed in the administrative record.

Section VIII: Safeguards, Deferrals, and Waivers

Section VIII recognizes that individuals serving as peer reviewers have a privacy interest in information about themselves that the government maintains and retrieves by name or identifier from a system of records. To the extent information about a reviewer (name, credential, affiliation) will be disclosed along with his/her comments or analysis, the agency must comply with the requirements of the Privacy Act, 5 U.S.C. 552a, as amended, and OMB Circular A-130, Appendix I, 61 Fed. Reg. 6428 (February 20, 1996) to establish appropriate routine uses in a published System of Records Notice. Furthermore, the peer review must be conducted in a manner that respects confidential business information as well as intellectual property.

Section VIII also allows for a deferral or waiver of the requirements of the Bulletin where necessary. Specifically, the agency head may waive or defer some or all of the peer review requirements of Sections II or III of this Bulletin if there is a compelling rationale for waiver or deferral. Waivers will seldom be warranted under this provision because the Bulletin already provides significant safety valves, such as: the exemptions provided in Section IX, including the exemption for time-sensitive health and safety information; the authorization for alternative procedures in Section IV; and the overall flexibility provided for peer reviews of influential scientific information under Section II. Nonetheless, we have included this waiver and deferral provision to ensure needed flexibility in unusual and compelling situations not otherwise covered by the exemptions to the Bulletin, such as situations where unavoidable legal deadlines prevent full compliance with the Bulletin before information is disseminated. Deadlines found in consent decrees agreed to by agencies after the Bulletin is issued will not ordinarily warrant waiver of the Bulletin's requirements because those deadlines should be negotiated to permit time for all required procedures, including peer review. In addition, when an agency is unavoidably up against a deadline, deferral of some or all requirements of the Bulletin (as opposed to outright waiver of all of them) is the most appropriate accommodation between the need to satisfy immovable deadlines and the need to undertake proper peer review. If the agency head defers any of the peer review requirements prior to dissemination, peer review should be conducted as soon as practicable thereafter.

Section IX: Exemptions

There are a variety of situations where agencies need not conduct peer review under this Bulletin. These include, for example, disseminations of sensitive information related to certain national security, foreign affairs, or negotiations involving international treaties and trade where compliance with this Bulletin would interfere with the need for secrecy or promptness.

This Bulletin does not cover official disseminations that arise in adjudications and permit proceedings, unless the agency determines that peer review is practical and appropriate and that the influential dissemination is scientifically or technically novel (i.e., a major change in accepted practice) or likely to have precedent-setting influence on future adjudications or permit proceedings. This exclusion is intended to cover, among other things, licensing, approval and registration processes for specific product development activities as well as site-specific activities. The determination as to whether peer review is practical and appropriate is left to the discretion of the agency. While this Bulletin is not broadly applicable to adjudications, agencies are encouraged to hold peer reviews of scientific assessments supporting adjudications to the same technical standards as peer reviews covered by the Bulletin, including transparency and disclosure of the data and models underlying the assessments. Protections apply to confidential business information.

The Bulletin does not cover time-sensitive health and safety disseminations, for example, a dissemination based primarily on data from a recent clinical trial that was adequately peer reviewed before the trial began. For this purpose, "health" includes public health, or plant or animal infectious diseases.

This Bulletin covers original data and formal analytic models used by agencies in Regulatory Impact Analyses (RIAs). However, the RIA documents themselves are already reviewed through an interagency review process under E.O. 12866 that involves application of the principles and methods defined in OMB Circular A-4. In that respect, RIAs are excluded from coverage by this Bulletin, although agencies are encouraged to have RIAs reviewed by peers within the government for adequacy and completeness.

The Bulletin does not cover accounting, budget, actuarial, and financial information including that which is generated or used by agencies that focus on interest rates, banking, currency, securities, commodities, futures, or taxes.

Routine statistical information released by federal statistical agencies (e.g., periodic demographic and economic statistics) and analyses of these data to compute standard indicators and trends (e.g., unemployment and poverty rates) is excluded from this Bulletin.

The Bulletin does not cover information disseminated in connection with routine rules that materially alter entitlements, grants, user fees, or loan programs, or the rights and obligations of recipients thereof.

If information is disseminated pursuant to an exemption to this Bulletin, subsequent disseminations are not automatically exempted. For example, if influential scientific information is first disseminated in the course of an exempt agency adjudication, but is later disseminated in the context of a non-exempt rulemaking, the subsequent dissemination will be subject to the requirements of this Bulletin even though the first dissemination was not.

Section X: OIRA and OSTP Responsibilities

OIRA, in consultation with OSTP, is responsible for overseeing agency implementation of this Bulletin. In order to foster learning about peer review practices across agencies, OIRA and OSTP shall form an interagency workgroup on peer review that meets regularly, discusses progress and challenges, and recommends improvements to peer review practices.

Section XI: Effective Date and Existing Law

The requirements of this Bulletin, with the exception of Section V, apply to information disseminated on or after six months after publication of this Bulletin. However, the Bulletin does not apply to information that is already being addressed by an agency-initiated peer review process (e.g., a draft is already being reviewed by a formal scientific advisory committee established by the agency). An existing peer review mechanism mandated by law should be implemented by the agency in a manner as consistent as possible with the practices and procedures outlined in this Bulletin. The requirements of Section V apply to "highly influential scientific assessments," as designated in Section III of the Bulletin, within six months of publication of the final Bulletin. The requirements in Section V apply to documents subject to Section II of the Bulletin one year after publication of the final Bulletin.

Section XII: Judicial Review

This Bulletin is intended to improve the internal management of the Executive Branch and is not intended to, and does not, create any right or benefit, substantive or procedural, enforceable at law or in equity, against the United States, its agencies or other entities, its officers or employees, or any other person.

Bulletin for Peer Review

I. Definitions.

For purposes of this Bulletin—
  1. the term "Administrator" means the Administrator of the Office of Information and Regulatory Affairs in the Office of Management and Budget (OIRA);
  2. the term "agency" has the same meaning as in the Paperwork Reduction Act, 44 U.S.C. § 3502(1);
  3. the term "dissemination" means agency initiated or sponsored distribution of information to the public (see 5 C.F.R. 1320.3(d) (definition of "Conduct or Sponsor")). Dissemination does not include distribution limited to government employees or agency contractors or grantees; intra- or interagency use or sharing of government information; or responses to requests for agency records under the Freedom of Information Act, the Privacy Act, the Federal Advisory Committee Act, the Government Performance and Results Act or similar law. This definition also excludes distribution limited to correspondence with individuals or persons, press releases, archival records, public filings, subpoenas and adjudicative processes. The term "dissemination" also excludes information distributed for peer review in compliance with this Bulletin, provided that the distributing agency includes a clear disclaimer on the information as follows:

> "THIS INFORMATION IS DISTRIBUTED SOLELY FOR THE PURPOSE OF PREDISSEMINATION PEER REVIEW UNDER APPLICABLE INFORMATION QUALITY GUIDELINES. IT HAS NOT BEEN FORMALLY DISSEMINATED BY [THE AGENCY]. IT DOES NOT REPRESENT AND SHOULD NOT BE CONSTRUED TO REPRESENT ANY AGENCY DETERMINATION OR POLICY."

For the purposes of this Bulletin, "dissemination" excludes research produced by government-funded scientists (e.g., those supported extramurally or intramurally by federal agencies or those working in state or local governments with federal support) if that information does not represent the views of an agency. To qualify for this exemption, the information should display a clear disclaimer that "the findings and conclusions in this report are those of the author(s) and do not necessarily represent the views of the funding agency";

4. the term "Information Quality Act" means Section 515 of Public Law 106-554 (Pub. No. 106-554, § 515, 114 Stat. 2763, 2763A-153-154 (2000));

5. the term "scientific information" means factual inputs, data, models, analyses, technical information, or scientific assessments based on the behavioral and social sciences, public health and medical sciences, life and earth sciences, engineering, or physical sciences. This includes any communication or representation of knowledge such as facts or data, in any medium or form, including textual, numerical, graphic, cartographic, narrative, or audiovisual forms. This definition includes information that an agency disseminates from a web page, but does not include the provision of hyperlinks to information that others disseminate. This definition does not include opinions, where the agency's presentation makes clear that what is being offered is someone's opinion rather than fact or the agency's views;

6. the term "influential scientific information" means scientific information the agency reasonably can determine will have or does have a clear and substantial impact on important public policies or private sector decisions; and

7. the term "scientific assessment" means an evaluation of a body of scientific or technical knowledge, which typically synthesizes multiple factual inputs, data, models, assumptions, and/or applies best professional judgment to bridge uncertainties in the available information. These assessments include, but are not limited to, state-of-science reports; technology assessments; weight-of-evidence analyses; meta-analyses; health, safety, or ecological risk assessments; toxicological characterizations of substances; integrated assessment models; hazard determinations; or exposure assessments.

II. Peer Review of Influential Scientific Information.

1. *In General*: To the extent permitted by law, each agency shall conduct a peer review on all influential scientific information that the agency intends to disseminate. Peer reviewers shall be charged with reviewing scientific and technical matters, leaving policy determinations for the agency. Reviewers shall be informed of applicable access, objectivity, reproducibility and other quality standards under the federal laws governing information access and quality.

2. *Adequacy of Prior Peer Review*: For information subject to this section of the Bulletin, agencies need not have further peer review conducted on information that has already been subjected to adequate peer review. In determining whether prior peer review is adequate, agencies shall give due consideration to the novelty and complexity of the science to be reviewed, the importance of the information to decision making, the extent of prior peer reviews, and the expected benefits and costs of additional review. Principal findings, conclusions and recommendations in official reports of the National Academy of Sciences are generally presumed to have been adequately peer reviewed.

3. *Selection of Reviewers*: a. *Expertise and Balance:* Peer reviewers shall be selected based on expertise, experience and skills, including specialists from multiple disciplines, as necessary. The group of reviewers shall be sufficiently broad and diverse to fairly represent the relevant scientific and technical perspectives and fields of knowledge. Agencies shall consider requesting that the public, including scientific and professional societies, nominate potential reviewers.

b. *Conflicts:* The agency—or the entity selecting the peer reviewers—shall (i) ensure that those reviewers serving as federal employees (including special government employees) comply with applicable federal ethics requirements; (ii) in selecting peer reviewers who are not government employees, adopt or adapt the National Academy of Sciences policy for committee selection with respect to evaluating the potential for conflicts (e.g., those arising from investments; agency, employer, and business affiliations; grants, contracts and consulting income). For scientific information relevant to specific regulations, the agency shall examine a reviewer's financial ties to regulated entities (e.g., businesses), other stakeholders, and the agency.

c. *Independence*: Peer reviewers shall not have participated in development of the work product. Agencies are encouraged to rotate membership on standing panels across the pool of qualified reviewers. Research grants that were awarded to scientists based on investigator-initiated, competitive, peer-reviewed proposals generally do not raise issues as to independence or conflicts.

4. *Choice of Peer Review Mechanism:* The choice of a peer review mechanism (for example, letter reviews or ad hoc panels) for influential scientific information shall be based on the novelty and complexity of the information to be reviewed, the importance of the information to decision making, the extent of prior peer review, and the expected benefits and costs of review, as well as the factors regarding transparency described in II(5).

5. *Transparency:* The agency—or entity managing the peer review—shall instruct peer reviewers to prepare a report that describes the nature of their review and their findings and conclusions. The peer review report shall either (a) include a verbatim copy of each reviewer's comments (either with or without specific attributions) or (b) represent the views of the group as a whole, including any disparate and dissenting views. The agency shall disclose the names of the reviewers and their organizational affiliations in the report. Reviewers shall be notified in advance regarding the extent of disclosure and attribution planned by the agency. The agency shall disseminate the final peer review report on the agency's website along with all materials related to the peer review (any charge statement, the peer review report, and any agency response). The peer review report shall be discussed in the preamble to any related rulemaking and included in the administrative record for any related agency action.

6. *Management of Peer Review Process and Reviewer Selection:* The agency may commission independent entities to manage the peer review process, including the selection of peer reviewers, in accordance with this Bulletin.

III. Additional Peer Review Requirements for Highly Influential Scientific Assessments.

1. *Applicability:* This section applies to influential scientific information that the agency or the Administrator determines to be a scientific assessment that:

(i) could have a potential impact of more than $500 million in any year, or

(ii) is novel, controversial, or precedent-setting or has significant interagency interest.

2. *In General:* To the extent permitted by law, each agency shall conduct peer reviews on all information subject to this Section. The peer reviews shall satisfy the requirements of Section II of this Bulletin, as well as the additional requirements found in this Section. Principal findings, conclusions and recommendations in official reports of the National Academy of Sciences that fall under this Section are generally presumed not to require additional peer review.

3. *Selection of Reviewers:* a. *Expertise and Balance:* Peer reviewers shall be selected based on expertise, experience and skills, including specialists from multiple disciplines, as necessary. The group of reviewers shall be sufficiently broad and diverse to fairly represent the relevant scientific and tech-

nical perspectives and fields of knowledge. Agencies shall consider requesting that the public, including scientific and professional societies, nominate potential reviewers.

b. *Conflicts:* The agency—or the entity selecting the peer reviewers—shall (i) ensure that those reviewers serving as federal employees (including special government employees) comply with applicable federal ethics requirements; (ii) in selecting peer reviewers who are not government employees, adopt or adapt the National Academy of Sciences' policy for committee selection with respect to evaluating the potential for conflicts (e.g., those arising from investments; agency, employer, and business affiliations; grants, contracts and consulting income). For scientific assessments relevant to specific regulations, a reviewer's financial ties to regulated entities (e.g., businesses), other stakeholders, and the agency shall be examined.

c. *Independence:* In addition to the requirements of Section II (3)(c), which shall apply to all reviews conducted under Section III, the agency—or entity selecting the reviewers—shall bar participation of scientists employed by the sponsoring agency unless the reviewer is employed only for the purpose of conducting the peer review (i.e., special government employees). The only exception to this bar would be the rare case where the agency determines, using the criteria developed by NAS for evaluating use of "employees of sponsors," that a premier government scientist is (a) not in a position of management or policy responsibility and (b) possesses essential expertise that cannot be obtained elsewhere. Furthermore, to be eligible for this exception, the scientist must be employed by a different agency of the Cabinet-level department than the agency that is disseminating the scientific information. The agency's determination shall be documented in writing and approved, on a non-delegable basis, by the Secretary or Deputy Secretary of the department prior to the scientist's appointment.

d. *Rotation:* Agencies shall avoid repeated use of the same reviewer on multiple assessments unless his or her participation is essential and cannot be obtained elsewhere.

4. *Information Access:* The agency—or entity managing the peer review—shall provide the reviewers with sufficient information—including background information about key studies or models—to enable them to understand the data, analytic procedures, and assumptions used to support the key findings or conclusions of the draft assessment.

5. *Opportunity for Public Participation:* Whenever feasible and appropriate, the agency shall make the draft scientific assessment available to the public for comment at the same time it is submitted for peer review (or during the peer review process) and sponsor a public meeting where oral

presentations on scientific issues can be made to the peer reviewers by interested members of the public. When employing a public comment process as part of the peer review, the agency shall, whenever practical, provide peer reviewers with access to public comments that address significant scientific or technical issues. To ensure that public participation does not unduly delay agency activities, the agency shall clearly specify time limits for public participation throughout the peer review process.

6. *Transparency:* In addition to the requirements specified in II(5), which shall apply to all reviews conducted under Section III, the peer review report shall include the charge to the reviewers and a short paragraph on both the credentials and relevant experiences of each peer reviewer. The agency shall prepare a written response to the peer review report explaining (a) the agency's agreement or disagreement with the views expressed in the report, (b) the actions the agency has undertaken or will undertake in response to the report, and (c) the reasons the agency believes those actions satisfy the key concerns stated in the report (if applicable). The agency shall disseminate its response to the peer review report on the agency's website with the related material specified in Section II(5).

7. *Management of Peer Review Process and Reviewer Selection:* The agency may commission independent entities to manage the peer review process, including the selection of peer reviewers, in accordance with this Bulletin.

IV. Alternative Procedures.

As an alternative to complying with Sections II and III of this Bulletin, an agency may instead: (i) rely on the principal findings, conclusions and recommendations of a report produced by the National Academy of Sciences; (ii) commission the National Academy of Sciences to peer review an agency's draft scientific information; or (iii) employ an alternative scientific procedure or process, specifically approved by the Administrator in consultation with the Office of Science and Technology Policy (OSTP), that ensures the agency's scientific information satisfies applicable information quality standards. The alternative procedure(s) may be applied to a designated report or group of reports.

V. Peer Review Planning.

1. *Peer Review Agenda:* Each agency shall post on its website, and update at least every six months, an agenda of peer review plans. The agenda

shall describe all planned and ongoing influential scientific information subject to this Bulletin. The agency shall provide a link from the agenda to each document that has been made public pursuant to this Bulletin. Agencies are encouraged to offer a listserve or similar mechanism to alert interested members of the public when entries are added or updated.

2. *Peer Review Plans:* For each entry on the agenda the agency shall describe the peer review plan. Each peer review plan shall include: (i) a paragraph including the title, subject and purpose of the planned report, as well as an agency contact to whom inquiries may be directed to learn the specifics of the plan; (ii) whether the dissemination is likely to be influential scientific information or a highly influential scientific assessment; (iii) the timing of the review (including deferrals); (iv) whether the review will be conducted through a panel or individual letters (or whether an alternative procedure will be employed); (v) whether there will be opportunities for the public to comment on the work product to be peer reviewed, and if so, how and when these opportunities will be provided; (vi) whether the agency will provide significant and relevant public comments to the peer reviewers before they conduct their review; (vii) the anticipated number of reviewers (3 or fewer; 4-10; or more than 10); (viii) a succinct description of the primary disciplines or expertise needed in the review; (ix) whether reviewers will be selected by the agency or by a designated outside organization; and (x) whether the public, including scientific or professional societies, will be asked to nominate potential peer reviewers.

3. *Public Comment:* Agencies shall establish a mechanism for allowing the public to comment on the adequacy of the peer review plans. Agencies shall consider public comments on peer review plans.

VI. Annual Reports.

Each agency shall provide to OIRA, by December 15 of each year, a summary of the peer reviews conducted by the agency during the fiscal year. The report should include the following: 1) the number of peer reviews conducted subject to the Bulletin (i.e., for influential scientific information and highly influential scientific assessments); 2) the number of times alternative procedures were invoked; 3) the number of times waivers or deferrals were invoked (and in the case of deferrals, the length of time elapsed between the deferral and the peer review); 4) any decision to appoint a reviewer pursuant to any exception to the applicable independence or conflict of interest standards of the Bulletin, including determinations by the Secretary pursuant to Section III(3)(c); 5) the number of peer review panels that were conducted in public and the number that allowed public comment; 6) the number of public comments provided on the agency's peer review plans; and 7) the number of peer reviewers that the agency used that were recommended by professional societies.

VII. Certification in the Administrative Record.

If an agency relies on influential scientific information or a highly influential scientific assessment subject to this Bulletin to support a regulatory action, it shall include in the administrative record for that action a certification explaining how the agency has complied with the requirements of this Bulletin and the applicable information quality guidelines. Relevant materials shall be placed in the administrative record.

VIII. Safeguards, Deferrals, and Waivers.

1. *Privacy:* To the extent information about a reviewer (name, credentials, affiliation) will be disclosed along with his/her comments or analysis, the agency shall comply with the requirements of the Privacy Act, 5 U.S.C. § 522a as amended, and OMB Circular A130, Appendix I, 61 Fed. Reg. 6428 (February 20, 1996) to establish appropriate routine uses in a published System of Records Notice.

2. *Confidentiality:* Peer review shall be conducted in a manner that respects (i) confidential business information and (ii) intellectual property.

3. *Deferral and Waiver:* The agency head may waive or defer some or all of the peer review requirements of Sections II and III of this Bulletin where warranted by a compelling rationale. If the agency head defers the peer review requirements prior to dissemination, peer review shall be conducted as soon as practicable.

IX. Exemptions.

Agencies need not have peer review conducted on information that is:

1. related to certain national security, foreign affairs, or negotiations involving international trade or treaties where compliance with this Bulletin would interfere with the need for secrecy or promptness;

2. disseminated in the course of an individual agency adjudication or permit proceeding (including a registration, approval, licensing, site-specific determination), unless the agency determines that peer review is practical and appropriate and that the influential dissemination is scientifically or techni-

cally novel or likely to have precedent-setting influence on future adjudications and/or permit proceedings;

3. a health or safety dissemination where the agency determines that the dissemination is time-sensitive (e.g., findings based primarily on data from a recent clinical trial that was adequately peer reviewed before the trial began);

4. an agency regulatory impact analysis or regulatory flexibility analysis subject to interagency review under Executive Order 12866, except for underlying data and analytical models used;

5. routine statistical information released by federal statistical agencies (e.g., periodic demographic and economic statistics) and analyses of these data to compute standard indicators and trends (e.g., unemployment and poverty rates);

6. accounting, budget, actuarial, and financial information, including that which is generated or used by agencies that focus on interest rates, banking, currency, securities, commodities, futures, or taxes; or

7. information disseminated in connection with routine rules that materially alter entitlements, grants, user fees, or loan programs, or the rights and obligations of recipients thereof.

X. Responsibilities of OIRA and OSTP.

OIRA, in consultation with OSTP, shall be responsible for overseeing implementation of this Bulletin. An interagency group, chaired by OSTP and OIRA, shall meet periodically to foster better understanding about peer review practices and to assess progress in implementing this Bulletin.

XI. Effective Date and Existing Law.

The requirements of this Bulletin, with the exception of those in Section V (Peer Review Planning), apply to information disseminated on or after six months following publication of this Bulletin, except that they do not apply to information for which an agency has already provided a draft report and an associated charge to peer reviewers. Any existing peer review mechanisms mandated by law shall be employed in a manner as consistent as possible with the practices and procedures laid out herein. The requirements in Section V apply to "highly influential scientific assessments," as designated in Section III of this Bulletin, within six months of publication of this Bulletin. The requirements in Section V apply to documents subject to Section II of this Bulletin one year after publication of this Bulletin.

XII. Judicial Review

This Bulletin is intended to improve the internal management of the executive branch, and is not intended to, and does not, create any right or benefit, substantive or procedural, enforceable at law or in equity, against the United States, its agencies or other entities, its officers or employees, or any other person.

National Environmental Policy Act

Citations:

42 U.S.C. §§4321-4347 (2000); enacted January 1, 1970 by Pub. L. No. 91-190; 83 Stat. 852.

Lead Agency:

Council on Environmental Quality, Old Executive Office Building, Room 360, Washington, DC 20502 (202) 456-6224 http://www.whitehouse.gov/ceq.

Overview:

The National Environmental Policy Act (NEPA) was the first federal statute to use the "impact statement" approach in federal regulation. Its purpose is to require federal agencies to analyze and consider the environmental impact of their actions in an open and public process. The Act also created the Council on Environmental Quality within the Executive Office of the President.

Environmental Impact Statements. The core of NEPA is found in section 102(2)(C) (codified at 42 U.S.C. §4332(2)(C) (2000)), which creates the environmental impact statement (EIS) requirement. The provision requires that:

> all agencies of the Federal Government . . . include in every recommendation or report on proposals for legislation and other major Federal actions significantly affecting the quality of the human environment, a detailed statement by the responsible official on—
>
> (i) the environmental impact of the proposed action,

(ii) any adverse environmental effects which cannot be avoided should the proposal be implemented,
(iii) alternatives to the proposed action,
(iv) the relationship between local short-term uses of man's environment and the maintenance and enhancement of long-term productivity, and
(v) any irreversible and irretrievable commitments of resources which would be involved in the proposed action should it be implemented.

The provision goes on to require the responsible federal official to consult with and seek comments from other affected agencies. Copies of the statements and relevant comments must be made public and must accompany the proposal through the agency review process.

Despite language in NEPA that might be construed otherwise, the Supreme Court has held that NEPA does not impose any substantive requirement on agencies to favor the environment in the agency's decisionmaking. *See Strycker's Bay Neighborhood Council, Inc. v. Karlen*, 444 U.S. 223 (1980). Notwithstanding the lack of substantive requirements, NEPA has been the source of an extremely large number of challenges to agency action, arguing either that the agency failed to prepare an EIS when NEPA required it or that the EIS that the agency prepared was inadequate. Even after more than 35 years, agencies frequently lose these suits, with the result that the agency action is enjoined until the agency fully complies with NEPA's procedural requirements.

Council on Environmental Quality Role. The Council on Environmental Quality (CEQ), created by title 11 of the Act, is the legal overseer of NEPA and in its early years was active in shaping NEPA law. Until 2000, it prepared extensive annual environmental quality reports pursuant to 42 U.S.C. §4341, which was effectively repealed in that year. The Council took the lead in developing appropriate procedures for EIS preparation. In President Nixon's Executive Order 11,514 (March 5, 1970), issued shortly after NEPA's passage, he gave CEQ the authority to issue guidelines to agencies for the preparation of EIS's. The CEQ's original guidelines (36 Fed. Reg. 7724-29, April 23, 1971) were nonbinding but were relied upon by most federal agencies when promulgating their own procedures. In 1977 President Carter significantly expanded CEQ's authority by giving it the power to issue binding regulations in Executive Order 11,991 (May 24, 1977). These regulations, issued on November 28, 1978 (43 Fed. Reg. 55,978-56,007), are codified at 40 C.F.R. Parts 1500-1508. The Supreme Court has since treated these regulations as deserving substantial deference. *See Andrus v. Sierra Club*, 442 U.S. 347 (1979).

The CEQ regulations cover many of the procedural issues that have emerged in the extensive litigation over the meaning of the Act's terms. The regulations provide comprehensive guidance on what constitutes a "major federal action" requiring an EIS, the preparation of draft, supplemental and final statements, page limits, recommended format and content (all in 40 C.F.R. Part 1502); the comment process (Part 1503), predecision referral of interagency disputes to CEQ (Part 1504); integration with agency decisionmaking (Part 1505); elimination of duplication with state and local requirements and procedures for filing with EPA (Part 1506); and agency compliance (Part 1507).

In addition to the regulations, CEQ also provided continuing guidance to agencies on implementation of NEPA. For example, in 1981 it published the *Memorandum to Agencies Containing Answers to 40 Most Asked Questions on NEPA Regulations.* In April 1981 it issued a *Memorandum for General Counsels, NEPA Liaisons and Participants in Scoping* on the subject of "scoping guidance." In 1983, after a solicitation of comments on the existing regulations and a two-year review process, the Council published a supplemental memorandum giving further guidance to agencies. In 1993, it issued a guidance memorandum on the subject of pollution prevention and NEPA. In 1997, it issued two guidance memoranda, one on cumulative effects analysis under NEPA and the other on considering environmental justice under NEPA. In 2002, CEQ established a NEPA Task Force to undertake a thorough review of NEPA implementation. The Task Force's issued its report, *Modernizing NEPA Implementation*, a year later. It contained recommendations designed to modernize the implementation of NEPA and make the NEPA process more effective and efficient.

The CEQ also compiles annual data on the number of environmental impact statements filed by agencies and the trends in NEPA litigation. This information is available online at: http://ceq.eh.doe.gov/nepa/nepanet.htm.

Originally, under 42 U.S.C. §4342, the CEQ consisted of three members appointed by the President with the advice and consent of the Senate, one of whom the President designated as Chairman. However, beginning in 1997, Congress inserted a provision in annual appropriations acts stating that, notwithstanding this section of NEPA, the CEQ would consist of one member appointed by the President with the advice and consent of the Senate, who should serve as chairman. In 2005, Congress made the change permanent. Pub. L. No. 109-54, Title III, August 2, 2005, 119 Stat. 543.

Legislative History:

Senators Jackson and Stevens introduced S. 1075, the original NEPA legislation, on February 18, 1969. It authorized the Secretary of the Interior to conduct a research program on environmental problems and created the Council on Environmental Quality. A hearing was held on April 16, 1969 during which witnesses (primarily Lynton Caldwell, professor of political science at Indiana University) urged the creation of an "action-forcing" mechanism, which later became the environmental impact statement. S. 1075 was reported with amendments and an accompanying report of the Senate Committee on Interior and Insular Affairs on July 9, 1969. The following day the Senate passed the bill unanimously.

The House of Representatives' subcommittee of the Committee on Merchant Marine and Fisheries held a series of hearings during May and June 1969 on various related bills. On July 1, 1969, Representative Dingell and others introduced H.R. 12,549, which became the leading House bill. It, however, lacked the impact statement requirement. On July 11, 1969, the full Committee reported H.R. 12,549. A supplemental report was filed on July 19. On September 23, 1969, the House passed the Senate bill, but only after substituting the text of the House bill in place of the Senate's language. The House then requested a conference.

On October 8, 1969, after listening to Senator Jackson address the differences between the two versions, the Senate voted to insist on its version and appointed conferees. On December 17, 1969 the conference committee reported out a substitute version of S. 1075. This compromise version accepted the Senate's environmental impact statement requirement, adding the language "to the fullest extent possible." That same day, the Senate approved the Conference Report. The House followed suit on December 23. The bill became Pub. L. No. 91-190 on January 1, 1970.

Section 201 of NEPA, 42 U.S.C. §4341, which required the President to transmit an annual report to Congress relating to the environment, was eliminated by the Federal Reports Elimination and Sunset Act of 1995, Pub. L. No. 104-66, §3003, 109 Stat. 707 (1995), as amended by Pub. L. No. 106-113, Div. B, §1000(a)(5), 113 Stat. 1536 (1999).

Section 202 of NEPA, 42 U.S.C. §4342, was effectively amended, although its language was not changed, by a series of annual riders to appropriation acts beginning in 1997 and culminating in a permanent rider to an appropriation act in 2005 that states "notwithstanding section 202 of the National Environmental Policy Act of 1970, the Council shall consist of one member, appointed by the President, by and with the advice and consent of the Senate, serving as chairman and exercising all powers, functions, and duties of the Council."[1] This was apparently the consequence of President Clinton's failure (or refusal) to appoint more than one member of the Council, *see* H.R. Rep. No. 104-628, 104th Cong., 2d Sess. 70 (1996).

Source Note:

There is an extensive literature of commentary, criticism, and analysis of NEPA and its implementation. Of course, the most authoritative pronouncements emanate from the Council on Environmental Quality. A selection of various books and articles on diverse aspects of NEPA practice and procedure is included in the Bibliography.

Bibliography:

I. Legislative History

1. *Conference Report on S.1075*, H.R. Rep. No. 91-765 (Dec. 17, 1969); *reprinted in* 1969 U.S. Code Cong. & Ad. News 2767.
2. *Congressional White Paper on a National Policy for the Environment submitted to the United States Congress under the Auspices of the Senate Committee on Interior and Insular Affairs and the House Committee on Science and Astronautics,* 90th Cong., 2d Sess. (Committee Print 1968).
3. House of Representatives Committee on Merchant Marine and Fisheries, *Report to Accompany H.R.12549,* H.R. Rep. No. 91-378 (July 11 & 19, 1969), 91st Cong., 1st Sess., *reprinted in* 1969 U.S. Code Cong. & Ad. News 2751.
4. *Joint House-Senate Colloquium to Discuss a National Policy for the Environment, Hearing before the Senate Committee on Science and Astronautics,* 90th Cong., 2d Sess. (Committee Print 1968).

---

[1] *See* Pub. L. No. 109-54, Title III, 119 Stat. 543 (2005); Pub. L. No. 108-447, Div. I, Title III, 118 Stat. 3332 (2004); Pub. L. No. 108-199, Div. G, Title III, 118 Stat. 408 (2004); Pub. L. No. 108-7, Div. K, Title I, 117 Stat. 514 (2003); Pub. L. No. 107-73, Title III, 115 Stat. 686 (2001); Pub. L. No. 106-377, § 1(a)(1), 114 Stat. 1441 (2000); Pub. L. No. 106-74, Title III, 113 Stat. 1084 (1999); Pub. L. No. 105-276, Title III, 112 Stat. 2500 (1998); Pub. L. No. 105-65, Title III, 111 Stat. 1375 (1997).

5. Senate Committee on Interior and Insular Affairs, *Report to Accompany S.*1075, S. Rep. No. 91-296 (July 9, 1969), 91st Cong., 1st Sess.
6. Staff of Subcommittee on Science, Research, and Development of the House Committee on Science and Astronautics, *Report of Managing the Environment*, 90th Cong., 2d Sess. (Committee Print 1968).

II. Other Government Documents Not Contained in Appendix (in chronological order)

1. Council on Environmental Quality, *Environmental Quality* (Annual Reports, 1970-1997 (when discontinued))(1993-1997), *available at* http://ceq.eh.doe.gov/nepa/reports/reports.htm).
2. *Hearings on Administration of the National Environmental Policy Act Before the Subcommittee on Fisheries and Wildlife Conservation, House Committee on Merchant Marine and Fisheries*, 91st Cong., 2d Sess. (Committee Serial 91-41, 1971) (2 parts).
3. Council on Environmental Quality, *Environmental Impact Statements: An Analysis of Six Years' Experience by Seventy Federal Agencies* (Mar. 1976).
4. *Hearings on National Environmental Policy Act Oversight Before the Subcommittee on Fisheries and Wildlife Conservation and the Environment, House Committee on Merchant Marine and Fisheries*, 94th Cong., 1st Sess. (Committee Serial 94-14, 1976).
5. Staff of Senate Committee on Interior and Insular Affairs, *Council on Environmental Quality: Oversight Report*, 94th Cong., 2d Sess. (Committee Print 1976).
6. Executive Order 11,514, *Protection and Enhancement of Environmental Quality*, March 5, 1970, *reprinted as amended* in Codification of Presidential Proclamations and Executive Orders, Jan. 20, 1961-Jan. 20, 1981, 717 (Office of the Federal Register, GSA, 1981) (Incorporates Executive Order 11,991, issued May 24, 1977).
7. *Hearings on CEQ Implementation of the National Environmental Policy Act Before the Subcommittee on Fisheries and Wildlife Conservation and the Environment, House Committee on Merchant Marine and Fisheries*, 95th Cong., 2d. Sess. (Committee Serial 95-35, 1978).
8. *Hearings on Implementation of the National Environmental Policy Act by the Council on Environmental Quality Before the Subcommittee on Toxic Substances and Environmental Oversight,* Senate Committee on Environment and Public Works, 97th Cong., 2d. Sess. (Committee Serial 97-H56, July 21, 1982).

9. Council on Environmental Quality, *Regulations for Implementing the Procedural Provisions of the National Environmental Policy Act,* 40 C.F.R. Parts 1500-1508 (July 1986).

10. *Hearings on Compliance with the National Environmental Policy Act of 1969 Before the Subcommittee on Hazardous Wastes and Toxic Substances,* Senate Committee on Environmental and Public Works, 100th Cong., 1st and 2d Sess. (S. Hrg. 100-509, Nov. 24, 1987; Jan. 14, 1988).

11. Council on Environmental Quality, *Memorandum to Heads of Departments and Agencies Regarding Pollution Prevention and the National Environmental Policy Act,* 58 Fed. Reg. 6478-81 (Jan. 29, 1993) (http://ceq.eh.doe.gov/nepa/regs/poll/ppguidnc.htm).

12. Council on Environmental Quality, *Incorporating Biodiversity Considerations Into Environmental Impact Analysis Under the National Environmental Policy Act,* January 1993 (http://www.eh.doe.gov/nepa/tools/guidance/Guidance-PDFs/iii-9.pdf).

13. Executive Order 12,852, *President's Council on Sustainable Development,* 58 Fed. Reg. 39,107 (July 19, 1993).

14. Executive Order 12,898, *Federal Actions to Address Environmental Justice in Minority Populations and Low Income Populations,* 60 Fed. Reg. 6381 (Feb. 11, 1994).

15. Council on Environmental Quality, *The Twenty-fifth Anniversary Report of the Council on Environmental Quality* (1994-1995).

16. *Hearing on the Application of the National Environmental Policy Act Before the Subcommittee on Oversight and Investigations,* Senate Committee on Energy and Natural Resources, 104th Cong., 1st Sess. (S. Hrg. 10481, June 7, 1995).

17. *Hearing on the Efforts By the Federal Land Management Agencies to Strengthen the National Environmental Policy Act Before the Subcommittee on Oversight and Investigations,* Senate Committee on Energy and Natural Resources, 104th Cong., 2d Sess. (S. Hrg. 104-775, Sept. 26, 1996).

18. Council on Environmental Quality, *Considering Cumulative Effects Under the National Environmental Policy Act* (Jan. 1997), *available at* http://ceq.eh.doe.gov/nepa/ccenepa/ccenepa.htm.

19. Council on Environmental Quality, *Guidance on NEPA Analyses for Transboundary Impacts* (July 1, 1997), *available at* http://ceq.eh.doe.gov/nepa/regs/transguide.html.

20. Council on Environmental Quality, *Environmental Justice Guidance Under the National Environmental Policy Act* (Dec. 10, 1997), *available at* http://ceq.eh.doe.gov/nepa/regs/ej/justice.pdf.

21. *Oversight Hearing on the Problems and Issues with the National Environmental Policy Act Before the House Committee on Resources,* House Committee on Resources, 105th Cong., 2d Sess. (Mar. 18, 1998).

22. Council on Environmental Quality, Memorandum for Heads of Federal Agencies: Designation of Non-Federal Agencies to be Cooperating Agencies in Implementing the Procedural Requirements of NEPA (July 28, 1999), *available at* http://ceq.eh.doe.gov/nepa/regs/ceqcoop.pdf.

23. Council on Environmental Quality, *Memorandum for Heads of Federal Agencies: Cooperating Agencies in Implementing the Procedural Requirements of the National Environmental Policy Act* (Jan. 30, 2002), *available at* http://ceq.eh.doe.gov/nepa/regs/cooperating/cooperatingagencies memorandum.html.

24. Council on Environmental Quality, *Memorandum to Heads of Federal Agencies: Reporting Cooperating Agencies in Implementing the Procedural Requirements of the National Environmental Policy Act* (Dec 23, 2004), *available at* http://ceq.eh.doe.gov/nepa/regs/connaughton.pdf.

25. Council on Environmental Quality, *Guidance on the Consideration of Past Actions in Cumulative Effects Analysis* (June 24, 2005), *available at* http://ceq.eh.doe.gov/nepa/regs/Guidance_on_CE.pdf.

26. Council on Environmental Quality, *Memorandum for Federal NEPA Contacts: Emergency Actions and NEPA* (Sept. 8 2005), *available at* http://ceq.eh.doe.gov/nepa/regs/Memo_to_NEPA_Contacts_September_8_05.pdf.

27. Council on Environmental Quality and Office of Management and Budget, *Memorandum on Environmental Conflict Resolution* (Nov. 28, 2005), *available at* http://ceq.eh.doe.gov/nepa/regs/OMB_CEQ_Joint_Statement.pdf.

III. Books and Articles

a. General Treatments

1. F. Anderson, D. Mandelker & D. Tarlock, *Environmental Protection: Law and Policy* Chapter 7 (Little, Brown & Co. 1990).

2. J. Battle, R. Fischman, M. Lipeles & M. Squillace, *Environmental Law: Environmental Decisionmaking: NEPA and the Endangered Species Act* (Anderson Publishing Co. 1994).

3. R. Clark, L. Canter, *Environmental Policy and NEPA: Past, Present, and Future* (1997).

4. V. Fogelman, *Guide to the National Environmental Policy Act: Interpretations, Applications, and Compliance* (1990).

5. D. Mandelker, *NEPA Law and Litigation* (Clark Boardman Callaghan 1992) (looseleaf).

6. W. Rodgers, Jr., *Environmental Law*, Chapter 9 (West Publishing Co. 1994).

b. Seminal Law Review Articles and Monographs

1. F. Anderson, *NEPA in the Courts: A Legal Analysis of the National Environmental Policy Act* (Johns Hopkins University Press 1973).

2. R. Andrews et al., *Substantive Guidance for Environmental Impact Assessment: An Exploratory Study* (The Institute for Ecology, Butler Univ., 1977).

3. Bardach and Pugliaresi, *The Environmental Impact Statement vs. The Real World,* 49 Pub. Interest 22 (1977).

4. Berg and Cramton, *On Leading a Horse to Water: NEPA and the Federal Bureaucracy,* 71 Mich. L. Rev. 511 (1973).

5. L. Caldwell, *A Study of Ways to Improve the Scientific Content and Methodology of Environmental Impact Analysis* (School of Public and Envtl. Affairs, Indiana Univ., 1982).

6. Comment, *NEPA's Forgotten Clause: Impact Statements For Legislative Proposals,* 58 B.U.L. Rev. 560 (1978).

7. Fergenson, *The Sin of Omission: Inaction as Action Under Section 102(2)(C) of the National Environmental Policy Act of* 1969, 53 Ind. L.J. 497 (1978).

8. Fisher, *The CEQ Regulations: New Stage in the Evolution of NEPA,* 3 Harv. Envtl. L. Rev. 347 (1979).

9. Leventhal, *Environmental Decisionmaking and the Role of the Courts,* 122 U. Pa. L. Rev. 509 (1974).

10. McGarity, *Courts, the Agencies and NEPA Threshold Issues,* 55 Tex. L. Rev. 801 (1977).

11. Murphy, *The National Environmental Policy Act and the Licensing Process: Environmentalist Magna Carta or Agency Coup de Grace?*, Report to the Administrative Conference of the U.S., 3 ACUS 363 (1975), *reprinted in* 72 Colum. L. Rev. 963 (1972).

12. Pridgeon, Anderson, Cornelia and Delphey, *State Environmental Policy Acts: A Survey of Recent Developments,* 2 Harv. Envtl. L. Rev. 419 (1978).

13. Reeve, *Scientific Uncertainty and the National Environmental Policy Act—The Council on Environmental Quality's Regulation 40 C.F.R. section 1502.22,* 60 Wash. L. Rev. 101 (1984).

14. Taylor, *Making Bureaucracies Think: The Environmental Impact Statement Strategy of Administrative Reform* (1984).

15. Weiss, *Federal Agency Treatment of Uncertainty in Environmental Impact Statements Under the CEQ's Amended NEPA Regulation §1502.22: Worst Case Analysis or Risk Threshold?*, 86 Mich. L. Rev. 777 (1988).

16. Yost, *The Governance of Environmental Affairs—Toward Consensus* (New York: Aspen Institute for Humanistic Studies, 1982).

c. More Recent Analyses

1. Andreen, *In Pursuit of NEPA's Promise: The Role of Executive Oversight in the Implementation of Environmental Policy*, 64 Ind. L.J. 205 (1989).

2. Battle, *A Transnational Perspective on Extending NEPA: The Convention on Environmental Impact Assessment in a Transboundary Context*, 5 Duke Envtl. L. & Pol'y F. 1 (1995).

3. Bear, *The National Environmental Policy Act: Its Origins and Evolutions*, 10 Nat. Resources & Env't 3 (Fall 1995).

4. Bear, *NEPA at 19.- A Primer on an "Old" Law with Solutions to New Problems*, 19 Envtl. L. Rep. 10,060 (1989).

5. Blomquist, *Supplemental Environmental Impact Statements Under NEPA: A Conceptual Synthesis and Critique of Existing Legal Approaches to Environmental and Technological Changes*, 8 Temple Envtl. L. & Tech. J. 1 (1989).

6. Blumm & Brown, *Pluralism and the Environment: The Role of Comment Agencies in NEPA Litigation*, 14 Harv. Envtl. L. Rev. 277 (1990).

7. Buccino, *NEPA under Assault: Congressional and Administrative Proposals Would Weaken Environmental Review and Public Participation*, 12 N.Y.U. Envtl. L.J. 50 (2003).

8. Caldwell, *Beyond NEPA: Future Significance of the National Environmental Policy Act*, 22 Harv. Envtl. L. Rev. 203 (1998).

9. Carlson, *NEPA and the Conservation of Biological Diversity*, 19 Envtl. L. 15 (Fall 1988).

10. Carroll, *International Application of the National Environmental Policy Act*, 4 ILSA J. Int'l. & Comp. L. 1 (1997).

11. Comment, *Supplements to Environmental Impact Statements: Implementation of the Standards Set by the Council on Environmental Quality*, 35 Me. L. Rev. 111 (1983).

12. Cooper, *Broad Programmatic, Policy and Planning Assessments under the National Environmental Policy Act and Similar Devices: A Quiet*

Revolution in an Approach to Environmental Considerations, 11 Pace Envt'l L. Rev. 89 (1993).

13. Davis, *The Fox Is Guarding the Henhouse: Enhancing the Role of the EPA in FONSI Determinations Pursuant to NEPA*, 39 Akron L. Rev. 35 (2006).

14. Flatt, *The Human Environment of the Mind: Correcting NEPA Implementation by Treating Environmental Philosophy and Environmental Risk Allocation as Environmental Values under NEPA*, 46 Hastings L. J. 85 (1994).

15. Fischman, *The EPA's NEPA Duties and Ecosystem Services*, 20 Stan. Envtl. L.J. 497 (1998).

16. Garver, *A New Approach to Review of NEPA Findings of No Significant Impact*, 85 Mich. L. Rev 191 (1986).

17. Herz, *Parallel Universes: NEPA Lessons for the New Property*, 93 Colum. L. Rev. 1668 (1993).

18. Ichter, *Beyond Judicial Scrutiny: Military Compliance with NEPA*, 18 Ga. L. Rev. 639 (1984).

19. Jacobs, *Compromising NEPA? The Interplay between Settlement Agreements and the National Environmental Policy Act*, 19 Harv. Envt'l L. Rev. 113 (1995).

20. Johnson, *NEPA and SEPA's in the Quest for Environmental Justice*, 30 Loy. L.A. L. Rev. 565 (1997).

21. Karkkainen, *Whither NEPA?*, 12 N.Y.U. Envtl. L.J. 333 (2004).

22. Karkkainen, *Toward a Smarter NEPA: Monitoring and Managing Government's Environmental Performance*, 102 Colum. L. Rev. 903 (2002).

23. Montange, *NEPA In An Era of Economic Deregulation: A Case Study of Environmental Avoidance at the Interstate Commerce Commission*, 9 Va. Envtl. L.J. 1 (1989).

24. Murchison, *Does NEPA Matter?—An Analysis of the Historical Development and Contemporary Significance of the National Environmental Policy Act*, 18 U. Rich. L. Rev. 557 (1984).

25. Poisner, *A Civic Republican Perspective on the National Environmental Policy Act's Process for Citizen Participation*, 26 Envt'l L. 53 (1996).

26. Symposium, *NEPA at Twenty: The Past, Present and Future of the National Environmental Policy Act*, 20 Envtl. L. No. 3 (1990).

27. Symposium, *Law-Science Cooperation Under the National Environmental Policy Act*, 15 Nat. Resources Law. 569 (1983).

28. Symposium, *Special Focus: Articles and Essays: NEPA at Twenty*, 25 Land & Water L. Rev. 1 (1990).

29. Tripp and Alley, *Streamlining NEPA's Environmental Review Process: Suggestions for Agency Reform*, 12 N.Y.U. Envtl. L.J. 74 (2003).

IV. Miscellaneous

1. Environmental Law Institute, *NEPA Deskbook* (3d ed. 2003).

Agency Regulations:

Federal agencies have promulgated their own individualized regulations, within the parameters set by the CEQ regulations. See the Code of Federal Regulations Index, ("environmental impact statements") for a list of citations to agency regulations.

Appendix:

1. National Environmental Policy Act, title 1, 42 U.S.C. §§4321, 4331-4347, 4365 (2000).
2. Council on Environmental Quality, 40 C.F.R. Parts 1500-1508.
3. Council on Environmental Quality, *Memorandum to Agencies Containing Answers to 40 Most Asked Questions on NEPA Regulations*, 46 Fed. Reg. 18,026 (March 23, 1981). (Note: The answer to Question #20 was rescinded. *See* 51 Fed. Reg. 15,625 (April 25, 1986); codified at 40 C.F.R. §1502.22 (1990)).

National Environmental Policy Act
Title 42, U.S. Code

§4321. Congressional declaration of purpose

SUBCHAPTER I - POLICIES AND GOALS

§4331. Congressional declaration of national environmental policy
§4332. Cooperation of agencies; reports; availability of information; recommendations;
international and national coordination of efforts
§4333. Conformity of administrative procedures to national environmental policy
§4334. Other statutory obligations of agencies
§4335. Efforts supplemental to existing authorizations

SUBCHAPTER II - COUNCIL ON ENVIRONMENTAL QUALITY

§4341. Omitted
§4342. Establishment; membership; Chairman; appointments
§4343. Employment of personnel, experts and consultants
§4344. Duties and functions
§4345. Consultation with Citizens' Advisory Committee on Environmental Quality and other representatives

* * *

SUBCHAPTER III - MISCELLANEOUS PROVISIONS

§4365. Science Advisory Board

Sec. 4321. Congressional declaration of purpose

The purposes of this chapter are: To declare a national policy which will encourage productive and enjoyable harmony between man and his environment; to promote efforts which will prevent or eliminate damage to the environment and biosphere and stimulate the health and welfare of man; to enrich the understanding of the ecological systems and natural resources important to the Nation; and to establish a Council on Environmental Quality.

(Pub. L. No. 91-190, Sec. 2, Jan. 1, 1970, 83 Stat. 852.)

SUBCHAPTER I - POLICIES AND GOALS

Sec. 4331. Congressional declaration of national environmental policy

(a) The Congress, recognizing the profound impact of man's activity on the interrelations of all components of the natural environment, particularly the profound influences of population growth, high-density urbanization, industrial expansion, resource exploitation, and new and expanding technological advances and recognizing further the critical importance of restoring and maintaining environmental quality to the overall welfare and development of man, declares that it is the continuing policy of the Federal Government, in cooperation with State and local governments, and other concerned public and private organizations, to use all practicable means and measures, including financial and technical assistance, in a manner calculated to foster and promote the general welfare, to create and maintain conditions under which man and nature can exist in productive harmony, and fulfill the social, economic, and other requirements of present and future generations of Americans.

(b) In order to carry out the policy set forth in this chapter, it is the continuing responsibility of the Federal Government to use all practicable means, consistent with other essential considerations of national policy, to improve and coordinate Federal plans, functions, programs, and resources to the end that the Nation may -

(1) fulfill the responsibilities of each generation as trustee of the environment for succeeding generations;

(2) assure for all Americans safe, healthful, productive, and esthetically and culturally pleasing surroundings;

(3) attain the widest range of beneficial uses of the environment without degradation, risk to health or safety, or other undesirable and unintended consequences;

(4) preserve important historic, cultural, and natural aspects of our national heritage, and maintain, wherever possible, an environment which supports diversity and variety of individual choice;

(5) achieve a balance between population and resource use which will permit high standards of living and a wide sharing of life's amenities; and

(6) enhance the quality of renewable resources and approach the maximum attainable recycling of depletable resources.

(c) The Congress recognizes that each person should enjoy a healthful environment and that each person has a responsibility to contribute to the preservation and enhancement of the environment.

(Pub. L. No. 91-190, title I, Sec. 101, Jan. 1, 1970, 83 Stat. 852.)

Sec. 4332. Cooperation of agencies; reports; availability of information; recommendations; international and national coordination of efforts

The Congress authorizes and directs that, to the fullest extent possible: (1) the policies, regulations, and public laws of the United States shall be interpreted and administered in accordance with the policies set forth in this chapter, and (2) all agencies of the Federal Government shall -

(A) utilize a systematic, interdisciplinary approach which will insure the integrated use of the natural and social sciences and the environmental design arts in planning and in decisionmaking which may have an impact on man's environment;

(B) identify and develop methods and procedures, in consultation with the Council on Environmental Quality established by subchapter II of this chapter, which will insure that presently unquantified environmental amenities and values may be given appropriate consideration in decisionmaking along with economic and technical considerations;(C) include in every recommendation or report on proposals for legislation and other major Federal actions significantly affecting the quality of the human environment, a detailed statement by the responsible official on -

(i) the environmental impact of the proposed action,

(ii) any adverse environmental effects which cannot be avoided should the proposal be implemented,

(iii) alternatives to the proposed action,

(iv) the relationship between local short-term uses of man's environment and the maintenance and enhancement of long-term productivity, and

(v) any irreversible and irretrievable commitments of resources which would be involved in the proposed action should it be implemented. Prior to making any detailed statement, the responsible Federal official shall consult with and obtain the comments of any Federal agency which has jurisdiction by law or special expertise with respect to any environmental impact involved. Copies of such statement and the comments and views of the appropriate Federal, State, and local agencies, which are authorized to develop and enforce environmental standards, shall be made available to the President, the Council on Environmental Quality and to the public as provided by section 552 of title 5, and shall accompany the proposal through the existing agency review processes;

(D) Any detailed statement required under subparagraph (C) after January 1, 1970, for any major Federal action funded under a program of grants to States shall not be deemed to be legally insufficient solely by reason of having been prepared by a State agency or official, if:

(i) the State agency or official has statewide jurisdiction and has the responsibility for such action,

(ii) the responsible Federal official furnishes guidance and participates in such preparation,

(iii) the responsible Federal official independently evaluates such statement prior to its approval and adoption, and

(iv) after January 1, 1976, the responsible Federal official provides early notification to, and solicits the views of, any other State or any Federal land management entity of any action or any alternative thereto which may have significant impacts upon such State or affected Federal land management entity and, if there is any disagreement on such impacts, prepares a written assessment of such impacts and views for incorporation into such detailed statement. The procedures in this subparagraph shall not relieve the Federal official of his responsibilities for the scope, objectivity, and content of the entire statement or of any other responsibility under this chapter; and further, this subparagraph does not affect the legal sufficiency of statements prepared by State agencies with less than statewide jurisdiction.[2]

(E) study, develop, and describe appropriate alternatives to recommended courses of action in any proposal which involves unresolved conflicts concerning alternative uses of available resources;

(F) recognize the worldwide and long-range character of environmental problems and, where consistent with the foreign policy of the United States, lend appropriate support to initiatives, resolutions, and programs designed to maximize international cooperation in anticipating and preventing a decline in the quality of mankind's world environment;

(G) make available to States, counties, municipalities, institutions, and individuals, advice and information useful in restoring, maintaining, and enhancing the quality of the environment;

(H) initiate and utilize ecological information in the planning and development of resource-oriented projects; and

(I) assist the Council on Environmental Quality established by subchapter II of this chapter. (Pub. L. No. 91-190, title I, Sec. 102, Jan. 1, 1970, 83 Stat. 853; Pub. L. No. 94-83, Aug. 9, 1975, 89 Stat. 424.)

---

[2] So in original. The period probably should be a semicolon.

Sec. 4333. Conformity of administrative procedures to national environmental policy

All agencies of the Federal Government shall review their present statutory authority, administrative regulations, and current policies and procedures for the purpose of determining whether there are any deficiencies or inconsistencies therein which prohibit full compliance with the purposes and provisions of this chapter and shall propose to the President not later than July 1, 1971, such measures as may be necessary to bring their authority and policies into conformity with the intent, purposes, and procedures set forth in this chapter.

(Pub. L. No. 91-190, title I, Sec. 103, Jan. 1, 1970, 83 Stat. 854.)

Sec. 4334. Other statutory obligations of agencies

Nothing in section 4332 or 4333 of this title shall in any way affect the specific statutory obligations of any Federal agency (1) to comply with criteria or standards of environmental quality, (2) to coordinate or consult with any other Federal or State agency, or (3) to act, or refrain from acting contingent upon the recommendations or certification of any other Federal or State agency.

(Pub. L. No. 91-190, title I, Sec. 104, Jan. 1, 1970, 83 Stat. 854.)

Sec. 4335. Efforts supplemental to existing authorizations

The policies and goals set forth in this chapter are supplementary to those set forth in existing authorizations of Federal agencies.

(Pub. L. No. 91-190, title I, Sec. 105, Jan. 1, 1970, 83 Stat. 854.)

SUBCHAPTER II - COUNCIL ON ENVIRONMENTAL QUALITY

Sec. 4341. Omitted

[This section, Pub. L. No. 91-190, Title II, §201, Jan. 1, 1970, 83 Stat. 854, which required the President to transmit to Congress annually an Environmental Quality Report, terminated, effective May 15, 2000, pursuant to Pub. L. No. 104- 66, §3003, as amended, set out as a note under 31 U.S.C. §1113.]

Sec. 4342. Establishment; membership; Chairman; appointments

There is created in the Executive Office of the President a Council on Environmental Quality (hereinafter referred to as the "Council"). The Council shall be composed of three members who shall be appointed by the President to serve at his pleasure, by and with the advice and consent of the Senate. The President shall designate one of the members of the Council to serve as Chairman. Each member shall be a person who, as a result of his training, experience, and attainments, is exceptionally well qualified to analyze and interpret environmental trends and information of all kinds; to appraise programs and activities of the Federal Government in the light of the policy set forth in subchapter I of this chapter; to be conscious of and responsive to the scientific, economic, social, esthetic, and cultural needs and interests of the Nation; and to formulate and recommend national policies to promote the improvement of the quality of the environment.

(Pub. L. No. 91-190, title II, Sec. 202, Jan. 1, 1970, 83 Stat. 854.)
[Pub. L. No. 109-54, Title III, Aug. 2, 2005, 119 Stat. 543, provided in part: "That notwithstanding section 202 of the National Environmental Policy Act of 1970 [sic; probably means section 202 of the National Environmental Policy Act of 1969, which enacted this section], the Council shall consist of one member, appointed by the President, by and with the advice and consent of the Senate, serving as chairman and exercising all powers, functions, and duties of the Council." Similar provisions were contained in the following prior appropriations Acts:
    Pub. L. No. 108-447, Div. I, Title III, Dec. 8, 2004, 118 Stat. 3332.
    Pub. L. No. 108-199, Div. G, Title III, Jan. 23, 2004, 118 Stat. 408.
    Pub. L. No. 108-7, Div. K, Title I, Feb. 20, 2003, 117 Stat. 514.
    Pub. L. No. 107-73, Title III, Nov. 26, 2001, 115 Stat. 686.
    Pub. L. No. 106-377, § 1(a)(1) [Title III], Oct. 27, 2000, 114 Stat. 1441, 1441A-45.
    Pub. L. No. 106-74, Title III, Oct. 20, 1999, 113 Stat. 1084.
    Pub. L. No. 105-276, Title III, Oct. 21, 1998, 112 Stat. 2500.
    Pub. L. No. 105-65, Title III, Oct. 27, 1997, 111 Stat. 1375.]

Sec. 4343. Employment of personnel, experts and consultants

(a) The Council may employ such officers and employees as may be necessary to carry out its functions under this chapter. In addition, the Council may employ and fix the compensation of such experts and consultants as may be necessary for the carrying out of its functions under this chapter, in accordance with section 3109 of title 5 (but without regard to the last sentence thereof).

(b) Notwithstanding section 1342 of title 31, the Council may accept and employ voluntary and uncompensated services in furtherance of the purposes of the Council.

(Pub. L. No. 91-190, title II, Sec. 203, Jan. 1, 1970, 83 Stat. 855; Pub. L. No. 94-52, Sec. 2, July 3, 1975, 89 Stat. 258.)

Sec. 4344. Duties and functions

It shall be the duty and function of the Council -

(1) to assist and advise the President in the preparation of the Environmental Quality Report required by section 4341 of this title;

(2) to gather timely and authoritative information concerning the conditions and trends in the quality of the environment both current and prospective, to analyze and interpret such information for the purpose of determining whether such conditions and trends are interfering, or are likely to interfere, with the achievement of the policy set forth in subchapter I of this chapter, and to compile and submit to the President studies relating to such conditions and trends;

(3) to review and appraise the various programs and activities of the Federal Government in the light of the policy set forth in subchapter I of this chapter for the purpose of determining the extent to which such programs and activities are contributing to the achievement of such policy, and to make recommendations to the President with respect thereto;

(4) to develop and recommend to the President national policies to foster and promote the improvement of environmental quality to meet the conservation, social, economic, health, and other requirements and goals of the Nation;

(5) to conduct investigations, studies, surveys, research, and analyses relating to ecological systems and environmental quality;

(6) to document and define changes in the natural environment, including the plant and animal systems, and to accumulate necessary data and other information for a continuing analysis of these changes or trends and an interpretation of their underlying causes;

(7) to report at least once each year to the President on the state and condition of the environment; and

(8) to make and furnish such studies, reports thereon, and recommendations with respect to matters of policy and legislation as the President may request.

(Pub. L. No. 91-190, title II, Sec. 204, Jan. 1, 1970, 83 Stat. 855.)

Sec. 4345. Consultation with Citizens' Advisory Committee on Environmental Quality and other representatives

In exercising its powers, functions, and duties under this chapter, the Council shall -

(1) consult with the Citizens' Advisory Committee on Environmental Quality established by Executive Order numbered 11472, dated May 29, 1969, and with such representatives of science, industry, agriculture, labor, conservation organizations, State and local governments and other groups, as it deems advisable; and

(2) utilize, to the fullest extent possible, the services, facilities, and information (including statistical information) of public and private agencies and organizations, and individuals, in order that duplication of effort and expense may be avoided, thus assuring that the Council's activities will not unnecessarily overlap or conflict with similar activities authorized by law and performed by established agencies.

(Pub. L. No. 91-190, title II, Sec. 205, Jan. 1, 1970, 83 Stat. 855.)

* * *

SUBCHAPTER III - MISCELLANEOUS PROVISIONS

Sec. 4365. Science Advisory Board

(a) Establishment; requests for advice by Administrator of Environmental Protection Agency and Congressional committees. The Administrator of the Environmental Protection Agency shall establish a Science Advisory Board which shall provide such scientific advice as may be requested by the Administrator, the Committee on Environment and Public Works of the United States Senate, or the Committee on Science, Space, and Technology, on Energy and Commerce, or on Public Works and Transportation of the House of Representatives.

(b) Membership; Chairman; meetings; qualifications of members. Such Board shall be composed of at least nine members, one of whom shall be designated Chairman, and shall meet at such times and places as may be designated by the Chairman of the Board in consultation with the Administrator. Each member of the Board shall be qualified by education, training, and experience to evaluate scientific and technical information on matters referred to the Board under this section.

(c) Proposed environmental criteria document, standard, limitation, or regulation; functions respecting in conjunction with Administrator.

(1) The Administrator, at the time any proposed criteria document, standard, limitation, or regulation under the Clean Air Act (42 U.S.C. 7401 et seq.), the Federal Water Pollution Control Act (33 U.S.C. 1251 et seq.), the Resource Conservation and Recovery Act of 1976 (42 U.S.C. 6901 et seq.), the Noise Control Act (42 U.S.C. 4901 et seq.), the Toxic Substances Control Act (15 U.S.C. 2601 et seq.), or the Safe Drinking Water Act (42 U.S.C. 300f et seq.), or under any other authority of the Administrator, is provided to any other Federal agency for formal review and comment, shall make available to the Board such proposed criteria document, standard, limitation, or regulation, together with relevant scientific and technical information in the possession of the Environmental Protection Agency on which the proposed action is based.

(2) The Board may make available to the Administrator, within the time specified by the Administrator, its advice and comments on the adequacy of the scientific and technical basis of the proposed criteria document, standard, limitation, or regulation, together with any pertinent information in the Board's possession.

(d) Utilization of technical and scientific capabilities of Federal agencies and national environmental laboratories for determining adequacy of scientific and technical basis of proposed criteria document, etc. In preparing such advice and comments, the Board shall avail itself of the technical and scientific capabilities of any Federal agency, including the Environmental Protection Agency and any national environmental laboratories.

(e) Member committees and investigative panels; establishment; chairmenship. The Board is authorized to constitute such member committees and investigative panels as the Administrator and the Board find necessary to carry out this section. Each such member committee or investigative panel shall be chaired by a member of the Board.

(f) Appointment and compensation of secretary and other personnel; compensation of members.

(1) Upon the recommendation of the Board, the Administrator shall appoint a secretary, and such other employees as deemed necessary to exercise and fulfill the Board's powers and responsibilities. The compensation of all employees appointed under this paragraph shall be fixed in accordance with chapter 51 and subchapter III of chapter 53 of title 5.

(2) Members of the Board may be compensated at a rate to be fixed by the President but not in excess of the maximum rate of pay for grade GS-18, as provided in the General Schedule under section 5332 of title 5.

(g) Consultation and coordination with Scientific Advisory Panel. In carrying out the functions assigned by this section, the Board shall consult and coordinate its activities with the Scientific Advisory Panel established by the Administrator pursuant to section 136w(d) of title 7.

(Pub. L. No. 95-155, Sec. 8, Nov. 8, 1977, 91 Stat. 1,260; Pub. L. No. 96-569, Sec. 3, Dec. 22, 1980, 94 Stat. 3,337; Pub. L. No. 103-437, Sec. 15(o), Nov. 2, 1994, 108 Stat. 4,593; Pub. L. No. 104-66, title II, Sec. 2021(k)(3), Dec. 21, 1995, 109 Stat. 728.)

Council on Environmental Quality Regulations
40 CFR Parts 1500-1508

§ 1500.1

PART 1500—PURPOSE, POLICY AND MANDATE

Sec.
1500.1   Purpose
1500.2   Policy
1500.3   Mandate
1500.4   Reducing paperwork
1500.5   Reducing delay
1500.6   Agency authority.

Authority: NEPA, the Environmental Quality Improvement Act of 1970, as amended (42 U.S.C. 4371 et seq.), sec. 309 of the Clean Air Act, as amended (42 U.S.C. 7609) and E.O. 11514, Mar. 5, 1970, as amended by E.O. 11991, May 24, 1977).

Source: 43 FR 55990, Nov. 28, 1978, unless otherwise noted.

Sec. 1500.1 Purpose.

(a) The National Environmental Policy Act (NEPA) is our basic national charter for protection of the environment. It establishes policy, sets goals (section 101), and provides means (section 102) for carrying out the policy. Section 102(2) contains "action-forcing" provisions to make sure that federal agencies act according to the letter and spirit of the Act. The regulations that follow implement section 102(2). Their purpose is to tell federal agencies what they must do to comply with the procedures and achieve the goals of the Act. The President, the federal agencies, and the courts share responsibility for enforcing the Act so as to achieve the substantive requirements of section 101.

(b) NEPA procedures must insure that environmental information is available to public officials and citizens before decisions are made and before actions are taken. The information must be of high quality. Accurate scientific analysis, expert agency comments, and public scrutiny are essential to implementing NEPA. Most important, NEPA documents must concentrate on the issues that are truly significant to the action in question, rather than amassing needless detail.

(c) Ultimately, of course, it is not better documents but better decisions that count. NEPA's purpose is not to generate paperwork—even excellent paperwork—but to foster excellent action. The NEPA process is intended to help public officials make decisions that are based on understanding of environmental consequences, and take actions that protect, restore, and enhance the environment. These regulations provide the direction to achieve this purpose.

Sec. 1500.2 Policy.

Federal agencies shall to the fullest extent possible:

(a) Interpret and administer the policies, regulations, and public laws of the United States in accordance with the policies set forth in the Act and in these regulations.

(b) Implement procedures to make the NEPA process more useful to decisionmakers and the public; to reduce paperwork and the accumulation of extraneous background data; and to emphasize real environmental issues and alternatives. Environmental impact statements shall be concise, clear, and to the point, and shall be supported by evidence that agencies have made the necessary environmental analyses.

(c) Integrate the requirements of NEPA with other planning and environmental review procedures required by law or by agency practice so that all such procedures run concurrently rather than consecutively.

(d) Encourage and facilitate public involvement in decisions which affect the quality of the human environment.

(e) Use the NEPA process to identify and assess the reasonable alternatives to proposed actions that will avoid or minimize adverse effects of these actions upon the quality of the human environment.

(f) Use all practicable means, consistent with the requirements of the Act and other essential considerations of national policy, to restore and enhance the quality of the human environment and avoid or minimize any possible adverse effects of their actions upon the quality of the human environment.

Sec. 1500.3 Mandate.

Parts 1500 through 1508 of this title provide regulations applicable to and binding on all Federal agencies for implementing the procedural provisions of the National Environmental Policy Act of 1969, as amended (Pub. L. 91-190, 42 U.S.C. 4321 et seq.) (NEPA or the Act) except where compliance would be inconsistent with other statutory requirements. These regulations are issued pursuant to NEPA, the Environmental Quality Improvement Act of 1970, as amended (42 U.S.C. 4371 et seq.) section 309 of the Clean Air Act, as amended (42 U.S.C. 7609) and Executive Order 11514, Protection and Enhancement of Environmental Quality (March 5, 1970, as amended by Executive Order 11991, May 24, 1977). These regulations, unlike the predecessor guidelines, are not confined to sec. 102(2)(C) (environmental impact statements). The regulations apply to the whole of section 102(2). The provisions of the Act and of these regulations must be read together as a whole in order to comply with the spirit and letter of the law. It is the Council's intention that judicial review of agency compliance with these regulations not occur before an agency has filed the final environmental impact statement, or has made a final finding of no significant impact (when such a finding will result in action affecting the environment), or takes action that will result in irreparable injury. Furthermore, it is the Council's intention that any trivial violation of these regulations not give rise to any independent cause of action.

Sec. 1500.4 Reducing paperwork.

Agencies shall reduce excessive paperwork by:

(a) Reducing the length of environmental impact statements (Sec. 1502.2(c)), by means such as setting appropriate page limits (Secs. 1501.7(b)(1) and 1502.7).

(b) Preparing analytic rather than encyclopedic environmental impact statements (Sec. 1502.2(a)).

(c) Discussing only briefly issues other than significant ones (Sec. 1502.2(b)).

(d) Writing environmental impact statements in plain language (Sec. 1502.8).

(e) Following a clear format for environmental impact statements (Sec. 1502.10).

(f) Emphasizing the portions of the environmental impact statement that are useful to decisionmakers and the public (Secs. 1502.14 and 1502.15) and reducing emphasis on background material (Sec. 1502.16).

(g) Using the scoping process, not only to identify significant environmental issues deserving of study, but also to deemphasize insignificant issues, narrowing the scope of the environmental impact statement process accordingly (Sec. 1501.7).

(h) Summarizing the environmental impact statement (Sec. 1502.12) and circulating the summary instead of the entire environmental impact statement if the latter is unusually long (Sec. 1502.19).

(i) Using program, policy, or plan environmental impact statements and tiering from statements of broad scope to those of narrower scope, to eliminate repetitive discussions of the same issues (Secs. 1502.4 and 1502.20).

(j) Incorporating by reference (Sec. 1502.21).

(k) Integrating NEPA requirements with other environmental review and consultation requirements (Sec. 1502.25).

(l) Requiring comments to be as specific as possible (Sec. 1503.3). (m) Attaching and circulating only changes to the draft environmental impact statement, rather than rewriting and circulating the entire statement when changes are minor (Sec. 1503.4(c)).

(n) Eliminating duplication with State and local procedures, by providing for joint preparation (Sec. 1506.2), and with other Federal procedures, by providing that an agency may adopt appropriate environmental documents prepared by another agency (Sec. 1506.3).

(o) Combining environmental documents with other documents (Sec. 1506.4).

(p) Using categorical exclusions to define categories of actions which do not individually or cumulatively have a significant effect on the human environment and which are therefore exempt from requirements to prepare an environmental impact statement (Sec. 1508.4).

(q) Using a finding of no significant impact when an action not otherwise excluded will not have a significant effect on the human environment and is therefore exempt from requirements to prepare an environmental impact statement (Sec. 1508.13).

[43 FR 55990, Nov. 29, 1978; 44 FR 873, Jan. 3, 1979]

Sec. 1500.5 Reducing delay.

Agencies shall reduce delay by:

(a) Integrating the NEPA process into early planning (Sec. 1501.2).

(b) Emphasizing interagency cooperation before the environmental impact statement is prepared, rather than submission of adversary comments on a completed document (Sec. 1501.6).

(c) Insuring the swift and fair resolution of lead agency disputes (Sec. 1501.5).

(d) Using the scoping process for an early identification of what are and what are not the real issues (Sec. 1501.7).

(e) Establishing appropriate time limits for the environmental impact statement process (Secs. 1501.7(b)(2) and 1501.8).

(f) Preparing environmental impact statements early in the process (Sec. 1502.5).

(g) Integrating NEPA requirements with other environmental review and consultation requirements (Sec. 1502.25).

(h) Eliminating duplication with State and local procedures by providing for joint preparation (Sec. 1506.2) and with other Federal procedures by providing that an agency may adopt appropriate environmental documents prepared by another agency (Sec. 1506.3).

(i) Combining environmental documents with other documents (Sec. 1506.4).

(j) Using accelerated procedures for proposals for legislation (Sec. 1506.8).

(k) Using categorical exclusions to define categories of actions which do not individually or cumulatively have a significant effect on the human environment (Sec. 1508.4) and which are therefore exempt from requirements to prepare an environmental impact statement.

(l) Using a finding of no significant impact when an action not otherwise excluded will not have a significant effect on the human environment (Sec. 1508.13) and is therefore exempt from requirements to prepare an environmental impact statement.

Sec. 1500.6 Agency authority.

Each agency shall interpret the provisions of the Act as a supplement to its existing authority and as a mandate to view traditional policies and missions in the light of the Act's national environmental objectives. Agencies shall review their policies, procedures, and regulations accordingly and revise them as necessary to insure full compliance with the purposes and provisions of the Act. The phrase "to the fullest extent possible" in section 102 means that each agency of the Federal Government shall comply with that section unless existing law applicable to the agency's operations expressly prohibits or makes compliance impossible.

PART 1501—NEPA AND AGENCY PLANNING

Sec.
1501.1 Purpose
1501.2 Apply NEPA early in the process.
1501.3 When to prepare an environmental assessment.
1501.4 Whether to prepare an environmental impact statement.
1501.5 Lead agencies.
1501.6 Cooperating agencies.
1501.7 Scoping.
1501.8 Time limits.

Authority: NEPA, the Environmental Quality Improvement Act of 1970, as amended (42 U.S.C. 4371 et seq.), sec. 309 of the Clean Air Act, as amended (42 U.S.C. 7609, and E.O. 11514 (Mar. 5, 1970, as amended by E.O. 11991, May 24, 1977).

Source: 43 FR 55992, Nov. 29, 1978, unless otherwise noted.

Sec. 1501.1 Purpose.

The purposes of this part include:

(a) Integrating the NEPA process into early planning to insure appropriate consideration of NEPA's policies and to eliminate delay.

(b) Emphasizing cooperative consultation among agencies before the environmental impact statement is prepared rather than submission of adversary comments on a completed document.

(c) Providing for the swift and fair resolution of lead agency disputes.

(d) Identifying at an early stage the significant environmental issues deserving of study and deemphasizing insignificant issues, narrowing the scope of the environmental impact statement accordingly.

(e) Providing a mechanism for putting appropriate time limits on the environmental impact statement process.

Sec. 1501.2 Apply NEPA early in the process.

Agencies shall integrate the NEPA process with other planning at the earliest possible time to insure that planning and decisions reflect environmental values, to avoid delays later in the process, and to head off potential conflicts. Each agency shall:

(a) Comply with the mandate of section 102(2)(A) to "utilize a systematic, interdisciplinary approach which will insure the integrated use of the natural and social sciences and the environmental design arts in planning and in decisionmaking which may have an impact on man's environment," as specified by Sec. 1507.2.

(b) Identify environmental effects and values in adequate detail so they can be compared to economic and technical analyses. Environmental documents and appropriate analyses shall be circulated and reviewed at the same time as other planning documents.

(c) Study, develop, and describe appropriate alternatives to recommended courses of action in any proposal which involves unresolved conflicts concerning alternative uses of available resources as provided by section 102(2)(E) of the Act.

(d) Provide for cases where actions are planned by private applicants or other non-Federal entities before Federal involvement so that:

(1) Policies or designated staff are available to advise potential applicants of studies or other information foreseeably required for later Federal action.

(2) The Federal agency consults early with appropriate State and local agencies and Indian tribes and with interested private persons and organizations when its own

involvement is reasonably foreseeable.

(3) The Federal agency commences its NEPA process at the earliest possible time.

Sec. 1501.3 When to prepare an environmental assessment.

(a) Agencies shall prepare an environmental assessment (Sec. 1508.9) when necessary under the procedures adopted by individual agencies to supplement these regulations as described in Sec. 1507.3. An assessment is not necessary if the agency has decided to prepare an environmental impact statement.

(b) Agencies may prepare an environmental assessment on any action at any time in order to assist agency planning and decisionmaking.

Sec. 1501.4 Whether to prepare an environmental impact statement.

In determining whether to prepare an environmental impact statement the Federal agency shall:

(a) Determine under its procedures supplementing these regulations (described in Sec. 1507.3) whether the proposal is one which:

Normally requires an environmental impact statement, or

Normally does not require either an environmental impact statement or an environmental assessment (categorical exclusion).

(b) If the proposed action is not covered by paragraph (a) of this section, prepare an environmental assessment (Sec. 1508.9). The agency shall involve environmental agencies, applicants, and the public, to the extent practicable, in preparing assessments required by Sec. 1508.9(a)(1).

(c) Based on the environmental assessment make its determination whether to prepare an environmental impact statement.

(d) Commence the scoping process (Sec. 1501.7), if the agency will prepare an environmental impact statement.

(e) Prepare a finding of no significant impact (Sec. 1508.13), if the agency determines on the basis of the environmental assessment not to prepare a statement.

(1) The agency shall make the finding of no significant impact available to the affected public as specified in Sec. 1506.6.

(2) In certain limited circumstances, which the agency may cover in its procedures under Sec. 1507.3, the agency shall make the finding of no significant impact available for public review (including State and areawide clearinghouses) for 30 days before the agency makes its final determination whether to prepare an environmental impact statement and before the action may begin. The circumstances are:

(i) The proposed action is, or is closely similar to, one which normally requires the preparation of an environmental impact statement under the procedures adopted by the agency pursuant to Sec. 1507.3, or

(ii) The nature of the proposed action is one without precedent.

Sec. 1501.5 Lead agencies.

(a) A lead agency shall supervise the preparation of an environmental impact statement if more than one Federal agency either:

(1) Proposes or is involved in the same action; or

(2) Is involved in a group of actions directly related to each other because of their functional interdependence or geographical proximity.

(b) Federal, State, or local agencies, including at least one Federal agency, may act as joint lead agencies to prepare an environmental impact statement (Sec. 1506.2).

(c) If an action falls within the provisions of paragraph (a) of this section the potential lead agencies shall determine by letter or memorandum which agency shall be the lead agency and which shall be cooperating agencies. The agencies shall resolve the lead agency question so as not to cause delay. If there is disagreement among the agencies, the following factors (which are listed in order of descending importance) shall determine lead agency designation:

(1) Magnitude of agency's involvement.

(2) Project approval/disapproval authority.

(3) Expertise concerning the action's environmental effects.

(4) Duration of agency's involvement.

(5) Sequence of agency's involvement.

(d) Any Federal agency, or any State or local agency or private person substantially affected by the absence of lead agency designation, may make a written request to the potential lead agencies that a lead agency be designated.

(e) If Federal agencies are unable to agree on which agency will be the lead agency or if the procedure described in paragraph (c) of this section has not resulted within 45 days in a lead agency designation, any of the agencies or persons concerned may file a request with the Council asking it to determine which Federal agency shall be the lead agency. A copy of the request shall be transmitted to each potential lead agency. The request shall consist of:

A precise description of the nature and extent of the proposed action.

A detailed statement of why each potential lead agency should or should not be the lead agency under the criteria specified in paragraph (c) of this section.

(f) A response may be filed by any potential lead agency concerned within 20 days after a request is filed with the Council. The Council shall determine as soon as possible but not later than 20 days after receiving the request and all responses to it which Federal agency shall be the lead agency and which other Federal agencies shall be cooperating agencies.

[43 FR 55992, Nov. 29, 1978; 44 FR 873, Jan. 3, 1979]

Sec. 1501.6 Cooperating agencies.

The purpose of this section is to emphasize agency cooperation early in the NEPA process. Upon request of the lead agency, any other Federal agency which has jurisdiction by law shall be a cooperating agency. In addition any other Federal agency which has special expertise with respect to any environmental issue, which should be addressed in the statement may be a cooperating agency upon request of the lead agency. An agency may request the lead agency to designate it a cooperating agency.

(a) The lead agency shall:

(1) Request the participation of each cooperating agency in the NEPA process at the earliest possible time.

(2) Use the environmental analysis and proposals of cooperating agencies with jurisdiction by law or special expertise, to the maximum extent possible consistent with its responsibility as lead agency.

(3) Meet with a cooperating agency at the latter's request.

(b) Each cooperating agency shall:

(1) Participate in the NEPA process at the earliest possible time.

(2) Participate in the scoping process (described below in Sec. 1501.7).

(3) Assume on request of the lead agency responsibility for developing information and preparing environmental analyses including portions of the environmental impact statement concerning which the cooperating agency has special expertise.

(4) Make available staff support at the lead agency's request to enhance the latter's interdisciplinary capability.

(5) Normally use its own funds. The lead agency shall, to the extent available funds permit, fund those major activities or analyses it requests from cooperating agencies. Potential lead agencies shall include such funding requirements in their budget requests.

(c) A cooperating agency may in response to a lead agency's request for assistance in preparing the environmental impact statement (described in paragraph (b)(3), (4), or (5) of this section) reply that other program commitments preclude any involvement or the degree of involvement requested in the action that is the subject of the environmental impact statement. A copy of this reply shall be submitted to the Council.

Sec. 1501.7 Scoping.

There shall be an early and open process for determining the scope of issues to be addressed and for identifying the significant issues related to a proposed action. This process shall be termed scoping. As soon as practicable after its decision to prepare an environmental impact statement and before the scoping process the lead agency shall publish a notice of intent (Sec. 1508.22) in the Federal Register except as provided in Sec. 1507.3(e).

(a) As part of the scoping process the lead agency shall:

(1) Invite the participation of affected Federal, State, and local agencies, any affected Indian tribe, the proponent of the action, and other interested persons (including those who might not be in accord with the action on environmental grounds), unless there is a limited exception under Sec. 1507.3(c). An agency may give notice in accordance with Sec. 1506.6.

(2) Determine the scope (Sec. 1508.25) and the significant issues to be analyzed in depth in the environmental impact statement.

(3) Identify and eliminate from detailed study the issues which are not significant or which have been covered by prior environmental review (Sec. 1506.3), narrowing the discussion of these issues in the statement to a brief presentation of why they will not have a significant effect on the human environment or providing a reference to their coverage elsewhere.

(4) Allocate assignments for preparation of the environmental impact statement among the lead and cooperating agencies, with the lead agency retaining responsibility for the statement.

(5) Indicate any public environmental assessments and other environmental impact statements which are being or will be prepared that are related to but are not part of the scope of the impact statement under consideration.

(6) Identify other environmental review and consultation requirements so the lead and cooperating agencies may prepare other required analyses and studies concurrently with, and integrated with, the environmental impact statement as provided in Sec. 1502.25.

(7) Indicate the relationship between the timing of the preparation of environmental analyses and the agency's tentative planning and decisionmaking schedule.

(b) As part of the scoping process the lead agency may:

(1) Set page limits on environmental documents (Sec. 1502.7).

(2) Set time limits (Sec. 1501.8).

(3) Adopt procedures under Sec. 1507.3 to combine its environmental assessment process with its scoping process.

(4) Hold an early scoping meeting or meetings which may be integrated with any other early planning meeting the agency has. Such a scoping meeting will often be appropriate when the impacts of a particular action are confined to specific sites.

(c) An agency shall revise the determinations made under paragraphs (a) and (b) of this section if substantial changes are made later in the proposed action, or if significant new circumstances or information arise which bear on the proposal or its impacts.

Sec. 1501.8 Time limits.

Although the Council has decided that prescribed universal time limits for the entire NEPA process are too inflexible, Federal agencies are encouraged to set time limits appropriate to individual actions (consistent with the time intervals required by Sec.

1506.10). When multiple agencies are involved the reference to agency below means lead agency.

(a) The agency shall set time limits if an applicant for the proposed action requests them: Provided, That the limits are consistent with the purposes of NEPA and other essential considerations of national policy.

(b) The agency may:

(1) Consider the following factors in determining time limits:

(i) Potential for environmental harm.

(ii) Size of the proposed action.

(iii) State of the art of analytic techniques.

(iv) Degree of public need for the proposed action, including the consequences of delay.

(v) Number of persons and agencies affected.

(vi) Degree to which relevant information is known and if not known the time required for obtaining it.

(vii) Degree to which the action is controversial.

(viii) Other time limits imposed on the agency by law, regulations, or executive order.

(2) Set overall time limits or limits for each constituent part of the NEPA process, which may include:

(i) Decision on whether to prepare an environmental impact statement (if not already decided).

(ii) Determination of the scope of the environmental impact statement.

(iii) Preparation of the draft environmental impact statement.

(iv) Review of any comments on the draft environmental impact statement from the public and agencies.

(v) Preparation of the final environmental impact statement.

(vi) Review of any comments on the final environmental impact statement.

(vii) Decision on the action based in part on the environmental impact statement.

(3) Designate a person (such as the project manager or a person in the agency's office with NEPA responsibilities) to expedite the NEPA process.

(c) State or local agencies or members of the public may request a Federal Agency to set time limits.

PART 1502—ENVIRONMENTAL IMPACT STATEMENT

Sec.
1502.1   Purpose
1502.2   Implementation
1502.3   Statutory requirements for statements
1502.4   Major Federal actions requiring the preparation of environmental impact statements
1502.5   Timing
1502.6   Interdisciplinary preparation
1502.7   Page limits
1502.8   Writing
1502.9   Draft, final, and supplemental statements
1502.10 Recommended format
1502.11 Cover sheet
1502.12 Summary
1502.13 Purpose and need
1502.14 Alternatives including the proposed action
1502.15 Affected environment
1502.16 Environmental consequences
1502.17 List of preparers
1502.18 Appendix
1502.19 Circulation of the environmental impact statement
1502.20 Tiering
1502.21 Incorporation by reference
1502.22 Incomplete or unavailable information
1502.23 Cost-benefit analysis
1502.24 Methodology and scientific accuracy
1502.25 Environmental review and consultation requirements.

Authority: NEPA, the Environmental Quality Improvement Act of 1970, as amended (42 U.S.C. 4371 et seq.), sec. 309 of the Clean Air Act, as amended (42 U.S.C. 7609), and E.O. 11514 (Mar. 5, 1970, as amended by E.O. 11991, May 24, 1977).

Source: 43 FR 55994, Nov. 29, 1978, unless otherwise noted.

Sec. 1502.1 Purpose.

The primary purpose of an environmental impact statement is to serve as an action-forcing device to insure that the policies and goals defined in the Act are infused into the ongoing programs and actions of the Federal Government. It shall provide full and fair discussion of significant environmental impacts and shall inform decisionmakers and the public of the reasonable alternatives which would avoid or minimize adverse impacts or enhance the quality of the human environment. Agencies shall focus on significant environmental issues and alternatives and shall reduce paperwork and the accumulation of extraneous background data. Statements shall be concise, clear, and to the point, and shall be supported by evidence that the agency has made the necessary environmental analyses. An environmental impact statement is more than a disclosure document. It shall be used by Federal officials in conjunction with other relevant material to plan actions and make decisions.

Sec. 1502.2 Implementation.

To achieve the purposes set forth in Sec. 1502.1 agencies shall prepare environmental impact statements in the following manner:

(a) Environmental impact statements shall be analytic rather than encyclopedic.

(b) Impacts shall be discussed in proportion to their significance. There shall be only brief discussion of other than significant issues. As in a finding of no significant impact, there should be only enough discussion to show why more study is not warranted.

(c) Environmental impact statements shall be kept concise and shall be no longer than absolutely necessary to comply with NEPA and with these regulations. Length should vary first with potential environmental problems and then with project size.

(d) Environmental impact statements shall state how alternatives considered in it and decisions based on it will or will not achieve the requirements of sections 101 and 102(1) of the Act and other environmental laws and policies.

(e) The range of alternatives discussed in environmental impact statements shall encompass those to be considered by the ultimate agency decisionmaker.

(f) Agencies shall not commit resources prejudicing selection of alternatives before making a final decision (Sec. 1506.1).

(g) Environmental impact statements shall serve as the means of assessing the environmental impact of proposed agency actions, rather than justifying decisions already made.

Sec. 1502.3 Statutory requirements for statements.

As required by sec. 102(2)(C) of NEPA environmental impact statements (Sec. 1508.11) are to be included in every recommendation or report.

On proposals (Sec. 1508.23).

For legislation and (Sec. 1508.17).

Other major Federal actions (Sec. 1508.18).

Significantly (Sec. 1508.27).

Affecting (Secs. 1508.3, 1508.8).

The quality of the human environment (Sec. 1508.14).

Sec. 1502.4 Major Federal actions requiring the preparation of environmental impact statements.

(a) Agencies shall make sure the proposal which is the subject of an environmental impact statement is properly defined. Agencies shall use the criteria for scope (Sec. 1508.25) to determine which proposal(s) shall be the subject of a particular statement. Proposals or parts of proposals which are related to each other closely enough to be, in effect, a single course of action shall be evaluated in a single impact statement.

(b) Environmental impact statements may be prepared, and are sometimes required, for broad Federal actions such as the adoption of new agency programs or regulations (Sec. 1508.18). Agencies shall prepare statements on broad actions so that they are relevant to policy and are timed to coincide with meaningful points in agency planning and decisionmaking.

(c) When preparing statements on broad actions (including proposals by more than one agency), agencies may find it useful to evaluate the proposal(s) in one of the following ways:

(1) Geographically, including actions occurring in the same general location, such as body of water, region, or metropolitan area.

(2) Generically, including actions which have relevant similarities, such as common timing, impacts, alternatives, methods of implementation, media, or subject matter.

(3) By stage of technological development including federal or federally assisted research, development or demonstration programs for new technologies which, if applied, could significantly affect the quality of the human environment. Statements shall be prepared on such programs and shall be available before the program has reached a stage of investment or commitment to implementation likely to determine subsequent development or restrict later alternatives.

(d) Agencies shall as appropriate employ scoping (Sec. 1501.7), tiering (Sec. 1502.20), and other methods listed in Secs. 1500.4 and 1500.5 to relate broad and narrow actions and to avoid duplication and delay.

Sec. 1502.5 Timing.

An agency shall commence preparation of an environmental impact statement as close as possible to the time the agency is developing or is presented with a proposal (Sec. 1508.23) so that preparation can be completed in time for the final statement to be included in any recommendation or report on the proposal. The statement shall be prepared early enough so that it can serve practically as an important contribution to the decisionmaking process and will not be used to rationalize or justify decisions already made (Secs. 1500.2(c), 1501.2, and 1502.2). For instance:

(a) For projects directly undertaken by Federal agencies the environmental impact statement shall be prepared at the feasibility analysis (go-no go) stage and may be supplemented at a later stage if necessary.

(b) For applications to the agency appropriate environmental assessments or statements shall be commenced no later than immediately after the application is received. Federal agencies are encouraged to begin preparation of such assessments or statements earlier, preferably jointly with applicable• State or local agencies.

(c) For adjudication, the final environmental impact statement shall normally precede the final staff recommendation and that portion of the public hearing related to the impact study. In appropriate circumstances the statement may follow preliminary hearings designed to gather information for use in the statements.

(d) For informal rulemaking the draft environmental impact statement shall normally accompany the proposed rule.

Sec. 1502.6 Interdisciplinary preparation.

Environmental impact statements shall be prepared using an inter- disciplinary approach which will insure the integrated use of the natural and social sciences and the environmental design arts (section 102(2)(A) of the Act). The disciplines of the preparers shall be appropriate to the scope and issues identified in the scoping process (Sec. 1501.7).

Sec. 1502.7 Page limits.

The text of final environmental impact statements (e.g., paragraphs (d) through (g) of Sec. 1502.10) shall normally be less than 150 pages and for proposals of unusual scope or complexity shall normally be less than 300 pages.

Sec. 1502.8 Writing.

Environmental impact statements shall be written in plain language and may use appropriate graphics so that decisionmakers and the public can readily understand them. Agencies should employ writers of clear prose or editors to write, review, or edit statements, which will be based upon the analysis and supporting data from the natural and social sciences and the environmental• design arts.

Sec. 1502.9 Draft, final, and supplemental statements.

Except for proposals for legislation as provided in Sec. 1506.8 environmental impact statements shall be prepared in two stages and may be supplemented.

(a) Draft environmental impact statements shall be prepared in accordance with the scope decided upon in the scoping process. The lead agency shall work with the cooperating agencies and shall obtain comments as required in Part 1503 of this chapter. The draft statement must fulfill and satisfy to the fullest extent possible the requirements established for final statements in section 102(2)(C) of the Act. If a draft statement is so inadequate as to preclude meaningful analysis, the agency shall prepare and circulate a revised draft of the appropriate portion. The agency shall make every effort to disclose and discuss at appropriate points in the draft statement all major points of view on the environmental impacts of the alternatives including the proposed action.

(b) Final environmental impact statements shall respond to comments as required in Part 1503 of this chapter. The agency shall discuss at appropriate points in the final statement any responsible opposing view which was not adequately discussed in the draft statement and shall indicate the agency's response to the issues raised.

(c) Agencies:

Shall prepare supplements to either draft or final environmental• impact statements if:

(i) The agency makes substantial changes in the proposed action that are relevant to environmental concerns; or

(ii) There are significant new circumstances or information relevant to environmental concerns and bearing on the proposed action or its impacts.

May also prepare supplements when the agency determines that the purposes of the Act will be furthered by doing so.

Shall adopt procedures for introducing a supplement into its formal administrative record, if such a record exists.

Shall prepare, circulate, and file a supplement to a statement in the same fashion (exclusive of scoping) as a draft and final statement unless alternative procedures are approved by the Council.

Sec. 1502.10 Recommended format.

Agencies shall use a format for environmental impact statements which will encourage good analysis and clear presentation of the alternatives including the proposed action. The following standard format for environmental impact statements should be followed unless the agency determines that there is a compelling reason to do otherwise:

(a) Cover sheet.
(b) Summary.
(c) Table of contents.
(d) Purpose of and need for action.
(e) Alternatives including proposed action (sections 102(2)(C)(iii) and 102(2)(E) of the Act).

(f) Affected environment.

(g) Environmental consequences (especially sections 102(2)(C)(i), (ii), (iv), and (v) of the Act).

(h) List of preparers.

(i) List of Agencies, Organizations, and persons to whom copies of the statement are sent.

(j) Index.

(k) Appendices (if any).

If a different format is used, it shall include paragraphs (a), (b), (c), (h), (i), and (j), of this section and shall include the substance of paragraphs (d), (e), (f), (g), and (k) of this section, as further described in Secs. 1502.11 through 1502.18, in any appropriate format.

Sec. 1502.11 Cover sheet.

The cover sheet shall not exceed one page. It shall include:

(a) A list of the responsible agencies including the lead agency and any cooperating agencies.

(b) The title of the proposed action that is the subject of the statement (and if appropriate the titles of related cooperating agency actions), together with the State(s) and county(ies) (or other jurisdiction if applicable) where the action is located.

(c) The name, address, and telephone number of the person at the agency who can supply further information.

(d) A designation of the statement as a draft, final, or draft or final supplement.

(e) A one paragraph abstract of the statement.

(f) The date by which comments must be received (computed in cooperation with EPA under Sec. 1506.10).

The information required by this section may be entered on Standard Form 424 (in items 4, 6, 7, 10, and 18).

Sec. 1502.12 Summary.

Each environmental impact statement shall contain a summary which adequately and accurately summarizes the statement. The summary shall stress the major conclusions, areas of controversy (including issues raised by agencies and the public), and the issues to be resolved (including the choice among alternatives). The summary will normally not exceed 15 pages.

Sec. 1502.13 Purpose and need.

The statement shall briefly specify the underlying purpose and need to which the agency is responding in proposing the alternatives including the proposed action.

Sec. 1502.14 Alternatives including the proposed action.

This section is the heart of the environmental impact statement. Based on the information and analysis presented in the sections on the Affected Environment (Sec. 1502.15) and the Environmental Consequences (Sec. 1502.16), it should present the environmental impacts of the proposal and the alternatives in comparative form, thus sharply defining the issues and providing a clear basis for choice among options by the decisionmaker and• the public. In this section agencies shall:

(a) Rigorously explore and objectively evaluate all reasonable alternatives, and for alternatives which were eliminated from detailed study, briefly discuss the reasons for their having been eliminated.

(b) Devote substantial treatment to each alternative considered in detail including the proposed action so that reviewers may evaluate their comparative merits.

(c) Include reasonable alternatives not within the jurisdiction of the lead agency.

(d) Include the alternative of no action.

(e) Identify the agency's preferred alternative or alternatives, if one or more exists, in the draft statement and identify such alternative in the final statement unless another law prohibits the expression of such a preference.

(f) Include appropriate mitigation measures not already included in the proposed action or alternatives.

Sec. 1502.15 Affected environment.

The environmental impact statement shall succinctly describe the environment of the area(s) to be affected or created by the alternatives under consideration. The descriptions shall be no longer than is necessary to understand the effects of the alternatives. Data and analyses in a statement shall be commensurate with the importance of the impact, with less important material summarized, consolidated, or simply referenced. Agencies shall avoid useless bulk in statements and shall concentrate effort and attention on important issues. Verbose descriptions of the affected environment are themselves no measure of the adequacy of an environmental impact statement.

Sec. 1502.16 Environmental consequences.

This section forms the scientific and analytic basis for the comparisons under Sec. 1502.14. It shall consolidate the discussions of those elements required by sections 102(2)(C)(i), (ii), (iv), and (v) of NEPA which are within the scope of the statement and as much of section 102(2)(C)(iii) as is necessary to support the comparisons. The discussion will include the environmental impacts of the alternatives including the proposed action, any adverse environmental effects which cannot be avoided should the proposal be implemented, the relationship between short-term uses of man's environment and the maintenance and enhancement of long-term productivity, and any irreversible or irretrievable commitments of resources which would be involved in the proposal should it be implemented. This section should not duplicate discussions in Sec. 1502.14. It shall include discussions of:

(a) Direct effects and their significance (Sec. 1508.8).

(b) Indirect effects and their significance (Sec. 1508.8).

(c) Possible conflicts between the proposed action and the objectives of Federal, regional, State, and local (and in the case of a reservation, Indian tribe) land use plans, policies and controls for the area concerned. (See Sec. 1506.2(d).)

(d) The environmental effects of alternatives including the proposed action. The comparisons under Sec. 1502.14 will be based on this discussion.

(e) Energy requirements and conservation potential of various alternatives and mitigation measures.

(f) Natural or depletable resource requirements and conservation potential of various alternatives and mitigation measures.

(g) Urban quality, historic and cultural resources, and the design of the built environment, including the reuse and conservation potential of various alternatives and mitigation measures.

(h) Means to mitigate adverse environmental impacts (if not fully covered under Sec. 1502.14(f)).

[43 FR 55994, Nov. 29, 1978; 44 FR 873, Jan. 3, 1979]

Sec. 1502.17 List of preparers.

The environmental impact statement shall list the names, together with their qualifications (expertise, experience, professional disciplines), of the persons who were primarily responsible for preparing the environmental impact statement or significant background papers, including basic components of the statement (Secs. 1502.6 and 1502.8). Where possible the persons who are responsible for a particular analysis, including analyses in background papers, shall be identified. Normally the list will not exceed two pages.

Sec. 1502.18 Appendix.

If an agency prepares an appendix to an environmental impact statement the appendix shall:

(a) Consist of material prepared in connection with an environmental impact statement (as distinct from material which is not so prepared and which is incorporated by reference (Sec. 1502.21)).

(b) Normally consist of material which substantiates any analysis fundamental to the impact statement.

(c) Normally be analytic and relevant to the decision to be made.

(d) Be circulated with the environmental impact statement or be readily available on request.

Sec. 1502.19 Circulation of the environmental impact statement.

Agencies shall circulate the entire draft and final environmental impact statements except for certain appendices as provided in Sec. 1502.18(d) and unchanged statements as provided in Sec. 1503.4(c). However, if the statement is unusually long, the agency may circulate the summary instead, except that the entire statement shall be furnished to:

(a) Any Federal agency which has jurisdiction by law or special expertise with respect to any environmental impact involved and any appropriate Federal, State or local agency authorized to develop and enforce environmental standards.

(b) The applicant, if any.

(c) Any person, organization, or agency requesting the entire environmental impact statement.

(d) In the case of a final environmental impact statement any person, organization, or agency which submitted substantive comments on the draft.

If the agency circulates the summary and thereafter receives a timely request for the entire statement and for additional time to comment, the time for that requestor only shall be extended by at least 15 days beyond the minimum period.

Sec. 1502.20 Tiering.

Agencies are encouraged to tier their environmental impact statements to eliminate repetitive discussions of the same issues and to focus on the actual issues ripe for decision at each level of environmental review (Sec. 1508.28). Whenever a broad environmental impact statement has been prepared (such as a program or policy statement) and a subsequent statement or environmental assessment is then prepared on an action included within the entire program or policy (such as a site specific action) the subsequent statement or environmental assessment need only summarize the issues discussed in the broader statement and incorporate discussions from the broader statement by reference and shall concentrate on the issues specific to the subsequent action. The subsequent document shall state where the earlier document is available. Tiering may also be appropriate for different stages of actions. (Section 1508.28).

Sec. 1502.21 Incorporation by reference.

Agencies shall incorporate material into an environmental impact statement by reference when the effect will be to cut down on bulk without impeding agency and public review of the action. The incorporated material shall be cited in the statement and its content briefly described. No material may be incorporated by reference unless it is reasonably available for inspection by potentially interested persons within the time allowed for comment. Material based on proprietary data which is itself not available for review and comment shall not be incorporated by reference.

Sec. 1502.22 Incomplete or unavailable information.

When an agency is evaluating reasonably foreseeable significant adverse effects on the human environment in an environmental impact statement and there is incomplete or unavailable information, the agency shall always make clear that such information is lacking.

(a) If the incomplete information relevant to reasonably foreseeable significant adverse impacts is essential to a reasoned choice among alternatives and the overall costs of obtaining it are not exorbitant, the agency shall include the information in the environmental impact statement.

(b) If the information relevant to reasonably foreseeable significant adverse impacts cannot be obtained because the overall costs of obtaining it are exorbitant or the means to obtain it are not known, the agency shall include within the environmental impact statement:

(1) A statement that such information is incomplete or unavailable; (2) a statement of the relevance of the incomplete or unavailable information to evaluating reasonably foreseeable significant adverse impacts on the human environment; (3) a summary of existing credible scientific evidence which is relevant to evaluating the reasonably foreseeable significant adverse impacts on the human environment, and (4) the agency's evaluation of such impacts based upon theoretical approaches or research methods generally accepted in the scientific community. For the purposes of this section, "reasonably foreseeable" includes impacts which have catastrophic consequences, even if their probability of occurrence is low, provided that the analysis of the impacts is supported by credible scientific evidence, is not based on pure conjecture, and is within the rule of reason.

(c) The amended regulation will be applicable to all environmental impact statements for which a Notice of Intent (40 CFR 1508.22) is published in the Federal Register on or after May 27, 1986. For environmental impact statements in progress, agencies may choose to comply with the requirements of either the original or amended regulation.

[51 FR 15625, Apr. 25, 1986]

Sec. 1502.23 Cost-benefit analysis.

If a cost-benefit analysis relevant to the choice among environmentally different alternatives is being considered for the proposed action, it shall be incorporated by reference or appended to the statement as an aid in evaluating the environmental consequences. To assess the adequacy of compliance with section 102(2)(B) of the Act the statement shall, when a cost-benefit analysis is prepared, discuss the relationship between that analysis and any analyses of unquantified environmental impacts, values, and amenities. For purposes of complying with the Act, the weighing of the merits and drawbacks of the various alternatives need not be displayed in a monetary cost-benefit analysis and should not be when there are important qualitative considerations. In any event, an environmental impact statement should at least indicate those considerations, including factors not related to environmental quality, which are likely to be relevant and important to a decision.

Sec. 1502.24 Methodology and scientific accuracy.

Agencies shall insure the professional integrity, including scientific integrity, of the discussions and analyses in environmental impact statements. They shall identify any methodologies used and shall make explicit reference by footnote to the scientific and other sources relied upon for conclusions in the statement. An agency may place discussion of methodology in an appendix.

Sec. 1502.25 Environmental review and consultation requirements.

(a) To the fullest extent possible, agencies shall prepare draft environmental impact statements concurrently with and integrated with environmental impact analyses and related surveys and studies required by the Fish and Wildlife Coordination Act (16 U.S.C. 661 et seq.), the National Historic Preservation Act of 1966 (16 U.S.C. 470 et seq.), the Endangered Species Act of 1973 (16 U.S.C. 1531 et seq.), and other environmental review laws and executive orders.

(b) The draft environmental impact statement shall list all Federal permits, licenses, and other entitlements which must be obtained in implementing the proposal. If it is uncertain whether a Federal permit, license, or other entitlement is necessary, the draft environmental impact statement shall so indicate.

PART 1503—COMMENTING

Sec.
1503.1   Inviting comments.
1503.2   Duty to comment.
1503.3   Specificity of comments.
1503.4   Response to comments.

Authority: NEPA, the Environmental Quality Improvement Act of 1970, as amended (42 U.S.C. 4371 et seq.), sec. 309 of the Clean Air Act, as amended (42 U.S.C. 7609), and E.O. 11514 (Mar. 5, 1970, as amended by E.O. 11991, May 24, 1977).

Source: 43 FR 55997, Nov. 29, 1978, unless otherwise noted.

Sec. 1503.1 Inviting comments.

(a) After preparing a draft environmental impact statement and before preparing a final environmental impact statement the agency shall:

(1) Obtain the comments of any Federal agency which has jurisdiction by law or special expertise with respect to any environmental impact involved or which is authorized to develop and enforce environmental standards.

(2) Request the comments of:

(i) Appropriate State and local agencies which are authorized to develop and enforce environmental standards;

(ii) Indian tribes, when the effects may be on a reservation; and

(iii) Any agency which has requested that it receive statements on actions of the kind proposed.

Office of Management and Budget Circular A-95 (Revised), through its system of clearinghouses, provides a means of securing the views of State and local environmental agencies. The clearinghouses may be used, by mutual agreement of the lead agency and the clearinghouse, for securing State and local reviews of the draft environmental impact statements.

(3) Request comments from the applicant, if any.

(4) Request comments from the public, affirmatively soliciting comments from those persons or organizations who may be interested or affected.

(b) An agency may request comments on a final environmental impact statement before the decision is finally made. In any case other agencies or persons may make comments before the final decision unless a different time is provided under Sec. 1506.10.

Sec. 1503.2 Duty to comment.

Federal agencies with jurisdiction by law or special expertise with respect to any environmental impact involved and agencies which are authorized to develop and enforce environmental standards shall comment on statements within their jurisdiction, expertise, or authority. Agencies shall comment within the time period specified for comment in Sec. 1506.10. A Federal agency may reply that it has no comment. If a cooperating agency is satisfied that its views are adequately reflected in the environmental impact statement, it should reply that it has no comment.

Sec. 1503.3 Specificity of comments.

(a) Comments on an environmental impact statement or on a proposed action shall be as specific as possible and may address either the adequacy of the statement or the merits of the alternatives discussed or both.

(b) When a commenting agency criticizes a lead agency's predictive methodology, the commenting agency should describe the alternative methodology which it prefers and why.

(c) A cooperating agency shall specify in its comments whether it needs additional information to fulfill other applicable environmental reviews or consultation requirements and what information it needs. In particular, it shall specify any additional information it needs to comment adequately on the draft statement's analysis of significant site-specific effects associated with the granting or approving by that cooperating agency of necessary Federal permits, licenses, or entitlements.

(d) When a cooperating agency with jurisdiction by law objects to or expresses reservations about the proposal on grounds of environmental impacts, the agency expressing the objection or reservation shall specify the mitigation measures it considers necessary to allow the agency to grant or approve applicable permit, license, or related requirements or concurrences.

Sec. 1503.4 Response to comments.

(a) An agency preparing a final environmental impact statement shall assess and consider comments both individually and collectively, and shall respond by one or more of the means listed below, stating its response in the final statement. Possible responses are to:

(1) Modify alternatives including the proposed action.

(2) Develop and evaluate alternatives not previously given serious consideration by the agency.

(3) Supplement, improve, or modify its analyses.

(4) Make factual corrections.

(5) Explain why the comments do not warrant further agency response, citing the sources, authorities, or reasons which support the agency's position and, if appropriate, indicate those circumstances which would trigger agency reappraisal or further response.

(b) All substantive comments received on the draft statement (or summaries thereof where the response has been exceptionally voluminous), should be attached to the final statement whether or not the comment is thought to merit individual discussion by the agency in the text of the statement.

(c) If changes in response to comments are minor and are confined to the responses described in paragraphs (a)(4) and (5) of this section, agencies may write them on errata sheets and attach them to the statement instead of rewriting the draft statement. In such cases only the comments, the responses, and the changes and not the final statement need be circulated (Sec. 1502.19). The entire document with a new cover sheet shall be filed as the final statement (Sec. 1506.9).

PART 1504—PREDECISION REFERRALS TO THE COUNCIL OF PROPOSED FEDERAL ACTIONS DETERMINED TO BE ENVIRONMENTALLY UNSATISFACTORY

Sec.
1504.1 Purpose
1504.2 Criteria for referral
1504.3 Procedure for referrals and response.

Authority: NEPA, the Environmental Quality Improvement Act of 1970, as amended (42 U.S.C. 4371 et seq.), sec. 309 of the Clean Air Act, as amended (42 U.S.C. 7609), and E.O. 11514 (Mar. 5, 1970, as amended by E.O. 11991, May 24, 1977).

Sec. 1504.1 Purpose.

(a) This part establishes procedures for referring to the Council Federal interagency disagreements concerning proposed major Federal actions that might cause unsatisfactory environmental effects. It provides means for early resolution of such disagreements.

(b) Under section 309 of the Clean Air Act (42 U.S.C. 7609), the Administrator of the Environmental Protection Agency is directed to review and comment publicly on the environmental impacts of Federal activities, including actions for which environmental impact statements are prepared. If after this review the Administrator determines that the matter is "unsatisfactory from the standpoint of public health or welfare or environmental quality," section 309 directs that the matter be referred to the Council (hereafter "environmental referrals").

(c) Under section 102(2)(C) of the Act other Federal agencies may make similar reviews of environmental impact statements, including judgments on the acceptability of anticipated environmental impacts. These reviews must be made available to the President, the Council and the public.

Sec. 1504.2 Criteria for referral.

Environmental referrals should be made to the Council only after concerted, timely (as early as possible in the process), but unsuccessful attempts to resolve differences with the lead agency. In determining what environmental objections to the matter are appropriate to refer to the Council, an agency should weigh potential adverse environmental impacts, considering:

(a) Possible violation of national environmental standards or policies.

(b) Severity.

(c) Geographical scope.

(d) Duration.

(e) Importance as precedents.

(f) Availability of environmentally preferable alternatives.

Sec. 1504.3 Procedure for referrals and response.

(a) A Federal agency making the referral to the Council shall:

(1) Advise the lead agency at the earliest possible time that it intends to refer a matter to the Council unless a satisfactory agreement is reached.

(2) Include such advice in the referring agency's comments on the draft environmental impact statement, except when the statement does not contain adequate information to permit an assessment of the matter's environmental acceptability.

(3) Identify any essential information that is lacking and request that it be made available at the earliest possible time.

(4) Send copies of such advice to the Council.

(b) The referring agency shall deliver its referral to the Council not later than twenty-five (25) days after the final environmental impact statement has been made available to the Environmental Protection Agency, commenting agencies, and the public. Except when an extension of this period has been granted by the lead agency, the Council will not accept a referral after that date.

(c) The referral shall consist of:

(1) A copy of the letter signed by the head of the referring agency and delivered to the lead agency informing the lead agency of the referral and the reasons for it, and requesting that no action be taken to implement the matter until the Council acts upon the referral. The letter shall include a copy of the statement referred to in (c)(2) of this section.

(2) A statement supported by factual evidence leading to the conclusion that the matter is unsatisfactory from the standpoint of public health or welfare or environmental quality. The statement shall:

(i) Identify any material facts in controversy and incorporate (by reference if appropriate) agreed upon facts,

(ii) Identify any existing environmental requirements or policies which would be violated by the matter,

(iii) Present the reasons why the referring agency believes the matter is environmentally unsatisfactory,

(iv) Contain a finding by the agency

whether the issue raised is of national importance because of the threat to national environmental resources or policies or for some other reason,

(v) Review the steps taken by the referring agency to bring its concerns to the attention of the lead agency at the earliest possible time, and

(vi) Give the referring agency's recommendations as to what mitigation alternative, further study, or other course of action (including abandonment of the matter) are necessary to remedy the situation.

(d) Not later than twenty-five (25) days after the referral to the Council the lead agency may deliver a response to the Council, and the referring agency. If the lead agency requests more time and gives assurance that the matter will not go forward in the interim, the Council may grant an extension. The response shall:

(1) Address fully the issues raised in the referral.

(2) Be supported by evidence.

(3) Give the lead agency's response to the referring agency's recommendations.

(e) Interested persons (including the applicant) may deliver their views in writing to the Council. Views in support of the referral should be delivered not later than the referral. Views in support of the response shall be delivered not later than the response.

(f) Not later than twenty-five (25) days after receipt of both the referral and any response or upon being informed that there will be no response (unless the lead agency agrees to a longer time), the Council may take one or more of the following actions:

(1) Conclude that the process of referral and response has successfully resolved the problem.

(2) Initiate discussions with the agencies with the objective of mediation with referring and lead agencies.

(3) Hold public meetings or hearings to obtain additional views and information.

(4) Determine that the issue is not one of national importance and request the referring and lead agencies to pursue their decision process.

(5) Determine that the issue should be further negotiated by the referring and lead agencies and is not appropriate for Council consideration until one or more heads of agencies report to the Council that the agencies' disagreements are irreconcilable.

(6) Publish its findings and recommendations (including where appropriate a finding that the submitted evidence does not support the position of an agency).

(7) When appropriate, submit the referral and the response together with the Council's recommendation to the President for action.

(g) The Council shall take no longer than 60 days to complete the actions specified in paragraph (f)(2), (3), or (5) of this section.

(h) When the referral involves an action required by statute to be determined on the record after opportunity for agency hearing, the referral shall be conducted in a manner consistent with 5 U.S.C. 557(d) (Administrative Procedure Act).

[43 FR 55998, Nov. 29, 1978; 44 FR 873, Jan. 3, 1979]

PART 1505—NEPA AND AGENCY DECISIONMAKING

Sec.
1505.1 Agency decisionmaking procedures.
1505.2 Record of decision in cases requiring environmental impact statements.
1505.3 Implementing the decision.

Authority: NEPA, the Environmental Quality Improvement Act of 1970, as amended (42 U.S.C. 4371 et seq.), sec. 309 of the Clean Air Act, as amended (42 U.S.C. 7609), and E.O. 11514 (Mar. 5, 1970, as amended by E.O. 11991, May 24, 1977).

Source: 43 FR 55999, Nov. 29, 1978, unless otherwise noted.

Sec. 1505.1 Agency decisionmaking procedures.

Agencies shall adopt procedures (Sec. 1507.3) to ensure that decisions are made in accordance with the policies and purposes of the Act. Such procedures shall include but not be limited to:

(a) Implementing procedures under section 102(2) to achieve the requirements of sections 101 and 102(1).

(b) Designating the major decision points for the agency's principal programs likely to have a significant effect on the human environment and assuring that the NEPA process corresponds with them.

(c) Requiring that relevant environmental documents, comments, and responses be part of the record in formal rulemaking or adjudicatory proceedings.

(d) Requiring that relevant environmental documents, comments, and responses accompany the proposal through existing agency review processes so that agency officials use the statement in making decisions.

(e) Requiring that the alternatives considered by the decisionmaker are encompassed by the range of alternatives discussed in the relevant environmental documents and that the decisionmaker consider the alternatives described in the environmental impact statement. If another decision document accompanies the relevant environmental documents to the decisionmaker, agencies are encouraged to make available to the public before the decision is made any part of that document that relates to the comparison of alternatives.

Sec. 1505.2 Record of decision in cases requiring environmental impact statements.

At the time of its decision (Sec. 1506.10) or, if appropriate, its recommendation to Congress, each agency shall prepare a concise public record of decision. The record, which may be integrated into any other record prepared by the agency, including that required by OMB Circular A-95 (Revised), part I, sections 6(c) and (d), and Part II, section 5(b)(4), shall:

(a) State what the decision was.

(b) Identify all alternatives considered by the agency in reaching its decision, specifying the alternative or alternatives which were considered to be environmentally preferable. An agency may discuss preferences among alternatives based on relevant factors including economic and technical considerations and agency statutory missions. An agency shall identify and discuss all such factors including any essential considerations of national policy which were balanced by the agency in making its decision and state how those considerations entered into its decision.

(c) State whether all practicable means to avoid or minimize environmental harm from the alternative selected have been adopted, and if not, why they were not. A monitoring and enforcement program shall be adopted and summarized where applicable for any mitigation.

Sec. 1505.3 Implementing the decision.

Agencies may provide for monitoring to assure that their decisions are carried out and should do so in important cases. Mitigation (Sec. 1505.2(c)) and other conditions established in the environmental impact statement or during its review and committed as part of the decision shall be implemented by the lead agency or other appropriate consenting agency. The lead agency shall:

(a) Include appropriate conditions in grants, permits or other approvals.

(b) Condition funding of actions on mitigation.

(c) Upon request, inform cooperating or commenting agencies on progress in carrying out mitigation measures which they have proposed and which were adopted by the agency making the decision.

(d) Upon request, make available to the public the results of relevant monitoring.

PART 1506—OTHER REQUIREMENTS OF NEPA

Sec.
1506.1 Limitations on actions during NEPA process
1506.2 Elimination of duplication with State and local procedures
1506.3 Adoption
1506.4 Combining documents
1506.5 Agency responsibility
1506.6 Public involvement
1506.7 Further guidance
1506.8 Proposals for legislation
1506.9 Filing requirements
1506.10 Timing of agency action
1506.11 Emergencies
1506.12 Effective date

Authority: NEPA, the Environmental Quality Improvement Act of 1970, as amended (42 U.S.C. 4371 et seq.), sec. 309 of the Clean Air Act, as amended (42 U.S.C. 7609), and E.O. 11514 (Mar. 5, 1970, as amended by E.O. 11991, May 24, 1977).

Source: 43 FR 56000, Nov. 29, 1978, unless otherwise noted.

Sec. 1506.1 Limitations on actions during NEPA process.

(a) Until an agency issues a record of decision as provided in Sec. 1505.2 (except as provided in paragraph (c) of this section), no action concerning the proposal shall be taken which would:

(1) Have an adverse environmental impact; or

(2) Limit the choice of reasonable alternatives.

(b) If any agency is considering an application from a non-Federal entity, and is aware that the applicant is about to take an action within the agency's jurisdiction that would meet either of the criteria in paragraph (a) of this section, then the agency shall promptly notify the applicant that the agency will take appropriate action to insure that the objectives and procedures of NEPA are achieved.

(c) While work on a required program environmental impact statement is in progress and the action is not covered by an existing program statement, agencies shall not undertake in the interim any major Federal action covered by the program which may significantly affect the quality of the human environment unless such action:

(1) Is justified independently of the program;

(2) Is itself accompanied by an adequate environmental impact statement; and

(3) Will not prejudice the ultimate decision on the program. Interim action prejudices the ultimate decision on the program when it tends to determine subsequent development or limit alternatives.

(d) This section does not preclude development by applicants of plans or designs or performance of other work necessary to support an application for Federal, State or local permits or assistance. Nothing in this section shall preclude Rural Electrification Administration approval of minimal expenditures not affecting the environment (e.g. long leadtime equipment and purchase options) made by non-governmental entities seeking loan guarantees from the Administration.

Sec. 1506.2 Elimination of duplication with State and local procedures.

(a) Agencies authorized by law to cooperate with State agencies of statewide jurisdiction pursuant to section 102(2)(D) of the Act may do so.

(b) Agencies shall cooperate with State and local agencies to the fullest extent possible to reduce duplication between NEPA and State and local requirements, unless the agencies are specifically barred from doing so by some other law. Except for cases covered by paragraph (a) of this section, such cooperation shall to the fullest extent possible include:

(1) Joint planning processes.

(2) Joint environmental research and studies.

(3) Joint public hearings (except where otherwise provided by statute).

(4) Joint environmental assessments.

(c) Agencies shall cooperate with State and local agencies to the fullest extent possible to reduce duplication between NEPA and comparable State and local requirements, unless the agencies are specifically barred from doing so by some other law. Except for cases covered by paragraph (a) of this section, such cooperation shall to the fullest extent possible include joint environmental impact statements. In such cases one or more Federal agencies and one or more State or local agencies shall be joint lead agencies. Where State laws or local ordinances have environmental impact statement requirements in addition to but not in conflict with those in NEPA, Federal agencies shall cooperate in fulfilling these requirements as well as those of Federal laws so that one document will comply with all applicable laws.

(d) To better integrate environmental impact statements into State or local planning processes, statements shall discuss any inconsistency of a proposed action with any approved State or local plan and laws (whether or not federally sanctioned). Where an inconsistency exists, the statement should describe the extent to which the agency would reconcile its proposed action with the plan or law.

Sec. 1506.3 Adoption.

(a) An agency may adopt a Federal draft or final environmental impact statement or portion thereof provided that the statement or portion thereof meets the standards for an adequate statement under these regulations.

(b) If the actions covered by the original environmental impact statement and the proposed action are substantially the same, the agency adopting another agency's statement is not required to recirculate it except as a final statement. Otherwise the adopting agency shall treat the statement as a draft and recirculate it (except as provided in paragraph (c) of this section).

(c) A cooperating agency may adopt without recirculating the environmental impact statement of a lead agency when, after an independent review of the statement, the cooperating agency concludes that its comments and suggestions have been satisfied.

(d) When an agency adopts a statement which is not final within the agency that prepared it, or when the action it assesses is the subject of a referral under Part 1504, or when the statement's adequacy is the subject of a judicial action which is not final, the agency shall so specify.

Sec. 1506.4 Combining documents.

Any environmental document in compliance with NEPA may be combined with any other agency document to reduce duplication and paperwork.

Sec. 1506.5 Agency responsibility.

(a) Information. If an agency requires an applicant to submit environmental information for possible use by the agency in preparing an environmental impact statement, then the agency should assist the applicant by outlining the types of information required. The agency shall independently evaluate the information submitted and shall be responsible for its accuracy. If the agency chooses to use the information submitted by the applicant in the environmental impact statement, either directly or by reference, then the names of the persons responsible for the independent evaluation shall be included in the list of preparers (Sec. 1502.17). It is the intent of this paragraph that acceptable work not be redone, but that it be verified by the agency.

(b) Environmental assessments. If an agency permits an applicant to prepare an environmental assessment, the agency, besides fulfilling the requirements of paragraph (a) of this section, shall make its own evaluation of the environmental issues and take responsibility for the scope and content of the environmental assessment.

(c) Environmental impact statements. Except as provided in Secs. 1506.2 and 1506.3 any environmental impact statement prepared pursuant to the requirements of NEPA shall be prepared directly by or by a contractor selected by the lead agency or where appropriate under Sec. 1501.6(b), a cooperating agency. It is the intent of these regulations that the contractor be chosen solely by the lead agency, or by the lead agency in cooperation with cooperating agencies, or where appropriate by a cooperating agency to avoid any conflict of interest. Contractors shall execute a disclosure statement prepared by the lead agency, or where appropriate the cooperating agency, specifying that they have no financial or other interest in the outcome of the project. If the document is prepared by contract, the responsible Federal official shall furnish guidance and participate in the preparation and shall independently evaluate the statement prior to its approval and take responsibility for its scope and contents. Nothing in this section is intended to prohibit any agency from requesting any person to submit information to it or to prohibit any person from submitting information to any agency.

Sec. 1506.6 Public involvement.

Agencies shall:

(a) Make diligent efforts to involve the public in preparing and implementing their NEPA procedures.

(b) Provide public notice of NEPA-related hearings, public meetings, and the availability of environmental documents so as to inform those persons and agencies who may be interested or affected.

In all cases the agency shall mail notice to those who have requested it on an individual action.

In the case of an action with effects of national concern notice shall include publication in the Federal Register and notice by mail to national organizations reasonably expected to be interested in the matter and may include listing in the 102 Monitor. An agency engaged in rulemaking may provide notice by mail to national organizations who have requested that notice regularly be provided. Agencies shall maintain a list of such organizations.

In the case of an action with effects primarily of local concern the notice may include:

(i) Notice to State and areawide clearinghouses pursuant to OMB Circular A-95 (Revised).

(ii) Notice to Indian tribes when effects may occur on reservations.

(iii) Following the affected State's public notice procedures for comparable actions.

(iv) Publication in local newspapers (in papers of general circulation rather than legal papers).

(v) Notice through other local media.

(vi) Notice to potentially interested community organizations including small business associations.

(vii) Publication in newsletters that may be expected to reach potentially interested persons.

(viii) Direct mailing to owners and occupants of nearby or affected property.

(ix) Posting of notice on and off site in the area where the action is to be located.

(c) Hold or sponsor public hearings or public meetings whenever appropriate or in accordance with statutory requirements applicable to the agency. Criteria shall include whether there is:

(1) Substantial environmental controversy concerning the proposed action or substantial interest in holding the hearing.

(2) A request for a hearing by another agency with jurisdiction over the action supported by reasons why a hearing will be helpful. If a draft environmental impact statement is to be considered at a public hearing, the agency should make the statement available to the public at least 15 days in advance (unless the purpose of the hearing is to provide information for the draft environmental impact statement).

(d) Solicit appropriate information from the public.

(e) Explain in its procedures where interested persons can get information or status reports on environmental impact statements and other elements of the NEPA process.

(f) Make environmental impact statements, the comments received, and any underlying documents available to the public pursuant to the provisions of the Freedom of Information Act (5 U.S.C. 552), without regard to the exclusion for interagency memoranda where such memoranda transmit comments of Federal agencies on the environmental impact of the proposed action. Materials to be made available to the public shall be provided to the public without charge to the extent practicable, or at a fee which is not more than the actual costs of reproducing copies required to be sent to other Federal agencies, including the Council.

Sec. 1506.7 Further guidance.

The Council may provide further guidance concerning NEPA and its procedures including:

(a) A handbook which the Council may supplement from time to time, which shall in plain language provide guidance and instructions concerning the application of NEPA and these regulations.

(b) Publication of the Council's Memoranda to Heads of Agencies.

(c) In conjunction with the Environmental Protection Agency and the publication of the 102 Monitor, notice of:

(1) Research activities;

(2) Meetings and conferences related to NEPA; and

(3) Successful and innovative procedures used by agencies to implement NEPA.

Sec. 1506.8 Proposals for legislation.

(a) The NEPA process for proposals for legislation (Sec. 1508.17) significantly affecting the quality of the human environment shall be integrated with the legislative process of the Congress. A legislative environmental impact statement is the detailed statement required by law to be included in a recommendation or report on a legislative proposal to Congress. A legislative environmental impact statement shall be considered part of the formal transmittal of a legislative proposal to Congress; however, it may be transmitted to Congress up to 30 days later in order to allow time for completion of an accurate statement which can serve as the basis for public and Congressional debate. The statement must be available in time for Congressional hearings and deliberations.

(b) Preparation of a legislative environmental impact statement shall conform to the requirements of these regulations except as follows:

(1) There need not be a scoping process.

(2) The legislative statement shall be prepared in the same manner as a draft statement, but shall be considered the "detailed statement" required by statute; Provided, That when any of the following conditions exist both the draft and final environmental impact statement on the legislative proposal shall be prepared and circulated as provided by Secs. 1503.1 and 1506.10.

(i) A Congressional Committee with jurisdiction over the proposal has a rule requiring both draft and final environmental impact statements.

(ii) The proposal results from a study process required by statute (such as those required by the Wild and Scenic Rivers Act (16 U.S.C. 1271 et seq.) and the Wilderness Act (16 U.S.C. 1131 et seq.)).

(iii) Legislative approval is sought for Federal or federally assisted construction or other projects which the agency recommends be located at specific geographic locations. For proposals requiring an environmental impact statement for the acquisition of space by the General Services Administration, a draft statement shall accompany the Prospectus or the 11(b) Report of Building Project Surveys to the Congress, and a final statement shall be completed before site acquisition.

(iv) The agency decides to prepare draft and final statements.

(c) Comments on the legislative statement shall be given to the lead agency which shall forward them along with its own responses to the Congressional committees with jurisdiction.

Sec. 1506.9 Filing requirements.

Environmental impact statements together with comments and responses shall be filed with the Environmental Protection Agency, attention Office of Federal Activities (A-104), 401 M Street SW., Washington, DC 20460. Statements shall be filed with EPA no earlier than they are also transmitted to commenting agencies and made available to the public. EPA shall deliver one copy of each statement to the Council, which shall satisfy the requirement of availability to the President. EPA may issue guidelines to agencies to implement its responsibilities under this section and Sec. 1506.10.

Sec. 1506.10 Timing of agency action.

(a) The Environmental Protection Agency shall publish a notice in the Federal Register each week of the environmental impact statements filed during the preceding week. The minimum time periods set forth in this section shall be calculated from the date of publication of this notice.

(b) No decision on the proposed action shall be made or recorded under Sec. 1505.2 by a Federal agency until the later of the following dates:

Ninety (90) days after publication of the notice described above in paragraph (a) of this section for a draft environmental impact statement.

Thirty (30) days after publication of the notice described above in paragraph (a) of this section for a final environmental impact statement. An exception to the rules on timing may be made in the case of an agency decision which is subject to a formal internal appeal. Some agencies have a formally established appeal process which allows other agencies or the public to take appeals on a decision and make their views known, after publication of the final environmental impact statement. In such cases, where a real opportunity exists to alter the decision, the decision may be made and recorded at the same time the environmental impact statement is published.

This means that the period for appeal of the decision and the 30-day period prescribed in paragraph (b)(2) of this section may run concurrently. In such cases the environmental impact statement shall explain the timing and the public's right of appeal. An agency engaged in rulemaking under the Administrative Procedure Act or other statute for the purpose of protecting the public health or safety, may waive the time period in paragraph (b)(2) of this section and publish a decision on the final rule simultaneously with publication of the notice of the availability of the final environmental impact statement as described in paragraph (a) of this section.

(c) If the final environmental impact statement is filed within ninety (90) days after a draft environmental impact statement is filed with the Environmental Protection Agency, the minimum thirty (30) day period and the minimum ninety (90) day period may run concurrently. However, subject to paragraph (d) of this section agencies shall allow not less than 45 days for comments on draft statements.

(d) The lead agency may extend prescribed periods. The Environmental Protection Agency may upon a showing by the lead agency of compelling reasons of national policy reduce the prescribed periods and may upon a showing by any other Federal agency of compelling reasons of national policy also extend prescribed periods, but only after consultation with the lead agency. (Also see Sec. 1507.3(d).) Failure to file timely comments shall not be a sufficient reason for extending a period. If the lead agency does not concur with the extension of time, EPA may not extend it for more than 30 days. When the Environmental Protection Agency reduces or extends any period of time it shall notify the Council.

[43 FR 56000, Nov. 29, 1978; 44 FR 874, Jan. 3, 1979]

Sec. 1506.11 Emergencies.

Where emergency circumstances make it necessary to take an action with significant environmental impact without observing the provisions of these regulations, the Federal agency taking the action should consult with the Council about alternative arrangements. Agencies and the Council will limit such arrangements to actions necessary to control the immediate impacts of the emergency. Other actions remain subject to NEPA review.

Sec. 1506.12 Effective date.

The effective date of these regulations is July 30, 1979, except that for agencies that administer programs that qualify under section 102(2)(D) of the Act or under section 104(h) of the Housing and Community Development Act of 1974 an additional four months shall be allowed for the State or local agencies to adopt their implementing procedures.

(a) These regulations shall apply to the fullest extent practicable to ongoing activities and environmental documents begun before the effective date. These regulations do not apply to an environmental impact statement or supplement if the draft statement was filed before the effective date of these regulations. No completed environmental documents need be redone by reasons of these regulations. Until these regulations are applicable, the Council's guidelines published in the Federal Register of August 1, 1973, shall continue to be applicable. In cases where these regulations are applicable the guidelines are superseded. However, nothing shall prevent an agency from proceeding under these regulations at an earlier time.

(b) NEPA shall continue to be applicable to actions begun before January 1, 1970, to the fullest extent possible.

PART 1507—AGENCY COMPLIANCE

Sec.
1507.1   Compliance
1507.2   Agency capability to comply
1507.3   Agency procedures

Authority: NEPA, the Environmental Quality Improvement Act of 1970, as amended (42 U.S.C. 4371 et seq.), sec. 309 of the Clean Air Act, as amended (42 U.S.C. 7609), and E.O. 11514 (Mar. 5, 1970, as amended by E.O. 11991, May 24, 1977).

Source: 43 FR 56002, Nov. 29, 1978, unless otherwise noted.

Sec. 1507.1 Compliance.

All agencies of the Federal Government shall comply with these regulations. It is the intent of these regulations to allow each agency flexibility in adapting its implementing procedures authorized by Sec. 1507.3 to the requirements of other applicable laws.

Sec. 1507.2 Agency capability to comply.

Each agency shall be capable (in terms of personnel and other resources) of complying with the requirements enumerated below. Such compliance may include use of other's resources, but the using agency shall itself have sufficient capability to evaluate what others do for it. Agencies shall:

(a) Fulfill the requirements of section 102(2)(A) of the Act to utilize a systematic, interdisciplinary approach which will insure the integrated use of the natural and social sciences and the environmental design arts in planning and in decisionmaking which may have an impact on the human environment. Agencies shall designate a person to be responsible for overall review of agency NEPA compliance.

(b) Identify methods and procedures required by section 102(2)(B) to insure that presently unquantified environmental amenities and values may be given appropriate consideration.

(c) Prepare adequate environmental impact statements pursuant to section 102(2)(C) and comment on statements in the areas where the agency has jurisdiction by law or special expertise or is authorized to develop and enforce environmental standards.

(d) Study, develop, and describe alternatives to recommended courses of action in any proposal which involves unresolved conflicts concerning alternative uses of available resources. This requirement of section 102(2)(E) extends to all such proposals, not just the more limited scope of section 102(2)(C)(iii) where the discussion of alternatives is confined to impact statements.

(e) Comply with the requirements of section 102(2)(H) that the agency initiate and utilize ecological information in the planning and development of resource-oriented projects.

(f) Fulfill the requirements of sections 102(2)(F), 102(2)(G), and 102(2)(I), of the Act and of Executive Order 11514, Protection and Enhancement of Environmental Quality, Sec. 2.

Sec. 1507.3 Agency procedures.

(a) Not later than eight months after publication of these regulations as finally adopted in the Federal Register, or five months after the establishment of an agency, whichever shall come later, each agency shall as necessary adopt procedures to supplement these regulations. When the agency is a department, major subunits are encouraged (with the consent of the department) to adopt their own procedures. Such procedures shall not paraphrase these regulations. They shall confine themselves to implementing procedures. Each agency shall consult with the Council while developing its procedures and before publishing them in the Federal Register for comment. Agencies with similar programs should consult with each other and the Council to coordinate their procedures, especially for programs requesting similar information from applicants. The procedures shall be adopted only after an opportunity for public review and after review by the Council for conformity with the Act and these regulations. The Council shall complete its review within 30 days. Once in effect they shall be filed with the Council and made readily available to the public. Agencies are encouraged to publish explanatory guidance for these regulations and their own procedures. Agencies shall continue to review their policies and procedures and in consultation with the Council to revise them as necessary to ensure full compliance with the purposes and provisions of the Act.

(b) Agency procedures shall comply with these regulations except where compliance would be inconsistent with statutory requirements and shall include:

Those procedures required by Secs. 1501.2(d), 1502.9(c)(3), 1505.1, 1506.6(e), and 1508.4.

Specific criteria for and identification of those typical classes of action:

(i) Which normally do require environmental impact statements.

(ii) Which normally do not require either an environmental impact statement or an environmental assessment (categorical exclusions (Sec. 1508.4)).

(iii) Which normally require environmental assessments but not necessarily environmental impact statements.

(c) Agency procedures may include specific criteria for providing limited exceptions to the provisions of these regulations for classified proposals. They are proposed actions which are specifically authorized under criteria established by an Executive Order or statute to be kept secret in the interest of national defense or foreign policy and are in fact properly classified pursuant to such Executive Order or statute. Environmental assessments and environmental impact statements which address classified proposals may be safeguarded and restricted from public dissemination in accordance with agencies' own regulations applicable to classified information. These documents may be organized so that classified portions can be included as annexes, in order that the unclassified portions can be made available to the public.

(d) Agency procedures may provide for periods of time other than those presented in Sec. 1506.10 when necessary to comply with other specific statutory requirements.

(e) Agency procedures may provide that where there is a lengthy period between the agency's decision to prepare an environmental impact statement and the time of actual preparation, the notice of intent required by Sec. 1501.7 may be published at a reasonable time in advance of preparation of the draft statement.

PART 1508—TERMINOLOGY AND INDEX

Sec.
1508.1   Terminology
1508.2   Act
1508.3   Affecting
1508.4   Categorical exclusion
1508.5   Cooperating agency
1508.6   Council
1508.7   Cumulative impact
1508.8   Effects
1508.9   Environmental assessment
1508.10 Environmental document
1508.11 Environmental impact statement
1508.12 Federal agency
1508.13 Finding of no significant impact
1508.14 Human environment
1508.15 Jurisdiction by law
1508.16 Lead agency
1508.17 Legislation
1508.18 Major Federal action
1508.19 Matter
1508.20 Mitigation
1508.21 NEPA process
1508.22 Notice of intent
1508.23 Proposal
1508.24 Referring agency
1508.25 Scope
1508.26 Special expertise
1508.27 Significantly
1508.28 Tiering

Authority: NEPA, the Environmental Quality Improvement Act of 1970, as amended (42 U.S.C. 4371 et seq.), sec. 309 of the Clean Air Act, as amended (42 U.S.C. 7609), and E.O. 11514 (Mar. 5, 1970, as amended by E.O. 11991, May 24, 1977).

Source: 43 FR 56003, Nov. 29, 1978, unless otherwise noted.

Sec. 1508.1 Terminology.

The terminology of this part shall be uniform throughout the Federal Government.

Sec. 1508.2 Act.

"Act" means the National Environmental Policy Act, as amended (42 U.S.C. 4321, et seq.) which is also referred to as "NEPA."

Sec. 1508.3 Affecting.

"Affecting" means will or may have an effect on.

Sec. 1508.4 Categorical exclusion.

"Categorical exclusion" means a category of actions which do not individually or cumulatively have a significant effect on the human environment and which have been found to have no such effect in procedures adopted by a Federal agency in implementation of these regulations (Sec. 1507.3) and for which, therefore, neither an environmental assessment nor an environmental impact statement is required. An agency may decide in its procedures or otherwise, to prepare environmental assessments for the reasons stated in Sec. 1508.9 even though it is not required to do so. Any procedures under this section shall provide for extraordinary circumstances in which a normally excluded action may have a significant environmental effect.

Sec. 1508.5 Cooperating agency.

"Cooperating agency" means any Federal agency other than a lead agency which has jurisdiction by law or special expertise with respect to any environmental impact involved in a proposal (or a reasonable alternative) for legislation or other major Federal action significantly affecting the quality of the human environment. The selection and responsibilities of a cooperating agency are described in Sec. 1501.6. A State or local agency of similar qualifications or, when the effects are on a reservation, an Indian Tribe, may by agreement with the lead agency become a cooperating agency.

Sec. 1508.6 Council.

"Council" means the Council on Environmental Quality established by Title II of the Act.

Sec. 1508.7 Cumulative impact.

"Cumulative impact" is the impact on the environment which results from the incremental impact of the action when added to other past, present, and reasonably foreseeable future actions regardless of what agency (Federal or non-Federal) or person undertakes such other actions. Cumulative impacts can result from individually minor but collectively significant actions taking place over a period of time.

Sec. 1508.8 Effects.

"Effects" include:

(a) Direct effects, which are caused by the action and occur at the same time and place.

(b) Indirect effects, which are caused by the action and are later in time or farther removed in distance, but are still reasonably foreseeable. Indirect effects may include growth inducing effects and other effects related to induced changes in the pattern of land use, population density or growth rate, and related effects on air and water and other natural systems, including ecosystems.

Effects and impacts as used in these regulations are synonymous. Effects includes ecological (such as the effects on natural resources and on the components, structures, and functioning of affected ecosystems), aesthetic, historic, cultural, economic, social, or health, whether direct, indirect, or cumulative. Effects may also include those resulting from actions which may have both beneficial and detrimental effects, even if on balance the agency believes that the effect will be beneficial.

Sec. 1508.9 Environmental assessment.

"Environmental assessment":

(a) Means a concise public document for

which a Federal agency is responsible that serves to:

(1) Briefly provide sufficient evidence and analysis for determining whether to prepare an environmental impact statement or a finding of no significant impact.

(2) Aid an agency's compliance with the Act when no environmental impact statement is necessary.

(3) Facilitate preparation of a statement when one is necessary.

(b) Shall include brief discussions of the need for the proposal, of alternatives as required by section 102(2)(E), of the environmental impacts of the proposed action and alternatives, and a listing of agencies and persons consulted.

Sec. 1508.10 Environmental document.

"Environmental document" includes the documents specified in Sec. 1508.9 (environmental assessment), Sec. 1508.11 (environmental impact statement), Sec. 1508.13 (finding of no significant impact), and Sec. 1508.22 (notice of intent).

Sec. 1508.11 Environmental impact statement.

"Environmental impact statement" means a detailed written statement as required by section 102(2)(C) of the Act.

Sec. 1508.12 Federal agency.

"Federal agency" means all agencies of the Federal Government. It does not mean the Congress, the Judiciary, or the President, including the performance of staff functions for the President in his Executive Office. It also includes for purposes of these regulations States and units of general local government and Indian tribes assuming NEPA responsibilities under section 104(h) of the Housing and Community Development Act of 1974.

Sec. 1508.13 Finding of no significant impact.

"Finding of no significant impact" means a document by a Federal agency briefly presenting the reasons why an action, not otherwise excluded (Sec. 1508.4), will not have a significant effect on the human environment and for which an environmental impact statement therefore will not be prepared. It shall include the environmental assessment or a summary of it and shall note any other environmental documents related to it (Sec. 1501.7(a)(5)). If the assessment is included, the finding need not repeat any of the discussion in the assessment but may incorporate it by reference.

Sec. 1508.14 Human environment.

"Human environment" shall be interpreted comprehensively to include the natural and physical environment and the relationship of people with that environment. (See the definition of "effects" (Sec. 1508.8).) This means that economic or social effects are not intended by themselves to require preparation of an environmental impact statement. When an environmental impact statement is prepared and economic or social and natural or physical environmental effects are interrelated, then the environmental impact statement will discuss all of these effects on the human environment.

Sec. 1508.15 Jurisdiction by law.

"Jurisdiction by law" means agency authority to approve, veto, or finance all or part of the proposal.

Sec. 1508.16 Lead agency.

"Lead agency" means the agency or agencies preparing or having taken primary responsibility for preparing the environmental impact statement.

Sec. 1508.17 Legislation.

"Legislation" includes a bill or legislative proposal to Congress developed by or with the significant cooperation and support of a Federal agency, but does not include requests for appropriations. The test for significant cooperation is whether the proposal is in fact predominantly that of the agency rather than another source. Drafting does not by itself constitute significant cooperation. Proposals for legislation include requests for ratification of treaties. Only the agency which has primary responsibility for the subject matter involved will prepare a legislative environmental impact statement.

Sec. 1508.18 Major Federal action.

"Major Federal action" includes actions with effects that may be major and which are potentially subject to Federal control and responsibility. Major reinforces but does not have a meaning independent of significantly (Sec. 1508.27). Actions include the circumstance where the responsible officials fail to act and that failure to act is reviewable by courts or administrative tribunals under the Administrative Procedure Act or other applicable law as agency action.

(a) Actions include new and continuing activities, including projects and programs entirely or partly financed, assisted, conducted, regulated, or approved by federal agencies; new or revised agency rules, regulations, plans, policies, or procedures; and legislative proposals (Secs. 1506.8, 1508.17). Actions do not include funding assistance solely in the form of general revenue sharing funds, distributed under the State and Local Fiscal Assistance Act of 1972, 31 U.S.C. 1221 et seq., with no Federal agency control over the subsequent use of such funds. Actions do not include bringing judicial or administrative civil or criminal enforcement actions.

(b) Federal actions tend to fall within one of the following categories:

(1) Adoption of official policy, such as rules, regulations, and interpretations adopted pursuant to the Administrative Procedure Act, 5 U.S.C. 551 et seq.; treaties and international conventions or agreements; formal documents establishing an agency's policies which will result in or substantially alter agency programs.

(2) Adoption of formal plans, such as official documents prepared or approved by federal agencies which guide or prescribe alternative uses of Federal resources, upon which future agency actions will be based.

(3) Adoption of programs, such as a group of concerted actions to implement a specific policy or plan; systematic and connected agency decisions allocating agency resources to implement a specific statutory program or executive directive.

(4) Approval of specific projects, such as construction or management activities located in a defined geographic area. Projects include actions approved by permit or other regulatory decision as well as federal and federally assisted activities.

Sec. 1508.19 Matter.

"Matter" includes for purposes of Part 1504: (a) With respect to the Environmental Protection Agency, any proposed legislation, project, action or regulation as those terms are used in section 309(a) of the Clean Air Act (42 U.S.C. 7609). (b) With respect to all other agencies, any proposed major federal action to which section 102(2)(C) of NEPA applies.

Sec. 1508.20 Mitigation.

"Mitigation" includes:

(a) Avoiding the impact altogether by not taking a certain action or parts of an action.

(b) Minimizing impacts by limiting the degree or magnitude of the action and its implementation.

(c) Rectifying the impact by repairing, rehabilitating, or restoring the affected environment.

(d) Reducing or eliminating the impact over time by preservation and maintenance operations during the life of the action.

(e) Compensating for the impact by replacing or providing substitute resources or environments.

Sec. 1508.21 NEPA process.

"NEPA process" means all measures necessary for compliance with the requirements of section 2 and Title I of NEPA.

Sec. 1508.22 Notice of intent.

"Notice of intent" means a notice that an environmental impact statement will be prepared and considered. The notice shall briefly:

(a) Describe the proposed action and possible alternatives.

(b) Describe the agency's proposed scoping process including whether, when, and where any scoping meeting will be held.

(c) State the name and address of a person within the agency who can answer questions about the proposed action and the environmental impact statement.

Sec. 1508.23 Proposal.

"Proposal" exists at that stage in the development of an action when an agency subject to the Act has a goal and is actively preparing to make a decision on one or more alternative means of accomplishing that goal and the effects can be meaningfully evaluated. Preparation of an environmental impact statement on a proposal should be timed (Sec. 1502.5) so that the final statement may be completed in time for the statement to be included in any recommendation or report on the proposal. A proposal may exist in fact as well as by agency declaration that one exists.

Sec. 1508.24 Referring agency.

"Referring agency" means the federal agency which has referred any matter to the Council after a determination that the matter is unsatisfactory from the standpoint of public health or welfare or environmental quality.

Sec. 1508.25 Scope.

Scope consists of the range of actions, alternatives, and impacts to be considered in an environmental impact statement. The scope of an individual statement may depend on its relationships to other statements (Secs.1502.20 and 1508.28). To determine the scope of environmental impact statements, agencies shall consider 3 types of actions, 3 types of alternatives, and 3 types of impacts. They include:

(a) Actions (other than unconnected single actions) which may be:

(1) Connected actions, which means that they are closely related and therefore should be discussed in the same impact statement. Actions are connected if they:

(i) Automatically trigger other actions which may require environmental impact statements.

(ii) Cannot or will not proceed unless other actions are taken previously or simultaneously.

(iii) Are interdependent parts of a larger action and depend on the larger action for their justification.

(2) Cumulative actions, which when viewed with other proposed actions have cumulatively significant impacts and should therefore be discussed in the same impact statement.

(3) Similar actions, which when viewed with other reasonably foreseeable or proposed agency actions, have similarities that provide a basis for evaluating their environmental consequences together, such as common timing or geography. An agency may wish to analyze these actions in the same impact statement. It should do so when the best way to assess adequately the combined impacts of similar actions or reasonable alternatives to such actions is to treat them in a single impact statement.

(b) Alternatives, which include:

(1) No action alternative.

(2) Other reasonable courses of actions.

(3) Mitigation measures (not in the proposed action).

(c) Impacts, which may be: (1) Direct; (2) indirect; (3) cumulative.

Sec. 1508.26 Special expertise.

"Special expertise" means statutory responsibility, agency mission, or related program experience.

Sec. 1508.27 Significantly.

"Significantly" as used in NEPA requires considerations of both context and intensity:

(a) Context. This means that the significance of an action must be analyzed in several contexts such as society as a whole (human, national), the affected region, the affected interests, and the locality. Significance varies with the setting of the proposed action. For instance, in the case of a site-specific action, significance would usually depend upon the effects in the locale rather than in the world as a whole. Both short- and long-term effects are relevant.

(b) Intensity. This refers to the severity of impact. Responsible officials must bear in mind that more than one agency may make decisions about partial aspects of a major action. The following should be considered in evaluating intensity:

(1) Impacts that may be both beneficial and adverse. A significant effect may exist even if the Federal agency believes that on balance the effect will be beneficial.

(2) The degree to which the proposed action affects public health or safety.

(3) Unique characteristics of the geographic area such as proximity to historic or cultural resources, park lands, prime farmlands, wetlands, wild and scenic rivers, or ecologically critical areas.

(4) The degree to which the effects on the quality of the human environment are likely to be highly controversial.

(5) The degree to which the possible effects on the human environment are highly uncertain or involve unique or unknown risks.

(6) The degree to which the action may establish a precedent for future actions with significant effects or represents a decision in principle about a future consideration.

(7) Whether the action is related to other actions with individually insignificant but cumulatively significant impacts. Significance exists if it is reasonable to anticipate a cumulatively significant impact on the environment. Significance cannot be avoided by terming an action temporary or by breaking it down into small component parts.

(8) The degree to which the action may adversely affect districts, sites, highways, structures, or objects listed in or eligible for listing in the National Register of Historic Places or may cause loss or destruction of significant scientific, cultural, or historical resources.

(9) The degree to which the action may adversely affect an endangered or threatened species or its habitat that has been determined to be critical under the Endangered Species Act of 1973.

(10) Whether the action threatens a violation of Federal, State, or local law or requirements imposed for the protection of the environment.

[43 FR 56003, Nov. 29, 1978; 44 FR 874, Jan. 3, 1979]

Sec. 1508.28 Tiering.

"Tiering" refers to the coverage of general matters in broader environmental impact statements (such as national program or policy statements) with subsequent narrower statements or environmental analyses (such as regional or basinwide program statements or ultimately site-specific statements) incorporating by reference the general discussions and concentrating solely on the issues specific to the statement subsequently prepared. Tiering is appropriate when the sequence of statements or analyses is:

(a) From a program, plan, or policy environmental impact statement to a program, plan, or policy statement or analysis of lesser scope or to a site- specific statement or analysis.

(b) From an environmental impact statement on a specific action at an early stage (such as need and site selection) to a supplement (which is preferred) or a subsequent statement or analysis at a later stage (such as environmental mitigation). Tiering in such cases is appropriate when it helps the lead agency to focus on the issues which are ripe for decision and exclude from consideration issues already decided or not yet ripe.

40 Frequently Asked Questions

March 16, 1981

Memorandum for Federal NEPA Liaisons, Federal, State, and Local Officials and Other Persons Involved in the Nepa Process

Subject: Questions and Answers About the NEPA Regulations

During June and July of 1980 the Council on Environmental Quality, with the assistance and cooperation of EPA's EIS Coordinators from the ten EPA regions, held one-day meetings with federal, state and local officials in the ten EPA regional offices around the country. In addition, on July 10, 1980, CEQ conducted a similar meeting for the Washington, D.C. NEPA liaisons and persons involved in the NEPA process. At these meetings CEQ discussed (a) the results of its 1980 review of Draft EISs issued since the July 30, 1979 effective date of the NEPA regulations, (b) agency compliance with the Record of Decision requirements in Section 1505 of the NEPA regulations, and (c) CEQ's preliminary findings on how the scoping process is working. Participants at these meetings received copies of materials prepared by CEQ summarizing its oversight and findings.

These meetings also provided NEPA liaisons and other participants with an opportunity to ask questions about NEPA and the practical application of the NEPA regulations. A number of these questions were answered by CEQ representatives at the regional meetings. In response to the many requests from the agencies and other participants, CEQ has compiled forty of the most important or most frequently asked questions and their answers and reduced them to writing. The answers were prepared by the General Counsel of CEQ in consultation with the Office of Federal Activities of EPA. These answers, of course, do not impose any additional requirements beyond those of the NEPA regulations. This document does not represent new guidance under the NEPA regulations, but rather makes generally available to concerned agencies and private individuals the answers which CEQ has already given at the 1980 regional meetings. The answers also reflect the advice which the Council has given over the past two years to aid agency staff and consultants in their day-to-day application of NEPA and the regulations.

CEQ has also received numerous inquiries regarding the scoping process. CEQ hopes to issue written guidance on scoping later this year on the basis of its special study of scoping, which is nearing completion.

NICHOLAS C. YOST
General Counsel

INDEX

1. Range of Alternatives
2. Alternatives Outside the Capability of Applicant or Jurisdiction of Agencies
3. No-Action Alternative
4. Agency's Preferred Alternative
5. Proposed Action v. Preferred Alternative
6. Environmentally Preferable Alternative
7. Difference Between Sections of EIS on Alternatives and Environmental Consequences
8. Early Application of NEPA
9. Applicant Who Needs Other Permits
10. Limitations on Action During 30-Day Review Period for Final EIS
11. Limitations on Actions by an Applicant During EIS Process
12. Effective date and Enforceability of the Regulations [omitted]
13. Use of Scoping Before Notice of Intent to Prepare EIS
14. Rights and Responsibilities of Lead and Cooperating Agencies
15. Commenting Responsibilities of EPA
16. Third Party Contracts
17. Disclosure Statement to Avoid Conflict of Interest
18. Uncertainties About Indirect Effects of a Proposal
19. Mitigation Measures
20. Worst Case Analysis
21. Combining Environmental and Planning Documents
22. State and Federal Agencies as Joint Lead Agencies
23. Conflicts of Federal Proposal With Land Use Plans, on Policies and Controls
24. Environmental Impact Statements on Policies, Plans or Programs
25. Appendices and Incorporation by Reference
26. Index and Keyword Index In EISs
27. List of Preparers
28. Advance or Xerox Copies of EIS
29. Responses to Comments
30. Adoption of EISs
31. Application of Regulations to Independent Regulatory Agencies
32. Supplements to Old EISs
33. Referrals
34. Records of Decision
35. Time Required for the NEPA Process
36. Environmental Assessments (EA)

37. Findings of No Significant Impact (FONSI)
38. Public Availability of EAs v. FONSIs
39. Mitigation Measures Imposed in EAs and FONSIs
40. Propriety of Issuing EA When Mitigation Reduces Impacts

Questions and Answers About the NEPA Regulations Range of Alternatives

1a. Q. What is meant by "range of alternatives" as referred to in Sec. 1505.1(e)?

A. The phrase "range of alternatives" refers to the alternatives discussed in environmental documents. It includes all reasonable alternatives, which must be rigorously explored and objectively evaluated, as well as those other alternatives, which are eliminated from detailed study with a brief discussion of the reasons for eliminating them. Section 1502.14. A decisionmaker must not consider alternatives beyond the range of alternatives discussed in the relevant environmental documents. Moreover, a decisionmaker must, in fact, consider all the alternatives discussed in an EIS. Section 1505.1(e).

1b. Q. How many alternatives have to be discussed when there is an infinite number of possible alternatives?

A. For some proposals there may exist a very large or even an infinite number of possible reasonable alternatives. For example, a proposal to designate wilderness areas within a National Forest could be said to involve an infinite number of alternatives from 0 to 100 percent of the forest. When there are potentially a very large number of alternatives, only a reasonable number of examples, covering the full spectrum of alternatives, must be analyzed and compared in the EIS. An appropriate series of alternatives might include dedicating 0, 10, 30, 50, 70, 90, or 100 percent of the Forest to wilderness. What constitutes a reasonable range of alternatives depends on the nature of the proposal and the facts in each case.

2a. Q. If an EIS is prepared in connection with an application for a permit or other federal approval, must the EIS rigorously analyze and discuss alternatives that are outside the capability of the applicant or can it be limited to reasonable alternatives that can be carried out by the applicant?

A. Section 1502.14 requires the EIS to examine all reasonable alternatives to the proposal. In determining the scope of alternatives to be considered, the emphasis is on what is "reasonable" rather than on whether the proponent or applicant likes or is itself capable of carrying out a particular alternative. Reasonable alternatives include those that are practical or fea-

910   NATIONAL ENVIRONMENTAL POLICY ACT

sible from the technical and economic standpoint and using common sense, rather than simply desirable from the standpoint of the applicant.

2b. Q. Must the EIS analyze alternatives outside the jurisdiction or capability of the agency or beyond what Congress has authorized?

A. An alternative that is outside the legal jurisdiction of the lead agency must still be analyzed in the EIS if it is reasonable. A potential conflict with local or federal law does not necessarily render an alternative unreasonable, although such conflicts must be considered. Section 1506.2(d). Alternatives that are outside the scope of what Congress has approved or funded must still be evaluated in the EIS if they are reasonable, because the EIS may serve as the basis for modifying the Congressional approval or funding in light of NEPA's goals and policies. Section 1500.1(a).

3. Q. What does the "no action" alternative include? If an agency is under a court order or legislative command to act, must the EIS address the "no action" alternative?

A. Section 1502.14(d) requires the alternatives analysis in the EIS to "include the alternative of no action." There are two distinct interpretations of "no action" that must be considered, depending on the nature of the proposal being evaluated. The first situation might involve an action such as updating a land management plan where ongoing programs initiated under existing legislation and regulations will continue, even as new plans are developed. In these cases "no action" is "no change" from current management direction or level of management intensity. To construct an alternative that is based on no management at all would be a useless academic exercise. Therefore, the "no action" alternative may be thought of in terms of continuing with the present course of action until that action is changed. Consequently, projected impacts of alternative management schemes would be compared in the EIS to those impacts projected for the existing plan. In this case, alternatives would include management plans of both greater and lesser intensity, especially greater and lesser levels of resource development.

The second interpretation of "no action" is illustrated in instances involving federal decisions on proposals for projects. "No action" in such cases would mean the proposed activity would not take place, and the resulting environmental effects from taking no action would be compared with the effects of permitting the proposed activity or an alternative activity to go forward. Where a choice of "no action" by the agency would result in predictable actions by others, this consequence of the "no action" alternative should be included in the analysis. For example, if denial of permission to build a railroad to a facility would lead to construction of a road and increased truck traffic, the EIS should analyze this consequence of the "no action" alternative. In light of the above, it is difficult to think of a situation where it would not be appropriate to address a "no action" alternative. Accordingly, the regulations require the analysis of the no action alternative even if the agency is under a court order or legislative command to act. This analysis provides a benchmark, enabling decisionmakers to compare the magnitude of environmental effects of the action alternatives. It is also an example of a reasonable alternative outside the jurisdiction of the agency which must be analyzed. Section 1502.14(c). See Question 2 above. Inclusion of such an analysis in the EIS is necessary to inform the Congress, the public, and the President as intended by NEPA. Section 1500.1(a).

4a. Q. What is the "agency's preferred alternative"?

A. The "agency's preferred alternative" is the alternative which the agency believes would fulfill its statutory mission and responsibilities, giving consideration to economic, environmental, technical and other factors. The concept of the "agency's preferred alternative" is different from the "environmentally preferable alternative," although in some cases one alternative may be both. See Question 6 below. It is identified so that agencies and the public can understand the lead agency's orientation.

4b. Q. Does the "preferred alternative" have to be identified in the Draft EIS and the Final EIS or just in the Final EIS?

A. Section 1502.14(e) requires the section of the EIS on alternatives to "identify the agency's preferred alternative if one or more exists, in the draft statement, and identify such alternative in the final statement. . . ." This means that if the agency has a preferred alternative at the Draft EIS stage, that alternative must be labeled or identified as such in the Draft EIS. If the responsible federal official in fact has no preferred alternative at the Draft EIS stage, a preferred alternative need not be identified there. By the time the Final EIS is filed, Section 1502.14(e) presumes the existence of a preferred alternative and requires its identification in the Final EIS "unless another law prohibits the expression of such a preference."

4c. Q. Who recommends or determines the "preferred alternative"?

A. The lead agency's official with line responsibility for preparing the EIS and assuring its adequacy is responsible for identifying the agency's preferred alternative(s). The NEPA regulations do not dictate which official in an agency shall be responsible for preparation of EISs, but agencies can identify this official in their implementing procedures, pursuant to Section 1507.3. Even though the agency's preferred alternative is identified by the EIS preparer in the EIS, the statement must be objectively prepared and not slanted to support the choice of the agency's preferred alternative over the other reasonable and feasible alternatives.

5a. Q. Is the "proposed action" the same thing as the "preferred alternative"?

A. The "proposed action" may be, but is not necessarily, the agency's "preferred alternative." The proposed action may be a proposal in its initial form before undergoing analysis in the EIS process. If the proposed action is internally generated, such as preparing a land management plan, the proposed action might end up as the agency's preferred alternative. On the other hand the proposed action may be granting an application to a non-federal entity for a permit. The agency may or may not have a "preferred alternative" at the Draft EIS stage (see Question 4 above). In that case the agency may decide at the Final EIS stage, on the basis of the Draft EIS and the public and agency comments, that an alternative other than the proposed action is the agency's "preferred alternative."

5b. Q. Is the analysis of the "proposed action" in an EIS to be treated differently from the analysis of alternatives?

A. The degree of analysis devoted to each alternative in the EIS is to be substantially similar to that devoted to the "proposed action." Section 1502.14 is titled "Alternatives including the proposed action" to reflect such comparable treatment. Section 1502.14(b) specifically requires "substantial treatment" in the EIS of each alternative including the proposed action. This regulation does not dictate an amount of information to be provided, but rather, prescribes a level of treatment, which may in turn require varying amounts of information, to enable a reviewer to evaluate and compare alternatives.

6a Q. What is the meaning of the term "environmentally preferable alternative" as used in the regulations with reference to Records of Decision? How is the term "environment" used in the phrase?

A. Section 1505.2(b) requires that, in cases where an EIS has been prepared, the Record of Decision (ROD) must identify all alternatives that were considered, ". . . specifying the alternative or alternatives which were considered to be environmentally preferable." The environmentally preferable alternative is the alternative that will promote the national environmental policy as expressed in NEPA's Section 101. Ordinarily, this means the alternative that causes the least damage to the biological and physical environment; it also means the alternative which best protects, preserves, and enhances historic, cultural, and natural resources.

The Council recognizes that the identification of the environmentally preferable alternative may involve difficult judgments, particularly when one environmental value must be balanced against another. The public and other agencies reviewing a Draft EIS can assist the lead agency to develop and determine environmentally preferable alternatives by providing their views in comments on the Draft EIS. Through the identification of the environmentally preferable alternative, the decisionmaker is clearly faced with a choice between that alternative and others, and must consider whether the decision accords with the Congressionally declared policies of the Act.

6b. Q. Who recommends or determines what is environmentally preferable?

A. The agency EIS staff is encouraged to make recommendations of the environmentally preferable alternative(s) during EIS preparation. In any event the lead agency official responsible for the EIS is encouraged to identify the environmentally preferable alternative(s) in the EIS. In all cases, commentors from other agencies and the public are also encouraged to address this question. The agency must identify the environmentally preferable alternative in the ROD.

7. Q. What is the difference between the sections in the EIS on "alternatives" and "environmental consequences"? How do you avoid duplicating the discussion of alternatives in preparing these two sections?

A. The "alternatives" section is the heart of the EIS. This section rigorously explores and objectively evaluates all reasonable alternatives including the proposed action. Section 1502.14. It should include relevant comparisons on environmental and other grounds. The "environmental consequences" section of the EIS discusses the specific environmental impacts or effects of each of the alternatives including the proposed action. Section 1502.16. In order to avoid duplication between these two sections, most of the "alternatives" section should be devoted to describing and comparing the alternatives. Discussion of the environmental impacts of these alternatives should be limited to a concise descriptive summary of such impacts in a comparative form, including charts or tables, thus sharply defining the issues and providing a clear basis for choice among options. Section 1502.14. The "environmental consequences" section should be devoted largely to a scientific analysis of the direct and indirect environmental effects of the proposed action and of each of the alternatives. It forms the analytic basis for the concise comparison in the "alternatives" section.

8. Q. Section 1501.2(d) of the NEPA regulations requires agencies to provide for the early application of NEPA to cases where actions are planned by private applicants or non-Federal entities and are, at some stage, subject to federal approval of permits, loans, loan guarantees, insurance or other actions. What must and can agencies do to apply NEPA early in these cases?

A. Section 1501.2(d) requires federal agencies to take steps toward ensuring that private parties and state and local entities initiate environmental studies as soon as federal involvement in their proposals can be foreseen. This section is intended to ensure that environmental factors are considered at an early stage in the planning process and to avoid the situation where the applicant for a federal permit or approval has completed planning and eliminated all alternatives to the proposed action by the time the EIS process commences or before the EIS process has been completed.

Through early consultation, business applicants and approving agencies may gain better appreciation of each other's needs and foster a decisionmaking process which avoids later unexpected confrontations.

Federal agencies are required by Section 1507.3(b) to develop procedures to carry out Section 1501.2(d). The procedures should include an "outreach program", such as a means for prospective applicants to conduct pre-application consultations with the lead and cooperating agencies. Applicants need to find out, in advance of project planning, what environmental studies or other information will be required, and what mitigation requirements are likely, in connecton with the later federal NEPA process. Agencies should designate staff to advise potential applicants of the agency's NEPA information requirements and should publicize their pre-application procedures and information requirements in newsletters or other media used by potential applicants.

Complementing Section 1501.2(d), Section 1506.5(a) requires agencies to assist applicants by outlining the types of information required in those cases where the agency requires the applicant to submit environmental data for possible use by the agency in preparing an EIS.

Section 1506.5(b) allows agencies to authorize preparation of environmental assessments by applicants. Thus, the procedures should also include a means for anticipating and utilizing applicants' environmental studies or "early corporate environmental assessments" to fulfill some of the federal agency's NEPA obligations. However, in such cases the agency must still evaluate independently the environmental issues and take responsibility for the environmental assessment.

These provisions are intended to encourage and enable private and other non-federal entities to build environmental considerations into their own planning processes in a way that facilitates the application of NEPA and avoids delay.

9. Q. To what extent must an agency inquire into whether an applicant for a federal permit, funding or other approval of a proposal will also need approval from another agency for the same proposal or some other related aspect of it?

A. Agencies must integrate the NEPA process into other planning at the earliest possible time to insure that planning and decisions reflect environmental values, to avoid delays later in the process, and to head off potential conflicts. Specifically, the agency must "provide for cases where actions are planned by . . . applicants," so that designated staff are available to advise potential applicants of studies or other information that will foreseeably be required for the later federal action; the agency shall consult with the applicant if the agency foresees its own involvement in the proposal; and it shall insure that the NEPA process commences at the earliest possible time. Section 1501.2(d). (See Question 8.)

The regulations emphasize agency cooperation early in the NEPA process. Section 1501.6. Section 1501.7 on "scoping" also provides that all affected Federal agencies are to be invited to participate in scoping the environmental issues and to identify the various environmental review and consultation requirements that may apply to the proposed action. Further, Section 1502.25(b) requires that the draft EIS list all the federal permits, licenses and other entitlements that are needed to implement the proposal.

These provisions create an affirmative obligation on federal agencies to inquire early, and to the maximum degree possible, to ascertain whether an applicant is or will be seeking other federal assistance or approval, or whether the applicant is waiting until a proposal has been substantially developed before requesting federal aid or approval.

Thus, a federal agency receiving a request for approval or assistance should determine whether the applicant has filed separate requests for federal approval or assistance with other federal agencies. Other federal agencies that are likely to become involved should then be contacted, and the NEPA process coordinated, to insure an early and comprehensive analysis of the direct and indirect effects of the proposal and any related actions. The agency should inform the applicant that action on its application may be delayed unless it submits all other federal applications (where feasible to do so), so that all the relevant agencies can work together on the scoping process and preparation of the EIS.

10a. Q. What actions by agencies and/or applicants are allowed during EIS preparation and during the 30-day review period after publication of a final EIS?

A. No federal decision on the proposed action shall be made or recorded until at least 30 days after the publication by EPA of notice that the particular EIS has been filed with EPA. Sections 1505.2 and 1506.10. Section 1505.2 requires this decision to be stated in a public Record of Decision.

Until the agency issues its Record of Decision, no action by an agency or an applicant concerning the proposal shall be taken which would have an adverse environmental impact or limit the choice of reasonable alternatives. Section 1506.1(a). But this does not preclude preliminary planning or design work which is needed to support an application for permits or assistance. Section 1506.1(d).

When the impact statement in question is a program EIS, no major action concerning the program may be taken which may significantly affect the quality of the human environment, unless the particular action is justified independently of the program, is accompanied by its own adequate environmental impact statement and will not prejudice the ultimate decision on the program. Section 1506.1(c).

10b. Q. Do these limitations on action (described in Question 10a) apply to state or local agencies that have statutorily delegated responsibility for preparation of environmental documents required by NEPA, for example, under the HUD Block Grant program?

A. Yes, these limitations do apply, without any variation from their application to federal agencies.

11. Q. What actions must a lead agency take during the NEPA process when it becomes aware that a non-federal applicant is about to take an action within the agency's jurisdiction that would either have an adverse environmental impact or limit the choice of reasonable alternatives (e.g., prematurely commit money or other resources towards the completion of the proposal)?

A. The federal agency must notify the applicant that the agency will take strong affirmative steps to insure that the objectives and procedures of NEPA are fulfilled. Section 1506.1(b). These steps could include seeking injunctive measures under NEPA, or the use of sanctions available under either the agency's permitting authority or statutes setting forth the agency's statutory mission. For example, the agency might advise an applicant that if it takes such action the agency will not process its application.

12a Q. What actions are subject to the Council's new regulations, and what actions are grandfathered under the old guidelines?

A. The effective date of the Council's regulations was July 30, 1979 (except for certain HUD programs under the Housing and Community Development Act, 42 U.S.C. 5304(h), and certain state highway programs that qualify under Section 102(2)(D) of NEPA for which the regulations became effective on November 30, 1979). All the provisions of the regulations are binding as of that date, including those covering decisionmaking, public participation, referrals, limitations on actions, EIS supplements, etc. For example, a Record of Decision would be prepared even for decisions where the draft EIS was filed before July 30, 1979.

But in determining whether or not the new regulations apply to the preparation of a particular environmental document, the relevant factor is the date of filing of the draft of that document. Thus, the new regulations do not require the redrafting of an EIS or supplement if the draft EIS or supplement was filed before July 30, 1979. However, a supplement prepared after the effective date of the regulations for an EIS issued in final before the effective date of the regulations would be controlled by the regulations.

Even though agencies are not required to apply the regulations to an EIS or other document for which the draft was filed prior to July 30, 1979, the regulations encourage agencies to follow the regulations "to the fullest extent practicable," i.e., if it is feasible to do so, in preparing the final document. Section 1506.12(a).

12b Q. Are projects authorized by Congress before the effective date of the Council's regulations grandfathered?

A. No. The date of Congressional authorization for a project is not determinative of whether the Council's regulations or former Guidelines apply to the particular proposal. No incomplete projects or proposals of any kind are grandfathered in whole or in part. Only certain environmental documents, for which the draft was issued before the effective date of the regulations, are grandfathered and [46 FR 18030] subject to the Council's former Guidelines.

12c Q. Can a violation of the regulations give rise to a cause of action?

A. While a trivial violation of the regulations would not give rise to an independent cause of action, such a cause of action would arise from a substantial violation of the regulations. Section 1500.3.

13. Q. Can the scoping process be used in connection with preparation of an environmental assessment, i.e., before both the decision to proceed with an EIS and publication of a notice of intent?

A. Yes. Scoping can be a useful tool for discovering alternatives to a proposal, or significant impacts that may have been overlooked. In cases where an environmental assessment is being prepared to help an agency decide whether to prepare an EIS, useful information might result from early participation by other agencies and the public in a scoping process.

The regulations state that the scoping process is to be preceded by a Notice of Intent (NOI) to prepare an EIS. But that is only the minimum requirement. Scoping may be initiated earlier, as long as there is appropriate public notice and enough information available on the proposal so that the public and relevant agencies can participate effectively.

However, scoping that is done before the assessment, and in aid of its preparation, cannot substitute for the normal scoping process after publication of the NOI, unless the earlier public notice stated clearly that this possibility was under consideration, and the NOI expressly provides that written comments on the scope of alternatives and impacts will still be considered.

14a. Q. What are the respective rights and responsibilities of lead and cooperating agencies? What letters and memoranda must be prepared?

A. After a lead agency has been designated (Sec. 1501.5), that agency has the responsibility to solicit cooperation from other federal agencies that have jurisdiction by law or special expertise on any environmental issue that should be addressed in the EIS being prepared. Where appropriate, the lead agency should seek the cooperation of state or local agencies of similar qualifications. When the proposal may affect an Indian reservation, the agency should consult with the Indian tribe. Section 1508.5. The request for cooperation should come at the earliest possible time in the NEPA process.

After discussions with the candidate cooperating agencies, the lead agency and the cooperating agencies are to determine by letter or by memorandum which agencies will undertake cooperating responsibilities. To the extent possible at this stage, responsibilities for specific issues should be assigned. The allocation of responsibilities will be completed during scoping. Section 1501.7(a)(4). Cooperating agencies must assume responsibility for the development of information and the preparation of environmental analyses at the request of the lead agency. Section 1501.6(b)(3). Cooperating agencies are now required by Section 1501.6 to devote staff resources that were normally primarily used to critique or comment on the Draft EIS after its preparation, much earlier in the NEPA process—primarily at the scoping and Draft EIS preparation stages. If a cooperating agency determines that its resource limitations preclude any involvement, or the degree of involvement (amount of work) requested by the lead agency, it must so inform the lead agency in writing and submit a copy of this correspondence to the Council. Section 1501.6(c). In other words, the potential cooperating agency must decide early if it is able to devote any of its resources to a particular proposal. For this reason the regulation states that an agency may reply to a request for cooperation that "other program commitments preclude any involvement or the degree of involvement requested in the action that is the subject of the environmental impact statement." (Emphasis added). The regulation refers to the "action," rather than to the EIS, to clarify that the agency is taking itself out of all phases of the federal action, not just draft EIS preparation. This means that the agency has determined that it cannot be involved in the later stages of EIS review and comment, as well as decisionmaking on the proposed action. For this reason, cooperating agencies with jurisdiction by law (those which have permitting or other approval authority) cannot opt out entirely of the duty to cooperate on the EIS. See also Question 15, relating specifically to the responsibility of EPA.

14b. Q. How are disputes resolved between lead and cooperating agencies concerning the scope and level of detail of analysis and the quality of data in impact statements?

A. Such disputes are resolved by the agencies themselves. A lead agency, of course, has the ultimate responsibility for the content of an EIS. But it is supposed to use the environmental analysis and recommendations of cooperating agencies with jurisdiction by law or special expertise to the maximum extent possible, consistent with its own responsibilities as lead agency. Section 1501.6(a)(2). If the lead agency leaves out a significant issue or ignores the advice and expertise of the cooperating agency, the EIS may be found later to be inadequate. Similarly, where cooperating agencies have their own decisions to make and they intend to adopt the environmental impact statement and base their decisions on it, one document should include all of the information necessary for the decisions by the cooperating agencies. Otherwise they may be forced to duplicate the EIS process by issuing a new, more complete EIS or Supplemental EIS, even though the original EIS could have sufficed if it had been properly done at the outset. Thus, both lead and cooperating agencies have a stake in producing a document of good quality. Cooperating agencies also have a duty to participate fully in the scoping process to ensure that the appropriate range of issues is determined early in the EIS process. Because the EIS is not the Record of Decision, but instead constitutes the information and analysis on which to base a decision, disagreements about conclusions to be drawn from the EIS need not inhibit agencies from issuing a joint document, or adopting another agency's EIS, if the analysis is adequate. Thus, if each agency has its own "preferred alternative," both can be identified in the EIS. Similarly, a cooperating agency with jurisdiction by law may determine in its own ROD that alternative A is the environmentally preferable action, even though the lead agency has decided in its separate ROD that Alternative B is environmentally preferable.

14c. Q. What are the specific responsibilities of federal and state cooperating agencies to review draft EISs?
A. Cooperating agencies (i.e., agencies with jurisdiction by law or special expertise) and agencies that are authorized to develop or enforce environmental standards, must comment on environmental impact statements within their jurisdiction, expertise or authority. Sections 1503.2, 1508.5. If a cooperating agency is satisfied that its views are adequately reflected in the environmental impact statement, it should simply comment accordingly. Conversely, if the cooperating agency determines that a draft EIS is incomplete, inadequate or inaccurate, or it has other comments, it should promptly make such comments, conforming to the requirements of specificity in section 1503.3.

14d. Q. How is the lead agency to treat the comments of another agency with jurisdiction by law or special expertise which has failed or refused to cooperate or participate in scoping or EIS preparation?
A. A lead agency has the responsibility to respond to all substantive comments raising significant issues regarding a draft EIS. Section 1503.4. However, cooperating agencies are generally under an obligation to raise issues or otherwise participate in the EIS process during scoping and EIS preparation if they reasonably can do so. In practical terms, if a cooperating agency fails to cooperate at the outset, such as during scoping, it will find that its comments at a later stage will not be as persuasive to the lead agency.

15. Q. Are EPA's responsibilities to review and comment on the environmental effects of agency proposals under Section 309 of the Clean Air Act independent of its responsibility as a cooperating agency?
A. Yes. EPA has an obligation under Section 309 of the Clean Air Act to review and comment in writing on the environmental impact of any matter relating to the authority of the Administrator contained in proposed legislation, federal construction projects, other federal actions requiring EISs, and

new regulations. 42 U.S.C. Sec. 7609. This obligation is independent of its role as a cooperating agency under the NEPA regulations.

16. Q. What is meant by the term "third party contracts" in connection with the preparation of an EIS See Section 1506.5(c). When can "third party contracts" be used?

A. As used by EPA and other agencies, the term "third party contract" refers to the preparation of EISs by contractors paid by the applicant. In the case of an EIS for a National Pollution Discharge Elimination System (NPDES) permit, the applicant, aware in the early planning stages of the proposed project of the need for an EIS, contracts directly with a consulting firm for its preparation. See 40 C.F.R. 6.604(g). The "third party" is EPA which, under Section 1506.5(c), must select the consulting firm, even though the applicant pays for the cost of preparing the EIS. The consulting firm is responsible to EPA for preparing an EIS that meets the requirements of the NEPA regulations and EPA's NEPA procedures. It is in the applicant's interest that the EIS comply with the law so that EPA can take prompt action on the NPDES permit application. The "third party contract" method under EPA's NEPA procedures is purely voluntary, though most applicants have found it helpful in expediting compliance with NEPA. If a federal agency uses "third party contracting," the applicant may undertake the necessary paperwork for the solicitation of a field of candidates under the agency's direction, so long as the agency complies with Section 1506.5(c). Federal procurement requirements do not apply to the agency because it incurs no obligations or costs under the contract, nor does the agency procure anything under the contract.

17a. Q. If an EIS is prepared with the assistance of a consulting firm, the firm must execute a disclosure statement. What criteria must the firm follow in determining whether it has any "financial or other interest in the outcome of the project" which would cause a conflict of interest?

A. Section 1506.5(c), which specifies that a consulting firm preparing an EIS must execute a disclosure statement, does not define "financial or other interest in the outcome of the project." The Council interprets this term broadly to cover any known benefits other than general enhancement of professional reputation. This includes any financial benefit such as a promise of future construction or design work on the project, as well as indirect benefits the consultant is aware of (e.g., if the project would aid proposals sponsored by the firm's other clients). For example, completion of a highway project may encourage construction of a shopping center or industrial park from which the consultant stands to benefit. If a consulting firm is aware that it has such an interest in the decision on the proposal, it should be disqualified from preparing the EIS, to preserve the objectivity and integrity of the NEPA process. When a consulting firm has been involved in developing initial data and plans for the project, but does not have any financial or other interest in the outcome of the decision, it need not be disqualified from preparing the EIS. However, a disclosure statement in the draft EIS should clearly state the scope and extent of the firm's prior involvement to expose any potential conflicts of interest that may exist.

17b. Q. If the firm in fact has no promise of future work or other interest in the outcome of the proposal, may the firm later bid in competition with others for future work on the project if the proposed action is approved?
A. Yes.

18. Q. How should uncertainties about indirect effects of a proposal be addressed, for example, in cases of disposal of federal lands, when the identity or plans of future landowners is unknown?
A. The EIS must identify all the indirect effects that are known, and make a good faith effort to explain the effects that are not known but are "reasonably foreseeable." Section 1508.8(b). In the example, if there is total uncertainty about the identity of future land owners or the nature of future land uses, then of course, the agency is not required to engage in speculation or contemplation about their future plans. But, in the ordinary course of business, people do make judgments based upon reasonably foreseeable occurrences. It will often be possible to consider the likely purchasers and the development trends in that area or similar areas in recent years; or the likelihood that the land will be used for an energy project, shopping center, subdivision, farm or factory. The agency has the responsibility to make an informed judgment, and to estimate future impacts on that basis, especially if trends are ascertainable or potential purchasers have made themselves known. The agency cannot ignore these uncertain, but probable, effects of its decisions.

19a. Q. What is the scope of mitigation measures that must be discussed?
A. The mitigation measures discussed in an EIS must cover the range of impacts of the proposal. The measures must include such things as design alternatives that would decrease pollution emissions, construction impacts, esthetic intrusion, as well as relocation assistance, possible land use controls that could be enacted, and other possible efforts. Mitigation measures must be considered even for impacts that by themselves would not be considered

"significant." Once the proposal itself is considered as a whole to have significant effects, all of its specific effects on the environment (whether or not "significant") must be considered, and mitigation measures must be developed where it is feasible to do so. Sections 1502.14(f), 1502.16(h), 1508.14.

19b. Q. How should an EIS treat the subject of available mitigation measures that are (1) outside the jurisdiction of the lead or cooperating agencies, or (2) unlikely to be adopted or enforced by the responsible agency?

A. All relevant, reasonable mitigation measures that could improve the project are to be identified, even if they are outside the jurisdiction of the lead agency or the cooperating agencies, and thus would not be committed as part of the RODs of these agencies. Sections 1502.16(h), 1505.2(c). This will serve to alert agencies or officials who can implement these extra measures, and will encourage them to do so. Because the EIS is the most comprehensive environmental document, it is an ideal vehicle in which to lay out not only the full range of environmental impacts but also the full spectrum of appropriate mitigation. However, to ensure that environmental effects of a proposed action are fairly assessed, the probability of the mitigation measures being implemented must also be discussed. Thus the EIS and the Record of Decision should indicate the likelihood that such measures will be adopted or enforced by the responsible agencies. Sections 1502.16(h), 1505.2. If there is a history of nonenforcement or opposition to such measures, the EIS and Record of Decision should acknowledge such opposition or nonenforcement. If the necessary mitigation measures will not be ready for a long period of time, this fact, of course, should also be recognized.

Note: Answer to Question 20 has been rescinded. See 51 Fed. Reg. 15625, April 25, 1986.

21. Q. Where an EIS or an EA is combined with another project planning document (sometimes called "piggybacking"), to what degree may the EIS or EA refer to and rely upon information in the project document to satisfy NEPA's requirements?

A. Section 1502.25 of the regulations requires that draft EISs be prepared concurrently and integrated with environmental analyses and related surveys and studies required by other federal statutes. In addition, Section 1506.4 allows any environmental document prepared in compliance with NEPA to be combined with any other agency document to reduce duplication and paperwork. However, these provisions were not intended to authorize the preparation of a short summary or outline EIS, attached to a detailed project report or land use plan containing the required environmental impact data. In such circumstances, the reader would have to refer constantly to the detailed report to understand the environmental impacts and alternatives which should have been found in the EIS itself.

The EIS must stand on its own as an analytical document which fully informs decisionmakers and the public of the environmental effects of the proposal and those of the reasonable alternatives. Section 1502.1. But, as long as the EIS is clearly identified and is self-supporting, it can be physically included in or attached to the project report or land use plan, and may use attached report material as technical backup. Forest Service environmental impact statements for forest management plans are handled in this manner. The EIS identifies the agency's preferred alternative, which is developed in detail as the proposed management plan. The detailed proposed plan accompanies the EIS through the review process, and the documents are appropriately cross-referenced. The proposed plan is useful for EIS readers as an example, to show how one choice of management options translates into effects on natural resources. This procedure permits initiation of the 90-day public review of proposed forest plans, which is required by the National Forest Management Act.

All the alternatives are discussed in the EIS, which can be read as an independent document. The details of the management plan are not repeated in the EIS, and vice versa. This is a reasonable functional separation of the documents: the EIS contains information relevant to the choice among alternatives; the plan is a detailed description of proposed management activities suitable for use by the land managers. This procedure provides for concurrent compliance with the public review requirements of both NEPA and the National Forest Management Act. Under some circumstances, a project report or management plan may be totally merged with the EIS, and the one document labeled as both "EIS" and "management plan" or "project report." This may be reasonable where the documents are short, or where the EIS format and the regulations for clear, analytical EISs also satisfy the requirements for a project report.

22. Q. May state and federal agencies serve as joint lead agencies? If so, how do they resolve law, policy and resource conflicts under NEPA and the relevant state environmental policy act? How do they resolve differences in perspective where, for example, national and local needs may differ?

A. Under Section 1501.5(b), federal, state or local agencies, as long as they include at least one federal agency, may act as joint lead agencies to prepare an EIS. Section 1506.2 also strongly urges state and local agencies and the relevant federal agencies to cooperate fully with each other. This should cover joint research and studies, planning activities, public hearings, environmental assessments and the preparation of joint EISs under NEPA and the relevant "little NEPA" state laws, so that one document will satisfy both laws.

The regulations also recognize that certain inconsistencies may exist between the proposed federal action and any approved state or local plan or law. The joint document should discuss the extent to which the federal agency would reconcile its proposed action with such plan or law. Section 1506.2(d). (See Question 23).

Because there may be differences in perspective as well as conflicts among federal, state and local goals for resources management, the Council has advised participating agencies to adopt a flexible, cooperative approach. The joint EIS should reflect all of their interests and missions, clearly identified as such. The final document would then indicate how state and local interests have been accommodated, or would identify conflicts in goals (e.g., how a hydroelectric project, which might induce second home development, would require new land use controls). The EIS must contain a complete discussion of scope and purpose of the proposal, alternatives, and impacts so that the discussion is adequate to meet the needs of local, state and federal decisionmakers.

23a. Q. How should an agency handle potential conflicts between a proposal and the objectives of Federal, state or local land use plans, policies and controls for the area concerned? See Sec. 1502.16(c).

A. The agency should first inquire of other agencies whether there are any potential conflicts. If there would be immediate conflicts, or if conflicts could arise in the future when the plans are finished (see Question 23(b) below), the EIS must acknowledge and describe the extent of those conflicts. If there are any possibilities of resolving the conflicts, these should be explained as well. The EIS should also evaluate the seriousness of the impact of the proposal on the land use plans and policies, and whether, or how much, the proposal will impair the effectiveness of land use control mechanisms for the area. Comments from officials of the affected area should be solicited early and should be carefully acknowledged and answered in the EIS.

23b. Q. What constitutes a "land use plan or policy" for purposes of this discussion?

A. The term "land use plans," includes all types of formally adopted documents for land use planning, zoning and related regulatory requirements.

Local general plans are included, even though they are subject to future change. Proposed plans should also be addressed if they have been formally proposed by the appropriate government body in a written form, and are being actively pursued by officials of the jurisdiction. Staged plans, which must go through phases of development such as the Water Resources Council's Level. A, B and C planning process should also be included even though they are incomplete. The term "policies" includes formally adopted statements of land use policy as embodied in laws or regulations. It also includes proposals for action such as the initiation of a planning process, or a formally adopted policy statement of the local, regional or state executive branch, even if it has not yet been formally adopted by the local, regional or state legislative body.

23c. Q. What options are available for the decisionmaker when conflicts with such plans or policies are identified?

A. After identifying any potential land use conflicts, the decisionmaker must weigh the significance of the conflicts, among all the other environmental and non-environmental factors that must be considered in reaching a rational and balanced decision. Unless precluded by other law from causing or contributing to any inconsistency with the land use plans, policies or controls, the decisionmaker retains the authority to go forward with the proposal, despite the potential conflict. In the Record of Decision, the decisionmaker must explain what the decision was, how it was made, and what mitigation measures are being imposed to lessen adverse environmental impacts of the proposal, among the other requirements of Section 1505.2. This provision would require the decisionmaker to explain any decision to override land use plans, policies or controls for the area.

24a. Q. When are EISs required on policies, plans or programs?

A. An EIS must be prepared if an agency proposes to implement a specific policy, to adopt a plan for a group of related actions, or to implement a specific statutory program or executive directive. Section 1508.18. In addition, the adoption of official policy in the form of rules, regulations and interpretations pursuant to the Administrative Procedure Act, treaties, conventions, or other formal documents establishing governmental or agency policy which will substantially alter agency programs, could require an EIS. Section 1508.18. In all cases, the policy, plan, or program must have the potential for significantly affecting the quality of the human environment in order to require an EIS. It should be noted that a proposal "may exist in fact as well as by agency declaration that one exists." Section 1508.23.

24b. Q. When is an area-wide or overview EIS appropriate?

A. The preparation of an area-wide or overview EIS may be particularly useful when similar actions, viewed with other reasonably foreseeable or proposed agency actions, share common timing or geography. For example, when a variety of energy projects may be located in a single watershed, or when a series of new energy technologies may be developed through federal funding, the overview or area-wide EIS would serve as a valuable and necessary analysis of the affected environment and the potential cumulative impacts of the reasonably foreseeable actions under that program or within that geographical area.

24c. Q. What is the function of tiering in such cases?

A. Tiering is a procedure which allows an agency to avoid duplication of paperwork through the incorporation by reference of the general discussions and relevant specific discussions from an environmental impact statement of broader scope into one of lesser scope or vice versa. In the example given in Question 24b, this would mean that an overview EIS would be prepared for all of the energy activities reasonably foreseeable in a particular geographic area or resulting from a particular development program. This impact statement would be followed by site-specific or project-specific EISs. The tiering process would make each EIS of greater use and meaning to the public as the plan or program develops, without duplication of the analysis prepared for the previous impact statement.

25a. Q. When is it appropriate to use appendices instead of including information in the body of an EIS?

A. The body of the EIS should be a succinct statement of all the information on environmental impacts and alternatives that the decisionmaker and the public need, in order to make the decision and to ascertain that every significant factor has been examined. The EIS must explain or summarize methodologies of research and modeling, and the results of research that may have been conducted to analyze impacts and alternatives.

Lengthy technical discussions of modeling methodology, baseline studies, or other work are best reserved for the appendix. In other words, if only technically trained individuals are likely to understand a particular discussion then it should go in the appendix, and a plain language summary of the analysis and conclusions of that technical discussion should go in the text of the EIS.

The final statement must also contain the agency's responses to comments on the draft EIS. These responses will be primarily in the form of changes in the document itself, but specific answers to each significant comment should also be included. These specific responses may be placed in an appendix. If the comments are especially voluminous, summaries of the comments and responses will suffice. (See Question 29 regarding the level of detail required for responses to comments.)

25b. Q. How does an appendix differ from incorporation by reference?

A. First, if at all possible, the appendix accompanies the EIS, whereas the material which is incorporated by reference does not accompany the EIS. Thus the appendix should contain information that reviewers will be likely to want to examine. The appendix should include material that pertains to preparation of a particular EIS. Research papers directly relevant to the proposal, lists of affected species, discussion of the methodology of models used in the analysis of impacts, extremely detailed responses to comments, or other information, would be placed in the appendix.

The appendix must be complete and available at the time the EIS is filed. Five copies of the appendix must be sent to EPA with five copies of the EIS for filing. If the appendix is too bulky to be circulated, it instead must be placed in conveniently accessible locations or furnished directly to commentors upon request. If it is not circulated with the EIS, the Notice of Availability published by EPA must so state, giving a telephone number to enable potential commentors to locate or request copies of the appendix promptly.

Material that is not directly related to preparation of the EIS should be incorporated by reference. This would include other EISs, research papers in the general literature, technical background papers or other material that someone with technical training could use to evaluate the analysis of the proposal. These must be made available, either by citing the literature, furnishing copies to central locations, or sending copies directly to commentors upon request.

Care must be taken in all cases to ensure that material incorporated by reference, and the occasional appendix that does not accompany the EIS, are in fact available for the full minimum public comment period. index

26a. Q. How detailed must an EIS index be?

A. The EIS index should have a level of detail sufficient to focus on areas of the EIS of reasonable interest to any reader. It cannot be restricted to the most important topics. On the other hand, it need not identify every conceivable term or phrase in the EIS. If an agency believes that the reader is reasonably likely to be interested in a topic, it should be included.

26b. Q. Is a keyword index required?

A. No. A keyword index is a relatively short list of descriptive terms that identifies the key concepts or subject areas in a document. For example it could consist of 20 terms which describe the most significant aspects of an EIS that a future researcher would need: type of proposal, type of impacts, type of environment, geographical area, sampling or modelling methodologies used. This technique permits the compilation of EIS data banks, by facilitating quick and inexpensive access to stored materials. While a keyword index is not required by the regulations, it could be a useful addition for several reasons. First, it can be useful as a quick index for reviewers of the EIS, helping to focus on areas of interest. Second, if an agency keeps a listing of the keyword indexes of the EISs it produces, the EIS preparers themselves will have quick access to similar research data and methodologies to aid their future EIS work. Third, a keyword index will be needed to make an EIS available to future researchers using EIS data banks that are being developed. Preparation of such an index now when the document is produced will save a later effort when the data banks become operational.

27a. Q. If a consultant is used in preparing an EIS, must the list of preparers identify members of the consulting firm as well as the agency NEPA staff who were primarily responsible?

A. Section 1502.17 requires identification of the names and qualifications of persons who were primarily responsible for preparing the EIS or significant background papers, including basic components of the statement. This means that members of a consulting firm preparing material that is to become part of the EIS must be identified. The EIS should identify these individuals even though the consultant's contribution may have been modified by the agency.

27b. Q. Should agency staff involved in reviewing and editing the EIS also be included in the list of preparers?

A. Agency personnel who wrote basic components of the EIS or significant background papers must, of course, be identified. The EIS should also list the technical editors who reviewed or edited the statements.

27c. Q. How much information should be included on each person listed?

A. The list of preparers should normally not exceed two pages. Therefore, agencies must determine which individuals had primary responsibility and need not identify individuals with minor involvement. The list of preparers should include a very brief identification of the individuals involved, their qualifications (expertise, professional disciplines) and the specific portion of the EIS for which they are responsible. This may be done in tabular form to cut down on length. A line or two for each person's qualifications should be sufficient.

28. Q. May an agency file xerox copies of an EIS with EPA pending the completion of printing the document?

A. Xerox copies of an EIS may be filed with EPA prior to printing only if the xerox copies are simultaneously made available to other agencies and the public. Section 1506.9 of the regulations, which governs EIS filing, specifically requires Federal agencies to file EISs with EPA no earlier than the EIS is distributed to the public. However, this section does not prohibit xeroxing as a form of reproduction and distribution. When an agency chooses xeroxing as the reproduction method, the EIS must be clear and legible to permit ease of reading and ultimate microfiching of the EIS. Where color graphs are important to the EIS, they should be reproduced and circulated with the xeroxed copy.

29a Q. What response must an agency provide to a comment on a draft EIS which states that the EIS's methodology is inadequate or inadequately explained? For example, what level of detail must an agency include in its response to a simple postcard comment making such an allegation?

A. Appropriate responses to comments are described in Section 1503.4. Normally the responses should result in changes in the text of the EIS, not simply a separate answer at the back of the document. But, in addition, the agency must state what its response was, and if the agency decides that no substantive response to a comment is necessary, it must explain briefly why.

An agency is not under an obligation to issue a lengthy reiteration of its methodology for any portion of an EIS if the only comment addressing the methodology is a simple complaint that the EIS methodology is inadequate. But agencies must respond to comments, however brief, which are specific in their criticism of agency methodology. For example, if a commentor on an EIS said that an agency's air quality dispersion analysis or methodology was inadequate, and the agency had included a discussion of that analysis in the EIS, little if anything need be added in response to such a comment. However, if the commentor said that the dispersion analysis was inadequate because of its use of a certain computational technique, or that a dispersion analysis was inadequately explained because computational techniques were not included or referenced, then the agency would have to respond in a substantive and meaningful way to such a comment.

If a number of comments are identical or very similar, agencies may group the comments and prepare a single answer for each group. Comments may be summarized if they are especially voluminous. The comments or summaries must be attached to the EIS regardless of whether the agency believes they merit individual discussion in the body of the final EIS.

29b. Q. How must an agency respond to a comment on a draft EIS that raises a new alternative not previously considered in the draft EIS?

A. This question might arise in several possible situations. First, a commentor on a draft EIS may indicate that there is a possible alternative which, in the agency's view, is not a reasonable alternative. Section 1502.14(a). If that is the case, the agency must explain why the comment does not warrant further agency response, citing authorities or reasons that support the agency's position and, if appropriate, indicate those circumstances which would trigger agency reappraisal or further response. Section 1503.4(a). For example, a commentor on a draft EIS on a coal fired power plant may suggest the alternative of using synthetic fuel. The agency may reject the alternative with a brief discussion (with authorities) of the unavailability of synthetic fuel within the time frame necessary to meet the need and purpose of the proposed facility.

A second possibility is that an agency may receive a comment indicating that a particular alternative, while reasonable, should be modified somewhat, for example, to achieve certain mitigation benefits, or for other reasons. If the modification is reasonable, the agency should include a discussion of it in the final EIS. For example, a commentor on a draft EIS on a proposal for a pumped storage power facility might suggest that the applicant's proposed alternative should be enhanced by the addition of certain reasonable mitigation measures, including the purchase and setaside of a wildlife preserve to substitute for the tract to be destroyed by the project. The modified alternative including the additional mitigation measures should be discussed by the agency in the final EIS.

A third slightly different possibility is that a comment on a draft EIS will raise an alternative which is a minor variation of one of the alternatives discussed in the draft EIS, but this variation was not given any consideration by the agency. In such a case, the agency should develop and evaluate the new alternative, if it is reasonable, in the final EIS. If it is qualitatively within the spectrum of alternatives that were discussed in the draft, a supplemental draft will not be needed. For example, a commentor on a draft EIS to designate a wilderness area within a National Forest might reasonably identify a specific tract of the forest, and urge that it be considered for designation. If the draft

EIS considered designation of a range of alternative tracts which encompassed forest area of similar quality and quantity, no supplemental EIS would have to be prepared. The agency could fulfill its obligation by addressing that specific alternative in the final EIS.

As another example, an EIS on an urban housing project may analyze the alternatives of constructing 2,000, 4,000, or 6,000 units. A commentor on the draft EIS might urge the consideration of constructing 5,000 units utilizing a different configuration of buildings. This alternative is within the spectrum of alternatives already considered, and, therefore, could be addressed in the final EIS.

A fourth possibility is that a commentor points out an alternative which is not a variation of the proposal or of any alternative discussed in the draft impact statement, and is a reasonable alternative that warrants serious agency response. In such a case, the agency must issue a supplement to the draft EIS that discusses this new alternative. For example, a commentor on a draft EIS on a nuclear power plant might suggest that a reasonable alternative for meeting the projected need for power would be through peak load management and energy conservation programs. If the permitting agency has failed to consider that approach in the Draft EIS, and the approach cannot be dismissed by the agency as unreasonable, a supplement to the Draft EIS, which discusses that alternative, must be prepared. (If necessary, the same supplement should also discuss substantial changes in the proposed action or significant new circumstances or information, as required by Section 1502.9(c)(1) of the Council's regulations.)

If the new alternative was not raised by the commentor during scoping, but could have been, commentors may find that they are unpersuasive in their efforts to have their suggested alternative analyzed in detail by the agency. However, if the new alternative is discovered or developed later, and it could not reasonably have been raised during the scoping process, then the agency must address it in a supplemental draft EIS. The agency is, in any case, ultimately responsible for preparing an adequate EIS that considers all alternatives.

30. Q. When a cooperating agency with jurisdiction by law intends to adopt a lead agency's EIS and it is not satisfied with the adequacy of the document, may the cooperating agency adopt only the part of the EIS with which it is satisfied? If so, would a cooperating agency with jurisdiction by law have to prepare a separate EIS or EIS supplement covering the areas of disagreement with the lead agency?

A. Generally, a cooperating agency may adopt a lead agency's EIS without recirculating it if it concludes that its NEPA requirements and its comments and suggestions have been satisfied. Section 1506.3(a), (c). If necessary, a cooperating agency may adopt only a portion of the lead agency's EIS and may reject that part of the EIS with which it disagrees, stating publicly why it did so. Section 1506.3(a).

A cooperating agency with jurisidiction by law (e.g., an agency with independent legal responsibilities with respect to the proposal) has an independent legal obligation to comply with NEPA. Therefore, if the cooperating agency determines that the EIS is wrong or inadequate, it must prepare a supplement to the EIS, replacing or adding any needed information, and must circulate the supplement as a draft for public and agency review and comment. A final supplemental EIS would be required before the agency could take action. The adopted portions of the lead agency EIS should be circulated with the supplement. Section 1506.3(b). A cooperating agency with jurisdiction by law will have to prepare its own Record of Decision for its action, in which it must explain how it reached its conclusions. Each agency should explain how and why its conclusions differ, if that is the case, from those of other agencies which issued their Records of Decision earlier.

An agency that did not cooperate in preparation of an EIS may also adopt an EIS or portion thereof. But this would arise only in rare instances, because an agency adopting an EIS for use in its own decision normally would have been a cooperating agency. If the proposed action for which the EIS was prepared is substantially the same as the proposed action of the adopting agency, the EIS may be adopted as long as it is recirculated as a final EIS and the agency announces what it is doing. This would be followed by the 30-day review period and issuance of a Record of Decision by the adopting agency. If the proposed action by the adopting agency is not substantially the same as that in the EIS (i.e., if an EIS on one action is being adapted for use in a decision on another action), the EIS would be treated as a draft and circulated for the normal public comment period and other procedures. Section 1506.3(b).

31a. Q. Do the Council's NEPA regulations apply to independent regulatory agencies like the Federal Energy Regulatory Commission (FERC) and the Nuclear Regulatory Commission?

A. The statutory requirements of NEPA's Section 102 apply to "all agencies of the federal government." The NEPA regulations implement the procedural provisions of NEPA as set forth in NEPA's Section 102(2) for all agencies of the federal government. The NEPA regulations apply to independent regulatory agencies, however, they do not direct independent regulatory agencies or other agencies to make decisions in any particular way or in a way inconsistent with an agency's statutory charter. Sections 1500.3, 1500.6, 1507.1, and 1507.3.

31b. Q. Can an Executive Branch agency like the Department of the Interior adopt an EIS prepared by an independent regulatory agency such as FERC?

A. If an independent regulatory agency such as FERC has prepared an EIS in connection with its approval of a proposed project, an Executive Branch agency (e.g., the Bureau of Land Management in the Department of the Interior) may, in accordance with Section 1506.3, adopt the EIS or a portion thereof for its use in considering the same proposal. In such a case the EIS must, to the satisfaction of the adopting agency, meet the standards for an adequate statement under the NEPA regulations (including scope and quality of analysis of alternatives) and must satisfy the adopting agency's comments and suggestions. If the independent regulatory agency fails to comply with the NEPA regulations, the cooperating or adopting agency may find that it is unable to adopt the EIS, thus forcing the preparation of a new EIS or EIS Supplement for the same action. The NEPA regulations were made applicable to all federal agencies in order to avoid this result, and to achieve uniform application and efficiency of the NEPA process.

32. Q. Under what circumstances do old EISs have to be supplemented before taking action on a proposal?

A. As a rule of thumb, if the proposal has not yet been implemented, or if the EIS concerns an ongoing program, EISs that are more than 5 years old should be carefully reexamined to determine if the criteria in Section 1502.9 compel preparation of an EIS supplement. If an agency has made a substantial change in a proposed action that is relevant to environmental concerns, or if there are significant new circumstances or information relevant to environmental concerns and bearing on the proposed action or its impacts, a supplemental EIS must be prepared for an old EIS so that the agency has the best possible information to make any necessary substantive changes in its decisions regarding the proposal. Section 1502.9(c).

33a. Q. When must a referral of an interagency disagreement be made to the Council?

A. The Council's referral procedure is a pre-decision referral process for interagency disagreements. Hence, Section 1504.3 requires that a referring agency must deliver its referral to the Council not later than 25 days after publication by EPA of notice that the final EIS is available (unless the lead agency grants an extension of time under Section 1504.3(b)).

33b. Q. May a referral be made after this issuance of a Record of Decision?

A. No, except for cases where agencies provide an internal appeal procedure which permits simultaneous filing of the final EIS and the record of decision (ROD). Section 1506.10(b)(2). Otherwise, as stated above, the process is a pre-decision referral process. Referrals must be made within 25 days after the notice of availability of the final EIS, whereas the final decision (ROD) may not be made or filed until after 30 days from the notice of availability of the EIS. Sections 1504.3(b), 1506.10(b). If a lead agency has granted an extension of time for another agency to take action on a referral, the ROD may not be issued until the extension has expired.

34a. Q. Must Records of Decision (RODs) be made public? How should they be made available?

A. Under the regulations, agencies must prepare a "concise public record of decision," which contains the elements specified in Section 1505.2. This public record may be integrated into any other decision record prepared by the agency, or it may be separate if decision documents are not normally made public. The Record of Decision is intended by the Council to be an environmental document (even though it is not explicitly mentioned in the definition of "environmental document" in Section 1508.10). Therefore, it must be made available to the public through appropriate public notice as required by Section 1506.6(b). However, there is no specific requirement for publication of the ROD itself, either in the Federal Register or elsewhere.

34b. Q. May the summary section in the final Environmental Impact Statement substitute for or constitute an agency's Record of Decision?

A. No. An environmental impact statement is supposed to inform the decisionmaker before the decision is made. Sections 1502.1, 1505.2. The Council's regulations provide for a 30-day period after notice is published that the final EIS has been filed with EPA before the agency may take final action. During that period, in addition to the agency's own internal final review, the public and other agencies can comment on the final EIS prior to the agency's final action on the proposal. In addition, the Council's regulations make clear that the requirements for the summary in an EIS are not the same as the requirements for a ROD. Sections 1502.12 and 1505.2.

34c. Q. What provisions should Records of Decision contain pertaining to mitigation and monitoring?

A. Lead agencies "shall include appropriate conditions [including mitigation measures and monitoring and enforcement programs] in grants, permits or other approvals" and shall "condition funding of actions on mitigation." Section 1505.3. Any such measures that are adopted must be explained and committed in the ROD.

The reasonable alternative mitigation measures and monitoring programs should have been addressed in the draft and final EIS. The discussion of mitigation and monitoring in a Record of Decision must be more detailed than a general statement that mitigation is being required, but not so detailed as to duplicate discussion of mitigation in the EIS. The Record of Decision should contain a concise summary identification of the mitigation measures which the agency has committed itself to adopt.

The Record of Decision must also state whether all practicable mitigation measures have been adopted, and if not, why not. Section 1505.2(c). The Record of Decision must identify the mitigation measures and monitoring and enforcement programs that have been selected and plainly indicate that they are adopted as part of the agency's decision. If the proposed action is the issuance of a permit or other approval, the specific details of the mitigation measures shall then be included as appropriate conditions in whatever grants, permits, funding or other approvals are being made by the federal agency. Section 1505.3 (a), (b). If the proposal is to be carried out by the federal agency itself, the Record of Decision should delineate the mitigation and monitoring measures in sufficient detail to constitute an enforceable commitment, or incorporate by reference the portions of the EIS that do so.

34d. Q. What is the enforceability of a Record of Decision?

A. Pursuant to generally recognized principles of federal administrative law, agencies will be held accountable for preparing Records of Decision that conform to the decisions actually made and for carrying out the actions set forth in the Records of Decision. This is based on the principle that an agency must comply with its own decisons and regulations once they are adopted. Thus, the terms of a Record of Decision are enforceable by agencies and private parties. A Record of Decision can be used to compel compliance with or execution of the mitigation measures identified therein.

35. Q. How long should the NEPA process take to complete?

A. When an EIS is required, the process obviously will take longer than when an EA is the only document prepared. But the Council's NEPA regulations encourage streamlined review, adoption of deadlines, elimination of duplicative work, eliciting suggested alternatives and other comments early through scoping, cooperation among agencies, and consultation with applicants during project planning. The Council has advised agencies that under the new NEPA regulations even large complex energy projects would require only about 12 months for the completion of the entire EIS process. For most major actions, this period is well within the planning time that is needed in any event, apart from NEPA.

The time required for the preparation of program EISs may be greater. The Council also recognizes that some projects will entail difficult long-term planning and/or the acquisition of certain data which of necessity will require more time for the preparation of the EIS. Indeed, some proposals should be given more time for the thoughtful preparation of an EIS and development of a decision which fulfills NEPA's substantive goals. For cases in which only an environmental assessment will be prepared, the NEPA process should take no more than 3 months, and in many cases substantially less, as part of the normal analysis and approval process for the action.

36a. Q. How long and detailed must an environmental assessment (EA) be?

A. The environmental assessment is a concise public document which has three defined functions. (1) It briefly provides sufficient evidence and analysis for determining whether to prepare an EIS; (2) it aids an agency's compliance with NEPA when no EIS is necessary, i.e., it helps to identify better alternatives and mitigation measures; and (3) it facilitates preparation of an EIS when one is necessary. Section 1508.9(a).

Since the EA is a concise document, it should not contain long descriptions or detailed data which the agency may have gathered. Rather, it should contain a brief discussion of the need for the proposal, alternatives to the proposal, the environmental impacts of the proposed action and alternatives, and a list of agencies and persons consulted. Section 1508.9(b).

While the regulations do not contain page limits for EA's, the Council has generally advised agencies to keep the length of EAs to not more than approximately 10-15 pages. Some agencies expressly provide page guidelines (e.g., 10-15 pages in the case of the Army Corps). To avoid undue length, the EA may incorporate by reference background data to support its concise discussion of the proposal and relevant issues.

36b. Q. Under what circumstances is a lengthy EA appropriate?

A. Agencies should avoid preparing lengthy EAs except in unusual cases, where a proposal is so complex that a concise document cannot meet the goals of Section 1508.9 and where it is extremely difficult to determine whether the proposal could have significant environmental effects. In most cases, however, a lengthy EA indicates that an EIS is needed.

37a. Q. What is the level of detail of information that must be included in a finding of no significant impact (FONSI)?

A. The FONSI is a document in which the agency briefly explains the reasons why an action will not have a significant effect on the human environment and, therefore, why an EIS will not be prepared. Section 1508.13. The finding itself need not be detailed, but must succinctly state the reasons for deciding that the action will have no significant environmental effects, and, if relevant, must show which factors were weighted most heavily in the determination. In addition to this statement, the FONSI must include, summarize, or attach and incorporate by reference, the environmental assessment.

37b. Q. What are the criteria for deciding whether a FONSI should be made available for public review for 30 days before the agency's final determination whether to prepare an EIS?

A. Public review is necessary, for example, (a) if the proposal is a borderline case, i.e., when there is a reasonable argument for preparation of an EIS; (b) if it is an unusual case, a new kind of action, or a precedent setting case such as a first intrusion of even a minor development into a pristine area; (c) when there is either scientific or public controversy over the proposal; or (d) when it involves a proposal which is or is closely similar to one which normally requires preparation of an EIS. Sections 1501.4(e)(2), 1508.27. Agencies also must allow a period of public review of the FONSI if the proposed action would be located in a floodplain or wetland. E.O. 11988, Sec. 2(a)(4); E.O. 11990, Sec. 2(b).

38. Q. Must (EAs) and FONSIs be made public? If so, how should this be done?

A. Yes, they must be available to the public. Section 1506.6 requires agencies to involve the public in implementing their NEPA procedures, and this includes public involvement in the preparation of EAs and FONSIs. These are public "environmental documents" under Section 1506.6(b), and, therefore, agencies must give public notice of their availability. A combination of methods may be used to give notice, and the methods should be tailored to the needs of particular cases. Thus, a Federal Register notice of availability of the documents, coupled with notices in national publications and mailed to interested national groups might be appropriate for proposals that are national in scope. Local newspaper notices may be more appropriate for regional or site-specific proposals.

The objective, however, is to notify all interested or affected parties. If this is not being achieved, then the methods should be reevaluated and changed. Repeated failure to reach the interested or affected public would be interpreted as a violation of the regulations. index

39. Q. Can an EA and FONSI be used to impose enforceable mitigation measures, monitoring programs, or other requirements, even though there is no requirement in the regulations in such cases for a formal Record of Decision?

A. Yes. In cases where an environmental assessment is the appropriate environmental document, there still may be mitigation measures or alternatives that would be desirable to consider and adopt even though the impacts of the proposal will not be "significant." In such cases, the EA should include a discussion of these measures or alternatives to "assist agency planning and decisionmaking" and to "aid an agency's compliance with [NEPA] when no environmental impact statement is necessary." Section 1501.3(b), 1508. 9(a)(2). The appropriate mitigation measures can be imposed as enforceable permit conditions, or adopted as part of the agency final decision in the same manner mitigation measures are adopted in the formal Record of Decision that is required in EIS cases.

40. Q. If an environmental assessment indicates that the environmental effects of a proposal are significant but that, with mitigation, those effects may be reduced to less than significant levels, may the agency make a finding of no significant impact rather than prepare an EIS? Is that a legitimate function of an EA and scoping?

A. Mitigation measures may be relied upon to make a finding of no significant impact only if they are imposed by statute or regulation, or submitted by an applicant or agency as part of the original proposal. As a general rule, the regulations contemplate that agencies should use a broad approach in defining significance and should not rely on the possibility of mitigation as an excuse to avoid the EIS requirement. Sections 1508.8, 1508.27.

If a proposal appears to have adverse effects which would be significant, and certain mitigation measures are then developed during the scoping or EA stages, the existence of such possible mitigation does not obviate the need for an EIS. Therefore, if scoping or the EA identifies certain mitigation possibilities without altering the nature of the overall proposal itself, the agency should continue the EIS process and submit the proposal, and the potential mitigation, for public and agency review and comment. This is essential to ensure that the final decision is based on all the relevant factors and that the full NEPA process will result in enforceable mitigation measures through the Record of Decision.

In some instances, where the proposal itself so integrates mitigation from the beginning that it is impossible to define the proposal without including the mitigation, the agency may then rely on the mitigation measures in determining that the overall effects would not be significant (e.g., where an application for a permit for a small hydro dam is based on a binding commitment to build fish ladders, to permit adequate down stream flow, and to replace any lost wetlands, wildlife habitat and recreational potential). In those instances, agencies should make the FONSI and EA available for 30 days of public comment before taking action. Section 1501.4(e)(2).

Similarly, scoping may result in a redefinition of the entire project, as a result of mitigation proposals. In that case, the agency may alter its previous decision to do an EIS, as long as the agency or applicant resubmits the entire proposal and the EA and FONSI are available for 30 days of review and comment. One example of this would be where the size and location of a proposed industrial park are changed to avoid affecting a nearby wetland area.

Negotiated Rulemaking Act

Citations:

5 U.S.C. §§561-570 (2000); enacted November 29, 1990, by Pub. L. No. 101-648, 104 Stat. 4969, renumbered August 26, 1992 by Pub. L. No. 102-354, 106 Stat. 944; amended by Pub. L. No. 104-320, §10, Oct. 19, 1996, 110 Stat. 3870.

Lead Agency:

The Act originally named the Administrative Conference of the United States as the lead agency for coordinating negotiated rulemaking, but the Conference was defunded by Congress in 1995, so in 1996 Section 569 of the Act was amended to require the President to designate an agency or interagency committee to facilitate and encourage agency use of negotiated rulemaking. The President then named the Regulatory Working Group, which had been established under Section 4(d) of Executive Order 12,866, 58 Fed. Reg. 51,735 (Sept. 30, 1993), as the lead agency.[1] However, it is not clear that the Regulatory Working Group as a functioning entity survived the change in administrations, despite its retention on paper and specific amendment in Executive Order 13,258, 67 Fed. Reg. 9385 (2002). Thus, there does not appear to be a lead agency for this Act.

Overview:

The Negotiated Rulemaking Act of 1990 establishes a statutory framework for agencies to formulate proposed regulations by using negotiated rulemaking. The Act supplements the rulemaking provisions of the Adminis-

---

[1] *See* Memorandum on the Designation of Interagency Committees to Facilitate and Encourage Agency Use of Alternate Means of Dispute Resolution and Negotiated Rulemaking, May 1, 1998, 1998 WL 214697.

trative Procedure Act by clarifying the authority of federal agencies to conduct negotiated rulemaking. It largely codifies the practice of those agencies that had previously used the procedure. While not requiring use of the technique, the Act provides each agency discretion with regard to using negotiated rulemaking.

Negotiated rulemaking (sometimes known as "regulatory negotiation" or "reg-neg") emerged in the 1980s as an alternative to traditional procedures for drafting proposed regulations. The essence of the idea was that in certain situations it is possible to bring together representatives of an agency and the various affected interest groups to negotiate the text of a proposed rule. The negotiators would try to reach a consensus through a process of evaluating their own priorities and making tradeoffs to achieve an acceptable outcome on the issues of greatest importance to them. If they do achieve a consensus, then the resulting rule is likely to be easier to implement and the likelihood of subsequent litigation is diminished. Even absent consensus on a draft rule, the process may be valuable as a means of better informing the regulatory agency of the issues and the concerns of the affected interests.

Negotiated rulemaking should be viewed as a supplement to the rulemaking provisions of the Administrative Procedure Act. This means that the negotiation sessions generally take place prior to issuance of the notice and the opportunity for the public to comment on a proposed rule that are required by the APA (5 U.S.C. §553). In some instances, negotiations may be appropriate at a later stage of the proceeding and have sometimes been used effectively in drafting the text of a final rule based on comments received.

In 1982 the Administrative Conference of the United States set forth criteria for identifying rulemaking situations for which reg-neg is likely to be successful (Recommendation 82-4, 47 Fed. Reg. 30,708 (July 15, 1982)). These criteria were intended to guide agencies in determining whether negotiated rulemaking would be appropriate for addressing particular regulatory problems. The Conference also suggested specific procedures for agencies to follow in applying this approach. Additional refinements, based on a study of initial agency experiences with reg-neg, were recommended in 1985 (Recommendation 85-5, 50 Fed. Reg. 52,895 (Dec. 27, 1985)).

Much of the Negotiated Rulemaking Act is permissive, incorporating many of the criteria and procedures suggested in the Conference recommendations. The drafters intended that the Act not impair any rights otherwise retained by agencies or parties, and section 561 expressly provides that the Act is not intended to limit innovation or experimentation with the negotiated rulemaking process. Although the Act plainly permits an agency to publish as its own the consensus proposal adopted by the negotiating committee, nothing in the Act requires the agency to publish either a proposed or final rule merely because a negotiating committee proposed it.

Following the recommendations of the Conference, section 563 of the Act lists several criteria for agencies to consider in determining whether to use negotiated rulemaking in any particular instance. It permits, but does not require, the use of outside impartial persons (referred to as "conveners") to assist the agency in identifying potential participants in the negotiation process. Section 564 requires public notice of planned negotiated rulemaking proceedings both in the Federal Register and in appropriate trade and specialized publications. Persons or interest groups believing that they are not adequately represented on the negotiating committee must be given an opportunity to apply for membership, though the agency retains discretion as to whether to grant such requests.

Section 565 outlines the process for establishing negotiating committees and makes clear that they are also to comply with the Federal Advisory Committee Act. At least one member of the committee must be a representative of the agency. If, after considering the public responses to the published notice of intent to establish a negotiating committee under the Act, the agency determines not to do so, then the agency must publish a notice of that fact and the reasons for its decision.

Section 566 addresses the procedures of the negotiating committee and provides for selection of a neutral "facilitator" or mediator to assist the committee in its deliberations.

Section 567 permits an agency to keep a negotiating committee in existence until promulgation of the final rule, but also allows earlier termination if the agency or the committee so chooses.

Section 568 addresses options for acquiring the services of conveners and facilitators.[2] Agencies are authorized to pay expenses of certain committee members in accordance with the Federal Advisory Committee Act.

Section 569 refers agencies considering negotiated rulemaking to consult the agency or committee identified by the President to facilitate and encourage negotiated rulemaking. It also permits an agency to accept and utilize gifts in support of negotiated rulemaking, if the gift would not "create a conflict of interest."

---

[2] *See also* Administrative Conference Recommendation 86-8, *Acquiring the Services of "Neutrals" for Alternative Means of Dispute Resolution*, 51 Fed. Reg. 46,990; Ruttinger, *Acquiring the Services of Neutrals for Alternative Means of Dispute Resolution and Negotiated Rulemaking*, 1986 ACUS 863.

To avoid creating new sources of potential litigation, section 570 provides that agency actions relating to the establishment, assistance, or termination of a negotiated rulemaking committee are not subject to judicial review. However, the Act does not affect the otherwise available judicial review of the *rules* promulgated through the negotiation process.

Under section 5 of the Negotiated Rulemaking Act of 1990, as originally enacted by Public Law 101-648, the provisions of the Act were to be repealed six years after the date of enactment (Nov. 26, 1996). Section 11(a) of the Administrative Dispute Resolution Act of 1996 (Pub. L. No. 104-320) repealed section 5 and permanently reauthorized the Act.

Legislative History:

The Senate's Select Committee on Small Business and Committee on Governmental Affairs held joint hearings on "regulatory negotiation" in July 1980. Legislation was introduced in September 1980 "to create a pilot program to encourage . . . the formation of regulatory negotiation commissions, comprised of representatives of business, public interest organizations, labor, State and local officials, and other interested persons, for the purpose of making recommendations to Federal agencies on regulatory policy." (H.R. 8240, 96th Congress) Other bills to establish a statutory framework for negotiated rulemaking were introduced in each subsequent Congress throughout the 1980s.

100th Congress. The first negotiated rulemaking bill to be acted upon was S.1504, introduced by Senator Carl Levin in the 100th Congress. The Senate Committee on Governmental Affairs held hearings on May 13, 1988, and the Senate passed the bill on September 30, 1988 (134 Cong. Rec. S13760 (1988); *see also* the report of the Senate Committee on Governmental Affairs, 100th Congress, 2d Session, S. Rep. No. 100-547). In the House, the Judiciary Subcommittee on Administrative Law and Governmental Relations held a hearing on August 10, 1988, on a companion bill, H.R. 3052, introduced by Representative Donald Pease. No further action was taken.

101st Congress. In the 101st Congress, identical bills, S. 303 and H.R. 743, were introduced on January 31, 1989 (135 Cong. Rec. S862 and H144 (1989). The Senate Committee on Governmental Affairs reported out S. 303 on July 13, 1989, and the Senate passed it on August 3, 1989 (see 135 Cong. Rec. S10060 (1989); see also the report of the Senate Committee on Governmental Affairs, 101st Congress, 1st Session, S. Rep. No. 101-97).

The House Subcommittee held a hearing on H.R. 743 on May 3, 1989, and on February 7, 1990, reported out the bill with amendments. The Committee on the Judiciary passed the bill on March 28, and the House passed it on May 1 (136 Cong. Rec. H1852 (1990); *see also* the report of the House Committee on the Judiciary, 101st Congress, 2d Session, H. Rep. No. 101-461). The Senate amended the bill further and passed S. 303 again on October 4 (136 Cong. Rec. S14580 (1990). The House accepted the Senate amendments, voting final passage on October 22 (136 Cong. Rec. H10966, Oct. 22, 1990). The bill was signed by President Bush on November 29, 1990.

During the period of Congressional consideration of the Negotiated Rulemaking Act, Congress passed three other pieces of legislation that mandated use of negotiated rulemaking: the Carl D. Perkins Vocational and Applied Technology Education Act Amendments (Pub. L. No. 101-392), the Hawkins-Stafford Elementary and Secondary School Improvements Amendments (Pub. L. No. 100-297), and the Price-Anderson Amendments Act of 1988 (Pub. L. No. 100-408). Each of these laws provided specific and widely differing procedures for negotiating rules.

102d Congress. The Administrative Procedure Technical Amendments Act of 1991, Pub. L. No. 102-354, 106 Stat. 944, was passed by the 102d Congress and signed into law on August 26, 1992. It recodified the existing Negotiated Rulemaking Act to a different subchapter to eliminate the duplication in section numbering with the Administrative Dispute Resolution Act.

104th Congress. On February 27, 1996, Representative Gekas introduced H.R. 2977, a predecessor for the measure that would eventually become Pub. L. No. 104-320. H.R. 2977 was referred to the House Committee on the Judiciary and the Subcommittee on Commercial and Administrative Law for consideration. The Committee on the Judiciary reported up the measure (H. Rep. 104-597), and the House passed an amended resolution on June 4. In the Senate, S. 1224 was incorporated into H.R. 2977 as an amendment. A Conference report was filed in the House, H. Rep. 104-841 to consider the House's objections to the amendments. On September 27, the House considered and passed H.R. 4194, substantially identical to H.R. 2977. The Senate considered and passed H.R. 4194 as amended three days later, and the House passed the amended resolution without objection. On October 19, 1996, President Clinton signed the bill into law.

Congress has used the Negotiated Rulemaking Act as a common reference for application of reg-neg procedures to other legislation. For example, see Agriculture, Rural Development, Food and Drug Administration, and Related Agencies Appropriations Act of 1997, Pub. L. No. 104-180, August 6, 1996, 110 Stat. 1,569, Section 734(d); or Health Insurance Portability and Accountability Act, Pub. L. No. 104-191, August 21, 1996, 110 Stat. 1,936, Section 216(b).

Significant Case Law:

EPA's final rule on asbestos-containing materials in schools was the first reg-neg rule to be challenged in court. The suit was brought by the Safe Buildings Alliance, a group representing former manufacturers of asbestos building products that are now illegal. Plaintiffs in the lawsuit claimed that the rule would encourage unnecessary removal of materials from buildings and would result in a chaotic situation. They sought a more objective standard—based on air monitoring, for example—rather than the professional judgment called for under EPA's rule. The Safe Buildings Alliance had been represented on the negotiating committee. Several other parties who were represented on the negotiating committee intervened *in support of the final rule* as published. These included the National Education Association, the American Association of School Administrators, and a group of state attorneys general.

In May 1988, the rule was upheld by the U.S. Court of Appeals for the D.C. Circuit, *Safe Buildings Alliance v. EPA*, 846 F.2d 79 (D.C. Cir. 1988). The court determined that EPA's regulation embodied a reasonable interpretation of the requirements of the Asbestos Hazard Emergency Response Act of 1986, Pub. L. No. 99-519, 15 U.S.C. §§2641-54 (2000). Neither the appeal nor the court's decision referred to the negotiation procedure that was followed. EPA's underground injection rule, based in part on negotiated rulemaking, was also challenged and essentially upheld by the D.C. Circuit, *Natural Resources Defense Council v. EPA*, 907 F.2d 1146 (D.C. Cir. 1990).

The Department of Education's regulations pertaining to the liability of student loan servicers were the first reg-neg rules in which the court actually discussed the negotiated rulemaking process. *USA Loan Services, Inc. v. Riley*, 82 F.3d 708 (7th Cir. 1996). The court determined that any promises made by the agency during negotiations regarding the outcome of the final rule were unenforceable under the Negotiated Rulemaking Act. *Id.* at 714. Furthermore, the reg-neg procedures were viewed as merely a consultative process since an agency is not bound by the consensus of the negotiations in determining the final rule. *Id.* at 715. This case is notable, however, because it referred to negotiated rulemaking as "a novelty in the administrative process," and because the court's discussion seemed critical of this new process, even as it upheld the legality of what was done. This decision has been criticized as narrow and erroneous.[3]

---

[3] *See* Philip J. Harter, *First Judicial Review of Reg Neg a Disappointment*, ADMIN. & REG. L. NEWS 1 (Fall 1996).

While Section 570 of the Act states that agency actions establishing negotiated rulemaking committees are not subject to judicial review, it also says that nothing in the section bars review of a rule otherwise subject to review. In *Center for Law and Educ. v. U.S. Dept. of Educ.*, 315 F. Supp. 2d 15 (D.D.C. 2004), *aff'd on other grounds*, 396 F.3d 1152 (D.C. Cir. 2005), the court held that this section precluded a challenge to a rule in which the plaintiff claimed that the composition of the rulemaking committee violated the requirements of the Federal Advisory Committee Act. The court of appeals affirmed the judgment of dismissal on the grounds that the plaintiffs lacked standing and did not reach the Section 570 question. Judge Edwards, however, wrote separately to state his view that, while he agreed that the plaintiffs lacked standing, he believed that Section 570 did not bar their challenge. He believed that the savings portion of the section allowed judicial review pursuant to the APA of a claim that the agency violated FACA in its establishment of the rulemaking committee.

Source Note:

In 1995, the Administrative Conference of the United States published a second edition of its *Negotiated Rulemaking Sourcebook*, a step-by-step guide to the conduct of negotiated rulemaking proceedings. The volume contains a discussion of when and how to use the procedure, along with sample notices and other documents that may be needed by an agency using the process. Numerous articles, both analytical and practical, are reprinted in the *Sourcebook,* including the Harter and Perritt reports to the Conference that furnished the research background for Conference Recommendations 82-4 and 85-5. An extensive bibliography is also included. The Table of Contents of the *Negotiated Rulemaking Sourcebook* is included in Appendix 2. While this book is out of print, it is still available in a number of libraries.

Bibliography:

I. Legislative History

1. *Conference Report to accompany H.R.2977, Administrative Dispute Resolution Act of 1996*, H. Rep. 104-841, 104th Cong., 2d Sess. (1996).
2. House Committee on the Judiciary, *Administrative Dispute Resolution Act of 1996 (H.R. 2977)*, H. Rep. 104-597, 104th Cong., 2d Sess. (1996).
3. House Committee on the Judiciary, *Negotiated Rulemaking Act of*

1990 (H.R. 743), H. Rep. 101-461, 101st Cong., 2d Sess. (1990).

4. *Negotiated Rulemaking Act of 1987: Hearing before the Subcommittee on Administrative Law and Governmental Relations of the House Committee on the Judiciary (H.R. 3052)*, 100th Cong., 2d Sess. (1988).

5. *Negotiated Rulemaking Act of 1989: Hearing before the Subcommittee on Administrative Law and Governmental Relations of the House Committee on the Judiciary (H.R. 743)*, 101st Cong., 1st Sess. (1989).

6. *President's Statement on Signing the Negotiated Rulemaking Act of 1990*, 26 Weekly Comp. Press Doc. 1945 (Nov. 29, 1990).

7. *Regulatory Negotiation: Joint Hearings Before the Senate Select Committee on Small Business and the Subcommittee on Oversight of Government Management of the Senate Committee on Governmental Affairs*, 96th Cong., 2d Sess. (1980).

8. Senate Committee on Governmental Affairs, *Negotiated Rulemaking Act of 1988 (S. 1504)*, Rep. 100-547, 100th Cong., 2d Sess. (1988).

9. Senate Committee on Governmental Affairs, *Negotiated Rulemaking Act of 1989 (S. 303)*, Rep. 101-97, 101st Cong., 1st Sess. (1989).

10. *Interstate Compacts; Reauthorization of the Negotiated Rulemaking Act: Hearings before the Subcommittee on Commercial and Administrative Law*, 104th Cong., 2d Sess. (1996).

11. *House Conference Report on the Administrative Dispute Resolution Act of 1996*, H.R. Conf. Rep. No. 841, 104th Cong., 2d Sess. (1996).

II. Other Government Documents

1. Administrative Conference of the U.S., *Negotiated Rulemaking Sourcebook* (David M. Pritzker and Deborah S. Dalton, eds.) (U.S. Government Printing Office 1995).

2. Administrative Conference of the U.S., Recommendation 82-4, *Procedures for Negotiating Proposed Regulations*, 47 Fed. Reg. 30,708 (July 15, 1982).

3. Administrative Conference of the U.S., Recommendation 85-5, *Procedures for Negotiating Proposed Regulations*, 50 Fed. Reg. 52,895 (Dec. 27, 1985).

4. Administrative Conference of the U.S., Recommendation 86-8, *Acquiring the Services of "Neutrals" for Alternative Means of Dispute Resolution*, 51 Fed. Reg. 46,990 (Dec. 30, 1986).

5. Philip J. Harter, *Negotiating Regulations: A Cure for Malaise,* Report to the Administrative Conference of the U.S., 1982 ACUS (Vol. 1) 301,

reprinted in 71 Georgetown L.J. 1 (1982).

6. Henry H. Perritt, Jr., *Analysis of Four Negotiated Rulemaking Efforts*, Report to the Administrative Conference of the U.S., 1985 ACUS 637, *revised version published as Negotiated Rulemaking Before Federal Agencies: Evaluation of Recommendations by the Administrative Conference*, 74 Geo. L.J. 1625 (1986).

7. Henry H. Perritt, Jr., *Use of Negotiated Rulemaking to Develop a Proposed OSHA Health Standard for MDA* (Report prepared for the Deputy Assistant Secretary of Labor, May 1988).

8. Executive Order 12,866, §4(d), Regulatory Planning and Review, 58 Fed. Reg. 51,735 (Oct. 4, 1993).

III. Books and Articles

The following books and articles have been written since the *Negotiated Rulemaking Sourcebook* appeared in 1995 with its extensive bibliography:

1. Danielle Holley-Walker, *The Importance of Negotiated Rulemaking to the No Child Left Behind Act*, 85 Nebr. L. Rev. 1015 (2007)

2. Robin McCall, *Dogs v. Birds: Negotiated Rulemaking at Fort Funston*, 13 Hastings W.-N.W. J. Envtl. L. & Pol'y 187 (2007).

3. Federal Administrative Dispute Resolution Deskbook (Marshall J. Breger, ed.) (ABA Press 2001).

4. Cary Coglianese, *Assessing the Advocacy of Negotiated Rulemaking: a Response to Philip Harter*, 9 N.Y.U. Envtl. L.J. 386 (2001).

5. Philip J. Harter, *Assessing the Assessors: the Actual Performance of Negotiated Rulemaking*, 9 N.Y.U. Envtl. L.J. 32 (2000).

6. Cary Coglianese, *Assessing Consensus: The Promise and Performance of Negotiated Rulemaking*, 46 Duke L.J. 1255 (1997).

7. Gary R. Dillinger, *Guidelines for Negotiated Rulemaking*, 25 Colo. Law 21 (1996).

8. Dennis H. Esposito & Kristen W. Ulbrich, *Negotiated Rulemaking in Environmental Law*, 46 R.I.B.J. 5 (1998).

9. Jody Freeman, *Collaborative Governance in the Administrative State*, 45 U.C.L.A. L. Rev. 1 (1997).

10. William Funk, *Bargaining Toward the New Millennium: Regulatory Negotiation and the Subversion of the Public Interest*, 46 Duke L.J. 1351 (1997).

11. Philip J. Harter, *First Judicial Review of Reg Neg a Disappointment*, 22 Admin. & Reg. L. News 1 (Fall 1996).

12. Philip J. Harter, *Fear of Commitment: An Affliction of Adolescents*, 46 Duke L.J. 1389 1997).

13. Ellen Siegler, *Regulatory Negotiation and Other Rulemaking Processes: Strengths and Weaknesses from an Industry Viewpoint*, 46 Duke L.J. 1429 (1997).

14. Patricia M. Wald, *ADR and the Courts: An Update*, 46 Duke L.J. 1445 (1997).

Appendix:

1. Negotiated Rulemaking Act, 5 U.S.C. §§561-70 (2000).
2. Administrative Conference of the U.S., *Negotiated Rulemaking Sourcebook* (David M. Pritzker & Deborah S. Dalton, eds) (1995), Table of Contents.
3. Administrative Conference Recommendation 82-4.
4. Administrative Conference Recommendation 85-5.

Negotiated Rulemaking Act

Title 5, U.S. Code

Subchapter III–Negotiated Rulemaking Procedure

§561. Purpose
§562. Definitions
§563. Determination of need for negotiated rulemaking committee
§564. Publication of notice; applications for membership on committees
§565. Establishment of committee
§566. Conduct of committee activity
§567. Termination of committee
§568. Services, facilities, and payment of committee member expenses
§569. Encouraging negotiated rulemaking
§570. Judicial review
§570a. Authorization of appropriations

Subchapter III–Negotiated Rulemaking Procedure

§561. Purpose

The purpose of this subchapter is to establish a framework for the conduct of negotiated rulemaking, consistent with section 553 of this title, to encourage agencies to use the process when it enhances the informal rulemaking process. Nothing in this subchapter should be construed as an attempt to limit innovation and experimentation with the negotiated rulemaking process or with other innovative rulemaking procedures otherwise authorized by law.

(Added Pub. L. No. 101-648, § 3(a), Nov. 29, 1990, 104 Stat. 4970, § 581, and renumbered § 561, Pub. L. No. 102-354, § 3(a)(2), Aug. 26, 1992, 106 Stat. 944.)

§562. Definitions

For the purposes of this subchapter, the term—
   (1) "agency" has the same meaning as in section 551(1) of this title;
   (2) "consensus" means unanimous concurrence among the interests represented on a negotiated rulemaking committee established under this subchapter, unless such committee—
      (A) agrees to define such term to mean a general but not unanimous concurrence; or

(B) agrees upon another specified definition;

(3) "convener" means a person who impartially assists an agency in determining whether establishment of a negotiated rulemaking committee is feasible and appropriate in a particular rulemaking;

(4) "facilitator" means a person who impartially aids in the discussions and negotiations among the members of a negotiated rulemaking committee to develop a proposed rule;

(5) "interest" means, with respect to an issue or matter, multiple parties which have a similar point of view or which are likely to be affected in a similar manner;

(6) "negotiated rulemaking" means rulemaking through the use of a negotiated rulemaking committee;

(7) "negotiated rulemaking committee" or "committee" means an advisory committee established by an agency in accordance with this subchapter and the Federal Advisory Committee Act to consider and discuss issues for the purpose of reaching a consensus in the development of a proposed rule;

(8) "party" has the same meaning as in section 551(3) of this title;

(9) "person" has the same meaning as in section 551(2) of this title;

(10) "rule" has the same meaning as in section 551(4) of this title; and

(11) "rulemaking" means "rule making" as that term is defined in section 551(5) of this title.

(Added Pub. L. No. 101-648, § 3(a), Nov. 29, 1990, 104 Stat. 4,970, § 581, and renumbered § 561, Pub. L. No. 102-354, § 3(a)(2), Aug. 26, 1992, 106 Stat. 944.)

§563. Determination of need for negotiated rulemaking committee

(a) Determination of need by the agency.—An agency may establish a negotiated rulemaking committee to negotiate and develop a proposed rule, if the head of the agency determines that the use of the negotiated rulemaking procedure is in the public interest. In making such a determination, the head of the agency shall consider whether—

(1) there is a need for a rule;

(2) there are a limited number of identifiable interests that will be significantly affected by the rule;

(3) there is a reasonable likelihood that a committee can be convened with a balanced representation of persons who—

(A) can adequately represent the interests identified under paragraph (2); and

(B) are willing to negotiate in good faith to reach a consensus on the proposed rule;

(4) there is a reasonable likelihood that a committee will reach a consensus on the proposed rule within a fixed period of time;

(5) the negotiated rulemaking procedure will not unreasonably delay the notice of proposed rulemaking and the issuance of the final rule;

(6) the agency has adequate resources and is willing to commit such resources, including technical assistance, to the committee; and

(7) the agency, to the maximum extent possible consistent with the legal obligations of the agency, will use the consensus of the committee with respect to the proposed rule as the basis for the rule proposed by the agency for notice and comment.

(b) Use of conveners.—

(1) Purposes of conveners.—An agency may use the services of a convener to assist the agency in—

(A) identifying persons who will be significantly affected by a proposed rule, including residents of rural areas; and

(B) conducting discussions with such persons to identify the issues of concern to such persons, and to ascertain whether the establishment of a negotiated rulemaking committee is feasible and appropriate in the particular rulemaking.

(2) Duties of conveners.—The convener shall report findings and may make recommendations to the agency. Upon request of the agency, the convener shall ascertain the names of persons who are willing and qualified to represent interests that will be significantly affected by the proposed rule, including residents of rural areas. The report and any recommendations of the convener shall be made available to the public upon request.

(Added Pub. L. No. 101-648, § 3(a), Nov. 29, 1990, 104 Stat. 4,970, § 583, and renumbered § 563, Pub. L. No. 102-354, § 3(a)(2), Aug. 26, 1992, 106 Stat. 944.)

5 U.S.C § 563 note:
The Director of the Office of Management and Budget shall—

(1) within 180 days of the date of the enactment of this Act [Oct. 19, 1996], take appropriate action to expedite the establishment of negotiated rulemaking committees and committees established to resolve disputes under the Administrative Dispute Resolution Act [Pub. L. 101–552, see Short Title note set out under section 571 of this title], including, with respect to negotiated rulemaking committees, eliminating any redundant administrative requirements related to filing a committee charter under section 9 of the Federal Advisory Committee Act (5 U.S.C. App.) and providing public notice of such committee under section 564 of title 5, United States Code; and

(2) within one year of the date of the enactment of this Act, submit recommendations to Congress for any necessary legislative changes.

(Added Pub. L. No. 104-320, §11(e), Oct. 19, 1996, 100 Stat. 3874.)

§564. Publication of notice; applications for membership on committees

(a) Publication of notice.—If, after considering the report of a convener or conducting its own assessment, an agency decides to establish a negotiated rulemaking committee, the agency shall publish in the Federal Register and, as appropriate, in trade or other specialized publications, a notice which shall include—

(1) an announcement that the agency intends to establish a negotiated rulemaking committee to negotiate and develop a proposed rule;

(2) a description of the subject and scope of the rule to be developed, and the issues to be considered;

(3) a list of the interests which are likely to be significantly affected by the rule;

(4) a list of the persons proposed to represent such interests and the person or persons proposed to represent the agency;

(5) a proposed agenda and schedule for completing the work of the committee, including a target date for publication by the agency of a proposed rule for notice and comment;

(6) a description of administrative support for the committee to be provided by the agency, including technical assistance;

(7) a solicitation for comments on the proposal to establish the committee, and the proposed membership of the negotiated rulemaking committee; and

(8) an explanation of how a person may apply or nominate another person for membership on the committee, as provided under subsection (b).

(b) Applications for membership or[4] committee.—Persons who will be significantly affected by a proposed rule and who believe that their interests will not be adequately represented by any person specified in a notice under subsection (a)(4) may apply for, or nominate another person for, membership on the negotiated rulemaking committee to represent such interests with respect to the proposed rule. Each application or nomination shall include—

(1) the name of the applicant or nominee and a description of the interests such person shall represent;

---

[4] So in original. Probably should be "on."

(2) evidence that the applicant or nominee is authorized to represent parties related to the interests the person proposes to represent;

(3) a written commitment that the applicant or nominee shall actively participate in good faith in the development of the rule under consideration; and

(4) the reasons that the persons specified in the notice under subsection (a)(4) do not adequately represent the interests of the person submitting the application or nomination.

(c) Period for submission of comments and applications.—The agency shall provide for a period of at least 30 calendar days for the submission of comments and applications under this section.

(Added Pub. L. 101-648, § 3(a), Nov. 29, 1990, 104 Stat. 4,972, § 585, and renumbered § 565 and amended Pub. L. 102-354, § 3(a)(2), (3), Aug. 26, 1992, 106 Stat. 944.)

§565. Establishment of committee

(a) Establishment.—

(1) Determination to establish committee.—If after considering comments and applications submitted under section 564, the agency determines that a negotiated rulemaking committee can adequately represent the interests that will be significantly affected by a proposed rule and that it is feasible and appropriate in the particular rulemaking, the agency may establish a negotiated rulemaking committee. In establishing and administering such a committee, the agency shall comply with the Federal Advisory Committee Act with respect to such committee, except as otherwise provided in this subchapter.

(2) Determination not to establish committee.—If after considering such comments and applications, the agency decides not to establish a negotiated rulemaking committee, the agency shall promptly publish notice of such decision and the reasons therefor in the Federal Register and, as appropriate, in trade or other specialized publications, a copy of which shall be sent to any person who applied for, or nominated another person for membership on the negotiating[5] rulemaking committee to represent such interests with respect to the proposed rule.

(b) Membership.—The agency shall limit membership on a negotiated rulemaking committee to 25 members, unless the agency head determines that a greater number of members is necessary for the functioning of the

---

[5] So in original. Probably should be "negotiated."

committee or to achieve balanced membership. Each committee shall include at least one person representing the agency.

(c) **Administrative support.**—The agency shall provide appropriate administrative support to the negotiated rulemaking committee, including technical assistance.

(Added Pub. L. No. 101-648, § 3(a), Nov. 29, 1990, 104 Stat. 4,972, § 585, and renumbered § 565 and amended Pub. L. No. 102-354, § 3(a)(2), (3), Aug. 26, 1992, 106 Stat. 944.)

§566. Conduct of committee activity

(a) **Duties of committee.**—Each negotiated rulemaking committee established under this subchapter shall consider the matter proposed by the agency for consideration and shall attempt to reach a consensus concerning a proposed rule with respect to such matter and any other matter the committee determines is relevant to the proposed rule.

(b) **Representatives of agency on committee.**—The person or persons representing the agency on a negotiated rulemaking committee shall participate in the deliberations and activities of the committee with the same rights and responsibilities as other members of the committee, and shall be authorized to fully represent the agency in the discussions and negotiations of the committee.

(c) **Selecting facilitator.**—Notwithstanding section 10(e) of the Federal Advisory Committee Act, an agency may nominate either a person from the Federal Government or a person from outside the Federal Government to serve as a facilitator for the negotiations of the committee, subject to the approval of the committee by consensus. If the committee does not approve the nominee of the agency for facilitator, the agency shall submit a substitute nomination. If a committee does not approve any nominee of the agency for facilitator, the committee shall select by consensus a person to serve as facilitator. A person designated to represent the agency in substantive issues may not serve as facilitator or otherwise chair the committee.

(d) **Duties of facilitator.**—A facilitator approved or selected by a negotiated rulemaking committee shall—

(1) chair the meetings of the committee in an impartial manner;

(2) impartially assist the members of the committee in conducting discussions and negotiations; and

(3) manage the keeping of minutes and records as required under section 10(b) and (c) of the Federal Advisory Committee Act, except that any per-

sonal notes and materials of the facilitator or of the members of a committee shall not be subject to section 552 of this title.

(e) **Committee procedures.**—A negotiated rulemaking committee established under this subchapter may adopt procedures for the operation of the committee. No provision of section 553 of this title shall apply to the procedures of a negotiated rulemaking committee.

(f) **Report of committee.**—If a committee reaches a consensus on a proposed rule, at the conclusion of negotiations the committee shall transmit to the agency that established the committee a report containing the proposed rule. If the committee does not reach a consensus on a proposed rule, the committee may transmit to the agency a report specifying any areas in which the committee reached a consensus. The committee may include in a report any other information, recommendations, or materials that the committee considers appropriate. Any committee member may include as an addendum to the report additional information, recommendations, or materials.

(g) **Records of committee.**—In addition to the report required by subsection (f), a committee shall submit to the agency the records required under section 10(b) and (c) of the Federal Advisory Committee Act.

(Added Pub. L. No. 101-648, § 3(a), Nov. 29, 1990, 104 Stat. 4,973, § 586, and renumbered § 566, Pub. L. No. 102-354, § 3(a)(2), Aug. 26, 1992, 106 Stat. 944.)

§567. Termination of committee

A negotiated rulemaking committee shall terminate upon promulgation of the final rule under consideration, unless the committee's charter contains an earlier termination date or the agency, after consulting the committee, or the committee itself specifies an earlier termination date.

(Added Pub. L. No. 101-648, § 3(a), Nov. 29, 1990, 104 Stat. 4,974, § 587, and renumbered § 567, Pub. L. No. 102-354, § 3(a)(2), Aug. 26, 1992, 106 Stat. 944.)

§568. Services, facilities, and payment of committee member expenses

(a) Services of conveners and facilitators.—

(1) In general.—An agency may employ or enter into contracts for the services of an individual or organization to serve as a convener or facilitator for a negotiated rulemaking committee under this subchapter, or may use the services of a Government employee to act as a convener or a facilitator for such a committee.

(2) Determination of conflicting interests.—An agency shall determine whether a person under consideration to serve as convener or facilitator of a committee under paragraph (1) has any financial or other interest that would preclude such person from serving in an impartial and independent manner.
(b) Services and facilities of other entities.—For purposes of this subchapter, an agency may use the services and facilities of other Federal agencies and public and private agencies and instrumentalities with the consent of such agencies and instrumentalities, and with or without reimbursement to such agencies and instrumentalities, and may accept voluntary and uncompensated services without regard to the provisions of section 1342 of title 31. The Federal Mediation and Conciliation Service may provide services and facilities, with or without reimbursement, to assist agencies under this subchapter, including furnishing conveners, facilitators, and training in negotiated rulemaking.
(c) Expenses of committee members.—Members of a negotiated rulemaking committee shall be responsible for their own expenses of participation in such committee, except that an agency may, in accordance with section 7(d) of the Federal Advisory Committee Act, pay for a member's reasonable travel and per diem expenses, expenses to obtain technical assistance, and a reasonable rate of compensation, if—

(1) such member certifies a lack of adequate financial resources to participate in the committee; and

(2) the agency determines that such member's participation in the committee

is necessary to assure an adequate representation of the member's interest.
(d) Status of member as federal employee.—A member's receipt of funds under this section or section 569 shall not conclusively determine for purposes of sections 202 through 209 of title 18 whether that member is an employee of the United States Government.

(Added Pub. L. No. 101-648, § 3(a), Nov. 29, 1990, 104 Stat. 4,974, § 588, and renumbered § 568 and amended Pub. L. No. 102-354, § 3(a)(2), (4), Aug. 26, 1992, 106 Stat. 944.)

§569. Encouraging negotiated rulemaking

(a) The President shall designate an agency or designate or establish an interagency committee to facilitate and encourage agency use of negotiated rulemaking. An agency that is considering, planning, or conducting a negotiated rulemaking may consult with such agency or committee for information and assistance.

(b) To carry out the purposes of this subchapter, an agency planning or conducting a negotiated rulemaking may accept, hold, administer, and utilize gifts, devises, and bequests of property, both real and personal if that agency's acceptance and use of such gifts, devises, or bequests do not create a conflict of interest. Gifts and bequests of money and proceeds from sales of other property received as gifts, devises, or bequests shall be deposited in the Treasury and shall be disbursed upon the order of the head of such agency. Property accepted pursuant to this section, and the proceeds thereof, shall be used as nearly as possible in accordance with the terms of the gifts, devises, or bequests.

(As amended Pub. L. No. 104-320, § 11(b)(1), Oct. 19, 1996, 110 Stat. 3,873.)

§570. Judicial review

Any agency action relating to establishing, assisting, or terminating a negotiated rulemaking committee under this subchapter shall not be subject to judicial review. Nothing in this section shall bar judicial review of a rule if such judicial review is otherwise provided by law. A rule which is the product of negotiated rulemaking and is subject to judicial review shall not be accorded any greater deference by a court than a rule which is the product of other rulemaking procedures.

(Added Pub. L. No. 101-648, § 3(a), Nov. 29, 1990, 104 Stat. 4,976, § 590, and renumbered § 570, Pub. L. No. 102-354, § 3(a)(2), Aug. 26, 1992, 106 Stat. 944.)

§570a. Authorization of appropriations

There are authorized to be appropriated such sums as may be necessary to carry out the purposes of this subchapter.

(Added Pub. L. No. 104-320, § 11(d)(1), Oct. 19, 1996, 110 Stat. 3,874.)

Administrative Conference of the U.S. Negotiated Rulemaking Sourcebook
(David M. Pritzker & Deborah S. Dalton, eds.) (1995)
Table of Contents

TABLE OF CONTENTS

Foreword xiii

Introduction .... xv.

Acknowledgments xvii

1. **What Is Negotiated Rulemaking?** I
   Why Use Negotiated Rulemaking; Benefits
   of Negotiated Rulemaking; Some Drawbacks;
   Criteria for Negotiated Rulemaking;
   Procedures; Federal Agency Experience

   Appendix:

   Procedures for Negotiating Proposed
   Regulations, Administrative Conference
   Recommendation 82-4 11

   Procedures for Negotiating Proposed
   Regulations, Administrative Conference
   Recommendation 85-5 15

   EPA Flow Chart for Negotiated Rulemaking 18

   Lee M. Thomas, The *Successful Use of
   Regulatory Negotiation by EPA*,
   13 Admin. L. News 1 (Fall 1987) 20

   Assessment of EPA's Negotiated Rulemaking
   Activities 23

2. **When to Use Negotiated Rulemaking** 37
   Evaluating a Rule's Suitability for
   Negotiated Rulemaking; How Is Negotiated
   Rulemaking Proposed?

Appendix:

    Selection Criteria (EPA) 42

    Notice of EPA Regulatory Negotiation Project 43

    Letter from John McGlennon 45

    Discussion on the Use of Consultation and
        Consensus-Building Processes 48

3. Statutory Basis for Negotiated Rulemaking 67

    Administrative Procedure Act; Federal
    Advisory Committee Act; Other Requirements

Appendix:

    Negotiated Rulemaking Act of 1990 76

    Federal Administrative Procedure Sourcebook,
    Chapter 4, Negotiated Rulemaking Act 84

    Statement of Senator Carl Levin (August 10,
        1988) 91

    Administrative Procedure Act §553 97

    Ex Parte Communications in Informal
        Rulemaking, Administrative Conference
        Recommendation 77-3 98

    Federal Advisory Committee Act 100

    Federal Advisory Committee Management Final
        Rule (GSA) 107

4. The Convening Process 123

> Selecting a Convenor; Steps in the Convening Process; Decision to Proceed; Final Convening Phase; Federal Advisory Committee Act

Appendix:

> Cover Letter for FACA Charter (EPA) 132
>
> Wood-Burning Stoves FACA Charter (EPA) 134
>
> Oil Spill Vessel Response Plans FACA Charter (Coast Guard) 136
>
> EPA Memorandum on Wood-Burning Stoves 138
>
> Notice of Intent to Form Advisory Committee on Wood-Burning Stoves (EPA) 141
>
> Notice of Establishment and Meeting of Wood-Burning Stoves Advisory Committee (EPA) 146
>
> Notice of Intent to Form Advisory Committee on Roadway Worker Protection (Federal Railroad Administration) 147
>
> Notice of Establishment and Meeting of Advisory Committee on Roadway Worker Protection (FRA) 154
>
> Notice of Meeting Schedule of Advisory Committee on Nondiscrimination in Air Travel (DOT) 159
>
> Notice of Intent to Form Advisory Committee on Safety Standards for Steel Erection (OSHA) 160
>
> Notice of Establishment of Steel Erection Advisory Committee (OSHA) 171

Notice of Meeting and Appointment of
Members of Steel Erection Advisory
Committee (OSHA) 173

Letter to OSHA on Negotiation for Benzene 183

Order of U.S. District Court, *California
v. Hodel* 188

5. **Orientation and Training of Participants** 193

Objectives; Content of Training Sessions

Appendix:

Agenda for Training Session (DOT) 196

Agenda for Training Session (EPA) 199

Agenda for Training Session (FCC) 205

6. **Negotiating the Rule** 207

Design of the Negotiations; Organizational
Meeting; Consensus; Structuring the
Negotiating Sessions; Meeting Management;
Deadlines; Coordination, Agency Review
and Concurrence

Appendix:

Notice of Meeting of Steel Erection
Advisory Committee (OSHA) 217

Notices of Meetings on Wood-Burning
Stoves (EPA) 218

Organizational Protocols for Wood-Burning
Stoves (EPA) 219

Organizational Protocols for Oil Spill
Vessel Response Plans (Coast Guard) 222

7. Concluding the Negotiations **229**

   Final Steps; Evaluation of the Rulemaking
   Effort

   Appendix:

   Notice of Results of Negotiation for Wood-
      Burning Stoves (EPA) 234

   Agreement on Wood-Burning Stoves (EPA) 240

   Notice of Proposed Rulemaking (Preamble)
      on Wood-Burning Stoves (EPA) 242

   Notice of Proposed Rulemaking (Preamble)
      on Flight Time Limitations (FAA) 250

   Notice of Meeting (After Comment Period)
      (FAA) 255

   Mediator's Summary Letter on Benzene
      Negotiations (OSHA) 256

   Cover Letter for Report on RCRA Permit
      Modification (EPA) 259

   Committee Statement on RCRA Permit
      Modification (EPA) 261

8. Resources and Logistics **267**

   Convenor and Mediator Services; Committee-
   Sponsored Research; Expenses for Training,
   Orientation and Meetings; Expenses of
   Participation; Reimbursement for Time

   Appendix:

Table of Costs of EPA Negotiations 274

Acquiring the Services of "Neutrals,"
Administrative Conference
Recommendation 86-8 275

George D. Ruttinger, *Acquiring the Services
of Neutrals for Alternative Means of
Dispute Resolution and Negotiated
Rulemaking* (Report to the Administrative Conference), 1986 ACUS 863 279

Commerce Business Daily Procurement Notice
(EPA) 324

Commerce Business Daily Procurement Notice
(Interior) 324

EPA Contract for Support Services 325

Interior Contract for Support Services 353

9. **Negotiated Rulemaking at State Level** 369

Negotiated Rulemaking; Policy Dialogues
and Other Consensus-Building Efforts

10. **Agency Experience with Negotiated Rulemaking** 375

Department of Agriculture 375

Department of Education 376

Department of Energy 379

Department of Health & Human Services 379

Department of Housing & Urban Development 380

Department of the Interior 380

Department of Labor 382

Department of Transportation. 383

Environmental Protection Agency 387

Farm Credit Administration 395

Federal Communications Commission 395

Federal Trade Commission 396

Interstate Commerce Commission 397

Nuclear Regulatory Commission 397

11. Sources of Assistance 399

Organizations with Experience in Negotiated Rulemaking or Mediation of Public Policy Disputes

12. Bibliography 411

13. Selected Articles 427

Index to Articles 427

Comprehensive Analyses

Philip J. Harter. *Negotiating Regulations: A Cure for Malaise,* 71 Geo. L. J. 1 (1982) 431

Philip J. Harter. *Regulatory Negotiation: Experienced Practitioner Offers Guidance* (two parts), 2 BNA ADR Report 62, 80 (February 18 and March 3, 1988) 544

Henry H. Perritt, Jr., *Negotiated Rulemaking Before Federal Agencies: Evaluation of Recommendation by the Administrative Conference* (excerpts), 74 Geo. L. J. 1625 (1986) 554

Henry H. Perritt, Jr., *Administrative ADR: Development of Negotiated Rulemaking and Other Processes (excerpts),* 14 Pepperdine L. Rev. 863 (1987) 603

Henry H. Perritt, Jr., *Use of Negotiated Rulemaking to Develop a Proposed OSHA Health Standard for MDA* (Report to Deputy Assistant Secretary of Labor, May 1988) 661

Lawrence Susskind & Gerard McMahon, *The Theory and Practice of Negotiated Rulemaking,* 3 Yale J. Reg. 133 (1985) 704

Owen Alpin et al., *Applying ADR to Rulemaking* (Administrative Conference Colloquium Proceedings), I Admin. L. J. 575 (1987) 737

Patricia M. Wald, *Negotiation of Environmental Disputes: A New Role for the Courts?* (excerpts), 10 Colum. J. Envtl. L. I (1985) 751

Philip J. Harter, The *Role of the Courts in Reg-Neg — A Response to Judge Wald,* 11 Colum. J. Envtl. L. 51 (1986) 767

William Funk, *When Smoke Gets in Your Eyes: Reg-Neg and the Public Interest — EPA's Woodstove Standards,* 18 Envtl. L. 55 (1987) 789

News and Shorter Articles

Neil Eisner, *Regulatory Negotiation: A Real World Experience,* 31 Fed. Bar News & J. 371 (1984) 833

Daniel J. Fiorino & Chris Kirtz, *Breaking Down Walls: Negotiated Rulemaking at EPA,* 4 Temple Envtl. L. & Tech. J. 29 (1985) 839

Daniel J. Fiorino, *Regulatory Negotiation as a Policy Process,* 48 Pub. Admin. Rev. 764 (1988) 849

Regulatory Negotiation: Four Perspectives, DR Forum (NIDR), p. 8 (Jan. 1986) 858

Lawrence Susskind & Laura Van Dam, *Squaring Off at the Table, Not in the Courts,* Tech. Rev., p. 37 (July 1986) 862

William H. Miller, *Bypassing the Lawyers,* Industry Week, June 23, 1986, p. 20 869

Mike McClintock, *Regulating Wood Stove Emissions,* Wash. Post, Sept. 25, 1986, (Wash. Home) p. 5 870

EPA Negotiates Proposed Rule on Asbestos in Schools, 1 BNA ADR Report 133 (July 9, 1987) 872

Participants and Facilitators Discuss Negotiation of EPA's Proposed Rule on Asbestos in Schools, 1 BNA ADR Report 154 (July 23, 1987) 875

Rena Steinzor & Scott Strauss, *Building a Consensus: Agencies Stressing "Reg-Neg" Approach,* Legal Times, Aug. 3, 1987, p. 16 880

Marshall J. Breger, Letter Replying to
Steinzor & Strauss, Legal Times,
Aug. 10, 1987 886

Marianne Lavelle, *"Reg-Neg" Revving Up
in D.C.*, Nat'l L. J., March 21, 1988,
p. 1 887

*Despite Impasse, Parties Praise DOT's
Non-discrimination Reg-Neg,* 2 BNA
ADR Report 117 (March 31, 1988) 890

Education *Law Calls for Test of Modified
Reg-Neg Process,* 2 BNA ADR Report
300 (Sept. 1, 1988) 894

Robert B. Reich, *Regulation by Confrontation
or Negotiation?*, Harv. Bus. Rev., p. 82
(May-June 1981) 896

Kathrin Day Lassila, *See You Later, Litigator,*
Amicus J. 5 (Summer (992) 908

Stephen B. Goldberg, *Reflections on Negotiated
Rulemaking,* 9 Wash. Lawyer (no. 1) 42
(Sept./Oct. 1994) 910

Ellen Siegler, *Regulatory Negotiations: A
Practical Perspective,* 22 Envtl. L. Rep.
(no. 10) 10647 (1992) 917

Recommendations of the Administrative Conference of the United States

Procedures for Negotiating Proposed Regulations (Recommendation No. 82-4).

[47 Fed. Reg. 30,708 (July 15, 1982)]

The complexity of government regulation has increased greatly compared to that which existed when the Administrative procedure Act was enacted, and this complexity has been accompanied by a formalization of the rulemaking process beyond the brief, expeditious notice and comment procedures envisioned by section 553 of the APA. Procedures in addition to notice and comment may, in some instances, provide important safeguards against arbitrary or capricious decisions by agencies and help ensure that agencies develop sound factual bases for the exercise of the discretion entrusted them by Congress, but the increased formalization of the rulemaking process has also had adverse consequences. The participants, including the agency, tend to develop adversarial relationships with each other causing them to take extreme positions, to withhold information from one another, and to attack the legitimacy of opposing positions. Because of the adversarial relationships, participants often do not focus on creative solutions to problems, ranking of the issues involved in a rulemaking, or the important details involved in a rule. Extensive factual records are often developed beyond what is necessary. Long periods of delay result and participation in rulemaking proceedings can become needlessly expensive. Moreover, many participants perceive their roles in the rulemaking proceeding more as positioning themselves for the subsequent judicial review than as contributing to a solution on the merits at the administrative level. Finally, many participants remain dissatisfied with the policy judgments made at the outcome of rulemaking proceedings.

Participants in rulemaking rarely meet as a group with each other and with the agency to communicate their respective views so that each can react directly to the concerns and positions of the others in an effort to resolve conflicts. Experience indicates that if the parties in interest were to work together to negotiate the text of a proposed rule, they might be able in some circumstances to identify the major issues, gauge their importance to the respective parties, identify the information and data necessary to resolve the issues, and develop a rule that is acceptable to the respective interests, all within the contours of the substantive statute. For example, highly technical standards are negotiated that have extensive health, safety, and economic effects; lawsuits challenging rules are regularly settled by agreement on a negotiated rule; public law litigation involves sensitive negotiation over rulelike issues; and many environmental disputes and policies have been successfully negotiated. These experiences can be drawn upon in certain rulemaking contexts to provide procedures by which affected interests and the agency might participate directly in the development of the text of a proposed rule through negotiation and mediation.

The Federal Advisory Committee Act (FACA) has, however, dampened administrative enthusiasm for attempts to build on experience with successful negotiations. Without proposing a general revision of FACA, the Administrative Conference urges that Congress amend the Act to facilitate the use of the negotiating procedures contemplated in this recommendation.

The suggested procedures provide a mechanism by which the benefits of negotiation could be achieved while providing appropriate safeguards to ensure that affected interests have the opportunity to participate, that the resulting rule is within the discretion delegated by Congress, and that it is not arbitrary or capricious. The premise of the recommendation is that provision of opportunities and incentives to resolve issues during rulemaking, through negotiations, will result in an improved process and better rules. Such rules would likely be more acceptable to affected interests because of their participation in the negotiations. The purpose of this recommendation is to establish a supplemental rulemaking procedure that can be used in appropriate circumstances to permit the direct participation of affected interests in the development of proposed rules. This procedure should be viewed as experimental, and should be reviewed after it has been used a reasonable number of times.

RECOMMENDATION

1. Agencies should consider using regulatory negotiation, as described in this recommendation, as a means of drafting for agency consideration the text of a proposed regulation. A proposal to establish a regulatory negotiating group could be made either by the agency (for example, in an advance notice of proposed rulemaking) or by the suggestion of any interested person.
2. Congress should facilitate the regulatory negotiation process by passing legislation explicitly authorizing agencies to conduct rulemaking proceedings in the manner described in this recommendation. This authority, to the extent that it enlarges existing agency rulemaking authority, should be viewed as an experiment in improving rulemaking procedures. Accordingly, the legislation should contain

a sunset provision. The legislation should provide substantial flexibility for agencies to adapt negotiation techniques to the circumstances of individual proceedings, as contemplated in this recommendation, free of the restrictions of the Federal Advisory Committee Act and any ex parte limitations. Legislation should provide that information tendered to such groups, operating in the manner proposed, should not be considered an agency record under the Freedom of Information Act.
3. In legislation authorizing regulatory negotiation, Congress should authorize agencies to designate a "convenor" to organize the negotiations in a particular proceeding. The convenor should be an individual, government agency, or private organization, neutral with respect to the regulatory policy issues under consideration. If the agency chooses an individual who is an employee of the agency itself, that person should not be associated with either the rulemaking or enforcement staff. The convenor would be responsible for (i) advising the agency as to whether, in a given proceeding, regulatory negotiation is feasible and is likely to be conducive to the fairer and more efficient conduct of the agency's regulatory program, and (ii) determining, in consultation with the agency, who should participate in the negotiations.
4. An agency considering use of regulatory negotiation should select and consult with a convenor at the earliest practicable time about the feasibility of its use. The convenor should conduct a preliminary inquiry to determine whether a regulatory negotiating group should be empanelled to develop a proposed rule relating to the particular topic. The convenor should consider the risks that negotiation procedures would increase the likelihood of a consensus proposal that would limit output, raise prices, restrict entry, or otherwise establish or support unreasonable restraints on competition. Other factors bearing on this decision include the following:
    (a) The issues to be raised in the proceeding should be mature and ripe for decision. Ideally, there should be some deadline for issuing the rule, so that a decision on a rule is inevitable within a relatively fixed time frame. The agency may also impose a deadline on the negotiations.
    (b) The resolution of issues should not be such as to require participants in negotiations to compromise their fundamental tenets, since it is unlikely that agreement will be reached in such circumstances. Rather, issues involving such fundamental tenets

should already have been determined, or not be crucial to the resolution of the issues involved in writing the proposed regulation.
- (c) The interests significantly affected should be such that individuals can be selected who will adequately represent those interests. Since negotiations cannot generally be conducted with a large number of participants, there should be a limited number of interests that will be significantly affected by the rule and therefore represented in the negotiations. A rule of thumb might be that negotiations should ordinarily involve no more than 15 participants.
- (d) There should be a number of diverse issues that the participants can rank according to their own priorities and on which they might reach agreement by attempting to optimize the return to all the participants.
- (e) No single interest should be able to dominate the negotiations. The agency's representative in the negotiations will not be deemed to possess this power solely by virtue of the agency's ultimate power to promulgate the final rule.
- (f) The participants in the negotiations should be willing to negotiate in good faith to draft a proposed rule.
- (g) The agency should be willing to designate an appropriate staff member to participate as the agency's representative, but the representative should make clear to the other participants that he or she cannot bind the agency.
5. If the convenor determines that regulatory negotiation would be appropriate, it would recommend this procedure to the agency. If the agency and the convenor agree that regulatory negotiation is appropriate, the convenor should be responsible for determining preliminarily the interests that will likely be substantially affected by a proposed rule, the individuals that will represent those interests in negotiations, the scope of issues to be addressed, and a schedule for completing the work. It will be important for potential participants to agree among themselves as to these matters, and their agreement can be facilitated by either the convenor or a possible participant conducting a preliminary inquiry among identified interests. Reasonable efforts should be made to secure a balanced group in which no interest has more than a third of the members and each representative is technically qualified to address the issues presented, or has access to qualified individuals.

6. The subject matter of the proposed regulation may be within the jurisdiction of an existing committee of a nongovernmental standards writing organization that has procedures to ensure the fair representation of the respective interests and a process for determining whether the decision actually reflects a consensus among them. If such a committee exists and appears to enjoy the support and confidence of the affected interests, the convenor should consider recommending that negotiations be conducted under that committee's auspices instead of establishing an entirely new framework for negotiations. In such a case, the existing committee could be regarded as a regulatory negotiation group for purposes of this recommendation. (Alternatively, the product of the committee could be used as the basis of a proposed regulation pursuant to Administrative Conference Recommendation 784.)[6]
7. To ensure that the appropriate interest have been identified and have had the opportunity to be represented in the negotiating group, the agency should publish in the *Federal Register* a notice that it is contemplating developing a rule by negotiation and indicate in the notice the issues involved and the participants and interests already identified. If an additional person or interest petitions for membership or representation in the negotiating group, the convenor, in consultation with the agency, should determine (i) whether that interest would be substantially affected by the rule, (ii) if so, whether it would be represented by an individual already in the negotiating group, and (iii) whether, in any event, the petitioner should be added to the negotiating group, or whether interests can be consolidated and still provide adequate representation.
8. The agency should designate a senior official to represent it in the negotiations and should identify that official in the *Federal Register* notice.
9. It may be that, in particular proceedings, certain affected interests will require reimbursement for direct expenses to be able to participate at a level that will foster broadlybased, successful negotiations. Unlike intervenors, the negotiating group will be performing a function normally performed within the agency, and the agency should consider reimbursing the direct expenses of such participants. The

---

[6] Federal Agency Interaction with Private Standard-Setting Organizations in Health and Safety Regulation, 1978 ACUS Recommendations and Reports 13, 1 CFR §305.784.

agency should also provide financial or other support for the convenor and the negotiating group. Congress should clarify the authority of agencies to provide such financial resources.
10. The convenor and the agency might consider whether selection of a mediator is likely to facilitate the negotiation process. Where participants lack relevant negotiating experience, a mediator may be of significant help in making them comfortable with the process and in resolving impasses.
11. The goal of the negotiating group should be to arrive at a consensus on a proposed rule. Consensus in this context means that each interest represented in the negotiating group concurs in the result, unless all members of the group agree at the outset on another definition. Following consensus, the negotiating group should prepare a report to the agency containing its proposed rule and a concise general statement of its basis and purpose. The report should also describe the factual material on which the group relied in preparing its proposed regulation, for inclusion in the agency's record of the proceeding. The participants may, of course, be unable to reach a consensus on a proposed rule, and, in that event, they should identify in the report both the areas in which they are agreed and the areas in which consensus could not be achieved. This could serve to narrow the issues in dispute, identify information necessary to resolve issues, rank priorities, and identify potentially acceptable solutions.
12. The negotiating group should be authorized to close its meeting to the public only when necessary to protect confidential data or when, in the judgment of the participants, the likelihood of achieving consensus would be significantly enhanced.
13. The agency should publish the negotiated text of the proposed rule in its notice of proposed rulemaking. If the agency does not publish the negotiated text as a proposed rule, it should explain its reasons. The agency may wish to propose amendments or modifications to the negotiated proposed rule, but it should do so in such a manner that the public at large can identify the work of the agency and of the negotiating group.
14. The negotiating group should be afforded an opportunity to review any comments that are received in response to the notice of proposed rulemaking so that the participants can determine whether their recommendations should be modified. The final responsibility for issuing the rule would remain with the agency.

Recommendations of the Administrative Conference of the United States

Procedures for Negotiating Proposed Regulations (Recommendation No. 85-5).

[50 Fed. Reg. 52,895 (Dec. 27, 1985)]

Negotiations among persons representing diverse interests have proven to be effective in some cases in developing proposals for agency rules. In 1982, the Administrative Conference of the United States adopted Recommendation 82-4, 1 CFR § 305.82-4, encouraging the use of negotiated rulemaking by federal agencies in appropriate situations.[7] The concept of negotiated rulemaking arose from dissatisfaction with the rulemaking process, which since the 1960's, in many agencies, had become increasingly adversarial and formalized—unlike the brief, expeditious notice and comment procedure envisioned in section 553 of the Administrative Procedure Act. Experience has now shown that negotiated rulemaking can be a practical technique in appropriate instances.

Since Recommendation 82-4 was adopted, its recommended procedures have been followed four times by federal agencies. The Federal Aviation Administration used negotiated rulemaking to develop a new flight and duty time regulation for pilots. The Environmental Protection Agency used negotiated rulemaking to develop proposed rules on nonconformance penalties for vehicle emissions and on emergency exemptions from pesticide regulations. The Occupational Safety and Health Administration encouraged labor, public interest, and industry representatives to negotiate a standard for occupational exposure to benzene. The benzene negotiations did not result in agreement among the parties on a proposed rule, but the other three negotiations did lead to substantial agreement resulting in two final rules (which have thus far not been challenged) and one draft rule which, after public comment, is pending before the agency.

The experience of these four cases has shown that the original recommendation was basically sound, and has provided a basis for the Administrative Conference to use in supplementing Recommendation 82-4.

---

[7] Recommendation 82-4 used the term "regulatory negotiation" to refer to this process. The present recommendation substitutes "negotiated rulemaking" to emphasize that it is addressing negotiation of rules, and not other uses of negotiations in the regulatory process.

It is important to view Recommendation 82-4 and the present recommendation, taken together, as a guide to issues to be considered rather than a formula to be followed. Negotiation is intrinsically a fluid process that cannot be delineated in advance. Accordingly, what will "work" in a particular case depends on the substantive issues, the perception of the agency's position by interested parties, past and current relationships among the parties, the authority of party representatives in the negotiations, the negotiating style of the representatives, the number and divergence of views within each constituency represented, and the skill of the participants and mediators. These factors are mostly dynamic and their character is likely to change during the negotiating process. Proponents of negotiated rulemaking must recognize the unavailability of neat formal solutions to questions of who should participate, how the negotiations should be conducted, or even the definition of "successful" negotiations.

Agencies undertaking negotiated rulemaking must be prepared to deal with these real world uncertainties by pursuing a thoughtfully flexible approach. Elements of Recommendation 82-4 and the present recommendation provide a conceptual framework within which to plan and conduct negotiations in a particular proceeding, but should not be taken as a formal model. An agency cannot merely transplant a pattern followed successfully by another agency, or even by itself on another occasion. Nevertheless, agencies that are considering negotiated rulemaking for the first time should find it helpful to discuss their plans with other agencies and persons experienced with the process.

Some agencies have indicated a concern about the effect of the Federal Advisory Committee Act on negotiated rulemaking proceedings. The four agency experiences reviewed by the Administrative Conference have not shown that the Act, as interpreted by the sponsoring agencies and participants, impeded effective negotiations. Under current judicial and agency interpretations of the Act, it appears that caucuses and other working group meetings may be held in private, where this is necessary to promote an effective exchange of views.

Another concern expressed by some agencies has been the potential costs associated with negotiated rulemaking. While aspects of the recommended process may entail some short-term additional costs, the Conference believe that potential long-range savings will more than offset the costs. Moreover, agencies should be aware of opportunities for assistance from within the government, for example, training provided by the Legal Education Institute of the Department of Justice, and mediation assistance by the Federal Mediation and Conciliation Service and the Community, Relations Service.

RECOMMENDATION

1. An agency sponsoring a negotiated rulemaking proceeding should take part in the negotiations. Agency participation can occur in various ways. The range of possibilities extends from full participation as a negotiator to acting as an observer and commenting on possible agency reactions and concerns. Agency representatives participating in negotiations should be sufficiently senior in rank to be able to express agency views with credibility.
2. Negotiations are unlikely to succeed unless all participants (including the agency) are motivated throughout the process by the view that a negotiated agreement will provide a better alternative than a rule developed under traditional processes. The agency, accordingly, should be sensitive to each participant's need to have a reasonably clear expectation of the consequences of not reaching a consensus. Agencies must be mindful, from the beginning to the end of negotiations, of the impact that agency conduct and statements have on party expectations. The agency, and others involved in the negotiations, may need to communicate with other participants—perhaps with the assistance of a mediator or facilitator—to ensure that each one has realistic expectations about the outcome of agency action in the absence of a negotiated agreement. Communications of this character always should consist of an honest expression of agency actions that are realistically possible.
3. The agency should recognize that negotiations can be useful at several stages of rulemaking proceedings. For example, negotiating the terms of a final rule could be a useful procedure even after publication of a proposed rule. Usually, however, negotiations should be used to help develop a notice of proposed rulemaking, with negotiations to be resumed after comments on the notice are received, as contemplated by paragraphs 13 and 14 of Recommendation 82-4.
4. The agency should consider providing the parties with an opportunity to participate in a training session in negotiation skills just prior to the beginning of the negotiations.
5. The agency should select a person skilled in techniques of dispute resolution to assist the negotiating group in reaching an agreement. In some cases, that person may need to have prior knowledge of the subject matter of the negotiations. The person chosen may be styled "mediator" or "facilitator," and may be, but need not be, the same

person as the "convenor" identified in Recommendation 82-4. There may be specific proceedings, however, where party incentives to reach voluntary agreement are so strong that a mediator or facilitator is not necessary.

6. In some circumstances, federal agencies such as the Federal Mediation and Conciliation Service or the Community Relations Service of the Department of Justice may be appropriate sources of mediators or facilitators. These agencies should consider making available a small number of staff members with mediation experience to assist in the conduct of negotiated rulemaking proceedings.

7. The agency, the mediator or facilitator, and, where appropriate, other participants in negotiated rulemaking should be prepared to address internal disagreements within a particular constituency. In some cases, it may be helpful to retain a special mediator or facilitator to assist in mediating issues internal to a constituency. The agency should consider the potential for internal constituency disagreements in choosing representatives, in planning for successful negotiations, and in selecting persons as mediators or facilitators. The agency should also recognize the possibility that a group viewed as a single constituency at the outset of negotiations may later become so divided as to suggest modification of the membership of the negotiating group.

8. Where appropriate, the agency, the mediator or facilitator, or the negotiating group should consider appointing a neutral outside individual who could receive confidential data, evaluate it, and report to the negotiators. The parties would need to agree upon the protection to be given confidential data. A similar procedure may also be desirable in order to permit neutral technical advice to be given in connection with complex data.

9. Use of a "resource pool" may be desirable, to support travel, training, or other appropriate costs, either incurred by participants or expended on behalf of the negotiating group. The feasibility of creating such a pool from contributions by private sources and the agency should be considered in the pre-negotiation stages.

Paperwork Reduction Act

Citations:

44 U.S.C. §§3501-3521 (2000 & Supp. II 2002); enacted December 11, 1980 by Pub. L. No. 96-511, 94 Stat. 2812, amended October 18, 1986 by Pub. L. No. 99-591, title I, §101(m), 100 Stat. 3341-308, 3341-335; amended and re-codified May 22, 1995 by Pub. L. No. 104-13, §2, 109 Stat. 163; amended Oct. 30, 2000, by Pub. L. 106-398, Sec. 1 [[div. A], title X, §§1064(a)-(b)], 114 Stat. 1654, 1654A-275; amended June 28, 2002, by Pub. L. No. 107-198, §§2-3, 116 Stat. 732; amended August 21, 2002, by Pub. L. No. 107-217, §3(l), 116 Stat. 1301; amended November 25, 2002 by Pub. L. No. 107-296, §1005(c), 116 Stat. 2273; amended December 17, 2002 by Pub. L. No. 107-347, title III, §305(c)(3), 116 Stat. 2961.

Lead Agency:

The Office of Information and Regulatory Affairs (OIRA), Office of Management and Budget, Eisenhower Executive Office Building, 1650 Pennsylvania Avenue NW, Washington, DC 20502, (202) 395-4852.

Overview:

The Paperwork Reduction Act has as its main purposes to "minimize the paperwork burden for individuals, small businesses, educational and non-profit institutions, Federal contractors, State, local and tribal governments, and other persons . . . ; ensure the greatest possible public benefit . . . of information collected. . . ; [and] and minimize the cost to the Federal Government of the creation, collection, maintenance, use, dissemination, and disposition of information . . . ." 44 U.S.C. §3501. The Act statutorily established the Office of Information and Regulatory Affairs (OIRA) in the Office of Management and Budget (OMB), and assigned it responsibility for coordinating government information policies, including approving agency collections of information. The Act applies to all agencies in the executive branch, as well as to the independent regulatory agencies. Only very narrow functions are exempted from its coverage: (1) federal criminal matters or actions; (2) civil and administrative actions, and investigations of specified individuals or entities; (3) compulsory process issued in connection with antitrust proceedings; and (4) federal intelligence activities carried out under presidential executive order. §3518.

Basic Clearance Requirement. The Act assigns to OIRA the function of approving information collections. The Act provides that agencies "shall not conduct or sponsor the collection of information" without first obtaining the actual or inferred approval of the OMB Director. §3507(a)(2). The Act (§3502(3)) defines "collection of information" as:

> The obtaining, causing to be obtained, soliciting, or requiring the disclosure to third parties or the public, of facts or opinions by or for an agency, regardless of form or format, calling for either—
>
> (i) answers to identical questions posed to, or identical reporting or recordkeeping requirements imposed on, ten or more persons, other than agencies, instrumentalities, or employees of the United States; or
>
> (ii) answers to questions posed to agencies instrumentalities, or employees of the United States which are to be used for general statistical purposes.

Note that the 1995 Amendments added "to third parties" in §3502(3) in order to overrule the holding of *Dole v. United Steelworkers of America*, 494 U.S. 26 (1990).

The Act forbids OMB to approve any information collection for a period of more than one year at a time. §3507(c)(3)(C). Failure to obtain OMB approval of a collection of information triggers operation of the Act's "public protection provision," §3512, which provides that no person shall be subject to any penalty for failing to comply with a collection of information that is subject to this subchapter if—(1) the collection of information does not display a valid control number assigned by the Director [of OMB] . . . ; or (2) the agency fails to inform the person who is to respond to the collection of information that such person is not required to respond to the collection of information unless it displays a valid control number.

Clearance Procedure. The Act provides a general set of clearance procedures for approving agency information collections, with more specific procedures prescribed for information collections imposed through notice-and-comment rulemakings.

Section 3507(d) of the Act prescribes the following procedure for information collections contained in rules promulgated following notice and comment:

- Each agency shall forward to OMB a copy of any proposed rule which contains a collection of information, and any information that OMB deems necessary to make the determination. This information must be transmitted no later than publication of the notice of proposed rulemaking (NPRM) in the Federal Register.
- Within 60 days after the notice of proposed rulemaking is published in the Federal Register, OMB may file public comments on the collection of information contained in the proposed rule.
- When a final rule is published in the Federal Register, the agency shall explain how any collection of information contained in the final rule responds to the comments filed by OMB or the public, and the reason the comments were rejected.
- If OMB has received notice and failed to comment on an agency rule within 60 days after the notice of proposed rulemaking, OMB may not disapprove any collection of information specifically contained in that rule.
- However, OMB may disapprove a collection of information where (A) the collection of information was not specifically required by an agency rule; (B) the agency failed to comply with the submission requirements; (C) OMB finds within 60 days after publication of the final rule that the agency's response to OMB's comments were unreasonable; or (D) OMB determines the agency has substantially modified the collection of information in the final rule without giving OMB 60 days to review the modified requirement.
- OMB's decision to disapprove the collection of information in the rule, and its reasons for that decision, must be made publicly available and include an explanation of the reasons for such decision. But OMB's decision to approve or not act upon a rule is not subject to judicial review.

OMB's regulations implementing the Act (5 C.F.R. Part 1320) have added certain requirements to the clearance process for collections of information contained in proposed agency rules (5 C.F.R. §1320.11), current agency rules

(5 C.F.R. §1320.12), and clearance of collections other than in proposed or current rules. 5 C.F.R. §1320.10.

- Agencies should submit collections of information contained in proposed rules to the Federal Register for public comment. The preamble to the Notice of Proposed Rulemaking shall state that the collection of information has been submitted for OMB review and direct that comments be filed with the desk officer for the agency in OIRA/OMB. (5 C.F.R. §1320.11(a)). OMB will provide at least 30 days for public comment. 5 C.F.R. §1320.11(e).
- Upon publication of the final rule, the agency shall explain how the collection of information in the final rule responds to comments, and identify and explain modifications made to the rule. 5 C.F.R. §1320.11(f).
- On or before the date of publication of the final rule, the agency will submit the final rule to OMB (Unless the approved proposed rule was not materially changed). OMB then has 60 days to approve, disapprove, or order a change in the final rule. (5 C.F.R. §1320.11(h)). If OMB approves, it will assign an OMB control number. 5 C.F.R. §1320.11(i).

For information collections that are *not* contained in new rules promulgated after notice and comment, there is a different process:

- On or before the day an information collection proposal is submitted to OMB for clearance, the agency must send a notice to the Federal Register, in which the agency advises the public that OMB approval has been requested and that the public has 30 to submit comments on the proposal to the OIRA/OMB desk officer for the agency. 5 C.F.R. §1320.10(a).
- Within 60 days after receipt of the agency's submission, OMB will notify the agency of its decision to approve or disapprove, in whole or in part, the information collection. OMB will provide at least 30 days for public comment before making a decision. 5 C.F.R. §1320.10(b).
- If OMB does not act within the 60-day period, the agency can ask OMB to assign the required control number (valid for one year in these circumstances), and OMB must do so without delay. 5 C.F.R. §1320.10(c).

OMB has also developed procedures that govern clearance for information collections in existing rules. §1320.12. The procedures are intended to prevent expiration of OMB approval for an information collection before the agency has undertaken the necessary administrative procedure to extend OMB's 3-year approval or effect a repeal or amendment of the rule containing the collection provision. The agency is required to seek public comment on the requirement and initiate the OMB review process not later than 60 days before the existing OMB approval expires. If OMB indicates disapproval of the existing information collection provision, OMB must publish an explanation in the Federal Register and instruct the agency to initiate a rulemaking to amend or rescind the provision, consistent with the APA or other applicable requirements.

Finally OMB regulations (§1320.6(e)) make clear that the public protection provision in §3512 of the Act does not preclude the government from imposing a penalty failing to comply with a collection of information that is mandated by statute, even in the absence of a valid OMB control number. Several courts have so held: *Salberg v. United States*, 969 F.2d 379, 384 (7th Cir. 1992); *United States v. Neff*, 954 F.2d 698, 699-700, (11th Cir. 1992); *United States v. Hicks*, 947 F.2d 1356, 1359 (9th Cir. 1991), *United States v. Kerwin*, 945 F.2d 92 (5th Cir. 1991); *United States v. Wunder*, 919 F.2d 34, 38 (6th Cir. 1990).

Alternative Procedures. The Act contains several variations from the general review procedures for review of agency information collections. Section 3507(j) establishes a "fast track" review procedure for emergency situations which is available on request by agency heads. OMB regulations provided a stringent test for granting such requests. *See* 5 C.F.R. §1320.13.

The Act also authorizes the OMB director to designate an agency senior official who "is sufficiently independent of program responsibility to evaluate fairly whether proposed information collection requests should be approved and has sufficient resources to carry out this responsibility effectively." 5 U.S.C. §3507(i). Such an official must comply with OMB's regulations in reviewing his or her agency's information collection provisions. 5 C.F.R. §1320.7.

OMB's general clearance procedures are subject to the Act's provision that independent regulatory agencies may, by majority vote, override an OMB decision disapproving a proposed information collection. 44 U.S.C. §3507(f); 5 C.F.R. §1320.15. The Act also contains the only extant statutory definition of "independent regulatory agency" in 44 U.S.C. §3502(5).

Agency Certifications. The regulations, (5 C.F.R. §1320.5(d)(1)) further describe the standard: an agency must show that all reasonable steps have been taken to ensure that the collection of information is the least burdensome necessary, that it is not duplicative of information otherwise accessible to the agency and that the collection of information has practical utility.

In addition, OMB has established general guidelines (5 C.F.R. §1320.5(d)(2)) that will be applied unless the agency can demonstrate the need for an exception to them. Among other things, OMB will generally not approve a collection of information that requires reporting more often than quarterly; that requires a response in fewer than 30 days; that requires respondents to submit more than one original and two copies of a document; that requires persons to retain records (other than health, medical, contract, grant, or tax records) for more than three years; is not a statistical survey designed to produce valid and reliable statistical results or requires the use of a statistical data classification that has not been reviewed and approved by OMB; includes a pledge of confidentiality that is not supported by authority established in statute or regulation, that is not supported by disclosure and data security policies that are consistent with the pledge, or which unnecessarily impedes sharing of data with other agencies for compatible confidential use; or requires respondents to submit proprietary, trade secret, or other confidential information unless the agency can demonstrate that it has instituted procedures to protect the information's confidentiality to the extent permitted by law.

Also pertinent to OMB's authority is section 3518(e) of the Act, which states:

> Nothing in [the Act] shall be interpreted as increasing or decreasing the authority of the President, the Office of Management and Budget or the Director thereof, under the laws of the United States, with respect to the substantive policies and programs of departments, agencies, and offices, including the substantive authority of any Federal agency to enforce the civil rights laws.

Information Management. The Paperwork Reduction Act also authorizes OMB to develop and implement uniform policies on information resources management by federal agencies. OMB has done this through Circular A-130, which sets out various policies agencies are to use in managing government information. Circular A-130, originally issued in 1985, 50 Fed. Reg. 52,730 (Dec. 24, 1985), has been amended, see 59 Fed. Reg. 37,906 (July 25, 1994) (Transmittal 2). This issuance incorporated and superseded Transmittal 1, 58 Fed. Reg. 36,066 (July 2, 1993).

Legislative History:

The Paperwork Reduction Act of 1980 replaced the Federal Reports Act of 1942 as the basic statute controlling paperwork requirements imposed on the public by the federal government. The Act was amended significantly in 1986 and in minor ways in ensuing years, and then amended and completely recodified in 1995.

The Paperwork Reduction Act was originally enacted as part of the regulatory reform movement of the 1970s. Reacting to growing public concern over the burden imposed by federal information collections, Congress established the Commission on Federal Paperwork in late 1974. The Commission, in its report in 1977, made 770 recommendations for reducing the federal paperwork burden. Legislation implementing some of the Recommendations was introduced in both the 95th and 96th Congresses, and the Paperwork Reduction Act was passed in November 1980, and signed by President Carter on December 11, 1980. (The legislative history of the 1980 Act was recounted by William Funk in *The Paperwork Reduction Act: Paperwork Reduction Meets Administrative Law*, 24 Harv. J. on Legis. 1 (1987).)

Conflicts over the interpretations of certain provisions of the Act resulted in amendments enacted in 1986. Among the amendments was language clarifying the relationship between the procedures required for clearance of information collections in proposed rules and other proposed information collections.

The 1995 amendments updated, strengthened and completely recodified the Paperwork Reduction Act of 1980. The goals were the same as the 1980 Act—to strengthen OMB and agency paperwork reduction efforts, to improve OMB and agency information resources management, and to encourage and provide for public participation in reduction efforts and management decisions. In order to achieve these goals, the 1995 Act clarified the scope of OMB review, enhanced opportunities for public participation, expanded the Act's public protection provisions, and specified the agency paperwork reduction responsibilities.

It also settled the major question of whether agency rules that require businesses or individuals to maintain information for the benefit of third parties or the public were covered by the Act. The Supreme Court had ruled in *Dole v. United Steelworkers*, 494 U.S. 26 (1990), that the Act did not so require. But the 1995 amendments make clear that it does now. This means that many agency rules containing such requirements not previously reviewed by OIRA will now have to be reviewed.

In 2002, Congress enacted the which added current section 1320 (and renumbered the old §3520 as §3521).

Bibliography:

I. Legislative History

1. *Paperwork and Redtape Reduction Act of 1979,* Hearings before Subcommittee on Federal Spending Practices and Open Government of the Senate Committee on Governmental Affairs, 96th Cong., 1st Sess. (1979).
2. *Paperwork Reduction Act of 1980,* Hearings on H.R. 6410 before a Subcommittee of the House Committee on Government Operations, 96th Cong., 2d Sess. (1980).
3. *Report on the Paperwork Reduction Act,* House Committee on Government Operations, H. Rep. No. 835, 96th Cong., 2d Sess. (1980).
4. *Report on the Paperwork Reduction Act of 1980,* Senate Committee on Governmental Affairs, S. Rep. No. 930, 96th Cong., 2d Sess. (1980), *reprinted in* 1980 U.S. Code Cong. & Ad. News 6241.
5. *The Federal Paperwork Burden: Identifying the Major Problems,* Hearings before the Subcommittee on Federal Expenditures, Research and Rules of the Senate Committee on Governmental Affairs, 97th Cong., 1st Sess. (1981).
6. *Implementation of the Paperwork Reduction Act of 1980,* Hearing before the Subcommittee on Legislation and National Security of the House Committee on Government Operations, 97th Cong. 1st Sess. (1981).
7. *Implementation of Paperwork Reduction Act of 1980,* Hearing before the Subcommittee on Federal Expenditures, Research, and Rules of the Senate Committee on Governmental Affairs, 97th Cong., 2d Sess. (1982).
8. *Oversight of the Paperwork Reduction Act of 1980,* Hearing before the Subcommittee on Information Management and Regulatory Affairs of the Senate Committee on Governmental Affairs, 98th Cong., 1st Sess. (1983).
9. *Report to Accompany S. 2230,* Senate Committee on Governmental Affairs, 99th Cong., 2d Sess. (1986).
10. 132 Cong. Rec. H10896 (daily ed. Oct. 15, 1986).
11. 132 Cong. Rec. S16739 (daily ed. Oct. 16, 1986) (remarks of Sen. Chiles).
12. 132 Cong. Rec. S16876 (daily ed. Oct. 17, 1986) (remarks of Sen. Roth).
13. *Reauthorization of the Paperwork Reduction Act,* Hearings before the Subcommittee on Government Information and Regulations, Senate Committee on Governmental Affairs, (June 12, 16, 1989).
14. *Reauthorization of OMB's Office of Information and Regulatory Affairs:* Hearings before the Senate Committee on Governmental Affairs, 101st Cong., 2d Sess. (Feb. 21-22, 1990).

15. *S. 1742, Federal Information Resources Management Act*, Senate Committee on Governmental Affairs, S. Rep. No. 101-487, 101st Cong., 2d Sess. (Oct. 2, 1990).

16. *H.R. 3695, Paperwork Reduction and Federal Information Resources Management Act of 1990*, House Committee on Government Operations, H. Rep. No. 101-927, 101st Cong., 2d Sess. (Oct. 23, 1990).

17. *Restraining Paperwork Burdens on Small Business: Implementation of the "Paperwork Reduction Act of 1980" and Recommendations to Make it More Effective*, Hearings before the House Committee on Small Business, 102d Cong., 1st Sess. (June 25, 1991).

18. *The Paperwork Reduction Act and Its Impact on Small Business*, Hearing before the House Committee on Small Business, 103d Cong., 1st Sess. (Oct 28, 1993).

19. *S. 560, Paperwork Reduction Act of 1994*, Senate Committee on Governmental Affairs, S. Rep. No. 103-392, 103d Cong., 2d Sess. (Sept. 30, 1994).

20. *The Paperwork Reduction Act*, Hearings before the House Committee on Small Business, 104th Cong., 1st Sess. (Jan.27, 1995).

21. *H.R. 830, Paperwork Reduction Act and Risk Assessment and Cost/Benefit Analysis for New Regulations*, Hearings before the Subcommittee on National Economic Growth, Natural Resources, and Regulatory Affairs, House Government Reform and Oversight Committee (Feb. 7, 1995).

22. *S. 244, Paperwork Reduction Act of 1995*, Senate Committee on Governmental Affairs, S. Rep. No. 104-8, 104th Cong., 1st Sess. (Feb. 14, 1995).

23. *H.R. 830, Paperwork Reduction Act of 1995*, House Committee on Government Reform and Oversight, H. Rep. No. 104-37 104th Cong., 1st Sess. (Feb. 15, 1995).

24. *Conference report on S. 244, Paperwork Reduction Act of 1995*, H. Rep. No. 104-99, 104th Cong., 1st Sess. (April 3 1995).

25. Small Business Paperwork Reduction Act Amendments of 1998: Report to Accompany H.R. 3310, H. Rep. No. 105-462, 105th Cong. (1998).

26. *Reinventing Paperwork?: The Clinton-Gore Administration's Record On Paperwork Reduction*, Hearing before the Subcommittee on National Economic Growth, Natural Resources, and Regulatory Affairs of the House Committee on Government Reform, 106th Cong., 2d. Sess. (April 12, 2000).

27. *Paperwork Inflation—Past Failures and Future Plans*: Hearing before the Subcommittee on Energy Policy, Natural Resources, and Regulatory Affairs, Committee on Government Reform, House of Representatives, 107th Cong. 1st Sess. (April 24, 2001).

28. *Paperwork Inflation—the Growing Burden on America:* Hearing before the Subcommittee on Energy, Policy, Natural Resources and Regulatory Affairs, Committee on Government Reform, House of Representatives, 107th Cong. 2d Sess. (April 11, 2002).

29. *Mid-Term Report Card: Is the Bush Administration Doing Enough on Paperwork Reduction?* Hearing before the House Subcommittee on Energy Policy, Natural Resources and Regulatory Affairs of the Committee on Government Reform, 108th Cong., 1st Sess. (April 11, 2003).

30. *Paperwork and Regulatory Improvements Act of 2003*, Hearing before the House Government Reform Committee, 108th Cong., 1st Sess. (July 22, 2003).

31. *What is the Bush Administration's Economic Growth Plan Component for Paperwork Reduction?* Hearing before the Subcommittee on Energy Policy, Natural Resources and Regulatory Affairs of the House Committee on Government Reform, 108th Cong., 2d Sess. (April 20, 2004).

32. United States Congress House Committee on Government Reform, Paperwork and Regulatory Improvements Act of 2004 (to accompany H.R. 2432) (including cost estimate of the Congressional Budget Office), H.R. Rep. No. 108-490.

33. *Less is More: The Increasing Burden of Taxpayer Paperwork*, Hearing before the House Subcommittee on Regulatory Affairs of the Committee on Government Reform, 109th Cong., 1st Sess. (May 25, 2005).

34. *Reducing the Paperwork Burden on the Public: Are Agencies Doing All They Can?* Hearing before the House Subcommittee on Regulatory Affairs of the Committee On Government Reform, 109th Cong., 1st Sess. (June 14, 2005).

35. *The Paperwork Reduction Act at 25: Opportunities to Strengthen and Improve the Law:* Hearing before the Subcommittee on Regulatory Affairs, Committee on Government Reform, House of Representatives, 109th Cong. 2d Sess. (March 8, 2006).

II. Other Government Documents

1. Commission on Federal Paperwork, *Final Summary Report* (1977).
2. Commission on Federal Paperwork, *The Reports Clearance Process* (1977).
3. U.S. General Accounting Office, *Implementing the Paperwork Reduction Act: Some Progress, But Many Problems Remain* (GAO/GGD 83-35, Apr. 20, 1983).

4. U.S. Small Business Administration, Office of Advocacy, *Small Business Paperwork: Problems and Progress* (1983).

5. Office of Management and Budget, Office of Information and Regulatory Affairs, *Information Collection Review Handbook* (Jan. 1989); *superseded by* OMB/OIRA, *The Paperwork Reduction Act, of 1995: Implementing Guidance* (Preliminary Draft, Feb 3, 1997).

6. OMB Bulletin 97-03, *Fiscal Year 1996 Information Streamlining Plan and Information Collection Budget*.

7. U.S. General Accounting Office, *Paperwork Reduction Act—Burden Increases and Unauthorized Information Collections*, Testimony of L. Nye Stevens, Director, Federal Management and Workforce Issues, General Government Division before the House Subcommittee on National Economic Growth, Natural Resources and Regulatory Affairs; and the Subcommittee on Government management, Information, and Technology of the Committee on Government Reform (GAO/T-GGD-9-78) (April 15, 1999).

8. U.S. General Accounting Office, *Paperwork Reduction Act: Burden Increases at IRS and Other Agencies* (GAO/T-GGD-00-114) (April 12, 2000).

9. U.S. Government Accountability Office, Paperwork Reduction Act: Changes Needed to Annual Report (GAO-02-651R) (April 29, 2002).

10. Paperwork Reduction Act: New Approach May Be Needed to Reduce Government Burden on Public (GAO-05-424) (May 20, 2005).

11. Office of Management and Budget, Office of Information and Regulatory Affairs, *Managing Information Collection: Information Collection Budget of the United States Government, Fiscal Year 2005* (May 2005), *available at* http://www.whitehouse.gov/omb/inforeg/2005_icb_final.pdf.

12. U.S. Government Accountability Office, *Paperwork Reduction Act: Subcommittee Questions Concerning the Act's Information Collection Provisions*, (GAO-05-909R) (July 19, 2005).

13. U.S. Government Accountability Office, *Paperwork Reduction Act: Increase in Estimated Burden Hours Highlights Need for New Approach* (GAO-06-974T) (July 18, 2006).

14. U.S. Government Accountability Office, *Federal Information Collection: A Reexamination of the Portfolio of Major Federal Household Surveys Is Needed* (GAO-07-62) (Nov. 2006).

15. Office of Management and Budget, Office of Information and Regulatory Affairs, *Managing Information Collection: Information Collection Budget of the United States Government, Fiscal Year 2006* (Revised version)

(Dec. 2006), *available at* http://www.whitehouse.gov/omb/inforeg/icb/fy2006_icb_revised.pdf.[1]

16. Office of Management and Budget, *Questions and Answers When Designing Surveys for Information Collections* (Jan. 2006), *available at* http://www.whitehouse.gov.omb.inforeg/pmc_survey_guidance_2006.pdf.

17. Relyea, *Paperwork Reduction Act Reauthorization and Government Information Management Issues*, Congressional Research Service (RL30590) (Jan. 4, 2007), *available at* http://www.fas.org/sgp/crs/secrecy/RL30590.pdf.

III. Books and Articles

1. Bardach, Self-Regulation and Regulatory Paperwork in *Social Regulation: Strategies for Reform*, ed. E. Bardach and R. Kagan (San Francisco: Institute for Contemporary Studies, 1982).

2. Funk, *The Paperwork Reduction Act: Paperwork Reduction Meets Administrative Law*, 24 Harv. J. on Legis. 1 (1987).

3. Indick, Greene, & Squire, *The Economic Growth and Regulatory Paperwork Reduction Act of 1996*, 114 Banking L.J. 298 (1997).

4. Levy, *The Paperwork Reduction Act of 1980: Unnecessary Burdens and Unrealized Efficiency*, 14 J.L. & Comm. 99 (1994).

5. Lubbers, *Paperwork Redux: The (Stronger) Paperwork Reduction Act of 1995*, 49 Admin. L. Rev. 111 (1997).

6. Neustadt, *Taming the Paperwork Tiger: An Experiment in Regulatory Management,* Regulation 28 (Jan./Feb. 1981).

7. Note, *A Limit to OMB's Authority Under the Paperwork Reduction Act in Dole v. United Steelworkers of America: A Step in the Right Direction*, 6 Admin. L. J. Am. U. 153 (1992).

8. O'Reilly, *Who's on First?: The Role of the Office of Management and Budget in Federal Information Policy*, 10 J. Legis. 95 (1983).

9. Perritt, *Electronic Acquisition and Release of Federal Agency Information*, Report to the Administrative Conference of the U.S., 1988 ACUS 601, *portions reprinted in* 41 Admin. L. Rev. 253 (1989).

10. Perritt, *Federal Agency Electronic Records Management and Archives*, Report to the Administrative Conference of the U.S., 1990 ACUS 389. *See also Electronic Records Management and Archives*, 53 U. Pitt. L. Rev. 963 (1992).

---

[1] For *Information Collection Budgets* from 1997-2005, see http://www.whitehouse.gov/omb/inforeg/infocoll.html.

11. Plocher, *The Paperwork Reduction Act of 1995: A Second Chance for Information Resources Management (Reauthorization of the 1980 Act)*, Gov't Info. Q. 271 (1997).

12. Rosacher and Davies, *An Analysis of Federal Income Tax Complexity Utilizing Internal Revenue Service Estimates for Taxpayer Paperwork Burden*, 45 Oil & Gas Tax Q. 791 (1997).

Agency Regulations:

Office of Management and Budget   5 C.F.R. Part 1320

Appendix:

1. Paperwork Reduction Act, 44 U.S.C. §§3501-3521 (2000 & Supp. II 2002).

2. Office of Management and Budget, Controlling Paperwork Burdens on the Public, 5 CFR Part 1320 (2007).

3. OMB Form 83-1, Paperwork Reduction Act Submission (rev. Feb 2004).

4. Memorandum for Chief Information Officers, From Steven D. Aitken, Acting Administrator, OIRA, Subject: Data Call for the FY 2007 Information Collection Budget (Sept. 29, 2006).

19

Paperwork Reduction Act

Title 44 U.S. Code

CHAPTER 35—COORDINATION OF FEDERAL INFORMATION POLICY

SUBCHAPTER I—FEDERAL INFORMATION POLICY

§3501. Purposes.
§3502. Definitions.
§3503. Office of Information and Regulatory Affairs.
§3504. Authority and functions of Director.
§3505. Assignment of tasks and deadlines.
§3506. Federal agency responsibilities.
§3507. Public information collection activities; submission to Director; approval and delegation.
§3508. Determination of necessity for information; hearing.
§3509. Designation of central collection agency.
§3510. Cooperation of agencies in making information available.
§3511. Establishment and operation of Government Information Locator Service.
§3512. Public protection.
§3513. Director review of agency activities; reporting; agency response.
§3514. Responsiveness to Congress.
§3515. Administrative powers.
§3516. Rules and regulations.
§3517. Consultation with other agencies and the public.
§3518. Effect on existing laws and regulations.
§3519. Access to information.
§3520. Establishment of task force on information collection and dissemination
§3521. Authorization of appropriations.

§3501. Purposes

The purposes of this subchapter are to—

(1) minimize the paperwork burden for individuals, small businesses, educational and nonprofit institutions, Federal contractors, State, local and tribal governments, and other persons resulting from the collection of information by or for the Federal Government;

(2) ensure the greatest possible public benefit from and maximize the utility of information created, collected, maintained, used, shared and disseminated by or for the Federal Government;

(3) coordinate, integrate, and to the extent practicable and appropriate, make uniform Federal information resources management policies and practices as a means to improve the productivity, efficiency, and effectiveness of Government programs, including the reduction of information collection burdens on the public and the improvement of service delivery to the public;

(4) improve the quality and use of Federal information to strengthen decisionmaking, accountability, and openness in Government and society;

(5) minimize the cost to the Federal Government of the creation, collection, maintenance, use, dissemination, and disposition of information;

(6) strengthen the partnership between the Federal Government and State, local, and tribal governments by minimizing the burden and maximizing the utility of information created, collected, maintained, used, disseminated, and retained by or for the Federal Government;

(7) provide for the dissemination of public information on a timely basis, on equitable terms, and in a manner that promotes the utility of the information to the public and makes effective use of information technology;

(8) ensure that the creation, collection, maintenance, use, dissemination, and disposition of information by or for the Federal Government is consistent with applicable laws, including laws relating to—

    (A) privacy and confidentiality, including section 552a of title 5;

    (B) security of information, including section 11332 of title 40; and

    (C) access to information, including section 552 of title 5;

(9) ensure the integrity, quality, and utility of the Federal statistical system;

(10) ensure that information technology is acquired, used, and managed to improve performance of agency missions, including the reduction of information collection burdens on the public; and

(11) improve the responsibility and accountability of the Office of Management and Budget and all other Federal agencies to Congress and to the public for implementing the information collection review process, information resources management, and related policies and guidelines established under this subchapter.

§3502. Definitions

As used in this subchapter—
(1) the term "agency" means any executive department, military department, Government corporation, Government controlled corporation, or other establishment in the executive branch of the Government (including the Executive Office of the President), or any independent regulatory agency, but does not include—
(A) the Government Accountability Office;
(B) Federal Election Commission;
(C) the governments of the District of Columbia and of the territories and possessions of the United States, and their various subdivisions; or
(D) Government-owned contractor-operated facilities, including laboratories engaged in national defense research and production activities;
(2) the term "burden" means time, effort, or financial resources expended by persons to generate, maintain, or provide information to or for a Federal agency, including the resources expended for—
(A) reviewing instructions;
(B) acquiring, installing, and utilizing technology and systems;
(C) adjusting the existing ways to comply with any previously applicable instructions and requirements;
(D) searching data sources;
(E) completing and reviewing the collection of information; and
(F) transmitting, or otherwise disclosing the information;
(3) the term "collection of information"—
(A) means the obtaining, causing to be obtained, soliciting, or requiring the disclosure to third parties or the public, of facts or opinions by or for an agency, regardless of form or format, calling for either—
(i) answers to identical questions posed to, or identical reporting or recordkeeping requirements imposed on, ten or more per-

sons, other than agencies, instrumentalities, or employees of the United States; or

(ii) answers to questions posed to agencies, instrumentalities, or employees of the United States which are to be used for general statistical purposes; and

(B) shall not include a collection of information described under section 3518(c)(1);

(4) the term "Director" means the Director of the Office of Management and Budget;

(5) the term "independent regulatory agency" means the Board of Governors of the Federal Reserve System, the Commodity Futures Trading Commission, the Consumer Product Safety Commission, the Federal Communications Commission, the Federal Deposit Insurance Corporation, the Federal Energy Regulatory Commission, the Federal Housing Finance Board, the Federal Maritime Commission, the Federal Trade Commission, the Interstate Commerce Commission, the Mine Enforcement Safety and Health Review Commission, the National Labor Relations Board, the Nuclear Regulatory Commission, the Occupational Safety and Health Review Commission, the Postal Rate Commission, the Securities and Exchange Commission, and any other similar agency designated by statute as a Federal independent regulatory agency or commission;

(6) the term "information resources" means information and related resources, such as personnel, equipment, funds, and information technology;

(7) the term "information resources management" means the process of managing information resources to accomplish agency missions and to improve agency performance, including through the reduction of information collection burdens on the public;

(8) the term "information system" means a discrete set of information resources organized for the collection, processing, maintenance, use, sharing, dissemination, or disposition of information;

(9) the term "information technology" has the meaning given that term in section 11101 of title 40 but does not include national security systems as defined in section 11103 of title 40;

(10) the term "person" means an individual, partnership, association, corporation, business trust, or legal representative, an organized group of individuals, a State, territorial, tribal, or local government or branch thereof, or a political subdivision of a State, territory, tribal, or local government or a branch of a political subdivision;

(11) the term "practical utility" means the ability of an agency to use information, particularly the capability to process such information in a timely and useful fashion;

(12) the term "public information" means any information, regardless of form or format, that an agency discloses, disseminates, or makes available to the public;

(13) the term "recordkeeping requirement" means a requirement imposed by or for an agency on persons to maintain specified records, including a requirement to—

(A) retain such records;

(B) notify third parties, the Federal Government, or the public of the existence of such records;

(C) disclose such records to third parties, the Federal Government, or the public; or

(D) report to third parties, the Federal Government, or the public regarding such records; and

(14) the term "penalty" includes the imposition by an agency or court of a fine or other punishment; a judgment for monetary damages or equitable relief; or the revocation, suspension, reduction, or denial of a license, privilege, right, grant, or benefit.

§3503. Office of Information and Regulatory Affairs

(a) There is established in the Office of Management and Budget an office to be known as the Office of Information and Regulatory Affairs.

(b) There shall be at the head of the Office an Administrator who shall be appointed by the President, by and with the advice and consent of the Senate. The Director shall delegate to the Administrator the authority to administer all functions under this subchapter, except that any such delegation shall not relieve the Director of responsibility for the administration of such functions. The Administrator shall serve as principal adviser to the Director on Federal information resources management policy.

§3504. Authority and functions of Director

(a)(1) The Director shall oversee the use of information resources to improve the efficiency and effectiveness of governmental operations to serve agency missions, including burden reduction and service delivery to the public. In performing such oversight, the Director shall—

(A) develop, coordinate and oversee the implementation of Federal information resources management policies, principles, standards, and guidelines; and

(B) provide direction and oversee—

(i) the review and approval of the collection of information and the reduction of the information collection burden;

(ii) agency dissemination of and public access to information;

(iii) statistical activities;

(iv) records management activities;

(v) privacy, confidentiality, security, disclosure, and sharing of information; and

(vi) the acquisition and use of information technology, including alternative information technologies that provide for electronic submission, maintenance, or disclosure of information as a substitute for paper and for the use and acceptance of electronic signatures.

(2) The authority of the Director under this subchapter shall be exercised consistent with applicable law.

(b) With respect to general information resources management policy, the Director shall—

(1) develop and oversee the implementation of uniform information resources management policies, principles, standards, and guidelines;

(2) foster greater sharing, dissemination, and access to public information, including through –

(A) the use of the Government Information Locator Service; and

(B) the development and utilization of common standards for information collection, storage, processing and communication, including standards for security, interconnectivity and interoperability;

(3) initiate and review proposals for changes in legislation, regulations, and agency procedures to improve information resources management practices;

(4) oversee the development and implementation of best practices in information resources management, including training; and

(5) oversee agency integration of program and management functions with information resources management functions.

(c) With respect to the collection of information and the control of paperwork, the Director shall—

(1) review and approve proposed agency collections of information;

(2) coordinate the review of the collection of information associated with Federal procurement and acquisition by the Office of Information

and Regulatory Affairs with the Office of Federal Procurement Policy, with particular emphasis on applying information technology to improve the efficiency and effectiveness of Federal procurement, acquisition and payment, and to reduce information collection burdens on the public;

(3) minimize the Federal information collection burden, with particular emphasis on those individuals and entities most adversely affected;

(4) maximize the practical utility of and public benefit from information collected by or for the Federal Government;

(5) establish and oversee standards and guidelines by which agencies are to estimate the burden to comply with a proposed collection of information;

(6) publish in the Federal Register and make available on the Internet (in consultation with the Small Business Administration) on an annual basis a list of the compliance assistance resources available to small businesses, with the first such publication occurring not later than 1 year after the date of enactment of the Small Business Paperwork Relief Act of 2002.

(d) With respect to information dissemination, the Director shall develop and oversee the implementation of policies, principles, standards, and guidelines to—

(1) apply to Federal agency dissemination of public information, regardless of the form or format in which such information is disseminated; and

(2) promote public access to public information and fulfill the purposes of this subchapter, including through the effective use of information technology.

(e) With respect to statistical policy and coordination, the Director shall—

(1) coordinate the activities of the Federal statistical system to ensure—

(A) the efficiency and effectiveness of the system; and

(B) the integrity, objectivity, impartiality, utility, and confidentiality of information collected for statistical purposes;

(2) ensure that budget proposals of agencies are consistent with system-wide priorities for maintaining and improving the quality of Federal statistics and prepare an annual report on statistical program funding;

(3) develop and oversee the implementation of Governmentwide policies, principles, standards, and guidelines concerning—

(A) statistical collection procedures and methods;

(B) statistical data classification;

(C) statistical information presentation and dissemination;

(D) timely release of statistical data; and

(E) such statistical data sources as may be required for the administration of Federal programs;

(4) evaluate statistical program performance and agency compliance with Governmentwide policies, principles, standards and guidelines;

(5) promote the sharing of information collected for statistical purposes consistent with privacy rights and confidentiality pledges;

(6) coordinate the participation of the United States in international statistical activities, including the development of comparable statistics;

(7) appoint a chief statistician who is a trained and experienced professional statistician to carry out the functions described under this subsection;

(8) establish an Interagency Council on Statistical Policy to advise and assist the Director in carrying out the functions under this subsection that shall—

    (A) be headed by the chief statistician; and

    (B) consist of—

        (i) the heads of the major statistical programs; and

        (ii) representatives of other statistical agencies under rotating membership; and

(9) provide opportunities for training in statistical policy functions to employees of the Federal Government under which—

    (A) each trainee shall be selected at the discretion of the Director based on agency requests and shall serve under the chief statistician for at least 6 months and not more than 1 year; and

    (B) all costs of the training shall be paid by the agency requesting training.

(f) With respect to records management, the Director shall—

(1) provide advice and assistance to the Archivist of the United States and the Administrator of General Services to promote coordination in the administration of chapters 29, 31, and 33 of this title with the information resources management policies, principles, standards, and guidelines established under this subchapter;

(2) review compliance by agencies with—

    (A) the requirements of chapters 29, 31, and 33 of this title; and

    (B) regulations promulgated by the Archivist of the United States and the Administrator of General Services; and

(3) oversee the application of records management policies, principles, standards, and guidelines, including requirements for archiving information maintained in electronic format, in the planning and design of information systems.

(g) With respect to privacy and security, the Director shall –
(1) develop and oversee the implementation of policies, principles, standards, and guidelines on privacy, confidentiality, security, disclosure and sharing of information collected or maintained by or for agencies; and
(2) oversee and coordinate compliance with sections 552 and 552a of title 5, sections 20 and 21 of the National Institute of Standards and Technology Act (15 U.S.C. 278g-3 and 278g-4), section 11331 of title 40 and subchapter II of this chapter, and related information management laws.

(h) With respect to Federal information technology, the Director shall—
(1) in consultation with the Director of the National Institute of Standards and Technology and the Administrator of General Services—
(A) develop and oversee the implementation of policies, principles, standards, and guidelines for information technology functions and activities of the Federal Government, including periodic evaluations of major information systems; and
(B) oversee the development and implementation of standards under section 11331 of title 40;
(2) monitor the effectiveness of, and compliance with, directives issued under subtitle III of title 40 and directives issued under section 322 of title 40;
(3) coordinate the development and review by the Office of Information and Regulatory Affairs of policy associated with Federal procurement and acquisition of information technology with the Office of Federal Procurement Policy;
(4) ensure, through the review of agency budget proposals, information resources management plans and other means –
(A) agency integration of information resources management plans, program plans and budgets for acquisition and use of information technology; and
(B) the efficiency and effectiveness of inter-agency information technology initiatives to improve agency performance and the accomplishment of agency missions; and
(5) promote the use of information technology by the Federal Government to improve the productivity, efficiency, and effectiveness of Federal programs, including through dissemination of public information and the reduction of information collection burdens on the public.

§3505. Assignment of tasks and deadlines

(a) In carrying out the functions under this subchapter, the Director shall –
(1) in consultation with agency heads, set an annual Governmentwide goal for the reduction of information collection burdens by at least 10 percent during each of fiscal years 1996 and 1997 and 5 percent during each of fiscal years 1998, 1999, 2000, and 2001, and set annual agency goals to—
(A) reduce information collection burdens imposed on the public that—
(i) represent the maximum practicable opportunity in each agency; and
(ii) are consistent with improving agency management of the process for the review of collections of information established under section 3506(c); and
(B) improve information resources management in ways that increase the productivity, efficiency and effectiveness of Federal programs, including service delivery to the public;
(2) with selected agencies and non-Federal entities on a voluntary basis, conduct pilot projects to test alternative policies, practices, regulations, and procedures to fulfill the purposes of this subchapter, particularly with regard to minimizing the Federal information collection burden; and
(3) in consultation with the Administrator of General Services, the Director of the National Institute of Standards and Technology, the Archivist of the United States, and the Director of the Office of Personnel Management, develop and maintain a Governmentwide strategic plan for information resources management, that shall include—
(A) a description of the objectives and the means by which the Federal Government shall apply information resources to improve agency and program performance;
(B) plans for—
(i) reducing information burdens on the public, including reducing such burdens through the elimination of duplication and meeting shared data needs with shared resources;
(ii) enhancing public access to and dissemination of, information, using electronic and other formats; and
(iii) meeting the information technology needs of the Federal Government in accordance with the purposes of this subchapter; and

(C) a description of progress in applying information resources management to improve agency performance and the accomplishment of missions.

(b) For purposes of any pilot project conducted under subsection (a)(2), the Director may, after consultation with the agency head, waive the application of any administrative directive issued by an agency with which the project is conducted, including any directive requiring a collection of information, after giving timely notice to the public and the Congress regarding the need for such waiver.

(c) Inventory of Major Information Systems. –

(1) The head of each agency shall develop and maintain an inventory of major information systems (including major national security systems) operated by or under the control of such agency.

(2) The identification of information systems in an inventory under this subsection shall include an identification of the interfaces between each such system and all other systems or networks, including those not operated by or under the control of the agency.

(3) Such inventory shall be—

(A) updated at least annually;

(B) made available to the Comptroller General; and

(C) used to support information resources management, including—

(i) preparation and maintenance of the inventory of information resources under section 3506(b)(4);

(ii) information technology planning, budgeting, acquisition, and management under section 3506(h), subtitle III of title 40, and related laws and guidance;

(iii) monitoring, testing, and evaluation of information security controls under subchapter II;

(iv) preparation of the index of major information systems required under section 552(g) of title 5, United States Code; and

(v) preparation of information system inventories required for records management under chapters 21, 29, 31, and 33.

(4) The Director shall issue guidance for and oversee the implementation of the requirements of this subsection.

§3506. Federal agency responsibilities

(a)(1) The head of each agency shall be responsible for –

(A) carrying out the agency's information resources management activities to improve agency productivity, efficiency, and effectiveness; and

(B) complying with the requirements of this subchapter and related policies established by the Director.

(2)(A) Except as provided under subparagraph (B), the head of each agency shall designate a Chief Information Officer who shall report directly to such agency head to carry out the responsibilities of the agency under this subchapter.

(B) The Secretary of the Department of Defense and the Secretary of each military department may each designate Chief Information Officers who shall report directly to such Secretary to carry out the responsibilities of the department under this subchapter. If more than one Chief Information Officer is designated, the respective duties of the Chief Information Officers shall be clearly delineated.

(3) The Chief Information Officer designated under paragraph (2) shall head an office responsible for ensuring agency compliance with and prompt, efficient, and effective implementation of the information policies and information resources management responsibilities established under this subchapter, including the reduction of information collection burdens on the public. The Chief Information Officer and employees of such office shall be selected with special attention to the professional qualifications required to administer the functions described under this subchapter.

(4) Each agency program official shall be responsible and accountable for information resources assigned to and supporting the programs under such official. In consultation with the Chief Information Officer designated under paragraph (2) and the agency Chief Financial Officer (or comparable official), each agency program official shall define program information needs and develop strategies, systems, and capabilities to meet those needs.

(b) With respect to general information resources management, each agency shall—

(1) manage information resources to—

(A) reduce information collection burdens on the public;

(B) increase program efficiency and effectiveness; and

(C) improve the integrity, quality, and utility of information to all users within and outside the agency, including capabilities for ensuring dissemination of public information, public access to government information, and protections for privacy and security;

(2) in accordance with guidance by the Director, develop and maintain a strategic information resources management plan that shall describe how

information resources management activities help accomplish agency missions;

(3) develop and maintain an ongoing process to—

(A) ensure that information resources management operations and decisions are integrated with organizational planning, budget, financial management, human resources management, and program decisions;

(B) in cooperation with the agency Chief Financial Officer (or comparable official), develop a full and accurate accounting of information technology expenditures, related expenses, and results; and

(C) establish goals for improving information resources management's contribution to program productivity, efficiency, and effectiveness, methods for measuring progress towards those goals, and clear roles and responsibilities for achieving those goals;

(4) in consultation with the Director, the Administrator of General Services, and the Archivist of the United States, maintain a current and complete inventory of the agency's information resources, including directories necessary to fulfill the requirements of section 3511 of this subchapter; and

(5) in consultation with the Director and the Director of the Office of Personnel Management, conduct formal training programs to educate agency program and management officials about information resources management.

(c) With respect to the collection of information and the control of paperwork, each agency shall—

(1) establish a process within the office headed by the Chief Information Officer designated under subsection (a), that is sufficiently independent of program responsibility to evaluate fairly whether proposed collections of information should be approved under this subchapter, to—

(A) review each collection of information before submission to the Director for review under this subchapter, including—

(i) an evaluation of the need for the collection of information;

(ii) a functional description of the information to be collected;

(iii) a plan for the collection of the information;

(iv) a specific, objectively supported estimate of burden;

(v) a test of the collection of information through a pilot program, if appropriate; and

(vi) a plan for the efficient and effective management and use of the information to be collected, including necessary resources;

(B) ensure that each information collection—

(i) is inventoried, displays a control number and, if appropriate, an expiration date;
(ii) indicates the collection is in accordance with the clearance requirements of section 3507; and
(iii) informs the person receiving the collection of information of—

    (I) the reasons the information is being collected;
    (II) the way such information is to be used;
    (III) an estimate, to the extent practicable, of the burden of the collection;
    (IV) whether responses to the collection of information are voluntary, required to obtain a benefit, or mandatory; and
    (V) the fact that an agency may not conduct or sponsor, and person is not required to respond to, a collection of information unless it displays a valid control number; and

(C) assess the information collection burden of proposed legislation affecting the agency;

(2)(A) except as provided under subparagraph (B) or section 3507(j), provide 60-day notice in the Federal Register, and otherwise consult with members of the public and affected agencies concerning each proposed collection of information, to solicit comment to—

(i) evaluate whether the proposed collection of information is necessary for the proper performance of the functions of the agency, including whether the information shall have practical utility;
(ii) evaluate the accuracy of the agency's estimate of the burden of the proposed collection of information;
(iii) enhance the quality, utility, and clarity of the Information to be collected; and
(iv) minimize the burden of the collection of information on those who are to respond, including through the use of automated collection techniques or other forms of information technology; and

(B) for any proposed collection of information contained in a proposed rule (to be reviewed by the Director under section 3507(d)), provide notice and comment through the notice of proposed rulemaking for the proposed rule and such notice shall have the same purposes specified under subparagraph (A)(i) through (iv);

(3) certify (and provide a record supporting such certification, including

public comments received by the agency) that each collection of information submitted to the Director for review under section 3507—

(A) is necessary for the proper performance of the functions of the agency, including that the information has practical utility;

(B) is not unnecessarily duplicative of information otherwise reasonably accessible to the agency;

(C) reduces to the extent practicable and appropriate the burden on persons who shall provide information to or for the agency, including with respect to small entities, as defined under section 601(6) of title 5, the use of such techniques as—

  (i) establishing differing compliance or reporting requirements or timetables that take into account the resources available to those who are to respond;

  (ii) the clarification, consolidation, or simplification of compliance and reporting requirements; or

  (iii) an exemption from coverage of the collection of information, or any part thereof;

(D) is written using plain, coherent, and unambiguous terminology and is understandable to those who are to respond;

(E) is to be implemented in ways consistent and compatible, to the maximum extent practicable, with the existing reporting and recordkeeping practices of those who are to respond;

(F) indicates for each recordkeeping requirement the length of time persons are required to maintain the records specified;

(G) contains the statement required under paragraph (1)(B)(iii);

(H) has been developed by an office that has planned and allocated resources for the efficient and effective management and use of the information to be collected, including the processing of the information in a manner which shall enhance, where appropriate, the utility of the information to agencies and the public;

(I) uses effective and efficient statistical survey methodology appropriate to the purpose for which the information is to be collected; and

(J) to the maximum extent practicable, uses information technology to reduce burden and improve data quality, agency efficiency and responsiveness to the public; and

(4) in addition to the requirements of this chapter regarding the reduction of information collection burdens for small business concerns (as defined in section 3 of the Small Business Act (15 U.S.C. 632)), make

efforts to further reduce the information collection burden for small business concerns with fewer than 25 employees.

(d) With respect to information dissemination, each agency shall—

(1) ensure that the public has timely and equitable access to the agency's public information, including ensuring such access through—

(A) encouraging a diversity of public and private sources for information based on government public information;

(B) in cases in which the agency provides public information maintained in electronic format, providing timely and equitable access to the underlying data (in whole or in part); and

(C) agency dissemination of public information in an efficient, effective, and economical manner;

(2) regularly solicit and consider public input on the agency's information dissemination activities;

(3) provide adequate notice when initiating, substantially modifying, or terminating significant information dissemination products; and

(4) not, except where specifically authorized by statute—

(A) establish an exclusive, restricted, or other distribution arrangement that interferes with timely and equitable availability of public information to the public;

(B) restrict or regulate the use, resale, or redissemination of public information by the public;

(C) charge fees or royalties for resale or redissemination of public information; or

(D) establish user fees for public information that exceed the cost of dissemination.

(e) With respect to statistical policy and coordination, each agency shall—

(1) ensure the relevance, accuracy, timeliness, integrity, and objectivity of information collected or created for statistical purposes;

(2) inform respondents fully and accurately about the sponsors, purposes, and uses of statistical surveys and studies;

(3) protect respondents' privacy and ensure that disclosure policies fully honor pledges of confidentiality;

(4) observe Federal standards and practices for data collection, analysis, documentation, sharing, and dissemination of information;

(5) ensure the timely publication of the results of statistical surveys and studies, including information about the quality and limitations of the surveys and studies; and

(6) make data available to statistical agencies and readily accessible to the public.

(f) With respect to records management, each agency shall implement and enforce applicable policies and procedures, including requirements for archiving information maintained in electronic format, particularly in the planning, design and operation of information systems.

(g) With respect to privacy and security, each agency shall—

(1) implement and enforce applicable policies, procedures, standards, and guidelines on privacy, confidentiality, security, disclosure and sharing of information collected or maintained by or for the agency; and

(2) assume responsibility and accountability for compliance with and coordinated management of sections 552 and 552a of title 5, subchapter II of this chapter, and related information management laws.

(h) With respect to Federal information technology, each agency shall—

(1) implement and enforce applicable Governmentwide and agency information technology management policies, principles, standards, and guidelines;

(2) assume responsibility and accountability for information technology investments;

(3) promote the use of information technology by the agency to improve the productivity, efficiency, and effectiveness of agency programs, including the reduction of information collection burdens on the public and improved dissemination of public information;

(4) propose changes in legislation, regulations, and agency procedures to improve information technology practices, including changes that improve the ability of the agency to use technology to reduce burden; and

(5) assume responsibility for maximizing the value and assessing and managing the risks of major information systems initiatives through a process that is—

(A) integrated with budget, financial, and program management decisions; and

(B) used to select, control, and evaluate the results of major information systems initiatives.

(i)(1) In addition to the requirements described in subsection (c), each agency shall, with respect to the collection of information and the control of paperwork, establish 1 point of contact in the agency to act as a liaison between the agency and small business concerns (as defined in section 3 of the Small Business Act (15 U.S.C. 632)).

(2) Each point of contact described under paragraph (1) shall be established not later than 1 year after the date of enactment of the Small Business Paperwork Relief Act of 2002.

§3507. Public information collection activities; submission to Director; approval and delegation

(a) An agency shall not conduct or sponsor the collection of information unless in advance of the adoption or revision of the collection of information—
- (1) the agency has—
    - (A) conducted the review established under section 3506(c)(1);
    - (B) evaluated the public comments received under section 3506(c)(2);
    - (C) submitted to the Director the certification required under section 3506(c)(3), the proposed collection of information, copies of pertinent statutory authority, regulations, and other related materials as the Director may specify; and
    - (D) published a notice in the Federal Register—
        - (i) stating that the agency has made such submission; and
        - (ii) setting forth—
            - (I) a title for the collection of information;
            - (II) a summary of the collection of information;
            - (III) a brief description of the need for the information and the proposed use of the information;
            - (IV) a description of the likely respondents and proposed frequency of response to the collection of information;
            - (V) an estimate of the burden that shall result from the collection of information; and
            - (VI) notice that comments may be submitted to the agency and Director;
- (2) the Director has approved the proposed collection of information or approval has been inferred, under the provisions of this section; and
- (3) the agency has obtained from the Director a control number to be displayed upon the collection of information.

(b) The Director shall provide at least 30 days for public comment prior to making a decision under subsection (c), (d), or (h), except as provided under subsection (j).

(c)(1) For any proposed collection of information not contained in a proposed rule, the Director shall notify the agency involved of the decision to approve or disapprove the proposed collection of information.

    (2) The Director shall provide the notification under paragraph (1), within 60 days after receipt or publication of the notice under subsection (a)(1)(D), whichever is later.

(3) If the Director does not notify the agency of a denial or approval within the 60-day period described under paragraph (2)—
   (A) the approval may be inferred;
   (B) a control number shall be assigned without further delay; and
   (C) the agency may collect the information for not more than 1 year.

(d)(1) For any proposed collection of information contained in a proposed rule—
   (A) as soon as practicable, but no later than the date of publication of a notice of proposed rulemaking in the Federal Register, each agency shall forward to the Director a copy of any proposed rule which contains a collection of information and any information requested by the Director necessary to make the determination required under this subsection; and
   (B) within 60 days after the notice of proposed rulemaking is published in the Federal Register, the Director may file public comments pursuant to the standards set forth in section 3508 on the collection of information contained in the proposed rule;

(2) When a final rule is published in the Federal Register, the agency shall explain—
   (A) how any collection of information contained in the final rule responds to the comments, if any, filed by the Director or the public; or
   (B) the reasons such comments were rejected.

(3) If the Director has received notice and failed to comment on an agency rule within 60 days after the notice of proposed rulemaking, the Director may not disapprove any collection of information specifically contained in an agency rule.

(4) No provision in this section shall be construed to prevent the Director, in the Director's discretion –
   (A) from disapproving any collection of information which was not specifically required by an agency rule;
   (B) from disapproving any collection of information contained in an agency rule, if the agency failed to comply with the requirements of paragraph (1) of this subsection;
   (C) from disapproving any collection of information contained in a final agency rule, if the Director finds within 60 days after the publication of the final rule that the agency's response to the Director's comments filed under paragraph (2) of this subsection was unreasonable; or

(D) from disapproving any collection of information contained in a final rule, if—

(i) the Director determines that the agency has substantially modified in the final rule the collection of information contained in the proposed rule; and

(ii) the agency has not given the Director the information required under paragraph (1) with respect to the modified collection of information, at least 60 days before the issuance of the final rule.

(5) This subsection shall apply only when an agency publishes a notice of proposed rulemaking and requests public comments.

(6) The decision by the Director to approve or not act upon a collection of information contained in an agency rule shall not be subject to judicial review.

(e)(1) Any decision by the Director under subsection (c), (d), (h) or (j) to disapprove a collection of information, or to instruct the agency to make substantive or material change to a collection of information, shall be publicly available and include an explanation of the reasons for such decision.

(2) Any written communication between the Administrator of the Office of Information and Regulatory Affairs, or any employee of the Office of Information and Regulatory Affairs, and an agency or person not employed by the Federal Government concerning a proposed collection of information shall be made available to the public.

(3) This subsection shall not require the disclosure of—

(A) any information which is protected at all times by procedures established for information which has been specifically authorized under criteria established by an Executive order or an Act of Congress to be kept secret in the interest of national defense or foreign policy; or

(B) any communication relating to a collection of information which is not approved under this subchapter, the disclosure of which could lead to retaliation or discrimination against the communicator.

(f)(1) An independent regulatory agency which is administered by 2 or more members of a commission, board, or similar body, may by majority vote void—

(A) any disapproval by the Director, in whole or in part, of a proposed collection of information of that agency; or

(B) an exercise of authority under subsection (d) of section 3507 concerning that agency.

(2) The agency shall certify each vote to void such disapproval or exercise to the Director, and explain the reasons for such vote. The Director shall without further delay assign a control number to such collection of information, and such vote to void the disapproval or exercise shall be valid for a period of 3 years.

(g) The Director may not approve a collection of information for a period in excess of 3 years.

(h)(1) If an agency decides to seek extension of the Director's approval granted for a currently approved collection of information, the agency shall—

> (A) conduct the review established under section 3506(c), including the seeking of comment from the public on the continued need for, and burden imposed by the collection of information; and
>
> (B) after having made a reasonable effort to seek public comment, but no later than 60 days before the expiration date of the control number assigned by the Director for the currently approved collection of information, submit the collection of information for review and approval under this section, which shall include an explanation of how the agency has used the information that it has collected.

(2) If under the provisions of this section, the Director disapproves a collection of information contained in an existing rule, or recommends or instructs the agency to make a substantive or material change to a collection of information contained in an existing rule, the Director shall—

> (A) publish an explanation thereof in the Federal Register; and
>
> (B) instruct the agency to undertake a rulemaking within a reasonable time limited to consideration of changes to the collection of information contained in the rule and thereafter to submit the collection of information for approval or disapproval under this subchapter.

(3) An agency may not make a substantive or material modification to a collection of information after such collection has been approved by the Director, unless the modification has been submitted to the Director for review and approval under this subchapter.

(i)(1) If the Director finds that a senior official of an agency designated under section 3506(a) is sufficiently independent of program responsibility to evaluate fairly whether proposed collections of information should be approved and has sufficient resources to carry out this responsibility effectively, the Director may, by rule in accordance with the notice and comment provisions of chapter 5 of title 5, United States Code, delegate to such official the authority to approve proposed collections of information in specific program areas, for specific purposes, or for all agency purposes.

(2) A delegation by the Director under this section shall not preclude the Director from reviewing individual collections of information if the Director determines that circumstances warrant such a review. The Director shall retain authority to revoke such delegations, both in general and with regard to any specific matter. In acting for the Director, any official to whom approval authority has been delegated under this section shall comply fully with the rules and regulations promulgated by the Director.
(j)(1) The agency head may request the Director to authorize a collection of information, if an agency head determines that—
    (A) a collection of information—
        (i) is needed prior to the expiration of time periods established under this subchapter; and
        (ii) is essential to the mission of the agency; and
    (B) the agency cannot reasonably comply with the provisions of this subchapter because—
        (i) public harm is reasonably likely to result if normal clearance procedures are followed;
        (ii) an unanticipated event has occurred; or
        (iii) the use of normal clearance procedures is reasonably likely to prevent or disrupt the collection of information or is reasonably likely to cause a statutory or court ordered deadline to be missed.
(2) The Director shall approve or disapprove any such authorization request within the time requested by the agency head and, if approved, shall assign the collection of information a control number. Any collection of information conducted under this subsection may be conducted without compliance with the provisions of this subchapter for a maximum of 180 days after the date on which the Director received the request to authorize such collection.

§3508. Determination of necessity for information; hearing

Before approving a proposed collection of information, the Director shall determine whether the collection of information by the agency is necessary for the proper performance of the functions of the agency, including whether the information shall have practical utility. Before making a determination the Director may give the agency and other interested persons an opportunity to be heard or to submit statements in writing. To the extent, if any, that the Director determines that the collection of information by an agency is unnecessary for any reason, the agency may not engage in the collection of information.

§3509. Designation of central collection agency

The Director may designate a central collection agency to obtain information for two or more agencies if the Director determines that the needs of such agencies for information will be adequately served by a single collection agency, and such sharing of data is not inconsistent with applicable law. In such cases the Director shall prescribe (with reference to the collection of information) the duties and functions of the collection agency so designated and of the agencies for which it is to act as agent (including reimbursement for costs). While the designation is in effect, an agency covered by the designation may not obtain for itself information for the agency which is the duty of the collection agency to obtain. The Director may modify the designation from time to time as circumstances require. The authority to designate under this section is subject to the provisions of section 3507(f) of this subchapter.

§3510. Cooperation of agencies in making information available

(a) The Director may direct an agency to make available to another agency, or an agency may make available to another agency, information obtained by a collection of information if the disclosure is not inconsistent with applicable law.

(b)(1) If information obtained by an agency is released by that agency to another agency, all the provisions of law (including penalties) that relate to the unlawful disclosure of information apply to the officers and employees of the agency to which information is released to the same extent and in the same manner as the provisions apply to the officers and employees of the agency which originally obtained the information.

   (2) The officers and employees of the agency to which the information is released, in addition, shall be subject to the same provisions of law, including penalties, relating to the unlawful disclosure of information as if the information had been collected directly by that agency.

§3511. Establishment and operation of Government Information Locator Service

(a) In order to assist agencies and the public in locating information and to promote information sharing and equitable access by the public, the Director shall—

   (1) cause to be established and maintained a distributed agency-based electronic Government Information Locator Service (hereafter in this

section referred to as the "Service"), which shall identify the major information systems, holdings, and dissemination products of each agency;
(2) require each agency to establish and maintain an agency information locator service as a component of, and to support the establishment and operation of the Service;
(3) in cooperation with the Archivist of the United States, the Administrator of General Services, the Public Printer, and the Librarian of Congress, establish an interagency committee to advise the Secretary of Commerce on the development of technical standards for the Service to ensure compatibility, promote information sharing, and uniform access by the public;
(4) consider public access and other user needs in the establishment and operation of the Service;
(5) ensure the security and integrity of the Service, including measures to ensure that only information which is intended to be disclosed to the public is disclosed through the Service; and
(6) periodically review the development and effectiveness of the Service and make recommendations for improvement, including other mechanisms for improving public access to Federal agency public information.
(b) This section shall not apply to operational files as defined by the Central Intelligence Agency Information Act (50 U.S.C. 431 et seq.).

§3512. Public protection

(a) Notwithstanding any other provision of law, no person shall be subject to any penalty for failing to comply with a collection of information that is subject to this subchapter if—
> (1) the collection of information does not display a valid control number assigned by the Director in accordance with this subchapter; or
> (2) the agency fails to inform the person who is to respond to the collection of information that such person is not required to respond to the collection of information unless it displays a valid control number.

(b) The protection provided by this section may be raised in the form of a complete defense, bar, or otherwise at any time during the agency administrative process or judicial action applicable thereto.

§3513. Director review of agency activities; reporting; agency response

(a) In consultation with the Administrator of General Services, the Archivist of the United States, the Director of the National Institute of Standards and Technology, and the Director of the Office of Personnel Management, the Director shall periodically review selected agency information resources management activities to ascertain the efficiency and effectiveness of such activities to improve agency performance and the accomplishment of agency missions.

(b) Each agency having an activity reviewed under subsection (a) shall, within 60 days after receipt of a report on the review, provide a written plan to the Director describing steps (including milestones) to—

  (1) be taken to address information resources management problems identified in the report; and

  (2) improve agency performance and the accomplishment of agency missions.

§3514. Responsiveness to Congress

(a)(1) The Director shall—

  (A) keep the Congress and congressional committees fully and currently informed of the major activities under this subchapter; and

  (B) submit a report on such activities to the President of the Senate and the Speaker of the House of Representatives annually and at such other times as the Director determines necessary.*

(2) The Director shall include in any such report a description of the extent to which agencies have—

  (A) reduced information collection burdens on the public, including—

    (i) a summary of accomplishments and planned initiatives to reduce collection of information burdens;

    (ii) a list of all violations of this subchapter and of any rules,

---

* TERMINATION OF REPORTING REQUIREMENTS

For termination, effective May 15, 2000, of provisions of law requiring submittal to Congress of any annual, semiannual, or other regular periodic report listed in House Document No. 103-7 (in which the 8th item on page 41 identifies an annual reporting requirement which, as subsequently amended, is contained in subsec. (a) of this section), see section 3003 of Pub. L. 104-66, as amended, set out as a note under section 1113 of Title 31, Money and Finance.

guidelines, policies, and procedures issued pursuant to this subchapter;

(iii) a list of any increase in the collection of information burden, including the authority for each such collection; and

(iv) a list of agencies that in the preceding year did not reduce information collection burdens in accordance with section 3505(a)(1), a list of the programs and statutory responsibilities of those agencies that precluded that reduction, and recommendations to assist those agencies to reduce information collection burdens in accordance with that section;

(B) improved the quality and utility of statistical information;

(C) improved public access to Government information; and

(D) improved program performance and the accomplishment of agency missions through information resources management.

(b) The preparation of any report required by this section shall be based on performance results reported by the agencies and shall not increase the collection of information burden on persons outside the Federal Government.

§3515. Administrative powers

Upon the request of the Director, each agency (other than an independent regulatory agency) shall, to the extent practicable, make its services, personnel, and facilities available to the Director for the performance of functions under this subchapter.

§3516. Rules and regulations

The Director shall promulgate rules, regulations, or procedures necessary to exercise the authority provided by this subchapter.

§3517. Consultation with other agencies and the public

(a) In developing information resources management policies, plans, rules, regulations, procedures, and guidelines and in reviewing collections of information, the Director shall provide interested agencies and persons early and meaningful opportunity to comment.

(b) Any person may request the Director to review any collection of information conducted by or for an agency to determine, if, under this subchapter, a person shall maintain, provide, or disclose the information to or for the agency. Unless the request is frivolous, the Director shall, in coordination with the

agency responsible for the collection of information—
(1) respond to the request within 60 days after receiving the request, unless such period is extended by the Director to a specified date and the person making the request is given notice of such extension; and
(2) take appropriate remedial action, if necessary.

§3518. Effect on existing laws and regulations

(a) Except as otherwise provided in this subchapter, the authority of an agency under any other law to prescribe policies, rules, regulations, and procedures for Federal information resources management activities is subject to the authority of the Director under this subchapter.
(b) Nothing in this subchapter shall be deemed to affect or reduce the authority of the Secretary of Commerce or the Director of the Office of Management and Budget pursuant to Reorganization Plan No. 1 of 1977 (as amended) and Executive order, relating to telecommunications and information policy, procurement and management of telecommunications and information systems, spectrum use, and related matters.
(c)(1) Except as provided in paragraph (2), this subchapter shall not apply to the collection of information—
(A) during the conduct of a Federal criminal investigation or prosecution, or during the disposition of a particular criminal matter;
(B) during the conduct of—
(i) a civil action to which the United States or any official or agency thereof is a party; or
(ii) an administrative action or investigation involving an agency against specific individuals or entities;
(C) by compulsory process pursuant to the Antitrust Civil Process Act and section 13 of the Federal Trade Commission Improvements Act of 1980; or
(D) during the conduct of intelligence activities as defined in section 3.4(e) of Executive Order No. 12333, issued December 4, 1981, or successor orders, or during the conduct of cryptologic activities that are communications security activities.
(2) This subchapter applies to the collection of information during the conduct of general investigations (other than information collected in an antitrust investigation to the extent provided in subparagraph (C) of paragraph (1)) undertaken with reference to a category of individuals or entities such as a class of licensees or an entire industry.

(d) Nothing in this subchapter shall be interpreted as increasing or decreasing the authority conferred by sections 11331 and 11332 of title 40 on the Secretary of Commerce or the Director of the Office of Management and Budget.
(e) Nothing in this subchapter shall be interpreted as increasing or decreasing the authority of the President, the Office of Management and Budget or the Director thereof, under the laws of the United States, with respect to the substantive policies and programs of departments, agencies and offices, including the substantive authority of any Federal agency to enforce the civil rights laws.

§3519. Access to information

Under the conditions and procedures prescribed in section 716 of title 31, the Director and personnel in the Office of Information and Regulatory Affairs shall furnish such information as the Comptroller General may require for the discharge of the responsibilities of the Comptroller General. For the purpose of obtaining such information, the Comptroller General or representatives thereof shall have access to all books, documents, papers and records, regardless of form or format, of the Office.

§3520. Establishment of task force on information collection and dissemination

(a) There is established a task force to study the feasibility of streamlining requirements with respect to small business concerns regarding collection of information and strengthening dissemination of information (in this section referred to as the "task force").
(b)(1) The Director shall determine—
    (A) subject to the minimum requirements under paragraph (2), the number of representatives to be designated under each subparagraph of that paragraph; and
    (B) the agencies to be represented under paragraph (2)(K).
(2) After all determinations are made under paragraph (1), the members of the task force shall be designated by the head of each applicable department or agency, and include—
    (A) 1 representative of the Director, who shall convene and chair the task force;
    (B) not less than 2 representatives of the Department of Labor, including 1 representative of the Bureau of Labor Statistics and 1 representative of the Occupational Safety and Health Administration;

(C) not less than 1 representative of the Environmental Protection Agency;

(D) not less than 1 representative of the Department of Transportation;

(E) not less than 1 representative of the Office of Advocacy of the Small Business Administration;

(F) not less than 1 representative of the Internal Revenue Service;

(G) not less than 2 representatives of the Department of Health and Human Services, including 1 representative of the Centers for Medicare and Medicaid Services;

(H) not less than 1 representative of the Department of Agriculture;

(I) not less than 1 representative of the Department of the Interior;

(J) not less than 1 representative of the General Services Administration; and

(K) not less than 1 representative of each of 2 agencies not represented by representatives described under subparagraphs (A) through (J).

(c) The task force shall—

(1) identify ways to integrate the collection of information across Federal agencies and programs and examine the feasibility and desirability of requiring each agency to consolidate requirements regarding collections of information with respect to small business concerns within and across agencies, without negatively impacting the effectiveness of underlying laws and regulations regarding such collections of information, in order that each small business concern may submit all information required by the agency—

(A) to 1 point of contact in the agency;

(B) in a single format, such as a single electronic reporting system, with respect to the agency; and

(C) with synchronized reporting for information submissions having the same frequency, such as synchronized quarterly, semiannual, and annual reporting dates;

(2) examine the feasibility and benefits to small businesses of publishing a list by the Director of the collections of information applicable to small business concerns (as defined in section 3 of the Small Business Act (15 U.S.C. 632)), organized—

(A) by North American Industry Classification System code;

(B) by industrial sector description; or

(C) in another manner by which small business concerns can more easily identify requirements with which those small business concerns are expected to comply;

(3) examine the savings, including cost savings, and develop recommendations for implementing—

(A) systems for electronic submissions of information to the Federal Government; and

(B) interactive reporting systems, including components that provide immediate feedback to assure that data being submitted—

(i) meet requirements of format; and

(ii) are within the range of acceptable options for each data field;

(4) make recommendations to improve the electronic dissemination of information collected under Federal requirements;

(5) recommend a plan for the development of an interactive Governmentwide system, available through the Internet, to allow each small business to—

(A) better understand which Federal requirements regarding collection of information (and, when possible, which other Federal regulatory requirements) apply to that particular business; and

(B) more easily comply with those Federal requirements; and

(6) in carrying out this section, consider opportunities for the coordination—

(A) of Federal and State reporting requirements; and

(B) among the points of contact described under section 3506(i), such as to enable agencies to provide small business concerns with contacts for information collection requirements for other agencies.

(d) The task force shall—

(1) by publication in the Federal Register, provide notice and an opportunity for public comment on each report in draft form; and

(2) make provision in each report for the inclusion of—

(A) any additional or dissenting views of task force members; and

(B) a summary of significant public comments.

(e) Not later than 1 year after the date of enactment of the Small Business Paperwork Relief Act of 2002, the task force shall submit a report of its findings under subsection (c) (1), (2), and (3) to—

(1) the Director;

(2) the chairpersons and ranking minority members of—

(A) the Committee on Governmental Affairs and the Committee on Small Business and Entrepreneurship of the Senate; and

(B) the Committee on Government Reform and the Committee on Small Business of the House of Representatives; and

(3) the Small Business and Agriculture Regulatory Enforcement Ombudsman designated under section 30(b) of the Small Business Act (15 U.S.C. 657(b)).

(f) Not later than 2 years after the date of enactment of the Small Business Paperwork Relief Act of 2002, the task force shall submit a report of its findings under subsection (c) (4) and (5) to—

(1) the Director;

(2) the chairpersons and ranking minority members of—

(A) the Committee on Governmental Affairs and the Committee on Small Business and Entrepreneurship of the Senate; and

(B) the Committee on Government Reform and the Committee on Small Business of the House of Representatives; and

(3) the Small Business and Agriculture Regulatory Enforcement Ombudsman designated under section 30(b) of the Small Business Act (15 U.S.C. 657(b)).

(g) The task force shall terminate after completion of its work.

(h) In this section, the term "small business concern" has the meaning given under section 3 of the Small Business Act (15 U.S.C. 632).

§3521. Authorization of appropriations

There are authorized to be appropriated to the Office of Information and Regulatory Affairs to carry out the provisions of this subchapter, and for no other purpose, $8,000,000 for each of the fiscal years 1996, 1997, 1998, 1999, 2000, and 2001.

Office of Management and Budget
5 C.F.R. Part 1320 (2007)
Controlling Paperwork Burdens on the Public

PART 1320—CONTROLLING PAPERWORK BURDENS ON THE PUBLIC

§ 1320.1 Purpose.
§ 1320.2 Effect.
§ 1320.3 Definitions.
§ 1320.4 Coverage.
§ 1320.5 General requirements.
§ 1320.6 Public protection.
§ 1320.7 Agency head and Senior Official responsibilities.
§ 1320.8 Agency collection of information responsibilities.
§ 1320.9 Agency certifications for proposed collections of information.
§ 1320.10 Clearance of collections of information, other than those contained in proposed rules or in current rules.
§ 1320.11 Clearance of collections of information in proposed rules.
§ 1320.12 Clearance of collections of information in current rules.
§ 1320.13 Emergency processing.
§ 1320.14 Public access.
§ 1320.15 Independent regulatory agency override authority.
§ 1320.16 Delegation of approval authority.
§ 1320.17 Information collection budget.
§ 1320.18 Other authority.

Appendix A to Part 1320 —Agencies With Delegated Review and Approval Authority

§ 1320.1 Purpose.

The purpose of this part is to implement the provisions of the Paperwork Reduction Act of 1995 (44 U.S.C. chapter 35)(the Act) concerning collections of information. It is issued under the authority of section 3516 of the Act, which provides that "The Director shall promulgate rules, regulations, or procedures necessary to exercise the authority provided by this chapter." It is designed to reduce, minimize and control burdens and maximize the practical utility and public benefit of the information created, collected, disclosed, maintained, used, shared and disseminated by or for the Federal government.

§ 1320.2 Effect.

(a) Except as provided in paragraph (b) of this section, this part takes effect on October 1, 1995.

(b)(1) In the case of a collection of information for which there is in effect on September 30, 1995, a control number issued by the Office of Management and Budget under 44 U.S.C. Chapter 35, the provisions of this Part shall take effect beginning on the earlier of:

(i) The date of the first extension of approval for or modification of that collection of information after September 30, 1995; or

(ii) The date of the expiration of the OMB control number after September 30, 1995.

(2) Prior to such extension of approval, modification, or expiration, the collection of information shall be subject to 5 CFR part 1320, as in effect on September 30, 1995.

§ 1320.3 Definitions.

For purposes of implementing the Act and this Part, the following terms are defined as follows:

(a) *Agency* means any executive department, military department, Government corporation, Government controlled corporation, or other establishment in the executive branch of the government, or any independent regulatory agency, but does not include:

(1) The General Accounting Office;

(2) Federal Election Commission;

(3) The governments of the District of Columbia and the territories and possessions of the United States, and their various subdivisions; or

(4) Government-owned contractor-operated facilities, including laboratories engaged in national defense research and production activities.

(b)(1) *Burden* means the total time, effort, or financial resources expended by persons to generate, maintain, retain, or disclose or provide information to or for a Federal agency, including:

(i) Reviewing instructions;

(ii) Developing, acquiring, installing, and utilizing technology and systems for the purpose of collecting, validating, and verifying information;

(iii) Developing, acquiring, installing, and utilizing technology and systems for the purpose of processing and maintaining information;

(iv) Developing, acquiring, installing, and utilizing technology and systems for the purpose of disclosing and providing information;

(v) Adjusting the existing ways to comply with any previously applicable instructions and requirements;

(vi) Training personnel to be able to respond to a collection of information;

(vii) Searching data sources;

(viii) Completing and reviewing the collection of information; and

(ix) Transmitting, or otherwise disclosing the information.

(2) The time, effort, and financial resources necessary to comply with a collection of information that would be incurred by persons in the normal course of their activities (e.g., in compiling and maintaining business records) will be excluded from the "burden" if the agency demonstrates that the reporting, recordkeeping, or disclosure activities needed to comply are usual and customary.

(3) A collection of information conducted or sponsored by a Federal agency that is also conducted or sponsored by a unit of State, local, or tribal government is presumed to impose a Federal burden except to the extent that the agency shows that such State, local, or tribal requirement would be imposed even in the absence of a Federal requirement.

(c) *Collection of information* means, except as provided in §1320.4, the obtaining, causing to be obtained, soliciting, or requiring the disclosure to an agency, third parties or the public of information by or for an agency by means of identical questions posed to, or identical reporting, recordkeeping, or disclosure requirements imposed on, ten or more persons, whether such collection of information is mandatory, voluntary, or required to obtain or retain a benefit. "Collection of information" includes any requirement or request for persons to obtain, maintain, retain, report, or publicly disclose information. As used in this Part, "collection of information" refers to the act of collecting or disclosing information, to the information to be collected or disclosed, to a plan and/or an instrument calling for the collection or disclosure of information, or any of these, as appropriate.

(1) A "collection of information" may be in any form or format, including the use of report forms; application forms; schedules; questionnaires; surveys; reporting or recordkeeping requirements; contracts; agreements; policy statements; plans; rules or regulations; planning requirements; circulars; directives; instructions; bulletins; requests for proposal or other procurement requirements; interview guides; oral communica-

tions; posting, notification, labeling, or similar disclosure requirements; telegraphic or telephonic requests; automated, electronic, mechanical, or other technological collection techniques; standard questionnaires used to monitor compliance with agency requirements; or any other techniques or technological methods used to monitor compliance with agency requirements. A "collection of information" may implicitly or explicitly include related collection of information requirements.

(2) Requirements by an agency for a person to obtain or compile information for the purpose of disclosure to members of the public or the public at large, through posting, notification, labeling or similar disclosure requirements constitute the "collection of information" whenever the same requirement to obtain or compile information would be a "collection of information" if the information were directly provided to the agency. The public disclosure of information originally supplied by the Federal government to the recipient for the purpose of disclosure to the public is not included within this definition.

(3) "Collection of information" includes questions posed to agencies, instrumentalities, or employees of the United States, if the results are to be used for general statistical purposes, that is, if the results are to be used for statistical compilations of general public interest, including compilations showing the status or implementation of Federal activities and programs.

(4) As used in paragraph (c) of this section, "ten or more persons" refers to the persons to whom a collection of information is addressed by the agency within any 12-month period, and to any independent entities to which the initial addressee may reasonably be expected to transmit the collection of information during that period, including independent State, territorial, tribal or local entities and separately incorporated subsidiaries or affiliates. For the purposes of this definition of "ten or more persons," "persons" does not include employees of the respondent acting within the scope of their employment, contractors engaged by a respondent for the purpose of complying with the collection of information, or current employees of the Federal government (including military reservists and members of the National Guard while on active duty) when acting within the scope of their employment, but it does include retired and other former Federal employees.

(i) Any recordkeeping, reporting, or disclosure requirement contained in a rule of general applicability is deemed to involve ten or more persons.

(ii) Any collection of information addressed to all or a substantial majority of an industry is presumed to involve ten or more persons.

(d) *Conduct or Sponsor.* A Federal agency is considered to "conduct or sponsor" a collection of information if the agency collects the information, causes another agency to collect the information, contracts or enters into a cooperative agreement with a person to collect the information, or requires a person to provide information to another person, or in similar ways causes another agency, contractor, partner in a cooperative agreement, or person to obtain, solicit, or require the disclosure to third parties or the public of information by or for an agency. A collection of information undertaken by a recipient of a Federal grant is considered to be "conducted or sponsored" by an agency only if:

(1) The recipient of a grant is conducting the collection of information at the specific request of the agency; or

(2) The terms and conditions of the grant require specific approval by the agency of the collection of information or collection procedures.

(e) *Director* means the Director of OMB, or his or her designee.

(f) *Display* means:

(1) In the case of forms, questionnaires,

instructions, and other written collections of information sent or made available to potential respondents (other than in an electronic format), to place the currently valid OMB control number on the front page of the collection of information;

(2) In the case of forms, questionnaires, instructions, and other written collections of information sent or made available to potential respondents in an electronic format, to place the currently valid OMB control number in the instructions, near the title of the electronic collection instrument, or, for online applications, on the first screen viewed by the respondent;

(3) In the case of collections of information published in regulations, guidelines, and other issuances in the Federal Register, to publish the currently valid OMB control number in the Federal Register (for example, in the case of a collection of information in a regulation, by publishing the OMB control number in the preamble or the regulatory text for the final rule, in a technical amendment to the final rule, or in a separate notice announcing OMB approval of the collection of information). In the case of a collection of information published in an issuance that is also included in the Code of Federal Regulations, publication of the currently valid control number in the Code of Federal Regulations constitutes an alternative means of "display." In the case of a collection of information published in an issuance that is also included in the Code of Federal Regulations, OMB recommends for ease of future reference that, even where an agency has already "displayed" the OMB control number by publishing it in the Federal Register as a separate notice or in the preamble for the final rule (rather than in the regulatory text for the final rule or in a technical amendment to the final rule), the agency also place the currently valid control number in a table or codified section to be included in the Code of Federal Regulations. For placement of OMB control numbers in the Code of Federal Regulations, see 1 CFR 21.35.

(4) In other cases, and where OMB determines in advance in writing that special circumstances exist, to use other means to inform potential respondents of the OMB control number.

(g) *Independent regulatory agency* means the Board of Governors of the Federal Reserve System, the Commodity Futures Trading Commission, the Consumer Product Safety Commission, the Federal Communications Commission, the Federal Deposit Insurance Corporation, the Federal Energy Regulatory Commission, the Federal Housing Finance Board, the Federal Maritime Commission, the Federal Trade Commission, the Interstate Commerce Commission, the Mine Enforcement Safety and Health Review Commission, the National Labor Relations Board, the Nuclear Regulatory Commission, the Occupational Safety and Health Review Commission, the Postal Rate Commission, the Securities and Exchange Commission, and any other similar agency designated by statute as a Federal independent regulatory agency or commission.

(h) *Information* means any statement or estimate of fact or opinion, regardless of form or format, whether in numerical, graphic, or narrative form, and whether oral or maintained on paper, electronic or other media. "Information" does not generally include items in the following categories; however, OMB may determine that any specific item constitutes "information":

(1) Affidavits, oaths, affirmations, certifications, receipts, changes of address, consents, or acknowledgments; provided that they entail no burden other than that necessary to identify the respondent, the date, the respondent's address, and the nature of the instrument (by contrast, a certification would likely involve the collection of "information" if an agency conducted or sponsored it as a substitute for a collection of information to collect evidence of, or to monitor, compliance with regulatory standards, because such

a certification would generally entail burden in addition to that necessary to identify the respondent, the date, the respondent's address, and the nature of the instrument);

(2) Samples of products or of any other physical objects;

(3) Facts or opinions obtained through direct observation by an employee or agent of the sponsoring agency or through nonstandardized oral communication in connection with such direct observations;

(4) Facts or opinions submitted in response to general solicitations of comments from the public, published in theFederal Registeror other publications, regardless of the form or format thereof, provided that no person is required to supply specific information pertaining to the commenter, other than that necessary for self-identification, as a condition of the agency's full consideration of the comment;

(5) Facts or opinions obtained initially or in follow-on requests, from individuals (including individuals in control groups) under treatment or clinical examination in connection with research on or prophylaxis to prevent a clinical disorder, direct treatment of that disorder, or the interpretation of biological analyses of body fluids, tissues, or other specimens, or the identification or classification of such specimens;

(6) A request for facts or opinions addressed to a single person;

(7) Examinations designed to test the aptitude, abilities, or knowledge of the persons tested and the collection of information for identification or classification in connection with such examinations;

(8) Facts or opinions obtained or solicited at or in connection with public hearings or meetings;

(9) Facts or opinions obtained or solicited through nonstandardized follow-up questions designed to clarify responses to approved collections of information; and

(10) Like items so designated by OMB.

(i) *OMB* refers to the Office of Management and Budget.

(j) *Penalty* includes the imposition by an agency or court of a fine or other punishment; a judgment for monetary damages or equitable relief; or the revocation, suspension, reduction, or denial of a license, privilege, right, grant, or benefit.

(k) *Person* means an individual, partnership, association, corporation (including operations of government-owned contractor-operated facilities), business trust, or legal representative, an organized group of individuals, a State, territorial, tribal, or local government or branch thereof, or a political subdivision of a State, territory, tribal, or local government or a branch of a political subdivision;

(l) *Practical utility* means the actual, not merely the theoretical or potential, usefulness of information to or for an agency, taking into account its accuracy, validity, adequacy, and reliability, and the agency's ability to process the information it collects (or a person's ability to receive and process that which is disclosed, in the case of a third-party or public disclosure) in a useful and timely fashion. In determining whether information will have "practical utility," OMB will take into account whether the agency demonstrates actual timely use for the information either to carry out its functions or make it available to third-parties or the public, either directly or by means of a third-party or public posting, notification, labeling, or similar disclosure requirement, for the use of persons who have an interest in entities or transactions over which the agency has jurisdiction. In the case of recordkeeping requirements or general purpose statistics (see §1320.3(c)(3)), "practical utility" means that actual uses can be demonstrated.

(m) *Recordkeeping requirement* means a requirement imposed by or for an agency on persons to maintain specified records, including a requirement to:

(1) Retain such records;

(2) Notify third parties, the Federal gov-

ernment, or the public of the existence of such records;

(3) Disclose such records to third parties, the Federal government, or the public; or

(4) Report to third parties, the Federal government, or the public regarding such records.

§ 1320.4 Coverage.

(a) The requirements of this part apply to all agencies as defined in § 1320.3(a) and to all collections of information conducted or sponsored by those agencies, as defined in § 1320.3 (c) and (d), wherever conducted or sponsored, but, except as provided in paragraph (b) of this section, shall not apply to collections of information:

(1) During the conduct of a Federal criminal investigation or prosecution, or during the disposition of a particular criminal matter;

(2) During the conduct of a civil action to which the United States or any official or agency thereof is a party, or during the conduct of an administrative action, investigation, or audit involving an agency against specific individuals or entities;

(3) By compulsory process pursuant to the Antitrust Civil Process Act and section 13 of the Federal Trade Commission Improvements Act of 1980; or

(4) During the conduct of intelligence activities as defined in section 3.4(e) of Executive Order No. 12333, issued December 4, 1981, or successor orders, or during the conduct of cryptologic activities that are communications security activities.

(b) The requirements of this Part apply to the collection of information during the conduct of general investigations or audits (other than information collected in an antitrust investigation to the extent provided in paragraph (a)(3) of this section) undertaken with reference to a category of individuals or entities such as a class of licensees or an entire industry.

(c) The exception in paragraph (a)(2) of this section applies during the entire course of the investigation, audit, or action, whether before or after formal charges or complaints are filed or formal administrative action is initiated, but only after a case file or equivalent is opened with respect to a particular party. In accordance with paragraph (b) of this section, collections of information prepared or undertaken with reference to a category of individuals or entities, such as a class of licensees or an industry, do not fall within this exception.

§ 1320.5 General requirements.

(a) An agency shall not conduct or sponsor a collection of information unless, in advance of the adoption or revision of the collection of information—

(1) The agency has—

(i) Conducted the review required in § 1320.8;

(ii) Evaluated the public comments received under § 1320.8(d) and § 1320.11;

(iii) Submitted to the Director, in accordance with such procedures and in such form as OMB may specify,

(A) The certification required under § 1320.9,

(B) The proposed collection of information in accordance with § 1320.10, § 1320.11, or § 1320.12, as appropriate,

(C) An explanation for the decision that it would not be appropriate, under § 1320.8(b)(1), for a proposed collection of information to display an expiration date;

(D) An explanation for a decision to provide for any payment or gift to respondents, other than remuneration of contractors or grantees;

(E) A statement indicating whether (and if so, to what extent) the proposed collection of information involves the use of automated, electronic, mechanical, or other technological collection techniques or other forms of information technology, e.g., permitting electronic submission of responses, and an explanation for the decision;

(F) A summary of the public comments received under §1320.8(d), including actions taken by the agency in response to the comments, and the date and page of the publication in the Federal Register of the notice therefor; and

(G) Copies of pertinent statutory authority, regulations, and such related supporting materials as OMB may request; and

(iv) Published, except as provided in §1320.13(d), a notice in the Federal Register—

(A) Stating that the agency has made such submission; and

(B) Setting forth—

(*1*) A title for the collection of information;

(*2*) A summary of the collection of information;

(*3*) A brief description of the need for the information and proposed use of the information;

(*4*) A description of the likely respondents, including the estimated number of likely respondents, and proposed frequency of response to the collection of information;

(*5*) An estimate of the total annual reporting and recordkeeping burden that will result from the collection of information;

(*6*) Notice that comments may be submitted to OMB; and

(*7*) The time period within which the agency is requesting OMB to approve or disapprove the collection of information if, at the time of submittal of a collection of information for OMB review under §1320.10, §1320.11 or §1320.12, the agency plans to request or has requested OMB to conduct its review on an emergency basis under §1320.13; and

(2) OMB has approved the proposed collection of information, OMB's approval has been inferred under §1320.10(c), §1320.11(i), or §1320.12(e), or OMB's disapproval has been voided by an independent regulatory agency under §1320.15; and

(3) The agency has obtained from the Director a control number to be displayed upon the collection of information.

(b) In addition to the requirements in paragraph (a) of this section, an agency shall not conduct or sponsor a collection of information unless:

(1) The collection of information displays a currently valid OMB control number; and

(2)(i) The agency informs the potential persons who are to respond to the collection of information that such persons are not required to respond to the collection of information unless it displays a currently valid OMB control number.

(ii) An agency shall provide the information described in paragraph (b)(2)(i) of this section in a manner that is reasonably calculated to inform the public.

(A) In the case of forms, questionnaires, instructions, and other written collections of information sent or made available to potential respondents (other than in an electronic format), the information described in paragraph (b)(2)(i) of this section is provided "in a manner that is reasonably calculated to inform the public" if the agency includes it either on the form, questionnaire or other collection of information, or in the instructions for such collection.

(B) In the case of forms, questionnaires, instructions, and other written collections of information sent or made available to potential respondents in an electronic format, the information described in paragraph (b)(2)(i) of this section is provided "in a manner that is reasonably calculated to inform the public" if the agency places the currently valid OMB control number in the instructions, near the title of the electronic collection instrument, or, for on-line applications, on the first screen viewed by the respondent.

(C) In the case of collections of information published in regulations, guidelines, and other issuances in the Federal Register, the information described in paragraph (b)(2)(i) of this section is provided "in a manner that is reasonably calculated to inform the public" if the agency publishes such information in theFederal Register(for example, in the case of a collection of information in a regulation, by publishing such information in the preamble or the regulatory text, or in a technical amendment to the regulation, or in a separate notice announcing OMB approval of the collection of information). In the case of a collection of information published in an issuance that is also included in the Code of Federal Regulations, publication of such information in the Code of Federal Regulations constitutes an alternative means of providing it "in a manner that is reasonably calculated to inform the public." In the case of a collection of information published in an issuance that is also included in the Code of Federal Regulations, OMB recommends for ease of future reference that, even where an agency has already provided such information "in a manner that is reasonably calculated to inform the public" by publishing it in theFederal Registeras a separate notice or in the preamble for the final rule (rather than in the regulatory text for the final rule or in a technical amendment to the final rule), the agency also publish such information along with a table or codified section of OMB control numbers to be included in the Code of Federal Regulations (see §1320.3(f)(3)).

(D) In other cases, and where OMB determines in advance in writing that special circumstances exist, to use other means that are reasonably calculated to inform the public of the information described in paragraph (b)(2)(i) of this section.

(c)(1) Agencies shall submit all collections of information, other than those contained in proposed rules published for public comment in theFederal Registeror in current regulations that were published as final rules in theFederal Register,in accordance with the requirements in §1320.10. Agencies shall submit collections of information contained in interim final rules or direct final rules in accordance with the requirements of §1320.10.

(2) Agencies shall submit collections of information contained in proposed rules published for public comment in theFederal Registerin accordance with the requirements in §1320.11.

(3) Agencies shall submit collections of information contained in current regulations that were published as final rules in theFederal Registerin accordance with the requirements in §1320.12.

(4) Special rules for emergency processing of collections of information are set forth in §1320.13.

(5) For purposes of time limits for OMB review of collections of information, any submission properly submitted and received by OMB after 12:00 noon will be deemed to have been received on the following business day.

(d)(1) To obtain OMB approval of a collection of information, an agency shall demonstrate that it has taken every reasonable step to ensure that the proposed collection of information:

(i) Is the least burdensome necessary for the proper performance of the agency's functions to comply with legal requirements and achieve program objectives;

(ii) Is not duplicative of information otherwise accessible to the agency; and

(iii) Has practical utility. The agency shall also seek to minimize the cost to itself of collecting, processing, and using the information, but shall not do so by means of shifting disproportionate costs or burdens onto the public.

(2) Unless the agency is able to demonstrate, in its submission for OMB clearance, that such characteristic of the collection of information is necessary to satisfy statutory requirements or other substantial need, OMB will not approve a collection of information—

(i) Requiring respondents to report information to the agency more often than quarterly;

(ii) Requiring respondents to prepare a

written response to a collection of information in fewer than 30 days after receipt of it;

(iii) Requiring respondents to submit more than an original and two copies of any document;

(iv) Requiring respondents to retain records, other than health, medical, government contract, grant-in-aid, or tax records, for more than three years;

(v) In connection with a statistical survey, that is not designed to produce valid and reliable results that can be generalized to the universe of study;

(vi) Requiring the use of a statistical data classification that has not been reviewed and approved by OMB;

(vii) That includes a pledge of confidentiality that is not supported by authority established in statute or regulation, that is not supported by disclosure and data security policies that are consistent with the pledge, or which unnecessarily impedes sharing of data with other agencies for compatible confidential use; or

(viii) Requiring respondents to submit proprietary, trade secret, or other confidential information unless the agency can demonstrate that it has instituted procedures to protect the information's confidentiality to the extent permitted by law.

(e) OMB shall determine whether the collection of information, as submitted by the agency, is necessary for the proper performance of the agency's functions. In making this determination, OMB will take into account the criteria set forth in paragraph (d) of this section, and will consider whether the burden of the collection of information is justified by its practical utility. In addition:

(1) OMB will consider necessary any collection of information specifically mandated by statute or court order, but will independently assess any collection of information to the extent that the agency exercises discretion in its implementation; and

(2) OMB will consider necessary any collection of information specifically required by an agency rule approved or not acted upon by OMB under §1320.11 or §1320.12, but will independently assess any such collection of information to the extent that it deviates from the specifications of the rule.

(f) Except as provided in §1320.15, to the extent that OMB determines that all or any portion of a collection of information is unnecessary, for any reason, the agency shall not engage in such collection or portion thereof. OMB will reconsider its disapproval of a collection of information upon the request of the agency head or Senior Official only if the sponsoring agency is able to provide significant new or additional information relevant to the original decision.

(g) An agency may not make a substantive or material modification to a collection of information after such collection of information has been approved by OMB, unless the modification has been submitted to OMB for review and approval under this Part.

(h) An agency should consult with OMB before using currently approved forms or other collections of information after the expiration date printed thereon (in those cases where the actual form being used contains an expiration date that would expire before the end of the use of the form).

§ 1320.6 Public protection.

(a) Notwithstanding any other provision of law, no person shall be subject to any penalty for failing to comply with a collection of information that is subject to the requirements of this part if:

(1) The collection of information does not display, in accordance with §1320.3(f) and §1320.5(b)(1), a currently valid OMB control number assigned by the Director in accordance with the Act; or

(2) The agency fails to inform the potential person who is to respond to the collection of information, in accordance with §1320.5(b)(2), that such person is not required to respond to the collection of information unless it displays a currently valid

OMB control number.

(b) The protection provided by paragraph (a) of this section may be raised in the form of a complete defense, bar, or otherwise to the imposition of such penalty at any time during the agency administrative process in which such penalty may be imposed or in any judicial action applicable thereto.

(c) Whenever an agency has imposed a collection of information as a means for proving or satisfying a condition for the receipt of a benefit or the avoidance of a penalty, and the collection of information does not display a currently valid OMB control number or inform the potential persons who are to respond to the collection of information, as prescribed in §1320.5(b), the agency shall not treat a person's failure to comply, in and of itself, as grounds for withholding the benefit or imposing the penalty. The agency shall instead permit respondents to prove or satisfy the legal conditions in any other reasonable manner.

(1) If OMB disapproves the whole of such a collection of information (and the disapproval is not overridden under §1320.15), the agency shall grant the benefit to (or not impose the penalty on) otherwise qualified persons without requesting further proof concerning the condition.

(2) If OMB instructs an agency to make a substantive or material change to such a collection of information (and the instruction is not overridden under §1320.15), the agency shall permit respondents to prove or satisfy the condition by complying with the collection of information as so changed.

(d) Whenever a member of the public is protected from imposition of a penalty under this section for failure to comply with a collection of information, such penalty may not be imposed by an agency directly, by an agency through judicial process, or by any other person through administrative or judicial process.

(e) The protection provided by paragraph (a) of this section does not preclude the imposition of a penalty on a person for failing to comply with a collection of information that is imposed on the person by statute— e.g., 26 U.S.C. §6011(a) (statutory requirement for person to file a tax return), 42 U.S.C. §6938(c) (statutory requirement for person to provide notification before exporting hazardous waste).

§ 1320.7 Agency head and Senior Official responsibilities.

(a) Except as provided in paragraph (b) of this section, each agency head shall designate a Senior Official to carry out the responsibilities of the agency under the Act and this part. The Senior Official shall report directly to the head of the agency and shall have the authority, subject to that of the agency head, to carry out the responsibilities of the agency under the Act and this part.

(b) An agency head may retain full undelegated review authority for any component of the agency which by statute is required to be independent of any agency official below the agency head. For each component for which responsibility under the Act is not delegated to the Senior Official, the agency head shall be responsible for the performance of those functions.

(c) The Senior Official shall head an office responsible for ensuring agency compliance with and prompt, efficient, and effective implementation of the information policies and information resources management responsibilities established under the Act, including the reduction of information collection burdens on the public.

(d) With respect to the collection of information and the control of paperwork, the Senior Official shall establish a process within such office that is sufficiently independent of program responsibility to evaluate fairly whether proposed collections of information should be approved under this Part.

(e) Agency submissions of collections of information for OMB review, and the accompanying certifications under §1320.9, may be made only by the agency head or the Senior Official, or their designee.

§ 1320.8 Agency collection of information responsibilities.

The office established under §1320.7 shall review each collection of information before submission to OMB for review under this part.

(a) This review shall include:

(1) An evaluation of the need for the collection of information, which shall include, in the case of an existing collection of information, an evaluation of the continued need for such collection;

(2) A functional description of the information to be collected;

(3) A plan for the collection of information;

(4) A specific, objectively supported estimate of burden, which shall include, in the case of an existing collection of information, an evaluation of the burden that has been imposed by such collection;

(5) An evaluation of whether (and if so, to what extent) the burden on respondents can be reduced by use of automated, electronic, mechanical, or other technological collection techniques or other forms of information technology, e.g., permitting electronic submission of responses;

(6) A test of the collection of information through a pilot program, if appropriate; and

(7) A plan for the efficient and effective management and use of the information to be collected, including necessary resources.

(b) Such office shall ensure that each collection of information:

(1) Is inventoried, displays a currently valid OMB control number, and, if appropriate, an expiration date;

(2) Is reviewed by OMB in accordance with the clearance requirements of 44 U.S.C. §3507; and

(3) Informs and provides reasonable notice to the potential persons to whom the collection of information is addressed of—

(i) The reasons the information is planned to be and/or has been collected;

(ii) The way such information is planned to be and/or has been used to further the proper performance of the functions of the agency;

(iii) An estimate, to the extent practicable, of the average burden of the collection (together with a request that the public direct to the agency any comments concerning the accuracy of this burden estimate and any suggestions for reducing this burden);

(iv) Whether responses to the collection of information are voluntary, required to obtain or retain a benefit (citing authority), or mandatory (citing authority);

(v) The nature and extent of confidentiality to be provided, if any (citing authority); and

(vi) The fact that an agency may not conduct or sponsor, and a person is not required to respond to, a collection of information unless it displays a currently valid OMB control number.

(c)(1) An agency shall provide the information described in paragraphs (b)(3)(i) through (v) of this section as follows:

(i) In the case of forms, questionnaires, instructions, and other written collections of information sent or made available to potential respondents (except in an electronic format), such information can be included either on the form, questionnaire or other collection of information, as part of the instructions for such collection, or in a cover letter or memorandum that accompanies the collection of information.

(ii) In the case of forms, questionnaires, instructions, and other written collections of information sent or made available to potential respondents in an electronic format, such information can be included either in the instructions, near the title of the electronic collection instrument, or, for on-line applications, on the first screen viewed by the respondent;

(iii) In the case of collections of information published in regulations, guidelines, and other issuances in the Federal Register, such information can be published in the Federal Register (for example, in the case of a collection of information in a regulation, by publishing such information in the preamble or the regulatory text to the final rule, or in a technical amendment to the final rule, or in a separate notice announcing OMB approval of the collection of information).

(iv) In other cases, and where OMB determines in advance in writing that special circumstances exist, agencies may use other means to inform potential respondents.

(2) An agency shall provide the information described in paragraph (b)(3)(vi) of this section in a manner that is reasonably calculated to inform the public (see §1320.5(b)(2)(ii)).

(d)(1) Before an agency submits a collection of information to OMB for approval, and except as provided in paragraphs (d)(3) and (d)(4) of this section, the agency shall provide 60-day notice in the Federal Register, and otherwise consult with members of the public and affected agencies concerning each proposed collection of information, to solicit comment to:

(i) Evaluate whether the proposed collection of information is necessary for the proper performance of the functions of the agency, including whether the information will have practical utility;

(ii) Evaluate the accuracy of the agency's estimate of the burden of the proposed collection of information, including the validity of the methodology and assumptions used;

(iii) Enhance the quality, utility, and clarity of the information to be collected; and

(iv) Minimize the burden of the collection of information on those who are to respond, including through the use of appropriate automated, electronic, mechanical, or other technological collection techniques or other forms of information technology, e.g., permitting electronic submission of responses.

(2) If the agency does not publish a copy of the proposed collection of information, together with the related instructions, as part of the Federal Register notice, the agency should—

(i) Provide more than 60-day notice to permit timely receipt, by interested members of the public, of a copy of the proposed collection of information and related instructions; or

(ii) Explain how and from whom an interested member of the public can request and obtain a copy without charge, including, if applicable, how the public can gain access to the collection of information and related instructions electronically on demand.

(3) The agency need not separately seek such public comment for any proposed collection of information contained in a proposed rule to be reviewed under §1320.11, if the agency provides notice and comment through the notice of proposed rulemaking for the proposed rule and such notice specifically includes the solicitation of comments for the same purposes as are listed under paragraph (d)(1) of this section.

(4) The agency need not seek or may shorten the time allowed for such public comment if OMB grants an exemption from such requirement for emergency processing under §1320.13.

§ 1320.9 Agency certifications for proposed collections of information.

As part of the agency submission to OMB of a proposed collection of information, the agency (through the head of the agency, the Senior Official, or their designee) shall certify (and provide a record supporting such certification) that the proposed collection of information—

(a) Is necessary for the proper performance of the functions of the agency, including that the information to be collected will have practical utility;

(b) Is not unnecessarily duplicative of information otherwise reasonably accessible to the agency;

(c) Reduces to the extent practicable and appropriate the burden on persons who shall provide information to or for the agency, including with respect to small entities, as defined in the Regulatory Flexibility Act (5 U.S.C. 601(6)), the use of such techniques as:

(1) Establishing differing compliance or reporting requirements or timetables that take into account the resources available to those who are to respond;

(2) The clarification, consolidation, or simplification of compliance and reporting requirements; or

(3) An exemption from coverage of the collection of information, or any part thereof;

(d) Is written using plain, coherent, and unambiguous terminology and is understandable to those who are to respond;

(e) Is to be implemented in ways consistent and compatible, to the maximum extent practicable, with the existing reporting and recordkeeping practices of those who are to respond;

(f) Indicates for each recordkeeping requirement the length of time persons are required to maintain the records specified;

(g) Informs potential respondents of the information called for under §1320.8(b)(3);

(h) Has been developed by an office that has planned and allocated resources for the efficient and effective management and use of the information to be collected, including the processing of the information in a manner which shall enhance, where appropriate, the utility of the information to agencies and the public;

(i) Uses effective and efficient statistical survey methodology appropriate to the purpose for which the information is to be collected; and

(j) To the maximum extent practicable, uses appropriate information technology to reduce burden and improve data quality, agency efficiency and responsiveness to the public.

§ 1320.10 Clearance of collections of information, other than those contained in proposed rules or in current rules.

Agencies shall submit all collections of information, other than those contained either in proposed rules published for public comment in the Federal Register (which are submitted under §1320.11) or in current rules that were published as final rules in the Federal Register (which are submitted under §1320.12), in accordance with the following requirements:

(a) On or before the date of submission to OMB, the agency shall, in accordance with the requirements in §1320.5(a)(1)(iv), forward a notice to the Federal Register stating that OMB approval is being sought. The notice shall direct requests for information, including copies of the proposed collection of information and supporting documentation, to the agency, and shall request that comments be submitted to OMB within 30 days of the notice's publication. The notice shall direct comments to the Office of Information and Regulatory Affairs of OMB, Attention: Desk Officer for [name of agency]. A copy of the notice submitted to the Federal Register, together with the date of expected publication, shall be included in the agency's submission to OMB.

(b) Within 60 days after receipt of the proposed collection of information or publication of the notice under paragraph (a) of this section, whichever is later, OMB shall notify the agency involved of its decision to approve, to instruct the agency to make a substantive or material change to, or to disapprove, the collection of information, and shall make such decision publicly available. OMB shall provide at least 30 days for public comment after receipt of the proposed collection of information before making its decision, except as provided under §1320.13. Upon approval of a collection of information, OMB shall assign an OMB control number and, if appropriate, an expiration date. OMB shall not approve any collection of information for a period longer than three years.

(c) If OMB fails to notify the agency of its approval, instruction to make substantive or material change, or disapproval within the 60-day period, the agency may request, and OMB shall assign without further delay, an OMB control number that shall be valid for not more than one year.

(d) As provided in §1320.5(b) and §1320.6(a), an agency may not conduct or sponsor a collection of information unless the collection of information displays a currently valid OMB control number and the agency informs potential persons who are to respond to the collection of information that such persons are not required to respond to the collection of information unless it displays a currently valid OMB control number.

(e)(1) In the case of a collection of information not contained in a published current rule which has been approved by OMB and has a currently valid OMB control number, the agency shall:

(i) Conduct the review established under §1320.8, including the seeking of public comment under §1320.8(d); and

(ii) After having made a reasonable effort to seek public comment, but no later than 60 days before the expiration date of the OMB control number for the currently approved collection of information, submit the collection of information for review and approval under this part, which shall include an explanation of how the agency has used the information that it has collected.

(2) The agency may continue to conduct or sponsor the collection of information while the submission is pending at OMB.

(f) Prior to the expiration of OMB's approval of a collection of information, OMB may decide on its own initiative, after consultation with the agency, to review the collection of information. Such decisions will be made only when relevant circumstances have changed or the burden estimates provided by the agency at the time of initial submission were materially in error. Upon notification by OMB of its decision to review the collection of information, the agency shall submit it to OMB for review under this part.

(g) For good cause, after consultation with the agency, OMB may stay the effectiveness of its prior approval of any collection of information that is not specifically required by agency rule; in such case, the agency shall cease conducting or sponsoring such collection of information while the submission is pending, and shall publish a notice in the Federal Register to that effect.

§ 1320.11 Clearance of collections of information in proposed rules.

Agencies shall submit collections of information contained in proposed rules published for public comment in the Federal Register in accordance with the following requirements:

(a) The agency shall include, in accordance with the requirements in §1320.5(a)(1)(iv) and §1320.8(d)(1) and (3), in the preamble to the Notice of Proposed Rulemaking a statement that the collections of information contained in the proposed rule, and identified as such, have been submitted to OMB for review under section 3507(d) of the Act. The notice shall direct comments to the Office of Information and Regulatory Affairs of OMB, Attention: Desk Officer for [name of agency].

(b) All such submissions shall be made to OMB not later than the day on which the Notice of Proposed Rulemaking is published in the Federal Register, in such form and in accordance with such procedures as OMB may direct. Such submissions shall include a copy of the proposed regulation and preamble.

(c) Within 60 days of publication of the proposed rule, but subject to paragraph (e) of this section, OMB may file public comments on collection of information provisions. The OMB comments shall be in the form of an OMB Notice of Action, which shall be sent to the Senior Official or agency head, or their designee, and which shall be made a part of the agency's rulemaking record.

(d) If an agency submission is not in compliance with paragraph (b) of this section, OMB may, subject to paragraph (e) of this section, disapprove the collection of information in the proposed rule within 60 days of receipt of the submission. If an agency fails to submit a collection of information subject to this section, OMB may, subject to paragraph (e) of this section, disapprove it at any time.

(e) OMB shall provide at least 30 days after receipt of the proposed collection of information before submitting its comments or making its decision, except as provided under §1320.13.

(f) When the final rule is published in theFederal Register,the agency shall explain how any collection of information contained in the final rule responds to any comments received from OMB or the public. The agency shall include an identification and explanation of any modifications made in the rule, or explain why it rejected the comments. If requested by OMB, the agency shall include OMB's comments in the preamble to the final rule.

(g) If OMB has not filed public comments under paragraph (c) of this section, or has approved without conditions the collection of information contained in a rule before the final rule is published in theFederal Register,OMB may assign an OMB control number prior to publication of the final rule.

(h) On or before the date of publication of the final rule, the agency shall submit the final rule to OMB, unless it has been approved under paragraph (g) of this section (and not substantively or materially modified by the agency after approval). Not later than 60 days after publication, but subject to paragraph (e) of this section, OMB shall approve, instruct the agency to make a substantive or material change to, or disapprove, the collection of information contained in the final rule. Any such instruction to change or disapprove may be based on one or more of the following reasons, as determined by OMB:

(1) The agency has failed to comply with paragraph (b) of this section;

(2) The agency had substantially modified the collection of information contained in the final rule from that contained in the proposed rule without providing OMB with notice of the change and sufficient information to make a determination concerning the modified collection of information at least 60 days before publication of the final rule; or

(3) In cases in which OMB had filed public comments under paragraph (c) of this section, the agency's response to such comments was unreasonable, and the collection of information is unnecessary for the proper performance of the agency's functions.

(i) After making such decision to approve, to instruct the agency to make a substantive or material change to, or disapprove, the collection of information, OMB shall so notify the agency. If OMB approves the collection of information or if it has not acted upon the submission within the time limits of this section, the agency may request, and OMB shall assign an OMB control number. If OMB disapproves or instructs the agency to make substantive or material change to the collection of information, it shall make the reasons for its decision publicly available.

(j) OMB shall not approve any collection of information under this section for a period longer than three years. Approval of such collection of information will be for the full three-year period, unless OMB determines that there are special circumstances requiring approval for a shorter period.

(k) After receipt of notification of OMB's approval, instruction to make a substantive or material change to, disapproval of a collection of information, or failure to act, the agency shall publish a notice in the Federal Register to inform the public of OMB's decision.

(1) As provided in §1320.5(b) and §1320.6(a), an agency may not conduct or sponsor a collection of information unless the collection of information displays a currently valid OMB control number and the agency informs potential persons who are to respond to the collection of information that such persons are not required to respond to the collection of information unless it displays a currently valid OMB control number.

§ 1320.12 Clearance of collections of information in current rules.

Agencies shall submit collections of information contained in current rules that were published as final rules in the Federal Register in accordance with the following procedures:

(a) In the case of a collection of information contained in a published current rule which has been approved by OMB and has a currently valid OMB control number, the agency shall:

(1) Conduct the review established under §1320.8, including the seeking of public comment under §1320.8(d); and

(2) After having made a reasonable effort to seek public comment, but no later than 60 days before the expiration date of the OMB control number for the currently approved collection of information, submit the collection of information for review and approval under this part, which shall include an explanation of how the agency has used the information that it has collected.

(b)(1) In the case of a collection of information contained in a published current rule that was not required to be submitted for OMB review under the Paperwork Reduction Act at the time the collection of information was made part of the rule, but which collection of information is now subject to the Act and this part, the agency shall:

(i) Conduct the review established under §1320.8, including the seeking of public comment under §1320.(8)(d); and

(ii) After having made a reasonable effort to seek public comment, submit the collection of information for review and approval under this part, which shall include an explanation of how the agency has used the information that it has collected.

(2) The agency may continue to conduct or sponsor the collection of information while the submission is pending at OMB. In the case of a collection of information not previously approved, approval shall be granted for such period, which shall not exceed 60 days, unless extended by the Director for an additional 60 days, and an OMB control number assigned. Upon assignment of the OMB control number, and in accordance with §1320.3(f) and §1320.5(b), the agency shall display the number and inform the potential persons who are to respond to the collection of information that such persons are not required to respond to the collection of information unless it displays a currently valid OMB control number.

(c) On or before the day of submission to OMB under paragraphs (a) or (b) of this section, the agency shall, in accordance with the requirements set forth in §1320.5(a)(1)(iv), forward a notice to the Federal Register stating that OMB review is being sought. The notice shall direct requests for copies of the collection of information and supporting documentation to the agency, and shall request that comments be submitted to OMB within 30 days of the notice's publication. The notice shall direct comments to the Office of Information and Regulatory Affairs of OMB, Attention: Desk Officer for [name of agency]. A copy of the notice submitted to the Federal Register, together with the date of expected publication, shall be included in the agency's submission to OMB.

(d) Within 60 days after receipt of the collection of information or publication of the notice under paragraph (c) of this section, whichever is later, OMB shall notify the agency involved of its decision to approve, to instruct the agency to make a substantive or material change to, or to disapprove, the collection of information, and shall make such decision publicly available. OMB shall provide at least 30 days for public comment after receipt of the proposed collection of information before making its decision, except as provided under §1320.13.

(e)(1) Upon approval of a collection of information, OMB shall assign an OMB control number and an expiration date. OMB shall not approve any collection of information for a period longer than three years. Approval of any collection of information submitted under this section will be for the full three-year period, unless OMB determines that there are special circumstances requiring approval for a shorter period.

(2) If OMB fails to notify the agency of its approval, instruction to make substantive or material change, or disapproval within the 60-day period, the agency may request, and OMB shall assign without further delay, an OMB control number that shall be valid for not more than one year.

(3) As provided in §1320.5(b) and §1320.6(a), an agency may not conduct or sponsor a collection of information unless the collection of information displays a currently valid OMB control number and the agency informs potential persons who are to respond to the collection of information that such persons are not required to respond to the collection of information unless it displays a currently valid OMB control number.

(f)(1) If OMB disapproves a collection of information contained in an existing rule, or instructs the agency to make a substantive or material change to a collection of information contained in an existing rule, OMB shall:

(i) Publish an explanation thereof in theFederal Register; and

(ii) Instruct the agency to undertake a rulemaking within a reasonable time limited to consideration of changes to the collection of information contained in the rule and thereafter to submit the collection of information for approval or disapproval under §1320.10 or §1320.11, as appropriate; and

(iii) Extend the existing approval of the collection of information (including an interim approval granted under paragraph (b) of this section) for the duration of the period required for consideration of proposed changes, including that required for OMB approval or disapproval of the collection of information under §1320.10 or §1320.11, as appropriate.

(2) Thereafter, the agency shall, within a reasonable period of time not to exceed 120 days, undertake such procedures as are necessary in compliance with the Administrative Procedure Act and other applicable law to amend or rescind the collection of information, and shall notify the public through theFederal Register.Such notice shall identify the proposed changes in the collections of information and shall solicit public comment on retention, change, or rescission of such collections of information. If the agency employs notice and comment rulemaking procedures for amendment or rescission of the collection of information, publication of the above in theFederal Registerand submission to OMB shall initiate OMB clearance procedures under section 3507(d) of the Act and §1320.11. All procedures shall be completed within a reasonable period of time to be determined by OMB in consultation with the agency.

(g) OMB may disapprove, in whole or in part, any collection of information subject to the procedures of this section, if the agency:

(1) Has refused within a reasonable time to comply with an OMB instruction to submit the collection of information for review;

(2) Has refused within a reasonable time to initiate procedures to change the collection of information; or

(3) Has refused within a reasonable time

to publish a final rule continuing the collection of information, with such changes as may be appropriate, or otherwise complete the procedures for amendment or rescission of the collection of information.

(h)(1) Upon disapproval by OMB of a collection of information subject to this section, except as provided in paragraph (f)(1)(iii) of this section, the OMB control number assigned to such collection of information shall immediately expire, and no agency shall conduct or sponsor such collection of information. Any such disapproval shall constitute disapproval of the collection of information contained in the Notice of Proposed Rulemaking or other submissions, and also of the preexisting information collection instruments directed at the same collection of information and therefore constituting essentially the same collection of information.

(2) The failure to display a currently valid OMB control number for a collection of information contained in a current rule, or the failure to inform the potential persons who are to respond to the collection of information that such persons are not required to respond to the collection of information unless it displays a currently valid OMB control number, does not, as a legal matter, rescind or amend the rule; however, such absence will alert the public that either the agency has failed to comply with applicable legal requirements for the collection of information or the collection of information has been disapproved, and that therefore the portion of the rule containing the collection of information has no legal force and effect and the public protection provisions of 44 U.S.C. 3512 apply.

(i) Prior to the expiration of OMB's approval of a collection of information in a current rule, OMB may decide on its own initiative, after consultation with the agency, to review the collection of information. Such decisions will be made only when relevant circumstances have changed or the burden estimates provided by the agency at the time of initial submission were materially in error. Upon notification by OMB of its decision to review the collection of information, the agency shall submit it to OMB for review under this Part.

§ 1320.13 Emergency processing.

An agency head or the Senior Official, or their designee, may request OMB to authorize emergency processing of submissions of collections of information.

(a) Any such request shall be accompanied by a written determination that:

(1) The collection of information:

(i) Is needed prior to the expiration of time periods established under this Part; and

(ii) Is essential to the mission of the agency; and

(2) The agency cannot reasonably comply with the normal clearance procedures under this part because:

(i) Public harm is reasonably likely to result if normal clearance procedures are followed;

(ii) An unanticipated event has occurred; or

(iii) The use of normal clearance procedures is reasonably likely to prevent or disrupt the collection of information or is reasonably likely to cause a statutory or court ordered deadline to be missed.

(b) The agency shall state the time period within which OMB should approve or disapprove the collection of information.

(c) The agency shall submit information indicating that it has taken all practicable steps to consult with interested agencies and members of the public in order to minimize the burden of the collection of information.

(d) The agency shall set forth in the Federal Register notice prescribed by §1320.5(a)(1)(iv), unless waived or modified under this section, a statement that it is requesting emergency processing, and the time period stated under paragraph (b) of this section.

(e) OMB shall approve or disapprove each such submission within the time period stated under paragraph (b) of this section, provided that such time period is consistent with the purposes of this Act.

(f) If OMB approves the collection of information, it shall assign a control number valid for a maximum of 90 days after receipt of the agency submission.

§ 1320.14 Public access.

(a) In order to enable the public to participate in and provide comments during the clearance process, OMB will ordinarily make its paperwork docket files available for public inspection during normal business hours. Notwithstanding other provisions of this Part, and to the extent permitted by law, requirements to publish public notices or to provide materials to the public may be modified or waived by the Director to the extent that such public participation in the approval process would defeat the purpose of the collection of information; jeopardize the confidentiality of proprietary, trade secret, or other confidential information; violate State or Federal law; or substantially interfere with an agency's ability to perform its statutory obligations.

(b) Agencies shall provide copies of the material submitted to OMB for review promptly upon request by any person.

(c) Any person may request OMB to review any collection of information conducted by or for an agency to determine, if, under this Act and this part, a person shall maintain, provide, or disclose the information to or for the agency. Unless the request is frivolous, OMB shall, in coordination with the agency responsible for the collection of information:

(1) Respond to the request within 60 days after receiving the request, unless such period is extended by OMB to a specified date and the person making the request is given notice of such extension; and

(2) Take appropriate remedial action, if necessary.

§ 1320.15 Independent regulatory agency override authority.

(a) An independent regulatory agency which is administered by two or more members of a commission, board, or similar body, may by majority vote void:

(1) Any disapproval, instruction to such agency to make material or substantive change to, or stay of the effectiveness of OMB approval of, any collection of information of such agency; or

(2) An exercise of authority under §1320.10(g) concerning such agency.

(b) The agency shall certify each vote to void such OMB action to OMB, and explain the reasons for such vote. OMB shall without further delay assign an OMB control number to such collection of information, valid for the length of time requested by the agency, up to three years, to any collection of information as to which this vote is exercised. No override shall become effective until the independent regulatory agency, as provided in §1320.5(b) and §1320.6(2), has displayed the OMB control number and informed the potential persons who are to respond to the collection of information that such persons are not required to respond to the collection of information unless it displays a currently valid OMB control number.

§ 1320.16 Delegation of approval authority.

(a) OMB may, after complying with the notice and comment procedures of the Administrative Procedure Act, delegate OMB review of some or all of an agency's collections of information to the Senior Official, or to the agency head with respect to those components of the agency for which he or she has not delegated authority.

(b) No delegation of review authority shall be made unless the agency demonstrates to OMB that the Senior Official or agency head to whom the authority would be delegate:

(1) Is sufficiently independent of program

Paperwork Reduction Act

responsibility to evaluate fairly whether proposed collections of information should be approved;

(2) Has sufficient resources to carry out this responsibility effectively; and

(3) Has established an agency review process that demonstrates the prompt, efficient, and effective performance of collection of information review responsibilities.

(c) OMB may limit, condition, or rescind, in whole or in part, at any time, such delegations of authority, and reserves the right to review any individual collection of information, or part thereof, conducted or sponsored by an agency, at any time.

(d) Subject to the provisions of this part, and in accordance with the terms and conditions of each delegation as specified in appendix A to this part, OMB delegates review and approval authority to the following agencies:

(1) Board of Governors of the Federal Reserve System; and

(2) Managing Director of the Federal Communications Commission.

§ 1320.17 Information collection budget.

Each agency's Senior Official, or agency head in the case of any agency for which the agency head has not delegated responsibility under the Act for any component of the agency to the Senior Official, shall develop and submit to OMB, in such form, at such time, and in accordance with such procedures as OMB may prescribe, an annual comprehensive budget for all collections of information from the public to be conducted in the succeeding twelve months. For good cause, OMB may exempt any agency from this requirement.

§ 1320.18 Other authority.

(a) OMB shall determine whether any collection of information or other matter is within the scope of the Act, or this Part.

(b) In appropriate cases, after consultation with the agency, OMB may initiate a rulemaking proceeding to determine whether an agency's collection of information is consistent with statutory standards. Such proceedings shall be in accordance with the informal rulemaking procedures of the Administrative Procedure Act.

(c) Each agency is responsible for complying with the information policies, principles, standards, and guidelines prescribed by OMB under this Act.

(d) To the extent permitted by law, OMB may waive any requirements contained in this part.

(e) Nothing in this part shall be interpreted to limit the authority of OMB under this Act, or any other law. Nothing in this part or this Act shall be interpreted as increasing or decreasing the authority of OMB with respect to the substantive policies and programs of the agencies.

APPENDIX A TO PART 1320—AGENCIES WITH DELEGATED REVIEW AND APPROVAL AUTHORITY

1. The Board of Governors of the Federal Reserve System

(a) Authority to review and approve collection of information requests, collection of information requirements, and collections of information in current rules is delegated to the Board of Governors of the Federal Reserve System.

(1) This delegation does not include review and approval authority over any new collection of information or any modification to an existing collection of information that:

(i) Is proposed to be collected as a result of a requirement or other mandate of the Federal Financial Institutions Examination Council, or other Federal executive branch entities with authority to require the Board to conduct or sponsor a collection of information.

(ii) Is objected to by another Federal agency on the grounds that agency requires information currently collected by the Board, that the currently collected information is being deleted from the collection, and the deletion will have a serious adverse impact on the agency's program, provided that such objection is certified to OMB by the head of the Federal agency involved, with a copy to the Board, before the end of the comment period specified by the Board on the Federal Register notices specified in paragraph (1)(3)(i) of this section 1.

(iii) Would cause the burden of the information collections conducted or sponsored by the Board to exceed by the end of the fiscal year the Information Collection Budget allowance set by the Board and OMB for the fiscal year-end.

(2) The Board may ask that OMB review and approve collections of information covered by this delegation.

(3) In exercising delegated authority, the Board will:

(i) Provide the public, to the extent possible and appropriate, with reasonable opportunity to comment on collections of information under review prior to taking final action approving the collection. Reasonable opportunity for public comment will include publishing a notice in the Federal Register informing the public of the proposed collection of information, announcing the beginning of a 60-day public comment period, and the availability of copies of the "clearance package," to provide the public with the opportunity to comment. Such Federal Register notices shall also advise the public that they may also send a copy of their comments to the Federal Reserve Board and to the OMB/OIRA Desk Officer.

(A) Should the Board determine that a new collection of information or a change in an existing collection must be instituted quickly and that public participation in the approval process would defeat the purpose of the collection or substantially interfere with the Board's ability to perform its statutory obligation, the Board may temporarily approve of the collection of information for a period not to exceed 90 days without providing opportunity for public comment.

(B) At the earliest practical date after approving the temporary extension to the collection of information, the Board will publish a Federal Register notice informing the public of its approval of the collection of information and indicating why immediate action was necessary. In such cases, the Board will conduct a normal delegated review and publish a notice in the Federal Register soliciting public comment on the intention to extend the collection of information for a period not to exceed three years.

(ii) Provide the OMB/OIRA Desk Officer for the Federal Reserve Board with a copy of the Board's Federal Register notice not later than the day the Board files the notice with the Office of the Federal Register.

(iii) Assure that approved collections of information are reviewed not less frequently than once every three years, and that such reviews are normally conducted before the expiration date of the prior approval. Where the review has not been completed prior to the expiration date, the Board may extend the report, for up to three months, without public notice in order to complete the review and consequent revisions, if any. There may also be other circumstances in which the Board determines that a three-month extension without public notice is appropriate.

(iv) Take every reasonable step to conduct the review established under 5 CFR 1320.8, including the seeking of public comment under 5 CFR 1320.8(d). In determining whether to approve a collection of information, the Board will consider all comments received from the public and other agencies. The Board will not approve a collection of information that it determines does not satisfy the guidelines set forth in 5 CFR 1320.5(d)(2), unless it determines that departure from these guidelines is necessary to satisfy statutory requirements or other substantial need.

Paperwork Reduction Act 1047

(v)(A) Assure that each approved collection of information displays, as required by 5 CFR 1320.6, a currently valid OMB control number and the fact that a person is not required to respond to a collection of information unless it displays a currently valid OMB control number.

(B) Assure that all collections of information, except those contained in regulations, display the expiration date of the approval, or, in case the expiration date has been omitted, explain the decision that it would not be appropriate, under 5 CFR 1320.5(a)(1)(iii)(C), for a proposed collection of information to display an expiration date.

(C) Assure that each collection of information, as required by 5 CFR 1320.8(b)(3), informs and provides fair notice to the potential respondents of why the information is being collected; the way in which such information is to be used; the estimated burden; whether responses are voluntary, required to obtain or retain a benefit, or mandatory; the confidentiality to be provided; and the fact that an agency may not conduct or sponsor, and the respondent is not required to respond to, a collection of information unless it displays a currently valid OMB control number.

(vi) Assure that each approved collection of information, together with a completed form OMB 83–I, a supporting statement, a copy of each comment received from the public and other agencies in response to the Board's Federal Register notice or a summary of these comments, the certification required by 5 CFR 1320.9, and a certification that the Board has approved of the collection of information in accordance with the provisions of this delegation is transmitted to OMB for incorporation into OMB's public docket files. Such transmittal shall be made as soon as practical after the Board has taken final action approving the collection. However, no collection of information may be instituted until the Board has delivered this transmittal to OMB.

(b) OMB will:

(1) Provide the Board in advance with a block of control numbers which the Board will assign in sequential order to and display on, new collections of information.

(2) Provide a written notice of action to the Board indicating that the Board approvals of collections of information that have been received by OMB and incorporated into OMB's public docket files and an inventory of currently approved collections of information.

(3) Review any collection of information referred by the Board in accordance with the provisions of section 1(a)(2) of this Appendix.

(c) OMB may review the Board's paperwork review process under the delegation. The Board will cooperate in carrying out such a review. The Board will respond to any recommendations resulting from such review and, if it finds the recommendations to be appropriate, will either accept the recommendations or propose an alternative approach to achieve the intended purpose.

(d) This delegation may, as provided by 5 CFR 1320.16(c), be limited, conditioned, or rescinded, in whole or in part at any time. OMB will exercise this authority only in unusual circumstances and, in those rare instances, will do so, subject to the provisions of 5 CFR 1320.10(f) and 1320.10(g), prior to the expiration of the time period set for public comment in the Board's Federal Register notices and generally only if:

(1) Prior to the commencement of a Board review (e.g., during the review for the Information Collection Budget). OMB has notified the Board that it intends to review a specific new proposal for the collection of information or the continued use (with or without modification) of an existing collection;

(2) There is substantial public objection to a proposed information collection: or

(3) OMB determines that a substantially inadequate and inappropriate lead time has

been provided between the final announcement date of the proposed requirement and the first date when the information is to be submitted or disclosed. When OMB exercises this authority it will consider that the period of its review began the date that OMB received the Federal Register notice provided for in section 1(a)(3)(i) of this Appendix.

(e) Where OMB conducts a review of a Board information collection proposal under section 1(a)(1), 1(a)(2), or 1(d) of this Appendix, the provisions of 5 CFR 1320.13 continue to apply.

2. The Managing Director of the Federal Communications Commission

(a) Authority to review and approve currently valid (OMB-approved) collections of information, including collections of information contained in existing rules, that have a total annual burden of 5,000 hours or less and a burden of less than 500 hours per respondent is delegated to the Managing Director of the Federal Communications Commission.

(1) This delegation does not include review and approval authority over any new collection of information, any collections whose approval has lapsed, any substantive or material modification to existing collections, any reauthorization of information collections employing statistical methods, or any information collections that exceed a total annual burden of 5,000 hours or an estimated burden of 500 hours per respondent.

(2) The Managing Director may ask that OMB review and approve collections of information covered by the delegation.

(3) In exercising delegated authority, the Managing Director will:

(i) Provide the public, to the extent possible and appropriate, with reasonable opportunity to comment on collections of information under review prior to taking final action on reauthorizing an existing collection. Reasonable opportunity for public comment will include publishing a notice in the Federal Register and an FCC Public Notice informing the public that a collection of information is being extended and announcing the beginning of a 60-day comment period, notifying the public of the "intent to extend an information collection," and providing the public with the opportunity to comment on the need for the information, its practicality, the accuracy of the agency's burden estimate, and on ways to minimize burden, including the use of automated, electronic, mechanical, or other technological collection techniques or other forms of information technology, e.g., permitting electronic submission of responses. Such notices shall advise the public that they may also send a copy of their comments to the OMB/Office of Information and Regulatory Affairs desk officer for the Commission.

(A) Should the Managing Director determine that a collection of information that falls within the scope of this delegation must be reauthorized quickly and that public participation in the reauthorization process interferes with the Commission's ability to perform its statutory obligation, the Managing Director may temporarily reauthorize the extension of an information collection, for a period not to exceed 90 days, without providing opportunity for public comment.

(B) At the earliest practical date after granting this temporary extension to an information collection, the Managing Director will conduct a normal delegated review and publish a Federal Register notice soliciting public comment on its intention to extend the collection of information for a period not to exceed three years.

(ii) Assure that approved collections of information are reviewed not less frequently than once every three years and that such reviews are conducted before the expiration date of the prior approval. When the review is not completed prior to the expiration date, the Managing Director will submit the lapsed information collection to OMB for review and reauthorization.

(iii) Assure that each reauthorized collection of information displays an OMB control number and, except for those contained in regulations or specifically designated by OMB, displays the expiration date of the approval.

(iv) Inform and provide fair notice to the potential respondents, as required by 5 CFR 1320.8(b)(3), of why the information is being collected; the way in which such information is to be used; the estimated burden; whether responses are voluntary, required, required to obtain or retain a benefit, or mandatory; the confidentiality to be provided; and the fact that an agency may not conduct or sponsor, and the respondent is not required to respond to, a collection of information unless it displays a currently valid OMB control number.

(v) Transmit to OMB for incorporation into OMB's public docket files, a report of delegated approval certifying that the Managing Director has reauthorized each collection of information in accordance with the provisions of this delegation. The Managing Director shall also make the certification required by 5 CFR 1320.9, e.g., that the approved collection of information reduces to the extent practicable and appropriate, the burden on respondents, including, for small business, local government, and other small entities, the use of the techniques outlined in the Regulatory Flexibility Act. Such transmittals shall be made no later than 15 days after the Managing Director has taken final action reauthorizing the extension of an information collection.

(vi) Ensure that the personnel in the Commission's functional bureaus and offices responsible for managing information collections receive periodic training on procedures related to meeting the requirements of this part and the Act.

(b) OMB will:

(1) Provide notice to the Commission acknowledging receipt of the report of delegated approval and its incorporation into OMB's public docket files and inventory of currently approved collections of information.

(2) Act upon any request by the Commission to review a collection of information referred by the Commission in accordance with the provisions of section 2(a)(2) of this appendix.

(3) Periodically assess, at its discretion, the Commission's paperwork review process as administered under the delegation. The Managing Director will cooperate in carrying out such an assessment. The Managing Director will respond to any recommendations resulting from such a review and, if it finds the recommendations to be appropriate, will either accept the recommendation or propose an alternative approach to achieve the intended purpose.

(c) This delegation may, as provided by 5 CFR 1320.16(c), be limited, conditioned, or rescinded, in whole or in part at any time. OMB will exercise this authority only in unusual circumstances.

1050

PAPERWORK REDUCTION ACT

PAPERWORK REDUCTION ACT SUBMISSION

Please read the instructions before completing this form. For additional forms or assistance in completing this form, contact your agency's Paperwork Clearance Officer. Send two copies of this form, the collection instrument to be reviewed, the Supporting Statement, and any additional documentation to: Office of Information and Regulatory Affairs, Office of Management and Budget, Docket Library, Room 10102, 725 17th Street NW, Washington, DC 20503.

1. Agency/Subagency originating request	2. OMB control number b. __ None a. __ __ __ __ - __ __ __ __ __ __ __
3. Type of information collection *(check one)* a. ☐ New collection b. ☐ Revision of a currently approved collection c. ☐ Extension, without change, of a currently approved collection d. ☐ Reinstatement, without change, of a previously approved collection for which approval has expired e. ☐ Reinstatement, with change, of a previously approved collection for which approval has expired f. ☐ Existing collection in use without an OMB control number	4. Type of review requested *(check one)* a. ☐ Regular b. ☐ Emergency - Approval requested by: ___/___/___ c. ☐ Delegated 5. Small entities Will this information collection have a significant economic impact on a substantial number of small entities? ☐ Yes ☐ No
3a. Public Comments Has the agency received public comments on this information collection? ☐ Yes ☐ No	6. Requested expiration date a. ☐ Three years from approval date b. ☐ Other Specify: ___/___

7. Title

8. Agency form number(s) *(if applicable)*

9. Keywords

10. Abstract

11. Affected public *(Mark primary with "P" and all others that apply with "X")* a. __ Individuals or households d. __ Farms b. __ Business or other for-profit e. __ Federal Government c. __ Not-for-profit institutions f. __ State, Local or Tribal Government	12. Obligation to respond *(Mark primary with "P" and all others that apply with "X")* a. __ Voluntary b. __ Required to obtain or retain benefits c. __ Mandatory

13. Annual reporting and recordkeeping hour burden
a. Number of respondents _____
b. Total annual responses _____
   1. Percentage of these responses collected electronically _____%
c. Total annual hours requested _____
d. Current OMB inventory _____
e. Difference _____
f. Explanation of difference
   1. Program change _____
   2. Adjustment _____
	14. Annual reporting and recordkeeping cost burden *(in thousands of dollars)*
	a. Total annualized capital/startup costs _____
	b. Total annual costs (O&M) _____
	c. Total annualized cost requested _____
	d. Current OMB inventory _____
	e. Difference _____
	f. Explanation of difference
	   1. Program change _____
	   2. Adjustment _____

15. Purpose of information collection *(Mark primary with "P" and all others that apply with "X")*
a. __ Application for benefits   e. __ Program planning or management
b. __ Program evaluation   f. __ Research
c. __ General purpose statistics   g. __ Regulatory or compliance
d. __ Audit
	16. Frequency of recordkeeping or reporting *(check all that apply)*
	a. __ Recordkeeping b. __ Third party disclosure
	c. __ Reporting
	   1. __ On occasion 2. __ Weekly 3. __ Monthly
	   4. __ Quarterly 5. __ Semi-annually 6. __ Annually
	   7. __ Biennially 8. __ Other (describe)

17. Statistical methods Does this information collection employ statistical methods? ☐ Yes ☐ No	18. Agency contact *(person who can best answer questions regarding the content of this submission)* Name: _____ Phone: _____

OMB 83-I

02/04

19. Certification for Paperwork Reduction Act Submissions

On behalf of this Federal agency, I certify that the collection of information encompassed by this request complies with 5 CFR 1320.9.

Note: The text of 5 CFR 1320.9, and the related provisions of 5 CFR 1320.8(b)(3), appear at the end of the instructions. The certification is to be made with reference to those regulatory provisions as set forth in the instructions.

The following is a summary of the topics, regarding the proposed collection of information, that the certification covers:

(a) It is necessary for the proper performance of agency functions;

(b) It avoids unnecessary duplication;

(c) It reduces burden on small entities;

(d) It uses plain, coherent, and unambiguous terminology that is understandable to respondents;

(e) Its implementation will be consistent and compatible with current reporting and recordkeeping practices;

(f) It indicates the retention period for recordkeeping requirements;

(g) It informs respondents of the information called for under 5 CFR 1320.8(b)(3):

    (i) Why the information is being collected;

    (ii) Use of information;

    (iii) Burden estimate;

    (iv) Nature of response (voluntary, required for a benefit, or mandatory);

    (v) Nature and extent of confidentiality; and

    (vi) Need to display currently valid OMB control number;

(h) It was developed by an office that has planned and allocated resources for the efficient and effective management and use of the information to be collected (see note in Item 19 of the instructions);

(i) It uses effective and efficient statistical survey methodology; and

(j) It makes appropriate use of information technology.

If you are unable to certify compliance with any of these provisions, identify the item below and explain the reason in Item 18 of the Supporting Statement.

Signature of Senior Official or designee	Date

OMB 83-I   02/04

Paperwork Reduction Act

Instructions For Completing OMB Form 83-I

Please answer all questions and have the Senior Official or designee sign the form. These instructions should be used in conjunction with 5 CFR 1320, which provides information on coverage, definitions, and other matters of procedure and interpretation under the Paperwork Reduction Act of 1995.

1. Agency/Subagency originating request

Provide the name of the agency or subagency originating the request. For most cabinet-level agencies, a subagency designation is also necessary. For non-cabinet agencies, the subagency designation is generally unnecessary.

2. OMB control number

a. If the information collection in this request has previously received or now has an OMB control or comment number, enter the number.
b. Check "None" if the information collection in this request has not previously received an OMB control number. Enter the four digit agency code for your agency.

3. Type of information collection (check one)

a. Check "New collection" when the collection has not previously been used or sponsored by the agency.
b. Check "Revision" when the collection is currently approved by OMB, and the agency request includes a material change to the collection instrument, instructions, its frequency of collection, or the use to which the information is to be put.
c. Check "Extension" when the collection is currently approved by OMB, and the agency wishes only to extend the approval past the current expiration date without making any material change in the collection instrument, instructions, frequency of collection, or the use to which the information is to be put.
d. Check "Reinstatement without change" when the collection previously had OMB approval, but the approval has expired or was withdrawn before this submission was made, and there is no change to the collection.
e. Check "Reinstatement with change" when the collection previously had OMB approval, but the approval has expired or was withdrawn before this submission was made, and there is change to the collection.
f. Check "Existing collection in use without OMB control number" when the collection is currently in use but does not have a currently valid OMB control number.

4. Type of review requested (check one)

a. Check "Regular" when the collection is submitted under 5 CFR 1320.10, 1320.11, or 1320.12 with a standard 60 day review schedule.
b. Check "Emergency" when the agency is submitting the request under 5 CFR 1320.13 for emergency processing and provides the required supporting material. Provide the date by which the agency requests approval.
c. Check "Delegated" when the agency is submitting the collection under the conditions OMB has granted

5. Small entities

Indicate whether this information collection will have a significant impact on a substantial number of small entities. A small entity may be (1) a small business which is deemed to be one that is independently owned and operated and that is not dominant in its field of operation; (2) a small organization that is any not-for-profit enterprise that is independently owned and operated and is not dominant in its field; or (3) a small government jurisdiction which is a government of a city, county, town, township, school district, or special district with a population of less than 50,000.

6. Requested expiration date

a. Check "Three years" if the agency requests a three year approval for the collection.
b. Check "Other" if the agency requests approval for less than three years. Specify the month and year of the requested expiration date.

7. Title

Provide the official title of the information collection. If an official title does not exist, provide a description which will distinguish this collection from others.

8. Agency form number(s) (if applicable)

Provide any form number the agency has assigned to this collection of information. Separate each form number with a comma.

9. Keywords

Select and list at least two keywords (descriptors) from the "Federal Register Thesaurus of Indexing Terms" that describe the subject area(s) of the information collection. Other terms may be used but should be listed after those selected from the thesaurus. Separate keywords with commas. Keywords should not exceed two lines of text.

10. Abstract

Provide a statement, limited to five lines of text, covering the agency's need for the information, uses to which it will be put, and a brief description of the respondents.

11. Affected public

Mark all categories that apply, denoting the primary public with a "P" and all others that apply with "X."

12. Obligation to respond

Mark all categories that apply, denoting the primary obligation with a "P" and all others that apply with "X."

a. Mark "Voluntary" when the response is entirely discretionary and has no direct effect on any benefit or privilege for the respondent.
b. Mark "Required to obtain or retain benefits" when the response is elective, but is required to obtain or retain a benefit.
c. Mark "Mandatory" when the respondent must reply or face civil or criminal sanctions.

13. Annual reporting and recordkeeping hour burden

a. Enter the number of respondents and/or recordkeepers. If a respondent is also a recordkeeper, report the respondent only once.
b. Enter the number of responses provided annually. For recordkeeping as compared to reporting activity, the number of responses equals the number of recordkeepers.
b1. Enter the estimated percentage of responses that will be submitted/collected electronically using magnetic media (i.e., diskette), electronic mail, or electronic data interchange. Facsimile is not considered an electronic submission.
c. Enter the total annual recordkeeping and reporting hour burden.
d. Enter the burden hours currently approved by OMB for this collection of information. Enter zero (0) for any new submission or for any collection whose OMB approval has expired.
e. Enter the difference by subtracting line d from line c. Record a negative number (d larger than c) within parentheses.
f. Explain the difference. The difference in line e must be accounted for in lines f.1. and f.2.
f.1. "Program change" is the result of deliberate Federal government action. All new collections and any subsequent revision of existing collections (e.g., the addition or deletion of questions) are recorded as program changes.
f.2. "Adjustment" is a change that is not the result of a deliberate Federal government action. Changes resulting from new estimates or action not controllable by the Federal government are recorded as adjustments.

14. Annual reporting and recordkeeping cost burden (in thousands of dollars)

The costs identified in this item must exclude the cost of hour burden identified in Item 13.

a. Enter the total dollar amount of annualized cost for all respondents of any associated capital or start-up costs.
b. Enter recurring annual dollar amount of cost for all respondents associated with operating or maintaining systems or purchasing services.
c. Enter total (14.a. + 14.b.) annual reporting and recordkeeping cost burden.
d. Enter any cost burden currently approved by OMB for this collection of information. Enter zero (0) if this is the first submission after October 1, 1995.
e. Enter the difference by subtracting line d from line c. Record a negative number (d larger than c) within parenthesis.
f. Explain the difference. The difference in line e must be accounted for in lines f.1. and f.2.
f.1. "Program change" is the result of deliberate Federal government action. All new collections and any subsequent revisions or changes resulting in cost changes are recorded as program changes.

PAPERWORK REDUCTION ACT

f.2. "Adjustment" is a change that is not the result of a deliberate Federal government action. Changes resulting from new estimations or actions not controllable by the Federal government are recorded as adjustments.

15. Purpose of information collection

Mark all categories that apply, denoting the primary purpose with a "P" and all others that apply with "X."

a. Mark "Application for benefits" when the purpose is to participate in, receive, or qualify for a grant, financial assistance, etc., from a Federal agency or program.

b. Mark "Program evaluation" when the purpose is a formal assessment, through objective measures and systematic analysis, of the manner and extent to which Federal programs achieve their objectives or produce other significant effects.

c. Mark "General purpose statistics" when the data is collected chiefly for use by the public or for general government use without primary reference to the policy or program operations of the agency collecting the data.

d. Mark "Audit" when the purpose is to verify the accuracy of accounts and records.

e. Mark "Program planning or management" when the purpose relates to progress reporting, financial reporting and grants management, procurement and quality control, or other administrative information that does not fit into any other category.

f. Mark "Research" when the purpose is to further the course of research, rather than for a specific program purpose.

g. Mark "Regulatory or compliance" when the purpose is to measure compliance with laws or regulations.

16. Frequency of recordkeeping or reporting

Check "Recordkeeping" if the collection of information explicitly includes a recordkeeping requirement.

Check "Third party disclosure" if a collection of information includes third-party disclosure requirements as defined by 1320.3(c).

Check "Reporting" for information collections that involve reporting and check the frequency of reporting that is requested or required of a respondent. If the reporting is on "an event" basis, check "On occasion."

17. Statistical methods

Check "Yes" if the information collection uses statistical methods such as sampling or imputation. Generally, check "No" for applications and audits (unless a random auditing scheme is used). Check "Yes" for statistical collections, most research collections, and program evaluations using scientific methods. For other types of data collection, the use of sampling, imputation, or other statistical estimation techniques should dictate the response for this item. Ensure that supporting documentation is provided in accordance with Section B of the Supporting Statement.

18. Agency contact

Provide the name and telephone number of the agency person best able to answer questions regarding the content of this submission.

19. Certification for Paperwork Reduction Act Submissions

The Senior Official or designee signing this statement certifies that the collection of information encompassed by the request complies with 5 CFR 1320.9. Provisions of this certification that the agency cannot comply with should be identified here and fully explained in item 18 of the attached Supporting Statement. NOTE: The Office that "develops" and "uses" the information to be collected is the office that "conducts or sponsors" the collection of information. (See 5 CFR 1320.3(d)).

Certification Requirement for Paperwork Reduction Act Submissions

5 CFR 1320.9 reads "As part of the agency submission to OMB of a proposed collection of information, the agency (through the head of the agency, the Senior Official, or their designee) shall certify (and provide a record supporting such certification) that the proposed collection of information--

"(a) is necessary for the proper performance of the functions of the agency, including that the information to be collected will have practical utility;

"(b) is not unnecessarily duplicative of information otherwise reasonably accessible to the agency;

"(c) reduces to the extent practicable and appropriate the burden on persons who shall provide information to or for the agency, including with respect to small entities, as defined in the Regulatory Flexibility Act (5 U.S.C. § 601(6)), the use of such techniques as:

"(1) establishing differing compliance or reporting requirements or timetables that take into account the resources available to those who are to respond;

"(2) the clarification, consolidation, or simplification of compliance and reporting requirements; or collections of information, or any part thereof;

"(3) an exemption from coverage of the collection of information, or any part thereof;

"(d) is written using plain, coherent, and unambiguous terminology and is understandable to those who are to respond;

"(e) is to be implemented in ways consistent and compatible, to the maximum extent practicable, with the existing reporting and recordkeeping practices of those who are to respond;

"(f) indicates for each recordkeeping requirement the length of time persons are required to maintain the records specified;

"(g) informs potential respondents of the information called for under §1320.8(b)(3); [see below]

"(h) has been developed by an office that has planned and allocated resources for the efficient and effective management and use of the information to be collected, including the processing of the information in a manner which shall enhance, where appropriate, the utility of the information to agencies and the public;

"(i) uses effective and efficient statistical survey methodology appropriate to the purpose for which the information is to be collected; and

"(j) to the maximum extent practicable, uses appropriate information technology to reduce burden and improve data quality, agency efficiency and responsiveness to the public."

NOTE: 5 CFR 1320.8(b)(3) requires that each collection of information:

"(3) informs and provides reasonable notice to the potential persons to whom the collection of information is addressed of:

"(i) the reasons the information is planned to be and/or has been collected;

"(ii) the way such information is planned to be and/or has been used to further the proper performance of the functions of the agency;

"(iii) an estimate, to the extent practicable, of the average burden of the collection (together with a request that the public direct to the agency any comments concerning the accuracy of this burden estimate and any suggestions for reducing this burden);

"(iv) whether responses to the collection of information are voluntary, require to obtain or retain a benefit (citing authority) or mandatory (citing authority);

"(v) the nature and extent of confidentiality to be provided, if any (citing authority); and

"(vi) the fact that an agency may not conduct or sponsor, and a person is not required to respond to, a collection of information unless it displays a currently valid OMB control number."

Paperwork Reduction Act

Supporting Statement for Paperwork Reduction Act Submissions

General Instructions

A Supporting Statement, including the text of the notice to the public required by 5 CFR 1320.5(a)(i)(iv) and its actual or estimated date of publication in the Federal Register, must accompany each request for approval of a collection of information. The Supporting Statement must be prepared in the format described below, and must contain the information specified in Section A below. If an item is not applicable, provide a brief explanation. When Item 17 of the OMB Form 83-I is checked "Yes", Section B of the Supporting Statement must be completed. OMB reserves the right to require the submission of additional information with respect to any request for approval.

Specific Instructions

A. Justification

1. Explain the circumstances that make the collection of information necessary. Identify any legal or administrative requirements that necessitate the collection. Attach a copy of the appropriate section of each statute and regulation mandating or authorizing the collection of information.

2. Indicate how, by whom, and for what purpose the information is to be used. Except for a new collection, indicate the actual use the agency has made of the information received from the current collection.

3. Describe whether, and to what extent, the collection of information involves the use of automated, electronic, mechanical, or other technological collection techniques or other forms of information technology, e.g., permitting electronic submission of responses, and the basis for the decision for adopting this means of collection. Also describe any consideration of using information technology to reduce burden.

4. Describe efforts to identify duplication. Show specifically why any similar information already available cannot be used or modified for use for the purposes described in Item 2 above.

5. If the collection of information impacts small businesses or other small entities (Item 5 of OMB Form 83-I), describe any methods used to minimize burden.

6. Describe the consequence to Federal program or policy activities if the collection is not conducted or is conducted less frequently, as well as any technical or legal obstacles to reducing burden.

7. Explain any special circumstances that would cause an information collection to be conducted in a manner:
* requiring respondents to report information to the agency more often than quarterly;
* requiring respondents to prepare a written response to a collection of information in fewer than 30 days after receipt of it;
* requiring respondents to submit more than an original and two copies of any document;
* requiring respondents to retain records, other than health, medical, government contract, grant-in-aid, or tax records, for more than three years;
* in connection with a statistical survey, that is not designed to produce valid and reliable results that can be generalized to the universe of study;
* requiring the use of a statistical data classification that has not been reviewed and approved by OMB;
* that includes a pledge of confidentiality that is not supported by authority established in statute or regulation, that is not supported by disclosure and data security policies that are consistent with the pledge, or which unnecessarily impedes sharing of data with other agencies for compatible confidential use; or
* requiring respondents to submit proprietary trade secrets, or other confidential information unless the agency can demonstrate that it has instituted procedures to protect the information's confidentiality to the extent permitted by law.

8. If applicable, provide a copy and identify the date and page number of publication in the Federal Register of the agency's notice, required by 5 CFR 1320.8(d), soliciting comments on the information collection prior to submission to OMB. Summarize public comments received in response to that notice and describe actions taken by the agency in response to these comments. Specifically address comments received on cost and hour burden.
Describe efforts to consult with persons outside the agency to obtain their views on the availability of data, frequency of collection, the clarity of instructions and recordkeeping, disclosure, or reporting format (if any), and on the data elements to be recorded, disclosed, or reported.
Consultation with representatives of those from whom information is to be obtained or those who must compile records should occur at least once every 3 years - even if the collection of information activity is the same as in prior periods. There may be circumstances that may preclude consultation in a specific situation. These circumstances should be explained.

9. Explain any decision to provide any payment or gift to respondents, other than reenumeration of contractors or grantees.

10. Describe any assurance of confidentiality provided to respondents and the basis for the assurance in statute, regulation, or agency policy.

11. Provide additional justification for any questions of a sensitive nature, such as sexual behavior and attitudes, religious beliefs, and other matters that are commonly considered private. This justification should include the reasons why the agency considers the questions necessary, the specific uses to be made of the information, the explanation to be given to persons from whom the information is requested, and any steps to be taken to obtain their consent.

12. Provide estimates of the hour burden of the collection of information. The statement should:
* Indicate the number of respondents, frequency of response, annual hour burden, and an explanation of how the burden was estimated. Unless directed to do so, agencies should not conduct special surveys to obtain information on which to base hour burden estimates. Consultation with a sample (fewer than 10) of potential respondents is desirable. If the hour burden on respondents is expected to vary widely because of differences in activity, size, or complexity, show the range of estimated hour burden, and explain the reasons for the variance. Generally, estimates should not include burden hours for customary and usual business practices.
* If this request for approval covers more than one form, provide separate hour burden estimates for each form and aggregate the hour burdens in Item 13 of OMB Form 83-I.
* Provide estimates of annualized cost to respondents for the hour burdens for collections of information, identifying and using appropriate wage rate categories. The cost of contracting out or paying outside parties for information collection activities should not be included here. Instead, this cost should be included in Item 13.

13. Provide an estimate for the total annual cost burden to respondents or recordkeepers resulting from the collection of information. (Do not include the cost of any hour burden shown in Items 12 and 14).
* The cost estimate should be split into two components: (a) a total capital and start-up cost component (annualized over its expected useful life) and (b) a total operation and maintenance and purchase of services component. The estimates should take into account costs associated with generating, maintaining, and disclosing or providing the information. Include descriptions of methods used to estimate major cost factors including system and technology acquisition, expected useful life of capital equipment, the discount rate(s), and the time period over which costs will be incurred. Capital and start-up costs include, among other items, preparations for collecting information such as purchasing computers and software; monitoring, sampling, drilling and testing equipment; and record storage facilities.
* If cost estimates are expected to vary widely, agencies should present ranges of cost burdens and explain the reasons for the variance. The cost of purchasing or contracting out information collections services should be a part of this cost burden estimate. In developing cost burden estimates, agencies may consult with a sample of respondents (fewer than 10), utilize the 60-day pre-OMB submission public comment process and use

Paperwork Reduction Act

existing economic or regulatory impact analysis associated with the rulemaking containing the information collection, as appropriate.
* Generally, estimates should not include purchases of equipment or services, or portions thereof, made: (1) prior to October 1, 1995, (2) to achieve regulatory compliance with requirements not associated with the information collection, (3) for reasons other than to provide information or keep records for the government, or (4) as part of customary and usual business or private practices.

14. Provide estimates of annualized costs to the Federal government. Also, provide a description of the method used to estimate cost, which should include quantification of hours, operational expenses (such as equipment, overhead, printing, and support staff), and any other expense that would not have been incurred without this collection of information. Agencies may also aggregate cost estimates from Items 12, 13, and 14 in a single table.

15. Explain the reasons for any program changes or adjustments reported in Items 13 or 14 of the OMB Form 83-I.

16. For collections of information whose results will be published, outline plans for tabulation and publication. Address any complex analytical techniques that will be used. Provide the time schedule for the entire project, including beginning and ending dates of the collection of information, completion of report, publication dates, and other actions.

17. If seeking approval to not display the expiration date for OMB approval of the information collection, explain the reasons that display would be inappropriate.

18. Explain each exception to the certification statement identified in Item 19, "Certification for Paperwork Reduction Act Submissions," of OMB Form 83-I.

B. Collections of Information Employing Statistical Methods

The agency should be prepared to justify its decision not to use statistical methods in any case where such methods might reduce burden or improve accuracy of results. When Item 17 on the Form OMB 83-I is checked, "Yes," the following documentation should be included in the Supporting Statement to the extend that it applies to the methods proposed:

1. Describe (including a numerical estimate) the potential respondent universe and any sampling or other respondent selection methods to be used. Data on the number of entities (e.g., establishments, State and local government units, households, or persons) in the universe covered by the collection and in the corresponding sample are to be provided in tabular form for the universe as a whole and for each of the strata in the proposed sample. Indicate expected response rates for the collection as a whole. If the collection had been conducted previously, include the actual response rate achieved during the last collection.

2. Describe the procedures for the collection of information including:
* Statistical methodology for stratification and sample selection,
* Estimation procedure,
* Degree of accuracy needed for the purpose described in the justification,
* Unusual problems requiring specialized sampling procedures, and
* Any use of periodic (less frequent than annual) data collection cycles to reduce burden.

3. Describe methods to maximize response rates and to deal with issues of non-response. The accuracy and reliability of information collected must be shown to be adequate for intended uses. For collections based on sampling, a special justification must be provided for any collection that will not yield "reliable" data that can be generalized to the universe studied.

4. Describe any tests of procedures or methods to be undertaken. Testing is encouraged as an effective means of refining collections of information to minimize burden and improve utility. Tests must be approved if they call for answers to identical questions from 10 or more respondents. A proposed test or set of test may be submitted for approval separately or in combination with the main collection of information.

5. Provide the name and telephone number of individuals consulted on statistical aspects of the design and the name of the agency unit, contractor(s), grantee(s), or other person(s) who will actually collect and/or analyze the information for the agency.

EXECUTIVE OFFICE OF THE PRESIDENT
OFFICE OF MANAGEMENT AND BUDGET
WASHINGTON, D.C. 20503

ADMINISTRATOR
OFFICE OF
INFORMATION AND
REGULATORY AFFAIR

September 29, 2006

MEMORANDUM FOR CHIEF INFORMATION OFFICERS

FROM: Steven D. Aitken   SDA
                 Acting Administrator

SUBJECT: Data Call for the FY 2007 Information Collection Budget

This memorandum provides instructions to the Chief Information Officer (CIO) on the preparation and submission of information to the OMB Office of Information and Regulatory Affairs (OIRA) that will be the basis for the Fiscal Year 2007 Information Collection Budget (ICB). This annual report describes the information collection burden imposed by the Federal government on the public and progress of the agencies towards the burden reduction goals set forth in the Paperwork Reduction Act of 1995 (PRA).

1. **When are responses to the memorandum due?** Submissions are due to OIRA no later than **Wednesday, November 22, 2006.**

2. **Who must respond to this memorandum?** The Chief Information Officers from the following agencies must comply with the requirements of this memorandum:

   Department of Agriculture
   Department of Commerce
   Department of Defense
   Department of Education
   Department of Energy
   Department of Health and Human Services
   Department of Homeland Security
   Department of Housing and Urban Development
   Department of the Interior
   Department of Justice
   Department of Labor
   Department of State
   Department of Transportation
   Department of the Treasury
   Department of Veterans Affairs
   Environmental Protection Agency
   Federal Acquisition Regulation (FAR Secretariat)

Federal Communications Commission
Federal Deposit Insurance Corporation
Federal Energy Regulatory Commission
Federal Trade Commission
National Aeronautics and Space Administration
National Science Foundation
Nuclear Regulatory Commission
Securities and Exchange Commission
Small Business Administration
Social Security Administration

If your agency is not listed here, you do not need to comply with this memorandum. However, agencies that sponsor information collections under the auspices of the E-gov series (i.e. collections beginning with the OMB prefix "4040") must also comply with this memorandum.

3. **What changes has OMB made to this data call since last year?**
The requirements of this memorandum are very similar to last year's bulletin. However, you should note the three changes below.

- During FY 2006, OMB and the General Services Administration (GSA) developed a new system for processing PRA information collection requests. It is referred to as "ROCIS," and it is a joint OMB/GSA system for use by all Federal agencies. OMB will use ROCIS to provide information to assist with the development of this year's ICB. See Questions 3 and 13 of Appendix B.

- This year, in Appendix A, we are asking agencies that generate burdens equal to or in excess of 10 million hours annually to provide OMB new initiatives which have resulted in a cumulative burden reduction level of approximately 1% of total agency burden. Agencies may submit between one and three initiatives that accomplish this goal. We are requesting that all other respondents provide a single primary burden reduction initiative. In addition, we are requesting that agencies provide an update on the status of burden reduction initiatives initially proposed in the FY 2005 ICB.

- In Appendix C, "Compliance with the Paperwork Reduction Act of 1995," OMB calls on agencies to review the procedures by which senior officials certify that the Act's standards have been met. OMB also reminds agencies of the importance of reviewing their websites to ensure that any information collections that are subject to the PRA have OMB approval.

4. **How does the ICB fit into OMB's "zero tolerance" approach to violations of the Paperwork Reduction Act?** The PRA requires that agencies obtain OMB approval for all collections of information. A collection of information without current OMB approval constitutes a violation of the PRA. Each year, OMB is

required to report to Congress PRA violations published in the Information Collection Budget.

Over the past several years, OMB has been working closely with agencies to address violations of the PRA. Our goal continues to be the elimination of all existing violations of the PRA as soon as possible. Throughout the year, we have been tracking violations for your agency. As part of the ICB process, we will verify this information with you. In addition, you **must** designate any transaction related to a violation, including an expiration, reinstatement, or approval, as a lapse in OMB approval in your response to Appendix B.

5. **How does the ICB fit into OMB's initiatives under the E-Government Act?**
The E-Government Act has implications for information collections covered by the Paperwork Reduction Act. While information is collected on this statute through other reporting mechanisms (i.e., the annual E-Gov Act Report), agencies should be cognizant of the E-Gov Act when preparing their ICB submission and work to coordinate agency efforts under both the PRA and the E-Gov Act.

6. **What must my agency's submission include?** The CIO's office is required to submit the following information:

   a. a detailed description of new agency initiatives to improve information collection in accordance with the instructions in Appendix A, as well as a description of progress made on past agency initiatives;

   b. your agency's comprehensive burden accounting, including aggregate burden totals, program changes broken into several categories, and examples of significant burden changes prepared in accordance with the instructions in Appendix B; and

   c. data regarding your agency's compliance with the information collection provisions of the Paperwork Reduction Act, prepared in accordance with the instructions in Appendix C.

   All submissions should be consistent with OMB fiscal and policy guidance.

7. **In what format should the CIO provide this information to OMB?** The information required under this memorandum should be sent electronically to Lorraine Hunt. (LHunt@omb.eop.gov). Where the Memorandum asks you to enter information in tables you should submit tables in the **format specified herein.**

   Please use Microsoft Excel for your submission. **We will not accept files in Microsoft Access.**

8. **Will OMB conduct hearings on my agency's submission?** OMB will schedule, as needed, hearings with an agency on its progress toward burden reductions goals and agency compliance with the Paperwork Reduction Act.

9. **Will OMB conduct training on this memorandum?** OMB has scheduled the following training sessions on this memorandum.

>Tuesday, October 10, 2006, 10:00 a.m. - noon
>Wednesday, October 18, 2006, 12:30 p.m. – 2:30 p.m.

Both training sessions will be held in the Eisenhower Executive Office Building, Room 450. All meeting attendees will need to provide security clearance information (full name, date of birth, Social Security number, and citizenship) to Lorraine Hunt (LHunt@omb.eop.gov or 202-395-3085) at least 48 hours in advance of the training session. Please plan to arrive early on the date of the training to ensure adequate time to pass through security.

10. **Who should I contact for further information?** Questions about specific agency matters should be directed to your agency's Desk Officer within OMB's Office of Information and Regulatory Affairs.

    Questions about this Memorandum should be directed to: Rachel Potter Phone: 202-395-5887. Email: rpotter@omb.eop.gov.

Attachments

Memorandum to Chief Information Officers
September 29, 2006
Appendix A

BURDEN REDUCTION INITIATIVE

1. **What is the purpose of this Appendix?** For the FY 2005 ICB, we asked agencies that generate burdens equal to or in excess of 10 million hours annually to provide OMB with up to three initiatives, which will result in a cumulative burden reduction level of approximately 1% of total agency burden. We requested that all other respondents provide a single primary burden reduction initiative. In the FY 2006 ICB, we published summary updates of progress made by the agencies in achieving these initiatives and reducing burden.
   This year, we are again asking agencies that generate burdens equal to or in excess of 10 million hours annually to provide OMB with new initiatives which have resulted in a cumulative burden reduction level of approximately 1% of total agency burden. Agencies may submit between one and three initiatives that accomplish this goal. We are requesting that all other respondents provide a single primary burden reduction initiative.

   All initiative submissions must include a listing of the overall burden reduction associated with each initiative, the OMB numbers of affected collections, and an estimate of the amount of the total burden reduction associated with each collection. Your submission will not be considered complete with out this information.

   We are also asking agencies to provide a status update on progress made on initiatives initially published in the FY 2005 ICB.

2. **What is an appropriate initiative in response to this bulletin?** We ask you to identify up to three initiatives to improve program performance by enhancing the efficiency of information collections and to reduce paperwork burden on the public. We seek initiatives that:

   a. Improve program performance by enhancing the efficiency of agency information collections (both within the agency and, in the case of related information collection activities, among agency components or across agencies);

   b. Significantly reduce the burden per response on the public; or

   c. Lead to a comprehensive review of an entire program (both within the agency and, in the case of related information collection activities, among agency components or across agencies), including regulations and procedures.

Please Note: Initiatives **MUST NOT** consist of methodological changes in the manner by which agencies estimate burden.

3. **What information about these initiatives must we submit?** We ask that your submission include:

   a. A complete and concise description of the programs that you will be affecting, including statutory and regulatory citations, a description of the affected public, and the agency structure that implements the program (both within the agency and, in the case of related information collection activities, among agency components or across agencies).

   b. Measurable objectives you expect to achieve through this initiative which must include estimates of expected burden reduction linked to specific collections which will be effected (the total estimated burden reduction for each initiative must be broken out by collection).

   c. Proposed timeline for actions that you will take.

   d. Perceived difficulties in accomplishing this initiative, including statutory or policy barriers.

4. **How should I report this information?** You should use Microsoft Word and follow the format below for each initiative:

   Agency:
   Initiative Title:
   Description: (The Description should consist of one concise paragraph clearly summarizing the initiative)
   Total Estimated Burden Reduction:
   Collections Affected: (Collections Affected must include OMB Numbers, Collection Titles, and the estimated level of burden reduction associated with each item.)
   Expected Date of Completion:
   Potential Hurdles to Completion:

5. **What information should I provide to update past Initiative(s)?** We will provide a file to you with the initiative(s) published in the FY 2006 ICB. You should verify that the initiative summary is correct and revise and update, as appropriate the burden reduction estimation, the OMB numbers of the affected collections, any hurdles to completion, and the status of the initiative. If the initiative has been completed, the expected completion date should contain the date(s) of OMB approval for the affected collections.

   For initiatives that were identified as "completed" in the FY 2006 ICB, you will not need to provide any further information.

Memorandum to Chief Information Officers
September 29, 2006
Appendix B

INFORMATION COLLECTION BUDGET (ICB)

1. **What is the purpose of this Appendix?** This appendix explains what information you will need to gather from within your agency to develop your Information Collection Budget (ICB) submission for FY 2007 and what you must submit to OMB.

    a. Part 1 discusses how you should begin working on your ICB submission and offers general ideas we would like you to keep in mind.

    b. Part 2 describes how to complete a chart which lists all of the transactions that affected your burden totals for FY 2006 and a chart that lists all of the expected transactions which you used to estimate your FY 2007 total burden.

    c. Part 3 describes how to complete a chart showing the changes in your agency's total burden from FY 2005 to FY 2006, broken down into different kinds of program changes and adjustments.

    d. Part 4 instructs you to describe a limited number of significant examples of your agency's paperwork reductions and increases for FY 2006 and planned reductions and increases for FY 2007, grouped by how or why the change occurred.

2. **How do I begin working on this portion of the ICB?** The ICB always contains a review of the previous fiscal year (FY 2006) and a look toward the next (FY 2007), with an emphasis on identification of significant changes in burden reduction.

    It is important for you to work with the program officials in your agency to verify the information that we send to you and to appropriately classify all the changes in information collection activities in FY 2006. As part of this process, you should make sure that you have a clear understanding of what a significant change is. (See Question 14 of this Appendix.) You should also make sure that program officials are working to resolve any outstanding violations.

    To provide information for FY 2007, it is also important to work with the program officials in your agency to identify all potential changes in information collection activities in FY 2007. Make sure you have, for each change, an OMB number (if assigned), the expected program change and/or expected adjustment for burden hours and costs. You will need this information to estimate your agency's FY 2007 total hour burden.

Part 2: A Comprehensive Accounting

3. **Is this accounting different than in previous years?** While the accounting scheme has not changed, the process by which you prepare burden spreadsheets will be affected by ROCIS – the new OMB/GSA system for processing PRA information collection requests – as explained below and in future OMB guidance.

4. **How will I report information on each transaction?** ROCIS will provide the information for Microsoft Excel files containing two tables similar to Figure 1. The spreadsheets will have columns 1, 2, 5, 6, and 7 already completed. You will need to complete the rest of the table by dividing net burden changes into program changes due to statutory changes or Agency Action. You will also need to indicate the changes that will be identified and described as significant burden changes (See Part 4 of this Appendix). For each transaction, the following information goes in the following columns:

   a. Columns 1 and 2 present the OMB number and the date of the OMB Notice of Action, respectively. The spreadsheets will contain this information.

   b. In column 3, the change in hour or cost burden due to program changes by the agency that were not attributed to statutory changes or lapses in OMB approval (see Question 7).

   c. In column 4, the change in hour or cost burden due to changes in statutory requirements for each transaction (see Question 5).

   d. In column 5, the change in hour or cost burden due to lapses in OMB approval. The spreadsheets will provide this information based on OMB's database on violations- including expirations, reinstatements, and approvals. You must verify this information and make sure it is consistent with the information provided in Appendix C (see Question 6).

   e. Column 6 will be provided by ROCIS. The sum of entries in columns 3, 4, and 5 should equal the entry in column 6.

   f. Column 7 will be provided in the spreadsheets, but you should verify the classification of the transaction and change accordingly (see Question 8).

   g. In Column 8, an "X" should be placed for each "significant burden change" as described in Part 4 of this Appendix. There should not be an X used for any transaction identified in Column 5, Changes Due to Lapse of OMB Approval.

Paperwork Reduction Act

h. In column 9, Event, ROCIS will provide information relating to the most recent action taken on the collection (e.g., discontinuation or expiration), or the type of transaction that the agency submitted for OMB review (new, existing collection in use without an OMB number, revision, extension, etc.)

FY 2006 CHANGES IN BURDEN HOURS

OMB #	Date	PROGRAM CHANGES			NET PROGRAM CHANGES	ADJUSTMENTS	EXHIBIT	EVENT
		Due to Agency Actions	Due to Statutory Changes	Due to Lapse of OMB Approval				
TOTAL		0	0	0	0	0		
(1)	(2)	(3)	(4)	(5)	(6)	(7)	(8)	(9)
TOTAL		0	0	0	0	0		

FY 2006 CHANGES IN COST BURDEN

OMB #	Date	PROGRAM CHANGES			NET PROGRAM CHANGES	ADJUSTMENTS	EXHIBIT	EVENT
		Due to Agency Actions	Due to Statutory Changes	Due to Lapse of OMB Approval				
TOTAL		0	0	0	0	0		
(1)	(2)	(3)	(4)	(5)	(6)	(7)	(8)	(9)
TOTAL		0	0	0	0	0		

FIGURE 1.

You should total columns 3 through 7 and enter the total at the bottom of each column

As we requested last year, you **must** include a **concise** statement to indicate **any** changes you make in the information provided by ROCIS. For example, if you reclassify a transaction from an adjustment to a program change, you should include a note stating "Data misclassified as adjustment." If you reclassify a transaction from "Due to Lapse of OMB Approval" to "Due to Agency Actions" because the collection was discontinued, you should include a note stating "Collection discontinued." This information can be provided either in the Event column or in a separate Notes column if the agency so chooses (although a Notes column is not featured in Figure 1, the agency could add it to the figure as a tenth column).

Note: See definition of "significant" in Question 14 below. If a program change is greater than 10,000 hours or has a cost change greater than $10,000,000, and you do not provide an exhibit (i.e., the change is not "significant" as described in question 13), you **must** also provide a concise statement in the Event or the Notes section. This will help streamline the review process for both the agencies and OMB.

Note: Because the new ROCIS systems does not calculate cost burden in thousands of dollars, we will not be reporting costs in thousands of dollars this year. This is a change from past years' practice. Agencies should report cost burden in the <u>actual</u> dollar amount.

5. **When can we attribute a program change to a new statutory requirement?**
You should only attribute a program change to a new statutory requirement when the information collection directly related to a statute enacted within the last five years (i.e., after January 1, 2002). This should not include increases in burden due to long-standing statutory mandates or recurring statutory requirements. You may, however, include changes if this is the first time your agency is implementing a statute that has been law for many years. Please consult your OIRA desk officer if you are uncertain.

6. **What changes in burden should be listed under lapses of OMB approval?**
This column should contain any change in burden that occurred when:

   a. your agency allowed an OMB approval for a collection to expire even though your agency continued to conduct or sponsor the collection; or

   b. OMB approved a collection that your agency has been conducting or sponsoring without prior OMB approval.

Your response to this section **must** include **all** transactions – expirations, reinstatements, or approvals – related to the violations reported to OMB in Appendix C.

Do not include collections that your agency has discontinued and for which OMB approval has expired. These changes should be listed as changes due to other agency actions.

7. **What changes in burden should be listed as changes due to other agency actions?** Under this category, you should list any other program changes that do not result from statutory obligation or a lapse in OMB approval. For example, if you eliminated a form or streamlined an information collection, the reduction should be listed as due to other agency actions.

This category should also include intentional expirations and discontinued collections. For example, if you allowed a collection to expire or discontinued a collection because a program has been completed (e.g., a one time survey), the transaction should be listed as due to other agency actions.

8. **What changes in burden should be counted as adjustments?** Adjustments are changes that do not affect the content of the information your agency collects or how it is collected. These changes may be due to factors over which your agency has no control such as population growth or economic expansion.

    Example: If burden increased because your agency took an action to collect information from a new segment of the economy, you should classify it as a **program change**. If, instead, burden went up because more businesses entered a segment of the economy from which your agency already collected information, you should classify it as an **adjustment**.

    Example: If you reported an increase in burden because your agency changed the way it estimates burden, you should classify it as an **adjustment**.

9. **How do I report to OMB transactions that we expect will affect burden during FY2007?** You should report every transaction that you expect will affect burden during FY 2007 in two tables in formats similar to Figures 1 and 2, excluding column 2 (Date). Please list expected transactions in order by OMB number. List new collections not yet assigned an OMB number at the bottom of the list with the appropriate four digit prefix. We will provide Excel charts to complete.

10. **Do I need to provide an entry for every transaction we expect during FY 2007?** No, you only need to provide an entry for transactions that will affect your total burden for FY 2007.

Part 3: Aggregate Burden Totals

11. **How do I report aggregate burden totals for FY 2006?** As part of the Microsoft Excel spreadsheet file that we provide to complete Part 2, we will include a table similar to that shown in Figure 2. The spreadsheet you work from will contain links to the totals from the spreadsheet on individual transactions for the Fiscal year (See Part 2, Figure 1, Appendix B). As you complete the spreadsheets for individual transactions, the totals from Columns 3, 4, 5, 6, and 7 of Figure 1, Appendix B will be entered in the fields 3, 4, 5, 6, and 7 of Figure 2. You should verify that these links are working correctly prior to submission.

    OMB will provide your agency's FY 2005 total burden for Field A at a later date. When OMB provides this data element to you, it may not be altered under any circumstance; it contains the total burden we reported for your agency in last year's ICB. As part of this process, you must make sure that the FY 2006 Total Burden (Field B) corresponds to the numbers provided to you at the end of the Fiscal Year as part of the monthly inventory of information collections. If there are discrepancies between your agency's records and our database, you will need to work with your OIRA desk officer to determine the cause of the discrepancy and the appropriate remedy.

12. **How do I report expected aggregate burden totals for FY 2007?** Again, the information you provide for FY 2007 in Part 2 should be used to complete the corresponding cells in Figure 2. Add the aggregate burden total for FY 2006 to the expected net program change for FY 2007 and the expected net adjustments for FY 2007 to get an expected aggregate burden total for FY 2007.

SUMMARY TABLE OF BURDEN CHANGES	Burden Hours (millions)	Cost Burden
FY 2005 Total Burden	A	
FY 2006 Program Changes Due to Agency Actions	3	
FY 2006 Program Changes Due to New Statutes	4	
FY 2006 Program Changes Due to Lapses in OMB Approval	5	
SUBTOTAL: FY 2006 Total Program Changes	6	
FY 2006 Adjustments	7	
FY 2006 Total Burden	B	
Expected FY 2007 Program Changes Due to Agency Actions		
Expected FY 2007 Program Changes Due to New Statutes		
Expected FY 2007 Program Changes Due to Lapses in OMB Approval		
SUBTOTAL: Expected FY 2007 Total Program Changes		
Expected FY 2007 Adjustments		
Expected FY 2007 Total Burden		

FIGURE 2. Aggregate Burden Totals Table

Part 4: Exhibits of Significant Burden Changes

13. **Will the preparation of exhibits be different than in previous years?** The process is unchanged with the exception that OMB will provide you with a formatted list of exhibits – generated by ROCIS and containing information in the database – that you will review, edit, and resubmit to OMB.

14. **What does "significant" mean?** Significant burden reductions are those that demonstrate the agency's adherence to the principles of the Paperwork Reduction Act and have a meaningful impact on the burden imposed on the public. Significant burden increases are generally those that have attracted attention and/or have a meaningful impact on the public. We request that you limit discussion to program changes of 10,000 hours and/or $10,000,000 or greater. If you do not provide an exhibit for a program change of 10,000 hours and/or $10,000,000 or greater, you must provide a concise note, in the Notes section of the spreadsheet (See Figure 1).

    Significant burden changes **do not** include **adjustments, only program changes**. In addition, please **do not** provide exhibits for the following types of burden changes, **regardless of their burden**:

    - elimination of pilot programs;
    - completion of one time surveys;
    - changes in burden associated with ongoing cyclical surveys; and
    - merged collections under a new OMB number where there has been no change in burden.

    If these burden changes are greater than 10,000 hours and/or $10,000,000 and are program changes, please use the Notes section of the spreadsheet to identify the type of collection.

15. **What kinds of burden reductions and increases should I describe?** We are splitting information on program changes into several categories. Please assign each change to only one of the following categories. If two or more categories could apply to a single change; select the category that is most appropriate.

    a. Burden <u>reductions</u> should be placed into one of the following six categories.

      Changing Regulations: reducing information collection burden by revising existing regulations to eliminate unnecessary requirements or by completely changing the way you regulate;

      Cutting Redundancy: reducing information collection burden by raising reporting thresholds to reduce the number of reports that need to be submitted, cutting the frequency of periodic reporting requirements, consolidating information collections, or working together with other agencies to share information across programs;

Changing Forms: reducing burden by simplifying and streamlining forms, making them easier to read and fill out and by making programs easier to apply for;

Using Information Technology and E-Government: reducing burden by putting in place electronic systems that can speed the exchange of information between the government and the public and allow respondents to use their own information technology to ease reporting burdens;

Statutory Reductions: reducing burden because of recently enacted statutes; and

Other: reducing burden through other agency efforts.

b. Burden <u>increases</u> should be placed into one of the following two categories:

Statutory Increases: Increasing burden due to new statutory requirements (see question 6 for more information; and

Other: Increasing burden due to other factors.

16. **What information do I need to describe these changes?** At a minimum you will need:

   a. the title of the collection and/or title of the initiative;

   b. a one- or two-sentence description of the purpose of the collection (including from whom you collect the information, what information you collect prior to the change, and, if the collection is not a recordkeeping requirement or a third-party disclosure, how your agency uses the information collected);

   c. a short concise description of what is or was changed, how it affected burden, and whether the change is or was part of a broader agency initiative;

   d. the change in burden (hours and costs, program changes only);

   e. for statutory increases and reductions, the full name of the statute and the public law number; and

   f. whether the changes or initiative reduced paperwork burden on small entities with fewer than 25 employees.

For your convenience, ROCIS will generate a list of exhibits with significant changes. You will need to carefully review the exhibits contained in this list to ensure that they are concise and accurate and edit them accordingly.

17. **How should I report this information?** This information will be reported in succinct "exhibits." Please adhere to the following requirements:

18. **May I include more than one example for each category? Do I need to include one example for each category?** You may include more than one example under each category, but you should try to have at least one example for your agency in each category. Do not include any examples more than once. Please try to limit the total number of examples to 15 per fiscal year.

19. **How does this tie in to the charts in Part 2?** For each example, identify the corresponding transaction in the charts for Part 2 by placing an "X" in column 8. If there is a burden change of 10,000 hrs and/or $10,000,000 or greater and it is not a change due to a violation and you are not providing an exhibit please provide a short note (e.g. elimination of one time survey).

19

Privacy Act

Citations:

5 U.S.C. §552a (Supp. IV 2004), enacted December 31, 1974 by Pub. L. No. 93579, §3, 88 Stat. 1897; significantly amended by Pub. L. No. 94183, §2(2), 89 Stat. 1057, December 31, 1975; Pub. L. No. 97--365, §2, 96 Stat. 1749, October 25, 1982; Pub. L. No. 97375, title II, §201(a), (b), 96 Stat. 1821, December 21, 1982; Pub. L. No. 97-452, §2(a)(1), 96 Stat. 2478, January 12, 1983; Pub. L. No. 98-477, §2(c), 98 Stat. 2211, October 15, 1984; Pub. L. No. 98-497, title I, §107(g), 98 Stat. 2292, October 19, 1984; Pub. L. No. 100503, §§28, 102 Stat. 25072514, October 18, 1988; and Pub. L. No. 101508, title VII, §7201(b)(1), 104 Stat. 1388(3), November 5, 1990; Pub. L. No. 103-66, title XIII, Ch. 2, subch. A, pt. V, §13581(c), 107 Stat. 611, August 10, 1993; Pub. L. No. 104-193, title I, §110(w), 110 Stat. 2175, August 22, 1996; Pub. L. No.104-226, §1(b)(3), 110 Stat. 3033, October 2, 1996; Pub. L. No.104-316, title I, §115(g)(2)(b), 110 Stat. 3835, October 19, 1996; Pub. L. No. 105-34, title IX, subtitle C, §1026(b)(2), 111 Stat. 925, August 5, 1997; Pub. L. No.105-362, title XIII, §1301(d), 112 Stat. 3292, November 10, 1998; Pub. L. No. 107-306, 116 Stat. 2390, November 27, 2002; Pub. L. No. 108-271, 118 Stat. 814, July 7, 2004.

Lead Agency:

Office of Management and Budget, Office of Information and Regulatory Policy, Old Executive Office Building, Washington, DC 20503 (202) 3955897 or (202) 395-3647.

Overview:

The Privacy Act of 1974 represents Congressional response to concerns about government uses of information collected about private individuals. The Act gives individuals greater control over gathering, dissemination, and ensuring accuracy of information collected about themselves by agencies. (*Miller v. U.S.*, 630 F. Supp. 347 (E.D.N.Y. 1986)). The main purpose of the Act is to forbid disclosure unless it is required by the Freedom of Information Act. (*Lovell v. Alderete*, 630 F.2d 428 (5th Cir. 1980)). To protect individual privacy, the Act constrains executive branch recordkeeping, defines the individual's right to access certain records, limits agency disclosure of records containing an individual's private information, establishes safeguards to protect records concerning individuals, and provides remedies for agency violation of the Act's provisions.

Scope. The Act covers records maintained by agencies as defined in FOIA. The Act applies to, including Cabinet level departments, independent regulatory agencies, military departments, and government corporations (5 U.S.C. §552a(a)(1)). It does not apply to the legislative branch, national banks (*U.S. v. Miller*, 643 F.2d 713 (10th Cir. 1981)), or Amtrak (*Ehm v. National R.R. Passenger Corp.*, 732 F.2d 1250 (5th Cir. 1984), *cert. denied*, 469 U.S. 982 (1984)). *See Alexander v. FBI*, 971 F. Supp. 603, 606-07 (D.D.C. 1997) (recognizing that definition of "agency" under Privacy Act is same as in FOIA and that courts have interpreted that definition under FOIA to exclude President's immediate personal staff and units within Executive Office of President whose sole function is to advise and assist President, but rejecting such limitation with regard to "agency" as used in Privacy Act due to different purposes that two statutes serve); *Shannon v. General Elec. Co.*, 812 F. Supp. 308, 313, 315 n.5 (N.D.N.Y. 1993) (noting that there is "no dispute" that GE falls within definition of "agency" subject to requirements of Privacy Act where, pursuant to contract, it operated Department of Energy-owned lab under supervision, control, and oversight of Department and where by terms of contract GE agreed to comply with Privacy Act).

A record is a collection or grouping of information about an individual that, for example, may include educational, financial, or biographical information together with personal identifiers such as names, photos, numbers, or fingerprints. (5 U.S.C. §552a(a)(4)). It does not apply to all government records and documents that may contain an individual's name or other private information. For example, it does not include private notes of a supervisor if such notes are not used by the agency to make decisions (*Johnston v. Horne*, 875 F.2d 1415 (9th Cir. 1989)), but such notes may become subject to the Act if they become part of an agency's decision. (*Chapman v. NASA*, 682 F.2d 526 (5th Cir. 1982), *cert. denied*, 469 U.S. 1038 (1984)). It also does not apply to information in documents obtained from independent sources of information, even though identical information may be in an agency's system of records (*Thomas v. DOE*, 719 F.2d 342 (10th Cir. 1983)).

The Act focuses on "systems of records" established, maintained, or controlled by an agency. A "system of records" is a group of any records where individual names or other individual identifiers can be used to retrieve the information (5 U.S.C. §552a(a)(5)). Agencies may maintain records covered by the Act only when they are relevant and necessary to accomplish the agency's purpose (5 U.S.C. §552(e)(1)). The D.C. Circuit addressed the "system of records" definition in the context of computerized information in *Henke v. United States Dep't of Commerce*, 83 F.3d 1453 (D.C. Cir. 1996), and noted that "the OMB guidelines make it clear that it is not sufficient that an agency has the *capability* to retrieve information indexed under a person's name, but the agency must *in fact* retrieve records in this way in order for a system of records to exist." *Id.* at 1460 n.12. The D.C. Circuit looked to Congress's use of the words "*is retrieved*" in the statute's definition of a system of records and focused on whether the agency "*in practice*" retrieved information. *Id.* at 1459-61.

Access to Records. Where the agency is authorized to keep records covered by the Act, an individual has a right of access to records concerning him or her. This is a central protection of the Act for individuals. The individual has a right to:

- Copy any or all of the record (§552a(d)(1));
- Request amendment of the record (§552a(d)(2)) and to file a concise statement of disagreement if the agency refuses to amend the record that will be provided to all persons to whom the record is disclosed (§552a(d)(4));
- Request an accounting from the agency on the date, nature, and purpose of each disclosure of the record (§552a(c)).

The individual has an absolute right to access and need not provide any reason for seeking access (*FTC v. Shaffner*, 626 F.2d 32 (7th Cir. 1980)).

Agency Requirements. For each system of records an agency maintains, it must:

- Publish in the Federal Register the name and location of the system; the categories of individuals contained in the system; the routine use of the records; agency policies concerning the records including storage, retrieval, access, retention and disposal; the person, including title and address, responsible for the system; the method used to notify individuals how to gain access to records about themselves;

and the sources or records in the system. Any new use of the system must be noticed for comment 30 days prior to implementing the new use. Exempt systems must also be noticed. (*See, e.g.*, §552a(b)(3), (e)(4) and (e)(11).)
- Maintain records in the system accurately, completely, and timely to ensure fairness to the individuals (§552a(e)(5));
- Establish rules and training for persons designing, developing, operating, or maintaining the system to ensure compliance with the Act and the agency's implementing policies (§552a(e)(9));
- Establish safeguards for the protection of records (§552a(e)(10));
- Inform government contractors of their duties under the Act (§552a(m)).

When the agency collects information that "may result in adverse determinations about an individual's rights, benefits, and privileges under Federal programs," the Act requires the information to be collected, to the "greatest extent practicable," directly from the affected individual (§552a(e)(2)). When requesting such information from individuals, the agency must disclose: (1) the authority under which collection is authorized (2) the principal purposes for which the information is needed; (3) the routine use of the information; and (4) consequences, if any, of not providing the information (§552a(e)(3)).

The Act mandates that information maintained in agency records be as relevant and as necessary as possible to accomplish the agency's purpose. It must also ensure fairness to the individual. In *DOE v. U.S.*, 821 F.2d 694 (D.C. Cir. 1987), the court sitting *en banc* held that an agency may leave information an individual considers damaging, together with the individual's explanation or disagreement with the accuracy of the information, in its records without making an explanation under section 552a(d)(4), concerning why it chose not to expunge the information as requested. The court found that the agency made a reasonable effort to determine the accuracy of the information and that an adjudication of the disputed facts was not necessary for the agency's purposes. The court said that in some cases, fairness may require a record to contain both versions of disputed fact. Strong dissents argued that fairness to the individual was the overriding concern under the Act, and that the harm to the individual is the same if disputed facts are unverified or substantiated.

Agencies are prohibited from maintaining records describing how an individual exercises First Amendment rights, unless such records are authorized by statute or are pertinent to and within the scope of authorized law enforcement activity (§552a(e)(7)). Such records are subject to the Act even if not kept in "a system of records." *Clarkson v. IRS*, 678 F.2d 1368, 1373-77 (11th Cir. 1982), *cert. denied*, 481 U.S. 1031. *Cf. Pototsky v. Dept of Navy*, 717 F. Supp. 20 (D. Mass. 1989). OMB guidelines call for the broadest reasonable interpretation of the prohibition.[1]

Exemptions from Access. The Act provides general (§552a(j)) and specific (§552a(k)) exemptions. These are exemptions allowing an agency to deny access to the record by the individual to whom the record pertains. The two types are different in nature and consequences and are discretionary on the agency's part. To be effective, the agency must first determine that a record or system of records meets the criteria for exemption under the Act and then publish the exemption as a rule under the APA's notice and comment provisions. Failure to set out reasons demonstrating that the exemption meets the requirements of the Act may leave the records subject to the Act. *Exner v. FBI*, 612 F.2d 1202 (9th Cir. 1980). The exemptions do not authorize the agency to use the record in a manner other than the manner originally set out in the Federal Register establishing the system of records. *DOE v. Naval Air Station*, 768 F.2d 1229 (11th Cir. 1985).

A general exemption denies access by an affected individual under virtually all the Act's provisions and is available for records maintained by the Central Intelligence Agency or by an agency whose principal functions are criminal law enforcement. The general exemption may not be used to exempt records compiled for a non-criminal or administrative purpose even if they are also a part of a system of records maintained by an agency qualified to assert the exemption. *Vymetalik v. FBI*, 785 F.2d 1090 (D.C. Cir. 1986).

The specific exemptions (§552a(k)(1)(7)) are available to any agency if the head of the agency promulgates rules pursuant to the noticeandcomment provisions of the APA (5 U.S.C. §553). The specific exemption is from a particular provision of the Act. The seven exemptions allowed are:

- FOIA (b)(1) exemptions (matters to be kept secret in the interest of national defense or foreign policy and properly classified by executive order);
- Investigatory material compiled for law enforcement purposes that does not fall within the general exemption;
- Material maintained to provide protective service to the President or pursuant to 18 U.S.C. §3056;
- Confidential investigatory records relating to employment or contracts;
- Statistical records required by statute;

---

[1] See the Appendix to this chapter.

- Testing and examination material related to federal employment;
- Evaluations related to military promotions obtained confidentially.

An individual may sue to challenge a denial of access to records based on the general or specific exemptions, and the court will determine the substantive and procedural propriety of the agency's assertion of the exemption. *Zeller v. U.S.*, 467 F. Supp. 487 (E.D.N.Y. 1979).

Restrictions on Disclosure. The Act prohibits disclosure of any record covered by the Act without the written request or prior written consent of the person whom the record concerns. (§552a(b)). The restriction on disclosure applies to any person or agency and includes any means of communication—written, oral, electronic or mechanical (OMB Privacy Act Guidelines, 40 Fed. Reg. 28,948 at 28,953 (July 9, 1975)). Information obtained (or released) through sources independent of agency records is not "disclosure" under the Act.

The general rule of nondisclosure is subject to 12 exceptions (§552a(b)(1)(12)). They are:

- Internal agency use on a need to know basis;
- Proper requests under FOIA;
- Routine use;
- Census Bureau activities;
- Statistical research where the recipient has given written assurance that records are not individually identifiable;
- National Archives preservation;
- Information to Congress;
- Information to the Comptroller General in performing GAO duties;
- Showing of compelling circumstances affecting the health or safety of an individual;
- Pursuant to court order (Subpoenas issued by clerks of courts are not "orders." *Stiles v. Atlanta Gas Light Co.*, 453 F. Supp. 798, 800 (N.D. Ga. 1978));
- To a consumer reporting agency in accordance with 31 U.S.C. §3711(f); and
- Use by "any governmental jurisdiction . . . for a civil or criminal law enforcement activity . . . " as long as a written request (1) is made by the head of the agency seeking the record, (2) specifies the portion of the record sought, and (3) describes the relevant enforcement

activity (*See DOE v. Naval Air Station*, 768 F.2d 1229 (11th Cir. 1985)).

"Routine use," considered generally the most important exception, is defined as "the use of such record for a purpose that is compatible with the purpose for which it was collected" (§552a(a)(d)). Each routine use is identified in the Federal Register notice upon establishment or revision of each system of records. (§552a(e)(4)(d)). This exception permits nonconsensual intra or interagency transfer of what is generally described as "housekeeping" information. Because the language is broad, the potential for abuse is considered great, and the courts have strictly required that the use be clearly and specifically identified in the rule adopted by the agency identifying the system of records (*Covert v. Harrington*, 876 F.2d 751 (9th Cir. 1989); *DOE v. Stephens*, 851 F.2d 1457 (D.C. Cir. 1988); *Zeller v. U.S.*, 467 F. Supp. 487 (E.D.N.Y. 1979)).

Review, Relief, Remedies. The Act provides that each agency shall promulgate rules that establish, among other things, procedures of notice, disclosure, and review of requests (§552a(f)). In the event that the rules are not followed or that a dispute persists, there are four civil actions: (1) a challenge for failure to provide access; (2) a challenge for refusal to amend; (3) a damages action for improper maintenance of the content of records; and (4) a damages action for other breaches of the Act or regulations issued thereunder that adversely affect the individual (§552a(g)(1)). The latter two actions require proof of damages and are limited to actual damages. A cause of action for monetary damages requires a showing of an agency's intentional or willful failure to maintain accurate records and that the violation of the Act caused the actual damages complained of *(Molerio v. FBI*, 749 F.2d 815 (D.C. Cir. 1984)). While "actual damages" may include physical and mental injury as well as "out-of-pocket" expenses (*Johnson v. Dept. of Treasury*, 700 F.2d 971 (5th Cir. 1983)), direct evidence of expense for psychiatric care or other pecuniary losses necessitated by the Act's violation is required (*Fitzpatrick v. IRS*, 665 F.2d 327 (11th Cir. 1982)). Remedies for failure to grant access or refusal to amend are injunctive.

An individual bringing a claim under section 552a(g)(1) must demonstrate a causal connection between the alleged violation and the harm suffered, but may not use the Privacy Act claim as the forum in which to prove the improper denial of entitlement to the individual's claims (*Gizoni v. Southwest Marine, Inc.*, 909 F.2d 385 (9th Cir. 1990)).

Criminal penalties are established for willful disclosure of records by those who know such disclosure is prohibited, willful maintenance of a system of records without meeting the appropriate notice requirements, and knowing and willful requests for records under false pretenses (§552a(i)). Each violation is classified as a misdemeanor, and the violator may be fined not more than $5,000. There have been at least two criminal prosecutions for unlawful disclosure of Privacy Act-protected records. *See United States v. Trabert*, 978 F. Supp. 1368 (D. Colo. 1997) (finding defendant not guilty; prosecution did not prove "beyond a reasonable doubt that Defendant 'willfully disclosed' protected material," evidence presented constituted, "at best, gross negligence," and thus was "insufficient for purposes of prosecution under §§ 552a(i)(1)"); *United States v. Gonzalez*, No. 76-132 (M.D. La. Dec. 21, 1976) (guilty plea entered). *See generally In re Mullins (Tamposi Fee Application)*, 84 F.3d 1439, 1441 (D.C. Cir. 1996) (per curiam) (concerning an application for reimbursement of attorney fees where Independent Counsel found no prosecution was warranted under Privacy Act because there was no conclusive evidence of improper disclosure of information).

The Act provides a 2year statute of limitations (§552a(g)(5)). The time begins to run when a reasonable person should have known of the alleged violation. *Rose v. U.S.*, 905 F.2d 1257, 1259 (9th Cir. 1990); *Diliberti v. U.S.*, 817 F.2d 1259, 1262 (7th Cir. 1987).

Computer Matching. The Act was amended in 1988 by Pub. L. No. 100503, the Computer Matching and Privacy Protection Act of 1988. The Office of Management and Budget issued final guidance implementing the amendment's provisions on June 19, 1989 (54 Fed. Reg. 25,818 (June 19, 1989)). The amendments added sections 552a(o)(q) to establish procedural safeguards affecting agencies' use of Privacy Act records when performing computerized matching programs. The amendments require agencies to conclude written agreements specifying terms and safeguards under which matches are to be done. They provide procedures for individuals whose information is contained in the affected records to use to prevent agencies from taking adverse actions unless they have independently verified the results of matching and given the individual advance notice. Oversight is established by requiring Federal Register notice of matching agreements, by requiring reports to OMB and Congress, and by requiring the establishment of internal "data integrity boards" to oversee and coordinate the agency's implementation of matching programs.

Relationship to FOIA. Two provisions relate to the Freedom of Information Act (5 U.S.C. §552). Section 552a(b)(2) exempts agencies from the requirement of obtaining an individual's consent to release of information subject to disclosure under FOIA. In 1984, Congress added provisions delineating an individual's access rights to records exempt from disclosure under

FOIA or the Privacy Act. An agency must give an individual access to a record if it is accessible under either act irrespective of whether it might be withheld under the other (§552a(t)). This gives maximum access to records by an individual whose personal information is contained therein. An accounting of the number of FOIA releases of Privacy Act information is not required (§552a(c)(1)). If released under FOIA, the agency is relieved from ensuring the accuracy, completeness, timeliness, and relevance of the record (§552a(e)(6)). If the system of records is made necessary by FOIA, the agency may exempt the system from the Privacy Act (§552a(k)(1)).

Social Security Numbers. The Act restricts use of an individual's Social Security account number. ((Section 7 of Pub. L. No. 93579, 88 Stat. 1896) (not codified as part of 5 U.S.C. §552a)). This provision applies to state and local governments as well as the federal government and makes it unlawful to deny any right, benefit, or privilege based on an individual's failure to disclose the Social Security account number, unless the disclosure was required by any federal, state, or local system of records in operation before January 1, 1975, or the disclosure is required by federal law. Since enactment, Congress has required disclosure in the Tax Reform Act of 1976, the Deficit Reduction Act of 1984, and the Debt Collection Act of 1982. In the Tax Reform Act of 1976, Congress declared it to be U.S. policy to use Social Security account numbers "in the administration of any tax, general public assistance, driver's license, or motor vehicle registration law. . ." Pub. L. No. 94-55, 90 Stat. 1520, 1711(1976), amending 42 U.S.C. §405(c)(2)).

Oversight:

The Act requires the Office of Management and Budget to develop guidelines and regulations for its implementation and to provide continuing assistance and oversight. The OMB guidelines are entitled to the usual deference accorded the interpretations of the agency charged with administration of a statute. (*Albright v. U.S.*, 631 F.2d 915, 919, n. 5 (D.C. Cir. 1980); *Quinn v. Stone*, 978 F.2d 126, 133 (3d Cir. 1992)). However, a few courts have rejected particular aspects of the OMB Guidelines as inconsistent with the statute. *See, e.g.*, *Kassel v. VA*, No. 87-217-S, slip op. at 24-25 (D.N.H. Mar. 30, 1992) (subsection (e)(3)); *Doe v. Chao*, 124 S. Ct. 1204, 1212, 1215 (2004) (disagreeing with dissent's reliance on OMB interpretation of damages provision since the Court does "not find its unelaborated conclusion persuasive").

The vast majority of OMB's Privacy Act Guidelines are published at 40 Fed. Reg. 28,948-78 (1975). However, these original guidelines have been supplemented in particular subject areas over the years. *See* Appendix I to

OMB Circular No. A130 (initially published at 50 Fed. Reg. 52,738, December 24, 1985; most recently revised at 61 Fed. Reg. 6,428 (Feb. 20, 1996)); *see also* 40 Fed. Reg. 56,741-43 (1975) (system of records definition, routine use and intra-agency disclosures, consent and congressional inquiries, accounting of disclosures, amendment appeals, rights of parents and legal guardians, relationship to FOIA); 48 Fed. Reg. 15,556-60 (1983) (relationship to Debt Collection Act); 52 Fed. Reg. 12,990-93 (1987) ("call detail" programs); 54 Fed. Reg. 25,818-29 (1989) (computer matching); 56 Fed. Reg. 18,599-601 (proposed Apr. 23, 1991) (computer matching); 61 Fed. Reg. 6,428, 6,435-39 (1996) ("Federal Agency Responsibilities for Maintaining Records About Individuals"). Thus, when researching in this area, it may be important to check on subsequent supplements.

In 1998, President Clinton called upon all federal agencies to take further privacy-protection steps within the next year. Memorandum on Privacy and Personal Information in Federal Records, 34 Weekly Comp. Pres. Doc. 870 (May 14, 1998), available in Westlaw, 1998 WL 241263 (May 14, 1998). Specifically, the President directed each agency to designate a senior official with responsibility for privacy policy, to apply the Principles for Providing and Using Personal Information that were developed through the Information Infrastructure Task Force under the auspices of the Department of Commerce in 1995, and to conduct a series of reviews of agency record systems in order to ensure compliance with Privacy Act requirements. The Privacy Act-related reviews, conducted in accordance with instructions issued by OMB, reported results to OMB. The memorandum also provided that OMB issue further guidance on the making of "routine use" disclosures under the Act.

Section 208 of the E-Government Act of 2002 (Pub. L. No. 107-347, 44 U.S.C. Ch 36) requires that OMB issue guidance to agencies on implementing the privacy provisions of the E-Government Act. Under this guidance (see Bibliography, below), agencies are required to conduct privacy impact assessments for electronic information systems and collections; make them publicly available; post privacy policies on agency websites used by the public; translate privacy policies into a standardized machine-readable format; and report annually to OMB on compliance with the E-Government Act.

In 2002, GAO conducted an extensive review of agency Privacy Act practices, and reported on its findings in June 2003. (*See Privacy Act: OMB Leadership Needed to Improve Agency Compliance*, GAO-03-304).

While most questions concerning the Act should first be directed to agency Privacy Act officers, important policy or litigation questions, or questions concerning the OMB Guidelines, may be directed to the Office of Information and Regulatory Affairs, OMB.

Legislative History:

The Act reflects the merger of seemingly disparate bills from the Senate and the House: S. 3418, introduced by Senator Ervin, and H.R. 16373, supported by the Administration. The Senate bill would have granted sweeping powers to a Federal Privacy Board for the oversight of collection, maintenance and dissemination of individually identifiable information by both the public and private sectors, while the House bill focused on access to and correction of records, as well as data collection and maintenance standards. The Senate approved its bill on November 21, 1974 after consideration and, on the same day, the House bill passed by a 353 to 1 vote, after two days of floor debate.

The bills were not reconciled by the usual conference committee because of the limited time available between the end of Thanksgiving recess and the end of the session. Instead, the respective staffs of the committees studied the differing bills, reported to the committees and, after informal meetings, reached an agreement. The description of the amendments that made the two bills identical (thus avoiding a conference committee) was inserted into the record of both sides, and both houses passed identical bills. Thus, many of the most important provisions of the bill are not explained by committee reports. The only record of the final negotiations leading to the bill actually adopted is a staff memorandum entitled "Analysis of House and Senate Compromise Amendments to the Federal Privacy Act" (*see* 120 Cong. Rec. 40,445, December 17, 1974; *see also Source Book on Privacy* at 858).

The final product included most of the fair information practices defined in the Senate version and the access and correction provisions of the House bill. None of the Senate provisions relating to a Federal Privacy Board was included. However, the Act provided for two important means of further development and oversight:

- It instructed OMB to develop guidelines for the implementation of the Act throughout the executive. branch; and
- The Privacy Protection Study Commission was created by the Act to study the issues raised by the Act and to recommend further legislation, and it subsequently completed its thorough and informative report, *Personal Privacy in an Information Society.*

The bill was signed by President Ford on December 31, 1974 and became effective September 1975.

Source Note:

The legislative history of the original Act is exhaustively collected in *Legislative History of the Privacy Act of 1974, S. 3418 (Pub. L. No. 93579): Source Book on Privacy* (1976) (See Bibliography). The Department of Justice's *Overview of the Privacy Act of 1974* is updated periodically and discusses the extensive case law under the Act. For the latest version (May 2004), see http://www.usdoj.gov/oip/04_7_1.html.

Bibliography:

I. Legislative History

1. Analysis of House and Senate Compromise Amendments to the Federal Privacy Act, 120 Cong. Rec. 12,243 (daily ed. Dec. 18, 1974); *id.* at 21,815 (daily ed. Dec. 17, 1974).
2. Joint Committee on Government Operations, *Legislative History of the Privacy Act of 1974, S. 3418 (Pub. L. No. 93579): Source Book on Privacy*, 94th Cong., 2d Sess., (September 1976) (available from the U.S. Government Printing Office).
3. H.R. Rep. No. 100-802, 100th Cong., 2d Sess. (1988), 134 Cong. Rec. S13001 (daily ed. Sept. 20, 1988).
4. S. Rep. No. 100516, 100th Cong., 2d Sess. (1988), 134 Cong. Rec. S13001 (daily ed. Sept. 20, 1988).
5. *Who Cares About Privacy? Oversight of the Privacy Act of 1974 by the Office of Management and Budget and by the Congress,* H.R. Rep. No. 98-455, 98th Cong., 1st Sess. (1983); *Hearings on Oversight of the Privacy Act of 1974 Before a Subcommittee of the House Committee on Government Operations,* 98th Cong., 1st Sess. (1983).

II. Other Government Documents

1. Office of Management and Budget, *Privacy Act Guidelines,* 40 Fed. Reg. 28,948 (July 9, 1975), supplemented at 56,741 (1975); 49 Fed. Reg. 12,338 (1984), and 54 Fed. Reg. 25,818 (1989).
2. Office of Management and Budget, *Implementation of the Privacy Act of 1974, Supplementary Guidance,* 40 Fed. Reg. 5,674 (December 4, 1975).
3. *Personal Privacy in an Information Society: The Report of the Privacy Protection Study Commission* (GPO, July 1977).

4. Office of Management and Budget, *Revised Supplemental Guidance for Conducting Matching Programs*, 47 Fed. Reg. 21,656 (May 19, 1982).

5. Office of Management and Budget, *Debt Collection Act Guidelines*, 48 Fed. Reg. 15,556 (April 11, 1983).

6. Office of Management and Budget, *Management of Federal Information Resources, Circular A130*, 50 Fed. Reg. 52,730 (Dec. 24, 1985), revised February 8, 1996, see http://www.whitehouse.gov/omb/circulars/a130/a130.html. *See also Proposed Revision of Circular A130*, 57 Fed. Reg. 18,296 (April 29, 1992).

7. U.S. General Accounting Office, *Computer Matching: Assessing its Costs and Benefits*, GAO/PEMD872 (Nov. 1986).

8. Office of Management and Budget, *Final Guidance on Privacy Act Implications of "Call Detail" Programs*, 52 Fed. Reg. 12,2903 (April 20, 1987).

9. Office of Management and Budget, *Final Guidance Interpreting the Provisions of Public Law No. 100—503, the Computer Matching and Privacy Protection Act of 1988*, 54 Fed. Reg. 25,818 (June 19, 1989).

10. U.S. General Accounting Office, *Peer Review: Compliance with the Privacy Act and the Federal Advisory Committee Act,* GAO/GG D91 48 (1991), *available at* http://www.gao.gov/new.items/d03304.pdf.

11. Memorandum on Privacy and Personal Information in Federal Records, 34 Weekly Comp. Pres. Doc. 870 (May 14, 1998).

12. Office of Management and Budget, *Guidance on Inter-Agency Sharing of Personal Data—Protecting Personal Privacy*, December 20, 2000 (M-01-05).

13. Office of Management and Budget, *Guidance for Implementing the Privacy Provisions of the E-Government Act of 2002* (September 26, 2003) (M-03-22).

14. U.S. Department of Justice, *Overview of the Privacy Act of 1974*, (May 2004), *available at* http://www.usdoj.gov/oip/04_7_1.html.

15. U.S. Government Accountability Office, *Privacy Act: OMB Leadership Needed to Improve Agency Compliance,* GAO-03-304 (2004).

16. Office of Management and Budget, FY 2005 Report to Congress on Implementation of the E-Government Act of 2002 (2006).

III. Selected Books and Articles

1. L. BeVier, *Information about Individuals in the Hands of Government: Some Reflections on Mechanisms for Privacy Protection*, 4 Wm. & Mary Bill Rights J. 455 (1991).

2. W. Challis & A. Cavoukian, *The Case for a U.S. Privacy Commissioner: A Canadian Commissioner's Perspective*, 19 J. Marshall J. Computer & Info. L. 1 (2000).

3. Coles, *Does the Privacy Act of 1974 Protect your Right to Privacy?: An Examination of the Routine Use Exemption*, 40 Am. U. L. Rev. 957 (1991).

4. J. Eden, *When Big Brother Privatizes: Commercial Surveillance, the Privacy Act of 1974, and the Future of RFID*, 2005 Duke L. & Tech. Rev. 20.

5. E. M. Grace, *Privacy vs. Convenience: Benefits and Drawbacks of Tax System Modification*, 47 Fed. Comm. L. J. 409 (1994).

6. H. Hong, *Dismantling the Private Enforcement of the Privacy Act of 1974: Doe v. Chao*, 38 Akron L. Rev. 71 (2005).

7. J. Kaplan & J. Mahoney, *Reckless Disregard: Intentional and Willful Violations of the Privacy Act's Investigatory Requirements*, 44 Fed. Law. 38 (May 1997).

8. F. Komuves, *We've Got Your Number: An Overview of Legislation and Decisions to Control the Use of Social Security Numbers as Personal Identifiers*, 16 J. Marshall J. Computer & Info. L. 529 (1998).

9. F. Lodge, Note, *Damages Under the Privacy Act of 1974: Compensation and Deterrence*, 52 Fordham L. Rev. 611 (1984).

10. Note, *Privacy Act: D.C. Circuit Review,* 56 Geo. Wash. L. Rev. 1028 (May and August 1987 and 1988).

11. M. Rotenberg, *The Privacy Law Sourcebook* (2000).

12. P. Schwartz, *Privacy and Participation: Personal Information and Public Sector Regulation in the United States*, 80 Iowa L. Rev. 553 (1995).

13. D. Solove, *Identity Theft, Privacy, and the Architecture of Vulnerability*, 54 Hastings L.J. 1227 (2003).

14. J. M. Sullivan, *Will the Privacy Act of 1974 Still Hold Up in 2004? How Advancing Technology Has Created a Need for a Change in the "System of Records" Analysis*, 39 Cal. W. L. Rev. 395 (2003).

15. T. Susman, *Privacy Act and the Freedom of Information Act: Conflict and Resolution,* 21 J. Marshall L. Rev. 703 (1988).

16. G. Trubow ed., *Privacy Law and Practice* (New York: Matthew Bender, 1990) (see especially Ehlke, *The Privacy Act of 1974,* Chap. 2).

17. J. Weiser, *Measure of Damages for Violation of Property Rules: Breach of Confidentiality*, 9 U. Chi. L. Sch. Roundtable 75 (2002).

IV. Selected Cases

1. *Stiles v. Atlanta Gas Light Co.*, 453 F. Supp. 798 (N.D. Ga. 1978).
2. *Zeller v. United States*, 467 F. Supp. 487 (E.D.N.Y. 1979).
3. *Albright v. United States*, 631 F.2d 915 (D.C. Cir. 1980).
4. *Lovell v. Alderete*, 630 F.2d 428 (5th Cir. 1980).
5. *Exner v. FBI*, 612 F.2d 1202 (9th Cir. 1980).
6. *United States v. Miller*, 643 F.2d 713 (10th Cir. 1981).
7. *Fitzpatrick v. United States*, 665 F.2d 327 (11th Cir. 1982).
8. *Clarkson v. IRS*, 678 F.2d 1368 (11th Cir. 1982).
9. *Johnson v. Department of the Treasury*, 700 F.2d 971 (5th Cir. 1983).
10. *Thomas v. DOE*, 719 F.2d 342 (10th Cir. 1983).
11. *Molerio v. FBI*, 749 F.2d 815 (D.C. Cir. 1984).
12. *Elm v. National R.R. Passenger Corp.*, 732 F.2d 1250 (5th Cir. 1984).
13. *DOE v. Naval Air Station*, 768 F.2d 1229 (11th Cir. 1985).
14. *Vymetalik v. FBI*, 785 F.2d 1090 (D.C. Cir. 1986).
15. *DOE v. United States*, 821 F.2d 694 (D.C. Cir. 1987).
16. *DOE v. Stephens*, 851 F.2d 1457 (D.C. Cir. 1988).
17. *Johnston v. Horne*, 875 F.2d 1415 (9th Cir. 1989).
18. *Pototsky v. Department of the Navy*, 717 F. Supp. 20 (D. Mass. 1989).
19. *Covert v. Harrington*, 876 F.2d 751 (9th Cir. 1989).
20. *Quinn v. Stone*, 978 F.2d 126, 133 (3rd Cir. 1992).
21. *Kassel v. VA*, No. 87-217-S (D.N.H. Mar. 30, 1992).
22. *United States v. Trabert*, 978 F. Supp. 1368 (D. Colo. 1997).
23. *United States v. Gonzalez*, No. 76-132 (M.D. La. Dec. 21, 1976).
24. *In re Mullins (Tamposi Fee Application)*, 84 F.3d 1439 (D.C. Cir. 1996).
25. *Alexander v. FBI*, 971 F. Supp. 603 (D.D.C. 1997).
26. *Shannon v. General Elec. Co.*, 812 F. Supp. 308 (N.D.N.Y. 1993).
27. *Henke v. United States Dep't of Commerce*, 83 F.3d 1453 (D.C. Cir. 1996).
28. *Falwell v. Executive Office of the President*, 113 F. Supp. 2d 967 (W.D. Va. 2000).
29. *Dale v. Executive Office of the President*, 164 F. Supp. 2d 22 (D.D.C. 2001).
30. *Trulock v. United States Dep't of Justice*, No. 00-2234, slip op. (D.D.C. Sept. 18, 2001).
31. *Tripp v. Executive Office of the President*, 200 F.R.D. 140 (D.D.C. 2001).

32. *Broaddrick v. Executive Office of the President*, 139 F. Supp. 2d 55 (D.D.C. 2001).

33. *Flowers v. Executive Office of the President*, 142 F. Supp. 2d 38 (D.D.C. 2001).

34. *Jones v. Executive Office of the President*, 167 F. Supp. 2d 10 (D.D.C. 2001).

35. *Sculimbrene v. Reno*, 158 F. Supp. 2d 26 (D.D.C. 2001).

36. *Schwarz v. United States Dep't of Treasury*, 131 F. Supp. 2d 142 (D.D.C. 2000).

37. *Cobell v. Norton*, 157 F. Supp. 2d 82 (D.D.C. 2001).

38. *Cready v. Principi*, 297 F. Supp. 2d 178 (D.D.C. 2003).

39. *Recticel Foam Corp. v. U.S. Dep't of Justice*, No. 98-2523, slip op. (D.D.C. Jan. 31, 2002).

40. *Caang v. Dep't of the Navy*, No. 00-0783, 2004 WL 882030 (D.D.C. Apr. 22, 2004).

41. *Maydak v. United States*, 363 F.3d 512 (D.C. Cir. 2004).

42. *Doe v. Chao*, 124 S. Ct. 1204 (2004).

Appendix:

1. Privacy Act, 5 U.S.C. §552a (Supp. IV 2004).

Privacy Act

Title 5, U. S. Code

Sec. 552a. Records maintained on individuals

(a) **Definitions.**—For purposes of this section—
  (1) the term "agency" means agency as defined in section 552(e) [1] of this title;
  (2) the term "individual" means a citizen of the United States or an alien lawfully admitted for permanent residence;
  (3) the term "maintain" includes maintain, collect, use, or disseminate;
  (4) the term "record" means any item, collection, or grouping of information about an individual that is maintained by an agency, including, but not limited to, his education, financial transactions, medical history, and criminal or employment history and that contains his name, or the identifying number, symbol, or other identifying particular assigned to the individual, such as a finger or voice print or a photograph;
  (5) the term "system of records" means a group of any records under the control of any agency from which information is retrieved by the name of the individual or by some identifying number, symbol, or other identifying particular assigned to the individual;
  (6) the term "statistical record" means a record in a system of records maintained for statistical research or reporting purposes only and not used in whole or in part in making any determination about an identifiable individual, except as provided by section 8 of title 13;
  (7) the term "routine use" means, with respect to the disclosure of a record, the use of such record for a purpose which is compatible with the purpose for which it was collected;
  (8) the term "matching program"—
    (A) means any computerized comparison of—
      (i) two or more automated systems of records or a system of records with nonFederal records for the purpose of—
        (I) establishing or verifying the eligibility of, or continuing compliance with statutory and regulatory requirements by, applicants for, recipients or beneficiaries of, participants in, or providers of services with respect to, cash or inkind assistance or payments under Federal benefit programs, or
        (II) recouping payments or delinquent debts under such Federal benefit programs, or

(ii) two or more automated Federal personnel or payroll systems of records or a system of Federal personnel or payroll records with nonFederal records,

(B) but does not include—

(i) matches performed to produce aggregate statistical data without any personal identifiers;

(ii) matches performed to support any research or statistical project, the specific data of which may not be used to make decisions concerning the rights, benefits, or privileges of specific individuals;

(iii) matches performed, by an agency (or component thereof) which performs as its principal function any activity pertaining to the enforcement of criminal laws, subsequent to the initiation of a specific criminal or civil law enforcement investigation of a named person or persons for the purpose of gathering evidence against such person or persons;

(iv) matches of tax information (I) pursuant to section 6103(d) of the Internal Revenue Code of 1986, (II) for purposes of tax administration as defined in section 6103(b)(4) of such Code, (III) for the purpose of intercepting a tax refund due an individual under authority granted by section 404(e), 464, or 1137 of the Social Security Act; or (IV) for the purpose of intercepting a tax refund due an individual under any other tax refund intercept program authorized by statute which has been determined by the Director of the Office of Management and Budget to contain verification, notice, and hearing requirements that are substantially similar to the procedures in section 1137 of the Social Security Act;

(v) matches—

(I) using records predominantly relating to Federal personnel, that are performed for routine administrative purposes (subject to guidance provided by the Director of the Office of Management and Budget pursuant to subsection (v)); or

(II) conducted by an agency using only records from systems of records maintained by that agency; if the purpose of the match is not to take any adverse financial, personnel, disciplinary, or other adverse action against Federal personnel;

(vi) matches performed for foreign counterintelligence purposes or to produce background checks for security clearances of Federal personnel or Federal contractor personnel; or

(vii) matches performed incident to a levy described in section 6103(k)(8) of the Internal Revenue Code of 1986;

(9) the term "recipient agency" means any agency, or contractor thereof, receiving records contained in a system of records from a source agency for use in a matching program;

(10) the term "non Federal agency" means any State or local government, or agency thereof, which receives records contained in a system of records from a source agency for use in a matching program;

(11) the term "source agency" means any agency which discloses records contained in a system of records to be used in a matching program, or any State or local government, or agency thereof, which discloses records to be used in a matching program;

(12) the term "Federal benefit program" means any program administered or funded by the Federal Government, or by any agent or State on behalf of the Federal Government, providing cash or inkind assistance in the form of payments, grants, loans, or loan guarantees to individuals; and

(13) the term "Federal personnel" means officers and employees of the Government of the United States, members of the uniformed services (including members of the Reserve Components), individuals entitled to receive immediate or deferred retirement benefits under any retirement program of the Government of the United States (including survivor benefits).

(b) Conditions of Disclosure.

No agency shall disclose any record which is contained in a system of records by any means of communication to any person, or to another agency, except pursuant to a written request by, or with the prior written consent of, the individual to whom the record pertains, unless disclosure of the record would be—

(1) to those officers and employees of the agency which maintains the record who have a need for the record in the performance of their duties;

(2) required under section 552 of this title;

(3) for a routine use as defined in subsection (a)(7) of this section and described under subsection (e)(4)(D) of this section;

(4) to the Bureau of the Census for purposes of planning or carrying out a census or survey or related activity pursuant to the provisions of title 13;

(5) to a recipient who has provided the agency with advance adequate written assurance that the record will be used solely as a statistical research or reporting record, and the record is to be transferred in a form that is not individually identifiable;

(6) to the National Archives and Records Administration as a record which has sufficient historical or other value to warrant its continued preservation by the United States Government, or for evaluation by the Archivist of the United States or the designee of the Archivist to determine whether the record has such value;

(7) to another agency or to an instrumentality of any governmental jurisdiction within or under the control of the United States for a civil or criminal law enforcement activity if the activity is authorized by law, and if the head of the agency or instrumentality has made a written request to the agency which maintains the record specifying the particular portion desired and the law enforcement activity for which the record is sought;

(8) to a person pursuant to a showing of compelling circumstances affecting the health or safety of an individual if upon such disclosure notification is transmitted to the last known address of such individual;

(9) to either House of Congress, or, to the extent of matter within its jurisdiction, any committee or subcommittee thereof, any joint committee of Congress or subcommittee of any such joint committee;

(10) to the Comptroller General, or any of his authorized representatives, in the course of the performance of the duties of the Government Accountability Office;

(11) pursuant to the order of a court of competent jurisdiction; or (12) to a consumer reporting agency in accordance with section 3711(e) of title 31.

(c) Accounting of Certain Disclosures.

Each agency, with respect to each system of records under its control, shall—
 (1) except for disclosures made under subsections (b)(1) or (b)(2) of this section, keep an accurate accounting of –
  (A) the date, nature, and purpose of each disclosure of a record to any person or to another agency made under subsection (b) of this section; and
  (B) the name and address of the person or agency to whom the disclosure is made;

(2) retain the accounting made under paragraph (1) of this subsection for at least five years or the life of the record, whichever is longer, after the disclosure for which the accounting is made;

(3) except for disclosures made under subsection (b)(7) of this section, make the accounting made under paragraph (1) of this subsection available to the individual named in the record at his request; and

(4) inform any person or other agency about any correction or notation of dispute made by the agency in accordance with subsection (d) of this section of any record that has been disclosed to the person or agency if an accounting of the disclosure was made.

(d) Access to Records.

Each agency that maintains a system of records shall—
(1) upon request by any individual to gain access to his record or to any information pertaining to him which is contained in the system, permit him and upon his request, a person of his own choosing to accompany him, to review the record and have a copy made of all or any portion thereof in a form comprehensible to him, except that the agency may require the individual to furnish a written statement authorizing discussion of that individual's record in the accompanying person's presence;
(2) permit the individual to request amendment of a record pertaining to him and—
(A) not later than 10 days (excluding Saturdays, Sundays, and legal public holidays) after the date of receipt of such request, acknowledge in writing such receipt; and
(B) promptly, either—
(i) make any correction of any portion thereof which the individual believes is not accurate, relevant, timely, or complete; or
(ii) inform the individual of its refusal to amend the record in accordance with his request, the reason for the refusal, the procedures established by the agency for the individual to request a review of that refusal by the head of the agency or an officer designated by the head of the agency, and the name and business address of that official;
(3) permit the individual who disagrees with the refusal of the agency to amend his record to request a review of such refusal, and not later than 30 days (excluding Saturdays, Sundays, and legal public holidays) from the date on which the individual requests such review, complete such review and make a final determination unless, for good cause shown, the

head of the agency extends such 30day period; and if, after his review, the reviewing official also refuses to amend the record in accordance with the request, permit the individual to file with the agency a concise statement setting forth the reasons for his disagreement with the refusal of the agency, and notify the individual of the provisions for judicial review of the reviewing official's determination under subsection (g)(1)(A) of this section;

(4) in any disclosure, containing information about which the individual has filed a statement of disagreement, occurring after the filing of the statement under paragraph (3) of this subsection, clearly note any portion of the record which is disputed and provide copies of the statement and, if the agency deems it appropriate, copies of a concise statement of the reasons of the agency for not making the amendments requested, to persons or other agencies to whom the disputed record has been disclosed; and

(5) nothing in this section shall allow an individual access to any information compiled in reasonable anticipation of a civil action or proceeding.

(e) Agency Requirements.

Each agency that maintains a system of records shall—

(1) maintain in its records only such information about an individual as is relevant and necessary to accomplish a purpose of the agency required to be accomplished by statute or by executive order of the President;

(2) collect information to the greatest extent practicable directly from the subject individual when the information may result in adverse determinations about an individual's rights, benefits, and privileges under Federal programs;

(3) inform each individual whom it asks to supply information, on the form which it uses to collect the information or on a separate form that can be retained by the individual

(A) the authority (whether granted by statute, or by executive order of the President) which authorizes the solicitation of the information and whether disclosure of such information is mandatory or voluntary;

(B) the principal purpose or purposes for which the information is intended to be used;

(C) the routine uses which may be made of the information, as published pursuant to paragraph (4)(D) of this subsection; and

(D) the effects on him, if any, of not providing all or any part of the requested information;

(4) subject to the provisions of paragraph (11) of this subsection, publish in the Federal Register upon establishment or revision a notice of the existence and character of the system of records, which notice shall include—

(A) the name and location of the system;

(B) the categories of individuals on whom records are maintained in the system;

(C) the categories of records maintained in the system;

(D) each routine use of the records contained in the system, including the categories of users and the purpose of such use;

(E) the policies and practices of the agency regarding storage, retrievability, access controls, retention, and disposal of the records;

(F) the title and business address of the agency official who is responsible for the system of records;

(G) the agency procedures whereby an individual can be notified at his request if the system of records contains a record pertaining to him;

(H) the agency procedures whereby an individual can be notified at his request how he can gain access to any record pertaining to him contained in the system of records, and how he can contest its content; and

(I) the categories of sources of records in the system;

(5) maintain all records which are used by the agency in making any determination about any individual with such accuracy, relevance, timeliness, and completeness as is reasonably necessary to assure fairness to the individual in the determination;

(6) prior to disseminating any record about an individual to any person other than an agency, unless the dissemination is made pursuant to subsection (b)(2) of this section, make reasonable efforts to assure that such records are accurate, complete, timely, and relevant for agency purposes;

(7) maintain no record describing how any individual exercises rights guaranteed by the First Amendment unless expressly authorized by statute or by the individual about whom the record is maintained or unless pertinent to and within the scope of an authorized law enforcement activity;

(8) make reasonable efforts to serve notice on an individual when any record on such individual is made available to any person under compulsory legal process when such process becomes a matter of public record;

(9) establish rules of conduct for persons involved in the design, development, operation, or maintenance of any system of records, or in maintaining any record, and instruct each such person with respect to such rules and the requirements of this section, including any other rules and procedures adopted pursuant to this section and the penalties for noncompliance;

(10) establish appropriate administrative, technical, and physical safeguards to insure the security and confidentiality of records and to protect against any anticipated threats or hazards to their security or integrity which could result in substantial harm, embarrassment, inconvenience, or unfairness to any individual on whom information is maintained;

(11) at least 30 days prior to publication of information under paragraph (4)(D) of this subsection, publish in the Federal Register notice of any new use or intended use of the information in the system, and provide an opportunity for interested persons to submit written data, views, or arguments to the agency; and

(12) if such agency is a recipient agency or a source agency in a matching program with a nonFederal agency, with respect to any establishment or revision of a matching program, at least 30 days prior to conducting such program, publish in the Federal Register notice of such establishment or revision.

(f) Agency Rules.

In order to carry out the provisions of this section, each agency that maintains a system of records shall promulgate rules, in accordance with the requirements (including general notice) of section 553 of this title, which shall –

(1) establish procedures whereby an individual can be notified in response to his request if any system of records named by the individual contains a record pertaining to him;

(2) define reasonable times, places, and requirements for identifying an individual who requests his record or information pertaining to him before the agency shall make the record or information available to the individual;

(3) establish procedures for the disclosure to an individual upon his request of his record or information pertaining to him, including special procedure, if deemed necessary, for the disclosure to an individual of medical records, including psychological records, pertaining to him;

(4) establish procedures for reviewing a request from an individual concerning the amendment of any record or information pertaining to the

individual, for making a determination on the request, for an appeal within the agency of an initial adverse agency determination, and for whatever additional means may be necessary for each individual to be able to exercise fully his rights under this section; and

(5) establish fees to be charged, if any, to any individual for making copies of his record, excluding the cost of any search for and review of the record. The Office of the Federal Register shall biennially compile and publish the rules promulgated under this subsection and agency notices published under subsection (e)(4) of this section in a form available to the public at low cost.

(g) (1) Civil Remedies.

Whenever any agency –

(A) makes a determination under subsection (d)(3) of this section not to amend an individual's record in accordance with his request, or fails to make such review in conformity with that subsection;
(B) refuses to comply with an individual request under subsection (d)(1) of this section;
(C) fails to maintain any record concerning any individual with such accuracy, relevance, timeliness, and completeness as is necessary to assure fairness in any determination relating to the qualifications, character, rights, or opportunities of, or benefits to the individual that may be made on the basis of such record, and consequently a determination is made which is adverse to the individual; or
(D) fails to comply with any other provision of this section, or any rule promulgated thereunder, in such a way as to have an adverse effect on an individual, the individual may bring a civil action against the agency, and the district courts of the United States shall have jurisdiction in the matters under the provisions of this subsection.

(2) (A) In any suit brought under the provisions of subsection (g)(1)(A) of this section, the court may order the agency to amend the individual's record in accordance with his request or in such other way as the court may direct. In such a case the court shall determine the matter de novo.

(B) The court may assess against the United States reasonable attorney fees and other litigation costs reasonably incurred in any case under this paragraph in which the complainant has substantially prevailed.

(3) (A) In any suit brought under the provisions of subsection (g)(1)(B) of this section, the court may enjoin the agency from withholding the

records and order the production to the complainant of any agency records improperly withheld from him. In such a case the court shall determine the matter de novo, and may examine the contents of any agency records in camera to determine whether the records or any portion thereof may be withheld under any of the exemptions set forth in subsection (k) of this section, and the burden is on the agency to sustain its action.

(B) The court may assess against the United States reasonable attorney fees and other litigation costs reasonably incurred in any case under this paragraph in which the complainant has substantially prevailed.

(4) In any suit brought under the provisions of subsection (g)(1)(C) or (D) of this section in which the court determines that the agency acted in a manner which was intentional or willful, the United States shall be liable to the individual in an amount equal to the sum of—

(A) actual damages sustained by the individual as a result of the refusal or failure, but in no case shall a person entitled to recovery receive less than the sum of $1,000; and

(B) the costs of the action together with reasonable attorney fees as determined by the court.

(5) An action to enforce any liability created under this section may be brought in the district court of the United States in the district in which the complainant resides, or has his principal place of business, or in which the agency records are situated, or in the District of Columbia, without regard to the amount in controversy, within two years from the date on which the cause of action arises, except that where an agency has materially and willfully misrepresented any information required under this section to be disclosed to an individual and the information so misrepresented is material to establishment of the liability of the agency to the individual under this section, the action may be brought at any time within two years after discovery by the individual of the misrepresentation. Nothing in this section shall be construed to authorize any civil action by reason of any injury sustained as the result of a disclosure of a record prior to September 27, 1975.

(h) Rights of Legal Guardians.

For the purposes of this section, the parent of any minor, or the legal guardian of any individual who has been declared to be incompetent due to physical or mental incapacity or age by a court of competent jurisdiction, may act on behalf of the individual.

(i) Criminal Penalties.

(1) Any officer or employee of an agency, who by virtue of his employment or official position, has possession of, or access to, agency records which contain individually identifiable information the disclosure of which is prohibited by this section or by rules or regulations established thereunder, and who knowing that disclosure of the specific material is so prohibited, willfully discloses the material in any manner to any person or agency not entitled to receive it, shall be guilty of a misdemeanor and fined not more than $5,000.
(2) Any officer or employee of any agency who willfully maintains a system of records without meeting the notice requirements of subsection (e)(4) of this section shall be guilty of a misdemeanor and fined not more than $5,000.
(3) Any person who knowingly and willfully requests or obtains any record concerning an individual from an agency under false pretenses shall be guilty of a misdemeanor and fined not more than $5,000.

(j) General Exemptions.

The head of any agency may promulgate rules, in accordance with the requirements (including general notice) of sections 553(b)(1), (2), and (3), (c), and (e) of this title, to exempt any system of records within the agency from any part of this section except subsections (b), (c)(1) and (2), (e)(4)(A) through (F), (e)(6), (7), (9), (10), and (11), and (i) if the system of records is—
    (1) maintained by the Central Intelligence Agency; or
    (2) maintained by an agency or component thereof which performs as its principal function any activity pertaining to the enforcement of criminal laws, including police efforts to prevent, control, or reduce crime or to apprehend criminals, and the activities of prosecutors, courts, correctional, probation, pardon, or parole authorities, and which consists of
        (A) information compiled for the purpose of identifying individual criminal offenders and alleged offenders and consisting only of identifying data and notations of arrests, the nature and disposition of criminal charges, sentencing, confinement, release, and parole and probation status; (B) information compiled for the purpose of a criminal investigation, including reports of informants and investigators, and associated with an identifiable individual; or (C) reports identifiable to an individual compiled at any stage of the process of enforcement of the criminal laws from arrest or indictment through

release from supervision. At the time rules are adopted under this subsection, the agency shall include in the statement required under section 553(c) of this title, the reasons why the system of records is to be exempted from a provision of this section.

(k) Specific Exemptions.

The head of any agency may promulgate rules, in accordance with the requirements (including general notice) of sections 553(b)(1), (2), and (3), (c), and (e) of this title, to exempt any system of records within the agency from subsections (c)(3), (d), (e)(1), (e)(4)(G), (H), and (I) and (f) of this section if the system of records is—

(1) subject to the provisions of section 552(b)(1) of this title;

(2) investigatory material compiled for law enforcement purposes, other than material within the scope of subsection (j)(2) of this section: Provided, however, That if any individual is denied any right, privilege, or benefit that he would otherwise be entitled by Federal law, or for which he would otherwise be eligible, as a result of the maintenance of such material, such material shall be provided to such individual, except to the extent that the disclosure of such material would reveal the identity of a source who furnished information to the Government under an express promise that the identity of the source would be held in confidence, or, prior to the effective date of this section, under an implied promise that the identity of the source would be held in confidence;

(3) maintained in connection with providing protective services to the President of the United States or other individuals pursuant to section 3056 of title 18;

(4) required by statute to be maintained and used solely as statistical records;

(5) investigatory material compiled solely for the purpose of determining suitability, eligibility, or qualifications for Federal civilian employment, military service, Federal contracts, or access to classified information, but only to the extent that the disclosure of such material would reveal the identity of a source who furnished information to the Government under an express promise that the identity of the source would be held in confidence, or, prior to the effective date of this section, under an implied promise that the identity of the source would be held in confidence;

(6) testing or examination material used solely to determine individual qualifications for appointment or promotion in the Federal service the disclosure of which would compromise the objectivity or fairness of the testing or examination process; or

(7) evaluation material used to determine potential for promotion in the armed services, but only to the extent that the disclosure of such material would reveal the identity of a source who furnished information to the Government under an express promise that the identity of the source would be held in confidence, or, prior to the effective date of this section, under an implied promise that the identity of the source would be held in confidence. At the time rules are adopted under this subsection, the agency shall include in the statement required under section 553(c) of this title, the reasons why the system of records is to be exempted from a provision of this section.

(l) Archival Records.

(1) Each agency record which is accepted by the Archivist of the United States for storage, processing, and servicing in accordance with section 3103 of title 44 shall, for the purposes of this section, be considered to be maintained by the agency which deposited the record and shall be subject to the provisions of this section. The Archivist of the United States shall not disclose the record except to the agency which maintains the record, or under rules established by that agency which are not inconsistent with the provisions of this section.

(2) Each agency record pertaining to an identifiable individual which was transferred to the National Archives of the United States as a record which has sufficient historical or other value to warrant its continued preservation by the United States Government, prior to the effective date of this section, shall, for the purposes of this section, be considered to be maintained by the National Archives and shall not be subject to the provisions of this section, except that a statement generally describing such records (modeled after the requirements relating to records subject to subsections (e)(4)(A) through (G) of this section) shall be published in the Federal Register.

(3) Each agency record pertaining to an identifiable individual which is transferred to the National Archives of the United States as a record which has sufficient historical or other value to warrant its continued preservation by the United States Government, on or after the effective date of this section, shall, for the purposes of this section, be considered to be maintained by the National Archives and shall be exempt from the requirements of this section except subsections (e)(4)(A) through (G) and (e)(9) of this section.

(m) Government Contractors.

(1) When an agency provides by a contract for the operation by or on behalf of the agency of a system of records to accomplish an agency function, the agency shall, consistent with its authority, cause the requirements of this section to be applied to such system. For purposes of subsection (i) of this section any such contractor and any employee of such contractor, if such contract is agreed to on or after the effective date of this section, shall be considered to be an employee of an agency.

(2) A consumer reporting agency to which a record is disclosed under section 3711(e) of title 31 shall not be considered a contractor for the purposes of this section.

(n) Mailing Lists.

An individual's name and address may not be sold or rented by an agency unless such action is specifically authorized by law. This provision shall not be construed to require the withholding of names and addresses otherwise permitted to be made public.

(o) Matching Agreements.

(1) No record which is contained in a system of records may be disclosed to a recipient agency or non Federal agency for use in a computer matching program except pursuant to a written agreement between the source agency and the recipient agency or nonFederal agency specifying—
    (A) the purpose and legal authority for conducting the program;
    (B) the justification for the program and the anticipated results, including a specific estimate of any savings;
    (C) a description of the records that will be matched, including each data element that will be used, the approximate number of records that will be matched, and the projected starting and completion dates of the matching program;
    (D) procedures for providing individualized notice at the time of application, and notice periodically thereafter as directed by the Data Integrity Board of such agency (subject to guidance provided by the Director of the Office of Management and Budget pursuant to subsection (v)), to—
        (i) applicants for and recipients of financial assistance or payments under Federal benefit programs, and

(ii) applicants for and holders of positions as Federal personnel, that any information provided by such applicants, recipients, holders, and individuals may be subject to verification through matching programs;

(E) procedures for verifying information produced in such matching program as required by subsection (p);

(F) procedures for the retention and timely destruction of identifiable records created by a recipient agency or nonFederal agency in such matching program;

(G) procedures for ensuring the administrative, technical, and physical security of the records matched and the results of such programs;

(H) prohibitions on duplication and redisclosure of records provided by the source agency within or outside the recipient agency or the nonFederal agency, except where required by law or essential to the conduct of the matching program;

(I) procedures governing the use by a recipient agency or nonFederal agency of records provided in a matching program by a source agency, including procedures governing return of the records to the source agency or destruction of records used in such program;

(J) information on assessments that have been made on the accuracy of the records that will be used in such matching program; and

(K) that the Comptroller General may have access to all records of a recipient agency or a nonFederal agency that the Comptroller General deems necessary in order to monitor or verify compliance with the agreement.

(2) (A) A copy of each agreement entered into pursuant to paragraph (1) shall—

(i) be transmitted to the Committee on Governmental Affairs of the Senate and the Committee on Government Operations of the House of Representatives; and

(ii) be available upon request to the public.

(B) No such agreement shall be effective until 30 days after the date on which such a copy is transmitted pursuant to subparagraph (A)(i).

(C) Such an agreement shall remain in effect only for such period, not to exceed 18 months, as the Data Integrity Board of the agency determines is appropriate in light of the purposes, and length of time necessary for the conduct, of the matching program.

(D) Within 3 months prior to the expiration of such an agreement pursuant to subparagraph (C), the Data Integrity Board of the agency may, without additional review, renew the matching agreement for a

current, ongoing matching program for not more than one additional year if—
(i) such program will be conducted without any change; and
(ii) each party to the agreement certifies to the Board in writing that the program has been conducted in compliance with the agreement.

(p) Verification and Opportunity to Contest Findings.

(1) In order to protect any individual whose records are used in a matching program, no recipient agency, nonFederal agency, or source agency may suspend, terminate, reduce, or make a final denial of any financial assistance or payment under a Federal benefit program to such individual, or take other adverse action against such individual, as a result of information produced by such matching program, until—
    (A) (i) the agency has independently verified the information; or
        (ii) the Data Integrity Board of the agency, or in the case of a nonFederal agency the Data Integrity Board of the source agency, determines in accordance with guidance issued by the Director of the Office of Management and Budget that—
            (I) the information is limited to identification and amount of benefits paid by the source agency under a Federal benefit program; and
            (II) there is a high degree of confidence that the information provided to the recipient agency is accurate;
    (B) the individual receives a notice from the agency containing a statement of its findings and informing the individual of the opportunity to contest such findings; and
    (C) (i) the expiration of any time period established for the program by statute or regulation for the individual to respond to that notice; or
        (ii) in the case of a program for which no such period is established, the end of the 30day period beginning on the date on which notice under subparagraph (B) is mailed or otherwise provided to the individual.

(2) Independent verification referred to in paragraph (1) requires investigation and confirmation of specific information relating to an individual that is used as a basis for an adverse action against the individual, including where applicable investigation and confirmation of—
    (A) the amount of any asset or income involved;
    (B) whether such individual actually has or had access to such asset

or income for such individual's own use; and

(C) the period or periods when the individual actually had such asset or income.

(3) Notwithstanding paragraph (1), an agency may take any appropriate action otherwise prohibited by such paragraph if the agency determines that the public health or public safety may be adversely affected or significantly threatened during any notice period required by such paragraph.

(q) Sanctions.

(1) Notwithstanding any other provision of law, no source agency may disclose any record which is contained in a system of records to a recipient agency or nonFederal agency for a matching program if such source agency has reason to believe that the requirements of subsection (p), or any matching agreement entered into pursuant to subsection (o), or both, are not being met by such recipient agency.

(2) No source agency may renew a matching agreement unless—

(A) the recipient agency or non-Federal agency has certified that it has complied with the provisions of that agreement; and

(B) the source agency has no reason to believe that the certification is inaccurate.

(r) Report on New Systems and Matching Programs.

Each agency that proposes to establish or make a significant change in a system of records or a matching program shall provide adequate advance notice of any such proposal (in duplicate) to the Committee on Government Operations of the House of Representatives, the Committee on Governmental Affairs of the Senate, and the Office of Management and Budget in order to permit an evaluation of the probable or potential effect of such proposal on the privacy or other rights of individuals.

(s) Biennial Report.

The President shall biennially submit to the Speaker of the House of Representatives and the President pro tempore of the Senate a report—

(1) describing the actions of the Director of the Office of Management and Budget pursuant to section 6 of the Privacy Act of 1974 during the preceding 2 years;

(2) describing the exercise of individual rights of access and amendment under this section during such years;

(3) identifying changes in or additions to systems of records;

(4) containing such other information concerning administration of this section as may be necessary or useful to the Congress in reviewing the effectiveness of this section in carrying out the purposes of the Privacy Act of 1974.

(t) Effect of Other Laws.

(1) No agency shall rely on any exemption contained in section 552 of this title to withhold from an individual any record which is otherwise accessible to such individual under the provisions of this section.

(2) No agency shall rely on any exemption in this section to withhold from an individual any record which is otherwise accessible to such individual under the provisions of section 552 of this title.

(u) Data Integrity Boards.

(1) Every agency conducting or participating in a matching program shall establish a Data Integrity Board to oversee and coordinate among the various components of such agency the agency's implementation of this section.

(2) Each Data Integrity Board shall consist of senior officials designated by the head of the agency, and shall include any senior official designated by the head of the agency as responsible for implementation of this section, and the inspector general of the agency, if any. The inspector general shall not serve as chairman of the Data Integrity Board.

(3) Each Data Integrity Board—

(A) shall review, approve, and maintain all written agreements for receipt or disclosure of agency records for matching programs to ensure compliance with subsection (o), and all relevant statutes, regulations, and guidelines;

(B) shall review all matching programs in which the agency has participated during the year, either as a source agency or recipient agency, determine compliance with applicable laws, regulations, guidelines, and agency agreements, and assess the costs and benefits of such programs;

(C) shall review all recurring matching programs in which the agency has participated during the year, either as a source agency or recipient agency, for continued justification for such disclosures;

(D) shall compile an annual report, which shall be submitted to the head of the agency and the Office of Management and Budget and made available to the public on request, describing the matching activities of the agency, including—

> (i) matching programs in which the agency has participated as a source agency or recipient agency;
>
> (ii) matching agreements proposed under subsection (o) that were disapproved by the Board;
>
> (iii) any changes in membership or structure of the Board in the preceding year;
>
> (iv) the reasons for any waiver of the requirement in paragraph (4) of this section for completion and submission of a costbenefit analysis prior to the approval of a matching program;
>
> (v) any violations of matching agreements that have been alleged or identified and any corrective action taken; and
>
> (vi) any other information required by the Director of the Office of Management and Budget to be included in such report;

(E) shall serve as a clearinghouse for receiving and providing information on the

accuracy, completeness, and reliability of records used in matching programs;

(F) shall provide interpretation and guidance to agency components and personnel on the requirements of this section for matching programs;

(G) shall review agency recordkeeping and disposal policies and practices for matching programs to assure compliance with this section; and

(H) may review and report on any agency matching activities that are not matching programs.

(4) (A) Except as provided in subparagraphs (B) and (C), a Data Integrity Board shall not approve any written agreement for a matching program unless the agency has completed and submitted to such Board a costbenefit analysis of the proposed program and such analysis demonstrates that the program is likely to be cost effective.

(B) The Board may waive the requirements of subparagraph (A) of this paragraph if it determines in writing, in accordance with guidelines prescribed by the Director of the Office of Management and Budget, that a costbenefit analysis is not required.

(C) A costbenefit analysis shall not be required under subparagraph (A) prior to the initial approval of a written agreement for a matching program that is specifically required by statute. Any subsequent written agreement for such a program shall not be approved by the Data Integrity Board unless the agency has submitted a costbenefit analysis of the program as conducted under the preceding approval of such agreement.

(5) (A) If a matching agreement is disapproved by a Data Integrity Board, any party to such agreement may appeal the disapproval to the Director of the Office of Management and Budget. Timely notice of the filing of such an appeal shall be provided by the Director of the Office of Management and Budget to the Committee on Governmental Affairs of the Senate and the Committee on Government Operations of the House of Representatives.

(B) The Director of the Office of Management and Budget may approve a matching agreement notwithstanding the disapproval of a Data Integrity Board if the Director determines that—

(i) the matching program will be consistent with all applicable legal, regulatory, and policy requirements;

(ii) there is adequate evidence that the matching agreement will be costeffective; and

(iii) the matching program is in the public interest.

(C) The decision of the Director to approve a matching agreement shall not take effect until 30 days after it is reported to committees described in subparagraph (A).

(D) If the Data Integrity Board and the Director of the Office of Management and Budget disapprove a matching program proposed by the inspector general of an agency, the inspector general may report the disapproval to the head of the agency and to the Congress.

(6) In the reports required by paragraph (3)(D), agency matching activities that are not matching programs may be reported on an aggregate basis, if and to the extent necessary to protect ongoing law enforcement or counterintelligence investigations.

(v) **Office of Management and Budget Responsibilities.**

The Director of the Office of Management and Budget shall—

(1) develop and, after notice and opportunity for public comment, prescribe guidelines and regulations for the use of agencies in implementing the provisions of this section; and

(2) provide continuing assistance to and oversight of the implementation of this section by agencies.

(Added Pub. L. No. 93579, Sec. 3, Dec. 31, 1974, 88 Stat. 1897; amended Pub. L. No. 94183, Sec. 2(2), Dec. 31, 1975, 89 Stat. 1057; Pub. L. No. 97365, Sec. 2, Oct. 25, 1982, 96 Stat. 1749; Pub. L. No. 97375, title II, Sec. 201(a), (b), Dec. 21, 1982, 96 Stat. 1821; Pub. L. No. 97452, Sec. 2(a)(1), Jan. 12, 1983, 96 Stat. 2478; Pub. L. No. 98477, Sec. 2(c), Oct. 15, 1984, 98 Stat. 2211; Pub. L. No. 98497, title I, Sec. 107(g), Oct. 19, 1984, 98 Stat. 2292; Pub. L. No. 100503, Sec. 26(a), 7, 8, Oct. 18, 1988, 102 Stat. 2507-2514; Pub. L. No. 101508, title VII, Sec. 7201(b)(1), Nov. 5, 1990, 104 Stat. 1388334; Pub. L. No. 10366, title XIII, Sec. 13581(c), Aug. 10, 1993, 107 Stat. 611; Pub. L. No. 104193, title I, Sec. 110(w), Aug. 22, 1996, 110 Stat. 2175; Pub. L. No. 104226, Sec. 1(b)(3), Oct. 2, 1996, 110 Stat. 3033; Pub. L. No. 104316, title I, Sec. 115(g)(2)(B), Oct. 19, 1996, 110 Stat. 3835; Pub. L. No. 10534, title X, Sec. 1026(b)(2), Aug. 5, 1997, 111 Stat. 925; Pub. L. No. 105362, title XIII, Sec. 1301(d), Nov. 10, 1998, 112 Stat. 3293; July 7, 2004, Pub. L. No. No. 108-271, 118 Stat. 814.)

Regulatory Flexibility Act

Citations:

5 U.S.C. §§601-612 (2000 and Supp. IV 2004); enacted September 19, 1980 by Pub. L. No. 96-354, 94 Stat. 1,164-1,170; amended by Pub. L. No. 104-121, Title II, §§241-245, March 29, 1996, 110 Stat. 864.

Lead Agency:

U.S. Small Business Administration, Office of Advocacy, 409 3rd Street SW, Washington, DC 20416, (202) 205-6533. http://www.sba.gov/advo.

Overview:

Requirements. The Regulatory Flexibility Act requires agencies to consider the special needs and concerns of small entities whenever they engage in rulemaking subject to the notice-and-comment requirements of the APA or other laws. In 1996, the Act's coverage was expanded to include interpretive rules promulgated by the Internal Revenue Service (IRS) that contain small entity information collection requirements. Each time an agency publishes a proposed rule (or IRS interpretive rule) in the Federal Register, it must prepare and publish a regulatory flexibility analysis (RFA) describing the impact of the proposed rule on small entities (including small businesses, organizations, and governmental jurisdictions), unless the agency head certifies that the proposed rule will not "have a significant economic impact on a substantial number of small entities."

The initial RFA, like the proposed rule itself, is subject to public comment, and the agency is encouraged to facilitate participation by small entities by providing actual notice of the proceeding to affected small entities, holding conferences and public hearings on the proposed rule as it affects small entities, and transmitting copies of its initial RFA to the Chief Counsel for Advocacy of the Small Business Administration.

Additional procedures are required to ensure small entities comment whenever either the Environmental Protection Agency (EPA) or the Occupational Health and Safety Administration (OSHA) promulgate rules. Prior to the publication of the initial RFA, EPA or OSHA must notify and provide the Chief Counsel with information regarding the potential impact of the proposed rule on small entities. The Chief Counsel then identifies individuals to represent small entities and gather comments and suggestions on the proposed rule. EPA or OSHA must also convene a regulatory review panel, consisting of employees from that agency, the Office of Management and Budget, and the Chief Counsel, to report on the agency's information and small entity representatives' comments and recommendations. This information becomes part of the rulemaking record, which can provide a basis for the agency to amend its initial proposed rule or RFA. The final rule adopted by any agency must be published with a final RFA that summarizes and responds to significant issues raised by the comments received.

The Act does not mandate any particular outcome in rulemaking; it encourages, but does not require, the "tiering" of government regulations through a number of techniques designed to make them less burdensome to small entities. An agency's initial RFA must identify any "significant alternatives" to the proposed regulation that might achieve its goals while minimizing the impact on small entities. Approaches suggested in the statute include modifying compliance or reporting timetables, simplifying compliance or reporting requirements, using performance rather than design standards, and exempting small entities from certain requirements. The final RFA must explain why any such significant alternatives to the rule were not adopted and the steps taken by the agency to minimize the affects of the rule on small entities.

Agencies must publish semiannual regulatory agendas identifying upcoming and current rulemaking proposals that may affect small entities. In addition, the Act directs agencies to apply regulatory flexibility analysis to their *existing* rules, initially evaluating them over a 10-year period and reviewing them periodically.

In 2002, President Bush signed Executive Order 13,272, titled "Proper Consideration of Small Entities in Agency Rulemaking." For the most part the Order simply restates the requirements of the Regulatory Flexibility Act, but the Order gives prominence to the role of the Chief Counsel for Advocacy of the Small Business Administration and specifically requires an agency to provide the Chief Counsel with a draft of any proposed rule that may have a significant economic impact on a substantial number of small entities at the same time the agency provides it to the Office of Information and Regulatory Affairs (OIRA) under E.O. 12,866 or, if the draft is not required to be sent to

OIRA, at a reasonable time prior to publication of the proposed rule. The Chief Counsel not only advises agencies as to his views on proposed rules, he also has from time-to-time participated in litigation as an amicus curiae is support of challenges to agency rules.

Coverage. The Act's limitations are important. It does not apply to the vast amount of administrative activity that is not rulemaking, from adjudication to the large variety of informal actions. Except for the limited set of IRS interpretive rules, the Act also does not reach rulemaking that is not subject to notice-and-comment, such as interpretive rules and other rules exempt from notice and comment by the provisions of section 553 of the APA.

Judicial Review. As originally enacted, the Act expressly prohibited judicial review of agency compliance with any of its requirements. Echoing the statutory language, most courts limited review to a determination under the APA of the reasonableness of a final rule based on the record before the agency, which included the regulatory flexibility analysis and any comments from small entities expressing the hardships associated with a proposed rule. *See, e.g., State of Michigan v. Thomas*, 805 F.2d 176 (6th Cir. 1986); *Thompson v. Clark*, 741 F.2d 401 (D.C. Cir. 1984).

In 1996, after noting that agencies were too often ignoring the requirements of the Act, Congress amended the Act to provide judicial review to small entities adversely affected or aggrieved by a final agency action. The amended Act permits review of agency compliance with certain sections of the Act and, without limiting the possibilities for relief, specifies the possibility of remanding the rule to the agency or deferring enforcement against the entity.

Courts are instructed to conduct their review in accordance with Chapter 7 of the APA. Accordingly, several courts have held that the standard of review for a final agency action is one of reasonableness, meaning that the agency must have made a reasonable, good-faith effort to carry out the requirements of the statute. *Associated Fisheries of Maine, Inc. v. Daley*, 127 F.3d 104, 114 (1st Cir. 1997); *see also Southern Offshore Fishing Association v. Daley*, 995 F. Supp. 1411 (M.D. Fla. 1998). Under the reasonableness standard, an agency need only consider significant alternatives to a rule, rather than all alternatives, when doing a final RFA. *Associated Fisheries*, 127 F.3d at 116. Similarly, an agency must make a reasonable effort to facilitate participation by small entities, but the method and manner of accomplishing this was left to agency discretion, since the Act only offered suggestions. *Id.* at 117. *Southern Offshore* applied the reasonableness standard and concluded that the agency's certification of no significant economic impact on a substantial number of small entities was unsatisfactory because the evidence contradicted many of the assumptions upon which the certification was based. *Southern Offshore*, 995 F. Supp. at 1436.

Several cases have involved challenges to the adequacy of an agency certification of no significant impact or final RFA by claiming that the agency failed to consider the effects of the proposed rule on a particular entity. The first case, *Mid-Tex Electric Cooperative, Inc. v. FERC*, 773 F.2d 327 (D.C. Cir. 1985), determined that the certification was appropriate because the agency need only consider the rule's direct impact on regulated entities and not the indirect impacts of the rule on entities not regulated by the agency. More recent cases have affirmed *Mid-Tex's* holding. *See, e.g., Cement Kiln Recycling Coalition v. E.P.A.*, 255 F.3d 855 (D.C. Cir. 2001); *Motor & Equipment Manufacturers Ass'n v. Nichols*, 142 F.3d 449, 467 (D.C. Cir. 1998); *United Distribution Cos. v. FERC*, 88 F.3d 1105, 1170 (D.C. Cir. 1996); *State of Colo. ex rel. Colorado State Banking Bd. v. Resolution Trust*, 926 F.2d 931 (10th Cir. 1991). *But see Federal Aeronautical Repair Station Ass'n, Inc. v. FAA*, 494 F.3d 161 (D.C. Cir. 2007).

In addition, when determining whether an impacted entity is a "small entity," the agency is required to use the definitions found in the Act, the references made therefrom to the Small Business Act, 15 U.S.C. §632, and definitions promulgated by the Small Business Association, 13 C.F.R. §121.201. *Northwestern Mining Ass'n v. Babbitt*, 5 F. Supp. 2d 9 (D.D.C. 1998).

Legislative History:

95th Congress.[1] The Act was introduced originally as S.1974 by Senators Culver and Nelson. Hearings on S.1974 as amended were held on October 7, 1977 and August 23, 1978 before the Senate Subcommittee on Administrative Practice and Procedure, which unanimously reported S. 1974 to the Judiciary Committee on September 9, 1978. The Senate passed the bill on October 14, 1978. In the House of Representatives, H.R. 11376, the companion bill to S. 1974, was introduced on March 8, 1978 by Representatives Kastenmeier and Baldus, but no further action was taken.

96th Congress.[2] On January 31, 1979, Senator Culver reintroduced his original bill as S. 299. Three similar bills were introduced in the House of Representatives: H.R. 1971 (companion bill to S. 299, on February 8, 1979), H.R. 1745 (a similar bill, but cast as an amendment to the Small Business

---

[1] Derived from Verkuil, *A Critical Guide to the Regulatory Flexibility Act*, 1982 DUKE L.J. 213, 227-29.

[2] *Id.* at 227-29.

Act, on January 31, 1979) and H.R. 4660 (an expansion of H.R. 1745, on June 28). The last bill became the principal bill in the House.

After extensive hearings, the Senate bill, S. 299, passed the Senate on August 6, 1980 in the form of a substitute, imprinted amendment intended to recodify the bill from 5 U.S.C. §§551, 552 to a new chapter within title 5 (sections 601-612). (*See* the Senate "Description of Major Issues" accompanying the amendment at 126 Cong. Rec. S10,934-43 (daily ed. Aug. 6, 1980)).

On September 8, 1980 the House of Representatives passed the Senate-passed version of S. 299 without amendment. The House held no separate hearings on the Senate bill; rather it simply adopted the Senate's "Description of Major Issues" and section-by-section analysis. The House did offer its own three-page "Discussion of the Issues" (126 Cong. Rec. H 8468-70 (daily ed. Sept. 8, 1980)).

President Carter signed the bill into law on September 19, 1980.

103rd Congress. Although Congress repeatedly held hearings on the Regulatory Flexibility Act and the effects of regulation on small entities, no amendments were proposed until the 103rd Congress. (*See Oversight of Regulatory Flexibility Act (Part 1): Hearings before the Subcommittee on Export Opportunities and Special Small Business Problems of the House Small Business Committee*, 97th Cong., 1st Sess. (1981).) Representative Ewing introduced the Regulatory Flexibility Act Amendments of 1993 as H.R. 830. Although H.R. 830 had over 250 cosponsors, the bill never progressed beyond the House Subcommittee on Administrative Law and Governmental Relations. The Senate passed a similar bill as an amendment to S. 4 which was considered in the House, H.R. 820, but this too failed to pass.

104th Congress. The Small Business Regulatory Enforcement Fairness Act of 1996 was originally introduced on June 16, 1995 by Senator Bond as S. 942 (141 Cong. Rec. 8560). It was referred to the Committee on Small Business, and hearings were held on February 28, 1996 (S. Hrg. 104-443). The Senate passed S. 942, as amended, on March 19, 1996. Three days later, the House began considering the measure as part of H.R. 3136. The bill was referred to the House Committees on Ways and Means, Budget, Rules, the Judiciary, Small Business, and Government Reform and Oversight for consideration. On March 27, the House Rules Committee reported up a resolution, H.R. Res. 391, which provided for the consideration of H.R. 3136 (H.R. Rep. No. 104-500). The next day, both the resolution and the bill passed the House, and the bill was read and passed without amendment by the Senate. President Clinton signed the bill into law on March 29, 1996.

Source Note:

One of the most extensive discussions of the Act's provisions is Paul Verkuil's 1982 *A Critical Guide to the Regulatory Flexibility Act*. Although it is somewhat dated and does not include a discussion of the 1996 Amendments, the Guide may still be useful in some regard since the Amendments changed very little of the previous substantive requirements of the Act. The annual reports issued by the Small Business Administration's Office of Advocacy contain a wealth of information on agency implementation of the Act, as well as on the Act's strengths and weaknesses as identified by that Office. These reports, along with a host of other Regulatory Flexibility Act documents, can be found at the Chief Counsel for Advocacy's Small Business Law Library website: http://www.sba.gov/advo/laws/law_lib.html#ex.

Bibliography:

I. Legislative History

1. *President's Statement on Senate Approval of S 299*, 16 Weekly Comp. Pres. Doc. 1,508 (Aug. 6, 1980).
2. *The Regulatory Flexibility Act: Hearings on S.1974 before the Subcomm. on Administrative Practices and Procedures of the Senate Comm. on the Judiciary*, 95th Cong., 1st Sess. (1977).
3. *The Regulatory Flexibility Act: Joint Hearings on S.1974 and S.3330 before the Subcomm. on Administrative Practice and Procedure, Senate Comm. on the Judiciary and Senate Select Comm. on Small Business*, 95th Cong., 2d Sess. (1978).
4. *Regulatory Reform: Hearings on S.104, S.262, S.299, S.755 and S.1291 before the Subcomm. on Administrative Practice and Procedure of the Senate Comm. on the Judiciary*, 96th Cong., 1st Sess. (1979).
5. *Report to Accompany H.R. 4660*, H. Rep. No. 519, 96th Cong., 1st Sess. (1979).
6. *Report to Accompany S.1974*, S. Rep. No. 1322, 95th Cong., 2d Sess. (1978).
7. *Report to Accompany S.299*, S. Rep. No. 878, 96th Cong., 2d Sess. (1980), *reprinted in* 1980 U.S. Code Cong. & Ad. News 2788.
8. *S.917 and S.942: Implementing the White House Conference on Small Business–Recommendations on Regulations and Paperwork: Hearings before the Senate Small Business Committee*, 104th Cong., 2d Sess. (1996).
9. *Providing for the Consideration of H.R. 3136, The Contract with America Advancement Act of 1996*, H.R. Rep. No. 500, 104th Cong., 2d Sess. (1996).

II. Other Government Documents

1. Food and Drug Administration, U.S. Dept. of Health and Human Services, *Flexible Regulatory Alternatives: A Guide for FDA Managers, Regulation Writers and Developers* (1981).
2. Government Accountability Office, *Regulatory Flexibility Act: Congress Should Revisit and Clarify Elements of the Act to Improve Its Effectiveness,* GAO-06-998T (July 20, 2006).
3. Office of Advocacy, U.S. Small Business Administration, *Annual Report of the Chief Counsel for Advocacy on Implementation of the Regulatory Flexibility Act* (1995-Present).
4. Office of Advocacy, U.S. Small Business Administration, *A Guide for Government Agencies: How to Comply with the Regulatory Flexibility Act* (May 2003).
5. Office of Advocacy, U.S. Small Business Administration, *Agency Compliance with Executive Order 13272: A Report to the Office of Management and Budget* (Sept. 2003).
6. *Reducing the Regulatory Burden on Small Business: Improving The Regulatory Flexibility Act, Hearing before the Committee on Small Business,* House of Representatives, 110th Cong., 1st Sess. (2007).
7. *Regulatory Flexibility Act: Joint Oversight Hearing on the Operation of the Act and on S.2170 before the Subcomm. on Regulatory Reform, Senate Comm. on the Judiciary and Subcomm. on Government Regulation and Paperwork, Senate Comm. on Small Business,* 97th Cong. 2d Sess. (1982).
8. *Regulatory Reform Initiatives: Hearings before the Senate Committee on Governmental Affairs,* 100th Cong., 2d Sess. (1988).
9. *The Regulatory Flexibility Act: Are Federal Agencies Using "Good Science" in Their Rule Making?: Joint Hearing before the Subcommittee on Government Programs and Oversight, Subcommittee on Regulation Reform and Paperwork Reduction of the Committee on Small Business,* House of Representatives, 105th Cong., 1st Sess. (1997).
10. U.S. Environmental Protection Agency, *EPA Guidelines for Implementing the Regulatory Flexibility Act* (Office of Policy, Planning and Evaluation, Apr. 1992).
11. U.S. General Accounting Office, *Regulatory Flexibility Act: Inherent Weaknesses May Limit Its Usefulness for Small Governments,* GAO/HRD-91-16 (Jan. 1991).
12. U.S. General Accounting Office, *Regulatory Flexibility Act: Key Terms Still Need to Be Clarified,* GAO-01-669T (April 24, 2001).
13. U.S. General Accounting Office, *Regulatory Flexibility Act: Status of Agencies' Compliance: Report to Congress* (March 1995).

14. U.S. General Accounting Office, *Regulatory Flexibility Act: Agencies' Use of the November 1996 Unified Agenda Did Not Satisfy Notification Requirements* (1997).

15. U.S. General Accounting Office, *Regulatory Flexibility Act: Agencies' Interpretations of Review Requirements Vary* (1999).

16. U.S. General Accounting Office, *Regulatory Flexibility Act: Implementation in EPA Programs Office and Proposed Lead Rule* (2000).

17. U.S. Regulatory Council, *Tiering Regulations: A Practical Guide* (March 1981).

18. U.S. Regulatory Council, *Tiering: A Practical Guide to the Use of Tiering as a Regulatory Alternative* (Project on Alternative Regulatory Approaches, Sept. 1981).

III. Books and Articles

1. Freedman, Singer, and Swain, *The Regulatory Flexibility Act: Orienting Federal Regulation Toward Small Business,* 93 Dick. L. Rev. 439 (1989).

2. Keith Holman, *The Regulatory Flexibility Act at 25: Is the Law Achieving its Goal?*, 33 Fordham Urb. L.J. 1119 (2006).

3. Jennifer McCoid, *EPA Rulemaking Under the Regulatory Flexibility Act: The Need for Reform,* 23 B.C. Envtl. Aff. L. Rev. 203 (1995).

4. Richard J. Pierce, Jr., *Small Is Not Beautiful: The Case Against Special Regulatory Treatment of Small Firms,* 50 Admin. L. Rev. 537 (1998).

5. Barry A. Pineles, *The Small Business Regulatory Enforcement Fairness Act: New Options in Regulatory Relief,* 5 Commlaw Conspectus 29 (1997).

6 Thomas O. Sargentich, *The Small Business Regulatory Enforcement Fairness Act,* 49 Admin. L. Rev. 123 (1997).

7. Michael See, *Willful Blindness: Federal Agencies' Failure to Comply with the Regulatory Flexibility Act's Periodic Review Requirement—and Current Proposals to Invigorate the Act,* 33 Fordham Urb. L.J. 1199 (2006).

8. Paul Verkuil, *A Critical Guide to the Regulatory Flexibility Act,* Report to the Administrative Conference of the U.S., 1981 ACUS 203, *reprinted in* 1982 Duke L.J. 213.

Appendix:

1. Regulatory Flexibility Act, 5 U.S.C. §§601-12 (2000 and Supp. IV 2004).

Note: for Executive Order 13,272, Proper Consideration of Small Entities in Agency Rulemaking, 67 Fed. Reg. 53,461 (Aug. 13, 2002), see Chapter 4 of this *Sourcebook*.

Regulatory Flexibility Act

Title 5, U.S. Code

§601. Definitions

For purposes of this chapter—
 (1) the term "agency" means an agency as defined in section 551(1) of this title;
 (2) the term "rule" means any rule for which the agency publishes a general notice of proposed rulemaking pursuant to section 553(b) of this title, or any other law, including any rule of general applicability governing Federal grants to State and local governments for which the agency provides an opportunity for notice and public comment, except that the term "rule" does not include a rule of particular applicability relating to rates, wages, corporate or financial structures or reorganizations thereof, prices, facilities, appliances, services, or allowances therefor or to valuations, costs or accounting, or practices relating to such rates, wages, structures, prices, appliances, services, or allowances;
 (3) the term "small business" has the same meaning as the term "small business concern" under section 3 of the Small Business Act, unless an agency, after consultation with the Office of Advocacy of the Small Business Administration and after opportunity for public comment, establishes one or more definitions of such term which are appropriate to the activities of the agency and publishes such definition(s) in the Federal Register;
 (4) the term "small organization" means any not-for-profit enterprise which is independently owned and operated and is not dominant in its field, unless an agency establishes, after opportunity for public comment, one or more definitions of such term which are appropriate to the activities of the agency and publishes such definition(s) in the Federal Register;
 (5) the term "small governmental jurisdiction" means governments of cities, counties, towns, townships, villages, school districts, or special districts, with a population of less than fifty thousand, unless an agency establishes, after opportunity for public comment, one or more definitions of such term which are appropriate to the activities of the agency and which are based on such factors as location in rural or sparsely populated areas or limited revenues due to the population of such jurisdiction, and publishes such definition(s) in the Federal Register;

(6) the term "small entity" shall have the same meaning as the terms "small business", "small organization" and "small governmental jurisdiction" defined in paragraphs (3), (4) and (5) of this section; and

(7) the term "collection of information" –

(A) means the obtaining, causing to be obtained, soliciting, or requiring the disclosure to third parties or the public, of facts or opinions by or for an agency, regardless of form or format, calling for either –

(i) answers to identical questions posed to, or identical reporting or recordkeeping requirements imposed on, 10 or more persons, other than agencies, instrumentalities, or employees of the United States; or

(ii) answers to questions posed to agencies, instrumentalities, or employees of the United States which are to be used for general statistical purposes; and

(B) shall not include a collection of information described under section 3518(c)(1) of title 44, United States Code.

(8) Recordkeeping requirement.—The term "recordkeeping requirement" means a requirement imposed by an agency on persons to maintain specified records.

(Added Pub. L. No. 96-354, § 3(a), Sept. 19, 1980, 94 Stat. 1165; as amended Pub. L. No. 104-121, Title II, § 241(a)(2), March 29, 1996, 110 Stat. 864.)

Note

Pub. L. No. 104-121, Title II, §§ 201 to 224, March 29, 1996, 110 Stat. 857-862, as amended by Pub. L. No. 110-28, Title VIII, § 8302, May 25, 2007, 121 Stat. 204, provides that:

Sec. 201. Short title.

This title [enacting sections 801 to 808 of this title and section 657 of Title 15, Commerce and Trade, amending sections 504, 601, 603 to 605, 609, 611, and 612 of this title, section 648 of Title 15, and section 2412 of Title 28, Judiciary and Judicial Procedure, enacting provisions set out as notes under this section and sections 504 and 609 of this title, and amending provisions set out as a note under section 631 of Title 15] may be cited as the "Small Business Regulatory Enforcement Fairness Act of 1996".

Sec. 202. Findings.

Congress finds that—
(1) a vibrant and growing small business sector is critical to creating jobs in a dynamic economy;
(2) small businesses bear a disproportionate share of regulatory costs and burdens;
(3) fundamental changes that are needed in the regulatory and enforcement culture of Federal agencies to make agencies more responsive to small business can be made without compromising the statutory missions of the agencies;
(4) three of the top recommendations of the 1995 White House Conference on Small Business involve reforms to the way government regulations are developed and enforced, and reductions in government paperwork requirements;
(5) the requirements of chapter 6 of title 5, United States Code [this chapter], have too often been ignored by government agencies, resulting in greater regulatory burdens on small entities than necessitated by statute; and
(6) small entities should be given the opportunity to seek judicial review of agency actions required by chapter 6 of title 5, United States Code [this chapter].

Sec. 203. Purposes.

The purposes of this title [Title II of Pub. L. No.104-121] are—
(1) to implement certain recommendations of the 1995 White House Conference on Small Business regarding the development and enforcement of Federal regulations;
(2) to provide for judicial review of chapter 6 of title 5, United States Code [this chapter];
(3) to encourage the effective participation of small businesses in the Federal regulatory process;
(4) to simplify the language of Federal regulations affecting small businesses;
(5) to develop more accessible sources of information on regulatory and reporting requirements for small businesses;
(6) to create a more cooperative regulatory environment among agencies and small businesses that is less punitive and more solution-oriented; and
(7) to make Federal regulators more accountable for their enforcement

actions by providing small entities with a meaningful opportunity for redress of excessive enforcement activities.

Subtitle A—Regulatory Compliance Simplification

Sec. 211. Definitions

For purposes of this subtitle [Pub. L. No. 104-121, §§211 to 216, which enacted subtitle A of this note and amended section 648 of Title 15]—
    (1) the terms "rule" and "small entity" have the same meanings as in section 601 of title 5, United States Code [this section];
    (2) the term "agency" has the same meaning as in section 551 of title 5, United States Code [section 551 of this title]; and
    (3) the term "small entity compliance guide" means a document designated and entitled as such by an agency.

Sec. 212. Compliance guides.

(a) Compliance guide.—
    (1) In general.—For each rule or group of related rules for which an agency is required to prepare a final regulatory flexibility analysis under section 605(b) of title 5, United States Code, the agency shall publish 1 or more guides to assist small entities in complying with the rule and shall entitle such publications "small entity compliance guides".
    (2) Publication of guides.—The publication of each guide under this subsection shall include—
        (A) the posting of the guide in an easily identified location on the website of the agency; and
        B) distribution of the guide to known industry contacts, such as small entities, associations, or industry leaders affected by the rule.
    (3) Publication date.—An agency shall publish each guide (including the posting and distribution of the guide as described under paragraph (2))—
        (A) on the same date as the date of publication of the final rule (or as soon as possible after that date); and
        (B) not later than the date on which the requirements of that rule become effective.
    (4) Compliance actions.—
        (A) In general.—Each guide shall explain the actions a small entity is required to take to comply with a rule.
        (B) Explanation.—The explanation under subparagraph (A)—

(i) shall include a description of actions needed to meet the requirements of a rule, to enable a small entity to know when such requirements are met; and

(ii) if determined appropriate by the agency, may include a description of possible procedures, such as conducting tests, that may assist a small entity in meeting such requirements, except that, compliance with any procedures described pursuant to this section does not establish compliance with the rule, or establish a presumption or inference of such compliance.

(C) Procedures.—Procedures described under subparagraph (B)(ii)—

(i) shall be suggestions to assist small entities; and

(ii) shall not be additional requirements, or diminish requirements, relating to the rule.

(5) Agency preparation of guides.—The agency shall, in its sole discretion, taking into account the subject matter of the rule and the language of relevant statutes, ensure that the guide is written using sufficiently plain language likely to be understood by affected small entities. Agencies may prepare separate guides covering groups or classes of similarly affected small entities and may cooperate with associations of small entities to develop and distribute such guides. An agency may prepare guides and apply this section with respect to a rule or a group of related rules.

(6) Reporting.—Not later than 1 year after the date of enactment of the Fair Minimum Wage Act of 2007 [May 25, 2007, the approval date of Pub. L. No. 110-28, Title VIII, subtitle A (§§8101 to 8104), 121 Stat. 188; for classification, see Tables], and annually thereafter, the head of each agency shall submit a report to the Committee on Small Business and Entrepreneurship of the Senate, the Committee on Small Business of the House of Representatives, and any other committee of relevant jurisdiction describing the status of the agency's compliance with paragraphs (1) through (5).

(b) Comprehensive source of information.—Agencies shall cooperate to make available to small entities through comprehensive sources of information, the small entity compliance guides and all other available information on statutory and regulatory requirements affecting small entities.

(c) Limitation on judicial review.—An agency's small entity compliance guide shall not be subject to judicial review, except that in any civil or administrative action against a small entity for a violation occurring after the effective date of this section [see section 216 of this note], the content of the small entity compliance guide may be considered as evidence of the reasonableness or appropriateness of any proposed fines, penalties or damages.

Sec. 213. Informal small entity guidance.

(a) General.—Whenever appropriate in the interest of administering statutes and regulations within the jurisdiction of an agency which regulates small entities, it shall be the practice of the agency to answer inquiries by small entities concerning information on, and advice about, compliance with such statutes and regulations, interpreting and applying the law to specific sets of facts supplied by the small entity. In any civil or administrative action against a small entity, guidance given by an agency applying the law to facts provided by the small entity may be considered as evidence of the reasonableness or appropriateness of any proposed fines, penalties or damages sought against such small entity.
(b) Program.—Each agency regulating the activities of small entities shall establish a program for responding to such inquiries no later than 1 year after enactment of this section [March 29, 1996], utilizing existing functions and personnel of the agency to the extent practicable.
(c) Reporting.—Each agency regulating the activities of small business shall report to the Committee on Small Business and Committee on Governmental Affairs of the Senate and the Committee on Small Business and Committee on the Judiciary of the House of Representatives no later than 2 years after the date of the enactment of this section [March 29, 1996] on the scope of the agency's program, the number of small entities using the program, and the achievements of the program to assist small entity compliance with agency regulations.

Sec. 214. Services of small business development centers.

(a) [Omitted. Amended section 648(c) of Title 15].
(b) Nothing in this Act [Pub. L. No. 104-121, March 29, 1996, 110 Stat. 847, for distribution of which see Short Title note set out under this section and Tables] in any way affects or limits the ability of other technical assistance or extension programs to perform or continue to perform services related to compliance assistance.

Sec. 215. Cooperation on guidance.

Agencies may, to the extent resources are available and where appropriate, in cooperation with the States, develop guides that fully integrate requirements of both Federal and State regulations where regulations within an agency's area of interest at the Federal and State levels impact small entities. Where regulations vary among the States, separate guides may be created for separate States in cooperation with State agencies.

§602. Regulatory agenda

(a) During the months of October and April of each year, each agency shall publish in the Federal Register a regulatory flexibility agenda which shall contain—
> (1) a brief description of the subject area of any rule which the agency expects to propose or promulgate which is likely to have a significant economic impact on a substantial number of small entities;
> (2) a summary of the nature of any such rule under consideration for each subject area listed in the agenda pursuant to paragraph (1), the objectives and legal basis for the issuance of the rule, and an approximate schedule for completing action on any rule for which the agency has issued a general notice of proposed rulemaking, and
> (3) the name and telephone number of an agency official knowledgeable concerning the items listed in paragraph (1).

(b) Each regulatory flexibility agenda shall be transmitted to the Chief Counsel for Advocacy of the Small Business Administration for comment, if any.

(c) Each agency shall endeavor to provide notice of each regulatory flexibility agenda to small entities or their representatives through direct notification or publication of the agenda in publications likely to be obtained by such small entities and shall invite comments upon each subject area on the agenda.

(d) Nothing in this section precludes an agency from considering or acting on any matter not included in a regulatory flexibility agenda, or requires an agency to consider or act on any matter listed in such agenda.

(Added Pub .L. No. 96-354, § 3(a), Sept. 19, 1980, 94 Stat. 1166.)

§603. Initial regulatory flexibility analysis

(a) Whenever an agency is required by section 553 of this title, or any other law, to publish general notice of proposed rulemaking for any proposed rule, or publishes a notice of proposed rulemaking for an interpretative rule involving the internal revenue laws of the United States, the agency shall prepare and make available for public comment an initial regulatory flexibility analysis. Such analysis shall describe the impact of the proposed rule on small entities. The initial regulatory flexibility analysis or a summary shall be published in the Federal Register at the time of the publication of general notice of proposed rulemaking for the rule. The agency shall transmit a copy of the initial regulatory flexibility analysis to the Chief Counsel for Advocacy of the Small Business Administration. In the case of an interpretative rule involving the internal revenue laws of the United States, this chapter applies to interpretative rules published in the Federal Register for codification in the Code of Federal Regulations, but only to the extent that such interpretative rules impose on small entities a collection of information requirement.

(b) Each initial regulatory flexibility analysis required under this section shall contain—

(1) a description of the reasons why action by the agency is being considered;

(2) a succinct statement of the objectives of, and legal basis for, the proposed rule;

(3) a description of and, where feasible, an estimate of the number of small entities to which the proposed rule will apply;

(4) a description of the projected reporting, recordkeeping and other compliance requirements of the proposed rule, including an estimate of the classes of small entities which will be subject to the requirement and the type of professional skills necessary for preparation of the report or record;

(5) an identification, to the extent practicable, of all relevant Federal rules which may duplicate, overlap or conflict with the proposed rule.

(c) Each initial regulatory flexibility analysis shall also contain a description of any significant alternatives to the proposed rule which accomplish the stated objectives of applicable statutes and which minimize any significant economic impact of the proposed rule on small entities. Consistent with the stated objectives of applicable statutes, the analysis shall discuss significant alternatives such as –

(1) the establishment of differing compliance or reporting requirements or timetables that take into account the resources available to small entities;

(2) the clarification, consolidation, or simplification of compliance and reporting requirements under the rule for such small entities;

(3) the use of performance rather than design standards; and

(4) an exemption from coverage of the rule, or any part thereof, for such small entities.

(Added Pub. L. No. 96-354, § 3(a), Sept. 19, 1980, 94 Stat. 1166; as amended Pub. L. No. 104-121, Title II, § 241(a)(1), March 29, 1996, 110 Stat. 864.)

§604. Final regulatory flexibility analysis

(a) When an agency promulgates a final rule under section 553 of this title,

after being required by that section or any other law to publish a general notice of proposed rulemaking, or promulgates a final interpretative rule involving the internal revenue laws of the United States as described in section 603(a), the agency shall prepare a final regulatory flexibility analysis. Each final regulatory flexibility analysis shall contain –
   (1) a succinct statement of the need for, and objectives of, the rule;
   (2) a summary of the significant issues raised by the public comments in response to the initial regulatory flexibility analysis, a summary of the assessment of the agency of such issues, and a statement of any changes made in the proposed rule as a result of such comments;
   (3) a description of and an estimate of the number of small entities to which the rule will apply or an explanation of why no such estimate is available;
   (4) a description of the projected reporting, recordkeeping and other compliance requirements of the rule, including an estimate of the classes of small entities which will be subject to the requirement and the type of professional skills necessary for preparation of the report or record; and
   (5) a description of the steps the agency has taken to minimize the significant economic impact on small entities consistent with the stated objectives of applicable statutes, including a statement of the factual, policy, and legal reasons for selecting the alternative adopted in the final rule and why each one of the other significant alternatives to the rule considered by the agency which affect the impact on small entities was rejected.
(b) The agency shall make copies of the final regulatory flexibility analysis available to members of the public and shall publish in the Federal Register such analysis or a summary thereof.
(Added Pub. L. No. 96-354, § 3(a), Sept. 19, 1980, 94 Stat. 1167; as amended Pub. L. No. 104-121, Title II, § 241(b), March 29, 1996, 110 Stat. 864.)

§605. Avoidance of duplicative or unnecessary analyses

(a) Any Federal agency may perform the analyses required by sections 602, 603, and 604 of this title in conjunction with or as a part of any other agenda or analysis required by any other law if such other analysis satisfies the provisions of such sections.
(b) Sections 603 and 604 of this title shall not apply to any proposed or final rule if the head of the agency certifies that the rule will not, if promulgated, have a significant economic impact on a substantial number of small entities. If the head of the agency makes a certification under the preceding sentence, the agency shall publish such certification in the Federal Register at the time

of publication of general notice of proposed rulemaking for the rule or at the time of publication of the final rule, along with a statement providing the factual basis for such certification. The agency shall provide such certification and statement to the Chief Counsel for Advocacy of the Small Business Administration.

(c) In order to avoid duplicative action, an agency may consider a series of closely related rules as one rule for the purposes of sections 602, 603, 604 and 610 of this title.

(Added Pub. L. No. 96-354, § 3(a), Sept. 19, 1980, 94 Stat. 1167; as amended Pub. L. No. 104-121, Title II, § 243(a), March 29, 1996, 110 Stat. 866.)

§606. Effect on other law

The requirements of sections 603 and 604 of this title do not alter in any manner standards otherwise applicable by law to agency action.

(Added Pub. L. No. 96-354, § 3(a), Sept. 19, 1980, 94 Stat. 1168.)

§607. Preparation of analyses

In complying with the provisions of sections 603 and 604 of this title, an agency may provide either a quantifiable or numerical description of the effects of a proposed rule or alternatives to the proposed rule, or more general descriptive statements if quantification is not practicable or reliable.

(Added Pub. L. No. 96-354, § 3(a), Sept. 19, 1980, 94 Stat. 1168.)

§608. Procedure for waiver or delay of completion

(a) An agency head may waive or delay the completion of some or all of the requirements of section 603 of this title by publishing in the Federal Register, not later than the date of publication of the final rule, a written finding, with reasons therefor, that the final rule is being promulgated in response to an emergency that makes compliance or timely compliance with the provisions of section 603 of this title impracticable.

(b) Except as provided in section 605(b), an agency head may not waive the requirements of section 604 of this title. An agency head may delay the completion of the requirements of section 604 of this title for a period of not more than one hundred and eighty days after the date of publication in the Federal Register of a final rule by publishing in the Federal Register, not later than such date of publication, a written finding, with reasons therefor, that the final rule is being promulgated in response to an emergency that makes timely compliance with the provisions of section 604 of this title impracticable. If the agency has not prepared a final regulatory analysis pursuant to section 604 of this title within one hundred and eighty days from the date of publication of the final rule, such rule shall lapse and have no effect. Such rule shall not be repromulgated until a final regulatory flexibility analysis has been completed by the agency.

(Added Pub. L. No. 96-354, § 3(a), Sept. 19, 1980, 94 Stat. 1168.)

§609. Procedures for gathering comments

(a) When any rule is promulgated which will have a significant economic impact on a substantial number of small entities, the head of the agency promulgating the rule or the official of the agency with statutory responsibility for the promulgation of the rule shall assure that small entities have been given an opportunity to participate in the rulemaking for the rule through the reasonable use of techniques such as –

(1) the inclusion in an advanced notice of proposed rulemaking, if issued, of a statement that the proposed rule may have a significant economic effect on a substantial number of small entities;

(2) the publication of general notice of proposed rulemaking in publications likely to be obtained by small entities;

(3) the direct notification of interested small entities;

(4) the conduct of open conferences or public hearings concerning the rule for small entities including soliciting and receiving comments over computer networks; and

(5) the adoption or modification of agency procedural rules to reduce the cost or complexity of participation in the rulemaking by small entities.

(b) Prior to publication of an initial regulatory flexibility analysis which a covered agency is required to conduct by this chapter—

(1) a covered agency shall notify the Chief Counsel for Advocacy of the Small Business Administration and provide the Chief Counsel with information on the potential impacts of the proposed rule on small entities and the type of small entities that might be affected;

(2) not later than 15 days after the date of receipt of the materials described in paragraph (1), the Chief Counsel shall identify individuals representative of affected small entities for the purpose of obtaining advice and recommendations from those individuals about the potential impacts of the proposed rule;

(3) the agency shall convene a review panel for such rule consisting wholly of full time Federal employees of the office within the agency responsible for carrying out the proposed rule, the Office of Information and Regulatory Affairs within the Office of Management and Budget, and the Chief Counsel;

(4) the panel shall review any material the agency has prepared in connection with this chapter, including any draft proposed rule, collect advice and recommendations of each individual small entity representative identified by the agency after consultation with the Chief Counsel, on issues related to subsections 603(b), paragraphs (3), (4) and (5) and 603(c);

(5) not later than 60 days after the date a covered agency convenes a review panel pursuant to paragraph (3), the review panel shall report on the comments of the small entity representatives and its findings as to issues related to subsections 603(b), paragraphs (3), (4) and (5) and 603(c), provided that such report shall be made public as part of the rulemaking record; and

(6) where appropriate, the agency shall modify the proposed rule, the initial regulatory flexibility analysis or the decision on whether an initial regulatory flexibility analysis is required.

(c) An agency may in its discretion apply subsection (b) to rules that the agency intends to certify under subsection 605(b), but the agency believes may have a greater than de minimis impact on a substantial number of small entities.

(d) For purposes of this section, the term "covered agency" means the Environmental Protection Agency and the Occupational Safety and Health Administration of the Department of Labor.

(e) The Chief Counsel for Advocacy, in consultation with the individuals identified in subsection (b)(2), and with the Administrator of the Office of Information and Regulatory Affairs within the Office of Management and Budget, may waive the requirements of subsections (b)(3), (b)(4), and (b)(5) by including in the rulemaking record a written finding, with reasons therefor, that those requirements would not advance the effective participation of small entities in the rulemaking process. For purposes of this subsection, the factors to be considered in making such a finding are as follows:

(1) In developing a proposed rule, the extent to which the covered agency consulted with individuals representative of affected small entities with respect to the potential impacts of the rule and took such concerns into consideration.

(2) Special circumstances requiring prompt issuance of the rule.

(3) Whether the requirements of subsection (b) would provide the indi-

viduals identified in subsection (b)(2) with a competitive advantage relative to other small entities.

(Added Pub. L. No. 96-354, § 3(a), Sept. 19, 1980, 94 Stat. 1168; as amended Pub. L. No. 104-121, Title II, § 244(a), March 29, 1996, 110 Stat. 867.)

§610. Periodic review of rules

(a) Within one hundred and eighty days after the effective date of this chapter, each agency shall publish in the Federal Register a plan for the periodic review of the rules issued by the agency which have or will have a significant economic impact upon a substantial number of small entities. Such plan may be amended by the agency at any time by publishing the revision in the Federal Register. The purpose of the review shall be to determine whether such rules should be continued without change, or should be amended or rescinded, consistent with the stated objectives of applicable statutes, to minimize any significant economic impact of the rules upon a substantial number of such small entities. The plan shall provide for the review of all such agency rules existing on the effective date of this chapter within ten years of that date and for the review of such rules adopted after the effective date of this chapter within ten years of the publication of such rules as the final rule. If the head of the agency determines that completion of the review of existing rules is not feasible by the established date, he shall so certify in a statement published in the Federal Register and may extend the completion date by one year at a time for a total of not more than five years.

(b) In reviewing rules to minimize any significant economic impact of the rule on a substantial number of small entities in a manner consistent with the stated objectives of applicable statutes, the agency shall consider the following factors—

    (1) the continued need for the rule;

    (2) the nature of complaints or comments received concerning the rule from the public;

    (3) the complexity of the rule;

    (4) the extent to which the rule overlaps, duplicates or conflicts with other Federal rules, and, to the extent feasible, with State and local governmental rules; and

    (5) the length of time since the rule has been evaluated or the degree to which technology, economic conditions, or other factors have changed in the area affected by the rule.

(c) Each year, each agency shall publish in the Federal Register a list of the rules which have a significant economic impact on a substantial number of small entities, which are to be reviewed pursuant to this section during the succeeding twelve months. The list shall include a brief description of each rule and the need for and legal basis of such rule and shall invite public comment upon the rule.

(Added Pub. L. No. 96-354, § 3(a), Sept. 19, 1980, 94 Stat. 1169.)

§611. Judicial review

(a)(1) For any rule subject to this chapter, a small entity that is adversely affected or aggrieved by final agency action is entitled to judicial review of agency compliance with the requirements of sections 601, 604, 605(b), 608(b), and 610 in accordance with chapter 7. Agency compliance with sections 607 and 609(a) shall be judicially reviewable in connection with judicial review of section 604.

(2) Each court having jurisdiction to review such rule for compliance with section 553, or under any other provision of law, shall have jurisdiction to review any claims of noncompliance with sections 601, 604, 605(b), 608(b), and 610 in accordance with chapter 7. Agency compliance with sections 607 and 609(a) shall be judicially reviewable in connection with judicial review of section 604.

(3) (A) A small entity may seek such review during the period beginning on the date of final agency action and ending one year later, except that where a provision of law requires that an action challenging a final agency action be commenced before the expiration of one year, such lesser period shall apply to an action for judicial review under this section.

(B) In the case where an agency delays the issuance of a final regulatory flexibility analysis pursuant to section 608(b) of this chapter, an action for judicial review under this section shall be filed not later than—

(i) one year after the date the analysis is made available to the public, or

(ii) where a provision of law requires that an action challenging a final agency regulation be commenced before the expiration of the 1-year period, the number of days specified in such provision of law that is after the date the analysis is made available to the public.

(4) In granting any relief in an action under this section, the court shall order the agency to take corrective action consistent with this chapter and chapter 7, including, but not limited to –

(A) remanding the rule to the agency, and

(B) deferring the enforcement of the rule against small entities unless the court finds that continued enforcement of the rule is in the public interest.

(5) Nothing in this subsection shall be construed to limit the authority of any court to stay the effective date of any rule or provision thereof under any other provision of law or to grant any other relief in addition to the requirements of this section.

(b) In an action for the judicial review of a rule, the regulatory flexibility analysis for such rule, including an analysis prepared or corrected pursuant to paragraph (a)(4), shall constitute part of the entire record of agency action in connection with such review.

(c) Compliance or noncompliance by an agency with the provisions of this chapter shall be subject to judicial review only in accordance with this section.

(d) Nothing in this section bars judicial review of any other impact statement or similar analysis required by any other law if judicial review of such statement or analysis is otherwise permitted by law.

(Added Pub. L. No. 96-354, § 3(a), Sept. 19, 1980, 94 Stat. 1169; as amended Pub. L. No. 104-121, Title II, § 242, March 29, 1996, 110 Stat. 865.)

§612. Reports and intervention rights

(a) The Chief Counsel for Advocacy of the Small Business Administration shall monitor agency compliance with this chapter and shall report at least annually thereon to the President and to the Committees on the Judiciary and Small Business of the Senate and House of Representatives.

(b) The Chief Counsel for Advocacy of the Small Business Administration is authorized to appear as amicus curiae in any action brought in a court of the United States to review a rule. In any such action, the Chief Counsel is authorized to present his or her views with respect to compliance with this chapter, the adequacy of the rulemaking record with respect to small entities and the effect of the rule on small entities.

(c) A court of the United States shall grant the application of the Chief Counsel for Advocacy of the Small Business Administration to appear in any such action for the purposes described in subsection (b).

(Added Pub. L. No. 96-354, § 3(a), Sept. 19, 1980, 94 Stat. 1170; as amended Pub. L. No. 104-121, Title II, § 243(b), March 29, 1996, 110 Stat. 866.)

Unfunded Mandates Reform Act

Citations:

2 U.S.C. §§1501-1571 (2000); enacted March 22, 1995 by Pub. L. No. 104-4, 109 Stat. 48.

Lead Agencies:

The Office of Information and Regulatory Affairs (OIRA) in the Office of Management and Budget (OMB), Eisenhower Executive Office Building, 1650 Pennsylvania Avenue NW, Washington, DC 20502, (202) 395-4852; Congressional Budget Office, Budget Analysis Division, 430 Ford House Office Building, Second and D Streets, SW, Washington, DC 20515-6925, (202) 226-2800.

Overview:

This legislation, which was enacted in 1995 with broad, bipartisan support, requires Congress and federal agencies (excepting independent agencies) to give special consideration to proposed legislation and regulations imposing mandates on state, local, and tribal entities. It also contains a special provision (added at the end of the legislative process) requiring agencies to prepare a special statement, in the nature of a regulatory impact analysis, for any proposed rulemaking that is likely to result in an expenditure by the private sector in excess of $100 million. The Act thus contains the only broad regulatory impact analysis requirement currently mandated by statute, and as such codifies many of the provisions in Executive Order 12,866. The Act's impact is, however, somewhat lessened because its provisions for judicial review of agency compliance with the Act are somewhat limited.

The Act's purpose was to help reveal, and ultimately limit the high (and often hidden) costs of federal mandates on state and local governments to undertake regulatory activity without sufficient federal compensation for this activity.

Title I of the Act modifies the legislative process by requiring any Congressional authorizing committee that approves a bill containing a federal mandate (with some exceptions) to identify that mandate in its committee report. The Congressional Budget Office must then estimate the overall impact of such mandates, and a point of order lies can be raised by any member against a bill that lacks such an estimate or if the bill contains an unfunded mandate exceeding $50 million burden on state and local governments or $100 million on the private sector.

Title II of the Act addresses agency regulations containing regulatory mandates of state, local and tribal governments and on the private sector. The key requirement is for a "statement to accompany significant regulatory actions." The statement is required in "any general notice of proposed rulemaking that is likely to result in the expenditure by State, local, and tribal governments, in the aggregate, or by the private sector, of $100,000,000 or more (adjusted annually for inflation) in any 1 year."[1]

The statement must include (1) citation to the law under which the rule is being promulgated; (2) "a qualitative and quantitative assessment of the anticipated costs and benefits of the Federal mandate. . . as well as the effect of the Federal mandate on health, safety, and the natural environment," along with an analysis of the availability of federal funds to help governments pay for the mandate; (3) estimates of future compliance costs and of disproportionate budgetary effects on regions or particular governments or segments of the private sector; (4) estimates of the effect on aspects of the national economy; and (5) a summary of the agency's consultations with elected representatives. The agency must also develop a plan to specially notify small governments of such requirements and develop a process to receive meaningful and timely input from elective officials. In that connection, an exemption from the Federal Advisory Committee Act is carved out for such consultations. A summary of this statement must appear in the notice of proposed rulemaking. However, the Act does

---

[1] In 2005, the inflation-adjusted amount on the original $100 million amount was $123 million. *See* Congressional Budget Office, Statement of Douglas Holtz-Eakin, Director, *A Review of CBO's Activities Under the Unfunded Mandates Reform Act*, before the Committee on Government Reform, U.S. House of Representatives (March 8, 2005), *available at* http://www.cbo.gov/showdoc.cfm?index=6141&sequence=0.

allow agencies to prepare the statement "in conjunction with or as a part of any other statement or analysis. . . ."

Before issuing a final rule that was subject to the above requirements, the agency must "identify and consider a reasonable number of regulatory alternatives and from those alternatives, select the least costly, most cost-effective or least burdensome alternative that achieves the objectives of the rule."

Judicial review of agency compliance with the Unfunded Mandates Reform Act is limited. The Act provides that judicial review of the agency statements accompanying significant regulatory actions is subject to review only under 5 U.S.C. §706(1)—which allows courts to "compel agency action unlawfully withheld or unreasonably delayed." This means that courts may compel the production of such agency statements but cannot review the contents of them. In fact, the Act makes clear that "the inadequacy or failure to prepare such statement (including the inadequacy or failure to prepare any estimate, analysis, statement or description) or written plan shall not be used as a basis for staying, enjoining, invalidating or otherwise affecting such agency rule."[2]

The Act requires OMB to submit annual reports to Congress on agency compliance with Title II of the Act, and OMB has submitted such reports since 1996.

Legislative History:

In the 103d Congress, eight bills were introduced that addressed the issue of unfunded mandates. This was directly in response to the pressure building over the previous fifteen years from State and local governments. Over those years, Congress continued a pattern of cutting federal funding while enacting statutes that passed costs onto State and local governments without providing funding to cover those costs. To demonstrate their dissatisfaction, the State and local governments declared October 27, 1993 "National Unfunded Mandates Day."

S. 993 had the strongest support in the 103d Congress. It was introduced by Senator Dirk Kempthorne as the Community Regulatory Relief Act, and

---

[2] *See* Allied Local and Regional Mfrs. Caucus v. EPA, 215 F.3d 61, 80 (D.C. Cir. 2000) (holding (1) that the Act precluded review of EPA's alleged failure to select the "least costly, most cost-effective or least burdensome alternative that achieves the objectives of the rule," [§ 1535(a)], and (2) that although the Act allowed limited judicial review of compliance with the requirement to prepare a written cost-benefit analysis, the Act did not apply because EPA estimated the total cost associated with the challenged rule to be only $32 million per year).

had more than fifty co-sponsors. However, S. 993 was not considered for a vote, and Congress adjourned without further consideration of the bill.

A new bill was introduced in the 104th Congress as S. 1 and H.R. 5, "The Unfunded Mandates Reform Act of 1995." It was rapidly reported out of committee in both houses. In February, the House passed H.R.5, and amended and passed S. 1. After disagreement between the House and Senate over amendments, the bill went to a conference committee (H.R. Rep. No. 104-76 (1995)). Both houses agreed to the conference report. The Senate vote was 91-9 and the House vote was 394-28.

On March 22, 1995, The Unfunded Mandates Reform Act of 1995 was signed into law by President Clinton as Pub. L. No. 104-4.

Bibliography:

I. Legislative History

1. *Impact of Federal Mandates on State and Local Governments,* Hearings before the Subcommittee on Human Resources and Intergovernmental Relations of the House Committee on Government Operations, 103d Cong. 1st Sess. (Oct. 25, 1993).

2. *Federal Mandates on State and Local Governments,* Hearings before the Senate Governmental Affairs Committee, 103d Cong. 1st Sess. (Nov. 3, 1993).

3. *Impact of Unfunded Mandates on State and Local Governments,* Hearings before the Subcommittee on Human Resources and Intergovernmental Relations of the House Committee on Government Reform and Oversight, 103d Cong. 2d Sess. (Feb. 26, 1994).

4. *Unfunded Federal Mandates: Who Should Pick Up the Tab?,* Hearings before the Subcommittee on Investigation and Oversight of the House Science Committee, 103d Cong. 2d Sess. (March 22, 1994).

5. *Unfunded Federal Mandates: Burdens and Costs in North Dakota,* Hearings before the Senate Governmental Affairs Committee, 103d Cong. 2d Sess. (April 5, 1994).

6. *Federal Mandate Reform Legislation,* Hearings before the Senate Governmental Affairs Committee, 103d Cong. 2d Sess. (April 28, 1994).

7. *Legislative Initiatives on Unfunded Mandates,* Hearings before the Subcommittee on Human Resources and Intergovernmental Relations of the House Committee on Government Reform and Oversight, 103d Cong. 2d Sess. (May 18, 1994).

8. *S.993, Federal Mandate Accountability and Reform Act of 1994*, Senate Committee on Governmental Affairs, S. Rep. No. 103-330, 103d Cong., 2d Sess. (Aug. 10, 1994).

9. *S.1, Unfunded Mandate Reform Act of 1995*, Senate Budget Committee and Senate Committee on Governmental Affairs, S. Rep. No. 104-2, 104th Cong., 1st Sess. (Jan. 12, 1995).

10. *H.R.5, Unfunded Mandate Reform Act of 1995*, House Rules Committee, and House Committee on Government Reform and Oversight, H.R. Rep. No. 104-1, pts.1 and 2, 104th Cong., 1st Sess. (Jan. 13, 1995).

11. *Ways to Reduce Unfunded Federal Mandates and Regulatory Burdens on the Aviation Industry Without Affecting the Safety of the Traveling Public,* Hearings before the Subcommittee on Aviation, House Transportation and Infrastructure Committee, 104th Cong., 1st Sess. (Feb. 1, 1995).

12. *S.1, Unfunded Mandate Reform Act of 1995*, Conference Committee Report, H. Rep. No. 104-76, 104th Cong., 1st Sess. (March 13, 1995).

13. *Hearings on S.1* before the Senate Budget Committee and the Senate Committee on Governmental Affairs, 104th Cong. 1st Sess, (Jan. 5, 1999).

14. *Hearings on H.R.5* before the House Rules, 104th Cong. 1st Sess, (Jan. 11, 1999).

II. OMB Reports to Congress on Unfunded Mandates[3]

1. Office of Management and Budget, *Agency Compliance With Title II of Unfunded Mandates Reform Act of 1995*, Report to Congress from the Director of OMB (March 22, 1996). These are annual reports. The 4th Annual Report was issued in October, 1999, *see* http://www.whitehouse.gov/OMB/inforeg/umra1999final.pdf. Citations to the most recent reports follow:

2. *Making Sense of Regulation, 2001 Report to Congress on the Costs and Benefits of Federal Regulations and Unfunded Mandates on State, Local, and Tribal Entities* (Dec. 2001), http://www.whitehouse.gov/omb/inforeg/costbenefitreport.pdf. Notice of availability of draft report and request for comments, 66 Fed. Reg. 22,041 (May 2, 2001); extended 66 Fed. Reg. 34,963 (July 2, 2001).

---

[3] These reports are required by the Regulatory Right to Know Act, 31 U.S.C. §1105 note, Pub. L. No. 106-554, §1(a)(3) [Title VI, §624], Dec. 21, 2000, 114 Stat. 2763, 2763A-161, and the Unfunded Mandates Reform Act, Pub. L. No. 104-4, Title II.

3. *Stimulating Smarter Regulation, 2002 Report to Congress on the Costs and Benefits of Federal Regulations and Unfunded Mandates on State, Local, and Tribal Entities* (Dec. 2002), *available at* http://www.whitehouse.gov/omb/inforeg/2002_report_to_congress.pdf. Notice of availability of draft report and request for comments, 67 Fed. Reg. 15,014 (Mar. 28, 2002).

4. *Informing Regulatory Decisions, 2003 Report to Congress on the Costs and Benefits of Federal Regulations and Unfunded Mandates on State, Local, and Tribal Entities* (Sept. 2003), *available at* http://www.whitehouse.gov/omb/inforeg/2003_cost-ben_final_rpt.pdf. Notice of availability of draft report and request for comments, 68 Fed. Reg. 15,772 (Apr. 1, 2003).

5. *Progress in Regulatory Reform, 2004 Report to Congress on the Costs and Benefits of Federal Regulations and Unfunded Mandates on State, Local, and Tribal Entities* (Dec. 2004), *available at* http://www.whitehouse.gov/omb/inforeg/2004_cb_final.pdf. Notice of availability of draft report and request for comments, 69 Fed. Reg. 7987 (Feb. 20, 2004).

6. *Validating Regulatory Analysis, 2005 Report to Congress on the Costs and Benefits of Federal Regulations and Unfunded Mandates on State, Local, and Tribal Entities* (Dec. 2005), *available at* http://www.whitehouse.gov/omb/inforeg/2005_cb/final_2005_cb_report.pdf. Notice of availability of draft report and request for comments, 70 Fed. Reg. 14,735 (March 23, 2005).

7. *2006 Report to Congress on the Costs and Benefits of Federal Regulations and Unfunded Mandates on State, Local, and Tribal Entities* (Jan. 2007), *available at* http://www.whitehouse.gov/omb/inforeg/2006_cb/2006_cb_final_report.pdf. Notice of availability of draft report and request for comments, 71 Fed. Reg. 19,213 (April 13, 2006).

8. *2007 Draft Report to Congress on the Costs and Benefits of Federal Regulations*, *available at* http://www.whitehouse.gov/omb/inforeg/2007_cb/2007_draft_cb_report.pdf. Notice of availability of draft report and request for comments, 72 Fed. Reg. 11,061 (March 12, 2007).

III. Other Government Documents

1. Advisory Commission on Intergovernmental Relations, *Federal Court Rulings Involving State, Local, and Tribal Governments Calendar Year 1994: A Report Prepared Under Section 304, Unfunded Mandates Reform Act of 1995.*

2. Richard S. Beth, *Mandates Information Act: Implications for Congressional Action on Legislation Containing Private Sector Mandates* (Con-

gressional Research Service Report 98-48) (May 15, 1998), http://www.opencrs.com/document/98-448.

3. William J. Clinton, Executive Order 12875, "Enhancing the Intergovernmental Partnership," 58 Fed. Reg. 58,093 (Oct. 23, 1993) (revoked by Executive Order 13,132, "Federalism," reprinted in this volume in Chapter 4).

4. Congressional Budget Office, *Preliminary Analysis of Unfunded Federal Mandates and the Cost of the Safe Drinking Water Act*, CBO Memorandum, (Sept. 1994).

5. Congressional Budget Office, *The Experience of the Congressional Budget Office During the First Year of the Unfunded Mandates Reform Act*, (Jan. 1997).

6. *1995 Unfunded Mandates Reform Act—An Overview of Effectiveness and Opportunities for Enhancement*, Hearing before the Rules Subcommittee on Technology and the House, 108th Cong, 1st Sess. (July 16, 2003).

7. Office of Management and Budget, Memorandum for the Heads of Executive Departments and Agencies, *Guidance for Implementing Title II of S.1*, from Alice M. Rivlin, OMB Director (with attached memorandum on same subject from OIRA Administrator Sally Katzen) (March 31, 1995).

8. Office of Management and Budget, Memorandum for the Heads of Departments and Agencies, *Guidelines and Instructions for Implementing Section 204, 'State, Local, and Tribal Government Input,' of Title II of P.L. 104-4*, from Alice M. Rivlin, OMB Director, September 21, 1995, 60 Fed. Reg. 50,651 (Sept. 29, 1995).

9. Office of Management and Budget, Memorandum for the Heads of Executive Departments and Agencies, and Independent Regulatory Agencies, *Guidance for Implementing E.O. 12,875, 'Reduction of Unfunded Mandates,'* from Leon E. Panetta, OMB Director (with attached memorandum from OIRA Administrator Sally Katzen) (Jan. 11, 1994).

10. *Passing the Buck, A Review of the Unfunded Mandates Reform Act*, Hearing before the Subcommittee on Oversight of Government Management, the Federal Workforce, and the District of Columbia of the Senate Committee on Homeland Security and Governmental Affairs, 109th Cong, 1st Sess. (April 14, 2005).

11. *The Tenth Anniversary of the Unfunded Mandates Reform Act*, Hearing before the House Committee on Government Reform, 109th Cong, 1st Sess. (March 8, 2005).

12. *The Unfunded Mandates Reform Act of 1995: One Year Later*, Hearing before the Subcommittee on Human Resources and Intergovernmental

Relations of the House Committee on Government Reform and Oversight, 105th Cong., 1st Sess. (March 22, 1996).

13. U.S. General Accounting Office, *Unfunded Mandates: Analysis of Reform Act Coverage,* Report to the Chairman, Subcommittee on Oversight of Government Management, the Federal Workforce, and the District of Columbia, Committee on Governmental Affairs, U. S. Senate (GAO-04-637) (May 2004).

14. U.S. General Accounting Office, *Unfunded Mandates Reform Act Has Had Little Effect on Agencies' Rulemaking Actions,* A Report to the Senate Committee on Governmental Affairs, (GAO/GGD-98-30) (Feb. 1998).

15. U.S. Government Accountability Office, *Unfunded Mandates: Opinions Vary About Reform Act's Strengths, Weaknesses, and Options for Improvement* (GAO-05-454) (March 31, 2005).

IV. Law Review Articles

1. R. Adler, *Unfunded Mandates and Fiscal Federalism: A Critique*, 50 Vand. L. Rev. 1137 (1997).

2. D. Cole & C. Comer, *Rhetoric, Reality, and the Law of Unfunded Federal Mandates,* 8 Stan. L. & Pol'y Rev. 103 (1997).

3. D. Dana, *The Case for Unfunded Environmental Mandates*, 69 S. Cal. L. Rev. 1 (1995).

4. D. Fort, Essay, *The Unfunded Mandates Reform Act of 1995: Where Will the New Federalism Take Environmental Policy?* 35 Nat. Resources J. 727 (1995).

5. D. Herzfeld, *Comment, Accountability and the Nondelegation of Unfunded Mandates: A Public Choice,* 7 Geo. Mason L. Rev. 419 (1999).

6. M. Jaber, *Comment, Unfunded Federal Mandates: An Issue of Federalism or a Brilliant Sound Bite,* 45 Emory L.J. 281 (1996).

7. T. Kaye, *Show Me The Money: Congressional Limitations on State Tax Sovereignty,* 35 Harv. J. on Legis. 149 (1998).

8. R. Lawton & B. Burns, *Models of Cooperative Federalism for Telecommunications,* 6 Alb. L. J. Sci. & Tech. 71 (1996).

9. S. Leckrone, *Note, Turning Back the Clock: The Unfunded Mandates Reform Act of 1995 and Its Effective Repeal of Environmental Legislation,* 71 Ind. L.J. 1029 (1996).

10. E. Luna, *The Impact of the Unfunded Mandates Reform Act of 1995 on Tribal Governments,* 22 Am. Indian L. Rev. 445 (1998).

11. R. Shaffer, *Comment, Unfunded State Mandates and Local Governments,* 64 U. Cin. L. Rev. 1057 (1996).

12. D. Troy, *The Unfunded Mandates Reform Act of 1995*, 49 Admin. L. Rev. 139 (1997).

13. E. Zelinsky, *The Unsolved Problem of the Unfunded Mandate*, 23 Ohio N.U. L. Rev. 741 (1997).

Appendix:

1. Unfunded Mandates Reform Act, 2 U.S.C. §§658, 1501-03, 1531-36, 1555, 1571 (2000).

2. Office of Management and Budget, Memorandum for the Heads of Executive Departments and Agencies, Guidance for Implementing Title II of S.1, from Alice M. Rivlin, OMB Director (with attached memorandum on same subject from OIRA Administrator Sally Katzen) (March 31, 1995).

3. Office of Management and Budget, Memorandum for the Heads of Departments and Agencies, "Guidelines and Instructions for Implementing Section 204, 'State, Local, and Tribal Government Input,' of Title II of P.L. 104-4," from Alice M. Rivlin, OMB Director, September 21, 1995 (60 Fed. Reg. 50,651, Sept. 29, 1995).

Unfunded Mandates Reform Act

Title 2, U.S. Code

§658. Definitions

For purposes of this part:

(1) Agency. The term "agency" has the same meaning as defined in section 551(1) of Title 5, but does not include independent regulatory agencies.

(2) Amount. The term "amount", with respect to an authorization of appropriations for Federal financial assistance, means the amount of budget authority for any Federal grant assistance program or any Federal program providing loan guarantees or direct loans.

(3) Direct costs. The term "direct costs"—

(A)(i) in the case of a Federal intergovernmental mandate, means the aggregate estimated amounts that all State, local, and tribal governments would be required to spend or would be prohibited from raising in revenues in order to comply with the Federal intergovernmental mandate; or

(ii) in the case of a provision referred to in paragraph (5)(A)(ii), means the amount of Federal financial assistance eliminated or reduced;

(B) in the case of a Federal private sector mandate, means the aggregate estimated amounts that the private sector will be required to spend in order to comply with the Federal private sector mandate;

(C) shall be determined on the assumption that—

(i) State, local, and tribal governments, and the private sector will take all reasonable steps necessary to mitigate the costs resulting from the Federal mandate, and will comply with applicable standards of practice and conduct established by recognized professional or trade associations; and

(ii) reasonable steps to mitigate the costs shall not include increases in State, local, or tribal taxes or fees; and

(D) shall not include—

(i) estimated amounts that the State, local, and tribal governments (in the case of a Federal intergovernmental mandate) or the private sector (in the case of a Federal private sector mandate) would spend—

(I) to comply with or carry out all applicable Federal, State, local, and tribal laws and regulations in effect at the time of the adoption of the Federal mandate for the same activity as is affected by that Federal mandate; or

(II) to comply with or carry out State, local, and tribal governmental programs, or private-sector business or other activities in effect at the time of the adoption of the Federal mandate for the same activity as is affected by that mandate; or

(ii) expenditures to the extent that such expenditures will be offset by any direct savings to the State, local, and tribal governments, or by the private sector, as a result of—

(I) compliance with the Federal mandate; or

(II) other changes in Federal law or regulation that are enacted or adopted in the same bill or joint resolution or proposed or final Federal regulation and that govern the same activity as is affected by the Federal mandate.

(4) Direct savings. The term "direct savings", when used with respect to the result of compliance with the Federal mandate—

(A) in the case of a Federal intergovernmental mandate, means the aggregate estimated reduction in costs to any State, local, or tribal government as a result of compliance with the Federal intergovernmental mandate; and

(B) in the case of a Federal private sector mandate, means the aggregate estimated reduction in costs to the private sector as a result of compliance with the Federal private sector mandate.

(5) Federal intergovernmental mandate. The term "Federal intergovernmental mandate" means—

(A) any provision in legislation, statute, or regulation that—

(i) would impose an enforceable duty upon State, local, or tribal governments, except—

(I) a condition of Federal assistance; or

(II) a duty arising from participation in a voluntary Federal program, except as provided in subparagraph (B); or

(ii) would reduce or eliminate the amount of authorization of appropriations for—

(I) Federal financial assistance that would be provided to State, local, or tribal governments for the purpose of complying with any such previously imposed duty unless such duty is reduced or eliminated by a corresponding amount;

or

(II) the control of borders by the Federal Government; or reimbursement to State, local, or tribal governments for the net cost associated with illegal, deportable, and excludable aliens, including court-mandated expenses related to emergency health care, education or criminal justice; when such a reduction or elimination would result in increased net costs to State, local, or tribal governments in providing education or emergency health care to, or incarceration of, illegal aliens; except that this subclause shall not be in effect with respect to a State, local, or tribal government, to the extent that such government has not fully cooperated in the efforts of the Federal Government to locate, apprehend, and deport illegal aliens;

(B) any provision in legislation, statute, or regulation that relates to a then-existing Federal program under which $500,000,000 or more is provided annually to State, local, and tribal governments under entitlement authority, if the provision—

(i)(I) would increase the stringency of conditions of assistance to State, local, or tribal governments under the program; or

(II) would place caps upon, or otherwise decrease, the Federal Government's responsibility to provide funding to State, local, or tribal governments under the program; and

(ii) the State, local, or tribal governments that participate in the Federal program lack authority under that program to amend their financial or programmatic responsibilities to continue providing required services that are affected by the legislation, statute, or regulation.

(6) Federal mandate. The term "Federal mandate" means a Federal intergovernmental mandate or a Federal private sector mandate, as defined in paragraphs (5) and (7).

(7) Federal private sector mandate. The term "Federal private sector mandate" means any provision in legislation, statute, or regulation that—

(A) would impose an enforceable duty upon the private sector except—

(i) a condition of Federal assistance; or

(ii) a duty arising from participation in a voluntary Federal program; or

(B) would reduce or eliminate the amount of authorization of appropriations for Federal financial assistance that will be provided to the private sector for the purposes of ensuring compliance with such duty.

(8) Local government. The term "local government" has the same meaning as defined in section 6501(6) of title 31.

(9) Private sector. The term "private sector" means all persons or entities in the United States, including individuals, partnerships, associations, corporations, and educational and nonprofit institutions, but shall not include State, local, or tribal governments.

(10) Regulation; rule. The term "regulation" or "rule" (except with respect to a rule of either House of the Congress) has the meaning of "rule" as defined in section 601(2) of title 5.

(11) Small government. The term "small government" means any small governmental jurisdictions defined in section 601(5) of title 5 and any tribal government.

(12) State. The term "State" has the same meaning as defined in section 6501(9) of title 31.

(13) Tribal government. The term "tribal government" means any Indian tribe, band, nation, or other organized group or community, including any Alaska Native village or regional or village corporation as defined in or established pursuant to the Alaska Native Claims Settlement Act (85 Stat. 688; 43 U.S.C. 1601 et seq.) which is recognized as eligible for the special programs and services provided by the United States to Indians because of their special status as Indians.

§1501. Purposes

The purposes of this chapter are—

***

(1) to assist Federal agencies in their consideration of proposed regulations affecting State, local, and tribal governments, by—
    (A) requiring that Federal agencies develop a process to enable the elected and other officials of State, local, and tribal governments to provide input when Federal agencies are developing regulations; and
    (B) requiring that Federal agencies prepare and consider estimates of the budgetary impact of regulations containing Federal mandates upon State, local, and tribal governments and the private sector before adopting such regulations, and ensuring that small governments are

given special consideration in that process; and
(2) to begin consideration of the effect of previously imposed Federal mandates, including the impact on State, local, and tribal governments of Federal court interpretations of Federal statutes and regulations that impose Federal intergovernmental mandates.

§1502. Definitions

For purposes of this chapter—
(1) except as provided in section 1555 of this title, the terms defined under section 658 of this title shall have the meanings as so defined; and
(2) the term "Director" means the Director of the Congressional Budget Office.

§1503. Exclusions

This chapter shall not apply to any provision in a bill, joint resolution, amendment, motion, or conference report before Congress and any provision in a proposed or final Federal regulation that—
(1) enforces constitutional rights of individuals;
(2) establishes or enforces any statutory rights that prohibit discrimination on the basis of race, color, religion, sex, national origin, age, handicap, or disability;
(3) requires compliance with accounting and auditing procedures with respect to grants or other money or property provided by the Federal Government;
(4) provides for emergency assistance or relief at the request of any State, local, or tribal government or any official of a State, local, or tribal government;
(5) is necessary for the national security or the ratification or implementation of international treaty obligations;
(6) the President designates as emergency legislation and that the Congress so designates in statute; or
(7) relates to the old-age, survivors, and disability insurance program under title II of the Social Security Act (42 U.S.C. 401 et seq.) (including taxes imposed by sections 3101(a) and 3111(a) of title 26 (relating to old-age, survivors, and disability insurance)).

§1531. Regulatory process

Each agency shall, unless otherwise prohibited by law, assess the effects of Federal regulatory actions on State, local, and tribal governments, and the private sector (other than to the extent that such regulations incorporate requirements specifically set forth in law).

§1532. Statements to accompany significant regulatory actions

(a) In general. Unless otherwise prohibited by law, before promulgating any general notice of proposed rulemaking that is likely to result in promulgation of any rule that includes any Federal mandate that may result in the expenditure by State, local, and tribal governments, in the aggregate, or by the private sector, of $100,000,000 or more (adjusted annually for inflation) in any 1 year, and before promulgating any final rule for which a general notice of proposed rulemaking was published, the agency shall prepare a written statement containing—
    (1) an identification of the provision of Federal law under which the rule is being promulgated;
    (2) a qualitative and quantitative assessment of the anticipated costs and benefits of the Federal mandate, including the costs and benefits to State, local, and tribal governments or the private sector, as well as the effect of the Federal mandate on health, safety, and the natural environment and such an assessment shall include—
        (A) an analysis of the extent to which such costs to State, local, and tribal governments may be paid with Federal financial assistance (or otherwise paid for by the Federal Government); and
        (B) the extent to which there are available Federal resources to carry out the intergovernmental mandate;
    (3) estimates by the agency, if and to the extent that the agency determines that accurate estimates are reasonably feasible, of—
        (A) the future compliance costs of the Federal mandate; and
        (B) any disproportionate budgetary effects of the Federal mandate upon any particular regions of the nation or particular State, local, or tribal governments, urban or rural or other types of communities, or particular segments of the private sector;
    (4) estimates by the agency of the effect on the national economy, such as the effect on productivity, economic growth, full employment, creation

of productive jobs, and international competitiveness of United States goods and services, if and to the extent that the agency in its sole discretion determines that accurate estimates are reasonably feasible and that such effect is relevant and material; and

(5) (A) a description of the extent of the agency's prior consultation with elected representatives (under section 1534 of this title) of the affected State, local, and tribal governments;

> (B) a summary of the comments and concerns that were presented by State, local, or tribal governments either orally or in writing to the agency; and
>
> (C) a summary of the agency's evaluation of those comments and concerns.
>
> (D) Promulgation. In promulgating a general notice of proposed rulemaking or a final rule for which a statement under subsection (a) of this section is required, the agency shall include in the promulgation a summary of the information contained in the statement.
>
> (E) Preparation in conjunction with other statement. Any agency may prepare any statement required under subsection (a) of this section in conjunction with or as a part of any other statement or analysis, provided that the statement or analysis satisfies the provisions of subsection (a) of this section.

§1533. Small government agency plan

(a) Effects on small governments. Before establishing any regulatory requirements that might significantly or uniquely affect small governments, agencies shall have developed a plan under which the agency shall—

> (1) provide notice of the requirements to potentially affected small governments, if any;
>
> (2) enable officials of affected small governments to provide meaningful and timely input in the development of regulatory proposals containing significant Federal intergovernmental mandates; and
>
> (3) inform, educate, and advise small governments on compliance with the requirements.

(b) Authorization of appropriations. There are authorized to be appropriated to each agency to carry out the provisions of this section and for no other purpose, such sums as are necessary.

§1534. State, local, and tribal government input

(a) In general. Each agency shall, to the extent permitted in law, develop an effective process to permit elected officers of State, local, and tribal governments (or their designated employees with authority to act on their behalf) to provide meaningful and timely input in the development of regulatory proposals containing significant Federal intergovernmental mandates.

(b) Meetings between State, local, tribal and Federal officers. The Federal Advisory Committee Act (5 U.S.C. App.) shall not apply to actions in support of intergovernmental communications where—

(1) meetings are held exclusively between Federal officials and elected officers of State, local, and tribal governments (or their designated employees with authority to act on their behalf) acting in their official capacities; and

(2) such meetings are solely for the purposes of exchanging views, information, or advice relating to the management or implementation of Federal programs established pursuant to public law that explicitly or inherently share intergovernmental responsibilities or administration.

(c) Implementing guidelines. No later than 6 months after March 22, 1995, the President shall issue guidelines and instructions to Federal agencies for appropriate implementation of subsections (a) and (b) of this section consistent with applicable laws and regulations.

§1535. Least burdensome option or explanation required

(a) In general. Except as provided in subsection (b) of this section, before promulgating any rule for which a written statement is required under section 1532 of this title, the agency shall identify and consider a reasonable number of regulatory alternatives and from those alternatives select the least costly, most cost-effective or least burdensome alternative that achieves the objectives of the rule, for—

(1) State, local, and tribal governments, in the case of a rule containing a Federal intergovernmental mandate; and

(2) the private sector, in the case of a rule containing a Federal private sector mandate.

(b) Exception. The provisions of subsection (a) of this section shall apply unless—

(1) the head of the affected agency publishes with the final rule an explanation of why the least costly, most cost-effective or least burdensome

method of achieving the objectives of the rule was not adopted; or

(2) the provisions are inconsistent with law.

(c) OMB certification. No later than 1 year after March 22, 1995, the Director of the Office of Management and Budget shall certify to Congress, with a written explanation, agency compliance with this section and include in that certification agencies and rulemakings that fail to adequately comply with this section.

§1536. Assistance to Congressional Budget Office

The Director of the Office of Management and Budget shall—

(1) collect from agencies the statements prepared under section 1532 of this title; and

(2) periodically forward copies of such statements to the Director of the Congressional Budget Office on a reasonably timely basis after promulgation of the general notice of proposed rulemaking or of the final rule for which the statement was prepared.

§1555. "Federal mandate" defined

Notwithstanding section 1502 of this title, for purposes of this subchapter the term "Federal mandate" means any provision in statute or regulation or any Federal court ruling that imposes an enforceable duty upon State, local, or tribal governments including a condition of Federal assistance or a duty arising from participation in a voluntary Federal program.

§1571. Judicial review

(a) Agency statements on significant regulatory actions

(1) In general. Compliance or noncompliance by any agency with the provisions of sections 1532 and 1533(a)(1) and (2) of this title shall be subject to judicial review only in accordance with this section.

(2) Limited review of agency compliance or noncompliance

(A) Agency compliance or noncompliance with the provisions of sections 1532 and 1533(a)(1) and (2) of this title shall be subject to judicial review only under section 706(1) of title 5, and only as provided under subparagraph (B).

(B) If an agency fails to prepare the written statement (including the preparation of the estimates, analyses, statements, or descriptions) under section 1532 of this title or the written plan under section 1533(a)(1) and (2) of this title, a court may compel the agency to prepare such written statement.

(3) Review of agency rules. In any judicial review under any other Federal law of an agency rule for which a written statement or plan is required under sections 1532 and 1533(a)(1) and (2) of this title, the inadequacy or failure to prepare such statement (including the inadequacy or failure to prepare any estimate, analysis, statement or description) or written plan shall not be used as a basis for staying, enjoining, invalidating or otherwise affecting such agency rule.

(4) Certain information as part of record. Any information generated under sections 1532 and 1533(a)(1) and (2) of this title that is part of the rulemaking record for judicial review under the provisions of any other Federal law may be considered as part of the record for judicial review conducted under such other provisions of Federal law.

(5) Application of other Federal law. For any petition under paragraph (2) the provisions of such other Federal law shall control all other matters, such as exhaustion of administrative remedies, the time for and manner of seeking review and venue, except that if such other Federal law does not provide a limitation on the time for filing a petition for judicial review that is less than 180 days, such limitation shall be 180 days after a final rule is promulgated by the appropriate agency.

(6) Effective date. This subsection shall take effect on October 1, 1995, and shall apply only to any agency rule for which a general notice of proposed rulemaking is promulgated on or after such date.

(b) Judicial review and rule of construction. Except as provided in subsection (a) of this section—

(1) any estimate, analysis, statement, description or report prepared under this chapter, and any compliance or noncompliance with the provisions of this chapter, and any determination concerning the applicability of the provisions of this chapter shall not be subject to judicial review; and

(2) no provision of this chapter shall be construed to create any right or benefit, substantive or procedural, enforceable by any person in any administrative or judicial action.

EXECUTIVE OFFICE OF THE PRESIDENT
OFFICE OF MANAGEMENT AND BUDGET
WASHINGTON, D.C. 20503

THE DIRECTOR

March 31, 1995

M-95-09

MEMORANDUM FOR THE HEADS OF EXECUTIVE DEPARTMENTS AND AGENCIES

FROM: Alice M. Rivlin
Director

SUBJECT: Guidance for Implementing Title II of S. 1

The President signed S. 1, the "Unfunded Mandates Reform Act of 1995," on March 22, 1995. Title II of this statute (P.L. 104-4) directs agencies, "unless otherwise prohibited by law, [to] assess the effects of Federal regulatory actions on State, local, and tribal governments, and the private sector ..." (Sec. 201). Title II also directs the Office of Management and Budget to submit to Congress each year "a written report detailing compliance by each agency during the preceding reporting period with the requirements of this title" (Sec. 208).

Within OMB, the Office of Information and Regulatory Affairs (OIRA) has the primary responsibility for monitoring agency compliance with this title. Sally Katzen, the OIRA Administrator, has prepared a memorandum providing guidance to agencies in complying with Title II.

I urge you to send Administrator Katzen's memorandum (attached) to the appropriate officials for their immediate attention.

Attachment

EXECUTIVE OFFICE OF THE PRESIDENT
OFFICE OF MANAGEMENT AND BUDGET
WASHINGTON, D.C. 20503

March 31, 1995

ADMINISTRATOR
OFFICE OF
INFORMATION AND
REGULATORY AFFAIRS

M-95-09

MEMORANDUM FOR THE HEADS OF EXECUTIVE DEPARTMENTS AND AGENCIES

FROM: Sally Katz
Administrator, Office of
Information and Regulatory Affairs

SUBJECT: Guidance for Implementing Title II of S. 1.

The President signed S. 1, the "Unfunded Mandates Reform Act of 1995, on March 22, 1995. Title II of this statute (P.L. 104-4) directs agencies to take a number of specific steps to assess the effects of Federal regulatory actions on State, local, and tribal governments, and the private sector. This memorandum summarizes the statutory requirements of Title II, and our role in overseeing agency compliance with it. This memorandum does not discuss Title I of the Act, which concerns mandates in legislation.

1. <u>Coverage</u>.

Title II applies to all Federal agencies, with the exception of the independent regulatory agencies (Sec. 3(1); Sec. 101(a), adding Sec. 421(1)).

Title II takes legal effect on the date of enactment, March 22, 1995 (Sec. 209).

2. <u>Judicial Review</u>.

Agency activities under Title II are subject to judicial review, as described in Section 401. The judicial review provisions "shall take effect on October 1, 1995, and shall apply only to any agency rule for which a general notice of proposed rulemaking is promulgated on or after such date" (Sec. 401(a)(6)).

An agency action can be challenged for failure to provide a statement required under Section 202 and a written plan required under Section 203(a), although the court will not have the authority to adjudge the adequacy of the analysis (Sec. 401(a)(2)). The court can compel an agency to prepare a required statement, but the absence or inadequacy of a statement cannot be used under any other Federal law as the basis for invalidating the rule (Sec. 401(a)(3)).

These statements will be considered part of the record of judicial review conducted under other provisions of Federal law (Sec. 401(a)(4)). The time for filing a petition for judicial review is the time set under other Federal law or 180 days after the final rule is promulgated, whichever is sooner (Sec. 401(a)(5)).

3. Section 201, "Regulatory Process."

Title II directs each agency, "unless otherwise prohibited by law, [to] assess the effects of Federal regulatory actions on State, local, and tribal governments, and the private sector (other than to the extent that such regulations incorporate requirements specifically set forth in law)."

4. Section 202, "Statements to Accompany Significant Regulatory Actions."

A. Required Written Statement. This section requires agencies to prepare a written statement before promulgating certain rules. This requirement builds on the assessment required by Section 6(a)(3)(C) of E.O. 12866.

Agencies are to include in the preamble to the published rulemaking "a summary of the information contained in the statement" (Sec. 202(b)).

In addition, OMB is to "collect from agencies the statements prepared under section 202," and "periodically forward copies" of these to the Congressional Budget Office "on a reasonably timely basis after promulgation" of the proposed or final rule (Sec. 206). We ask that you provide two copies of these statements to us as part of your submission under E.O. 12866 -- one, for our review and files; one, for transmission to CBO.

(1) Types of Rulemaking Covered. Section 202 applies to "any general notice of proposed rulemaking" or "any final rule for which a general notice of proposed rulemaking was published"[1] that "includes any Federal mandate that may result

---

[1] As the Conference Report states, "[i]t is the intent of the conferees that the rulemaking process shall follow the requirements of section 553 of title 5, United States Code, and shall be subject to the exceptions stated therein. When a general notice of proposed rulemaking is promulgated, such notice shall be accompanied by the written statement required by section 202. When an agency promulgates a final rule following the earlier promulgation of a proposed rule, the rule shall be accompanied by an updated written statement. In all cases, the exceptions stated in section 553 shall apply, including for good cause."

in the expenditure by State, local, and tribal governments, in the aggregate, or by the private sector, of $100,000,000 or more (adjusted annually for inflation) in any 1 year .... ."

(2) **Exemptions**. As a general limitation, Section 202 requires preparation of an estimate or analysis, "[u]nless otherwise prohibited by law". The Conference Report states that Section 202 "does not require the preparation of any estimate or analysis if the agency is prohibited by law from considering the estimate or analysis in adopting the rule."

Section 202 also does not apply to interim final rules or non-notice rules issued under the "good cause" exemption in 5 U.S.C. 553(b)(B). Nor does it apply to situations in which the agency has, under 5 U.S.C. 553(a), claimed an exemption. At the same time, if an agency waived the exemption and follows the informal rulemaking procedures in 5 U.S.C. 553, Section 202 would appear to apply.

Moreover, Section 202 is limited to what is defined in the Act as a "Federal mandate." As a general matter, a Federal mandate includes Federal regulations that impose enforceable duties on State, local, and tribal governments, or on the private sector, but excludes those related to certain kinds of Federal assistance and financial entitlements.[2]

---

[2] "Federal mandate" is a precisely defined term (Sec. 3(1); Sec. 101(a), adding Sec. 421(6)) that includes a "Federal intergovernmental mandate" (Sec. 421(5)) and a "Federal private sector mandate" (Sec. 421(7)).

"Federal intergovernmental mandate" includes a regulation that "would impose an enforceable duty upon State, local, or tribal governments," with two exceptions. It excludes "a condition of Federal assistance." It also excludes "a duty arising from participation in a voluntary Federal program," unless the regulation "relates to a then-existing Federal program under which $500,000,000 or more is provided annually to State, local, and tribal governments under entitlement authority," if the provision would "increase the stringency of conditions of assistance" or "place caps upon, or otherwise decrease the Federal Government's responsibility to provide funding" in a situation in which the State, local, or tribal governments "lack authority" to adjust accordingly.

"Federal private sector mandate" includes a regulation that "would impose an enforceable duty upon the private sector, except (i) a condition of Federal assistance; or (ii) a duty arising from participation in a voluntary Federal program."

B. **Content of Required Statement.** For regulations covered by Section 202, each agency is to prepare a written statement and include it in the rulemaking record. This statement may be prepared "in conjunction with or as part of any other statement or analysis" carried out by the agency, as long as it "satisfies the provisions" of Section 202(a) (Sec. 202(c)).

(1) **Authorizing Legislation.** The agency is to identify the "provision of Federal law under which the rule is being promulgated" (Sec. 202(a)(1)). As a general matter, if the rule is being issued pursuant to a statutory or judicial deadline, the agency should so state.

(2) **Cost-Benefit Analysis.** The agency is to provide a "qualitative and quantitative assessment of the anticipated costs and benefits of the Federal mandate, including the costs and benefits to State, local, and tribal governments or the private sector" (Sec. 202(a)(2)). This assessment is to include "the effect of the Federal mandate on health, safety, and the natural environment". This builds on the assessment required under Section 6(a)(3)(C) of E.O. 12866.

To the extent an agency determines that "accurate estimates are reasonably feasible," the assessment is also to include estimates of "future compliance costs of the Federal mandate" (Sec. 202(a)(3)(A)). For intergovernmental mandates, the assessment is to include an analysis of the extent to which the costs "may be paid with Federal financial assistance (or otherwise paid for by the Federal Government)" and "the extent to which there are available Federal resources to carry out the intergovernmental mandate" (Sec. 202(a)(2)(A) & (B)).

(3) **Macro-economic Effects.** The agency is also to estimate "the effect" of the regulation "on the national economy, such as the effect on productivity, economic growth, full employment, creation of productive jobs, and international competitiveness of United States goods and services, if and to the extent that the agency in its sole discretion determines that accurate estimates are reasonably feasible and that such effect is relevant and material" (Sec. 202(a)(4)).

We would note that such macro-economic effects tend to be measurable, in nation-wide econometric models, only if the economic impact of the regulation reaches 0.25 percent to 0.5 percent of Gross Domestic Product (in the range of $1.5 billion to $3 billion). A regulation with a smaller aggregate effect is highly unlikely to have any measurable impact in macro-economic terms unless it is highly focused on a particular geographic region or economic sector.

(4) **Summary of State, Local, and Tribal Government Input.** The agency is to describe the "extent of the agency's prior

- 5 -

consultation with elected representatives" under Section 204, summarize their comments and concerns, and summarize its evaluation of these comments and concerns (Sec. 202(a)(5)). Section 204, which in essence codifies Section 1 of E.O. 12875, is discussed below.

(5) "Least Burdensome Option or Explanation Required." For those regulations for which an agency prepares a statement under Section 202, "the agency shall [1] identify and consider a reasonable number of regulatory alternatives and [2] from those alternatives select the least costly, most cost-effective or least burdensome alternative that achieves the objectives of the rule" (Sec. 205(a)). This builds on the assessment of feasible alternatives required in Section 6(a)(3)(C)(iii) of E.O. 12866.

This selection of the "least costly, most cost-effective or least burdensome alternative" is to be done "for State, local, and tribal governments, in the case of a rule containing a Federal intergovernmental mandate" and for "the private sector, in the case of a rule containing a Federal private sector mandate" (Sec. 205(a)(1)-(2)).

If the agency does not select the least burdensome option, the agency head needs to publish "with the final rule an explanation of why the least costly, most cost-effective or least burdensome method of achieving the objectives of the rule was not adopted" (Sec. 205(b)(1)).

The agency need not comply with Section 205(a) if its provisions "are inconsistent with [the] law" under which the agency is issuing the rule (Sec. 205(b)(2)). We would also note that, while an agency's identification and selection of the least burdensome option in compliance with Section 205, may -- for purposes of presentation and clarity -- be included as part of the statement required under Section 202, this identification and selection is not subject to judicial review (Sec. 401).

5. Section 203, "Small Government Agency Plan."

Section 203 builds upon the policy objectives of the Regulatory Flexibility Act. It provides that "[b]efore establishing any regulatory requirements that might significantly or uniquely affect small governments, agencies shall have developed a plan under which the agency shall--

"(1) provide notice of the requirements to potentially affected small governments, if any;

"(2) enable officials of affected small governments to provide meaningful and timely input [therein]; and

"(3) inform, educate, and advise small governments on compliance with [such regulatory] requirements."

We have two suggestions. First, the "notice" to affected small governments should involve a more targeted effort than formal publication in the Federal Register.

Second, an outreach effort to enhance "meaningful ... input" and to "advise small governments on compliance" can further agency efforts to carry out Section 204. You may wish to consult with the Chief Counsel for Advocacy, in the Small Business Administration. In cooperation with a number of agencies, he has been working to improve outreach efforts, and will be able to share the pluses and minuses of various approaches.

6. Section 204, "State, Local, and Tribal Government Input."

Agencies are, "to the extent permitted in law, [to] develop an effective process to permit elected officers of State, local, and tribal governments ... to provide meaningful and timely input in the development of regulatory proposals containing significant Federal intergovernmental mandates" (Sec. 204(a)). Under this process, meetings are exempt from the Federal Advisory Committee Act (Sec. 204(b)).

The President is to issue guidelines for appropriate implementation of this section no later than six months from the date of enactment (Sec. 204(c)). Until that time, I suggest that you review the procedures you have developed to comply with E.O. 12875 and the Guidance for Implementing E.O. 12875, Section 1, that we sent you on January 11, 1994.

That Guidance suggests that intergovernmental consultations should take place as early as possible, and be integrated into the ongoing rulemaking process. It suggests that agencies should consult with the heads of governments, program and financial officials, and Washington representatives and elected officials. To facilitate these consultations, the Guidance suggests that agencies should estimate the direct costs to be incurred by the affected governments, and make reasonable efforts to disaggregate these cost estimates.

7. Section 207, "Pilot Program on Small Government Flexibility."

OMB, "in consultation with Federal agencies," is to establish pilot programs in at least two agencies "to test innovative, and more flexible regulatory approaches that (1) reduce reporting and compliance burdens on small governments; and (2) meet overall statutory goals and objectives" (Sec. 207(a)).

Those of you who would like to undertake such a pilot program should contact us to discuss your projects. You may

- 7 -

already be considering such an effort in the context of replying to the President's March 4 Memorandum, entitled "Regulatory Reinvention Initiative," or as part of your efforts to improve regulations as part of the Reinventing Government process.

8. <u>OMB Reports</u>.

OMB is to submit certain reports to Congress. Within one year, OMB is to "certify to Congress, with a written explanation, agency compliance with [Section 205] and include in that certification agencies and rulemakings that fail to adequately comply with [Section 205]" (Sec. 205(c)). More generally, every year, OMB is to provide to Congress a written report "detailing compliance by each agency during the preceding reporting period with the requirements of this title" (Sec. 208).

We will be reviewing your Section 202 statements during our reviews conducted under E.O. 12866. We will supplement this information with requests to you to learn about compliance with other provisions in Title II.

* * * * *

If you have any questions, please let us know. We will, of course, provide additional guidance as experience and need dictate.

EXECUTIVE OFFICE OF THE PRESIDENT
OFFICE OF MANAGEMENT AND BUDGET
WASHINGTON, D.C. 20503

THE DIRECTOR

September 21, 1995

M-95-20

MEMORANDUM FOR THE HEADS OF DEPARTMENTS AND AGENCIES

FROM: Alice M. Rivlin
Director

SUBJECT: Guidelines and Instructions for Implementing Section 204, "State, Local, and Tribal Government Input," of Title II of P.L. 104-4

On March 22, 1995, President Clinton signed into law the "Unfunded Mandates Reform Act of 1995" (P.L. 104-4) (the "Act"). Section 204(a) of the Act requires that --

> "Each agency shall, to the extent permitted in law, develop an effective process to permit elected officers of State, local, and tribal governments (or their designated employees with authority to act on their behalf) to provide meaningful and timely input in the development of regulatory proposals containing significant Federal intergovernmental mandates."[1]

Section 204(b) of the Act provides an exemption from the Federal Advisory Committee Act (5 U.S.C. App.) for intergovernmental consultations involving intergovernmental responsibilities or administration.

---

[1] The Act's consultation requirement builds on that set forth by President Clinton on October 26, 1993, in Executive Order No. 12875. In order "to reduce the imposition of unfunded mandates upon State, local, and tribal governments," the Executive order requires agencies, when they seek to impose unfunded mandates upon State, local, or tribal governments through a regulation, to provide to the Director of the Office of Management and Budget "a description of the extent of the agency's prior consultation with representatives of affected State, local, and tribal governments, the nature of their concerns, any written communications submitted to the agency by such units of government, and the agency's position supporting the need to issue the regulation containing the mandate" (Sec. 1(a)(2)).

- 2 -

Section 204(c) requires the President to issue guidelines and instructions to Federal agencies "for appropriate implementation" of both of these provisions "consistent with applicable laws and regulations." In accordance with the President's delegation of authority,[2] OMB is today issuing those guidelines and instructions.[3]

I. THE PROCESS FOR INTERGOVERNMENTAL CONSULTATION.

It is important that this intergovernmental consultation process not only achieves meaningful input, but also builds a better understanding among Federal, State, local, and tribal governments. As described in Part II, below, the process required by the Federal Advisory Committee Act is not to act as a hindrance to full and effective intergovernmental consultation.

A. What Agencies are Covered?

The process for intergovernmental consultation called for by Section 204(a) applies to all Federal agencies (as defined in 5 U.S.C. 551(1)), with the exception of independent regulatory agencies.

B. When Should Intergovernmental Consultations Take Place?

Intergovernmental consultation should take place as early in the regulatory process as possible. Except where the need for immediate agency action precludes prior consultation, consultation should occur before publication of the notice of proposed rulemaking or other regulatory action proposing a significant Federal intergovernmental mandate. Consultation should continue after publication of the regulatory action initiating the proposal. Except in exceptional circumstances where the need for immediate action precludes prior consultation, consultation must occur prior to the formal promulgation in final form of the regulatory action.

---

[2] See 60 Fed. Reg. 45039 (August 29, 1995).

[3] Portions of these guidelines and instructions are based on OMB Memorandum M-94-10, entitled "Guidance for Implementing E.O. 12875, 'Reduction of Unfunded Mandates,'" issued by Director Leon E. Panetta on January 11, 1994. These guidelines and instructions are not intended, and should not be construed, to create any right or benefit, substantive or procedural, enforceable at law by a party against the United States, its agencies, its officers, or its employees. Neither are these guidelines and instructions intended, nor should they be construed, to limit the availability of any exclusion from the Federal Advisory Committee Act contained in that Act or any applicable regulations.

- 3 -

C. With Whom Should Agencies Consult?

The statute directs agencies to develop an effective process to ensure that "elected officers of State, local, and tribal governments (or their designated employees with authority to act on their behalf)" who wish to provide meaningful and timely input are able to do so.

Each agency needs to develop an intergovernmental consultation process for that agency. To do so, the agency should first develop a proposal for that process, and consult with State, local, and tribal governments (as appropriate) concerning this proposed process, as soon as possible.

One approach an agency may wish to adopt is to designate a person or an office through which intergovernmental consultation should be coordinated. Another approach is for an agency to instruct those responsible for developing a rule to seek out the views of elected officers or their designated employees. An agency may also wish to develop other effective means of generating meaningful input or expand those that it already has. An agency will be able to obtain the fullest range of meaningful input from State, local, and tribal governments by undertaking the following kinds of consultation.

(1) Heads of Government.

Agencies should seek to consult with the highest levels of the pertinent government units, e.g., the Office of the Governor, Mayor, or Tribal Leader (or their designated employees with authority to act on their behalf). These officials are the ones elected to represent the people and are the ones that the public holds directly accountable for the actions of those government units.

(2) Both Program and Financial Officials.

Many regulatory agencies have functional counterparts in State, local, and tribal governments, e.g., those government officials who implement or enforce regulatory responsibilities required in whole or in part by the Federal agency. These local officials tend to be those most familiar with the Federal agency's regulatory program, and should be consulted as a source of important information concerning the likely effects of, or effective alternatives to, Federal regulatory proposals.

In addition, agencies should consult with those State, local, and tribal officials most directly responsible for ensuring the funding of compliance with the Federal mandate, e.g., the applicable treasury, budget, tax-collection, or other financial officials. These officials are institutionally responsible for

- 4 -

balancing the competing claims for scarce State, local, or tribal resources.

(3) Washington Representatives.

It is also important that Federal agencies consult with Washington representatives, where available, of associations representing elected officials. These Washington representatives often know which local elected officials are the most knowledgeable about, interested in, or responsible for, implementing specific issues, regulations or programs, and can ensure that a broad range of government officials learn of and provide valuable insight concerning a proposed intergovernmental mandate.

(4) Small Governments.

Agencies should make special efforts to consult with officials of small governments, and to develop a plan for such consultation under section 203 of Title II of the Act. Agencies may wish to consider several mechanisms for reaching small governments, including special task forces, periodic mailings through small government associations, or communication through rural development councils.

D. How Much Consultation Should There Be?

The scope of intergovernmental consultation should be based on common sense and be commensurate with the significance of the action being taken. The more costly, the more potentially disruptive, the more broadly applicable, the more controversial the proposed Federal intergovernmental mandate -- the more consultation there should be. An agency should decide the extent of its consultation on a case-by-case basis; a one-size-fits-all prescription is neither appropriate nor desirable.

E. What Should Be the Content of Consultation?

Agencies should seek views of State, local, and tribal governments regarding costs, benefits, risks, and alternative and flexible methods of compliance regarding their regulatory proposals. Agencies should also seek views on potential duplication with existing laws or regulations at other levels of government, and on ways to harmonize their rules with State, local and tribal policies and programs.

To assist with these consultations, agencies should first estimate the direct costs to be incurred by the State, local, or tribal governments in complying with the mandate and then inform the affected governmental units of these cost estimates. Estimates should cover both up-front and recurring costs, for a reasonable number of years after the rule is to be put into effect. To the extent practicable, agencies should make reasonable efforts to disaggregate these cost estimates as they affect the various levels of government, or otherwise provide the criteria by which those affected can disaggregate the cost estimates in order to determine the potential costs to themselves. Where quantitative estimates are not feasible, agencies should work with other levels of government to discern and discuss qualitative costs.

Agencies should also consult on and estimate the benefits expected from the mandate for States, localities, tribes, and their residents and businesses. Estimates should cover both up-front and recurring benefits for a reasonable number of years after the rule is to be put into effect. To the extent practicable, agencies should make reasonable efforts to disaggregate these benefit estimates as they affect the various levels of government, or otherwise provide the criteria by which those affected can disaggregate the benefit estimates in order to determine the potential benefits to themselves. Where quantitative estimates are not feasible, agencies should work with other levels of government to discern and discuss qualitative benefits.

Agencies should also, during the consultative process, seek views on the expected method of compliance. Governmental units may have suggestions as to how to achieve the Federal regulatory objective in a way that is more effective, efficient, flexible, and consistent with State, local, and tribal governmental regulatory and other functions.

F. How Should Agencies Integrate These Intergovernmental Consultations into the Rulemaking Process?

It is important for agencies to integrate these consultation activities into the ongoing rulemaking process. The cost and benefit estimates, any additional viable suggestions received during the pre-notice consultations, and the agency plan to carry out intergovernmental consultation should be included in the preamble to the notice of proposed rulemaking. Publication of the cost and benefit estimates and the intergovernmental consultation plan in the **Federal Register** will assure that those governmental units that are not contacted directly will have access to the same cost and benefit estimates as those who were contacted directly, and have the opportunity to make their concerns known. Similarly, and consistent with E.O. 12875, any preamble transmitted to the **Federal Register** on or after October 2, 1995, should include, as of the particular stage of the rulemaking, the extent of the agency's prior consultations with representatives of affected State, local, and tribal governments, the nature of their concerns, any written communications submitted to the agency by such units of government, and the agency's position supporting the need to issue the regulation containing the mandate.

G. What Compliance Reports Should Agencies Submit to OMB?

Under Section 208 of the Act, OMB is required to submit a report to Congress on agency compliance with the requirements of Title II of the Act, which includes the intergovernmental consultation requirement, on or before March 22, 1996, and annually thereafter. Accordingly, agencies should provide the Administrator of the Office of Information and Regulatory Affairs, by January 15, 1996, and annually on that date thereafter, a written report of each agency's compliance with Title II of the Act. The report should include a description of the process established by the agency to ensure meaningful input, as well as a description of agency consultations with State, local, and tribal governments for each proposed and final rule "containing significant Federal intergovernmental mandates." As part of the report to be submitted by January 15, 1996, agencies should also describe the plans they have developed to consult with small governments, under Section 203 of Title II of the Act.

II. THE EXEMPTION FROM THE FEDERAL ADVISORY COMMITTEE ACT

In order to facilitate the consultation process, section 204(b) of the Act provides an exemption from the Federal Advisory Committee Act ("FACA") (5 U.S.C. App.) "for the exchange of official views regarding the implementation of public laws requiring shared intergovernmental responsibilities or administration."[4] This exemption applies to all Federal agencies subject to FACA, and is not limited to the intergovernmental consultations required by Section 204(a) but instead applies to the entire range of intergovernmental responsibilities or administration. In accordance with the legislative intent, the exemption should be read broadly to facilitate intergovernmental communications on responsibilities or administration.

This exemption applies to meetings between Federal officials and employees and State, local, or tribal governments, acting through their elected officers, officials, employees, and Washington representatives, at which "views, information, or advice" are exchanged concerning the implementation of intergovernmental responsibilities or administration, including those that arise explicitly or implicitly under statute, regulation, or Executive order.[5]

---

[4] House Conference Report 104-76 (March 13, 1995), p. 40.

[5] Specifically, this exemption from FACA applies where --

"(1) meetings are held exclusively between Federal officials

- 7 -

The scope of meetings covered by the exemption should be construed broadly to include any meetings called for any purpose relating to intergovernmental responsibilities or administration. Such meetings include, but are not limited to, meetings called for the purpose of seeking consensus; exchanging views, information, advice, and/or recommendations; or facilitating any other interaction relating to intergovernmental responsibilities or administration.

The guidance given above should help determine when a meeting qualifies under Section 204(b) of the Act for an exemption from the FACA. We also note that meetings that do not meet these guidelines for an exemption may nonetheless not be subject to the FACA in the first instance. Accordingly, to determine whether there is even a need for an exemption from the FACA, agencies should also consult the FACA itself, as well as the General Service Administration's regulations at 41 C.F.R. Subpart 101-6.10, and the court decisions construing the FACA.

* * * * *

It is important that agencies make their best efforts to implement these guidelines and instructions. As the Conference Report stated, "an important part of efforts to improve the Federal regulatory process entails improved communications with State, local, and tribal governments. Accordingly, this legislation will require Federal agencies to establish effective mechanisms for soliciting and integrating the input of such interests into the Federal decision-making process."[6]

If agencies have any questions concerning these guidelines and instructions, they should contact the Administrator of the Office of Information and Regulatory Affairs, or her staff. OMB will provide additional guidance as experience and need dictate.

---

and elected officers of State, local, and tribal governments (or their designated employees with authority to act on their behalf), acting in their official capacities; and

"(2) such meetings are solely for the purposes of exchanging information, or advice relating to the management or implementation of Federal programs established pursuant to public law that explicitly or inherently share intergovernmental responsibilities or administration."

[6] House Conference Report 104-76 (March 13, 1995), p. 40.